SMALL-SCALE INDUSTRIES AND ENTREPRENEURSHIP

IN THE TWENTY-FIRST CENTURY

SMALL-SCALE INDUSTRIES AND ENTREPRENEURSHIP

IN THE TWENTY-FIRST CENTURY

- The Entrepreneur
- Entrepreneurship
- Small Enterprises
- Problems
- Opportunities
- Challenges

Dr. Vasant Desai
Director,
Visvesvaraya Institute of
Socio-economic Research (VISER),
Mumbai.

Himalaya Publishing House
ISO 9001:2015 CERTIFIED

First Edition	**: 1994**	**Reprint**	**: 2004**
Reprint	**: 1995**	**Reprint**	**: 2005**
Second Edition	**: 1996**	**Seventh Edition**	**: 2006**
Third Edition	**: 1997**	**Reprint**	**: 2007**
Reprint	**: 1998**	**Eighth Edition**	**: 2008**
Fourth Revised Edition	**: 1999**	**Reprint**	**: 2009**
Reprint	**: 1999**	**Ninth Revised Edition**	**: 2011**
Fifth Revised and Updated Edition	**: 2000**	**Edition**	**: 2013, 2014, 2015**
Reprint	**: 2000**	**Edition**	**: 2017, 2020, 2022**
Sixth Revised Edition	**: 2001**	**Edition**	**: 2023**
Reprint	**: 2002-2003**	**Edition**	**: 2026**

Published by : Mrs. Meena Pandey
for **HIMALAYA PUBLISHING HOUSE PVT. LTD.,**
Vishal Industrial Estate, 1st Floor, Office No. 63/64,
Bhandup Village Road, Subhash Nagar (Opp. CEAT Tyres),
Nahur (W), Mumbai - 400 078. **Phone:** 022-35131464/65/66/67
E-mail: himpub@bharatmail.co.in; **Website:** www.himpub.com

Branch Offices :

New Delhi : Pooja Apartments, 4-B, Murari Lal Street, Ansari Road, Darya Ganj,
New Delhi - 110 002. Phone: 011-23270392, 23278631; Fax: 011-23256286

Nagpur : Kundanlal Chandak Industrial Estate, Ghat Road, Nagpur - 440 018.
Mobile: 09325409992, 09325908881

Bengaluru : Plot No. 91-33, 2nd Main Road, Seshadripuram, Behind Nataraja Theatre,
Bengaluru - 560 020. Phone: 080-41138821; Mobile: 09379847017, 09379847005

Hyderabad : No. 3-4-184, Lingampally, Besides Raghavendra Swamy Matham, Kachiguda,
Hyderabad - 500 027. Phone: 040-27560041, 27550139

Chennai : No. 34/44, Motilal Street, T. Nagar, Chennai - 600 017. Mobile: 09380460419

Pune : First Floor, Laksha Apartment, No. 527, Mehunpura, Shaniwarpeth
(Near Prabhat Theatre), Pune - 411 030.
Phone: 020-24496323, 24496333; Mobile: 09370579333

Cuttack : Plot No. 5F-755/4, Sector-9, CDA Markat Nagar, Cuttack - 753 014,
Odisha. Mobile: 09338746007

Kolkata : 3, S.M. Bose Road, Near Gate No. 5, Agarpara Railway Station, North 24 Parganas,
West Bengal - 700 109. Mobile: 09674536325

DTP by : Sunanda

Printed at : Geetanjali Press Pvt. Ltd., Nagpur. On behalf of HPH (P).

PREFACE

Globalisation has become the hallmark of the 21st century. Clearly, globalisation has the potential to make all people better. To make this promise a reality, however, we must find a way to carefully manage the process

Globalisation is characterised by an increase in flow of trade, capital and information, as well as mobility of individuals, across brooders. It is not a new phenomenon – globalisation has progressed throughout the course of record history, although not in a steady or linear fashion.

In the new millennium, the economy continues to be in the throes of momentous change: the progressive reduction of barriers to capital flows and international trade the spread of market-based economy in key sector and the exciting possibilities of beneficial change brought by transformative technologies. These changes have provided great opportunities for the Indian corporate sector, and it is poised to brave the challenges in the new competitive global arena landscape and capitalise on these opportunities. The imperative to compete in the global arena demands a radical shift in business outlook that transcends a simple reliance on export as an indicator of an organisation's international credentials. I am confident that the Indian entrepreneurial class will demonstrate resilience of sprite in achieving this.

The millennium has opened up many an opportunities to entrepreneurs and accelerated the process of wealth creation. This Globalisation Process has also touched small-scale industries as well. The individuals will look for new anchor that will add meaning to their life as institutions like government, political parties, religion, etc., which are supposed to play that role, continue to erode in authority. The emergence of the "individual-in-control" will have tremendous implications for determining the behaviour pattern of all institutions and social mores in the future. Finally, the emergences of the internet and the revaluation in the telecommunication industry is going to change the landscape of your whole operating field. It is going to affect the way work, the way we move, the way we transact or in short the way we conduct our whole life. The century and the new millennium has owned with the above realities.

Small and medium enterprises (SMEs) too are quickly gearing up to meet the emerging challenges in the global economy through constant innovation and adoption of cutting-edge technology to prove superior customer solution. As in the past SME's motivation for undertaking this proactive transformation is guided by its *raison d'etre,* the Indian industry, and a desire to acquire the requisite competencies to play an important role in the emergence of a globally competitive Indian corporate sector. In the process SME would continue to be spurred by the imperative for driving organisational growth and shareholder value, and create economic and intellectual capital that benefits all stakeholders.

Will we drive towards an edge of chaos or will there be more opportunity for all of us? The past decade of liberalisation and globalisation has seen several paradigm shift. From a fear of foreign capital (remember FERA), we are now going all out to woo FDI. From bank nationalisation and direct credit, it's M&A season for a new breed or private banks and competition for funds. Government monopolies are being dismantled. Yesterday's luxuries have become necessities. The consumer is the king .

Against this background, "Small-scale Industries and Entrepreneurship" in the 21st century, is a subject of great importance.

New Opportunities

Literate on entrepreneurs and small-scale industries has been growing in recent years. Though there have been numerous articles in various journals on entrepreneurial development, especially in India and quite a few edited books containing contributed articles on different topics. It is, therefore, no exaggeration to say that there has not been a single comprehensive, critical analytical book on the subject, explaining, analysing and assessing the various aspects of the subject. This book is an attempt to fill this gap. It is also intended to help evolve a perspective of development of the vital sector of the national economy.

The 21st century and the new millennium has ushered in with high hopes and immense opportunities. New opportunities are opening up in the field of small-scale sector in India and the world over. To foster managerial and the organisational excellence, the study is designed for entrepreneurs who needs to understand the application excellence, the study is designed for entrepreneurs who needs to understands the application of special skills to lead them to excel in their work. The study will help to attain a good grasp of the fundamentals of financial management, marketing strategy and make optimal operational and strategic decisions in their industries. The study help to emerge victorious by strategy, decision-making and teamwork.

As an applied science, management education is expected to have close interaction with the education apart from various enterprise business world. In our country this may be partly true in the case of large organisation but nothing is mentioned, or discussed, in these institution about Small-scale Enterprises (SSEs), although the contribution of this sector to the economy in terms of employment output and export to include service activities too. However, pretty little is being done in the area of small business development programmers organised by industrial development agencies. It is time we sit back and look at management education as it relates to small business.

The picture of the entrepreneur that is drawn here has of necessity been painted with a broad brush. It could not be otherwise if the analysis were to be confined to a single volume. The purpose is to describe the essential features of an entrepreneur and entrepreneurship to provide a sense of direction for planners and policy-makers, on the one end, and the emerging crop of young entrepreneur, both men and women educated-uneducated, professional and non-professional, to reap immense benefits and decide the future-course of action on the other. In fact, this book *"Small-scale Industries and Entrepreneurship"* is neither a fresh beginning nor is the last word. Subsequent studies will elaborate on many of the issues raised here.

We need people who can become entrepreneurs. Having recognised that the qualities of entrepreneurship can be inculcated, we have to re-examine our activities towards entrepreneurship development. In India entrepreneurship development programmers are of short-term nature in general, primarily intended to produce quick 'entrepreneurs'. As Prof. Malcolm Harpers (of Canfield School of Management) study shows, a majority of such programmers all over the world have a duration of three weeks. Training in entrepreneurship and management education are covered in this period.

The vibrancy of an economy depends on the constant flow of entrepreneurs who can take up challenges in both business and agriculture. This can be achieved only in the long-run. As noted by Richard Morse of East-West Central, Hawaii, entrepreneurial education should start in schools.

School level education can however, be an introduction to business, At a higher level management education is unavoidable for serious businessmen. Business schools are the Best agencies to after long-term management education to potential small entrepreneurs. These institutions with a discipline structure have already the framework; they only have to redefine the target market and reorient the course. They have to cater to the small business managers too. Management institutions have to be a direct source of training for both existing and potential entrepreneurs.

Admitted, this is too short a period to have any strong foundation in management education. These short courses are catering to a small market segment. What about the bigger segment of the market whose wants remain unsatisfied, or where the demands is not created yet?

From all points of view this book provides a new insight into small-scale industry which is playing a catalytic role in the rapid development of the country. This will not only continue to assist the students to prepare for the examination but also inspire them to be young small entrepreneurs by exposing them to the varied aspect of small-scale industries, and entrepreneurship. There is an urgency in this book that affects the future of each one of us, and hence society.

Organisation of the Book

Small-scale industries and entrepreneurship has been of the most popular subjects that has aroused the interest of students and young entrepreneurs in large measure. The importance of the subject is magnified manifold in today's economic climate.

The book consists of **THIRTY-THREE** chapters and project work has been divided into three sections. Section I deals with multidimensional aspect of small-scale industries, Rural Industries, Industrial Estates, Organisation Ownership Finance, Taxation, Marketing, Problems and Prospects.

Section II provides an insight into the concept of the Entrepreneur, Entrepreneurship, Characteristics, Classification, Role, Environment, Entrepreneurial Development and Training, Institutions and Opportunities and Challenges. Project work is provided in Section III.

Acknowledgements

My debt to those who have helped me in one way or the other is large indeed. While I take this opportunity to thank all of them, they are too numerous to be mentioned in a brief preface. I would like to acknowledge my deep sense of gratitude to many veteran entrepreneurs, and professional managers for their guidance. Thanks are also due to late B.N. Nilaver, Mrs. Phalguni Ravi, K.N. Pandey, Anuj Pandey, Neeraj Pandey, and Manish Desai for their suggestions for effecting a number of stylistic improvements.

As usual Mr. K. N. Pandey provided the much needed inspiration, motivation and support in this exercise.

No words can adequately express my debt gratitude to my late father, Shri Ranganath Balwant Mutalik Desai, and my late mother Smt. Laxmi Devi, for generating in me a perennial interest in higher studies.

I will be failing in my duty if I do not mention here the tremendous cooperations I received from my wife, Mrs. M. V. Desai in the completion of this book and I wish to thank for her patience, continuous support, encouragement, her understanding and love helped to bring this efforts to fruition.

Mumbai **Vasant Desai**

ENTREPRENEURIAL MISSION STATEMENT

- The entrepreneur lives and work in an environment that is fiercely competitive. It is, therefore, crucial that the entrepreneur sharpens his/her cutting edge to stay ahead.
- The entrepreneur as the engine of economic growth, job creation and prosperity, always served the society. Customer priority and quality are his mission and passion.
- The entrepreneur shall adopt organisational structures to speed up communication, decision-making, job creation, income generation creation.
- The entrepreneur displays courage to take risk of putting his own money into an idea; courage to take on the competition and courage to take a leap into an unknown future and create new enterprises/business. This creative process is the lifeblood of the strong enterprises that derive growth and propel the nation forward.
- The entrepreneurial activities blossom and thrive under conditions where citizen participate and compete in the marketplace under conditions of equity and are not unduly burdened by regulation.
- The entrepreneur will always strive for a natural and sustainable enhancement of entrepreneurial society.
- Entrepreneurism is the lifeblood of any economy; but in India, where first generation innovators are still battling the odds to make on the global economy, enterprise in an idea whose true potential; is yet to be realised. Ironically, Indian entrepreneurism is more about overcoming barriers — be it finance, bureaucracy, and infrastructure — than about achieving the fruits of liberalisation. That is not an inspiring image for a country that dream soft begging a critical component of tomorrow's knowledge economy; of creating vibrant digital valleys; and of having its own Bill Gates and Michael Dells. Yet the changing Indian economy arena is always a busy with the news of mavericks that have discovered bold new ways of competing. And they have done so in areas that have been extremely tough to compete in, dominated as they are by mighty multinationals.
- Entrepreneurism triggered by liberalisation and the advent of the brainpower industry, demands the systematic development if business cluster in India, or geographical concentrations of competitiveness where technology diffusion is rapid and supply-chains are short and efficient. Clusters, where the levels of competitiveness are always high, are the educational institutes and research centres, and a good quality of life, to thrive. A hassle-free environment can leverage the diverse capabilities of Indian entrepreneurism.

Ground Reality

"Simulating a business situation in a classroom is very ineffective and is a very bad simulation. You can't simulate management that way, because management has to be about what's happening on the ground, not what's happening in executive offices."

— Henry Mintzberg, Management Guru

CONTENTS

SECTION-I

SMALL-SCALE INDUSTRIES

I.	**Small-scale Industries**	**1 – 2**
1.	Introduction	3 – 11
2.	The Concept of Small-scale Industry	12 – 24
3.	Characteristic of Small-scale Industries	25 – 33
4.	The Role of Small-scale Industries	34 – 42
5.	Policies Governing Small-scale Industries	43 – 55
6.	Rural Industries and Rural Artisans	56 – 70
7.	Ancillary Industries	71 – 76
8.	Industrial Estate	77 – 86
9.	Organisational Structure of Small-scale Industries	87 – 100
10.	Ownership Pattern in Small-scale Industry	101 – 117
11.	Finance for Small-scale Industries	118 – 142
12.	Working Capital Management	143 – 165
13.	Taxation Benefits	166 – 184
14.	Marketing Mechanism in Small-scale Industries	185 – 207
15.	Export Potentials of Small-scale Industries	208 – 221
16.	Problems of Small-scale Industries	222 – 234
17.	Prospects for Small-scale Industries	235 – 249

SECTION-II

ENTREPRENEURSHIP – THE ROAD TO REAL INDIA

- **Entrepreneurship – The Road To Real India** **250 – 256**

  The Road to Real India

  Credo of Entrepreneurs

  Entrepreneurs Who Changed the Pace of Corporate India

18. The Concept of Entrepreneurship 257 – 277
19. Development of Entrepreneurs 278 – 288
20. Evaluation of Entrepreneurs in India 289 – 300
21. Characteristics of Entrepreneurs 301 – 321
22. Classification and Types of Entrepreneurs 322 – 338
23. Women Entrepreneurs 339 – 353
24. The Role of Entrepreneurs 354 – 373
25. Entrepreneurial Environment 374 – 386
26. Identification of Opportunities 387 – 405
27. Converting Business Opportunities into Reality 406 – 434
28. Location Issues 435 – 448
29. Environmental Problems 449 – 456
30. Entrepreneurial Development 457 – 468
31. Entrepreneurial Training 469 – 485
32. Institutions in Aid of Entrepreneurship Development 486 – 504
33. All About Relevant Acts 505 – 531

SECTION-III

PROJECT WORK

- **Project Work** **531 – 566**

  The Case Study

  The Scope of the Project Work

  A New Case Studies

  Appendix **567 – 570**

BRIEF CONTENTS

SECTION-I : SMALL-SCALE INDUSTRIES 1 - 2

CHAPTER 1 : INTRODUCTION 3 - 11

Growth is Lifeblood of Small-scale Industries and Entrepreneur — Growing an Entrepreneurial Economic — Conclusion

CHAPTER 2 : THE CONCEPT OF SMALL-SCALE INDUSTRY 12 - 24

Introduction — SSI Units — Conclusion — Annexure-I

CHAPTER 3 : CHARATERISTIC OF SMALL-SCALE INDUSTRIES 25 - 33

Introduction — Characteristics of Small-scale Industries — Importance of Small Enterprises — Advantages of Small-scale Enterprises — Challenges and Opportunities — Small is Beautiful, but What is Really Beautiful is the Appropriate Small-scale is Efficient — Conclusion

CHAPTER 4 : THE ROLE OF SMALL-SCALE INDUSTRIES 34 - 42

Introduction — Vision of Small Industires — Small Industries Make a Big Difference to India's Economy — New Trade-boosting Measures — Conclusion

CHAPTER 5 : POLICIES GOVERNING SMALL-SCALE INDUSTRIES 43 - 55

Introduction — New Policy for Small and Tiny Sector — Salient Features of New Policy — Thrust Areas of the Policy for Small Enterprises — Expert Committee on Small Enterprises – New Policy Directives 1997 — Conclusion

CHAPTER 6 : RURAL INDUSTRIES AND RURAL ARTISANS 56 - 70

Introduction — Types of Rural Industries — Khadi and Village Industries — Strategy of Rural Industrialisation — Conclusion — Annexure-I — Annexure-II

CHAPTER 7 : ANCILLARY INDUSTRIES 71 - 76

Introduction — Conclusion

CHAPTER 8 : INDUSTRIAL ESTATE 77 - 86

Introduction — Software Technology Parks — Rural Industrial Estates — Lessons of Experience — Conclusion

CHAPTER 9 : ORGANISATIONAL STRUCTURE OF SMALL-SCALE INDUSTRIES 87 - 100

Introduction — A Preview of Tomorrow's Organisations — Conclusion

CHAPTER 10 : OWNERSHIP PATTERN IN SMALL-SCALE INDUSTRY 101 - 117

Introduction — Ownership of Organisation — Sole-proprietorship — Partnership Organisation — Joint-stock Companies — The Cooperative — Conclusion

CHAPTER 11 : FINANCE FOR SMALL-SCALE INDUSTRIES 118 - 142

Introduction — Means of Finance — Institutional Support Structure — Finance of Industrial Estate — FDI Not Enough — SMEs Deserve Better — Conclusion — Annexure-I

CHAPTER 12 : WORKING CAPITAL MANAGEMENT 143 - 165

Introduction — Composition of Working Capital — Factors Determining the Amount of Working Capital — Working Capital Finance and the Tandon Committee Uniform-Recommendations — Aligning Credit with Priority Industries — Norms for Inventory and Receivables — Term Loans to Small-scale Industries — Suggestion of Improving Facilities for Institutional Finance — Conclusion — Annexure-I

CHAPTER 13 : TAXATION BENEFITS 166 - 184

Introduction — Taxation Support for Small-scale Sector — Expenditure on Scientific Research — Small-scale Industries in Rural Areas — Guidelines for the Merger of Sick Units — Modvat and Small Industries — Conclusion

CHAPTER 14 : MARKETING MECHANISM IN SMALL-SCALE INDUSTRIES 185 - 207

Introduction — The Principal Marketing Functions — Supply-chain Management – Four Steps to Success — Conclusion

CHAPTER 15 : EXPORT POTENTIAL OF SMALL-SCALE INDUSTRIES 208 - 221

Introduction — Components of Exports — Infrastructural Set-up — Conclusion — Annexure-I

CHAPTER 16 : PROBLEMS OF SMALL-SCALE INDUSTRIES 222 - 234

Introduction — External vs. Internal Problems — Inspector Raj: The Great Survivor — The Management — Education — A Social Resource — Conclusion

CHAPTER 17 : PROSPECTS FOR SMALL-SCALE INDUSTRIES 235 - 249

Introduction — Well-designed Programme — Develop Capabilities — Recommendations of the Abid Hussain Committee — Prospects in the 21st century — Managing into the 21st Century: Fanning the Entrepreneurial Flame — Conclusion

SECTION-II : ENTREPRENEURSHIP – THE ROAD TO REAL INDIA 250 - 256

The Road to Real India — Credo on Entrepreneurs — Entrepreneurs Who Changed the Pace of Corporate India

CHAPTER 18 : THE CONCEPT OF ENTREPRENEURSHIP 257 - 277

Introduction — A Complex Phenomenon — The Six Pillars of Enterprise Governance — Fostering Entrepreneurship — Small-scale Industries as Seed-beds of Entrepreneurship — Conclusion

CHAPTER 19 : DEVELOPMENT OF ENTREPRENEURS 278 - 288

Introduction — The Entrepreneur: Other Definitions — Conclusion

CHAPTER 20 : EVALUATION OF ENTREPRENEURS IN INDIA 289 - 300

Introduction — An Analytical Perspective — The Emerging Models — Conclusion — Annexure-I — Annexure-II

CHAPTER 21 : CHARACTERISTICS OF ENTREPRENEURS 301 - 321

Introduction — Conclusion — Annexure-I — Annexure-II — Annexure-III — Annexure-IV

CHAPTER 22 : CLASSIFICATION AND TYPES OF ENTREPRENEURS 322 - 338

Introduction — Classification of Entrepreneurs — Information: Strategic Catalyst of Entrepreneurial Transformation — Conclusion

CHAPTER 23 : WOMEN ENTREPRENEURS 339 - 353

Introduction — Women of Substance — Women Entrepreneurs — Angels in Business — Conclusion

CHAPTER 24 : THE ROLE OF ENTREPRENEURS 354 - 373

Introduction — Entrepreneurial Qualities — Managers and Entrepreneurs — Conclusion

CHAPTER 25 : ENTREPRENERIAL ENVIRONMENT 374 - 386

Introduction — Private Enterprise and Development — Political Environment — Social Environment — Technological Environment — Legal Environment — Cultural Environment — The Green Arm of the Law — Conclusion

CHAPTER 26 : IDENTIFICATION OF OPPORTUNITIES 387 - 405

Introduction — An Illustration: Choice of a Product — Project Ideas – Scanning of Business Environs and Identifying a Project — Importance of Project Identification — Project Profile — Conclusion

CHAPTER 27 : CONVERTING BUSINESS OPPORTUNITIES INTO REALITY 406 - 434

Introduction — Selection of A Small-scale Industry — Conclusion — Annexure-I

CHAPTER 28 : LOCATION ISSUES 435 - 448

Introduction — Location — Selection of Most Economic Site — Factors Influencing the Location of Projects — Butibori – A New Industrial Area — Industrial Location Policy for BMR Modified — Conclusion — Annexure-I

CHAPTER 29 : ENVIRONMENTAL PROBLEMS 449 - 456

Introduction — Polluting Units — Conclusion

CHAPTER 30 : ENTREPRENEURIAL DEVELOPMENT 457 - 468

Introduction — Approaches to Entrepreneurship Development — Human Resources Development — Entrepreneurship Development Programme — Structuring Entrepreneurial Development Programmes — Conclusion

CHAPTER 31 : ENTREPRENEURIAL TRAINING 469 - 485

Introduction — What is Training? — Specialised Institutions: For Entrepreneurial Training — Financial and Technical Support Programmes for Entrepreneurship Development — Training Programme: Course Content and Curriculum — Conclusion

CHAPTER 32 : INSTITUTIONS IN AID OF ENTREPRENEURSHIP DEVELOPMENT 486 - 504

Introduction — Focus of EDPs — Entrepreneurship Development Programme Organisations — Management Development Institute (MDI) — The National Institute for Entrepreneurship and Small Business Development (NIESBUD) — Institutes for Entrepreneurship Development — Science and Technology Entrepreneurship Parks (STEPs) — EDPs of SIDBI — Role of NAYE (National Alliance of Young Entrepreneurs) — Conclusion — Annexure-I — Annexure-II — Annexure-III

CHAPTER 33 : ALL ABOUT RELEVANT ACTS 505 - 531

Introduction — Industrial Development (Regulation) Act (IDRA) — Factories Act, 1948 — Income-tax Act — The Industrial Employment (Standing Orders) Act, 1946 — The Indian Trade Union Act, 1926 — The Payment of Wages Act, 1936 — The Workmens Compensation Act, 1923 — The Employees State Insurance Act, 1948 — The Employees Provident Fund Act, 1952 — The Indian Boilers Act, 1923 — The Indian Electricity Act, 1910 — Intellectual Property Rights — Indian Patent Act, 1970 — Regulatory Laws for SSI Units — Conclusion — Annexure-I — Annexure-II — Annexure-III — Annexure-IV

SECTION-III : PROJECT WORK 532 - 566

The Case Study — The Scope of the Project Work — A New Case Studies

APPENDIX 567 - 570

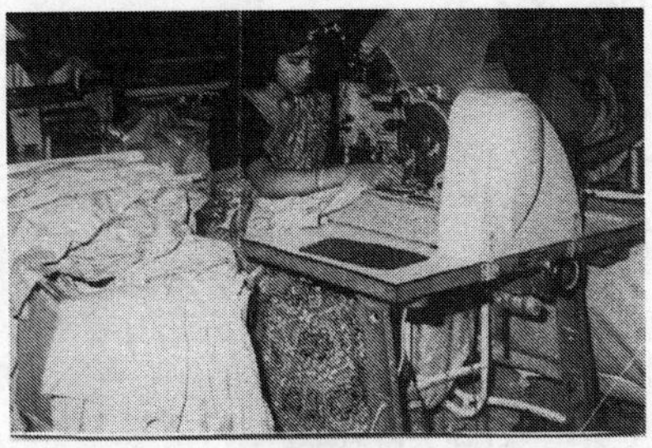

I SECTION

SMALL-SCALE INDUSTRY

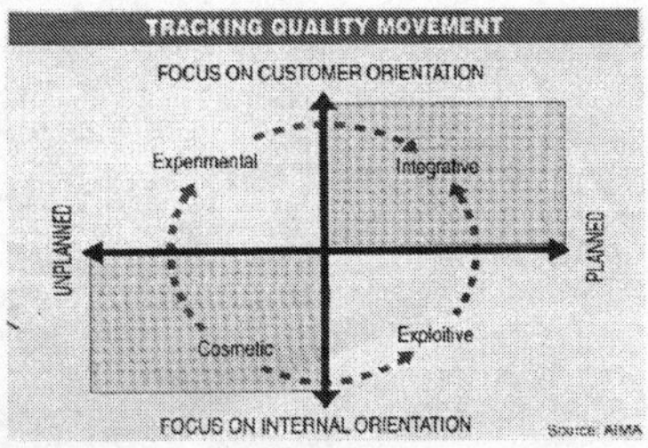

A rewarding feature of economic development in India has been the impressive growth of modern small-scale industries. The small enterprises have by now established their competence to manufacture a wide variety of sophisticated goods in different product-lines requiring a high degree of ski and precision. They have made a notable contribution in realising the principal objectives of expanded employment opportunities, adoption of modern techniques and dispersal of industries in small towns and rural areas. This has been possible as a result of the successful implementation of the programmes for assistance of small-scale industries. The diversified, rapid growth of these industries is a significant feature of India's economic development in recent years.

The small-scale industry has emerged as the most dynamic sector of the Indian industrial economy accounting for over 45 per cent of the total value of industrial production. Over 33 per cent of the country's exports and more importantly providing employment opportunities to over 322.28 lakh people in 133.68 lakh units have been the focus area of this sector. Further, MSME sector has consistently registered a higher growth rate than the rest of the industrial sector. There are over 6,000 products ranging from traditional to high-tech items, which are manufactured by the MSMEs in India. Added to in the MSMEs provide the maximum opportunities for self-employment and jobs after agriculture. All along, it has shown the growing spirit of entrepreneurship. Empirically, small-scale industries have contributed over 200 lakh entrepreneurs. If we add, entrepreneurs from small businesses, the growth of entrepreneurs increases manifold. Thus, small business is the seed bed for entrepreneurship. What is true of these entrepreneurs is that they continue to strive to excel in their fields. They have been learning failures, which do not dampen their spirits. Instead in their characteristic fashion, these enterprising businessmen/ businesswomen have swept them aside to continue on the winning track. Many have grown big. In other words, small business is the open university for entrepreneurs to translate their vision, innovative ideas into a reality and stand out distinctively in the society. In the process, they not only produce wealth, service but also create employment opportunities to others. Small business is thus the seed of entrepreneurial dreams. Today, the entrepreneur remains the backbone of society, to be more specific, economic society.

Some Key Parameters of Enterprises

S. No.	Parameters	Tiny	Small	Medium	Large
1.	Investment in Plant and Machinery	Up to ₹ 25 lakh	Up to ₹ 100 lakh to ₹ 300 lakh	Up to ₹ 5 crore	Above ₹ 5 crore
2.	Employment	Lesss than 5	Less than 100	Less than 200	Above 500 200
3.	Production	Tiny	Small	Medium	Large
4.	Technology	Nil	Low	Medium	High
5.	Brands		Nil	Rarely Few	Good
6.	Organisation	Proprietary partnership	Proprietary Pvt. Ltd. Cos.	Partnership	Public Limited
7.	Management	Direct	Direct	Professional	Organised
8.	Gestation	Nil	Short	Medium	Long
9.	Human Resources Development	Nil	Nil	Fair	Good
10.	Profits	Low	Good	V.Good	Huge

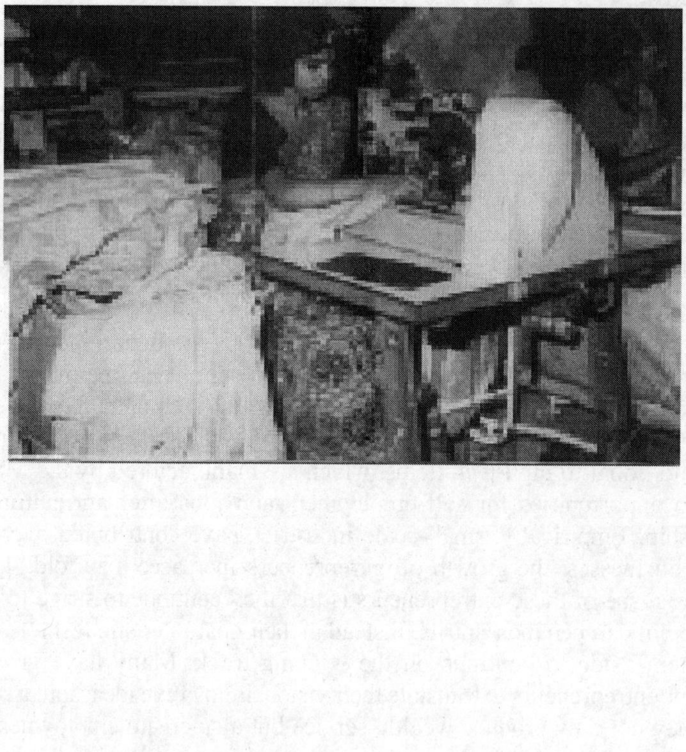

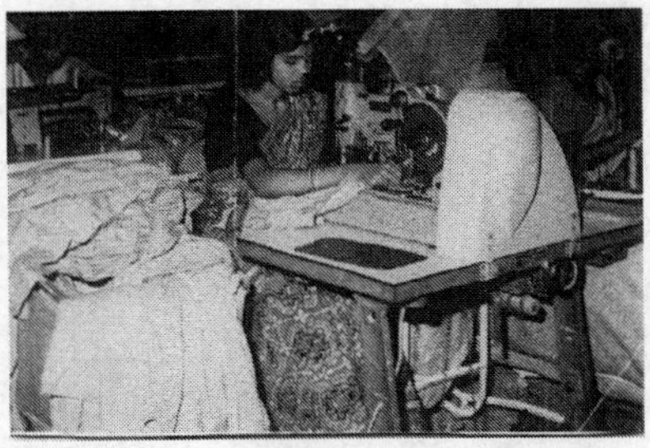

1 CHAPTER INTRODUCTION

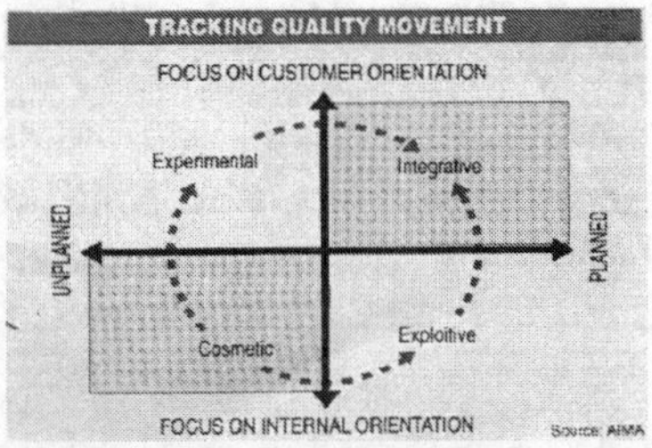

The success of a company is defined not just by the bottom line of its balance sheet, but also by its contribution to nation-building.

LEARNING OBJECTIVES

- To provide exposure to the students, teachers and entrepreneurs to the entrepreneurial culture and at the same give insight into rich material in the book, so as to awaken the entrepreneurial traits.
- In introduction one sets an insight of the rich entrepreneurial culture.
- Growth is lifeblood of entrepreneurs.
- Role of entrepreneur in an innovative economy.
- Core competitiveness.
- Education and managing change.
- Fostering entrepreneurship.
- Small- and medium-scale industries (SMIs) can contribute significantly to social and economic development objectives such as labour absorption, income distribution, rural development, poverty eradication, and regional balance. The objectives of the study were to review the performance of the SMI sector, analyse the constraints confronting the sector, examine the strengths and weaknesses of SMI support schemes and policies, and identify appropriate strategies for promoting SMIs.

The small-scale sector, the world over, is playing a vital role in the growth of the national economies. Small and Medium Enterprises (SMIs) have been rightly considered as the engine of growth in most countries. They enhance balanced regional industrial development; and they act as a nursery for entrepreneurship.

As we venture further into the 21st century, many of the rules that have guided business decisions and actions are history – ancient history – when measured in internet time. Electronic business is upsetting established companies and channels and creating new ones. Industries are consolidating with mega mergers across national boundaries. And the globalisation of information and currency markets is making national economies and worldwide industries increasingly – and almost instantly – interdependent. Understanding and responding to this kind of dramatic 'discontinuous' change is crucial to the success of business and government in the coming years.

But something equally important is being lost in the midst of such intense focus on the accelerating pace of change at the start of the new millennium. We need to rediscover the principles and values that stand the test of time.

GROWTH IS LIFEBLOOD OF SMALL-SCALE INDUSTRIES AND ENTREPRENEUR

The key to creating and sustaining business growth is to combine distinctive insight and foresight into developing our markets and meeting the evolving needs of our consumers. We do this by creatively applying technology and knowledge that push the boundaries of the possible. Applying state-of-the-art technology to create and deliver value-for-money products to consumers, will be the key to unlocking this market potential. Delivering value for money will also require a cost-effective chain.

Everyone is talking of the challenges and opportunities of the new millennium that is upon us but if one were to look at the events of the last decade of the twentieth century, one could almost believe that the new millennium for India began in 1991. Since those momentous days when the government took the most radical steps in over four decades to loosen the economy and create the condition for competition and allow global influences to wash over shores, we have not looked back. The pages of the financial media offer the reader exciting glimpses of the new world that the Indian economy, or at least the organised urban part of it, is carving out of the opportunities that economic reforms throwing up.

Basically, therefore, a new ethos is emerging. In India companies can grow large, afford to pay globally competitive incomes and also create wealth for the shareholders and the nation of an unprecedented kind. The ethos should be enough to bring the best talent back home. Government need not appeal to patriotism other emotional factors to reserve the brain-drain. The marketplace is doing the job wonderfully.

GROWING AN ENTREPRENEURIAL ECONOMIC

Starting a business requires courage even in the best of times; courage to take the risk of putting your own money into an idea; courage to take on the competition and courage to take a leap into an unknown future. Throughout the world, millions of entrepreneurs display such courage as they create new business. This creative process is the lifeblood of the strong private sectors that drive growth and propel nations forward.

How can policymakers ensure that entrepreneurship thrives in their countries? Their first effort must be to establish an environment in which entrepreneurship can flourish. Secondly, they must instill the values of entrepreneurship in future generations through sound educational policies and programmes.

Experience has shown that nations that support their courageous entrepreneurs have grown and prospered over the last 30 years, while nations that have placed barriers to the growth of their small business enterprises have been rated low on the performance graph. Even among countries that previously discouraged or prohibited such activity in favour of the government as the driving force for economic growth, there is now growing recognition of the importance of fostering entrepreneurial activity.

Professor Alan Gibb, Chairman of the Small Business Centre at Durham University, Business School in the United Kingdom describes the need for entrepreneurship education:

> *While the word 'Entrepreneurship' is ambiguous enough to embrace industry, business management, and new venture creation as well as the development of personal and social skills, there is increasingly more precise emphasis upon entrepreneurship. This seems to be in recognition of the need for societies, organisations and individual citizen to develop the capacity to enjoy and cope with an increasingly competitive, uncertain and complex world involving higher rates of innovation and change.*

Government play its most important role in helping its entrepreneurs blaze a trail of prosperity by implementing policies that create a business-friendly environment. These conditions must be in place before sustained growth and progress can be achieved.

What are the right elements? The answer, of course, will not be exactly the same for every country, but there are some basic principles that serve as a framework. Policymakers should focus their efforts on three key areas:

1. A market-oriented environment
   (i) Private property rights
   (ii) Legal system, and
   (iii) Government administration.
2. Business training, and
3. Finance and credit assistance.

The empirical studies show that entrepreneurship thrives under conditions where people participate and compete in the marketplace under conditions of equality and are not unduly burdened by regulation. Under such an environment entrepreneurs can apply the creative process that drives economic growth and propels their country forward.

In the process of industrial development especially in small business, the entrepreneurship has acquired special significance in the context of economic growth in a rapidly changing socio-economic and socio-cultural climates, both in developed and developing countries. The experience in the industrialised countries like the United States of America, Germany, Japan and the United Kingdom are authoritatively cited in support of this claim. An indepth study of the subject thus becomes not only relevant but also necessary.

The Importance of an Entrepreneur

An entrepreneur is one of the important segments of economic growth. Basically, an entrepreneur is a person who is responsible for setting up a business or an enterprise. In fact, he is one who has the initiative, skill for innovation and who looks for high achievements. He is a catalytic agent of change and works for the good of the people. He puts up new greenfield projects that actually creates wealth, opens up employment opportunities and fosters other sectors.

An entrepreneur is one of the most important inputs in the economic development of a country or of regions within the country. Entrepreneurial competence makes all the difference in the rate of economic growth. In India, state and private entrepreneurship coexists. The small-scale industrial sector and business are left completely to private entrepreneurs. It is, therefore, in this context that an increasingly important role has been assigned to the identification and promotion of entrepreneurs for this sector.

The Need

The need for a broad-based entrepreneurial class in India arises from the need to speed up the process of activating the factors of production, leading to a higher rate of economic growth, dispersal of economic activities, development of backward and tribal areas, creation of employment opportunities, improvement in the standard of living of the weaker sections and involvement of all sections of the society in the process of growth.

Several factors go into making of an entrepreneur. Individuals who initiate, establish, maintain and expand new enterprises constitute the entrepreneurial class. The socio-political and economic conditions, the availability of industrial technology and know-how, state-of-the-art and culture of business and trading, existence of markets for products and services and the incentives and facilities available for starting an industry or business, all have a bearing on the growth of entrepreneurship. A conducive environment is created through the policies and interest of the government in economic and industrial development.

Who is an Entrepreneur?

The entrepreneur brings in overall change through innovation for the maximum social good. Human values remain sacred which inspire him to serve the society. He has firm belief in social betterment and he carries out this responsibility with conviction. In the process, he accelerates personal, economic as well as human development. The entrepreneur is a visionary and an integrated man with outstanding leadership qualities. With a desire to excel, he gives top priority to research and development. He always works for the well-being of the society. More importantly, entrepreneurial activities encompass all fields/sectors and fosters a spirit of enterprise for the welfare of mankind.

Entrepreneur is one of the most important inputs in the economic development of a country or of regions within the country. Entrepreneurial competence makes all the difference in the rates of economic growth. In India, state and private entrepreneurship coexist. The small-scale industrial sector and business are left completely to private entrepreneurs. It is, therefore, in his context that an increasingly important role has been assigned to the identification and promotion of entrepreneurs for this potential sector.

Basic Qualities

An entrepreneur who has a high level of administrative capability, flair and ability for decision-making, computational skills, those pertaining to an organisation and delegation with sound technical knowledge and strategic communication stands a much better chance of success than his counterpart who possesses none of these basic qualities. It is the possession of these qualities which confers an advantage on some people in becoming an entrepreneur. Besides these qualities, however, the entrepreneur also needs either to be himself a generalist so that he can discharge his function without delegation, or to possess the skills mentioned above.

Technocrat Entrepreneur

Here is a case of a technocrat entrepreneur, who took to jobbing through a mechanical workshop. Mr. Saha is one of the first technocrats who was assisted by a bank under its special scheme. He is highly qualified mechanical engineer, with postgraduate degrees and diplomas in industrial management and industrial engineering from some leading universities of the world, including the famous MIT. He also has had considerable amount of practical experience in leading companies in the United States, Britain, and India. At the time he approached the bank for assistance to start his own industry, he was drawing a salary of about ₹ 2,500 per month. Quite an impressive background indeed.

The project submitted by Mr. Saha envisaged the manufacture of a stationary item – staple removers and job work on ancillary items and precision turned and pressed parts. The machinery required by him was: a power press, an automat and tool room equipment, i.e., a lathe, a milling machine, a shaping machine, a bench grinder, etc. The project was estimated to cost asunder:

		₹
Plant and machinery		1,36,000
Working capital		56,000
Deposit for shed		10,000
	Total	**2,02,000**

Of this amount, the borrower offered to bring in ₹ 10,000. The bank sanctioned the remaining amount by way of:

		₹
Loan against hypothecation of Machinery		1,36,000
Cash credit against hypothecation of stock		30,000
Clean loan		26,000
	Total	**1,92,000**

The entrepreneur anticipated an annual sales of ₹ 4.72 lakh with a pretax profit of ₹ 83,000.

Small-scale Industries

Small-scale industries play a key role in the industrialisation of a developing country. This is because they provide immediate large-scale employment and have a comparatively higher labour-capital ratio; they need a shorter gestation period and relatively smaller markets to be eonomic; they need lower investments, offer a method of ensuring a more equitable distribution of national income and facilitate an effective mobilisation of resources of capital and skill which might other wise remain unutilised; and they stimulate the growth of industrial entrepreneurship and promote a more diffused pattern of ownership location.

Box 1.1 Small Industry Clusters in India

India is a nation on the move. Its liberalised and open economic policies have shown results. New avenues have opened up for business activity, there is an aroma of all-round professionalism in the air. And the world is taking notice.

In this progressive economic scenario, one sector that has emerged as the most happening, is the small-scale sector.

It is here that the SSI sector has dared to dream. With a vision to foster the growth of the small-scale sector resulting in sustained employment generation, accelerated economic growth and in fact, to act as a nursery for entrepreneurial development.

As a result of these initiatives, the SSI sector has leapfrogged like never before.

- An average growth of 7.4% by SSI sector in comparison to 4.7% of industry in general.
- Employment generation for over lakh persons every year.
- 95% of India's industrial unit IN SSI sector with 40% value addition in the manufacturing sector.
- SSI share in total exports is around 35%.
- SSI contributes 6.29% to GDP.

The small-scale sector has stimulated economic activity of a far reaching magnitude and has played a significant role for attaining the following major objectives:

Elimination of economic backwardness of rural and underdeveloped regions in the country.

Attainment of self-reliance.

Reduction of regional imbalances.

Reduction of disparities in income, wealth and consumption.

Mobilisation of resources of capital and skills and their optimum utilisation.

Creation of greater employment opportunities and increased output, income and standard of living.

Meeting a substantial part of the economy's requirements for consumer goods and simple producer goods.

Provide employment and a steady source of income to the low-income groups living in rural and urban areas of the country.

Provide substitutes for various industrial products now being imported into the country, and

Improve the quality of industrial products manufactured in the cottage industry sector and to enhance both production and exports.

The development of these industries would be beneficial to the developing countries and assist them in improving their economic and social well-being. This would create greater employment opportunities and assist in entrepreneurship and skills development, and ensure better use of the scarce financial resources and appropriate technology.

India is ranked among the ten most industrialised countries in the world. The country has derived its economic strength from the growth of small industries (excluding powerlooms and handlooms) throughout its length and breadth. The pivotal role the small industries play in the economy of India can be judged by looking at the statistical data: more than 55 per cent of the total production in India today is from small-scale sector.

Core Competitiveness

The liberalisation process in India is at a very interesting stage at the moment; there is an enormous growth in the country, yet the full force of global competition is still not being felt. Many shackles of the old licence raj have been removed. And there is tremendous consumer demand. These three forces together make a recipe for extraordinary growth. But the question is whether this growth can be sustained when competition in India has changed significantly. It is not business as usual.

In the changed scenario, Indian entrepreneur/intrapreneur will be required to have an analytical orientation along with a commitment to introspection and self-development, and enforce learning through uncomfortable situations.

An entrepreneur's task will include:

Exploiting opportunities that are increasingly becoming global

Customising at low cost

Learning to manage and work in highly volatile environments, political and otherwise, and to scale down or scale up operations, according to the need

Learning to become part of the globals intellectual chain

Being less dependent on governments, the role of which is increasingly being challenged in every sphere

Realising that a job is no longer an entitlement or a right

Being able to convert data into knowledge

Looking at strategy as a resource mobilisation and resource leverage

Developing capacity for knowledge in action, and

Developing education, particularly management education, for a framework for sustaining change.

The alternative is downsizing or restructuring – five years later.

Education and Managing Change

Education is the cheapest, the best and the least threatening way of providing a framework that makes people reflect deeply on how they run a business and, at least intellectually, accept the need for change. There are different kinds of education — one that provides new information and another that teaches new skills. But large-scale transformation necessitates a new set of values, and new standards of behaviour, which are the most difficult to achieve.

Managers need new information and skills to develop a new point of view on how the world works. Management, in future, is going to demand fairly sophisticated technical knowledge. Businesses are getting to be more sophisticated technically, and those without proper training are going to find it difficult to understand the nuances of the business. The perfect knowledge base for a manager is his capacity to learn, but not any substantive knowledge.

Prospects

Employment generation, dispersal of industries in rural and semi-urban areas, utilisation of local resources and skills and development and widening of entrepreneurial base figure prominently in our Plan priorities. Similarly, maximisation of exports has assumed added importance in the context of current balance of payments position. The prospects for export of non-traditional items such as ready-made garments, leather and marine products, processed foods, plastics and engineering goods, etc., have improved. The growing dependence of large and medium industries on the small-scale sector for meeting their requirements of parts, components and intermediaries coupled with the policy of achieving higher level of indigenisation of items hither to imported, has created a more congenial climate for the repaid growth of the SSI sector. Further, the Government of India has recently modified the definition of small-scale and ancillary units and raised the ceilings on investment from ₹ 35 lakh to ₹ 60 lakh for small-scale units, which can go up to ₹ 75 lakh in the case of export-oriented units committing to export 30% of their production from third year onwards, and from ₹ 45 lakh to ₹ 75 lakh in the case of ancillary units. This revision will facilitate modernisation and technology upgradation of the SSI units. In this scenario, the small-scale sector will have greater opportunities for playing a more active and diversified role.

Fostering Entrepreneurship

Entrepreneurial development is a subject that has assumed great importance and is bound to be one of the dominant topics of discussion during the decades to come. This is and it should be in the context of rapid industrialisation in India. But to create an atmosphere of spontaneous will to cooperate is not all that easy. Resistance to change can be resolved by involving people in the process. The remedy lies in fostering an entrepreneurial spirit among the people.

An entrepreneur is one of the most important as well as significant inputs in the economic development of a country or of a region within a country. Entrepreneur competence makes all the difference to the rate of economic growth. The need for a broad-based entrepreneurial class in India arises from the need to speed up the process of activating the factors of production, dispersal of economic activites, creating employment opportunities – all of which are capable of leading to a higher rate of economic growth. It is now well recognised that entrepreneurs can be developed through appropriatly designed entrepreneurship development programmes. Entrepreneurial management requires policies, programmes and practise in major areas of development on a sustained basis. The entrepreneur and entrepreneurship are the catalystic agents of development and change.

The Future is Small

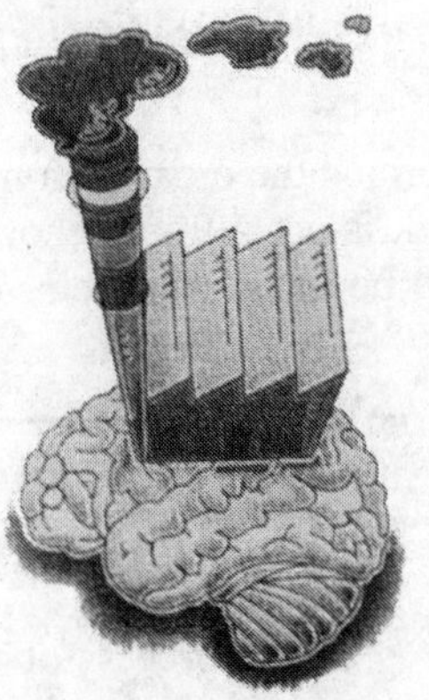

The process of globalisation has not only introduced new dynamism, opened up new opportunities, as well as has changed the business environment fundamentally in four ways. One, it has broken down barriers by connecting people across the world. Two, it has created information equality. Third, it has created a medium for a type of industry to expand globally with a speed and at costs inconceivable only a few years ago (and that type of industry is based on ideas – and not iron and steel of the early 20th century corporation). Finally, information technology has opened up revolutionary ways of understanding, interacting, and servicing the customer.

So, the successful organisation of the future will be one that is able to make the most of the new opportunities that technology offers; reconfigure itself quickly enough in response to market turbulence. Those could also be the so-called old economy companies, but chances are slim. Just like unprecedented wealth creation by industries lured labour into the industrial economy, the technology age will draw talent away from old economy. Not incidentally, the contribution of *fortune 500* companies to the American GDP has been declining over the past 30 years.

To capitalise on the opportunities of the new economy, organisations would need to be configured differently. They will be smaller, have smaller workforces and lifespans. Since their raw material will be ideas floating anywhere in the world, their core activity will involve identifying and implementing them. To facilitate sourcing of ideas, the 21st century corporation will build around itself a galaxy of satellite firms. Teams will consist of highly skilled people, and be deployed project-to-project. New companies will be incubated within the organisation and spun off later to realise wealth for its creators.

Outsourcing will become the norm. Already, companies have started farming out routine tasks like accounting, IT maintenance, and housekeeping. Tomorrow, the list could include activities such as manufacturing, servicing, and even selling. The corporate core would confine itself to research and development, branding, marketing, finance, and people management. The middle management would have almost completely disappeared. Management thinker, Peter Drucker, goes as far as to say that profit-making will not be the organisation's main goal anymore. Rather, it will be to create wealth for the society.

Trends Driving the Changes

The 21st century is a time of great change, growth and learning.

Bill Gates predicts that by 2050, half of the working population would be working from home. I see four trends driving the changes:

Telecommunications and computers will increasingly enable people – including farmers, fishermen, and small traders – to change the way they work. As the use of technology spreads, many more will do so.

Getting financed will be easier for small enterprises. Many banks recognise the opportunities for micro-lending. Therefore, many more smaller ventures will be born.

There will be increased participation in decision-making at the grassroot levels. Not only will this be propelled by the first two trends, but it will also be reinforced by the belief that empowerment will improve productivity.

The fourth is downsizing of large enterprises, which will result in the growth of small enterprises and solo workers.

Putting all this together, I see three kinds of workplaces in which the majority of people will work 25 years into the future. The first is small enterprises in both rural and urban settings. In many of these enterprises, the members will not work on the premises. They will, like the *dabbawallahs* of Mumbai, be out in the streets or, like the members of milk cooperatives, on their farms. There will be at least three significant changes in the way such enterprises will operate: One, much large numbers of women will participate in them. Two, computers and communication technologies will play an important role in their operations. And, there the governance systems in these enterprises will be participatory: there may be one owner, or many owners, but the workers will be involved in many decisions.

The second important workplace will be the home. More housewives will get involved with ways to supplement the family income, and many more people will choose to or be compelled to break out in their own. Most of these people will create work spaces in their homes to carry out their work efficiently.

This inexorable trend towards smaller, and even one-person organisations, will create a need for these micro-enterprises to network with each other. Some of this networking will take place over telephones and computers. But I imagine that a lot of it will have to be done face-to-face periodically. Therefore, another important workplace will be spaces in which meetings and workshops will take place.

Organisation change with their environment. The rise of the knowledge-entrepreneur has transformed the organisation's character. Equality is assured, wealth is shared, ideation is not just encouraged but required, and work is not a 9 to 5 chore, but a microcosm of entrepreneurship. Transnational competition is also forcing Indian businesses to be more like them, in size, systems, reach, innovation and people practices.

CONCLUSION

The small-scale industrial sector and related businesses are left completely to private entrepreneurs. It is, therefore, in this context that an increasingly important role has been assigned to the identification and promotion of entrepreneurs for this sector.

The need for the broad-based entrepreneurial class in India arises from the need to speed up the process of activating the factors of production, leading to a higher rate of economic growth, dispersal of economic activities, development of backward and tribal areas, creation of employment opportunities, improvement in the standard of living of the weaker sections of the society and involvement of all sections of the society in the process of growth.

Several factors go into the making of an entrepreneur. Individual who initiate establish, maintain and expand new enterprises constitute the entrepreneurial class. The socio-political and economic conditions, the availability of industrial technology and know-how, state-of-the-art and culture of business and trading, existence of markets for products and services and the incentives and facilities available for starting an industry or business, all have a bearing on the growth of entrepreneurship. A conducive environment is created through the policies and interest of the government in economic and industrial development.

All in all, small-scale industries is the beehive of entrepreneurship, innovation, and development. Both are interlinked, as well as foster integrated development. Small-scale industries and entrepreneurship are the two faces of the same coin, i.e., *industrial development.*

Challenging the Status Quo

"Leaders challenge the *status quo*. They constantly ask questions: "Is this good engough? Is there something better we should — or could — be doing?" In fact, one hallmark of a leader is that he or she as never satisified with the *status quo*. They believe that continuous learning and improvement are a critical part of a dynamic equation."

— ***Ned Barnholt, Chairman, Agilent***

Smooth Transition

"Most corporations take 'Six Sigma' naturally through its phases. They often start it as a quality improvement tool. Then, after a few years of using it for cost reduction, they start to see it as a tool for value-creation, It's a very natural process of unfolding as a company starts to use it."

— ***Mikei Harry, Architect of Six Sigma Initiative***

Dynamics of Change

"It is important for everyone in the company to understand that change is possible; there is an understandable process that exits to achieve it and everybody thinks enough of your role in the change process to come and talk directly with you."

— James Kits, CEO, Gillette

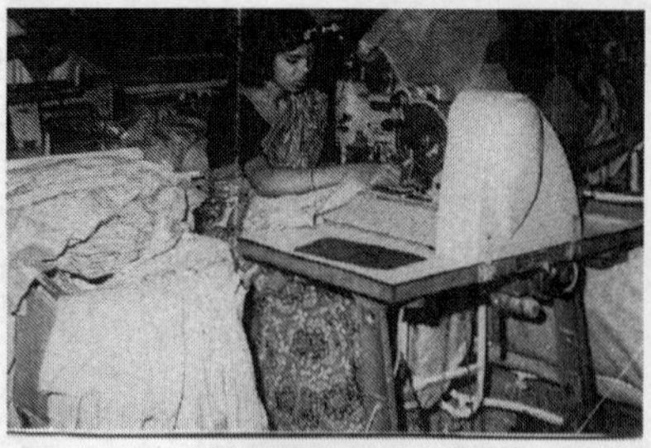

2 CHAPTER

THE CONCEPT OF SMALL-SCALE INDUSTRIES

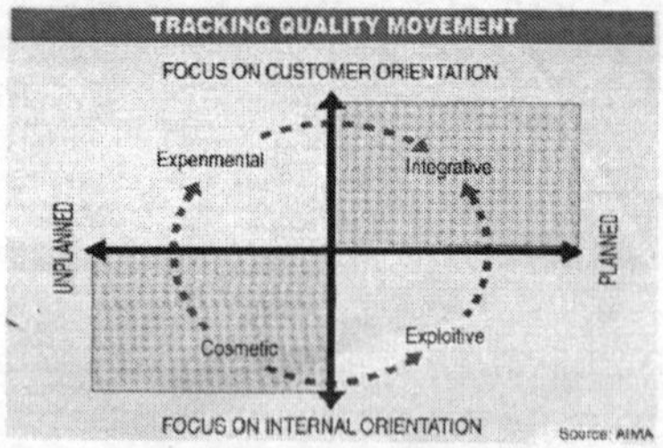

"Indian economy has been undergoing a transition phase and all the related sectors of the economy were witnessing the challenges of change in the liberalised era.In this backdrop the biggest challenge for SSIs in the emerging market scenario is to fully exploit the benefits of their product and process innovation capabilities on sustainable basis. WTO norms in areas such as safety, environment, labour and patenting are also assuming great importance."

LEARNING OBJECTIVES

- To provide exposure to the concept of small-scale industry so as to understand its significance in the Indian economy.
- The study encompasses a wide range of associated subjects, such as:
- Scope, product range, classification, and composition.
- Small-scale vs. Ancillary industries.
- Legal framework and planned promotion.
- The development of modern small-scale industries has been one of the most significant and characteristic features of industrial development in India.
- A thrust and directive has accordingly been given to the development of these industries by providing suitable policy framework supported by institutional arrangements and extension services throughout the country.

INTRODUCTION

More recently, enhancing small-scale industries has been viewed as an effective way of fostering the private sector's contribution to both growth and equity objectives of development.

Small-scale industries play a key role in the industrialisation of a developing country. This is because they provide immediate large-scale employment and have a comparatively higher labour-capital ratio: they need a shorter gestation period and relatively smaller markets to be economic; they need lower investments, offer a method of ensuring a more equitable distribution of national income and facilitate an effective mobilisation of resources of capital and skill which might otherwise remain unutilised; and they stimulate the growth of industrial entrepreneurship and promote a more diffused pattern of ownership and location.

The Meaning of Small

Use of 'Small' as a designation in the industry differentiates one set of industries from others. Comparatively its small in operation, employment, products, capital, technology, etc. Thus, this small sector share unique problems compared to others. In the case of manufacturing units, small industries are to be expected to have a unique set of problems in relation to their 'smallness' that differentiates them from medium and large manufacturing units. At the same time, the small sector has unique advantages. And, as such, *small* is not only beautiful, but also beneficial, efficient and reliable.

Definition of Micro, Small and Medium Enterprises in India:

There was a longstanding demand from entrepreneurs, small industry associations and related stakeholders for a single comprehensive legislation. The "Micro, Small and Medium Enterprises Development (MSMED) Act, 2006" is the first Act for micro, small and medium enterprises which, *inter alia,* provides for establishment of a statutory National Board for micro, small and medium enterprises, filling of memoranda, measures for promotion, development and enhancement of competitiveness of micro, small and medium enterprises, credit facilities, procurement preference and provisions related to delayed payments to micro and small enterprises. The medium sector has been defined for the first time in India and micro enterprises have been defined for the first time in this Act.

Under the MSMED Act, 2006, the concept of 'Enterprises'. Enterprises have been classified broadly into two distinctive categories, namely enterprises engaged in the manufacture/production of goods pertaining to any industry; and enterprises have been defined in terms of investment in plant and machinery/equipment excluding land and buildings.

Micro, small and medium enterprises as per MSMED Act, 2006, are defined based on their investment in plant and machinery (for manufacturing enterprise) and on equipments for enterprises providing or rendering services. **The present ceilings on investment for enterprises to be classifed as micro, small and medium enterprises are as follows:**

Enterprises to be classified as micro, small amd medium enterprises are as follows:

Classification	Manufacturing Enterprises*	Service Enterprises**
Micro	₹ 2.5 million/₹ 25 lakh	₹ 1 million/₹ 10 lakh (US$ 20,000) (US$ 50,000)
Small	₹ 50 million/₹ 5 crore (US$ 1 million)	₹ 20 million/₹ 2 crore (US$ 0.4 million)
Medium	₹ 100 milllion/₹ 10 crore (US$ 2 million)	₹ 50 million/₹ 2 crore (US$ 1 million)

* Investment limit in plant and machinery

** Investment limit in equipments

*** ₹ 50 = 1 US$

The term *"village industries"* has been redefined in amended KVIC Act, 1956 as "any industry located in a rural area which produces any goods or renders any service with or without the use of power and in which the fixed capital investment per head of artisan or worker does not exceed ₹ one lakh (₹ one lakh and fifty thousand in case of village industry located in a hilly area) or such other sum as may, be notification in the Official Gazette, be specified from time-to-time by the Central Government".

Scope of Small Industry

The importance of small-scale enterprises is a global phenomenon encompassing both the developing and developed countries. *Norman McRae* (1979) predicts that the age of the mammoth corporation was over and the future lay with small, dynamic, efficient production groups that could respond quickly to customers' needs. Globally, the emphasis is on the small enterprises holding the key to growth with equity and proficiency.

In India, small industry refers to manufacturing activity. Recently, it has also come to include, to a limited extent, servicing activities such as repair and maintenance shops and few community services. It does not include wholesale and retail trading as is done in Japan or UK.

Table 2.1 Scope of Small Industry in Select Countries

Country	Terminology	Scope
Japan	Small Enterprise (wholesale and retail)	Manufacturing, mining, services, trading
India	Small-scale Industry (SSI)	Manufacturing, repair and maintenance
Korea	Small Enterprise	Manufacturing, mining, construction, commerce
USA/Canada	Small Business	Manufacturing, services, trading (limited)
UK	Small Firms	Manufacturing, commerce (both retail and wholesale), construction, mining, transport
Indonesia	Small Industry	Manufacturing services

As is clear from the above table, the scope of the small industry in India is rather narrow as compared to other countries like Japan, UK and the USA. The question is: Is the scope of activities in the right perspective?

Product Range

Manufacturing over 6,000 items involving very simple to highly sophisticated technologies and offering opportunities for the utilisation of local resources and skills, the sector has emerged as a major supplier of a variety of products for mass consumption as well as parts and components to the large industry sector. Apart from handicrafts and other traditional products, small-scale units manufacturing some of the high-value-added and sophisticated products like electronic typewriters, electronic survey equipments, security and fire alarm systems, television sets and other consumer durables. Many such products are used as original equipment items by the manufacturers in the large industry sector. The sector has the flexibility of responding to varied needs of the economy.

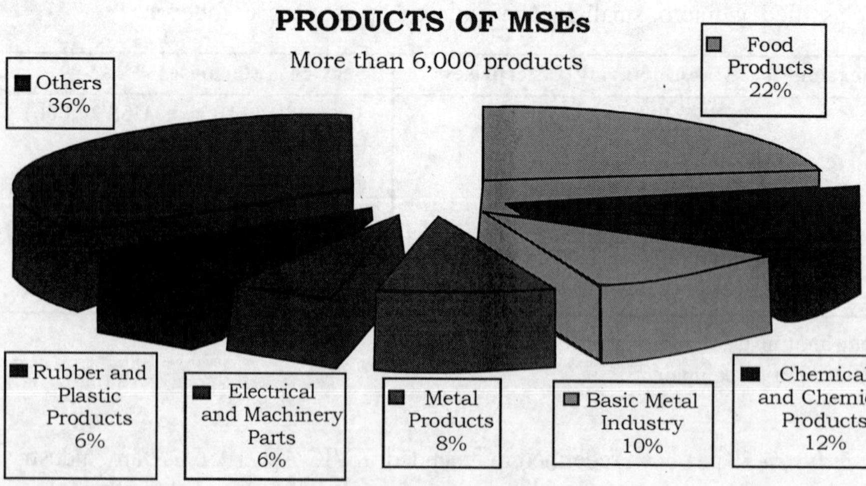

Sandwich Bottom Cookwares on Display

Display of Indian Merchandise for a Leading Departmental Store of France

The sector covers a wide spectrum with two clearly identifiable segments, viz., modern small-scale industries, including tiny units and powerlooms and traditional industries like khadi and village industries, handlooms, handicrafts, sericulture and the coir industry. Both the segments have their own special characteristics in terms of capital/labour intensity, locational orientation, manufacturing processes and skill requirements. Among the traditional industries, the share of the handloom subsector in employment is estimated at 125 lakh persons followed by handicrafts are 58 lakh persons. The handloom subsector which has a complement of 30 lakh looms and a workforce of 74 lakh in the weaving segment.

Classification

Small-scale industries are broadly classified into two sectors:

Traditional Industries

(1) Khadi and Village Industries (96)

(2) Handlooms,

(3) Handicrafts,

(4) Coir, and

(5) Sericulture

Manufacturing Sector Composition

In the Indian set up, the industry universe can be divided into various segments: factory sector (large-scale units – non-SSIs); factory sector (small-scale units), and the Village and Small Industries sector (VSI). As mentioned earlier, SSI units are defined on the basis of investment in plant and machinery with upper ceilings and no minimum investment is prescribed at the lower-end. The VSI sector covers a wide range of industries that differ from one another in terms of the nature of products manufactured, techniques used, scale of production, location and marketing, etc.

The VSI sector has further been divided into two broad subsectors, *viz.*:

Modern Small-scale Industries, and

Traditional Industries

SSIs (both in the factory/non-factory sectors) and powerloom units are covered under modern small-scale industries; while traditional industries include segments like handlooms, khadi and village industries, handicrafts, sericulture (silk) and coir. Traditional industries are generally artisan-based, located mostly in rural, semi-urban areas and have a nominal investment in plant and machinery. Modern SSIs are mostly those units that use power-driven machinery and possess better production

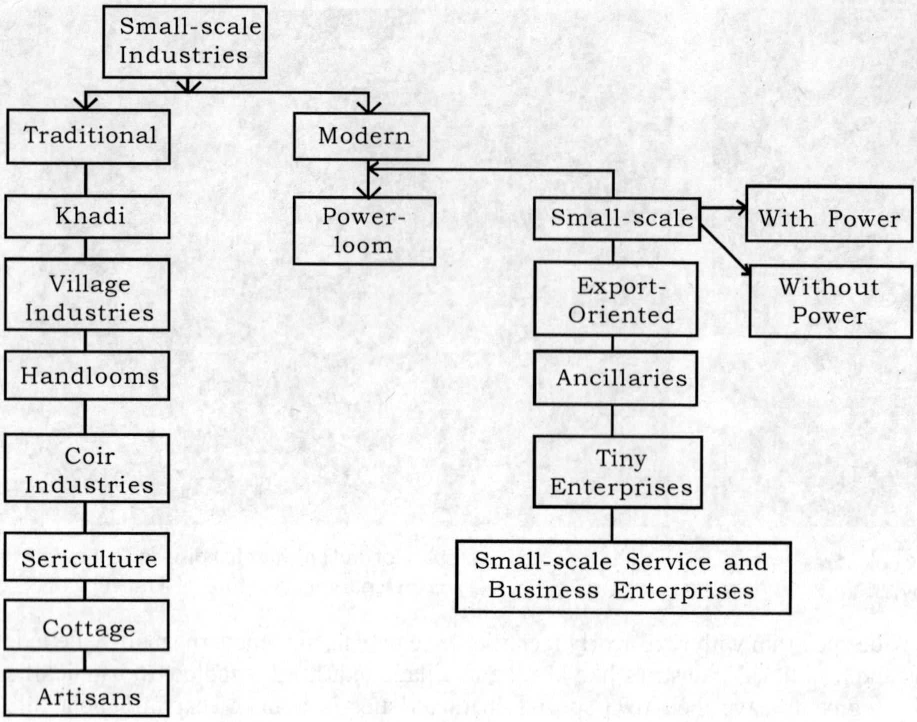

Fig. 2.1 Traditional Industries

techniques as compared to traditional sector units. These units are generally located in close proximity to large industrial centres or urban areas.

Furthermore, SSI units under SIDO comprise the residual industrial units that are not covered by any assistance programme of the sector-specific statutory bodies, namely, handicraft, handloom, sericulture and coir. However, some units under the Khadi and Village Industries Commission (KVIC) are registered with the State Directorate of Industries as SIDO units (as seen in the shaded portion in Fig. 2.2). Various segments of the industry universe and the corresponding data sources are also indicated.

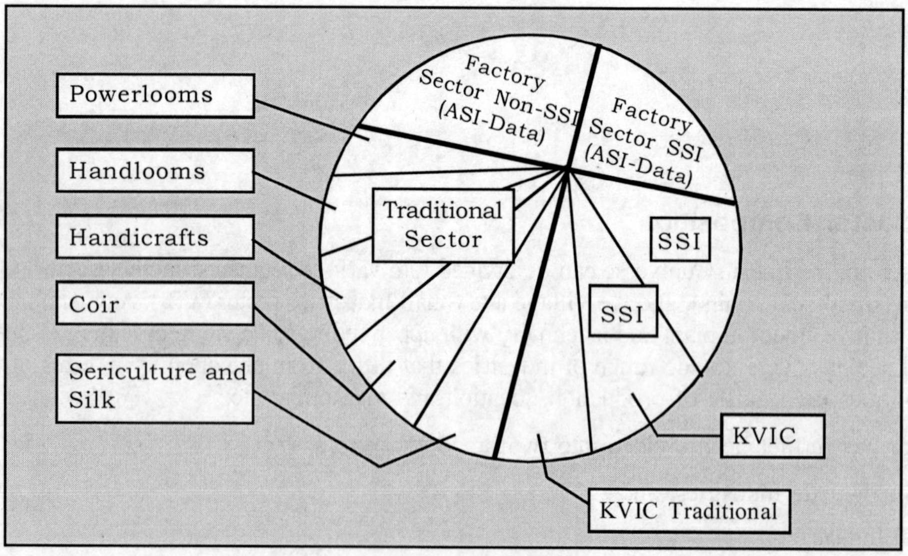

Fig. 2.2 Industry Universe Segments

SSI UNITS

(1) Small-scale industrial undertakings,
(2) Export-oriented SSI units,
(3) Ancillary industrial undertakings,
(4) Tiny enterprises,
(5) Small-scale Services and Business enterprises, and
(6) Powerlooms.

According to the second SSI Census, 50.2 per cent of the units were engaged in manufacturing assembly only. Of the total SSI units, 96.2 per cent were SSI units, 0.5 per cent were ancillary, 0.7 per cent were export-oriented and 2.5 per cent small service establishments.

Of the SSI units, 95.9 per cent units were tiny enterprises and 87.8 per cent units employed less than 10 workers.

The classification of the size, structure of manufacturing units in terms of the monetary value of paid-up capital or fixed assets or plant and machinery is problematic for a number of reasons including difficulties of measurement and poor data availability.

State-of-the-art Paper Machine in Operation

Smallness by itself does not identify any set of unique problems common to all small businesses. Instead, smallness identifies a hodgepodge of businesses ranging from family-owned neighbourhood stores to venture-capital-owned, innovative computer manufacturing firms. Identification of problems common to such widely differing business entities clearly is difficult. Policymakers have the choice either of becoming mired in a plethora of minute by prescribing policies for each retail store, service station, or computer manufacturing firm almost individually, or of seeking a new, more useful segmentation of the small industry sector that identifies common problems amenable to policy prescriptions.

Concept of Small Enterprises

Amber Charkha Kendra of Khadi and Village Industries Commission

The definition of small enterprises varies from one country to another. In most of the countries of the world, the criterion for defining a small enterprise is related to the size of employment. For instance, in the US, small business is one which has employment of less than 500 people. In UK, it is less than 20 skilled workers, in Germany less than 300 workers, in Sweden and Italy less that 50 and 500 people respectively. In some countries, both employment and investment are taken into account.

In Japan, the investment in industrial undertaking should not exceed 100 million employing not more than 300 employees. In South Korea, investment limit is 2 lakh dollars and employment limit being 200 people.

The definition of the small industry is an important aspect of the government policy as it identifies the target groups. The first official criterion for small-scale industry dates back to the Second Five Year Plan when it was in terms of gross investments in land, building, plant and machinery and the strength of the labour force. Subsequently, on the recommendation of the Federation of Association of Small Industries of India (FASII), an apex level organisation of the small-scale industry, was set up under the aegis of the Ford Foundation team, wherein, only the investment in fixed assets in plant and machinery, whether held in ownership terms or by lease or by hire purchase, instead of fixing the limit on overall investment, was considered for granting the status of a SSI unit. From time-to-time, there have been many changes in the ceiling limit of investment in plant and machinery. In the beginning, for a small-scale industry, the investment level was ₹ 5 lakh and employment limit of less than 50 persons when using power and less than 100 persons without using power.

The term 'small-scale industries' has been defined in three ways. The conventional definition includes cottage and handicraft industries which employ traditional labour-intensive methods to produce traditional products, largely in village households. They employ none or only a few hired hands. The handloom textile industry is an example. Though once famous, this sector has been steadily declining.

Different segments of SSIs have been defined asunder:

Ancillary Industrial Undertaking: An industrial undertaking which is engaged or is proposed to be engaged in the manufacture or production of parts, components, subassemblies, tooling or intermediates, or the rendering of services is termed as ancillary undertaking. The ancillary undertaking has to supply or render or propose to supply or render not less than 50 per cent of its production or services, as the case may be, to one or more other industrial undertakings. The investment in plant and machinery whether held in ownership terms or on lease or on hire purchase, should not exceed ₹ 30 million.

Tiny Enterprises: A unit is treated as tiny enterprise where investment in plant and machinery does not exceed ₹ 25 million, irrespective of the location of the unit.

Women Entrepreneurs' Enterprises: An SSI unit/industry related service or business enterprise, managed by one or more women entrepreneurs in proprietary concerns, or in which she/they individually or jointly have a share capital of not less than 51 per cent as partners/shareholders/directors of Private Ltd., company/members of cooperative society is treated as women entrepreneurs' enterprise.

Small-scale (industry-related) Service and Business Enterprises (SSSBEs): Enterprises rendering industry-related service/business with investment up to ₹ 0.5 million in fixed assets, excluding land and building, are called SSSBEs.

Export-oriented Units (EOU): A unit with an obligation to export at least 30 per cent of its annual production by the end of third year of commencement of production and having investment ceiling in fixed assets – plant and machinery – up to ₹ 30 million is regarded as an EOU.

The definition of SSI is linked to the question of ownership. SSI units cannot be controlled or owned or be a subsidiary of any other industrial undertaking. This implies that in proprietary/partnership firms, the combined investment of all the units set up by the same proprietor/partners should not exceed the total investment limit fixed for an SSI. As regards the formation of an SSIs as a limited company, the equity investment by other companies in SSIs should not exceed 24 per cent.

The objectives of such classificatory changes are aimed at:

Facilitating and boosting the growth of SSI in the private sector.

Promoting SSIs within the framework of the social and economic policy of the country.

Encouraging technology modernisation among existing units.

Aiding technically qualified entrepreneurs to set up new units with advanced technology.

Improving product standards.

Creating opportunities for in-house R&D.

Providing greater thrust to export.

Table 2.2 Comparative Standing Based on Quantitative and Qualitative Parameters

		Small-scale	Medium/Large	Public Sector
A.	**Quantitative**			
1.	Investment	Small	Medium to Large	Huge
2.	Capital Employed	Small	Medium to Large	Medium
3.	Turnover	Small	Good to Excellent	Fair to Good
4.	Profit	Small	Good	Poor
5.	Number of Employees	Small	Good	Large
B.	**Qualitative**			
1.	Technology Employed	Poor	Good	Medium
2.	Complexity of Organisation	Simple	Professional	Bureaucratic (Line Organisations) Core Sector

3.	Importance to the National Economy	Very Good	Good	
4.	Pay-scales	Poor	Good	Average
5.	Productivity	Poor	Average to Fair	Poor
6.	Quality	Poor	Average to Fair	Average

Table 2.3 Comparative Standing Average Per Unit

		Small	Medium	Large
		(₹ lakh)	(₹ crore)	
1.	Capital	0.16	0.96	27.50
2.	Net worth	0.20	1.35	109.05
3.	No. of Employees	6	490	2882
4.	Value of Output	7.38	8.60	313.88
5.	Annual Consumption of Raw Materials	5.50	5.44	149.10
6.	Gross Fixed Assets	1.59	3.37	249.61
7.	Investment in Plant and Machinery	0.60	2.38	175.19
8.	Long-term Borrowings	0.96	1.48	53.36
9.	Working Capital	1.23	1.82	31.19
10.	Profit after Tax	0.02	0.24	17.66

The operational definition for policy purposes includes all those undertaking having an investment in fixed assets in plant and machinery, whether held on ownership terms or by lease or by hire purchase, not exceeding ₹ 60 lakh. Both ancillary units and tiny units also come under the umbrella of small-scale industries. A tiny unit is one whose investment in fixed assets in plant and machinery does not exceed ₹ 5 lakh. An ancillary undertaking is one whose investment in plant and machinery does not exceed ₹ 75 lakh and is engaged in: (a) the manufacture of parts, components, subassemblies, toolings or intermediate, or (b) the rendering of services of supplying 1/3rd per cent of their total service or production, as the case may be, to other units for production of other articles. The operational definition is considered relevant for discussion in academic circles as well as policy decisions.

Table 2.4 Investment Ceiling in Plant and Machinery

(₹ Million)

Year	SSI		Ancillary	
	Nominal	Real*	Nominal	Real*
1966	0.75	0.95	1.00	1.26
1975	1.00	0.58	1.50	0.87
1980	2.00	0.85	2.50	1.05
1985	3.50	1.06	4.50	1.34
1991	6.00	1.18	7.50	1.48
1997	30.00	3.17	30.00	3.17
1998	10.00	1.13	30.00	3.28
1999	10.00	1.11	30.00	3.45
2000	10.00	1.34	30.00	3.55
2001	10.00	1.40	30.00	3.85
2002	10.00	1.41	30.00	4.00
2003	10.00	1.98	30.00	4.10

* The nominal asset value have been deflated by the wholesale price index (WPI) for machinery and transport equipment at 1970-71 prices.

(**Source:** Ministry of Industry, GoI.)

The third definition of small-scale industries relates to national income accounting. This includes all manufacturing and processing activities, including maintenance and repair services, undertaken by both household and non-household small-scale manufacturing units, which are not registered under the Factories Act.

Accordingly, a small industry is defined as 'a unit engaged in manufacturing, servicing, repairing, processing and preservation of goods having investment in plant and machinery, at an original cost not exceeding ₹ 5 crore'. On the other hand, an ancillary undertaking is defined as 'a unit having investment in fixed assets in plant and machinery not exceeding ₹ 7.5 crore and engaged in the manufacture of parts, components, subassemblies, tooling or intermediates or rendering of services and supplying or proposing to supply or render 50 per cent of their production of other articles, provided that no such undertaking shall be subsidiary of or owned or controlled by any other undertaking'.

The Government of India announced a new policy for small and micro sector and raised the investment limits to ₹ 25 lakh, irrespective of location of the unit.

The government has accepted the recommendation of the Abid Hussain Committee regarding enhancement in investment ceiling and raised the same for the small-scale sector.

The investment limit for the ancillary sector and for export-oriented units had been raised from ₹ 75 lakh to ₹ 3 crore.

The investment ceiling for the tiny sector had also been increased five-fold to ₹ 25 lakh from the prevailing ₹ 5 lakh.

The decision to enhance the investment limits after a revision in 1991, was taken for five reasons:

(i) the erosion of the rupees' value due to inflation,

(ii) devaluation,

(iii) the effect of foreign exchange fluctuation,

(iv) the increased international prices of capital goods, and

(v) the need to upgrade and modernise the technology base to keep it competitive.

For non-SSI units opting to manufacture items reserved for the small-scale sector, the export obligation has been reduced from 75% to 50%. Thus, non-SSI export units who were earlier allowed to sell only 25% of their produce in the domestic tariff area (DTA), will now be able to sell 50% of their produce.

The measures are expected to help the small-scale units expand, diversify, undertake technology upgradation and modernisation to remain competitive, while enabling them to avail special benefits. The sector could now grow vertically and compete successfully in the market with large units.

However, those who are opposed to increase in investment limits argue that by increasing the limit to ₹ 3 crore, the government is allowing backdoor entry to large and medium-scale companies in sectors reserved for small units.

To ensure that large units don't corner the available bank finance, it has been decided that out of the funds formally available to the SSI sector, 40% will be reserved for units with investment in plant and machinery up to ₹ 5 lakh, 20% for units with investment between ₹ 5 lakh and ₹ 25 lakh and the remaining 40% for other SSI units.

In fact, the restrictions on investment were proving as *disincentive* for growing units. The recommendations of the committee may enable to create a better environment for the small-scale sector to face the challenges with confidence and avail of new opportunties coming in their way.

SSI Investment Cap – Cut to ₹ 1 crore

The government has issued a notification, scaling down the investment limit in the fixed assets in the plant and machinery for small-scale/ancillary industrial undertaking, whether held on ownership terms or on leased or on hire purchase to ₹ 1 crore. However, the investment limit for tiny units will continue to be ₹ 25 lakh.

All these efforts are marginal and related to the money aspect of machinery and plant. The investment limits always overlooked very many investment aspects of small-scale enterprises.

SMEs in Other Countries

In India, there exists no definition of medium enterprises and as such, there is no specific definition for small and medium enterprises (SMEs). What prevails here, is only the concept of small-scale, ancillary and tiny industry which are related to the historical value of the investment in plant and machinery.

In other countries, SMEs are defined on the basis of both quantitative and qualitative elements, such as, the number of workers employed and/or annual turnover or the level of fixed investment. However, employment is an omnipresent criterion for determining the size of the unit in these countries. The prevailing definitions in some countries are listed in Table 2.5.

Table 2.5 Definition of SMEs in Asia and other Countries

Country	Category of Industry	Criteria/Country's Official Definition	Measure
North America USA	Very Small Enterprise, Small Enterprise,	<20 employees 20-99 employees 100-499 employees	Employment
Canada	Medium Enterprise	Independent firms having <200 employees	Employment
Latin America Mexico	Manufacturing Micro Small	<15 employees and gross income/sales <US $1,75,000 15-99 employees and gross income/sales <US $1,75,000	Employment and gross income/sales
	Medium	100-249 employees and gross income/sales <US $35,00,000	
Europe Belgium	SME	Annual staff average of 50 employees, annual turnover (VAT excluded) ECU-4.2 million, balance sheet total of ECU 2.1 million	Employment and annual turnover
Denmark	Manufacturing	<500 employees. Production units with more than 5 employees	Employment
France Germany Greece	SME SME Small Enterprises Medium Enterprises	10-499 employees <500 employees <50 employees 10-100 employees	Employment Employment Employment Employment
Ireland	SME	<500 employees	Employment
Italy Netherlands	Small Enterprises Small Enterprises Medium Enterprise	<200 employees <10 employees 10-100 employees	Employment Employment
Portugal	SME	<500 employees <Esc 2,400 million in sales (value for 1993) more than 50 per cent of any company (nor does it hold more than 50 per cent of any other company)	Employment and sales value is not controlled
Spain	Small Enterprises Medium Enterprises	<200 employees <500 employees	Employment Employment
Sweden	SME	Autonomous firms with <200 employees	Employment
Switzerland	SME	No fixed definition	
United Kingdom	SME	No fixed definition	
Asia China	SME	Depends on product group usually <100 employees: investment ceiling 30 million	Employment and investment Yuan (US $8 million)
Indonesia	SME	<100 employees	Employment
Japan	Manufacturing Wholesale Trade, Retail Trade and Services	<300 employees or asset capitalisation <100 million yen <50 employees or asset capitalisation <30 million yen <50 employees or asset capitalisation < 10 million yen	Employment and assets

Korea	Manufacturing Services	<300 employees <20 employees	Employment
Malaysia	SMIs	<75 full-time workers or with a shareholder fund of <RM 2.5 million (US $1 million)	Employment and
	SIS	Manufacturing establishments employing between 5 and 500 employees or with a shareholder fund up to RM 5,00,000.	shareholder fund
	MIS	Manufacturing establishments employing between 50 and 75 full-time employees or with shareholders' fund between RM 50,000 to RM 2.5 million	
Singapore	Manufacturing Services	<S $ 12 million fixed assets <100 employees	Fixed assets Employment
Taiwan	SMEs	In manufacturing, mining and construction-invested capital is <NT $40 million or regular employees to be <200	Employment or invested capital
	SSEs	In manufacturing and construction sales turnover <NT $120 million or regular 20	Employment or sales turnover
Thailand	Labour intensive sectors Capital intensive sectors	<200 employees <100 employees	Employment
Vietnam	SME	No fixed definition generally <200 employees	Employment
Brunei	SME	0-100 employees	Employment
Hong Kong	SME	Manufacturing enterprises with fewer than 100 employees and non-manufacturing enterprises with fewer than 50 employees	Employment
Australia	Manufacturing Services	Small enterprises <100 employees Medium enterprises <20 employees	Employment Employment

Sources:

1. Handbook on Foreign Direct Investment by Small and Medium-sized enterprises. Lessons from Asia, UNCTAD, Geneva, 1998.
2. Globalisation and Small and Medium Enterprises (SMEs)-Vol.I Synthesis Report OECD.
3. Industry Division, Government of Hong Kong, Special Administrative Region.
4. Small and Medium Business Administration, Government of Korea.

Legal Framework

Legal framework is an edifice to carry on the industrial activities in a systematic and satisfying manner, efficiently and fruitfully as far as possible. What is good to industries in general also hold good for small-scale industries, both modern as well as traditional:

The legal framework aims at promoting systematic and rapid development of small-scale industries and also helps in attaining certain socio-economic activities without disturbing the environment.

The legal framework stands in consonance with the aims and objective of the country's aims at attaining rapid growth in the small-scale sphere.

The small-scale sector in its broad perspective is governed by the following legislative measures (modified from time-to-time):

(1) The Companies Act, 1956;

(2) The Industries (Development and Regulation) Act, 1951;

(3) The Monopolies and Restrictive Trade Practices Act, 1969, and

(4) The Foreign Exchange Regulation Act, 1974.

However, an attempt is made in this chapter to trace the evolution of the legal concept of the modern small-scale industry and analyse the definition or the concept of small-scale industry. An attempt is also made to have a critical analysis of the legal framework of modern small enterprises so that an appropriate industrial environment is created, enabling the attainment of socio-economic objectives of India's Five Year Plans.

Empirical studies have shown that small-scale enterprises are an important vehicle for meeting the growth and equity with social justice objectives of developing economies. In the Indian context, they play a key role in the economic development of the country. What is more, they also act as a breeding ground for entrepreneurs. In the post-independence period, as many as 20 million entrepreneurs have established enterprises in this sector and contributed to the advancement of the industry in the country. More importantly, it is a stepping stone for entrepreneurs to grow from small to big. It provides inplant training to millions of entrepreneurs and motivates them to become innovative entrepreneurs to improve the economy. As such, development of small-scale industries should be given special attention.

Planned Promotion

Planned promotion of small industries with a comprehensive assistance programme is the basic postulate of the strategy of industrial growth in developing countries. Their governments, therefore, lay special emphasis on programmes for nurturing and nourishing small industries. In many countries, this has now become one of the basic tenets of economic policies. This should not, however, be construed as an unmistakable sign of the underdeveloped character of the national economies, because small industries have always existed in all countries – industrialised and industrialising – and in all economies – advanced as well as backward. A casual look at the composition of the industrial sector in any country is enough to prove the fact that a great majority of its industrial enterprises are concentrated in the small-scale sector. That is not without significance; because in the ultimate analysis, the small industry is really the mother of the large industry. This is very often forgotten, and mainly on account of the fact that it is the few giants that catch and hold the eye by virtue of their size. Again, the giants have the necessary means and resources to project images that cast long shadows on the entire industrial structure. We find such industrial giants in the advanced world. They are not only flourishing but are becoming super-giants through mergers and conglomerations. A discerning observer will not fail, however, to notice that this trend has not hindered the growth of small-scale industries. This too is in the nature of things, for the small-scale industry is not antithetical to large industry and the large industry is not and cannot be substitute for the small industry. Each sector has a distinctive field of its own and it is quite possible to demarcate these respective fields for further development. What is needed is strategic and intelligent planning.

CONCLUSION

Experience worldwide shows that the development of small-scale industries is one of the most cost-effective ways of creating employment, spreading the industry, catalysing research and development and allowing entrepreneurial talent to grow. As a corollary, many developing countries have encouraged small enterprises in the belief that they use more labour per unit of capital than large firms, use capital more productively and thus combine abundant labour with scarce capital more efficiently. But, however, there is no one definition of the small-scale industry. It varies from country-to-country. Even in India, the definition has moved from labour to capital. Yet, there exist four types of small-scale industries, namely, modern small-scale industry, cottage industry (tiny sector), village industry and ancillaries. Again, there are handlooms, powerlooms, khadi, handicrafts, etc. Another distinction is made of agro-industries and technology-oriented units.

Small labour-intensive industries have been favoured basically to create employment in an economy with abundant unskilled labour. In addition, a low capital requirement given an appropriate market environment, is believed to stimulate growth of numerous indigenous enterprises with wide regional dispersal. This helps promote balanced growth, more equitable distribution, promotion of national heritage, development of artistic tastes as well as diversification of the industrial structure which often leads to increased utilisation of national resources. The process also helps in developing entrepreneurial and managerial skills and boost capital formation. It also harmonises artistic talent with modern and efficient technology.

The modern small-scale industries, because of their cost-effective substitutability with and complementarity characteristic to large industries, are emerging as a dominant layer in the industrial development of the country. Advances in information technology have made it possible for small firms to gain access to global information and computer links across the globe. Technology transfer across the countries is sure to influence the small-scale sector in India, making them more cost and quality-conscious to withstand competition.

The current definition refers only to investment in plant and machinery and does not take into account the investment in land and building. This has been deliberately done, for land values so widely in the country that no meaningful figure can be given if the definition covers the value of land.

ANNEXURE-I

The definition of a small and medium enterprise varies from country-to-country

The EU's definition of SME is based on the number of people employed in the enterprise. A microenterprise has a headcount of less than 10, and a turnover or balance sheet total of not more than two million euros. A small enterprise has a headcount of less than 50, and a turnover of balance sheet total of not more than ten million euros. A medium-size enterprise has a headcount of less than 250 and a turnover of not more than fifty million euros or a balance sheet total of not more than forty-three million euros.

In UK, Sections 247 and 249 of the Companies Act, 1985, define an SME as a small company that has a turnover of not more than £5.6m, a balance sheet total of not more than £2.8 not more than 50 employees. A medium-size company has a turnover of not more than £22.8m, a balance sheet total of not more than £11.4m and not more than 250 employed. It is worthnoting that even within UK, this definition is not universally applied.

In the US, SME means an organisation of up to 1,500 employees and turnover of $0.75-29m, depending upon the type of business. In the US, a government department called the Small Business Administration (SBA) sets the definition of small business. The SBA uses the term "size standards" to indicate the largest a concern can be in order to still be considered a small business, and therefore able to benefit from small business targeted funding. The concern cannot be dominant in its field, on a national basis. It must also be independently owned and operated. Unlike UK and the European Union, Which have simple definitions applied to all industries, the US has chosen to set size standards for each individual NAICS code industry. This variation is intended to better reflect industry differences. The most common size standards are 500 employees for most manufacturing and mining industries or 100 employees for wholesale trade industries, $6m of annual receipts for most retail and service industries or $28.5m of annual receipts for most general and heavy construction industries or $12m of receipts for all special trade contractors or $0.75m of receipts for most agricultural industries.

In Australia, microenterprise is that which employs less than five employees and those employing between 5-19 personnel are small and the medium enterprises are those that employ 20-200 employees.

In China, for defining an SME, the categorisation is sector-specific and is divided between small and medium segments. In the industrial sector, those employing between 200-2,000 people and having sales between 30-300m yuan or assets in the range of 40-400m yuan are considered small and those above this are medium-level enterprises. Similarly, for construction industry, one of their huge employers, the employee strength between 600-3,000 and sales and assets level of 30-300m yuan and 40-400m yuan respectively are considered small and those having more than this are considered medium.

Malaysia follows a different benchmarks for the SME companies. on the basis of employees, a company is categorised as micro, if it employs less than five persons, irrespective of the sector. Small enterprises are those which have between 5 and 19 persons, in the case of primary agriculture and services sector and between 5 and 50 people in the manufacturing sector. And medium enterprises are those that have less than 50 employees in agriculture or services, and in case of manufacturing sector enterprises, they should employ less than 150 employees. On the basis of turnover, the microenterprises have a turnover of less than RM 2,00,000 in case of agriculture and services sector and RM 2,50,000 in case of manufacturing companies. Medium enterprises are those that have sales between RM 1m-RM 5m in the agriculture and services sector and between RM 10m and RM 25m in the manufacturing sector. Rest of the companies in between these levels are characterised as small enterprises.

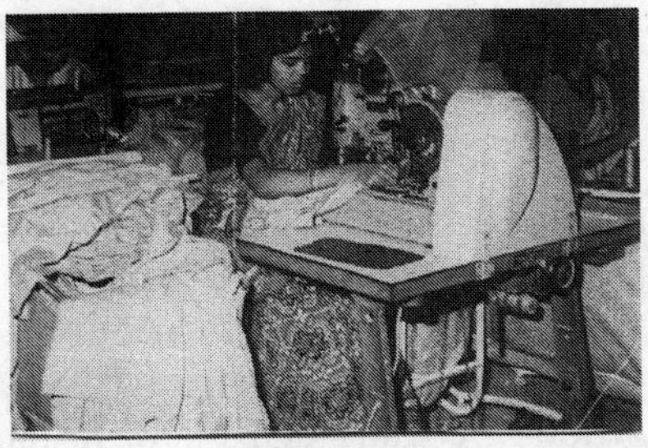

3 CHAPTER

CHARACTERISTICS OF SMALL-SCALE INDUSTRIES

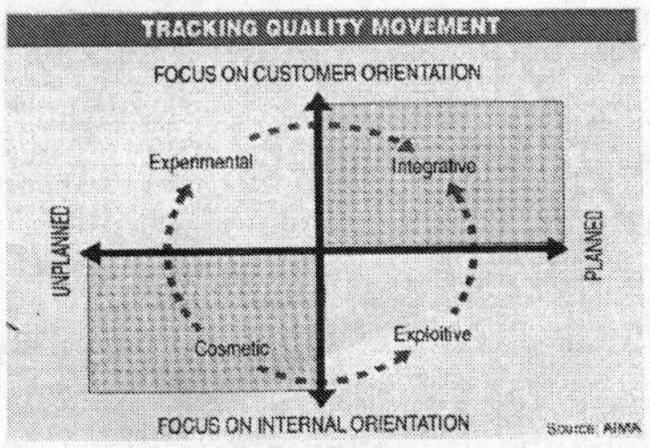

"Knowledge base has virtually become the lifeline for the free market economies. With the removal of the last vestiges of the quantitative restrictions and a number of other WTO agreements coming into force, there are widespread apprehensions about the future prospects of the SSIs."

LEARNING OBJECTIVES

The learning objective is an indepth study of unique characteristics of small-scale industry.

The chapter encompasses the followig topics:

- Small-scale industry is a key link in economic development.
- Distinctive features of small-scale industries.
- Small is beautiful, efficient and creative.
- Characteristics of small-scale industries.
- Importance of small enterprises.
- Advantages of small enterprises.
- Challenges and opportunities.
- Agenda for growth.
- Small-scale industries have high potential for employment generation.
- Small business holds the key to rapid economic growth.
- Small is beautiful.

INTRODUCTION

The small-scale industry is a significant segment of the Indian economy. The basic objectives underlying the development of small and medium-scale industries are: increase in the supply of manufactured goods, promotion of capital formation, the development of indigenous entrepreneurial talents and skills and the creation of employment opportunities. In addition, they include such socio-economic goals as decentralisation and dispersal of manufacturing activities from the metropolitan to the non-metropolitan and rural areas, the reduction of regional economic imbalances within a country and the diffusion of entrepreneurial and managerial abilities and skills as well as of technology on a broader canvas.

Small-scale industries constitute a key link in the process of socio-economic transformations of underdeveloped social structures. It is, no doubt, true that in the case of the dominantly rural countries, processes of transformation either germinating within the rural segment or bringing the latter within its orbit of influence will play a crucial role and should, therefore, occupy an important position in their development strategy. It is, however, equally true that both rural and urban processes are inseparably interwoven in the socio-economic fabric of the country and strategies of rural development cannot be operationalised outside that total developmental process, thus, straddling the rural-urban continuum.

Small-scale industries likewise permit the tapping of resources which otherwise would remain idle including entrepreneurship, capital, labour and raw materials. With proper orientation and support, these industries may attract people who, because of lack of technological and managerial know-how and ignorance of prospects offered by industry, would remain in their present occupations or engaged in less risky activities such as commerce and the real estate. Small-scale industries most often mobilise family as well as other savings which may otherwise be spent on luxuries or channeled to non-productive ventures. They may also utilise materials available in small concentrations, low-grade materials as well as byproducts. It may be mentioned further that small-scale factories are more capable than large-scale plants of taking advantage of semi-skilled labour, including traditional skills. As such, they are much less dependent on highly skilled workers.

Distinction between Industries (Medium and Large) and Small-scale Industries

Medium and Large Industries	Small-scale Industries
Under Industries Development and Regulation Act (IDRA), 1951, all the industrial undertakings (large and medium) included in Schedule of the Act are subject to licensing and registration with the government within a prescribed time limit.	Industrial undertaking covered by the small-scale sector required to be registered as SSI units with the Director of Industries or State and Union territories for the purpose of allocation of scarce raw materials, power supply, taxation as also for statistical purposes.
No new industrial unit could be established or substantial expansion and diversification to produce new items by existing units can be effected without a licence.	SSI undertakings are, however, outside the purview of IRA, being in the decentralised sector. For their expansion and diversification, they are governed by the rules and regulations enacted by the State Governments and directives issued by the Director of Industries.
Government could order an investigation in respect of any scheduled industry or undertaking if, in its opinion, there had been unjustifiable fall in the volume of production in the industry or undertaking or marked deterioration in quality or increase in price without any justification or cause serious injury or damage to consumers.	Government intervention is somewhat less pronounced as compared with units under the IDTA. However, the Small Industries Development Organisation (SIDO) has been entrusted with the main task of development of the small-scale industry in India. SIDO acts as a policy formulating, coordinating and monitoring agency for the development of small-scale industries.
In the event of an industry not carrying out the directions, the government could takeover its management.	SSI units are not generally governed by the government directives such as takeover by the government, in the event of deterioration of output, quality, etc.
Though the Industries Development and Regulation Act (IDRA) does not distinguish between large and medium units, normally an undertaking whose investment is more than ₹ 50 lakh and less than ₹ 5 crore is considered a medium industrial undertaking, and those with investment of ₹ 5 crore and above are reckoned as large industrial undertakings.	An undertaking with fixed investments in plant and machinery not exceeding ₹ 100 lakh is a small-scale unit. The investment limit is ₹ 125 lakh for ancillary industries. Those units with an investment of less than ₹ 25 lakh in plant and machinery are classified as the tiny sector within the overall framework of small-scale industries.
Organisationally, by and large, medium-scale units are closely held and private limited, whereas large units are normally public limited. Public ownership has given added status to large industrial undertakings.	Ownership of small-scale industries, by and large, is proprietary or based on the partnership. The ownership and control the small-scale industry vests in the hands of a few proprietors who have a major stake in the undertaking promoted or purchased by them.

Engaged in manufacturing and processing activities on a large-scale (mass production), large/medium units generally have higher input of technology and capital. Relatively they are more capital intensive.	Generally, SSI units are in less capital-intensive/intermediate technology areas, which are labour-intensive. There are also 843 industries which are reserved exclusively for the small-scale sector. While by the very definition, SSI units cannot be capital-intensive, they have later, entered into technologically sophisticated lines like electronics.
Large units converge more around metropolitan and urban areas, where all the basic infrastructural facilities are available. (they are, by and large, infrastructure-oriented).	SSI units are more amenable to dispersal and decentralised growth. As such, they are located in cities as well as in rural and semi-urban centres with minimum availability of infrastructural facilities.
The very large industries generally belong to the MRTP group or foreign companies; medium industries, by and large, are the outgrowth of SSI units.	Rural industries are indigenous in character, catering to the local needs and as such have no links with bigger companies.
Large and medium industrial undertakings have a greater exposure to professional management.	By and large, rural industries adhere to the age-old techniques and tools. Professionalisation has scope. It is a way of life. Modern management techniques have no impact.
Large and medium industries are basically market-oriented. They produce goods for the masses.	Traditional industries basically cater to the needs of the local people, in some cases to the needs of the cities. Some of the artistic goods manufactured in this sector have a good export potential. However, the benefit goes to the intermediary rather than to the producer.
These industries are prone to modern technology aimed at increased productivity and attractive wages.	Rural industries are prone to artistic creation aimed at depicting Indian culture and heritage. They offer resistance to change.
Different jobs are handled by a chain of specialised and/or professional skilled people.	All work from bringing raw material to marketing is done by the household. No specialisation is in their activities. Invariably the members of the family are all skilled workers in their vocation.
Training is imparted in specialised institutions and modern modes of management are implemented to derive varied benefits.	Training is generally imparted from father to son. It is a tradition rather than a work process. Skills are perfected over the years of work.
Large and medium industrial undertakings are capital-intensive, per employee investment being over ₹ 25,000.	In the case of rural industries, per worker investment is very low, varying from nil to ₹ 600. These industries are basically labour-intensive. These industries possess an enormous employment potential. Rural industries are consumption-oriented and/or service industries and as such they have no gestation period at all. The artisans engaged in the main and subsidiary activities commence their earnings from the start.
Comparatively a long gestation period.	Comparatively a short gestation period. One can commence commercial production within six months or so.

It isn't Whether You're Big or Small. It's How You Grow?

Enterprises of every size want to succeed. But doing it takes the proper resources. Process and management will act faster and increase enterprises competitive edge.

Resources not only help you move forward, but also let you make the most of success. One of the potential resources is knowledge of business.

CHARACTERISTICS OF SMALL INDUSTRIES

Although there is no such thing as the typical small industries, they do share many unique characteristics. Small is a relative term. These characteristics are:

(1) Capital investment is small.

(2) Most have fewer than 10 workers.

(3) Generally, engaged in the production of light consumer goods, processing, etc.

Ready-made garments business has seen a new dimension to its growth with several jeans manufacturers starting operations in Dharavi

(4) Located in rural and semi-urban areas.

(5) There is plethora of one-person firm.

(6) Virtually all these firms are privately owned and are organised as sole proprietorships.

(7) Proprietor and family workers generally form the largest component of the small-industry labour force.

(8) Hired workers are unorganised.

(9) The average person does not work full-time in one activity over the entire year.

(10) Fixed assets form the largest component of small units.

(11) Most of the funds come from the entrepreneur's savings.

(12) According to the available evidence, the small-scale industrial activity has been growing at a faster rate even than large-scale industries.

(13) The incidents of infant mortality are also highest.

(14) Very few of the small-scale industries have grown up to medium and large industries.

(15) Small-scale industrial activity is a beehive of entrepreneurship.

(16) Most of the small-scale industries, especially chemical units, have been polluting the environment.

(17) Exploitation of natural resources is another characteristic of small-scale industries.

(18) Human resources is exploited (child and women in particular) instead of developing it.

(19) Due to various constraints, corruption and cheating is a common feature.

(20) Small-scale industries are quality conscious.

(21) Most of them desire to make huge profits in a short time by hook or crook.

(22) Invariably both organisation and management are very poor and negligible in many cases.

(23) Financial discipline is very weak and rules and regulations are not adhered to.

(24) Urban units are overcrowded, unclear and lack strategic foundation, and

(25) Among the small-scale industries, the slowest growing segment is the one-person firm.

Box 3.1 Characteristics of Small-scale and Large-scale Entrepreneurs

Characteristics of Small-scale Entrepreneurs

(1) They are young men.

(2) They are energetic/zealous/enthusiastic.

(3) They have minimum basic education.

(4) They are pleasant mannered.

(5) They are hardworking.

(6) They are determined.

(7) They are systematic.

(8) They are self-made men.

(9) They are self-confident.

(10) They are disciplined.

(11) They follow planned approach.

(12) They are trained/experienced.

(13) They have entrepreneurial zeal.

(14) They have meagre capital.

(15) Their area of operation is small.

(16) Generally, they deal in one product.

(17) They employ few people.

(18) Their turnover is small.

(19) They are flexible, and

(20) They are determined people.

Characteristics of Large-scale Enterprise

(1) Promoted and professionally managed through employed persons.

(2) Large capital.

(3) Capital contributed by a large section of shareholders.

(4) Shares are registered in the share markets/stock exchanges.

(5) Large assets.

(6) Assets acquired on classified credit.

(7) Engaged in diversified activities.

(8) Promote and push goods in the markets.

(9) Huge turnover/sales/profits.

(10) Easy access to institutional finance.

IMPORTANCE OF SMALL ENTERPRISES

In a labour-abundant and capital-scarce country like India, small-scale industries have come to occupy a significant position in the planned industrialisation of the economy. Most small-scale industries have a low capital intensity and high potential for employment generation. Besides, they possess location flexibility, which serves as an effective instrument for achieving a wide dispersal of industries. Further, small-scale units serve as a means of bringing forth indigenous entrepreneurship and savings lying dormant, particularly in semi-urban and rural areas.

The small-scale sector has a high potential for employment, dispersal of industries, promoting entrepreneurship and earning and bringing foreign exchange into the country. The following points further demonstrate the importance of small-scale industries:

(1) Small is Beautiful: 'Small is beautiful', said E.F.Schumacher. He maintains that man's current pursuit of profit and progress, which promotes giant organisations and increased specialisation, has in fact resulted in gross inefficiency, environmental pollution and inhuman working conditions. Schumacher emphasised on small working units, communal ownership and regional workplaces, utilising local labour and resources. For him, emphasis should be on a person and not on products.

(2) Innovative and Productive: It is the small units which are highly innovative though they do not maintain their own research and development wings. "...a disproportionate share of innovation success in business seems to come from 'skunk works', tiny groups that tend to out-perform the much larger labs that often have a cast of hundreds."

(3) Individual Tastes, Fashions and Personalised Service: Small firms are quick in studying changes in tastes and fashions of consumers and in adjusting the production process and subsequent production accordingly.

Small firms seem to have an edge in industries that call for personalised service, attention to detail and the flexibility to adapt quickly to changes in the business or technological environment. For instance, in the garments and electronic fields, the small units have ruled the roost, a chorus of garment and TV industry voices says that big companies delegate responsibility down the line and cannot swiftly change the trace when necessary. Says a garment exporter: "...the garment business is personalised, oriented to changing fashions and has to be tightly controlled. Professional managers do not have the motivation for all this. And most people in the electronic business agree that big firms have so far had limited success because of their lack of flexibility".

(4) Symbols of National Identity: Small enterprises are almost always locally owned and controlled, and they can strengthen rather than destroy the extended family and other social systems and cultural traditions that are perceived as valuable in their own right as well as symbols of national identity.

(5) Happier in Work: People who work in small enterprises are happier in their work rather than those who work in large ones in spite of lower wages and inadequate standards of safety, comfort and welfare facilities.

(6) Always Winners of the Game: Small enterprises and new entrepreneurs were at the forefront of practically every business boom of the last decade, whether it was computers, consumer electronics (television, fridge, etc.), garments, diamond exports or advertising. And they frequently put the established large industrial house in the shade with the quality of their performance, their ability to seize business opportunities and their aggressive feeding of burgeoning markets.

(7) Dispersal Over Wide Areas: It is only small-scale units which have a tendency to disperse over wider areas. According to the second All India Census of small-scale units, 62.19 per cent of the units are located in backward areas.

Small-scale industries play a key role in the industrialisation of a developing country. This is because they provide immediate large-scale employment and have a comparatively higher labour-capital ratio; they need a shorter gestation period and relatively smaller markets to be economic; they need lower investments, offer a method of ensuring a more equitable distribution of national income in and facilitate an effective mobilisation of resources of capital and skills which might otherwise remain unutilised; and they stimulate the growth of industrial entrepreneurship and promote a more diffused pattern of ownership and location.

Table 3.1 Competitive Advantages of Small Business

Advantage	Outcomes	Examples
1. (a) Ability to perceive opportunities (b) Action orientation	1. (a) Innovation and Technological Development	1. (a) Silicon Valley (California) (b) Route 128,(Boston) (c) Research Triangle Park (Raleigh N.C.)
2. (a) Ability to mobilise local resources (b) Risk Management	2. (a) Development of venture capital fund	2. (a) Informal credit market in India
3. (a) Ability to utilise resources efficiently (b) Increased resource specialisation (c) Better managerial control	3. (a) Higher Profitability (b) Lower factor costs, particularly labour costs	3. (a) Bolton Report 1971 Wilson Committee 1979 (UK) (b) A large percentage of new employment in US (c) Salaries in small-scale sector in Japan are almost half of that in the large industries.
4. Ability to react to rapidly changing environment	4. (a) Greater innovative capabilities (b) Better equipped to complete in the growing service industry and in knowledge intensive-industries	4. (a) A large number of high tech, industries have been set up by entrepreneurs in the small-scale sector.

ADVANTAGES OF SMALL-SCALE ENTERPRISES

Small enterprises have distinct advantages: both economic and social. Some of these are:

(a) Some small-scale industries do not require a high level of technology,

(b) They are generally labour-intensive and do not require a large amount of capital. The energy of unemployed and underemployed people may be used for productive purposes in an economy in which capital is scarce,

(c) Projects related to these industries can be undertaken in a short period and hence can increases production both in the short and the long run.

(d) Most developing countries are rich in certain agricultural, forest and mineral resources; and small-scale enterprises can be based on the processing of locally-produced raw materials.

(e) It is possible both to save and to earn foreign exchange by producing and exporting goods from local resources.

(f) Small-scale industrial enterprises are the training ground for local entrepreneurs on decision-making. From small-scale industrial enterprises, knowledge and skills can be transferred to other enterprises; and small enterprises may grow into medium-sized enterprises.

(g) By creating opportunities for the small businesses, small industrial enterprises can bring about a more equitable distribution of income which is socially necessary and desirable;

(h) These enterprises in developing countries help to create economic stability in society by diffusing prosperity and by checking the expansions of monopolies.

(i) The development of small-scale enterprises will create jobs in the rural areas of the developing countries where unemployment and underemployment are high. This will help in reducing the exodus of workers from the rural to the urban areas in search of jobs.

(j) Small-scale enterprises will make possible a transfer of manufacturing activities from the congested metropolitan to the non-metropolitan and rural areas. The dispersal of manufacturing away from the metropolitan areas is a policy of the governments of many developing countries. This will also help in bringing about a geographical diffusion of skill and technology in a country.

(k) Apart from the linkages between agricultural or rural development and small-scale industrial enterprises, there is an essential linkage between large-scale enterprises and small-scale enterprises in the sense that the former create opportunities or facilities for the growth of the latter. For instance, the growth of the large motor industry creates opportunities for the setting up of small service and repair stations which are spread across the country. Certain large-scale industries also subcontract work to small producers.

(l) Small-scale enterprises have their own place in a country's economy. Imperfect competition protects the small firms' markets and enables them to exist even where they are not efficient in terms of cost.

(m) The development of small-scale enterprises can be a part of integrated rural development programmes on which a good deal of emphasis has been recently placed in the developing countries of Asia. Due attention needs to be given to the industrial and non-agricultural components or activities in the context of rural development programmes.

This apart, the small enterprises have the following advantages too:

(a) Small Enterprises (SEs) create immediate and permanent employment at a relatively small capital cost;

(b) They meet a substantial part of increased demand for consumer goods including mass consumption goods;

(c) They facilitate mobilisation of resources of capital and skills which often would remain inadequately utilised;

(d) They bring integration with rural economy on the one hand and large-scale enterprise on the other;

(e) They offer a method of ensuring equitable distribution of national income;

(f) They involve a short gestation period;

(g) They do not require as heavy and costly infrastructure as larger enterprises;

(h) They have a favourable capital output ratio;

(i) The products of these enterprises earn a substantial exchange; and

(j) They assist in dispersal and avoid problems which unplanned urbanisation tends to create.

Due to all these advantages, the development of small enterprises has been assigned a crucial role in India's Five Year Plans. With a view to protect, support and promote small enterprises to become self-supporting and to facilitate balanced growth of the small and large sector, a number of policies and promotional measures have been taken by the government. These measures include reservation of certain items for exclusive production in the small-scale sector, and exclusive purchase under the stores purchase policy and differential excise duty. Promotional measures have included development of entrepreneurship backed by a package of consultancy services, improvement in techniques, institutional support in respect of supply of credit and raw materials, factory accommodation in industrial estates, capital subsidy and rebates on sales of certain products.

The small-scale sector has stimulated economic activity of a far-reaching magnitude and has played a significant role in attaining the following major objectives:

Elimination of economic backwardness of rural and underdeveloped regions in the country.

Attainment of self-reliance.

Reduction of regional imbalances.

Reduction of disparities in income, wealth and consumption.

Mobilisation of resources of capital and skills and their optimum utilisation.

Creation of greater employment opportunities and increased output, income and standards of living.

Meeting a substantial part of the economy's requirements for consumer goods and simple producer goods.

Provides employment and a steady source of income to the low-income groups living in rural and urban areas of the country.

Provides substitutes of various industrial products now being imported into the country, and

Improves the quality of industrial products manufactured in the cottage industry sector and enhance both production and exports.

The development of these industries would be beneficial to the developing countries and assist them in improving their economic and social well-being. This would create greater employment opportunities, assist in entrepreneurship and skills development and ensure better use of the scarce financial resources and appropriate technology.

CHALLENGES AND OPPORTUNITIES

In the emerging scenario, characteristic of a liberalised regime, unrestricted competition from multinationals entering the consumer durables and non-durables market segments with their internationally known brand names, technological superiority and intensive marketing efforts would offer formidable challenge to the small-scale sector. Added to this is the large-scale exports of agricultural commodities in processed and semi-processed form by large export houses and multinationals leaving gaps in the supply of these resources which have traditionally been the input for tiny industries. Besides, liberalisation in imports of capital goods and related components, it is feared, would exert pressures on the existing markets of ancillaries and SSI vendors.

Yet, the winds of change have also opened up new vistas for the larger and progressive small-scale units. They have the flexibility and adaptability to switch over to low-volume specialised markets and diversify into differentiated products with appropriate manufacturing processes. The other small-scale and tiny units operating in the decentralised sector could gain through linkages with large enterprises or export houses. Foreign Direct Investment (FDI) will have the spin-off effects of linkages with small-scale units which can provide the supply base to large undertakings. These units as suppliers to duty-free licenceholders could avail of the benefits of deemed exports under the new EXIM policy. Entering into buyback arrangements for labour-intensive activities like reprocessing and repackaging for exportable goods and qualifying as ancillaries to large industrial houses having foreign collaboration through equity/technology transfers, modernisation and quality upgradation, could also be more rewarding options. Having attained superior quality standards, some of the more enterprising small-scale firms could even upgrade themselves as suppliers of components and finished products of Multinational Corporation (MNC) affiliates in the newly industrialised Asian countries. Prompted by the inherited advantages of advanced technologies through the MNC route, the more dynamic ones could move over onto developing new technologies and processes which could even be exported to other developing countries and become active global players by entering into joint ventures with small and medium enterprises in these countries.

Indian industry is at the crossroads where on the one hand, it has to integrate itself with the global markets, while on the other, it has to face competition in the domestic market from international suppliers. Technology, product quality, factor productivity and competitive marking techniques and management practices alone seem to hold the key for the future of the Indian small-scale industry. On moving from a protected economy to a market-oriented economy, some amount of transitional problems seem unavoidable. But given the intrinsic strength of the sector and several support services available to it, the sector can look forward to a level of sustained development in the coming years.

Agenda for Growth

- The Aim: to become a key player in the Indian economy in fostering entrepreneurship, creating employment opportunities, increasing industrial production and accelerating the process of sustainable development.
- The sector will bank upon the strategic business development plan, which draws on its core strength.
- To use modern technology in maintaining quality and in increasing productivity.
- To introduce new product-lines to garner a higher share in exports.
- To integrate with the medium and large enterprises, and
- To promote entrepreneurship, stress will be on human resources and development at the grassroot level.

SMALL IS BEAUTIFUL, BUT WHAT IS REALLY BEAUTIFUL IS THE APPROPRIATE SCALE, SMALL IS EFFICIENT

Small-scale enterprises is the beehive of entrepreneurship, innovation, growth and development. Of late, most of the Asian countries have adopted deliberate policy of promoting and encouraging small enterprises as a strategy for the accelerated industrialisation. India too has also given highest priority for fostering the development of the small-scale sector.

Small-scale enterprises/entrepreneur is no longer fighting a local battle, but a global war. In such a global competitive scenario, small enterprises may emerge victories by changing the tactics of warfare. First, by getting a clear vision of the future, mission of intent, purpose of the enterprise, values that guides goal to reach and the strategy to achieve the goal that its vision provides. Second, being armed with robust processes. Third, ensuring a strategic infrastructure. Fourth, ensuring timely implementation. And fifth, with people focussed on total customer satisfaction.

To enable small-scale enterprises to succeed, and excel, it is necessary to provide them with the basic tools and techniques of modern management. Efficiency proceeds professionalisation, technological reorientation, adequate training and adequate timely credit and other financial services.

CONCLUSION

The small enterprises must be developed along with large units. From the viewpoint of long-term perspectives, however, the capacity of small manufacturers to become economically viable, technically progressive and efficient and to develop competitive strength shall be the only justification for their continuance. In the intervening period, the government should help create conditions to facilitate their smooth growth.

The small-scale sector has a distinct advantage of low investment with a high potential for employment generation. It is also expected to bring about the dispersal of industries in rural and semi-urban areas with the concomitant advantage of equitable distribution of national income.

Empirical evidence indicates that the small-scale industry can be an important vehicle for meeting the growth and equity objections of developing economies. The government would therefore, be fair to foster entrepreneurship and should help to creatre a conducive environment to facilitate rapid growth of efficient small-scale enterprises in the country. Small-scale industries have a unique role to play in the industrial development of the country.

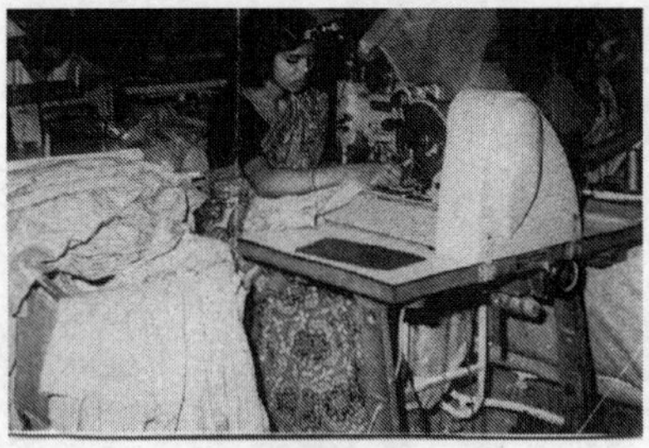

4 CHAPTER
THE ROLE OF SMALL-SCALE INDUSTRIES

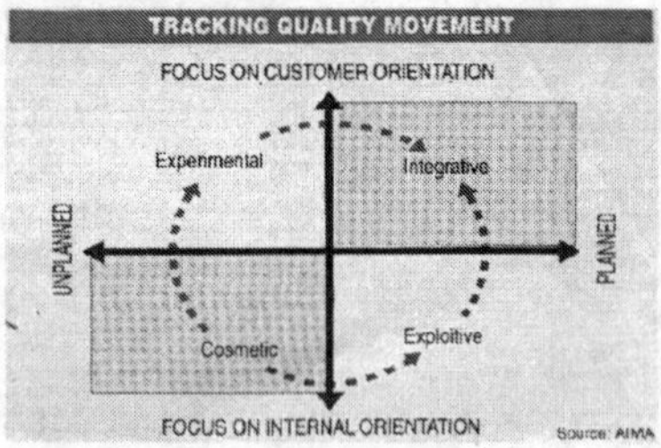

"The importance of the SSI sector is well-recognised from its contribution to the socio-economic objectives of growth in generation of employment, output, exports and in its fostering of entrepreneurship. Currently, the sector accounts for around 95 per cent of the industrial units in the country, contributing to 40 per cent of the manufacturing sector output and to approximately one-third of the nation's exports."

LEARNING OBJECTIVES

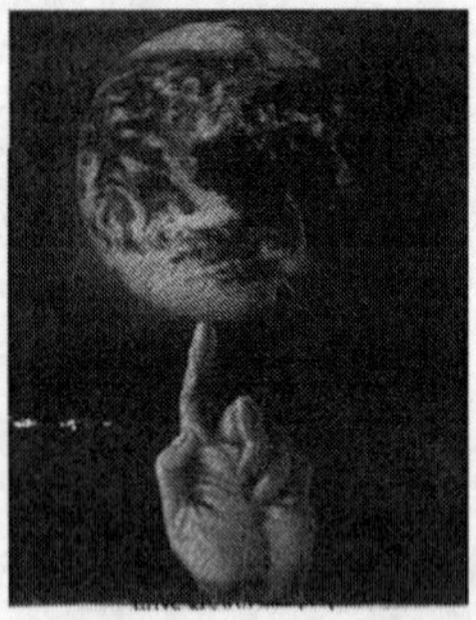

- To provide an insight on the role of small-scale industries in the accelerated growth of the economy and as well as a seed bed of entrepreneurship in the country.
- The chapter covers the following topics:
- Vision of small industries.
- The role of small-scale industry in planned development.
- Objective of the programme.
- SSI is quickly gearing up to meet the emerging challenges in the global economy through constant innovation and adoption of cutting-edge technology to provide superior customer solutions. As in the past, SSIs motivation for undertaking this proactive transformation is guided by its *raison d'etre,* the Indian industry, and a desire to acquire the requisite competencies to play a facilitating role in the emergence of a globally competitive Indian corporate sector. In the process, SSI would continue to be spurred by the imperative for driving organisational growth and shareholder value, and create economic and intellectual capital that benefits all stakeholders.

INTRODUCTION

Small-scale industries contribute significantly to social and economic development objectives such as – labour absorption, income distribution, rural development, poverty eradication, regional balance and promotion of entrepreneurship. In fact, they play an important role in the process of a country's industrial development.

Particularly in developing countries, small labour-intensive industries have been favoured basically to create employment opportunities in an economy with abundant unskilled labour, even though such industries may not always be supported on grounds of economic efficiency. In addition, a low capital requirement, given an appropriate market environment, is believed to stimulate growth of numerous indigenous industries with wide regional dispersal. This helps to promote balanced growth, ensure more equitable income distribution, as well as diversification of the industrial structure which often leads to increased utilisation of national resources. The process, if properly nurtured, can help the entrepreneurial class and boost capital formation as well as lead to the growth of industries in the small-scale sector in both urban and rural areas. Such a process creates the basis for transformation of technology management and pave the way for creative development while sustaining national heritage and skills. It will also contribute to the growth of the right type of entrepreneurship in the country.

Box 4.1 The SSI Preserve

- Ice cream
- Bread
- Biscuits
- Pastry
- Pickles and chutneys
- Vinegar
- Rice milling
- Dal milling
- Confectionery excluding chocolates, toffees and chewing gum
- Rapeseed oil, Mustard oil, Sesame oil and Groundnut oil except solvent extract
- Sweetened cashew products
- Poultry feed except in pellet form
- Ground and processed spices except spice oil and also resin spices
- Tapioca sago
- Tapioca flour, and
- Synthetic syrups

The major objective of the chapter is to evaluate the role of small-scale industries in the country's growth experience.

Empirical studies have shown that small-scale enterprises are an important vehicle for meeting the growth and equity with social justice-potential objective of developing economies. In the Indian context, they play a key role in the economic development besides acting as a breeding ground for the entrepreneur. In the post-independence period, as many as 18 million entrepreneurs have established enterprises in this sector and contributed to the advancement of industry in the country. More importantly, it is a stepping stone for entrepreneurs to grow from small to big. It provides inplant training to millions of entrepreneurs and motivates them to become innovative entrepreneurs contributing substantially to the national economy. As such, development of small-scale industries should be given special attention.

Promotion of small-scale industries has been one of the main strategies for economic development in developing countries since the 1950s. The special feature of the planning in India is that it does not stop at giving conceptual emphasis to the growth of small-scale industries, but it has in particular drawn up a concrete and constructive planned programme to attain the planned objectives. The development of small-scale industries as the focal point of industrial development is substantial evidence of the awareness of the government to propagate and develop this sector for the ultimate objective of tackling the all-prevailing and ever-growing problem of unemployment.

Agriculture supplies certain indispensable primary requisites – food for the population, raw materials for industries and surplus products for exports. No country, which aspires to be reasonably self-supporting, can do without agriculture. At the same time, no nation in modern times has grown rich through agriculture alone. With the growth of civilisation and the multiplication of human wants, the occupations associated with manufacturing industries have increased in importance and are very remunerative. *Industrialisation has become a necessity and is virtually synonymous with civilisation.* Small-scale industries play an important role in the productive activities of developed as well as developing countries.

VISION OF SMALL INDUSTRIES

Vision formulation for small industries is a must –

- If a small industry wants to run a marathon, it requires a value system. A value system is what separates the men from the boys. It provides energy and enthusiasm in moments of tribulation.
- Adhere to the value system and culture of the enterprise.
- It is possible for professionals to stay back in this country and create wealth leveraging sweat equity.
- It is possible to conduct business honestly.
- Sharing wealth with employees only increases your own wealth.
- Investors reward you if you adhere to the best principles of enterprise governance and level with the investors at all points of time.
- It is also possible to benchmark against global standards from India.
- You create incentives for innovation within an enterprise by rendering your own innovation obsolete.
- It is possible for two fiercely competing orgnisations to maintain an open, harmonious and even information-sharing relationship.
- Imbibe and inculcate skills and discipline on an ongoing basis
- Strive to innovate and update technology on and on.
- Putting maximum public good ahead of private good in every decision you make, in fact, will result in enriching the private good. This is what differentiates the developed world from the developing world.
- Do set benchmarks and base incentives around milestones.
- Forge an alliance with your team-members and strengthen it.
- It is possible to inspire a multitude of entrepreneurs to take a plunge in building a new economy in the new millennium.
- The importance of maintaining high ethical standards in business and focussing on the social responsibilities of an enterprise will become important in this millennium.
- Constant innovation and the ability to use technology to enhance customer interface in terms of better, cheaper more products and varied choices. In a business environment that is complex and everchanging, innovative managers could well emerge as the differentiating variable for the successful organisation. Not surprisingly, their predictions cover more than one certainty;
- Intellectual capital, not physical assets, will drive the new economy.
- The Net will usher in an era of connectedness between companies, suppliers, employees, customers and other stakeholders.
- Command and control-structures will be replaced by team-structures even as the number of part-timers increases.
- Companies will have to not just make good products and deliver good services, but also practise good governance.
- Creativity, flexibility and adaptability will be the parameters that decide who wins.
- The value chain will be redfined with the customer's core need at one extreme, and the company's core offering at another.
- People will focus on work and more on getting the most out of life, making worklife management a crucial organisational issue.

Japan – Home of the Small-scale Sector

Japan is an outstanding example of those who have achieved rapid industrialisation through the small and medium industries. Commenting on industrial productivity, the *Economist* (August 2, 1980) observed.

> *".......The Japanese work more entrepreneurially in smaller teams. Components flow into each big Japanese factory from many tiny mini-firms, which operate under the big factory's financial umbrella; along the automated production line, the factory's 'permanent' workers, in teams of six or seven, are responsible for jointly checking each product as it passes through their station; at the end of the line, the completed product may be backed by a separate 5-10 employees mini-firm."*

This is a salient feature of Japanese industrial production in rural and urban areas. The small-scale sector in Japan plays a catalytic and predominant role in the accelerated growth of its industry; and this has been made possible by a long span of regulated and indisciplined process of industrial development backed by progressive legislation.

A renowned economist hold the view that small industries are the key to speedy development and full employment. "No sector of our economy holds greater promise than the sector made up of small and medium industries...." Medium and small industries may very well provide one of the answers to economic development and full employment.

Indian Experience

India is predominantly an agricultural country. A proper development of small-scale industries is vital for the healthy growth of our economy. The country can profit by Japan's bold experience in this direction, spread over more than three decades.

Villages and small industries in their different aspects are an integral and continuing element, both in the economic structure and in the scheme of national planning. The primary object of developing small industries in rural areas is to generate better employment opportunities, raise incomes and standards of living, and bring about the growth of a more balanced and integrated rural economy. The prevailing scarcity of capital for the promotion of large-scale industries and a plentiful supply of labour favour the development of small-scale industries. Besides, the setting up of small but efficient units of production as suitable locations throughout the country would reduce the cost of transport involved in the haulage of raw materials or finished products of centralised industries. The low purchasing power of the mass of the people tends to restrict the market and the scale of production in certain spheres; and the needs of the people have, therefore, to be met in several ways by production on a small and often, on a semi-mechanised scale. Small-scale industries are also essential for providing subsidiary or alternate occupations and the utilisation of local raw materials constitute a progressive and efficient decentralised sector which comprises of large-scale industries. Small units exist and thrive even in highly industrialised countries. In Japan, for example, the small units serve as *feeders* to the larger ones. These small units operate along side large-scale industries either on their own or in conjunction with larger units.

Structure Features

Small-scale industries may be classified under three broad categories:

(1) Some industries are started on a small-scale, but they are likely to develop into medium-sized units within a short time. Like medium-scale industries, these are capital-intensive with relatively large investments in block assets; and are generally in the corporate sector, organised as public or private limited companies or as cooperative societies. In these concerns, borrowed capital is higher than owned capital. These concerns are in an advantageous position to offer adequate security by way of block assets or stocks. They are also able to provide the necessary information for the consideration of loan applications. The concerns in this group are comparatively well-managed and have a good sales turnover; they can be generally considered creditworthy for institutional financing. In India, some of the industries that come under this group are the companies or concerns which manufacture biscuits, paints, pens, engine oils, grinding wheels, automobile spares, etc.

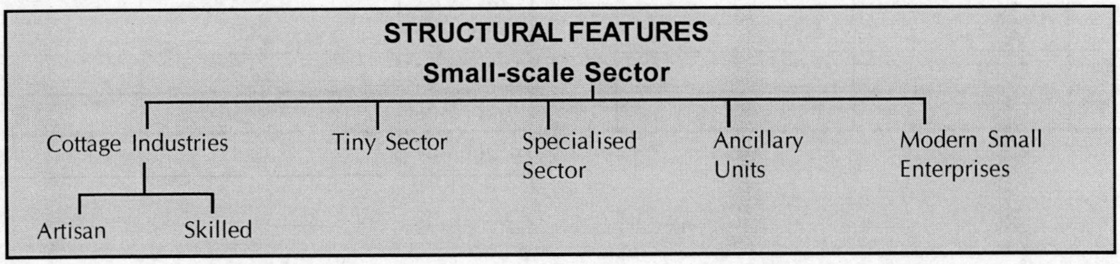

(2) Under the second category some units started on a small-scale and are likely to remain so for a long time in view of the specialised nature of demand for their products. Though specialised types of machines are required by this sector, they do not require any large-scale investment in block assets. Generally, these are organised as non-corporate concerns, partnerships, proprietory or joint family concerns. These concerns have little block assets to offer as security, though they maintain sufficient stocks. They do not have godown facilities, and their transactions are mostly on a small-scale. Nor do they have sufficient credit to raise finance on hypothecation from institutional agencies, for pledge arrangements are inconvenient to them. Their own resources are blocked either in holding stock or in giving short-term credits ranging from three to six months to their customers. Their principal requirement, therefore, is ***working capital.*** With little scope for attracting outside capital, they usually borrow either from relatives or from moneylenders, finance secured from institutions being quite meagre. Units producing agarbatties, bolts, nuts, oil stoves, wire nails, etc., come under this category.

(3) The third category covers concerns which began as cottage industries but later developed into small-scale industries or as feeder units to large-scale industries. This group, however, forms the smallest segment among the small-scale industries. Such concerns are mostly organised as proprietory or *partnership concerns.* Borrowed capital is relatively insignificant in their resources and the availability of institutional finance negligible. Being more labour-intensive, the tangible assets of these units are limited; their management as well as maintenance of records are rather poor, and an assessment of the market prospects for their products, etc., is rather difficult. Under these circumstances, finance has to be provided primarily on the basis of judgement of the integrity and expertise of the management; and not unnaturally, institutional agents are reluctant to meet their financial requirements. Units producing toys, confectionery, coil springs, etc., come under this category.

Role of Small-scale Industry in Planned Development

In a developing economy, it is the small-scale industry that constitutes the backbone of its economic structure. Its development creates vast employment opportunities for the people, effects decentralisation of industries by the creation of industrial estates and makes possible a redistribution of economic power and income.

Till independence, only cottage industries, village industries, rural industries or agro-based industries were considered to be small industries. The National Planning Committee, set up in 1938 under the Chairmanship of Pandit Jawaharlal Nehru, constituted a panel to study this problem. With the dawn of the planned era in the country, the government has been following a policy of promotion as well as protection of the small-scale industries sector; the protection would be gradually reduced as and when promotional activities begin to produce results.

The main objectives of the development of small-scale industries are: to create vast employment opportunities for the people; to effect decentralisation of industries by creating industrial estates; to effect a redistribution of economic power as well as income; and to raise the standard of living of the people. These objectives mainly follow the principles of the ideal goal of a welfare state. The objectives in theory aim at developing the country on the basis of the priniciples of social justice and social welfare.

Comparative Growth Rates

Year	Growth Rate of MSE Sector (%)	Overall Industrial Sector (%)
2002-03	8.68	5.70
2003-04	9.64	6.90
2004-05	10.88	6.90
2005-06	12.32	8.40
2006-07	12.60	11.5
2007-08	13.00	8.00

Contribution of MSEs in GDP

Year	Contribution of MSE (%) at 1999-2000 price in	
	Total Industrial Production	Gross Domestic Product (GDP)
1999-00	39.74	5.86
2000-01	39.71	6.04
2001-02	39.12	5.77
2002-03	38.89	5.91
2004-05	38.62	5.84
2005-06	38.56	5.83
2006-07	38.57	5.94

Table 4.1 MSEs Performance: Units, Investment, Production, Employment and Exports

Sr. No.	Year	Total MSEs (lakh numbers)	Fixed Investment (₹ crore)	Production (₹ crore)		Employment (lakh person)	Exports (₹ crore)
				Current Prices	Constant Prices (1993-94)		
1	1990-91	67.87	93555	78802	847228	158.34	9664
2	1991-92	70.63	100351	80615	87355	165.99	1388
		(4.07*)	(7.26)	(2.30)	(3.1)	(4.83)	(43.66)
3	1992-93	73.51	109623	84413	92246	174.84	17784
		(4.07)	(9.24)	(4.71)	(5.6)	(5.33)	(28.10)
4	1993-94	76.49	115795	98796	98796	182.64	25307
		(4.07)	(5.63)	(17.04)	(7.1)	(4.46)	(42.30)
5	1994-95	79.60	123790	122154	108774	191.40	29068
		(4.07)	(6.9)	(23.64)	(10.1)	(4.79)	(14.86)
6	1995-96	82.84	125750	147712	121175	197.93	36470
		(4.07)	(1.58)	(20.92)	(11.40)	(3.42)	(25.46)
7	1996-97	86.21	13.060	167805	134892	205.86	39248
		(4.07)	(3.82)	(13.60)	(11.32)	(4.00)	(7.26)
8	1997-98	89.71	133242	187217	146262.9	213.16	44442
		(4.07)	(2.05)	(11.57)	(8.43)	3.55)	(13.23)
9	1998-99	93.36	135482	210454	157525.1	220.55	48979
		(4.07)	(1.68)	(12.41)	(7.7)	(3.46)	(10.21)
10	1999-00	97.15	139982	233760	170379.2	229.10	54200
		(4.07)	(3.32)	(11.07)	(8.16)	(3.88)	(10.21)
11	2000-01	101.1	146845	261297	184401.4	238.73	69797
		(4.07)	(4.90)	(11.78)	(8.23)	(4.21)	(28.78)
12	2001-02	105.21	154349	282270	165613	249.33	71244
		(4.07)	(5.11)	(8.03)	(6.06)	(4.44)	(2.07)
				AT 2001-2 prices			
13	2002-03	109.49	162317	314850	306771	260.21	86013
		(4.07)	(5.16)	(11.54)	(8.68)	(4.36)	(20.73)
14	2003-04	113.95 (4.07)	170219 (4.87)	364547 (15.78)	336344 (9.64)	271.42 (4.31)	97644 (13.52)
15	2004-05	118.59	178699	429796	372938	282.57	124417
		(4.07)	(5.27)	(15.83)	(10.88)	(4.11)	(27.42)
16	2005-06	123.44	188113	497886	418884	299.85	150242
		(4.07)	(5.27)	(15.83)	(12.32)	(4.44)	(20.76)
17	2006-07	128.44	213219	585112	471663	312.52	177600
		(4.07)	(8.68)	(17.53)	(12.60)	(4.23)	(24.54)
18	2007-08	133.68	238975	695126	532979	322.28	1,99,500
		(4.08)	(12.08)	(18.80)	(13.00)	(3.12)	12.3

Objective of the Programme

The main objectives of the programme of the development of small-scale industries, therefore, are the creation of maximum amount of job opportunities, including self-employment; ventures with small doses of investment; production of consumer goods on a large-scale; mobilisation of local skills and capital; and dispersal of units into semi-urban and rural areas.

The 1956 Industrial Policy Resolution put forth arguments in favour of small-scale industrial units: (a) the employment argument, (b) the equality argument, (c) the latent resources argument, and (d) the decentralisation argument.

The Employment Argument: The argument is based on the assumption that small-scale industrial units are labour-intensive comparatively and thus create more job opportunities per unit of capital employed. It is argued, therefore, that leaving aside highly capital-intensive industries involving the most sophisticated technology and the building up of economic and social infrastructural facilities, it is the small enterprises which help enlargement of job opportunities. This is particularly important for a labour-surplus economy like India suffering from acute problems of unemployment, underemployment and seasonal unemployment. Besides, it is argued that most of the small enterprises are as mentioned earlier either proprietary concerns or partnership undertakings where the employer-employee relationships are personal and hence harmonious. This factor helps in the maintenance of industrial peace.

The Equality Argument: The equality argument suggests that the income generated in a large number of small enterprises is dispersed more widely in a community than income generated in a few large enterprises. Thus, the income benefit of small enterprises is derived by large segment of the population, while large enterprises encourage monopoly capital and concentration of economic power. In this way, small enterprises bring about an equalitarian distribution of income and wealth than do the large-scale enterprises.

The Latent Resource Argument: This argument suggests that small enterprises are able to tap latent resources like entrepreneurial ability, hoarded wealth, etc. Small enterprises encourage the growth of a class of small enterprises which introduces a *dynamic element* in the economy. The growth of a very large number of small firms during the three-and-a-half decades of planning highlights the fact that given a favourable environment, the latent resources of entrepreneurship can be tapped by the growth of small enterprises only.

The need for broad-basing the entrepreneurial class in India arises from the need to speed up the process of activating the factors of production leading to a higher rate of economic growth, dispersal of economic activities, development of backward and tribal areas, creation of employment opportunities, improvement in the standard of living of weaker sections of the society in the process of economic growth.

The Decentralisation Argument: This argument impresses the necessity of dispersal of industries. Location of large enterprises is conditioned by inflexible environment factors. Location of large enterprises is conditioned by inflexible environmental factors. If the industrialisation is to progress in an atmosphere of decentralisation, setting up of small-scale industrial units must be encouraged as their locational requirements are often flexible. Decentralisation also helps in tapping local resources, such as – raw materials, idle savings, local talents, etc., and also helps industrialisation of backward areas.

SMALL INDUSTRIES MAKE A BIG DIFFERENCE TO INDIA'S ECONOMY

It is a truism that small industries are the engines of growth in any economy. They are the job providers and the technological innovators. They have been gearing up to occupy a prominent place in the global market today.

Small is beautiful, efficient, innovative and creative where pursuit for progress is endless and growth is their way of life.

Small-scale industries contribute as much as 45 per cent of industrial production, 65 per cent of services, 80 per cent of employment generation and 35 per cent to India's exports. Over the years, the percentage in contribution by the SSI sector has been showing an increase.

NEW TRADE-BOOSTING MEASURES

- 894 items being shifted to the free list from the current negative list and another 414 items being placed in the SIL list. After this, only 667 items will remain in the restricted list.
- Creation of free trade zones on the existing global parameters.
- Duty exemption scheme made more flexible. Exporters will now be permitted to import any prescribed duty free input without approaching the DGFT.
- Pre-export DEPB credit entitlement has been increased from 5% to 10% of previous year's export performance.
- Threshold limit for zero duty EPCG scheme has been brought down from ₹ 20 crore to ₹ 1 crore for chemicals, plastics and textiles.
- No additional customs duty on import of capital goods under zero duty EPCG scheme in marine and electronics sectors.
- Duty free import consumables up to certain limits for gems and jewellery, handcraft and leather sectors.
- Value addition for rupee exports to Russia reduced from 100% to 33%.
- Special green cards for exporters exporting 50 per cent of their production.
- Green card will entitle them to various facilities.
- Extension of the period for fulfilment of past export obligation with respect to advance license and EPCG schemes.
- Institution of ombudsman for faster, resolution of exporters' problems.
- Net foreign exchange earnings as a percentage of exports made uniform at 20 per cent for both EOUs and EPZs.
- The entitlement of domestic tariff area sales for EOUs and EPZs increased to 50 per cent of f.o.b. value of the previous year.

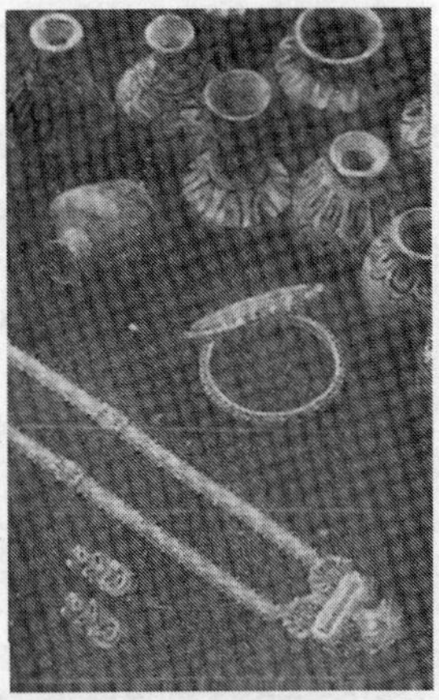

Products of Gems and Jewellery Sector

A Hardware Unit

Drug and Pharmaceutical Unit

Reforms in SSI

Box 4.2 Impact of Reforms on Small-scale Industries

Industry groups	De-regulation and De-licensing	Other Reforms
Auto Ancillary	Earlier 'mindset' on getting 5 per cent to 6 per cent growth in sales has given way to achieving attractive 30 per cent to 35 per cent growth rates.	Improved productivity
	New greenfield projects were on increase indicating a higher demand for intermediate goods manufactured by the SSI sector. Labour productivity in the new units comparable to international levels.	Enlarged equity base.
Lock-making: Cycle Lock	Business remained more or less stagnant. A few units had sought adoption of new technology. Absorption of unskilled labour.	With the exports of bicycles, the units had benefitted and turnover had increased.

Cotton Hosiery	Increased turnover. Growth in employment	Improved capacity utilisation. Increased use of machines and technology brought in quality consciousness for adoption of ISO 9000. Increased machinery and technology imports. Increased profitability.
Glass and Glass Products	Increased factor efficiency and capacity utilisation.	Better profit margin and more exportable surplus; improved viability of units. Substantial impact on improving product quality; progress was made to obtain ISO 9000.
Scientific Instruments	Competition within units led to improving products, quality and diversification.	Better profit margin for the exporting units.
Leather footwear	Increased production. Rise in the prices consequent upon decontrol. Increased employment	Increased exports, profit margin and viability.
Cardigan, Sweater, shawls, etc.	Not available	Increased production, exports, profit-margin. Graduation from small to medium and large industries by raising investment. Improved viability.

Reforms in SSI have touched small-scale industries (SSIs), but marginally, in the form of a relaxation of the investment limit of ₹ 60 lakh to ₹ 3 crore for garment units exporting over 50 per cent of their output. A second reform: non-SSI units are allowed into the sectors reserved for SSIs on a case-by-case basis, provided they export over 75 per cent of their production. The unfinished agenda is fundamental: dereserve the bulk of items earmarked for SSIs today. After all, 233 of the 1,096 reserved products are not even manufactured today while another 692 are produced in negligible quantities. And for the 171 items that they do make, SSIs get purchase and price preferences, subsidised loans, and tax exemptions at the state level. So long as small units did benefit from these steps, they would have been vindicated. But, as a 1993 study of SSI performance by the NCAER concludes, SSI units have simply been pitchforked into direct competition with large-scale companies instead of complementing them. Not only do many corporates continue to manufacture the same products – reservation only prevents them from expanding their capacities – they also market these products, outsourced from SSI units, under their own brandnames, thus moping up the margins.

Besides, the incentives structure is proving a honeytrap for SSI units, preventing them from growing and achieving economies of scale for fear of losing out on the benefits. In any case, points out the NCAER study, only 3 per cent of the country's 25.71 lakh SSI units have actually received the incentives. The case for reforms: dereserve the products reserved for the SSI sector, starting with the 925 items that are hardly produced at present. And second, limit the incentives to the tiny sector-units with investments of under ₹ 5 lakh – so that SSI units can be modernised and become bigger. As reforms have already proved, the greatest beneficiaries of the withdrawal of protection have been those who were protected.

CONCLUSION

In developing countries, small-scale industries can play a main role in the achievement of national economic and socio-political objectives. The principal economic objectives of a number of developing countries include an increase in the supply of manufactured goods, promotion of capital formation, development of indigenous enterprises and skills and creation of employment opportunities. Their main socio-economic goals include decentralisation of manufacturing activity and reduction in regional imbalances within the country. Their major socio-political aims include wide distribution of socio-economic and political power, creation of opportunities for people with initiative, to rise by their own ability and hardwork and development of entrepreneur-managers who not only acquire economic independence but learn to take initiative, to be self-reliant and acquire the knowledge to organise and operate a factory or other small-scale enterprise. Achievement of these objectives is seen as desirable in almost all developing countries, though the relative importance of these objectives varies from country-to-country, depending on the differences in the socio-economic and political complexes.

In India, the state has taken a greater interest in the development of small-scale industries. It renders two kinds of assistance to them, *viz.,* financial and non-financial. The state assists the small-scale industries to: (i) improve their techniques of production and management; (ii) provide credit facilities, both for investment and for working capital, (iii) to provide common services facilities. In order to coordinate these activities, the Central Government set up a Small-scale Industries Board, appointed a Development Commissioner for small-scale industries and established Regional Small Industries Service Institutes and a National Small Industries Corporation.

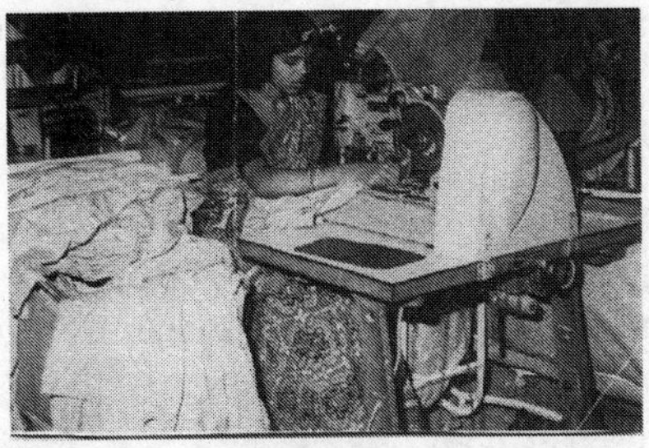

5 CHAPTER

POLICIES GOVERNING SMALL-SCALE INDUSTRIES

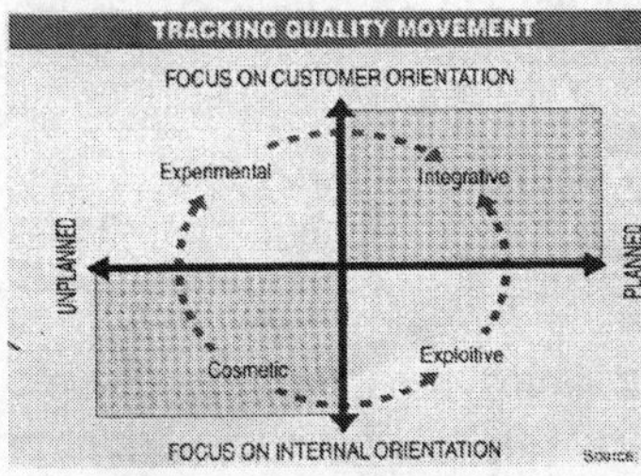

"The small-scale sectors contribution towards nation-building is quite unique and significant. Employment in the village and small industries sector is estimated to be around ₹ 655 lakh. Exports from the VSI sector are around ₹ 92,588 crore."

LEARNING OBJECTIVES

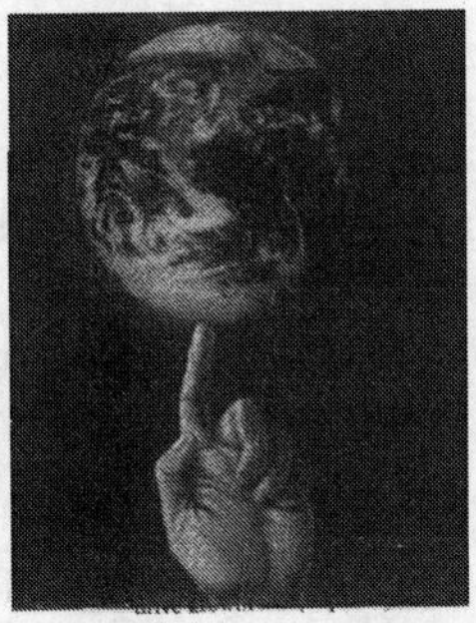

- To discuss the varied policies governing small-scale industries.
- The chapter covers the following topics:
- New policy for small and tiny sector.
- Salient features.
- Thrust areas.
- Assessment.
- Policy measures for promoting and strengthening of small, tiny and village enterprises have been announced on 6th August, 1991 in which special emphasis has been laid on infrastructure facilities, marketing and exports, modernisation, technological and quality upgradation, promotion of entrepreneurship and simplification of rules and procedures for which the Central, State Governments, and other non-governmental organisations have to attempt collectively so as to provide employment to the teeming millions and earn the valuable foreign exchange needed by the country. As a follow-up measure of the policy for small, tiny and village industries, the following new initiatives have been taken.

INTRODUCTION

Industrial development plays a crucial role in India's development strategy, particulary with regard to the objectives of structural diversification, modernisation and self-reliance. The progress of industrialisation over the last forty-three years has been a striking feature of the Indian economic development. More importantly, industrial policies lay stress on the strategy of development.

In increasing industrial production, diversifying the base of industrial production as well as increasing employment opportunities, industries have been playing an important role in India. The time has come when industries have to improve their productivity and efficiency by adopting modern technology and thereby reduce their cost of production and produce quality goods at competitive prices. There is ample scope for the existing industries to double their production and register three-fold increase in exports. What is lacking in organisation, professionalisation, planning and coordinated efforts. Even entrepreneurial visions have to be sharpened and given full support.

The promotion of industries has been regarded as an important element of the development strategy underlying our Five Year Plans. The rationale behind such an approach is that industries provide substantial scope for increasing employment as they are labour-intensive, and they require comparatively less capital. They have lesser gestation periods and can easily be set up in rural and backward areas. They need relatively smaller markets to be economical and hence they have an advantage in being set up as *ancillary units*. They stimulate growth of entrepreneurship, promote a more decentralised pattern of ownership, diversification of economic activities, introduce new products to enrich the living standard of people and equitable dispersal of industries throughout rural and designated backward areas. A laudable goal, but easier said than done.

Policies constitute the framework or guidelines for appropriate decisions at varied levels. They generally consist of statements that affect the working of a sector of the economy. The working of small-scale industries too is moulded by a number of policies, which are the base for effective plan development.

The living standards of the people in this world vary considerably. Generally speaking, industrialised countries are known as developed countries, in which industrial development is based on modern technology and research. The countries in which agriculture predominates are referred to as underdeveloped/developing countries. Underdeveloped countries are those where even agriculture is quite traditional. Developing countries have accepted mechanisation as a way of life and have concentrated on developing large industries.

The president of the World Bank once pointed out that over 40 per cent of the people in developing countries live in absolute poverty. Their life is so degraded by disease, illiteracy, malnutrition and squalor that the attainment and availability of even the basic necessities seems to be difficult for them in the near future.

For a developing country like India, the growth of industries is of great significance. Apart from increased production, the growth of industries helps to serve as an important milestone in the country's march towards industrial democracy. This movement has to be fostered by all-round efforts, so that a new class of talented entrepreneurs, endowed with initiative and enterprise, comes to the fore in this country.

To sustain the pace of industrial growth and ensure that it is enhanced, it is necessary to create a conducive environment and industrial climate. All along, new institutions need to be created, infrastructure to be developed and technical and financial support to be provided on an ongoing basis. Truly, entrepreneurial training should also receive attention. The programmes and policies progressively broadened the very notion of industrial development, till it became synonymous with the 'development of a better life'. Thus, policies and programmes form the crux of the development process, in particular in harnessing entrepreneurial spirit and channeling for the rapid growth of the economy.

The scope for investment opportunities to entrepreneurs is enormously vast. Theoretically, an entrepreneur has an infinitely wide choice with respect to his projects. In identifying a feasible and promising product which is likely to benefit the society immensely, an entrepreneur has to understand the policies which govern entrepreneurship.

In this chapter, the following factors which have bearing in identifying *prima facie* feasible and promising investment opportunities are discussed. The critical factors are:

1. Industrial Policy Resolution
2. Import Export Policy 1994-97.
3. The Pricing Policy
4. The Textile Policy

5. Policy for Development of Handloom Industry
6. Policy for Khadi and Village Industries
7. Industrial Estates Programme.
8. Promotion of Ancillary Industries

NEW POLICY FOR SMALL AND TINY SECTOR

The industrial policy would reflect the direction and pattern of industrial development the country desires to have to help realise the economic, social and political objectives of national development by means of industrialisation. Thus, the industrial development of a country will be guided and fostered by the industrial policy.

The industrial policy would indicate the respective roles of the public, private, joint and cooperative sectors and also of the large, medium and small-scale sectors and will underline the national priorities. It would express government's policy, etc., in respect of the industrial sector.

A number of policy statements on industrial development have been made by the Government of India after independence, starting with the Industrial Policy of 1948.

Policy for Small Enterprises

Although the Industrial Policy Resolution of 1948 laid stress on the importance of small enterprises, especially cottage and village industries, the Industrial Resolution of 1956 laid down the role to be assigned to an approach of the government towards small-scale industries in the country.

Among other things, the Industrial Policy Resolution of 1956 has assigned the following tasks to the small-scale industries:

(i) To create on a big scale employment opportunities for people with a relatively low capital investment per head;

(ii) To make an attempt to meet a substantial part of domestic demand for consumer goods and even part of capital goods;

(iii) To bring about mobilisation of capital and entrepreneurial skills in vast areas of the country, especially in rural areas which otherwise would be lying unused;

(iv) To provide assistance to a larger number of entrepreneurs, artisans and craftsmen in getting employment, income and reasonable standard of living;

(v) To make available foreign market for the products of small-scale industries by taking measures to make them export-oriented.

(vi) To remove disparities in regional industrial development in areas where such services do not exist or are thoroughly inadequate so that small-scale industries may develop there, providing employment and income to people in the area.

The Industrial Policy Resolution of 1956 has also entrusted the following role to small-scale industries.

".....heavy industries in the public sector may obtain some of their requirements of the lighter components from the private sector, while the private sector in turn would rely for many of its needs on the public sector. The same principle would apply with even greater force to the relationship between large-scale and small-scale industries."

"The Government of India would, in this context, stress the role of cottage, village and small-scale industries in the development of the national economy. In relation to some of the problems that need urgent solution, they offer some distinct advantages. They provide immediate employment opportunities to a large number of people; they offer a method of ensuring equitable distribution of national income and they facilitate an effective mobilisation of resources of capital and skill which might otherwise remain unutilised. Some of the problems that unplanned urbanisation tends to create will be avoided by the establishment of small industrial prouction all over the country."

In the subsequent policy statements, the state followed a policy of supporting small enterprises in the country.

The First Statement, 1991

The small enterprises have emerged as a dynamic and vibrant sector of the economy. At present, it accounts for 55 per cent of industrial production, 40 per cent of exports and above 88 per cent of manufacturing employment. Though their relative importance tends to vary inversely with the level of development, their contribution remains significant in the country. The small-scale enterprises have also been playing a more significant role in creating balanced economic and social development in the country. Over the years, small enterprises have emerged as the leaders in the industrial sector in India. In recognition of their significance and stature, the new government announced policy measures for promoting and strengthening small, tiny and village enterprises on August 6, 1991 for the first time in the post-independence period. The new policy on tiny, small and village enterprises envisages almost a u-turn in policy stimulants and structure of both micro and small enterprises in the country.

Objectives

The primary objective of the small-scale industrial policy during the nineties was to impart more vitality and growth impetus to the sector so that the sector could contribute in terms of growth output, employment and export.

The other objectives are:

(i) To decentralise and delicense the sector;

(ii) To deregulate and debureaucratise it;

(iii) To review all statutes, regulations and procedures and affect suitable modifications wherever necessary;

(iv) To promote small enterprises, especially industries in the tiny sector.

(v) To motivate small and sound entrepreneurs to set up new green enterprises in the country;

(vi) To involve traditional and reputed voluntary organisations in the intensive development of Khadi and Village Industries (KVIs) through area approach;

(vii) To maintain a sustained growth in productivity and attain competitiveness in the market economy, especially in the international markets;

(viii) To industrialise backward areas of the country; and

(ix) To Accelerate the process of development of modern small enterprises, tiny enterprises and village industries through appropriate incentives, institutional support and infrastructure investments.

The total approach of the new policy is towards creating an atmosphere conducive to the development of entrepreneurship and technological progress.

SALIENT FEATURES OF NEW POLICY

The salient features are mentioned below:

- Equity participation up to 24 per cent by other industrial undertakings (including foreign companies).
- Legislation to limit financial liability of new and non-active partner/entrepreneurs to the capital invested.
- Hike in investment limit for tiny sector from ₹ 2 lakh to ₹ 5 lakh.
- Service sector to be recognised as tiny sector.
- Support from National Equity fund for projects up to ₹ 10 lakh.
- Single Window Loans to cover projects up to ₹ 20 lakh. Banks to be involved too.
- Relaxation of certain provisions of labour laws.
- Subcontracting exchanges to be set up by industry association.
- Easier access to institutional finance.
- Factoring services through SIDBI to overcome the problem of delayed payments. Also, legislation to ensure payment of bills.

- Women enterprises redefined.
- Marketing of mass consumption items by National Small Industries Corporation under common brand name.
- Composite loans under the single window scheme also to be given by banks.
- Tiny sector to be accorded priority in government purchase programme.
- Priority to SSIs and tiny units in allocation of indigenous raw materials.
- Promise to deregulate and debureaucratise small and tiny sector.
- PSUs and NSIC to help market products through consortia approach both domestically and internationally.
- Janata cloth scheme to be replaced by a new schema which will provide funds for loom modernisation.
- Compulsory quality control for products that pose risk to health and life.
- Legislation to ensure payment of small-scale industries bills.
- A special monetary agency to be set up for the small-scale sector's credit needs.
- A new scheme of integrated infrastructural development to be implemented.
- A technology development cell to be set up.
- Incentives and services package to be delivered at the district level.
- An export development centre to be set up.
- Khadi and Village Industries Commission (KVIC) and boards to be expanded.
- Investment limit of ancillary units and export-oriented units raised to ₹ 75 lakh, and
- Traditional village industries would be given greater thrust.

In pursuance of the objectives of the policy statement, the Government of India has decided to take a series of initiative in respect of the policies related to the following areas:

Small-scale Industries

(i) Financial Support
(ii) Infrastructure Facilities
(iii) Marketing and Exports
(iv) Modernisation
(v) Promotion of Entrepreneurship
(vi) Simplification of Rules and Procedures
(vii) Tapping Resources.

Tiny Sector

(i) Investment
(ii) Broadening the concept of the service sector
(iii) Location, and
(iv) Simplification of Rules

Handloom Sector

(i) Project Package Scheme
(ii) Welfare Package Scheme
(iii) Organisation and Development Scheme, and
(iv) NHDC as a Nodal Agency.

Handicraft Sector

(i) Extending services like supply of raw materials, etc.
(ii) Market Development Support, and
(iii) Expansion of Training Facilities.

Other Village Industries

(i) Improving Quality
(ii) Enquiring better flow of credit from financial institutions
(iii) Thrust on the traditional village industries
(iv) Setting of functional industrial estates, and
(v) Upgrading the training programmes and coordinating with development programmes.

THRUST AREAS OF THE POLICY FOR SMALL ENTERPRISES

The new policy for small enterprises has several welcome features and indicates a reorientation of policy on crucial issues like speedy modernisation, upgradation of technology, availability of cheap, adequate and timely credit and quality control and work towards drawing them into the main stream of industrialisation.

The principal thrust of the new industrial policy for small enterprises is to speed up their modernisation and draw them into the mainstream of industrialisation. This is a welcome departure from the previous policy of merely fostering their unstructured growth through incentives and concessions. More significantly, the new policy created scope for expanded investment in the small-scale sector.

The integration of the Indian economy with the global economy will call for greater exposure of small and medium-sized industries to international and domestic competition and appropriate development of the skills and management capabilities of small entrepreneurs.

Payment Mechanism

The new policy seeks to improve the payments mechanism as also introduce legislation to enforce payments on time. This is necessary to ensure that small industries do not get into the grip of the large buyer enterprises which may also control them through equity and technology. In less trying times than the present, the shift from cheap credit to prompt payment would have meant immense relief to small enterprises. But the steep hike in lending interest rates and the virtual credit squeeze that has flowed from the first steps to adjustment raise doubts about the nature of trade-offs that small enterprises will be forced to accept. The new policy assigns industry associations a key role in quality counselling and establishing common testing facilities to ensure standardised production by the small industry. Should not industry associations be involved in ensuring smooth payment by their constituents to the weaker partners in modernisation? The policy talks of establishing and 'export development centre', but does not address the issue of export marketing. This is a significant omission, considering the fact that access to imported inputs are contingent upon exports affected by manufacturers.

Factoring Services

Factoring has recently been introduced by the State Bank of India in western India in collaboration with the Small Industries Development Bank of India (SIDBI). Similar service reportedly has been set up in the South by Canara Bank in collaboration with SIDBI. It is, however, doubtful if the factoring services as now visualised by SIDBI and the commercial banks will be able to solve the problem of delayed payment to small industries.

At present, these factoring services accept only receivables against 'first rate large and medium enterprises'. In no case, such enterprises can be accused of delayed payment. In this context, the promised legislation to ensure prompt payment of bills will meet one of the acutely felt needs of small suppliers of goods and services to both private and public sector enterprises.

The proposed Limited Partnership Act, which has been in demand for a decade or more will also help in enhancing the availability of risk capital for the small-scale sector. Further, the Act will limit the financial liability of the new inactive partners putting in the capital investment.

Resources for SSI

The most important change for the modern small-scale sector is the provision of additional finance by permitting limited liability for new non-active partners and by permitting up to 24 per cent equity investment by other industrial undertakings. This could encourage indirect ownership of small units by larger corporate entities. This already exists to a substantial degree as companies trying to cut costs, farm out production and also circumvent the reservation policy with regard to small units. The new policy in effect legitimises this kind of activity and must, therefore, be questioned. There is admittedly a great deal of merit in encouraging ancillarisation as it promotes the greater use of labour-intensive techniques of production and also broad-based entrepreneurship. However, it is quite a different thing to have what are nominally small-scale units which actually operate as part of large industrial conglomerates while enjoying all the benefits meant to encourage small-scale units. Is this aspect of the policy meant to help small or large ones?

Timely and Adequate Credit

The encouraging feature of the new policy is that it recognises the fact that small units require timely credit and financing arrangement rather than cheap credit. The scope of the single window clearance, which has been enlarged to cover project costs up to ₹ 20 lakh and working capital up to ₹ 10 lakh make things easier at the entry point. The point is to ensure that units once set up are allowed to function smoothly by the timely provision of additional credit. But it is not clear how this will be ensured. The setting up of a special monitoring agency is of little help unless it has the powers to force commercial banks to lend the additional credit required. In the final analysis, the new policy is only as good as its implementation. Considering that more than one-third of manufacturing output originates in the small-scale sector, and more than 40 per cent of total exports, this sector deserves at least as much encouragement as the large industrial sector. It must be borne in mind that the solution to industrial unemployment in the country is far more likely to come from small units than from an increasingly capital-intensive large industrial sector.

Nodal Agency

The Small Industry Development Organisation (SIDO) has been recognised as the nodal agency to support the SSIs in export promotion. An 'export development centre' was to be set up in a network of field offices to further augment export activities of this sector. A technology development cell would also be set up in SIDO to provide technology inputs for improving productivity and competitiveness of SSI products.

Regulatory provisions relating to the management of private limited companies are being libralised. The Limited Partnership Act will be introduced to enhance the supply of risk capital to the small-scale sector. Such an Act would limit the financial liability of the new and non-active partners to the capital invested. The policy has not spelt out their programme of action to free the small-scale sector from the harassment from some 57 inspectors who call on regularly on small units. An action programme would have eased the tension of the harassed entrepreneur.

To facilitate location of industries in backward areas and to promote stronger linkages between agriculture and industry, a new scheme of integrated infrastructural development for small-scale industries would be implemented with the active participation of state governments and financial institutions.

A technology development cell would be set up in the Small Industries Development Organisation which would provide technology inputs to improve productivity.

Marketing

Marketing promotion would be undertaken through cooperative, public sector institutions, other professional and marketing agencies backed up by such incentives as considered necessary.

The National Small Industries Corporation (NSIC) would concentrate on marketing of mass consumption items under a common brand name. An export development centre would be set up in SIDO to serve the small-scale industries through its network of field offices to promote exports.

Raw Material

Based on the capacity needs, tiny/small-scale units would be given priority in the allocation of indigenous raw materials.

Besides this, adequate and equitable distribution of imported raw materials would also be ensured for this sector. It has been felt that marketing has been a big hurdle in the promotion of tiny and the small sector. Now market promotion would be undertaken through cooperative/public sector institutions and other specialised promotional marketing agencies.

Quality

To improve the quality of goods and services of small-scale units, industry associations would be encouraged and supported to establish quality counselling and other testing facilities. Technology information centres, to provide up to date knowledge on technology and market would also be established. Compulsory quality control would be enforced.

Additional employment opportunities would be generated through training of multidisciplinary managers to suit the special requirements of the small-scale sectors. Indian Institute of Technology and selected regional/other engineering colleges would serve as technological information, design and development centres for the SSIs in their respective command areas.

Rules and procedures related to establishment and functioning of SSIs will be simplified. Any complaint regarding submission of returns, etc., would be attended to within a specified timeframe of three months.

Missing Aspects

The most regrettable feature of the new policy is the absence of any provision for restoring health and vitality to viable sick units. The policy is also silent about the future of young men and women, who staked everything that their parents or guardians could mobilise for setting up units which had to be closed down for bonafide reasons. They are already involved in cases for recovery of income tax, sales tax and other statutory levies and bank loans.

While bankruptcy in small businesses is not unknown in most industrialised countries, entrepreneurs, whose units had to be closed, can start up again with the financial support of institutions including commercial banks. In India, this is impossible. The National Alliance of Young Entrepreneurs (NAYE) has therefore, recommended that a Statutory Board of Settlement or Board of Litigation be set up to arbitrate and decide as to the extent and manner in which an entrepreneur can be called upon to finally discharge liabilities decided by it. If banks or large undertakings, which are declared insolvent, can get away by paying only 10 or 15 per cent of their accepted liabilities, there is no reason why small entrepreneurs cannot be give similar benefits.

The policy is also silent on price preference to small-scale and tiny industries by Central, State Governments and public sector enterprises. Nor does it mention whether existing purchase preferences for goods of the small-scale sector including tiny enterprises will continue. This has caused serious misapprehensions in the minds of non-tiny small industries.

The policy is also silent on vital components of management and entrepreneurial development on the one hand and integration of tiny and village industries with other industries. In fact, the policy for the small and tiny sector can only be part of the industrial policy. A better linkage with the other components is very vital, otherwise corporate bodies and multinationals will override this sector.

Apprehensions

Much avoidable controversy has been generated by introducing in the policy provision for unrestricted holding of up to 24 per cent equity participation in the small sector by other industrial undertakings. It has been clarified by an official spokesman that the permission for introduction of foreign capital will be automatic.

The government's hope that domestic large industries will not dominate the small-scale sector is not based on rational grounds. Once large companies get into unit producing items reserved for the small-scale sector, such units will totally become captive. There is no way the government can prevent their total domination over such small units once large undertakings, particularly India, have a financial stake.

It is also not desirable to allow foreign and domestic large companies in low-capital, labour-intensive consumer goods industries reserved for the small sector. The government and the representatives of micro- and small enterprises should carefully look into the items reserved for the small sector and decide on the items in which such investments can be permitted without causing any hardship to indigenous small entrepreneurs. Such permissions need to be necessarily accorded on a selective basis. It is not without reason that captains of large industries are so jubilant over the policy which will permit inroads now by the front door.

Tiny Sector

The policy statement gives a new thrust for the development of tiny enterprises which accounts for nearly 90 per cent of all small-scale units. The investment ceiling has been raised from ₹ 2 lakh to ₹ 5 lakh. A significant feature of the policy is the due recognition. In order to strengthen the tiny sector, it has been decided to recognise all industry-related services and business enterprises irrespective of their location as small-scale industries. Their investment ceiling would correspond to those of tiny enterprises.

While the small-scale sector (other than tiny enterprises) would be mainly entitled to one-time benefit (like preference in land allocation/power connection, access to facilities for skill/technology upgradation), the tiny enterprises would also be eligible for additional support on a continuing basis, including easier access to institutional finance, priority in the government purchase programme and relaxation from certain provisions of labour laws.

Handloom Sector

Schemes for the handloom sector will be redesigned keeping in mind the local and regional needs. Substantial funds will be provided for modernisation of looms, training, provision of better designs, provision of better dyes and chemicals and marketing assistance. Spinning capacity in the cooperative sector will be increased. National Cooperative Development Corporation will provide more assistance for this in the form of seed money, both for cotton growers, 'spinning mills and weavers' spinning mills.

The Janata cloth scheme which sustains weavers often on a minimum level of livelihood will be phased out by the terminal year of the Eighth Plan and replaced by the 'omnibus project package scheme' under which substantial funds will be provided for modernisation of looms, training, provision for better designs, provision for better dyes and chemicals and marketing assistance.

The role of the National Handloom Development Centres (NHDCs) is also being enhanced. It would now be a nodal agency for increasing supply of hank yarn and of dyes and chemicals. The spinning capacity will also be increased and the National Cooperative Development Corporation (NCDC) will provide more assistance in the form of seed money, both for cotton growers' spinning mills and weavers' spinning mills.

For the handicraft sector, 'craft development centres' are proposed to be set up which would ensure of raw materials, design and technical guidance, market support, training and procuring of related input in an integrated and area-based manner. Measures are also proposed to be initiated to increase exports from this sector through new marketing channels like trading companies and departmental stores.

Village Industries

Intensive development of KVIs through area approach with tie-up with DRDA, TRYSEM and ongoing development programmes relating to weaker sections like scheduled castes, scheduled tribes and women would be extended throughout the country. The traditional village industries would be given greater thrust.

Involvement of traditional and repute voluntary organisations will be encouraged for this purpose. However, the key components of the policy with regard to the handloom and handicraft sectors can be assessed only after one knows how exactly the new packages for these sectors will operate. The new policy's success depends substantially on the quality of the service provided by bodies like the small-scale industries development organisations, the process-cum-product development centres, the National Small Industries Corporation, etc., whose track record does not inspire confidence.

Box 5.1 New Policy Measures and SSIs

Sl.No.	Policy Changes	Effect on SSIs
1.	**Industrial Policy:**	
	Exemption from industrial licensing requirements affected through competition from new units	Although SSIs are not covered by this measure, the small industry is likely to be being set up in the delicensed sector
	Upward revision of investment ceilings in plant and machinery for SSIs, ancillary	To improve technology and products standardisation. This measure has brought in

	and exporting units in 1991 and again in 1997	competition from large-scale units, which have now come within the enhanced investment bracket of ₹ 30 million
	Relaxation in the manufacture of reserved items by large-scale units with 50% export obligations	Introduced new market competition to domestic sales and exports
	Environmental clearances before setting up of industrial products.	Provided relief to units for low-polluting items as an NOC is no longer required. Only an application form is to be filed with the pollution control authority
2.	**Foreign Direct Investment:**	
	Equity participation up to 24% in SSI by other undertakings including foreign investor companies	Inflow of new capital results in better financial strength, upgradation of technology and promotion of exports
	Beyond 24% is considered for reserved items manufacturing with 50% export obligations	
	100% foreign equity permitted for export-oriented Units/Export Processing Zones	
3.	**Technology Transfer:**	
	Foreign technology agreements and extensions	Product innovation and improvement in design leading to an increase in sales
	Removal of restrictions for use of foreign brand name/trademark for internal sale.	Increasing sales by protecting against piracy
	Amendment of the Indian Intellectual Property Rights (IPR) laws	
4.	**Trade Liberalisation:**	
	Reduction in customs duties on various items.	Improved access to imports of raw material.
	Duty reduction on import of capital goods and liberalisation of procedure	Modernisation of manufacturing processes
	Quality Certification Scheme of assistance for ISO 9000 series.	Improvement in export competitiveness
	Liberalisation of export procedures and incentives for exporters	Boosting of exports
	Removal of items from the negative list.	Increasing export opportunities.
	Liberalisation of the import of consumer goods	More competition in the electronics and white goods sector.

Assessment

Thus, the MRTP asset limit has been done away with a foreign equity participation hiked to 51 per cent for all but 18 industries. Yet, these policies have left the small-scale industries (SSI) untouched. (The SSI contributes over 30 per cent of GNP of exports and employs four million people in 1.9 million units – 17 per cent of which are sick or bankrupt).

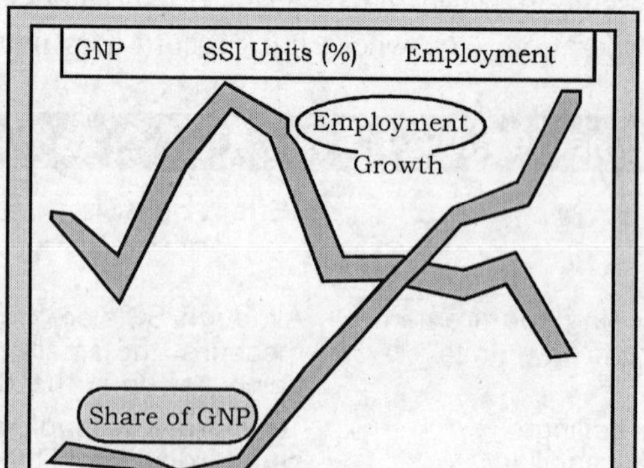

Has the four-decade old experiment of promoting SSIs by reserving employment-intensive industries for them and granting excise credits and interest subsidies to them been worth it?

The government has now come out with a lacklustre SSI policy. True, by raising asset limits and allowing 24 per cent equity participation by other industrial undertakings, the policy will help larger units in the small sector. But the majority will be unaffected, since 95 per cent of SSIs have below ₹ 2 lakh worth of assets.

But the point is that the sector is neither short of funds nor sick (see chart New Policy Measures and SSIs). The 17 per cent sickness is due to two reasons. One, because finance was given to intrinsically enviable units by nationalised banks seeking to fulfil their priority sector lending targets. Two, as benefits have, by definition, been reserved for low asset companies, it has forced several companies to remain small and vulnerable to market forces.

So if, as the data show, the sector is healthy, doesn't it make sense to let it be apart from fixing the cause of sickness by proper evaluation and monitoring of loans – a job that the Small Industries Development Board of India should do but has not?

The answer is no. There lies the fundamental problem of reservation that should have been addressed by the new policy. Currently, the SSI classification is given to 836 high-employment low-technology items. It has thus helped the growth of sectors which would in any case have remained small, such as boot polish and umbrellas. Sure, there would be marketing synergies in items like umbrellas but these would have been exploited by large firms using small firms as contract suppliers, even if the sector had been dereserved.

On the other hand, SSI benefits do not go to companies which commit large amounts to technology and capital, yet remain small in employee size. These have a significant contribution to make to the economy and need to be encouraged with cheap credits and access to the best domestic and foreign technology.

This strategy has paid-off spectacularly in Japan. For example, in the Tokyo industrial district of Otaku, well known for its innovative small factories, 95 per cent of the 9,000 companies have fewer than 30 employees. Overall in Japan, 75 per cent of industrial output comes from small or mid-sized companies. The experience of Germany and Italy is similar.

Quite simply, the small-scale does not need reservation of items. Where the technology is low and capital investment small, as in paints and dye-stuffs, natural economic forces will ensure that the bulk of production comes from small companies even if there is no SSI reservation for such items.

On the other hand, where technology is high and capital investment large, an item which could overtime become viable needs encouragement with subsides until it becomes large enough to be on its own.

The most sensible policy would be to deserve all items for the small-scale sector and provide subsidies to any small unit with turnover below a certain level (Say, ₹ 1 crore) and for affixed number of years after start-up (say three years). This would ensure that a small company gets the support it needs, until it reaches a viable level of sales. Thereafter, it would have to fend itself for itself with its increasing sales and market share, helping it to spread its fixed costs and obtain higher margins.

What has emerged is an SSI policy that makes for little change.This is a mistake in the context of the rapid, technology-inspired growth that the country needs. One expected much more from the new government after its bold industrial policy and budget.

EXPERT COMMITTEE ON SMALL ENTERPRISES – NEW POLICY DIRECTIVES 1997

An expert committee on small enterprises constituted in December 1995 under the Chairmanship of Shri Abid Hussain, Vice-chairman, Rajiv Gandhi Institute of Contemporary Studies, New Delhi, submitted its report in January 1997. The Committee gave important recommendations having a bearing on the small-scale sector. Some of the recommendations pertaining to cluster development, technology support, infrastructure development and SSI associations related issues are given below:

Cluster Developments:

- State governments to identify existing clusters and promote joint ventures between themselves/local authorities and business associations.

Technology Support:

- The ongoing process of economic reforms has facilitated large companies to enter into strategic alliances and joint ventures with overseas companies and MNCs can acquire equal or majority control to enable transfer of technology and tacit knowledge to Indian counterparts for product innovation. SSIs, on the contrary, are handicapped as the investment climate is not supportive enough to attract foreign as well as domestic investment from other companies into the SSI units as equity holding of other companies is capped at 24 per cent. To overcome the problem of technology lag for SSIs is to establish long-term alliances with large companies through the process of ancillarisation. The competitive strength of SSIs become fragile because of technological obsolescence and low quality products as per international standards. The expert committee recommended various steps to overcome this problem, including amending/repealing such laws as those that act as barriers to technological progress. In this direction, it was further recommended that the Department of Science and Technology should initiate a new scheme in the Ninth Five Year Plan to form 50 R&D associations with interested small-scale units as members, based around identified clusters and provide funding. It was also recommended that a National Research Institute be established to promote schemes for assisting technology upgradation and research and development for small-scale enterprises. This institute would operate as a networking institution and a clearing house for policy studies and technology issues that are raised by the small-scale industry.

Box 5.2 Small Industry Clusters In India

States	Clusters
Tamil Nadu (8)	1. Artificial Diamonds (Tiruchirapalli) 2. Hosiery (Tirupur) 3. Leather (Chennai) 4. Match Box/Fireworks (Sivakasi) 5. Engineering Industry (Tiruchirapalli) 6. Agricultural Pumps (Coimbatore) 7. Diesel Engines (Coimbatore) 8. Rigs (Tiruchengod)
Haryana (12)	9. Automobile Components (Gurgaon) 10. Automobile Components (Faridabad) 11. Handlooms (Panipat) 12. Scientific Instruments (Ambala) 13. Shoddy Yarn (Panipat) 14. Foundary (Samalkha) 15. Leather Footwear-Juti (Rewari) 16. Nuts/Bolts (Rohtak) 17. Cane Products (Mohindergarh) 18. Engineering Industry (Pinjore) 19. Mixiers and Grinders (Ambala) 20. Mushroom Cutivation (Sonipat)
Uttar Pradesh (13)	21. Electronics (Noida) 22. Sports Goods (Meerut) 23. Brassware (Moradabad) 24. Carpets (Bhadoi) 25. Glass Works (Shikhohabad/Ferozabad) 26. Hosiery (Kanpur) 27. Leather (Kanpur) 28. Leather footwear (Agra) 29. Ceramic Industry (Khurja) 30. Essential Oils (Kannauj) 31. Foundry (Agra) 32. Petha Sweets (Agra) 33. Locks (Aligarh)
Himachal Pradesh (7)	34. Paper (Solan) 35. Food Products (Kullu and Sirmaur) 36. Woollen Shawls (Kulu) 37. Light Engineering (Parwanoo) 38. Textiles (Baddi Barotiwala-Solan) 39. Cement (Kala Amb-Sirmaur) 40. Induction furnace (Solan and Sirmaur)
Gujarat (20)	41. Petrochemical Industry (Vadodara) 42. Brass Parts (Jamnagar) 43. Diamonds (Surat) 44. Machine Tools (Rajkot) 45. Read-ymade Garments (Ahmedabad) 46. Oil Paint (Vallabh Vidyanagar) 47. Salt and Salt based (Bhavnagar) 48. Chemicals (Vapi/Ankleshwar) 49. Chemical (Nandesari) 50. Diesel Engines (Rajkot) 51. Engineering Industry (Makarpura) 52. Flooring Tiles (Morbi) 53. Isabagol (Unjh-Mehsana) 54. Oil Mills Manufacture (Amrelli-Junagarh, Rajkot) 55. Sarees (Pattola Patan-Mehsana) 56. Textile Processing (Getpur) 57. Textiles (Surat) 58. Tuhar Dal (Vasad Kheda) 59. Wall Clocks (Morbi) 60. Weights and Measures (Savarkundla)
Punjab (14)	61. Agricultural Implement (Patiala Bhadson) 62. Automobile Components (Ludhiana) 63. Electric Fans (Ludhiana) 64. Hand Tools (Jallandhar) 65. Hosiery (Ludhiana) 66. Machine Tools (Batala) 67. Rubber Goods (Jallandhar) 68. Shoddy Yarn (Amritsar) 69. Sports Goods (Jallandhar) 70. Woollen Shawls (Amritsar) 71. Wheat Threshers (Moga) 72. Bicyle Parts (Ludhiana) 73. Diesel Engines (Phagwara) 74. Re-rolling Steel Mills (Mandi Govindgarth) 75. Sewing Machine Components (Ludhiana)
Maharashtra (24)	76. Automobile Components (Aurangabad) 77. Automobile Components (Pune) 78. Bed Spread (Sholapur) 79. Brass Goods (Bhandara) 80. Electronics (Pune) 81. Electronics (Mumbai) 82. Food Products (Pune) 83. Ganesh Statues (Pen Panvel) 84. Kumkum [Kem Sholapur (District)] 85. Lakh (Bhandara) 86. Ready-made Garments (Mumbai) 87. Silver Ornaments (Huppari) 88. Beedi (Bhandarage/Shinnar) 89. Chuna Bhatti (Rajura) 90. Foundry (Kolhapur) 91. Kaju (Vauguria Ratnagi) 92. Chemicals (Vashi) 93. Chappals (Kolhapur) 94. Diesel Engines (Kolhapur) 95. Powerlooms

	(Bhivandi) 96. Powerlooms Text Processing (Bhiwandi Malagarh) 97. Sarees (Paithan) 98. Sarees P. Looms (Nagpur) 99. Shipping Industry (Malegaon)
Assam (1)	100. Brass and Bell Metal (Hajo)
West Bengal (9)	101. Electric Fans (Calcutta) 102. Fishing Hooks (Bankura) 103. Handlooms (Agar Purulia (District) 104. Hosiery (Calcutta) 105. Leather (Howrah) 106. Wooden Handicraft (Bankura) 107. Foundary (Howrah) 108. Locks (Howrah) 109. Battery Unit (Howrah)
Karnataka (4)	110. Electronics (Bangalore) 111. Food Products (Karnataka) 112. Handmade Garments (Bangalore) 113. Silk (Mysore)
Orissa (3)	114. Handmade Silver Jewellery (Cuttak) 115. Handicrafts (Pipli) 116. Tusser, Silk (Sambhalpur)
Rajasthan (14)	117. Handmade Paper (Jaipur) 118. Handtools (Nagpur) 119. Lacquar Craft (Jaipur) 120. Marble Cutting (Kishangarh) 121. Screen Printing (Balhotra/Pali) 122. Textile Hand Printing (Sanganer) 123. Woollen Carpets (Jaipur) 124. Cement (Sirohi) 125 Gems & Jewellery (Jaipur) 126. Oils Mills (Alwar, S Madhopur Bharatpur) 127. Papad Mangodi (Bikaner) 128. Spinning and Processing (Bhilwara) 129. Statue Murticar (Jaipur)) 130. Textile Processing (Jodhpur)
Delhi (3)	131. Hosiery (Delhi) 132. Ready-made Garments (Delhi) 133. Stone Crushers (Rajoukri)
Madhya Pradesh (2)	134. Ready-made Garments (Indore) 135. Engineering Industry (Bhopal)
Andhra Pradesh (1)	136. Electronics (Hyderabad)
Kerala (2)	137. Sea Food Processing (Coastal Kerala) 138. Rubber (Kottayam)

(**Source:** UNIDO Report on Restructuring and Modernisation of SME Clusters in India, 1997.)

Infrastructure Development

- Private sector to be encouraged in the development of industrial parks. States to provide an opportunity by inviting private sector participation in upgradation and management of existing industrial parks.
- State governments to set up State Industrial Parks Promotion Authorities (SIPAs) which would regulate the setting up of these parks and assist and negotiate with the private sector for their participation.

SSI Associations Related Issues

- Dissemination of information/advisory services through the centres which may be set up in collaboration with SIDBI/state government. This may *inter alia* help in tapping the export potential of the SSI sector.
- For emerging needs of the SSI sector in the light of the opening up of the economy, there is need for having common facility centres at district/cluster level which will be set up on professional lines to help small units and help saving on costs (large number of associations have very thin and non-professional secretariats).
- To set up companies to market products of member units, common testing centres, etc.

CONCLUSION

Though conceptually sound, the new policy for small-scale industrial units including the tiny sector opens the flood gates for large industries and foreign companies, thus minimising the natural growth of entrepreneurship at the grassroot level. More importantly its success depends to a greater degree on the quality of the downstream action that is required. And the merit of the policy depends on its implementation, as well as in plugging the loopholes. The policy is expected to provide fresh stimulus for growth and international competitiveness of the small sector, if it is matched with timely technological upgradation, professional management, innovative ideas, entrepreneurial vision and well trained manpower. The need of the hour is an agenda for growth of small enterprises and industries in the tiny sector as a viable phenomenon. This apart, developing entrepreneurship and promoting responsible and innovative management must be the guiding principles of the new policy for the small enterprises. It calls for a sincere attempt to foster development and growth.

It has to be commended for its innovative features such as strengthening of micro (tiny) enterprises, removal of locational constraints, broadcasting of the concept of the small industry by including industry-related services and small business, ensuring access to need-based finance and promising deregulated and debureaucratised small business administration. However, the success of the policy will depend on its effective implementation.

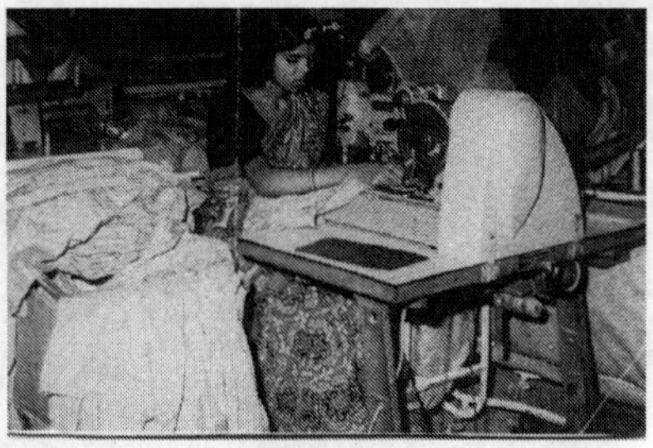

6 CHAPTER RURAL INDUSTRIES AND RURAL ARTISANS

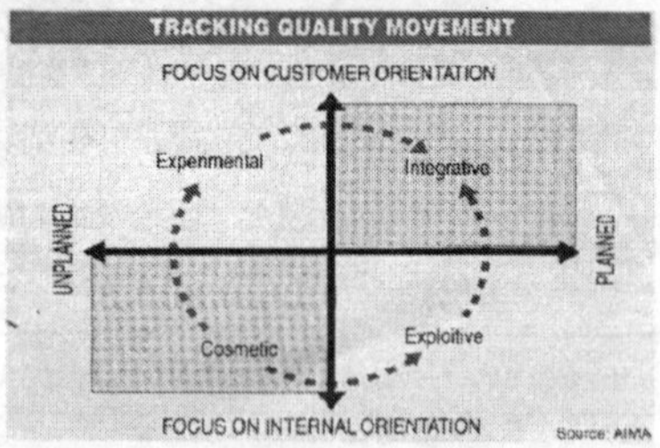

The movement that turned the charkha is inspiring a booming Indian rural industry.

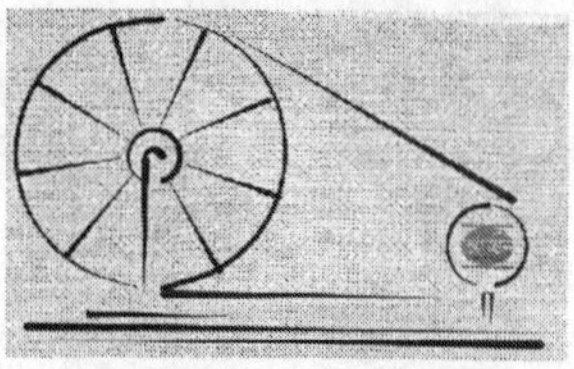

LEARNING OBJECTIVES

- To provide an insight into rural industries and rural artisans in India.
- Village and cottage industries and the SSI sector are an integral part of each other. The Planning Commission considers the village and small industries sector in its entirety and its definition includes traditional sectors, such as Khadi, Village Industries, Handlooms, Sericulture, Handicrafts, Coir and the modern sector including powerlooms and SSI.
- The chapter deals with:
- Benefits of rural industrialisation.
- Types of rural industries – Traditional and others.
- Importance of rural industrialisation.
- Strategy for rural industrialisation.
- Towards rural prosperity.

INTRODUCTION

Promotion of rural industries has been the central objective of many strategies adopted to bring about an equitable distribution of income through raising the productive capacity of rural people and increasing their participation in the process of development. Rural industrialisation is interlinked with agricultural activity.

What is a Rural Industry?

Rural industry embraces different kinds of village and small industries. The cottage industries are an important component of the rural industry. By the term 'rural industry' is meant an industry appropriate for the rural areas as demarcated by the census records. The concept here has a special demographic undertone. The rural industry serves the requirements of rural people as well as other markets. By and large, the financial needs of rural industry are small. More importantly, they function in the absence of infrastructural facilities and are environmentally-friendly.

Rural Artisans

Rural artisans are creative workers living in rural areas, playing a key role in the growth of the rural economy. An artisan is a doer, skilled craftsman of either gender.

He may be a machinist, operator, driver, mechanic, minder, or simply a craftsman.

An artisan has been defined as an "artmaster", designer or draftsman. He may be an artificer, tradesman, technician, skilled or semi-skilled worker or a pastmaster.

He may be proficient, journeyman or an apprentice. The categories of craftsmen specifically mentioned are: turner, potter, joiner, cabinet maker, carpenter, carver, woodworker, etc. He can be an architect, master mason, house-builder, brick layer, smith, blacksmith, coppersmith, to name a few.

Benefits of Rural Industrialisation

1. Rural industries provide additional employment opportunities, raise production and improve economic conditions in rural areas.
2. They are labour-intensive in terms of providing additional employment to men and women. They ensure decentralisation of economic power and elimination of monopolistic exploitation.
3. Decentralised production through network of well-knit rural industries obviates the necessity of complicated managerial and competitive marketing techniques, thus, reducing the costs on account of overheads.
4. Rural industrialisation leads to the development of rural areas thereby lessening the disproportionate growth in large cities, reducing the growth of slums, social tensions, exploitation and environmental pollution.
5. Rural industries will strive to build-up village republics and human resources development.
6. Rural industrialisation provides ample scope for the promotion of artistic achievement and creativity that has been suppressed in rural areas.

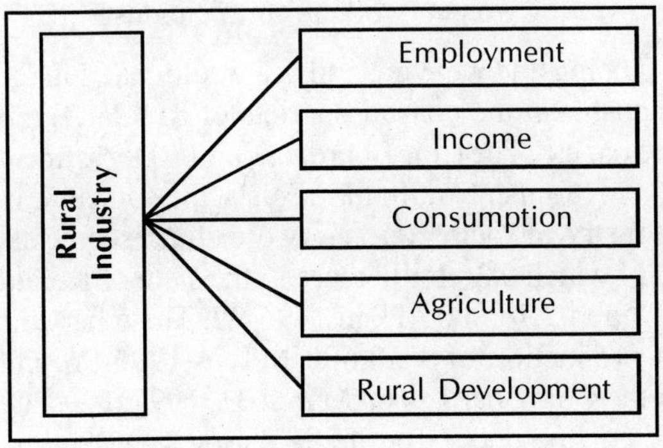

Although agriculture is the mainstay of the economy, rural industry is a complementary industry. The pressure of population on land is already high and increasing. In the process, it has resulted in a large surplus of labour, both educated as well as uneducated in rural areas. Agriculture alone cannot absorb the entire surplus force and hence the need for rural industries. If we consider rural industry as a mainstay, agriculture is an important part of this process. Rural industrialisation aims at the maximum productive employment of local resources, revival and development of traditional industries and skills, establishment of new units and integration of agricultural and industrial development to local prosperity, progressively narrow down the disparities between urban and rural incomes and prevent migration of rural population. More so, rural industrialisation has been assigned a crucial role in the development of industrially backward areas in rural India.

TYPES OF RURAL INDUSTRIES

By and large, rural industries are interlinked with agricultural activities, rural development and the service sector. They may also be grouped into small-scale industry, tiny industry and rural artisan (self-employed). The scope for process industry is vast and unexplored. The need of the hour is the proper organisation of rural industries and strategically integrate them into the rural ethos and development.

Powerlooms

The unorganised powerloom sector largely meets the requirements of the country's population. This sector contributes approximately 54 per cent to the total cloth production (excluding the cloth produced by non-SSI, weaving and hosiery/ knitting units).

There are 15,23,336 powerloom units in the country. The powerloom sector in India manufactured 10 billion square metres of cloth and employed 7.08 million persons. In view of the rising export share of this sector, the government has increased the export quota of fabrics and ready-made garments for powerloom units [exporting to quota countries covered by the Multi-fibre Agreement (MFA)].

Traditional Industries

Handicrafts: Handicrafts embody the traditional skills of artisans who use a variety of materials – wood, metal, clay ivory, cloth, etc., to produce consumer articles as well as decorative or artistic products. Today, only artistic and decorative articles are classified as handicrafts. The All India Handicrafts Board is responsible for the development of this industry, while the Handlooms and Handicrafts Export Promotion Corporation promotes exports from this subsector. This industry alone employs 7.6 million persons according to the Annual Report of Handicrafts Board, and is of special significance in the country's economy as regards foreign exchange earnings.

The promotion of handicrafts industries rests with state governments but various schemes at the Central level are directed by the Development Commissioner (Handicrafts). The important products from this sector are hand knitted carpets, printed textiles, art, metalwares, etc. The main item of exports are zari and zari goods, art, metalwares, woodwares, hand printed textiles, scarves and embroidered/crocheted goods and gems and Jewellery.

Handlooms: Handlooms form a part of India's heritage and exemplify the richness and artistry of the weavers. The handloom industry is the largest direct and indirect employer (more that 3.0 million weavers and 12.4 million other persons) among the traditional industries. The production of handloom fabrics is 7,862 million square metres and contributed to nearly 23 per cent of total cloth produced in the country. The hand weaving of cloth from yarn (produced by the mills) form an important segment of rural industry with respect to geographical spread, employment and exports.

The Handloom (Reservation of Articles for Production) Act, 1985, aimed at protecting the interests of weavers. Under this Act, 11 textile articles are presently reserved for exclusive production by handloom units.

Sericulture: India is the second largest producer of silk in the world. There are four main varieties of silk produced in the country, viz.: mulberry (91.7 per cent), eri (6.1 per cent), tasar (1.6 per cent) and muga (0.6 per cent). Sericulture is an agro-industrial activity based on mulberry and non-mulberry silk production and provides gainful occupation to about 6 million persons in the rural and semi-urban areas. There is substantial involvement of women workers in this industry.

Coir: Coir, obtained for coconut husk, involves operations like netting, spinning and weaving and is a traditional cottage industry located in coconut producing states. It forms an important cottage industry in the coastal districts of Kerala, Tamil Nadu, Karnataka, Andhra Pradesh, West Bengal, Orissa, Maharashtra, Assam, Goa, etc. The Coir Board, under the Department of Small-scale Industries and Agro and Rural Industries (SSI and A&RI), Government of India, assists the industry in increasing exports and in improving the quality of coir products. The coir industry in India consists two distinct segments, viz.: white and brown fibre. This sector employs a total of 0.5 million persons, of which 0.36 million are in the state of Kerala itself. The production of coir fibre was 2,63,300 metric tonnes (MT) in 1995-96 and 2,76,000 MT in 1996-97. The other coir products, such as, coir yarn, rope, curled and rubberised coir registered a production of 1,38,600 MT in 1995-96 and 1,47,300 MT during 1996-97. Out of a total of 6,531 coir units registered with the Coir Board as on March 31, 1997, the state of Kerala alone accounted for 5,124 registered coir units. Exports of coir and coir products from India during 1995-96 and 1996-97 were valued at ₹ 2,070 million and ₹ 2,130 million, respectively.

Khadi and Village Industries: Handwoven cloth from hand spun yarn is known as khadi. Along with certain specific village industries such as food processing, forest-based raw materials such as food processing, forest-based and other miscellaneous manufacturing activities, Khadi comes within the purview of the statutory body known as the Khadi and Village Industries Commission (KVIC). This agency operates under the department of SSI and A&RI in the Ministry of Industry. The Khadi and Village Industries (KVI) sector has much scope for utilising local silks and resources by providing employment to rural artisans and women workers in the rural and semi-urban areas.

The KVI sector employed a total of 6 million persons. The production of khadi cloth is 125 million square metres (msqm). The production originating from village industries was valued at ₹ 4,150 crore.

Rural and Urban Distribution of Enterprises

The state-wise distribution of 14.50 million enterprises (according to the 1994-95 CSO Survey of Manufacturing Enterprises), as furnished in Appendix 2.4, shows that of the total enterprises located in rural areas, Uttar Pradesh shared 17.49 per cent; West Bengal 14.59 per cent; Orissa 12.59 per cent, Bihar 10.95 per cent and Andhra Pradesh 9.19 per cent of enterprises.

The CSO Survey of Enterprises (1994-95) indicated that 72.37 per cent of enterprises operated in rural areas while the Second Census revealed that 42.2 per cent of the units were in rural areas. The industry group-wise distribution or units in rural areas both from SIDO Census and the CSO Survey is presented in Table 6.1.

Due to the government's promotional policies, with particular reference to the growth of backward areas and dispersal of units, industrialisation has taken place in various parts of the states including backward areas.

Table 6.1 Dispersal of Enterprises: Rural Areas

Industrial Groups	Manufacturing Enterprise Survey 1994-95	Percentage to Total	Second All India SSI	Percentage to Total Census 1987-88
Food Products	1,950.60	18.58	60.78	24.75
Beverages, Tobacco and Tobacco Products	1,145.03	10.91	1.78	0.72
Cotton Textiles	636.36	6.06	0.40	0.16
Wool, Silk and Synthetics Fibre Text	211.13	2.01	0.44	0.18
Jute, Hemp and Mesta Textiles	80.38	0.77	0.06	0.02
Hosiery and Garments	835.96	8.14	21.51	8.76
Wood Products	2,441.49	23.26	30.54	12.44
Paper Products and Printing	51.72	0.49	5.47	2.23
Leather Products	121.10	1.15	13.94	5.68
Rubber and Plastic Products	68.46	0.65	6.65	2.71
Chemical and Chemical Products	23.85	0.23	7.60	3.09
Non-metallic Mineral Products	744.922	7.10	17.45	7.11
Basic Metal Industries	7.05	0.07	2.09	0.85
Metal Products	249.49	2.38	22.55	9.18
Machinery and Parts Except Elect.	51.72	0.49	7.32	2.98
Electrical Machinery and Parts	6.71	0.06	1.47	0.60
Transport Equipments and Parts	7.80	0.07	2.95	1.20
Miscellaneous Mfg. Industries	688.81	6.56	2.00	0.82
Other Repair Services	252.12	2.40	3.07	1.25
Repair Services	897.58	8.55	37.43	115.24
Services (not else where classified)	6.80	0.07	0.07	0.03
Total	**10,497.08**	**100.00**	**245.57**	**100.00**

(**Source:** CSO-manufacturing Enterprise Survey 1994-95; DG (SSI);Second All India SSI Census).

Table 6.2 Details of Rural Industries Programme

States	Districts	Agency
Madhya Pradesh	Betul and Dhar	Centre for Entrepreneurship Development, Madhya Pradesh (CEDMAP), Bhopal
Chhattisgarh	Raipur	Centre for Entrepreneurship Development, Madhya Pradesh (CEDMAP), Bhopal
Jharkhand	Hazaribagh and Koderma	Nav Bharat Jagriti Kendra (NBJK), Hazaribagh.
	Palamu	ACIL Navsarjan Rural Development Foundation (ANARDE Foundation), Mumbai.
	Ranchi	Society for Human Ability and Right Endeavour (SHARE), Ranchi
Bihar	Bhagalpur	Science and Technology Entrepreneurship Development Project (STEDP), Bhagalpur
	Buxar	Asian Society for Entrepreneurship Education and Development (ASEED), New Delhi.
	Vaishali and Muzaffarpur	EDA Rural Systems, Gurgaon
Orissa	Mayurbhanj, Balasore, Bhadrak and Jaipur	Organisation for Social Change and Rural Development (OSCARD), Bhubaneswar.
	Nayagarh and Keonjhar	Centre for Development Research and Training (CENDRET), Bhubaneswar
Uttar Pradesh	Mirzapur	Asian Society for Entrepreneurship Education and Development (ASEED), New Delhi.
	Pratapgarh	Society for Entrepreneurship, Environment and Human Resource Development (SEEHURD), New Delhi
	Etah	Integrated Management Group (IMG), Lucknow.
	Ghazipur	Purvanchal Grameen Kalyan Sansthan (PGKS), Ghazipur
	Varanasi (Rural) Jaunpur	IEDUP, Lucknow.
Tamil Nadu	Salem and Namakkal	Industrial and Technical Consultancy Organisation of Tamil Nadu Ltd. (ITCOT), Chennai.
Rajasthan	Alwar	Matashree Gomati Devi Jan Seva Nidhi, Fort Road, Rajgarh, Alwar
	Bharatpur	Lupin Human Welfare Research Foundation (LHWRF), Bharatpur
	Jaipur, Ajmer and Dausa	EDA Rural Systems, Gurgaon.
	Jhalawar	Shri Pramod Paliwal, Indian Institute for Rural Development (IIRD), Jaipur
Karnataka	Bijapur and Shimoga	Association of Women Entrepreneurs of Karnataka (AWAKE), Bangalore
	Dharwad and Hassan	Centre for Entrepreneurship Development of Karnataka (CEDOK), Dharwad
	Udupi	Rural Development and Self-employment Training Institute (RUDSETI), Ujire, Karnataka.
Assam	Barpeta	Indian Institute of Entrepreneurship (IIE), Guwahati, Assam.
Himachal Pradesh	Kangra and Kullu	Himachal Consultancy Organisation Ltd., (HIMCON), Shimla.
Andhra Pradesh	Anantapur, Warangal, Chittoor, Karimnagar, Vizianagaram and East Godavari	Andhra Pradesh Industrial Technical Consultancy Organisation Ltd., (APITCO), Hyderabad.
	Nellore	Shri M.V. Ramanan, Principal Director, Andhra Pradesh Productivity Council, Hyderabad.

West Bengal	Malda and Murshidabad	Shri Sanjay Sinha, Director, EDA Rural Systems, Gurgaon.
	Howrah	West Bengal Consultancy Ltd., (WEBCON), Kolkata.
	Midnapore	Midnapore Planning and Development Society (MPDS), Midnapore.
Sikkim	East and South District	Sikkim Consultancy Centre (SICON).
Gujarat	Bhachau region of Kutch District	Shri Pramod Paliwal, Indian Institute for Rural Development (IIRD), Jaipur.
Tripura	West Tripura District	Tripura Industrial Development Corporation (TIDC).

Source: SIDBI.

Importance of Rural Industrialisation

Rural industrialisation is important not only as a means of generating employment opportunities in the rural areas with low capital cost and raising the retail income of the people, but because it contributes to the development of agriculture and urban industries. Without rural industrialisation, it would be considerably more difficult to solve the problem of agricultural unemployment and widespread underemployment. Rural industrialisation promotes rural industry. The development of rural industries increases the level of income in rural areas, and tends to break down the old self-sufficiency of the family and to lessen its cohesiveness creating opportunities for youth, women and the able bodied as well in changing the pattern of leisure life and work. Rural industrialisation should be looked upon not merely as a way of containing the rural workers and stopping them from migrating to urban areas by providing them some kind of remunerative employment in the villages, but as a dynamic element in the process of raising productivity and income levels of the workers in rural areas.

The main characteristics of these industries are to develop local initiative, cooperation and spirit of self-reliance in the economy and at the same time, help in the utilisation of the available manpower for processing locally available raw materials by adopting simple techniques.

These are capable of offering employment opportunities at the place of residence to a large section of the population.

The village industries are an antidote to the widespread problems of disguised unemployment or underemployment.

These decentralised industries require less gestation period on the one hand and produce goods of common necessities on the other. These industries have the capacity to correct regional imbalances by initiating industrial activities on dispersed basis in the most neglected, backward inaccessible areas where perhaps the large-scale sector is unable to penetrate.

Being small, these activities can ensure maximum participation of workers in management thus ensuring a feeling of involvement which is so uncommon with the large-scale sector.

These industries possess an additional advantage wherein the maximum participation of womenfolk can be ensured.

Rural industrialisation has taken roots in the rural economy in India. This is so because simple forms of manufacturing typical of consumer goods industries and varied service industries, are everywhere developed before the more complex process involved in the production of capital goods, and because the size of the home market at the time of industrialisation prohibits the establishment of optimum-sized plants in the production of certain capital goods.

Towards Rural Prosperity

Rural industrialisation is a key to rural development and rural prosperity. It constitutes a significant link in the process of socio-economic transformation of rural areas. Primarily, it provides additional opportunities of employment, income, better standard of living and thereby enriches the cultural heritage of the various social structures in rural areas. Rural industries programme should not be drawn in isolation. It should be drawn up keeping in mind the long-term industrial development plan under a broad framework for developing not only manufacturing industries but also industry-related activities to generate income and employment in the country, particularly targeted towards vulnerable sections of the society in backward regions. The development of rural industries should also take into account enriching of the environment particularly the ecosystem in the rural hinterland. Yet another policy measure adopted and implemented shall be to use products manufactured by rural industries in preference to imported goods, particularly in the urban market segment. This will open up a vast market both in urban as well as rural areas for the goods manufactured by rural industries and pave the way for its rapid growth in the coming years.

A Mass Movement

The programme for rapid growth of rural industries should be launched like a mass movement, with emphasis on the rural brand. Efforts should be made to carry the message of rural development to the rural people. This apart, a sure market is created for the rural consumer goods, and the urban and international markets are developed for artistic works. Rural industrialisation is an integral part of the overall rural economy and it will hasten the integrated rural development.

The traditional village industries and crafts continue to play a pivotal role in providing new markets, particularly in case of handicrafts, handlooms and other varied crafts. However, till today, the rural potential has not been effectively utilised. Besides, a number of industrial activities have begun to play a significant role in employment generation and income in rural areas. Most of these activities have been economically more rewarding than the traditional ones, and have been providing remunerative employment and shown relatively better growth potential. The emerging pattern of rural industries and their relative performance, therefore, indicate that rural industrialisation is an effective means for the generation of growth and employment in rural areas by utilising the potential of new industries and of the existing traditional ones.

KHADI AND VILLAGE INDUSTRIES

The development of khadi and village industries provide opportunities for work, albeit part-time work, in certain cases, and thereby helps to mitigate the severity of rural unemployment and underemployment. With this end in view, the Khadi and Village Industries Commission (KVIC) was established in April 1957, under the Khadi and Village Industries Commission Act, 1956.

Under the guidance of Mahatma Gandhi, provisional activities of khadi were started in 1922, when they were symbolic of the 'fight for freedom'. The khadi programme was thus closely linked with the struggle for freedom. The All India Congress Committee, then known as the All India Spinners' Association (AISA), was established in 1925 to organise hand-spinning and hand-weaving. This was followed by the establishment of another organisation in 1935, called the All India Village Industries Association (AIVA), to monitor and look after other village industries such as hand-pounding of paddy, ghana oil palm gur, bee-keeping, hand-made paper, etc. The establishment of the Khadi Commission was the culmination of the efforts to organise cottage/village industries during the freedom movement. In 1951, the Sarva Seva Sangh took over the work of AISA and AIVA, as a part of an integrated plan for rural industrialisation.

The Government of India evolved a general policy framework for the development of these industries. In the First Plan, these industries were treated as an integral part of agriculture; and emphasis was on local consumption. In the Second Plan, on the advice of the Village and Small-scale Industries Committee (Karve), 1955, and in consonance with the Industrial Policy Resolution of 1956, Khadi and Village Industries programmes were made an integral part of the whole plan for the country's industrialisation. The Third Plan retained the emphasis on these programmes while highlighting the need for an integrated approach. In the successive plans, emphasis and policy shifted from one of protection of such industries to positive forms of assistance – such as improving skills, supplying technical guidance, better equipments and adequate credit with a view to increasing productivity and reducing cost.

The government is committed to the encouragement of the production of textile and textile products in the khadi sector. Considering its large employment potential, it would be the endeavour of the government to make the products of this sector more competitive and of better quality.

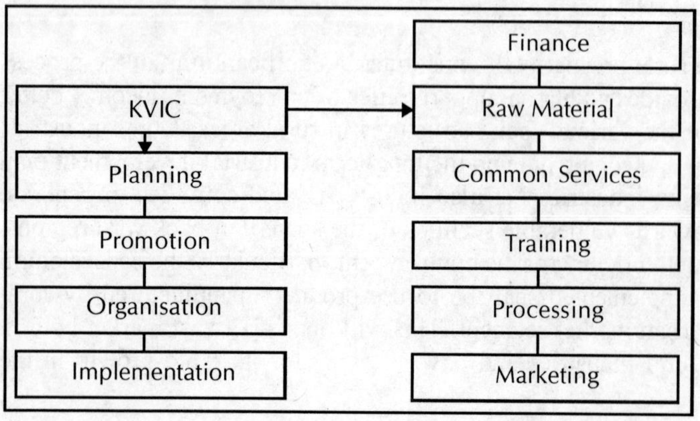

The infrastructure for the distribution of controlled cloth, particularly in rural areas, will be strengthened and streamlined. State governments will be encouraged to open more rural outlets and exercise stricter control over distribution.

Functions of KVIC

The functions of KVIC also comprise building up a reserve of raw materials and implements for supply to producers, creation of common service facilities for processing, marketing and training:

To promote the sale and marketing of khadi products of village industries or handicraft, the KVIC may forge lines with established marketing agencies wherever necessary and feasible.

The KVIC is also charged with the responsibility of encouraging and promoting research in the production techniques employed in the khadi and village industries sector and providing facilities for the study of the problems relating to it, including the use of non-conventional energy and electric power with a view to increasing productivity, eliminating drudgery and otherwise enhancing their competitive capacity and to arrange for the dissemination of salient results obtained from such research.

Further, the KVIC is entrusted with the task of providing financial assistance to institutions or persons engaged in the development and operation of khadi and village industries and guiding them through supply of design, prototypes and other technical information.

In implementing KVI activities, the KVIC plans to initiate steps to ensure genuineness of the products and to set up standards of quality and ensure that the products of these industries do conform to the standards including issue of certificates or letters of recognition to the concerned.

The KVIC may also undertake directly or through other agencies, studies concerning the problems of Khadi or Village Industries, besides experiments or pilot projects for the development of these industries and Rural Artisans and Rural Industries.

The KVIC is authorised to establish and maintain separate organisations for the purpose of carrying out any or all of the above matters besides carrying out any other matters incidental to its activities.

STRATEGY OF RURAL INDUSTRIALISATION

The framework of a strategy of rural industrialisation should consist of attempts towards rejuvenation of traditional village industries by bringing improvement in their technology, dispersal of modern manufacturing activity in the countryside with or without a linkage to the existing village industries as also production of any type of commodities that would cater to the needs of the country's population and that may or may not be based on the local resources. The rural industries would continue to be a supplementary source of income as well as part/fill-time employment activity for the rural artisans, landless labourers, women and educated unemployed. Progressive expansion and modernisation of rural industry could be best brought out by the establishment of small industrial units along with the necessary service in large villages and small towns located all over the country.

The non-traditional industries also seem to be capable of breaking the caste-industry nexus and reducing the rigidities of social stratification in rural areas. Their entrepreneurs come from a wider cross-section of rural society, while the caste-industry identification has been more or less complete in the traditional industries. In fact, the growth of rural industries, based primarily on traditional occupations, may well accentuate the social distance among the caste groups, despite the betterment they may bring about in the economic conditions of artisans and craftsmen. No doubt, even non-traditional activities exhibit concentration by social groups, though to a smaller extent than the traditional industries; but such concentration is primarily based on class distinction in terms of ownership resources, rather than on the traditional caste-occupation association.

Most rural industries, however, have a limited capacity for generating even subsistence income for those engaged in them and have not shown a very encouraging record of growth in the recent past. Only blacksmithy, carpentry and handloom have shown a good promise in sofar as the value added per worker and their dependents. The new industries – wire-meshing, lampshade and hub-brush manufacturing meet the criterion easily; and food and oil products, the old industries which run on modern lines and on a larger scale, have brought prosperity and affluence to their entrepreneurs.

The basic reason for their low income-generating capacity lies in their tiny size in terms of their physical volume of output. Most units are run on a household basis, and do provide full employment to all the household workers, low level of productivity, prevalence of traditional technology, lack of knowledge of the new innovations and development in the field of production, inadequate infrastructure, inadequate finance, absence of marketing skills, lethargy, inefficiency, non-availability of skills and entrepreneurial ability, including administrative snags have been enumerated as *constraints* in the task.

The supply of raw materials, which mostly are a free gift of nature, has already started posing a problem, and is likely to taper off with the passage of time. It is, therefore, essential to concentrate on the development of such traditional rural industries as they have a positive income elasticity of demand for their products and are not faced with the danger of inevitable extinction, such as have potential for technological flexibility which is necessary before they are able to cope with the changes in the demand pattern. Blacksmithy, carpentry, handloom and leather products fit quite well in this category. In order, however, that rural industrialisation becomes an effective tool for the development of rural areas as well as for the better integration of the rural and urban sectors, equal emphasis should be laid on the development of non-traditional industries in this area. Many of them may not be linked with rural areas in terms either of use of local materials or of having a local market, but would be effective in providing productive employment to the rural labour.

Rural industrialisation should be looked upon as a dynamic process in raising productivity and income levels of people in rural areas. It should also be looked upon as means of rural development. The first issue relates to the treatment of rural industrialisation as an aspect of industrial location or as a programme primarily for the development of rural areas. The long-term strategy of rural industrialisation would require not merely the development of traditional rural industries, but also a programme of inducing increasingly a larger component of modern consumer and other industries in rural areas. The promotion and development of 'dynamic' rural industries, no doubt, needs emphasis, but in the interest of long-term growth on a sustained basis, rural industrialisation should be looked upon as an integral part of the programme of rural development. It means effective linkages with both medium and large industries in urban areas.

Further, it is important not only to accelerate development of rural areas but also to reduce the economic and technological gap between rural and urban areas, and seek to achieve a greater degree of integration between the two. The development of low technology and low productivity industries located in rural areas should generate not only linkages, to the extent possible, in the villages, but become a link in rural-urban integration. Besides reducing the income gap between the two sectors, it is also desirable that rural industries use technologies which are in line with the technological pattern of the emerging industrial structure in the country as a whole. The upgradation of relatively modern-technology industries in rural areas alone are likely to make rural industries an integral part of the industrialisation process in the country. The technology used in rural industries varies the terms of these of machinery, equipment, non-human energy, and therefore, of capital intensity; but by and large, the activities in which mechanical devices and capital equipment are used yield a reasonable income only to those who are engaged in them. At the same time, the use of such devices and equipment does not turn these industries 'capital intensive' nor does it reduce the employment potential. It only makes employment more effective in terms of income generation.

One of the reasons which accounts for the fact that the productivity and income aspects of rural industries have received less attention than employment creation lies in the assumption that these industries are subsidiary activities on the part of the households, for which agriculture or some other activities is their main occupation; and that, therefore, they only reduce underemployment and supplement their income from their major activity. In fact, however, this assumption is not valid. For the households and workers engaged in rural industries, their occupation in them is their sole or at least the main source of income. Most of them do not even have another activity as a subsidiary occupation. These industries will, therefore, have to be seen as the effective means of providing full employment and as the only source of income for those engaged in them. The need for industrial employment on a full-time basis is likely to increase, for the development of agriculture, even if rapid, will absorb only a part of the increasing rural labour force.

It is necessary to spell out the concept of rural industrialisation. It begins with the assessment of resources, human and material, locally available in a selected area. Assessment is also made of the pattern of demand. Present and future and an area-wise production plan is formulated for ensuring minimum needs of the people by using local resources, skills and appropriate technology.

As rural industries play an important role in the national economy, particularly in the rural economy, modernisation and improvement of efficiency of these industries has assumed greater importance. The main element in the success of the modernisation programme is to train and bring awareness about new technology to the people who will implement it. As rural industries increase in progress, in number and diversity, and as their share of industrial production begins to grow, it becomes even more important that they improve efficiency in their operations. Five main elements in the success of these programmes are: the orientation of rural entrepreneurs and rural artisans to a more forward-looking approach and flexibility of loan basis to meet the cost of modernisation and the role of appropriate technology and marketing in modernisation and improvement efficiency of rural industries. The basic objective of the programme is to set the rural industries – traditional and non-traditional – on a path of growth so that they are able to complete, on more equal terms with the urban industries.

Innovation Process

Innovation processes fail to take-off because of the inadequate strength of linkages among the various institutional actors and the subcritical mass of resources allocated to them. In today's era of globalisation and liberalisation, with increased competition, industries cannot afford to continue to use obsolete technology. Indeed, they need to be able to use technology as a competitive weapon. In this context, R&D organisations and educational institutions, for their very survival, cannot remain insulated and aloof from industry. Gone too are the days of grants and subsidies. R&D organisations have to earn their expenses and working with industry is perhaps a pragmatic approach to generate revenue while simultaneously establishing credibility.

It is common knowledge that establishing strong linkages with R&D institutes is an effective way to complement and supplement the technological capabilities of a firm. Most firms recognise the importance of linkages and explicitly incorporate their establishment in their corporate objectives. However, due to lack of practical and realistic interventions, the establishment and utilisation of such linkages tend to be very weak. One of the key problems that leads to the withering away of the linkage establishment objectives appears to be the lack of a methodology to assess the potential of the actors within a national technology infrastructure and the strengths of their linkages with a firm. Unfortunately, the literature on management of technology has not paid adequate attention to the assessment of a national technology infrastructure.

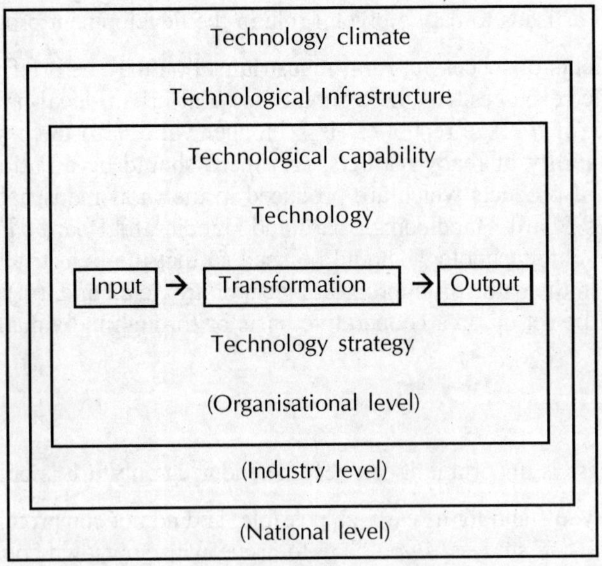

Fig. 6.1 Technology system structure

Table 6.3 Technology Assessment Criteria

Criteria	Evaluation attribute
Technoware level	Material, labour and energy productivity, quality of output, pollution characteristics, scale of operation, proximity to the state-of-the-art.
Humanware level	Operation and maintenance skill level.
Infoware level	Level of operation and maintenance documentation, proximity to the state-of-the-art.
Orgaware level	Level of relevant organisational system, proximity to the state-of-the-art.
Cost	Unit cost of technoware and humanware.
Interaction	The type of interaction the technology has with other technologies, currently being used by the organisation.

Table 6.4 Indicators of the Assessment of the Strength of Linkage

Types of Linkage	Possible Indicators
Technical linkage	Equipment-hours shared and the total cost of sharing as per cent of total cost of innovation, Person-hours shares, number of interactions made and the total cost of sharing as per cent of total cost of innovation, documents developed jointly, systems developed jointly.
Financial linkages	Ratio of outside sponsorship to in-house project development.
Market linkage	Extent of involvement of marketing personnel in idea generation, preliminary assessment, concept development, product development, testing, trial launching and final launching.

Organisational linkage	Mobilising support for a shared goal. Number of outside members (from other organisations of technical infrastructure) in the management and other committees percentage of outside members in various committees.
Generating commitment through superordinate goal	Availability of charismatic product champion, cohesive strength of design team.

Necessary Corrective Action

Rural industrialisation constitutes the key link in the process of socio-economic transformation of underdeveloped rural areas as well as social structures. In view of its importance and problems, it is necessary to take some corrective actions to rejuvenate rural industries and rural artisans to play a pivotal role in the development process.

Some of the necessary ingredients of successful rural industrialisation may be briefly stated as follows: (i) the industry should be based on locally available resources, (ii) there should be rural-urban, local-national and wherever possible, even foreign trade, linkages. The concept of 'village republics' is no longer valid, (iii) there should be comprehensive planning, especially with regard to the availability of ready markets, (iv) there should be a nationwide organisation, with separate sections for each product or group of products which are produced in the rural industrial sector. The existing organisations like the Khadi and Village Industries Board, Handlooms Board and Handicrafts Board can be utilised for the products which they are already handling, (v) up to date technology should be used so that the industrial units can be competitive; obsolete technologies should not be adopted in the name of 'appropriate technology', etc., and, (vi) while the government may provide necessary benefits, the units should be set-up on a cooperative basis or through individual enterprise and not by government departments.

Moral Economics

"While success is important, it can become enduring only if it is built on a strong foundation of values.

Define what you stand for as early as possible, and do not compromise with it for any reason. You can't enjoy the fruits of success if you have to argue with your own conscience."

— Azim Premji, Chairman, Wipro Ltd.,

Paradigm Shift

"The 21st century innovator has to know technology, not just what to do with it, but a lot more. He has to know how to solve a business problem. That does not mean that electrical and chemical engineers are not needed. They will be important, but they will need special training to understand the world from a different perspective."

— Nick Donofrio, Senior V-P, IBM

Growth Curve

"Leadership development has benefited me immensely and that is why it is a very high priority area. Leadership development is about helping people grow, and if I can get people as individuals growing, then I've got a company that grows."

— James McNerney Jr, CEO, 3M

CONCLUSION

The programme of rural industrialisation has endeavoured to take industrial and manufacturing activity to the rural areas through a process of *dispersal* as also developing on sound footing the existing traditional units, thereby creating an industrial climate in the countryside. For effecting this creation of growth centres and provision of infrastructural facilities in the rural areas should be planned carefully. Setting up of nucleus plants in districts or potential block level will promote as many, ancillary, small and cottage units, as possible. The interlinkages will strive for integrated industrial development in rural areas. Development of focal points in specific regions by providing different kinds of complementary facilities on the lines of Punjab is considered worth-emulating. This will facilitate better balancing, greater optimal use of resources, better control and higher productivity and profitability. And setting up of agro-industrial service complexes and non-traditional industries in a planned manner will lead to gradual urbanisation of the rural areas. This will in turn stop migration from the villages and may enable return the flow of skilled manpower to rural areas. Rural industrialisation is, therefore, an integral part of rural development. A cluster of villagers' approach would also be beneficial if adopted sagaciously and without undue interference of exogenous elements. Thus, rural industrialisation provides the necessary impetus to rapid rural development.

ANNEXURE-I

SAXENA'S SUCCESS

Name and Address of the Entrepreneur	:	Shri Amit Saxena No. 2 Lakhawali Estate, N.H. 8, Bhuwana, Udaipur -313 00 (Rajasthan).
Name of the Activity	:	Artworks-Interior Shopping
Project Cost	:	₹ 8.00 lakh.
Commencement of Production	:	1999-2000
Annual Turnover	:	₹ 30.00 lakh
Employment Generated	:	21 persons
Monthly Income	:	₹ 12,500

Artwork is a team of young and qualified professionals, engaged in interior decoration and manufacturing of high quality furniture, doors, windows, partitions, wall panelling, false ceilings, wardrobe, shutters, etc. The team ensures services after the sales, which is one of the fundamental principles of marketing system. The current installed capacity of the unit is 750 doors per month.

The name behind this success story is Shri Amit Saxena, a born enterperneur. His artwork is a unit assisted under MMS of KVIC. With his own capital of ₹ 2.25 lakh he ventured for making his art of wood into an art of living for others and himself too. He has his unit working in full swing in the village Bhuvana in Udaipur district.

He could do it when his project costing worth ₹ 8.00 lakh was considered by the State Bank of Jaipur and Bikaner.

New Fatehpura branch in January 2000 and he also received his MMS share of ₹ 2.00 lakh under the KVIC. Shri Saxena is a successful proprietor of artworks ever since it came into being with the aid from KVIC under its MMS.

Artwork is now in the process of acquiring ISO-9001:2000 Certification.

BHARATI's PAYS HER DUES!

Name and Address of the Entrepreneur	:	Smt. Bharati Gaind, Villl. Jandli, Distt. Ambala, Haryana.
Name of the Activity	:	Manufacturing of Plaster of Paris
Project Cost	:	₹ 7.23 lakh
Commencement of Production	:	1999-2000
Annual Turnover	:	₹ 10.00 lakh
Employment Generated	:	11 Persons
Monthly Income	:	₹ 13,000

First it was her husband Shri Bharati Bhutan who used to mould beautiful statues and decorative articles from Plaster of paris (PoP) at his residence on a small-scale. As his professional skills didn't bring in enough, his wife Bharati joined him in the entrepreneurship. Her aptitude for some creative activity seemed to be the only input in the beginning.

When Shri H.P. Joshi, supervisor, KVIC, Ambala on a fine morning happened to see those statues lined up for drying outside their house, he asked the couple to submit a suitable project for sanction under REGP.

Overwhelmed by the never expected motivation, that too from someone quite a stranger to the couple, Smt. Bharati arranged for a piece of land in the village Jandli near Ambala. Punjab National Bank was a next step, which gladly considered the project and sanctioned ₹ 6.87 lakh. Smt. Bharati arranged ₹ 36,000 from her own savings.

Bharati Arts and Crafts is the sign board now that makes the passers-by to peep into the shop and eye those nicely moulded and painted statues. Some even bow before them with great respect as if they are true Gods!

Smt. Bharati is quite proud of her success. She says, "I hardly expected that our creativity so easily would be an economically viable activity and settle us with enough to feed the family; these dump statues have brought smiles on the faces of the 11 others and their families. Our *bhakti* to our creative work has paid us much more than we ever imagined".

It's just the truth. The Bhakti Arts and Crafts supplies statues all over India. Its book show a record of demands for statues worth ₹ 8.00 lakh accomplished and those at the receiving end are proud to own those beautiful *shilpas.*

Those dump statues have now a job to do. They are campaigning for the REGP programme under KVIC that taught them to speak!

Shri Shiv Khera says, 'Success comes not to those who do different things; but to those who do things differently'.

That's why Smt. Bharati gained speaks less and does more.

FROM PARTNERSHIP TO PROPRIETORSHIP

Name and Address of the	: Shri Pavan Katyal,
Entrepreneur	: VPO Kutana, Distt. Rohtak.
Name of the Activity	: Manufacturing of Pressure Cookers
Project Cost	: ₹ 9.93 lakh
Commencement of Production	: 2000-2001
Annual Turnover	: ₹ 15.60 lakh
Employment Generated	: 9 persons
Monthly Income	: ₹ 1,50,000

Those with proven success in the normal course tend to expand their family units in the next layer, i.e., to partnership firms. But Pavan Katyal has a different story to tell.

He had to discontinue his partnership firm over some dispute and start his own one-man show activity that involved cumbersome shuttling between Rohtak and Delhi to sell his utensils. He also joined M/s. Maruti Metal in Sampla near Rohtak to learn how to produce the vessels and pressure cookers, though he knew how to sell them.

The three years rigour at last borne fruits when he came in touch with Shri Misra, Coordinator, KVIC who persuaded him to set-up his own industrial unit in the nearby rural area. Shri Katyal found himself in high spirits when the Central Bank of India, Rohtak branch accepted his project for setting up his manufacturing unit, and sanctioned ₹ 8.90 lakh. M/s. Laxmi Metal Industries came into the form in March 2001.

His unit, working successfully under Margin Money Scheme of KVIC, has a record production of cookingware worth ₹ 15.60 lakh during 2001-02 with gainful jobs to nine persons. Surely, the cookers have relieved him of tensions and released much of his financial pressures.

Shri Katyal now sports a smile and working shine in his eyes. He must be thanking REGP next to his trade partnership that changed his course of life.

ANNEXURE-II

Major Crafts Practised in Different States

States	Major Crafts
Andhra Pradesh	Carpets, ikat, himroo, lace, kalamkari, banjara embroidery, brassware, bidri, silver filigree, woodwork, nirmal work, jewellery, etc.
Assam	Cane and bamboo, brass and bell metal, ivory, pottery, solapith, fibre (kuhila), Jewellery, Mirijimask.
Bihar	Folk painting (madhubani), sikki, lacquerware, aplique, woodwork, papier machine, brass and bell metal, carpet and durries.
Gujarat	Embroidery, applique, bead work, handprinting, bandhani, durries, namdahs, shawls, wood carving, lacquer, marquetry, patara, silver smithy and agate.
Haryana	Durries, carpets, drugget, embroidery, brassware, moorah, jewellery, pottery, toys and dolls.
Himachal Pradesh	Shawls, rugs, namdahs, chamba rumals, costumes, metal craft, jewellery, woodcraft and paintings.
Jammu and Kashmir	Shawls, embroidery, namdahs, chain stitched rugs, carpets, wood carving, papier machine, metalware, widkerwork, turquoiseware jewellery.
Karnataka	Wood carving, wood inlay, lacquerware, bidriware, stone carving, embroidery, durries, matweaving, jewellery, pottery, painting, ivory.
Kerala	Wood carving, ivory, horn carving, bell metal, koftgiri, lace, matweaving, fibre crafts, cane and bamboo, lapidiary, coconut stem and shell articles.
Madhya Pradesh	Handprinted textiles, wood craft, dhokra, papier machine, lacquerware, jewellery, nag dolls, terracotta.
Maharashtra and Goa	Copperware, silver jewellery, bidriware, leather craft, agate, sisal work, folk painting (worli), paithani.
Manipur	Cane and bamboo, embroidery, bell metal, artistic weaving.
Meghalaya	Cane and bamboo, carpets, musical instruments, jewellery, fibre crafts, textiles.
Nagaland	Textiles, cane and bamboo, wood work, pottery, jewellery.
Orissa	Ikat, applique, stone carving, folk painting (pattachitra), silver filigree, dhokra, horn carving, grass and solapith crafts.
Punjab and Chandigarh	Embroidery (phulkari), carpets, durries, jewellery, ivory inlay, leather jooties, wood turning and lacquewa.
Rajasthan	Handprinted textiles, bandhani, carpets, art metalware, wood carving, ivory, folk painting, embroidery (textiles and leather), jewellery, stone carving, pottery, etc.
Sikkim	Carpets, lepcha weaving, cane and bamboo, wood carving and folk painting.
Tamil Nadu	Bronze casting and wood carving, grass and fibre articles, cane articles, pottery and clay crafts, embroidery and shell crafts.
Tripura	Cane and bamboo, wood craft, textiles crafts, sitalpati, bell metal, jewellery.
Uttar Pradesh	Carpets, art metalware, handprinted textiles, embroidery, wood carving, stone inlay, zardozi, jewellery, pottery.
West Bengal	Cane and bamboo, sitalpati, embroidery (kantha), artistic weaving (jamdani), solapith, shell products, horn crafts, clay craft, papier machine, pattachitra, jewellery, ivory, bell metal.
Andaman and Nicobar	Cane and bamboo, shell crafts, coconut shell crafts, mat making.
Arunachal Pradesh	Textiles crafts, carpets, cane and bamboo, wood carving, painting.
Delhi	Lace, embroidery, zari, hand printing, jewellery, woodware, ceramics and pottery, stoneware, metalware, etc.
Mizoram	Artistic textiles, woodware, cane and bamboo, stoneware, etc.
Pondicherry	Cane, bamboo and straw, art textiles, carpet, etc.

(**Source:** Press Information Bureau, Government of India (press release dated December 14, 2000).

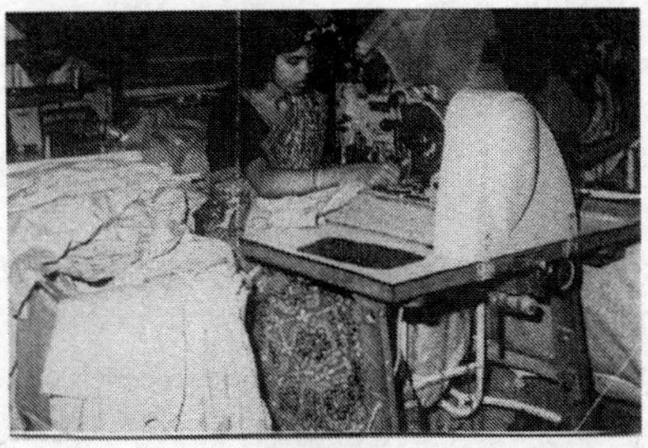

7 CHAPTER

ANCILLARY INDUSTRIES

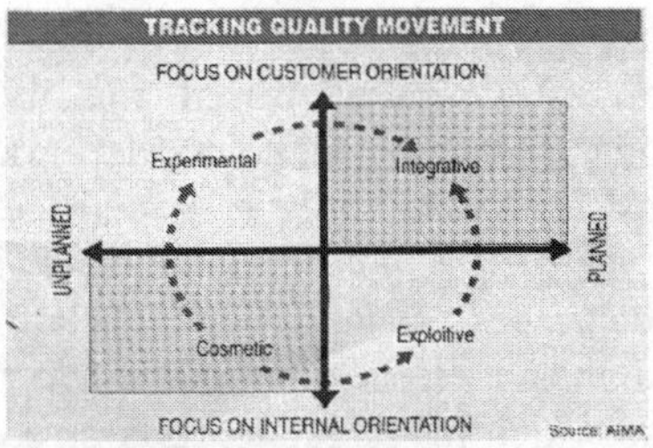

An 'Indian' enterprise would, as its fundamental orientation, favour value chains within India by supporting their competitiveness wherever feasible. Therefore, it is crucial to support the growth and vitality of 'Indian' enterprises that stand out by their approach and commitment to the Indian economy rather than merely by the source of their capital

LEARNING OBJECTIVES

- The student of small-scale industry and entrepreneurship should also know about varied aspect of ancillarisation.
- Ancillarisation is a continuous process and the chapter highlights on:
- Development of ancillary industries and their advantage.
- Benefits of ancillarisation.
- Factors affecting ancillarisation.
- The new millennium is the centre of small business and ancillarisation to usher into it one should constantly expand knowledge of potential new businesses and their technology. Empirical evidence indicates that ancillary industries can be an important vehicle for meeting the growth and equity objectives of developing countries. Improved policies and carefully crafted projects can play an important role in ensuring that the potential contribution of small enterprises to the development process is fully realised.

INTRODUCTION

A balanced industrial development, consistent with social justice, calls for diffused ownership and control and also decentralised growth of industries. This is possible only if new entrepreneurship is developed. The process of *ancillarisation* is one of the most handy methods of encouraging new entrepreneurs to set up small-scale units. This is so because the running of an ancillary industry does not give rise to complex problems which the uninitiated new entrepreneur, will have to face if he is to run an independent manufacturing unit. Also, ancillarisation makes it possible for him to establish a coherent relationship with small and large units. It is these circumstances that ancillaries can provide a strong and widespread base for industrial development.

Industries in India are classified under three heads: large-scale, medium-scale and small-scale. Some economists call small-scale industries cottage industries or village industries. In an underdeveloped economy, with an abundance of labour, it is the small-scale industry which forms the backbone of the economic structure. Japan is an outstanding example of this type. It has shown that small-scale industries can be made to serve and function as the backbone of large industrial enterprises.

In the initial stages of industrial development, emphasis was on establishing large and medium-scale units with provisions of manufacturing within the works. This *vertical integration* resulted is avoidable over investment in the projects and the creation of large unutilised capacity for a number of items. However, the modern economic policy reportedly puts great emphasis on economic interdependence between various sectors of the economic system. The need for coexistence of industries having variance in size as well as products and intersectoral cooperation among them has been recognised for the growth of the industrial sector. This intersectoral cooperation known by different terminologies, viz., ancillarisation, subcontracting, vendor-vendee relations, preferred supplies, etc., has become an inescapable part of large industrial projects. In short, ancillarisation has become an economic compulsion for industrial growth. In simple terms, ancillary industries are those which manufacture parts or components for supply to other firms which manufacture or assemble end-products. The main motivation for ancillary promotion lies in its effect on cost reduction, quality improvement and management efficiency. Ancillaries could be large or medium-sized or small-scale industries. The parent unit is assured of quality product while it also helps in modernising the small-scale ancillary units apart from helping them with raw materials, technical know-how and quality control guidance. Ancillarisation is thus the most effective way of helping the smaller units to cater to the demands of larger units. The assured orders and technical help from large parent units would help the smaller units to work profitably.

The importance of ancillaries is not continued extended to the developing countries where they play a specially significant role. Even in highly industrialised countries like Japan, USA, UK, West Germany, etc., the network of ancillaries is widespread in recognition of their contribution to output as well as employment. In Japan, medium and small-sized companies account for 75 per cent of the employment in the manufacturing industry and 50 per cent of the industrial output. About 60.7 per cent of the small units operate as subcontractors. There is in fact a widespread and distinctive division of labour called '*Shitauka relationship*', in which the small and medium subcontractors manufacture and process components for products produced by large enterprises. An average large-scale unit has about 24 small suppliers. The proportion of subcontractors in the total output is 46 per cent in textiles, 26 per cent in machinery, 25 per cent in transport equipments and electrical appliances and 20 per cent in automobiles. In USA small firms employing less than 500 workers account for over three-fourths of the new jobs created every year. The number of ancillaries to Ford Motor Company is 50,000, to Du Pont 30,000, to General Motors Corporation 26,000 and to US Rubber Company 14,000 units. Raytheon Company, one of the largest electronics manufacturers, purchases over 57 per cent of its requirements from ancillary units. Ancillaries are most widespread in the British Automobile Industry and fairly widespread in other industries. This underscores the importance of ancillaries in an industrial economy.

WHAT ARE ANCILLARY INDUSTRIES?

Ancillary industries are undertakings having investment in fixed assets in plant and machinery not exceeding ₹ 75 lakh and engaged in:

The manufacture of parts, components, subassemblies, toolings or intermediates; or

The rendering of services, supplying, rendering or proposing to supply or render 30% of their production of the total services, as the case may be, to other units for production of other articles; provided that no such undertaking shall be subsidiary of or owned or controlled by any other undertaking.

All the service-oriented enterprises are now eligible to be registered as small-scale establishments and are entitled for the same concessions and incentives as are available to small-scale industries and ancillary industries as defined above.

The government has issued clarifications and explanations on definition of ancillaries from time-to-time. These are as follows: (i) units producing intermediates will be recognised as ancillary units, (ii) units providing servicing facilities, e.g., sand blasting, machining, pressure cleaning and grinding will be recognised as ancillary units; (iii) the concept of parent units will also include small-scale industries also. Thus, one small industry can function as ancillary to another, (iv) a unit to be recognised as ancillary should supply or propose to supply at least 50 per cent of its production to one or more parent units, (v) in calculating the value of plant and machinery, the original price paid by the owner, irrespective of whether the plant and machinery are new or secondhand will be taken into account, (vi) the cost of equipment such as tools, jigs, dies, moulds and spare parts for maintenance and the cost of consumable stores, so also installation cost will be excluded in computing the value of plant and machinery, (vii) in the case of imported machinery, import duty will be excluded but not miscellaneous expenses like transportation charges from port to site of factory demurrage and premium paid for import entitlement. However, shipping charges, customs clearance charges and sales tax will be included in computing the cost of machinery, etc., (viii) the cost of generation sets, extra transformers, etc., as well as bank charges, service charges to National Small Industries Corporation or State Small Industries Corporation will be excluded. The ancillary units pertaining to 26 specified industries are provided facilities such as technical assistance, supply of machinery through NSIC, allotment of factory sheds in industrial estates, etc. It may be noted that the objective of ancillary development cannot be different from the overall objective of small-scale industries. However, the growth of ancillary industries has the following in-built advantages: (i) complementary in terms of output and bringing about a reduction in the cost of production, (ii) development of specialisation in specific fields, (iii) creation of cadres of single disciplined experts, (iv) reduction in the gestation period of production of small-scale units, (v) affecting rapid dispersal of industrial activities in various regions so as to achieve equitable distribution of economic power, (vi) providing an effective solution to the marketing problem of small-scale units, and (vii) indirect development of tertiary activities in areas where ancillary industries have been set up.

Development of Ancillary Industries in India

In the post-independence era, during the initial plan period, the main objective of the industrial policy was to develop heavy machine-building industry. As for example, the 1948 Industrial Policy Resolution had laid down that besides arms and ammunition, atomic energy and railway transport which would be the monopoly of the Central Government, the state would be exclusively responsible for the establishment of new undertakings in six basic industries. In the early period of industrialisation, most of the industries had to depend on imports or in-house production of components required for the final product. In short, in the immediate post-independence period, the emphasis was on the establishment of large industries without simultaneous and due stress on the dispersal through small-scale industries. The study group appointed to examine working of the Industries (Development and Regulation Act), 1951 observed that the actual implementation of the industrial policy had not been up to the expectations and declared objectives of policy, and had created certain anomalies. The Industrial Policy Statement before the Parliament on 23-12-77 observed that the growth in per capita national income had been inadequate with the increase in unemployment, widening of rural-urban disparities, the stagnation in real investment and widespread industrial sickness. The 1977 industrial policy laid special attention on the development of the tiny sector. The salient features of the 1977 industrial policy where the expansion of the list of items reserved for the small-scale sector (from 180 items to over 500 items), the establishment of District Industries Centres, creation of separate wing in the Industrial Development Bank of India (IDBI) to deal exclusively with the credit requirements of small-scale, village and cottage industries.

The strategy for ancillary development was originally outlined with the objective of: (i) development of employment opportunities coupled with growth of entrepreneurship in different fields and in different parts of the country; (ii) dispersal of industrial activities in various regions bringing out the desired equitable distribution of economic power; (iii) increase in productivity of the small-scale units; (iv) growth of a low cost economy through reduction in costs brought about by appropriate technology followed by ancillary units; (v) development of a single or multidisciplined expertise in different fields to bring about economies of scale, and (vi) a somewhat special objective of ancillary development is to provide an effective solution to the marketing problems of small enterprises in the initial period or before they reach the break even point.

The development of ancillary industries has assumed added importance in the country like India with large regional imbalances. The Chakravarty Committee on Backward Areas (1981) classified 155 districts as backward out of 326 districts, which the committee took up for analysis. The National Committees on the Development Backward areas had recommended that the industrial dispersal policy for medium and large industrial units should be such as would lead the establishment of industrial units far away from the present agglomeration since small units on their own cannot bear the cost of developing infrastructure in the backward areas without the support of large units. Already the Government of India has decided to locate at least one major industry in each district in order to achieve the objective of decentralised industrialisation of India. In India, rich farmers and several others in rural areas have gathered substantial amount of investible sources but they are not finding any suitable outlet. Small industrial units are inadequately profitable and highly risky as reflected in the magnitude of industrial sickness among small-scale units. The concept of the joint sector should help in creating basic infrastructure in the backward areas and motivating local rich towards enough investible resources to start industrial units in these areas. However, for this development, the development of ancillary industries is necessary. The potential entrepreneurs in thousands of scattered villages in the country suffer from isolation paradox. In isolation, they dare not invest their funds in industrial activities which involve some risk, at least initially. The establishment of large and medium-scale industrial units would have catalytic effect. Rural potential entrepreneurs both financial resources and or with technical qualification – would come forward with their savings for investment in industrial projects provided they are assured support by large and small-scale units through marketing support and technical guidance to produce quality goods.

Generally speaking, the quality of entrepreneurship that is required for managing an ancillary unit is different from that which is required for managing a small-scale unit. In an ancillary unit, the entrepreneurship can be transplanted or even injected into a technologist who can produce a few items to the exact specifications of the large-scale producer. In fact, many entrepreneurs engaged in ancillary production are either related to the owners of large-scale units or are experienced technologists who can fabricate a product as required. The usual types of skills required for a small-scale industrialist, namely, ability to market the products and raise finance for the purpose, are not so important in an ancillary producer, who often receives help by way of detailed drawings and other specifications from the large-scale manufacturers; and his main task is to turn out products according to these specifications. It is rue that the ancillary producer revives assistance from the large-scale producer either by way of advance payment or by supply of scarce raw materials and other goods.

A major problem faced by ancillary units is their vulnerability to variations in demand. When the large-scale manufacturer producing an end-product faces slackness in demand, the ancillary unit supplying the components is hit hard and may have to remain a practically idle unit till the demand for the end-product revives. Since the production apparatus in the ancillary units is highly specialised and tailored to meet the requirements of a particular assembly, it is not possible to switch over to any other items without incurring losses on account of machinery installed.

An ancillary unit, therefore, is a 'captive unit' with no alternative outlet. Its difficulties are often aggravated by delay in the payment of bills. During the times of financial stringency, there is a tendency on the part of the parent firms to squeeze the ancillary units by giving themselves the credit through non-payment of bills. A survey of industries in Japan revealed that only 8 per cent of the firms received payment within 60 days and that the remaining 92 per cent received it after the lapse of 60 days to 150 days. In this particular respect, therefore, ancillary units are in a more vulnerable position than small-scale industrial units. A small-scale industrial unit producing consumer items or other products will be able to make quick adjustments in its production plan as well as product design in order to minimise the adverse impact of a fall in demand. It may consider diversifying its activity with marginal additions to its machinery and/or equipment. It may even supply its products to other markets, if the traditional markets fail. But ancillary units are tied to the 'apron string' of one or two specific large-scale units and often find it extremely difficult to make such adjustments. As a result, they are very adversely affected.

While ancillary units suffer from these disabilities, they are free from the usual worries about the marketing of their products. An ancillary unit produces for a predetermined market because its production is affected against advance orders. It may be provided with scarce raw materials or even finance by the parent firm, depending upon the type of relationship between the two. And during periods of rising demand and plentiful orders, the ancillary units can continue to operate with hardly any problem.

In India, unlike other countries, the ancillaries sponsored by large units suffer from a major handicap. They lean too heavily on the large units. This dependence may be unavoidable in the initial stage of development; but the ancillary is able to stand on its own legs after a time, which would be possible only if the accent is placed on product improvement, cost reduction and the development of export outlets, especially when the ancillary product is able to meet the requirements of the replacement market abroad.

Advantages of Ancillary Units

A firm producing final products has a choice either to manufacture components and use specialised equipment to produce that product or purchase components from other units. Some of the large and medium units prefer buying certain requirements like tooling and fabricating of components of machinery from other units of small ancillaries even though the facility for manufacturing them is available within their own unit. For example, if the demand for such components is small, the scale of economies and cost saving would not be realised. In such a case, it would be advantageous to buy such inputs from secialised subcontractor firms. Such units having lower input costs by achieving economies of scale in the form of lower wages and capital costs reduce costs.

Benefits of Ancillarisation

The subcontracting process leads to reduction in overhead/infrastructural costs and in this way it enables the parent unit to increase production without a corresponding increase in capital investment, transport cost and additional layout force. The owner of a noted engineering works (an ancillary to Premier Automobiles Ltd., Bajaj Auto, TELCO, etc.), says in this regard that wages and overhead costs of such units are much lower than those of big firms. Also, greater attention is paid by the owner to production in small firms. Another major advantage of smaller firms/units is the absence of unions and greater freedom from labour disputes and strikes. According to Mr. Dua, former Managing Director of Maharashtra Small-scale Industries Development Corporation, *"Increasing problems in large-scale units along with an increase in social overheads, of which labour is one, led firms to farm out production in the seventies".* He also added that if the large units want to take advantage of economies of scale and the use of machinery, they needed to get the work done from ancillaries.

In fact, MRTP licensing laws act as a contributory factor in the development of subcontracting or ancillarisation. It has been noted that because of capacity restrictions under this Act, big firms have begun to off load components and subassemblies to ancillaries to release internal capacity. The rise in the cost of capital has been another reason for the growth of ancillaries. The extension of excise taxes to a large number of additional items also added to the growth of ancillaries. Also, small-scale units were either exempted from excise duties or were subject to relatively lower rates of excise which, in turn, gave a significant stimulus for the larger units to subcontract their production to smaller units.

The Various Forms of Emergence of Ancillary Units

The process takes place in many ways and the nature of manufacturing technology determines the various forms of subcontracting. The first criterion is where the large units provide raw materials to the small firms where the product is processed and the marketing of the finished product or output is being done by the large units. This way the large or medium firms give boost to the existing small and ancillary units. There is much specialisation and trade among the surrounded units, culminating in the final assembly of the bicycle in one of the firms and its marketing under a trademark. About 80 per cent of the value of the final bicycle consists of such purchase components. Similarly, in the leather industry, there is a higher rate of growth of small and ancillary units which serve large shoe firms like Bata. The large units provide leather and other inputs and designs to the small units which then process the leather for resale to the larger firms. Thus, these units with low capital, salary and inventory costs have comparative cost advantages relative to large firms, quite apart from concessions and tax advantages as small-scale units.

The other form of subcontracting is one where economies of scale in production is high and the rate of technological obsolescence is also very high. For example, in the electronics industry where production of components like chips, capacitor, transistor and television picture tubes are capital-intensive processes requiring high technology, it is observed that the assembling of these components to produce the final products is highly labour and skill-intensive. Hence, this operation can be farmed out to the small and even household units.

There is another form of such relationships where large and medium industries are established, first where most of its requirements are either met in-house or brought from outside sources. After the unit settles down, it starts encouraging ancillarisation (it takes 5-10 years). Among the public sector enterprises, HMT, BHEL, ITI, etc., have been successful in such kind of subcontracting processes. The public sector procurement of inputs from ancillary units and small-scale units should be enhanced and integrated.

Factors Affecting Ancillarisation

Recently, there has been a growing trend towards ancillarisation, thanks to the series of the rapid developments that have taken place in the industrial structure in this country. In the first place, the size of the operations of several industrial units has increased enormously, with the result that they are compelled to subcontract some of the items of production to ancillaries. During the 1950s, when these industrial units were set up for the production of all the components, it was to ensure that the stipulated targets might be met in terms of the licenses granted to them. In those days, there were few ancillary units adequately equipped to produce the components according to specifications. But during the 1960s, a large number of small-scale units, which were capable of producting a variety of items emerged, with the result that large-scale manufacturers developed enough confidence in them to assign the production of these specific items to these units.

Second, it was more convenient for large-scale manufacturers to get the ancillary units to produce certain items for them. With the growing complexity of the management, the large-scale manufacturer could now concentrate on the problems of organisation, marketing, finance, etc., rather than fritter away his energies on finding raw materials and framing production plans for the manufacture of the several minor items which go into the final assembly. For example, a bicycle manufacturer does not have to bother about buying and stocking the rubber used in the production of pedals; he prefers to get this item supplied to him by an ancillary unit.

Third, large-scale manufacturers can economise on transport costs, storage space, etc., by subcontracting rather than by producing the same components themselves.

Fourth, it is economic to have some items manufactured by ancillary units because the cost of these items is higher when they are fabricated by large-scale manufacturers.

Finally, by subcontracting, a large-scale manufacturer is able to insulate himself against fluctuations in the prices of raw materials over a period of time by entering into contracts for the supply of these items. A more accurate assessment of the input cost as well as the returns on manufacture is possible if the components are available at fixed prices. All these facts underscore the point that the development of ancillaries and their growing popularity have been well supported by economic and management considerations.

Although large units in the public and private sectors have been enjoined to promote the growth of ancillary units, the results achieved so far have not been satisfactory. Only about 300 out of 5,000 and odd large units in the country have, till date, taken measures to obtain their requirements from ancillaries. There are some 3,18,000 registered small-scale industrial units, of which only 7,607 are ancillary units. Several factors have contributed to the slow growth of ancillaries. In the first place, there has been a lack of mutual confidence. Very often, one hears complaints from large units that the small-scale sector does not adhere to quality specifications, standards and delivery schedules, while the small units complain of indifference on the part of large units, irregularity in the placing of orders and delay in the payments of bills.

Second, the tender system followed by large units while awarding contracts for their purchases has placed overemphasis on cost often at the risk of quality, apart from the fact that this contract system has encouraged cut-throat competition among small-scale units.

Third, there has never been a proper liaison between small and large units. Only recently have some organisations in the private sector – commercial banks, financial institutions and chambers of commerce embarked on schemes which promote the ancillaries.

In this context, it may be noted that, in several European countries, formal subcontracting exchanges, which act as clearing houses for the large-scale sector in locating sources of supply and for potential small entrepreneurs in locating outlets for their products, have been functioning with considerable success. In India, similar subcontract exchanges have been recently set up in Mumbai, Chennai and Kolkata.

Paradigms of success

"You should dare to dream, define what you stand for, never lose your zest and curiosity, always strive for excellence, build self-confidence, learn to work in teams, take care of yourself, preserve, have a broader social vision and finally never let success go to your head."

— Azim Premji, Chairman, Wipro

CONCLUSION

The ancillary industries are a key component of the concept of small-scale industries. They play a key role in the accelerated development of large and medium industries, by fostering a link of togetherness. In the process, they have every potential to grow bigger. To facilitate and accelerate the process of ancillarisation, it is necessary that entrepreneurs are provided with the source of information and right contact points.

He dared.
He cared.
He shared.
The visionary,
who believed that work was the
only form of worship,
and excellence the only offering acceptable to God.

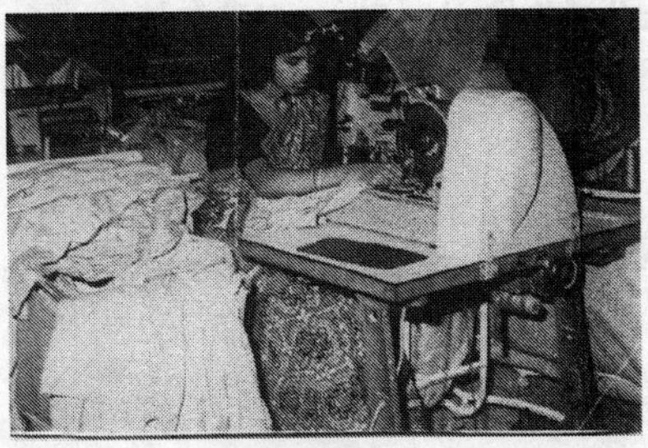

8 CHAPTER

INDUSTRIAL ESTATES

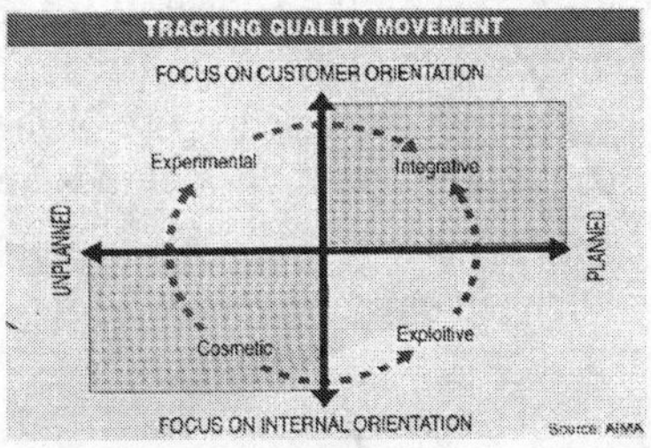

Enterprise cannot however, become competitive in isolation in view of their linkages with the broader economy for supply of cost-effective inputs, as well as for growth in demand for their output.

LEARNING OBJECTIVES

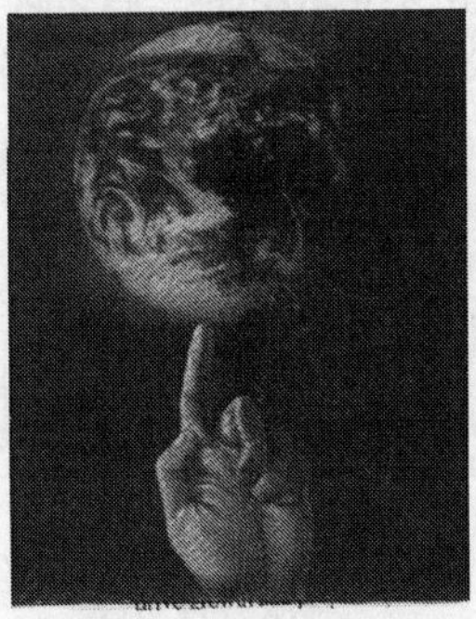

- To provide an insight into a key input of industrialisation. The chapter discusses the key issues:

  An industrial estate is a tract of land which is subdivided and developed according to a comprehensive plan for the use of a community of industrial enterprises.

  — Bredo

Types

I. Functional Basis: (i) General Industrial Estates, and (ii) Special or Specific Industrial Estates.

II. Organisational Basis: (i) Government Industrial Estates, (ii) Cooperative Industrial Estates, (iii) Corporation Industrial Estates, and (iv) Private Industrial Estates.

Objectives

(1) To provide accommodation and infrastructural facilities, (2) To assist in the setting up and development of small-scale industries, (3) To facilitate process of dispersal of industries, (4) To assist ancillary industries, and (5) To assist in the development of entrepreneurship.

Causes for Poor Performance

(i) Lack of essential infrastructural facilities, (ii) Lack of common facilities, (iii) Lack of realistic survey, (iv) Lack of clear idea about relevance of product to the area, and (v) Lack of local involvement.

INTRODUCTION

An industrial estate is a well planned unit with ready-built in factory space which is let out on rent or sold to industrialists. This enable small industrialists who have no capital to build their own premises or do not want to do it right in the beginning to acquire factory space at a reasonable rent.

Meaning of Industrial Estates

The concept of industrial estate is as old as the steam engine. The term *industrial estate* is defined to indicate the provision of the basic infrastructure for the rapid development of the area.

According to P.C. Alexander, an industrial estate is "a group of factors, constructed on an economic scale in suitable sites with facilities of water, transport, electricity, steam, bank, post office, canteen, watch and ward and first aid; and provided with special arrangements for technical guidance and common service facilities".

The United Nations has defined an industrial estate as "a planned clustering of enterprises, offering standard factory buildings erected in advance of demand and variety of services and facilities to the occupants".

In the view of William Bredo, "an industrial estate is a tract of land which is subdivided and developed according to a comprehensive plan for the use of the community of industrial enterprises. The plan must make detailed provision for streets and roads, transportation facilities and installation of utilities. The plan may provide for the erection of factory buildings in advance of sale or lease to occupants".

Planned clustering and a group character of industrial enterprises are important attributes of the programme of industrial estates.

Philosophy of Industrial Estates

The philosophy of the programme of industrial estate rests primarily on two major advantages, namely, economies of scale and economies of agglomeration. Considerable economies of scale may be released by industrial estates in providing infrastructural facilities to industrial occupants. Up to certain limits, it may be expected that costs of estate development and administration decline per unit of each facility, with the increasing size of the estate. The entire argument of the economies of scale for an industrial estate is based on what P. S. Florence pointed out way back that "a localisation of many medium or small plants offers similar economies to those found within a single large plant". Economies of scale are said to arise because an estate sheltering a large number of small enterprises, all of them enjoying the advantages in common in the form of overheads, take the character of a single firm.

According to Paul N. Rosenstein Rodan, the industrial estate constitutes a strong inducement to invest because it can capture the otherwise volatile external economies of agglomeration. An industrial estate, where a number of industrial enterprises are clustered together would, in effect, become a complex of interdependent and interrelated industries. Such a complex is expected to have advantages of agglomeration and external economic, which are necessary for the growth of individual industrial units. The external economies can be said to accrue from the environmental facilities in the form of improved services, both human and material. Broadly, external economies are derived from the availability of trained workers, access to improved production equipment and facilities, improved location with respect to raw material and markets and access to superior transportation facilities.

For an individual entrepreneur, the industrial estates can save a great deal of effort, trouble and expenses in erecting a factory. The selection of a well located industrial site, the formalities of acquiring suitable land, getting the building plans approved by local authorities, securing supply of water, power, gas and other facilities present formidable difficulties to and require considerable time from the entrepreneurs. The speed with which an industrialist starts in production is usually a significant element and is especially vital in developing countries.

Equally significant is the advantage of an initial economy in investment. When the industrialist can obtain the use of land and industrial buildings on rental or on hire-purchases, without large cash outlays, his financial position gets strengthened. Renting a factory premises permits a capital cost to be converted into an operational expenditure and releases resources for purchase of machinery and for working capital, which is of particular importance in an underdeveloped country like India, where inevitable resources happen to be scarce. Industrial estates thus become an effective instrument of mobilising investments in small blocks of capital and of facilitating entry into the industry. In the opinion of Mr. O.P. Mathur, industrial estates also serve as risk-absorbing devices because the capital investment of the entrepreneurs for starting enterprises in the estates gets considerably reduced with the provision of a large variety of facilities and services by the sponsors.

Industrial estates, by bringing together people engaged in the same or similar types of economic activity, having to deal with common problems and aiming at common objectives, may be expected to develop a community of interest among those people and promote the spirit of cooperation and combined effort. They can provide for a better division of labour by securing common technical, repair and information services, which could not pay for one industrial unit alone but do pay for a cluster of industrial units. They can also organise housing, transportation and social amenities for workers, which no single industrial project can do effectively.

Economics of Industrial Estates

As examined earlier in the chapter, in a programme of industrial estates created by public investments, it aims at inducing directly productive private investment and enterprise. Private investment and enterprise are usually motivated by profit. Agriculture, trade or cottage and village industries happen to be the traditional economic activities. Entrepreneurs engaged in these economic pursuits have to be attached to the modern small industry. Potential entrepreneurs will not be attracted to establish their industrial enterprises, unless they are expected to bring them a rate of return higher than that in the alternative economic pursuits.

Industrial estates by reducing the risk and by raising the profit for potential entrepreneurs can serve as a nursery for new entrepreneurs. Both economies of scale and external economies of agglomeration should improve the economic efficiency of industrial enterprises accommodated in industrial estates. Normally, industrial enterprises accommodated in the industrial estates should prove more efficient than their counterparts outside the estates.

Types of Industrial Estates

The seneric term ***industrial estate*** covers all the four variants of the concept, namely industrial areas, industrial estates, industrial townships and galas.

An industrial area is one, wherein the infrastructure facilities and services are provided but factory accommodation is constructed by entrepreneurs. In an industrial estate, both infrastructural facilities and factory accommodation are provided by the sponsoring authority.

In an industrial township, besides the infrastructure facilities and factory sheds having accommodation and other civic amenities associated with a town are also provided.

In galas, space is provided in a big building to set-up small-scale industries along with infrastrucural facilities.

On the basis of functions, industrial estates are classified into: (a) conventional (general) type, and (b) special type. General type industrial estates provide accommodation to a wide variety and range of industrial concerns while, special type estates attempt the establishment of industrial units, which are vertically or horizontally interdependent. In India, general type estates are very popular.

On the basis of the organisational set-up, industrial estates are classified into: (a) government, (b) private, (c) cooperative, and (d) municipal estates.

There are a number of other variants of industrial estates such as:

Ancillary Industrial Estate – only small industries which are ancillary to a particular large industry are housed in this estate just like the one attached to Hindustan Machine Tools (HMT), Bangalore.

Functional Industrial Estate – this is a small and fully serviced unit which serves as a reception centre for displaced small firms. It also serves as 'a pilot-cell' for small firms going into production and is a base for expansion into larger factories.

The Workshop-bay – this is usually located in the shopping centres to provide space for repair shops and enterprises such as job printing.

Rakhial Industrial Area

It is one of the five major satellite industrial areas around Ahmedabad. Industry presence began in this areas 50 years ago but it was in the early sixties that Rakhial began to look like an industrial area. Here, you have human habitation, old and new, like Amraiwadi, Saraspur, Bapunagar and Gomtinagar surrounding the industrial pocket. Gujarat being one of the leading industrially developed states in the country, has innumerable industrial estates but not all of them are properly maintained. Street lights, greenery, drainage, roads, planning are some of the basic requirement which should be given to the estates.

The Rakhial industrial area consists of several segments of small-scale industries. It is situated about 10 kms from the city and is well connected to the Bombay-Udaipur Highway. The main objectives of the industrial estates have been the development of backward areas and rapid development of small-scale industries.

Rakhial area consists mainly of these industries with negligible pollution. This is because the engineering units form more than 35 per cent of the total units in the area.

One of the unique features of this industrial area is its foundry culture. There are more than 350 units and total output of castings in the area is estimated to be around 15,000 tonnes. From humble beginnings, the foundries have moved to advanced technologies bringing in speed and accuracy. There is no advance booking here; the traders fetch stock on ready availability. Majority of the foundry units produce textile castings followed by motor body, pumps, castings and sanitaryware. Talking about foundries here, it is interesting to note the dominance of Panchals in this area. They are technocrats, workers as well as owners themselves. Living in the nearby areas, most of them can be found in their factories from 7 a.m. in the morning till late in the night.

Close upon the castings, there has been a proliferation of engineering units, of course largely foundry based. Machining, fabrication, sheet metal work, etc., are required for processing the casting into finished products. Most of these are textile loom parts. In fact, the Rakhial industrial zone could rightly be called a paradise for the small-scale and foundry-based engineering sector.

An interesting aspect of the Rakhial engineering units is that inherently and still, there are a lot of Panchals and owner operators who personally attend to all the technical processes. It follows that the Panchal generally lives on the premises or in the nearby settlements, and is a permanent resident-cum-industrial producer.

Even though the area was actually not planned to be one of the industrial zones, the amenities seem to be in good shape except the roads. In Rakhial, the lights are good enough and water supply is reliable to a certain extent. But what disturbs the industrialists and transporters frequenting here is the state of roads. Upgradation of rainwater drainage system needs immediate attention. There are several other reasons why the small-scale industries are preferred in Rakhial. In Vatva or Naroda, the price of the land is very high thereby reducing the working area.

Rakhial's market is mostly outside Gujarat especially in the south. As Rakhial is nearest to the city, people can go there more often. Therefore, the proximity of the place makes it a zone inviting further development. One of the major reasons that industrial estates normally do not succeed is lack of economic study. The availability of raw materials in the area which could be exploited, manual skill, market for the products locally, potential entrepreneurs, demand for manufacturing space, types of industries viable for the area should be taken into account before venturing into an industrial estate.

Quality-consciousness, which was lacking earlier in small industrial zones consisting of small-scale industries has to be implemented. Thanks to liberalisation, today no material, however low the cost may be, is accepted without cost analysis and chemical composition reports. Impurity in any form in either the raw materials or the finished products is rejected straightaway. One of the reasons is the severe competition in terms of price as well as the quality factor.

Good manpower availability, fine record of industrial peace, well networked transportation are the plus points except for being a little communally sensitive. During the times of such flare-ups due to the settlements around, Rakhial still has plots of land available which points out the fact that there is ample scope for further development.

SOFTWARE TECHNOLOGY PARKS

To encourage software development, the government has chalked out plans of setting up software technology parks (STPs). Today, there are seven major parks in the country, which collectively host about 700 software-development firms – 400 of which were export software. However, 80 per cent of the exports from the STPs are made by big companies, which numerically constitute a mere 10 per cent of the population. The STPs provide an incubating infrastructure for small developers by making equipment acquisition easier through various loan, lease, and use-and-return schemes.

With the banking and finance sector adopting around 9 per cent of the total infotech products and services, it appears that this sector has finally realised the importance of adopting the technology. More and more banks are introducing value-additions like ATMs, credit cards, phone-banking and even internet-banking. Spearheading this movement is the ICICI Bank, which has introduced infinity – its internet-banking service.

The industry has to get its priorities right to position the country as a player of significance in the sector.

The bank already has a website through its homepage www. icicibank.com. The site offers information about regulations pertaining to NRI accounts and as a result, the bank has been receiving an overwhelming response following visits from the NRI community for deposits remitted home. This is useful even for the domestic customers as they need not visit the bank for routine transactions. All the user has to do is to click on the bank's website and request for a cheque book. It gets couriered to him within a couple of hours. Infinity also allows transaction tracking which enables retrieval of transaction details based on cheque number, amount, and date. Security is the key concern in internet banking. But to access the Net and use its banking services, one needs effective telephone connections. The Mahanagar Telephone Nigam Ltd., (MTNL) has been providing efficient phone services in Delhi and Mumbai. Besides the regular services one needs effective telephone connections. Besides the regular service, it is on its way to introducing Wireless in Local Loop solution (WLL) in a big way. Intelligent network (IN) services are also being offered at certain exchanges. Recently, the Delhi High Court gave a decision in favour of MTNL on its cellular foray. This has set the stage for it to offer cost-effective cellular services to subscribers in Delhi and Mumbai. However, the ruling has been challenged by private cellular service providers. Using its infrastructure, MTNL may also plan to become private ISP and cash in on the emerging opportunity.

Objectives of Industrial Estates

The principle object of the progamme of industrial estates is to provide factory accommodation to small-scale industries at suitable sites with facilities of water, electricity, steam, transport, banks, post offices, canteens, watch and ward, first aid, etc., and thus create a healthy atmosphere for the development of industries. The industrial estates bring a number of industrial units together and facilitate establishment of common facility centres, introduction of modern techniques, collective purchase of raw materials and sale of finished goods, besides fostering a cooperative spirit of interdependence between them.

The programme also aims at the dispersal of industries to comparatively underdeveloped regions by development of these industrial growth centres and thus it helps in raising the living standard of the people in those areas. Industrial estates provide an ideal tool for interpreted industrial development.

The objectives of underlying the establishment of industrial estates in India are as follows:

(i) to encourage the growth of small-scale industries;

(ii) to shift small-scale industries from congested areas to estate premises with a view to increasing their productivity;

(iii) to achieve decentralised development in small towns and large villages;

(iv) to provide accommodation and infrastructural facilities to the entrepreneurs;

(v) to encourage growth of ancillary industries in the townships, surrounding major industrial undertakings, both in public and private sectors; and

(vi) to foster the development of industry as well as entrepreneurship by providing economies and incentives.

Industrial Estates in India

Industrial estates programme in India is perhaps the biggest undertaker by any developing country. The idea of establishing industrial estates as a measure for the development of small-scale industries was first adopted in India by the Small Scale Industries Board at its meeting held in January 1955. The first industrial estate in India was set up at Rajkot in September 1955.

The main objective of this programme is to encourage and support the creation, expansion and modernisation of small-scale industries through provision of factory accommodation, common service facilities and assistance and serving throughout all stages of establishment and operation and to develop a subcontracting relationship between the small and large-scale industries and specialised manufacturing activities. Subsequently, the programme also assumed the role of regional development through provision of built-in factory accommodation with the requisite facilities and services in semi-urban, rural and backward areas.

The programme also worked towards the growth of ancillary industries in townships surrounding major industrial undertakings both in the public and private sector.

The programme of industrial estates, which was initiated towards the end of the First Five Year Plan, (i.e., 1955), touched a new height in target achievement in each successive Five Year Plan.

The second Five Year Plan laid down the objectives of the industrial estates ".... to provide conditions favourable to working efficiency, maintenance of uniform standards in production and economic utilisation of materials and equipments. The principal objective is to enable a number of small-scale units to have the advantage of common services and other facilities such as – good site, electricity, water, gas steam, compressed air, railway sidings, watch and ward, etc. Being located near one another, some units may be better able to use the goods and services of others so that they become interdepedent and complementary". Though the primary objective of the programme focussed on the rapid development of small-scale industries, dispersal of industry to rural and underdeveloped areas to raise their levels of industralisation and general economic development also have come to be regarded as one of the most important objectives. With the progress of the scheme, additional objectives like relieving the cities of congestion and overcrowding, slum clearance, promotion of small industrial units as ancillary to large industrial units, work for students in universities and polytechniques in the pattern of 'earn while you learn' have been tagged to the programme.

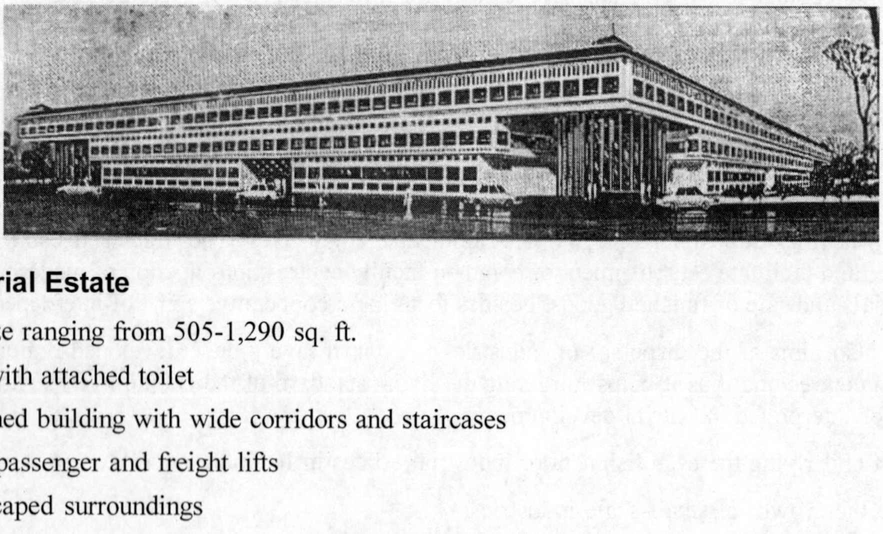

A Modern Industrial Estate

Units of size ranging from 505-1,290 sq. ft.

Each unit with attached toilet

Well-designed building with wide corridors and staircases

Automatic passenger and freight lifts

Well-landscaped surroundings

Dish antenna and cable television system provided, and

Sample unit ready for display.

Organisation

The industrial estates could be broadly divided into two groups:

(1) Those organised by the government, and

(2) Those by private agencies including cooperative societies and joint stock companies.

The establishment of industrial estates is primarily the responsibility of the state government. The role of the Central Government is mainly that of laying down policies for the guidance of the state governments and advancing funds for implementation of this programme. The selection of site and construction of factory sheds and their allotment and subsequent problems of management are left to the state governments.

Size

Size of a shed in an industrial estate would range from 700 sq.ft. to 15,000 sq.ft. depending on the state.

Allotment of Sheds

Generally, they are allotted to bonafide small-scale industrial units according to industrial priorities as fixed by the Industries Department of the state government concerned. Normally, industries using modern techniques, power, transport, technical know-how and manufacturing items which are important from the point of view of national economy and export-oriented industries, are given preference in the industrial estate. Since imported raw materials become scarce, industries using such raw material are usually not given preference.

Tenancy

Factory premises are generally allotted on rental basis. However, they may be allotted on hire-purchase or outright sale basis at the discretion of the state government.

RURAL INDUSTRIAL ESTATES

Over the years, the industrial estate programme has made considerable progress, but it is not uniform. The performance of rural industrial estates is not satisfactory. Of the total number of 705 industrial estates completed, 210 estates have been set-up in rural areas, 179 in semi-urban areas and 316 in urban areas with a population of above 50,000. Further, out of 3,725 sheds completed in rural industrial estates, 3,043 are occupied, as compared to 9,811 out of 10,562 sheds in urban industrial estates with an occupancy percentage of 81.7 and 92.9 respectively. The reasons for the low utilisation of rural industrial estates are wrong choice of location and site, inadequate infrastructural facilities, lack of local entrepreneurs and reluctance on the part of entrepreneurs from urban areas to go to rural and backward areas, etc.

In order to ensure full utilisation of sheds in the industrial estates, the state governments have been advised by the Central Government from time-to-time provide essential facilities like electricity, water, etc., which were found lacking; to set up coordination committees of the Department of Industries, PWD, Electricity Board, etc., for cutting down the procedural delays; to provide incentives and inducements to the entrepreneurs to occupy sheds in industrial estates situated in rural and backward areas and take up techno-economic surveys before setting up any industrial estate in future.

The programme is reviewed periodically at the meetings of the Advisory Committees attached to the Small Industries Service Institutes, the meetings held to discuss the annual plans of the state governments and at the meeting with State Directors of Industries and suitable directives are issued for better functioning of this important programme.

Essentials to Make Industrial Estates Programme Successful

(i) Existence of large number of small firms or artisan shops in appropriate industrial sector.

(ii) Entrepreneurs willing and able to take advantage of facilities.

(iii) A nucleus of skilled workers.

(iv) Government agencies with skills and funds to plan and administer the programme.

(v) Financial units willing to give credit to the units.

(vi) Availability of adequate infrastructure.

LESSONS OF EXPERIENCE

According to the Development Commissioner of Small Scale Industries, the following lessons of experience would be drawn for future:

1. Industrial estates have to be properly coordinated with the broader development programme. They have to be not only an integral part of the industry development programme but also of the overall economic development programme of the area/region.
2. They should be planned with a view to developing them into focal points of healthier industrial growth in an area rather than as a cluster of merely inward looking group of production units. They are to be so designed and managed that they may later be in a position to provide necessary common service facilities, technical advice, guidance, etc., to other industrial units in the area.
3. Homogeneity (rather than heterogeneity) is to be guiding criterion while selecting industrial units. This would lead to better planning and utilisation of common facilities, inter-firm cooperation and interlinked development.
4. While planning an industrial estate, due consideration is to be given to 'secondary growth' effect in order to regulate any haphazard growth around the estates.
5. Location of an industrial estate is to be decided only on techno-economic considerations. A techno-economic feasibility study should always precede the setting up of an estate.
6. While planning industrial estates in an area, uniform pattern need not be followed. The organisational structure in a particular area/region may be adjusted taking into consideration factors such as – special requirements of an area, economic environments, availability of skills, talents and enterprise, level of development of the region, etc.
7. Instead of building sheds in advance of demand, they may be built on expressed demand as revealed at the time of conducting techno-economic or feasibility studies.
8. Elaborate and costlier construction has to be avoided and instead functional types of sheds at cheaper rates may be provided.
9. When private initiative is ready or the success of industrial estates has been demonstrated by one or more examples, the government may confine its role to prescribing minimum factory standards, etc., and increasingly associate the entrepreneurs in the work of construction and maintenance of buildings.
10. To keep construction costs to the minimum, adequate attention should be paid to reduce cost by improving design efficiency, increasing size coverage and reducing to the minimum the areas allotted for non-factory purposes. The scope for reducing expenditure and non-development and administrative activities in the estates may also be explored and the consequent implications of the cost of construction on rent may be kept in view.
11. In backward and rural areas, greater efforts would have to be made to stimulate local entrepreneurship. The industrial estates in such areas have to play a promotional role and act as pace-setters in the process of industrial development. Besides guiding the entrepreneurs in selecting the right lines of manufacture, it may also be necessary to offer additional incentives for locating industrial units. These incentives may be in the shape of concessional credit, rebates in various taxes, preferential allotment of scarce raw materials, etc. The industrial estates in backward areas have also to be nursed over long periods and provided with adequate inducements to counter-balance the inherent disadvantages from which they suffer. The concessions could be given preferably as a 'package deal' on a tapering basis.
12. The selection of products to be manufactured in the industrial estates should be in accordance with other development programme, *viz.:* mechanisation of agriculture, utilisation of agricultural produce, electrification, item of mass consumption, etc.
13. Marketing of goods produced by the units in the estates may be undertaken by the Industries Development Corporations through setting up of showrooms, emporia and arrangements for securing government supply orders.
14. While general purpose industrial estates are very useful for backward and rural areas, in urban areas, functional or special type of industrial estates may be preferred in view of the emphasis on modernisation, ancillary developments, etc.

Special Economic Zones

The export processing zones of Kandla, Santacruz (Mumbai), Kochi and Surat are converted to SEZs along with setting up of new SEZs at: (i) Positra in Gujarat, (ii) Nanguneri in Tamil Nadu, (iii) Kakinad-Visakhapatnam in Andhra Pradesh, (iv) Paradeep in Orissa, (v) Kulpi in West Bengal, and (vi) Bhadohi in Uttar Pradesh.

The special features in SEZ as compared to EPZ are asunder:

No minimum export performance (EP) or Net Foreign Exchange earning as percentage of exports (NFEP), unlike EPZ units.

Monitoring of performance of SEZ units by a committee headed by Development Commissioner of Customs. Separate monitoring is being done in EPZ.

Duty with interest to be recovered in case of failure in achieving positive NFEP under Custom Act to be in proportion to shortfall, unlike in EPZ.

Unlimited DTA sales on full duty; for EPZ only 50 per cent of export on concessional duty.

No linkages with positive NFEP for domestic sale for SEZ units. In EPZ sales are subject to achievement of NFEP.

Duty free material to be utilised over five years, unlike in EPZ where it is one year.

Subcontracting facility available to SEZ jewellery units which is not available to EPZ units.

All imports on self-certification unlike in EPZ where attestation of Development Commissioner required for import of capital goods.

No routine examination by Customs of export and import cargo in SEZ, unlike EPZ.

100 per cent FDI investment through automatic route available to manufacturing SEZ units. In EPZ, FIPB approval required.

Procedural simplification for operations like record keeping, inter-unit transfer, subcontracting, disposal of obsolete material and waste and scrap.

Other facilities like tax holiday, 100 per cent foreign equity participation, retention of 70 per cent of export earnings in EEFC account, etc., are common for both SEZ and EPZ.

Facilities at SEZs

SEZ units may import or procure from the domestic source, duty free, all their requirements of capital goods, raw materials, consumables, spares, packing materials, office equipment, DG sets, etc., for implementation of their project in the zone without any licence or specific approval.

Supplies from the domestic source by SEZ units treated as deemed exports and the domestic supplies are eligible for deemed export benefits.

Central sales tax paid on domestic purchases reimbursed to the units by the Development Commissioner.

SEZ units eligible for a corporate tax holiday up to 2010, as per the provisions of Section 10A of the Income Tax Act.

SEZ units may sell their products in the domestic market in accordance with the import policy on payment of applicable duties.

Part of production or production process may be undertaken by SEZ units, including jewellery units, for exports through other SEZ units, or in the domestic area.

100 per cent foreign direct investment is freely allowed in the manufacturing sector in SEZ units under automatic route, except arms and ammunitions, explosive, atomic substance, narcotics and hazardous chemicals, distillation and brewing of alcoholic drinks and cigarettes, cigars and manufactured tobacco substitutes.

Goods imported/procured locally duty free could be utilised over the approval period of 5 years.

Customs clearance facility available in the zone to SEZ units, at no extra charge.

All support facilities like banking, post office, clearing agents provided in the service centres located in the zone.

Developed plots and ready-built space available for establishing units in SEZs.

CONCLUSION

An industrial estate is a method of organising, housing and servicing industry for an orderly development. Industrial estates are for two types, *viz.:* galas varying from 200 sq. feet to 2,000 sq. feet in area in a building and each unit is housed on a separate plot of land. The majority of the small-scale industries in metropolitan areas are housed in galas, in private or public industrial estates over the years, and industrial estates have played a catalytic role in promoting industries, especially in the small-scale sector in a big way. It is considered as a multipurpose tool supposed to take care of provisions of suitable factory premises, utilities, facilities and services, economy in the investment on social overheads and the increased scope for inter-servicing and inter-trading, development of complimentarity in production and creation of the spirit of cooperation, decentralisation of the industry for development of backward areas, moral industrialisation, achieving a specific loactional pattern, town planning, etc. In short, it accelerates the integrated development of small-scale industries in the country.

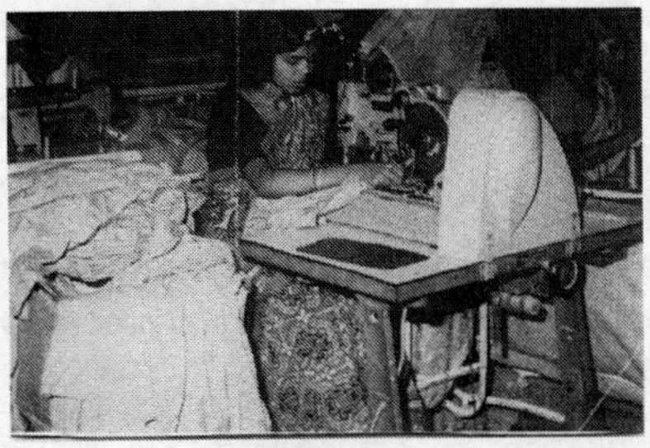

9 CHAPTER
ORGANISATIONAL STRUCTURE OF SMALL-SCALE INDUSTRIES

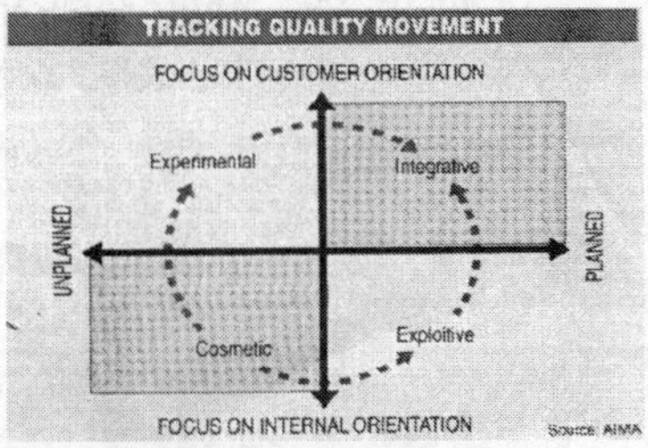

To capitalise on the opportunities of the new economy, organisations would need to be configured differently. They will be smaller, have smaller workforces and lifespans. Since their raw material will be ideas floating anywhere in the world, their core activity will involve identifying and implementing them.

LEARNING OBJECTIVES

- To provide exposure to organisational structure of small-scale industries.
- Organisation is a key input. And, the choice of a proper organisation determines the success of the enterprise.
- The chapter deals with the need, importance, principles, steps and other related issues.
- Importance, principles.
- Formal and informal.
- Steps in organisation.
- Ownership.
- Lines and functional.
- Tomorrows organisation.
- Organisational structure in the 21st century.

Core Priorities

"The primary purpose of an organisation is not, as many of us believe, to meet customer needs, foster innovation, or make a better world. Rather, organisations are set up, first and foremost, to fulfil the perceived desires and priorities of a 'core group' of people. As such, the success or failure of an organisation is determined by the behaviour of this key set of individuals."

— ***Art Kleiner, Organisational Learning Consultant***

INTRODUCTION

The choice of a proper form of organisation is crucial for the success of a business enterprise. Every entrepreneur has to decide, at the outset, about the type of organisation which he would select for his private enterprise. It is an important entrepreneurial decision. Choice of a proper organisation is by and large influenced by the socio-cultural norms and the prevailing environment.

The form of organisation chosen influences the success or failure of the enterprise.

The decision of an entrepreneur depends on a number of variable factors. Among the many, the following factors are given weightage in making a choice of a suitable form of organisation which is most suited to one's enterprise. The deciding ten core factors are:

Type of business – service, trade, manufacturing.

Selection of industry and the area of operation.

Scope of operation, value of business and the size of the market, including its likely growth potential.

Amount of capital funds required – initial capital, working capital.

Possibility of raising resources from the market – institutions, subsidies and other incentives.

Costs and procedures and relative freedom from government regulation.

Comparative tax advantages, etc.

Size of the risk.

Continuity of the enterprise, and

Degree of direct control and adaptability of administration.

By and large, the final organisational choice is a compromising one that is most suitable to the entrepreneur's needs. The above ten factors are the major factors that will influence the choice of a proper form of an organisation, which will withstand all the stresses and pressures and strive for its smooth progress on an ongoing basis.

The aim of entrepreneurial development programmes in India should not be to treat the small entrepreneurs as small, but to help the more promising and efficient ones amongst them to grow big. This would mobilise the productive resources of the country, contain the monopoly of a few large enterprises and increase income, profits and employment. The objective is to accelerate the process of innovative entrepreneurial development in the country. Herein, choice of organisation also depends on the entrepreneurial skills and vision.

Business Occupations

Business occupations may be classified into four broad categories: (a) Agriculture, (b) Industry, (c) Commerce, and (d) Professions (see Fig. 9.1). Agriculture and industry involve the production of goods and materials, while commerce is mainly concerned with their distribution. The professions provide technical support to production and distribution.

Need for an Organisation

Behind every enterprise/entrepreneur – successful or otherwise, lies the most intricate instrument the world has ever evolved – *an organisation*. It is this instrument which transcends its immediate use and reveals qualities and forms that lie hidden in the inert matters around it.

"An organisation is the formation of an effective machine, the management of an effective executive and the administration of an effective direction. Administration determines the goals; the management strives towards it. Administration determines the organisation: the management uses it. An organisation is a machine of the management in its achievement of the ends determined by its administration. An organisation tries to establish an effective behavioural relationship among selected employees and in selected workplaces in order that a group may work together effectively."

– ***Sheldon***

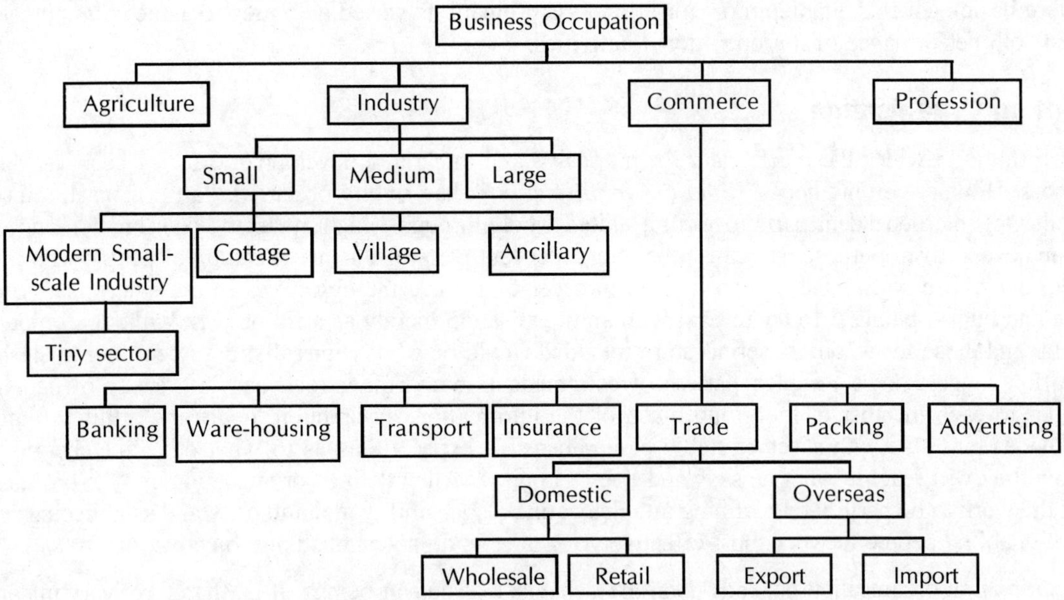

Fig. 9.1 Classification of Business Occupation in India

Organisation is one of the basic inputs for an enterprise/venture or business. An entrepreneur has to select a much suited organisation to achieve his goals.

Organisation is defined as a system in which individuals and groups operating at different levels perform the tasks assigned to them within the framework of delegated authority and responsibility which are rationally coordinated to achieve the desired organisational goals. It is an effective mechanism with which an entrepreneur directs, coordinates and controls the activities of man, machine, money and materials. The success and failure of an enterprise depends upon an organisation.

An organisation involves:

(i) A determination and an enumeration of the activities necessary for the achievement of the goals of an enterprise.

(ii) A grouping of these activities and assigning authority and responsibility to a particular position; and

(iii) A coordination of authority relationship so that the efforts of individuals are directed towards achieving the corporate goals.

An entrepreneur who has a high level of administrative capability, flair and ability for decision-making, computational skills, delegation and organisational skills, is good at communication and has sound technical knowledge stands a much better chance of success than his counterpart who possesses none or a low level of these basic qualities. It is the possession of these scarce qualities which confers an advantage on some people in becoming an entrepreneur. Besides these qualities, however, the entrepreneur also needs either to be himself a generalist so that he can discharge his function without delegation, or to possess delegation and organisational skills.

A proper organisation would assist in the most effective use of the physical assets – plants and machinery, tools, material and supplies – and the human resources of the industry so that the unit may be perpetuated and the objectives, including that of profit achieved. The need for organisation grows with the increase in the size of the unit. An organisation involves a division of work among people whose efforts must be coordinated to achieve specific objectives and implement predetermined strategies. An organisation is thus the foundation upon which the whole management structure is built.

The concept of organisation has five basic elements, namely:

(i) The assembly of men, materials, machines and money to produce a product in the unit accordance with the plan;

(ii) The identification and grouping of the work, i.e., work division and work allotment;

(iii) Definition of responsibility for every function;

(iv) Delegation of appropriate authority; and

(v) The establishment of structural relationships.

These five basic elements enable an organisation to coordinate its varied activities to achieve its objective. Moreover, they ensure smooth performance of the operational activities.

Definition of an Organisation

An organisation provides the mechanism for purposive and integrated development. It has been variously defined by different authors. Dimmock in his book, *"Public Administration"*, has rightly observed: "an organisation is the systematic bringing together of interdependent parts to form a united whole through which authority, coordination and control may be exercised to achieve a given purpose. (Because the interdependent parts of this are made up of people who must be directed and motivated and whose work must be coordinated in order to achieve the objectives of the enterprise, an organisation is both structure and human beings). To try to deal with an organisation merely as a framework without considering the people who make it up and those for whom its services are intended would be wholly unrealistic". According to Herbert Simon, the term organisation suggests "the complex pattern of communication and other relations in a group of human beings. This pattern provides to each member of the group much of the information, assumption, goals and attitudes that enter into his decisions, provides him also with a set of stable comprehensible expectations as to what other members of the group are doing, and how they will react to what he says and does". Louis A. Allen defined organisation as "the process of identifying and grouping the work to be performed, defining and delegating responsibility and authority and establishing relationships for the purpose of enabling people to work most effectively together in an accomplishing objectives".

The success of an organisation depends upon the behaviour of human beings. It is, therefore, very important to view it not merely as a simple physical structure of relationship but as a complex structure influenced by social and psychological behaviour and by informal groups governing the interactions of human beings.

An *organisational structure* is a framework which holds the various functions together according to the pattern, order, topical and legal arrangements and in-built relationships. According to the same authors, an organisation is a system with such inputs as men, materials, machines, goods and services, profits, etc.

Importance of an Organisation

Organisation is the foundation of management. It is a process in which individuals interact to accomplish definite objectives. Organisation has the following advantages:

(i) It encourages specialisation and ensures higher productivity;

(ii) It streamlines the process of activities and ensures their smooth functioning. Duplication of and consequent confusion as well as wasted efforts are likely to be removed if there is an adequate organisation and a fixing of responsibility;

(iii) It fosters coordination of various activities in an integrated manner towards the attainment of specific objectives;

(iv) It facilitates precise and effective delegation of authority;

(v) It ensures proper direction, motivation, coordination and control;

(vi) It aids in the expansion and growth of an enterprise. A sound organisational plan avoids all the pitfalls of rapid growth;

(vii) It provides for the optimum use of technological improvements and manpower for higher growth; and

(viii) An effective organisation promotes growth and diversification through decentralisation and divisionalisation on geographical or on product basis.

Formal and Informal Organisation

An organisation is broadly classified into *formal* and *informal* organisation.

The formal organisation is one resulting from planning where the pattern or structure is predetermined to carry out specific jobs or achieve goals. The structure, procedural rules, membership and work process of formal group/organisation are explicitly stated in clear terms. It is based on the delegation of authority with official leadership.

The informal organisation develops when people work together towards a specific objective or goal. In this organisation, people with common interests generally get together and work. It represents the pattern of interpersonal and intergroup relations which develop within a formal organisation without any prescribed position, duties, responsibility, authority, etc. By and large, the informal group develops its own leaders. It has a natural existence and performs unique functions.

Principles of Organisation

While choosing his viable organisational structure, every person, whether a small entrepreneur or a large one, must first determine the scientific principles on which it has to be based. The fifteen basic principles laid down by Urwick will serve as guidelines in determining the organisational pattern best suited for a unit. These fifteen principles are: (i) Objective; (ii) Specialisation; (iii) Coordination; (iv) Clear unbroken line of authority; (v) Responsibility; (vi) Efficiency; (vii) Delegation; (viii) The span of control; (ix) Balance; (x) Communication; (xi) Personal ability; (xii) Flexibility; (xiii) Grouping; (xiv) Definiteness, and (xv) Continuity.

Steps in Organising

The process of organisation follows the formulation of objectives. The work is then divided into component activities, which are then grouped into practical units of similar activities which are then divided into component activities. George R. Terry states: "*Organising is the establishing of effective behavioural relationships among selected work persons and workplaces in order that the group may work together efficiently*".

Briefly, following are the logical steps involved in organising:

(i) Identifying the activities in order to attain the objectives of the unit;

(ii) Determining the activities which are needed to execute plans and policies with a view to attaining objectives;

(iii) Classifying and grouping these activities on the principles of functions, products, and (a) grouping activities into individual jobs; (b) grouping jobs and people into section; (c) grouping sections into departments, and (d) grouping departments into administrative units.

(iv) Defining responsibility and accountability so that each person knows what is expected of him in terms of attainment of the unit's objectives;

(v) Delegating the requisite authority and adequate facilities enable each one to carryout his responsibility; and

(vi) Establishing clear structural relationships among individuals and groups.

The organisational structure of a small-scale industry differs from that of other business organisations. Its outstanding feature is the personal character of the organisation and management.

In analysing the organisational structure of a small-scale industry, we may broadly discuss the pattern of ownership (social organisation) and input organisation, i.e., the physical aspect of an organisation covering production, marketing, planning and control.

Functions of an Organisation

There are three kinds of works which must be performed whenever an organisation comes into being, *viz.:* division of labour, combination of labour and coordination, i.e., the *work,* the *people* and the *relationship* between them. These are known as the *fundamentals* in every successful organisation.

1. **Division of Labour:** Since an organisation is a structure of human association for the achievement of common goals, it involves individuals and groups of individuals. When two or more individuals join together to perform certain tasks, it follows that some division of work is done. Properly or improperly, fairly or unfairly, work is divided among those who participate in a productive organisation. With effective planning and organisation in an enterprise, the division of labour leads to a fixing of responsibility, the delegation of authority, specialisation and other conceptual schemes which are frequently called the *principles of an organisation.*
2. **Combination of Labour:** With work divided and assigned to the members of an organisation, their activities are grouped together, forming operations which are arranged to establish systems and procedures. From a structural point of view, this grouping of activities results in units, departments and divisions of an organisation. The basis for this grouping of activities may be the skills of the workers, the tools and machinery used, the nature of the product, the materials employed or some other element. Whether it is logical or not, there is always some reason for the arrangement of tasks in a work\place.
3. **Coordination:** This all-inclusive principle emerges because of the need in every organisation for the integration of activities and the coordination of individuals and groups of individuals performing their tastes. Coordination is

achieved through leadership; and in the structural sense, it involves the fixing of responsibility and the delegation of authority. It establishes controls which provide for an efficient scheduling and performance of activities.

The Genesis

This section highlights the role of an organisation in moulding entrepreneurship. Such a pivotal position of entrepreneurs will remain unchallenged in the 21st century in the midst of development in science and technology. In a way, it is a pace-setter for assigning a new role to the entrepreneur which has been provided by management thinkers and writers. Alvin Brown aptly observes that "Organisation will be of scant avail unless it is understood and practised by all the members of an enterprise. It will not be understood and practised unless it is set down in plain words for them to read and re-read. A transient communication will not suffice. The record of organisation must be durable and references thereto encouraged, so that its prescriptions may grow into the consciousness of those whom it is to guide".

Legal Status

The firms classified under the five types of ownership are recognised by Indian law. The simplest is an *individual proprietor*. The joint family is a partnership consisting entirely of family members and governed by traditional law in respect of the division of profits, inheritance and dissolution. A private limited company is a partnership in which the liability of the partners is limited to what they have invested in the firm. A public limited company is a firm in which equity shares have been sold to the public.

Ownership Organisation

The first and foremost question in organising a small-scale industry is that of ownership, which is represented by the right of an individual or a group of individuals to acquire legal title to assets for the purpose of controlling an industrial operation and enjoying the gains or profits flowing from such activities.

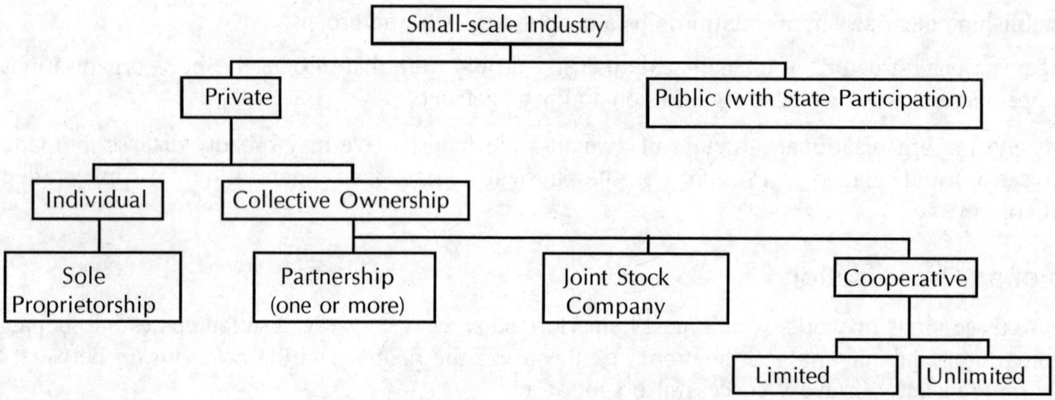

Fig. 9.2 Form of Ownership Organisation in a Small-scale Industry

The process of an organisation consists in making a rational division of work into groups of activities for the accomplishment of a task. The various stages of this process are:

(a) Determination of objectives;

(b) Enumeration of activities;

(c) Classification;

(d) Fitting individual (workers) into functional activities; and

(e) Assignment of authority for action.

Line Organisation

A *line organisation* is the basic framework of an organisation. It is the backbone of organisational hierarchy. Mr. Lundy has observed that "line organisation is characterised by direct lines of authority flowing from the top to the bottom of the organisational hierarchy and lines of responsibility flowing in an opposite but equally direct manner". Under this type, various activities are organised in groups and controlled by a manager, who is responsible to the top man. In this type of organisation, authority flows from the top to bottom, while responsibility flows bottom to top.

Advantages

(i) It is simple to form and easy to operate;

(ii) In it, line executives enjoy decision-making powers;

(iii) It has a systematic organisational structure;

(iv) It maintains a balance between authority, responsibility and accountability;

(v) Discipline can be maintained easily; and

(vi) Communication is easy and quick.

Disadvantages

(i) It becomes autocratic or dictatorial;

(ii) It suffers from lack of specialisation;

(iii) There is an overload of responsibility;

(iv) It hampers initiative;

(v) There is absence of coordination among different departments; and

(vi) It is unstable.

Functional Organisation

The simplest type of departmentation is the functional type of structure which consists of grouping all similar activities into major departments. It was originated by F.W.Taylor with a view to bringing about a specialisation of management activities. Under functional foremanship, office work is separated from shop or plant work. Fig. 9.3 depicts a functional structure in operation.

Advantages

(i) It promotes a better division of labour;

(ii) It ensures proper communication;

(iii) It offers a good scope for specialisation;

(iv) It promotes coordinated work; and

(v) It ensures systematic organisation.

Disadvantages

(i) The unity of command is absent;

(ii) There is a tendency towards over-specialisation;

(iii) In this type of organisation, it is difficult to pinpoint responsibility;

(iv) It is costly;

(v) There is no continuity of authority; and

(vi) Lower potency for developing managers for promotion.

The importance of sound organisational structure for a small-scale industry can hardly be over-emphasised. It facilitates sound administration, makes growth and diversification possible, provides for the optimum use of technological improvements and stimulates independence, creative thinking and initiative through well-defined areas of work (Figs. 9.3 and 9.4).

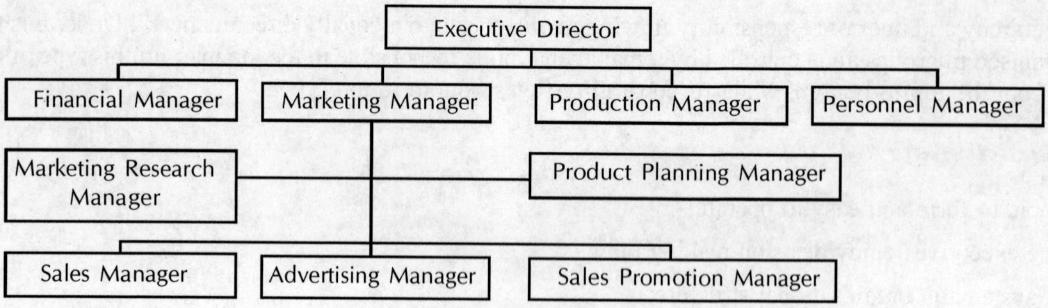

Fig. 9.3 Functional Structure

Note: In a pure functional organisation, we have multiple and divided responsibility. Although there is a need for functionalisation, it is probably never used in its pure form. A practical approach to functionalisation is reflected in the line and staff organisation, which is necessary for a large enterprise.

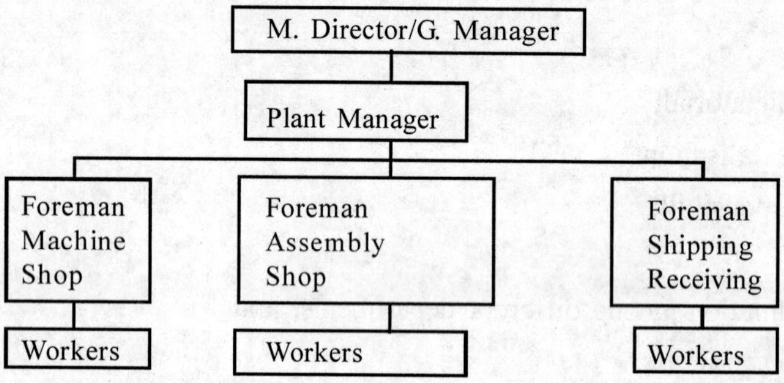

Fig. 9.4 A Simple Organisation

Note: (a) Production, Distribution and Finance are basic or primary functions and are known as line functions.
(b) Personnel, Engineering, Accounting, Legal Advice are staff functions.

Growth of the Undertaking

Figures 9.2 to 9.6 illustrate the various phases of a typical small-scale unit from the smallest beginnings to a size suitable for control as a single unit under the organisational structure of an entrepreneur.

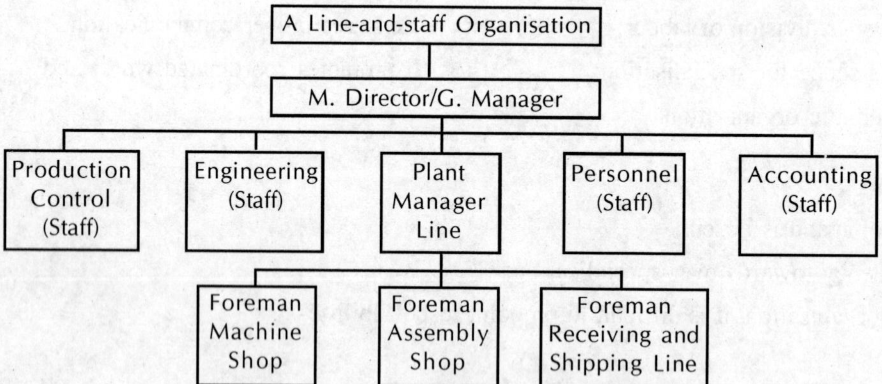

Fig. 9.5 A Simple Line-and-staff Organisation

Note: (i) Line portion maintains stability and discipline. (ii) Staff or functional portion provides expert knowledge and advice. (iii) Advantages of specialisation without disadvantages of Taylor's functional organisation. (iv) Staff organisations within themselve are organised on a line basis. (v) Line division ensures the performance of primary operations and procedures. It enjoys executive authority. (vi) Staff or service division is assigned the responsibility of providing solution to the problems and necessary facilitating services. It is an appendix and a necessary adjunct to line division, and (vii) Usually staff division has no direct aruthority on workers. Hence, no danger of multiple bosses and divided responsibility.

The One-man Small-scale Industry

Figures 9.3 to 9.5 represent the various phases in the growth of an individual small-scale entrepreneur. The first traces of a vertical organisation and specialisation in the work of management can be seen in Figure 9.3. The owner entrepreneur has a part-time clerk, who relieves him of some of the routine work of correspondence, accounts, records, etc. In this case, the owner-industrialist is a planner as well as a salesman. He alone determines the objectives and goals, enumerates and classifies various activities, distributes work among skilled and unskilled workers and attends to all other work. The authority for action is direct, and he shares the profit/loss of the industry with no one. Detailed accounting is done by him in his traditional way.

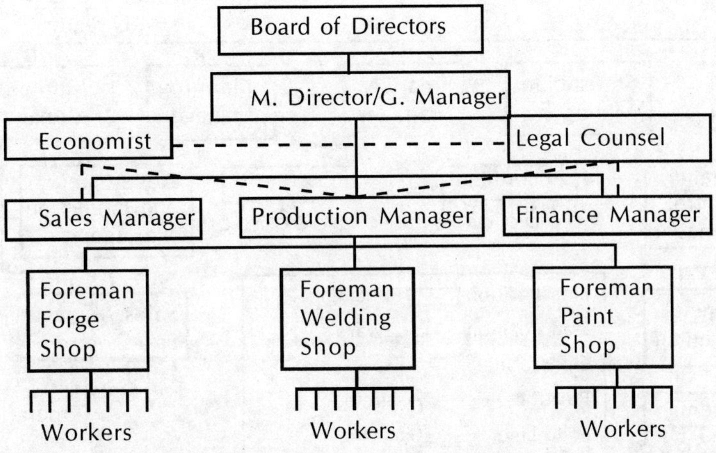

Fig. 9.6 Line-and-staff Organisation Chart

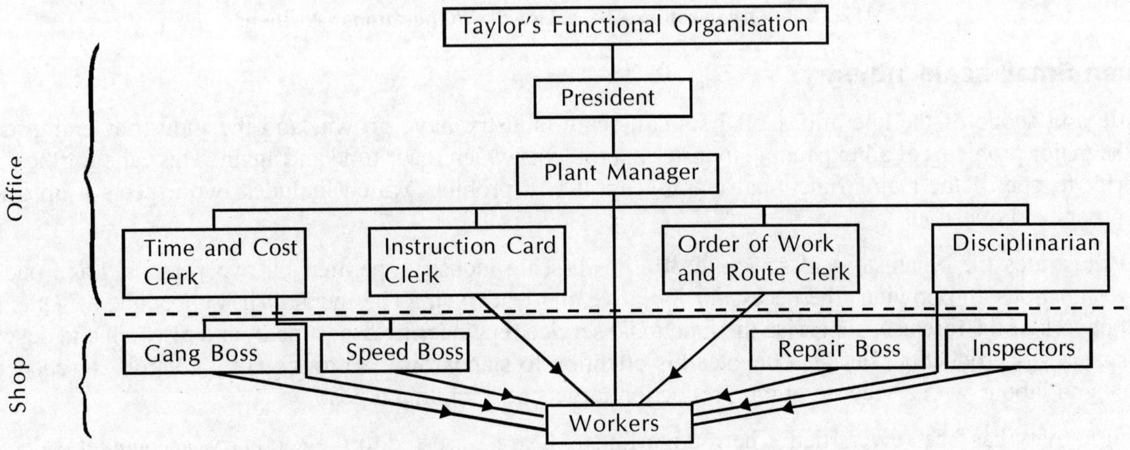

Fig. 9.7 Taylor's Functional Organisation

Note: (i) Office work is separated from shop work. (ii) Time and Cost Clerk, Instruction Card Clerk, Order of Work and Route Clerk and Disciplinarians operate at office level. (iii) Gang Boss, Speed Boss, Repair Boss and Inspectors are at the shop floor level. (iv) Taylor separated mental and clerical functions from shop or production functions. (v) There are eight boss for each worker – each boss telling the worker what to do. (vi) Functional specialisation creates difficulty about control and coordination. We have overlapping authority and responsibility. The chain of command is broken.

In some industries, the scale of operations is bigger than in the first phase, which calls for line support from the functional staff. In Fig. 9.4, there are three clerks, each one concerned with certain aspects of routine work, *viz.:* labour and personnel, sales and purchase accounts. The owner-entrepreneur has appointed a salesman to promote sales. He has also appointed two foremen to look after production. This involves a second-degree delegation of authority with regard to certain aspects of production.

The scale of the operations of the owner-industrialist is quite large and called for functional management. In Fig. 9.5, the industrial entrepreneur still performs all the functions in his own capacity. He has six persons reporting directly to him. He has appointed a chief salesman to organise and supervise the work related to sales, purchase, wages and accounts. The two foremen look after production. We see here the beginning of specialisation in production with the appointment of an engineer. The engineer, with his supporting staff, provides varied functional services to keep the channels of production clear of any defects. He also provides service in the event of a break down. Even then, the individual entrepreneur is responsible for providing leadership, direction and initiative in all the functional activities of his industry. This is the beginning of second-degree delegation, although the control still vests completely in the individual entrepreneur.

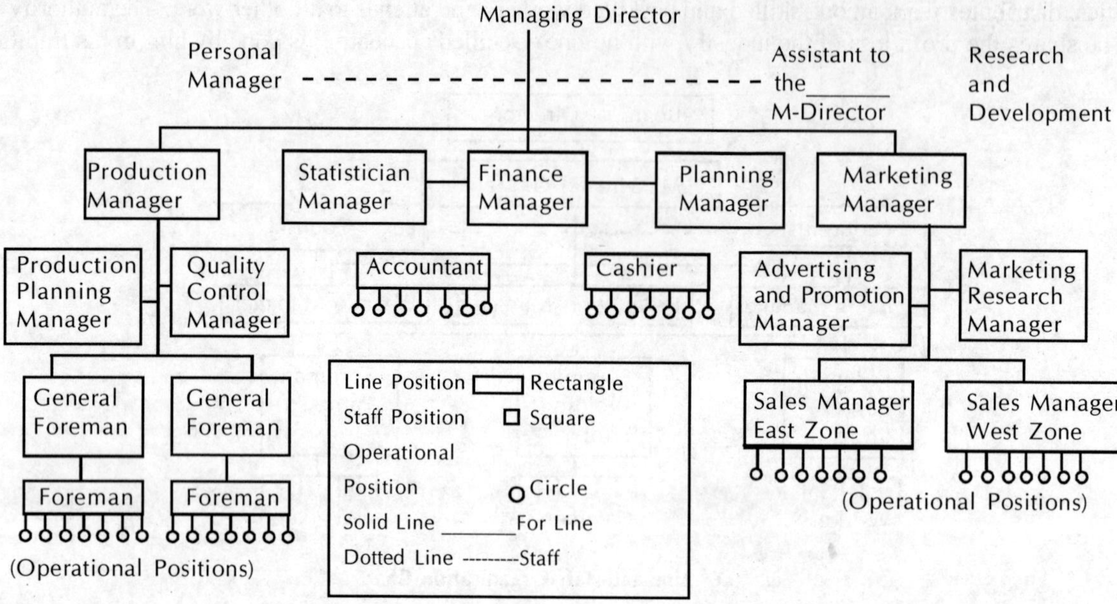

Fig. 9.8 Organisation Chart: Line/Staff/Operational Positions

The Two-men Small-scale Industry

The scale and scope of the operations of the small-scale industry have grown, and the industrial entrepreneur has encountered the major problems of all expanding industries, problems which recur time and again. This calls for the delegation of real authority to one of the major functional employees. It is a problem which includes two aspects – an impersonal question and a personal question.

Fig. 9.9 illustrates the organisational structure of a small-scale industry operated by two persons. Each one of them looks after two functions and provides the necessary initiative and leadership. The industry has appointed a works manager to look after the work of the foremen, supervise the functional service (engineering department) and research and development. He not only supervises production, but also devotes his attention to standardisation and quality control. He cooperates the work machines and labour with a view to attain production targets at a minimum cost.

Industrial activity has been diversified. The routine functions are entrusted to the secretary, accountant, sales director, etc. The industrialist has opened a new branch for export and import. He has also sought the services of a legal adviser in all legal matters connected with the operation of his industry.

Apparently, the functioning of the small-scale industry is organised on the basis of their functional activities. The owner industrialist still provides the necessary leadership and initiative. The overall control is in his hands. In many cases, key positions like those of the works managers, the Sales Director and the Accountant, are held by his close relatives (brothers or sons), while other routine matters are looked after by employees whose services are hired. For the first time, the small-scale industrialist appoints a young and well-qualified man to attend to the personnel problems of his industry. To make the delegation of authority really effective, the small-scale entrepreneur should not only pay due attention to principles of delegation, but also recognise the obstacles standing in the way of true delegation of authority. He should create an atmosphere in which the line staff are prepared to give and accept authority and responsibility enthusiastically. This is the beginning of delegation and an appreciation of modern management methods with a view to maximising profits.

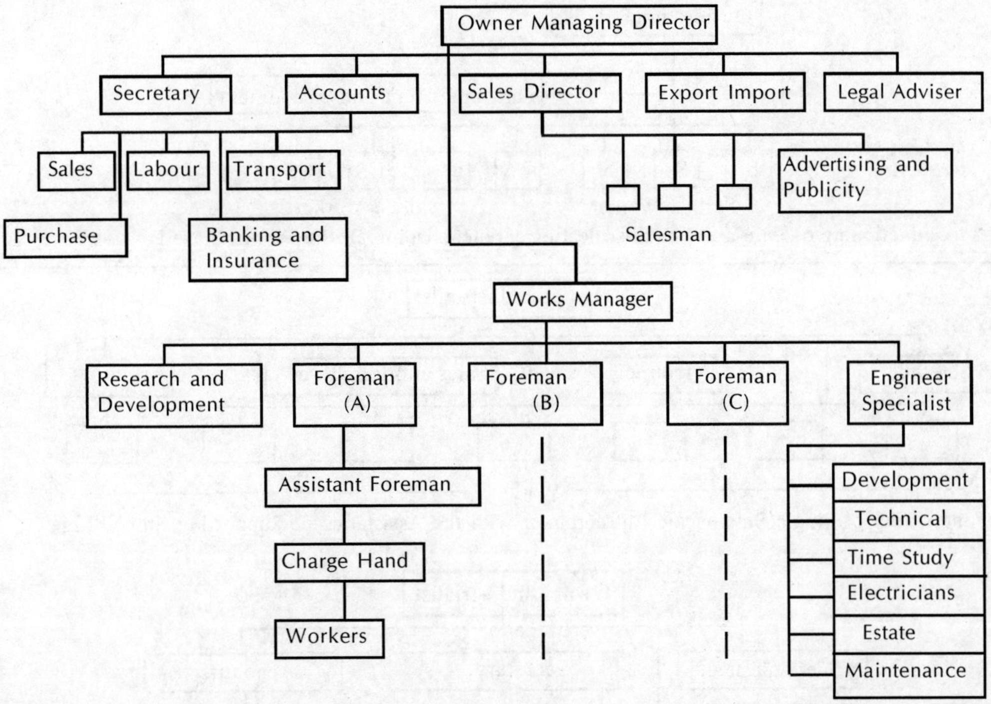

Fig. 9.9 Small Entrepreneur-owner Functioning with the Support of a Works Manager: Two-men Control

Table 9.1 Enterprises Registered with Different Agencies

(in '000)

Industry	Rural	Urban	Total	Per cent to Total
Under Factories Act/Bidi and Cigar Act	7.50	9.01	16.51	0.11
State Department of Industry	68.25	108.56	176.81	1.22
Khadi and Village Industries Commission	87.93	2.38	90.31	0.62
Handicraft Development Commission	0.69	0.90	1.59	0.01
Handloom Development Commission	12.45	1.35	13.80	0.10
Powerloom Textile Commission	2.31	11.52	13.83	0.10
Coir Board	5.85	0.19	6.04	0.04
Silk Board	0.44	0.03	0.47	0.00
Others	442.35	821.98	1,264.33	8.71
No Agency	9,821.12	2,992.69	12,813.81	88.35
Multiple Agencies	32.93	52.25	85.18	0.59
Not Reported	15.26	6.17	21.43	0.15
Total	10,497.80	4,007.03	14,504.11	100.00
Percentage Share	72.37	27.63	100.00	

(**Source:** CSO, Manufacturing Enterprise Survey, 1994-95)

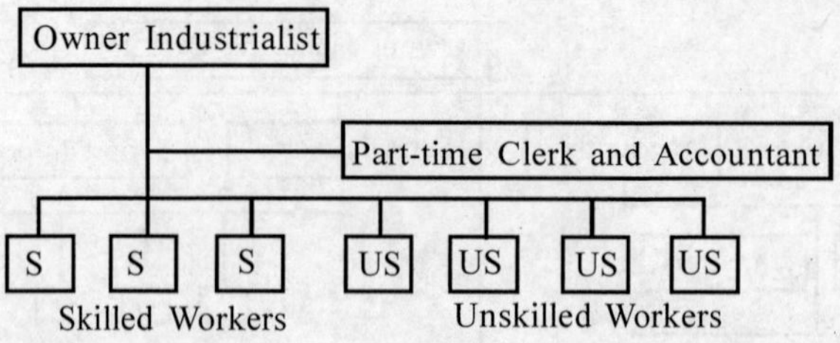

Functioning of One-man Small-scale Entrepreneur Doing all the Work: Phase I

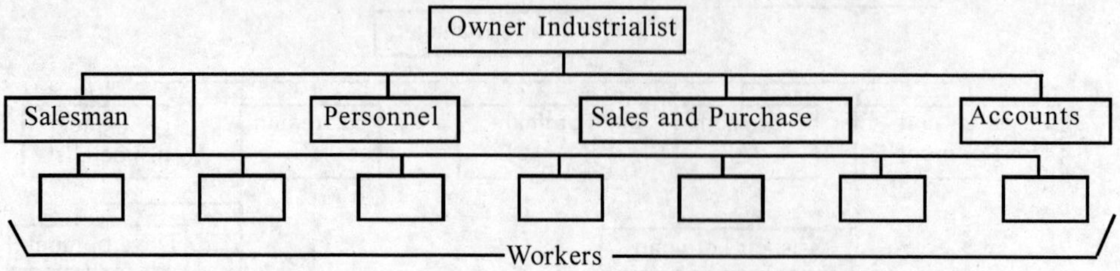

Functioning of Single Small-scale Entrepreneur with the Assistance of Supporting Staff: Phase 2.

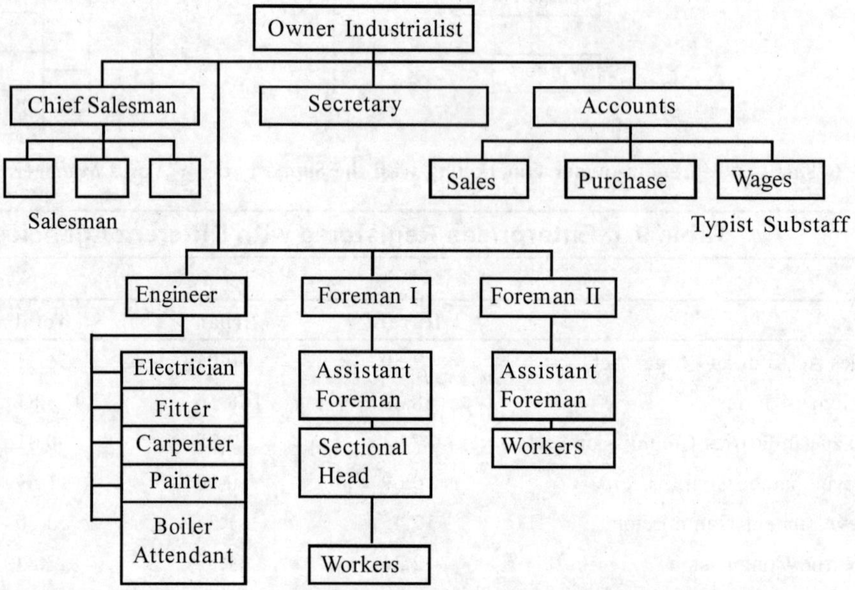

Small-scale Industrialist Functioning with the Assistance of Technical Supporting Staff: Phase 3.

A PREVIEW OF TOMORROW'S ORGANISATIONS

Organisations as we know them today will disintegrate in the future. The new structures will be more fluid. Departments, units, and divisions are expected to disappear and give way to multi-disciplinary and multi-skilled teams. Here is a look at two organisations that have started making their moves towards the future:

Polaris Software: In June 2001, Polaris moved away from the strategic business unit structure to a process-driven structure. The traditional Strategic Business Unit (SBU) structure had been adequate for growth till that point (₹ 250 crore), but to grow further, the Chennai-based company realised that it needed to increase synergy within the organisation to elevate the thinking of employees from a divisional level to the organisational level.

Three basic processes of the organisation were identified: getting customers, servicing customers and getting knowledge. According to IIM-A professor Ashok Korwar, who is the brain behind the design, "The idea was to identify the three constants Polaris had going forward into an uncertain world". The organisation has now been divided into SRDUs (Strategic Relationship and Delivery Units) and SPUs (Strategic Practice Units) and the GSOs (General Sales Organisations). It is up to the GSO to get new customers. After that the SRDUs are the customer focused units – a single point of control responsible for project delivery.

The new system is a radical departure from Polaris' earlier structure comprising SBUs, which were more competency and market focussed, with minimal cross-selling. SPUs will concentrate on leveraging Polaris' horizontal and vertical competencies to disseminate these competencies in the organisation. The focus is clearly to build knowledge in practice areas.

The SRDUs have the flexibility to pull in competence from all over the organisation. It will pull in resources as per the project requirement. Says CEO Arun Jain: "We are entering a knowledge-based era, where we cannot forecast what will happen, but we can ensure that our structure gives our people the ability to cope with challenges".

Around 30 SRDUs focus on consistency of delivery on projects, in an effort to sustain long-term partnerships with clients. The company will have around 12 vertical SPUs spread across industrial competencies and around 22 horizontal SPUs across technological competencies. These SPUs will form the second organisational pillar and will fuel the growth engine, while the SRDU will provide the cash engine for growth.

Andersen – At Andersen, the structure is even more flexible based totally on the client's needs. Teams are continuously formed and disbanded depending on the nature of the project. The teams are given full access to the capabilities of the firm. The structure provides for a mix of focus on multiple roles through clients, industry, solutions, and internal processes. Care, however, is taken to ensure that the solution and markets chosen are consistent with the company's capabilities. At the end of the day, the firm says, clients want solutions to their issues. A major focus, then, is to find the optimal alignment between client needs and organisational capabilities.

To enable this kind of integration, Andersen uses world-class tools, frameworks and methodologies. However, doing so involves managing an apparent paradox: that of being focused and integrated at the same time. It is integrated around the market and clients, but willing to accept the inherent boundaries that define focus, and clients, but willing to accept the inherent boundaries that define focus, and simultaneously, cross-organisational boundaries.

Organisational Structure

Six futuristic organisation models at work elsewhere in the world are mentioned below:

The Amoeba Organisation

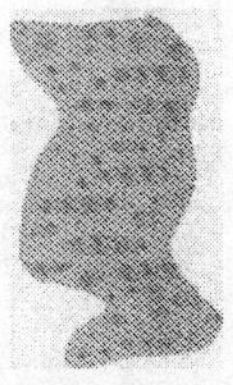

Self-learning horizontal teams are fluid, based on emerging products.

Employee 'move around' until they find the products where they can add the most value

Guided by "waterline" Principles (If risky areas, check with key people)

Ranks and titles avoided – leadership is defined by followers

The Abacus Organisation

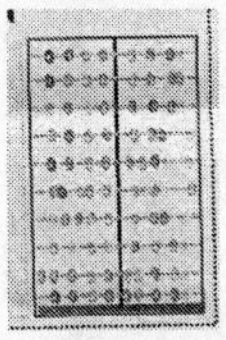

Abacus-like matrix structure of product areas (product) and geography (countries)

Networks transfer knowledge, provide support, and open communications.

Able to escalate globally through sharing information

The Molecular Organisation

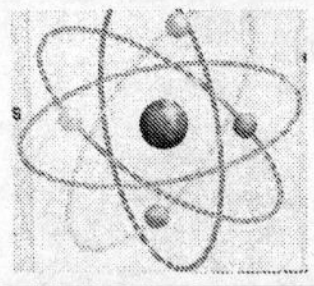

Customer focussed business units with all functions represented

Entire enterprise represented at tactical, coordinate and strategic level

The Pizza Organisation

Competency based, people are resources

Resources are the Pizza base, competencies and responsibilities are toppings

Reinventing seflin to a flatte organisation, and outward focus through project teams

Support service, like HR, are matrixes to foster team-development

Culture of teaming spreads from the top of the organisation

The EcoNets Organisation

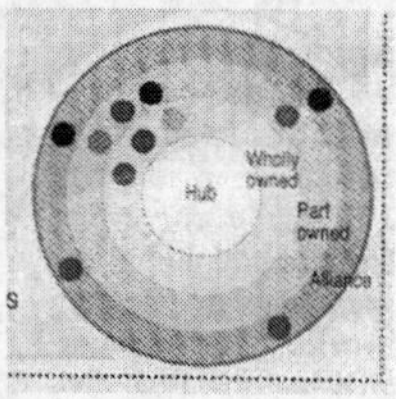

The EcoNet structure looks like this (small circles represent businesses)

Markets are more efficient portfolio managers at a time when the world is moving fast

Small is beautiful: emphasis on speed and boldness in decision-making, culture, and remuneration, therefore, access to talent

The Spaghetti Organisation

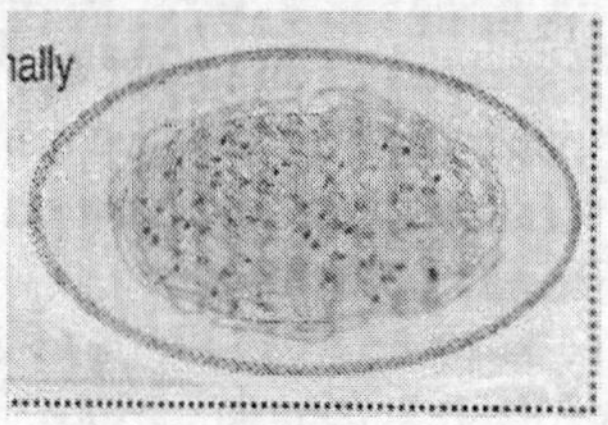

No titles, no departments, no personal office space

Small management teams sponsor and lead projects

Key is the information system and knowledge base

Physically and organisationally informal

Initiatives intertwine in this open environment

CONCLUSION

Finally, the small entrepreneur has to select a viable structure that is most suited to achieve his objectives or goals. In the words of Peter Drucker: "Organisation is not an end itself, but a means to an end of business performance and business results. Organisational structure is an indispensable means, and the wrong structure will seriously impair business performance and may even destroy it... Organisational structure must be designed so as to make possible attainment of the objectives of the business for five, ten, fifteen years hence". This may be achieved by activities analysis, decision analysis and relations analysis – all on a continuing basis. All in all, the organisational structure must contain the least possible number of management levels, and forge the shortest possible chain of command. It must also make possible the training and testing of tomorrow's top entrepreneurs.

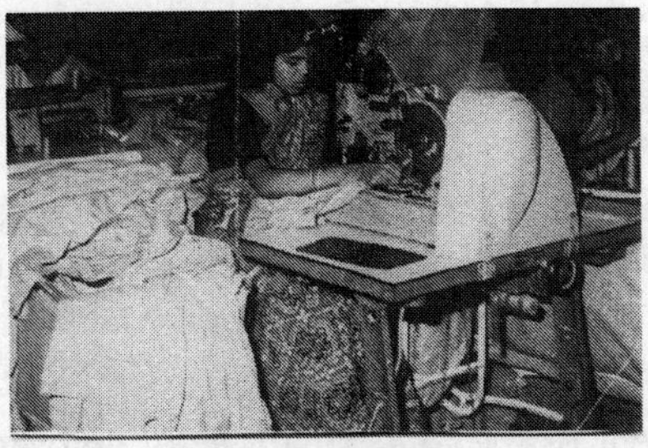

10 CHAPTER

OWNERSHIP PATTERN IN SMALL-SCALE INDUSTRY

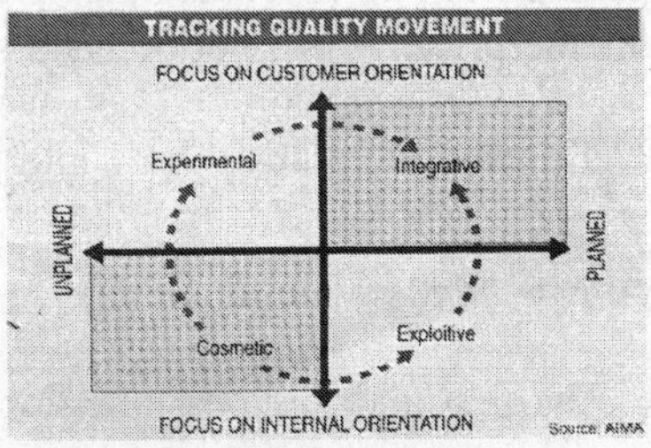

Management thinker, Peter Drucker, goes as far as to say that profit-making will not be the organisation's main goal anymore. Rather, it will be to create wealth for the society. May be. But the 21st century organisations will still be about what they are today: people, customers, and wealth.

Entrepreneurs have a number of legal forms of business to choose from. Entrepreneurs should determine which business form is best for them based on their short and long-term needs. In choosing a form of ownership, entrepreneurs must remember that there is no single best form; what is best depends on the business particularly circumstances.

LEARNING OBJECTIVES

The learning objective is an indepth discussion of the ownership pattern in small-scale industry.

The chapter discusses and analyses the ownership pattern in small-scale industry.

- Organisation is one of the key input of small-scale industry.
- Ownership of organisation.
- Policy decision.
- Over 80 per cent of small-scale industries are proprietory enterprises.
- Ownership pattern.
- State policy.
- Sole proprietorship – merits and demerits.
- Partnership – basic features, advantages and disadvantages.
- Joint-stock companies.
- Cooperative enterprises – advantages and disadvantages.
- Need of the hour is professional ownership.

INTRODUCTION

Behind every enterprise/entrepreneur – successful or otherwise, lies the most intricate instrument the world has ever evolved, an **organisation**. It is this instrument which transcends its immediateness and reveals qualities and forms that lie hidden in the inert matters around it. An organisation is one of the basic inputs for an enterprise/venture or business. An entrepreneur has to select a much suited organisation to achieve his goals.

According to the second Census of small-scale industries, about 80.5 per cent of the total small-scale units were proprietory, followed by partnership (16.8%), limited companies (2.1%), cooperatives (0.3%), and others (0.3%).

The Genesis

This section highlights the role of an organisation in moulding entrepreneurship. Such pivotal positions of entrepreneurs will remain unchallenged in the 21st century in the midst of all feats of development in science and technology. In a way, it is the pace-setter for assigning new roles to an entrepreneur which have been provided by management thinkers and writers. *Alwin Brown* aptly observes that, "Organisation will be of scant avail unless it is understood and practised by all the members of an enterprise. It will not be understood and practised unless it is set down in plain words for them to read and re-read. A transient communication will not suffice... The record of organisation must be durable and references thereto encouraged, so that its prescriptions may grow into the consciousness of those whom it is to guide".

OWNERSHIP OF ORGANISATION

The first and foremost question in organising a small-scale industry is that of ownership, which is represented by the right of an individual or a group of individuals to acquire legal title to assets for the purpose of controlling an industrial operation and enjoying the gains or profits flowing from such activities.

Small industrial units are, by and large, started by persons who value independence and are desirous of obtaining the highest rewards for their initiative, innovation, technical skills, business acumen and experience. As Nihal Singh has aptly observed: "The owner of a small industry values his undertaking for the job it provides him as well as for any return it may make on his invested capital". The chief forms of an ownership organisation are:

(i) Sole Proprietorship;

(ii) Partnership;

(iii) Cooperative Society; and

(iv) Joint-stock Company.

Policy Decision

Every entrepreneur has to make policy decisions in all vital areas of business activities. He has to organise and manage his business affairs on scientific lines. He has to make a decision either as manufacturer of some product or as the distributor of the products made by others. Whatever activity he chooses, he will be confronted with numerous problems and his ultimate success will depend upon his entrepreneurial ability. He will have to make a policy decision about the form of organisation. Should he start his enterprise as a sole proprietory concern, partnership or any other form of organisation suited to the needs of his business? He will also have to decide about the size of his business. Should it be a small-scale industry or a large-scale industry? He should also decide whether to register the small-scale industry with the appropriate authorities or not.

Ownership Organisation Decision

The entrepreneur's choice of the type of organisation will depend upon the nature of business, scale of operation, capital requirements, ownership rights such as – control and decision-making opportunities and the impact of taxation. The entrepreneur should understand the impact of these factors on his business and should fully decide whether to operate his business as a one-man firm, a partnership or a company. In general, an entrepreneur wishing to start an industry on his own will prefer to organise it on a small-scale if he has limited capital and skill, and cater to the local market. If the entrepreneur is unable to control all the operations, he will seek out other people willing to join him as a partner. In this way, new ability and more capital

Table 10.1 Distribution of Units by Types Organisation (Prop. Partnership, etc.), Fixed Investment Slabs and Their Production and Employment During 1987-88

Type of Organisation

S.No.	Investment In P&M	Proprietory			Partnership			Limited Co.			Cooperative			Others		
	Slabs (₹ lakh)	No. of Units	Production (₹ lakh)	Employment (Nos.)	No. of Units	Production (₹ lakh)	Employment (Nos.)	No. of Units	Production (₹ lakh)	Employment (Nos.)	No. of Units	Production (₹ lakh)	Employment (Nos.)	No. of Units	Production (₹ lakh)	Employment3 (Nos.)
(1)	(2)	(3)	(4)	(5)	(6)	(7)	(8)	(9)	(10)	(11)	(12)	(13	(14)	(15)	(16)	(17)
1.	0-10	466245	1100.73	17887536	91291	1397598	1040646	6655	261811	156714	1579	11792	18487	1154	18391	21571
2.	10-5	1341	43142	27649	3428	204653	94672	1471	9312	50497	46	790	1783	131	7304	4469
3.	15 and above	1130	84814	39099	330	405444	153325	41557	599043	231801	77	5738	7179	332	63215	20382
Total		**468717**	**1228329**	**1854284**	**98049**	**2007695**	**1288643**	**12283**	**953977**	**439012**	**1702**	**18320**	**37449**	**1617**	**88910**	**46422**

(*Note:* Total does not tally due to rounding up of decimal figures.)

Table 10.2 Distribution of Units by Types Organisation (Prop. Partnership, etc.), Fixed Investment Slabs and Their Production and Employment During 1987-88

Type of Organisation

S.No.	Investment In P&M	Proprietory			Partnership			Limited Co.			Cooperative			Others		
	Slabs (₹ lakh)	No. of Units	Production (₹ lakh)	Employment (Nos.)	No. of Units	Production (₹ lakh)	Employment (Nos.)	No. of Units	Production (₹ lakh)	Employment (Nos.)	No. of Units	Production (₹ lakh)	Employment (Nos.)	No. of Units	Production (₹ lakh)	Employment3 (Nos.)
(1)	(2)	(3)	(4)	(5)	(6)	(7)	(8)	(9)	(10)	(11)	(12)	(13	(14)	(15)	(16)	(17)
1.	0-5	463966	1054481	1759122	86428	1232416	971226	5481	200269	131437	1553	10756	29780	10080	14479	19246
2.	5-10	3180	81954	52192	7159	331102	157697	2238	145445	73497	75	1880	2700	180	9453	9279
3.	10 and above	1571	91893	42970	4462	444166	159720	456.4	608269	234078	74	5690	4969	357	64977	17987
Total		**468717**	**1228328**	**1854284**	**98049**	**2007685**	**1288643**	**12283**	**953983**	**439012**	**1702**	**18326**	**37449**	**1617**	**88909**	**46422**

(**Note:** Total does not tally due to rounding up of decimal figures.)

will be brought into the business. Partnerships are common in commercial business. Partnership is not a legal entity; the partners are personally responsible for all the activities performed by them in the name of the firm. The risks associated with unlimited liability can be avoided and large amount of capital can be brought into the business by forming a limited company. If the capital requirements are not very large, a private limited company may be formed; and to meet the needs of a large amount of capital to run a large business, a public company will have to be formed.

A survey of small-scale industries in Greater Bombay shows the organisational structure of small business units. The sole proprietorship is the most popular form of small business ownership. According to the Survey, 78.5 per cent of the total units were of private proprietorship type, joint family and partnership accounting together for about 1 per cent of the total. Even in the case of joint family and partnership, many a times a single entrepreneur controls the enterprises.

The type of organisation suited for the small-scale units depends upon several factors such as – the nature and type of industry, the extent of capital, the nature of skills required and the capacity to offer livelihood to the participating factors. Sole proprietorship is, however, the dominant form in small business enterprises.

Forms of Business, Their Pros and Cons

	Sole Proprietorship	Partnership	Pvt. Ltd., Company
Flexibility	Most flexible: you are the sole person in charge	Less flexible as areas of responsibility are defined	Same as partnership. May vary from case-to-case
Capital Risk	Very high, proprietor bears all the risk	Lower: shared by partners	Same as partnership depending on number of directors
Liability	Unlimited, extending to personal assets of proprietor	Unlimited, extending to personal assets of partners	Limited to company assets
Formation	Simplest; no legal requirements	Through partnership deed, though not compulsory	Through the articles of association and MoA
Exit option	On death of proprietor or closure	As per Partnership Act or through deed of dissolution	Compulsory wind-up under court of law or voluntary dissolution through shareholders resolution
Inheritance	Depends on the will of sole proprietor	Deed to specify who will be entitled to partner's share of profits	Shares transferred to legal heirs

Table 10.3 Ownership Pattern of the Unorganised Sector

(in million)

	Manufacturing Enterprises Survey 1994-95				Second All India Census 1987-88	
Ownership	**Rural**	**Urban**	**Enterprises**	**Percentage to total**	**SIDO Unit***	**Percentage to total**
Proprietory	10.34	3.81	14.15	96.65	0.47	81.03
Partnership	0.11	0.16	0.27	1.86	0.10	17.24
Cooperatives	0.00	0.00	0.00	0.00	0.00	0.00
Public Sector	0.00	0.00	0.00	0.00	0.00	0.00
Ltd.Cos.	0.00	0.00	0.00	0.00	0.1	1.73
Others	0.00	0.00	0.00	0.00	0.00	0.00
Not Reported	0.04	0.03	0.07	0.49	0.00	0.00
Total	**10.49**	**4.00**	**14.49**	**100.00**	**0.58**	**100.00**

*Include SSI units registered under the Factories Act.

(**Source:** CSO – Manufacturing Enterprise Survey 1994-95; DC (SSI): Second All India SSI Census.)

State Policy

It is the policy of the government, both at the Centre and in the states, to encourage and promote cooperative enterprises of all types. The registrar of Cooperative Societies in each state is concerned with the administration, supervision, coordination and development of cooperative societies, assisted by Deputy Registrars, Assistant Registrars and Inspectors. The Registrar offers assistance and guidance in the formation of all types of cooperatives and keeps a vigilant eye on their stability, administration, working, financial accounting, etc., through instructions, regulations, inspection, audits and other checks.

A few small-sale industries are in the public sector.

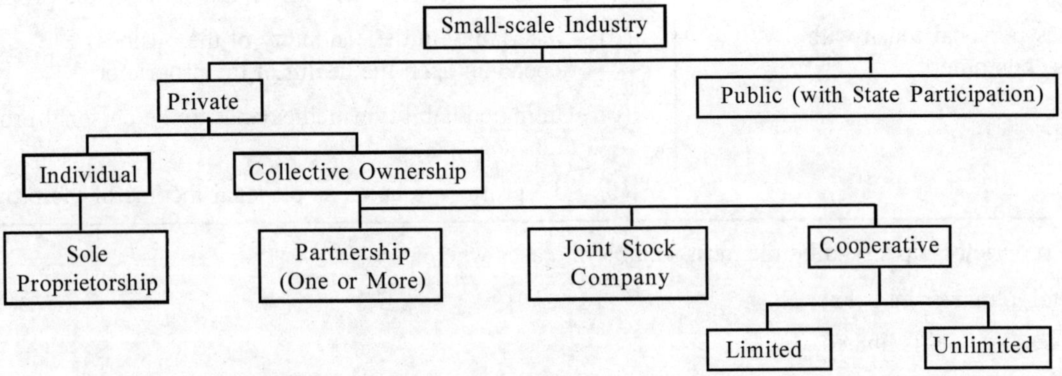

Fig. 10.1 Organisational Structure of Small-scale Industries in India

SOLE PROPRIETORSHIP

"Sole proprietorship is a form of a business organisation in which an individual invests his own capital, uses his own skill and intelligence in the management of its affairs and is solely responsible for the results of its operation." The individual, with the assistance of other workers or by his own labour and capital, may run the industry. This form of organisation is also known as *individual entrepreneurship* – the oldest and the most soughtafter form of enterprise in the field of the small-scale industry, and the easiest and simplest form of entrepreneurship for industrial activity with his own savings or with funds borrowed from his friends or relatives. The industry may be started either in a portion of the entrepreneur's own house or in rented premises. There are no legal formalities to be gone through except those required for a particular type of industry. For example, if the entrepreneur decides to start a small engraving industry, he has no legal formalities to comply with. He and his family members may run the industry in their own residence. In this form of ownership, the liability is unlimited. The small industrialist and the industry are highly interrelated and integrated. If the industry prospers, the entrepreneur is the sole beneficiary and *vice versa*. Moreover, he enjoys full control over the affairs of the industry. He is the sole authority to decide, plan and control. In short, the entrepreneur is his own master in this form of an organisation. The important features of a sole proprietorship are:

(a) Sole ownership;

(b) One-man control;

(c) Unlimited risk;

(d) Undivided risk;

(e) No separate entity of the firm, and

(f) No government regulations.

Sole Proprietorship Firm

Advantages	Disadvantages
(a) The profits accrue to the sole proprietor	(a) Limited amount of capital depending on the ability of the individual
(b) It ensures flexibility in managerial decision	(b) Managerial support for others is nil
(c) Decision-making is faster	(c) Success or failure depends on the skills of the proprietor
(d) It ensures personal touch with workers, customers	(d) Uncertainty in the continuity of the business depending upon the health of the proprietor
	(e) Unlimited liability which extends to the personal property also, and
	(f) The profits are taxed as personal income of the proprietor.

The sole proprietorship would be the most suitable in cases where:

(a) Capital requirement is low;

(b) Business activity is limited;

(c) Element of risk is minimum, and

(d) Individual can manage the show and also satisfy customers.

Merits

Following are the merits or advantages of the sole proprietorship form of an organisation:

(i) Easy and Simple Formation: The greatest advantage of this form of organisation is that it can be easily established. Unlike other forms, no elaborate legal formalities are necessary for its formation. One can form it easily in a simple manner and at the same time, one can close it down whenever he may choose to do so. There are no legal formalities for expansion, contraction or dissolution of the business. Thus, it is the most flexible type of business enterprise.

(ii) Smooth Management: Another merit of this form of organisation is that the management of the concern can be carried on smoothly. There is no one to oppose and hence there is no room for any friction.

(iii) Promptness in Decision-making: The sole proprietor is free to conduct the affair of his business and he enjoys individual responsibility. For this reason, he is able to make quick decisions without any delay and hesitation. Such promptness in decision-making is essential, for the smooth conduct of business operations.

(iv) Direct Motivation and Incentive to Work: The sole proprietor has to assume all the risks and is entitled to receive all the profits; therefore, he takes pains to work hard as there is direct relationship between effort and the rewards.

(v) Personal Touch with Customers: A sole trader is always able to maintain close and personal touch with his customers which may not be possible in other types of organisations. Thus, he is able to maintain goodwill and cater to the tastes of the consumers. This personal touch adds to the success of the business.

(vi) Secrecy: An individual entrepreneur is able to maintain complete secrecy about important matters relating to his business and thus safeguard business secrets from his competitors.

(vii) Social Advantages: This form provides employment opportunities to many. It ensures diffusion of business ownership and thus concentration of wealth and power in the hands of a few is avoided. Further, it helps in the development of several essential qualities in entrepreneurs, such as drive, initiative, hardwork, assumption of responsibilities, tact and self-reliance, etc. The preservation of a single proprietorship offers the best promise of securing motivation and widespread ownership and control the industry.

Limitations

Sole proprietorship has several limitations which are as follows:

(i) Limited Financial Resources: The greatest limitation of this form of organisation is that the capital available for the business remains very limited. An individual cannot possess enormous savings and he can borrow only limited funds from his friends and relatives. He may not have enough credit to borrow huge sums from either banks or financial institutions. This limits the size as well as profits of the business.

(ii) Limited Managerial Ability: An individual cannot be expected to possess knowledge of every branch of management. Now, when the management is highly specialised and business is becoming more and more complex, nobody can claim to be an expert on all the subjects. An individual may have limited knowledge and ability to take correct decisions. He may take a wrong decision which ultimately may prove to be detrimental for the business. Few persons are qualified by training or experience to handle alone the varied problems of purchasing, merchandising, advertising, customer relations and financing.

(iii) Unlimited Liability: Another great limitation is that the liability of the sole trader is unlimited. It implies that there is always a risk that he may lose the capital invested in his business as well as his personal property. In the event of some disaster, his creditors can satisfy their claims out of his personal property also. Thus, the entire risk has to be borne by one person alone but in a way unlimited liability may be of help too. The sole trader may get more credit for the creditors, as the limit of credit may extend to the value of property owned by him, and it will not be limited to the extent of capital invested by him in business only.

(iv) Lack of Continuity: There is always lack of continuity or stability in such business. The mortality rate of such a business has also been high. If the owner falls ill or he is away, the business stops. In case he dies, the business may not flourish or may have to be rebuilt.

In spite of the above limitations, this form of business organisation occupies a prominent place in the business world. In advanced countries as well as in developing countries like India, it is playing an important role. This form is ideal for small ventures and may be more than a match for larger enterprises. It is more suitable for concerns where: (i) capital required is small, (ii) risk involved is not heavy, (iii) goods of artistic nature are to be produced, (iv) personal touch with customers is necessary, (v) an individual is able to control the affairs, (vi) prompt decision is needed, (vii) scale of production is relatively small, and (viii) operation is simple in character not needing highly skilled management.

This form of organisation is quite popular in the small-scale industry. Nearly 61 per cent of the small-scale industries are *proprietory concerns*. The most important factor in the formation of proprietory concerns is non-interference from others. Further, an entrepreneur is not bound by law to publish annual accounts or to keep accounts except to the extent it may be necessary to do so for income-tax and other related purposes. He need not disclose any confidential information. Besides, this form of organisation is simple and no legal formalities are required for its formation.

PARTNERSHIP ORGANISATION

A partnership is a relationship between two or more persons (not exceeding 20) to share the profits as well as losses of a business. The terms of the partnership are incorporated in engagement called a *partnership deed*. Such a deed indicates the name and location of the business, nature of business, share of each partner, powers, duties and obligations of the partners, manner in which profits/losses would be shared among partners, provisions for retirement/expulsion of partner and dissolution of partnership. It is advisable to seek the assistance of legal experts in preparing a partnership deed. While registration of a partnership concern is not compulsory, it is advisable to register it with the Registrar of firms of the areas.

Partnership organisation grew and gained importance as an individual is not competent enough to possess enormous capital and knowledge or competence to manage everything. With the expansion of business and enlargement of the scale of its operations, it became necessary for a group of persons to join hands together and supply the necessary capital and skills. Often it is found that a person may be having a huge capital but may not possess the required skills. On the other hand, there may be another person who may be highly successful in its efficient conduct. Thus, partnership organisation has grown out of the necessity to arrange more capital, provide better skills, control and management, to take advantage of high degree of specialisation and division of labour and to share the risks.

In India, partnership organisations are governed by the Indian Partnership Act, 1932. Section 4 of this Act defines a partnership as "the relation between persons who have agreed to share profits of a business carried on by all or any of them acting for all". Persons who enter into partnership are collectively known as 'firm' but individually known as 'partner'. If we analyse this definition carefully, the following points emerge as the main elements of partnership: (i) Partnership is the relation between persons, i.e., at least two persons must be there to constitute a partnership, (ii) there should be an agreement between them. This also means that persons should be legally competent to enter into a contract, and (iii) they should carry on some business. It implies that an agreement to run a charitable institution will not constitute a partnership. Business here necessarily implies a lawful business, (iv) their motive for carrying on business should be to share the profits, (v) the business must be carried on by all or any of them acting for all. Thus, one or some partners can represent the firm and bind it by his/their actions in the usual course of business.

Basic Features

The partnership organisation has some basic or fundamental features which have been discussed below, with special reference to the position of partnership in India.

1. Number of Persons: There should be at least two persons to form a partnership organisation. In India, there is no upper limit prescribed under the Partnership Act, but a limit has been put under the Companies Act indirectly. Under this Act, a partnership consisting of more than 20 persons for a general business and 10 persons for a banking business would be illegal. Thus, the upper limit of the number of partners in a general business is 20 and in the banking business it is 10.

2. Contractual Relationship: Partnership is the result of contractual relationship between two or more persons. There must be an agreement between persons who wish to form partnership. It is a fundamental feature of the partnership organisation. For example, a manager of a firm may get his remuneration which may be based on the profits of the firm, but on that account, he cannot be taken as a partner as the element of agreement is not there. Similarly, two or more persons may be sharing the gains of a property jointly held and on that account alone, there cannot, the law does not interfere with its formation or dissolution. On that very basis, no partners agree for the same. Similarly, if a partner dies, the firm is dissolved as one of the contracting parties is dead. Thus, it has been rightly said that a partnership arises from contract and not from status.

3. No Legal Distinction between Firm and its Partners: It has been mentioned earlier that persons entering into a partnership are individually known as 'partners' and collectively as a 'firm'. Since a partnership is merely an association of persons, no separate legal entity or fictitious person is created. This implies that the law does not make any distinction between the firm and the partners who compose it. Any partner can bind the firm with his acts on behalf of the firm. But at the same time, a partner is free to undertake personal business or enter into personal contract.

4. Unlimited Liability: Just like sole proprietorship, the liability of the owners of the firm is unlimited. But the difference between the two is that in the case of the former, all risk is to be shouldered by one person alone but in the case of a partnership, it is to be borne by two or more persons. This means that a partner is not only liable to the extent of capital he has invested in the firm but he may be called upon to meet the liability to of his personal property also. If need be, the creditors of the firm can claim debt out of the personal property of the partners. In such an eventuality, the partner looses the capital invested in the firm as well as his personal property.

Box 10.1 Typecasting the Partner

Legally, any partner is just that – a partner – with rights to all the benefits and responsible for all liabilities, as defined in the partnership deed. But commercially, a partner could be of various types:

Working partner. Contributes to capital and takes active part in the day-to-day management of the firm.

Sleeping or dormant partner. Only contributes to capital and takes no part in the management of the firm.

Secret partner. Contributes capital and may or may not take an active part in the management of the firm. However, his connection with the firm is not known to the outside world.

Limited partner. His liability is limited to the extent of his share in the capital expenditure and profits of the firm. He is not entitled to an active part in the management of the firm.

Partner in profits only. Shares only the profits of the firm, not its losses. But he bears unlimited liability for its debts.

Nominal or ostensible partner. Does not contribute to capital, has no share in the firm's profits or losses. He only lends his name. Again, he could be a partner by estoppel (who represents himself as partner) or by non-declaration (who doesn't deny that he's not a partner). The first is liable to those who lend to the firm on the basis of this representation; the second is liable to third parties who lend on the basis of such non-declaration.

Minor partner. A minor cannot be a partner because he is not qualified to enter into a contract. But he may be admitted to the benefits of a partnership. On turning major, if he chooses to stay with the firm, his liability becomes unlimited retrospectively. He then also has a say in the running of the firm.

Advantages of Partnership Organisation

A partnership organisaton has certain advantages as compared to the sole proprietorship or the joint-stock company organisation. We discuss below its main advantages:

(i) Easy Formation: A partnership can be easily formed as no legal formalities are to be observed to establish it. At the same time, unlike a company, not much of the expenses are incurred for its formation.

(ii) Flexibility: A partnership organisation is a highly flexible as well as a mobile organisation. Changes can be introduced without much difficulty. The necessary additional capital can be raised, new partners can be introduced, the place and object of the firm can be changed. Business of the firm can also be expanded or contracted according to the needs.

(iii) Pooling of Resources and Skill, etc.: Unlike sole proprietorship under a partnership, several persons pool in their capital, resources, skills expertise, experience and services, etc. Two or more persons are always better than one and in that sense partners strive to work with zeal of the better. It enables combination of such individuals who may not be in a position to do anything alone.

(iv) Division of Risk: Under a partnership, the risks of business are divided among the partners and that way they are not to be shouldered by one person alone. Thus, it is more useful for risky business.

(v) Strong Credit Position: Unlimited liability of the partners enhances the creditworthiness of the firm. The credit can be extended to it to the limit of the value of property owned by the partners, and not confined to the extent of capital contributed by the partners. Further, it puts a check on the speculative and reckless activities of the partners. The partners always remain vigilant and behave cautiously.

(vi) Less Incidence of Tax: As compared to the joint-stock company, the burden of taxes on a firm or its partners individually is lower.

(vii) Encouragement of Mutual Trust, Personal Element in Business, etc.: Patners act in cooperation and thus mutual faith, trust and goodwill are maintained. They maintain personal relations with each other and take personal care to promote the business of the firm. This personal element in business, which is not found in a company, is highly useful. The existence of partnerships rests on mutual faith and goodwill and that way it encourages the spirit of helpfulness and instils qualities of honesty, sincerity, responsibility, initiative and self-reliance, etc.

Disadvantages of Partnership Organisation

While the partnership organisation has the above advantages, it has the following serious limitations which cannot be ignored:

(i) Limited Resources: In spite of pooling of resources by several partners, it is not possible to raise huge amount of capital and engage specialists required for modern business or industrial units. Partners may be rich but their capacity to contribute capital is limited as compared to the needs of modern industrial complexes. Undoubtedly, a joint-stock company may raise more capital as against a partnership firm.

(ii) Unlimited Liability: One of the serious limitations of a partnership organisation is that the liability of partners is not limited. The partners, like the sole trader, but unlike the shareholders of a company, may be personally held liable for the debts of the firm. Their private property also remains at stake. Moreover, liability is cumulative. Further, a partner may also be called upon to compensate for the misdeeds and dishonesty of his fellow partners along with his own acts.

(iii) Instability: Theoretically, it may appear that the partnership organisation is more stable than the sole proprietorship but in practice it is not so. It is often found that the business of a firm comes to an end on account of petty quarrels along the partners. If a partner is dishonest and short-tempered, it may become difficult for other partners to carry on business with him. Any misunderstanding may prove ruinous for it. It is also unstable because death, retirement, lunacy, and insolvency of a partner may dissolve the partnership. It is quite true that partnership provides better means to perpetuate itself "but existence of that 'self' at any given time is more precious".

(iv) Lack of Harmony of Interest: Unlike a sole proprietorship, it is not possible to maintain harmony of interest among the partners. There is always the possibility of friction. The partners may follow a conservative policy to avoid risk of their private property. Their combined judgement often may not prove useful. If mutual cooperation is lacking, prompt decision may also not be possible. There is the possibility of leakage of business secrets and matters which may affect the business adversely.

Box 10.2 Doing a Good Deed

However, informal the arrangement, close the friendship, at the end of the day, it is your partnership deed that decides your status in the firm. Putting it all on paper systematically will go a long way in defining your working and financial relationship. This is what lawyers and chartered accountants suggest:

- Commission terms of each partner should be clearly stated.
- Money spent over the sanctioned amount should be approved by all partners.
- The firm shall not be liable for loans raised as personal debt and other personal obligations.
- If a partner is declared insolvent, or is incapacitated, the business shall not be dissolved.
- Duration of the partnership should be clearly specified.
- The course of action in the event of death should be clearly mentioned whether the partnership will continue, or be terminated, or whether a new deed will be drawn up.
- In the case of a managing partner, everything the person has to contribute in terms of labour, time and capital should be spelt out.
- Regular maintenance of books of accounts should be insisted upon
- Access to books of accounts and correspondence should be stated.
- Signing authority should be shared between the partners.

About 35 per cent of the small-scale industries in India are partnership concerns of which, 21 per cent are joint-family partnerships and 14 per cent partnership concerns. Very often, small entrepreneurs with business acumen and training are handicapped by lack of capital; or there may be need of a wealthy man with managerial capacity. Partnership organisations grew essentially out of the failures and limitations of the sole proprietorship form of organisation. The formation and management of a partnership organisation is governed by the provisions of the Indian Partnership Act of 1932. According to it, "a partnership is the relation between persons who have agreed to share the profits of a business carried on by all or by any one of them acting for all". A partnership deed is essential for this type of organisation. The Partnership Act, 1932, outlines the rights and duties of a partner the liability of a partnership is unlimited.

The ownership pattern of small units is given in Table 10.3. As indicated in the table, 61 per cent of the units are single proprietory small-scale industrial units, followed by family partnerships, i.e., businesses which are owned by two or more members of the family. Only 14 per cent of the small-scale units are non-family partnerships, where the ownership is held by a small group which does not constitute a family. Among the small-scale industrialists, there is a strong tendency to keep the business within the family. As a general rule, a non-family partnership is restricted to craftsmen pooling their resources; alternatively, it may be a venture of the group of merchants. An industry-wise analysis shows that in the printing presses, general engineering and soap industries, 20 per cent of the units fall in the category of non-family partnerships. In these cases, a large amount of capital investment is necessary, and the family resources are generally too meagre for such a venture. The capital resources are increased by converting the industrial unit into a non-family partnership.

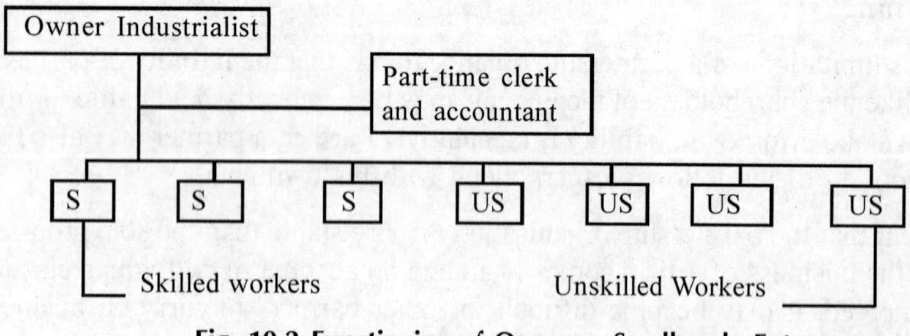

Fig. 10.2 Functioning of One-man Small-scale Entrepreneur doing all the work: Phase I

A partnership concern would be most suitable where:

(a) the size of the business is relatively small.

(b) the capital requirement is not much, and

(c) there is need for variety of skills for managing different types of activities.

In hosiery, leather goods, wooden furniture industries – wherein capital investment is less and one can develop the business by productively utilising one's skills with the cooperation of workers – a very large percentage of units come under the category of individual proprietorship.

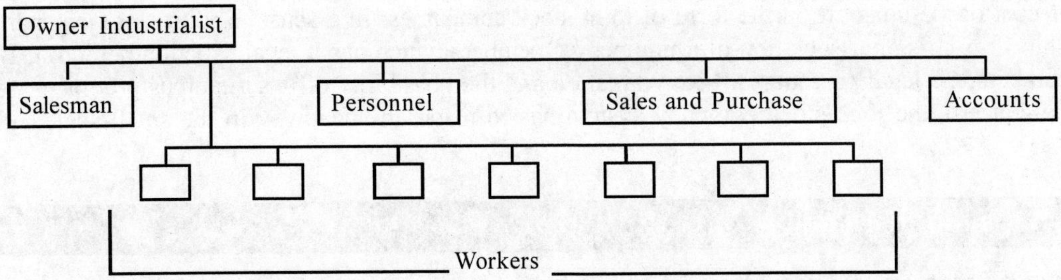

Fig. 10.3 Functioning of a Single Small-scale Entrepreneur with the Assistance of Supporting Staff: Phase 2

Table 10.4 Small Units Classified According to the Types of Ownership

Industry	Single	Partnership					
	Proprie-torship	Family and others	Family	Non-family	Co-operatives	Jt. stock	Total
1. Flour Mills	36.4	49.1	-	14.5	-	-	100.0
2. Printing presses	52.0	28.0	-	20.0	-	-	100.0
3. Leather – footwear	62.0	32.0	2.0	4.0	-	-	100.0
4. Light engineering	48.0	36.0	4.0	12.0	-	-	100.0
5. Electrical goods	25.0	65.0	4.0	6.0	-	-	100.0
6. Wooden furniture and fixtures	60.0	30.0	1.0	8.0	1.0	-	100.0
7. Hosiery	63.0	25.0	-	11.0	1.0	-	100.0
8. General engineering	558.0	18.0	-	20.0	1.0	3.0	100.0
9. Soap	27.0	53.0	-	20.0	-	3.0	100.0
10. Electroplating	40.0	39.0	8.0	13.0	-	-	100.0
11. Foundaries	43.0	43.0	-	14.0	-	-	100.0
12. Oil mills	15.0	70.0	-	12.0	2.0	11.0	100.0
13. Drugs	60.0	35.0	-	3.0	-	-	100.0
14. Utensils	55.0	38.0	-	6.0	10		100.0

JOINT-STOCK COMPANIES

The growth of the joint-stock company constitutes an important step in the historical evolution of forms of ownership of business enterprises. With the enlargement of the scale of business operations, it became difficult for a sole trader or partnership firm to cope with the problem of finding more resources and arranging for more specialised management.

The development of joint-stock companies has taken place almost in all the countries of the world but the nomenclature differs. There may be technical points of difference but the basic characteristics are almost the same everywhere. We call it joint-stock company in England and in India. In the USA, it is known as a 'corporation'.

Definition: A company is a voluntary association of persons who contribute to its capital but their liability remains limited. It carries on business for profit as a legal entity. It can sue and be sued on its own name. Thus, a corporation is an artificial being, invisible, intangible and existing only in the contemplation of law. Being a mere creation of law, it possesses only those properties which the charter of its creation confers upon it, either expressly or as incidental to its very existence.

Salient Features

A joint-stock company has a separate legal entity quite apart for that of the members comprising the organisation unlike a partnership. In other words, a joint-stock company is considered to be a 'person' in the eyes of law. As such a company possesses the right to own and transfer any property and to sue and be sued, in its own name.

In India, only 3 per cent of the units are in the form of joint-stock companies. In a sense, a joint-stock company is an extension of the partnership firm; it is an association of a number of members which has a legal sanction behind it. Because of the complicated and cumbersome legal procedures, heavy taxation and the possibility of unscrupulous promoters securing capital for an undesirable concern, the joint-stock company system has to made any headway in the small-scale industries sector.

Illustration **It's all in the Family**

The amalgamation group is possibly among the largest privately-held business houses in the country. The company in the group which went public in 1978, Bimetal Bearings Limited, did so only because it had to bring down its foreign shareholding. Although these shares are briskly traded, the family holds about 70 per cent of the equity. Other publicly-held companies are: T.Stanes of Coimbatore; the two plantation companies (Unitea and SAE), and Amalgamations Repco Limited.

The holding company, Amalgamations Private Limited, has two directors, Sivasailam and Krishnamurthy. The shares of the holding company are divided equally among Anantharamakrishnan's four children – two sons and two daughters. Sivasailam and Krishnamurthy, the two sons, are the chairman and vice-chairman of the group. One of Sivasailam's sons-in-law, K.S.Sundaram, runs Addisons Paints and the other son-in law, N.Venkatramani, heads India Pistons. Each company in the group is managed by its own board. Generally, there are very few outsiders on the Board.

Both the brothers also look after some of the group companies directly. For instance, Sivasailam monitors TAFE and Amco Batteries on day-to-day basis, while Krishnamurthy is involved in Simpsons, Bimetal Bearings and Shardlow. But it is clearly Sivasailam who has the greater say.

Third generation: The third generation in the business consists of Srinivasan, (who is married to Venu Srinivasan of the TVS Group), an MBA from Wharton University USA, is General Manager (Planning and Coordination) in TAFE. The younger daughter, Jayshree Venkatraman (Married to M.S. Venkatraman of WS Industries), who has an MBA from the International Management Institute, Delhi, has been inducted as an executive assistant to the chief executive of Amco. Krishnamurthy has no children.

Obviously, in a group like this, the chairman is the power centre. He deals with the banks, the government and makes all the initial preparations for collaborations. Krishnamurthy, who describes his role as a supportive one, is in charge of group industrial relations. If there are any disagreements, the decisions taken by the chairman prevail. "Sivasailam himself feels that the unique strength lies in this togetherness under the umbrella of amalgamations. We offer limitless opportunities to talented professionals. The family should induct and retain them. But the direction should come from the family", he says.

Simpson's Amalgamations and 'J'

Nobody quite knew who he was. But Simpson, who hailed from Scotland, chose to set up a company in Madras in 1840 to build horse-drawn coaches and carriages for the affluent. The star achievement of the company in the 19th century was to build a carriage for the use of the Prince of Wales during his visit to India in 1876. In the early 1900s, Simpson actually built a motor car and ran it on Mount Road. The company, however, confined itself to the car trade and opened many workshops and branches. It was only during the fifties, under the Indian management, that the company began to manufacture diesel engines.

In 1930, a 25-year-old unassuming accountant joined Simpson S. Ananthakrishana was known to his English colleagues as simply J. nickname stuck and no one knows why. By 1938, J. was ready to start a business of his own. He formed Amalgamations (Private) Limited that year. Why he chose that particular name is again not known. He then established Sri Rama Vilas Service (SRVS) which went on to run a large fleet and a cargo service. The same year an agency, Speed-A-Way, was established to distribute automobile spare parts.

Historical Move: In what we referred to in modern parlance as a historical move, J. acquired Simpson in 1941. And W.W. Ladden, then chairman of the company, voluntarily opted to serve under J. Simpson became a subsidiary of Amalgamations. In the next 25 years, both Amalgamations and Simpson began to acquire and promote companies at a blistering pace.

J was a true visionary who realised that after independence, it would be necessary to be manufacturing goods. He established units to manufacture paints, pistons, batteries and tractors, among other things. He bought a publishing house which owned a newspaper (The Mail). In 1961, he acquired interests in several plantations.

When J passed away in 1964, he left a highly diversified business house which featured among the top twenty in the country.

A private limited company can be formed by minimum two and maximum by fifty members. The members of the company have to subscribe to the Memorandum of Association (MoA) which would indicate the name of the company, the registered address of the company, share capital, liability of members, objects of the company, etc. It is advisable to seek the assistance of a legal expert/firm of auditor in preparing the memorandum.

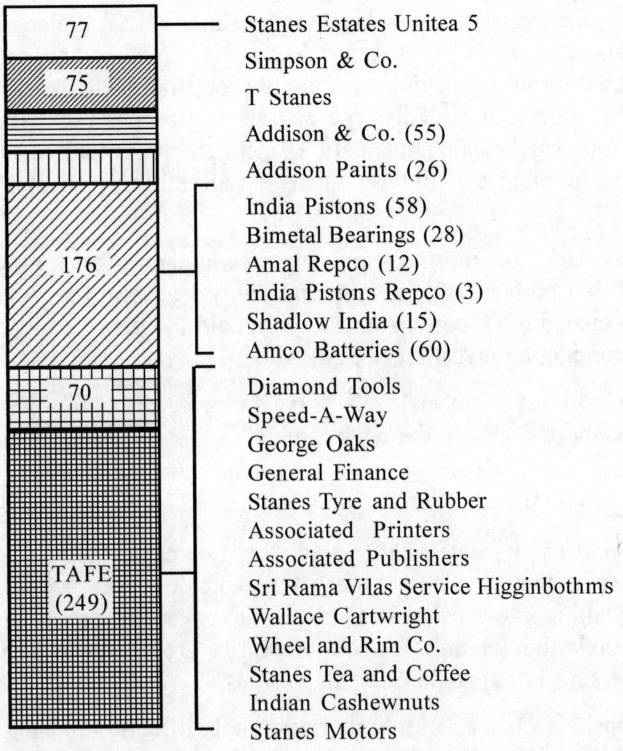

Fig 10.4 The Amalgamations Group at a Glance

Advantages	Disadvantages
(a) The liability of the members is limited (b) More resources can be made available to the enterprise (c) More persons available for management. A professional manager may be included.	(a) It attracts higher level of taxation (b) The formalities to be completed are more as compared to the partnership concern.

A private limited would be most suitable where:

(a) The size of the business is fairly large;

(b) The capital requirement is fairly high, and

(c) There is need for a variety of skills for managing the different types of activities.

Legislation

While it is not necessary to obtain a licence under the Industrial (Development and Regulations) Act, 1951, for the setting up of a small-scale industry, small-scale units are now generally required to get themselves registered with the State Directors of Industries/District Industries Centre. This also entitles them to obtain creation facilities from the government like quota for raw materials, etc. There are two stages of registration – provision and final registration. The provisional registration which can be obtained before a unit is actually set up is valid for six months, subject to a renewal thereafter. The final registration can, however, be obtained after the commencement of production.

THE COOPERATIVE

A cooperative society is essentially an association of persons who join together on a voluntary basis for the furtherance of their common economic interests. The International Labour Organisation (ILO) defines a cooperative "an association of persons, usually of limited means, who voluntarily join together to achieve a common economic end through the formation of a democratically controlled business organisation, making an equitable contribution to the capital required and accepting a fair share of the risks and benefits of the undertaking". This type of organisation has not made any appreciable impact on the small-scale industrial sector. Of the total small-scale units, only 0.7 per cent are organised as cooperative societies. These are mainly in such industries as wooden furniture and fixtures, utensils, agricultural hand tools and implements, printing and washing soaps.

In the Indian context, a study of 100 most outstanding enterprises indicates that family-run firms continue to dominate the corporate scene – an indication that professional management has yet to gain the respectability and confidence that it commands abroad. This is no doubt changing. The government could hold the process by reducing the burden of wealth tax which prevents individuals from accumulating investible wealth.

The choice of an organisation is to attain higher levels of performance through efficiency and innovation. It keeps on changing with the needs of the hour and changes in the environment.

Advantages and Disadvantages

Each form of organisation or unit has its own relative merits and demerits. Which type of an organisation would be suitable in a particular case or whether there is really a need for switching over from one form to another form of the organisation should be decided after taking into consideration all the factors stated above. What is, however, important is the organisational or administrative set-up within the unit. As your enterprise grows, it cannot apparently remain as a 'one-man show'. It is essential that suitable persons are appointed for the various key functions in the enterprise.

An entrepreneur will have to make a choice of an organisation only after scrutinising their merits and demerits while keeping in mind his goals and objectives. The choice of an organisation should always foster growth and development, it should be efficient, flexible and growth-oriented.

Organisational Reality	Immediate Objective
IR disputes and disharmony; climate of distrust within the organisation.	To build harmony and trust among the organisational members which will later be harnessed for productive and profitable purposes.
A conservative organisation (say in engineering industry) facing increased competition for domestic and international players	To bring in sufficient organisation wise awareness about the emerging realities and prepare a ground for meeting competitors face-to-face.
A conservative organisation in a traditional indsutry in famous for paternalistic approach to organisational members (e.g., Textiles, Jute).	To raise the organisation's ability to confront the changing environment and to manage the complexities of change).
Monopoly situation and no serious complaints on product quality.	To take proactive measure within the organisation which will create entry-barriers for potential competitors.

Chart 10.1 briefly indicates the comparative advantages and disadvantages of different types of organisation of industries/ business enterprises.

Chart 10.1 Small Units Classified According to the Types of Ownership

Merits	Demerits
A. Sole Proprietorship	**A. Sole Proprietorship**
1. Objectives of the firm are formulated in an informal manner by the entrepreneur	1. There is no plan and policy about objectives.
2. Specialisation is restricted to the entrepreneur	2. No scope for developing skill, knowledge, aptitude and ability.
3. Authority and responsibility are centred round the entrepreneur	3. No scope for coordination of activities.
4. Quick and prompt decisions	4. Limited managerial ability
5. Maximum flexibility in operations.	5. Lack of continuity, and
	6. Instability.
B. Partnership	**B. Partnership**
1. Objectives of the unit are clearly stated	1. Lack of harmony in the event of mutual distrust
2. Better specialisation through division of labour	2. Restricted growth.
3. Line of authority specified	3. Lack of public confidence
4. Authority and responsibility are defined.	4. Communication gaps.
5. Continuity of work	
6. Flexibility in operation	
C. Private Limited Company	**C. Private Limited Company**
1. Clear-cut plan and policy	1. Lack of regulation may lead to mismanagement
2. Objectives are formally formulated	
3. Effective coordination.	
4. Better specialisation through division of labour.	
5. Authority and responsibility are defined in definite terms.	
6. Span of control is well organised.	
7. Coordination of activities	
8. Flexible and dynamic.	
D. Cooperative	**D. Cooperative**
1. Objectives are clearly stated	1. Lack of authority and repressibility.
2. Democratic organisation	2. No coordination
3. Excessive state regulation	3. Excessive state regulation
	4. No scope for specialisation
	5. Authority and responsibility are not defined
	6. Lack of continuity
	7. Work is not properly divided.

Which type of company? Seven factors to consider before you start your business

	Sole proprietorship	Partnership
Flexibility	This is as flexible as you can get. You are the sole person in charge.	Less flexible than proprietorship, as the areas of responsibility are somewhat defined. But there may be some heads wearing more than one hat.
Capital risk	Very high, as the proprietor bears all the risk. The returns too are all his.	Lower than sole proprietorship, as the capital is shared by the partners.
Liability	Unlimited, extending to personal assets of the sole proprietor.	Unlimited, extending to the personal assets of the partners.

Formation	Simplest. No legal requirements.	Through a partnership deed, though not compulsory. If there is no deed, the partnership is governed by the Indian Partnership Act, 1932.
Exit option	On death of the sole proprietor, or if he decides to close down the business.	As per the Indian Partnership Act, or through a deed of dissolution which has to be accepted by all partners.
Inheritance	Depends on the will of the sole proprietor.	The partnership deed can specify whether the business will carry on in the event of the death of a partner, and who will be entitled to his share of profits, or whether a new deed will be drawn up, or the partnership will stand dissolved.
Goodwill	May or may not be mentioned in the books of accounts.	Has to be mentioned in the books of accounts. Method of calculation is subjective and open to debate.

Comparative Study of Business Organisation (Forms of Organisation)

Features	I Sole Trader	II Partnership	III Company
1. Formation	Very easy – no legal formalities.	Easy, simple and optional registration.	Private Co. Compulsory Registration Simple formation Public Co. Compulsory Registration, Difficult formation
2. Membership	One man show.	Minimum – 2 Maximum – 10 in Banking 20 in Trading	Private Co. Minimum 2, Maximum 50 Public Co. Minimum 7, Maximum nil – unlimited number
3. Legal Position	No separate legal life	No separate legal life.	Separate and distinct legal person created by law.
4. Stability or continuity of life	Unstable organisation. Terminable by death or insolvency of the owner.	More stable than sole trader. But terminable by death or insolvency of any partner.	Perpetual existence, very stable, permanent life, continuity not affected by death of members.
5. Relation between ownership and management	Control, management and risk lie where ownership lies. Owner has full control	Owners are also the managers and risk bearers. Every partner is entitled to manage the business of the firm.	Private Co. Control, risk ownership generally go together. Public Co. Complete separation of management from ownership. Representative management.
6. Capital-raising owner	Very limited – owner's savings and borrowing. Good for small business.	Limitation on capital. Enough for medium size business. We have pooling of capital on a limited scale.	Private Co. Suitable for medium six concerns. Public Co. Any amount of capital can be raised. Good for medium and large-scale business.
7. Management by experts	The proprietor enjoys supreme voice in management. But one man cannot manage a big business efficiently. No management by experts possible. Hired experts may be costly.	Management united in the partners. But it acts as a limiting factor for further expansion. Limited division of work and specialisation in management. Professional management may not be feasible.	In a company, on account of separation of management from ownership, there is ample scope for division of labour in management and this helps maximum specialisation in management. Professional management is a noteworthy feature of a company.
8. Liability of members	Unlimited liability. No distinction between the owner's business and private assets. Entire private property is in danger.	Unlimited liability – joint and several. It discourages wealthy persons to enter into a partnership with poor persons.	Limited liability – limited by face value of shares Members know the expected total loss or liability Private property free from any danger. It attracts capital.

9. Constitution	Most elastic or flexible organisation, changes at owner's will. There is no need of written constitution.	Changes only by the consent of all partners. Partnership agreement can be changed at the will of all partners.	Private Co. is an elastic organisation. But constitution of a public company is inelastic. Important constitutional changes in all companies require sanction of the government court. Members' consent is not enough.
10. Business secrecy	No need of publicity of accounts and affairs. Full secrecy and confidential character. Suitable for a family business.	No need of publicity of accounts and affairs. Very suitable for keeping business secrets within a family circle.	Private Co. Preparation and circulation of annual accounts and auditors' report compulsory. But profit and loss account need not be published.
11. Government control and regulation	No separate legislation subject to common law and Insolvency Act. Free from government control and regulation.	Separate legislation. But registration optional, very limited government control and regulation.	Public Co. Compulsory preparation filing and publicity of Annual A/c. Full publicity. Private Co. It enjoys considerable freedom from excessive legal control and regulation. Public Co. It is subject to excessive legal control and regulation. All companies governed by the Companies Act, very big legislation – from the cradle to the grave. Detailed control and regulation.
12. Marketable share.	No share as such. Owner may sell his business at anytime.	No transfer or sale of share without consent of all partners.	Private Co. Transfer of shares restricted by Articles of Association. No stock exchange quotation Public Co. Free transferability of shares as per transfer procedure. Stock exchange quotation provides easy marketability.
13. Owner personal Interest and attention	Maximum personal interest as no sharing of profits, maximum personal attention and touch in relation to employees and customers. It is a personal organisation. Quick decision and prompt action. Direct communication and good human relations.	Efforts and Rewards directly connected. Hence, considerable personal interest and attention to secure economy and efficiency. Good personal relations with employees and customers. It is a personal organisation. Quick decision, prompt action, good communication and human relations.	A company is an artificial person created by law. It is an impersonal organisation. Ownership is separated from management. Personal interest and attention of owners not possible. A large-scale organisation is ruled by law. Considerable red-tapism. Absence of human touch. Mechanical behaviour. No personal considerations. Delayed Action.
14. Tax liability	Personal income tax very high on large incomes – 70 to 80 per cent. But suitable for small business. Tax on small income is low.	Heavy personal tax on large incomes – 70 to 80 per cent. But suitable for small business. We have progressive income tax, rising with income, unless the firm is registered under Income Tax Act.	A company is a separate legal person subject to flat corporation tax at basic rate about 55 per cent abroad. Lower tax liability induces people to prefer a Ltd. company, even a family concern.

(**Note:** This table also gives answer to the choice of organisation.)

CONCLUSION

By and large, a bulk of the small-scale industries are proprietary units. In order to strive ahead in a competitive environment, the small-scale industries need to develop a professional management culture, which involves continuous efforts at improving strategies on an ongoing basis. To be professional means broad basing of its ownership and organisation. There is a need of professional ownership for the sustained growth of small-scale industries in India in the coming years.

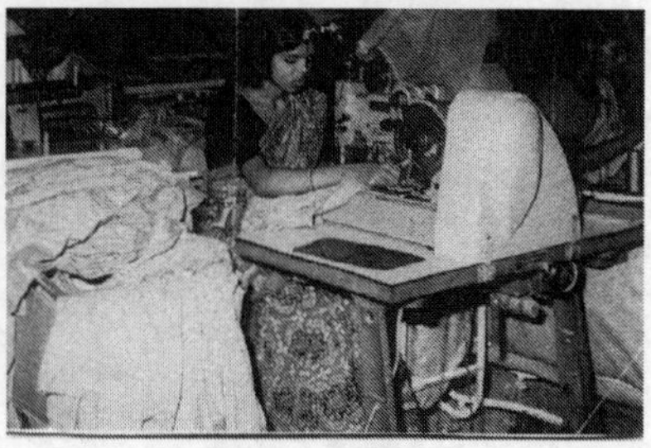

11 CHAPTER

FINANCE FOR SMALL-SCALE INDUSTRIES

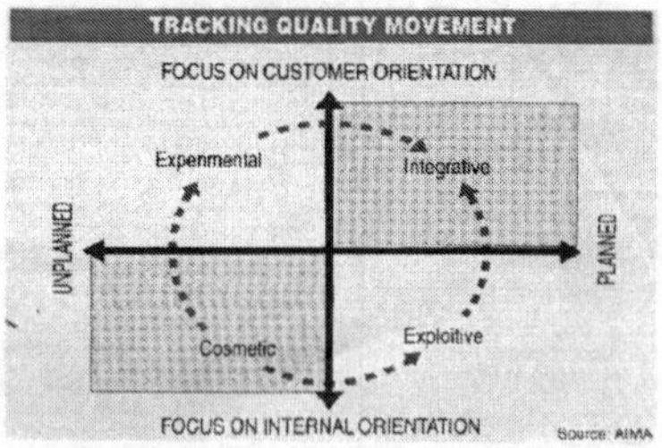

The health of a small-scale enterprise, its smooth operation and economic viability depend upon the capacity to generate and mobilise financial resources.

LEARNING OBJECTIVES

- Provides an insight into the need and the supply of finance to small-scale industries.
- India has evolved a sound institutional set up for financing of the SSI sector. New industrial policy was announced as part of the structural reforms in 1991, which eliminated various controls on the industrial sector, provided a greater role for the private sector and encouraged inflow of foreign investment and technology, but also contained specific initiatives for the development of the SSI sector.
- There are multiple institutions in the public, private and cooperative sectors of the Indian economy that cater to the credit needs of the SSI sector, both for fixed assets creation as well as for working capital. Consequent to the nationalisation of major banks in 1969, banking policy mandated that at least 40 per cent of bank credit should be directed towards the priority sector constituting agriculture, SSI and individual service and business sectors. Preferential treatment was also provided to the SSI sector via lower rates of interest on bank credit. The Small Industries Development Bank of India (SIDBI) was set up in April 1990 as the principal financial institution for promotion, financing and development of the SSI sector and for coordinating the activities of other institutions engaged in similar activities. A Fair Practices Code has also been adopted by SIDBI which, *inter alia,* clearly sets out the procedures that would be followed in respect of loan applications, appraisals and disbursements.

INTRODUCTION

Finance is a key input of production, distribution and development. It is, therefore, aptly described as the 'lifeblood' of industry and is a pre-requisite for accelerating the process of industrial development.

During the pre-independence period, financial constraints had hampered the rapid development of industries in the country. After independence, the government has built up a network of specialised financial institutions with a fairly big capital base to provide financial assistance to all types of industries, including small-scale industries.

A growing economy needs the support of a financial structure which is responsive to the needs of development. In India, in the process of financial deepening, commercial banks had to shoulder special responsibilities for meeting the financial needs of diverse sectors of the economy, at various stages of development. In the process, they have evolved various modes and instruments of financing, fashioned various organisational innovations, moved away from traditional commercial banking and evolved into development banks, responsive to socio-economic needs.

Finance is now made available to entrepreneurs on a totality basis by commercial banks, except in cases where the State Financial Corporation (SFCs) and other similar financing agencies step into meet their medium-term requirements. An appropriate type of credit is granted for the construction of the factory building, the purchase of plant, machinery and equipment, and for working capital requirements. In deserving cases, loan are advanced for the expansion, renovation and modernisation of plant and machinery. Banks and financial institutions provide the export finance needed by small industries for letters of credit, issuance of guarantees and extension of pre-shipment and post-shipment credit facilities. The interest rate structure is generally graded on a slab basis, with a favourable bias towards the smaller loans. Institutional support and economic factors are stimulating entrepreneurial activity and thus generating more robust economic development.

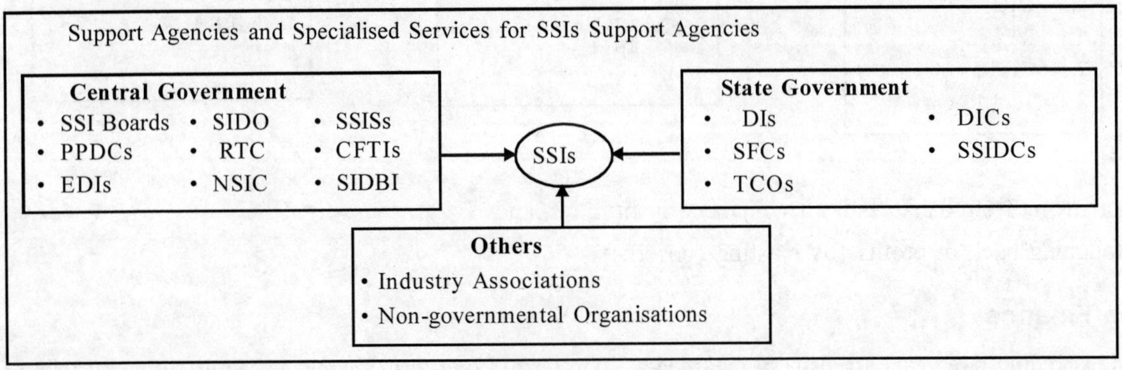

Types of Industrial Finance

Depending upon the nature of the activity, the entrepreneurs require three types of finances, *viz.,* short-term, medium-term and long-term finances. The distinctive features of these are enumerated below:

Short-term Finance

Short-term finance usually refers to the funds required for a period of less than one year. Short-term finance is usually required to meet variable, seasonal or temporary working capital requirements.

Borrowing from banks is a very important source of short-term finance. Other important sources of short-term finance are trade credit, instalment credit and customer advances.

Medium-term Finance

The period of one year to five years may be regarded as a medium-term. Medium-term finance is usually required for permanent working capital, small expansions, replacements, modifications, etc.

Medium-term finance may be raised by:

(i) Issue of shares;

(ii) Issue of debentures;

Providers of Finance and Specialised Suport Services (At the Apex Level: SIDBI)

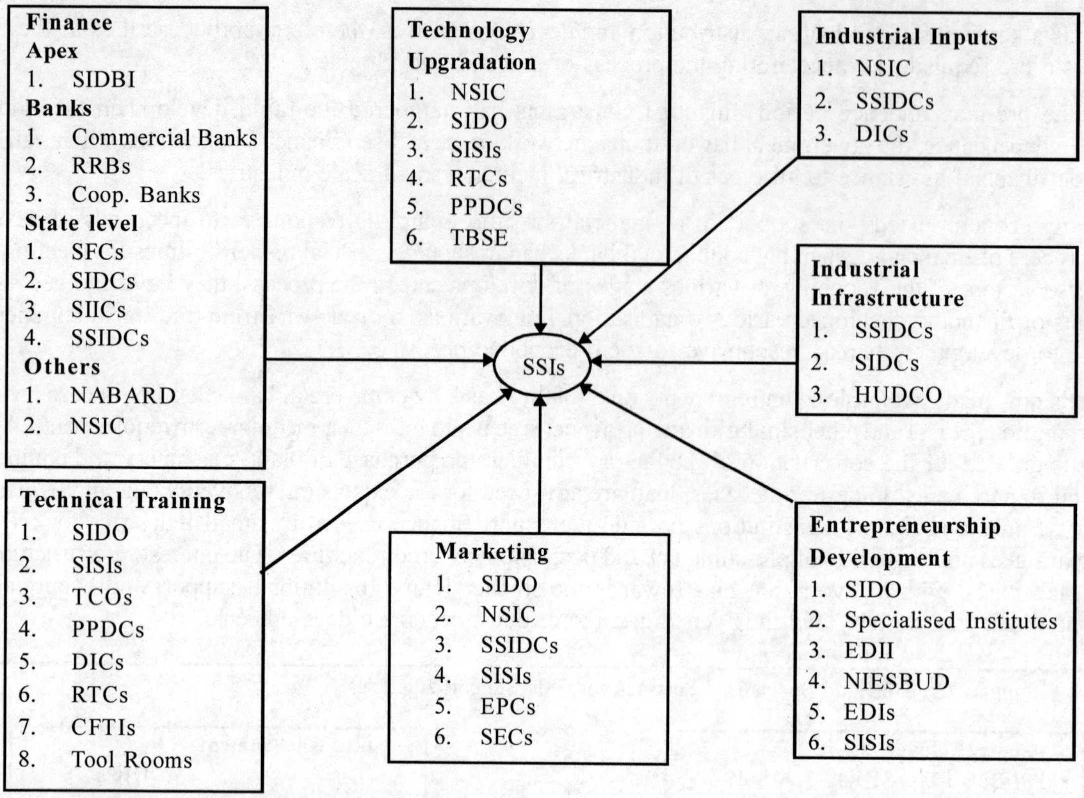

(iii) Borrowing from banks and other financial institutions, and

(iv) Ploughing back of profits (by existing concerns).

Long-term Finance

Period exceeding five years are usually regarded as long-term. Long-term finance is required for procuring fixed assets for the establishment of a new business, for substantial expansion of exsting business, modernisation, etc.

The important sources of long-term finances are:

(i) Issue of shares;

(ii) Issue of debentures;

(iii) Loans from financial institutions, and

(iv) Ploughing back of profits (by existing concerns).

Table 11.1 Types of Finance

Short-term	Medium-term	Long-term
(i) Bank credit	(i) Issue of shares	(i) Issue of shares
(ii) Trade credit	(ii) Issue of debentures	(ii) Issues of debentures
(iii) Instalment credit	(iii) Loans from banks and other financial institutions	(iii) Loans from financial institutions
(iv) Customer advances	(iv) Public deposits (for existing concerns)	(iv) Ploughing back of profits (for existing concerns)
	(v) Ploughing back of profits (for existing concerns)	

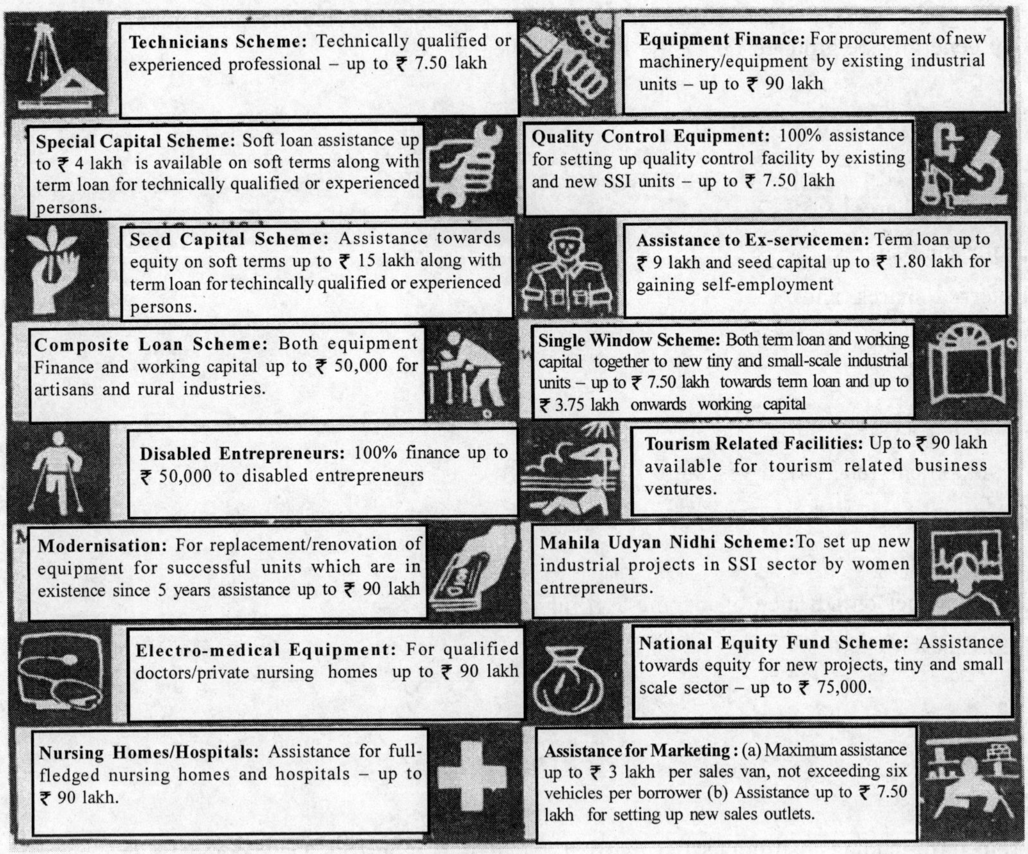

MEANS OF FINANCE

A characteristic feature of small-scale units is that the personal funds of entrepreneurs form a substantial proportion of the total assets. Most of the units are not corporate entities. The owners of small units, therefore, run a considerably higher risk than those of corporate units. The sources that ususally provide the working capital requirements are commercial banks, special agencies like the State Industrial and Investment Corporation of Maharashtra (SIICOM), the Gujarat Industrial Investment Corporation (GIIC) and cooperative banks. Indigenous bankers and moneylenders also advance loans for working capital needs. The fixed capital needs are usually met by State Government (under the State Aid to Industries Acts/Rules), State Finanacial Corporations (SFCs), National Small Industries Corporation (NSIC) which supplies machinery on hire-purchase basis, State Small Industries Corporations (SSICs), State Industrial Development Corporations (SIDCs), the State Bank of India and subsidiaries and other commercial banks.

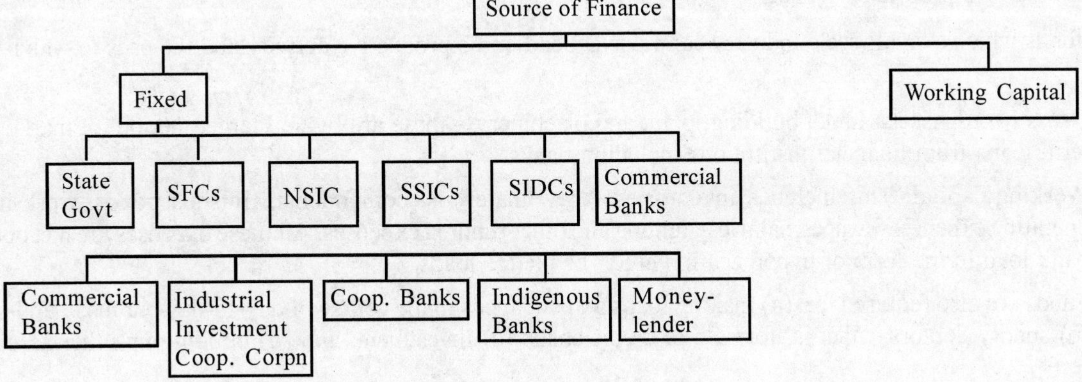

Fig. 11.1 Sources of Finance for Small-scale Sector

Broadly speaking, the various sources from which a small industry can raise funds are enumerated in its balance sheet. These sources may generally be grouped under the following heads:

I. Internal

A. Paid-up Capital

(i) Ordinary shares
(ii) Preference shares
(iii) Deferred shares, and
(iv) Forfeited shares

B. Reserve Surplus

(i) Capital reserves
(ii) Development rebate reserves, and
(iii) Others

C. Provisions

(i) Taxation (net on advance of income-tax), and
(ii) Depreciation

II. External

D. Borrowings

(i) From banks
(ii) From term-lending institutions like IDBI, IFCI, ICICI, Industrial Development Corporations, etc.
(iii) From government and semi-government agencies, and
(iv) Others

E. Trade Dues and Other Current Liabilities

(i) Sundry creditors, and
(ii) Others

F. Miscellaneous

All these sources of finance are not available to all small units. Much would depend on the status, character and the period of time the units have been in operation. For example, a new small unit has no reserves to provide for depreciation. Theses are built-up in gradual stages out of the funds set apart in the course of current operations.

Moreover, the funds which a small-scale industry can raise depends upon the character of the company – whether it is a private limited or a proprietory concern.

The funds which a small-scale industry can raise depend on its productive activity and the uses to which these funds are put:

(i) Gross Fixed Assets: Land, building, plant and machinery – these are by and large, met out of market borrowings or term loans from financial institutions including banks.

(ii) Working capital: This includes inventories – raw materials, components, finished goods, work-in-progress and operating expenses – wages, salaries, lighting and other running expenses. All these expenses are met out of commercial bank loan in the form of hypothecation credit or pledge loans.

(iii) Funds are also required for: (a) making loans and advances in the course of day-to-day purchase-and-sale operations: (b) sundry debtors – that is, for sale of credit basis; (c) investment, and (d) building up other assets.

Analysis of Financial Ratios

The financial data of small units were worked out in terms of some of the important conventional ratios. Most of the ratios, however, do not indicate any definite relationship with credit facilities. A detailed discussion of this aspect has been undertaken in the technical volume. It will be sufficient to mention here that comparatively high inventory-to-sales ratios were recorded by units which received institutional credit facilities. The average net working capital needs of small units, which are also given, shows that the units which received credit facilities need a comparatively high average working capital. A major proportion of the net working capital, however, was accounted for by inventories. The figures given in the statement do not, by themselves, point to any firm conclusions regarding the face of inventories among the factors to be taken into account by banks while examining the credit proposals of small-scale units.

Balance Sheet of Institutional and Non-institutional Borrowings

The survery also gives information on the balance sheet of institutional and non-institutional borrowings of small units. It shows that institutional borrowings per unit varied from one unit to another, and were the highest in the cases of the following categories of units:

(i) Those units whose assets exceeded ₹ 10 lakh;

(ii) Those units which manufacutred electronic and elctrical goods:

(iii) Units of six to ten years' standing:

(iv) Those which employed hundreden one and more persons;

(v) Public limited companies.

(vi) Units which were registered, and

(vii) Units located in industrial estates.

It may be pointed out here that those units which had high savings per unit institutional borrowings recorded high inventory ratios. The average non-institutional borrowings per unit in respect of respective classifications were the highest in the case of units which –

(a) borrowed from banks/cooperatives;

(b) whose assets were above ₹ 10 lakh and which employed hundreden one or more persons;

(c) were private limited companies, registered units and located in industrial estates, and

(d) belonged to the manufacturing group, including chemicals, dyes, etc.

The statement also shows that both large and small units in the sample borrow from institutional and non-institutional sources. However, the extent of reliance on non-institutional sources was lower in the case of large units than in that of small units. At the same time, even the smaller units obtained a major portion of their credit needs fron institutional lenders. Further, the average non-institutional borrowings formed a major proportion of average borrowings (institutional and non-institutional) on the part of units which did not approach any commercial bank/coopertive for credit or which did not get any institutional credit even though they asked for it. High proportions of average institutional borrowings were noticed in the case of units with assets over ₹ 10 lakh; which manufactured electronic and electrical goods; which had been operating for five years; which were public limited companies; which employed more than hundreden one persons; which were registered units and which were relatively high on the part of modern, younger and larger small-scale industrial units.

According to a recent study of small private limited companies, conducted by the Reserve Bank of India in 1987, these companies relied on external sources for financing assets. Of the total resources of ₹ 2,708 crore, external sources contributed as much as ₹ 1,610 crore (77.5 per cent) to asset formation. Of this amount, borrowings constituted more than 55.8 per cent while trade dues and other current liabilities contributed about 38.0 per cent. Bank borrowings, in particular, accounted for more than one-third of the total external resources. Among the internal resources, depreciation provision amounting to ₹ 408 crore constituted that main source. It representsed 87.18 per cent of the total internal resources.

While assessing the resources of a concern, we have to bear in mind the following factors: whether it is a new concern or a long-established concern; whether it is a private company or a proprietory concern; what is the nature of activity – is it manufacturing or trading; whether the purpose of raising resources is modernisation and expansion of business, or the establishment of a new concern to increase in turnover.

The expansion or diversification of business involving an addition to plant and machinery should be met out of owned funds – that is, out of depreciation and provisions – or out of increase in capital, out of term loans. The ability of a concern to raise resoures from all or some of these sources depends upon its strength, character and standing in the market. If the purpose is a mere increase in the turnover of the business which involves a larger inventory and increased operating expenses, the additional funds should be raised by way of bank loans.

Table 11.2 Sources and Uses of Funds of 1,125 Selected Small Private Limited Companies

	(₹ Crore)	% share in the total
Sources of Funds		
Internal Sources	**468**	**22.52**
A. 1. Paid-up capital	9	0.43
B. Reserve and Surplus	13	0.58
2. Capital reserve	5	
3. Development rebate reserve	16	
4. Others	2	
C. Provisions	446	21.46
5. Depreciation	408	19.63
6. Taxation (net of advance of income-tax)	17	0.82
7. Other current	10	0.48
8. Non-current	11	0.53
External Sources	**1,610**	**77.48**
D. Paid-up capital	100	4.81
9. Net issues	100	4.81
10. Premium on shares	-	-
E. Borrowings	**898**	**43.21**
11. From banks	543	26.13
12. From Industrial Finance Corporation and State Financial Corporations	-	-
13. From other institutional agencies	27	1.30
14. From government and semi-government agencies	5	0.24
15. From others	323	15.54
F. Trade dues and other liabilities	**611**	**29.40**
16. Sundry creditors	575	27.67
17. Others	36	1.73
G. Miscellaneous non-current liabilities		-
18. Total	2,078	100.00
Uses of Funds		
H. Gross fixed assets	**710**	**34.17**
19. Land	31	1.49
20. Buildings	140	6.74
21. Plant and machinery	420	20.21
22. Capital work-in-progress	2	0.10
23. Others	116	5.58
I. Inventories	**514**	**224.73**
24. Raw materials, components, etc.	290	13.96
25. Finished goods	193	9.29

	26. Work-in-progress	27	1.30
	27. Others	59	2.84
J.	*Loans and other advances and other debtor balances*	**744**	**35.80**
	28. Sundry debtors	598	28.77
	29. Others	146	7.02
K.	*Investments*	37	1.78
L.	*Other assets*	7	0.34
M.	*Cash and bank blances*	80	3.85
	30. Total	**2,078**	**100.00**

From a banker's point of view, there are well-established guidelines for assessing the credit requirements of a concern. A banker analyses the balance sheet and evaluates the turnover of funds, sales and other operating results in assessing the viability of a unit.

There are certain established ratios. For example:

(a) The debt equity ratio;

(b) Turnover to net worth;

(c) Return on capital employed;

(d) Net profit as a percentage of net worth;

(e) Dividend paid to shareholders, and

(f) Ratio of current assets to current liabilities.

A banker has to go behind these figures and assess the technical and managerial competence of a management, and the integrity of the men running a concern, in order to decide whether credit should or should not be advanced. Credit is a very important element in the process of economic development. It stimulates economic activity, particularly in countries which are short of capital and entrepreneurial talent. Because of the dearth of these two basic elements in the process of development, bankers who create credit have been assigned a vital role in stimulating the process of development.

INSTITUTIONAL SUPPORT STRUCTURE

Small Scale Industries Board is an apex advisory body constituted by the Government of India to render advice on all the issues pertaining to the SSI sector. The Board was constituted in 1954 to facilitate coordination and provide inter-institutional linkages for the development of the sector. Since 1997, the Union Industries Minister is the Chairman of the Board. Prior to that, the Board which consisted of, *inter alia*, State Industries Ministers, select Members of Parliament, secretaries of various departments of Central Government, Heads of financial institutions, industrial associations and eminent experts in the SSI field, was headed by the Prime Minister of India.

The Department of SSI and Agro and Rural Industries (SSI and A&RI) was created under the Ministry of Industry, Government of India, to formulate policy framework and initiate appropriate programmes and schemes for the promotion of SSIs in the country. The range of functions of the department included the setting up of a network of institutions to render services of a varied nature like techno-economic and managerial aspects, training, testing facilities, marketing assistance, etc. These activities are supported by a host of other Central/state departments, agencies and autonomous institutions all over the country.

The office of the Development Commissioner (Small Scale Industries), known as the Small Industries Development Organisation (SIDO) was set up in 1954 upon the recommendations of the Ford Foundation team of the Government of India. The team also suggested the creation of a suport network for exclusive development of SSIs. Since 1991, SIDO is functioning under the Department of SSI and A&RI. It is the nodal agency for implementation of Central Government policies and plays a constructive role in strengthening of the SSI sector. The organisation functions through a network of Small Industry Service Institutes and a host of other field centres. The major SSI-related activities of SIDO include evolving all India policies and programmes, coordinating policies and programmes of state governments, liaisoning with different state and Central ministers, Planning Commision, RBI and Financial Institutions. SIDO also provides a comprehensive range of extension services through allied institutions and monitors government-sponsored programmes.

At the state level, the Commissioner/Directorate of Industries implements policies for the promotion and development of small-scale, cottage, medium and large-scale industries. The Central policies for the SSI sector serve as the guidelines but each state evolves its own policy and package of incentives. The state department also oversees activities of the field offices, *viz.,* District Industries Centres (DICs), etc. In addition, State Financial Corporations, State Small Industries Development Corporations and technical consultancy organisations operate at the state level to assist the promotion and development of SSIs. Other regional level agencies include State Infrastructure Development Corporations, State Cooperative Banks, Regional Rural Banks, State Export Corporations, Agro Industries Corporation and Handloom and Handicrafts Corporations. For the purpose of Human Resources Development, there is a network of specialised institutes associated with SIDO. At the grassroot level, NGOs play an important role for the development of tiny units.

Industry associations provide support to the SSI sector and offer a common platform to raise industry-related issues. Government policies, in recent years, have stressed the increasing role of industry associations in the setting up of common facilities and other ventures in the areas of technology, marketing and other support services.

Institutional Credit Framework

The Government of India and Reserve Bank of India have been instrumental in devising a multi-agency approach/ system to ensure credit dispensation to different sectors of the economy, including the SSI sector. The distinctive feature of the multi-agency set-up is that each of the major institutions caters to the needs of a particular segment of the economy, e.g., agriculture, industry, exports, housing, etc. India has a well-developed network of financial institutions that provide credit to the SSIs. These include banks, financial institutions set-up at the national and state levels to channelise credit to the SSI sector, and other specialised agencies catering to specific sectors.

SIDBI is an all-India principal financial institution for promotion, finance and development of the SSI sector in India. Public sector banks with their extensive network of branches operating nationwide are also important channels of credit dispensation to the sector. SFCs and twin function SIDCs at the state level are the main source of long-term finance for the SSI sector. NABARD provides refinance to commercial banks against loans for farm and non-farm activities and extends resource support to RRBs and Cooperative Banks to help Tiny, Cottage and Village Industries. Various Statutory Boards/ Corporations, like KVIC, NSIC, Coir Board, Silk Board, Handloom and Handicraft Boards, etc., provide assistance for the promotion of industries under their purview. NEDFI has been created to look after the financing aspects of the industries, including SSIs, in the North-eastern Region of the country.

Since 1991, in the wake of trade and investment liberalisation and financial sector reforms, there has been a gradual change in the credit delivery system in the country. Due to increased competition, the financial institutions have tried to improve their operational efficiency. The setting up of new private sector banks has also helped in enhancing the flow of credit to different sectors. The institution-wise status of credit deployment and the operational strategies for the small-scale sector is described in the following paragraphs.

Schemes of Assistance

Within the broad framework, the following financial assistance is offered by the SFCs, SIDC and commercial banks. It includes financing –

- of new projects in the small and medium size category.
- for modernisation of small and medium industries.
- for rehabilitation of small and medium industries, and
- of import of capital equipment.

In view of the financial constraints being faced by SFCs, SIDCs and commercial banks, it is of interest to the borrowers to know the extent of refinancing assistance being extended by the IDBI for the aforesaid purposes. In terms of the currently prevailing guidelines, the following refinance assistance is extended:

	Category	Percentage of Refinance
●	Small-scale Units	
	– SFCs and SIDCs	85
	– Commercial Banks	60
●	Medium-size Units	
	– SFCs and SIDCs	75
	– Commercial Banks	60
●	Foreign currency loans by SIDCs	100

Financial Assistance to Small-scale Units

Rupee loans to the small-scale units are granted at concessional rates of interest. Non-commitment charge is levied on loans up to ₹ 5 lakh to units in the small-scale sector. Commitment charge at the rate of one per cent is levied on all other rupee loans after an initial grace period of 12 months from the date of sanction. However, units located in the category 'A' backward areas are totally exempted from commitment charges on rupee loans, and the units located in the category 'B' and category 'C' backward areas are eligible for 50 per cent concession on the commitment charges.

The small industrial undertakings are considered favourably and allowed a debt-equity ratio extending up to 2.5 per cent. The promoter's contribution norm varies between 12.5 per cent to 22.50 per cent, depending on the location of the project and status of the entrepreneurs.

Repayment schedule is fixed by the primary lending institutions after taking into consideration the profitability and debt-servicing capacity of the assisted units. The maximum repayment period shall, however, not exceed 10 years from the date of sanction.

Credit Facilities to Small-scale Industries

The small-scale industrial sector raises working credit and term capital required by it from commercial banks, cooperative banks, regional rural banks and State Financial Corporations: the banking system provides mainly working capital and the State Financial Corporation, mainly investment capital. Assistance is also available to the small-scale industrial sector from the National Small Industries Corporation (NSIC) at the national level and the State Small Industries Development Corporation (SSICs) at state level in the form of supply of machinery on hire-purchase basis. The Small Industries Development Bank of India (SIDBI), the National Bank for Agriculture and Rural Development (NABARD) and the Industrial Reconstruction Bank of India (IRBI) provide refinance facilities to banks and financial corporations for financing the small-scale industrial sector. The credit provided by banks to this sector was treated as credit to 'Priority Sector'. The commercial banks are required to lend 40% of their total loans of which 15% to 16% is required to be in the form of direct agricultural advances and the rest can be to the small-scale industry, small business, small transport operators, indirect agricultural loans, etc.

Commercial banks and financial institutions have played a significant role in supporting the SSI movement in India. Banks have continuously been evolving special schemes and approaches to suit the rapidly growing and changing needs of the sector. Provision of liberal credit facilities to the small-scale units has been a hallmark of banking support to the SSI over the years. As a large number of units suffer mainly because of their initial investment by way of equity being low, State Bank of India, a pioneer in extending financial support to the SSI set-up its own equity fund with the objective of providing equity assistance to new entrepreneurs. Under the scheme, assistance is provided to new units by way of interest free loans to fill the shortfall in equity. The loans are repayable over a period of five to seven years after an initial moratorium period of five to seven years.

Outstanding advances to small-scale industries by all scheduled commercial banks increased from ₹ 16,590.14 crore as on June 1991 to ₹ 59,200 crore by March 2003 and further to ₹ 1,29,414 crore by end of March 2007. However, the outstanding advances of Regional/Rural Banks (RRBs) to artisans, village and cottage industries slightly decreased from ₹ 282.04 crore as on March 1990 to ₹ 912.50 crore as on March 2003. Recently, the Reserve Bank appointed a One-man High Level Committee (S.L. Kapoor Committee) to suggest measures for further improving the delivering system and simplification of procedures for credit to the SSI sector. Out of 126 recommendations, submitted by the Committee covering a wide range of areas, the Apex Bank has accepted 35 recommendations for immediate implementation by the commercial banks (including RRBs). Some of the important recommendations accepted by RBI are furnished below:

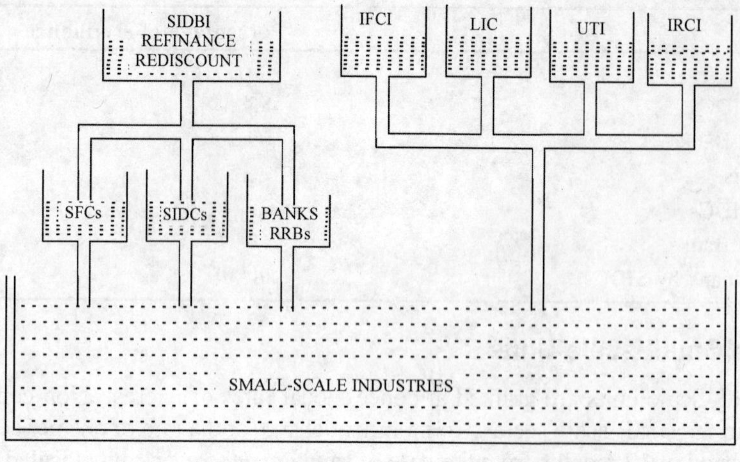

Fig. 11.2 Flow of Credit to Small-scale Industries

Table 11.2 Credit to SSI Sector: Public Sector Banks

Year	Net Bank Credit Sector	Credit to Priority	Credit to SSI		% Share of SSI Credit		Credit to Tiny Sector	
			SSI Accounts	Amount (₹ lakh)	Net Bank Credit	Priority Sector	Amount (₹ lakh)	% to SSI
1	2	3	4	5	6	7	8	9
1994-95	140714	52945.0	30.19	21561	15.30	40.72	5869	27.22
1995-96	169038	61794.0	32.25	25843	15.29	41.82	7734	29.93
1996-97	184381	69609.0	33.77	29485	15.99	42.35	8183	27.76
1997-98	189684	79131.2	31.44	31542	16.60	39.86	9515	30.17
1998-99	218219	91318.6	29.64	38109	17.50	41.73	10273	26.76
1999-00	339477	114611.0	93.91	48483	14.28	42.30	28837	18.23
2000-01	292943	154414.0	22.72	55972	15.20	36.24	24742	44.20
2001-02	349064	171484	19.00	54268	13.8	32.31	26019	43.26
2002-03	485271	199786	17.00	52646	10.8	28.68	27030	42.96
2003-04	560819	244456	17.00	58311	10.4	22.18	26937	42.32
2004-05	717419	307046	17.09	67999	9.5	20.08	27555	38.82
2005-06	1017656	409748	17.29	82434	8.1	19.85	28457	34.14
2006-07	1313640	521376	16.85	102550	7.8	19.68	35892	35.00
2007-08	1364268	608963	39.12	14865	10.9	24.41	49055	33.00

Box 11.1 S.L. Kapur Committee Recommendations Accepted by RBI

- Delegation of more powers to branch managers to grant *ad hoc* (funds for meeting temporary requirement for a specific pupose beyond the sanctioned limit).
- Further simplification of application forms
- Freedom to banks to decide their own norms for credit requirements
- Opening of more specialised branches by the commercial banks
- Enhancement in the limit for composite loans to ₹ 5 lakh (from ₹ 2 lakh at present)
- Strengthening the recovery mechanism by seeking resource to Lok Adalat (a forum providing non-legal remedies and facilitating working out of compromises and appointing/designating officers exclusively dealing with the recovery)
- Banks pay more attention towards meeting the credit requirement of industrially underdeveloped states
- Special programmes for training branch managers for appraising small projects, and
- Banks to make customer grievance machinery more transparent and simplify the procedure for handling complaints and monitoring thereof.

The SFCs have accorded high prority to the development of small-scale industries and bulk of their sanctions have flown to this segment which is a priority sector. More than 71.3 per cent of the assistance extended by SFCs during 2000-01 went to the SSI sector.

The evolution of the bank's policy framework towards the small-scale industries sector is as follows:

(a) Liberalised Scheme: Soon after its establishment by takeover of the undertaking of the Imperial Bank of India, in July 1955, the State Bank of India prepared a 'liberalised' scheme for financing small-scale industries, which was operated initially at nine pilot centres. Under the scheme, the Bank, for the first time in this country, introduced the concept of need-based approach to financing small-scale industries, which was a radical departure from the security-oriented approach. The Bank also showed readiness to meet all the genuine credit requirements of the unit once the viability of the scheme was proved. The concept of margins was kept flexible and linked, not with the saleability of raw materials but with the ability of the borrower to meet the margins. Collateral security was relegated to the background and no unit with a viable scheme was denied credit for want of collateral security.

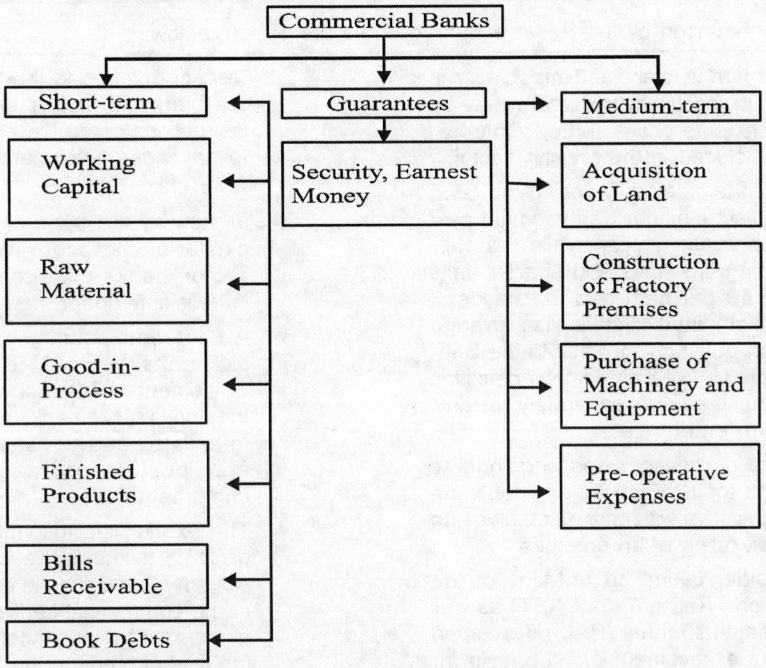

Fig. 11.3 Types of Assistance Extended by Banks

(b) Entrepreneur Scheme: In 1967, a novel scheme known as 'Entrepreneur Scheme' for providing financial assistance to technically qualified entrepreneurs was evolved. Under this scheme, 100 per cent finance was provided to the entrepreneurs, without insisting on any minimum equity contribution, where he is unable to bring any contribution. The scheme covers all technically-qualified persons, as also persons who have technical experience and skill but may not have received any formal technical education. Later, the scheme was extended to cover persons with management qualifications, chartered accountants, cost accountants, etc., who had taken up industrial activity. Though normally, a ceiling of ₹ 2,00,000 was placed on such loans, in exceptional cases, relaxations were permitted up to ₹ 5,00,000 and even higher.

(c) Financing of Artisans and Craftsmen: Initially, the State Bank was concentrating its assistance mainly on the small-scale industries in the organised modern sector. But with its expanding network of branches in the rural areas, the Bank had to take increasing interest in financing rural industries and artisans. The Scheme of Rural Industries Project was introduced by the Government of India in 1962, with the object of nurturing rural crafts as reducing imbalance between urban and rural areas, by bringing about a wider dispersal of small industries. In 1969, the Bank introduced a special scheme of financing artisans and craftsmen in rural industrial projects, in coordination with the government to give liberal credit assistance up to ₹ 75,000 to such artisans. The special features of the scheme were: its simplicity in terms and conditions and procedures and the coordination between the Bank and the government in identifying eligible artisans and in follow-up and recovery, etc.

(d) **Employment-oriented Lending:** With emphasis shifting to the increasing employment potential in the country, through formulation of employment-oriented lending schemes, the Bank, in 1971, started financing tiny economic activities like manufacture of foootwear, khadi, basket-making, etc. In 1972, introduction by the Government of India of the Differential Interest Rates Scheme for financing the weaker sections of society for productive activities at a highly concessionary rate of interest of 4 per cent per annum, gave a fillip to the financing of cottage industries and rural artisans. In the process, a large number of small units in the decentralised sector have been covered by the Bank.

(e) **Special Cells for Village Industries:** With the objective of promoting village industries and providng financial assistance to a large number of village artisans, the Bank set up, in 1977, a special Village Industries Division in each of its local Head Offices. This division evolves schemes of financial assistance to village industries and assists in the implementation of schemes and monitoring their progress.

Box 11.2 Policy Package for Stepping Up Credit to Small and Medium Enterprises

Major policy measures announced by the Reserve Bank of India are set out below:

- Units with investment in plant and machinery in excess of SSI limit and up to ₹10 crore may be treated as medium enterprises (MEs). Only SSI financing will be included in the priority sector.
- Banks may fix self-targets for financing the SME sector so as to reflect a higher disbursement over the immediately preceding year, while the sub-targets for financing tiny units and smaller units to the extend of 40 per cent and 20 per cent, respectively, may continue. Banks may arrange to compile data on outstanding credit to the SME sector as on March 31, 2005 as per new definition and also show the break-up separately for tiny, small and medium enterprises.
- Banks may initiate necessary steps to rationalise the cost of loans to the SME sector by adopting a transparent rating system with cost of credit being linked to the credit rating of an enterprise.
- Banks may consider taking advantages of the Credit Appraisal and Rating Tool (CART) as well as a Risk Assessments Model (RAM) developed by SIDBI for risk assessment of proposals for SMEs.
- Banks may consider the ratings developed by National Small Industries Corporation as per availability and wherever appropriate structure their rates of interest depending on the ratings assigned to the borrowing SME units.
- In order to increase the outreach of formal credit to the SME sector, all banks, including Regional Rural Banks may make concerted efforts to provide credit cover on an average to at least five new small/medium enterprises at each of their semi-urban/urban branches per year.
- Based on the guidelines earlier issued by the Reserve Bank in July 2005, the Boards of banksmay formulate comprehensive and more liberal policies than the existing policies in respect of loans to the SME sector. Till such time the banks formulate such a policy, the current instructions of the Reserve Bank will be applicable to advances granted/to be granted by banks to SME units.
- In view of the benefits accruing on account of cluster-based approach for financing the SME sector, banks may treat it as a thrust area and increasingly adopt the same for SME financing.
- A debt restructuring mechanism for nursing of sick units in the SME sector and a One-time Settlement (OTS) Scheme for SME accounts in the books of the banks as on March 31, 2004 were formulated and advised to all commercial banks and public sector banks respectively, for implementation.
- The existing institutional arrangements for review of credit to the SSI sector such as the Standing Advisory Committee in the Reserve Bank and cells at the commercial bank's head office level as also at important regional centres to review periodically the flow of credit to the SME sector, including tiny sector as a whole.
- Banks may ensure specialised SME branches in identified clusters/centres with preponderance of medium enterprises to enable the SME entrepreneurs to have easy access to the bank credit and to equip bank personnel to develop requisite expertise. The existing specialised SSI branches may also be redesignated as SME branches.
- For wider dissemination and easyaccessibility, the policy guidelines formulated by Boards of banks as well as instructions/guidelines issued by the Reserve Bank may be displayed on the respective websites of the banks as well as website of SIDBI. The banks may also prominently display all the facilities/schemes offered by them to small entrepreneurs at each of their branches.

(f) **Technical Consultancy Cell:** With a large increase in the Bank's coverage of small-scale units, the need for providing technical and managerial guidance to small-scale industries came into sharp focus. In 1973, the Bank, therefore, decided to set up its own Technical Consultancy Cells in each of its local Head Offices to provide such assistance to the borrowers. Suitable persons were selected from among the technically and professionally qualified official of the Bank for this purpose. The Bank entered into an agreement with a reputed business and industrial consultancy organisation to provide intensive training to these officials in consultancy work for a period of one to two years. The subjects covered include – financial analysis and appraisal, financial management, production planning and control, inventory control, budgetary control and costing, marketing, etc.

(g) **Technical Counselling and Management Appreciation Programmes:** Studies conducted by the Bank on the causes of sickness in small-scale industries revealed the necessity for providing counselling and consultancy cells were further strengthened by recruiting additional officials. The officials of the cell provide consultancy and counselling assistance to entrepreneurs who need these. The Bank has also published counselling booklets for use of small-scale industrialists on certain aspects of small industry management, including maintenance of an accounting system. In order to upgrade the managerial skills of small-scale industrialists, the Bank has also been conducting short-duration "Management Appreciation Programmes" for small-scale industrialists in various parts of the country, with particular emphasis on backward and remote areas.

(h) **Equity Support to Small-scale Units:** The Bank's experience with small industry financing indicates that despite the provision of liberal credit facilities, a large number of small-scale units suffer mainly because their initial investment by way of equity is low. Studies conducted by the Bank also indicated that inadequate equity-base was one of the major reasons for sickness in the small-scale sector. As one of the measures for preventing sickness in this sector, the Bank had, in 1975, recommended to the creation of a National Equity Fund to provide equity-support to new small-scale units. The State Bank of India, on its part, set up its own Equity Fund in 1978, with an initial contribution of ₹ 10 million from its profits, with the objective of providng equity assistance to new entrepreneurs eligible for financial assistance under the Entrepreneur Scheme and to other educational entrepreneurs, including those undergoing training under the Bank's Entrepreneurial Development Programme. Preference under the scheme is given to units in the backward areas, tiny sector units in the rural areas and export-oriented units in the small-scale sector. Assistance under the scheme is provided to new units by way of interest-free loans ranging from ₹ 5,000 to ₹ 50,000 to meet the shortfall in equity. The loans are repayable after an initial moratorium period of five to seven years, in a further period similar in essence.

(i) **Entrepreneurial Development:** In 1978, the Bank also launched an ambitious programme of entrepreneurial development in the country, with the object of accelerating industrial development in the backward areas with no traditions of industrialisation. The entrepreneurial development programmes conducted by the Bank include a specialised selection process based on psychological tests, group discussions and interviews and intensive training programmes of one month's duration. The training aims at development of entrepreneurial motivation, economic insight and management skills, creating confidence through direct experience, supply of information about the region, industry a potential, etc. The programme also includes practical training in small industrial units to impart industrial experience and develop confidence. After the training, in the support phase of the programmes, the bank provides to the entrepreneurs continuous counselling and consultancy services free of charge, in areas like project selection, preparation of project report, market surveys, project validation, etc.

Small Industries Development Bank of India

The Small Industries Development Bank of India (SIDBI), as an all India principal financial institution, was set up under the SIDBI Act, 1989 and commenced operations from April, 1990. SIDBI was delinked from IDBI to provide greater functional autonomy and operational flexibility in 2000.

SIDBI serves as a principal financial institution for:

- Promotion
- Financing
- Development of industries in the small-scale sector, and
- Coordinating the functions of institutions engaged in similar activities.

Channels of SIDBI Assistance

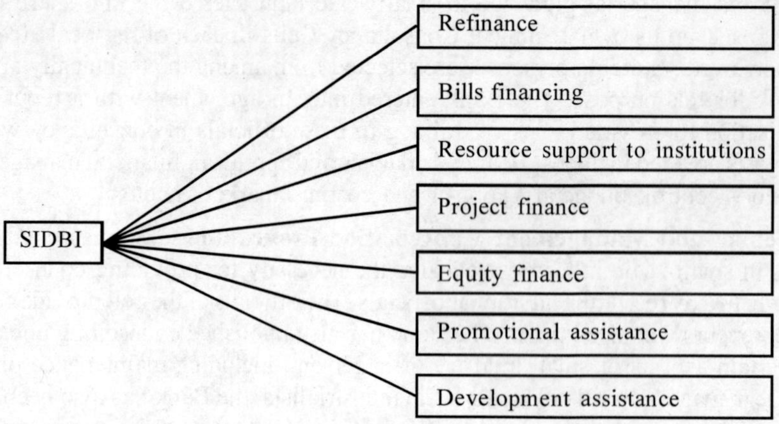

Fig. 11.4 Types of Assistance

Indirect Finance: By way of refinance and bills rediscounting through 894 primary lending institutions having 65,000 outlets across the country.

Direct Finance: Through SIDBI's own 38 offices by means of several tailor-made schemes to reach assistance to specific target groups.

Promotional and Development Activities

These involve accredited non-government organisations, voluntary organisations, scientific and research institutions, technology institutions, management institutions, etc.

Besides financing, SIDBI provides developmental and support services to the SSI sector. These initiatives of the Bank aim at improving the inherent strength of the SSI units on the one hand, and employment generation, economic rehabilitation of the rural poor on the other. Over the years, SIDBI's promotional and development initiatives have crystallised into five thrust areas:

Box 11.3 Schemes for Mitigating the Problems of the SSI Sector

Sl. No.	Problem No.	Schemes Operated by SIDBI
1.	Delayed Payment of Bills	Direct Discounting of Bills (Components) Scheme
		Direct Discounting of Bills (Equipment) Scheme
		Direct Factoring Services
		Bills Rediscounting Scheme (Equipment)
		Bills Rediscounting Scheme Against Inland Supply Bills of SSI
2.	Obsolescence of Technology	Technology Development and Modernisation Fund (TDMF) Scheme (Direct Assistance)
		Refinance Scheme for Technology Development and Modernisation
		ISO 9000 Scheme (Direct Assistance)
		Refinance Scheme for Acquisition of ISO 9000 Series Certification by SSI units
3.	Working Capital Availability	Single Window Scheme
		Composite Loan Scheme } Through PLIs
		Working Capital Term Loan
		Short-term Loan } Direct Assistance
4.	Marketing Inadequacies	Scheme for Financing Activities relating to Marketing of SSI products
5.	Lack of Suitable Infrastructure	Scheme of Direct Assistance for Development of Industrial Infrastructure for SSI sector
		Scheme of Integrated Infrastructural Development (IID)

6.	Insufficient Export Credit	Pre-shipment Credit in Foreign Currency Scheme for Export Bills Financing Rupee Pre-shipment/Post-shipment Credit Foreign Letters of Credit
7.	Human Resources	Entrepreneurship Development Programmes Small Industries Management Assistants' Programme Skill-cum-techonolgy Upgradation Programme

1. Enterprise Promotion
   (i) Rural Industries Programme
   (ii) Mahila Vikas Nidhi
   (iii) Entrepreneurship Development Programmes
   (iv) Mass Media
2. Human Resources Development
3. Technology Upgradation
4. Environment and Quality Management, and
5. Information Dissemination.

In the context of the emerging scenario of liberalisation and market orientation of the economy, SIDBI is gearing up itself to meet the enhanced and varied requirements of the small-scale sector. The Bank has striven in the last eight years to meet the objectives for which it has been set up. With a view to foster faster growth of this sector and to provide a cutting edge for development, the Bank has endeavoured to consolidate traditional products and has created new products that are relevant and impactful. The assistance provided by SIDBI, as it has evolved over the years, meets almost all the requirements of SSIs covering a wide spectrum of units from 'hi-tech' state-of-the-art units to traditional units.

The Small Industries Development Bank of India's promotional and developmental initiatives are aimed at improving the inherent strength of the SSI units on the one hand and employment generation as well as economic rehabilitation of the poor on the other. These initiatives centre around certain thrust areas like Enterprise Promotion (with emphasis on rural industrialisation), Human Resources Development, Technology Upgradation, Special Programmes on Environment and Quality Management and Information Dissemination. For the upliftment of the rural poor, the Bank operates a series of special schemes likes Micro Credit, Mahila Vikas Nidhi, Entrepreneurship Development Programmes, Rural Industries Programme, etc. The Bank operates its schemes in collaboration with a vast network of PLIs, reputed NGOs, Technology and Management Institutional and International Development Agencies.

Micro Credit has emerged as a powerful tool of empowering the poor people to alleviate their poverty. While there has been massive expansion of formal credit network in India, there still remains a perceptible gap in financing the genuine credit needs of the poor especially in rural areas. Under its Micro Credit Scheme, SIDBI provides assistance to well managed NGOs for on lending to the rural poor with an emphasis on women entrepreneurs. So as to provide undivided attention to this category of borrowers, the Bank has launched a separate outfit known as SIDBI Foundation for Micro Credit. With a thrust on institutional development, the SIDBI Foundation strives to create a coherent policy framework for accelerating the micro credit movement in the country.

Thus, SIDBI is poised to play its apex role more effectively while serving the SSI sector with the required financial and support services.

The Indian financial system is undergoing metamorphic changes. The coming years would be crucial for SIDBI mainly on account of the accelerated pace of deregulation of financial sector, softer interest rate and anticipated decline in availment of refinance by banks, which hitherto formed major portion of the Bank's business. SIDBI has been taking steps to effectively address the challenges with alternative business strategies. Direct financing is going to be a major focus area of the Bank. In this direction, SIDBIs thrust would be on financing of infrastructure, marketing, technology upgradation and services sector. As far as low cost funds for the Bank are concerned, considerable interest savings are expected on account of repayment of high cost borrowings. SIDBI would also mobilise resources at cost-effective yet competitive rates through issue of Capital Gains Bond.

SIDBIs future strategy would be to continue its focus in the areas of raising cost-effective resources, improved customer-service, building quality long-term assets, containing non-performing assets and bringing greater value to the shareholders.

Financial Assistance to Medium-scale Units

The medium-scale units are also eligible for concessional interest of 12.50 per cent per annum for units located in any industrially backward areas. However, in respect of units located in non-backward areas, the applicable rate of interest shall be 14 per cent per annum.

No commitment charges shall be levied on medium-scale units located in the category 'A' backward areas. In respect of loans to units in the category 'B' and the category 'C' backward areas, the concessional commitment charge at the rate of 0.50 per cent per annum shall be levied after allowing the normal period of a grace of six months from the date of sanction. Other units located in non-backward areas shall pay commitment charges at the rate of one per cent per annum.

The debt-equity ratio allowed to medium-scale units and the repayment schedule of medium-scale units shalll also be determined after taking into consideration their profitability and debt servicing capacity, subject to the condition that the maximum repayment period does not exceed 10 years from the date of sanction.

Assistance to Small and Medium-scale Units for Modernisation

The primary objective of this scheme is to encourage industrial units overcome the backlog of modernisation and to adopt improved and updated technology and methods of production and prevent mechanical and technological obsolescence. Modernisation may include replacement or renovation of plant and machinery or acquisition of balancing equipment for fuller and more effective utilisation of installed capacity.

Units to be eligible for modernisation assistance should have been in existence for a period of at least five years. In the case of replacemnet or renovation, the machinery should have been in use at the unit for a period of at least five years. Proposals for modernisation assistance should establish the benefits that would accrue by way of reduction in the unit cost of production, technology improvement, improved productivity, both in quality and quantity, better profitability, etc. The cost of acquisition of technical know-how would also be eligible. The project proposals should clearly bring out these aspects. Other things being equal, export-oriented and import-substitution schemes will be accorded higher priority.

The modernisation programmes should primarily aim at:

- Upgradation of process, technology and product;
- Export-orientation
- Import-substitution;
- Energy-saving;
- Anti-pollution measures;
- Conservation/substitution of scarce raw materials and other inputs including recycling/recovery of wastes and by-products;
- Improvement in capacity utilisation within the existing capacity, through increase in productivity and de-bottlenecking, and
- Improvements in material handling.

Irrespective of the location of the unit, interest at the rate of 11.5 per cent per annum shall be charged on all rupee loans for modernisation purposes. A commitment charge at the rate of 0.5 per cent per annum shall be levied on the undisbursed rupee loans after an initial grace period of six months from the date of sanction.

In regard to debt-equity ratio, a more flexible approach is adopted by the primary lending institutions. A reasonable equity base will, however, be required to be maintained to ensure servicing of the loans. Similarly, no fixed guidelines have been stipulated for the promoter's contribution norm. Modernisation assistance being financial assistance to existing units, internal accruals would also form a part of promoters' contribution.The exact promoters' contribution would be decided on a case-to-case basis depending on the financial status of the unit and the ability of its promoters to mobilise and induct additional resources.

Rehabilitation Assistance to Small and Medium-scale Units

The scheme for rehabilitation covers all small and medium-scale industrial units, including ancillary units and units in cottage and village industries which have been assisted by SFCs and SIDCs or are self-financed and which are classified as sick. It is not necessary that the past loans extended by SFCs or SIDCs should have been refinanced by IDBI. Rehabilitation loans extended by commercial banks to such units will also be eligible for refinance under the scheme. The objective is to rehabilitate sick industrial units in the portfolio of SFCs and SIDCs.

Eligibility Criteria

Under this scheme, a unit will be classified as sick if it has incurred cash losses during the previous accounting year and is likely to incur cash losses in the current year and there is erosion in its net worth to the extent of 50 per cent or more. The unit should be capable of being revived with reasonable financial support and relief and within a reasonable period of time. Usual norms of debt equity ratio and promoter's contribution would not be insisted upon and would depend on merits of each cases.

Rehabilitation assistance would be for the following purposes:

- Margin money for additional term loan and working capital requirements under the rehabilitation programmes;
- Working capaital term loans, if any, granted by banks to meet irregularities in the unit's working capital account;
- Payment of statutory liabilities, payment of pressing creditors, etc., (to the extent possible such dues should be liquidated over a period of time, in instalments);
- Cash loss, if any, that may be incurred during the implementation of the nursing programmes;
- Overdue instalments not recovered from the unit, but agreed to be funded into a separate term loan account; and minimum capital expenditure required for restarting the unit on a viable level.

In order to encourage the rehabilitation of sick units, the rate of interest on rehabilitation assistance has been fixed at 11.5 per cent per annum, irrespective of the location of the units. Such units have also been totally exempted from any liability on account of commitment charges on undisbursed financial assistance.

Similar to modernisation cases, a flexible approach is adopted in regard to debt-equity ratio and promoter's contribution. These norms shall be determined on a case-to-case basis depending on the health of the unit and the projected profitability and debt-serving capacity. The repayment period shall, however, not exceed a maximum of 10 years from the date of sanction.

FINANCING OF INDUSTRIAL ESTATE

Financial institutions have commenced extending direct assistance for financing of industrial estates. Such ventures costing up to ₹ 300 lakh are covered under the IDBI's refinance scheme where primary lending is affected through the SFCs, SIDCs and commercial banks. Industrial estates costing in excess of ₹ 300 lakh are extended direct financial assistance by all India financial institutions.

The main aspects considered in the proposals for setting up of industiral estates are suitability of the location, availability of power, water, raw materials, skilled and unskilled labour, transport and communication facilities, market for the products of industries to be set-up in the estate and the potential for overall economic growth. Significant emphasis initially is therefore laid on physical survey of the size and its proper designing.

Size of Industrial Estate

The size of the estate should preferably be not less than 15 acres of land where the cost is up to ₹ 300 lakh and not less than 25 acres of land where the cost is more than ₹ 300 lakh. The size results in individual units deriving the advantage of some economy in overhead expenses and sharing of some common facilities. However, it may not always be practical to insist on the minimum size of land and the financial institutions may, under such circumstances, relax the minimum areas where the estate is in urban areas or if the estate is proposed in a multistoreyed building.

The institutions also desire that the project acquires adequate reserve land at the begining itself as the cost of acquiring adjacent land at a later date might become prohibitive. Twice the estimated initial capacity for sheds booked/expected to be booked is considered a fair reserve area over the present requirements. This is not, however, taken as an inflexible norm and for large estates, particularly in urban and semi-urban areas, the reserve may be less, say equal to the area initially required.

Expenditure Eligible for Assistance

The cost of industrial estate for the purposes of financing is confined to the cost of site development, laying of roads, arrangements for water supply, power transmission and electrification, construction of sheds and construction of blocks for essential amenities such as – sanitation, watch and ward scheme, canteen, compound walls, administrative building, etc.

Expenditure on housing and power generation are not included in financing of industrial estates for the reason that assistance is separately available to units from various state and Central Government schemes for captive power generation plants and housing:

- Cost of improving land, laying of roads, arrangement for water supply, electrification, etc. 15%
- Cost of construction of sheds 75%
- Cost of essential amenities like sanitary blocks, watch and ward, compound walls, canteen, etc. 5%
- Cost of administrative building 3%
- Cost of stamp duty, registration charges, preliminary expenses, etc. 2%

Eligibility Criteria for Assistance

Financial assistance is given to establish industrial estates either in the corporate sector or the co-operative sector. The organisation may be a public or private limited company, partnership, joint Hindu Family concern, sole proprietorship or even a local body.

However, industrial estates established by state/Central Government which are financed out of budgetary allocations are not eligible for financial assistance under this scheme.

Financing Norms

The all-India financial institutions stipulate a promoter's contribution norm of 20 per cent (of the total project cost) for industrial estates set up in a notified less developed districts/areas and a 22.5 per cent norm (of the total project cost) in other cases. In respect of estates costing less than ₹ 300 lakh, the following margins have been stipulated by IDBI to make them eligible for refinance:

(a) 15 per cent margin for estates set up by technicial entrepreneurs or unemployed engineers where the sheds are to be acquired by them on rental/hire basis.

(b) 20 to 30 per cent margin for cooperative estates where the sheds are entirely by small-scale units.

(c) 30 to 35 per cent margin for estates set up by joint-stock companies whose shareholders occupy a majority of the sheds, and

(d) 40 to 50 per cent margin for estates set up by proprietary and partnership concerns.

The prescribed debt-equity ratio financing of industrial estates is a maximum of 2:1. This is, however, relaxed up to a maximum debt-equity ratio of 3:1 in respect of comparatively small estates in the private sector where the total investment does not exceed ₹ 10 lakh and for estates in the cooperative sector.

Interest and commitment charges are levied on industrial estates on the same lines as applicable to other industrial projects, being dependent on the location of the project.

Repayment Schedule

In respect of loans being refinanced by the IDBI, a repayment period of seven to ten years including an initial moratorium of two to three years is prescribed. The period many be extended up to twelve years in exceptional cases. Where assistance is directly rendered by all-India financial institutions, the repayment period may extend up to fifteen years, including an initial moratorium of two to three years.

Security

In determining the repayment scheme, a debt-service coverage ratio of 2:1 is generally adopted. This ratio is, however, relaxed up to 1.25:1 in respect of loans to industrial estates promoted with government assistance provided that payment of dues to financial institutions by way of principal and interest will have precedence over the dues to the government against loans received from it. Government's acceptance of this condition has to be obtained in writing.

The financial institutions stipulate that the sheds constructed in the industrial estate should be allotted only on a rental basis. No hire-purchase or outright sale is permitted in order to enable mortgage of sheds with the lending institutions towards the security for the loans. Where for any reason the mortgage of land and sheds constructed in the industrial estate is not possible, an unconditional guarantee of the government/bank for repayment of loan and payment of interest is insisted upon here.

Credit Dispensation

Availability of timely and adequate financial assistance is *sine qua non* for the growth of any sector, including SSIs. A multiagency credit structure, to fulfil the financial needs of units in the SSI sector, has got evolved in the country over the years. While there has been a substantial increase in the quantum of assistance extended to the SSI sector through the institutional set-up in the country over the years, there have also been some constraints relating to the timeliness and adequacy of credit as well as complexities of systems and procedures related thereto. In order to examine various aspects of credit dispensation, the Government of India/Reserve Bank of India constituted various Committees from time-to-time:

- Study Group to frame guidelines for follow-up of bank credit (Tandon Committee), 1974.
- Working Group to review the system of Cash Credit (Chore Committee), 1979.
- Committee on the financial system (Narasimham Committee-I), 1991.
- Committee to examine the adequacy of Institutional Credit to the SSI sector and related aspects (Nayak Committee), 1992.
- Expert Committee on Small Enterprises (Abid Hussain Committee), 1997
- Committee on Banking Sector Reforms (Narasimham Committee-II), 1998.
- Working Group for harmonising the role and operations of DFIs and Banks (Khan Working Group), 1998.
- High level Committee on Credit to SSIs (S.L. Kapur Committee), 1998.

Finance to the small-scale sector is inadequate availability of start-up finance for first generation entrepreneurs from the banking channels is not forthcoming. Working capital is inadequate and not coming easily long-term credit is not forthcoming.

Of the various suggestions received on improving the flow of credit to the SSI sector, the following merit consideration:

- Extending the limit of loans up to ₹ 0.2 million as against the present limit of ₹ 25,000 for exemption from collaterals. The exemption limit is already available in the case of beneficiaries under PMRY up to ₹ 0.1 million.
- Providing banks/SFCs with tax incentives; lower rates of taxes based on the proportion of funds deployed in the SSI sector, alternatively a lower SLR for banks having deployed funds in the sector, could be considered.
- Restructuring of SFCs/SIDCs.
- Instituting Credit Insurance or Credit Guarantee Scheme, which might cover lending risks and serve as substitute to the collateral security thereby facilitating easier access to risk-free credit. Similar schemes are prevalent in Japan (Credit Insurance Corporation of Japan) and USA (Small Business Administration). In the Union Budget 1999-2000, a new credit insurance scheme was proposed to be launched. Positive aspects of the schemes operating abroad can be included in the proposed scheme.
- Developing the business of discounting the bills of the SSIs in underdeveloped regions.
- Creating a facilitating environment enabling financial institutions to take up factoring services on a large-scale.
- Setting up of more specialised branches of banks for lending to SSIs in areas with larger concentration/clusters of small industries.
- Examining the feasibility of introducing a credit rating scheme for SSIs.

- Facilitating SIDBI to mobilise low cost funds, both in the domestic market and abroad, through measures such as floatation of tax-free bonds, support for resource raising from international funding agencies, etc.
- SIDBI might introduce new instruments/products which would encourage the PLIs to provide increased credit to the sector and commence merchant banking services for expanding equity assistance to the sector.

There is a need to formulate those policies would provide sufficiently strong incentives (and penalties) for banks and other players in the business of credit provision to the SSI sector. The policy environment would have to change in such a way that banks would view lending to the SSI sector as an opportunity rather than as a constraint.

Key Findings of Nayak Committee

Banks have insufficiently serviced the working capital needs of the SSI sector and in particular, village and tiny enterprises. The SSI sector has been getting 8.1 per cent of its annual turnover by way of working capital advanced from the banks. Of this, the tiny units, village industries and artisan units were receiving only 2.7 per cent of their annual turnover by way of working capital advances from the banks.

The need for specialised bank branches for SSIs, the absence of which, in the past, has led to serious bottlenecks, *viz.*: (a) arbitrary reductions in credit limits applied for, (b) inordinate delays and irregularity in the sanction of working capital, and (c) scarce availability of the assistance for start-up, expansions and diversifications.

The system of providing term credit and working capital by two kinds of institutions, *viz.,* Banks and SFCs has given rise to a host of problems of coordination between them.

Key findings of the S.L. Kapur Committee

An unsatisfactory performance by commercial banks in respect of SSI financing persisted with regard to: (a) non-adherence to working capital norms suggested by Nayak Committee; and (b) poor flow of credit to tiny units.

The loan application forms prescribed by banks for small loans were very complicated. There was no separate earmarking of funds by banks for working capital loans.

Bank staff/Management was not well-trained in the task of appraising the SSI projects.

The SFCs and other state-level institutions should be restructured as per recommendations made by the Khan Working Group.

SSIs should get special treatment in the matter of interest rates and they should normally get credit at Primary Lending Rate (PLR).

The existing Credit Guarantee Scheme being operated by Deposit Insurance and Credit Guarantee Corporation (DICGC) should be scrapped and be replaced by a more objective and suitable scheme to be operated by a new Guarantee Corporation. The Reserve Bank of India should take the initiative for setting up it in SIDBI. The proposed Corporation cover only those loans which are sanctioned by Public Sector Banks/Financial Institutions and where the principal amount sanctioned does not exceed ₹ 10 lakh.

The Reserve Bank of India might consider, in consultation with the Government of India, the need to set-up a Small Industries Infrastructure Development Fund, for development of industrial areas in and around metropolitan cities, urban and semi-urban areas which were not covered by RIDF of NABARD, to start with, a corpus of such funds, say ₹ 100 crore.

Credit Penetration in SMEs

Small and Medium Enterprises (SMEs) are not able to exploit their potential due to the low Credit Penetration into the segment. Almost 90 per cent of the units are not registered and close to 95 per cent of them do not have access to any kind of formal institutional credit. According to the Third All-India Census of small-scale industries, only 17.9 per cent had availed of credit of these 14.9 per cent could have had access to institutional credit. The report of the Committee on Financial Sector Assessment (CFSA) points to both a decline in the share of credit to SSIs and a widening of the credit gap to unreasonable levels. Further, the SME sector is underserved, especially in terms of working capital and trade finance.

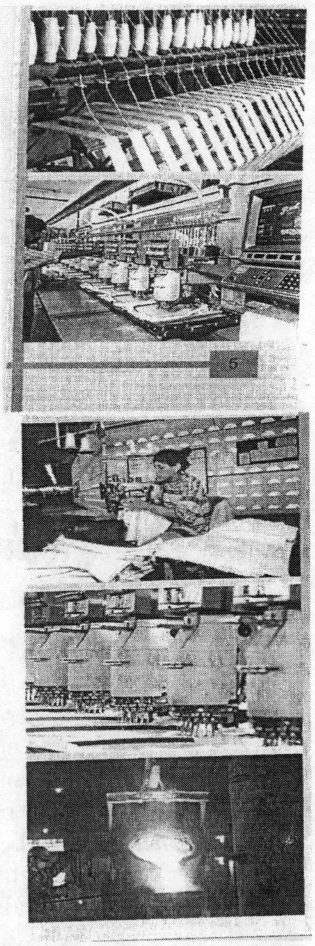

The CFSA report goes a step further and points out that even in case where credit is available for investment, the loan tenures are far too short to pay-off any sizable investment. Also, small-scale units do not have access to competitive rates which are usually reserved for blue-chip companies. The practices is that when banks lend to SSI, banks charge a commission for the additional risk and apply tougher screening measures, which drive up costs.

The CFSA has made an attempt to gauge the extent of the credit gap by assuming the credit that would have been available, if the share of small-scale credit in total available, if the share of small-scale credit in total bank credit remained at 13 per cent, its average share during credit 1998-2007. Figures shows that credit gap expressed as a per cent of the actual lending to SSI has steadily increased from 9 per cent in 2002 to nearly 100 per cent the period.

The report cites three reasons for banks increasing reluctance to lend to SSIs. One, banks' consider them high-risk borrowers, as they have insufficient assets, high vulnerability to market reflections and high mortality rates. Second, there are issues related to high transaction costs, as the small amount of credit used by each unit raise administrative costs. Third, there are difficulties in assessing the creditworthiness of the units, due to lack of accounting records or financial statements.

The third factor is especially relevant in the Indian contexts, where the growing sophistication of lending technologies has become a barrier to accessing credit for a small units, which are dependent on relationship lending – where decisions are based on soft information gathered by the lender on the borrower.

In relationship lending, the banker has personal knowledge of a borrower's managerial skills and business strategy of the loan firms over a period. This substituted for transparency of records. But as lending technologies of large banks become dependent on quantifiable transactions-based information, which is electronically stored and communicated across the institutions, the credit flows based on relationship lending are bound to fall, states the report.

Experts have stressed on the need to regenerate SME financing. According to firm Size and Business Environmental in SME Financing, a World Bank study, SME across the world face similar problems, due to inversely related factors, the problem areas being financing and regulatory policies.

Financing agencies are focusing on a cluster approach to achieve the twin objectives of their own business growth and development of the SME sector. The objective is to ensure that the fruit of development are spread across a vast majority of entrepreneurs and community and balanced regional development.

Regenerating SME financing in India is essential as the sector serves as a Greenfield for nurturing entrepreneurial talent. An increased focuses by Indian banks and financial institutions on providing microfinance, factoring assistance, etc., at a reasonable cost will go a long way in making SMEs domestically and globally competitive, lending to economic growth.

Going forward, to ensure better accessibility of credit by SMEs, banks ability to quickly evaluate the creditworthiness of small and medium enterprises will be critical. Due to limiting factors of financial statement lending and asset-based lending, consumer lending may be considered by banks in the case of SMEs. To make this a more effective option, it may be combined with relationship lending, universally the most popular lending technique for SMEs where information and documentation are quite inadequate. Under relationship lending, a lender's decision in substantial part is based on the proprietary information about the firm and its owner, acquired by the loan officer through a variety of sources.

FDI NOT ENOUGH

Small Enterprises Need Local Equity

The government has clarified the ambiguity over Foreign Direct Investment (FDI) norms for Micro and Small Enterprises (MSEs). They can have foreign investment up to the applicable spectral limit. Though this opens another option for this generally capital starved sector, a rush of FDI is unlike anytime soon. What is needed is some way of revitalising the smaller exchanges, which would allow MSEs to raise risk capital from local investors who are likely to be more appreciative. Most micro small enterprise lack access to any sort of formal funds, and are forced to rely on costly informal credit. Ironically, this is largely because organised lenders do not find them creditworthy, as many of them would not have the balance sheet strength to meet the basic eligibility conditions. The truth is functional MSEs are meeting the far more exacting terms of informal credit. If this informal credit could be substituted FDI, small and micro enterprise would see a sharp jump in their profitability. The large interest component of their profit and loss account would disappear and minus the debt, the balance sheet would look too good. The ability to plough back profit would allow them to expand and reap economies of scale. However, for the very reason MSEs cannot access formal credit, they are unlike to interest some investors in an overseas country. The FDI that they may attract is likely to be venture capital type, which is very expensive and therefore may entail huge dilution by the promoter.

Micro and small enterprises need smaller local exchanges where they can raise capital easily from investors who are likely to appreciate them better because of promxity. Access to the bigger national exchanges is difficult for smaller enterprises and they are also unlikely to get a good valuation. Despite SEBI's efforts, the regional exchanges have been a non-starter. The next best solution is for existing profitability exchanges to develop the regional markets or invest in the regional exchanges and put in place a variable business sold for them. The obvious way of doing that is to allow more equity exchanges. The competition would encourage product innovation and diversification.

SMEs DESERVE BETTER

They Drive India's Growth To Prosperity

The move by capital market regulator SEBI to ease stock listing and trading norms for small and medium enterprises (SMEs) can be but one step towards removing the panoply of constraints that they face on a daily basis. Finance, or the lack of it, at the right price and on time is, after all, a recurring problem. It make sense to exempt, SMEs from the eligibility criteria for initial public offering and follow-on offers. But, in tandem, what is required is to remove routine informational rigidities between SMEs and lenders and potential investors. It's the untoward presence of huge informational asymmetries that intrinsically heighten credit risk and transaction costs for the SME sector. Bank, of course, are required to meet the credit needs of SMEs as a part of their priority sector lending requirements. Also, the RBI has directed all banks to introduce standardised credit appraisal systems. Yet, SME lending by banks barely adds up to 2% of the gap. Worse, some studies suggest that banks seems to be stepping up lending for microfinance and self-help groups (as part of their priority sector lending) at the expense of SMEs. Hence, the need for institutional reform to rev up informational systems on SMEs.

What is required is a more responsive policy mechanism to finance SMEs. SEBI's new guidelines for listed SMEs have rightly done away with the standard requirement of disclosing quarterly result; semi-annual figures would do, the intention being to reduce costs and overheads. But concurrently, what is necessary is an array of advisory and business development services focused on SMEs; the ideas is to improve credit and business-performance information. We need a thriving SME sector to boost entrepreneurship and risk-taking pan-India, and spur innovation and growth. Hence, the need for proactive policy support for SME clusters to shore up demand and supply of finance. Actually, there seems scope for innovative financial products to reduce credit risks for SMEs and boost investor comfort. Additionally, there's the need to address the problem of delayed payments and rationalise the tax regime for SMEs. Equity finance for SMEs deserves a leg up.

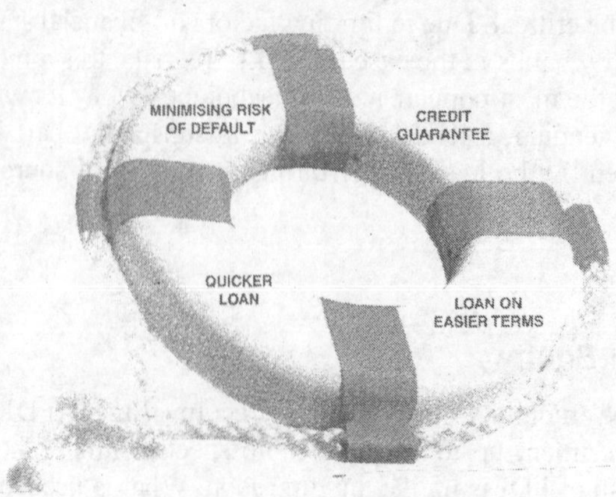

CONCLUSION

The opening up of the banking sector and greater disintermediation have facilitated the access of these SSI units, particularly the larger among them, to a variety of financial services. Private sector banks are also in the process of evolving special innovative schemes to attract the more efficient SSIs especially the export-oriented units. The pattern of financing these small-scale units is gradually changing in favour of specialised, target-specific financial services, with the introduction of new financial products. The financial institutions including SFCs/SIDCs and public sector banks are preparing themselves to provide a diversified range of services to various target groups including – venture capital, leasing, equipment finance, export finance, factoring services, etc., and private sector banks are carving out *niche* areas within the sector to give specialised sevice with innovatively designed financial instruments. The access of SSIs to the capital market has also improved with the formulation of boughtout deals on Over The Counter Exchange of India (OTCEI) by merchant bankers, providing yet another avenue to them for raising resources. Strategic alliances between institutions, banks and professional bodies of industries would also enable SSIs to receive specialised non-fund based services, e.g., technology tie-ups, quality improvements, etc., as well as finance under a common umbrella. These would result in speedy project appraisals and better project monitoring.

Finance is available for a project. But there is need for prudent financial management. All along there is need for planning the flow of funds for the smooth functioning of a project. A successful project is one which generates its own finances to a greater extent for its diversified activities. Internal resources will serve as a backbone of a project.

The generation of internal resources not only benefit the enterprise, but also the entrepreneur, shareholder and the society. Above all, prudent internal resources may also assist the natural growth of the capital market.

Finance, which has been aptly described as the 'lifeblood' of industry, is a prerequisite for the mobilisation of real resources to organise production and marketing. Depending upon the nature of the activity to be financed, business requires short-term, medium-term and long-term finance.

Financial mangement is an integral part of the industry and ranks equally in importance with other key components like production and marketing. Capital and finance form the bed rock foundatin for industrial development. They are provided by a number of financial institutions. The saga of industrial development in the post-independence period is the story of these core institutions.

Keeping in view the dynamics of the sector and expectations of the stakeholders, the financial institutions (FIs) are adopting a multifaceted approach to source and manage its business by bracing up its physical infrastructure; centralising several operational and non-operating process to increase efficiency; introducing hybrid channel arrangements; increasing the delivery network and many more similar steps. Efforts would continue to be made to augment the flow of credit to the sector and align FIs strategies in tune with the national and international systems.

Bring service enterprises at par with manufacturing sector enterprises in SME sector for priority treatment is a landmark development for the sector as also for the FIs. The Micro Small and Medium Enterprises Development Act, 2006 further opens new vistas of business opportunities for the FIs.

Realising the need to meet the growing demands of the sector, SDBI has changed its business model, with thrust on direct credit to emerge as one-stop shop for SMEs. The changes business model is also expected to supplement the Bank's refinance as well as resource support operations.

Given the sizable exposure in the SLFIs, the performance of SFCs/SIDCs would be closely monitored by the Bank. A based approach would continue to be adopted to address the problems being faced by the SFCs.

Towards improving flow of credit to SME sector and support Government of India and RBI in their endeavour to achieve this goal, SDBI has felt a need to develop specialised officers within the banking system, who will have a comprehensive knowledge about the sector, its problem, opportunity, etc. In this context, the Bank has initiated the process of setting up a training institute exclusively for bankers, SME entrepreneurs and policymakers.

Further, the FIs proposes to set up, knowledge hubs, to provide key inputs on industry-wise information, outlook, prospects, issues and concern, etc., to act as catalysts for extension of assistance to units in the SME sector. These will be web-based knowledge hubs (industrty specific, supported by academic institutions).

ANNEXURE-I

Safety Cover by CGTMSE Makes Loan Easier for MSEs

Collateral free loans sanctioned to MSE entrepreneurs for start ups, expansion, modernisation, diversification, etc., are eligible for coverage under the Credit Guarantee Scheme. The main objectives of this schemes is to allow micro and small enterprises access to credit easily. Benefits of this scheme include:

- MSEs are also able to get quicker loans as most of the procedural aspects like assessing and creating mortgage of the collateral security tech is eliminated.
- MSEs can avail of a collateral free loan either for acquisition of capital goods or for working capital or even both.
- Loans under the Credit Guarantee Scheme are available on softer terms as compared to standard loans since a major part of risk of default is passed on to the CGTMSE.

However, the loan amount, tenure of the loan, interest rate, promoter's contribution, debt equity ratio, repayment terms and other terms and conditions of the loan will vary from bank-to-bank and will depend on the internal policies of each Members Lending Institution (MLI).

The following criteria are applicable while applying for a loan under this scheme:

- Only micro and small enterprises engaged in the manufacturing and service sectors as defined by the MSMED Act (excluding the retails sector) are eligible to be covered under the scheme.
- Credit facility extended jointly by SDBI and a bank, out of the MSE Fund for North East Region (NER) which has been created by SIDBI, is eligible for coverage subject to conditions.
- Guarantee will be extended for a maximum of ₹ 100 lakh per borrower even if the credit extended is more than ₹ 100 lakh.
- The entire credit facility has to be given without collateral and/or third party guarantee. Loans may be secured against the primary security which has been defined under the scheme,
- The rate of interest charged to the unit should not exceed 3% above the Prime Lending Rate (PLR) of the lending institutions.
- The dues of the borrowing unit to the lending institution should not have become bad or doubtful of recovery as on date of issue of guarantee cover.

Where to obtain these loans?

CGTMSE has 97 Member Lending Institutions including all Public Sector Banks, SBI and Associates, select private sector/foreign/regional rural banks, NSIC, NEDFI, SIDBI, TIIC and DFC.

The Reserve Bank of India has recently issued guidelines making it mandatory for all scheduled commercial banks including Rural Regional Banks (RRBs) and Local Areas Banks, not to obtain collateral security in case of loans of up to ₹ 5 lakh granted to units in the MSE sector.

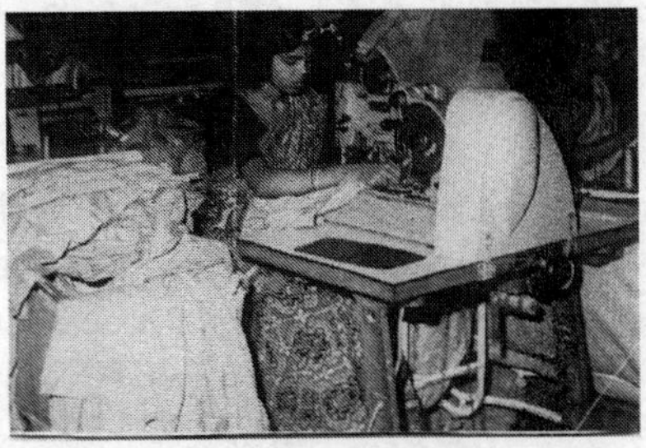

12 CHAPTER

WORKING CAPITAL MANAGEMENT

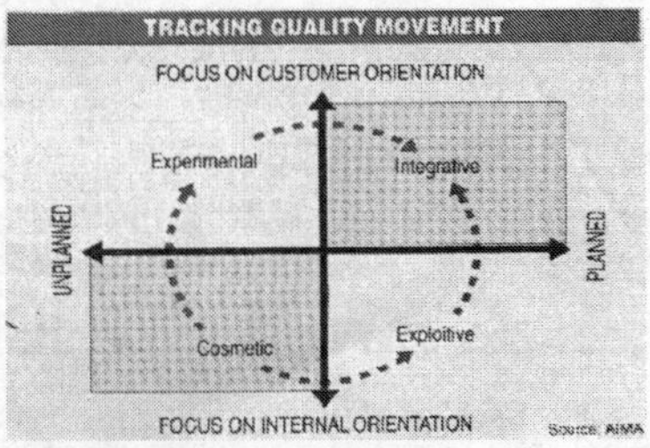

The majority see the obstacles; the few see the objectives; history records the successes of the latter; while oblivion is the reward of the former.

LEARNING OBJECTIVES

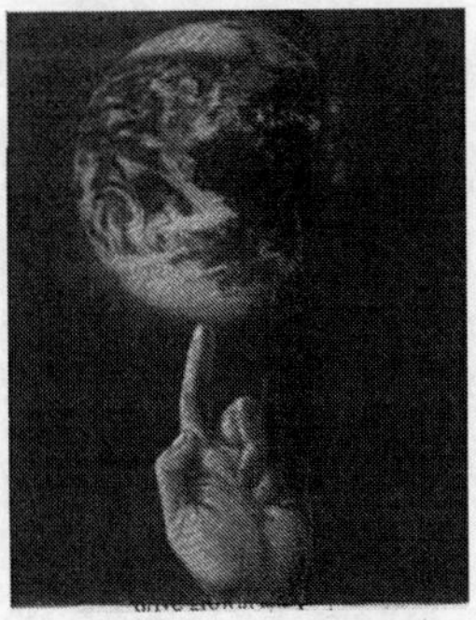

Working capital management is important for small-scale industries owing to resource crunch.

An enterprise needs finance, long-term or short-term. Finance could be raised through external or internal sources. Finance raised through external sources could be in the form of equity share capital, preference share capital, term loans or debentures. Long-term loans means the loans raised for acquiring fixed-assets for the enterprise and its main sources can be financial institutions, commercial banks, public deposits, etc. Internal sources include ploughing of profits which is a technique of raising finance out of accumulated profits not distributed as dividends.

Working capital implies that part of capital which is required to run day-to-day operations of an enterprise. Working capital can be gross or net working capital. Former refers to the total amount of current assets while latter means current assets minus current liabilities. The quantum of working capital required will be influenced by the nature of the enterprise, i.e., manufacturing relating or service enterprise. Mostly, SSIs have weaker working capital base as their money remains blocked in inventory, debtors or so.

The short-term sources of finance are commercial banks who lend money in the form of cash credit, overdraft, public deposits, demand loans, etc. Factoring has also come up as a tool which helps the entrepreneur in collecting his money choked in his debtors. Factor could be financial institution who helps the supplier companies to secure finance against the book debts and thus saves him from the effort of collecting the book debts.

INTRODUCTION

The management of working capital is an integral part of overall corporate management. In simple terms, working capital is the amount of funds which a small-scale industry must have to finance its day-to-day operations. It may also be regarded as that portion of an industry's total capital which is employed in short-term operations. Included in these operations are such items as stocks of raw materials and supplies needed for manufacture, stocks of finished goods awaiting sale, semi-processed items or components that will soon merge as final products, sundry debtors representing pending collections against credit sales and short-term investments.

Definition

In simple terms, working capital is the amount of funds which a small-scale enterprise must have to finance its day-to-day operations. It is a short-term finance, an effective utilisation of working capital results in the maximisation of productivity and profits. A proper management of working capital synchronises the cash receipts and cash outlay, and a unit may function with minimum cash reserves.

The Accounting Principles Board of the American Institute of Certified Public Accountants, USA, has defined working capital as follows: "Working capital, sometimes called networking capital, is represented by the excess of current assets over current liabilities and identifies the relatively liquid portion of total enterprise capital which constitutes a margin of buffer for maturing obligations within the ordinary operating cycle of the business."

Objectives of Working Capital

An essential pre-condition for successful financial management is the establishment of sound and consistent asset management policies, covering fixed as well as current assets. An effective utilisation of working capital results in the maximisation of productivity and profits. Profitability and solvency are the twin objectives of working capital management; and these can be achieved by striving to maintain a correct ratio between working and fixed capital. Such ratios will ensure a smooth and rapid flow of funds and enhance the efficiency and profitability of the enterprise. A proper management of working capital synchronises the cash receipts and cash outlay, and a unit may function with minimum cash reserves.

The objectives of working capital are:

(1) The management wants maximum productivity and profits in the employment of capital. This is possible by striving to maintain a correct ratio between working capital and fixed capital.

(2) The management has another objective and that is, to maintain a smooth and rapid flow of funds in order to enhance the efficiency of working capital or profitability of the enterprise.

(3) If cash receipts and cash outlay synchronise, there is no need to maintain a cash reserve. In business, it would be a miracle to have such perfect coincidence and coordination between receipts and payments. Hence, an enterprise must have a sufficient cash reserve to meet all normal as well as abnormal cash needs.

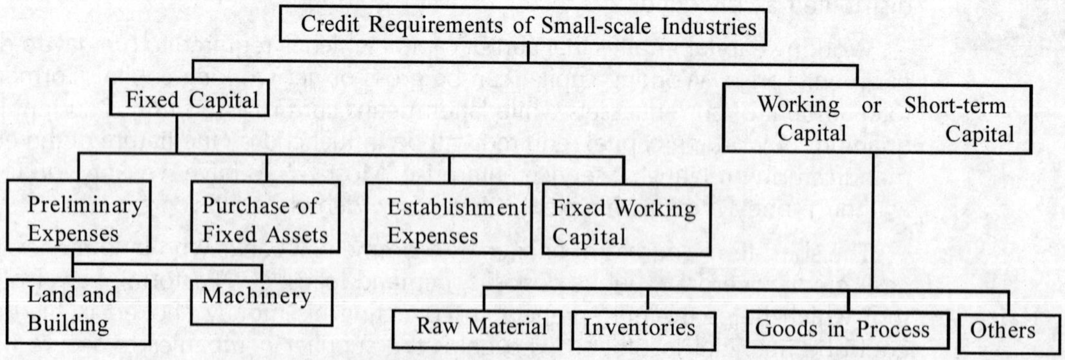

Fig. 12.1 Credit Requirements of Small-scale Industries

COMPOSITION OF WORKING CAPITAL

For a proper appreciation and understanding of it, a closer look at the composition of working capital is necessary. The following are the constituent parts of working capital:

Current Assets

Inventories

Raw materials, components, etc.

Work-in-progress

Finished goods

Others

Loans and advances and other debtor balances

Sundry debtors or trade debtors

Others, including prepayments

Investments

Government securities, semi-government securities } not applicable in the case of a small-

Industrial securities and others scale industry

Cash and bank balances

Fixed deposits with banks

Other bank balances } not applicable in case of smaller of

Cash in hand the small-scale industries

Advance of income-tax (net of tax provisions)

Current Liabilities

This includes borrowings for banks other than those against own debentures and other mortgages.

Other borrowings such as public deposits, loans, etc., other than those against own debentures and other mortgages at deferred payment liabilities (not applicable in the case of a large number of small-scale industries). They also include trade dues and other current liabilities, sundry creditors or trade creditors. Others include advances received, provisions, taxation (net of advance of income-tax) and other current provisions.

The purpose of working capital is to achieve cash realisation, which is precisely explained below:

Cash and Bank

Short-term Loan...

Investment...

Sundry Debtors...

Finished Goods...

Work-in-Progress..

Raw Materials...

Stocks...

Gross or Net?

The concept of working capital is broadly understood in 'gross' and 'net' concept. The financial is the 'gross' concept. The 'gross working capital' is represented by the sum total of all the current assets of the enterprise, while the net working capital (which is also known as the accounting concept) is the difference between both current assets and the current liabilities. In short, the gross and the net working capital concepts present two distinct and important facets of working capital management.

Net Working Capital

It represents the excess of total current assets over total current liabilities, and is measured by the current ratio. This indicates that current asset has an edge over current liabilities, *viz.,* current assets< current liabilities.

Unit has the current ratio of a large ratio 2:1 which indicates greater solvency, while a very low ratio indicates insolvency.

Net Working Capital = Current assets – Current liabilities

= (cash + marketable + accounts + bills + inventories securities) receivables

Minus (-)

(accounts + notes and bills + expenses + temporary loans payable)

Gross Working Capital

It is equal to the total sum of current assets and may represent both owned capital and loan capital.

The concept of gross capital is a financial concept, while that of net capital is an accounting concept. The distinction between gross and net working capital is summarised in Table 12.1.

Table 12.1. Net vs. Gross Working Capital

Net Working Capital	Gross Working Capital
Net Working Capital = Current Assets minus Current Liabilities	Gross Working Capital = Total Current Assets only
Increase in bank loans cannot increase net working capital, retained profit, sale of fixed assets will increases net working capital.	Every increase in borrowing will increase the gross working capital. Under net concept, no change in working capital.
Net concept suitable for sole trader and partnership, where ownership, management and control are united	Gross concept is suitable for companies where we have separation of ownership from management. Managers are uninterested in the ownership of current or fixed assets.
Net concept gives qualitative information about the company finances indicating its net liquidity. Long usage sanctions this concept.	Gross concept gives only quantitative information about the company finances – total circulating assets.
It is a concept very popular in accounting system.	It is a concept very popular in financial management circles.
It can point out the true financial position of a company even though both have the identical total capital	*It cannot reveal the true financial position of a company.*

	A Ltd.	B Ltd.		A Ltd.	B Ltd.
	₹	₹		₹	₹
Share Capital	20L	20L	Share capital	20L	20L
Reserves	20L	20L	Reserves	20L	20L
Loans	10L	10L	Loans	10L	10L
	50L	50L		50L	50L
Net Working Capital =	30L	10L	Gross Working Capital	50L	50L
A Ltd., is better than B Ltd., as it has larger net working capital			Both have identical gross working capital		

The Paradigm Shift in Working Capital		
	The Old	**The New**
Bank Finance	• Maximum Permissible Bank Finance • Rigid Receivables Norms • Loan and Cash Credit Component • Fixed Prime Lending Rates	• Current-ratio Financing • Cash-flow Financing. Flexible Norms • Increasing Loan Component • Variable Prime Lending Rates • Short-term Foreign Current Loans
Non-bank Finance (short-term)	• Trade Credit • Bill Discounting • Inter-corporate Deposits • Public Deposits • Commercial Paper	• Trade Credit • Bill Discounting • Inter-corporate Deposits • Public Deposits • Commercial Paper • Euro-commercial Paper • Factoring
Non-bank Finance (long-term)	• Non-convertible Debentures • Equity	• Non-convertible Debentures • Equity • Floating Rate Notes • Note Issuance Facility • Revolving Underwriting Facility • Dutch Auction Notes

Total Working Capital

Total working capital has two components – physical working capital (defined above) and financial working capital. Financial working capital includes cash in hand and at bank and net amount receivable (i.e., difference of amount receivable and payable) at the end of the accounting year. However, fixed deposits, for more than one year are not to be included in cash in hand and at bank. Long/medium-term borrowings taken for purchase of fixed assets are not to be included in the amount payable.

Productive Capital

Productive capital is the sum of fixed capital and total working capital.

Objectives of Working Capital

An essential precondition for a successful financial management is the establishment of sound and consistent asset management policies, covering fixed as well as current assets. An effective utilisation of working capital results in the maximisation of productivity and profits. Profitability and solvency are the twin objectives of working capital management; and these can be achieved by striving to maintain a correct ratio betweenh working and fixed capital. Such ratio will ensure a smooth and rapid flow of funds and enhance the efficiency and profitability of the enterprise. A proper management of working capital synchronises the cash receipts and cash outlay, and a unit may function with a minimum cash reserve.

The success of a small-scale industry depends on the availability of adequate working capital, which ensures the purchase of raw materials at competitive prices and payment for labour.

The Time Span

The two concepts of gross working capital and net working capital point to two distinct but interwoven sets of activity, namely, short-term and long-term financial operations respectively. The management of current assets involves short-term, financial consideration, whereas the management of networking capital covers an extended time span, i.e., long-term financial considerations.

To obtain working capital, entrepreneurs should approach one of the commercial banks (State Bank of India or any of its subsidiaries, other nationalised banks, private sector banks, etc.)

Banks provide credit facilities to meet working capital requirements to facilitate production as per the manufacturing needs of the industrial unit.

Broadly speaking, working capital facilities could be classified as:

(i) Lock and key pledge of stocks;

(ii) Factory/mundy type/hypothecation advances (pending statement on stocks held by the unit to be intimated to the bank);

(iii) Advances against stock-in-process;

(iv) Advances against bills (when finished goods are supplied on credit);

(v) Clean advances (contingent needs); and

(vi) Packing credit to exporters to execute export orders.

As already stated earlier, banks provide both term-loan and working capital together in composite loans and also give small loans. Some entrepreneurs also depend on friends, relatives and other sources for their increasing requirements of working capital.

In order to get a loan from a commercial bank, the entrepreneur has to fill in an application form as per the specimen provided by the financial institutions, including banks and submit it to the bank along with the following documents:

(i) Authentic copies of Balance Sheets and Profit and Loss Accounts (if the industrial concern is a limited company or an industrial cooperative society);

(ii) A statement of assets and liabilities in the prescribed form in the case of partnership and proprietary concerns;

(iii) Proforma statements in all other cases;

(iv) Copies of the affidavit in regard to the size of the unit; and

(v) Technical feasibility report from the Small Industries Service Institute, the Director of Industries, if obtained, may also be enclosed.

The total cost of the SSI project is computed as under:

(i) The cost of fixed assets proposed to be acquired;

(ii) Total working capital requirements (for the first year of production); and

(iii) Preliminary and preoperative expenses. Provision should be made for escalation of costs.

The following are the sources for meeting the above cost of the project:

(i) Your own capital, seed capital assistance from State Government/Development Corporations;

(ii) Loans/deposits from your friends and relatives, which can be held for long periods, say, three years;

(iii) Medium-term loans (for fixed assets) from the banks/term-lending institutions;

(iv) Working capital loan from the bank;

(v) Credit on purchases; and

(vi) IDBI bill discounting for purchase of machinery on deferred payment guarantee.

Profitability estimates may be worked out using the format of the bank. The schedule of repayment proposed to be adopted should be based on the profit accounts. Cost over-run and time over-run are common in most SSI units. Careful planning must be done to overcome them so that the bank can process as the working capital loan pragmatically.

The Working Capital Cycle

The operating cycle begins with the arrival of the stock, and ends when the cash is received.

The cash cycle begins when cash is paid for materials, and ends when cash is collected from receivables.

It has been rightly stressed that small-scale enterprises will have to learn to manage with a lower level of current assets to be globally competitive. Efficient working capital management techniques are those that compress the operating cycle. The length of the operating cycle is equal to the sum of the lengths of the inventory period and the receivables period. Besides, innovative financial instruments can also be deployed to churn over the current asset portfolio with greater speed. The entrepreneur may resort to bill discounting, factoring, etc.

Both core and variable working capital are supported by a mix of spontaneous current liabilities (trade credit and provisions for taxation), short-term financing (bank finance and short-term marketable securities), and long-term financing (long-term debt and equity). Since trade credit and accruals for tax payments are determined by exogenous factors, the crucial aspect for any working capital financing strategy is determining the proportion of current assets that is to be funded by short-term sources of finance.

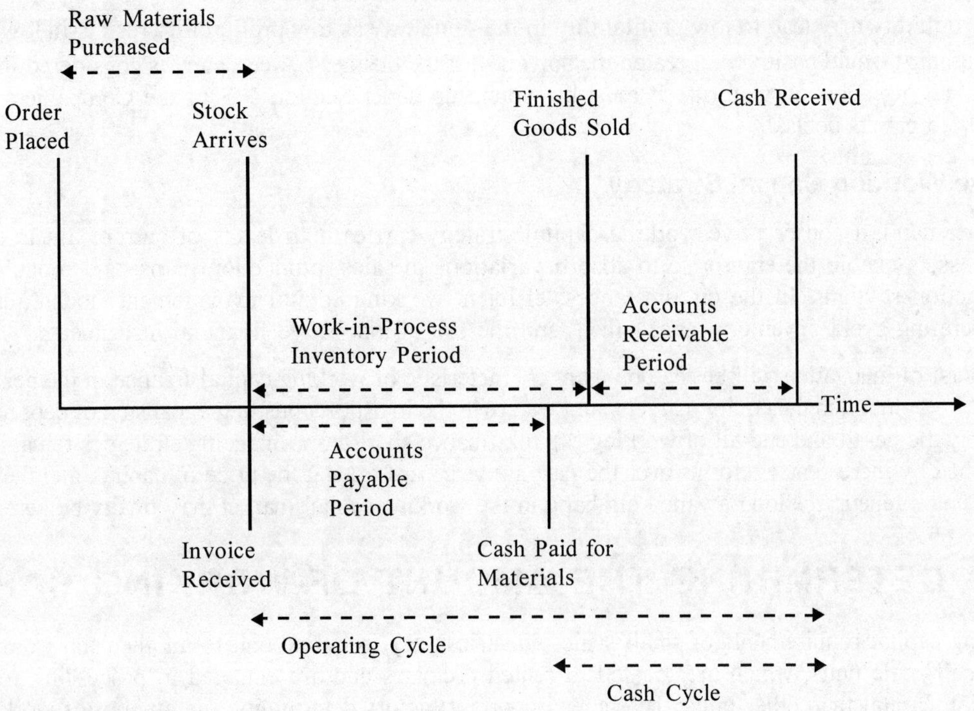

Adequacy of Working Capital

Working capital should be adequate for the following reasons:

(i) It protects a business from the adverse effects of shrinkage in the values of current assets.

(ii) It is possible to pay all the current obligations promptly and to take advantage of cash discounts.

(iii) It ensures to a greater extent the maintenance of a company's credit standing and provides for such emergencies as strikes, floods, fires, etc.

(iv) It permits the carrying of inventories at a level that would enable a business to serve satisfactory needs of its customers.

(v) It enables a company to extend favourable credit terms to customers.

(vi) It enables a company to operate its business more efficiently because there is no delay in obtaining materials, etc., because of credit difficulties.

(vii) It enables a business to withstand periods of depression smoothly.

(viii) There may be operating losses or decreased retained earnings.

(ix) There may be excessive non-operating of extraordinary losses.

(x) The management may fail to obtain funds from other sources for purposes of expansion.

(xi) There may be an unwise dividend policy.

(xii) Current funds may be invested in non-current assets.

(xiii) The management may fail to accumulate funds necessary for meeting debentures on maturity.

(xiv) There may be increasing price necessitating bigger investments in inventories and fixed assets.

When working capital is inadequate, a company faces the following problems:

(i) It is not possible for it to utilise production facilities fully for want of working capital.

(ii) A company may not be able to take advantage of cash discount facilities.

(iii) The creditworthiness of the company is likely to be jeopardised because of lack of liquidity.
(iv) A company may not be able to take advantage of profitable business opportunities.
(v) The modernisation of equipments and even routine repairs and maintenance facilities may be difficult to administer.
(vi) A company will not be able to pay its dividends because of the non-availability of funds.
(vii) A company cannot afford to increase its cash sales and may have to restrict its activities to credit sales only.
(viii) A company may have to borrow funds at exorbitant rates of interest.
(ix) Its low liquidity may lead to low profitability in the same way as low profitability results in low liquidity.
(x) Low liquidity would positively threaten the solvency of the business. A company is considered illiquid when it is not able to pay its debts on maturity. It must be wound up under Section 433 of the Companies Act, 1956, upon its inability to pay its debts.

An Aggressive Working Capital Strategy

On the other hand, a conservative working capital strategy carries high levels of current assets in relation to sales. Surplus current assets enable the enterprise to absorb variations in sales, production plans, and procurement time without disrupting production rhythms. In the circumstances, efficient working capital management techniques are those which compress the operating cycle, inventory management and the use of innovative financial instruments.

A frantic burst of innovation will be the dominant characteristic of working capital finance in the next millennium. There has already been a revolution in the equity markets, and we are in the midst of a bustling expansion of debt markets. Yet, as bank finance was simply the be-all and end-all of working capital, finance short-term, financing strategies remained static. No longer the forces unleashed by incremental reforms over the past six years are freeing the price of capital, and the interlocking money markets. For the entrepreneur, the long-awaited big bang in the working capital market may finally be here.

FACTORS DETERMINING THE AMOUNT OF WORKING CAPITAL

The working capital requirements of small-scale industries vary from one unit to another and from one type of unit to another type. Small-scale units, which are located in rented premises and are engaged in processing works, need a larger amount of working capital than other units. The other important factors determining the amount of working capital are:

(i) Size of the Small-scale Unit: The amount of working capital depends directly upon the volume of business. The bigger the size of a unit, the larger the amount of the working capital and *vice versa.*

(ii) Process of Production: Simple short-period processes of production require a smaller amount of working capital and *vice versa.*

(iii) Proportion of Raw Materials to Total Cost: The price of raw materials and the quantity required determine the amount of working capital.

(iv) Terms of Purchase and Sales: The amount of working capital varies directly with the use of credit and *vice versa.*

(v) Turnover of Inventories: If inventories are large and their turnover is slow, a small-scale industry will need a bigger amount of working capital. If they are small and their turnover is quick, the unit will require a smaller amount of working capital.

(vi) Importance of Labour: Small-scale and cottage industries are labour-intensive units and therefore require a larger amount of working capital.

(vii) Cash Requirements: The amount of working capital required varies directly with the cash requirement of a unit.

(viii) Seasonal Variations: Seasonal small-scale industries require a large amount of working capital during the season in which the scale of operations is higher.

(ix) Banking Facilities: If a small-scale unit has a good banking connection, it may have minimum margin of regular working capital over current liabilities.

(x) Growth and Expansion: The requirement of working capital varies directly in proportion to the growth and expansion of a small-scale unit.

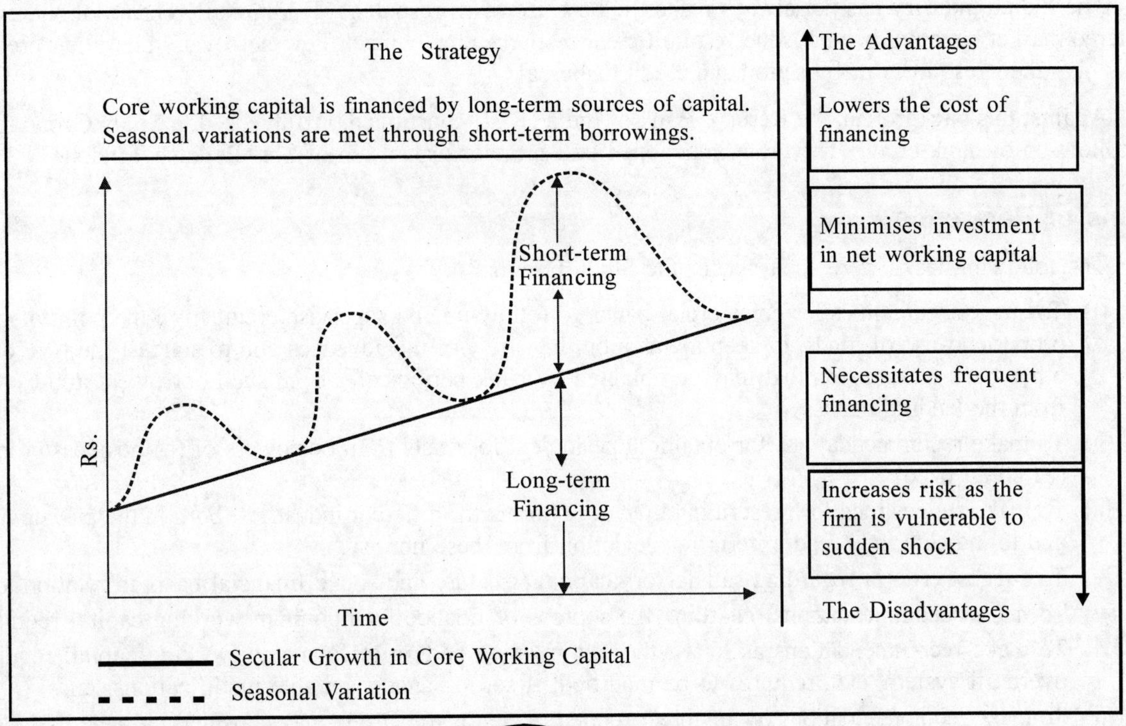

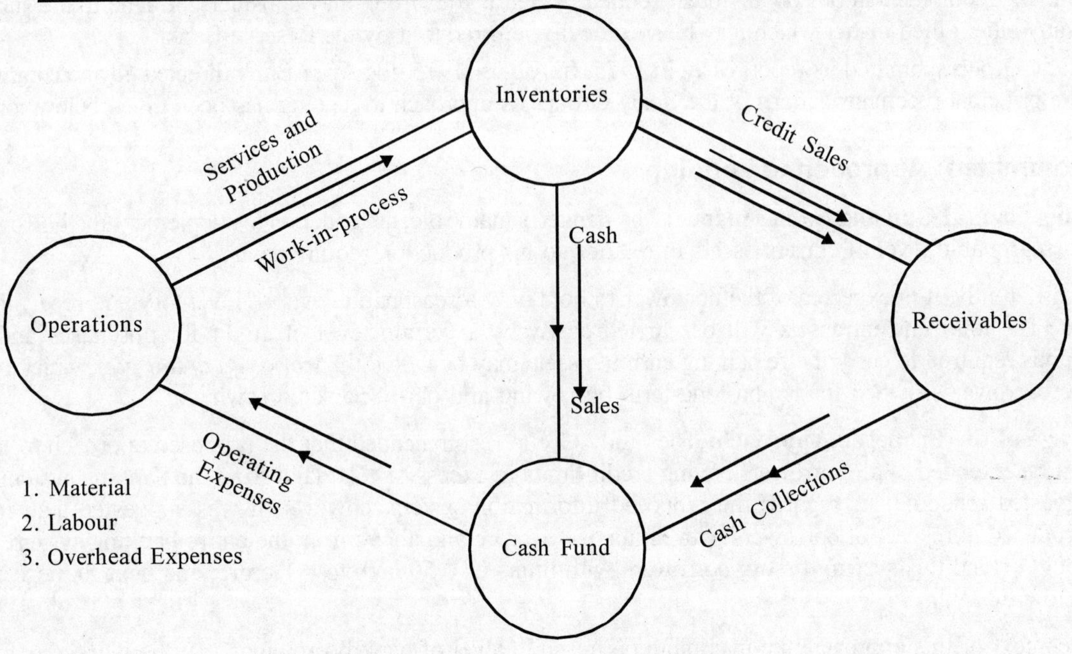

Fig. 12.2 Flow of Gross Working Capital

WORKING CAPITAL FINANCE AND THE TANDON COMMITTEE UNIFORM-RECOMMENDATIONS

Following the nationalisation of major commercial banks, the banking system was asked to adopt a new approach as a credit agency, based on development and on potential rather than on security only, to assist the weaker sections of society and later on, to lend to the public sector also. While assistance to the new credit users has gone up substantially since nationalisation, the bulk of bank credit continues to go to the organised industry, although its share as a percentage of the total credit has diminished.

The Indian industry has not always made the best use of its resources. Traditionally cheap labour, cheap money and a sheltered market have not been conducive to efficient resource employment. Few borrowers plan their credit needs; and few banks plan their resources mobilisation and credit disbursal.

Against this background, the Reserve Bank of India (RBI) constituted, in July 1974, a Study Group to frame guidelines for follow-up of bank credit. The group functioned under the chairmanship of Shri Prakash Tandon.

Terms of Reference

The following tasks were spelt out for the Study Group:

(i) To suggest guidelines for commercial banks to follow-up and supervise credit from the point of view of ensuring a proper end-use of funds, to keep a watch on the safety of the advances and to suggest the type of operational data other trans information that may be obtained by bank periodically from such borrowers and by the Reserve Bank from the lending banks:

(ii) To make recommendations for obtaining periodical forecasts from borrowers of (a) business/production plans, and (b) credit need;

(iii) To make suggestions for prescribing inventory norms for different industries, both in the private and public sectors, and to indicate the broad criteria for deviation from these norms;

(iv) To suggest criteria regarding satisfactory capital structure and sound financial basis in relation to borrowings;

(v) To make recommendations regarding the sources of finance for minimum working capital requirements;

(vi) To make recommendations as to whether the existing pattern of financing working capital requirements by cash/overdraft system, etc., requires to be modified; if so, to suggest suitable modifications; and

(vii) To make recommendations on any other related matter as the Group may consider germane to the subject of enquiry or any other allied matter which may be specifically referred to it by the Reserve Bank.

The Study Group submitted its report early in 1975. In August 1975, the Apex Bank directed all the commercial banks to implement the principal recommendations of the Study Group. Its approach to lending has been given below for a fuller study.

Tandon Committee: Approach to Lending

Working Capital Gap and Bank Finance: The banker's main role, as lender, is to supplement the borrower's resources in carrying a reasonable level of current assets in relation to his production requirements.

Stated differently, it is expected of the borrower to hold only a reasonable level of inventory and receivables, according to the norms. The total current assets will be carried partly by a certain level of credit for purchases and other current liabilities. Funds required to carry the remaining current assets may be called the *working capital gap,* which may be bridged partly by the borrower's owned funds and long-term borrowing and partly bank borrowings.

Coverage of the Proposed Approach: The Study Group recommended that the proposed approach to lending and the style of credit be extended to all borrowers having credit limits in excess of ₹ 10 lakh from the banking system in accordance with the suggested schedule. As regards the proposed information system, however, it was suggested that, to start with, it might be introduced in respect of borrowers with limits of ₹ 1 crore and above from the entire banking system. Progressively, the bank should extend this system, first to borrowers with limits of ₹ 50 lakh to ₹ 1 crore, and next to those enjoying limits of ₹ 10 lakh to ₹ 50 lakh.

In the context of this approach, the maximum permissible level of bank borrowings may be worked out in three ways:

(i) The bank may workout the working capital gap, i.e., total current assets *less* current liabilities other than bank borrowings, and finance a maximum of 75 per cent of gap: the balance should come out of long-term funds, i.e., owned funds and term borrowings;

(ii) The borrower should provide for a minimum of 25 per cent of the total current assets out of long-term funds, i.e., owned funds *plus* term borrowings. A certain level of credit for purchases and other current liabilities will be available, and the bank will provide the balance. The total current liabilities, inclusive of bank borrowings, should not exceed 75 per cent of the current assets; and

(iii) Same as in (ii) above, but excluding the core current assets from the total current assets on the theory that the core current assets should be financed out of long-term funds, i.e., owned funds *plus* term borrowing.

These three alternatives may be illustrated by taking the following example of a borrower's financial position, projected as at the end of the next year.

The existing net working capital (i.e., excess of current assets over current liabilities) exceeds 25 per cent of the working capital gap (in the First Method) or 25 per cent of the total current assets/real current assets (in the Second and Third Methods), the contribution of long-term sources should ordinarily be to the extent of the already existing net working capital.

The first method would mean that the banker financing up to a maximum of 75 per cent of the working capital gap of 220, i.e., 165 and the borrower providing at least 55 out of his long-term funds, i.e., owned funds *plus* long-term borrowings. This method will give a minimum current ratio of 1:1.

The second method would mean that the borrower would finance a minimum of 25 per cent of total current assets (92) through long-term funds and the gap, i.e., the maximum of 128 (278-150) would be provided by the bank. This will give a current ratio of at least 1.3:1.

Current Liabilities		**Current Assets**	
Creditors for purchases	100	Raw materials	200
Other current liabilities	50	Stocks-in-process	20
	150	Finished goods	90
Bank borrowings, including bills discounted with bankers	200	Receivables including bills discounted with bankers	50
		Other current assets	10
	350		370

* As per suggested norms or past practice, whichever is lower, in relation to projected production for the next year.

1st Method		**2nd Method**		**3rd Method**	
Total current assets	370	Total current assets	370	Total current assets	370
Less: current liabilities other than bank borrowings	150	25% of above from long-term sources	92	*Less:* Core current assets (illustrative figure) from long-term sources	95
Working capital gap	220		278	Real current assets	275
25% of above from long-term sources	55	*Less:* current liabilities other than bank borrowings	150	25% of above from long-term sources	69
Maximum bank borrowings permissible	165		128		206
		Working capital gap	220	Less: current liabilities other than bank borrowings	150
		Maximum bank borrowings permissible	128		56
				Working capital gap	220
				Maximum bank borrowings permissible	56
Excess borrowing	35	Excess borrowing	72	Excess borrowing	144
Current ratio	1.17:1	Current ratio	1.33:1	Current ratio	2.79:1

The third method would mean a further reduction in bank borrowing and the strengthening of the current ratio.

It is important to note that, in computing the level of bank finance, the classification of current assets and current liabilities should be made in terms of the usually accepted approach of the banker and not in terms of the definitions in the Companies Act. For instance, the instalments of term loans payable within 12 months from the date of the balance sheet are classified by the banker as current liabilities, while they are not so in the balance sheet prepared in accordance with the requirements of the Companies Act. These differences in classification have been brought out in the form for the analysis of the balance sheet prescribed by the Reserve Bank under its Credit Authorisation Scheme.

The third method is ideal, for it provides the largest multiplier of bank finance: the next best method from this point of view is the second one. However, to avoid hardship to borrowers, a beginning should be made with the first method before moving on to the next two methods. It is necessary, though, to have a time-bound programme. Banks should initiate immediate action to place all borrowers, say, those having credit limits in excess of ₹ 10 lakh from the banking system, on the first method, beginning with the borrowers with a weak financial position, as early as possible, say, within a period of about one year. At that stage, the Reserve Bank may review the system and chalk out a further programme for a switchover to the second and third methods, in stages, in the light of the circumstances then prevailing.

Implementation

As regards the proposed programme of change, the chairmen of banks were actually in favour of the banks, straightaway switching over to the second method for the reason that some of the borrowers already fulfil the requirements of the first method. Although most of them accepted the concept underlying the third method, they pointed out that much ground work would be necessary to workout the core current assets for various industries which would require detailed studies before the method could be accepted and used.

Lending up to 75 per cent of the working capital gap as in the first method is liberal, and this should be considered as the upper limit. The limit of 75 per cent has been suggested as the first step in order to facilitate the financial structuring of new companies, the setting up of projects in backward areas and for flexibility in the restructuring of existing companies with a weak financial base. As mentioned earlier, banks starting with the first method, should gradually reach the ideal of the third. It should be understood that the aim should be to move forward and that the borrowers who already fall in the third or the second category should not increase their dependence on bank borrowings and revert to the second or first category respectively. In other words, their existing current ratio should not be impaired. Also, if the credit needs of such borrowers increase in future they should be allowed to slip back from a higher to a lower category.

ALIGNING CREDIT WITH PRIORITY INDUSTRIES

The concept of bank forming only a position of the working capital gap could also be used as an instrument for influencing the directional flow of credit. It should be possible for the concerned authorities to define, from time-to-time, the order of priorities in the economy for different industries. Monetary authorities should lay down different scales of financing as a percentage of the working capital gap for different scales of financing as a percentage of the working capital gap for different classes of industries as an important instrument of economic policy, for aligning credit with the priorities for industries. The relevant percentage may be comparatively low for low-priority industries. Also, when a manufacturer has reached a stable level of production for a reasonable number of years, there is no reason why bank finance should continue to be made available to him on the same scale, because, if a portion of the finance earlier made available is withdrawn from him, such funds would be available for the promotion of new economic activity. A part of the working capital bank finance should, therefore, be considered as assistance only for a limited period, in the same manner as term loans for initial investment.

Funded Debt-equity Relationship

The question arises whether there should be a reasonable relationship between the equity and total term loans (i.e., those from the financial institutions and banks). Term lending institutions insist upon a certain relationship between funded debt and equity according to certain accepted norms, and see to it that long-term funds are adequate enough to provide for a margin for working capital purposes. No change is suggested in this practice. However, in future, while funding new projects, these institutions may provide for margins on the basis as suggested here. It will be useful if the bank which finances working capital requirements is associated at this stage in determining working capital and margin requirements. If this is done, there will be no need to deviate from the standard of relationship between funded debt and equity – a procedure which term lending institutions normally follow.

In the case of old units, it may be necessary to transfer, as mentioned earlier, a part of the present cash credit borrowing to a term loan repayable over a period in order to bring financing in line with the proposals suggested here. In some of these cases, the funded debt and equity relationship may not immediately conform to the normals laid down by term lending institutions, and borrowers may have to be given time to bring the position to normal over a period. The banks will, however, have to ensure that, in such cases, the total outside liabilities to owned funds relationship is acceptable to them.

Additional Requirement of Credit

Another question to be considered is how to take care of a request for additional credit from a borrower who already has an excess borrowing under any of the methods outlined above. Such a need for additional credit normally arises with an increase in production activity. If additional fund needs are on a regular basis, the borrower should bring and ensure similar contributions required under the relevant method of lending. He may do this from retained earnings or by raising additional equity or by issuing debentures or by bringing in more funds in any other suitable manner for the purpose. In very exceptional cases, when the borrower is not able to raise the requisite funds immediately in the aforesaid manner, banks may consider giving a term loan to a reasonable extent, provided that the cash generation capacity of the borrower is sufficiently good to take care of the amortisation of the existing term obligations as already stipulated and also the proposed additional loan within a short period acceptable to the bank. When, however, the additional fund need is for a short duration (e.g., for executing a large export order or a government contract) and cannot be met from the existing credit arrangement, it should be possible to consider additional credit for such a need without necessarily insisting on the similar contribution already mentioned to enable the borrower to complete the specific transactions/contracts on the clear understanding that he would return to the stage in the relevant method of lending within the stipulated period.

Apart from excess borrowing under any of the methods of lending, there may be excess borrowing representing the excess of inventory and receivables *vis-a-vis* the relative norms. In such cases, it should not be granted until such time as the current assets levels are brought down to the required levels. The grant of additional facilities on a purely temporary basis, however, may be considered but only as an exception, say, for the purpose of executing an export order.

Proposed Style of Credit

Once the quantum of bank funds to finance a reasonable level of current assets is agreed to, the style of extending bank credit should be changed.

The drawbacks of the cash credit system of lending are well known, but may be reiterated here:

(i) A bank has no control over the level of advances in cash credit accounts. No notice is required for drawing under limits that may remain unutilised for long periods.

(ii) A bank is thus in no position to foresee demand for credit. This hampers its credit planning.

(iii) The cost of the operation of the system to the banker, on account of attendant uncertainties, is high because, whatever chances he may take in *overselling* credit, there will always be a limit to how far he will *oversell*. And this was indeed what happened in the 1973-74 *credit crisis* when some banks found themselves heavily *over sold.*

It has been found in practice that the level of borrowing by industrial units during the course of a year fluctuates from month-to-month, depending on the scheduling of purchases of raw materials and the despatch of finished goods. It has also been observed that the outstanding in a cash credit account, particularly in non-seasonal industries, do not fall below a certain level which represents the stable fund requirements during the year. The Tandon Committee suggests that, instead of making available the entire credit limit as a cash credit for a year, it may be bifurcated into a loan and a demand cash credit, which should be reviewed annually.

The loan component should be the minimum level of borrowing which the borrower expects to use throughout the year, while the cash credit part would take care of his fluctuating requirements. As the loan carries interest throughout the year, it will induce a discipline in the customer to plan his needs carefully to ensure that as little of it as possible lies idle – ideally none.

Non-seasonal industries as well as most agro-based industries with some degree of seasonality can conform to the suggested system without difficulty. In industries which have a very high degree of seasonality, the assessment of bank finance, i.e., the overall credit limit, may have to be made on the basis of monthly cash budgets, as is being done at present for the sugar industry by certain banks, and thereafter drawings may be regulated by updated monthly cash budgets.

As the intention of introducing the new concept is to bring in a discipline in the system, the demand cash credit should be charged a slightly higher rate of interest than the loan component. This approach will give the borrower an incentive for good planning. Cash credit, in any case, involves additional cost and uncertainty to the banker; and therefore, a slightly higher rate is not a penalty. The term loan representing excess borrowing, to be amortised, as mentioned earlier, should also be at a slightly higher rate than the cash credit rate.

Information System

In order to ensure that customers do not use the new cash credit facility in an unplanned manner and credit the same problems as were faced under the old system, the Committee recommends that the financing should be placed on a quarterly budgeting reporting system for operational proceeds.

Bill Finance

There is an advantage in shortening the transaction cycle. A movement towards a cash and carry system should be considered. It may be mentioned that this system is already being followed. However, a further detailed study of its implications may be necessary. While this may therefore be the direction of change, it may sometimes be necessary for manufacturing units to extend credit to maintain sales. In such cases, apart from loan and demand cash credit, a part of the total credit requirement, within the overall eligibility, may be provided by way of bill limits to finance receivables. It is desirable that, as far as possible, receivables should be financed by way of bills rather than by cash credit against book debts, though the latter cannot be altogether eliminated, particularly when the period of credit is short and the amount is small. These bills may be on a demand basis or on a usance basis, depending on the marketing practice in the industry. Some of the advantages of a bill arising out of the sale of goods over the cash credit against book debts are:

(i) The transaction is easily identifiable;

(ii) There is a definite date of repayment;

(iii) The bill will carry more than one signature if it is on a usance basis;

(iv) It represents an easily shiftable asset; and

(v) When goods are sold on credit to a wholesaler instead of to a user-industry, bank finance for the transaction would in effect be credit for trading purposes; in such cases, bank finance by way of bill discounts would make for improvement in the quality of statistics in regard to the financing of trade. From the standpoint of monetary policy, such an arrangement would lend itself to better control.

The committee is of the view that, to the extent feasible, the banking system should move towards financing the purchases, who is in fact the debtor, rather than the seller, who is the creditor. In other words, the seller should be paid-off immediately after the sale, and bank credit may be extended only to the purchaser. As regards the financing of the purchaser, however, there are two different points of view. One view is that purchases should, as far as possible, be on the basis of bills, for the following reasons:

(i) The amount should be drawn only at the time of actual need. The end-use of credit is automatically taken care of;

(ii) Credit to the purchaser is directly related to his actual need, which is not the case with the seller's bills, where credit is extended as a measure of sales promotion, irrespective of the purchaser's ability to pay or his need for credit; and

(iii) A bill imposes discipline in resect of payments for purchases – it ensures timely payment to suppliers, which a system of book entries does not always ensure.

It has been argued on the other side that, under the revised system, the cash credit mode of financing is superior to bill financing in respect of the borrower's purchase operations for the following reasons:

(i) Drawals for non-approved purposes will be detected by the new information system proposed and by a scrutiny of cheques, the end-use of credit will be effectively taken care of by the proposed information system;

(ii) The cost of operations to the borrower and the banker will be higher: the borrower will have to pay more for the cost of stamp duty, while the banker's administrative cost will go up because of additional paperwork without the assistance of mechanisation or computerisation;

(iii) The advantages of centralised borrowing by way of a close watch over aggregate outstandings, debit and credit summations and borrowing trends would be lost.

(iv) In view of the foregoing, without attempting a definitive view on the subject, the Tandon Committee suggested that each bank might take its own decision, in consultation with the borrower, considering the size of his operations, the individual transactions and the administrative set-up in the bank.

The Mechanics of Lending

The mechanics of lending in the framework should be as under:

(i) Since the banker should be concerned with the borrower's tool operations and not merely inventories or receivables, an examination of the borrower's operational plan for the next year assumes special significance. It is in the customer's own interest to plan his operations, if he is to be assured by the banker of adequate credit to meet his genuine production needs;

(ii) Financial analysis should cover an examination of the borrower's past and current financial position, profitability, production operations for the next year and projected financial position at the end of the next year;

The borrower should, therefore, furnish an operating statement and a funds flow statement for the whole year, (i.e., the next year) and also a projected balance sheet at the end of the next year, along with an application for advance or renewal. Any assumptions underlying the statements should be explained to and examined by the banker;

(iii) The current asset position should be examined to ensure conformity with inventory and receivable norms in relation to the projected production;

(iv) The working capital gap should be computed, the extent of bank finance will be arrived at and the overall credit limit should be fixed on the basis indicated earlier; the fixation of a total limit is necessary for purposes of the registration of the charge with the Registrar of Companies, credit authorisation from the Reserve Bank documentation, etc.

In settling the quantum of bank finance, the operating funds flow and projected financial statements provided by the customer may have to be amended.

This would lead to an understanding between the banker and the customer on the financial needs arising from the next year's operations, covering both long-term and short-term finance, as well as the projected disposition of the resources generated.

(v) In respect of existing advances, excess finance over and above the permissible level should be identified and placed on a repayment basis, to be adjusted over a period of time, taking into account the customer's cash accruals and obligations and his capacity to raise additional equity;

(vi) The agreed quantum of bank finance will be made available in separate accounts; the minimum fund requirements during the year by way of a fixed loan for 12 months and the balance, by way of cash credit and/or bills;

(vii) There should be no rigidity but flexibility in the matter of the bifurcation of the limit between loan and cash credit, guided by the customer's past plans, how they compared with the actual pattern of drawings and the expectation for the next year. For purposes of credit authorisation from the Reserve Bank, the banker should apply only for the total limit and not for the two limits separately;

(viii) Quarterly, budget and performance data should be furnished in the prescribed forms. The quarterly operating statement and funds flow statement should constitute a segment of the annual plan submitted earlier, and the banker should see to it that the quarterly plan is more or less in line with earlier expectations. Fund needs, no directly linked to production needs – such as for investments in or loans to subsidiary firms or other companies, etc., – should be evident from the quarterly funds flow statement, and the banker should take a stand on what is not permissible;

(ix) Actual drawings within the sanctioned limit should be determined by the customer's inflow and outflow of funds as reflected in the quarterly funds flow statement. The deficit in cash during the quarter should be the level of additional demand cash credit bank borrowings required in the quarter. The permissible level of drawings in any quarter within the sanctioned limit should be the level at the end of the previous quarter, plus or minus the deficit or surplus shown in the funds flow statement. It must be borne in mind that the peak requirement within the quarter may conceivably be greater than is shown in the funds flow statement, which should only show the movement of funds between the two dates. If so, the borrower should specifically indicate his peak requirement to the banker.

(x) Within the overall permissible level of drawing, the day-to-day operations in the account should be regulated on the basis of drawing power (subject to the margins stipulated by the banker against the different components of inventory and receivables) on the basis of monthly stock statements, which should continue to be submitted. The drawing power remaining after providing for the fixed loan – vide item (vi) above and excess finance, if any, placed on repayment basis – vide item (v) above – will be the drawing power available for the demand cash credit account/ bill on account of purchases; and

(xi) No budget or plan, however carefully compiled, would always be correct. Variances are bound to arise. It is therefore suggested that there should be flexibility in permitting drawings. Variance to the extent of say, $\pm$ 10 per cent should be permissible. Beyond this, the banker and customer should discuss the reasons for the variance.

The system suggested here is only an aid to a better understanding of the customer's acceptable requirements. There would still be need for the banker's judgement.

It may be stated that the Study Group views its recommendations regarding inventory/receivable norms and the mechanics of lending as a package; it is an integrated scheme, and the borrower is expected to subject himself to the entire discipline envisaged by it.

NORMS FOR INVENTORY AND RECEIVABLES

For an efficient management of assets, the Tandon Committee suggested norms for raw materials, stock-in-process, finished goods and receivables. These norms represent the maximum levels of holding inventory and receivables in each industry.

Coverage: These norms are made applicable to all industrial borrowers, including small-scale industries, with aggregate limits from the banking system in excess of ₹ 10 lakh and extended progressively to small borrowers.

Objective: The norms for the four kinds of current assets are related to consumption/cost of production/cost of sales respectively. If the carryover of any one kind of asset is higher than the relative norm level, the surplus is treated as 'excess' carryover to be shed off, failing which an amount equivalent to the value thereof would be treated as excess borrowing; and a levy of penal rate of interest is suggested on such excess borrowing. Again, such excess holding cannot be set off against any shortfall in the holding of other assets, for the norms represent the maximum permissible levels of holding; and they are not *entitlements*. Lending banks are expected to scrutinise the periodical stock and receivable statements to determine whether the borrowers comply with the aforesaid stipulation.

Experience shows that while norms are reckoned in sanctioning credit limits, these are not uniformly complied with subsequently through the medium of monthly stock statements. Although both Tandon Committee and the Reserve Bank of India had hoped, while introducing the report, that excess current asset holding would be adjusted in two months, this has not happened. In fact, the Reserve Bank itself has had to adopt a flexible approach by permitting, *inter se*, raising of norm levels and adjustments of these levels of different assets.

Given the manufacturing cycle of a borrower, starting with raw materials to stocks-in-process, and further to finished goods, it is only logical to think of a combined norm for all the three items in relation to the value of output. A lending bank ought to scrutinise the levels of each kind of current assets in the ordinary course of its vigil on the borrower's operations but also to treat any of them as excess holding even as the overall level is considered reasonable and consistent with production is to make things unnecessarily complicated; and this serves no worthwhile purpose. The prime concern of the bank should be the holding of current assets in relation to turnover so that the total finance locked up may be reduced. Combined norms maybe developed for different industries from the Reserve Bank of India's studies on company finances. These may be revised from time-to-time to meet the objectives of national economic policies and/or bring them in tune with the policy approach to individual industry groupings. Thus, the suggested modification of laying down a combined norm for inventories in relation to the value of output, and receivables to sales as at present, would make things pragmatic, without jeopardising the interests of the lending bank and without hurrying any macro-economic objectives.

Management

Effective financial management is based on three factors: analysis of past performance; planning for further activities and control of current activity. Control is achieved by implementing decisions in accordance with the agreed plans. Accordingly, financial planning is of crucial importance in a small unit.

An effective working capital management calls for an understanding of cash requirements at varying stages of design, development, production and marketing. The overall efficiency of the working capital is judged by the annual results it produces.

A short-run financial management is built around two prime ingredients – profits and cash management. The objectives of cash planning are to indicate:

(i) What are the amounts of each needed to make a profit in short-time?

(ii) How much of cash requirements can be met out or the cash generated from current income?

(iii) What is the magnitude of the ebb and flow of cash emanating from operation, and what are the sizes and frequencies of the resulting cash surpluses and deficits?

(iv) What are the sources of cash (that is, borrowing) and under what conditions or in what context are they available?

Timely and rewarding short-term outlets will have to be found for surpluses, and appropriate external financing arrangements will have to be made for meeting deficits, to ensure that operations continue unhindered and planned profits are realised.

It is evident that if the advance signals thrown up by cash planning are constructively acted upon, most of the problems of cash surpluses and deficits would be resolved by suitable and marginal readjustment in internal operations, without affecting the short-run profit goals.

Scientific Approach to Working Capital

A scientific approach to working capital involves a study of the factors which affect the need for working capital – the terms offered by suppliers, the terms offered to customers, the average period of lead time for various inventory items, the seasonal fluctuations in sales, the production cycle, the level of stock and other influencing factors. These factors may be used to relate the balance sheet items to sales volumes. The relationship yield measures which may serve among other things, as tools for the prediction of future working capital needs.

For a scientific study of the working capital problem, a mathematical model may be developed to state the important quantitative relationships among different variables. In order to construct such a model, it is necessary to make an objective study of the situation. In the case of working capital, the relevant factors which should be studied are the relationships that exist between the amounts of current assets and current liabilities, and the volume of sales.

In developing the model, the first step is to analyse the relevant factors of a company's situation. This involves an examination of the records, a study of actual procedures and consultation with company officials.

The suggested method of forecasting working capital need is an improvement on the methods which are currently employed by companies. The use of the model would result in a more accurate forecast, allow for improvement through observation and experience, and act as a useful tool for the assessment of the size of the working capital.

The use of the working capital model is appropriate for many types of business. In companies which manufacture different types of products involving different materials or different processes, separate submodels may be constructed, and these may be combined in the final analysis. Where conditions are changing rapidly, the effects of the changes can be estimated objectively.

As long as the general pattern of the production and financial process does not change substantially, the model will hold good. When any change occurs, a re-study of the pertinent items would be sufficient.

The Suggested Norms are as Follows:

Suggested Norms for Inventory and Receivables

Industry	Raw Materials (including stores and other items used in the process of manufacture)	Stocks-in-process	Finished Goods	Receivables* and bills purchased and discounted
(1)	(2)	(3)	(4)	(5)
(i) Cotton and Synthetic Textiles	(i) Cotton 2 (Bombay and Ahmedabad areas) 2 (Eastern areas – Bihar, Orissa, West Bengal and Assam) 2 (Other raw materials)	¾ (Composite textile mills) ½ (other mills)	2¼	2¼

(ii) Man-made Fibre	(ii) 1½	½	1¾	1¾
(iii) Jute Textiles	(iii) 2½	¼	1 (for domestic sales) and 1½ (for exports)	1½
(iv) Rubber Products	(iv) 2	¼	-	1¾
(v) Fertilisers	(v) ¾ (Units near refinery)	Negligible	1(Where stock and in plant site)	1¼
(a) For nitrogenous plants	1½ (Units away from refinery)		1½ (Where stocks are also in upcountry centres)	
(b) For phosphatic plants	2 (Units in port areas) 3(Units away from port areas)	Negligible	1 (where stocks are in plant site) 1½ (where stocks are also in upcountry centres)	1¼
(vi) Pharmaceuticals	(vi) 2¾	½	2	1¼
(vii) Dyes and Dyestuffs	(vii) 2¼	1	¾	2¼
(viii) Basic Industrial Chemicals	(viii) 2¾	¼	1	1¾
(ix) Vegetable and hydrogenated oil	1	Negligible	¾	¾
(x) Paper	2-6 Bamboo and Wood (to be built-up in stages from November to May and thereafter to be brought down) 2¼ Chemicals	Negligible	1(for controlled sales) and ¾ (for free sales)	¾
(xi) Cement	2¼ Gypsum 1¼ Limestone ¾ Coal 1½ Packing material	½	1	1
(xii) Engineering Automobiles and ancillaries	2¼	¾	2½	2½
(xiii) Engineering Consumer Durables	2¼	¾	2½	2½
(xiv) Engineering Ancillaries (other than Automobile Ancillaries) and Component Suppliers	2	¾	2½	2½
(xv) Engineering machinery manufacturers and other Capital Equipment Suppliers (other than Heavy Engineering)**	2¾	1¼	3½	3½

Notes:

(i) Raw material are expressed as so many months' consumption. They include stores and other items used in the process of manufacture

(ii) (a) Stock-in-processes are expressed as so many months' cost of production.

(b) In individual cases, the bank may deviate from the norm for stocks-in-process if it is satisfied that the actual process time involved in any particular unit, say, in view of the nature of production, past experience and technology employed, is more than the suggested norm.

(iii) (a) Finished goods and receivables are expressed as so many months' cost of sales and sales respectively. These figures represent only the average levels. Individual items of finished goods and receivables may be for different periods, which may exceed the indicated norms so long as the overall average level of finished goods and receivables does not exceed the amounts as determined in terms of the norms.

*(b) the norm prescribed for receivables relates only to inland sales on short-term basis (i.e., excluding receivables arising out of deferred payment sales and exports).

(iv) Stocks of spares are not included for norms, since in financial terms they are not significant in many industries. Banks will ascertain the requirements of spares for individual units. They should, however, keep a watchful eye to ensure that spares do not exceed 5% of the total inventories.

**(v) Heavy engineering will include the supply of whole or substantial plants involving a long manufacturing period, i.e., sugar, cement, steel and textile plants.

(**Source:** Report of the Study Group, RBI, 1975, pp. 20-21.)

Illustration: ABC Industry

Established - 1969	
Manufacture of automobile spare parts and nuts and bolts	
Investment in Plant and Machinery	₹ 15 lakh
Bankers	Bank of Bombay
Capital	₹ 5 lakh
Reserves	₹ 3 lakh
Net worth	₹ 8 lakh

(₹ *in lakh*)

Current Liabilities		**Current Assets**	
Creditors for Purchases	55	Raw materials	120
Other Current Liabilities	25	Stocks-in-progress	20
	80	Receivables	30
Borrowing	120	Finished goods	40
(i) Long-term	50	Other current assets	10
(ii) Short-term	70		
	200		220

1st Method	
Total	220
Current Assets	
Less: Current liabilities other other than bank borrowings	80
Working Capital gap	140
25% of above from long-term sources	35
Maximum bank borrowings permissible	105
Excess Borrowings	15
Current ratio	1.19:1

2nd Method	
Total	220
Current Assets 25% of above from long-term sources	55
	165
Less: Current liabilities other than bank borrowings	80
Working Capital gap	85
	140
Maximum bank borrowings permissible	85
Excess Borrowings	35
Current ratio	1.33:1

3rd Method	
Total	220
Current Assets	
Less: Core current assets	55
	165
25% of above from long-term sources	41
	124
Less: Current liabilities	80
other than bank borrowings	44
Working capital gap	140
Maximum bank borrowings permissible	44
Excess Borrowings	96
Current ratio	2.12:1

In most cases, this type of working capital model can be developed easily. It would enable managers to forecast the level for each working capital item and ensure that the necessary resources are available. In addition, the model could establish working capital standards. A comparison of the actuals with the standards would provide a measure of efficiency of financial management.

It is evident that if the advance signals thrown up by cash planning are constructively acted upon, most of the problems of cash surpluses and deficits would be resolved by suitable and marginal readjustments in internal operations, without affecting the short-run profit goals.

TERM LOANS TO SMALL-SCALE INDUSTRIES

For several reasons, the somewhat comprehensive criteria which are applied to term-loan applications from medium and large-scale industries cannot be used in respect of term-loan proposals from small-scale industries. These industries find it difficult to secure adequate finance from institutional sources even for their working capital requirements because of their own inherent limitations on the one hand and generally high standards applied by the lending institutions to borrowers on the other. Organised credit institutions have generally been wary of lending to these industries because, in their eyes, they are generally not of much risk. By and large, small units have a low capital to turnover ratio, as a result of which the available block capital security is inadequate in relation to a given level of production; their markets are somewhat narrow, the prospects for business frequently uncertain, and their rate of mortality rather high. Banks, therefore, find it difficult to assess their creditworthiness. In these circumstances these industries deserve special treatment, because of their relatively high employment potential.

Difficulties in Procuring Institutional Finance: Small-scale industries are generally not regarded as sufficiently creditworthy because they are not able to satisfy the criteria laid down by lenders. The grant of medium- and long-term loans involves not only an assessment by the lending agency of the creditworthiness of the borrowers and the security offered by them, but also an observance of rules and regulations governing such advances. The financial position of a borrowing concern should be fairly sound and should show profit, or should have the prospect of improving its earning capacity, if financial assistance is granted; the equipment and technical processes employed in the production of goods and services should be efficient; the unit concerned should have an assured market or should produce items which are required by a big industry; and the borrowing concern should be owned by men of integrity and business standing. An assessment of the risk factor in advancing to small industries naturally poses a problem for the lender. Some of the more important difficulties are listed below:

(i) Some rigidity in the approach on the part of lending institutions in dealing with borrowers and the absence of a close association with them;

(ii) The complicated nature of the information required for the borrowers;

(iii) Strict requirements of security and a rigid prescription of acceptable collateral; and

(iv) Delay involved in the sanction of loans.

The institutions which normally respond to some extent to the needs of small-scale industries are the smaller banks, whose field of activity is restricted to a small area. These banks are often managed by local men who unlike the branch agents of big banks are able to develop informal relationships with the small industrialists. In view of their personal contact with customers, local banks are able to adopt a flexible attitude and expeditiously dispose of the applications for loans. However, the resources of these banks are limited; and unless bigger banks take a promotional view in the initial stages and extend the much-needed assistance to small industries, the latter would be forced to borrow from on institutional lenders, the disadvantages of which need no elaboration here. As a consequence, they would fail to raise their standard of operations, which alone can help them to develop and become creditworthy. On their part, the small industrialists should appreciate the fact that banks have to operate on business principles and cannot lower their lending standards to any appreciable extent in order to meet their financial needs. They should, therefore, makes earnest efforts to meet the requirements of lending institutions.

Application Forms: It is usual for some credit institutions to require an applicant for finance to fill in a very elaborate questionnaire. In this connection, it is suggested that, in the first instance, only such information may be obtained as would enable the lending institutions to judge whether a unit is creditworthy and the project for which finance is required is *prima facie* feasible. In other words, the information called for should be comprehensive enough, without being too detailed, to assist lending institutions to judge whether a proposal should be accepted for further detailed examination. In the preparation of the application form, the fact that most of the small industrialists do not have audited or published accounts, has been taken into account, and this would explain why Section B of the form dealing with the financial position of the borrower is somewhat more detailed. If, on an examination of this application, it is found that there is a *prima facie* case for the acceptance of the proposal, additional information in greater detail may be obtained either by a supplemental questionnaire or by the interview method, which may be suitably adopted by the investigator, having regard to the circumstances in each individual case. The intention for an experienced official should be to gather supplemental information or help the applicant in filling up the form.

Audited Accounts: As many industrial units are either proprietary or partnership concerns, it is usually difficult to obtain financial statements from them in an acceptable form. In such cases, some latitude may be shown to deserving units. For example, when a concern is unable to furnish audited account for the last few years, the latest account should be audited and presented to the lending institution.

Personal Inspection: Before a loan appraisal is completed, it is desirable that an experienced officer of the financing institution should inspect the concern so that a proper evaluation may be made of the proposal in the beginning. Small industrialists do not often know how to present their case to the satisfaction of the lending institution. It will, therefore, be useful if the latter, having regard to the circumstances of each case, provides the requisite guidance to the unit. Sometimes, slight modifications in the project, if agreed to be one unit, may make the application for a loan acceptable.

SUGGESTION OF IMPROVING FACILITIES FOR INSTITUTIONAL FINANCE

If institutional credit is to play a vital role in catering to the requirements of these industries, measures will have to be taken to overcome the difficulties pointed out here. This calls for a responsive cooperation between the lenders and the borrowers. The nature of adjustment in attitudes and other matters necessary on the part of the lending institutions on the one hand and borrowing units on the other is indicated below:

A. Lending Institutions

Some suggestions, which may be useful for lending institutions catering to the needs of small-scale industries, are given below:

(1) Lenders should take into account not only the value of the security offered but also the character and technical ability of the borrower, the prospects for the industry, the nature and quality of goods produced, etc.;

(2) The acceptance of only a few commodities as security and that too, on a pledge basis, makes it difficult for industries to become eligible for advances from lending institutions. Wherever possible, factory type advances may be given;

(3) Small and medium-sized banks which, individually, cannot afford to maintain a technical staff (engineers, business technicians, etc.), may join together and set-up a common advisory board for the purpose. One of the solutions is to utilise the services of the State Department of Industries and the Small Industries Service Institutes which, under instructions from the Government of India, offer assistance to credit institutions in the matter of technical appraisal of projects;

(4) Lending institutions may maintain personal contacts with borrowing units through periodical visits, etc., and

(5) In order to solve the problem of the paucity of technical data required for an appraisal of the creditworthiness of an industrial unit, it would be advisable to make use of the available official data on small-scale industries.

Some of the sources that may be tapped for this purpose are:

(a) Data released by the Development Commissioner and the Ministry of Commerce and Industry.

(b) Reports on studies conducted by the Small Industries Service Institutes, and

(c) Industry reports prepared by the Economic Investigation Division of the Central Small Industries Organisation.

The division also offers investment guidance and advice on the prospects for various industries. Moreover, it has been taken up the preparation of Industry Prospect Sheets on a large number of industries, which are miniature analysis of planning reports, and contain information on the technical feasibility of an industry, its competitiveness and the size of this investment, its supply-demand position, etc. As these sheets generally become outdated with the lapse of time, they have to be used with due caution, available from all these sources may be supplemented by the date furnished by the borrowers.

(6) The interest charges should be reasonable and the period of repayments should be determined with reference to the earning capacity of a unit. The first instalment may be claimed after a year or two to enable the borrower to stabilise his position and strengthen his repaying capacity. The margin of security should be liberal; varying between 25 per cent and 50 per cent, consistent with the safety of the loan.

(7) To enable financial institutions to liberalise their lending criteria, the Government of India has introduced the Credit Guarantee Scheme, operated by the Reserve Bank of India, which enables them to avail themselves of the guarantee facilities to cover a part of their risk. The maximum amount of loss recoverable under the scheme is ₹ 1 lakh, which is substantial in relation to the size of a small unit. Such guaranteed loans, if given on a term basis, are eligible for the refinance facilities offered by the Refinance Corporation.

(8) The different agencies may supplement one another's resources and share the risks collectively by participating in the loans of other agencies. Participation on the part of commercial banks and State Financial Corporations and of bigger and smaller banks would be useful. Such participation loans can also be covered under the Credit Guarantee Scheme referred to above, provided that one of the participant institutions is an eligible institution and undertakes to assume the risk of loss of loans to the extent of at least 25 per cent.

(9) Lending institutions should be practical and flexible in their attitude rather than strictly legal, with a view to enabling the borrowing units to overcome any temporary difficulties. While resorting to legal action or recourse to security should not be delayed once it becomes clear that the loan cannot be recovered, such a drastic step should not be

taken immediately on a default in payment of interest or instalment occurs. Not infrequently, defaults occur due to circumstances beyond the borrower's control. Timely advice and guidance and even the provision of additional financial assistance where so warranted, would enable him to tide over the crisis. Only when other avenues have been explored without result, or the borrower is considered to be recalcitrant or dishonest, should the lending institution force a closure.

B. Small-scale Industries

There are joint directions in which small-scale industries may improve their method of operation, etc., and make their proposals acceptable to lending institutions. These are:

(i) It may not be usually possible for small industries to furnish financial and other data in a thorough and detailed manner. In such cases, as much information as is available on the following aspects of the concern may be given to lending institutions:

Details of the nature of the industry and its products;

Data regarding performance, estimated cost of production and selling price;

Estimates regarding market prospects, capital invested, proportion of borrowed capital; and

Purpose of the loan, result expected from the investment, etc.

(ii) Concerns should, in their own interest and in order to facilitate the assessment of loan proposals by lending institutions, try to maintain audited accounts;

(iii) The units must be able to produce acceptable evidence for verification of the value of assets offered as security;

(iv) Loans sanctioned should not be used for purposes other than those for which they have been advanced; and

(v) In cases where the prospects of an industrial concern depend on a single individual, and where the loan is given on personal security or guarantee, the lender's interest may be safeguarded by insuring the life of such an individual during the loan period. Policies may be specifically devised for the purpose at special rate, somewhat on the lines of fire insurance. The premiums may be borne by the lending institutions or partly by them and partly by the borrowers.

CONCLUSION

The working capital management is an integral part of the overall management of small-scale industries. There is a need for greater coordination between of small-scale industries and financial institutions. Towards this direction, the Small Industries Development Bank of India (SIDBI) is shaped to provide a strong support to small-scale industries.

It is essential that financial institutions should safeguard their interests with adequate security. At the same time, small industrial concerns should not, as far a s possible, be denied the assistance they deserve or need. *Lack of finance is often not the cause but the result of difficulties in other areas.* In such cases, what is needed is measure to set right those factors which would render financial assistance fruitful. It is common knowledge that small-scale sector needs non-financial assistance, marketing assistance, technical guidance and training in management, etc. In order to assist it, the government has already established special institutions like the Small Industrial Service Institutes, the National Small Industries Corporation and industrial estates with necessary facilities. It has also arranged training programmes for small entrepreneurs; but the scope of operations of these need to be expanded. Above all, there is need for greater coordination at all levels between the financial and non-financial institutions and agencies engaged in the promotion of small-scale industries.

In the present Indian context, the socio-economic obligations of a banker include identification of project ideas, formulation of projects, location of managerial talent and provision of technical and managerial guidance to new ventures with a view to broad-basing entrepreneurial talent and assisting in the creation of more employment opportunities in the country. The banker who controls credit is a 'supply leader' as opposed to his erstwhile role of a 'demand follower'. He is no longer a 'wholesale' banker sitting in an ivory tower. His new role as an agent of economic development is to assist in the development growth of economic activities.

Planning and control of working capital centres around cash planning which includes setting of cash policies and procedures and the control over cash and credit. Cash is of course the very sensitive component of working capital. The working capital has, therefore, to be managed properly, especially by the small-scale industries, because over or under circulation may create volatile problems.

ANNEXURE-I

Required Documents for Procuring Business Loans

Sole Proprietorship/Partnership Firm

- Proof of identity (Copy of Sales Tax/VAT/Service Tax/PAN ID/IT return of the Concern/Water/Electricity/ Muncipal Tax Bill in the Name of the Concern)
- Proof of individual identity (Copy of Passport/Voter's Identity Card/Photo PAN Card/Driving License/ MAPIN Card)
- Pan Number/Form 60 of the Concern Financial Documents (Copy of P&L Accounts and Balance Sheet for last two years, audited by a CA; Copies of IT returns for the last two years)
- Proof of residential address (Copy of Passport/Voter's Identity Card/Driving License/Ration Card/Life Insurance Policy/Electricity Bill/Telephone Bill)
- Bank Statements for last 6 months
- Partnership deed (Required only in case of Partnership Firm)
- Two passport size photographs
- Proof of place of business

For Private Limited Company

- Proof of identify (Copy of Sales Tax/VAT/Service Tax/Excise Registration or Registration under Shops and Establishment Act or PAN ID/IT return of the Concern or Water/Electricity/Municipal Tax Bill in the Name of the Concern)
- Memorandum and Articles of Association (Copy of Certificate of Incorporation)
- Board Resolution (Copy of Annual Return establishing the shareholding pattern)
- Proof of individual identity for the authorised signatories and 2 directors, including the Managing Director (Copy of Passport/Voter's Identity Card/Photo PAN Card/Driving License/MAPIN Card)
- List of Directors
- Copy of form 32 filed with RoC
- PAN Card/Form 60 of the Concern
- Financial Documents (Copy of P&L Accounts and Balance Sheet for last two years, audited by a CA, and Copies of IT returns for the last two years)
- Bank statements for last 6 months
- Proof of place of Business
- Two passport size photographs

Steps to Obtain a Business Loan

1. Gather information: Obtain information on the type of loan you are looking for.
2. Application and assessment: Submit the required documents so that the lending institution can evaluate your financial status and your ability to repay.
3. Approval: On approval of the loan, you will receive a Facility Offer Letter
4. Receiving the money: The approval amount will be deposited into an agreed bank account
5. Making payments: Instruments will be deducted directly from a designated bank account.

According to the Code of Banks Commitment to Micro and Small Enterprises, once the loan is sanctioned, the Bank has to supply authenticated copies of all the loan documents executed along with a copy of each of all enclosed documents quoted in the loan document and the list thereof.

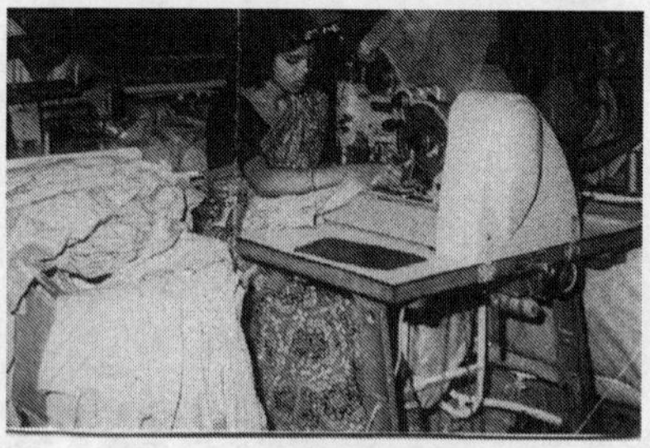

13 CHAPTER

TAXATION BENEFITS

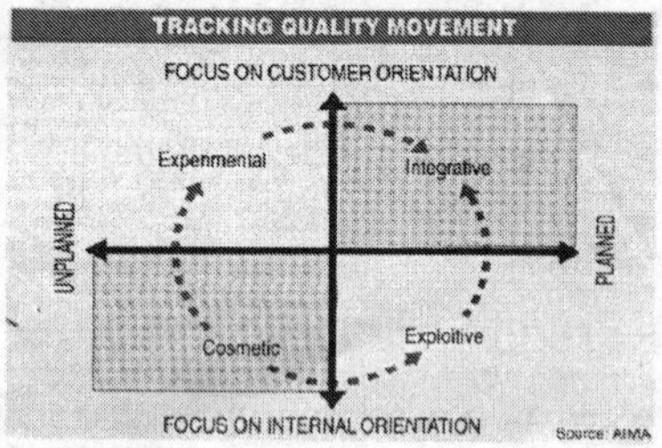

The measure of success is not whether you have a tough problem to deal with, but whether it is the same problem you have last year.

LEARNING OBJECTIVES

The learning objectives is to ascertain the taxation support to small-scale industry.

The chapter covers the following topics:

- The taxation policy aims at the accelerated growth of small-scale industries.
- Taxation support to small business.
- Tax Holiday.
- Depreciation.
- Rehabilitation allowance.
- Expenditure on scientific research.
- Patent rights and copyright.
- Export market development allowance.
- Investment allowance.
- Small-scale industries in rural areas, backward areas.
- Other concessions.
- Merger of sick enterprises.
- Modvat and small industries.
- Excise concessions.
- Promotional measures.

INTRODUCTION

In most developing countries, the taxation policy aims at the promotion of agriculture and industry. Industrial development may, however, be stimulated by means of reduction in the normally applicable tax liability in the form of either an exemption from income-tax on the amount invested or a concession in the tax rate. In the early stages of the developmental programmes for small-scale industries, the government had provided a number of taxation benefits with adequate incentives. In fact, special tax concessions to small-scale industries are desirable for the accumulation of capital and for directing it into the right channels. In the present context of rapid economic development, particularly in the rural hinterland, taxation benefits must be viewed in relation to the need for increasing investments in both small-scale and ancillary industries and discouraging speculative investments in unproductive activities. At the same time, there is need for increasing the productivity of the various factors of production utilised in the industrial advancement of the country.

Taxation benefits relate to:

(i) Income-tax:

(ii) Excise duty;

(iii) Sales tax;

(iv) Electricity duty; and

(v) Octroi.

Apart from these, small-scale industries are entitled to Central capital and transport subsidies.

TAXATION SUPPORT FOR SMALL-SCALE SECTOR

Small-scale entrepreneur are confronted with a number of problems right from the inception of their enterprises and these are inadequate credit facility, infrastructural bottlenecks, technology obsolescence, competitive environment, etc. Small-scale units deserve to be given preferential treatment while framing taxation policy. These units need to be provided support and assistance to tide over the crucial initial stage to enable them to survive and prosper. In order to safeguard and promote interests of small-scale units the government can provide them concession in tax liability or can exempt them from tax payments. In the small-scale sector various tax benefits offered by the government are in the form of direct and indirect tax. Various benefits under the taxation system can be as under:

Tax Benefits to Small-scale Industries

- Excise and Custom Duty
- Income Tax
- Sales Tax
- Other Taxes

Concessions in matters of taxation for industries have three supportive roles, *viz.,* marketing support, investment support and raw materials support. Concessions in excise duties and sales-tax primarily aim at marketing support.

The Government of India announces from time-to-time various incentive schemes for promotion of industries, particularly in industrially backward areas and other special regions with the intention of reducing regional imbalances. The package of incentives and facilities currently available from the Central Government are discussed hereunder.

Fiscal incentives are provided in the form of exemptions, rebate, refund or postponement of direct or indirect taxes leviable on production or profits, besides special tax concessions. Such measures include: (i) Income tax concessions, (ii) Customs duty drawbacks, (iii) Exemption and preferential treatment in respect of Excise duty, (iv) Exemption from Sales Tax, and (v) Tax holiday for new industrial units, etc.

Tax Incentives/Concessions/Deduction from Profits and Gains

- IT Section 80HH: 20 per cent for 10 years for industries to be set up under the Factories Act in backward areas.
- IT Section 80HHA: 20 per cent for 10 years for SSI units to be set up in rural areas.
- IT Section 80-I: 20 per cent for 7 to 9 years for SSI units to be set up under Factories Act, 25 per cent for 11 years in case of cooperative societies, 35 per cent for companies.

- IT Section 80-IA: 25 per cent for 10 years for industries to be set up under Factories Act, 100 per cent for 5 years and 25 per cent for next 5 years for backward areas only.
- IT Section 80-1B: The small-scale units commencing production between April 01, 1995 and March 31, 2000 are allowed a deduction of 25 per cent of their profits (30 per cent for companies) for a period of 10 years.

Incentives for Exports including Duty Drawbacks

The following tax incentives on exports are offered by the government:

- Deduction in respect of profits and gains from projects outside India (Section 80 HHB).
- Deduction in respect of Export Turnover (Section 80 HHC).
- Deduction in respect of earnings in convertible foreign exchange (Section 80 HHD).
- Deduction for consultancy exports (80 O).
- Deduction for export of Computer Software (Section 80 HHE), and
- Ten Year Tax Holiday for newly established industrial undertaking in the Free Trade Zones, or Electronic Hardware Technology Parks and Software Technology Parks (Section 10 A).
- Ten Year Tax Holiday for newly established 100 per cent Export Oriented Undertakings (Section 10 B).
- Duty drawback facilities are provided in two ways: (i) Drawback of the whole of import duty on imported articles, components and raw materials, and excise duty paid on excisable components used in the manufacture of the product when it is exported, and (ii) Drawback of 90 per cent of duty paid on imported article when it is re-exported.

Exemptions and Preferential Treatment from Excise Duties

For SSIs having clearances in the preceding financial year not exceeding ₹ 30 million, the present rates of excise duty are as under:

Clearances	Rate of Duty for SSIs availing Modvat Credit	Rate of Duty for SSIs availing Modvat Credit
Not exceeding ₹ 10 million	Nil	60% of normal rate
₹ 10 to 30 million	Normal	Normal
Goods for capital consumption	Nil	Nil

Note: Commodity specific exemption for small-scale units, namely articles of plastics/cosmetics and toilet preparation, tread rubber, air-conditioning and refrigeration, machinery and parts have been merged with the General SSI Exemption Scheme with effect from April 01, 2000.

Exemption from Sales Tax

- No liability under State Sales Tax law for import of the goods into the export of goods out of the territory of India.
- Export sales have been exempted from levy of Sales Tax under Central Sales Tax Act, 1956.

Every year SSI office formulates pre-budget proposals in consultation with the Technical Divisions of this office and appropriate suggestions/modifications in respect of direct and indirect taxes are sent to the Ministry of Finance for their consideration.

The Small-scale Exemption Scheme for small-scale industries was introduced in 1986. Under this scheme, excise exemption and concessional rates of excise duty to small-scale units till 31st March, 1993 was as follows:

Value of Clearances in a Financial Year	Rate of Duty
Up to ₹ 20 lakh	Fully exempt
Above ₹ 20 lakh, and Up to ₹ 75 lakh	Normal duty reduced by 10% age points subject to a minimum duty of 5% *advalorem*.
Above ₹ 75 lakh	Normal duty.
Eligibility limit	₹ 200 lakh

* In case of units which produce more than one item falling under different chapter headings of Central Excise Tariff, the limit of exemption can go up to ₹ 30 lakh.

In the budget proposed for 1993-94, the excise concessions have further been liberalised as per details given below:

(a)

Value of Clearance	Excise Duty
Not exceeding ₹ 30 lakh	Nil
Exceeding ₹ 30 lakh but not exceeding ₹ 50 lakh	Normal duty minus 10% age point (Subject to 5% minimum *advalorem* duty)
Exceeding ₹ 50 lakh but not exceeding ₹ 75 lakh	Normal duty minus 5% age point (subject to 5% minimum *advalorem* duty)
Exceeding ₹ 75 lakh	Normal duty

(b) Removal of the existing distinction between one chapter clearances and more than one chapter clearances.

(c) Withdrawal of higher notional credit of 5%.

(d) Full excise duty exemption to unregistered units for value of clearances not exceeding ₹ 30 lakh in each financial year.

(e) Eligibility limit – ₹ 200 lakh.

In the Union Budget for 1993-94, a five-year tax holiday has been granted for new industrial undertakings located in all the North Eastern States, Jammu and Kashmir, Himachal Pradesh, Sikkim, Goa and Union Territories of Andaman and Nicobar Islands, Dadra and Nager Haveli, Daman and Diu, Lakshadweep and Pondicherry.

This step aims to give a stimulus to new investments in these states in which all the districts are industrially backward.

The taxation benefits available to small-scale industries are enumerated below:

I. Excise and Customs Duty

Excise benefits offered are as under:

(a) The benefits of excise exemption was provided on a turnover of ₹ 30 lakh in 1986 and it was raised to ₹ 50 lakh for small-scale industries in 1998-99. A flat rate of excise duty @ 5% *advalorem* is imposed on value based product between ₹ 50 lakh and ₹ 100 lakh of annual turnover.

(b) SSI may opt for MODVAT (Modified Value Added Tax) with concession in normal rate of duty. In the Central budget of 1998-99 MODVAT credit was raised to 100% while in the budget 1999-2000 the MODVAT adjustment allowed to manufacturing units has been made at 95%.

(c) Before 1998-99 small-scale industries were not eligible for exemption from excise duty on products bearing brand name of another producer. However, Union budget 1998-99 provided for duty exemption to SSI units producing products under another brand name in the rural areas.

(d) Exemption provided to SSI units based on the product-line has now been extended to cover cotton yarn, which does not contain synthetic staple fibre.

(e) With effect from June 1, 1999 factories falling under the category of small-scale units can remit excise duty on a monthly basis instead of each time goods are cleared from the factory premises. This applies to small-scale units having turnover between ₹ 50 lakh to ₹ 1 crore.

Other Proposals

1. Rationalisation of Duty Structure

(i) Central Excise: 11 major *advalorem* rates have been merged into following three new rates.

Merit Rate – 8% (merging existing rates of 5%, 8%, 19% and 22%)

Central Rate – 16% (merging rates of 13%, 15% and 18%)

Demerit Rate – 24% (merging existing rates of 25%, 30%, 32% and 40%)

(ii) Customs: 7 major *advalorem* rates of basic customs duty merged into following 5 rates. 5%- No change

15% – (merging existing 10% rates)

25% – (merging existing rates of 20% and 25%)

35% – (merging existing rates of 30% and 35%)

40% – No change.

2. Expert Committee to Review Central Excise Exemptions

An expert committee would set up to examine and review on where the exemption should be retained and where they should be integrated into the new structure.

3. Customs

(i) A surcharge @ 10 per cent of basic duty has been imposed across the board except on gold and silver, crude and petroleum products, items attracting 40 per cent rate of basic duty and certain GATT bound items.

(ii) Special additional duty of 4 per cent shall continue (though there was a proposal for the abolition of the same in pre-budget proposals).

(iii) Special custom duty of 5 per cent has been withdrawn.

(iv) A basic duty of 5 per cent has been imposed on a number of commodities by withdrawing exemptions. However, special additional duty of 4 per cent is exempted on such goods on which this 5 per cent has been imposed for the first time.

Tax Holiday

New industrial undertakings, including small-scale industries, are exempted from the payment of income-tax under Section 80J of the Act on their profits up to 6 per cent per annum of the capital employed. Deduction at the rate of 6 per cent (7.5 per cent for companies) from the total income is allowed in the assessment year in which the unit begins to manufacture, provided that the conditions specified in Section 80J are fulfilled by small-scale industries. This concession is for five years from the commencement of production. Small-scale units should satisfy the following conditions before they become eligible for tax benefits:

(i) They should not have been formed by the splitting or reconstitution of an existing unit, and

(ii) They should employ 10 or more workers in a manufacturing process with power or 20 more persons without power.

Depreciation

Under Section 32 of the Income Tax Act, a small-scale industry is entitled to a deduction on depreciation account on buildings, furniture, plant and machinery at the prescribed rates. In the case of small-scale industries, the deduction from the actual cost of plant and machinery is allowed up to ₹ 20 lakh in the case of any machinery or plant hired by a unit, the actual cost thereof the owner of such machinery or plant. The depreciation is calculated on the reducing balance system. Full depreciation is available for a year irrespective of the actual number of days for which the asset is used so long as it is used for the purpose of business or profession at any time during the year. In the case of assets acquired before the accounting year, depreciation is to be calculated on the written down value. For plant and machinery used in factories working a double or triple shift, an additional allowance called *extra shift allowance*, is available. Any machinery or plant costing less than ₹ 750 is allowed to be written off completely in the year in which it was first used in business.

Deduction when Disallowed

The deduction of depreciation allowance will not be allowed in respect of:

(i) Any machinery or plant installed in any office premises to any residential accommodation, including any accommodation in the nature of a guest house;

(ii) Any machinery or plant in respect of which the deduction by way of development rebate is allowable under Section 33, and

(iii) Any machinery or plant installed after 31st March, 1976.

For the purpose of this Section, an industrial undertaking is deemed to be a small-scale industrial undertaking if the aggregate value of the machinery and plant installed on the last day of the year for the purpose of the business of undertaking does not exceed ₹ 7.5 lakh.

Conditions to be Fulfilled

The following conditions have to be fulfilled for eligibility:

(i) The assets should be owned by an assessee;

(ii) The assets should actually be used for the purpose of the assessee's business or profession;

(iii) The prescribed particulars should be furnished as required under Section 34 (I) of the Act. If they are not furnished, the income-tax officer would be justified in refusing to grant such allowance;

(iv) The aggregate of the initial depreciation and normal depreciation over the year should not exceed the actual cost to the assessee of the building, machinery, plant or furniture, and

(v) Depreciation allowance is granted only for building, machinery, plant and furniture and not for any other capital asset.

The word 'plant' is defined by Section 43(3) to include ships, vehicles, books, scientific apparatus and surgical instruments. Rebate as specified below, is allowed under Section 33, in addition to normal depreciation.

In the case of machinery or plant:

(i) Thirty-five per cent of the actual cost, if it was installed before 1st April, 1970 and 25 per cent of such cost if it was instilled after 31st March, 1970, and

(ii) Where the machinery or plant was installed after 31st March, 1967, being an asset representing expenditure of a capital nature on scientific research related to the business carried on by a unit, development rebate is given at the specified rates.

Rehabilitation Allowance

Under Section 33B, a rehabilitation allowance is granted to any small-scale industrial undertaking in India, whose business is discontinued on account of:

(i) Flood, typhoon, hurricane, cyclone, earthquake or other natural upheaval;

(ii) Riot or civil disturbance;

(iii) Accidental fire or explosion; and

(iv) Action by an enemy or action taken in combating an enemy.

Provided that this rehabilitation allowance is used for business purposes within three years. The re-established, reconstructed or revived unit is allowed a deduction of a sum, by way of rehabilitation allowance, equivalent to 60 per cent of the amount of the deduction allowance to the unit.

EXPENDITURE ON SCIENTIFIC RESEARCH

Under Section 35, the following deductions in respect of scientific research are allowed:

(i) Any expenditure (not being in the nature of capital expenditure incurred on scientific research related to the business, and

(ii) Any sum paid to a scientific research association which has as its object the undertaking of a scientific research, or to a university, college or other institutions to be used for scientific research.

Patent Right and Copyright

Under Section 35A, any expenditure of a capital nature, incurred after 28th February, 1966 on the business, shall be allowed, subject to and in accordance with the provisions of this section.

Export Markets Development Allowance

If a domestic company, whether directly or in association with any other person, has after 20th February, 1969, incurred any expenditure on this account (not being in the nature or capital expenditure or personal expenses), a deduction of a sum equal to one and one-third time the amount of such expenditure incurred during the previous year shall be allowed under Section 35B.

The expenditure incurred, wholly and exclusively, on the following items is eligible for deduction:

(i) Advertisement or publicity outside India;

(ii) Obtaining information regarding markets outside India;

(iii) Maintenance of a branch office or agency for the promotion of sales abroad;

(iv) Preparation and submission of tenders, samples or technical information;

(v) Travelling outside India for the promotion of sales;

(vi) Performance of services outside India in connection with, or incidental to the execution of any contract for the supply of such goods, services or facilities outside India, and

(vii) Such other activities as may be necessary for the promotion of sales outside India.

Amortisation of Certain Preliminary Expenses

Under Section 35D, Indian companies and resident persons are allowed deduction for the specified expenditure:

(i) Before the commencement of business;

(ii) After the commencement of the business in connection with the extension of an individual undertaking or in connection with the setting up of a new industrial unit;

(iii) Expenditure in connection with the preparation of a feasibility report necessary for the business;

(iv) Engineering services relating to the business; and

(v) Legal charges for drafting any agreements.

The aggregate amount of expenditure allowed to be deducted is limited to 2.5 per cent of the total cost of the project.

Under Section 80HH, a newly-established small-scale industrial unit located in a backward area, is allowed a deduction of 20 per cent on its profits and gains, provided that:

(i) It has begun, or begins, to manufacture or produce articles after 31st December, 1970 in any backward area;

(ii) It has bot been formed by the splitting up or reconstitution of a business already in existence in any backward area;

(iii) It has not been formed by the transfer to a new business machinery or plant previously used for any purpose in backward area; and

(iv) It employs ten or more workers in the manufacturing process carried on with the aid of power, or employs twenty or more workers in the manufacturing process carried on without the aid of power.

The deduction shall be allowed for ten years, beginning with the commencement of production.

Investment Allowance

Rate of Deduction: It was in 1976 that the concept of investment allowance was introduced, replacing the initial depreciation allowance. One of the most valuable tax concessions offered to small-scale industrial undertakings under the Income-tax Act is the deduction, by way of investment allowance, granted under Section 31A. The investment allowance is allowed at the rate of 25 per cent of the cost of acquisition of a new plant or machinery installed, unlike the development rebate, which was allowed at different rates, ranging from 10 per cent to 40 per cent.

Items of Low Priority: Eleventh Schedule: Although the benefit of investment allowance has been made available for the articles or things except certain articles and things of low priority specified in the Eleventh Schedule, a special dispensation has been provided for the plant and machinery installed in small-scale industrial undertakings. Such machinery and plants are eligible for investment allowance irrespective of whether they are used for the purpose of the business of construction, manufacture or production of low priority items listed in the Eleventh Schedule. Small-scale industrial undertakings are, in comparison with other industries, at an advantage in claiming a deduction of investment allowance.

Here when Forfeited: In order to avail itself of the benefit of investment allowance, a small-scale industrial units must put to use machinery or plant either in the year of installation or in the immediate following year; otherwise the benefit will be forfeited.

Conditions to be Fulfilled: An Investment Allowance Reserve (IAR must be created during the relevant financial year. This reserve is required to be utilised for the acquisition of machinery or plant for the purpose of the business of the small-scale industrial undertaking. Its utilisation for distribution by way of dividends or profits or for remittance outside India is prohibited.

When Withdrawable: The investment allowance will be withdrawn:

(i) If machinery or plant is sold or otherwise transferred by the assessee to any person (other than the Government, a local authority, a corporation or a government company) at any time before the expiry of eight years from the end of the financial year in which it was acquired or installed. It is not withdrawn if the sale or transfer is made in connection with the amalgamation of a partnership firm into a company or where a firm is succeeded by a company in the business carried on by it.

(ii) If a small-scale industrial undertaking ceases to be a small-scale industrial unit by virtue of the total value of the machinery or plant installed exceeding ₹ 10 lakh.

SMALL-SCALE INDUSTRIES IN RURAL AREAS

The Finance (No.2) Act of 1977 has inserted a new Section, 80HHA in the Income Tax Act, 1961, under which the tax-payers are entitled to claim a deduction from the gross total income to the extent of 20 per cent of the profits and gains derived by them from small-scale industrial undertakings newly set up in any rural area, and which begin manufacturing activity after 30th September, 1977. The expression *rural area* means any area defined under the Explanation to Section 35CC(I) of the Act. The small-scale industrial units engaged in mining are not allowed this tax concession. The deduction of profits and gains derived by an assessee from small-scale industrial undertakings will be allowed in computing the total income in each of the ten assessment years in which the small-scale industrial undertaking begins to manufacture or produce articles. For the purpose of this section, the term small-scale industrial undertaking will have the same meaning as assigned to it under Section 32(2) of the Act.

Conditions to be Fulfilled

The conditions for eligibility are:

(i) The small-scale industrial undertaking should not be formed by splitting up or by reconstructing a business already in existence in a rural area or any other area. In other words, machinery and plant must be newly acquired and put to use in its business for the first time, and the business should not have been in existence prior to the establishment thereof in the rural area.

(ii) It should not be formed by transfer to a new business of machinery or plant previously used for any purpose. This condition will not apply in cases in which the total value of machinery or plant or a part so transferred does not exceed 20 per cent of the total value of machinery or plant used in the business.

(iii) It should employ ten or more workers in the manufacturing process carried on with the aid of power or twenty or more workers in a manufacturing process carried on without the aid of power. When an industrial undertaking is located in a rural area which is also a backward area, the assessee has the choice of claiming the deduction to the extent of 20 per cent of the profits from the new business in the small-scale sector for the first 10 years either under Section 80HH or under 80HHA, but not under both the Sections.

Small-scale Industries in Backward Areas

The small-scale industries, which have been newly established in the backward areas specified in the English Schedule to the Income-tax Act and which produce or manufacture any article or thing in backward areas, are entitled to the benefit of deduction from gross total income to the extent of 20 per cent of their profits and gains. This deduction is allowed for ten assessment years beginning with the assessment year in which the small-scale industrial unit begins to manufacture or produce goods. The small-scale industrial units also fulfil the other conditions prescribed in Section 80HH of the Act before it can avail itself of this tax concession. If it has already been established in a non-backward area and shifts to a backward area, the profits derived from the industrial undertaking in the backward area subsequent to shifting would qualify for this tax concession for a period of 10 years. The small-scale industry engaged in the business of mining is not entitled to claim the benefit of this concession, even though it may have been established in a backward area.

Other Concessions

Publication of Books: A small-scale industry engaged in the business of publication of books is entitled to claim a deduction of a sum equal to 20 per cent of the profits and gains derived from such business under Section 80QQ of the Act. 'Books' for the purpose of this Section do not include newspapers, journals, magazines, diaries, bochures, pamphlets and other publications of similar nature.

Small-scale industrial undertakings are also entitled to claim the various tax benefits granted to other tax-payers, such as rehabilitation allowance, expenditure on specific research, mobilisation of the cost of patents and copyrights, agricultural development allowance of expenses by way of contribution for rural development and other deductions allowed in computing the taxable income from business, in addition to the tax concessions admissible in respect of capital gains.

Small-scale industrial undertakings should plan in such a way that it should be possible for them to avail themselves of the tax concessions to the maximum extent so that the aim of the government to encourage more and more small-scale industries to establish in rural and backward parts of the country may be fulfilled.

In addition, deductions are available in respect of:

(i) Inter-corporate dividends (Sec.80M);

(ii) Royalties from any company in India (Sec.80M);

(iii) Dividend from certain foreign companies (Sec.80N);

(iv) Royalties, etc., from certain foreign companies (Sec.80O);

(v) Income of Cooperative Societies (Sec. 80P);

(vi) Profits and gains of the business from the publication of books (Sec. 80QQ); and

(vii) Carry forward and set-off of business losses (Sec. 72).

Tax Benefits for Amalgamation of Sick Units: Sickness in an industry, whether large or small, is quite widespread in the country and has become a national problem which has caused a great deal of concern. It is estimated that the aggregate amount involved in the sick units is more than ₹ 2,000 crore.* The policy of the government has been to encourage the amalgamation of sick units with profit-making larger units. For this purpose, some tax concessions have been announced to include healthy units to take over sick units are discussed below:

What is Amalgamation? The Income-tax Act defines the amalgamation of companies as a merger of one or more companies with another company or a merger of two more companies to form another concern, in such a manner that all the property and liabilities of the amalgamating company become the property and liabilities of the amalgamated company, and the shareholders, holding not less than nine-tenths of the shares in the amalgamating company, become the shareholders of the amalgamated company, by the virtue of amalgamation. However, the shares which are already held immediately before the amalgamation by, or by a nominee of the amalgamated company or its subsidiary, are not to be taken into account for arriving at 90 per cent of the shares held. An 'amalgamating company' is a company which merges and the company with which it merges or which is formed as a result of the merger is the 'amalgamated company'. There can be no amalgamation when a company is wound up and another company purchases the assets of that company or receives its assets as a result of the distribution made by the company in liquidation. It is essential that all these conditions are satisfied before an amalgamation is said to have been effected.

Business Losses and Tax: The assessees are permitted to carry forward and set off business losses against income under the provision of Section 72 of the Income Tax Act. Under the existing provision of this Act, the business loss of a year, which cannot be set off against the other income of the assessee for the relevant year, is allowed to be carried and set off

* Of this amount, small-scale units account for about ₹ 800 crore, or 40 per cent of the total.

against the profits of the following assessment year from any business in which he is engaged. If the loss cannot be wholly set off against the profits, the amount of loss not so set off is allowed to be carried forward to the following assessment year, and so on up to a maximum of eight assessment years immediately succeeding the assessment year for which the loss was first computed. The concession is allowed only when the assessee continues to carry on business in which the loss was originally computed. Further, the assessee who has incurred the loss has the right to carry forward the same; and a successor in business, if any, cannot claim the right to carry forward the loss incurred by his predecessor. Again, if the business of an assessee is taken over by another, the unabsorbed depreciation allowance due to the predecessor in business is not allowed to be carried forward by the successor in business and set off against his profits in subsequent years. In view of these provisions, no unit was prepared to take over a sick unit because the accumulated loss and unabsorbed depreciation allowance of the amalgamating company could not be carried forward and set off by the amalgamated company against its profit.

Incentives for Amalgamation: The Finance (No. 2) Act of 1977 has inserted Section 72A in the Income-tax Act, relaxing the aforesaid provisions relating to carry forward and set off accumulated business loss and unabsorbed depreciation allowance in certain cases of amalgation. Section 72A provides that when there has been an amalgamation of a company owing to an industrial undertaking or a relationship with another company, and when the Central Government, on the recommendation of the specified authority, has made a declaration to that effect and that, thereupon notwithstanding anything contained in any other provision of the Income-tax Act, the accumulated loss and unabsorbed depreciation of the amalgamating company will be the loss or the allowance for depreciation of the amalgamated company for the previous year in which the amalgamation was effected. It therefore, follows that, as the unabsorbed loss of the amalgamating company is considered to be the loss for the previous year in which the amalgamation was affected, the amalgamated company will have the right to carry forward the loss for a period of eight assessment years immediately succeeding the assessment year in which the amalgation was effected. The government will make this declaration in respect of the amalgamation provided:

(i) That immediately preceding the amalgamation, the amalgamating company was not financially viable by reason of its liabilities, losses and other relevant factors;

(ii) That the amalgamation was in the public interest, and

(iii) That such other conditions as the Central Government may by notification in the Official Gazette specify to an amalgamation which would facilitate the rehabilitation or revival of the business of the amalgamating company.

Even after the said declaration by the Central Government, the concessions in respect of the accumulated loss and the unabsorbed depreciation allowance will not be granted to the amalgamated company unless the following further conditions are fulfilled:

(i) During the assessment year, for which such set off or allowance is claimed, the business of the amalgamating company is carried on by the amalgamated company without any modification, or with such modifications or reorganisations as may be approved by the Central Government to enable the amalgamated company to carry on such business more economically or more efficiently.

(ii) The amalgamated company furnishes, along with its return of income for the assessment year for which such set off or allowance is claimed, a certificate from the specified authority to the effect that adequate steps have been taken by the company for the rehabilitation or revival of the business of the amalgamated company. The term 'accumulated loss' for the purpose of this provision means so much of the loss of the amalgamating company under the head 'profits and gains of business or profession' as has not been sustained in speculative business, and which the amalgamating company would have been entitled to carry forward and set off under provisions of Section 72 if the amalgamation had not been affected. Similarly, 'unabsorbed depreciation' means so much of the allowance for depreciation of the amalgamating company which remains to be allowed and which would have been allowed to the amalgamating company under the provisions of the Income-tax Act if the amalgamation had not been affected. The term 'specified authority' means such authority as the Central Government may by notification in the Official Gazette specify for the purpose of this provision. The Central Government has recently notified an Inter Ministerial committee as the specified authority which consists of Secretaries of the Department of Industrial Development, the Department of Company Affairs, Ministry of Labour, the Department of Economic Affairs and the Chairman of the Central Board of Direct Taxes.

Under the existing provisions, the 'specified authority' can make a recommendation to the Central Government under Section 72A only after the company, which had accumulated losses and unabsorbed depreciation, had amalgamated with the other company. In these circumstances, the companies seeking amalgamation were not in a position to know in advance whether, after amalgamation, they would be entitled to the tax benefits offered under Section 72A. This lacuna has now been removed by the Finance Act of 1978, which has amended Section 72A. By virtue of this amendment, a unit seeking amalgamation with another unit will now be informed in advance whether, after the amalgamation, it will be entitled to benefits under this Section.

GUIDELINES FOR THE MERGER OF SICK UNITS

In February, 1978, the Central Government announced certain guidelines for the merger of sick industrial units with healthy ones. The specified authority has to scrutinise the proposals for amalgamation and recommend the grant of the tax concessions offered by the government. The guidelines are for the purpose of determining whether a scheme of amalgamation can be considered to be in the public interest or not. According to the guidelines, the amalgamating company should have employed at least 100 workers during the accounting year in which the amalgamation is affected as well as in the two preceding years. Alternatively, the fair market value of the fixed assets (excluding land), as on the date of amalgamation, should not be less than ₹ 50 lakh. However, these general criteria may be relaxed if the sick unit is engaged in the manufacture of mass consumption goods or goods which have a high priority, or a unit which has an industrial capacity which is required for the manufacture of such goods. Special consideration will also be given to those sick units which are located in any rural or backward area, or in any city or town a population of less than one million.

The amalgamated company should have formulated a satisfactory programme for the rehabilitation or revival of the sick units, after taking into account the interest of the workers employed by the amalgamating unit. It should also have the necessary managerial and financial resources to execute the programme. If either the amalgamating or the amalgamated company owns an industrial undertaking governed by the Monopolies and Restricted Trade Practices Act, amalgamation will be recommended by the specified authority only after the requirements of this have been satisfied and certain other conditions have been fulfilled. If the amalgamated company is a foreign majority company, the amalgamation will be recommended only if it conforms to the provisions of the Foreign Exchange Regulation Act (FERA) and fulfil certain other conditions. Although a formal recommendation to the Central Government under Section 72(A)(1) of the Act will be made by the specified authority only after the amalgamation has been affected, an application for the approval of the scheme may be made to the specified authority even before such amalgamation actually takes place.

Other Provisions

The other provisions of the Income-tax Act containing tax concessions for companies in the course of amalgamation are summarised as follows:

(1) There will be no computation of any profit under Section 41 (2) of the Income-tax Act in the case of an amalgamating company with reference to the consideration receivable by it in respect of any building, machinery or plant or furniture transferred by it to the amalgamated company. The profit under Section 41(2) of the Income-tax Act is the excess of sale proceeds or money receivable by the assessee in respect of any building, machinery or plant or furniture over the written down value thereof , to the extent of the depreciation allowance actually granted on such assets. A corollary to this, there will also be no computation of any 'terminal allowance', (i.e., the allowance for the net capital loss, if any, suffered on the transfer of an asset eligible for depreciation) in respect of such assets.

(2) As a corollary to the above provision, the actual cost as also the written down value of the building, machinery, plant or furniture transferred by the amalgamating company of the amalgated company, will be taken in the assessment of the amalgated company to be the same as in the case of the amalgating company. Further, for the purpose of the provisions in the Income-tax Act that the aggregate amount of the depreciation allowed for year-to-year in respect of any asset will be limited to its actual cost, the depreciation actually allowed to the amalgamating company in respect of such assets is equal to the actual cost of the asset in the hands of the amalgamating company, and the amalgamated company will not be entitled to any further depreciation on such assets.

(3) When the amalgamating company transfers to the amalgamated company special capital assets used by it for scientific research in connection with its business, or for promoting family planning amongst its employees, or any capital assets of the nature of the patent rights or copyrights, the amalgamated company will be entitled to amortise the capital costs of such assets against its profits under the existing provision of the law in this behalf, as if the amalgamation has not taken place.

(4) No capital gain or loss will be computed in the case of the amalgamating company in respect of any capital assets transferred by it to the amalgamated company.

(5) For the purpose of computing, in the case of the amalgamated company, any capital gains or loss in respect of assets which were transferred to it by the amalgamating company and are subsequently sold or otherwise transferred by the amalgamating company to any other person, 'the cost of acquisition' of such assets will be taken to be the same as in the hands of the amalgamating company.

Such capital gains will be computed by taking the cost of acquisition thereof to be the cost of acquisition of the shares in the amalgamating company.

(6) An amalgamating company, which is a closely held company, will not be liable to any gift tax in respect of the assets transferred by it to the amalgamated company. (Widely held companies have already been exempt from gift tax under the Gift-tax Act.)

(7) Where, in a scheme of amalgamation, the amalgamating company sells or otherwise transfers to the amalgamated company any ship, aircraft, machinery or plant in respect of which an investment allowance has been allowed to the amalgamating company under Sub-Section (1) of Section 32A:

(a) The amalgamated company shall continue to fulfil the conditions mentioned in Sub-Section(4) of Section 32A in respect of the reserve created by the amalgamating company and in respect of the period within which such ship; aircraft, machinery or plant shall not be sold or otherwise transferred; and in default of any of these conditions, the provisions of Sub-Section (4A) of Section 155 will apply to the amalgamated company as they would have applied to the amalgamating company had it committed the default; and

(b) The balance of investment allowance, if any, still outstanding to the amalgamating company in respect of such ship, aircraft, machinery or plant will be allowed to the amalgamating company in accordance with provisions of Sub-Section (3), subject to the provisions that the total period for which the balance of investment allowance shall be carried forward in the assessment of the amalgamating company and the amalgamated company shall not exceed the period of 8 years specified in Sub-Section(3), and provided that the amalgamated company shall be treated as the assessee in respect of such ship, aircraft, machinery or plant for the purpose of this Section.

(8) Where the amalgamating company sells or otherwise transfers to the amalgamated company any ship, machinery or plant in respect of which a development rebate has been allowed to the amalgamating company, the amalgamated company would continue to enjoy the benefits of the development rebate provided that it satisfies the conditions specified in Sub-Sections 34 (3) (a) and (b). The amalgamated company is allowed to carry forward the unabsorbed development rebate; but the total period for which the amount of this rebate is carried forward in the assessment of the amalgamating company and the amalgamated company should not exceed eight years.

The objectives of Section 72A in the Income-tax Act of 1977 are in keeping with the approach adopted by the government to help accelerate the rehabilitation of sick units. It remains to be seen, however, how far the concerned industries take advantage of the scheme of amalgamation and tax incentives offered to them. The Section has empowered the Central Government to lay down any other conditions that may be necessary by a notification in the Official Gazette. It is hoped, however, that such further conditions will not hamper but will speed up the process of amalgamation. As stressed by the Chokshi Committee on Direct Tax Laws, such further notifications, which may be issued by the Central Government, should apply only prospectively to the schemes of amalgamation which may be submitted for approval after the date of the issue of the notification.

In the guidelines recently issued by the government, it has been indicated that an application for the approval of a scheme for amalgamation may be made to the specified authority even before such amalgamation has actually taken place, and if the specified authority is satisfied, it may make a formal recommendation to the government to make a declaration under Sub-Section (1) of Section 72A. The Chokshi Committee has recommended that the substances of the assurance should be incorportated by a specific provision in the law to permit an application for amalgamation to the Central Government. After the application has been approved, the concerned companies may go ahead with the scheme, obtain the court's approval for it and implement it accordingly. It is, however, felt that with the right spirit of flexibility in the administration of the scheme, a codification of the substance of the assurance may not be necessary. The Chokshi Committee has suggested that the two proceedings, one before the specified authority and the other before the Central Government, should be coalesced. The Section should provide for a declaration to be issued by the Central Government or, alternatively, by the specified authority that an application by an amalgamated company be treated as a single proceeding. A consideration of this recommendation may, perhaps be necessary in the interest of expediting the process of amalgamation. The Committee has also suggested that the Section should spell out the conditions relating to the employment of workers, the use of productive capacity and the finance to be raised. A certification in regard to these matters would help in the simplification of the amalgamation process.

The amalgamation company has, with its return of income, to furnish a certificate from the specified authority to the effect that adequate steps have been taken by it for the rehabilitation or revival of the business of the amalgamating company. Here, again, the issue of such a certificate by the specified authority is subject to its satisfaction as to the method and manner in which the business operations are carried on by the unit. These checks are considered essential by the Government; otherwise the objects for which the scheme of amalgamation has been formulated may not be achieved, and the tax benefits may be misused.

MODVAT AND SMALL INDUSTRIES

The long-term fiscal policy has envisaged that the best solution to the vexatious question of taxation of inputs and the cascading effect of this on the value of the final product would be to extend the present system of proforma credit to all excisable commodities with the exception of a few sectors. This scheme has been referred as Modified Valued Added Tax (ModVat) Scheme. It is a good beginning.

It is intended to greatly expand the scope of the provisions for set-offs for excise and countervailing duties paid on inputs, with a view to coming as close to a generalised set-off for excise (and countervailing duty) taxation of inputs as is administratively feasible. The basic approach will be to move towards an extension of the present system of proforma credit to all excisable commodities with the exception of a few like petroleum, tobacco and textiles. This programme will be implemented in a phased manner over a period of some years, taking due account of the revenue implications, the need to revise administrative procedures and the lessons from experience gained in the early stages of the reforms.

It must be emphasised that the ModVat programme is intended to be broadly revenue neutral. It is not the purpose to use ModVat to give substantial net reliefs on excise. The loss of duty on inputs will be recouped through higher excise taxation of final products. Indeed, shifting the effective burden of excise taxation away from inputs and onto final products is at the heart of the proposed reform. Apart from reducing distortionary effect on production and thus increasing the competitiveness of the Indian industry, the shifting of excise to final products will help in tailoring excise duties in such a manner that the well-off bear a higher proportionate burden than the poor.

For the progress towards a generalised system of reliefs on input taxation, it will be necessary to coordinate this move with the fiscal concession to Small-scale Industries (SSIs). At present, input purchases from SSIs do not qualify for set-off for the good reason that excise is not generally paid on them. Introduction of ModVat will require further rationalisation of excise concession to SSI units and other excise exemptions. This will be done in a phased way.

ModVat credit is allowed at the rate of 100 per cent of duty paid on inputs, be it excise duty or special duty or additional duty of customs. It also covers capital goods purchased and used by the manufacturers.

Reform of Excise Concession of Small-scale Producers

An established feature of the excise duty structure is the concession schemes for small-scale producers. These have been granted in recognition of the employment potential of the small-scale sector and also the vital role of this sector in industrial development. The eligibility criteria for exemptions and concessions to small-scale units have varied overtime. However, the multiplicity of the criteria has been reduced considerably in recent years and there are at present two major schemes of concessions for the small-scale sector, namely: (i) a general scheme applicable to specified groups of commodities and (ii) for commodities coming under Tariff Item 68 of the Excise Tariff. There are also a few special schemes applicable to particular commodities.

Government attaches high priority to the growth of small-scale industries in view of their employment intensity, particularly in traditional sectors. Fiscal policy will continue to encourage growth of this sector through excise concessions. An important objective will be to provide an environment for the growth of these industries, while at the same time, ensuring that tax concessions are not used as loopholes by large-scale units for abuse. The modifications made in the last Budget were designed to remove the disincentives of growth and promote efficient expansion of the small-scale sector.

The recently submitted report of the Technical Study Group (TSG) on Central Excise Tariff has identified certain areas for further reform. For example, it has been noticed that a large number of small-scale units had been set up by large companies, solely to avail of concessions for small-scale units without additing significantly to employment or output. It has also been noted that the vast majority of small-sale units (over 90 per cent) have investment in plant and machinery of less than one lakh rupees. In respect of such units, it is particularly desirable to ensure that the fiscal environment is conducive to their growth. The TSG report is under consideration of the government and changes in respect of the small-scale sector as well as other areas of excise will be announced as necessary. As a step towards simplification of the existing concessions, the government also intends to move towards a uniform system of excise concessions for all commodities irrespective of the tariff classification.

Union Budget for 2002-03 – Issues Pertaining to SSI Sector

"As hon'ble members are aware, small-scale industries are now subject to increasing competition with the completion of trade liberalisation. A new approach to the promotion of small-scale industries therefore, has already been adopted.

Adequate credit flow is essential for the small-scale sector. The net bank credit outstanding to small-scale industries increased from ₹ 45,789 crore on March 31, 2000 to ₹ 48,445 crore on March 31, 2001. In order to further increase the flow of credit:

- The limit for composite loans has been increased from ₹ 2 lakh to ₹ 5 lakh.
- 391 specialised branches of public sector banks have been opened for small-scale industries as of September 30, 2001.
- The exemption limit for collateral security has been increased from ₹ 25,000 to ₹ 5 lakh. The project cost limit under the National Equity Fund has been increased from ₹ 25 lakh to ₹ 50 lakh.
- The extension of credit to SSI has already been facilitated through the Credit Guarantee Scheme and the Credit Linked Capital Subsidy Scheme for Technology Upgradation.
- Encouraged by the Kisan Credit Card Scheme, public sector banks have now decided to introduce a scheme called Laghu Udyami Credit Card (LUCC) Scheme for providing simplified and borrower friendly credit facilities to small businessmen, retail traders, artisans and small entrepreneurs, professionals and other self-employed persons, including those in the tiny sector.

Members will recall that last year I had announced the dereservation of 14 items in the footwear, leather goods and toy sectors. The government has been engaged in discussions with stakeholders in respect of certain other items in the reserved list. Over 50 items of knitwear, certain agricultural implements, auto components, some chemical and drugs, and others will now be dereserved. My colleague, the Minister of Small Scale Industries will announce the details of these items separately.

"...The National Innovation foundation was set up in March 2000 with a corpus of ₹ 20 crore, in order to build a national register of outstanding traditional knowledge and grassroot innovations. This initiative has shown good results. In the second annual campaign NIF has received more than 11,000 entries from all over the country, up from 948 entries in the first year. Encouraged by this enthusiastic response I propose to set up a micro venture capital fund for small innovations to be initiated by the Small Industries Development Bank of India (SIDBI), in cooperation with the National Innovation Foundation, to facilitate the transition of innovations into enterprises."

"...Mr. Speaker, Sir, the Indian textile industry occupies an important place in our economy. It is the second largest provider of employment after agriculture. The MFA will be phased out by 2004. Domestic market has already been opened up. Our textile industry has to prepare itself for the challenges ahead. I have carved out a special package of incentives for the textile industry."

"...I have already mentioned the need to provide incentives for fresh investments in the industrial sector. To give impetus to such investment, I propose to allow additional depreciation at the rate of 15% of new plant and machinery acquired on or after 1st April, 2002 for setting up a new industrial unit, or for expanding the installed capacity of the existing units by at least 25%."

"...The small-scale industry sector has been making an important contribution to economic growth, and deserves continued support. In order to enable the Small Industries Development Bank of India (SIDBI) to augment its resources and provide cheaper credit to the small-scale sector, I propose to allow capital gains exemption under Section 54EC of the Incom-tax Act to amounts invested in bonds issued by SIDBI."

"...In my Budget for 2000-2001, I had announced the setting up of a Credit Guarantee scheme for small-scale industries. Accordingly, the Credit Guarantee Fund Trust for Small Industries has been constituted. I propose to grant full exemption from tax to the income of this Trust."

Policy Initiatives on Small-scale Industries in 2002-03

- Fifty-one items were dereserved in May 2002.
- In the Union Budget 2002-03, income-tax exemption was granted to the income of the Credit Guarantee Fund Trust for Small Industries for 5 years.
- In the Union Budget 2002-03, the general SSI Excise exemption Scheme has been extended to air guns, air rifles and air pistols (not covered under the Arms Act, 1959); articles of apparel, knitted or crocheted; marble and Bengal lights.
- National Awards for scheduled commercial banks were constituted by the Ministry of Small-scale Industries for best performance in terms of lending to SSIs. The first ever Awards were given away in the 3rd SSI Convention on August 28, 2002.
- A Biotechnology Cell has been created in the Ministry of SSI under the Chairmanship of Development Commissioner (Small-scale Industries) to facilitate the development and promotion of biotechnology-based industries in the small-scale sector.
- For technology upgradation and quality improvement in SSI sector, the scope of the ongoing ISO 9000 reimbursement scheme has been enlarged to include reimbursement of expenses for ISO 14001 Environment Standard with effect from October 28, 2002.

CONCLUSION

Tax concessions have two important objectives, *viz.,* to promote investment in small-scale industries and to provide relief to them. Tax concessions are used to stimulate the establishment or expansion of small-scale industries in a desirable manner. They are granted on the basis of product-line, and the concessions refer to excise duties, sales taxes on specific input such as – capital equipment, intermediate goods, etc. Of all the privileges that small-scale industrial firms enjoy, excise duty concessions are probably the most important, which give small enterprises an important competitive edge. In addition, tax concessions are also provided for new investments in particular industries or specific localities. The idea is to stimulate investments in specific directions which in the eyes of the government are particularly helpful from a macro-economic development standpoint. Lowering of tariffs and sales tax concession enables the small-scale industry to push up their share in the domestic and international markets. Thus, taxation concessions not only stimulate growth of small-scale industries but also stimulate entrepreneurship production and marketing of quality goods. There is an increase in employment, industrial production, national income and in return increased revenue to the exchequer, which will offset the loss on account of tax concessions.

During the last one year, the Centre has initiated a number of changes in the policies and programmes. In view of these, the next few years are of crucial importance to the small-scale industries. To achieve sustained economic growth, it is necessary to develop the infrastructure, particularly essential facilities like — railway, communication, power, road transport, etc. In addition, the policies and programmes for this sector should emphasise rationalisation on the fiscal and taxation regime, provision of appropriate infrastructure, the introduction of modern management techniques, upgradation of skills of artisans and propagation of appropriate technology and the adoption of a coherent marketing strategy both for internal and export marketing. The policies should not, on the other hand, be such as would discourage the natural growth in size of tiny and small industries. The organisational set-up will have to be revamped to meet the changing higher technological needs in terms of a well-programmed human resources development. Adequate and well organised programmes of extension, training and entrepreneurial motivation will have to be undertaken. R&D efforts will have to be stepped up and commercial production and distribution of improved tools and equipment undertaken. Special programmes and taxation incentives should be provided to the tiny sector having investment below ₹ 5 lakh.

The future of the small-scale industries by and large depends upon the industrial policy pursued by the government during the nineties. The small-scale sector requires the active support of the government. *It is, therefore, necessary to adopt a policy conducive to the growth of this sector, so as to enable it to enter the 21st century with confidence and bright prospects.

* Taxation benefits be adequate, meaningful and free from undue harassment. It should aim at motivating an entrepreneur to go to set-up an SSI.

ANNEXURE

Comprehensive Policy Package for SSI Sector and Tiny Sector

SSI SECTOR

Policy Support

- The investment limit for the SSI sector will continue to be ₹ 10 million.
- The Ministry of SSI and ARI will bring out a specific list of hi-tech and export-oriented items which would require the investment limit to be raised to ₹ 50 million to admit suitable technology upgradation and to enable them to maintain their competitive edge.
- The Limited Partnership Act will be drafted quickly and get enacted. An attempt will be made to bring the Bill before the next session of the Parliament.

Fiscal Support

- To improve the competitiveness of the Small-scale Sector, the exemption limit for excise duty has been raised from ₹ 5 million to ₹ 10 million.

Credit Support

- The composite loans limit has been raised from ₹ 1 million to ₹ 2.5 million.
- The Small-scale Service and Business (Industry Related) Enterprises (SSSBEs) with a maximum investment of ₹ 1 million will qualify for priority lending.
- The eligibility limit for coverage under the recently launched (August 2000) Credit Guarantee Scheme has been revised to ₹ 2.5 million from the present limit of ₹ 1 million.
- Under the National Equity Fund (NEF) Scheme, the project cost limit will be raised from ₹ 2.5 million to ₹ 5 million. The soft loan limit will be retained at 25 per cent of the project subject to a maximum of ₹ 1 million, per project. Assistance under the NEF will be provided at a service charge of 5 per cent per annum.
- The Department of Economic Affairs will appoint a Task Force to suggest the revitalisation/restructuring of the State Financial Corporations.
- The Nayak Committee's recommendations with regard to the provision of 20 per cent of the projected turnover as working capital is being recommended to the financial institutions and banks.

Infrastructural Support

- The Integrated Infrastructure Development Scheme will progressively cover all areas in the country with a 50 per cent reservation for rural areas.
- Regarding the upgradation of the industrial estates, that are languishing, the SSI Ministry will draw up a detailed scheme for consideration of the Planning Commission.
- A plan scheme for cluster development will be drawn up.
- The funds available under the non-lapsable pool for the North East will be made use of for Industrial Infrastructure Development in the North East region including Sikkim, for the setting up of incubation centres and for cluster development.

Technological Support and Quality Improvement

- Capital subsidy of 12 per cent of investment in technology in select sectors. An inter-ministerial committee of experts will be set-up to define the scope of technology upgradation and sectoral priorities.
- To encourage total quality management, the scheme of granting ₹ 75,000 to each unit for obtaining ISO-9000 certification will continue for the next six years, i.e., till the end of the Tenth Plan.
- The setting up of incubation centres in sunrise industries will be supported.
- The TBSE set-up by SIDBI will be strengthened so that it functions effectively as a Technology Bank. It will be properly networked with NSIC, SIDO (SENET Programme) and APCTT.
- SIDO, SIDBI and NSIC will jointly prepare a compendium of available technologies for the R&D institutions in India and abroad and circulate this among the industry associations for the dissemination of the latest technology-related information.
- Commercial banks are being requested to develop schemes to encourage investment in technology upgradation and harmonise the same with SIDBI.

- A one time capital grant of 50% will be given to small-scale industries associations which wish to develop and operate testing laboratories, provided they are of international standards.

Marketing Support

- SIDO will have a Market Development Assistance Programme, similar to the one operating in the Ministry of Commerce. It will be a plan scheme.
- The Vendor Development Programme, Buyer-seller Meets and Exhibitions will take place more often and at dispersed locations.

Streamlining Inspections/Rules and Regulations

- To minimise harassment to the SSI sector a group will be set-up to recommend within 3 months, the means for streamlining inspection. This will include a repeal of laws and regulations applicable to the sector that have since become redundant.
- Self-certification will be progressively encouraged in lieu of inspections, which should be prescribed under the following three conditions:
  - On receipt of specific complaint;
  - Selection of unit for sample check (Say 10 per cent of total units); and
  - For audit and safety purposes.

Entrepreneurship Development

- Capacity building in the SSI sector, both for entrepreneurs as well as workers will be given top priority. The Ministry of SSI and Labour Ministry will jointly workout the strategy.

Facilitating Prompt Payment

- The Reserve Bank of India is being requested to appoint a Task Force to go into the question of strengthening and popularising factoring services, without recourse to the SSI suppliers. The Task Force shall give its report within six months of its constitution.
- RBI is being requested to take up with the banks the question of sub-allocating the overall limits to the large borrowers specifically for meeting the payment obligations in respect of purchases from the SSIs, either on a cash basis or on bills basis.

Rehabilitation of Sick Units

- RBI is being requested to draw up revised guidelines for the rehabilitation of currently sick but potentially viable SSI units. Such guidelines should be detailed, transparent and non-discretionary.

Promoting Rural Industries

- To support the Handloom Sector the "Deendayal Hathkarga Protsahan Yojna" has been announced. The scheme has a total financial impliction of ₹ 4.47 billion and will provide comprehensive financial and infrastructural support to weavers.
- The government is working out new comprehensive package to strengthen Khadi and Village Industries that will further upgrade the skills of khadi workers.

Improving Data Base

- A fresh Census of small-scale industries will be conducted covering *inter alia*, the incident of sickness.

TINY SECTOR

Policy Support

- The investment limit for the tiny sector will continue to be ₹ 2.5 million.
- Under the Prime Minister's Rozgar Yojna, which facilitates the setting up of micro enterprises and generates employment for the educated unemployed, the family income eligibility limit of ₹ 24,000 per annum being revised to ₹ 40,000 per annum.

Credit Support

- The Nayak Committee's recommendations regarding the provision of 20 per cent of the projected turnover as working capital is being recommended to the financial institutions and banks. In respect of tiny units also 20 per cent of the projected annual turnover would qualify for working capital loan.
- The National Small Industries Corporation will continue to give composite loans up to ₹ 2.5 million to the tiny sector and continue to charge one per cent concessional interest rate.
- SIDBI will continue to give concessional rate of refinance to the tiny sector which is now at 10.5 per cent as compared to 12 per cent for the SSI sector. This policy will continue.

In the National Equity Fund Scheme, the project cost limit will be raised from ₹ 2.5 million to Rs. 5.0 million. The soft loan limit will be retained at 25 per cent of the project cost subject to a maximum of ₹ 1.0 million per project. Assistance under the NEF will be provided at a service charge of 5 per cent per annum. Under the National Equity Fund Scheme, 30 per cent of the investment will be earmarked for the tiny sector.

Infrastructure Support

The Integrated Infrastructure Development (IID) Scheme will progressively cover all areas in the country with 50 per cent reservation for rural areas. Under this scheme, 50 per cent of the plots will be earmarked for the tiny sector (as against the 40 per cent done earlier).

Under the National Programme for Rural Industrialisation, cluster development is being taken up by KVIC, SIDO, SIDBI and NABARD. The major beneficiaries of the cluster development programme will be tiny sector units. The sponsoring organisation for each cluster will provide for design development, capacity building, technology intervention and consortium marketing. A cluster development fund will be created under the plan.

Technological Support

Under the capital subsidy of scheme of 12 per cent for investment in technology upgradation in select sectors, preference will be given to the tiny sector.

Marketing Support

Preference will be given to the tiny sector while organising buyer-seller meets, vendor development programmes and exhibitions.

(**Source:** Office of the DC (SSI)

New Package for Khadi and Village Industries

Options of Rebate and MDA

Market Development Assistance (MDA) at the rate of 20 per cent of the annual turnover has been introduced as an option in place of rebate to the institutions for producing innovative designs and marketable products.

Additional Working Capital

The term loan of ₹ 3 billion given to Khadi Institutions is being converted into working capital. Further, a fresh line of credit of ₹ 2.5 billion as working capital would be provided to those institutions that are willing to switch from Rebate Scheme to MDA Scheme.

Insurance Cover to Khadi Artisans

Insurance cover for khadi artisans against death, disability and disease will be provided.

Quality

The quality of products of this sector will be certified through labs accredited by NABI.

- To create Packaging and Design Facilities, Brand Building Exercise, in the form of Heritage Khadi, standard logo and standard design of sales outlets.
- To undertake marketing blitz and campaigns through the use of multimedia and sustained publicity.

Cluster Development Programme

To create common facilities for innovation, technology upgradation, packaging, processing, testing and e-commerce.

Focus on Core Areas

An amount of ₹ 2.75 billion has been earmarked for a few selected areas where there exists a competitive advantage, namely herbal cosmetic and medicines, honey, organic foods, edible oils and essential oils to begin with.

Source: Office of the DC (SSI)

Measures taken for Development of North Eastern Region

- Small Industry Service Institutes (SISIs) have been set-up in all the North Eastern States to provide assistance/consultancy services to prospective and existing entrepreneurs, conduct entrepreneurship development, management development and skill development programmes for SSI entrepreneurs and also to provide common facilities through workshops/laboratories attached to SSIs.
- The Prime Minister's Rozgar Yojana (PMRY) has been liberalised for the North Eastern Region. The family income limit for each beneficiary and his/her spouse has been enhanced from ₹ 24,000 to ₹ 40,000 per annum and the age limit for eligibility has also been enhanced from 35 years to 40 years. Activities like horticulture, piggery, poultry, fishing and small tea gardens have also been included as economically viable activities, which are distinctive for the North Eastern Region.
- Under the Integrated Infrastructure Development (IID) Scheme meant for improvement of infrastructure in rural and backward areas for SSIs, one IID Centre has been sanctioned for Assam in the district of Darang (Village Dalgon) and another for Manipur in the district of Chandel (Village Moreh).
- Indian Institute of Entrepreneurship (IIE), Guwahati was set-up in 1994 as a full-fledged institute to act as a catalyst to encourage entrepreneurial development in the North East. The institute organises training programmes and undertakes research and consultancy services in the field of small industry and entrepreneurship.
- Transport Subsidy Scheme was introduced in 1971, with a view to promoting industrialisation in hilly, remote and inaccessible areas. Under the scheme, transport subsidy ranging from 50 per cent to 90 per cent is admissible on the transport cost incurred on movement of raw materials and finished goods from the designated rail heads/ports up to the location of industrial units and *vice versa*. The scheme has been extended up to March 31, 2007 for North Eastern Region.
- Industrial undertakings set up in Integrated Infrastructural Development Centres and Industrial Growth Centres to be notified by the Central Government are exempt from income-tax for ten consecutive assessment years. A similar benefit is given to such other industries in the North Eastern Region as are notified by the Central Government. The above are effective from April 1, 2000.
- A Tool Room and Training Centre at Guwahati to create facilities for manufacture of quality tools and dies and for training in tool making is under implementation.
- On June 1, 1998 the Government of India has notified the Central Capital Investment Subsidy Scheme for industrial units in the North Eastern Region. A scheme of interest subsidy on the working capital loans for industrial units in the North Eastern Region called the Central Interest Subsidy Scheme, 1977 has also been notified on February 18, 1999 with a view to accelerating the industrial development in the region.

(Source: Office of the DC (SSI)

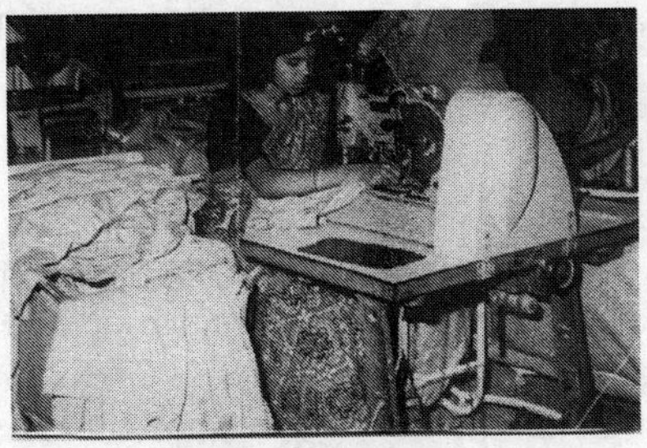

14 CHAPTER

MARKETING MECHANISM IN SMALL-SCALE INDUSTRIES

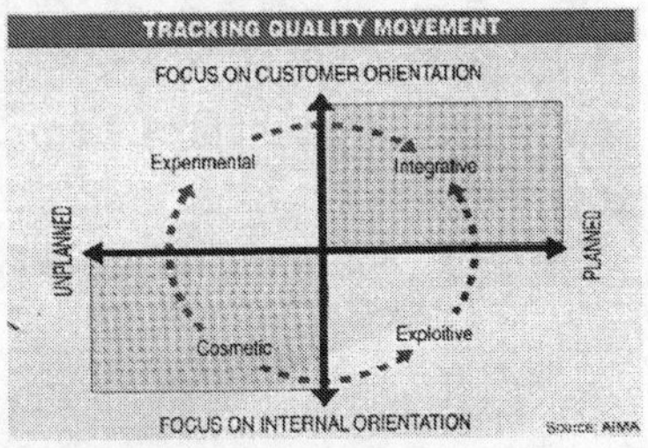

Vitality of companies operating in an economy makes the decisive difference in the capacity of a country to create wealth and to upgrade the basis of competition from comparative factor advantages to innovative capability that enables the highest order of value capture.

LEARNING OBJECTIVES

The chapter covers the following topics:

- Studying of this chapter, enables you to understand
- The principal functions of marketing.
- Responsibilities of the management.
- Marketing mix, segmentation and assessment.
- Institutional marketing.
- Marketing problems.
- Sales management, and
- Marketing plan.

Marketing is "the process of planning and executing the conception, pricing, promotion and distribution of ideas, goods and services to create exchange that satisfy individual and organisational objectives".

INTRODUCTION

Marketing occupies an important place in the management of a small-scale industry. It is a key factor in determining the success of an industrial concern. Traditionally, marketing consisted of 'those efforts which affect transfers in ownership of goods and care for their physical distribution'. In economic terms, marketing covers those activities which relate to the creation of time, place and possession of activities. Marketing is defined as the process of exchange between seller and buyer. P. Kotler defines marketing as a 'human activity directed at satisfying needs and process'. The American Marketing Association (AMA) defines market as 'the performance of business activities that direct the flow of goods and services from producer to consumer or user'.

The salient features of marketing are:

(i) It is a creative function;

(ii) It promotes trade and employment;

(iii) It coordinates finance, production and distribution and determines and directs the scale and value of the total efforts;

(iv) There is an emphasis on what the consumer wants; and

(v) There is an emphasis on the social good, on increasing employment and on giving the consumer the chance to decide.

The small industries in India generally suffer from many ailments where marketing is concerned. The most important are:

(i) Lack of brand names and places of respectability for goods of the small-scale industry;

(ii) Identification of proper markets and consumers;

(iii) Research and market investigations and services;

(iv) Standardisation and quality improvement;

(v) Introduction of goods in foreign markets; and

(vi) Raw materials.

Marketing mechanism in small-scale industries involves all the activities undertaken in the transferring of goods and titles thereto from the producer to consumers. The efficiency of marketing determines the sales and profits of the small-scale industries. In fact, these industries are able to prosper with a very significant marketing system. The marketing mechanism differs from one industry to another. While tiny industries and ancillary units opt for simple mechanisms, some others opt for full-scale marketing mechanisms, usually adopted by medium and large-scale units. In some other cases, marketing of goods is entrusted to marketing agencies, which are specialised in such operations. The significance of marketing for the small-scale industry is the very basis of its industrial activity. Thus, marketing is the key factor for the success of small-scale industries.

Marketing Process: Marketing involves three basic inputs: the product, promotional methods and the distribution system. These three are the core of the marketing programme and must be integrated to achieve maximum consumer satisfaction and optimum profits. The marketing process brings together producers and customers – the two important segments in any exchange. An exchange or a transaction takes place when a market offering is acceptable to the customer who is prepared to give something in return for the product he purchases.

THE PRINCIPAL MARKETING FUNCTIONS

A marketing function may be defined as a major specialised activity or group of activities performed in the marketing of goods and services. Although the performance of a specific function may be inescapable, it is frequently transferable: in other words, it has to be performed by someone regardless of his official title and responsibilities. Another characteristic of a function is that, whereas its purpose may be unchanging, its content, in terms of the number and kinds of activities involved, may be subject to constant change. Newer and better ways of doing things and carrying out traditional functions are continually being developed.

Traditionally, some seven or eight so-called marketing functions have been listed and normally include: (a) the exchange functions of buying and selling, (b) the physical distribution functions of transporting, warehousing and handling goods between producer and customer, (c) what are usually described as the 'facilitating' functions which take in product standardisation and simplification, commercial and market information, financing and risk-bearing. (It is questionable whether risk-bearing, in the true entrepreneurial sense of commiting one's own resources to a speculative venture, really belongs in any list of marketing functions, and risk bearing is a responsibility jointly undertaken by the managers of a business or solely by the chief executive).

This kind of analysis is inadequate as a description of modern marketing activities since it fails to distinguish clearly between major functions and the specialised activities which comprise the different functions. Under the modern marketing concept, there are four principal functions – marketing research and information, product planning, selling and distribution and advertising and promotion. Table 14.1 sets out those major functions and the specialised activities involved in each segments.

Table 14.1 The Principal Marketing Functions

Specific Function	Activities involved
Marketing Information and Research	Economics, business, trade, industry, consumer, user, product, sales and advertising research and analysis. Information handling the data processing. Marketing operations research and competitive intelligence.
Product Planning	Determining and developing the company's product mix. Matching the products specifications, packaging, pricing, performance and servicing to customer needs through product and service improvements and new product development.
Sales and Distribution	Field selling/Selection of distribution channels/Warehousing/Transport/Sales analysis/Sales reporting/Sales forecasting/Sales budgets and quotas/ Merchandising/Sales communications.
Advertising and Promotion	Advertising to the customer or user in all media (press, television, cinema, radio, outdoor posters, etc.), Consumer promotion directed at the customer or user, e.g., reduced price offers, branded pack offers, premiums, competitions, couponing, etc. Point-of-purchase display materials. Trade promotion, e.g., incentive schemes, display competitions, sales contest.

(**Source:** Extracted from Marketing in a Competitive Economy, by Lesile Rodger.)

Responsibilities of Management

The major responsibilities of general management are to establish marketing objectives, to make policy decisions and communicate these decisions to the managers of the operating (or implementing) divisions of the company and to establish standards for measuring and guiding its overall performance. The responsibilities of operational or line management are to plan programmes, methods and procedures and implement the decisions necessary to achieve the stated objectives; to organise and coordinate the activities and resources necessary to carry out the programmes; and to see that operating results conform as nearly as possible to agreed plans and standards of performance.

Dressing up a New Generation (children are the new target buyers for Apparel Makers)

The production division is responsible for the manufacturing aspects of marketing – organising men, materials, machines and time to produce the requisite qualities and quantities at specified times and at a designated cost to meet market requirements and sales forecasts. Quality control, production programming and raw materials procurement are included here.

The financial or accounting division of the company is concerned with the financial aspects of marketing-budgetary control, standard costing and profit planning. Business is based on the rigorous discipline of money and a major criterion of performance, but not necessarily the only one, must be profit earned. Nothing that a company produces makes money for the company until it is sold and paid for.

The marketing division is responsible for the sales, marketing research, product-planning and development, distribution and promotional aspects of marketing, for the detailed implementation of marketing and advertising plans and programmes and for achieving designated marketing goals. In some companies, the sales distribution functions are separated from the research, product planning and promotion functions – the latter group sometimes being designated as 'marketing services'. This does not matter so long as both the sales division and the 'marketing services' division are coordinated by the same individual, irrespective of the latter's title, i.e., Marketing Director, Sales Director or Commercial Director.

Finally, the Personnel and Administration Division of the company, if this is separated from general management, is responsible for those aspects of marketing dealing with job evaluation, selection and recruitment, executive training and general administrative procedures laid down in the company policy.

The line-up of the management and the four basic operating divisions of a company as described above is depicted in Fig. 14.1.

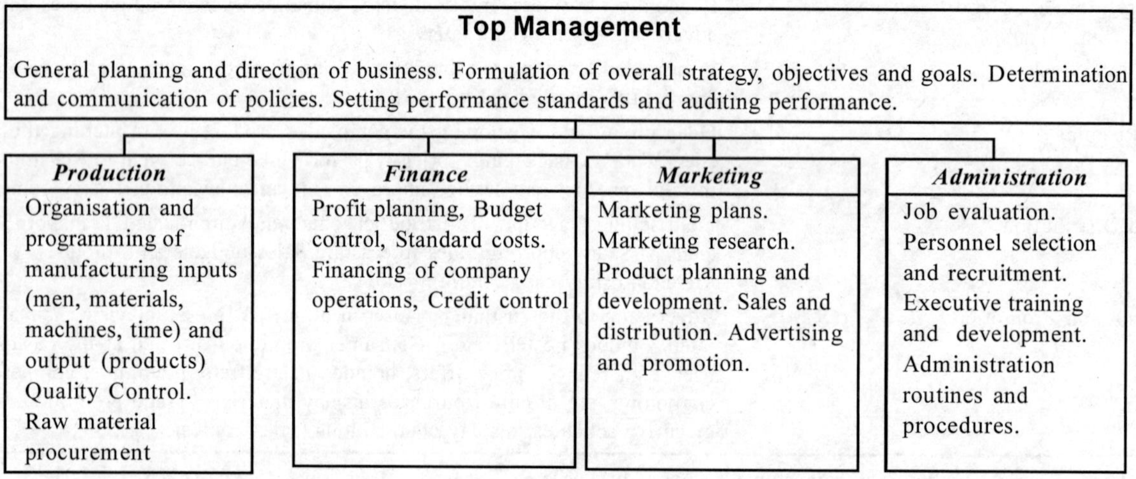

Fig. 14.1 The Responsibilities of Top Management and Four Opening Divisions of a Company

Marketing is nothing more nor less than the profitable matching of total company resources against market requirements and opportunities. Production requirements are dependent upon the solution given to this commercial equation; in other words, a company should make what can be profitably sold. What is absolutely certain is that, if it remains unsold, it cannot yield a profit. In the divisions, the business function has been more concerned with matching total company resources against production requirements, that is the company has attempted to sell what it wanted to make. The task of marketing management is to identify, assess and realise market opportunities and potentials.

Marketing management is responsible for creating customers by persuading them through advertising and personal salesmanship that the company's products or services match their indicated needs and preferences more closely than competitor's offerings, by developing products and services through technical and market research which appear to offer profitable sales opportunities, and at a price, time and place the customers want.

The marketing process starts with knowledge of the customer and his needs and ends with a customers purchase and the satisfaction of those needs. Through technical product research and customer research, generalised needs are translated into specific product sales opportunities. Product planning identifies and specifies the particular product-price-package combinations to exploit these opportunities. Products are engineered or formulated (a number of variations of a single prototype may be made up), screened and tested with customers for overall acceptance and perfomance. Final decisions have to be taken on packaging design, pricing and trade terms. Assuming that one product stands out as eminently suitable in all major respects, the next step is to prepare a marketing plan, in writing, setting down all the relevant facts about the product, the market, and the competition, the company's marketing objectives and sales goals and the means by which they are to be achieved.

Applying the Marketing Concept

The marketing concept is applicable to all business organisations irrespective of size or nature of the goods and services marketed. Difference in the types of goods supplied in the size and characteristics of the consumer or user markets for the various classes of goods, in the purposes for which they are acquired and in the methods by which they are distributed, do not invalidate the universal applicability of the marketing concept to business.

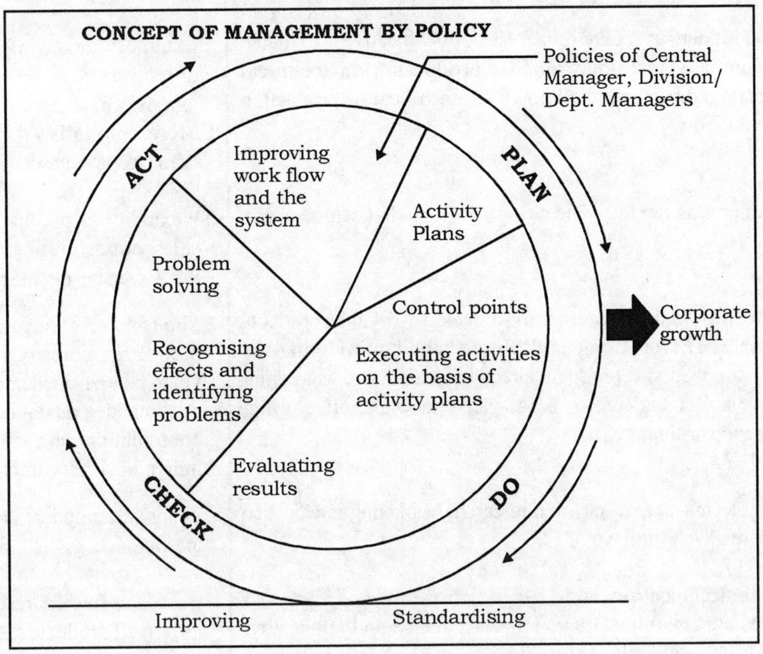

Fig. 14.2 Concept of Management by Policy

As between large and small firms, and as between producers of consumer goods and producers of industrial goods, there may be differences in the permissible scale of marketing effort and in the specific types of marketing techniques that are appropriate to the particular industry or market. A far more fundamental difference, irrespective of size or type of business, is the attitude of management. The following chart attempts to highlight some of the major differences that might be expected to be reflected in business operations according to whether the management ends to think in terms of production or in terms of marketing.

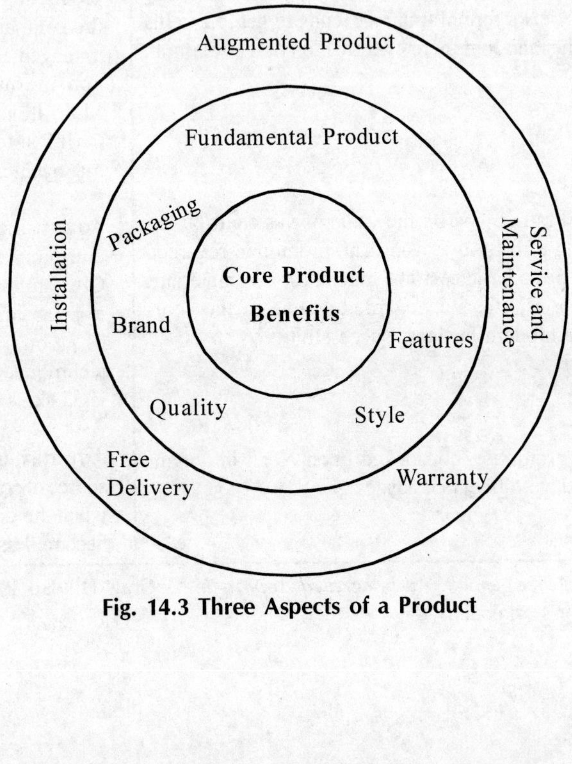

Fig. 14.3 Three Aspects of a Product

Basic Differences Between Production-oriented and Marketing-oriented Organisation

Business Function or Activity	Company Perspective: Production	Company Perspective: Marketing
Top Management	Technological considerations predominate. Production and engineering personnel in highest level executive positions.	Customer considerations paramount. Marketing personnel in highest level executive positions.
Objectives	Internal influences predominate. Business objective is to match total company resources against production on technical efficiency and methods be known for technical or production and know-how.	External market influences predominate. Business objective is to match total company resources against market requirements and opportunities. More emphasis on market strategy and planning. Want to be regarded as style and market leader.
Manufacturing	Production less flexible. The company sells what can be made.	Flexibility in production so as to match product to sales opportunities. The company manufactures what can be profitably sold.
Marketing	Aims to fulfil existing needs and develop workable products to meet these needs. Company's future bound up with markets already supplied and products already in existence. Marketing function not considered to be as valuable as manufacturing, engineering or finance.	Seeks to create markets and develop saleable products. Company's future bound up with markets yet to be identified and developed, and with products not yet in existence. Marketing considered to be coordination with manufacturing, finance and other major business functions.
Research	Leads in technical and scientific research. Marketing intelligence system relatively undeveloped.	Leads in analytical and marketing research. Market intelligence system well developed.
Product Planning	Based on technical research, suggestion for new or improved products system from functional performance and application are prime considerations. Engineering consideration tends to predominate. Laboratory testing more prominent than sales or market. Packaging viewed as a shipping and protective device. Chief concern in engineering, materials handling and packaging machinery.	Based on market research. Suggestions for new or improved products stem from research into customer needs. Performance and applications are prime considerations regarded to be almost as important. Sales and market testing are an integral part of planning. Packaging viewed as a sales tool in terms of user convenience and advertising and promotional effectiveness.
Sales Organisation	Salesman regarded as an order-getter for the factory. Salesman lacks the professional status of the engineer, chemist, lawyer or accountant. Less likely to be promoted to the top management. He lacks formal training, tends to get left to his own devices as the man 'out there'. Motivation of the salesman minimal.	Salesman regarded as an order-maker who keeps the factory running and provides employment to production workers. He is accorded high status in the company and more likely to be promoted to top management positions. Salesman given formal and continuous internal and on-the-job training. Motivation of sales organisation given high priority. Chief sales executive regarded as part of the management team.
Advertising and promotion	Emphasis on cost rather than on the value of this contribution to the total selling effort. Advertising and promotion regarded as an extra cost, not a basic cost like machines, raw materials, research laboratories, etc. Not regarded as one of the skills required to run a modern business successfully.	Advertising and promotion is an integral part of the company's marketing effort and a basic cost. Outstanding advertising and promotion considered to be as equally important to the successful running of a business as outstanding manufacturing technique, technical research ability or financial and legal skills.
	Advertising and promotion not looked upon as an important source of competitive differential advantage.	Advertising and promotion regarded as a potential source of competitive differential advantage particularly when the differences is own and competitive products become less and less distinguishable.

Source: F.F. Mayseer, *Modern Marketing Management: An Integrated Approach,* McGraw-Hill Book Co. Inc., 1961, pp. 10-11. The data above has been adapted from the author's original.

Marketing Mix

A successful marketing strategy depends upon a marketing mix of all the marketing elements and resources.

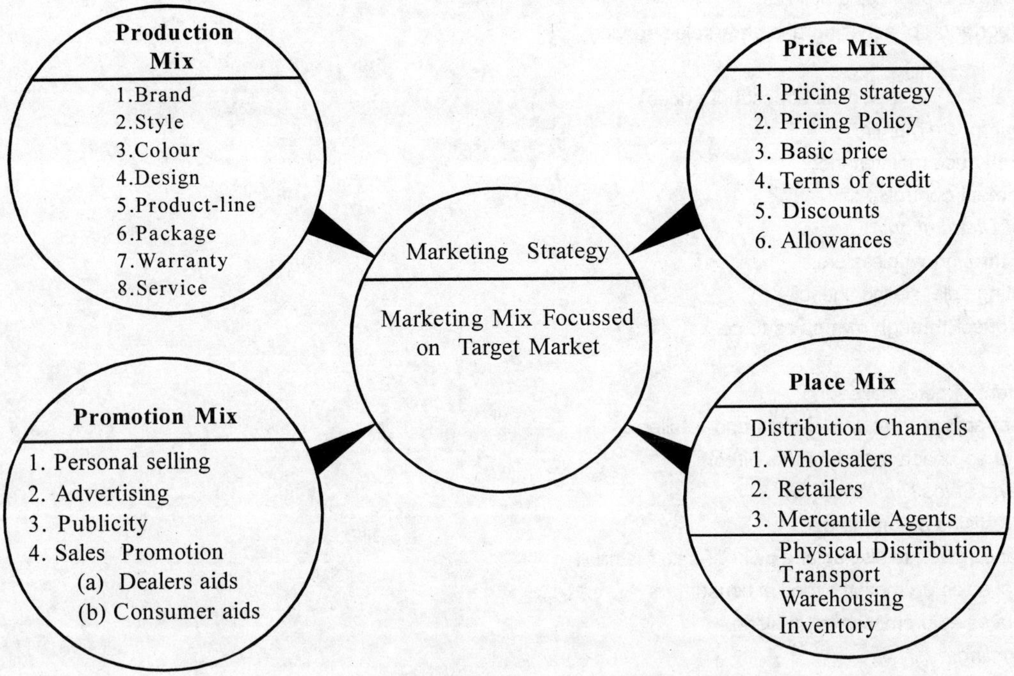

Fig. 14.4 Elements of Marketing Mix

The basic marketing mix is the blending of four inputs or submixes which form the core of the marketing system: (i) Product mix, (ii) Place mix, (iii) Promotion mix, and (iv) Price mix. The outputs are optimum productivity and satisfaction.

Marketing Process

Marketing involves three basic inputs: the product, the promotional methods and the distribution system. These three are the core of the marketing programme and must be integrated to achieve maximum consumer satisfaction and optimum profits. The marketing process brings together producers and customers – the two important segments in any exchange. An exchange or a transaction takes place when a market offering is acceptable to the customer who is prepared to give something in return for the product he purchases.

The marketing process starts with knowledge of the customer and his needs and ends with a customer's purchase and the satisfaction of those needs. Through technical product research and customer research, generalised needs are translated into specific product sales opportunities. Product planning identifies and specifies the particular product-price-package combinations to exploit these opportunities. Products are engineered or formulated (a number of variations of a single prototype may be made up), screened and tested with customers for overall acceptance and performance, final decisions have to be taken on packaging design, pricing and trade terms. Assuming that one product stands out as eminently suitable in all major respects, the next step is to prepare a marketing plan, in writing, setting down all the relevant facts about the product, the market and competition, the company's marketing objectives and sales goals and the means by which they have to be achieved.

Box 14.1 Elements of the Marketing Mix

1. *General Planning:*
   (-) Establishing an acceptable and possible rate of growth.
   (-) Determining the size and extent of market where business may function profitably.
   (-) Determining the cost and expenses needed for the business operations.
   (-) Estimating the finance needed.

2. *Product Planning:*
   - (-) Determining the product or service offered.
   - (-) The possible improvement and innovation in the product.
   - (-) The brand and packaging policies.
   - (-) The importance of servicing and after-sales service.
3. *Pricing:*
   - (-) The level and psychological aspects of prices.
   - (-) The appropriate margin.
   - (-) Research price maintenance.
   - (-) Government control, if any.
4. *Channels of Distribution:*
   - (-) Selling through wholesalers.
   - (-) Appointing sole selling agencies.
   - (-) Selling direct through own sales force.
5. *Sales Force:*
   - (-) The extent of personal selling.
   - (-) Extent of approach to wholesalers and retailers.
   - (-) Extent of approach to consumers direct.
6. *Advertising and Sales Promotion:*
   - (-) The advertising programme.
   - (-) Importance given to display and point-of-sale material.
   - (-) Extent of sales promotion aimed at consumers.
   - (-) Extent of sales promotion to dealers.
7. *Physical Handling:*
   - (-) Transportation.
   - (-) Warehousing.
   - (-) Inventory policies.
   - (-) Possible reduction in costs.
8. *Marketing Research:*
   - (-) Sales analysis.
   - (-) Field surveys.
   - (-) Use of outside agencies.

Market Segmentation

No organisation can effectively serve all sections of the market. This is so, because customers are numerous, widely spread over and differ in their buying practices/requirements and perceptions. This is more relevant to SSI units, in view of their resource constraints. It is, therefore, essential to first decide which segments of the market the organisation would be in the best position to serve. This can be facilitated through market segmentation.

India has many diversities with regard to consumption patterns. Thus, in reality, it is a conglomeration of several markets in which people tend to differ. People can be regrouped demographically, economically and socially, but even within these groups, each set of consumers can be differentiated further. For instance, individuals sharing a common demographic profile may show variations in terms of a cultural and demographic mosaic. The marketer has to recognise all these differences since each individual represents a unique opportunity.

Segmentation is dynamic and extends beyond the traditional two-dimensional classification. We need to treat it as three-four or five-dimensional segmenting. Many intelligent companies have been able to do beyond tow-dimension. However, it is only the gut feeling of the marketer that will help him into the fourth and fifth dimensions of segmenting. Thus, segmentation itself becomes a multi-dimensional issue, and a marketer has to face a complex matrix in terms of positioning products.

Segmentation or subdivision of the market is based upon the modern marketing concept, i.e., market-oriented strategy and philosophy. Segmentation places special emphasis on the demand side of the market. It is a more rational and more precise adjustment of the product and marketing effort is tuned to the consumer or user's needs and requirements. Segmentation implies that there are several demand schedules and not necessarily a single demand schedule or curve. For each demand schedule representing of group of buyers with similar needs and characteristics, we can prepare a separate and precise market offering or marketing mix.

Market segmentation is a method for achieving maximum market response from limited marketing resources by recognising *differences* in the characteristics of the various parts of the market. In a sense, market segmentation is the strategy of *divide and conquer*, i.e., dividing markets in order to conquer them. Its philosophy is something for everybody, within practicable limits. Marketing strategy is adjusted to inherent differences in buyer behaviour. For different groups of customers, i.e., market segments, we have different sets of marketing strategies. Segmentation strategy is an answer to the question: "To whom should we sell our products, and what should we sell them?" It is a strategic choice concerned with "doing the right things" as opposed to the tactical choice, "doing things right".

Market segmentation enables the marketers to give better attention to the selection of customers and offer an appropriate marketing mix for each chosen segment, or a group of buyers having homogeneous demand. Each subdivision or segment can be selected as a market target to be reached with a distinct marketing mix.

Marketers must go beyond the age-old classifications based on consumer locations, age-profiles, gender, and economic strata, among others, and take into account several other factors that differentiate the markets.

Table 14.2 Stages of Development in Marketing Management

Production Orientation	Sales Orientation	Customer/ Market Orientation
Market is viewed as dependent variable and production capacity as the independent variable. Production Deptt. → Market	Market as dependent variable and sale department capacity as the independent variable. Sales Deptt. → Market	Market and the firm are mutually interdependent; firm is highly dependent on market; it is an extension of the market. Market → Firm
Emphasis is on the production process – on technical unit. Focus is on problems of manufacturing/finance.	Emphasis is on own products of the firm – on sales.	Emphasis is on the customer needs and wants – on demand. Focus is on problems of marketing.
Marketing means: 'Sell what is produced'.	Marketing means: 'A good proudct does not sell by itself. It has to be pushed. Customers have to be manipulated.'	Marketing means: 'Targeting on customer needs/present or future purchasing patterns of demand.'
Prevalent in a situation of absolute scarcity, or during the seller's market.	Prevalent in a situation of surplus production surplus capacity, or when the market has not been surveyed properly.	Prevalent in a situation of relative affluence or during the buyer's market.
Prevalent in the West prior to 1930. Prevalent in areas, e.g., developing nations a production economy stage.	Prevalent in the West during 1930-1950 and when demands is declined in certain industries.	Prevalent in the developed and affluent countries since 1955.
Production was the centre of the universe.	Salesmanship and promotion acted as the focus of marketing universe.	Customer satisfaction is the focus of the marketing universe.
It was summed that the best product could attract buyers automatically. Consumer choice could be based on quality in relation to price.	It is assumed that goods are not bought. They have to be sold at any cost, and profit is through sales volume.	It is assumed that goods are bought and not sold and profit is through customer satisfaction only.
No need of aggressive salesmanship and publicity. Company sells what it can make.	Special selling efforts and promotion to capture and maintain demand.	If demand clicks with supply, no special selling effort are necessary, problem is only of distribution, i.e., serving of demand. Company makes what it can sell.

Note: Since 1965, under environmental approach, marketing concept has been widened in the West. Government, market and pressure groups influence the firm and its marketing strategy. The firm has to adopt socially responsible marketing strategies. It has to cater to the needs of consumers as well as society – market needs in a social framework. It has to ensure quality of life, e.g., absence of food , air and water pollution. Consumerism and government should achieve consumer protection and environmental protection. The firm now aims at benefits for both sides, i.e., customer satisfaction and profitability. Societal or social marketing concept appeared in many affluent countries from 1965. It is slowly spreading over also in other developing countries. It is now said that the so-called affluent countries have become really effluent countries. Developing countries should not be effluent countries.

Market Assessment

Successful innovation is a necessary condition for effective marketing. '*Innovate or perish*' is a current slogan which has a rich meaning for business operating in an economy with customer-oriented marketing. An innovation is considered as a successful invention. An innovation is the act of developing a novel ideal into a process or product. For an innovation to be successful, the new product or new process must be feasible and must have commercial acceptability. The successful innovation passes through three stages: (i) idea or invention, (ii) implementation of the idea, and (iii) market acceptance. Implementation refers to the development of the idea or invention from its conceptual stage to an output – a developed product or service. Market acceptance is the third stage and it is the most critical to any successful innovation. A firm can control partially the first two stages. However, the acceptance decision is an external factor and it depends upon consumers and their reactions. Markets rely on all modes of promotion or marketing communication to exert influence on consumer behaviour and induce the potential customers to adopt the innovation.

In this changing world, attitudes, habits, preferences, values and trends change. A change in income, or instance, alters the demand pattern to unrecognisable dimensions. There are a number of variables which have a direct bearing on the demand pattern of a product. It is therefore, necessary to gather data and information on these variables to the extent possible with a view to making sound decisions. A sound decision based on sound facts should certainly reduce the risk. This is the role of marketing research.

Marketing research is needed to determine the kind of product you should manufacture on the basis of the needs, uses and preferences of the consumers; what size, package and presentation will be most effective in persuading the consumer to choose your products; the number of units that may be sold; the time and season for peak sales, optimum price, sales promotion methods and so on.

In other words, marketing research involves and study of consumer preferences, habits and attitudes; it helps to decide how immediate market operation should be directed. It also involves an examination of trends so that the subsequent findings indicate the future pattern of the market and assist in planning future programmes.

In a free economy, the consumer has the right to choose and the prerequisites of his choice are free competition and enough production to meet the demand – that is the demand does not exceed the supply. His second right is to be informed of the products, its characteristics and its capacity to satisfy his needs. His third right is that the product. Finally, he has the right to benefit from technological progress in terms of the satisfaction of his needs at reasonable cost. Therefore, any marketing research programme must begin with ascertaining the need, habits and preferences of consumers.

How to Grow A Stagnant Market
Promote the product, rather than specific brands, to convey the generic benefits
Break down usage barriers by eliminating the misconceptions that consumers have about it
Break the limitations of existing offerings to present new reasons to use the product
Offer added benefits that require increased usage of the product for better effect
Attach unique attributes to each brand to build customer involvement and increase usage
Offer entry to new customers at a price-per-unit that makes purchasing the product possible.
Identify the key benefits, and make the USP of new brands in order to win over customers
Use countrywide sampling activity to acquaint potential customers and back-up with advertising to convert intent to purchase
Multiply both brands and segments to add value

A System

Marketing is a system of integrated activities defined to develop strategies and plans including marketing mixes to the satisfaction of customer wants to selected market segments or targets. It is an ongoing process involving a set of multi-directional as well as multi-dimensional activities. Marketing is a matching process by which a producer provides marketing mix (product, price, promotion and physical distribution) that meets consumer demand of a target market within the limits of society.

Promotion is the process of marketing communication involving information, persuasion and influence. It is a systematic attempt to move forward from a stage of awareness to purchase action.

Of late, marketing management has been given much importance, especially by the SSI sector. This could be attributed to the vastly different market situations existing now. The demand for most products then exceeded the supply and anybody having the resources could normally do well. In a competitive environment, small-scale industries face marketing problems from stage-to-stage.

Some of the factors which contribute to marketing problems of the small-scale industry could be identified as under:

(i) Increasing competition from within the small-scale sector as well as from large industries with established brand names and marketing set up;

(ii) Consumer awareness, even in rural and semi-urban areas, for quality goods;

(iii) The need to set up distribution networks for reaching out widely dispersed markets, and

(iv) Inability of the SSI units to exploit the export markets.

Considerable difficulty is being experienced by small-scale industrial units in marketing their products due to their size, limited scale of operations and inability to set up an adequate network of retail outlets. With a view to facilitating the marketing efforts of small-scale units, it is considered desirable to encourage the operations of marketing organisations specially engaged in promotion of sales of products – cottage, tiny and small-scale industrial units. Any requests from such marketing organisations for financial assistance to meet their working capital needs should, therefore, be favourably considered by banks with due regard to the performance of such organisations in respect of recycling of bank credit.

The requirement, therefore, of systematic marketing efforts for survival and growth of small-scale industries, cannot be overemphasised. Basically, marketing involves:

- Finding out what consumers want;
- Planning and developing a product or service to satisfy these wants, and
- Determining the best way to price, promote and distribute that product or service.

The various activities required to be looked into in detail for arriving at a sound marketing strategy comprise product planning, market segmentation, market research, sales promotion, advertising, pricing and distribution. However, depending upon the product, the market and the environmental conditions, the intensity of usage of these activities will differ.

Marketing begins with the choice of a product and its planned production.

Product planning concerns itself with the creation of a product which is in demand in the market. It includes:

(i) Selection and development of a new product;

(ii) Product differentiation;

(iii) Packaging;

(iv) Branding;

(v) Value analysis; and

(vi) Product modification.

The proposed product can be a totally new product or an existing product with some modifications. It can also be a duplication of a competitor's product. The selection of product is an important process both for few and existing units. For an existing unit, it is important because old products cannot survive indefinitely as every product has a life cycle. Product life cycle consists of four stages: introduction, growth, maturity and decline. Depending upon the product, the cycle may vary from some months to even a few decades. Graphically, the product life cycle can be shown as under:

Table 14.3 Promotion Strategy

Push Strategy	*Pull Strategy*	*Push-Pull Strategy*
It is called a pressure strategy. Emphasis is on personal selling at all stages in distribution. We have aggressive and high pressure salesmanship. Conditions favouring push strategy: 1.Quality product with unique product features and talking points for salesmen 2.High-priced product, and 3.Higher profit margins to resellers. Advertising plays a minor role in the push strategy.	It is called a suction strategy. Emphasis is on extensive advertising to generate consumer demand. Product is literally pulled through the marketing channel by the consumer. Salesmen are mere order takers and distributing agents. Less emphasis on personal selling at all stages in distribution. Lower trade margins are offered to resellers. Lower retail prices but higher turnover rates. Heavy emphasis on consumer advertising and large investments required.	In the consumer goods market very large companies generally adopt a push-pull or a combination strategy to sell their products. Salesmen are employed to push products through the marketing channels. Extensive advertising is also employed to accelerate sales and to increase the market share. We need extensive promotion expenditures and only very big national companies can resort to combination strategy. All tools of promotion work together as a total communication process.

Note:

1. Strategy lay down plan of action to secure an advantage over competitors, demonstrate attractiveness to buyers and try to achieve fuller exploitation of company resources.
2. Pull strategy given emphais on mass promotion. Push strategy gives emphasis on personal selling.
3. Conditions indicating a favourable opportunity to promote are: 1. A favourable trend in demand, 2. Major product differences, 3. Hidden qualities (purity in drugs, cleaning power in detergents, flavour in foods), 4. Emotional buying motives to change the psychological climate or buyer's predisposition. Promotion strategy is expected to exploit such opportunities partly through information, partly through motivation and partly using promotion as a form of non-price competition.
4. In the push strategy, the middlemen have an active role for creating demand. In the pull strategy, he is responsible for the serving demand.

Table 14.4 Promotion Plans

Advertising Plan	Publicity Plan	Personal Selling Plan	Sales Promotion Plan
An advertising plan covers advertising: 1. Targets. 2. Objectives. 3. Strategy 4. Appeal 5. Copy theme. 6. Media schedule 7. Budget. 8. Methods for measuring advertising results.	A publicity plan covers: 1. Targets and objectives. 2. Schedule of company products and events with news value. 3. Media possibilities. 4. Budget 5. Means of measuring the results of publicity	A personal selling plan covers: 1. Sales targets. 2. Objectives. 3. Strategies. 4. Major appeals. 5. Budget. 6. Methods of measuring personal selling results.	A sales promotion plan covers: 1. Sales promotion targets. 2. Objectives. 3. Strategies. 4. Schedules of events. 5. Budget. 6. Methods of measuring the results of sales promotion.

Note:

1. Objectives indicate where a firm wants to go: strategy shows the way or means of going there and achieving objectives.
2. Promotion plans should be: (1) relevant, (2) practical, (3) complete and detailed. They should include specific costs and schedules of activities. They should be coordinated. They should allocate responsibilities and give necessary authority to those who are required to carry out each part of the plan.
3. Typical promotion objectives are: (1) increase sales, (2) improve market share, (3) create or improve brand recognition, acceptance, insistence, etc., (4) inform and educate the market, (5) create a competitive difference, and (6) create a favourble climate for future sales. Please note that promotion is only one tool to achieve these objectives.
4. A strategy is a plan for achieving objectives through the use of scarce resources in the face of intelligent competition.

A segmentation of the market may be done on the basis of consumer goods, both durable and non-durable. It may even be done in terms of producer goods in some cases. Let us take the example of durable goods. One proposes to manufacture builder's hardware. The different segments of the market in this case are house-builders aristocratic middle-class, lower middle-class, lower class; houses in hilly areas and so on. Officer's, shops and other similar buildings are other examples. The railways require this hardware for their wagons. Shipbuilders constitute another segment of the market.

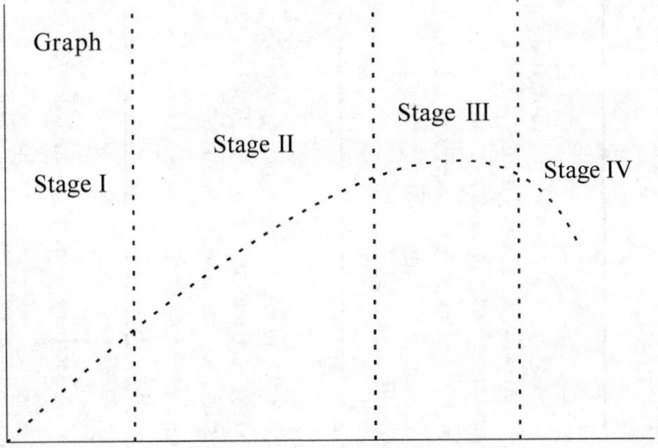

Fig. 14.5 Product Life Cycle

The advantages of segmentation of the market are:

(i) Narrowing the range of products;
(ii) Ease in preparing the design of the product, its colour scheme, shape, size and the type of package it may require;
(iii) Ease in determining the trade channels and avenues for direct selling;
(iv) Ease in preparing sales forecasts;
(v) Ease in planning, marketing programmers; and
(vi) Ease in selecting the media for appeals that will be most effective for promotion, e.g., displays, etc.

Buying Behaviour

Buying behaviour is the most important factor in conducting marketing; and yet it is the most complicated. Quite often, consumers, when questioned, give evasive answers which they feel they should rather than state the actual facts. Put in psychological terms, shyness, reticence, subconscious blocks, etc., of the respondents create complications. It is, therefore, essential that the information and data gathered through market research should be read with other available information.

Box 14.2 The Profits Models

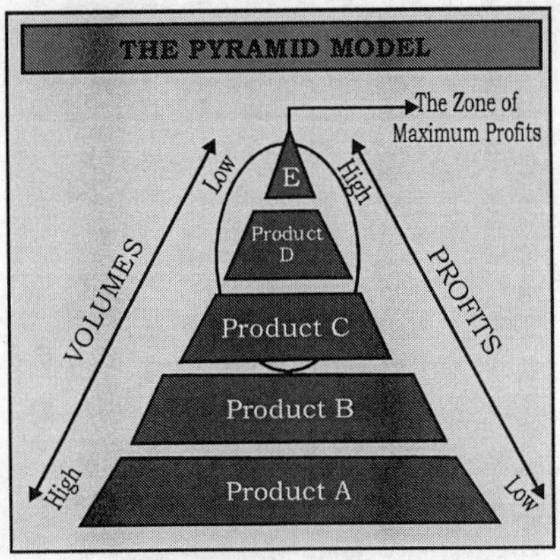

Profits And price. An inter-play of these 2 Ps makes the Product Pyramid the ideal profits model in the automobiles market. MUL uses it, and Fiat is planning to model its own business on it. The Product Pyramid posits the existence of distinct customer segments, exhibiting varied purchase-behaviour. In effect, customer preferences vary in terms of style, colour, features, and price.

The base of the Pyramid is occupied by low-price, high-volume products – like the Maruti 800 – where the margins are slim. The apex of the Pyramid is occupied by high-price, low-volume products – such as the Maruti Esteem VX.

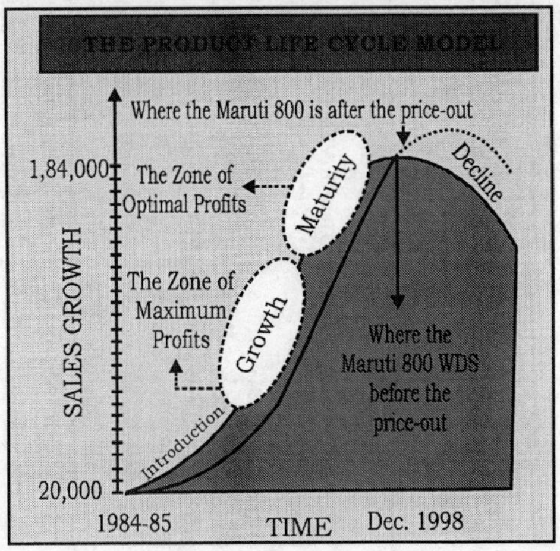

Although profits are concentrated near the top, the base plays a crucial role. It creates an entry-barrier for competitors, and insulates the profitable area near the top from competition.

The Pyramid is a profit's model for companies with multiple products aimed at multiple segments. The profits associated with each product follow models of their own. In the specific case of cars, the decline as the product nears the end of the maturity phases. MUL's decision to drop the prices of all the versions of the Maruti 800 came at this stage. The respite that this price-cut is expected to provide is aimed at extending the maturity phase of the product even as MUL shifts its investments to create the next-generation best-seller.

Tabel 14.5 Types of Communication (Promotion) Influencing Various Stages in Buyer Behaviour

Components or Dimensions of Attitude	Movement towards purchase (Six Stage Sequence)	Types of Communication Relevant at each Stage
1.The Conative (Behavioural) Dimension It is the region of drives or motives, i.e., activated unsatisfied wants. Advertisements and sales promotion must stimulate and direct desires so as to motivate the consumer to buy a product. The buyer should be made ready to respond and he should have the conviction that the purchase would be wise. Purchase is the last step converting this attitude into actual purchase.	↑ 6 Purchase Convictions	Point-of-purchase Material, Retail Store Advertising, Special Deals, 'Last Chance offer', Price Appeals, Testimonials, Source Credibility, i.e., expertness and trustworthiness of the sources, personal selling, interpersonal communication, word-of-mouth and communication are essential in evaluation and adoption stages. Believability of company as a communicator is called *source credibility*.
2.The Affective (Feelings and Emotions) Dimension It is the region of feelings and emotions. Consumer moves from knowledge to liking and preference, he develops a favourable attitude towards the product (liking) and then develops the point of reference. Promotion tools must stress the affective aspect of behaviour, i.e., the area of feeling and emotions must be tapped. Advertisements and sales promotion will change emotions and feelings.	↑ 4 Preference 3 Liking	Competitive Advertising, Argumentative Advertising Copy, Image Advertising, Status, Glamour Appeals, Stress on changing emotions and feelings of buyers. Opinion leaders are used as a good source of information and opinion – to change attitude of buyer through interpersonal communication.
3.The Cognitive Dimension It is the region of awareness and knowledge. Promotion tools must emphasise the cognitive aspects of buyer behaviour in order to create awareness and knowledge. Advertising provides adequate information and facts.	↑ 2 Knowledge 1 Awakened	Announcements Advertising, Descriptive Advertising Copy, Classified Advertisements, Slogans, Jingles, Sky Writing, Television, Radio Advertisements. Mass media must be adopted to create awareness, provide knowledge and information.

Note:

1. Buying process involves a six-stage sequence related to three basic psychological states: (1) The cognitive dimension (awareness and knowledge), (2) The affective dimension (liking and preference), and (3) The cognitive dimension (conviction and purchase).
2. A firm does not have separate strategies of advertising, selling and sales promotion. It has one promotional mix and this mix is an integral part of the overall marketing plan. The elements of promotion mix are no independent strategies. Each one supports the other. They are complementary tools of promotion. Taken together, advertising, personal selling and sales promotion are the 'three musketeers' of marketing programmes. Their motto is 'All for one and one for all'. An integrated marketing mix means this, and nothing short of this can be thought by a marketer.
3. Promotion plan should be in harmony with overall corporate objective, policies, organisation and its competence. Promotional plan should be evaluated against specific promotional objectives as well as against the rest of the marketing mix.
4. The proper coordination and integration of selling, advertising and sales promotion produces a far more efficient programme than an attempt to carry out these activities without regard to their effects upon each other.
5. Movement towards purchase is upwards. It starts from awareness and ends at purchase action or decision, and
6. The company reputation, created through advertising and other form of mass communication, can enhance the effectiveness of the salesmen. Company image is the personality or reputation of the company as perceived by customers, prospects, supplied shareholders and the general public company image is created by communications, particularly through public relations.

One has to design the marketing research programmes according to one's specific objectives – for example, for introducing a new product or for diversifying products to meet the challenge of the competitors in the line, or for making alternative products available in the market to serve the same need. The conduct of marketing research is a specialised job.

Marketing Research and Small-scale Industry

Marketing research is a very important tool for small-scale units. It fills the gap between the development of a product and its ultimate sale to the consumer. Combined with test-marketing, it makes it possible for an entrepreneur not to get involved in heavy promotional expenditure on a wrong product. It keeps him posted with information about his stocks and purchases, and about the sales of representative sample of retailers in different regions, consumer preferences and demand for his product.

Marketing research should be used by small-scale industries not only when things are going wrong but when the prospects are bright. Marketing research continuously strives to answer six important questions of marketing mechanism, viz.:

What does the market buy?
Why does it buy?
Who buys it?
How does it buy?
When does it buy?, and
Where does it buy?

At macro and micro-levels, marketing research enables the small entrepreneur to produce quality goods, sell them in the market and make adequate profits. It is a behavioural science; motivational studies would, therefore, help the small-scale units to diversify their products and/or improve their quality. It enables the small entrepreneur to plan to organise, to stimulate, to coordinate and to control production, finance, sales, advertising and profits. It enables him to improve upon the presentation and packaging of his product, to train and encourage his salesmen and coordinate the double action sales and advertising.

Since large number of small-scale industries in India are proprietary and partnership concerns, market research is carried out by the proprietor in a very rudimentary manner. The need of the hour is scientific marketing research to promote research which is therefore one of the important objectives of a progressive sales management and sales promotion.

Demand Forecasting

Estimation of future demand is an essential input for commercial feasibility and analysis.

There are a number of techniques available for forecasting demand. The selection of the technique(s) for a particular forecasting should be made considering the characteristics of the forecasting situation and the purpose of forecasting.

Survey Method: One widely-used method of estimating future demand is the survey method. This involves collective relevant information from the consumers (including potential consumers) or from people having intimate knowledge like dealers of the product, people with expert knowledge, etc.

Consumer survey is the most direct method in the sense that it directly asks the consumers about their intention to purchase. If the number of consumers of the product is very small, the survey may cover all the consumers (census method) and a reasonably accurate estimate may be obtained. But when the number of consumers is very large, it would not be possible to gather information from all of them. Hence, under such cases, a representative sample may be taken for the survey.

Statistical Methods: Some statistical methods are widely used for demand forecasting. If historical data (time series data) are available about the demand for a product, the method of *trend projection* may be employed to estimate the future demand. For example, if the demand for a product has been rising at the rate of 12%-15% per annum, during the previous five or six years, it may be expected that in the next few years also, the same trend would continue provided the relevant environmental factors do not change much. However, in many cases, such consistent trends may not be observed and hence in such cases, trend projection involves application of statistical methods.

Another important statistical method used in demand forecasting is the *Regression* method. This method may be used in cases where a definite relationship between the relevant variable affecting the income and the demand is established. For example, if the relationship between the consumer income and the demand for the product can be clearly defined, it may be used to estimate the demand of the product at various levels of consumer incomes. Some knowledge of statistics is necessary to understand this method clearly.

The *Leading Indicator* method can be used for demand forecasting in a number of cases. This method is based on the fact that some factors move up or down ahead of others and by observing their movements, the events which follow them may be predicted. For example, rain can be forecasted by observing the cloud formation. Similarly, changes in barometric reading help forecast changes in weather. The principle used in demand forecasting by the leading indicator method is the same. For example, government permission to increase automobile accessories and diesel/petrol.

Marketing Organisation

In a large number of proprietary small-scale organisations, the marketing functions are invariably carried out by the proprietor himself. However, in case of modernised, multi-product, global units, marketing organisations are developed in three basic systems. The first is a geographic break down of authority and responsibility, resulting in the establishment of sales areas and territories. Area managers are responsible for sales in their areas.

The second is to develop an organisation along product-lines, in which case each manufacturer is charged with effecting sales of a particular product or a group of products.

The third is to develop an organisation in accordance with the customer class.

The marketing organisation, by and large, depends upon the nature and extent of marketing functions to be discharged, the areas to be covered, competitiveness, special problems, size of sales and product-lines, size of sales force, area of operation and channels of distribution.

Institutionalised Marketing for Entrepreneurs

Before they come up, and for their sustenance, small industries need various supporting services, efficiently organised and promptly extended. Marketing guidance and assistance in one such service, which is increasingly accepted by newly established small units in areas which are far away from developed metropolitan cities. These industries are often not in a position to carry on market research, which is an essential prerequisite in the marketing process. To encourage the small entrepreneur to take up the production and marketing of new products, the governments in the developing countries and their specialised institution collect, collate and disseminate up to date and reliable market intelligence on a regular basis in the absence of which an entrepreneur would often operate either in the dark or wander on an punchers sea. As a matter of fact, manufacturing units should be guided into the unexplored areas of assumed profits. This is the rationale behind the Market Intelligence Bureau, which collects and disseminates relevant information about potential and profitable market areas.

The production and financial capacity of small industries are limited; so are their sustaining powers and competitive strength. They can compete individually if the product is special, and demand outstrips supply. In the case of products which are not special, and in lines where competition, particularly from the large-scale sector, is fierce, individual marketing becomes difficult. To contend against established large and even small units is not an easy job. The very small size of operations turns out to be a handicap. But if several small units decide to pool their resources, their confined aggregate capacity would be larger than that of even the largest industrial unit. In fact, in some lines of production, the total installed capacity in the small-scale sector is higher than that in the large sector. Small units can then compete collectively and secure a share of the market, which is legitimately theirs. However, a collective of this type can succeed only if the participants are prepared to sacrifice a part of their individuality. This is more true of foreign markets, where one has to contend not only against all the other countries, but also against a vast, domestic market. Extensive organisation is needs to reach potential areas, and to hold one's own against the unfair competition from the large-scale sector. It is in this context that the consortium idea, which is still in an embryonic stage in India, is relevant. Government purchase from small industries would also go up tremendously if small entrepreneurs adopt this consortium approach. They would eliminate to a great extent competition amongst themselves in their own sector and face confidently competition from other quarters.

Box 14.3 Marketing

Marketing is one of the major stumbling blocks for small-scale industries. Most of the problems which they face in marketing their product are enumerated below:

(i) Lack of standardisation;
(ii) Poor Designing;
(iii) Poor quality;
(iv) Lack of quality control;
(v) Lack of precision;
(vi) Poor bargaining power;
(vii) Lack of service after sales;
(viii) Scale of production;
(ix) Brand preferences;
(x) Distribution contacts;
(xi) Lack of marketing knowledge;
(xii) Competition;
(xiii) Ignorance and potential markets;
(xiv) Unfamiliarity with export activities – procedures and market know-how;
(xv) Financial weakness; limited resources;
(xvi) Limited local market; heavy dependence on middlemen;
(xvii) Lack of advertisement in building a brand image;
(xviii) Lack of testing equipment;
(xix) Absence of a marketing strategy;
(xx) Ill-equipped marketing organisation;
(xxi) Lack of liaison;
(xxii) Delayed payments, and
(xxiii) Weak bargaining position.

As mentioned earlier, because of his weak financial base a small industrialist cannot afford to spend as heavily as a large unit does on marketing his products. A rare exception is the pharmaceutical industry, in which the gap between the manufacturing cost and the selling price is very large. This is a special situation, in which marketing techniques are different, and therefore the cost of marketing is very high, particularly the marketing cost of those drugs for which there is stiff competition. The small industrialists in this line have to follow this trend in order to survive.

In the absence of a marketing channel of their own, many small units sell their products to large selling houses. Voltas, for instance, markets a number of products produced by small units. Similarly, the Bata Shoe Company sells shoes manufactured by the small sector. As a result, small units invariably get a raw deal. The large companies make handsome profits from marketing the products of small units by charging a much higher price from the consumer. In this respect, there is a need for a large number of marketing consortia, whose primary responsibility will be to assist small units.

Some small industries have good prospects of selling their products in international markets. If they cannot develop a consortium for the export of their products, they should at least associate with and support an export house. If marketing is a war, it is most fierce in the international fields. Well equipped and highly professionalised export houses are indeed necessary, if the products of small industries are to be established in overseas markets. India has not made any serious inroads into these markets, not because her products do not conform to specification or are not competitively priced, but because her export ability – the organised power to export – is somewhat low. There is a distinct need of large, strong, high voltage and high resources export houses, which have specialised in the promotion of the export of the products of small industries, individually small units may succeed when entrepreneurs have a high degree of marketing competence. But this is not true of most small units. They should not, therefore, enter the foreign markets on their own.

Exports have their own attractions; but unfortunately, very few entrepreneurs care to equip themselves adequately to export successfully and satisfactorily. The complaint one hears from foreign buyers of Indian goods, particularly against manufacturers in the small-scale sector, bear testimony to this fact, though it may be conceded that some small Indian entrepreneurs do enjoy a high reputation abroad; but their number is woefully small. In these circumstances, the small entrepreneur should help build-up the right type of export houses which have specialised in the promotion of the products of small industries in foreign markets in the existing pattern, their operations likely to be of real benefit to small exporting units. Hence, the need for specialised export houses capable of promoting and pushing the products of small industries in overseas markets.

To establish contacts and secure government contracts for the supply of goods and services appears to be simple enough task; but is not really so. The government is a demanding customer. The risks are great; and the job calls for competent marketing skills and expertise. Contract interpretation and proposal preparation are difficult jobs. To the extent an entrepreneur succeeds in these two tasks, his penetration in the Government Purchasing Department is assured. The quality norms and reliability levels are relatively higher of government purchase because the purpose of government buying is quite different from that of private buying. The government's purchases are not for resale but for use. Therefore, the products must have a high degree of reliability. This can be ensured if quality control is enforced and if there is a high sense of business. Unfortunately, the purchase administration in several government departments and establishments is corrupt, and the competition is not between the good product and competitive price but between corruption and corruptibility. However, this is not always the case.

Leaving aside this consideration, the small industries, because of their very smallness, suffer from a major handicap. The quantity required by the government's purchasing authorities is quite large and beyond their capacity, though within the competence, of individual small industrial units. If they work in concert, however, and develop a reliable and promotional marketing organisation, not only would their purpose be served, but they would also collectively become a force that cannot be easily ignored.

India, like many developing countries, is deficient in efficient marketing organisations. There are scarcely any marketing enterprises which are engaged in meaningful market research on a continuing basis. For example, there are very few distributing organisations which have undertaken promotional functions. There is just a begining of designning the products after a study of customer requirements. Very few so-called marketing organisations possess adequate resources to spends on advertising and so stimulate interest of prospective customers. In a developing country, its economy can be greatly expanded improved and diversified by efficient marketing organisations, manned by expert personnel. Small industries need them more. If their share in domestic, government and foreign markets is to be secured and expanded, the small entrepreneur should develop a new attitude and assist in the process of building up powerful and prosperous organisations.

Sales Management

Sales management in its broader perspective includes all such marketing activities as advertising, sales promotion, marketing research, marketing analysis, physical distribution, pricing and product merchandising. In the words of Leslie M. Dawson: "A business tends to be more responsive to the accentuation of human values occurring in society, and perhaps, to move from a marketing orientation to a broader human orientation, the concept of sales management is one which focussed on the total development of individual members of the selling force. This does not necessarily imply a lesser contribution to profitability by the sales manager than has been true in the past. It does, however, imply a keener scrutiny of profits, particularly as to the distinction between the short-run and the long-run. Aggressive sales management techniques may appear to boost short-run profit; but in the light of negative consequences of loyalty, enthusiasm, self-respect, and *espirit de corps* within the sales force, their effect on long-run profit can never be clear and may well be negative. Thus, in the long-run, the total development approach may be desirable not only for humanistic reasons but also from a profit standpoint."

Marketing Plan

The marketing plan is the key document which sets down precisely who is to do what, when, where and how. There must be liaison with production to determine product requirements and scheduling; ample stocks of the product must be available at the times required by the sales advertising. The advertising and promotional programme must be worked out in detail – the amount of money to be spent, the media to be used, the kind of advertising to be run. What is to be the basis of the advertising appeal, to reach what kind of audience and with what degree of frequency and impact? Are there to be any introductory and product sales targets which must be set by sales territory and by individual sales representatives. Physical distribution facilities have to be organised, delivery schedules worked out and so on. The financial people have to provide costing and profit estimates based on proposed expenditures and forecasted sales volume. Every part of the marketing plan has to be costed out and budgets prepared.

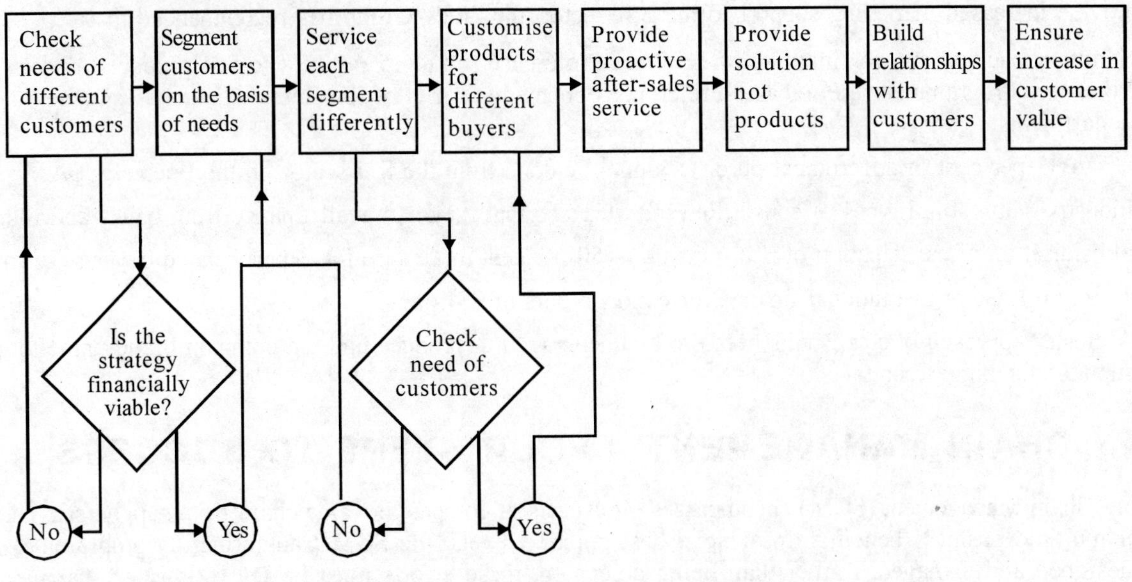

Fig. 14.6 How to Add Value in Industrial Marketing

The next stage is the implementation of the paper plan through coordination and interaction of the physical field selling and distribution effort and the company's advertising and promotional activities. The functions of the former are to see to it that the company's distributions and sales targets are met, that wholesale, retail and direct customers are efficiently survived and at all times carry adequate stock to meet their anticipated requirements, and that customer information is given as feedback regularly to the sales management in the form of daily, weekly or monthly reports. An efficient field intelligence system is of the utmost importance in keeping the headquarters appraised of the latest situation, expect developments in the market and in checking and controlling actual field performances against planned performance.

Advertising and sales promotion activities run parallel with the physical selling and distribution operations, and include advertising and display material aimed directly at the consumer user; trade and technical press advertising to distributors, trade buyers, professional groups, etc., direct main, trade receptions, and planned sales presentations to trade buyers, committees or associations; consumer and trade incentive schemes, such as special offers, bonuses, competitions, premiums, etc.

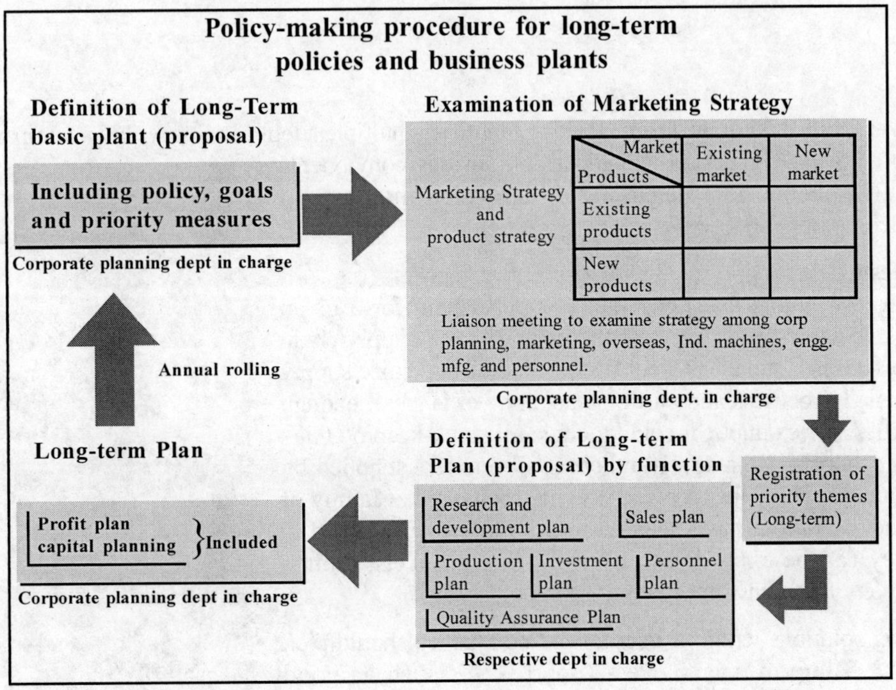

To provide increased marketing support to the SSI sector, the Study Group has recommended that:

- Statutory backing and continuation of the Price Preference (up to 15 per cent to SSI products) under Government Purchases Programme and Purchases Preference Scheme in respect of 358 items on purchases made by government departments.
- Up to 33 per cent of government purchases may be done from the SSI sector on the lines of USA.
- Industry status to all types of consortium industries so that they can avail finance from banks and FIs.
- Subsidisation of participation of SSI units up to 50 per cent in air fare for export related buyer-seller meets.
- Timely release of institutional finance for export orders of SSI units.
- A cluster approach of small units needs to be encouraged to produce under a common brand name to qualify as a supplier for bigger contracts.

SUPPLY CHAIN MANAGEMENT – FOUR STEPS TO SUCCESS

Supply Chain Management (SCM) encompasses all aspects of company's value chain from suppliers to customers and can deliver multiple business benefits. To achieve best-practice levels, the SCM transformation programmes need to be carefully designed and managed. Rather than being delegated, these efforts must be led by the top management or the entrepreneur.

Four steps to success are as follows:

Step 1:

Set Aspirations and Direction: Typically, companies have more than one supply chain, each of which addresses a different market segment and therefore requires a different transformation approach. For example, a watch manufacturer can have three product-lines: one for the low-cost mass market, one for the brand-conscious upmarket consumer, and a third as a customised fashion statement for the elite. Each product-line serves a distinct segment with different customer expectations and with different costs to meet them. Clearly, a one-size-fits-all approach to designing the supply chains will not work for such distinct segments.

For each supply chain, top management must launch the transformation effort by defining stretch aspirations along with multiple dimensions; extent of inventory, response time to customers, level of stock-outs at the front-line, extent of distribution costs, etc.

Step 2:

Priorities Levers and Design Solution: Having identified multiple supply chains within a company and set improvement aspirations for each of them, companies should design various components of each supply chain (i.e., define how the physical, information and financial flows would work from supplier to customer).

Rather than design the supply chain for the entire market, (e.g., all plants, suppliers and distributors that constitute a supply chain for a given segment), companies should develop and test the solution on a supply chain microcosm. A microcosm is a supplier-to-consumer slice of the entire supply chain, which contains all processes and participants, and yet is small enough to ensure manageability. For example, it could include all stock-keeping units within one family of products, a plant, a warehouse, all retailers supplied by that warehouse, and the suppliers that provide raw materials to that family of products. Once the new solutions have been designed and pressure tested in the microcosom, they can be expanded to overall other products, plants, warehouses and markets that constitute the entire supply chain.

While designing solutions within a microcosm, companies should pick the right subset of 3-5 improvement levers (not 15-20), such as good forecasting processes for the fashion industry, efficient and effective logistics infrastructure management for basic materials supply chains, production management for engineered goods, etc. Clearly, these 3-5 levers vary according to the type of supply chain, level of aspiration relative impact of each improvement lever and the starting position of the company, and must be thoughtfully chosen. Our experience suggests that a detail fact-based diagnostic of underlying root causes helps the companies to identify the right subset of levers.

Step 3:

Provide Appropriate IT and Organisational Support: While it is a key enabler of the supply chain solution, it is not the silver bullet. It is, therefore, prudent to define the IT architecture only after the basic supply chain blueprint for a company is ready, and the prototype IT tools have been tested within a microcosm using simple applications such as spreadsheets.

On the organisational front, most Indian companies operate their supply chains suboptimally – as fragmented pieces controlled by multiple functional departments (e.g., sales, distribution, manufacturing, purchasing, etc.). Given the critical need for cross-functional integration in successful SCM, the transformation effort must be managed by a cross-functional team of star line managers, and in some cases, by a full-time supply chain manager. Equally importantly, the top management across areas (CEO, CFO and relevant functional heads) must actively drive the supply chain transformation process and stay involved in ongoing management of the supply chain.

Step 4:

Monitor Performance: While a new supply chain design may be state-of-the-art, it may not provide the desired results if the metrics for the stakeholders are not appropriately defined. A balanced set of metrics, encompassing 'outputs' (e.g., inventories, service levels and lead times) and 'inputs' (e.g., forecasting, production, sourcing and dispatch accuracies) is crucial towards ensuring large, sustainable benefits. Here again, our experience suggests that a comprehensive set of metrics does not exist in several companies, or is incorrectly defined and monitored only intermittently.

Overall, supply chain transformation programmes are complex and need significant CEO attention and organisational energy. However, the pay-offs from doing it right are immense: not just to reduce costs and to improve customer-service levels, but also to potentially redefine competitive position.

E-MARKETING

E-MARKETING is traditional marketing using electronic methods. It affects traditional marketing in two ways. First, it increases efficiency in established marketing functions. Second, the technology of e-marketing transforms many marketing strategies. The transformation results in new business models that add customer value and/or increase company profitability.The internet serves as an efficient marketing planning tool for both secondary and primary data collection… One of the most important applications of electronic marketing involves customer relationship management. The power is shifting away from firm's to the person in control of the mouse, but fortunately companies are using technology to discover and meet the needs of these savvy and demanding customers. The internet is a rapidly changing medium, enterprising entrepreneurs constantly have cool new ideas.

Online Marketing Tips for Small Business

- If you don't have a website, get one. If you do, invest in it.
- Making your website user-friendly and well-structured helps search engines find and index it easily.
- Use search marketing to reach out to customers looking for local services.
- Management your RoI. This concept is not unique to online marketing, but it's far easier to manage with online tools.
- With search marketing, you can bid to appear only against specific search queries from relevant audience.
- Write 'must-click' ads. Convey product benefits clearly, get to the point, and include a strong call to action.
- Determine the goal: Increased traffic to your website, conversions, or brand awareness? Then measures success.
- Track the impact of your marketing with free online tools. This way you can make sure you're paying for the results.

- You can pause, cancel or resume campaigns at the click of a mouse. Use this to your advantage.
- Depending on your kind of business, you could create marketing campaigns in different languages, or ones that target particular countries or cities.

Trade Fair

The trade fair is an exclusive meeting ground for businessmen/women, entrepreneurs, manufacturers, suppliers and distributors. It is a platform for entrepreneurs who have the potential to succeed, but not the exposure. Here, they can show their products, widen and test markets, enter into business deals with prospective partners, get exposure among their counter-partners and buyers, and exploit unique networking opportunities.

Apart from sales and networking the trade fair facilitate banker-entrepreneur interactions for quicker loan processing. Budding entrepreneurs could seek advice and assistance from entrepreneurs who are successfully running their businesses.

CONCLUSION

Industrial liberalisation, globalisation, marketing economy and heightened competition is changing all this permanently. While labour laws have become antiquated and virtually ineffective, government policies which encourage dispersal of industries into backward area locations have helped improve matters. Market forces are now compelling modernisation, productivity improvement and value of additional efficiency like never before. Some parts of the country where industry had been severely affected by obscurantist trade unionism, are today showing heightened pragmatism to generate and safeguard employment as well as to attract new investments. Industrially better endowed states do not seem to appreciate that in order to stay ahead in the game of economic and industrial development, only one thing counts – efficiency of value addition and an enabling climate along with a degree of reassurance about the future.

With market forces changing rapidly, marketing has been seen as a change agent – a means of continuous adjustment and adaptation. This refers to significant orientation in marketing management and priorities. The imperatives of market exploitation demand – understanding meaningful marketing facts, observations and opinions. The dynamics of successful marketing calls for selecting the right question, getting answers, organise, evaluate and form strategies to deal with competition and technological changes. Marketing perspective focuses on what we want to find, how and where we find and what we believe it means to the business. It is an integrated approach to generate market power by critical analysis of the market logistically, segment proportion of the customers, understanding profile of customers and the competitors, finding new products and services, customer preferences, customer records as to retention and defection, etc.

Since, the marketplace in the decade has been registering rapid transformation, we are witnessing that the business events reflect a distinct pace and capacity for expansion. The moments signal continuous shift in the way of performing – both in style and behaviour. Market is now being defined and perceived as a group of competitors. Hence, there is an entrepreneurship surge in the market – the triumph of the entrepreneur. It suggests great opportunities in the fast growing market where there are many underserved market niches. Marketers are always competing to locate the markets that will value the products and would pay for them. It calls for concentrating on market efforts of targeting and positioning the product. "ME TO" profile of a market man is the formidable force enabling him to acquire distinct competence and chalk out specific strategies for business emphasis. The competing dynamics is resulting in reinventing the marketer. It is the only stimulus today in the development of "new" market concepts. Today 'operating salesman' is reborn as a marketer because he is to take strategic decisions in the new market requirements.

Market focus therefore demands –

- Perceiving market as market intelligence;
- Targeting customers;
- Managing for profitability and not sales volume alone;
- Building customer relationship and loyalty; and
- Growing with the market.

So, '*Compete*' is the buzzword. It is forcing market operators to develop innovative strategies to sway over the market.

Today's salesman, *nay* the marketing man, must always edge closer to the market call to transcend the adventurous customers and excel by solving daunting problems continuously to be different in the market.

Marketing information will become a highly valued asset in today's information age. Monitoring and scanning scenario building and continuous planning would be the marketing priority. As the future will occupy a prominent position in marketing research concerns, marketing research is expected to change both in technique and orientation. Marketing intelligence, therefore, will be a critical factor to be given greater attention to. While assessing the strategic situation, executives will be focussing on marketing factors and strategies, corporate affairs and public relations activities. Marketing environment is expected to be paradoxical – keenly competitive, but exhibiting more cooperation, making marketing more important in the management hierarchy.

Marketing intelligence is supposed to explore real demand of the customers and the steps the competitions are taking to fulfil the same. Marketing intelligence is a way to understand the customers' perception of values and purchase preference. It shall be imperative for the organisations to be alert about competition's approach towards marketing determinants like dependability and reliability, consumer-friendly features, technical specification, high quality and service uniqueness.

In the year ahead, industrial location will be guided primarily by commercial considerations and sustainability rather than by regulatory social demands alone. An investment which does not maximise the generation of surpluses cannot contribute to the country's social goals. Thus, location in backward regions where there is a great deal of willingness and native skill amongst the first generation workers proves very attractive to the decaying environment of cities where industry has been traditionally located.

In the current rising wave of economic growth and liberalisation and in the absence of systematic market research, capacities far in excess of demand have been set up in many industries. Thus, in addition to some of the old and obsolete industries, many relatively new investments have either turned sick or have shut down. The government has taken several imaginative measures to revive many of these. The Board for Industrial Finance and Reconstruction (BIFR) was created to expedite revival schemes.

The Indian economy and the business environment, currently undergoing important structural changes, will grow faster than ever and will encounter myriad complexities of a free enterprise system. The private sector, which had always clamoured for freedom to conduct its affairs, is now face-to-face with the realities of standing more or less on its own. We had not realised that change would be upon us as fast as it has.

Business now has an opportunity to transform individuals and organisations into vibrant and competitive entities. Industries which cannot generate surplus can neither have any place in our country or can they achieve the goal of a more egalitarian society. It is through productive endeavours and mutual cooperation of those engaged in the industry and agriculture, that the larger issues of population control, unemployment and poverty alleviation can be effectively tackled.

The era of mutual distrust, government controls and disruptive trade union movements must, under these changing circumstances, recede into the background. Our economy, to get progressively drawn into the sphere of a new international trade and export, will have to grow faster.

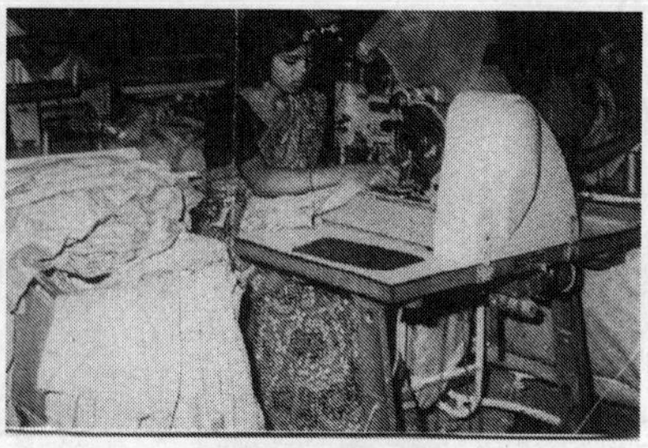

15 CHAPTER

EXPORT POTENTIALS OF SMALL-SCALE INDUSTRIES

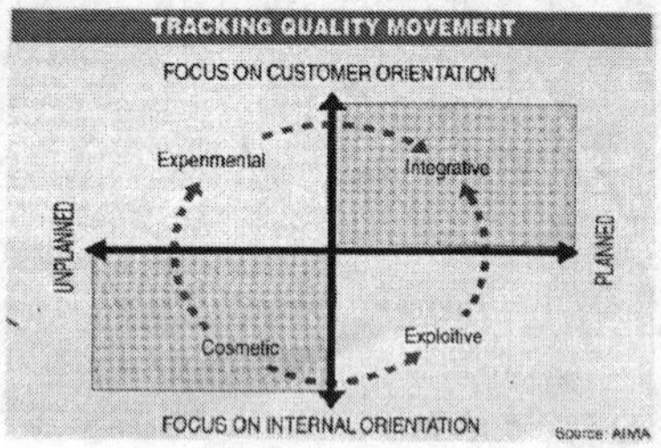

The information technology has metamorphosed the 'market'. We are now in the era of customer-driven market. It is time now for a new formula – formula of '4Cs' as envisioned by Robert Lauterborn, Professor of Advertising at the University of North Carolina, Chapel Hill. In short '4Ps' 'Product', 'Price', 'Placement', and 'Promotion', are the things of the millennium that has gone by. The formula for success in the new context is: (i) Consumer wants and needs, (ii) Cost to satisfy the wants and needs, (iii) Convenience to buy, and (iv) Communication to buy.

LEARNING OBJECTIVES

The small-scale enterprises have a high potential and capability to export to developing as well as developed countries. As on March 2009, SME sectors exports were around ₹ 2,32,580 crore or 30.4 per cent of total countries exports. With new technology and networking SME sector can grow even at a greater rate.

- The wide variety of products of small-scale industries have a great export potential.
- Differentiate standardisation from customisation of products/services.
- Analyse product strategies including new product development, pricing policy, production policy, distribution policy, branding strategies, etc.
- Explain pricing discussions including dumping and countertrade.
- Discuss price/distribution strategies and different types of marketing intermediaries.
- Describe the promotion strategies including advertising, personal selling, sales promotion and public relations strategies.
- Assess the export potential for small-scale industries including Gems and Jewellery.
- Discuss 'Export-import' Policy.

INTRODUCTION

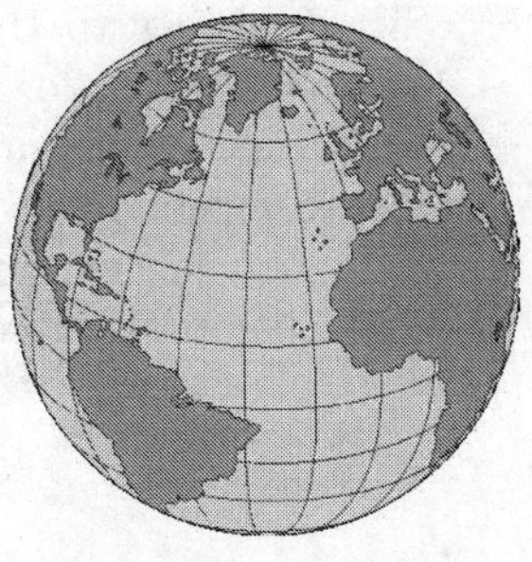

In the achievement of the strategic objectives of a self-reliant and dynamic economy, the government considers a substantial expansion in export earnings to be of great importance. Exports enable the country to pay for critical imports – machinery, metals, petroleum, fertilisers and new technological inputs and step up the pace of economic development, put the resources of those goods in which India has a long-term comparative advantage. This apart, exports are an important instrument for the creation of employment opportunities in small-scale industries, cottage industries and in the agricultural sector as well as in the medium and large industrial sectors.

Although the quickening pace of industrialisation in the nineteenth century has opened up vast markets for the commodities produced by developing countries, the volume of their exports began to decline with the changes in the economic climate in the middle of the twentieth century.

In order to achieve national objectives, the government adopted a new and scientific approach to its export policy, which has been made an integral part of the country's overall strategy for economic development. The new export policy aims at consciously and systematically developing the export of items in which India has a comparative advantage and which promises long-term growth prospects. More practically, stress has been laid on greater participation by the small-scale sector and the labour-intensive sector in the export trade with a view to providing wider employment opportunities to the people.

Export promotion of products manufactured in the small-scale sector has been given considerable importance, and efforts are being made to increase its share in total exports.

COMPONENTS OF EXPORTS

The main components of exports of products manufactured in the small-scale sector are: khadi and handloom, processed foods, engineering goods, computers, handicrafts including gems and jewellery, garments (all types), project exports, consultancy exports, ancillary exports outsourcive, export services, and so on.

Exports from the SSI Sector

The value of exports from the small-scale industries (SSI) sector has been rising from year-to-year. The value increased from ₹ 1,643 crore in 1980-81 to ₹ 22,250 crore in 1993-94. The share of exports from the small-scale sector as percentage of India's total exports also rose from 24.5 per cent in 1980-81 to 33.9 per cent in 1996-97. This increase in SSI exports is mainly due to the promotional measures undertaken by the government as well as entrepreneurial push.

If exports of powerlooms, handicrafts, handlooms and khadi are included, the share of the SSI sector is likely to be nearly half of the total. Even in the global market, the SSI units have been successful in enlarging their share every year. This goes to prove that the SSI sector is quite significant in the everchanging economic scenario. Fig. 15.1 bring out the growth of SSI exports during the 80s and 90s.

An analysis of the data on product group-wise exports shows that the entire exports of sports goods are from the SSI sector. The substantial shares of the SSI sector in the total exports of other commodity groups are: woollen garments (95 per cent), ready-made garments (90 per cent), processed tobacco, snuff and bidi (70 per cent), processed food (65 per cent), finished leather and leather products (52 per cent), basic chemicals, pharmaceuticals and cosmetics (44 per cent) and marine products (44 per cent). Data on exports, as available from various Export Promotion Councils, are presented in Appendix 2.20.

Factors Affecting SSI Exports

(i) **Technological Constraints:** The technology used by small-scale units in India is of low to medium quality. The products of the SSI sector in terms of quality are not comparable to products from foreign countries. Research and Development which are crucial for producing high technology products has not been the focus of the Indian SSI sector. A large number of SSIs in India manufacture products for the domestic market only and exports from the larger ones among the SSI units have a low skill and technology content. In order to step up its exports, it is, therefore, important for the SSI sector to undertake research and development and focus on technology based product-lines.

(ii) Size Constraints: The small size of the SSI units limits their activities mainly to production for the domestic market, as the resources required for venturing into exports, is beyond the capacity of the lower end units.

(iii) Inability to Undertake Promotional Activities: Enterprises undertaking advertising and promotional activities perform better than others in the international markets because of their conscious building of brand images and trade names and to maintain quality as well as satisfactory after-sales services. Due to lack of resources for competing with multinationals in the international market, many of the SSIs sell their products to trading agencies or merchant exporters to avoid international competition. Similarly, it is difficult for SSIs to establish their own marketing channels in foreign countries or to establish formal links with marketing companies to promote exports.

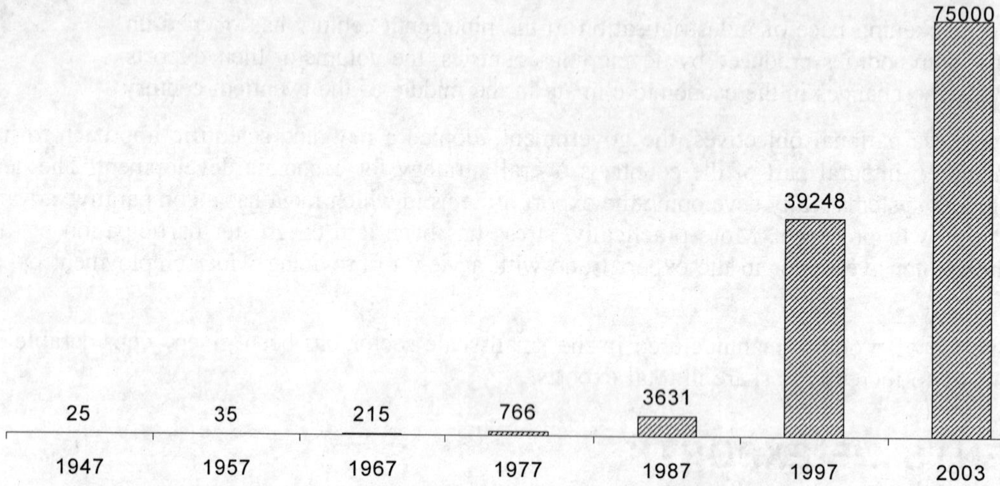

Fig. 15.1 SSI Exports (₹ in crore)

Export Prospects

Tech Mart India '96, Pragati Maidan, New Delhi

Container handling at one of the ports

The small-scale sector in India now produces a wide range of products, from simple consumer goods to such sophisticated products as scientific and precision instruments, hearing aids, electronic components, taperecorders, television sets, etc. With a lower level of labour costs than in the Western countries, India enjoys an advantage in exporting both traditional and non-traditional labour-intensive products. This apart, there is favourable climate for SSI exports in foreign markets because frequent wage hikes and pollution hazards in industrialised countries tend to favour imports from developing countries, particularly the import of SSI products.

In order to promote exports, the government has drawn up a number of schemes for promotion of exports from the SSI sector, which includes organisation of specialised training programmes on packaging for exports in collaboration with the Indian Institute of Packaging, Bombay, assistance to SSI units for participation in the international and internal exhibitions, dissemination of export information at the doorstep of SSI units through Technological Information Promotions Systems (TIPS) and incentives for quality production in the SSI sectors.

In order to strengthen the export production base, manufacturers of items reserved for SSI sectors are permitted to increase their capacity by way of investment in plant and equipment beyond ₹ 100 lakh provided they undertake a minimum export of 76 per cent of their annual production.

The new revised export and import policy extends equal opportunity to small and medium exports. Bulk of the country's exports, in terms of value, are taking place through export trading/star trading/superstar trading houses and such status is granted on the basis of prescribed export performance level and all exporters, including small and medium exporters, are extended equal treatment.

If the status is claimed in terms of FOB value of exports, double weightage is given to the export of products manufactured by the Small Scale Industry (SSI), handloom and handicrafts including sports goods, hand-knitted carpets and silk products.

If the status is claimed in terms of Net Foreign Exchange (NFE) earned, double weightage is given to the export products manufactured by SSI and triple weightage is given to the NFE earned on the exports of hand-knotted carpets and silk products manufactured by the handloom and handicrafts sectors.

Such status holders are extended equal treatment for getting transferable special import licence valid for the import of specified items of the negative list of import. Under the duty exemption scheme, SSI units have been extended the facility to give the bank guarantee wherever applicable, at 50 per cent of the normal requirement.

Table 15.1 SSI Exports

(₹ Crore)

Year	Total Exports	SSI Exports	3 as% of 2
1980-81	6,711	1,643	24.5
1981-82	7,806	2,071	26.5
1982-83	8,803	2,071	23.2
1983-84	9,771	2,164	22.1
1984-85	11,744	2,553	21.7
1985-86	10,895	2,773	25.5
1986-87	12,452	3,631	29.2
1987-88	15,674	4,535	28.9
1988-89	20,232	5,681	28.1
1989-90	27,658	7,990	28.9
1990-91	32,553	9,64	30.0
1991-92	44,041	13,883	31.5
1992-93	53,688	17,784	33.3
1993-94	69,751	25,307	36.4
1994-95	82,674	29,068	35.2
1995-96	1,06,353	36,470	34.3
1996-97	1,18,817	39,248	33.4
1997-98	1,30,100	44,442	34.1
1998-99	1,39,752	48,979	35.0
1999-2000	1,59,561	54,200	33.4
2000-01	2,03,571	69,797	34.3
2001-02	2,09,018	71,244	34.2
2002-03	2,55,137	86,013	33.7
2003-04	2,93,367	97,644	33.5
2004-05	3,75,340	1,24,417	33.1
2005-06	4,56,418	1,50,242	32.9
2006-07	5,71,779	1,77,600	32.8
2007-08	6,55,864	2,13,500	32.5
2008-09 (Projected)	7,66,935	2,32,850	30.4

Table 15.2 Export Thrust Areas

City	State	Commodity
Tirupur	Tamil Nadu	Knitwear and hosiery
Moradabad	Uttar Pradesh	Brassware
Ludhiana	Punjab	Heavy machinery, Hosiery
Surat	Gujarat	Handloom
Alleppey	Kerala	Coir
Jallandhar	Punjab	Sports goods
Ranipet/Ambur	Tamil Nadu	Leather
Nagpur	Maharashtra	Handtools
Vishakapatnam	Andhra Pradesh	Marine products
Meerut	Uttar Pradesh	Sport goods
Aligarh	Uttar Pradesh	Brass locks
Agra	Uttar Pradesh	Leather footwear
Khurja	Uttar Pradesh	Pottery
Kanchipuram	Tamil Nadu	Silk
Sivakasi	Tamil Nadu	Safety matches
Salem	Tamil Nadu	Handtools
Ambala	Haryana	Scientific instruments
Jamnagar	Gujarat	Brass parts
Rajkot	Gujarat	Engine pumps
Vapi-Ankleshwar	Gujarat	Chemicals
Batala	Punjab	Machine tools
Bhagalpur	Bihar	Weaving

Box 15.1 Our Heritage

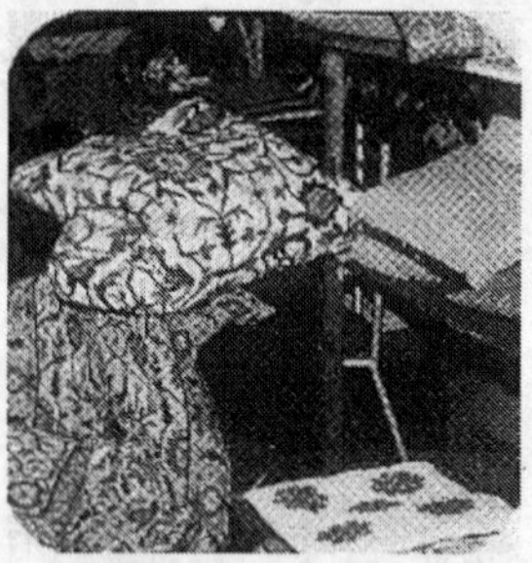

India's handicrafts have been renowned from time immemorial for their intricate workmanship and exclusive designs. The sector has got a significant boost over the last decade from the efforts of the Export Promotion Council for Handicrafts (EPCH), which has been actively working to promote India's arts and crafts in overseas markets. The EPCH has been organising the IHGF since 1994 under the aegis of the Development Commissioner (Handicrafts), Ministry of Textiles. The institutionalisation of IHGF over the past 10 years and its role as a "one-stop sourcing centre" for buyers has made it the largest gifts and handicrafts exhibition of South-East Asia. The basic objective of IHGF is to display under one roof the range of handicrafts available in India. The fair presents a huge business opportunity to exhibitors and offers overseas buyers the opportunity to directly interact with the manufacturers.

For several centuries, almost every region of India has had its own distinct form of art and craft. Handicrafts production predominantly happens in the small-scale and medium sector. It plays a vital role in the economic development of India by providing employment at the village and town level. The office of the Development Commissioner (Handicrafts) in the Textiles Ministry has played a key role in the rise of this sector by providing regular assistance to the industry for further growth. Today, it is estimated that over 60 lakh artisans are involved in producing and creating Indian handicrafts.

The strength of the Indian handicrafts industry lies in its low capital investment, abundant skilled manpower, negligible import content and high export potential. The other strength of the industry is the rich "hidden treasures" that are to be found across India.

The marketing approach adopted by EPCH lays considerable emphasis on development, presentation, packaging, production and finishing techniques for the products. The National Centre for Design and Product Development is equipped with the latest methods of design computing. Assisted by a team of Indian and foreign designers, the centre is expected to be fully operational during the 10th Plan. The integrated design and technology project in the cane and bamboo sector implemented in the North-East by the Office of the Development Commissioner (Handicrafts), under a UNDP-assisted programme, had tremendous impact and opened up immense export opportunities in the North-East. EPCH has taken this mission forward with the support of the Ministry of Commerce for promoting exports from the North-East.

An analysis of the export trend of handicrafts shows 48 per cent of the total exports of the country emanating from four centres of production, Moradabad, Saharanpur, Jodhpur and Narsapur. Moradabad is the centre for art metalware production, which accounted for exports worth ₹ 2,165.21 crore (23.12 per cent of total handicraft exports) in 2002. Saharanpur is known for its wooden wares. The export of woodware in 2002 was ₹ 511.35 crore, or 18.47 per cent of exports. Jodhpur is famous for textiles, embroidered goods, art metalware and woodware while Narsapur is known for lace and crochet. This category last year accounted for 20 per cent of total exports, amounting to ₹ 2,477.75 crore.

The handicrafts sector received a major boost with the opening in 2005 of the India Exposition Mart in Greater Noida, on Delhi's outskirts. The mart will provide marketing support to cottage and small-scale handicrafts exporters and serve as a centralised facility and a permanent contact point (open throughout the year) for foreign buyers.

To boost India's handicraft industry, EPCH has also finalised plans for the opening of permanent showrooms and warehouses in the US and the Netherlands. It intends to double the export of handicrafts from India in the next five years with integrated tie-ups with international marketers. The proactive approach of EPCH, strongly supported by the Development Commissioner (Handicrafts), Ministry of Textiles, in association with industry, the government and overseas buyers, will project India as the preferred handicrafts destination. It will also increase employment generation, earning of foreign exchange and safeguard India's cultural heritage.

LUDHIANA

Export thrust: Machine tools

No. of Units: NA

Export earnings: ₹ 75 crore

Infrastructure problems: Lack of roads and waste disposal systems; power shortage; inadequate communication and transport infrastructure.

Government initiative: None

Exporters' choice: Want government to help.

SURAT

Export thrust: Diamonds

No. of Units: NA

Export earnings: ₹ 4,000 crore (approx.)

Infrastructure problems: No direct international access; absence of good hotels and recreational facilities; poor roads; power shortage; poor sewage disposal systems.

Government initiative: None

Exporters' choice: Need government help, but some are relocating to world-class facilities set up by themselves outside the city.

MORADABAD

Export thrust: Brassware

No. of Units: 900

Export earnings: ₹ 800 crore

Infrastructure problems: Power shortage; no direct access to Mumbai port, absence of factory stuffing; inadequate telecom, transportation, education and health facilities.

Government initiative: Plans for ₹ 2,500 crore infrastructure upgradation. Blueprint not yet ready

Exporters' choice: Major private sector investments not possible, exporters ready for limited involvement.

TIRUPUR

Export thrust: Knitwear
No. of Units: 3,500
Export earnings: ₹ 2,400 crore
Infrastructure problems: Lack of water, roads and sewage facilities; power shortage; educational facilities almost non-existent.
Government initiative: ₹ 2,500 crore infrastructure plan identified.
Exporter's choice: Willing to share the infrastructure cost. ₹ 1,317 crore upgradation scheme already underway.

International Subcontracting

Due to enormous costs, firms in the Western countries prefer to subcontract the manufacture of spares, components and parts of a machine to developing countries before they are fitted into the final product. As a result, motor car parts are manufactured in many countries before they are assembled in one country. Semiconductors, tubes and electronic components are manufactured in developing countries for the parent firm in the developed country. Many textile firms in Europe airlift cloth to Morroco, Malaysia and Indonesia, where it is converted into garments, bedding, rugs, towels and upholstery. Watchmakers in Europe fly jewels to Mauritius for precision drilling. Also, sports materials and kits for games like basket-ball and cricket are manufactured in different countries. With the development of technical skills in India in recent years, the small-scale sector is in a position to undertake the manufacture of all these items. There is a vast scope for expanding the export of several non-traditional products. The role of the small-scale sector in the export field can hardly be overemphasised.

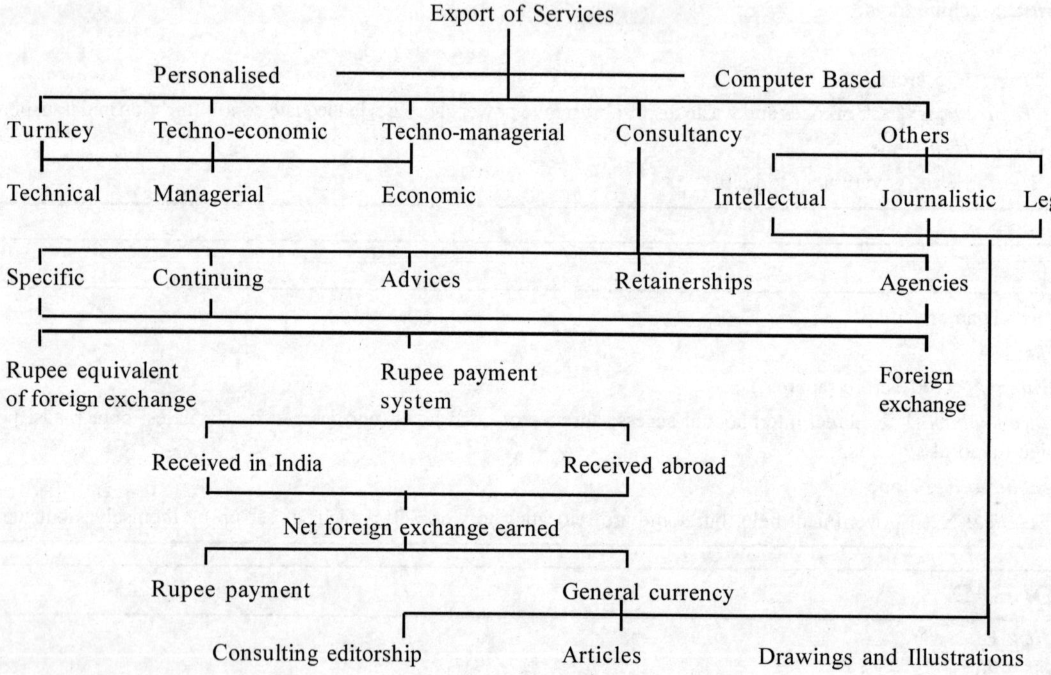

Units in the small and medium-scale industries are playing an important role in raising the level of industrial production in the country in a variety of fields, especially engineering, chemical, sports goods, textiles, etc. Similarly, the export of the products of the medium and small-scale sectors has increased substantially and now account for about 1/8th of the country's total exports. The government continues to encourage export production in the small and medium sectors by facilitating the availability of the necessary inputs, finance, market intelligence, etc. The importance of the development and expansion of this sector gives due weight in the formulation of export policies, the extension and establishment of institutional framework and the infrastructural facilities. Public sector organisations play a special role in providing the necessary guidance and inputs to both small and medium exporters.

Box 15.2 Planning to Export

With renewed emphasis on the country's export efforts, a number of policies concerning special economic zones (SEZs) are being fine-tuned. It was the 2000-1 EXIM Policy which for the first time talked about setting up of SEZs with a view to provide an internationally competitive and hassle-free environment for exports. This and other extensive information is now available on www. sezindia. nic.in, a website set up and managed by the department of commerce, under the Ministry of Commerce and Industry. The website has separate sections on setting up of SEZs, criteria for approval, application criteria, facility for developers, policy related to an SEZ developer, and a list of operational and approved SEZs. The website informs visitors that all the import/export operations of SEZ units would be on a self-certification basis, and though these have to be a net foreign exchange earner, they shall not be subject to any predetermined value addition or minimum export performance requirements. The high-point of the website is the FAQs section, which lists almost every bit of information a visitor needs to know about SEZs, and the low-point in the section on 'Articles', which lists just three clippings from newspapers and that too, of 2001 vintage! But this is no way undermines the basic information dissemination objective of the website.

Export Promotion Measures

To ensure a secured base for India's export, the government initiated various measures that would: (i) strengthen export production, (ii) encourage capacity expansion in export-oriented industries, (iii) augment bargaining power of our exporting community, (iv) encourage entry of our products in the new markets of both developed and developing countries, and (v) improve our inherent competitive strength through imparting greater relative price stability of the Indian economy. One of the most important features of government's measures has been to provide a stable base, uncertainties are removed and exporters are encouraged to take a long-term view about international marketing. Another noteworthy aspect of these measures has been to make export promotion truly a national effort by involving various agencies of the Central Government, public sector organisations, state governments, financial institutions and other national agencies engaged in different types of economic activities.

Quality Control

Closely allied to the programme of modernisation is the question of maintaining the quality of the product. Overseas buyers do not differentiate between goods manufactured by a small-scale unit and a large-scale unit. All they care about is the quality of the product. The quality of the products delivered to customers should conform to the sample design originally shown to them. The products, moreover, should be used at the time specified therein. Recognising that individual entrepreneurs are not in a position to establish laboratories to test their products, the Small Industries Development Organisation has set up four Regional Testing Centres at New Delhi, Kolkata, Mumbai and Chennai to provide general as well as product-oriented testing facilities for mechanical, metallurgical, chemical and electrical products. In the course of time these Regional Testing Centres plan to open sub-centres in other parts of the country to cover small units in the remotest parts.

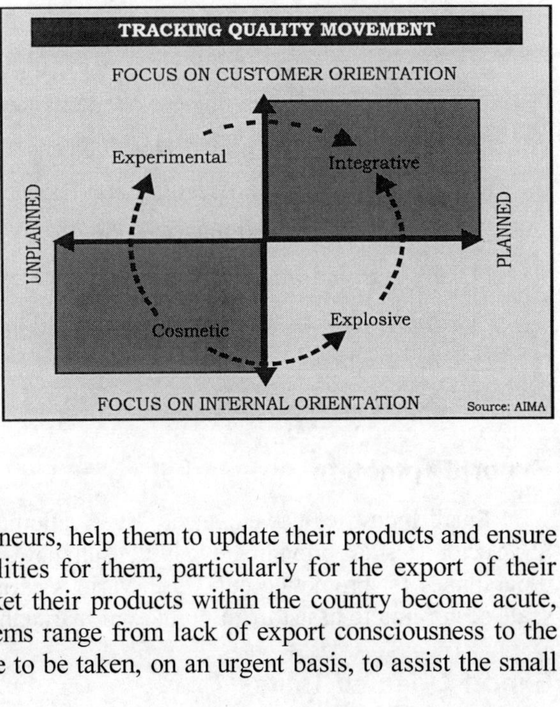

Marketing

Attempts have been made to obtain raw materials for small entrepreneurs, help them to update their products and ensure their quality. But not enough has been done to provide marketing facilities for them, particularly for the export of their products. The problems which small entrepreneurs face when they market their products within the country become acute, varied and complex when they enter international markets. These problems range from lack of export consciousness to the absence of infrastructural facilities in marketing abroad. Here, steps have to be taken, on an urgent basis, to assist the small entrepreneurs.

Export Consortia

One way of overcoming the problems of marketing is through the increasing participation of small entrepreneurs. They can adopt a group approach by forming themselves into export houses or export groups to maximise the opportunities available in the marketing of their products. Their combined efforts may lead to, among other things, better packaging methods and overseas publicity campaigns. It is essentially with a view to encouraging small-scale industrialists to join together for this purpose that the Union Government has announced liberal concession for small-scale export consortia.

INFRASTRUCTURAL SET-UP

The government has established adequate and appropriate institutions, mainly to assist export promotion in particular. They are:

1. 18 Export Promotion Councils, for the promotion of specific commodities of groups;
2. Commodity Boards for coffee, tea, cardamom, rubber, coir, silk, handicrafts and handloom;
3. The Board of Trade; Advisory Council of Trade; Zonal Committees;
4. Chamber of Commerce and Industry and Associations of Trade and Industry;
5. The Trade Development Authority (TDA);
6. The Federation of Indian Export Organisation (FIEO);
7. Export Processing Zone;
8. Indian Institute of Trade;
9. Export Inspection Council;
10. Indian Council of Arbitration;
11. State Trading Corporation of India;
12. The Minerals and Metals Trading Corporation;
13. Export Houses and Trading Houses;
14. Free Trade Zones;
15. 100% Export-oriented Units
16. Trade Fair Authority of India (TFAI), to concentrate exclusively on fairs and exhibitions in furtherance of exports directly and derive immense benefits to the sector.
17. Marine Products Export Development Authority, Cochin;
18. Agricultural and Processed Food Products, Export Development Authority, New Delhi;
19. Export Credit Guarantee Corporation of India Limited;
20. Projects and Equipment Corporation of India Ltd.;
21. Spices Trading Corporation of India Ltd.;
22. Tea Trading Corporation of India Ltd.;
23. Export-import Bank of India.

Export Promotion and Marketing

Small Industries Development Organisation (SIDO) is functioning as a Nodal Agency for promotion of exports of the SSI Sector. Besides providing export consultancy and export market intelligence, SIDO is also organising specialised training programmes for promoting exports in various parts of the country. With a view to augmenting the exports from the small-scale sector and to assist them in internal marketing, SIDO has been implementing the following schemes:

Export Oriented Units

The scheme of 100 per cent Export Oriented Units (EOUs) was introduced in 1980 with the objective of generating additional production capacity for exports by providing appropriate policy framework and incentives. The predominance of small-scale enterprises in EOUs and their key role in generating additional production capacity, producing quality goods and enlarging. The scope for export is well recognised. The scheme needs to be reviewed and streamlined, so that it plays a pivotal role in enhancing exports.

The growth of EOUs is imbalanced.

Five states – Andhra Pradesh, Tamil Nadu, Maharashtra, Gujarat and Karnataka account for more than half the number of EOUs in the country. Between August 1991 to April 1997, these five state received investment of ₹ 28,177 crore spread over 18,91,000 units.

The level of export performance for the purpose of export house recognition shall be as per the following table:

Table 15.3 Level of Export Performance

Category	FOB Criterion		NFE Criterion	
	Average FOB value of exports made during the preceding three licensing years	FOB value of exports made during the preceding licensing year	Average net foreign exchange value of exports made during the preceding three licensing years	Net foreign exchange value of export made during the preceding licensing year
Export Houses	20 crore	30 crore	16 crore	24 crore
Trading Houses	100 crore	150 crore	80 crore	120 crore
Star Trading Houses	500 crore	750 crore	400 crore	600 crore
Super Star Trading Houses	1,500 crore	2,250 crore	1,200 crore	1,800 crore

Problems

The small-scale sector is beset with a number of problems. Basically, the three aspects that affect the SSI exports relate to:

(a) Availability of raw materials;

(b) Quality control; and

(c) Marketing facilities.

A major difficulty facing the small-scale industry is the procurement of raw materials, both imported and indigenous. Big industries have resources to maintain special staff for liaison with the various government agencies and are able to use their influence to expedite their applications and obtain raw materials on a priority basis. In this respect, though small-scale industries get some government help, the small medium-scale industries with no special staff to liaise with the government agencies are left with inadequate supplies and often they have to resort to open market purchases at very high prices.

Another major problem facing the small-scale sector is that at least 40 per cent of them are connected with the company organisation. Only few companies have detailed sales plans, and only 50 per cent of the units allocate and control department costs. Application of modern methods of management would enable small-scale industries to lower production costs, standardise and improve the quality of their products and achieve sustained growth, thus consequently making the products more competitive overseas.

The procedures for claiming export assistance have been considerably streamlined. However, the dynamism and sense of dedication should percolate to the working levels of the ITC office and sustained dialogue maintained with the industry not excluding the smaller units to evaluate and assess what has been done and what remains to be done.

Export Processing Zones

Special incentives for companies to undertake manufacturing of export items have been provided by the Government of India through the establishment of Export Processing Zones or through 100 per cent Export Oriented Units set up outside the EPZs, EPZs and EoUs fall under the purview of the Ministry of Commerce, Government of India.

EPZs are special areas designated for providing export production or the processing of manufactured products at a low cost. Each EPZ provided basic infrastructural facilities at reduced rates and included other incentives like developed land sites, standard designed factory buildings, roads, power, water and drainage. Other provisions included banking, post offices and custom clearing agents. Units located in EPZs/EOUs are permitted to sell up to 25 per cent of the value of production in the Domestic Tariff Area.

The Government of India has established 7 EPZs across the country. The Kandla Free Trade Zone, the Santacruz Electronics Export Porcessing Zone and the Falta EPZ were set up in 1965, 1974 and 1984 respectively. The EPZs set up at Chennai, Cochin, Visakhapatnam and NOIDA are of more recent origin.

Special Economic Zones

The Government of India declared a new liberalised customs framework for the Special Economic Zones (SEZs) with a view to boosting exports by making necessary changes in the EXIM Policy with effect from November 1, 2000. The SEZ scheme envisaged a simple and transparent policy and procedures for the promotion of exports with minimum paperwork. This will make the customs process in the SEZs free of controls to a great extent and will provide for green channel clearances. The important features of the scheme are as follows:

The SEZ area shall be deemed to be a foreign territory for the purpose of duties and taxes.

Goods supplied to SEZ from Domestic Tariff Area (DTA) will be treated as deemed export and goods brought from SEZ will be treated as deemed import.

Goods may be imported procured from DTA duty free for the purpose of manufacture of goods and services, production, assembling, trading, repair, reconditioning, re-engineering, packaging or in connection therewith and export thereof.

Prospects

With the functioning of District Industries Centre and by reserving 827 items for production in the small-scale sector, there will be greater industrial production in the small-scale sector as a result of which there will be more avenues of employment. It is further necessary to find more outlets for this increased production as there are limitations to absorb all the production in India.

In harnessing the growing international market, the small-scale units should maintain high quality of the goods and channelise their products through the Export Promotional Agencies. Exports of small-scale industries are going to play a crucial role in the export performance during the Sixth Five Year Plan.

Export Management: In the seventies, the small-scale sector emerged as a principal contributor to the country's exports. The pattern and direction of trade have been diversified, and an increasing number of small-scale units have switched over to non-traditional exports and export-oriented industries to cater to the specific needs of the export market. These industries have played a very significant role in pushing up exports through large-scale undertakings. These developments have called for the organisation of exports on sound lines. Export management in the small sector calls for professionalisation and sound organisation. The basic principles of export management are:

(i) Planning;

(ii) Organisation;

(iii) Building a team;

(iv) Executive action; and

(v) Management control.

Planning

Planning for export, even though extremely difficult, is the most important function. It involves forecasting, programming, procedures and budgeting. While forecasting leads to objectives and potential, programming spells out the ways of accomplishing them. A properly prepared programme spells out the ways of accomplishing them. A properly prepared programme becomes an administrative tool of much significance. Procedures help in the performance of work in a uniform manner. Budgeting in export marketing is a vital element in planning.

Organisation

A sound export organisation determines the economy and effectiveness with which the export business is managed and operated. The three basic activities of an export organisation are:

(a) Designing organisation components, that is, identifying the work that has to be performed to reach the objective and grouping this work in well-balanced jobs, territories, divisions and other operational segments.

(b) Defining and delegating responsibility and authority, and

(c) Establishing relationships.

The organisation chart indicates all the important functions of an export activity. Since many a small unit may not be in a position to have a specialised organisation of this type, efforts should be made by a group of small-scale industries to form a consortium to promote their exports on a larger scale.

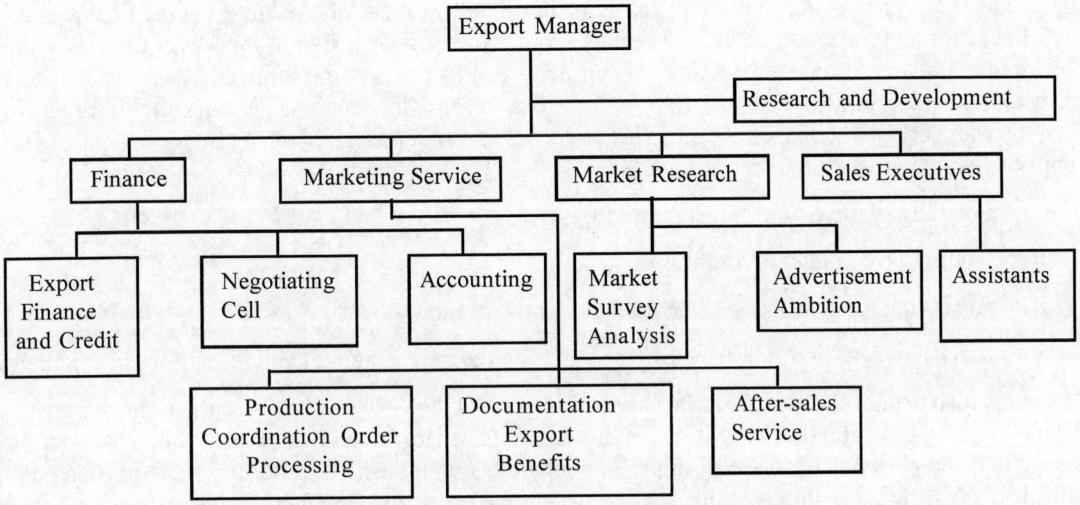

Fig. 15.2 Organisation Chart for a Small-scale Unit

The future of exports of the small-scale sector hinges on their concentrating as subcontractors and vendors. For growth of exports during the Tenth Plan, the Study Group has made the following recommendations:

Strengthening the international linkages;

Encouraging brand building to create a distinct identity;

Buyer-seller meets to be oganised in target markets;

Upgrading technology with the help of international experts wherever it is needed;

Encouraging consortia approach in selected clusters to meet bulk orders;

Focus on product design. Avail of updated market information;

Indian Trade Missions abroad to play an active role in popularising Indian products;

Timely availability of finance; and

Laws and rules to be simplified.

CONCLUSION

The exports of small-scale sector have been continuously expanding. As such, the share of the small-scale sector in the total exports showed a perceptible increase over the years. However, the increase was generally larger among the small-scale industries. The share of exports of the smaller sector among the small-scale industries – with less than ₹ 2 lakh fixed capital – declined sharply. Those industries which showed improvement in exports had relatively lesser dependence on exports in their total output. Hence, the export performance of these industries was only a subsidiary function, while catering to the domestic market constituted their major activity. At the same time, the smaller among the small-scale industries had a high degree of dependence on export.

CONCLUSION

Small-scale units are flexible in product adaptation because of their small size. That is why the items which are frequently modified according to the customer's demand can be produced by them and should be undertaken for export production.

The export market is a highly competitive market. It would, therefore, not be worthwhile to try to export the products of all the SSI units. It is desirable to identify some and to select a few export-worthy SSI units. This should be done on a continuing basis. Once the products and units have been identified, every effort should be made to develop the exports of the products of these units.

The small-scale sector, which is rightly called the unorganised sector, require organisational assistance, particularly in the marketing of its products abroad. Some of the State Export Corporations have rendered useful services in an organised way to market the products of the SSI units situated in their respective states. But most of the states either do not have any State Export Corporation or, when they have one, the desired services are not available. Merchant exporters and some of the export houses have no doubt played an important role in exporting the products of small-scale units; but this is insignificant in view of the large export potential of this sector. Small-scale units producing identical products should form a consortium of their own to market their products. But no satisfactory progress has so far been achieved in this system which is developed in marketing the exportable products of the SSI units abroad in a bigger way, the small-scale units should organise and mount their own export marketing effort. For this purposes, arrangements should be made by public institutions to render package assistance in respect of:

(i) Locating markets and buyers abroad;

(ii) Getting price indications and samples;

(iii) Arranging exhibitions of their products abroad; and

(iv) Advising identified export-worthy SSI units on the trade practices and formalities in the buying countries.

The study also brings into focus that export performance of industries with high capital intensity was remarkable during the period, while the share of labour-intensive industries in the total export showed a declining tendency throughout the period. The share of highly labour-intensive industries in the total export also showed a sharp fall. Though it may be admitted that the export performance of capital-intensive industries has enlarged the scope for employment generation both directly and indirectly through employment linkages, additional employment creation would have been much higher had the labour-intensive industries showed better export performance.

The expansion of export of semi-processed and manufactured goods during the period under study had benefitted mostly the large-scale capital intensive industries and larger among the small-scale industries. It is true that small-scale and labour-intensive industries could expand their exports to an extent and thereby contribute towards the avowed objective of reduction in inequality of wealth and economic power, but the inequality would have been reduced by a large extent, had these industries strived to secure a larger share in the total exports of semi-processed and manufactured goods.

Small-scale industries are not in a position to achieve the necessary thrust in marketing their products in competitive international markets. Since the small units' resources are quite meagre, they cannot go in for an aggressive drive in marketing their products in competition with large-scale and/or multinational units. The small-scale units do not only require professional managerial supports, they also need the active support of financial institutions. In particular, the commercial banks and the newly constituted Export-Import Bank of India can play a very crucial role in promoting export of the small-scale units.

Small-scale industries are poised for a leap under the Eighth Five Year Plan, and the SSI sector offers immense scope. It is, therefore, necessary for the small-scale units to increasingly exploit export demand for their products as a supplementary demand outlet. Given the inherent potential of India, government's new thrust of export promotion, stability of policies, simplified procedures and the national commitment to rapid economic growth, the government is confident that it shall be possible for India to overcome the present situation and to attain a sustained growth in export to meet not only important requirements but also the needs for development. In harnessing the growing international market, the small-scale units should maintain the high quality of the goods and channelise their products through the Export Promotional Agencies. Exports of small-scale industries are going to play a crucial role in the export performance.

ANNEXURE-I

The Handicrafts Sector has Emerged as a Prime Foreign Exchange Earner for India

The handicrafts sector has emerged as one of the most important foreign exchange earners for India on a sustained basis. The progress in terms of product range, number of companies and value of exports has been tremendous. In 1990-91, the export of handicrafts, excluding hand-knitted carpets, stood at ₹ 713 crore. This rose to ₹ 6,955 crore in 2000-01 and ₹ 8,343 crore in 2002-03. When compared with the export figures of previous year, the growth has been to the tune of 23.25 per cent, which is one of the highest in the export sector. Indian handicrafts are exported mainly to the American and European continents and the Far East. Hand-printed textiles, shawls, zari goods, imitation jewellery, embroidered and crocheted goods are exported to the US, UK, Germany, Canada, Japan and Saudi Arabia. The US is the largest buyer, with 32 per cent of India's total exports, followed by UK (11 per cent), Germany (11 per cent), France (5 per cent); Canada, Japan, Italy, the Netherlands (each sharing 3 per cent of India's exports), and Australia, Switzerland and Saudi Arabia (each with 2 per cent). The share of all other countries in India's export is 23 per cent. Special promotions in the Latin American countries, South Africa and new destinations in EU countries and the US are being targeted by EPCH as potential markets.

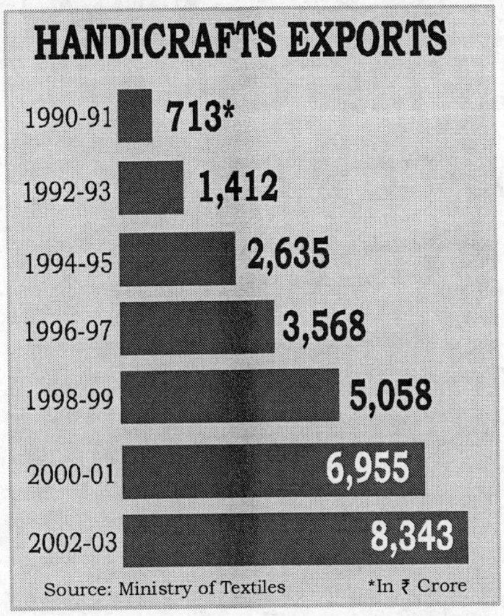

The handicrafts sector plays a key role in the economy by providing employment to lakh and generating foreign exchange

Bamboo and cane handicrafts from India's north-eastern states

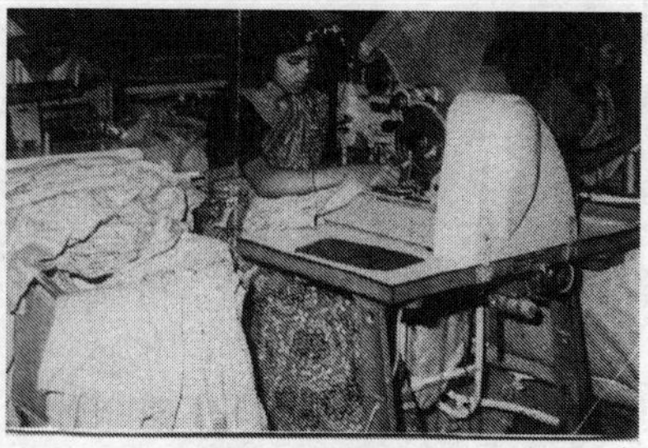

16 CHAPTER

PROBLEMS OF SMALL-SCALE INDUSTRIES

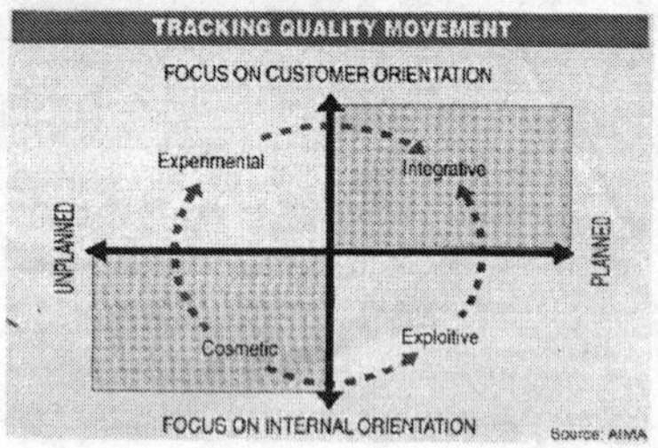

"Look failure in the eye, have faith, do not submit, stand tall, overcome, and live knowing that failing in life is the key to rising above."

LEARNING OBJECTIVES

The learning objective is to discuss and analyse the multi-complex problems faced by the small-scale industry.

Problems are an integral part of a small and medium enterprises (SMEs). They exit and it is the challenge to the entrepreneur to find appropriate solutions to overcome and grow with confidence. The chapter makes an indepth study of problems of small-scale industries.

- Problems galore.
- External vs. Internal problems of small industries.
- Teething problems.
- Licence and sanctions.
- Inspector Raj.
- Financial problems – Availability, cost and timely.
- Locational problems.
- Raw material.
- Technology.
- Marketing.
- Labour.
- Training.
- High infant mortality.
- Management.
- Coordination and Integration.
- Developing industrial and entrepreneurial culture.
- Education - A Social Resource.
- Knowledge is power.

INTRODUCTION

Recognising the important role that small industries play in the national economy, the Central and state governments have taken active steps to promote and foster their growth. These measures have been particularly effective; but many of the problems of production, distribution and finance still continue to afflict the small-scale sectors. While some of them are more or less common to a wide range of small industries, others have particular relevance to a group of small industries and the industries situated in rural and backward areas. As part of the programme, steps to improve the prospects and position of such industries have been conducted on an all-India and a regional basis so as to build up data on the economic and statistical background against which plans of development may be framed. These surveys, which have been carried out by the Economic Investigation Team attached to Small Industries Services Institutes in each state, have thrown valuable light on the various difficulties and problems faced by different small industries, and have recommended measures to overcome them.

EXTERNAL vs. INTERNAL PROBLEMS

We may divide the problems of small industries into two groups – external and internal. As is obvious, external problems are those which result from factors beyond the control of the industrialist, the availability of power and other infrastructure facilities required for the smooth running of small-scale industries; while internal problems are those which are not influenced by external forces. The internal problems affecting the small-scale industries relate to organisation, structure, production channel, distribution channel, technical know-how, training, industrial relations and inadequacy of management, etc. However, it is not our intention here to suggest that the two kinds of problems are mutually exclusive, they are corelated.

The problems of industries, whether in the small-scale sector or in the organised sector, are almost identical. However, the organised industry is financially very strong and its resources are large; it can therefore face its problems more effectively. Because of its weak financial structure, the resources of the small-scale sector are limited. The large-scale sector can employ trained and experienced managers: in the small industry, the proprietor or the partners, or if the unit is a company, its Director or Directors, have to take care of all the problems by himself or themselves. The large-scale sector can influence its raw material suppliers, its customers and at times even the government in framing its policies; but the small entrepreneur is helpless in this respect. He, therefore, has to lookafter the entire spectrum of problems despite the great limitations under which he functions.

In Indian context, small industries problems do have two phases. Many of the problems are internal and these are compounded with external problems.

A few of the internal problems are:

- Most of these units are set up by individual promoters or entrepreneurs. They come with personal egos and ideas, proprietorial attitudes and ineffective delegation. In short it is a one man show.
- The progress of the company depends heavily on mindset, courage and vision of the owners. This is at times influenced by personnel and family requirements.
- The organisational structure is not built, targets and budgets are not worked out. The systems and procedures are not defined or transparent. Planning is not corporated and dealings are informal.
- This is lack of professional expertise, with not much of real accountability.
- The emphasis is on short-term gain even at the cost of quality. Rather, a penny wise and pound foolish approach.
- Though personal loyalty may exist, logical reasoning, career plan and motivation are somewhat lacking. While pay scales are generally lower, goodwill and job security are less existent.
- In many instances, business ideas and exposures are not up to date and adequate, rules and regulations are less understood, product and market knowledge are not up to the mark, business remains confined within local or regional market.

But even then, many such industries do survive, mainly because of a few excellent individuals, either the owner or a trusted lieutenant. Most of them remain limited in their progress, due to in access of the right corporate approach and team-work.

A few major external problems and issues are suggested below;

(a) Surveys of the material and human resources of the countries to identify the regions or areas for the development of small-scale and medium-scale industrial enterprises;
(b) Identification of industrial projects for development;
(c) Project preparation and evaluation;
(d) Financial or credit support and investment promotion;
(e) Consultancy and counselling services;
(f) Technology development and applications, such as, the designing of prototype machines for products identified according to country resources and requirements;
(g) Development of infrastructure of various kinds in the appropriate areas;
(h) Entrepreneurship development;
(i) Industrial training and skill formation;
(j) Linkages between large industries and small industries and the creation of subcontracting facilities at the national, regional and international levels;
(k) Quality control and testing facilities;
(l) Market promotion, both domestic and export;
(m) Procurement of new materials and equipments;
(n) Scientific and industrial research;
(o) Information collection and dissemination on technology, markets, etc.;
(p) Identification of and assistance to enterprises which are experiencing difficulties;
(q) Management and reorganisation or restructuring of small and/or medium-scale enterprises through various schemes;
(r) Productivity increases through modernisation;
(s) Incentive measures by industry and by area;
(t) Local initiative;
(u) Creation of institutions and changes in prevailing institutional arrangements;
(v) Regional and international technical and financial assistance;
(w) Cooperation among the developing countries.

Teething Troubles

From the moment a small industrialist conceives the idea to start his own unit, he has to workhard against heavy odds. The first step, *viz*., the preparation of a project report, calls for the collection of data on the marketability of the product chosen, the availability of raw materials, the manufacturing techniques involved, the choice of machinery and location. While a large unit can afford to pay a fat fee to a consultant for the preparation of a project report, the small industrialist has generally to rely on himself.

Licence

The next problem is to obtain the permission of, and licence from, the Industries Department of the State, local bodies, etc. But despite the policy of the government, petty officials are often unhelpful – they have other ideas. A lot of time and energy is wasted in persuading these officials to perform their duties. It is also true that the small in the small-scale sector does not know how to make an approach and avail itself of the various facilities announced by the Central and state governments. Alternatively, it is not in a position to communicate with the well organised, urbanised bureaucracy. These are the major handicaps which hinder the growth of the small-scale sector in the country. If the production programme calls for imported machinery or raw materials, the small industrialist has the additional problem of obtaining suitable licences and of going through import procedure which keep on changing frequently because of the changes in the government's policy; as a result people generally cannot understand them easily; and corruption takes deep roots in the economy. At almost every stage, the small entrepreneur has to tip people; only the courageous and influential can face up to the corrupt and emerge successful. Though the government often states its support and commitment to the rapid development of small-scale industries, it holds them to random by implementing wrong policies. For example, the Government of Maharashtra distributed cement at ₹ 120 per bag, which is beyond the means of a small entrepreneur. Anyone who wants to stand on his own legs cannot hopes to achieve his objective in the normal course; he can only do so at enormous cost and/or with the government's patronage.

Table 16.1 Problems of Enterprises

Internal	External
(1) Choice of an Idea	(1) Infrastructural
(2) Feeble Structure	(a) Location
(3) Faulty Planning	(b) Power
(4) Poor Project Implementation	(c) Water
(5) Poor Management	(d) Post Office, etc.
(6) Poor Production	(e) Communication
(7) Quality	(2) Financial
(8) Marketing	(a) Capital
(9) Inadequate Finance	(b) Working Capital
(10) Labour Problems	(c) Long-term Funds
(11) Capacity Utilisation	(d) Recovery
(12) Lack of Vertical and Horizontal Integration	(3) Marketing
(13) Inadequate Training in Skills	(4) Taxation
(14) Poor and Loose Organisation	(5) Raw Material
(15) Lack of Strategies	(6) Industrial and Financial Regulations
	(7) Inspections
	(8) Technology
	(9) Policy
	(10) Competitive and Volatile Environment

INSPECTOR RAJ: THE GREAT SURVIVOR

Ministry	No. of inspectors	Work Done
Industry	5	Check registration, inventories, tax payment quality control, safety equipment
Home	2	Check fire protection facilities and compliance with Explosives Act
Planning and Statistics	1	Collect data on production, manpower, man-hours utilised and lost
Finance	12	Five for income tax (three of them checking the same records for three different departments); seven from excise department
Separate Revenue	5	Enforcement, verification and recovery of sales tax; enrolment of professional tax; weights and measures
Revenue Department (State Government) tax	1	Registration of professional
Labour	8	Checking compliance with different labour laws, checking the same records
Municipal Corporations	2	Municipal bye-laws
Power and Energy	1	Electricity connections
Health and Family Welfare	2	Hygiene and Occupational health

Urban Affairs and Employment	1	Sanitation
Environment and Forests	2	Pollution control
Communications	1	Telecom facilities
Local Self-government Food and	2	Octroi and mass raids
Drug Administration	1	Safety standards

The licence-quota raj may be over but the inspector raj still reigns supreme. Industry may have been delicensed in 1991 but is still highly regulated. Each industrial unit is visited by between 40 and 60 inspectors in the course of a month. The following is an illustrative, and not an exhaustive, list of inspectors. There may be several more inspectors depending on the kind of manufacturing activity. As a result, small and medium enterprises are forced to shell out bribes to these officers or else face harassment.

Finance

Small units, as is well known, are not exclusively and not even mainly dependent on government assistance. Most of these units owe their origin to the spurt in the demand of their products either in the local market, the neighbouring or distant markets, or in a combination of markets. (Generally speaking, the demand starts initially from the local market or neighbouring market and then is picked up from the regional and distant markets.)

The initial investment of these small units comes mainly from within, most of them invest their own funds or borrowed funds (mainly from relatives, friends and professional lenders). Much less comes from banks and government channels.

The small units depend more on their own funds and borrowed funds from non-banking and non-government sectors because of the fact that institutional lenders like banks and government financial corporations are generally reluctant to advance money to these small units, since they have yet to establish themselves.

These small units are not in a position to offer the guarantee required by the banking sector. Even when small loans can be raised from government agencies, the procedure is so cumbersome that most of the entrepreneurs, who are either illiterate or semi-literate, hesitate to make use of these facilities. And since the finance they acquire is on a small-scale, entrepreneurs prefer to put in their own rather than borrowed funds. For example, skilled persons, who become potential entrepreneurs of small industries in due course, have generally saved some money in the past while they were employed in other firms as wage workers. In fact, it is the ambition of most skilled workers that they should start their own business (especially in the engineering trade) after a few years of service, when they have gained the requisite experience, studied the market trends and accumulated some savings.

The skilled-worker-entrepreneur generally gets some assistance from his previous masters – depending on their relationship with these masters. Also, as these *mistry*-entrepreneurs are already known in the market, because of their having worked in a particular area over the years, they develop links with the local market which help them to buy inputs and their products.

In this way, a number of factors work together and enable the new entrepreneurs to raise the initial capital needed for the starting of small units from sources other than government agencies. Of course, over a period of time, institutional finance is available for further expansion: but the extent to which they avail themselves of this finance depends upon the rate of growth of small units as well as the contacts they have built up with institutional ledgers. Many established small units hesitate to approach institutional lenders. Many established small units hesitate to approach institutional financial agencies (including government agencies) because of their traditional tie-up with non-institutional bodies and also because of their lack of training, especially in financial matters. This fact is supported by the Moga study conducted under the supervision of Mr.V.S. Mahajan. The finding of the study is that almost all the 300 and odd small units engaged in the production of agricultural implements were started with the entrepreneurs' own funds and with funds borrowed from relatives and friends, and that the nationalised banking sector and State Financial Corporations have contributed precious little.

Small-scale industrialists do not have sufficient funds of their own for fixed capital investment, nor can they obtain the necessary resources from institutional agencies if the latter are doubtful of the farmer's ability to repay the loans in time. The shortage of funds makes it difficult for them to install modern machinery and tools and to maintain well organised and full-equipped factories. Moreover, they cannot buy and store good quality raw materials or stock their financed products, pack their goods attractively, have any sales organisation of their own or furnish security deposits, whenever necessary. State Finance Corporations take several months to take decisions on extending term loans. If one is in a hurry to commence a project, loan is applied for which would be repaid out of the State Finance Corporation's sanctioned loan. Banks also are not quick enough in the disposal of loan applications. They too take anything from one to three months to clear a project and sanction advance facilities. Their assistance is hardly available for initial capital or for future expansion. It is available only for the working capital needs of small-scale units.

Financial institutions ask for a lot of information and data. They are hardly ever satisfied with whatever information the prospective borrower supplies and go on raising queries, often not at one time, but in instalments with wide gaps. This makes matters very difficult for the small industrialist, particularly when he lacks knowledge in this field, and he has to deal with both the State Finance Corporation and the bank. Quite often, a few back out at this stage and give up the project. If only the bureaucracy were helpful, a major problem of the small industrialist would be solved.

Location

Banks and other financial institutions have not shed their traditional attachment to liquidity and safety of resources. On their part, the small entrepreneurs have no knowledge of the availability of varied financial assistance from various sources. With proper education and training, the small entrepreneur may seek better financial assistance. The choice of location, and getting water and power connections, also call for a great deal of effort on his part. It is not easy to decide on location, for the choice involves consideration of the availability of infrastructural facilities, the cost and tenure of acquisition, the availability of labour and proximity of the markets. Once the location is chosen, one has to go ahead to select and purchase a plot of land and construct a shed or to take it on rent or on ownership basis. At the same time, arrangements have to be made to select and procure machinery and to get it installed.

Raw Materials

In view of the rising tempo of industrial activity, the shortage of the right type of raw material at standard prices has affected the entire industrial sector. Because of their smallness and weak financial position, small-scale industries have to utilise the services of middlemen to get raw materials on credit. Such an arrangement, however, results in higher costs and is particularly disadvantageous when raw materials are imported, for the profit margins of middlemen are rather high. Their meagre resources induce small industrialists to use cheap and inferior materials, which naturally affect the quality of their finished products. Moreover, the irregular supply of certain raw materials adversely affects their production programmes.

The raw material problem has been extremely acute for steel-based industries like bicycles and their spare parts, sewing machines and spare parts, automobile leaf springs, agricultural implements, etc. The shortage of special steel, such as – chrome-vanadium steel and chorme-silicon steel is even greater. Manufacturers complain that since some companies supply steel only in wagon-loads, they cannot obtain their requirements. Even when some units can buy wagon-loads, there have been complaints of inordinate delays between the placing of orders and the receipt of supplies. It appears that, although the quota for small-scale industries has been raised, the actual supply has not matched the quota. It is alleged that dealers deliberately delay supplies till the expiry of the quota certificate and sell the material in the open market at inflated prices. As a result, entrepreneurs are compelled to purchase defective imported material or scrap metal from local dealers. Even when quotas are issued to them, they cannot obtain their raw material requirement through the normal channels at controlled prices. They are forced to buy these materials in the black market at prohibitive prices which upset all their cost calculations. In the face of any infrastructural crisis, the small-scale sector is the first casualty.

The industrialist should, therefore, make a proper study of the raw materials market. The selecting of right material and obtaining quotations so as to get it at an economic price are his most immediate problems. Moreover, the choice of raw materials or correct specifications is very important from the point of view of quality control. Sometimes, a sample of the material has to be tested in a laboratory on each occasion, because different batches of raw material may vary in quality.

The availability of raw materials has been a great problem in our country. Some of them are chronically in short supply; some are very scarce at times and abundant at others; and there are great price variations. Manufacturers and suppliers very frequently create artificial scarcities and rig up prices. Even the government is at fault, sometimes deliberately because it is politically motivated, and often throws the trade into complete confusion by frequent changes in policy, especially in regard to controls. Quite often, the announced objective of the control policy is defeated by unscrupulous elements with the connivance of bureaucrats, who exploit the situation at the cost of the buyers. In such circumstances, everyone wants to protect himself by resorting or stock-piling for a rainy day. (The problems of overstocking are discussed separately).

The small-scale units in the rubber industry are facing serious difficulties because of the imbalance between the demand for and the supply of raw materials, they lead to unduly high prices. During the past five years, the consumption of natural rubber has gone up from 1.33 lakh tonnes to 1.73 lakh tonnes – on an average, by 8,000 tonnes per annum; but the increase in domestic production has been for 1.43 lakh tonnes to 1.48 lakh tonnes 1,000 tonnes a year. Imports have been channelled through the State Trading Corporation, but they have failed to remedy the situation because of their inadequacy. The current price of RMA-I grade, around Rs. 15,000 tonnes, exceeds the government's fixed price of ₹ 8,2250 by a wide margin. Unless the situation is rectified soon and concerted measures taken on a long-term basis, widespread shortages of several consumer goods using rubber as a basic raw material would develop and exports would suffer.

In view of the serious shortage of raw materials, the industry feels that sizable imports will have to be continued for several years despite the efforts which have been made to produce natural rubber in new areas. Long-term arrangements with some of the neighbouring countries – with Malaysia, Thailand, Indonesia, Vietnam and Sri Lanka – should be made. A buffer stock of rubber, too ought to be built-up.

The rubber industry is strongly of the opinion that the State Trading Corporation has not been of much help in containing prices or in ensuring an adequate supply of rubber. Imports, therefore, should be canalised. Imports, by actual users, it has been stressed, ought to be exempted from custom duty. Since domestic natural rubber does not attract any excise duty, imports too ought not to be subjected to a countervailing duty. In view of the attractive prices which the producers are able to receive for natural rubber, the cess charged from the industry for the ostensible purpose of fostering the cultivation of rubber should be dispensed with.

The Estimated Committee of Parliament has expressed its dissatisfaction over the fact that small-scale industries, which had been assigned an increasingly important role in the plans in achieving wider employment opportunities and an intensified development of new industries, were suffering from chronic shortages of essential raw materials. In its 14th report on the Industries Ministry, the committee has recommended that, considering the small-scale sector's contribution to industrial production and national economy, its raw materials requirements should be given the highest priority. As a matter of fact, these requirements should be the first charge on the availability of such materials, consistent with the needs of such other important and strategic sectors as public utilities, defence and oil exploration. According to the committee, the government had not been able to assess the demand of the small-scale sector. It has, therefore, called upon the government to evolve a mechanism for a demand survey of the sector at least in so far as scarce raw materials are concerned.

Meanwhile the committee reiterated that, as far as possible, excise duty should be levied at the basic input stage or at the end product stage. In its 12th report on the action taken by the government on the recommendation made by it, the Committee has stated that the government should try out such a scheme on an experimental basis, to begin with, for a selected number of commodities, before gradually extending it in the light of the experience gained. It has favoured a one-stage imposition of excise duty with a view to curbing evasion of payments, reducing scope for harassment and minimising administrative expenditure.

Technology

Technology is the case of all industries. The growth of small-scale industries in India has not been very satisfactory despite the various provisions for its promotion in the industrial policy of the country. One of the major handicaps of the small-scale sector has been the absence of the latest technology which alone can ensure quality and high rate of productivity. The small industrialist, therefore, should keep himself abreast of developments in technology, so as to:

(i) Remain in the market;

(ii) Improve the quality of his products;

(iii) Lower the cost of production; and

(iv) Pass on the benefits to the consumer.

Unless he takes to this policy, he may soon find himself squeezed out of business. It is even advisable for the small entrepreneur to give a lead in research and development, which may not always be very expensive. Even without the facility of a sophisticated laboratory and gadgets, by using his intellectual capabilities and utilising the knowledge gained by others, it is possible for him to stumble upon some new ideas, provided that he is development-oriented and is capable of innovation.

Marketing

Marketing is one of the major stumbling blocks for small-scale industries. The many problems which they face in marketing their products are enumerated below:

(i) Lack of standardisation;
(ii) Poor designing;
(iii) Poor quality;
(iv) Lack of quality control;
(v) Lack of precision;
(vi) Poor finish;
(vii) Poor bargaining power;
(viii) Lack of service after sales;
(ix) Scale of production;
(x) Brand preferences;
(xi) Distribution contacts;
(xii) Lack of knowledge of marketing;
(xiii) Competition;
(xiv) Ignorance of potential markets;
(xv) Unfamiliarity with export activities – procedures and market know-how, and
(xvi) Financial weakness.

As mentioned earlier, because of his weak financial base, a small industrialist cannot afford to spend as heavily as a large unit does on marketing his products. A rare exception is the pharmaceutical industry, in which the gap between the manufacturing cost and the selling price is very large. This is a special situation, in which marketing techniques are different, and therefore the cost of marketing is very high, particularly the marketing cost of those drugs for which there is stiff competition. The small industrialists in this line have to follow this trend in order to survive in the global market.

In the absence of a marketing channel of their own, many small units sell their products to large selling houses. Voltas, for instance, markets a number of products produced by small units. Similarly, Bata Shoe Company sells shoes manufactured by the small-scale sector. As a result, small units invariably get a raw deal. The large companies make handsome profits from marketing the products of small units by charging a much higher price from the consumer. In this respect, there is a need for a larger number of marketing consortia, whose primary responsibility will be to assist small units.

Recoveries

One of the most difficult problems of the small industrialist today is recoveries from sales. It is an established practice for buyers to expect credit from sellers. This practice is forced upon the small industrialist by the larger ones. Initially, credit was available for a month or two; but with a very tight money market, a situation has developed in which buyers do not pay their suppliers for over 12 months, and get away with it.

The financial assistance availed of by the small unit with great difficulty for a bank is taken advantage of by its customers, who do not pay their dues in time. The bank may, if at all, extend further assistance: but this assistance, after all, is not limitless. The New Bill Market Scheme of the Reserve Bank of India has not touched this problem. The only way out of this situation is for the Central Government to introduce measures to curb the practice and save the small industrialist.

Labour

Handling labour, which is a major contributor to industrial production, is one of the most difficult tasks of the industrialist because of the human element involved in it. One has to keep abreast of the maze of labour laws, which keep changing from time-to-time. Labour today is fully aware of its rights. It has, therefore, to be handled with patience and understanding. Unfortunately, trade unionists politicalise the problems of labour, and at times even create a problem where there was none before. To protect their vested interests, politicians often prevent a settlement of a dispute between labour and employers, and thus work against the interests of both. It is very important, therefore, to evolve a code of conduct for trade unionists to protect the interests of labour as well as of employers; this will add to the general prosperity and well-being of both.

Faulty Planning

The most important one is faulty planning and inadequate appraisal of projects. No proper viability studies, technical or economic, are carried out before units are sponsored.

The report of the study team of the State Bank of India (1975), which examined the difficulties and problems of the small sector, came to the conclusion that over 40 per cent of the sample units examined by it were started with feasibility studies or detailed project reports.

P. Ravindra, owner of a small-scale fabrication plant in the industrial estate in Jogeshwari, a Mumbai suburb, confirmed this view: "Very few entrepreneurs launch their operations on the basis of a careful plan," he said. "Some are over-enthusiastic about their projects and jump headlong into the business without surveying the market for their products or evaluating the stability of raw material prices. By the time they start production, most of their earlier guesses and hopes are belied. The fact is that very few small industrialists have a clear conception of business. Most of us have had to learn the hard way. Yet some never learn and start milking their companies. This is how the sickness spreads."

Even when detailed project reports are prepared, inexperienced entrepreneurs may 'build' sickness into their units from the conception stage itself. For example, they may opt for an improper location, employ inadequately experienced consultants, choose inappropriate technology, underestimate the fixed and operational costs involved in the manufacture of their products, and embark on a project without a proper market survey.

Given the general spread of sickness in the small-scale sector, it seems that government agencies have not properly scrutinised project proposals. In fact, T. Ragupati, a faculty member of the Industrial Development Department, Small Industries Extension Training Institute, Hyderabad, places the blame squarely on government agencies.

"The sickness among new small-scale units is attributable to their indiscriminate promotion by government agencies in order to achieve employment targets fixed under plan programmes. During the Fifth Plan, and in later years, there was an increased emphasis on providing job opportunities by developing small-scale and tiny units. It resulted in hastily prepared and implemented programmes for the promotion of these units.

"Campaigns were undertaken by the promotional agencies to select unemployed educated and technically qualified persons as entrepreneurs in promoting small industries. Financial agencies like banks were subjected to pressures to finance without adequate evaluation of the projects. This appears to be the principal factor for the ever-rising incidence of sickness among newly promoted industries, particularly in backward areas."

High Infant Mortality

Due to this indiscriminate sponsoring of small units, 'infant mortality' among them is fairly high. The 1972 census estimated that 35 per cent of all the small units were dead before they started. The current figure is bound to be of a similar, if not of a much greater magnitude.

Another consequence of this indiscriminate promotion without proper scrutiny is the spread of numerous malpractices in the name of the small-scale sector. It is common knowledge that some entrepreneurs have a vested interest in remaining small so that they may avail themselves of such government concessions as quotas for scarce raw materials, tax rebates and power subsidies.

At end-March 2007, credit extended by scheduled commercial banks to 1,14,132 sick SSI units was at ₹ 5,267 crore. Of the sick SSI units 4,287 units with their outstanding bank credit at ₹ 427 crore were found to be viable. Of these, banks placed 588 units under the nursing programmes, involving an outstanding credit of ₹ 269 crore. In all, 109,011 units with outstanding credit of ₹ 4,757 crore were found non-viable.

On the other hand, some large business houses have been known to use small-scale units as front companies to indulge in various malpractices and defraud the government.

Even viable small-scale units are struggling for survival. The Industrial Policy Resolution, 1948, has noted that "the healthy expansion of cottage and small-scale industries depends on a number of factors, such as – the provision of raw materials, cheap power, technical advice, organised marketing of their products and wherever necessary, safeguards against intensive competition by large-scale manufacturers".

The growth of small-scale industries in India was largely included by the promotional policies of the government since the beginning of the Third Five Year Plan. A large number of units flourished under various incentive schemes. But this was followed, with certain lags, by high rates of failures or closures of these units. Certain patterns of concentration of 'births' and 'deaths' have generally been observed.

THE MANAGEMENT

The area in which small-scale industries have encountered the greatest difficulty is that of management. A well-organised industry owes its success mainly to its good management. A successful manager is one who has anticipated his problems and prepared himself to face them squarely and in good time. He should have foresight, so that he may prepare his organisation to face the coming events. He gauges the strength and weakness of his organisation, and appraises the new situation, and to meet it, he works out a strategy. This strategy makes demands on his organisation's strength in terms of the resources that are at its command, whether in men, materials or money – the three 'Ms' of industry. He takes stock of those resources which are readily available and identifies those not so readily available. He gathers all the resources and puts them into productive activity. Each step in the functions of the manager is fraught with uncertainties and difficulties. He has to take calculated decisions, upon which depends the results of his endeavours.

Traditionally, the management of enterprises has been in the hands of the families of business communities, and the managerial talent was handed down the family ladder. It had been accepted that people from other communities are incapable of taking up these responsibilities. There is some substance in this, for in a traditionally business family, the prospective manager was initiated into the responsibilities of his profession at an early age. However, this traditional practice has not been free from its own aberrations. In the final analysis, the success of any business depends on the earnestness with which he applies himself to learn out of his own experience. Tradition has not made a systematic study of the management of enterprises. It exists and suffers from individual whims and fancies. It has never bothered to foster or train new entrepreneurs, nor welcomed newcomers because of fear of competition rather than for any other reason. By and large, its objective is limited to earning quick profits for the owners of the industry, often at the cost of the future of the industry itself, with which the owners do not identify themselves.

Modern management, however, has overcome the shortcomings of the old system. It makes a proper and systematic study of the subject. Regular courses are now conducted at university levels. By applying the principles of management learnt in such a course and with no-the-job training available, today's professional managers are at much better advantage than those who had traditional training alone.

The functions of management lie in the collection of relevant material and utilising them to take quick decisions for the attainment of desired goals. Management is a skill which, like any other skill, can be acquired. The success of an industry is largely determined by a satisfactory management of finance, inventory, budgeting, marketing, accounting and manpower. These areas are deeply studied, and the information collected is utilised to plan and control the activities of a unit. The management of finance and inventory, by far, is the most important of all. Many units get sick because of an improper handling of these areas of management.

Coordination and Integration

Purposeful coordination and integration of such supporting institutions will go a long way in making these institutions a valuable resource that can go into the small industry, leading to its accelerated growth. Again, such assistance should be easily and constantly made available to the small entrepreneur and this could be possible only if the service institutions are organised regionally, if not locally. Further, the assistance should also be prompt and efficient. Promptness would go a long way in saving time, which amounts to slackening on expenses, and consequently, improving profitability. It should also be equally efficient. The diagnosis should be correct and the remedies should be effective. Efficiency, therefore, means correct diagnosis and effective remedies. The whole object of assistance to small entrepreneurs is to improve vitality as well as competitive ability of their industrial units. This is important because enterprising service institutions and innovative local entrepreneurship can together change the environment and the horizon of the small industries sector in the developing economies. Infrastructure is thus acquiring a wider connotation and greater significance than ever before. It is essential for the developing countries to realise this and prepare themselves to face the new challenges that await them on the horizon of industrial transformation.

How to Help Small Firms

While there are no simple solutions and remains to be learned about how to create a favourable environment for small enterprises, several countries, with assistance from the World Bank during the last five years, have employed a more market-oriented approach to fostering them. It is too early to evaluate the results, but the response so far has been encouraging.

Essentially, the approach entails the following measures: (i) to reduce subsidies and policy preferences which favour large industry and discriminate against small; (ii) to enhance the availability and efficient utilisation of inputs commonly needed by small firms, and (iii) to increase the range of marketing opportunities. Fundamental to the market-oriented approach is the view that small enterprises will thrive, if they are economically efficient, without a plethora of special subsidies and government interventions.

Develop Industrial Culture

One more requisite for the growth of small industries is the right kind of education. Industrialisation ushers in a new culture. It revolutionises the society. Industry demands a new sense of values – individual as well as social. Industrial productive process and marketing practices in modern times call for attitudes and approaches different from those of conventional agriculture and traditional arts and crafts. Though man invented the machine, the latter eventually tends to discipline its creator. Modern industry, therefore, leads to a different kind of behaviour of man – individually and collectively. Punctuality in attendance, continuous vigilance, sense of economy, attitude of productivity, pride in the job and awareness of schedules are some of the virtues of the industrial culture. Agriculture is more individualistic. Industry is more collectivist. So, new attitudes and tendencies have to be socially developed and this new culture has to be imbibed amongst all those who are concerned with the various operations in the industry. In marketing, one has to contend and compete with many other rivals and as such, enterprise, aggressiveness and such other qualities have to be cultivated by him.

Industry as well as marketing are becoming progressively scientific and technological, which again lead to a kind of specialisation and professionalism. This process further gains momentum when mechanisation, sophistication and automation follow. Change in quality and magnitude, change in processes and practices, change in designs and patterns – in fact, all kinds of changes take place in an emerging and existing industrialist society. Small industries cannot afford to be oblivious of this factor.

Small industries need to be progressively modernised. Modernisation demands not merely on modern machinery and advanced technology, but a different psychology. The social mind must become progressively modern and rational. The society ought to exhibit new character, new discipline, and new temper. The traditional values and conventional attitudes ought to undergo a radical transformation. New abilities and capabilities must be systematically developed and should become the order of the day. Modern industrial culture must replace the traditional culture associated with agriculture. This will emerge mainly through the system of education if it is attuned to the needs of modern industrialisation. The greatest obstacle in the way of industrial progress is the paucity of modern skills and capabilities. Education must instill a spirit of inquiry, pride in enterprise and optimism towards innovative change. The educational system, then, has to be built up on different lines, with accent on achievement, innovation and enterprise. Without such an educational system, the entrepreneurial base will remain narrow and education will provide the requisite and appropriate impulse and motivation, which in turn will breed industrial entrepreneurship and infuse service institutions with a sense of purpose and a spirit of achievement. If the state governments take care of education, service institutions and entrepreneurship, they will ensure the emergence and progress of the small industries.

EDUCATION – A SOCIAL RESOURCE

If there is something like industrial culture, it can only be massively and rapidly spread with education. Education is a social resource which motivates a community into certain activities in preference to others. Education in an industrialising society is bound to be different from what it is in a predominantly agricultural society. Education is, after all, for equipping the young generation of today for facing the tasks of tomorrow. When industry depends on science and technology, as well as effective execution and management, the object and content of education must, in essence, be to appreciate the needs of tomorrow and to provide the requisite skill to fulfil these needs. In most developing societies, the educational system is largely irrelevant to the needs of today and tomorrow. The arch of industry would need the foundation of modern education that will support modern industry with the resultant industrial culture. Systems of education have, therefore, to be imaginatively and objectively evolved so as to stimulate and motivate the young men of the developing countries to face the industrial tasks in the small industry. The tasks have to be faced mostly by the individual entrepreneur and so the need for the right type of education relevant to these tasks is assuredly most imperative.

Problems Faced By Small-scale Enterprises

Small-scale enterprise quite face distinctive problems. These are:

1. Difficulty in obtaining credit from commercial banks because of their general inability to provide security.
2. Inability to offer liberal credit terms in the sale of their products.
3. Absence of management expertise. Often management is by one person who performs a number of functions usually with no formal training.
4. Difficulty in competing with imported products due to high production costs.
5. Difficulty with competition from other local entrepreneurs in the same line of business competing for the limited local market.
6. Difficulty in obtaining industrial land in towns and cities. The shortage of industrial land is giving rise to more and more backward operations.
7. Under capitalisation.
8. Difficulty in identifying appropriate technology and technical assistance.
9. The manner in which both the needs of the economy and linkage with existing industry can best be served.
10. Bureaucratic red-tape and regulations.
11. Surveys of the material and human resources of the countries to identify the regions or areas for the development of small-scale and medium-scale industrial enterprises;
12. Identification of industrial projects for development;
13. Project preparation and evaluation;
14. Financial or credit support and investment promotion;
15. Consultancy and counselling services;
16. Technology development and applications such as the designing of prototype machines for products identified according to country resources and requirements;
17. Development of infrastructure of various kinds in the appropriate areas;
18. Entrepreneurship development;
19. Industrial training and skill formation;
20. Linkages between large industries and small industries and the creation of subcontracting facilities at the national, regional and international levels;
21. Quality control and testing facilities;
22. Market promotion, both domestic and export;
23. Procurement of raw materials and equipment;
24. Scientific and industrial research;
25. Information collection and dissemination of technology, markets, etc.;
26. Identification of and assistance to enterprises which are experiencing difficulties;
27. Management and reorganisation or restructuring of small- and/or medium-scale enterprises though various schemes;
28. Productivity increases through modernisation;
29. Incentive measures by industry and by area;
30. Local initiative;
31. Creation of institutions and changes in prevailing institutional arrangements;
32. Regional and international technical and financial assistance, and
33. Cooperation among the developing countries.

CONCLUSION

Whether in the small industry or the large industrial sector, problems always exist. Some face problems as if they are a challenge because that is the road to advancement. If there is no problem or challenge, we tend to feel complacent, which is the beginning of our degeneration. The problems of small industries should, therefore, be treated in this spirit. This, of course, does not mean that the government, the local bodies, financial institutions and banks should create unnecessary obstacles in the path of industrialists; nor that industrialists should function in isolation. Rather, they should be increasingly aware of the fact that they are a part of a larger society, each section of which has its own strong and weak points.

In the post-independence period, the governments at the Centre and the state have established a number of specialised institutions to cater to the varied needs of small-scale units. These promotional institutions assist all and sundry in setting up small units with a view either to fulfilling their objective or over-reach their target; but they do not ensure the provision of adequate working capital, raw materials, power supply; nor do they help them in developing marketing outlets for the sale of their products. This situation has arisen because of the absence of a meaningful coordination among the concerned agencies.

The entrepreneur needs to reorient his attitude and develop special leadership qualities necessary for taking decisions based on wider implications rather than trodding the narrow path of urge satisfying action alone. His problem, therefore, is one of growing from professional entrepreneur into a professional manager and finally into an administrator in order to successfully come out of the growth crisis, which he starts facing once his enterprise grows from a small business into a large enterprise.

The problems of entrepreneurs are multidimensional. These can be solved by the coordinated efforts of entrepreneurs, coordinated functioning of promotional agencies, and governmental assistance without red-tape or bureaucratic delays. The entrepreneur has to be educated; and he should have a proper training in acquiring the necessary skills in running an enterprise. In fact the entrepreneur is the kingpin of the industrial spectrum.

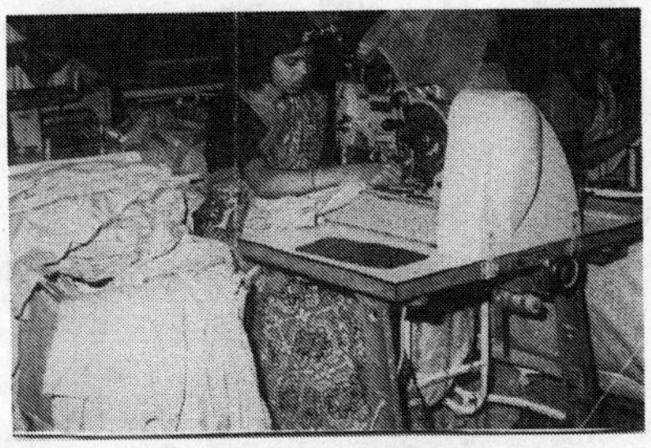

17 CHAPTER

PROSPECTS FOR SMALL-SCALE INDUSTRIES

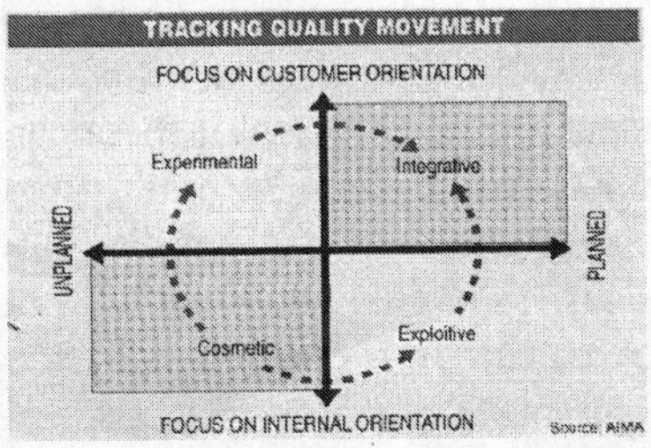

Sabeer Bhatia *Netpreneur*

Everything from land to gold is cyclical but the returns from businesses are unmatched. Not to mention the thrill of making your dream work.

LEARNING OBJECTIVES

The learning objective is to look ahead and analyse the potential and prospects for small-scale industries.

The chapter looks at the key issues related to its prospects.

- Small-scale industries has vast potential.
- Inappropriate support.
- Development challenges.
- Follow economies of scale.
- Well-designed programme.
- Developing capabilities.
- Creativity should be given full support.
- Innovation is key to small-scale growth.
- Industrial integration.
- Developing appropriate technology.
- Organise service agencies.
- Institutional infrastructure.
- Recommendations.
- Fanning the entrepreneurial flame.
- Prospects in the 21st century.

INTRODUCTION

The small-scale industrial sector has vast potential in terms of employment, output, export promotion, expansion of base for indigenous entrepreneurship and dispersal of industries and entrepreneurship skills in rural as well as backward areas. The small-scale industries sector showed remarkable progress during the 1980s. This sector reportedly accounts for nearly 35 per cent of the gross value of output in the manufacturing sector and over 40 per cent of the total exports from the country. The level of employment in this sector has been over 140 lakh and increasing by 3.5 per cent per annum. With the opening of the economy and rapid stride in liberalisation, the small-scale industries sector is at the threshold of major challenges which need to be addressed squarely. The strategy, therefore, should be one of making the best of the available resources, opportunities and entrepreneurial skills to expand the scope of its activities horizontally and gain vertical integration.

In Perspective

The decade poses a challenge to the Indian economy and in particular, to the small-scale industries. Looking ahead, the development can never be a smooth process. Dynamic as it is, the process of development has its own problems and its own challenges. In the past, the industry has prospered in a somewhat secure environment enjoying protection in different ways. Recently, however, the environment has changed and the industry had to face major changes which have come about in greater frequency. Some of these changes have been brought about by internal factors, whereas others have been induced by international changes. In the last few years, small industry has learned to live with uncertainties such as inflation, demand recession and market instability. As we look into the future, it may have to endure a situation which is prone to frequent changes. In a situation like this, strategies have to be continuously reviewed and changed from time-to-time. Solutions for many of the problems faced by the small industry, whether of an operational nature or otherwise, have been found by development finance institutions. At this juncture in the country's development, it would seem useful to carefully review the past, analyse the present and reassess some of the basic elements of the environment for the growth of the small industries in the 1990s and the coming decades.

The small-scale sector which entered the seventies in a relatively small way is moving into the eighties in a big way. The small sector has rightly been recognised as an important sector of the economy and has assumed growing significance from the point of view of rapid industrialisation and reduction of inter-regional disparities.

Motivating and encouraging planned small-scale industrial development is a complex task, more so in a country of our size with wide variations in physical conditions and levels of development. It calls for action on many fronts. Besides the development of infrastructure, various facilities and incentives have to be offered by the government for accelerating industrial growth and achieving balanced regional development. Efforts in these directions have continued since the advent of planning and these have been increasingly intensified. A number of institutions have also been set up to speed up this process.

In order, however, to hasten the pace of industrialisation and to sustain it at an appropriate level, it is also necessary that the facilities available in different parts of the country and the incentives offered by the state government are made widely known to encourage the entrepreneurs to make investments in required directions through setting up new industries and by undertaking expansion and diversification of the existing units.

Inappropriate Support

While inappropriate regulations may distort their structure, it is also clear that specific government measures of support to small enterprises may, unless carefully designed, actually discourage or even prevent their efficient operation. Public support for small enterprises is frequently justified, for example, on the basis that they act as a 'breeding ground' for entrepreneurs. This argument needs to be looked into closely, however. Clearly, entrepreneurship is an essential element in economic development; risks must be taken in introducing innovations; businessmen are more likely to take risks, and usually better at gauging them than public servants. They are able to 'think small' and, as 'economic lubricants' to search for identity and fill needs likely to be overlooked by the public sector. Moreover, businessmen are more likely to terminate activities which the public will not pay for.

Nevertheless, certain limitations must be recognised if programmes to assist small enterprises are to be appropriately designed. Most fundamentally, entrepreneurs are by definition self-reliant, energetic and innovative, and do not generally need to be coddled by promotion programmes. It has, in any event, proven extremely difficult for the public sector to devise programmes that can develop entrepreneurship. Not all – or even most – artisans and petty traders are capable of developing the capacity to innovate by taking the special courses that have sometimes been provided under government auspices.

In general, the skill and aptitudes of most proprietors of small firms are best utilised if concentrated on a narrow range of activities, leaving the more innovative entrepreneurial functions to other organisations such as trading companies or larger firms which then subcontract to smaller ones. As economies develop and their structures change, many independent artisans may, in fact, be absorbed into larger organisations as workers and supervisors. The exceptionally entrepreneurial small businessman will usualy survive (and eventually stop being small) if he is left free to operate, subject only to the basic ground rules of public safety.

Follow Economies of Scale

Industrial development everywhere has proved beyond doubt that something like economies of scale do exist. What is economy of small-scale is dis-economy of large-scale and *vice versa.* The economies of scale would undergo a change with the advance of science and the progress of technology. Yesterday's economies of large-scale may become very productive economies of small-scale today or tomorrow. Thus, the concept of economies of scale is a changing concept, depending upon the dynamics of science and technology as well as the stage of economic growth and marketing prospects. Small industries make their appearance in the initial stages of industrialisation in any economy. When they grow in volume and strength, some of them taking their cue from the unmistakable signs of expanding markets at home or abroad develop by vertical or horizontal integration and become either medium or large industries. But this process does not create a dent in the ranks of small industries, because when small units grow to medium and medium into large, the number of small industries also grow – perhaps even in geometrical progression. One cannot conceive of any national economy merely based on a few large industries. An economy having a strong and broad base of small industries and an apex consisting of large industries, with some middle layers of medium industries can be said to have a pyramidal structure and it is this type of economy that processes in ample measure the elements of stability and dynamism. This is very true in the present-day context, and in respect of both the developed and the developing economies.

But that is the techno-economic aspect of industrialisation. In underdeveloped countries, one must not think of development on techno-economic considerations alone. There are certain social compulsions also, which assert themselves through political exigencies. It is the complex of techno-socio-politico-economic obligations that ultimately determine the pattern of industrialisation, particularly in the developing countries. Here modern technology is more or less conspicuous by its absence. The standard of living is generally not much above the subsistence level. Economy, in general, is still primitive – predominantly agricultural but the expectations of the masses are rising high and they produce from time-to-time political upheavals, small or great, shaking in the process the foundations of the national institutions. Mere industrialisation based strictly on techno-economic imperatives may make the develoment lop-sided and may, in its wake, usher in focus that will create social and political tensions. Mere renunciation of social objectives would not keep these forces in check. People would expect and demand positive action to scale down regional imbalances and remove social inequalities. In addition to all this, hunger and poverty stare right into the eyes of that vast mass of humanity which inhabits the underdeveloped world.

WELL-DESIGNED PROGRAMME

Broad programmes designed to provide equal incentives and access to scarce resources for all enterprises, irrespective of size, are likely to be more beneficial in the long-run than special programmes tailored exclusively to suit small-scale enterprises, which, as seen, can often yield perverse results.

A well-designed programme is likely to include many of the following components:

Credit: The availability of credit to small enterprises can often be increased by removing or at least raising the interest rate ceilings and permitting a 'spread' that makes it worthwhile for banks to lend to small enterprises; or by increasing the number and range of intermediaries allocating foreign exchange for investment. Refinancing facility can be useful, as can credit guarantee schemes (with costs passed on to borrowers) and training of local bank staff in simplified project appraisal and supervision methods. More importantly, credit should be made available at the appropriate time.

Important Raw Materials: Reform of trade regimes may be necessary to remove abuses of the import licensing system. It is not uncommon, for instance, for middlemen to find their way on the allocation lists and then resell their supplies at black market prices to small enterprises that desperately need imported input to survive in business but lack of influence over the licensing authorities. Freer access to foreign sources and lower levels of protection for domestic alternatives would be desirable. If possible, attempts should be made to reduce the years of middlemen in procuring raw materials for an enterprise.

Labour: The objective here is to increase labour skills and mobility by supplementing on-the-job training and by reducing labour market rigidities (particularly those affecting wages) which prevent the free flow of workers. Useful advice and assistance in training can often best be provided by the suppliers and customers of small enterprises, but governmental vocational training programmes can also be adapted to small-scale enterprise needs and circumstances (through such media as mobile demonstration units and night schools). In-plant training is much suited in this direction.

Technology and Equipment: Changing policies that have the effect of subsidising imported machinery would stimulate domestic engineering industries and machine shops, which are potentially important in helping small-scale enterprises improve their equipment. Technology should not be complicated. It should be easy but productive.

Buildings and Utilities: 'Industrial estates' are valuable to small enterprises but generally are subsidised and sometimes are built above the necessary standards. Removing the subsidies, levying charges adequate to recover costs and thereby permitting wider replication, and adopting appropriate, more modest standards are likely to produce economic rewards in the long-run. 'Sites and service' programmes for small enterprises, under which they build their own specifications, also are useful.

Advisory Services: Advisory services are needed but should be charged for on a full-cost basis so that the providing agencies – or preferably consulting firms – have ready evidence from the market of their utility. Public technical assistance institutions are more likely to be useful and responsive if they are specialised than if they seek to cover all areas of need. Also, their utility is more likely to be assured if their intended beneficiaries are adequately represented on their governing bodies.

Markets: The demand for small enterprise products and services would be increased by eliminating 'unfair' competition in the form of subsidies given to the large-scale industry. Often barriers to the trading companies which market the products of small firms exist and should be removed. Export markets can be tapped more fully by ensuring that small firms as well as large firms benefit from import duty rebates or exemptions on imported materials and components that are incoporated into exported products. Governments can also directly enlarge the markets for small enterprises by subcontracting maintenance and repair services that public agencies might otherwise perform themselves. Domestic market should be competitive but protected from foreign goods. Export market should be open to small-scale enterprises, especially set up for this purpose.

This list is not, of course, exhaustive. The best overall tonic for small enterprise is likely to be an economic climate, combining minimum regulation with maximum openness.

DEVELOP CAPABILITIES

Advanced economies have grown through the centuries with the development and diversification of the industry and the resultant commerce. Every country slowly, and many times unknowingly, develops a sense of proportion. This sense ultimately determines, along with the economies of scale, the scale of economies. This sense of economic proportion brings with it the consciousness of capabilities – technological, managerial, financial and organisational. The advanced economies in the developed countries are due to the advanced and developed capabilities. So long as such capabilities have not been developed, large projects and larger conglomerates would prove to be sterile, difficult to establish and much more rigorous to manage. Any national industrial economy must develop, as far as possible, naturally. On its birth, it must be properly protected and nourished. Then, with the passage of time, it will grow into healthy proportions. It will outgrow the gestation stage and eventually become self-reliant, self-sustained and self-accelerating, with stout muscles and stronger nerves. The national enterprises, which is equivalent to the sum total of the entrepreneurial, managerial, financial and technological capabilities is the growth of time; therefore, small industries in underdeveloped countries when they are emerging out of traditional agricultural economy provide a cradle for modern medium and larger industries.

The sense of economic proportion at any point of time determines the direction of economic development. There are several constraints which influence the process of industrialisation. The underdevelopment of a country is really the reflection of inadequate development of entrepreneurship in that country. When entrepreneurial growth is accelerated, modern industrial development automatically gathers momentum. Narrow or non-existent entrepreneurial base explains the non-development or slow development of industries in various countries. How to broaden and strengthen the entrepreneurial base in the society is the real challenge facing the developing countries today.

Industrial Integration

In the initial period, national entrepreneurship can certainly be nurtured and nourished in the small-scale sector much more assuredly than in any other sector. Small-scale industry assumes a special role in this context in the industrialising economies of Afro-Asian countries. When small businesses, enterprises and industries first make their appearance, they have to be properly and carefully nurtured. They also have to be protected from unequal competition and unfair practices of other sectors of the industry. This period of teething troubles and protection will depend upon several factors, such as the access to and availability of raw materials, credit on equitable basis, etc. There have to be several levels of organisation of monitoring and supporting services that can rush to the help of small industries in time of need.

There are distinctive functional characteristics of the small industry which mark it out from the large industry. These characteristics provide a rationale to policies which are aimed at making the small industries economically viable, financially prosperous, technically modern and commercially competitive. If the small industry is not progressively modernised, it will not remain competitive. It has to produce goods which are technological competent and which would be available to the customer at a competitive price. Unless small industries fulfil these two criteria, they will act as a drag on any economy and such dead weight cannot be suffered and sustained for long by any society in any country. The small industry has also to get itself more and more integrated with the large industry – the large and the small industries must play complementary and supplementary roles. In course of time, the fields of small and large industries must become distinct and definite and at the same time, an organic and integral relationship must be developed between them. The small industry, besides producing consumers' goods with their distinctive excellence, should also manufacture parts, components and subassemblies required by large industries; and wherever feasible and possible, finished products too. The small industry is not merely an appendage of the large industry. It is in one way independent of and in another sense, ancillary to the large industry. Together they should produce goods economically and excellently and serve the socio-politico-economic objective of the society.

There is really no conflict between the large-scale and the small-scale industries. If sometimes there is an apparent conflict, it is due to the inequitable access to and availability of resources required for production and sometimes, due to the preponderating influence that is brought to bear on national governments by the lobbies of large industries. The large and small entrepreneurs together constitute the national business and industrial community. This business community and the national government must always keep in mind the integrated national economic perspective. Such a perspective, if borne in mind, would eliminate conflicts and pave the way for the smooth functioning of both the sectors and ensure national prosperity. It is a lack of this perspective on the part of several national governments as well as most of the entrepreneurs both in the large and the small-scale sectors – that impedes or distorts development in the right direction and also vitiates the sense to economic proportion.

Develop Appropriate Technology

The underdeveloped countries face a number of problems which are both serious and complex. The problem of unemployment is one of them which demands early and effective solution. Blind imitation and wholesale adoption of the established technology from industrialised countries may aggravate the problem of unemployment in several Afro-Asian countries. The traditional agricultural economies are capital-short and labour affluent, while the industrialised countries are enormously capital-affluent and relatively labour-short. Whether or not the technology which is being developed in the advanced countries with the help of scientific discoveries and invention is in its original form really going to benefit the underdeveloped countries a fundamental issue the economic, scientific and technological genius of Africa and Asia should address itself. Development is a means that should lead to the efflorescence of human qualities of the vast manpower sheltered in these two ancient continents. Small industries would offer at least a partial remedy for the mounting problem of unemployment in these societies. Perhaps a new type of technology would have to be developed which will take cognisance of millions of idle hands and at the same time, will facilitate production of goods of comparable quality at a reasonable cost. Such a technology should be developed through the small industry. However, the development of such a technology, which can be legitimately termed as 'appropriate technology', is not entirely in the hands of small industries. It is scientific capability and innovative talent that could really provide a solution. Necessity is the mother of invention. Perhaps the urgent necessity of developing a new type of technology, appropriate to the economic facts and factors of Asia and Africa, may give both to that bonny and brainy baby – a new technology. We all have to pray for its birth at no distant date.

Organise Service Agencies

The basic characteristic of the small industry is the identity of management and ownership. But economy is constantly becoming more and more complex due to advances in science and technology. Furthermore, small industries have to face competition from units in their own category, from medium and large industries and from units in their own category, from medium and large industries and from industries in other countries. It is here that the owner-managed small industries suffer. They neither possess the specialisation nor the expertise which is required at such times. Smallness itself conditions their capability and manoeuvrability, which are so very essential to face squarely the suddenly developing situation that demands correct reading and instate decision. The capacity to absorb shocks from an error of judgement or from a miscalculation is probably the lowest in the small-scale sector. In fact, the small industry can safely be defined as one that has the least capacity to absorb an error. An error not only proves to be costly but sometimes even fatal. Accidents, however small, prove disastrous to the small industry because of its initial limited strength – financial, managerial, organisational, technological, administrative and competitive. This characteristic of small industries makes it obligatory on the part of any national government to organise service agencies.

Problem of small units are individual and like a human patient, they also have to be treated individually. Prescriptions have to be given after correctly diagnosing the constitutional and other maladies. Different maladies at different times affect the small units, but they all have to be attended to promptly and efficiently. When such small industrial units multiply and they must multiply with the progress of the national economy, the problem of the small-scale sector in any country collectively assumes gigantic proportions. If, therefore, the national small-scale industry is to be protected and promoted during the gestation period, very large organisations have to be established providing specialised knowledge and services and that too with countrywide coverage. These organisations must be action-oriented, achievement-mixed, and service-motivated. The administration of these organisations must be honest as well as efficient. Their personnel must be imbued with a sense of purpose with a feeling of involvement and with pristine conscientiousness. Such personnel will have to be specially trained and suitably motivated. Mere borrowing of expertise from the large-scale sector will not go very far. Expert knowledge is necessary, but it has to be integrated with a special aptitude for small-scale industries.

Institutional Infrastructure

Growth of small-scale industries requires infrastructural facilities on an increasing scale, appropriate and integrated institutional structure and prompt and adequate provision of finance. In developing countries, the accent should be on a comprehensive planning as possible. This itself envisages an efficient institutional structure. In fact, institutions, specially brought into being to assist small-scale industries, themselves constitute one of the most valuable resources, since it is these institutions that are expected to make the manifold deficiencies and weakness of small entrepreneurs all over the country and their performance would be judged by how much they stimulate and accelerate the development of small industries. Institutions have an inherent tendency to be static and sluggish, regulative and restrictive, conservative and assertive. Institutions formed for servicing and assisting small-scale industries must, on the contrary, be inherently developmental: that is being promotional, innovative and creative, progressive and productive. Their performance should be periodically reviewed and their programmes continually redefined and streamlined so that the changing needs of the growing number and multiplying lines of small industries will be adequately and effectively satisfied. These institutions must themselves show the *spirit of enterprise*. They should be able to take calculated risks and venture to make necessary experiments, which in turn, will enable them to gather experience and inspire confidence. They must be far ahead of and above the generality of small entrepreneurs. Such service institutions, manned by dedicated and devoted personnel and supported by the state, will be welcomed by all small entrepreneurs and will certainly accelerate the development of the small industry in any country.

Infrastructure facilities do not mean mere economic amenities such as – water, power, accommodation, communication and transport, but should also include service institutions capable of providing financial, managerial, technological and marketing expertise most satisfactorily and economically. This is because the small industry needs well-planned, closely-integrated and strategically coordinated assistance. Supporting and monitoring service have, therefore to be provided to nurture and nourish the small industry in its infancy. In fact, a favourble atmosphere has to be created so that the energy and vitality of the small industry will not unnecessarily get dissipated, when it is important to conserve them for production and marketing. This can be achieved if various types of facilities are made available to the small entrepreneur by specialised institutions imbued with a sense of pose and the spirit of enterprise. Many a time, it so happens that such facilities and services are not made available simultaneously as a result of which, despite a plethora of organisations, hardships of the small industry persist and frustration sets in. If the facilities and services are offered as a package progress is bound to be fast, and the small industry will improve considerably if the assisting institutions function in a coordinated manner. Unfortunately, this rarely happens in the developing countries.

Findings of a Research Study

The findings of a research study conducted by the NCAER in 1993 are as follows:

- Of the small-scale units studied, 61 per cent found the service from government agencies to be poor or unsatisfactory;
- 40 per cent found the service from private agencies to be poor or unsatisfactory;

- 93 per cent depend on themselves for advice in decision-making; only 10 per cent had undergone one or more types of training;
- 92 per cent have no quality markings;
- 56 per cent had no greater managerial problems;
- Small-scale units have developed in clusters spontaneously in small towns where infrastructure has not developed correspondingly; and
- The major problems are administrative bottlenecks, procedures, finance, infrastructure, marketing, training and counselling.

Table 17.1 Select Cluster Development

Small-scale Industry	District/Region
Leather footwear	Agra, Kanpur, Kolkata, Ambur, Ranipet
Sports goods	Meerut, Jallundhar
Glass and ceramics	Nagpur, Batala, Khurja, Farukabad
Locks	Firozabad, Aligarh
Woollen and cotton hosiery	Tirupur, Ludhiana, Kolkata, Delhi
Scientific instruments	Ambala, Ajmer
Safety matches	Sivakasi, Sattur, Kovilpatti, Ludhiana
Bicycles and parts	Jamnagar, Hajo (Assam), Moradabad, Kolhapur, Agra, Rajkot, Coimbatore
Brass parts	Ghaziabad, Mumbai, Pune, Bangalore
Diesel engines and parts	Delhi
Electronics	Mumbai, Delhi
Domestic electrical appliances	Morvi
Wall clocks	Vapi, Ankaleshwar
Powerlooms	Mumbai, Bangalore, Chennai, Ambala
Pens	Surat, Bhiwandi, Ichalkaranji, Goregaon
Carpets and Coir	Panipet, Allepey

RECOMMENDATIONS OF THE ABID HUSSAIN COMMITTEE

An expert committee with 11 members and headed by Abid Hussain was constituted on December 1995 by the government to study the status of small-scale enterprises and to suggest measures by which these units could grow and remain competitive in the changing economic environment. The committee has proposed highly debatable and sweeping reforms in the small-scale sector to make it globally competitive. Major recommendations *inter alia* include:

- Abolition of the policy of reservation for SSIs.
- Scrapping of 24% equity participation ceiling by large companies and foreign investors in SSI units.
- Transitional package of ₹ 2,500 crore (by setting up of a corpus of ₹ 500 crore on annual basis) to provide consessional funding for the SSIs affected by dereservation.
- Earmarking 70% priority sector lending allocated to the small sector for the tiny enterprises.
- Specialised commercial bank branches for SSIs for easy credit facilities.
- Reduction of credit cost of SSIs
- Responsibility of developing SSIs on states, with the centre to confine itself to broad policy-making.
- Widening the concept of the small-scale sector to include small businesses and service enterprises.
- Setting up of SSI clusters with modern infrastructural facilities.
- Revitalisation of district industries centres and coverting them into district enterprise promotion agencies (DEPAs) with participation from business associations, government agencies and banks.
- Corporatisation of government extension agencies. Restructuring the state financial corporations (SFCs) and SIDCs.

- Separate law for small enterprises also covering labour related regulations for putting an end to the inspector raj.
- Restoration of excise exemption on branded goods.
- Excise incentives for graduating tiny and small-scale units, and
- Credit rating for small business to enable them to avail funds at lower costs.

In recent times, a lot of management thought in India has been directed at enterprise governance, with its emphasis on the role of the entrepreneur, business strategy, etc. It is found that transformational entrepreneurs are responsible for creating and sustaining an environment at fostering a constant and positive climate for rapid growth. Small-scale enterprises have a key role to play in the new millennium.

The Future Growth Fields

Perhaps equally important as the 100 best jobs are 100 companies that eptiomise how the business world is going to look in the next century. These companies represent the future career opportunities and the overall dramatic changes that will impact every aspect of our lives.

They include a diverse range such as – environmental services, health care delivery, trucking, connectivity hardware, education, telephony, computer software, facilities management, organ transplantation and companies with high social utility.

Many of the Quantum 100 companies are focussed on improving the global village. You'll find a company that destroys hazardous materials and creates basic elements that can be reused by industry; another manages public schools and another company that makes building material that is stronger than oak out of soyabeans and old newsprint.

The Top Six Growth Fields

Listed below are six fields showing promise of future growth potential into the twenty-first century

Health care

Technology will continue to create new breakthroughs in patient treatments. Revolutions in health care will continually create new opportunities at all employment levels.

Robotics

Experts project a new generation of robots that can see, hear, feel and obey. The demand for engineers, technicians, installers and repair people will steadily increase.

Computer graphics

CAD (computer-aided design) and CAI (computer-aided imagery) will be two of the fastest-growing fields into the year 2000 and beyond. They will revolutionise design in manufacturing, fashion, film and video.

Information technology

Advances in telecommunications, fibre optics, mega communication mergers, and the internet all make for an explosion of jobs in this fast-growing field.

Biotechnology

Solving medical problems with the new technology is the new frontier into the next century. Individuals with backgrounds in science, biology, engineering and chemistry will have unlimited opportunities in this field into the next century.

Lasers

They will be used in a variety of ways ranging from health care and communications to manufacturing. For individuals in this field who have laser knowledge, opportunities will remain plentiful.

Based on the research of Carol Kleiman, Author of the 100 *Best Jobs for the 1990s and Beyond,* A David Silver, Author of *Quantum Companies and the US Bureau of Labour and Statistics.*

The 100 Best Jobs Going into the Next Century

There is a change in emphasis from white-collar, professionally based jobs to computer-oriented, technically based jobs. In fact, some researchers predict that by the turn of the century, eight of ten jobs will not require a bachelor's degree.

Technical jobs, many of which are still emerging, will be the fastest growing segment of the new world of work. It is predicted that these jobs will offer salaries competitive with current white-collar professional pay scales.

In order to keep up, thinking will have to shift as well. Previous definitions of career success will need to be reassessed. The old drumbeat of having to be a doctor or lawyer to have a sense of honour and fulfilment is very limited. Social status will be redefined not by education but the ability to adapt to technology and contribute to society in a rapidly changing information age. Employers will increasingly favour not those with advanced graduate degrees but those with four-year degrees and technical expertise and those with two-year technical degrees. A four-year liberal arts college degree will not become a thing of the past, but knowledge of technology will be the key factor in the hiring processes of most enterprises.

Our changing world has dictated the best jobs going into the next century. For example, 186 million baby boomers will be in their fifties. The greying population will open new demands in health care, retirement-related industries and travel and leisure. Jobs will be further influenced by the information technology explosion and new breakthroughs in genetics, bioengineering, robotics and environmental research. Further influences will be the fact that women, minorities and immigrants will account for 80% of Indian labour force growth. White men, who for decades were the majority, will make up only 15 per cent of new entrants into the workforce.

The 100 Best Jobs

This table represents the 100 best jobs going into the next century in alphabetical order

Accountant/auditor	Engineer	Ophthalmic laboratory technician
Actor/director producer	Environmental scientist	Optician
Advertising and marketing account	Farm manager	Paralegal
supervisor	Financial planner	Paramedic
Agricultural scientist	Firefighter	Peripheral electronic data processing
Aircraft technician	Flight attendant	equipment operator
Appliance/power tool repairer	Flight engineer	Pharmacist
Architect	Food scientist	Photographer/camera operator
Arts administrator	Healthy services administrator	Physical therapist/physician
Automotive mechanic	Home health aide	Physician's assistant
Bank loan officer	Hotel manager/assistant	Physicist/astronomer
Bank marketer	Human resources manager executive	Pilot
Carpenter		Paediatrist
Chemist	Industrial designer	Police officer
Clerical supervisor/office manager	Information systems manager	Psychologist/counseller
Commercial/graphic-artist	Insurance claim examiner	Public relations specialist
Computer operator	Insurance salesperson	Radio/TV news reporter
Computer programer	Interior designer	Radio/TV service technician
Computer service technician	Investment banker	Radiologic technologist
Computer systems-analyst	Labour relations specialist	Real estate agent/broker
Cook/chef	Landscape architect	Real estate appraiser
Corporate financial analyst	Lawyer	Registered nurse
Corporate personnel trainer	Librarian	Reporter/correspondent
Corrections officer/guard/jailer	Licensed practical nurse	Restaurant/food service
Cosmetologist	Management consultant	Retail salesperson
Court reporter	Manufacturing specialist	Secretary/administrator
Database manager	(CAD, CAM CAI)	Social worker
Dental hygienist	Manager	Speech pathologist/audiologist
Dentist	Mathematician/statistician	Teacher/professor
Drafter	Medical records administrator	Travel agent
Economist	Occupational therapist	Truck driver
Editor/writer	Office/business machine-repairer	Underwriter
Education administrator	Operations manager/manufacturing	Veterinarian
Employment interviewer	Operations/systems-research analyst	Wholesale sales-representative

(**Source:** *The 100 Best Jobs for the 1990s and Beyond* by Carol Kleiman, Published by Dearborn Financial Publishing, Inc., Chicago.)

Future Strategy

Promotional and developmental efforts by SIDBI continued to be an integral part of its overall strategy for the qualitative growth of the small-scale sector. The effectiveness of the developmental efforts is proposed to be evaluated in an independent manner. The RIP which started in November 1993 has shown good promise. With the active participation of state governments, business-oriented voluntary organisations and technology institutions, it expects to promote about 10,000 substainable rural enterprises during 1995-96. The funding support to well-run VOs for on-lending to rural poor in many cases for a mass based activity such as – carpet weaving in Orissa, fisheries in Kerala, tasar silk in Bihar, micro fibre tiles in Rajasthan and wool spinning in Himachal Pradesh will be stepped up. Besides, VOs and SHGs would be provided with training and managerial support for a more effective saving and credit operation. The 'Udyog Sadhana' would be extended to a few more states and efforts would be made to utilise the reach and effectiveness of television for spreading the entrepreneurship message. The awareness on ISO-9000 created through 60 programmes will be made use of for extending direct financial assistance to over 100 small entrepreneurs for acquisition of ISO-9000 series certificate. Services of Technology Bureau for Small Enterprises would be made use of in an increasing scale. A beginning will also be made for institutionalising the successful training programmes for entrepreneurs and managers by creation of exclusive small industry divisions in leading management and technical institutes. Initiatives in the area of environment management will be stepped up. Responsive industry associations will be encouraged to run industrial clinics for providing industry-specific counselling in the area of technology, finance and legal matters. The bank proposes to strengthen its links and financial collaborations with several international agencies so as to be able to design and implement more support programmes for the small-scale sector.

Unless we emphasis on total industrial upliftment, India cannot expect to emerge as an industrially developed nation. And in our targeted direction, the revised role of management education and application will be of paramount importance.

Small firms working together in flexible networks have been highly successful in responding to new production and market needs. According to a ILO study, the high road to small industry development lay through acquisition of collective ability to respond to new and changing customer preferences. In an ideal case a cluster of small firms needs to include in one and the same geographical area, all the activities required for development, manufacturing and commercialisation of a product.

PROSPECTS IN THE 21ST CENTURY

The problems faced by the SSI entrepreneurs make the situation quite a difficult one. The nineties would ensure a bright future for the small industry only if a conscious and sincere effort is initiated for overcoming hardships faced by this sector. The entrepreneurs, particularly from the SSI sector, have to lay more emphasis on the quality of this production. The gospel truth is, better quality and better productivity. The process should start with the top and work down to the middle management, first-line management and finally to the first-line the employees. Edwards Deming, an authority on quality, has given the following checklist:

- Build quality into the process; don't rely on inspection.
- Foster teamwork and dismantle the barriers that divide and disparate departments.
- Establish long-term ties with select suppliers; don't award contracts on price tag alone.
- Provide managers and workers the training they need to fully participate in the improvement process, and
- Have the top management chart a company-wide strategy for continuous improvement of products and services.

This process in the coming decades with go a long way in enhancing the prestige of Indian entrepreneurs.

Yet another area wherein the entrepreneurs have to devote sufficient attention is Research and Development (R&D). Innovation is the real step towards continued progress. The full benefits of R&D could percolate to the production process only if technical skills of entrepreneurs engaged in the production process are also upgraded. Likewise, marketing skills and innovative financial skills should be sharpened to reap the desired benefits both in the short- and long-run. The government and industrial as well as entrepreneurial associations should, therefore, aim at improving technical skills, entrepreneurial skill and work culture. This will go a long way in putting the Indian industry on a sound and strong pedestal or edifice.

The present trend does indicate qualitative and quantitative growth in terms of industrial production, exports, investments, modernisation and upgradation of technology, etc., but there is need also to give shape to the policy frameworks adopted till now.

The next decade would witness certain changes in the structure of small industry; if the present developments are any indication. Location-wise, small units would be established outside the metropolitan areas and mainly in small towns or large villages, thus providing more opportunities for convergence of agriculture and industry. The entrepreneurs are likely to play a pivotal role in accelerating the industrial process in the country.

Table 17.2 Progress of Growth Centres

State	Growth Centres – At Different Stages of Progress	Growth Centres Progress yet to Commence
Andhra Pradesh	Hidupur, Vizianagaram-Bobbilli, Ongole	Khamman
Arunachal Pradesh	Niklok, Ngordung	
Assam	Chariduar, Matia	
Bihar	Begusarai, Bhagalpur, Chhapra, Hazaribagh and Muzaffarpur	Darbhanga
Goa	Electronic City	
Gujarat	Gandhidham, Palnpur and Vagra	
Haryana	Bawal and Saha	
Himachal Pradesh	Kangra	
Jammu and Kashmir	Samba	Ompura-Lassipora
Karnataka	Dharwad, Raichur and Hassan	
Kerala	Alappuzha, Mallappuram, Kannur-Kozhikode	
Madhya Pradesh	Boraj, Chainpua, Ghirongi, Kheda, Sitalpur and Siltara	
Maharashtra	Akola, Chandrapur, Dhule, Nanded and Ratnagiri	
Manipur	Lamlai-Napet	
Meghalaya	Mendipathar	
Mizoram		Luangmual
Nagaland	Ganeshnagar	
Orissa	Chatrapur and Duburi	Jharsuguda
Pondicherry		Polagam-Karaikal
Punjab	Bhatinda and Phatankot	
Rajasthan	Abu Road, Bikaner, Bhilwara, Dholpur and Jhalawar	
Tamil Nadu	Erode and Tirunelveli	
Tripura		Boodhjung Nagar
Uttar Pradesh	Bachouli-Buzung, Banthata, Chaudarpur, Khurja, Mingra-Sathria and Sahjanwa	Dibiapur
West Bengal		Bolpur Jalpaiguri and Malda

(**Source:** Ministry of Industry, Government of India.)

Prospects and Outlook

The process of liberalisation and economic reforms while creating tremendous opportunities for the growth of SSIs have thrown up new challenges to the sector. Building competitive strengths, technology upgradation and quality improvement are the vital issues which need to be addressed so as to build capabilities of the sector to withstand emerging pressures and ensure sustained growth. Also, the sector needs to reposition itself to meet expanding demands for ancillarisation, sub-contracting and job work from large industrial units/MNCs requiring higher standards of quality, economies of scale and strict delivery schedules. There is also a need for integration of the sector with the overall domestic economy and global markets by gearing itself to greater interdependence and networking. The following important expedient issues, which emerged, can contribute to the competitive advantage of the SSI sector.

- Extension of the definition of SSIs to cover service/tertiary sector enterprises in its ambit with an increased investment ceiling.
- National debate on the issue of dereservation of items reserved for exclusive manufacture by SSIs in the backdrop of diverse views on the policy of dereservation.
- Revisiting the laws governing SSIs and making them simpler so as to enable small entrepreneurs to comply with the simplified procedures.
- Extending required institutional support and infrastructural facilities to natural clusters already in existence to get a boost in the form of joint ventures between state authorities and industry/business associations.
- Collection and updation of data through census of SSI units which could be followed regularly though sample surveys to fill the gaps in availability of information on the SSI sector. Participation by Industry associations could be helpful in this direction so as to improve the reliability and regularity in flow of data from SSI units to the government departments and other related agencies.
- Banks/FIs need to devise ways and means to fulfil the sectoral requirements as per the Ninth Five Year Plan (1997-2002) estimates for additional working capital funds in the range of ₹ 1,420 billion to ₹ 1,460 billion and additional long-term credit of the order of ₹ 345 billion to ₹ 365 billion.
- Restructuring of SFCs/SIDCs, instituting Credit Insurance or Credit Guarantee Scheme, creating a facilitating environment, enabling institutions to take up discounting of bills, factoring services and introduction of innovative instruments/products which would help PLIs to provide increased credit to the sector. To improve the attitude and mindset of entrepreneurs, development of human resources, greater linkage between the manufacturers and research/technical institutions and support initiatives by industry associations are necessary.
- Prioritise the efforts on the setting up of growth centre and infrastructural development centres to make available adequate infrastructure facilities for the promotion of industries, particularly SSIs and growth of exports.
- For appropriate understanding of demand conditions and supply-side management, there is need for building an authentic information base, participation in trade fairs and exhibitions, warehousing/storage facilities and evolving a mechanism to address the market problems of the tiny sector.
- Extended financial assistance for locational shift of affected units in addition to the provision of infrastructual facilities to enable SSIs to conform to envionment cleanliness norms and pollution control measures, and
- A proactive role from industry associations has been expected in the areas such as – building up of common use/comprehensive information bases and dissemination thereof and setting up of marketing and testing facilities. State authorities might take part in designing a support mechanism by way of providing financial assistance for this purpose.

Inadequate infrastructure has severely undermined the growth potential of various sectors, including the SSI sector. In order to reap full benefits of the market reforms and liberalisation, concerted steps for increasing the SSI related infrastructure, as also marketing infrastructure, would give an impetus to the growth prospects of the sector. Further, to encourage cooperation amongst small-scale enterprises and research and development institutions, the evolution of specific schemes could strengthen long-term linkages between the industry and R&D and enhance the productivity of the sector.

In the current scenario for the SSI sector to achieve economic efficiency and international quality standards, there is an imminent need to upgrade its technology. While the setting up of the Technology Bank, as announced in the comprehensive policy package for SSIs, would facilitate technology transfer and match making, creation of a separate Small Industries Development Fund at the earliest would meet the much needed financial requirements of the sector for mass scale technology upgradation. The suggested fund would also provide access of resources for infrastructure, marketing development and other similar requirements of the sector. These measures are expected to help in accelerating the pace of growth of the sector.

As is known, the process of liberalisation and globalisation has necessitated technological upgradation and the building of appropriate marketing and other related infrastructure. Entrepreneurs need to hasten the transition from existing levels to higher standards in terms of quality and design in order to become internationally competitive. Thereafter, constant adaptation and innovation would hold the key to sustained competitiveness. In order to do so, there is a need for internalising, not only new technology, but also effective management techniques and economies of scale. The government has already enhanced the limit of investment in plant and machinery in select subsectors of the SSI sector to facilitate their vertical expansion and building of competitive strength. To continue the momentum in this direction, the creation of a category of Medium Enterprises would be a step forward. With the continuance of the incentive/support measures available to the tiny and small enterprises, the creation of a separate new category of medium enterprises would not really affect the interests of the small and tiny units. On the contrary, such an initiative would help in broadening the scope of existing SSIs to graduate into medium enterprises and provide the economy with the much needed growth impetus. This would also be in tandem with the global phenomena of SMEs. The SMEs, as compared to small-scale units, would be better equipped in terms of their corporatisation and, in turn, would have smooth integration with broader markets in the era of globalisation. These steps are expected to go a long way in enabling the sector retain its pre-eminent position and contribute in the growth process in a larger way in the years to come.

MANAGING INTO THE 21ST CENTURY: FANNING THE ENTREPRENEURIAL FLAME

Balancing the spirit of the entrepreneur with the reality of big business takes more than a single simple policy or strategy. What is required is a flexible, dynamic structure that pays heed to the importance of the people within and is based on a value set that is clear and agreeable to all.

Lotus Employee Handbook, therefore, devotes a full page to our corporate values, placing importance on the attributes of honesty, ethics, fairness and integrity, as well as on teamwork, cooperation, creativity and initiative and on having a sense of humour.

Be a Leader: This does not mean being just a manager. Leadership begins with setting examples in terms of personal characteristics like honesty and fairness.

Be a Felicitator: Management should demonstrate a commitment to communication throughout the organisation. This means being accessible and listening to people in the lower realms of the organisation.

Be Deliberate: When calling and conducting meetings (the greatest time waster in companies), be result-oriented. Use firm agendas and strive for specific objectives.

Be Explicit: In assigning responsibility, get people to take responsibility for small tasks as well as for big projects.

Be Decisive: If someone isn't working out, and you have exhausted all possibilities, break quickly and clearly. Indecision can be bad for everyone.

If these attributes are combined with sincerity and integrity, the result should be a business clutter that stimulates innovation and *esprit de corps* at every corporate level, whether developing a new product, building a new headquarter or contributing to the neighbouring community.

For people in communication and creative businesses, it is a major breakthrough, because it puts a powerful weapon into the hands of the people who develop concepts; the ability to execute those concepts so that they can be evaluated and appreciated by peers and by clients. The dream is to make information accessible and understandable to more people by bringing the benefits of computing closer and closer to the individual.

Most developing countries are characterised by rapidly growing population and labour force. While much of the labour force will be absorbed in traditional agriculture, it is clear that an increasing amount of labour will seek employment in non-farm occupations – roughly two out of every three job-seekers over the next 25 years. Some of the jobs may be found in villages and small towns, closely linked to developments in agriculture. A growing number, however, will have to be in the larger towns and cities.

Absorbing the growing labour force in productive employment is one of he principal challenges of development. Most new labour force entrants will be poor and unskilled, coming from rural areas and city slums. Their number and lack of skills mean that in most countries, the process of absorption will take place in conditions in which real urban wages for the great majority will not increase substantially because of the pressures of population growth and migration.

Capital is scarce in most developing countries. Depending upon a country's resources, capital has to be used as efficiently as possible to expand the demand for labour. Small-scale enterprises (SSEs) usually generate more jobs per unit of investment than do larger firms, which suggests that SSE development can be an important component of the attack on poverty. The small entrepreneurs themselves do not usually have resources and prosperity; if they have any, it is often precarious, but they provide a livelihood for many others in need.

In developing countries, small enterprises started with groups of rational small businesses set up by sole proprietors in retail trade, services and consumer industries. However, with changes in the socio-economic environment, such entrepreneurs have been confronted with the choice of either remaining as they are or being swept out of the market competition or making necessary changes and innovations so as to continue to survive. Also, they face the prospect of either remaining small or to be willing to expand and/or diversify.

However, the development process itself has given time to new economic opportunities for entrepreneurs, including small business entrepreneurs. With the growth of economy and the political and economic compulsions and the desire to become self-reliant, the need arises for enterprises that cater to the multiple demands of economy for low gestation, employment-oriented and medium-based enterprises. In addition, development within the agricultural sector has also resulted in the creation of agro-business activities like food processing and wood-based industries. Similarly, small-scale businesses have emerged in diverse areas of activity, ranging from cottage industries to metallurgy and engineering, electronics and the like.

CONCLUSION

Small-scale industries play a key role in the industrialisation of a developing country. This is because they provide immediate large-scale employment and have a comparatively higher labour, capital ratio; they need a shorter gestation period and relatively smaller markets to be economic; they need lower investments, offer a method of ensuring a more quotable distribution of national income and facilitate an effective mobilisation of resources of capital and skill which might otherwise remain unutilised; and they stimulate the growth of industrial entrepreneurship and promote a more diffused pattern of ownership and location.

Small enterprises represent the fountain head of vitality for the national economy. At the end of the Seventh Plan, small-scale industrial sector including village industries accounted for over 55 per cent of the gross value of output in the manufacturing sector and over 40 per cent of the total exports from the country. It also provided direct employment to 245 lakh people. What is more, certain groups of small enterprises such as – electronics, engineering and leather have made impressive progress. The small-scale sector has also achieved a high degree of sophistication and made significant progress in quality upgradation and standardisation. They have also given fillip to entrepreneurship development. Small enterprises are able to successfully adapt to the changing situations and possess creative strength. Therefore, much is expected of them as the driving power behind the continued development of the Indian economy.

In India, the promotion of small-scale industries has continued to be an important element in the national development strategy, particularly because of their very favourable capital output ratio and high employment intensity.

The government is determined to promote forms of industrialisation in the country which will generate economic viability in the villages. The promotion of suitable industries in rural areas will be accelerated to grenerate higher employment and higher per capita income for the villagers without disturbing the ecological balance. Handlooms, handicrafts, khadi and other village industries will receive greater attention to achieve a faster rate of growth in the villages.

Industrialisation plays an important role in correcting regional imbalance and reviving industrial growth to lead the economy once again to the take-off stage. To achieve this goal, the government decided to encourage dispersal of the industry and the setting up of units in industrially backward areas. Special growth and perfomance-oriented concessions and facilities were to be reportedly offered for this purpose.

Numerous incentives have been provided to industries from time-to-time. It is the government's considered view that all incentives to the industry must be peformance-oriented. It is, therefore, proposed that a periodic assessment be made of the impact of these incentives to see the extent to which they fulfilled their initial purpose. Unless it is apparent that the incentives are serving the intended purpose, the system will be reviewed.

Finally, it has been emphasised that industrial development must be viewed in the broader context of generating higher production and employment. Overcoming the problems of poverty and backwardness needs a multi-pronged approach. Creation of new focal points of industrial growth which have the maximum effect on the equality of life is an integral part of this approach. This will have to be based on the utilisation of local materials and locally available manpower. The ripple effect of substantial investments in backward districts in the past has in many cases not been adequate, mainly because such investments did not have effective linkages with local resources. The government, therefore, proposes to encourage investments by public and private sectors which will meet these criteria and will also promote a network of ancillary industries.

Although the prospects for small-scale industries are plenty, the new industrial policy hampers its sustained growth in the nineties. On the contrary, the policy is oriented towards development of large-scale industries, in particular, multinationals based on technology as well as finance imported from advanced countries, while showing lip sympathy to the small-scale sector. The need of the hour is an appropriate industrial policy conducive for the development of small-scale industries. The high potentials inherent in the small-scale sector are yet to be properly understood and analysed.

In the 50 years of independence, the small-scale sector has acquired a prominent place in the socio-economic development of the country. Its performance is creditable, yet a proper and innovative approach still alludes. The sector needs many corrective steps to succeeded in the 21st century. The key to success for small-scale enterprise would lie in looking at the globe as a market and reposition itself as a means to get into the global marketplace and succeed out there.

No Place for Lone Rangers

"The challenges ahead are so complex that no individual will be able to face them alone. While most of our education is focused in individual strength, teaming with others is equally important. You cannot fire a missile from a canoe. Unless you will be restricted network of people with complimentary skills, you will be restricted by your own limitations."

— Azim Premji, Chairman, Wipro Ltd.

Carly's Vision

"You have to have strategic vision and peripheral vision. Strategic vision is the ability to look ahead and peripheral vision is the ability to look around, and both are important."

— Carly Fiorina, Chairman, Hewlett Packard.

II SECTION

ENTREPRENEURSHIP – THE ROAD TO REAL INDIA

Overcoming the Risk Factor

"Over 35% of the start-ups in Silicon Valley are by Indians. We need to have similar risk-taking ability within the country as well. Entrepreneurs need more than technical talent. What they need is the indefatigable energy and optimism that enables them to take the road less travelled and convert their dreams into reality."

— ***Azim Premji, Chairman, Wipro***

Entrepreneurial development is a complex phenomenon. Productive activity undertaken by an entrepreneur and constant endeavour to sustain and improve it are the outward expressions of this process of the development of his personality.

Such a process is crystallisation of social milieu from which he comes, what the family imbibes, make-up of his mind, personal attitudes, caste system, educational level, parental occupation and so on.

The words *entrepreneur, intrapreneur* and *entrepreneurship* have acquired special significance in the context of economic growth in rapidly changing socio-economic and socio-cultural climates, particularly in industry, both in developed and developing countries. The experience in the industrialised countries like the United States of America, Germany, Japan and the United Kingdom are authoritatively cited in support of this claim. An in-depth study of the subject thus becomes not only relevant but also necessary.

An entrepreneur is one of the important segments of economic growth. Basically, an entrepreneur is a person who is responsible for setting up a business or an enterprise. In fact, he is one who has the initiative, skill for innovation and who looks for high achievement. He is a catalytic agent of change and works for the good of people. He puts up new greenfield projects that actually creates wealth, opens up employment opportunities and fosters other sectors in terms of economic feasibility.

Urges of an Entrepreneur

An urge to exercise power over things and objects persists among all human beings. The urge may vary in degree from person-to-person. This urge is an intrinsic quality of an entrepreneur. Sociologists consider him as a sensitive energiser – in the modernisation of societies. The psychologists look upon him as an 'entrepreneurial man', his motivations and aspirations are conducive to development. Political scientists regard him as a leader of the system. To economists, he is the harbinger of economic growth. He combines entrepreneurial drive with leadership and innovativeness.

The entrepreneur is a critical factor in the socio-economic change, who envisages new opportunities, new techniques, new lines of production, new products and coordinates all other activities.

Who is an Entrepreneur?

The entrepreneur brings in overall change through innovation for the maximum social good. Human values remain on top priority and inspires him to serve society. He has firm belief in social betterment and he carries out this responsibility with conviction. In the process, he accelerates personal, economic as well as human development. The entrepreneur is a visionary and an integrated man with outstanding leadership qualities. With a desire to excel, the entrepreneur gives top priority to research and development. He always works for the well-being of the society. More importantly, entrepreneurial activities encompass all fields/sectors and fosters a sport of enterprise for the welfare of mankind.

Importance of an Entrepreneur

The entrepreneur is one of the most important inputs in the economic development of a country or of regions within the country. Entrepreneurial competence makes all the difference in the rate of economic growth. In India, state and private entrepreneurship coexist. The small-scale industrial sector and business are left completely to private entrepreneurs. It is, therefore, in this context that an increasingly important role has been assigned to the identification and promotion of entrepreneurs for this sector.

The need for a broad-based entrepreneurial call in India arises from the need to speed up the process of activating the factors of production, leading to a higher rate of economic growth, dispersal of economic activities, development of backward and tribal areas, creation of employment opportunities, improvement in the standard of living of the weaker sections of the society and involvement of all sections of the society in the process of growth.

Several factors go into the making of an entrepreneur. Individuals who initiate, establish, maintain and expand new enterprises constitute the entrepreneurial class. The socio-political and economic conditions, the availability of industrial technology and know-how, state-of-the-art and culture of business and trading, existence of markets for products and services and the incentives and facilities available for starting an industry or business, all have a bearing on the growth of entrepreneurship. A conducive environment is created through the policies and interests of the government in economic and industrial development.

The Objective of Foresight

The goal of competition for industry foresight is, at one level, simple: to build the best-possible assumption-base about the future and, thereby, develop the prescience to proactively shape industry evolution. Competition for industry foresight is, essentially, competition to establish one's company as the intellectual leader in terms of influence over the direction and shape of industry transformation. Industry foresight gives a company the potential to get to the future first and stake out a leadership position. It allows a company to control the evolution of its industry and, thereby, its own destiny. It helps managers answer three critical questions: what new types of customer benefit should we seek to provide in five, then, or 15 years? What new competencies will we need to build or acquire to offer those benefits to the customer? And how will we need to reconfigure the customer interface over the next several years?

Essentially, a point of view about the future is a point of view about benefits, competencies, and the customer interface. Motorola has such a point of view. It dreams of a world in which telephone numbers will be assigned to people rather than places; where small hand-held devices will allow people to stay in touch no matter where they are; and where the new communicators can deliver video-images and data and voice-signals. For this world to become a reality, Motorola knows that it will have to strengthen its competence in digital compression, flat-screen displays, and battery technology. The company also knows that to capture a significant share of a burgeoning market, it will have to substantially increase the familiarity of its brand with customers around the world.

Dynamic Strategies

"The challenge of the future is to handle business strategies and brand strategies in a dynamic environment. You have to use all the tools in your brand portfolio in order to stay relevant, in order to adapt your offering to the emerging trends in some markets."

— ***David Aaker, Marketing Guru***

Tech Tack

"In the 21st century real growth and prosperity will depend on how a business problem is meshed with technology. Technology is pushing itself to solve business problems and create better innovative applications, that's where invention will occur."

— ***Nick Donofrio, Senior V-P, IBM***

Box 1 The World Needs

The World Today is looking for
Entrepreneurs who are visionaries
Entrepreneurs who are honest
Entrepreneurs who are innovative
Entrepreneurs who are optimistic
Entrepreneurs who are enterprising
Entrepreneurs who are foresighted
Entrepreneurs who are trustworthy
Entrepreneurs who practice fair play
Entrepreneurs who stand integrity
Entrepreneurs who are tolerant
Entrepreneurs who are inspirers
Entrepreneurs who are dynamic
Entrepreneurs who are transparent
Entrepreneurs who recognise talent
Entrepreneurs who have a fixed aim
Entrepreneurs who are ambitious
Entrepreneurs who are committed
Entrepreneurs who are compassionate
Entrepreneurs who are good time managers
Entrepreneurs who are good strategist
Entrepreneurs who are empowering people
Entrepreneurs who are customer-friendly
Entrepreneurs who neither brag nor run
Entrepreneurs who neither flag nor flinch
Entrepreneurs who know their message and tell
Entrepreneurs who know their place and fill in
Entrepreneurs who know their business and attend to it
Entrepreneurs who will not lie, shirk or dodge
Entrepreneurs who are not too crazy

Amit Burman

Adi Godrej

Narayana Murthy

Entrepreneurs who are not too lazy to work
Entrepreneurs who will prosper with society
Entrepreneurs who will lead and motivate
Entrepreneurs who always dream for change
Entrepreneurs who live for their principles
Entrepreneurs who will stand for the right
Entrepreneurs who care for the society
Entrepreneurs who stand for values
Entrepreneurs who set ambitious goals
Entrepreneurs who strive for quality products
Entrepreneurs who practise business ethics
Entrepreneurs who have sound knowledge
Entrepreneurs who lead by caring and sharing

Bill Gates

Box 2 Entrepreneurs Who Changed the Face of Corporate India

Late Cowasjee Nanabhai Davar (1814-1873)

The Inspiration to Invest: Cowasjee Davar inaugurated India's industrial revolution. In 1854, he set-up India's first steam-powered textile mill in Bombay. Capitalised at ₹ 5 lakh, the Bombay Spinning and Weaving Company paid a 10 per cent dividend for six years straight. Davar set the stage for the safety of industrial capital in India. Galvanised by his example, others too made industrial investments. Among them were: Wadias and the Tatas.

Late Sir Jamsetji Nusserwanji Tata (March 3, 1839-May 19, 1904)

The Father of India's Industrial Revolution: J.N. Tata was the first Indian to understand the significance of the industrial revolution. At his Swadeshi Textile Mill, he instituted pension funds and accident compensation. He believed India's progress hinged around steel, hydroelectric power, and technical education. The industrialist in Jamsetji Tata was a pioneer and a visionary, possessed of a spirit of entrepreneurial adventure and acumen never seen before or since in a native of colonial India. The nationalist in him believed unwaveringly that the fruits of his business success would enrich a country he cared deeply about. These attributes, by themselves, would have been enough to mark him as an extraordinary figure. But what made Jamsetji Tata truly unique, the quality that places him in the pantheon of modern India's greatest sons, was his humaneness. He inspired creation of the Indian Institute of Science, formerly Tata Institute, in Bangalore. In 1900, when he was 60, he set up Jamshedpur Steelworks after learning steel-making in Europe. He was the giant who touched tomorrow.

Late V.O. Chidambaram Pillai (September 5, 1872-November 18, 1936)

The Steamships That Cried Freedom: Pillai was a nationalist who entered business to prove a point as much as to make profits. His Swadeshi Steam Navigation Company Ltd., broke the monopoly of British shipping in coastal trade with Ceylon. VOC, as he was popularly called, was a radical Congressman who was arrested in March 1908 on charges of sedition. He was finally released in 1912. Pillai inspired an entire generation of conservative southerners to plunge into business.

Late Rai Bahadur Mohan Singh Oberoi (August 15, 1898-May 3, 2002)

The Brown Sahib's Opportunity: In 1934 Oberoi mortgaged his wife's jewels while scratching together ₹ 20,000 to buy his British partner's stake in the Clarke's Hotel, Simla. He put in money while the Brits pulled their out, and a decade later, he was the first Indian to run a hotel chain. In 1965, he opened the first five-star international hotel in India in Delhi. Thirty-four hotels in seven countries later, Oberoi was the first real Indian multinational.

Late J.R.D. Tata (July 29, 1904-November 29, 1993)

A Visionary of the New Generation: Late Jehangir Ratanji Dadabhoy Tata (Popularly known as JRD) is a visionary industrialist of the 20th century.

Titan of the Times. J.R.D. Tata left an indelible mark on industry. He built the industry on the cornerstones of integrity and honesty. He played a critical role in increasing India's scientific, medical and artistic quotient.

Born in Paris on July 29, 1904, Jehangir Ratanji Dadabhoy Tata was the second child of Ratanji Dadabhoy Tata and his French wife Sooni. JRD was barely 34 when he took over as the fourth chairman of a 13-company group with sales of ₹ 280 crore. India's industrial revolution mirrored his entrepreneurship as he set up businesses ranging from trucks to locomotives, cement to pharmaceuticals, hi-tech enterprises like TCS to agri-businesses and services including airlines and hotels. When he stepped down in March 1991, the conglomerate earned ₹ 10,627 crore.

Late Henning Holck Larsen (July 4, 1907-July 27, 2003)

The Dane Who Never Went Home: One of a small flock of Europeans who refused Quit India, Larsen and his partner Soren K. Toubro – both came here to set up a cement plant for a British employer – set up a company in 1938 that became India's pre-eminent engineering giant. Larsen knew independent India offered much scope for his company and his skills, worth ₹ 5,400 crore today. Larsen's push to manufacture it all in India sparked off an engineering boom that hasn't quit. From nuclear plants to new expressways, Larsen's stamps on India is indelible. His spirit continues to find expression in the products we make, in the projects we execute, and indeed in everything we do, as we make the things that make India proud.

Dr. Verghese Kurien (November 26, 1921)

Father of the Unlikely Entrepreneur: Dr. Kurien created Operation Flood, the largest dairy development programme in the world. He made India the world's largest milk producer. But most importantly, he put economic power in the hands of the producers, all 10 million families at last count. The Kaira District Cooperative Milk Producers' Union, or Amul, as India knows the giant, is modern and fleet enough to lord it over an array of multinational competitors. Humble farmers, and cowherds – they all have a stake in one of the world's best dairy operations.

Karsanbhai Khodidas Patel (March 10, 1944)

The Power of the Grassroots: Patel knew no marketing, had no management qualifications and no collaborator, Indian or foreign, when he created the first Indian brand to humble the best multinationals. The saga of this Gujarat government chemist began with a 12-yard shed in his backyard in 1969. Worth ₹ 2,440 crore today, Nirma's cut-price detergent shook the likes of Lever. Patel, who speaks little English, inspired legions of Davids to do entrepreneurial battle with India's corporate Goliaths.

Late Aditya Vikram Birla (November 14, 1943-October 1, 1995)

The First Mogul of Globalisation: When MIT graduate Aditya Vikram Birla returned to India to be a part of his grandfather G.D. Birla's sprawling empire in the 1960s, he could have gone with the flow. But when it took Indian bureaucrats 11 years to clear a refinery project, Birla did not believe it worth his while to work the licence raj. Instead long before globalisation became a buzzword, he spread outward, setting up a textile mill in Thailand; later the world's largest palm oil refinery in Malaysia. When he died in 1995, his group had 17 companies in 14 countries.

"The late Aditya Vikram Birla inherently believed in the trusteeship concept of management. Simply put, he said that the wealth that one generates and holds is to be held in trust for its stakeholders."

This meant not only rewarding shareholders and employees, but reaching out to communities.

Late Dhirubhai Hirachand Ambani (1932-2002)

The Saga of New India: Truly an entrepreneur for the tumultuous, new India. Poor son of Gujarat village school teacher, he reached Aden at the age 17 and worked as petrol station attendant. Mixing grand opportunism with extreme guile, he clambered his way up, manipulating the licence raj to his advantage. He created an equity cult by going to millions of small investors when the big bankers refused him money. He adapted as easily to liberalisation. At ₹ 60,000 crore, there's quite simply nothing larger than Reliance in India today.

Dhirubhai always encouraged people to think big, think fast, think ahead. He often said "Our dreams have to be bigger. Our ambitions higher. Our commitment deeper. And our efforts greater. This is my dream for Reliance and for India."

N.R. Narayana Murthy (August 20, 1946)

Messiah of the new middle-class: Nagavara Ramarao Narayana Murthy is the messiah of the new India, who along with his associates with middle-class ethics, value system and global ambitions created a new kind of an enterprise in India. Narayana Murthy and six colleagues quit Patni Computers and each contributed ₹ 10,000 to set-up the new firm in 1981 in an apartment of capital led to sharing wealth in creating rupee and dollar millionaires, including drivers and peons. He has honesty strived to inspire unaccountable thousands of good way to make money. Thus, N.R. Narayana Murthy is stepping into mentoring entrepreneuring and encouraging research and innovation. He firmly believes that entrepreneursing is an effective instrument for creating jobs, and is the best way to solve poverty in India. The Corpns of Catamaran will be ₹ 600 crore or about $130 million and is operational in 2010.

He did it with middle-class values – hardwork, humility, honesty and innovation – and inspired uncountable thousands on the good way to make money. And as the thousands clamouring to get into Infosys indicate, there is no better employer around.

One of India's most successful entrepreneurs and mentor has turned into a Venture Capital is along with Mrs. Sudha Murthy to fund start-ups mainly in India. The idea is to encourage young Indian entrepreneurs with brilliant ideas. The new Venture Capital (VC) is named 'Catamaran' and will help entrepreneurs across sectors such as health care, retail, technology, education and nutrition's with early stage and seed investments. The Corpns of catamaran will be ₹ 600 crore or about $ 130 million and is operational in 2010. Thus, N. R. Narayana Murthy is stepping into mentoring entrepreneurs and encouraging research and innovation. He firmly believes that entrepreneurship is an effetive instrument for creating jobs and is the best way to solve poverty in India.

Kiran Mazumdar Shaw (March 23, 1953)

Biotech Baroness: It's rare for a women to be the CEO of a company that leads its industry. It's rarer still for that woman to also have pioneered the industry. But then, Kiran Mazumdar Shaw is no ordinary woman. When she returned from UK with a master's degree in brewing (her father R.I. Mazumdar was India's first brewmaster), she was all of 25 years old. Her original idea was to take up a job as a brewmistress. But fate willed otherwise. As it happened, she couldn't find a job. Far from being deterred, the young Mazumdar launched her own company with Biocon, an Irish firm, to manufacture enzymes for packaged fruit juices. Now Biocon is moving into even greener pastures. It will use its technology to manufacture recombinant human insulin. It is a multi-billion dollar market that is expected to revolutionise diabetes treatment and the product will pit Biocon with MNCs like Eli Lilly. Her dream: To propel Biocon into the world's top 10 biotech firms.

It is Kiran's people-centric nature that makes her rise above mundane things like gender differentiation. Her style is hands on and she usually puts in 15 hours of work daily.

Faquir Chand Kohli (February 28, 1924)

Father of Indian Software Industry: As an electrical engineer, F.C. Kohli was an unlikely candidate to be India's software revolutionary. But, as it turned out, J.R.D. Tata couldn't have picked a better man to lead the Tata group's foray into the then esoteric software business. When Kohli took over the reins at Tata Consultancy Services in 1969, the electrical engineer from the Massachusetts Institute of Technology only had experience in managing power plants. Worse, computer technology wasn't really a priority for the government. Kohli battled on, managing to get a modest share of the software boom that had begun in the US in the early 60s. The arrival of Rajiv Gandhi and his technology-friendly team opened up opportunities for TCS, and a horde of other software wannabes. Today, TCS is Asia's largest software and services company, and set to cross the $1 billion turnover mark (₹ 4,700 crore) in 2001-02.

Late P.C. Mahalanobis (June 29, 1893-June 28, 1972)

India's Quality Guru: Prasanta Chandra Mahalanobis was India's answer to the American quality guru Edwards W. Deming. Just like his American peer, Mahalanobis was a statistician. And like Deming, Mahalanobis (called 'Professor' by his friends) sought to create prosperity through the use of statistics. When Mahalanobis was in his late 20s, he set up the Statistical Laboratory within the Physics department of Calcutta's Presidency College. By 1931, it became the Indian Statistical Institute, and in 1959 it was a national institution. Mahalanobis also showed India the use of sample surveys, by employing them to study Bengal's jute production and yield in 1937. Statisticians today consider that Professor's greatest contribution. But in popular memory, the Cambridge graduate is best remembered for his seminal work on the Five Year Plan. While the decay of Nehru's command capitalism may be at the root of India's economic problems, the Mahalanobis model did give a newly independent India a spring-board to prosperity. It's a pity that the expected leap did not take place.

Desh Bandhu Gupta

Standing Tall: His medium build, silver hair and soft spoken manner make him look more like a college professor than a business tycoon. Yet, Desh Bandhu Gupta, the founder and chairman of Lupin Ltd., one of India's most successful pharmaceutical companies, provides ample evidence that one should never judge a person merely by appearance. Though his company now has a market capitalisation of ₹ 6,000-7,000 crore, and annual sales of ₹ 3,775 crore, Gupta has not forgotten that Lupin was started in 1968 with an initial investment of just ₹ 5,000! But his close confidantes point out that the company's CSR programmes give him much more satisfaction than market leadership in one more product, one more country.

In the field of generics (off-patent), the competition will keep on increasing. So, Lupin is trying to carve out certain riches, concentrating on drugs that are technologically difficult to manufacture.

They are also moving towards their own drug molecules, which will help them to stay ahead of the competition. The company is under professional and not a part of the Family.

Lupin is at the very forefront of successful Indian (pharma) companies. Of course, many first generation companies find it difficult to transition to the second or third generation. But Lupin has overcome this hurdle with Gupta's children – Son Nilesh and daughter Vinita.

Azim Hasham Premji (July 24, 1945)

Creator of the New Wealth: Azim Hasham Premji is not an entrepreneur by choice. In 1966, at the age of 21, he was practically overnight thrust into the role of the Chief Executive Officer (CEO) of a company about $ 4 million in sales then and not in the best shape. In the following year Azim Premji diversified and entered the knowledge economy in 1979. From then on, he led his way to software superpower status his vision, determination has created new wealth and newer opportunities. The big opportunities are driven by changes in the world that we live in. We have to seize these opportunities. Premji is a picture of clam. A lot of that has to do with his empowerment strategy. Heads of division and companies prepare their own business plans. Premji is a champion of integrity. Above all, Azim Premji invitingly serves as an inspiration for hundreds of techies – around the country and within his company – to strike out on their own.

18 CHAPTER

THE CONCEPT OF ENTREPRENEURSHIP

Entrepreneurship is the key to economic growth. A country that fosters innovation and entrepreneurship will emerge the strongest in the future.

LEARNING OBJECTIVES

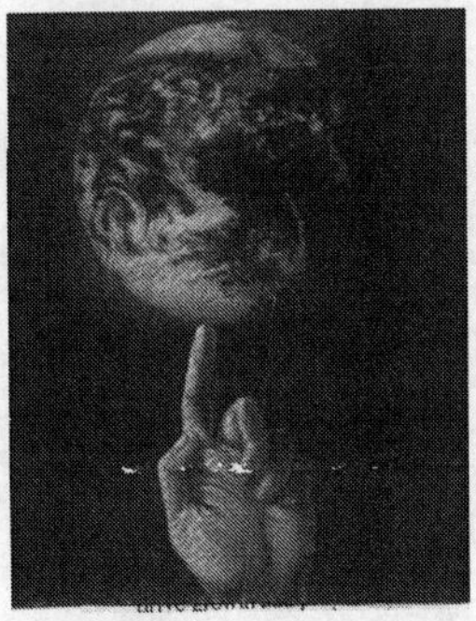

The chapter provides an insight into the concept of entrepreneurship.

- A Complex Phenomenon
- Enterprise Governance
- Empowering Entrepreneurship
- Stimulation of Entrepreneurship
- Definition
- Concept of Entrepreneurship
- Phases of Entrepreneurship Development
- Fostering Entrepreneurship
- Entrepreneurship and Economic Growth
- SSI as Seed-beds of Entrepreneurship
- Factors Influencing Entrepreneurship
- Operational Problems
- Obstacles
- Success of Entrepreneurship
- Entrepreneurship Management
- Vision for the Future

INTRODUCTION

Entrepreneurship introduces a critical element of dynamism into an economic system. It is no coincidence that the world's leading economy, the USA, is believed to be the most entrepreneurial society in the world. The process of globalisation and liberalisation has introduced two sets of changes–the first is the obvious introduction of dynamism into the system through the process of globalisation. While new opportunities have opened up in international markets, the bar has been raised in the domestic market through international products and services being available to Indian consumers. The domestic market will no longer be lower-risk. It will force Indian entrepreneurs to regain their spirit of innovation.

The more subtle change is social: increase in literacy levels, greater consumer awareness, enhanced media penetration, and basic changes in family structure. These changes are bound to result in a higher level of entrepreneurial activity in the future.

In keeping with the demands for greater innovation in Indian enterprises, several have fundamentally redesigned structures. There are no easy answers to how the rate of change in entrepreneurial activity can be increased. The solutions to eliminate some of the structural constraints to entrepreneurship are really no different from the solutions to driving higher economic growth rates. Entrepreneurship extends beyond a conventional business and economic perspective. Creativity, innovation, and bringing a vision to life are as much entrepreneurial activities in a social sphere and have the same impact on society as does business entrepreneurship to the economy.

Indians have always been entrepreneurs: we have all heard about businesses growing from father-to- son or the rags-to-riches story in conventional industry. But recently there has been a shift in the nature of Indian entrepreneurship. It has come to stand for something that is out of the box and globally-oriented. It began with the infotech revolution a decade ago. Now all the signs point to another industry joining this new wave of Indian enterprise. Venture capitalists and economic forecasters believe biotechnology is India's next big thing, its new IT.

A COMPLEX PHENOMENON

The concept of entrepreneurship is a complex phenomenon. Broadly, it relates to the entrepreneur, his vision and its implementation. The key player is the entrepreneur. Entrepreneurship refers to a process of action an entrepreneur (person) undertakes to establish his/her enterprise. It is a creative and innovative response to the environment.

Entrepreneurship is thus a cycle of actions to further the interests of the entrepreneur. In this chapter, the concept of entrepreneurship and the related issues are analysed, discussed and deliberated.

One of the qualities of entrepreneurship is the ability to discover an investment opportunity and to organise an enterprise, thereby contributing to real economic growth. It involves taking of risks and making the necessary investments under conditions of uncertainty and innovating, planning and taking decisions so as to increase production in agriculture, business, industry, etc.

Entrepreneurship is a composite skill, the resultant of a mix of many qualities and traits. These include imagination, readiness to take risks, ability to bring together and put to use other factors of production, capital, labour, land, as also intangible factors such as the ability to mobilise scientific and technological advances.

A hard practical approach is necessary to be able to implement and manage a project by securing the required licences, approvals and finance from governmental and financial agencies. The personal incentive is to make profits from the successful management of the project. A sense of cost-consciousness is even more necessary for the long-term success of the enterprise. However, both are different sides of the same coin. Entrepreneurship lies perhaps more in the ability to minimise the use of resources and to put them to maximum advantages. Without an awareness of quality and desire for excellence, consumer acceptance cannot be achieved and sustained. Above all entrepreneurship today is the product of teamwork and the ability to create, build and work as a team. The entrepreneur is the maestro of the business orchestra, wielding his baton to which the band is played.

THE SIX PILLARS OF ENTERPRISE GOVERNANCE

In this global age, leaders in the business world can come from anywhere. The best ideas will dominate, regardless of their national origins. It is in this competitive global regime that the best hopes and aspirations of India rest.

A well-run enterprise embraces and practices a sound Predictability-Sustainability-Profitability-Derisking (PSPD) model. A good forecasting system for sales based on data gathered ensures predictability.

Sustainability is achieved by motivated salespeople who make sales happen; by production people ensuring that quality products are delivered on time; and by billing and collecting on time.

Every enterprise must focus on high profitability in order to ensure the best returns for its shareholders. Indeed, profitability is crucial for the long-term success of a corporation.

The enterprise must have a good derisking approach that recognise, measure and mitigates risk along every dimension. Take them you must, but carefully thought out risks.

Enterprise governance is focus on maximising shareholder value while ensuring fairness to all stakeholders. In these days of free following global capital, in order to attract capital, corporations have to adhere to the best global standards of enterprise governance.

The foundation of enterprise governance philosophy is the belief that it is better to lose crore of rupees than to act in ways that make one loose a night's sleep.

It is a good practice to underpromise and over-deliver, it is best to deliver bad news to the stakeholders proactively. This creates goodwill as they understand that ups and downs are inevitable in every business. What they value is honest and open management.

Quick progress comes in an environment that respects competence, where there is competition and where there are no prejudices. Infoscions (those associated with Infosys) have respect our competitors and a sense of humility about what we have achieved. The success is generally ephemeral. We are only as good as the results we produce and we believe in a long-term approach: our strategies and policies reflect that.

The enterprises have an important duty to contribute to society. No enterprise can sustain its progress unless it makes a difference to its context. The six pillars of enterprise governance are:

- I want to emphasise the importance of being trustworthy in your dealings. It is on such foundations that great organisations are created.
- Fear is natural, but do not let your actions be totally governed by it. Just as fear may sometimes be the voice of your institution, it might also be an invitation to explore yourself and the world.
- A supportive family is the bedrock upon which lives and careers are built.
- Learn how to manage yourself separating the merits and demerits of a decision from the accompanying feelings. Infoscions call this 'being transaction-oriented'.
- Live your life and lead your career in a way that makes a difference to your society.
- Follow your bliss. All else will follow.
- So, choose a worthy dream for yourself. Go after it confidently but always ensure that you are following your bliss.

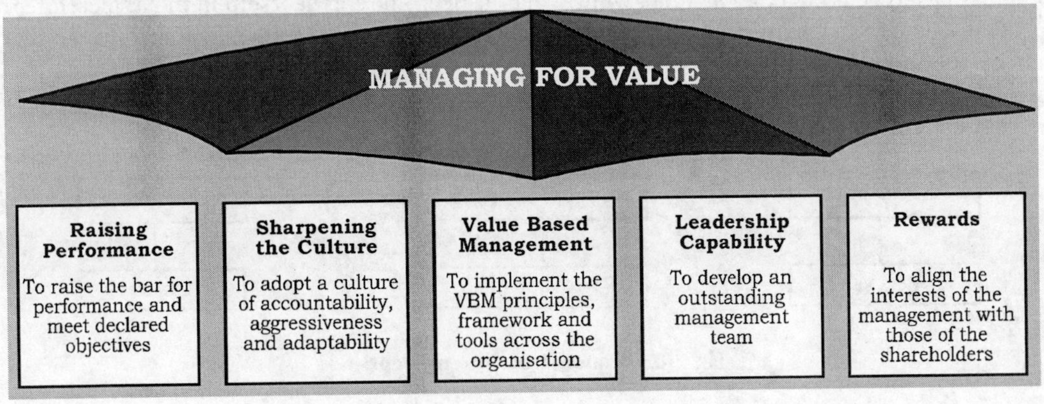

Empowering Entrepreneurship

In the new competitive environment, it is necessary to grow out of a mindset that thinks only of control. Organisations have to learn to treat their employees not as mere implementors of decisions, but as entrepreneurs – thus, intrapreneurs – who can all contribute to the growth of the company. But entrepreneurial freedom is more than just the decentralisation or delegation of work.

Treating employees as entrepreneurs means both the ownership of work as well as opportunities for self-management. Not only does an entrepreneur has more freedom, he also has greater responsibility for successful performance. Thus, to stimulate entrepreneurs, organisations must develop systems that combine rewards for creativity and risk-taking with accountability for performance.

Treating support functions as profit centres – which charge for the services they render to the line function – has at least three advantages. First, it makes these functions more accountable for their performance. Second, since the line functions pay for their services, they will make more specific demands on them. and, lastly, it will stir entrepreneurial initiative, which is often dormant in support functions.

Finally, the appropriation of the free-market model to the small-scale world has critical imitations for the role of the entrepreneur in an enterprise. To build an empowered and entrepreneurial organisation, intrapreneurs must learn to adopt a hands-off approach. In a liberalised organisation, the role of the intrapreneurs is akin to that of a venture capitalist who supports and strategies organisational initiatives without interfering in the day-to-day management of the enterprise. Without this strategic shift, it is impossible for an organisation to derive the full benefits of liberalisation.

What is Entrepreneurship?

Entrepreneurship is the propensity of mind to take calculated risks with confidence to achieve a predetermined business or industrial objective. In substance, it is the risk-taking ability of the individual, broadly coupled with correct decision-making. When one witnesses a relatively larger number of individuals and that too generation after generation in a particular community, who engage themselves in the industrial or commercial pursuits and appear to take risks and show enterprise, it is acknowledged to be a commercial class. The commercial class is a myth just like that of the so-called martial race. There are neither, for all-time, martial races nor commercial classes. Communities, which in the course of history once appeared to be martial in spirit have, in later periods, emerged as mercantile societies. Those who were once more concerned with and relished in trade, later in history, seem to have taken to the profession of the sword. Today, it is quite evident to anyone that national communities which have developed worldwide industrial and consequent commercial interests are militarily powerful: nay, great industrial powers have today become super-military powers as well. Enterprise finds manifestation in different ways. The capacity to take risk independently and individually, with a view to making profits and seizing an opportunity to make more earning in the market-oriented economy, is the dominant characteristic of modern entrepreneurship. Enterprise, ready for the pursuit of business and responsive to profit by way of producing and or marketing goods and commodities, to meet the expanding and diversifying actual and potential needs and demands of the customers, is what constitutes *entrepreneurial stuff.* But this kind of sensitivity of enterprising citizens throws up a species of entrepreneurs, who are mostly mercantile in outlook and performance. In underdeveloped countries like India, a new species of entrepreneurs is desirable, because here the economic progress has to be brought about along with social justice. Entrepreneurship in India, therefore, has to subserve the national objective. There is an apparent conflict between social objectives and economic imperatives. This conflict has to be resolved first by the individual entrepreneur in his own mind and make economic growth, which induces industrial development, as one of the instruments of attaining the social objective. A high sense of responsibility is thus an essential attribute of emergent entrepreneurship in India.

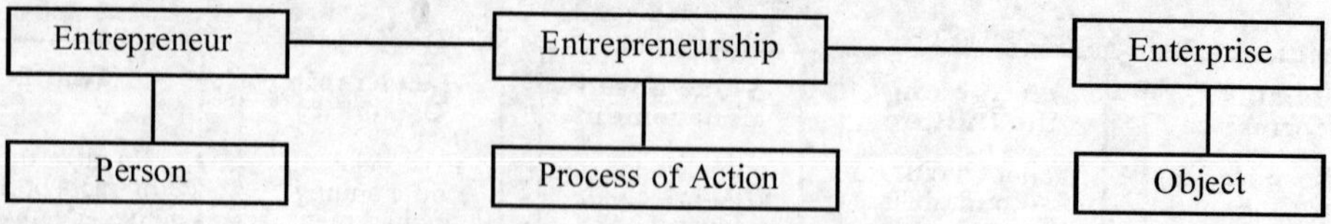

Fig. 18.1 Concept of Entrepreneurship

Stimulation of Entrepreneurship

Entrepreneurship development is probably one of the most elusive, complicated and perplexing issues in the promotion and growth of small enterprises. Recently, a number of development agencies have been involved. However, in spite of all these efforts, there have been only a few partially successful programmes and many colossal failures in the field.

The stimulation of entrepreneurship is a function of both internal and external variables. The presence of certain personal qualities in an individual is a requisite. Some of the findings about entrepreneurs in Nepal are as follows:

(a) Mainly there are two types of entrepreneurs: the government and private individuals.
(b) In a family-run business, the entrepreneur is owner as well as manager. Entrepreneurs are frequently found to have parents who were engaged in business-related occupations. Membership in certain types of communities (Mewass, Marwadies, Gurung, etc.), is highly correlated with entrepreneurship.
(c) Many people who migrated from the hills to the southern part of the country (Terai), and returned have become entrepreneurs, and
(d) In the family, a change is taking place. Now the educated young members are becoming entrepreneurs rather than the head of the family who is generally old.

Box 18.1 Entrepreneurship

From a humble, but profitable, canteen in Hostel at IIT Bombay to three successful start-ups (including Aspect Development, which was sold to i2 technologies in 1999 for $ 9.8 bn), to a fourth, Symphony Technology Group – the beat never slows for Romesh Wadhwani, nor does his quest to make others step to this drummer. When a man of such tremendous entrepreneurial spirit – not to mentions personal wealth-pledges "many millions" of his fortune of build an entrepreneurial network in India, it's not something to be taken lightly. The vehicle of his dream is the Wadhwani Foundation.

Romesh's reasoning is simple: If the Indian diaspora in the US can start about 30% of the companies in Silicon Valley, why can't Indians in India do the same thing? The end result isn't just personal success, it's also the creation of hundreds and thousands of much-needed jobs. "The divide between social and for-profit entrepreneurship is superficial, " says Laura Parkings, executive director of the Foundation. "So many of the skills required are the same."

It's this belief that will fuel the Foundation's three-fold attack on the risk-averse attitude of Indians. The beginning is from education. The '01 Global Entrepreneurship Monitor noted that "the prevalence rate (of entrepreneurial activity) is lowest among those that do not have any formal education and significantly higher among those with professional degrees". It goes on to suggest that the inclusion of entrepreneurship curricula at all levels of education in India, particularly for professional degree programmes may stimulate start-up activity.

That's where the National Entrepreneurship Network (NEN) comes in. NEN builds on the premise that high quality entrepreneurial education and research can increase the success of individuals in all fields. "The purpose of the NEN is to make it possible for millions of Indians like me to start and build large and successful business all over India, in all kinds of industries; businesses that create join for tens of millions of professional workers", says Romesh Wadhwani. To sow the seed of an enterprise, the Foundation is launching a competition to select five Indian academic institutes to form the base of an entrepreneurial network. In five years, "we hope to have entrepreneurship development centres in 100s of institutes". The competition will begin with a by-invitation list of 250 institutes, to be pruned to five. Thirty semi-finalists will first submit plans for proposed activities like curricula development, courses, skill-building exercises, networking events and entrepreneurial activities. These will be studied by a panel of judges which includes HSBC's Naina La Kidwi, Sunil Mittal of Brahma, Harsh Mariwala of Marico, and Jaithirth Rao of Mphasis among others. Each of the five will receive non-financial support and seed funding of $10 to 50,000. Each will have a year to develop further proposals for entrepreneurial activity, depending on which they will be eligible for funding of $ 2,50,000 to $ 1m. "Introducing entrepreneurship as a viable career choice for all sectors is very important", says Laura. Adds Mr. Wadhwani, "The key here is to train managers, engineers and others to be entrepreneurs, to encourage them to take risks in the expectation of large rewards, to teach them the tools and help them find the talent and resources they need to succeed, and to provide access to mentors and role models to guide them."

To this end, the contest will include hotel and Mphasis, fashion and design, and technology and management institutes.

Alongside, IIM Bangalore has been roped in to conduct the National Entrepreneurship Survey (NES). NES will attempt to understand the barriers to entrepreneurship and prioritise the conditions needed for such activity to thrive. For instance, explains Laura, "how important was a knowledgeable Diaspora to the success of Indians in the Silicon Valley". Or how seminal are issues like venture capital, infrastructure, FDI or educational levels of the labour force. Executed annually, NES will seek to build a systematic knowledge base and be a resource for developing policies that encourage and support entrepreneurship.

Finally, the foundation plans to set up a Global Entrepreneurship Forum to bring together researchers, entrepreneurs, policymakers, NGOs and funding agencies among others. Not only will the forum provide a platform for discussion of the issues affecting emerging markets, it also hopes to inform and influence policy. And while the Wadhwani Foundation doesn't expect financial returns, this is not charity. "In every venture there is a bottom line. It's about creating value", says Laura.

Definition

Entrepreneurship is a multidimensional task defined differently by different authorities. Centillon was the first to use the term 'entrepreneur'. He portrayed an entrepreneur as one discharging the faction of direction and speculation. J.B. Say, moving along in the French (Cantillon) tradition, was the first to assign the entrepreneur a position in the economic process. According to him, an entrepreneur's function is to combine the factors of production into a producing organism, but to Adam Smith, the father of political economy, the entrepreneur was a proprietary capitalist, a supplier of capital and at the same time, working as manager, intervening between the labour and the consumer. Adam Smith also treated him with the capitalist. Schumpeter was decidedly the first economic thinker to have assigned the entrepreneur a key role in the process of economic development . In Schumpeter's system, entrepreneurship is essentially a creative activity. The entrepreneur is the innovator who introduces something new into the economy. The innovation may be a method of production not yet tested by experience in the branch of manufacture concerned or a product with which consumers are not yet familiar, or a new source of raw material or of a market hitherto unexploited or other innovations in the strict sense of the term.

According to him, entrepreneurs are business leaders and not simple owners of capital. They are men of vision, drive and talent, who spot out opportunities and promptly seize them for exploitation. It will not be out of place to mention here that the innovator's concept of entrepreneurship cannot be exclusively depended upon in underdeveloped countries. In these countries, business leaders who promote many large and small enterprises and adapt Western techniques of production and distribution to the prevailing conditions in their own industires are entrepreneurs of no mean significance. They may not be innovators in the true sense of the term but they are men of great vision and effective industrial leaders who transform the economic landscape of their countries. People like Jamsetji Nusserwanji Tata, M. Visvesvaraya, G.D. Birla, Jamnalal Bajaj, Laxmanrao Kirloskar and other visionaries, builders and thinkers laid the foundation for a modern industrialised India. Professor Bert F. Hoselitz calls them imitative entrepreneurs, and regards their existence as quite purposeful in a mixed economy. " Coupled with all historical experiences of Western Europe, it appears to be safe to assume", he writes, that "small and medium-scale entrepreneurs are likely to play an important role in developing countries for several decades, provided these developing nations permit a private sector of enterprise in the industrial, commercial and financial field at all".

Besides, in South-East Asian countries, at the pretake-off stage, the need is for more promoters, risk takers and business organisers than fair innovators. In the emerging countries, employment creation is a far more immediate goal for the entrepreneurs than technological innovation. As Professor Jan Tinbergen points out: "The best entrepreneur to any developing country is not necessarily the man who use much capital, but rather the man who knows how to organise the employment and training of his employees. Whoever concentrates on this is rendering a much more important service to this country than the man who uses huge capital".

Concept of Entrepreneurship

From classical economics to the post-Keynesian analysts, the topic of the entrepreneur has been surveyed and observations, theories and pronouncements advanced. Not only were pure economists involved in this endeavour, but also prominent social theorists such as Marx, Weber, Sombard and Veblen.

In general, contemporary economists agree that the entrepreneur is a business leader and that his role in fostering economic growth and development is a pivotal one. At present, however, there is no consensus as to what constitutes the essential activity which makes the entrepreneur a crucial figure, while some economists have identified the basic entrepreneurial requirements of production resources, the provision of capital or the introduction of innovations. Professor James R. Omps of the International Institute of Entreprenology, Honolulu, Hawaii, in his paper entitled "*Entreprenology, the Critical Factor in Nation Development*", has this to say:

"In all crisis situations, there is one critical factor. There is one factor in each situation that can be cited as being the straw that broke the camel's back! In listing some of today's possible critical factors, such familiar words and phrases as limited natural resources... food.... energy all would emerge. A question may be phrased thus:

"What is the critical factor?"

Over-population?

Food shortages?

Energy shortages?

Lack of technology? and

All of the above?

"Many factors have been proposed... and yet is it possible that the most critical factor has not been recognised? What is this factor that has either been stifled or totally ignored? It is a relatively untapped source... that of qualified individuals with peculiarly unique aptitudes for innovation ... for change aptitudes, in other words, for using present-day technology in ways yet unheard of or perhaps even unthought of. The critical factor is a dire shortage of the appropriate economic innovator and implement... the entreprenologists."

In the words of A.H. Cole, entrepreneurship is the purposeful activity of an individual or a group of associated individuals, undertaken to initiate, maintain or organise a profit-oriented business unit for the production or distribution of economic goods and services.

Frank H. Knight seriously questioned the unimportance of entrepreneurship in his publication 'Risk, Uncertainty and Profit' (1921) and expressed views similar to these of Cantillon. Knight emphasised that many uncertainties of economic life can be insured but some uncertainties are such which can never be reduced to objective measurement because they involve unprecendented situations. Knight remarked that "The only 'risk' which leads to profits is a unique uncertainty resulting from an exercise of ultimate responsibility which in its very nature cannot be insured not capitalised nor salaried." Thus, he draws a distinction between the ordinary risk and uncertainty. A risk can be insured, whereas uncertainty is a risk which cannot be calculated and cannot be insured. *He showed that the man who earns positive profits in this "uncertainty" about the future and guesses the price at which will he sell the output is to an entrepreneur*. In spite of some criticism, Knight could provide with a satisfactory explanation of entrepreneurship.

McClelland described the innovative characteristics of entrepreneurial role – Entrepreneurial role, by definition, involves doing things in a new and better way. A businessman who simply behaves in a traditional way is not an entrepreneur. Moreover, entrepreneurial role calls for decision-making under uncertainty. If there is no significant uncertainty and the action involves applying known and predicable results, then entrepreneurship is not at all involved.

D.C. McClelland, like others, identified two characteristic of entrepreneurship. First, doing things in a 'new and better way'. This is synonymous with the innovative characteristics given by Schumpeter and secondly, decision-making under uncertainty, i.e., risk as identified by Cantillon. McClelland more explicitly emphasised the need for achievement or achievement-orientation as the most directly relevant factor for explaining economic behaviour. This motive is defined as tendency to strive for success in situations involved and of one's performance in relation to the same standard of excellence.

As per **Casson,** entrepreneurship consists of an eccentric evaluation of economic events which other people are unwilling to support. As per **Janil and Stevenson**, "Entrepreneurship is a process by which individuals – either on their own or inside organisation – persue opportunities without regard to the sources they currently control." Although English classical economsits failed to recognise entrepreneurship as a moving force towards the development of an economy but some of them like Israel Kirzner and Mark Casson did have their strong views about entrepreneurship. As **Kirzner** puts it, "Entrepreneurship means alertness towards profit opportunities."

Friedrich Von Hayek (1899-1922) **Ludwig Von Mises** (1881-1973), Keynes defined entrepreneurship and assigned a role played by entrepreneurship. Thus, entrepreneurship came up as a theory which has the ability to mobilise the resources and combine them to initiate change in production.

In other words, entrepreneurship means the function of creating something new, organising and coordinating and undertaking risk and handling economic uncertainty. Higgins defines the term as, "Entrepreneurship is meant the function of seeing investment and production opportunity, organising an enterprise to undertake a new production process, raising capital, hiring labour, arranging for the supply of raw materials and selecting top managers for day-to-day operation of the enterprise."

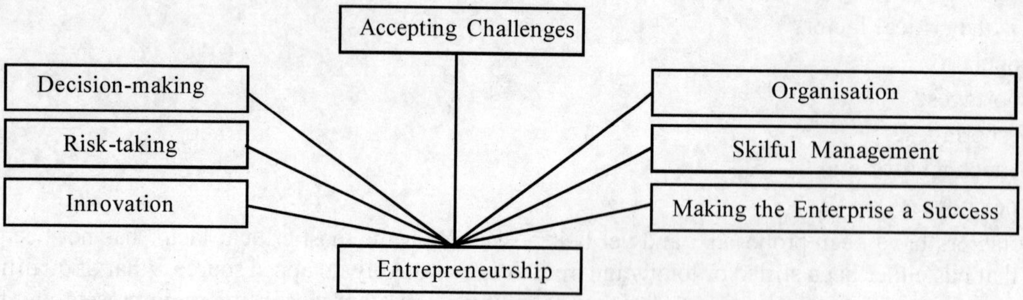

Fig. 18.2 Characteristics of Entrepreneurship

According to Peter Drucker, "Entrepreneurship is neither a science nor an art. It is a practice. It has a knowledge base. Knowledge in entrepreneurship is a means to an end. Indeed what constitutes knowledge in practice is largely defined by the ends, that is, by the practice." Entrepreneurship is considerably less risky, if the entrepreneur is methodical and does not violate elementary and well known rules.

Innovation and entrepreneurship are thus needed in society as much as in the economy, in public service institutes as much as in business. It is precisely because innovation and entrepreneurship are not 'root and branch' but 'one step at a time', a product here, a policy there, a public service yonder; because they are not planned but focussed on this opportunity and that need; because they are tentative and will disappear if they do not produce the expected and needed results; because, in other words, they are pragmatic rather than dogmatic and modest rather than grandiose – that they promise to keep any society, economy, industry, public service or business flexible and self-renewing.

Thus, entrepreneurship is a complex phenomenon. "Some think of entrepreneurs primarily as innovators, some chiefly as managers of enterprise, some as bearers of risks and others place major emphasis on their function as mobilisers and allocators of capital." In the Indian context, however, an entrepreneur may at best be defined as a person (or a group of persons) responsible for existence of new business enterprises.

Box 18.2 Entrepreneurship: Some Important Definitions

Joseph Alois Schumpeter	:	Schumpeter described entrepreneurship as a process to shatter (1883-1950) the *status quo* through new combinations of resources and new methods of commerce.
Richard Cantillon	:	Entrepreneurship is a matter of foresight and willingness to assume risks, which is not necessarily connected with the employment of labour in some productive process.
Leon Walrus	:	Entrepreneurship is not itself a factor of production, but rather a function that can be carried on by an agent.
William Diamond	:	Entrepreneurship is equivalent to 'enterprise' which involves the willingness to assume risks in undertaking an economic activity particularly a new one.
Jaffrey A. Timmons	:	Entrepreneurship is the ability to create and build something from practically nothing. A human creative activity.
Janil and Howard Stevenson	:	Entrepreneurship is a process by which individuals – either on their own or inside organisation – persue opportunities without regard to the sources they currently control.
Isrel Kizner	:	Entrepreneurship means alertness towards profit opportunities.
Arthur H. Cole	:	Entrepreneurship is the purposeful activity of an individual or a group of associated individuals, undertaken to initiate, maintain or aggrandise profit by production or distribution of goods and services.
Everett E. Heggins	:	Entrepreneurship is meant the function of seeking investment and production opportunity, organising an enterprise to undertake a new production process, raising capital, hiring labour, arranging the supply of raw materials, finding site, introducing a new technique and commodities, discovering new sources of raw materials and selecting top managers of day-to-day operations of the enterprise.

Peter F.Drucker (1909-2005) :	Entrepreneurship in neither a science nor an art. It is a practice. It has knowledge base. Knowledge in entrepreneurship is a means to an end. It is not just about making money. It is about imagination, flexibility, creativity, willingness of think conceptually, readiness to take risks, ability to mobilise agents of production and capacity to see change as an opportunity. It is also about marrying passion and process with a good dose of perseverance.
M.Low. and J.MacMillan :	Entrepreneurship is the creation of a private economic organisation (or network of organisations) for the purpose of gain or growth under conditions of risk and uncertainty.
H.Aldrich and C.Zimmer :	The definition of entrepreneurship includes more than the mere creation of a business, it also includes the generation and implementation of an idea.
Robert Ronstadt :	Entrepreneurship is the dynamic process of creating incremental wealth. The wealth is created by individuals who assume the major risks in terms of equity, time, and/or career commitment or provide value for some product or service.
Robert D. Hisrich :	Entrepreneurship is the process of creating something new with value by devoting the necessary time and effort, assuming the accompanying financial, psychic, and social risk and receiving the resulting rewards of monetary and personal satisfaction and independence.
John J. Kao :	Entrepreneurship is the attempt create value through regulation of business opportunity, the management of risk-taking appropriate to the opportunity, and through the communicative and management skills to mobilise human, financial, and material resources necessary to bring a project to fruition.
Robert K. Lamb :	Entrepreneurship is that form of social decision which is performed by economic innovators.
V.R. Gaikwad :	Entrepreneurship connotes innovativeness, an urge to take risk in face of uncertainties and an intuition.
Musscleman and Jackson :	Entrepreneurship is the investing and risking of time, money and effort to start a business and make it successful.
H.N. Pathak :	Entrepreneurship involves, (i) perception of an opportunity, (ii) organising an industrial unit, and (iii) running the industrial unit as a profitable, going and growing concern.

The Global Entrepreneurship Monitor: Entrepreneurship, the process of planning, organising, operating and assuming the risk of a business venture, is now a mainstream activity.

The culture of entrepreneurship is deeply rooted: Entrepreneurs are celebrated role models, failure is seen as a learning experience, and the entrepreneurial career option is regarded as attractive. In today's economic environment, entrepreneurship is a key component of globalisation.

Box 18.3 My Best Lesson in Leadership

What's the secret to building a great organisation? How do you sustain consistent growth, profits, and service in an industry that can, literally, change overnight? And how do you build a culture of commitment and performance? I can answer all that in two words: be Yourself.

That's both a simple and a profoundly difficult goal. It means spending less time building an organisation in which personality counts as much as quality and reliability. Southwest Airlines has the reputation being the wild-and-crazy guy of commercial aviation. Yet, in many ways, we are the most conservative company in our industry. We have always paid as much attention to out financial fitness in good times as in bad. But you can't lead by just the numbers.

As far too many companies, when you come into the office, you put on a mask. You look different, talk different, and act different, which is why most business encounters are bland and impersonal. But we try not to hire people who are humourless, self-centred, or complacent. So, when they come to work, we want them – not their corporate clones. They are what makes us different from other airlines and, in most enterprises, different is better.

Culture defines personality: If you create an environment where people truly participate, you don't need control. They know what needs to be done, and they do it. We're not looking for blind obedience. We're looking for people who, on their own initiative, want to be doing what they're doing because they consider it to be a worthy objective. They know that our company's success rests with them – not with me.

Personality is strategy: Over the years, we've developed not only a different strategy, but also a different strategic planning-process. Basically, we just don't do it. In an industry where a two-week plan is likely to become obsolete, to spend days debating whether we're to serve Trenton, New Jersey, in 2005 is a meaningless exercise. So, rather than trying to predict what we'll do, we try to define who we are, and what we want in terms of market niche, operational strategy, and financial health. Obviously, you manage a $25-billion company differently than you do a $25 million company. But you change practices – not principles. You remember that systems are not masters. And that nothing comes ahead of your people.

Working for a worthy cause: Because our low-fare strategy is central to who we are, our employees are enormously cost conscious. But you need to spend more time on the intangibles than on the tangibles to create that kind of buy-in. We're not afraid to talk to our people with emotion. One of our managers once said: "The important thing is to take a brick-layer and make him understand that he's building a home." So, we constantly hold up examples of customer-experiences and employee-efforts to make a difference.

Building employee-partnerships: Our most important tools for building employee-partnerships are job-security and a stimulating work-environment. And, as it turns out, providing job-security imposes additional discipline because, if your goal is to avoid lay-offs, you hire sparingly. But it's not enough to try to assure people a job; equally important is allowing them to feel liberated when they come to work. To foster problem-solving and cooperation, for example, we have the Walk-a-mile programme, in which any employee can do another's job for a day.

Training is another way you forge partnerships. Our most important training is in how to lead. My best lesson in leadership came during my early days as a trial lawyer. Wanting to learn from the best, I went to see two of the most renowned litigators in San Antonio try cases. One sat there, never objected to anything, was very gentle with witnesses, and established a rapport with the jury. The other was an aggressive, thundering help-raiser. And both seemed to win every case. That's when I realised that there are many different paths – not one right path. That's true of leadership as well.

People with different personalities, different approaches, and different values, succeed not because one set of values or practices is superior, but because their value and practices are genuine. And when you and your organisation are true to yourselves–when you deliver both results and a singular experience–customers can spot it from 30,000 feet.

Herb Kelleher

Box 18.4 Trends Driving Entrepreneurship

Smaller Government :

As the size of the state as an employer shrinks it will spur private enterprise

Easier Money:

With banking getting more entrepreneur-friendly and venture capitalists spreading their wings, money will be more accessible

Nuclear Families:

With more women working a double income in the family will allow more budding entrepreneurs to take the plunge.

Less Economic Controls:

As bottlenecks and entry barriers come down further it will make the entrepreneurs' life easier.

Technology :

With new technologies come new opportunities

Growing Services:

The low-capital option for small-scale entrepreneur

Instant Gratification:

An instant-mix generation that will reach out for quick success

Just-do-it effect:

Entrepreneurial successstories in the peer group will spur more to take the risk

Growing Consumer Class:

More types of consumers lead to more entrepreneurial opportunities

Globalisation:

As barriers come down opportunities will increase.

How will the new entrepreneurs realise their ambitions? What are the fundamental changes urging them to strike out on their own in increasing numbers. An irreverent take on the times: By Ninan and Jayanto.

Features of Entrepreneurship

Entrepreneurship is the tendency of a person to organise the business of his own and to run it profitably, using various traits like leadership, decision-making, innovation, managerial calibre, etc. Entrepreneurship is a set of activities performed by an entrepreneur. In a way, entrepreneur precedes entrepreneurship. The main features of entrepreneurship are as follows:

(i) Economic Activity: Although classical economists like Adam Smith and Richard Cantillon and many others didn't recognise entrepreneurship as an economic activity but since last few decades entrepreneurship is catching up and is primarily becoming an economic function because it involves creation and operation of an enterprise.

Schumpeter's argument was that all important changes in the economy are set-off by an entrepreneur and then these changes slowly work themselves through economic system, in the form of a business cycle.

(ii) Innovative Activity: According to Schumpeter, entrepreneurship is essentially a creative and an innovative activity. There are five ways of being innovative.

(a) The introduction of a new good;
(b) The introduction of a new method of production;
(c) Opening of a new market;
(d) The conquest of a new source of supply of raw material;
(e) The creation of a new organisation of an industry.

Phases of Entrepreneurship Development

Broadly, entrepreneurship development consists of the three following phases:

(a) **Initial Phase** – Creation of awareness about the entrepreneurial opportunities based on survey.
(b) **Development Phase** – Implementation of training programmes to develop motivation and management skill.
(c) **Support Phase** – Infrastructure support of counselling and assisting to establish a new enterprise and to develop existing units.

Box 18.5 CEO Survival Kit

Digital devices rule Chugh's life. Not surprising. His company helps machines talk to one another.

Cellphone: Nokia 6210. It is my constant companion, as my wife says. I largely use it for phone calls and SMS, especially during long, laborious meetings.

Laptop: Toshiba Tecra 8100 – It is the key to my survival. I use it in the office, in flight, any time I am away from home, at least three to four hours a day. I have dispensed with the desk-top PC (After all) our business runs off the net.

PDA: I rely on my good old Palm IIIxE. I store schedules when I travel, and some spreadsheets. A true friend away from home.

Telephone: Cisco 7960 IP phone. Just one integrated infrastructure. No complex manuals, just simple English.

Manoj Chugh, CEO, Cisco India.

Causes of Slow Growth

Entrepreneurship growth is slow in India and women's entrepreneurship is still slower and negligible due to the discouraging social factors such as unfavourable family background, lack of education, dual role of women, lack of aptitudes and training, absence of individualistic spirit, lack of freedom to choose a job according to ability, influence of sex, caste, kinship, custom and family burden, etc. All these retarding causes are due to the unfavourable socio-economic conditions and tradition-bond society.

The retarding economic factors for entrepreneurship growth are inadequate infrastructural facilities, shortage of capital and technical know-how, transport and communication facilities, absence of cheaper and regular supply of power and raw materials. These constraints are existing more in rural areas. The environmental factors discouraging entrepreneurship are unstable state governments, lack of security, absence of ideal market conditions and business and corruption in administration.

Entrepreneurship Stimulants

A variety of social, economic, political and cultural factors are stimulating entrepreneurial activity and thus generating more robust economic development. These stimulants are as follows:

- An increasing focus on capital formation. Availability of capital is a stimulant to an entrepreneur to start a new firm and/or give birth to a new idea.
- The ability to transform scientific and technical developments through new institutional development is a second stimulant.
- A third stimulant is the supportive government programmes.
- Availability of required training and input is ranked fourth.
- A collaborative relationship between business and research and their direct attempts to transfer technology to the marketplace may provide stimulus to a number of entrepreneurs who seek the opportunity to commercialise their ideas, and
- Finally, an endeavour to create an environment conducive to innovation will provide a much needed stimulant to entrepreneurial activities.

The innovation centre provides technological evaluation, entrepreneurial assessment and other related levels of assistance to entrepreneurs.

FOSTERING ENTREPRENEURSHIP

Fuelling ambitions and dreams. Helping insightful, imaginative business ideas glide smoothly over tough passages, breathing life into promising business ventures. Encouraging foresight and drive complementing acumen and enterprise with a steady flow of resources. *For effective management, it is imperative to foster and stimulate entrepreneurship and industrial culture to accelerate the process of industrialisation.*

Innovation is success in business and especially in the small-scale industry, innovation is the path to success. This is widely understood by small, medium and large companies alike. Innovation is particularly important for an operating system so that information can flow without hindrances.

Strategic Phases of Management

- Calibrate strategies constantly with board members.
- Share the company's progress towards set objectives with employees.
- Award employee stock options on a case-by-case basis.
- Stimulate growth by tapping employee's experience and abilities.
- Prepare written short-term and long-term plans.
- Ensure collaborative decision-making among the top management
- Turn between two and five top managers into entrepreneurs.
- Add to the number of management levels only as sales grow.
- Establish entrepreneurial competencies in finance, marketing and operations, and
- Involve the board of directors in all matters of management.

Entrepreneurship and Economic Growth

Economic development of any region is an outcome of purposeful human activity. Men assume various roles in the development process, namely, as organiser of human capital, natural material resources, worker and consumer. He stands at the centre of the whole process of economic development. According to Schumpeter, economic development consists of "employing resources in a different way", in doing a new combination of means of production. The entrepreneur locates ideas and puts them into effect in the process of economic development.

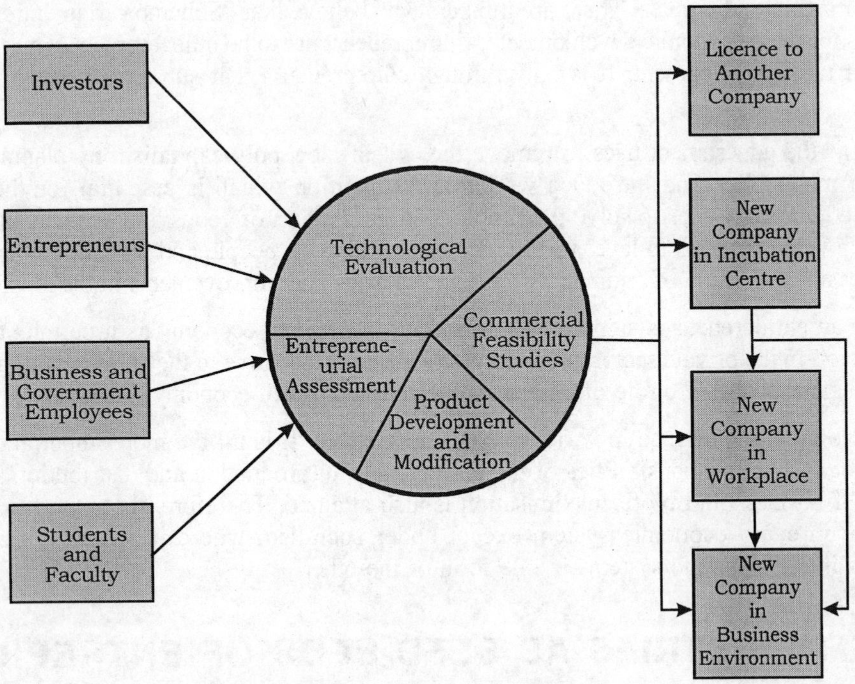

Fig. 18.3 Innovation Centre

According to Baumol, an entrepreneur is a Shumpeterian innovator and something more than a leader. The entrepreneur, according to him, occupies a crucial place in the process of economic development.

Schumpeter further says that economic growth depends on the rate of applied technical progress (i.e., innovation) and rate of technical process in the economic field which in turn depends on the supply of entrepreneurs in the society. Thus, the entrepreneur becomes the agent of change in society.

In the Schumpeterian model, entrepreneur is an innovator and the supply of 'innovative entrepreneurs' depends on the necessary social and economic overheads. These economic and social overheads are very poor in backward regions which cause a short supply of entrepreneurs. In this connection, we can refer to David McClelland who explained the development of entrepreneurship in terms of human motivation to achieve or need for achievement (N Ach). McClelland's hypothesis is that a society with a generally high level of achievement will produce more energetic entrepreneurs, who in turn accelerate the process of economic development.

In the Indian context, entrepreneurship has yet another dimension. An entrepreneur may not necessarily be an 'innovator' but an 'imitator' who would copy the organisation, technology, products of innovators from other developed regions. His role as an imitator is likely to be guided and controlled by the various constraints and conditions peculiar to this area of operation and the factors under which he conducts his minimal modest industrial activity.

Other social scientists, notably Max Weber, have talked of the importance of entrepreneurship and expressed the view that creative and entrepreneurial energies are generated by the adoption of exogenously supplied beliefs which in turn produce intense efforts in occupational pursuits and accumulation of productive assets leading to the manufacture of goods and services. According to him, entrepreneurs are a product of the particular social conditions in which they live and it is the society which shapes the personality of individual entrepreneurs.

John Kunkel believes that the behavioural pattern of individuals is important for development and such a pattern can be influenced by external stimulus so as to alter it in the manner we want it. In other words, if we want more people in society to behave as entrepreneurs, we can bring about such behaviour on their part by appropriate alterations in the social environment so as to influence them to take to entrepreneurial pursuits. Like Weber, Cochran and Young underscore the importance of society in shaping the entrepreneur's personality and consider that ingredients in the emergence of entrepreneurs are cultural values, role expectations, social tensions and inter-group relations in society.

The entrepreneurs are an important source of economic development. It is, therefore, suggested that there must be a motivational training programme to develop entrepreneurs and measures to be taken to modify the environment to stimulate entrepreneurial behaviour among individuals. There are thinkers who believe that "Schumpeterian entrepreneurs are needed in underdeveloped countries for rapid economic development". Entrepreneurs are to be innovators who must change the production function and bring about rapid development. It is only through entrepreneurs that substantial development can be brought about.

In a mixed economy, the government tries to remove the evil of monopoly capitalism by placing some restrictions. It may curb the growth of monopolies and introduce workable competition which is essential for the optimum use of the available resources. Mixed economy tries to solve the problem of distribution of goods and services in a better way than the capitalist economy. The government tries to level up the incomes of the poor people and level down those of the rich people. This is done by fiscal measures, fixation of minimum wages and salaries and improvements in the environment by the people.

The role played by an entrepreneur is significantly important in a mixed economy as it permits the growth of both the public and the private sector. In the private sector, profit motive acts as an incentive to the entrepreneur and market mechanism plays its own role and this establishes the role of an entrepreneur in the mixed economy.

Entrepreneurship has great importance in various economic systems. It is all the more important under capitalism and mixed economy where not only the responsibilities of the entrepreneur in production and distribution are recognised but the objective of the growth of business and profit maximisation is also attained. Therefore, the importance of entrepreneurship stands beyond challenge in every economic system except under socialism where it appears in a different form. Yet, entrepreneurship prevails in all economic systems in one form or the other.

SMALL-SCALE INDUSTRIES AS SEED-BEDS OF ENTREPRENEURSHIP

Small-scale industries contribute significantly to the strengthening of the industrial structure, many articles can be produced economically on a small-scale, with some even more economically than on a larger scale, efficient small-scale industries can be linked with large enterprises in complementary relationship, e.g., subcontracting. One of the most obvious benefits of such a relationship is that it expands the industrial base by efficiently utilising resources, scarce otherwise.

Also, small-scale industries may serve as seed-beds of entrepreneurship. They serve an emerging industrialising country not only by their output of goods but also by functioning as a nursery of entrepreneurial and managerial talent. The almost infinite diversity of products and services that may be developed and produced by the small-scale industry sector also demands a commensurate development of skills – a desirable basis for long-term development of a diversified industrial structure in the regions. Already skilled technicians, foremen and workers are induced and are often able to set up their own small-scale industrial enterprises. Generally, they offer the most promising means of promoting entrepreneurship among the people from different walks of life, especially those with limited financial resources and scant technical and managerial experience, thus establishing a wide base for rapid industrialisation. This role of small-scale industries is of decisive importance in any economy, where the industrial structure consists of a few large-scale and medium-sized industries (many of which are foreign-owned) on the one hand, and of a large number of traditional industries such as – artisans, handicrafts and cottage industries on the other.

The lack of a middle group of modern small-scale industries is a factor of imbalance in the industrial structure. Such lack also contributes to the stagnation of the economy as a whole. As a general rule, neither the government nor foreign investors are interested in owning and operating small-scale establishments. Therefore, to promote small-scale industries is to promote rural industrial private enterprises, specifically to create a new class of indigenous industrialists throughout the country.

Small-scale industries play a useful role in regional development and industrial dispersal. Indeed, one of the pivotal problems confronting many countries in the world today in the task of social modernisation is how to disperse sources of economic activities so that development should become general rather than concentrated in larger cities and capital. In a country that sanctions free enterprise, the movement of economic activities cannot be easily directed as the government would want them to be. Instead, we witness the tendency of capital to centralise itself in already developed areas.

Table 18.1 Sources of Entrepreneurial Emergence and Motivation

Author	Entrepreneurial Phenomenon	Source of Entrepreneurial Emergence	Motive Force
1. Cochran, T.C.	Individual	Society's 'Model', personality determined by its cultural values, role expectations and social sanctions	'Social acceptance' of entrepreneurial role
2. McClelland, D.C.	Religious and social groups	Individuals with high achievement, creative	Child-rearing practices and climate
3. Schumpeter, J.A.	Individual	Extraordinary individuals	Innate urge to do something newer
4. Hoselitz, B.F.	Group	Culturally marginal groups	Gaining social recognition
5. Weber, M.	Status Groups	Extraordinary individuals	Religious beliefs – Calvinist ethic
6. Frank, H. Night	Individual	Risk leads to profits	Risk-taking in uncertain situation
7. Peter F. Drucker	Group	It is a practice	Knowledge as a means
8. Arthur H.Cole	Individual/Group	Purposeful activity	Profit-oriented
9. Fradrik Barth	Group	Connectivity	Social justice
10. The Economist	Group	Innovation/Promoting Development	Technology/knowledge

Factors Influencing Entrepreneurship

Peter Heydeman, the Science Counsellor in the US Embassy, is very much impressed with the role of small businesses play in the process of innovation in the US economy. He explained how 'incubators' are used successfully in the United States to encourage small entrepreneurs.

The problem is how best to help small entrepreneurs translate the results of laboratory research into a commercial product. Simply put, 'incubators' are very basic facilities offering shared secretarial services, space for conducting a retail or manufacturing business, and a few simple machine tools. But, and this is very important, incubators offer advice and consultation on subjects with which the most budding entrepreneurs are unfamiliar: business and finance planning, market development, government regulations. Incubators have indeed greatly helped small manufacturers to develop new products. Recent studies show that such enterprises are the main source of innovation in the US industry.

The idea of incubators of technology is relatively new, "five or six years old", says Heydeman. This is because until recently it was felt that the US industry would forever remain in the forefront, without any competition. But things changed rapidly. So, realising that "the 6,000 plus national laboratories could not possibly service all the one-and-a-half million or so small entrepreneurs, individual American states took it upon themselves to help local industry through their technology support and development organisations.

Incubators are very often attached to state university systems as universities have much of the technical and non-technical information that needs to be fed to the entrepreneurs. Moreover, state universities have increasingly come to believe that apart from their traditional role, they must also promote industrial activity in their areas of operation.

State authorities in turn help by enabling businessmen cut through red-tape, provide low-interest loans to develop prototypes, undertake market research and generally assist in bringing a new product to the consumer. "Some notion of the magnitude of this support can be had from the fact that last year alone, the federal and state governments together spent more than $2,000 million in encouraging small business." Many private sector companies also provide incubator facilities, though at a comparatively higher cost.

Another important aspect of incubators is that experts do not make any business decisions for their clients. They only provide guidelines and advice on product development, engineering, pilot production and in identifying markets.

Among the businesses in which incubators are making a significant contribution, says Heydeman, "are light manufacturing in mature technologies, retail and wholesale trade and, finally research and development in emerging technologies".

The success rate of incubators has been salutary in the number of new jobs created, the enlarged tax base for state revenues and in the export of manufactured. In short, incubators are bringing new vigour and vitality to America's industrial renaissance and are once more giving the country a competitive edge.

Operational Problems

The task before the national leadership today is to industrialise a predominantly agricultural society, where capital is scarce and layout is plentiful. Again, the modern industry implies a style and a method of work which are quite at variance with the traditional culture and modes of social behaviour in the underdeveloped countries. So, the whole structure of society has to undergo a considerable structural and institutional change commensurate with the needs of the situation.

The gap between the indigenous arts and even the improved crafts, on the one hand, and the imported and also the indigenous technology on the other, is wide enough and is further widening day-after-day with the explosion of innovative research. Furthermore, the economy has been historically and unavoidably polarised between a few mighty industrial centres and the far-flung rural areas. With all the progress during the two decades and a half, the national economy is beset with all kinds of shortages and scarcities of inputs, most vital to new entrepreneurs, when they launch their small or tiny units. Besides, they have, at times, to contend and compete with the well-established small, medium or large industrial units in the same lines of production. Newly emerging industries, particularly of the first generation entrepreneurs, even in the underdeveloped economies, are slowly but certainly tending to become high investment industries and the entrepreneurs have to battle against the formidable force of hostile elements, such as: (i) erratic shortages of raw materials, (ii) flourishing black market, (iii) rigged up prices by monopolists, (iv) administrate maldisribution, (v) gap between official promise and performance, (vi) inefficiency of industrial management, (vii) irresponsible attitude to work, (viii) rising cost of capital and credit, (ix) deficient and arrogant institutional banking, (x) inadequacy of common service, (xi) primitive wholesale and retail trade outlets and others. New entrepreneurship in India has to be cradled in this environment.

The present stage of entrepreneurship development programmes as a factor contributing to the industrialisation of backward and other areas needs a proper direction and organisation for making it more effective and purposeful. The contribution of entrepreneurship development programmes is very uneven among different regions and definite programmes need to be chalked out to bring about some degree of uniformity and upgradation. Before these problems are tackled, some important issues need immediate attention, for example, (i) structure and composition of entrepreneurship development programmes; (ii) areas of operation; (iii) fixing of priorities; (iv) follow-up; (v) spatial dispersal of the entrepreneurship development programmes; (vi) training of trainees; and (vii) financing pattern.

Apart from these, some of the operational problems experienced in the course of implementing the entrepreneurship development programmes are listed below:

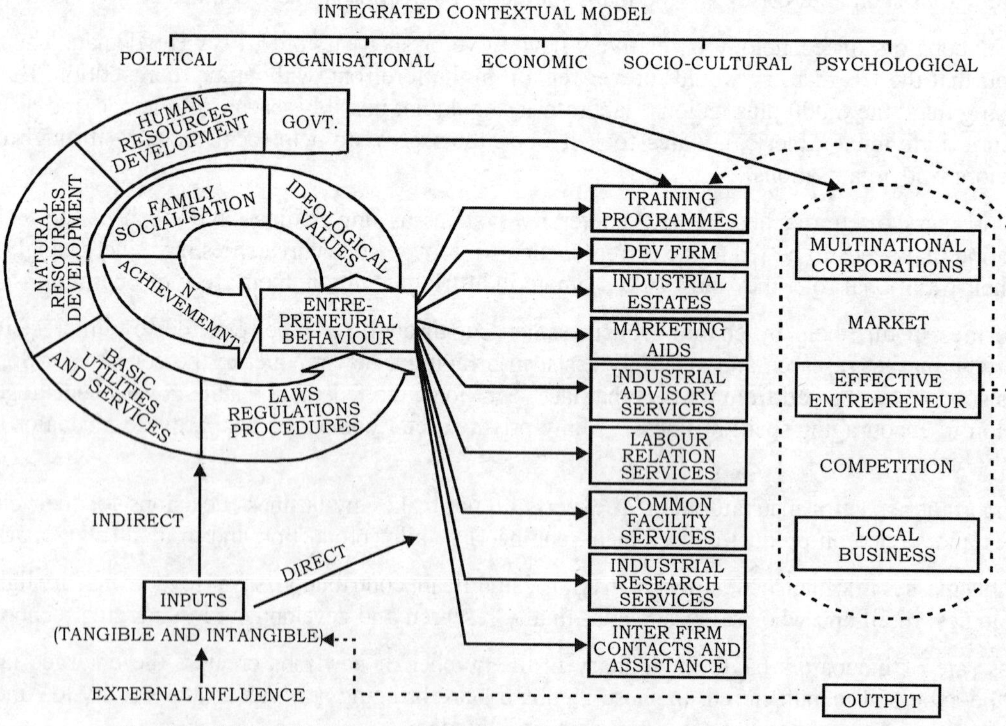

Fig. 18.4 A Model of factors influencing the emergence of entrepreneurship

(**Source:** Adapted from Abdul Aziz Mahumud, *Developing Effective Indigenous Entrepreneurs*. Malaysian Management Review, April 1974, Vol. 9, No.1.)

Box 18.6 Entrepreneurship Beyond Borders

The ability to spot opportunities and do business beyond borders is increasingly becoming the defining trend that will separate the entrepreneur from the rest. Government deregulation is opening national borders for commerce. Trading and investing beyond national borders is now common and is either the salvation or the death knell of the Indian economy. We have an enviable domestic market and that in itself is a threat unless domestic enterprises shake themselves out of their comfort zones and gear up to face the pressures of competition from across the border, now made easier, thanks to the World Trade Organisation (WTO).

India and other developing countries will continue to oppose and seek amendments to the WTO proposals that prohibit developing countries from following the same policies that developed countries pursued to make their domestic enterprises internationally competitive. But the WTO threats are real. The trick, if one is to survive and prosper, will be to identify emerging threats before they become real and then prepare for them. It will be equally important to learn to spot opportunities before they arise, and take advantage of them. Success comes to those who are able to take advantage of opportunity. Alexander Graham Bell said: "When one door closes, another door opens; but we often look so long and so regretfully upon the closed door that we do not see the one that open for us." In business, opportunity knocks once; it usually does not lean on the doorbell.

Competition from across the border will affect high-cost producers, and perhaps even decimate entire industries, especially in the small-scale sector. India already finds itself in a situation of jobless growth. Where will new jobs be generated?

However, the alternative for job-seekers is to create their own jobs. Entrepreneurship in India (outside of family-controlled businesses) is largely necessity-based, not opportunity-driven. Entrepreneurs in this country have traditionally not been looked up to as role models. It is still widely believed that you cannot become a successful entrepreneur in this country without bending the rules. But this view is slowly changing, thanks to the success of Indian entrepreneurs in the infotech industry. They have fired the imagination of a whole new generation, and entrepreneurship is now a desired career option. Industries where entrepreneurship has flourished are IT, drugs, and pharmaceuticals.

The comparable advantage of developing countries will expand beyond low labour costs. This trend is a clear warning to those who are basking in the comfort of apparent demand for their products and services. If the industry is so complacent, then where is the opportunity for innovation?

(1) Past experience has shown that the supporting agencies/organisations either tend to be slipshod in the first phase or are less interested in the third phase which means that the programme fails to tap the entrepreneurial potential of the area or the trained entrepreneurs do not receive the support and counselling which they need most.

(2) Most of the existing support organisations meant for maintenance operations are not for innovative functions. There is also an element of cynicism. A reorientation in the attitude of supporting organisations is called for.

(3) Poor investment on the part of institutions as also trainees and wrong selection of target groups contributed largely to the failure of the number of entrepreneurship development programmes.

(4) Experiences reveal that entrepreneurial failures are mostly due to incompetence and poor management.

(5) It is also said that there is an inability to identify the needs of institutions and differences of opinion prevailed amongst the practitioners and also amongst the trainees.

(6) It is also stated that there is a low institutional commitment for local support to the entrepreneurs. There is also a very low level of involvement in the marketing of products of the units.

(7) Non-availability of various inputs, i.e., raw materials, power, etc., and infrastructure support combined with poor follow-up by the primary monetary institutions resulted in the failure of the entrepreneurship development programmes.

(8) It is also stated that there is ill-planned training methodology, inconsistency in the programme design, its content, sequence and theme and the focus of the programme is not clear.

(9) Training institutions do not have much concern for the objective of identification and selection of entrepreneurs and the follow-up after training.

(10) Some of the institutions are still debating whether to have a proper identification and selection of entrepreneurs for preparing successful entrepreneurs.

(11) Those involved in and concerned with the selection and follow-up activities have either limited manpower support or a narrow linkage with other support agencies.

(12) It is also said that there is no standard curricula even in terms of broad module being adopted by interventions.

(13) A majority of the institutions engaged in the entrepreneurship development programmes are themselves not convinced of what they are doing as the task is delegated by the government. As a result, the social objective aimed at is not achieved.

(14) Perpetual ambiguity in the objectives of entrepreneurship development programmes seems to have percolated to the grassroot level with significant deterioration in terms of content and interest.

(15) It has also been realised that absence of an appropriate industrial and commercial climate coupled with lack of information and access to relevant technology has acted as a great handicap, and

(16) Mechanical implementation of entrepreneurship development programmes, as it is happening in many cases, will not solve the problem. The mechanical approach may help entrepreneurs to initiate the entrepreneurial development activity but they may not be able to manage it and expand it successfully.

Obstacles Inhibiting Entrepreneurship

There are a variety of obstacles which inhibit entrepreneurship an unwillingness to devote organisational abilities to business purposes, restrictive effects of customs and tradition, lack of response to monetary incentives, low status of businessmen, high risks involved in new enterprises, absence of vertical mobility in the social structure, market imperfections which deny potential entrepreneurs, the resources they need for organising new production units, and arbitrary changes in the administration of laws by the government, all of which make the environment too uncertain for entrepreneurs. N.H. Leff has put it as follows: "Absence of entrepreneurship (in LDCs) is generally attributed to alleged socio-cultural rigidities."

Robert L. Garner has observed that "development is a state of mind. People have to develop themselves before they can change their physical environment and this is a slow process.... it involves change in relations between classes and races. It requires improvement of governmental organisations and operations; the extension of social institutions, schools, courts and health services. Habits of thoughts and conduct are the most stubborn obstacles to development."

Motives, abilities and a congenial environment, which promote entrepreneurship, are lacking in India. If the motives and abilities are weak, then it becomes all the more essential to have a more congenial environment. But in India the congenial environment is also lacking. The stimulation of entrepreneurial abilities is a complicated long-run sociological problem. The social organisations represented by such major institutions as caste, joint family, rural village, and school are more favourable for the development of entrepreneurship. In India all these are not conducive to the development of entrepreneurship.

In underdeveloped countries, the functions of a given person in entrepreneurial capacity include innovation, promotion, capital provision and risk-bearing, management, assembling materials and labour.

He lacks the help of markets for components, materials, labour, capital markets which have already standardised products and trained workers. He also lacks the communication network, specialised industrial newspapers and magazines. Sociologists and anthropologists distinguish many types of family in terms of who lays down the law and where the newly married couples live. The vertical family under which young adults continue to live with one set of parents after marriage and contribute earnings to a common pool, has a distinctly inhibiting effect on many of the factors affecting economic development such as mobility, saving, risk-taking, even willingness to work more for high price.

Labour supply curves may bend backward with more respect to wage increases because of limit on economic aspirations or because the personal incentive is dulled by the necessity to contribute all the work while sharing its fruits. The incentive to take risks in entrepreneurship is blunted in the same way. The institutional framework of a community determines the scope of an individual's efforts. If the institutions are favourable, willingness to make effort is encouraged and grows; and if this willingness is strong, institutions will be remodelled to accommodate themselves.

If religious attitudes and institutions encourage discipline, hardwork, efficiency, honesty and thrift among its followers, the social climate will impel people to apply their minds to increasing productivity to acquire wealth and to improve their social prestige and power. Most religions, as prevailing in India, consider the existing order of the universe as sacred and try to make people believe like that. Ethical beliefs discourage the spirit of enquiry, experimental and scientific outlook among members of the society. A religion which permits and encourages rationality and scientific attitude is conducive to technological improvements and dynamism in social relations and in social attitude. A desire to discover the causes of things is the most effective motivating force behind inventions, discoveries and innovations in physical as well as in social sheers.

The Success of Entrepreneurship

The success of entrepreneurship and enterprise solely depends on innovation, technological advancement and systematic commercialisation for the good of the society. The significance of entrepreneurship as one of the important keys to economic development hardly needs to be emphasised where motivation of development is present among the people, and entrepreneurial energy acts as stimulant where motivation is lacking, it acts as a lubricant.

The development of entrepreneurship in backward and rural areas with a view of broad-basing their existing skills and utilising local raw materials would help attain the growth rate visualised for the industry.

Hitherto, much as we wanted to spread small and rural industry in backward and rural areas, the efforts have not been as intensive as we propose doing in the coming years.

Development of local skills, productive utilisation of local raw materials and wastes, and encouragement to entrepreneurs in backward and tribal areas are new directions of future small industry development. In this programme, it is employment and not investment which is an important criterion, so that the facilities of consessional finance and capital subsidy made available to the backward and tribal areas would reach a larger number of persons and thereby provide larger employment. The generalised assistance programmes so far worked out has to be given an appropriate shape according to the condition of the backwardness or tribal social structures of the area. Where necessary, the scheme may have to be modified so that the plan allocations earmarked for the development of backward and tribal areas are utilised.

If enterprises are to expand, entrepreneurship should also develop. If entrepreneurship is important, then organisations and society might find ways to encourage it. Both the enterprise and entrepreneurship need to be nurtured, supported, cultivated, developed and built-up. These infrastructural institutional support provide a strong impetus to the development of new enterprise. More importantly, supportive entrepreneurial climate with a 'can do' attitude among the educational service and the professional consultants combined with assistance in training, finance, venture capital, research and development, government incentive and subsidies and local advisory services be created.

Entrepreneurial Management

Entrepreneurship is not 'natural', it is not 'creative'. It is work. Entrepreneurship and innovation can be achieved in any business. But they must be striven for. They can be learnt, but they require effort.

Specifically, entrepreneurial management in an existing business requires policies and practices in four major areas:

1. The organisation must be made receptive to innovation and willing to perceive change as an opportunity rather than as a threat. It must be organised to do the hardwork of the entrepreneur. Policies and practices are needed to create an entrepreneurial climate.
2. Systematic measurement or at least appraisal of a company's performance as entrepreneur and innovator is mandatory, as well as built in learning to improve performance.
3. Entrepreneurial management requires specific practices pertaining to organisational structure, to staffing and managing, and to compensation, incentives, and rewards.
4. There are some 'don'ts', things not to do in entrepreneurial management:
   (a) not to mix managerial units and entrepreneurial ones, and
   (b) innovative efforts that take the existing business out of its own field are rarely successful. Innovation should not be 'diversification'.

A business that wants to be able to innovate, wants to have a chance to succeed and prosper in a time of rapid change, has to build entrepreneurial management into its own system. It has to adopt politics that create throughout the entire organisation the desire to innovate the habits of entrepreneurship and innovation.

Next Big Leap

By the first phase of liberalisation, modern management practices began to establish themselves in some family-run firms. As society and the economy changed, it was no longer enough to keep old files going: it was obvious they needed to be recreated to fit the new moulds.

The biggest warning to the business family was served by the rise of the Indian middle-class. With new money and new desires borne on satellite television, new markets were created by a rising tide of entrepreneurs. Many were people who came from communities not previously known for entrepreneurship. They were sons of austere middle-class clerks, bankers, professionals and farmers.

The first wave of entrepreneurship spread to small towns where business folk churning out things like bicycle parts and gaskets began to reach out to the world beyond. They created some of the markets we take for granted today: from housing finance to cheap television sets to private airlines. They were pathbreakers.

But the flaws of liberalisation also meant that to be really successful, the new breed of entrepreneur need to know how to work the system. The result is that many of the people who came out of nowhere since the late 1980s excel at schmoozing their way to the top.

It is time for all of India's entrepreneurs, new and old, to shrug off the chains-perceived or otherwise. While there are a lot of infrastructural problems that must be solved, there is no denying the fact that we need to do much more ourselves. Thinking global is not just about setting up operations in other countries or acquiring companies. It is about having the passion, the zeal, the confidence to beat anybody and everybody, whether at home or in the new markets beyond our shores.

Every point of growth that we witness today is qualitatively better than all the growth we witnessed in the era since independence. That's because everything the Indian entrepreneur achieves today is in the face of increasing competition.

Vision for Future

The entrepreneurship that contributes in a modest way to critical economic and social needs of the country and always strive to attain global leadership in all of its major initiative. This is the vision for future.

Pursuing this vision, over the next few years, entrepreneurs will pursue a strategy of:

- Reinforcing competitive advantage of existing business through new capacities and synergistic acquisitions.
- Scaling sizable opportunities in the core sectors.
- Forward integrating into retailing transportation fuels and creating new customer experiences.
- Addressing the significant information and communications market opportunity in India and in the world.
- Leveraging its strong balance sheet, cash flows and managerial capacity to create value by adding new capacities, acquisitions and turnaround of underperforming assets.
- Developing strategic alliances in technology and product-market domains with global majors.
- Fostering new higher educational institutions for knowledge creation and sharing.
- Leveraging its formidable strengths beyond Indian borders.
- Reorienting the best practices to enhance productivity and quality (Q).
- In addition to manufacturing products venture into developing manufacturing systems.
- From having a manufacturing orientation to providing technical solutions.
- From being an intermediate goods producer to being a final goods and services provider.
- From licensing technology to developing technology.
- From being an intellectual property user to an intellectual property creator.
- In addition to operating in India to being a global company.
- From building financial equity to fostering social equity.

This change will entail creating new organisational competencies such as:

- Creating a customer-centric organisation.
- Developing new products and technologies.
- Exploring and producing new products to meet the new generation's expectations.
- Fostering and sustaining globally-oriented management talent.

- Training the human resources to harness the opportunities.
- Encouraging entrepreneurship.
- Focusing on Research and Development for sustainable development.
- Imbibing new technology to enhance the value of the product.
- Focusing on business ethics in managing the enterprises.
- Managing customer-oriented supply chains.
- Developing and protecting intellectual capital.
- Managing strategic technology and product-market relationships.

CONCLUSION

Entrepreneurship is an attitude of the mind can take risks but calculated ones; a true entrepreneur is one who can see possibilities in a given situation where others see none and has the patience to workout the idea into a scheme to which financial support can be provided. It is one of the catalytic activities fostering initiative, promoting and maintaining economic activities for the production and distribution of wealth. In developing countries, there is no dearth of ideas but there is a real scarcity of men with the right blend of vision and practical sense to becomes successful entrepreneurs. The objective of the programme is to identify such people and to provide them with the support needed to make them a success. They then become 'demonstration models' to the community; and once a right climate is generated, entrepreneurship becomes a way of life.

Industrial growth in a country is achieved through a 'mix' of the large and small industry; the entrepreneurship for the former comes through the large companies often in collaboration with the multinationals. Simultaneously, economic growth also depends upon the level of development and use of information system in the country.

In fact, the small-scale industry sector is considered as an ideal nursery for the rapid growth and development of entrepreneurship. But, alas, there are only a handful of entrepreneurs in the true sense of the term in this sector. The men who will set up small industry units have to come from within the country and the community; they are 'local' in the true sense and their success, therefore, has a much greater impact on generating the right climate for successful entrepreneurship.

Programmes for developing entrepreneurship must recognise that, ultimately, the change they seek to induce is attitudinal; it is more than just providing information, land or money. It is to provide new goals so that a motivated young person is no longer content to take up a secure job which will assure him a modest income but seeks bigger challenges in setting up and running his own business. The risks are greater but so are the rewards, both in monetary sense and psychologically, in the feeling of confidence and pride it generates in the person. It is through the effort of such persons that a small industry can become a dynamic sector of the economy and hence, the effort made to develop such persons is worth the money and labour. The need of the hour is the growth of entrepreneurship in the country to accelerate the process of economic growth. According to Peter Drucker, the entrepreneurial strategy is as important as purposeful innovation and entrepreneurship in a normal, steady and an ongoing basis. Just as management has become the specific organ of all contemporary institutions, and the integrating organ of our society and of organisations, so innovative and entrepreneurship have to become an integral life — sustaining activity in our organisations, our economy and our society.

This requires executives in all institutions to make innovation and entrepreneurship a normal, ongoing, *everyday activity, a practice in their own work and in that of their organisation. Entrepreneurship is the cornerstone of the emerging economic scene in the world.*

19 CHAPTER

DEVELOPMENT OF ENTREPRENEURS

Innovate or perish

"The world is a lot more competitive than most people think, particularly in a high-technology area. If a company takes its eye off improving its products, if it tries to do anything that would be viewed as an exercise of power, it'll be displaced very rapidly."

— ***Bill Gates, Chairman, Microsoft Corporation***

LEARNING OBJECTIVES

The chapter provides an indepth analysis of the concept of entrepreneurs and the related theories.

- The Entrepreneur
- Theories
- Principles
- Modern Concept
- The New Concept
- Catalytic Agent of Change

What is most important is the creation of conducive and healthy environment for the growth of small enterprises. The new entrepreneurs also should imbibe in themselves the issues such as social responsibility, consumer satisfaction, quality consciousness and their obligations to the nation.

INTRODUCTION

An entrepreneur is the one of the important segments of economic growth. Basically, an entrepreneur is a person who is responsible for setting up a business or an enterprise. In fact, he is one who has the initiative, skill for innovation and who looks for high achievements. He is a catalytic agent of change and works for the good of people.

An urge to exercise power over other things and objects persists among all human beings. The urge may vary in degree from person to person. This urge is an intrinsic quality of an entrepreneur. Sociologists consider him as a sensitive energiser – in the moderation of societies. The psychologists look upon him as an 'entrepreneurial man', his motivations and aspirations being conducive to development. Political scientists regard him as a leader for the system. To economists, he is an *harbinger* of economic growth.

The entrepreneur is a critical factor in the socio-economic change. He is the key man who envisages new opportunities, new techniques, new lines of production, new products and coordinates all other activities.

The term 'entrepreneur' is defined in a variety of ways. Yet no consensus has been arrived at on the precise skills and abilities that make a person a successful entrepreneur.

Revival of Entrepreneurial Spirit

The entrepreneurial spirit is being revived in India. A search and guest for a better way of life, for creating employment, for creating a meaningful project, for the benefit of the maximum, for eradication of poverty, for the excitement that is inherent risk of a new enterprise, is a strong motivational urge being felt by many entrepreneurs. So, during these times, small enterprise must be given the opportunity to continue to be a great source of growth. This opportunity must be backed by guidance, assistance and capital. More importantly, an entrepreneurial climate must be created to support the entrepreneurial growth strategy. Through this effort, the existing enterprise can have a positive impact on the economic growth of a region/ country by creating new enterprises/business under the corporate umbrella. It means the development of the economy has to be interlinked with entrepreneurship, research, innovation and entrepreneurship.

Entrepreneur: Definition

The word 'entrepreneur' is derived from the French verb *entreprendre*. It means 'to undertake'. In the early 16th century, the Frenchmen who organised and led military expeditions were referred to as 'entrepreneurs'. Around 1700 A.D., the term was used for architects and contractors of public works. Quesnay. F. (1694-1774) regarded the rich farmer as an entrepreneur who manages and makes his business profitable by his intelligence, skills and wealth.

In many countries, the entrepreneur is often associated with a person who starts his own, new and small business. Business encompasses manufacturing, transport, trade and all other self-employed vacations in the service sector. But not every new small business is entrepreneurial or represents entrepreneurship.

The term 'entrepreneur' was applied to business initially by the French economist, Richard Cantillon, in the 18th century, to designate a dealer who purchases the means of production for combining them into marketable products. Another Frenchman, Jean Baptiste Say, an industrialist expanded Cantillon's ideas and conceptualised the entrepreneur as *an organiser of a business firm, central to its distributive* and *production functions*. Beyond stressing the entrepreneur's importance to the business, Say did little with his entrepreneurial analysis.

According to him, 'an entrepreneur is the economic agent who unites all means of production, the labour force of the one and the capital or land of the others and who finds in the value of the products which results from their employment, the reconstitution of the entire capital that he utilises and the value of the wages, the interest and the rent which he pays as well as profit belonging to himself. He emphasised the functions of coordination, organisation and supervision. Further, it can be said that the entrepreneur is an organiser and speculator of a business enterprise. The entrepreneur lifts economic resources out of an area lower into an area of higher productivity and greater yield.

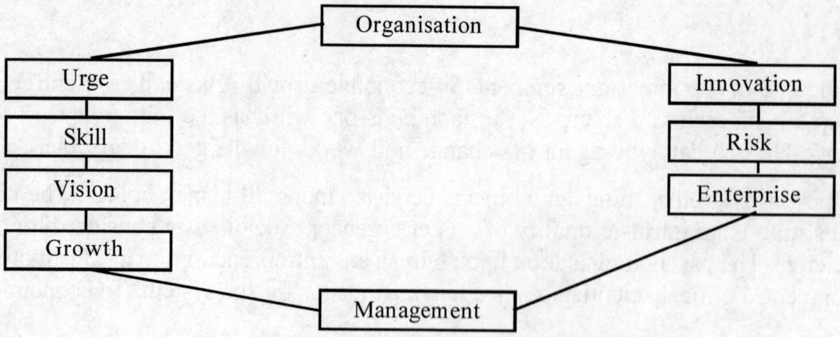

Fig. 19.1 Basis of an Entrepreneur

The concept of entrepreneurship did not find any unique place in the writings of Adam Smith, David Ricardo, J.S. Mill, Karl Marx and others. It was just elevated to the four factors of production and the important functions of entrepreneur, *viz.*, designing, directing, leading and coordinating are ignored in the literature of these writers.

Box 19.1 Success Story in Entrepreneurship

When Vikas Gutgutia landed in Delhi 10 years back with ₹ 5,000 in his pocket, one couldn't have imagined that he would go on to establish himself as the country's first branded florist. But success didn't come overnight. With little capital to invest, he had to go through the grind. His floriculture background helped as he hails from a family engaged in cultivating flowers in the Bihar-West Bengal border. On reaching Delhi from Kolkata in October 1994, a friend helped him get a place on rent to sell flowers – but since the property was disputed he had to literally sell flowers on the pavement for a year, till he earned enough money to establish the first Ferns N.Petals (FNP) outlet. Today, with over 28 outlets – the company's turnover is pitched at ₹ 15 crore for the ongoing financial year. The total floral market in India is worth ₹ 500 crore. "Our company has 10 per cent of the country's entire share – which includes the organised and unorganised sector," Vikas added. FNP has now become a one-stop wedding shop – where depending on the budget they can plan weddings, which includes the decorations, catering, entertainment and even printing cards. People are willing to splurge when it comes to celebrations. For a wedding in the Munjal family, the cost of flowers used in the decorations was around ₹ 7 lakh. Vikas's only aspiration now is to see his brand identified whenever anyone thinks of flowers. "When one thinks of a soft-drink the two names which flash in the mind are either Coke or Pepsi. In the same line I would want people to think of Ferns N.Petals when they think of flowers or decorations," says Vikas.

THE ENTREPRENEUR: OTHER DEFINITIONS

Quesnay, F. recognised a rich farmer as an entrepreneur who manages and makes his business by his intelligence and wealth.

Adam Smith described entrepreneur as a person who only provides capital without taking active part in the leading role in an enterprise.

Richard Cantillon considered all persons engaged in economic activity as entrepreneurs.

He defined "Entrepreneur" as the agent who purchases means of production in order to combine them to produce a product to sell at prices that are uncertain at the moment at which he consists himself to his cost.

Jean Baptiste Say opined that the entrepreneur was a person endowed with the qualities of judgement, perseverance and a knowledge of the world as well as of business. The definition included bringing together the factors of production.

French tradition regarded an entrepreneur as a person translating a profitable idea into a productive activity.

Karl Marx regarded the entrepreneur as a social parasite.

Joseph Alois Schumpeter recognised that a person who introduces innovative changes is an entrepreneur. He treated the entrepreneur as an integral part of economic growth. The fundamental source of disequilibrium was the entrepreneur.

Frank Young describes entrepreneur as a change agent.

Noah Webster thinks entrepreneur is one who assumes the risk and management of business.

Francis A. Walker observes that the true entrepreneur is one who is endowed with more than average capacities in the risk of organising and coordinating the various other factors of production.

Peter F. Drucker defines an entrepreneur as one who always searches for change, responds to it and exploits it as an opportunity. Innovation is the specific tool of entrepreneurs, the means by which they exploit change as an opportunity for a different business or service.

Arthur Dewing conceptualised the function of the entrepreneur as one that promotes ideas into business.

Clarence H. Dantrof considers the entrepreneur as a person who makes decisions under alternative courses of action.

The entrepreneur has become the focal point in economic activities. He is viewed as an initiator of action, a stimulant of socio-economic change and development.

Robert D. Hisrich says, "The person who is going to establish a successful new business venture must also be a visionary leader – a person who dreams great dreams. Although there are many definitions of leadership, the one that best describes the needed entrepreneurial leadership is: a leader is like a gardener. When you want a tomato, you take a seed, put it in fertile soil and carefully water it under tender care. You don't manufacture tomatoes, you grow them".

Martin Luther King said, "I have a dream and thousands followed in spite of overwhelming obstacles. In order to establish a successful new business venture, the entrepreneurial leader must have a dream and work against an obstacle to achieve it." The entrepreneur is one who is distinguished as a person who undertakes to organise, manage and assume the risk of running a factory and/or a business or an enterprise.

Entrepreneurship is neither a science nor an art. It is a practice. It has a knowledge base. Knowledge entrepreneurship is a means to an end. Indeed, what constitutes knowledge in practice is largely defined by the ends, that is, by practice.

According to E.E. Hagen, an entrepreneur is an economic man who tries to maximise his profits by innovations. Innovations involve problem-solving and the entrepreneur gets satisfaction from using his capacities in attacking problems.

The New Encyclopaedia Britannica considers an entrepreneur as 'an individual who bears the risk of operating a business in the face of uncertainty about the future conditions'. Leading economists of all schools, including Karl Marx, have emphasised the contribution of the entrepreneurs to the development of economics, but Joseph Schumpeter, who argues that the rate of growth in an economy depends to a great extent on the activities of entrepreneurs, has probably put greater emphasis on the entrepreneurial function than any other economist.

Schumpeter`s Definition of an Entrepreneur

Joseph A. Schumpeter (1883-1950) for the first time put the human agent at the centre of the process of economic development and assigned a critical role to entrepreneurship in his theory of economic development. According to Schumpeter "The Entrepreneurship is essentially a creative activity or it is an innovative sanction."

He also writes: "The entrepreneur in an advanced economy is an individual who introduces something new in the economy – a method of production not yet tested by experience in the branch of manufacture concerned, a product with which consumers are not yet familiar, new source of raw material or of new markets and the like." Schumpeter further states that the entrepreneur's function is to "reform or revolutionise the pattern of production by exploiting an invention or more generally, an untried technological possibility for producing a new commodity....."

The process of innovation may be in the form of: (a) Introduction of new product, (b) Use of new method of production, (c) Opening of new market, (d) The conquest of new source of supplying raw material, or (e) A new form of organisation. Hence, Joseph A. Schumpeter depicted an entrepreneur not only a premier agent of production who brings together all factors production but also provides a sound management and control for the survival as well as the growth of the production unit.

Briefly, an entrepreneur is one who innovates, raises money, assembles inputs, chooses managers and sets the organisation going with his ability to identify them. Innovation occurs through (i) the introduction of a new quality in a product, (ii) a new product, (iii) a discovery of fresh demand and a fresh source of supply, and (iv) by changes in the organisation and management.

In the case of a developing economy like ours, the concept is being understood differently. Entrepreneur in a developing economy is one who starts an industry (old or new), undertakes risk, bears uncertainties and also performs the managerial functions of decision-making and coordination. He also puts the new process based on technological research into operation. Even if he imitates any technique of production from a developed economy, he is called an entrepreneur. In point of fact, entrepreneurship in developing economies is one form of labour that tells the rest of the labour what to do and sees to it that it gets things done. Unlike in the developed industrial world, emphasis is not put (nor is there any need for it) only on 'Schumpeterian innovations" in the case of developing countries.

Schumpeter's entrepreneur only exists if the factors of production are combined for the first time. To him, maintenance of a combination is not entrepreneurial activity. As such, he differs from the Theory of Rent enunciated by Ricardo. Ricardo included the term 'entrepreneurial ability' as an independent factor of production. To Ricardo, profit is the reward for entrepreneurial ability.

Drucker's Views of an Entrepreneur

Peter Drucker defines an entrepreneur as one who always searches for change, responds to it and exploits it as an opportunity. Entrepreneurs innovate.

Peter Drucker has aptly observed that, "Innovation is the specific tool of entrepreneurs, the means by which they exploit changes as an opportunity for a different business or a different service. It is capable of being presented as a discipline, capable of being learned and capable of being practiced. Entrepreneurs need to search purposefully for the sources of innovation, the changes and their symptoms that indicate opportunities for successful innovation. And they need to know and to apply the principle of successful innovation".

Systematic innovation, according to him, consists in the purposeful and organised search for changes and in the systematic analysis of the opportunities, such changes might offer scope for economic and social innovation.

According to Drucker, three conditions have to be fulfilled:

- Innovation is work. It requires both knowledge and ingenuity. It makes great demands on diligence, persistence and commitment.
- To succeed, innovation must build on their strengths.
- Innovation always has to be close to the market, focussed on the market, indeed it is market-driven.

Specially, systematic innovation means monitoring six sources for innovative opportunity.

The first three sources lie within the enterprise, whether it be a business or a public service institution or within an industry or service sector. They are, therefore, visible primarily to people within that industry or service sector. They are basically symptoms. But they are highly reliable indicators of changes that have already occurred or can be made to occur with little effort. These source areas are:

- The unexpected – unexpected success, unexpected failure and unexpected external event.
- The incongruity – between reality as it actually is and reality as it is assumed to be or as it 'ought to be'.
- Innovation in industry structure or market structure that catches everyone unawares.

The second set of sources for innovative opportunity, a set of three, involves changes outside the enterprise or industry:

- Demographic (population changes).
- Changes in perception, mood and meaning, and
- New knowledge, both scientific and non-scientific.

Principle of Innovations

According to Drucker, the principle of innovation requires a few 'do's' and a few 'don'ts'. He also enumerates what he calls 'conditions'.

The 'Do'*s*'

1. Purposeful, systematic innovation begins with an analysis of opportunities. It begins with thinking through what he has called the sources of innovative principles.

2. Innovation is both conceptual and perceptual. The second imperative of innovation is to go out to look, to ask and to listen.
3. An innovation to be effective has to be simple and it has to be focussed. It should do only one thing, otherwise it confuses. If it is not simple, it won't work.
4. Effective innovations start small. They are not grandiose. They try to do one specific thing, and
5. A successful innovation aims at leadership.

The 'Don'ts'

1. The first is simply not to try to be clear. Innovations have to be handled by ordinary human beings. In other words, anything too clear, whether in design or in execution, is almost bound to fail.
2. Do not diversify. Innovations that stray from a core are likely to become diffuse. They remain ideas and do not become innovations.
3. Finally, do not try to innovate for the future. Innovate for the present.

According to Drucker, three conditions have to be fulfilled. All three are obvious, but often go disregarded:

1. Innovation is work. It requires knowledge and great ingenuity. When all is said and done, innovation becomes hard, on purposeful work, making very great demands on diligence, on persistence and on commitment.
2. To succeed, innovators must build on their strengths.
3. Finally, innovation always has to be close to the market, focussed on the market, indeed market-driven.

Modern Concept

The term 'entrepreneur' in the modern sense came into use in the late 18th century with the advent of the Industrial Revolution in England. It was during this period that people demonstrated an innovative spirit. They developed inventions and made an appreciable amount of discoveries in a variety of productive occupations. Their innovative behaviour engaged them in doing new and useful things or old things in an improved way. The invention of colour photography and colour television, for example, were the responses of innovative efforts of the individual who conceived the idea, developed it and pursued it to its ultimate success. These innovators came to be known as entrepreneurs.

Box 19.2 Rags to Riches

Affability and humility of Jayaram Banan, owner of Sagar Ratna, the most successful chain of South Indian restaurants in and around Delhi, hides the struggles of the past. Son of a truck driver from Mangalore, Banan ran away from home at the age of 14 with just ₹ 200, to escape his father's wrath after he failed his eighth standard exam, and landed up in a Mumbai canteen as a trolley boy. Eight years later, Banan came to Delhi at the urging of his brother and took up a canteen contract with a small firm. His efficiency earned him the contract of Dabur's industrial canteen at Ghaziabad. There has been no looking back since then. He was soon in a position to fulfil his dream of owning a restaurant. The first Sagar Ratna restaurant was opened on 4th December, 1986 in Defence Colony and the rest as the saying goes – is history. Banan now owns 24 Sagar Ratnas spread as far-away from Delhi to Ludhiana and Lucknow. Today, it's a favourite joint with the Capital's who's who such as George Fernandes, L.K. Advani, Sheila Dikshit. Last year, Banan entered the multicuisine, non-vegetarian segment with the Swagat brand. Banan is now in the process of forming a company. His ultimate dream – to own a five-star hotel. Well, nothing seems impossible for this man.

The term 'entrepreneur', as mentioned earlier, is subject to a number of definitions. The entrepreneur is often thought of as a risk-taker. Schumpeter argued that his sole function was innovation. Arthur Dewing conceptualised the function of the entrepreneur as one that promotes ideas into business. Evans views the entrepreneur as a person who has the task of determining the kind of business to be operated. To Danhof, an entrepreneur is a person who makes decisions under alternative courses or action.

Walker's Views on Entrepreneur

According to Francis A. Walker, the true entrepreneur is one who is endowed with more than average capacities in the task of organising and coordinating the various other factors of production. He should be pioneer, a captain of the industry. The supply of such entrepreneurship is however quite limited and an enterprise in general consists of several grades of organisational skills and capability. The more efficient entrepreneurs receive a surplus reward over and above the managerial wages and this sum constitutes true profit ascribable to superior talent.

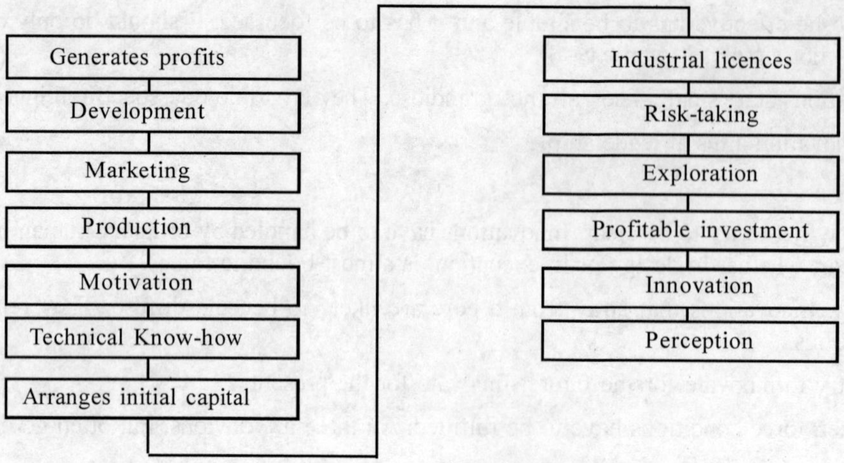

Fig. 19.2 Flow Chart of an Industrial Entrepreneur

New Concept of Entrepreneur

The term 'entrepreneur" has been defined as one who detects and evaluates a new situation in his environment and directs the making of such adjustments in the economic systems as he deems necessary. He conceives of an industrial enterprise for the purpose, displays considerable initiative, grit and determination in bringing his project to fruition, and in this process, performs one or more of the following:

(i) perceives opportunities for profitable investments:
(ii) explores the prospects of starting such a manufacturing enterprise;
(iii) obtains necessary industrial licenses;
(iv) arranges initial capital;
(v) provides personal guarantees to the financial institutions;
(vi) promises to meet the shortfalls in the capital, and
(vii) supplies technical know-how.

Activities of Entrepreneurs

Following are the major activities of entrepreneurs:

1. Perceiving the need and analysing own-self in relation to one's life goals.
2. Scanning the environment for opportunities.
3. Identification of product/project.
4. Conducting market survey.
5. Identification of technology, plant and equipment.
6. Determination of source of finance.
7. Preparation of project report business plan.
8. Arranging finance, infrastructure and utilities.
9. Project implementation.
10. Marketing and sales management.
11. Management of enterprise.

Box 19.3 The Culture of Leadership

Genuine leadership is based on values like honesty, integrity and trust. These strong personal values bring life to initiatives and transform seemingly routine activities into programmes that make a meaningful contribution to the individual and the organisation. Great leaders transmit these values to the rest of the organisation and thus institutionalise leadership itself. This creates a leadership 'culture' which continues indefinitely.

An enduring and universal quality that great leaders possess is innovative and passionate communication. They have an impeccable sense of timing and seem to know exactly how to communicate to get the appropriate level of attention. Communication is more than what is said, it's about how it is said; and this begins at the top of the organisation.

Great leaders are almost fanatical about growing talent and building great teams. They connect with potential leaders on a personal level and spend time – teaching, educating and developing talent. At the same time, great leaders also believe in moving their best people, not hoarding them. They truly believe that if they choose the right people, set the right strategy, provide opportunities, coach, mentor, communicate and set appropriate short-term and long-term stretch goals, the cycle of great leadership can be maintained.

By moving their best people into areas and geographies for which they have little experience, leaders are taking a huge organisational risk. However, almost always, taking risks is less risky than not taking any. Leaders have a very clear sense of the competencies and capabilities that emerging talent needs, and have more clarity around the experiences that are required for success.

By giving these opportunities to emerging talent, taking risks with them and having the faith and the confidence to take these risks, leaders foster reciprocity and solidify a relationship that no incentive or reward scheme can replicate. There is a key difference between an incentive or a reward scheme and the kind of emotional, obligatory responsibility that reciprocal relationships bring. Both are effective and both are necessary in the business environment today. But the latter is more enduring and, in the end, more powerful. Reciprocity instils a strong sense of pride and desire to give something back to the organisation. This is how leadership 'culture' is built.

A Catalytic Agent of Change

An entrepreneur is an important input in the economic development of a country or of regions within the country.

Entrepreneurial competence makes all the difference in the part of the economic growth. In India, state and private entrepreneurship coexist. The small-scale industrial sector and business are left completely to private entrepreneurs. It is, therefore, in this context that an increasingly important role has been assigned to the identification and promotion of entrepreneurs for this sector.

The need for a broad-based entrepreneurial class in India arises from the need to speed up the process of activating the factors of production, leading to higher rate of economic growth, dispersal of economic activities, development of backward and tribal areas, creation of employment opportunities, improvement in the standard of living of the weaker sections of the society and involvement of all sections of the society in the process of growth.

Several factors go into the making of an entrepreneur. Individuals who initiate, establish, maintain and expand new enterprises constitute the entrepreneurial class. The socio-political and economic conditions, the availability for industrial technology and know-how, state-of-the-art and culture of business and trading, existence of markets for products and services and the incentives and facilities available for starting an industry or business, all have a bearing on the growth of entrepreneurship. A conducive environment is created through the policies and interest of the government is in economic and industrial development.

Box 19.4 Welcome the New Entrepreneur

The late 1990s saw educated professionals starting upon their own. The future will stem from that core. A highly educated man or woman, who not only knows how to take risks but takes them at a pace quicker than ever before. A person conversant in global trends and processes, confident of enduring failure. From the peson who raked in the money, the entrepreneur is becoming the champion of knowledge in the institution. The age of the fixit general manager, the overbearing Lala, the chairman in his ivory-tower, is done.

"In the future, entrepreneurism will not be about manipulation of the environment but about the difference in customer service an enterprise can bring about," says Dr. C. Srinivasan, Managing Director, at Kearney Consultants. "A lot of the uniqueness of the offering will be motivated by the individual entrepreneur." It is knowledge that will provide the competitive edge to the organisation. Obviously, managing this resource will be a critical function of the entrepreneur. Being tech-savvy will come naturally. The entrepreneurs may not have to be a deep expert but will have an appreciation of what technology can or cannot do. All this will be possible because financing will not be an entrepreneur's sole concern. The start-up of the future will be a collaborative effort shared with VCs and others. With outsourcing making increasing economic sense, entrepreneurs will increasingly partner suppliers. Getting along with people, the ability to work with others as equals, will be of prime concern to the new entrepreneur in the coming days of growing pluralism in not just business but also in society. Unlike the old days, no entrepreneur of the coming era can harbour hopes of being lord of all that he or she surveys.

It is now well recognised that entrepreneurial business can be developed through appropriately-designed entrepreneurship development programmes. These programmes broadly envisage a three-tiered approach: developing achievement motivation and sharpening of entrepreneurial traits and behaviour, project planning and development and guidance on industrial opportunities, incentives and facilities and rules and regulations, and developing managerial and operational capabilities. Various techniques and approaches have been developed and adopted to achieve these objectives, keep in view the target-groups and/or target-areas.

New Generation of Entrepreneurs

As the economy opens up, it is inevitable that a whole new generation of entrepreneurs should come to the fore. By early next century, those whom we haven't heard of today would have emerged as players to reckon with on the industrial scene.

There are two reasons why this should happen. It is implicit in the very nature of a free market system, which by virtue of competition ensures that the big don't necessarily remain big. There is also the fact that India with its long entrepreneurial history is particularly suited for such competition to evolve. Indeed, Indian entrepreneurs overseas do very well wherever they happen to be. However, in this country rules and laws have tended to curb entrepreneurial ability. While we acknowledge that the government's role must be to ensure that business is conducted in a manner conducive to social good, within the framework of social priorities, enterprise must be allowed to flourish.

The other side of competitive coin is that failure too are inevitable and businesses can collapse. If the failure is because the promoters have siphoned off funds from the company, it is inexcusable. If it is the outcome of competitive forces, we must accept this as the cost we have to pay for a free market.

History has shown that societies which are more open have advanced technologically more rapidly. Political controls and free markets cannot coexist. And the example of Eastern Europe bears testimony to this. Since we have committed ourselves already to the democratic system, we must take steps to encourage the entrepreneurial drive and create an environment conducive to its growth.

An ideal entrepreneur is one who combines values in the market economy; that profits do not somehow preclude ethical behaviour; that growth is possible even if political patronage is not used to vend rules and cut corners, and quite simply that pursuit of wealth can be grateful and mannerly one. He takes with him the interest of his people, his country, his natural resources, the ecology and sees that his enterprise becomes a catalytic agent of development. There is thus a need of true entrepreneurs, who do not for incentives, infrastructure, government support; but build his enterprises, harness the resources and develop. They adopt a responsible value-driven corporate philosophy for their enterprises and/or business activities. As such, there is no dispute among economists and social thinkers about the urgent need for the emergence of an entrepreneurial society as a forerunner of accelerated development of the economy in an integrated manner.

The ethos of entrepreneurial culture runs through the business society in the 21st century. Indeed entrepreneurial culture lays a strong foundation for a well regulated, sustainable and environmentally friendly society.

Box 19.5 New Generation

Aruna Kashinath, Managing Partner, Polaris

Computing on IBM 1401 mainframes, working with punch cards and being content with 60K of memory space, that's the early memories Aruna Kashinath has of working in the IT sector way back in 1978. A masters in statistics from Bombay University, the 47-year-old managing partner of Polaris Software Lab joined the IT industry much before it became a happening sector and she's been a part of several generations of computing. "Curiosity, coupled with a personal belief in making life more efficient brought me into IT, much against my father's advice," she says.

Working initially at ORG Systems, ABC Consultants and JK Straw Products, Kashinath developed the IT infrastructure at these companies and then moved to Polaris in 1991, which was just being set up.

She joined as a systems manager because she was "curious to know how an IT services company can be a viable business model and because there was a lot of hunger and aspiration and a sense of entrepreneurship at the company". Since then she has been an integral part of Polaris and is part of the business leadership team.

In first few years she consolidated the company's business with Citibank and then she was responsible for setting up its development centre at Noida. Later she got busy with the company's forays in the European and the US market. In between she created the Enterprise Information System business for Polaris, which incorporates everything from ERP, CRM and SCM to business intelligence and enterprise portals practice. A managing partner since 2001, Kashinath also heads the retail subsidiary of Polaris and is on the boards of other Polaris subsidiaries.

It's quite believable when she says, "I can't afford the luxury of having time for unwinding and spend almost eighteen hours a day working". Polaris earns 88% of its revenues from the banking sector, but Kashinath's chosen to move out of the mainstream. She now leads the company's initiatives in the non-banking sector and emerging fields. "We need to replicate our success in the banking sector in the new areas where we are getting into," says Kashinath and going by her previous accomplishments, Polaris knows she can do it.

(**Source:** *The Economic Times,* 10 June, 2004.)

Box 19.6 Free Agent Nation

While entrepreneurship and self-employment have been around, Free Agency stems from a new set of new environmental factors: economical, social and cultural circumstances.

In the Free Agent economy, individuals matter more than organisations, because they last a lot longer than organisations.

Secondly, in the knowledge economy, workers own the means of production.

Thirdly, there has been significant shift in the long-term power arrangement between individuals and organisations.

Fourthly, Free Agency is also altering the shape of business. The shift is towards small organisations, wherein transparency and integrity is more.

Fifthly, the best leaders are motivated by their intrinsic sense of doing great things and of changing the world.

Sixthly, technology plays a big role in bringing about change.

Seventhly, the post-information age economy requires greater artistic capabilities, emotional capabilities and more importantly the ability to see the big picture the ability to do things that are novel rather than routine.

Finally, talented individuals are far more powerful than large organisations — and they don't work for them.

— ***Daniel Pink***
Free Agent Nation

(**Source:** *The Economic Times,* 7 May, 2004.)

Box 19.7 Starting Up Isn't Easy

Doing business in India is a pain. Nepal or Bhutan make more sense, reckons the World Bank

Doing business in India continues to be an extremely difficult proposition, contends Simeon Djankov, Manager, Monitoring Analysis and Public Unit at the World Bank. Djankov should know, after all, as the author of the recent World Bank study on *Doing Business in 2005,* he has studied in minute detail the regulatory cost of doing business in as many as 145 countries. The parameters, which among others include entry regulations (cost of starting a business), employment regulations (hiring and firing of workers), property regulations (registering and transfer of property), and bankruptcy regulation (closing of banks), clearly indicate that the business of doing business is still a costly affair.

Take the issue of starting a business, for instance, both in terms of the time required and the cost involved. While it needs just five days to start a business in the US and just two in Australia, in India it takes as many as 89 days. What really hurts is that even in neighbours Pakistan, Nepal and Bangladesh, it takes just 24, 21 and 35 days respectively to start up. The reasons for such delay, as Djankov points out, are simply too many rules and regulations, and too much paperwork.

Starting a business in India is also a costly affair. On an average it would cost an entrepreneur nearly half his total income (or 49.5 per cent of the gross national income per capita), which is 100 times more when compared to setting up a business in the US. Again poorer cousins Bhutan, Pakistan and Sri Lanka are better off.

Even running a business in India can be expensive. Firing costs, calculated in terms of the notice period that has to be given to a worker, are on the higher side. Firms in India have to give an average notice of 79 weeks, compared to eight weeks in the US and virtually no time in New Zealand. While China may be lagging behind India in terms of giving termination notice – 90 days – that does not provide a true picture, says Djankov. "There are a number of other work contracts available in China, which require little or no termination notice," he adds.

But where India lags behind most countries is in the time needed to register property and in the actual cost of registration. In both cases, costs are extremely prohibitive and not for the faint-hearted. For instance, while it takes only one day to register property in Norway, 49 days in Pakistan and 44 days in Bhutan, it takes 67 days to register property in India. And the registration costs too are huge – 13.9 per cent of the total value of the property. It is only 5 per cent in the US, 3.1 per cent in China, 4.2 per cent in Pakistan and 1 per cent in Bhutan. Even in other regulatory issues such as the time required to go through insolvency (10.3 years), and contract enforcement (425 days), India clearly remains a laggard.

So, what should India do to put things in order? "India desperately needs to bring in administrative reforms", contends Djankov. In simple terms it means bringing in a more flexible labour policy, reform the painfully-slow judiciary and drastically cut down red-tapism, to allow much-needed foreign direct investment to flow in.

CONCLUSION

The rapid growth of intrapreneurs owes basically to rapid and diversified growth of enterprise. The main objective is to grow far faster than it is possible, to unleash the core strength – its entrepreneurial spirit – in full force, to face new global competition and to exploit huge new opportunities profitably. Intrapreneurs are generated by totally decentralising the decision-making process, bank-rolling powerful business ideas, working with new generation of entrepreneurs. In the process, entrepreneurial talents are spotted and new ventures are set up on an ongoing basis. By spinning off each individual business as a separate enterprise the intrapreneurial culture is developed for the benefit of industrial growth in the country.

The rapid economic development process depends upon the proper functioning of enterprises, which *inter alia* depends upon entrepreneurship. India has great entrepreneurial and commercial reserves. India could be Asia's greatest economic miracle, if entrepreneurial efforts are given a chance, but it is being crippled by its unscrupulous politicians. This necessitates a proper understanding of the concept at its micro-level. The need of the hour is scientific outlook, structural adjustment and scientific management. Though a comprehensive knowledge of rules, regulations, incentives and procedures is quite essential, the development of innovative, professional management skills in the faculty of planning, budgeting, organisation, marketing research, research and development and training will produce a band of dedicated and innovative entrepreneurs to set up new ventures and make them a success. The need is to create an entrepreneurial climate, sharpen the entrepreneurial skills and stimulate the entrepreneurial spirit for bringing about economic development through new and mature enterprises.

20 CHAPTER

EVOLUTION OF ENTREPRENEURS IN INDIA

"The essence of entreprenership consists in the alertness of market participants to profits opportunities. A typical entrepreneur, according to Kirzer (1979) is the arbitrageur, the person who discovers opportunity at low prices and sells the same items at high prices because of inter-temporal and inter-spatial demands....."

LEARNING OBJECTIVES

The evolution of entrepreneurs in India is the story of the legends as well as the professionals. Entrepreneurial class is getting broad based.

The entrepreneur continues to:

- Inspiring people to play their designated roles is the most effective way to achieve results
- Delegation of responsibility must be accompanied by complete trust if it is to be successful
- Power must be tampered with accountability for individuals to meet organisational goals
- Freedom to take decisions must be backed by a top-down belief in catalysing consensus
- Interpersonal relationships are more useful than organisational systems in cementing deals
- Ideas must be allowed to breakthrough barriers and present themselves to decision-makers

INTRODUCTION

The story of business in India is the history of the business families. They are the proudest institution, symbolising courage, innovation, commonsense, energy and enterprise, aspiration and adventurousness. The seeds of entrepreneurship were sown in the 1860s – when the first Cotton mill came up in Mumbai. Over the years, entrepreneurship multiplied in all direction – manufacturing to service, trade to export, health to care, knowledge to information, technology to bio-technology.

The entrepreneurs have indulged in asset-building, wealth creation and creating mega-empires.

History of Entrepreneurship in India

In the historical past Indian communities consists of four main casts, *viz.,* the Brahmins, the Kshtriyas, the Vaishyas and the Shoodras. The caste groups were rigidly separated on a functional basis. The Brahmins were the learned men assist the Kshtriyas (rulers) in administration and the Shoodras were involved in agricultural occupation. The Vaishya community were engaging in trade and commerce and industrial productive activities. The brief description of entrepreneurship during the past is as follows:

1. The industrial activity was influenced by the caste system.
2. The skill for any enterprise was inherited from ancestors.
3. The trading/merchantile class use to take care of providing forward and backward linkage to craftsmen and skilled artisans.
4. There were no formal organisational units. All family members use to associate themselves in production process of an enterprise.
5. Supply of a product was mainly on the basis of demand for the same. The merchantile class use to help in getting orders from buyer and communicate it to the producer.

The industrial activity consist of small and cottage industries in India received a blow during the British regime. But Trade and Commerce prevalent in India especially in Western parts. There were instances in which the entrepreneurs achieved success in opening the textile mills at Bombay (Coasjee Davar, 1854) and Ahmedabad (Ranchodlal Chotalal, 1861). During 1850-1880, Indian entrepreneurship was extended to textiles, shipping, iron and steel and hydroelectric systems.

Present Scene

Over the last 60 years, India has seen the entrepreneur evolve in different roles. The modern entrepreneurs are wealth creators, communicators, entertainers, etc. The third millennium rightly belongs to Indian entrepreneurs.

Late Shri G.D. Birla (1894-1983)

With liberalisation setting in, it was bound to be sooner, rather than later, that a new business class would emerge. Never could we have predicated that Azim Premji, who inherited a vegetable oil company, could beat traditional industrialists in becoming the richest Indian. And that a school teacher's son, Narayana Murthy, would own the most valued company in the country, Infosys. Such twists of fate, possible only in today's India, were a far cry a decade ago.

Late Shri J.R.D. Tata (1904-1993)

That it has been possible for these transformations to occur is largely on account of the fact that there has been a shift in the way of conducting business over the last 50 years. Using Alvin Toffler's terminology, one of the main aspects of change has been that India has moved from essentially being a primary economy through a secondary phase to a tertiary one. In other words, it has moved from an agricultural economy to an industrial one to a service-driven one. This shift is reflected in the country's GDP figures as well. According to the Statistical Outline of India, 1999-2000, agriculture contributed 55.8 per cent and in 1950-51, industry 15.2 per cent, and services 29 per cent. Today, the figures tell another story – the contribution from agriculture has halved to 25.3 per cent, that from industry has doubled to 30.1 per cent, and the share of services has gone up to 44.6 per cent.

Before 1943, the Indian business scene was completely dominated by British companies. Apart from a few Parsi families, notably the Tatas in steel and the Wadias in shipbuilding, and scattered Gujarati and

Aditya Birla was the first Indian industrialist with a global vision

Bohri Muslim businessmen, Indians had to be content with the crumbs. Manufacturing was closed to all but a handful of Indian business houses with large financial resources and a working relationship with British companies. Trading was the only viable option, with jute and cotton-broking in Calcutta another possible alternative.

In such a bleak scenario, the Birla Jute Mill, which was started in 1919, marked the entry of the Birla family, essentially traders, into industrial manufacturing. More business opportunities surfaced when business opportunities surfaced when World War II ended in 1945. Reconstruction after the war required cement, steel, and other infrastructure industries. However, it was only after independence in 1947 that the Indian industry began to expand in the core sector.

Box 20.1 Leadership Secrets

Entrepreneurial spirit: A leader senses, targets and accomplishes his goals with unswerving faith and resolve. Hurdles on the road to entrepreneurial initiative need to be steadfastly surmounted through self-belief, conviction and a never-say-die attitude.

Innovation: The very quality that makes a team deliver successfully overtime is innovation. A leader realises that the timeless adage 'change is the only constant' holds true throughout the life of an organisation.

Empowerment of people: This is the cornerstone of management thinking at every successful organisation. A good leader encourages his people to participate in decision-making and is open to their ideas and suggestions.

Simplicity: This ensures that the ideas of the leader will reach and be understood by each member of his team. The virtue of simplicity, coupled with assertiveness, determines the effectiveness of a leader.

Quality: Maintaining quality at work is an infallible way of ensuring an organisation's success. Demanding perfection while realising each team-member's limitations is the essence of good leadership.

Risks: Leaders always take risks. They never hesitate to take decisions. The key to success is the ability of a leader to take unambiguous decisions, right or wrong. The need to act and implement practical initiatives quickly should take precedence over intellectual debates.

Contextual: Leadership is contextual. There is no single leadership style that works everywhere. A successful leader adapts his or her style to the organisation and uses it for the company's and employees' benefit. A good leader, therefore, is one who understands the organisation and its employees, creates goals accordingly and executes them effectively.

Success Mantras: Successful leaders have had their success mantras analysed, dissected and, if proven effective, adopted. A lot of effort has been made by experts and researchers to unravel the qualities and secrets of leadership. Others have diligently worked towards emulating them. Nevertheless, good leaders are as rare today as ever.

Commonsense: Success as a leader, therefore, does not come from specialised training or education. It comes from common sense and from the ability to learn from others. Examples of successful leadership are visible in plenty all around us – in different situations, in different social groups, as also in different organisations. The trick is to comprehend the behavioural patterns of these people that lead them to be exceptionally brilliant as leaders.

Ethics: Leadership is built on trust. Leaders need to ensure that their conduct inspires the confidence of the people they lead. They must consistently espouse and act upon their values, standards and principles in their public as well as private lives.

Knowledge: Knowledge helps develop perspective. It also opens up the mind and removes biases. And it is this that helps leaders to see the big picture and develop an agenda that is aligned not only to the present but also to the future.

The ability to listen: Almost everyone can hear. But few really listen, especially when they are at the top. Good leaders need to be patient listeners – they must listen to their colleagues and collaborators, to markets and constituencies, and ultimately, to themselves. This feedback is vital to their staying on course to success.

Decisiveness: Good leaders listen to all but do what they think is best for their companies. Leaders must rely on their intuition while making key decisions.

Communication: Through communication, leaders inform, convince, unite, motivate, and direct their flock. The power to inform and persuade is critical to winning the hearts and minds of employees – something that is essential to leading organisations effectively.

Exemplification: Credibility comes from walking the talk. Stepping back while others take risks simply doesn't work for leaders. They must be where they are expected to be – ahead, in front, leading the charge.

The ability to think differently: For instance, a leader who's able to ask "What can I get out of my team?" instead of a "What does my team want from me?", is the one whose team-members go out of their way to help him realise his vision. The key, therefore, is to think differently and be innovative in one's approach to handling people in an organisation.

Trusting by delegation: Allocating tasks to team-members with complete empowerment earns their trust. Once that is done, a sense of belonging sets in. Delegation is not just about assinging tasks. If team-members believe that the leader trusts them, they go out of their way to do the tasks they are set with greater efficiency. A leader must be liberal in appreciating such extra effort – this goes a long way in acting as a morale-booster for the team-members and, in turn, helps increase the productivity and efficiency of the organisation.

Decision-making: Decisiveness is one of the key traits a leader must possess. Indecision is the biggest risk in business and a leader cannot afford to be fickle-minded.

Faith: Great leaders display unwavering faith in their dreams and remain focused with a strong will to pursue those dreams. They give due credit for success to their coworkers while taking responsibility for failures. Good leaders are also those who remain humble in their disposition because humility allows them to learn even from subordinates who may have a few good lessons to teach.

Finally, as a Chinese proverb goes: "All things come to the person who is modest and kind at a high position." A team will support a leader only if he is modest and kind. A humane leader undisputedly commands more respect from his team than a merely proud one.

In 1947, India had inherited a shrivelled industrial economy after nearly 200 years of British rule. If anything was available, it was shortage. The government's idea was that a rationing of resources might work and hence it adopted socialist policies. Through the 1960s, the Indian government was in the throes of the licence raj, also known as the Industrial Development and Regulation Act, and business houses were hostage to the Monopolies and Restrictive Trade Practices (MRTP) Act. Indira Gandhi's retrograde policies sent the Indian industry into a tailspin for nearly 20 years. There were problems aplenty – licences, red tapes, quotas. Indian business was characterised by high taxes, low productivity, strict licensing and a parallel economy called the black market.

Late Ashok Birla

However, while the world, and particularly the economies of East Asia, spurred themselves on with free market regimes, India sank deeper into socialism. Business houses were prevented from developing global production capacities and vertical expansion by MRTP. A high tax bracket of 99 per cent constrained capital formation. Foreign investment was largely banned and hard currency shortages made even foreign travel a rare luxury. And then there was a long waiting period to obtain approval from the government to set up a new business, with the added risk of the idea being given away to the small-scale sector. Setting up new industries required licences, which were nearly impossible for new entrepreneurs to get. A licence was the first step to a fortune in an economy governed by controlled production, controlled markets and controlled competition. Some of the dominant business groups of the 1960s were Tata, Mafatlal, Sarabhai and Walchand Hirachand.

N.R. Narayana Murthy

The decade beginning 1970 was the most politically turbulent in India's post-independence history. It was during this period that the Foreign Exchange Regulation Act (FERA) and MRTP came into force. In fact, MRTP crippled the nascent attempt of the Indian industry to build plants of global size with large economies of scale. In spite of the odds, G.D. Birla and J.R.D. Tata have gone down in Indian corporate history as the men who created the country's two largest industrial empires, comprising companies such as Grasim, Hindalco, Tata Steel and Telco. This period also witnessed the emergence of a new entrepreneur class – those who started their business with small-scale licences and grew to become large corporates. Karsanbhai Patel and his soap manufacturing company Nirma would be worth a mention. Hence, though growth did occur it was rather slow as all industries were asset-based, the main inputs coming from raw materials, finance and asset-creation.

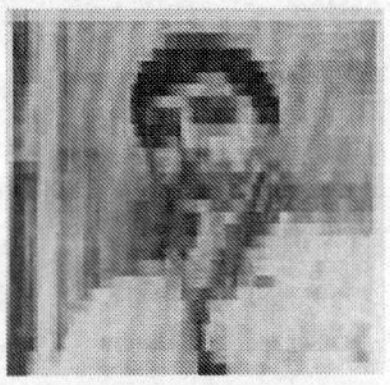

Sabeer Bhatia

It was only in the 1980s that things began to change. The new leaders began to forge a *laissez-faire* economic policy. But four decades of Nehruvian socialism had built a steel grid of bureaucratic control over the private sector that could hardly be dismantled overnight. But the seeds were planted by him in two things; he wanted to modernise India and he introduced computerisation in the public sector, irrespective of whether the computers were being used or not.

Azim Premji

Raising finance was essential. The two main areas that were available for financing were the capital market and savings. With a high tax bracket, starting a business from savings was essentially ruled out. Government financial institutions, banks and mutual funds on an average held 35-40 per cent of the equity of blue chip companies. Dhirubhai Ambani and Aditya Birla realised the importance of raising money from the public. In 1977, Reliance had its first IPO. In 1990, Hindalco was the first company to raise capital at a premium of ₹ 100 per share in the domestic market.

Emergence of New Breed of Entrepreneurs

Sabeer Bhati

Finance Minister V.P. Singh's 1985 budget was a benchmark for economic liberalisation. Manmohan Singh's sweeping reforms in 1991 budget was the precursor. Till the latter's 1991 budget, there was still too much government involvement in business activities. Foreign equity participation was still limited to 40 per cent. The system of seeking permits and licences had to be discontinued if India wanted to integrate with the global economy. However, globalisation and privatisation appeared on the government's agenda only in 1992.

Economic liberalisation was a mixed blessing for most big Indian business houses. It was between 1991 and 1995 that the Indian economy entered a new orbit of high growth. Liberalisation kick-started the stock market, drew foreign investment, all but abolished industrial investment, and gave groups like Tata, Birla and Reliance more room to grow. With Indian companies allowed to tap foreign equity and debt funds, Grasim floated a $90-million global depository receipt issue in late 1992. It became the second Indian company to do so after Reliance Industries. Hindalco followed shortly after with a $110-million Euro issue. With foreign direct investment pouring in, Indian companies without deep pockets were vulnerable. The takeover of Parle by Coca-Cola was the first warning signal that a market economy could cut both ways.

The second aspect of change is that today there are many avenues of finance that are available to the entrepreneur. It is not just the family unit that is used to raise funds. Now even someone with a bunch of ideas can get funding. With institutions such as HDFC and ICICI having had a change of heart towards financing by 1997, it was possible for the professional to look towards entrepreneurship. Ashoka Wadhwa left his secure job with Arthur Andersen to set up his own outfit, *Ambit*.

Sabeer Bhatia

With the consumer today dictating terms, the change that we are seeing today is taking place a lot faster. The move is quite obvious away from asset-based towards knowledge-based industries.

AN ANALYTICAL PERSPECTIVE

India's business system has, almost unnoticed, undergone a virtual transformation since independence. This is not so much due to the evolution of the country's public sector, which was almost non-existent in 1947, as it is because of the convulsions in the private sector itself. Perhaps the most conspicuous feature of India's business life on the eve of independence was the predominance of a handful of business families. R.K. Hazari, the economist, estimated that most of the manufacturing companies in 1947 were controlled by just 18 Indian families – and two British business houses. Between them, they manufactured, practically, all the industrial products that India then made, and they were all involved in our international trade too.

Technically, these business houses did not own the companies that constituted their empires, but, for all practical purposes, the companies belonged to them. These families were able to exercise control over their companies because of the managing agency system. While the family was the pivot around which the system revolved, the *modus operandi* was simple. When a family with adequate financial strength and business standing decided to enter a business, it would do two things simultaneously. One, it would declare itself to be a managing agency; usually, a partnership of family members. Two, it would allot to the members of the family, and their relatives, a large enough number of shares such that they could control the nascent concern.

The Family and the Agency System

Although the new company would be an independent corporate entity under the Indian Companies Act, with the promoting family having a controlling stake in it, it was a mere formality for its shareholders to entrust the task – through a formal resolution at their very first meeting – of managing it to the managing agency.

The big four: *J.N. Tata and his three partners, his sons Ratan and Dorab (seated) and his own cousin 'RD', father of JRD Tata*

Moreover, the terms and conditions under which this would be done would be so wide-ranging that, in effect, it would mean the complete surrender of the rights and responsibilities for critical decisions and strategic actions to the managing agents. Even though the company would have a board of directors, its members, hand-picked by the managing agents, would be no more than a decorative facade. Corporate management at the time of independence was, thus, a strange combination of family control and joint stock companies.

Born along with the processes of industrialisation around the mid-19th century, the managing agency system became firmly entrenched in this country because of two factors. First, the sources of finance in pre-independence India were limited to a few families which had accumulated capital through their trading operations. Secondly, the system was eminently consistent with the joint family system, which has remained a feature of our social structure over the decades. Since the head of the promoting family of a joint stock company was, usually, also the head of the managing agency, the system entailed little, or no threat to his authority.

In that sense, the structure of business management was coterminous with the structure of family management in this country. That India did not have an investor class, and stock market operations were yet to gather sufficient momentum only provided reinforcement to the managing agency system of family control. However, the system was open to abuse, and most of the managing agents did misuse their privileges, providing fodder for sharp, and persistent, attacks on this form of management for more than half a century before independence. But it survived because of the social and economic realities of the Indian situation. Of course, the clamour became increasingly virulent as India's destiny passed into her own hands.

The Family and the Financial Institution

Destined for greatness: ***Young Birla with his father Aditya Vikram, great-grandfather G.D.Birla, and grandfather B.K.Birla***

INDIA'S TOP 25 BUSINESS FAMILIES

GROUP 2001 TOP 25 GROUPS—2001	2001 SALES T/O	2001 NET PROFIT
RELIANCE GROUP [AMBANI]	59,592.35	4,222.79
TATA GROUP	30,200.08	1,091.57
ADITYA BIRLA GROUP	16,905.91	1,306.35
B.K. BIRLA GROUP	5,389.87	123.55
THAPAR GROUP*	5,331.29	-406.87
BAJAJ GROUP	5,273.74	223.68
MAHINDRA & MAHINDRA GROUP	4,966.03	204.92
OM PRAKASH JINDAL GROUP	4,489.61	162.72
HINDUJA (ASHOK LEYLAND) GROUP	4,107.16	196.04
HERO (MUNJALS) GROUP	3,898.72	254.33
C.K. BIRLA GROUP	3,412.66	-24.44
ESSAR (RUIA) GROUP	3,405.53	-261.63
ISPAT (MITTALS) GROUP	3,382.36	-521.25
RPG ENTERPRISES GROUP	3,336.98	-135.26
CHIDAMBARAM M.A. GROUP	3,295.02	106.09
VIDEOCON GROUP	3,244.05	154.52
TVS IYENGAR GROUP	3,213.5	132.68
WIPRO GROUP	3,135.54	657.42
GODREJ GROUP	3,125.3	34.66
LALBHAI GROUP	2,909.24	-295.76
MURUGAPPA CHETTIAR GROUP	2,799.92	94.44
RUCHI GROOUP	2,727.92	20.25
WADIA (BOMBAY DYEING) GROUP	2,654.69	43.18
NIRMA GROUP	2,429.22	249.71
HARI SHANKAR SINGHANIA GROUP	2,266.86	-19.03

Source: CMIE Figures in ₹ Crore
This listing takes into account the sales turnover of listed companies only
* The Thapar have now split into four factions : IM. BM. LM and MM Thapar, but the data has not divided the turnovers accordingly.

Yet, the (New) Government of India chose to impose only cosmetic restrictions on managing agents and, by implication, on family control over the nation's business when the Indian Companies Act was amended in 1956. For, the government was acutely aware that the ground realities that continued to provide nourishment to family business would take time to change. Instead of submitting to the liberal rhetoric that sought the immediate abolition of the managing agency system, it therefore left the arrangement, more or less, undisturbed for, eventually, 15 more years. If the government had hoped that, during the interregnum, the situation would change to the extent that it would render painless the demise of the system, its thesis was borne out by events. Eventually, the managing agency system did die unwept, unsung, and unnoticed on April 1, 1970, yielding to a new system and provided for a functional chairman-cum-managing director and a board of directors as the decision-makers in a company.

Initially, it appeared that the change was merely one form as the erstwhile managing agents quickly embraced new designations.

Gradually, however, it became clear that the end of the system would have a profound impact on not only the structure of the corporate sector, but also its composition. In fact, the smoothness of the transition to the new system was not due to legal reasons alone; it was also a reflection of a new set of social and economic forces that the business family would have to contend with. Perhaps the most important change was the nation's resolve to accelerate the pace of economic development as reflected by the Five Year Plans. In most cases, the nature of the projects that the private sector was expected to implement to accomplish the Plans' objective was such that no business family could finance them on its own. With the passage of time, the family as a source of industrial finance ceased to be as indispensable as it had been before independence. In the meantime, new sources of industrial finance emerged, most of which were under government control, on which the business families had no choice but to depend. And, in most cases, their dependence was so great that, in effect, the financial institutions and not the business families themselves – ended up acquiring a controlling interest in companies.

Family Controlled Business – Birla Group

C.K. Birla Group
Hindustan Motors,
Orient Paper & Industries,
Hyderabad Industries,
National Engineering
Industries

B.K. Birla Group
Century Textiles & Industries,
Century Enka,
Manjushree Plantations,
ECE
Kesoram Industries,
Akzo Nobel Chemicals

M.P. Birla Group

Vindhya Telelinks
Birla Ericsson Optical
Universal Cables
Birla Corporation
Indian Smelting & Refining Company

K.K. Birla Group

Zuari Industries
Chambal Fertilisers & Chemicals
Texmaco
The Hindustan Times
Upper Ganges Sugar & Industries
Oudh Sugar Mills
New India Sugar Mills
Gobind Sugar Mills
Sutlej Industries
Indian Steamship Company

Aditya Birla Group

Grasim Industries
Indian Rayon
Hindalco
Indo Gulf
Birla Global Finance
HGI Ind. & Essel Mining
Tanfac Industries
Indal
PSI Data Systems
Bihar Caustic
Idea Cellular
Birla Sunlife Group

S.K. Birla Group

Birla VXL
Mysore Cements
Saurashtra Chemicals
XPRO India
Cimmco Birla

Yash Birla Group

Zenith
Birla Yamaha
Dagger Forst Tools
Birla Perucchini
Birla Kennamental
Birla Transasia Carpets
Birla 3M

As family-owned businesses increase in size, their requirements increase too. Business groups, like the Tatas, the R.P. Goenka Group, and the Mahindra Group, for instance, have exhibited five years average sales growth-rates of 19 per cent, 17 per cent, and 21 per cent, respectively. They will, therefore, require a larger number of professional managers, a more robust organisational structure, better-defined policies and practices, more capital, and heightened visibility. In short, they will have to rethink the way they conduct their business.

THE EMERGING MODELS

Having attained maturity in the pre-liberalisation era, family-owned businesses are, often, centred around the vision and style of the founder. Many of these leaders end to be authoritarian and control-oriented, viewing the business as an extension of themselves, and their families, rather than as an independent entity. The leader makes most of the decisions, especially when it comes to portfolio management. And these decisions are made with inputs only from members of the family or a small number of trusted managers – or even just gut-feel.

Some Observations

The term 'entrepreneur' has now been attributed to all small industries, small business, traders and industrialists. All people who are gainfully engaged in work – manufacturing, distribution or service and other sectors – are called entrepreneurs. Again, even the founder, creator and risk-taker are called entrepreneurs. Each of these terms focus on some aspects of some entrepreneurs. They have some attributes, but they are not entrepreneurs in the strict sense. Many successful people have been good at copying and/or imitating others. For example, the first commercial production of two-wheelers is to be called an effort of the entrepreneur, who has visualised the importance in modern times for the benefit of the maximum risk taken in manufacturing, marketing, etc. And all subsequent scores of people engaged in manufacturing, distribution, financing, etc., are just imitators. Likewise, a brothelkeeper or a call girl business organiser cannot be an entrepreneur, though he takes risks, creates a market and get a reward more than visualised. So also, a bootlegger, drug peddler, black marketeer, etc. These occupations are not for the social good. They violate business ethics. The term 'entrepreneur' is to be understood in its totality and not in fabricated manner. Innovation precedes the entrepreneur and runs parallel with entrepreneurship. The term 'entrepreneur' can only be understood with a bearing on economic, psychological, sociological and cultural bearings. The social responsibility is essentially a part of entrepreneurial outlook on life.

Box 20.2 Knowledge – The Real Wealth of Nations

The turn of the millennium will be the first globally shared moment in history. The onset of the 21st century and the third millennium will see the end of the era of standalone computers. The transition from computations to connections connecting all to all — humans, bots, objects and machines, is expected to gather pace.

The millennium difference will probably be best reflected in the inverted pricing and the law of plentitude associated with a network economy that flies in the face of received economic theory.

The domination matter is of mind over giving way to intellectual empowerment through informations. The 'find, nurture, destroy' syndrome is expected to result in well calibrated technological breakthroughs that are regular, systematic and exponential, ensuring that inverted pricing has come to stay and that it is embedded in billions of objects, the expanding communications network will make sure that audio communication would soon be drowned by digital communication, when each of these billions of chips communicate with some other chips. It would be one delightfully chirpy world. And, when this happens, as it will, sooner than later, we would be totally integrated into a Network Economy.

Clearly, the new millennium seems to belong to those endowed with skills in multiple disciplines and cross specialisations, and capable of responding to the information network. The products of such knowledge workers would nowhere be better reflected than in the structuring of economic organisations.

The corporations of the future will be dominated by ideas. Enterprises will increasingly give way to intelprises (intellectual+enterprises), and intelpreneurs (intelligence+entrepreneurs) will take a march over other entrepreneurs. These new leaders would naturally prefer the intelplace (intelligence+marketplace) to the current marketplace. And, internet is the domain of interaction for the intelprises.

They will not seek to optimise. Instead, they will be hardwired to innovate and measure their performance thereof. They will not seek to perfect the known. Instead, they will seek to create wealth by imperfectly seeking the unknown.

The knowledge workers and intelligent corporations will perceive in networking an opportunity to create new organisations, redesign business processes, and develop dynamic structures resembling biological growth in technological systems.

Knowledge workers-managers, executives, entrepreneurs will make a departure from the existing norms and structure their strategic visioning and planning processes around a learning and performance framework, rather than just a product/ performance only framework. The choice for him/her would not be how to do the job right, but what would be the right job to do.

Concomitantly, the greatest challenge in the new millennium for economies, businesses and humans alike will be skill formation. Successful workers of a networked world must possess a good deal of formal education and the ability to acquire and to apply theoretical and analytical knowledge. The mind-set of a knowledge worker is the habit of continuous learning. Facilitation of continuous knowledge tools would be the greatest need.

As Peter F. Drucker says, "the productivity of knowledge work still abysmally low will become the economic challenge of the knowledge society. On it will depend the competitive position of every single country, every single industry, every single institution within society...Learning will become the tool of the individual – available to him or her at any age – if only because so much skill and knowledge can be acquired by means of the new learning technologies".

The state-of-the-future of economies/corporations would hinge on its intangible, intellectual competence; not on its ability to learn, but its ability to apply learning efficiently and effectively.

A lesson at the fag end of the millennium that all economies/corporations will do well to learn/remember is that non-linear, explosive growth is possible only when an economy/corporation focuses upon knowledge, not technology, innovation, not solutions, value-systems, not value chains, customer success, not satisfaction, and collaboration, not competition.

Effective knowledge management and expeditious knowledge deployment have the potential of creating distinctive competencies, unique market positioning and sustianed growth. It would be difficult to replicate success strategies such as these since the benefits of a network economy invariably are garnered by the first entrants.

(**Source:** *The Economic Times*)

A Classic Example

Since the dawn of civilisation, there have appeared, at periodic intervals, men who have led mankind, shaping the future out of the lessons of the past and the experiences of the present. This involves visionaries, builders, thinkers and scientists, men who saw ahead of their times and whose prescience benefitted not only the country of their birth, but all mankind. In this illustratious company of uncommon people, a special place is occupied by an Indian who was born one hundred and fifty years ago – Jamshetji Nusserwanji Tata. His inspired vision of modern industrialised India was to sustain economic growth to support freedom. To breathe life into his dream, he set about to create steel, electric power and scientific-cum-technical education – the vital ingredients of economic growth. Today, the Tatas cover a bright landscape in Indian economy. To this day, Jamshetji Tata's industrial philosophy, including his firm belief in the principle of trusteeship, his insistence on absolute standards of integrity and realisation that to survive and prosper, free enterprise must serve the needs of society, these were all remarkably in tune with modern thinking and the ethical and social standards of the most advanced societies of today.

Jamshetji Tata, Jamnalal Bajaj, Laxamanrao Kirloskar and Ghanshyamdas Birla are some of the entrepreneurs in their truest sense.

Entrepreneurship is not just a way to increase the level of innovation and productivity of organisations, although it will do that. More importantly, it is a way of organising vast business so that work becomes a joyful expression of ones' contribution to society.

The concept of entrepreneur and entrepreneurship incorporates basic qualities of leadership, innovation, enterprise, hardwork, vision and maximisation of profits. He is an able motivator and brings in change for the betterment of the society. All his socio-economic, organisational and managerial qualities are always directed towards the well-being of the society/community. He is committed to progress. He is a catalytic agent of development and change. Personal satisfaction and monetary rewards are blended with social betterment and welfare of mankind.

The concepts of entrepreneur and entrepreneurship have been investigated from economic, social, political, cultural and managerial points.

CONCLUSION

The process of restructuring of economy and the society must give a visible evidence. The society in a country or in a locality must show readiness to shed inertia and pulsate with new vigour and urge. Self-reliance, enterprise, innovation and attitudinal change are the attributes of a development-oriented society. These propensities need cultivation, if economic growth is to become a reality. Basically the task is to change the stratified socio-economic structure in the underdeveloped regions. This can only be achieved if a change is brought about in social attitude and behaviour. A developmental mind has to be cultivated in the society of the underdeveloped areas, shedding lethargy, apathy and traditional psychology. Further, a new industrial culture has to emerge in the backward regions, reflecting the urge and willingness to observe the industrial disciplines and readiness to seek self-employment and gainful employment opportunities.

Business families have diversified and moved with the times. In the process, they have given rise to the healthy growth of professional managers and entrepreneurs.

A number of entrepreneurial managers have attempted to identify the true nature of entrepreneur, entrepreneurship in the post-industrial revolution. The definition has, therefore, undergone changes with the changes in the socio-economic environment and will continue to undergo changes with the changing times. However, some basis concepts of innovation, risk taking, vision and organising skills continue to be the four pillars on which the edifice of entrepreneurial concept has to be perceived from time-to-time.

An ideal entrepreneur is one who combines values in the market economy that profits do not somehow preclude ethical behaviour, that growth is possible even if political patronage is not used to bend rules and cut corners, and quite simply that pursuit of wealth can be grateful and mannerly. As such, there is no dispute among thinkers about the emergence of an entrepreneurial society as a forerunner to all round development in an integrated manner.

To succeed, you need continuous innovation. And to have continuous innovation, you need to tap the thinking of every one in your organisation. To win today is not the same thing as winning tomorrow. The leader of tomorrow must ensure that everyone in his organisation is heard.

Leadership is understood in terms of three set of skills – identify, build and drive. Leaders should be able to identify opportunities and threats.

What leaders should understand now is to identify real opportunities, where the real innovations are talking place. One of the things I talk about here is social product development because the idea of connecting people now, finding out what people's talents are and what they can contribute, is the way forward in terms of leadership characteristics. They should form the use of communities. Again, it's not only enough to see an opportunity, but leaders, should be able to build the infrastructure, and talent that's required to take advantage of that opportunity.

— ***Barry F. Cohen***

ANNEXURE-I

Lessons from a Winner

Azim Premji, chairman and managing director, Wipro outlines the lessons he has learnt along the way in building an Indian institution which is to be second to none in the world. – I hope you will find them useful.

The first lesson is you must always have the courage to think big. A vision that is beyond what seems to be achievable has a tremendous capacity to ignite the collective imagination and passion of your team. It must not be an impossible dream and one must be prepared to work for it with a single-minded dedication. If the vision is powerful enough, it enables you to tap inner strengths, resources and potential that you didn't know existed. It can create enthusiasm that is contagious to those working with you and build the resilience to take risks.

As someone said, ships are safe in the harbour. But that is not what they were designed for. A vision cannot be safe. Strategies must derisk it.

Second, you must never compromise on fundamental value, no matter what the situation is. It not only leads to success, but also makes success worthwhile. The only way to create an organisation based on values is to demonstrate them transparently and walk the talk. All actions with integrity can stand public scrutiny.

Third, you must build tremendous self-confidence. It is needed most when things do not look very bright. But if you are convinced you are right, then go ahead and do what you set out to do. Ignore any pessimists you may meet along the way. To my mind, self-confidence is absolutely fundamental to success. If you don't have confidence in yourself, there is no way that you can expect your employees, your customers and your investors to have confidence in you.

Fourth, you must surround yourself with the best of people. Even if you have the acknowledge that some of them may be better than you. An organisation doesn't really accomplish anything. Plans do not accomplish anything. Organisations succeed or fail because of the people involved. Look for people who have the capacity to anticipate and see around corners. Also look for people with loyalty, integrity, a high-energy drive, emotional maturity and an overpowering desire to get things done.

Fifth, you must have an obsessive commitment to quality. Customers want more quality for less cost. That is an absolute global truth. One of the greatest contributions of globalisation has been demand for higher quality. Quality is an absolute prerequisite for survival, leave alone success. Like integrity, there can be no compromise in quality.

Sixth, you must play to win. Too long, we have suffered from an ideological hangover, which made people feel a little guilty about making profits or succeeding. Playing to win is one of the finest thing you can do. Playing to win stretches you and everyone around you. It gives you a new sense of direction and energy. Playing to win does not mean playing dirty. If you cut corners along the way, you will miss out on the personal satisfaction of winning. Because, winning means reaching the depth of your own potential and utilising it to its fullest. Ultimately, your only competition is yourself.

Lastly, the most important facilitator of success is the blessing of a force beyond us. We can call it luck, we can call it God. As a non-religious person, I attribute most of my success to the "Force beyond me". Let me illustrate this with a touching story.

One night, a man had a dream. He dreamt he was walking along the beach with the Lord. Across the sky flashed scenes from his life. For each scene, he saw two sets of footprints in the sand, one belonging to him and the other to the Lord. When the last scene flashed before him, he looked back at the footprints in the sand. He found that many times along the path of his life there was only one set of footprints. He also noted that it happened at the most difficult and saddest times in his life. This really disturbed him and he questioned the Lord thus: "Lord, you said that once I decided to follow you, you would walk with me all the way. But I have noticed that during the most troublesome times in my life, there is only one set of footprints. I don't understand why when I needed you the most, you would leave me." The Lord smiled and gently replied, "My precious, precious child, I love you and I would never leave you. During your times of trial and suffering, when you see only one set of footprints, I carried you in my arms."

ANNEXURE-II

Of Wealth and Legacy

Immortality can be bought; Alfred Nobel used his 'WILL' to do it. What would Bill Gates do? Would the world the world's richest man use his 'will and final testament' as the ultimate software tool to empower the human individual? Would his claim to global leadership, eventually, be less about the man-machine interface, and more about the mind he devotes to his legacy?

Gates' is a mind that has given him $46.6 billion (over ₹ 2 lakh crore) in just a quarter of a century. He owns about a tenth of Microsoft. He has three children, Jennifer, Rory and Phoebe – and he intends leaving them $10 million (₹ 45 crore) each in his will. About 0.02 per cent, each "I don't think it would be very useful for my children if they learn about life having so much money," Gates is on record as saying.

The man also hopes to give away most of his wealth during his own lifetime, to make the world 'measurably healthier'. Here's businessman, you'd think, who consider his own do-good efforts more effective than anything 'the people' can undertake. But in 2001, Gates intervened with a resounding 'No!' in the debate ragging in the US over whether 'estate tax' by which the government takes more than half a wealthy person's wealth upon demise should be abolished. Pay the country back, he urged, for enabling your wealth.

"A hypothetical case may illustrate what I mean: suppose two foetuses are summoned to appear before God, and he tells them that they are the next two birth on Earth and will go – one to Ethiopia and other one to the US. He goes on to say that his treasury is running a bit low, and he wants them to help replenish it, so he is going to auction off the opportunity to be born in the US. He asks each of them to write down and hand him a sheet on which they setforth the per cent of the net worth they will have when they die which they will commit to bequeath to God's treasury. He promises that the one who writes down the highest number will be born in the US. Would either of them put down a number as low as 55 per cent?"

A cleverly reasoned argument. But of obvious US-conception, ironically. In poor countries, giving children a headstart is needed just to give them a global 'equal start'. So, will Gates' notions of a good legacy win a global following? It's still open to debate. Hypothetically, it would take something that can resound with true intellectual power for long after he's gone.

21 CHAPTER

CHARACTERISTICS OF ENTREPRENEURS

The Mark of a Leader

"No matter what the external climate, corporate leaders must be able to find creative ways to restructure their businesses to accommodate new realities while continuing to motivate and energise their people and inspire innovative thinking. They should also have the ability to scan the environment for future opportunities and quickly learn from what they see."

— Ned Barnholt, Agilent Technologies Chief

LEARNING OBJECTIVES

"The challenge today is to sustain continuity. How you manage your people is critical for that"

B.K. Modi
Chairman, Modi Xerox

The principle objective is to dwell on the unique characteristics of entrepreneurs – small and big, men and women and a host of others.

The chapter dwells on:

- Characteristics of successful entrepreneurs.
- Entrepreneurial Initiative.
- Motivation.
- What makes an entrepreneur?
- Qualities of an entrepreneur.
- Entrepreneurial skills.
- Need for skills.

The success of an enterprise entirely depends on the entrepreneurial characters.

INTRODUCTION

An entrepreneur who has a high level of administrative capability, flair and ability for decision-making, computational skill, delegation skill, organisational skill, good at communication and has a sound technical knowledge stands a much better chance of success than his counterpart who possesses none or a low level of these basic qualities. It is the possession of these scarce qualities which confers an advantage on some people in becoming an entrepreneur. Besides these qualities, however, the entrepreneur also needs either to be himself a generalist so that he can discharge his function without delegation, or to process delegation and organisational skills.

The entrepreneurial qualities are to some extent innate. But not all of them are entirely innate. Some can be enhanced by training, or simply by experience. For example, analytical ability and computational skills can be enhanced by education at school and university, while practical knowledge and foresight skills can be enhanced by the general experience of everyday life. Entrepreneurial careers will be strongly influenced by the desire to enhance qualities which are scarce, yet difficult to obtain through delegation because of the problems involved in screening for them. Of the two indispensable qualities of the entrepreneur, imagination is almost entirely innate, while foresight, though to some extent innate, can be enhanced by a varied experience. Imagination and foresight are the scarce qualities which are difficult to analyse and quantify. Delegation skill and organisation skill, though to some extent innate, can be enhanced by a varied experience. Imagination and foresight are the scarce qualities which are difficult to analyse and quantify. Delegation skill and organisation skill, though not essential, are highly desirable whenever large-scale decision-making is contemplated. These too are qualities which can be enhanced through experience.

Box 21.1 How to be a Great Manager

Management consultant Peter Stark suggested the following if you want to make it to the top in management:

- Develop positive vision. See success before it arrives. Example: Successful managers – when visualising themselves walking across a high wire – see themselves walking to the other side. Managers who struggle usually have their focus on not falling off the rope.
- Think big. Look for ideas that will be contagious and excite people.
- Encourage others to do their best. Successful managers believe that people do want to make a significant contribution. Coach, counsel and develop people to live up to their potential.
- Set and maintain high expectations for all who work with you. Mediocrity does not generate a highly motivated work force.
- Overuse polite phrases. Unsuccessful managers don't seem to find the time to say "please" and "thank you".

(**Source:** The Manager's Advisor, Peter Barron Stark & Associates. (Communication Briefinas))

Characteristics of Entrepreneurs

The characteristics of an entrepreneur that contribute to success are the result of his achievement motivation. The characteristics of achievement motivated persons as identified by McClelland have been discussed in the chapter on "Future of Entrepreneurship in India". A successful entrepreneur must be a person with technical competence, initiative, good judgement, intelligence, leadership qualities, self-confidence, energy, attitude, creativeness, fairness, honesty, tactfulness and emotional stability.

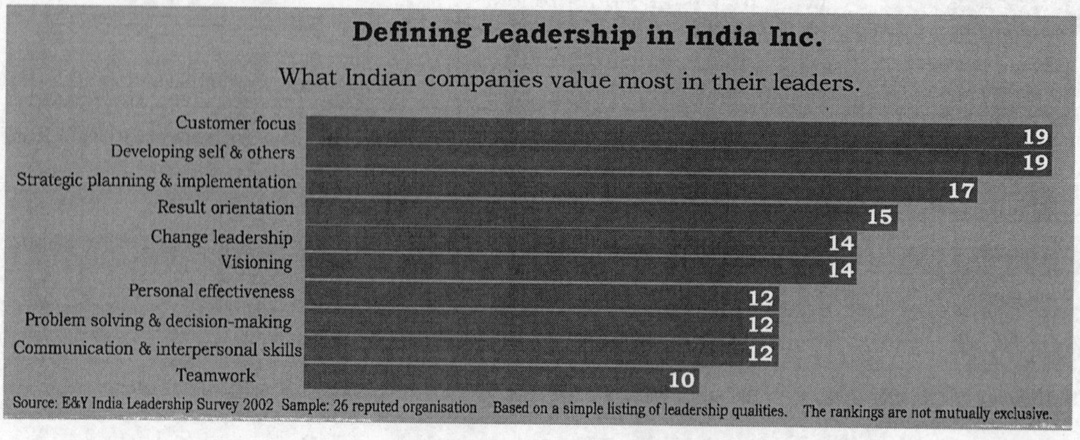

1. *Mental ability:* Mental ability consists of intelligence and creative thinking. An entrepreneur must be reasonably intelligent, and should have creative thinking and must be able to engage in the analysis of various problems and situations in order to deal with them. The entrepreneur should anticipate changes and must be able to study the various situations under which decisions have to be made.
2. *Clear objectives:* An entrepreneur should have a clear objective as to the exact nature of the business, the nature of the goods to be produced and subsidiary activities to be undertaken. A successful entrepreneur may have the objective to establish the product, to make profit or to render social service.
3. *Business secrecy:* An entrepreneur must be able to guard business secrets. Leakage of business secrets to trade competitions is a serious matter which should be carefully guarded against by an entrepreneur. An entrepreneur should be able to make a proper selection of his assistants.
4. *Human relation ability:* The most important personality factors contributing to the success of an entrepreneur are emotional stability, personal relations, consideration and tactfulness. An entrepreneur must maintain good relation with his customers if he is to establish relations that will encourage them to continue to patronise his business. He must also maintain good relations with his employees if he is to motivate them to perform their jobs at a high level of efficiency. An entrepreneur who maintains good relations with customers, employees, suppliers, creditors and the community is much more likely to succeed in his business than the individual who does not invest in maintaining these relations.
5. *Communication ability:* This ability pertains to communicate effectively. Good communication also means that both the sender and the receiver understand each other and are being understood. An entrepreneur who can effectively communicate with customers, employees, suppliers and creditors will be more likely to succeed than the entrepreneur who does not.
6. *Technical knowledge:* An entrepreneur must have a reasonable level of technical knowledge. This is the one ability that most people are able to acquire if they try hard enough.

An entrepreneur who has a high level of administrative ability, mental ability, human relations ability, communication ability and technical knowledge stands a much better chance of success than his counterpart who possesses low levels of these basic qualities. Brilliant men with first class degrees from university hesitate becoming entrepreneurs because the one thing they cannot be taught is coping with human emotions.

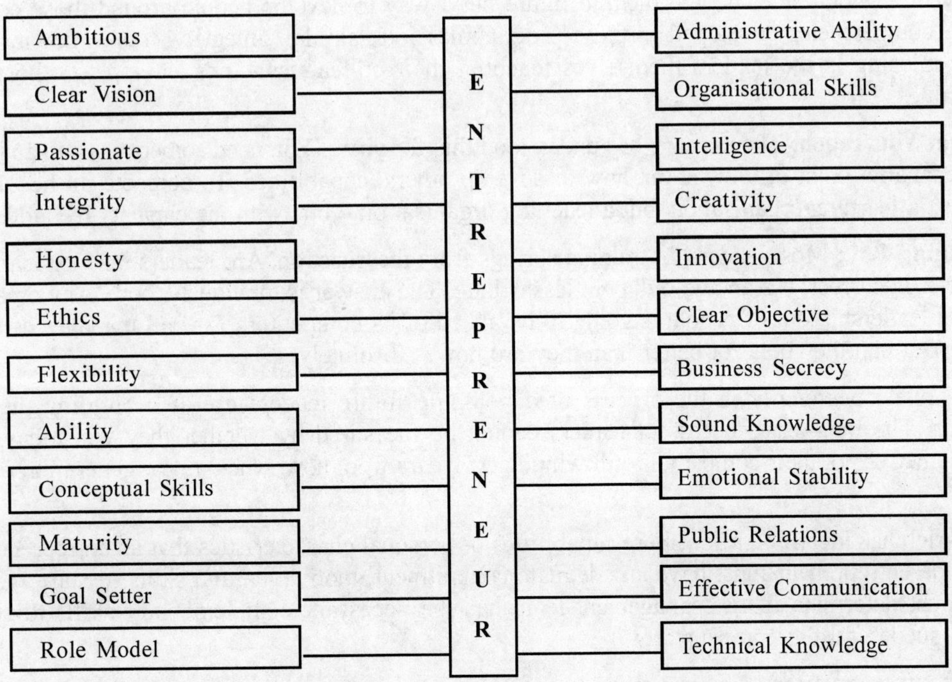

Fig. 21.1 Characteristics of an Entrepreneur

The Mark of a Leader

What separates winning organisations from the also-rans? Winning organisations share certain financial attributes. Companies consistently ranked in the top quartile of the S&P 500 maintain annual revenue growth of 12 per cent and 16 per cent operating returns on assets. Gains achieved by simply slashing payroll and expenses are seldom sustained in the long-run. Likewise, erstwhile winners who fail to keep pace with change, and thereby destroy billions of dollars in shareholder value, are severely punished.

Companies such as General Electric, Allied Signal, PepsiCo, Intel, and others are led by people who personally and methodically nurture the development of other leaders at all levels of the organisation. Even if you, as a leader, are smart enough to anticipate and prepare for massive economic and social shifts, you cannot response to the ground-level demands of the moment without the energy, commitment, and ability of people throughout the organisation. Effective leaders recognise that the ultimate test of leadership is sustained success, which demands the constant cultivation of future leaders.

Three Keys for Leading: The ability to develop the leadership of others needs 3 things: a teachable point of view, a story for your organisation, and a well-defined teaching methodology.

To succeed as a leader, you must be able to talk clearly and convincingly about who you are, why you exist, and how you operate. This means you need to have ideas on proucts, services, distribution channels, customers and growth. But you also need something I call e^3: emotional, energy and edge. Winning leaders seem naturally to generate positive emotional energy in others. They also have the edge to face reality, and take tough decisions. All 3 components of leadership – good ideas, appropriate values, and positive energy and edge – are part of the package you resent to those you hope to develop. How you apply these essential elements of leadership has changed in important ways in recent years.

The basic cognitive form in which people organise their thinking is the narrative story. There are 3 kind of stories that leaders can tell. There's the "who I am" story, in which leaders describe themselves. There's the "who we are" story, in which you articulate for your constituents what their identity is. But the most important leadership tale is the "where we are going" story. To be a great teacher, you have to be a great learner. Most effective teachers and leaders will tell you that they grow as much as those they teach and lead. The process of teaching can be quite simple; it starts with having a conscious system for interacting with people.

Learning to Teach: The current conventional wisdom in leadership – development programmes is to develop a set of competencies for what a good leader is, and then, to figure out a way to develop people around those competencies. At the end of the day, the competencies developed in these programmes look similar: integrity, trust, knowing how to overcome resistance. What's missing is the leaders themselves teaching their colleagues – not leaving to others, or talking about somebody else's values.

Practice What You Teach: The military has understood this for years. You need someone who has hands-on expertise, credibility, and a teachable point of view about how to develop others' capabilities. To compete in the 21st century, leaders need to build not just a learning organisation, but a teaching organisation – one with the capacity to build leaders.

Making Training Pay: Most leadership training springs from the question. Are leaders born or made? and is designed to prove that the latter is correct. It's an age-old, pointless debate. The answer is, obviously, both. Any organisation that takes the time to get more leadership out of people is going to be ahead of its competitors. Are all manager candidates for the top job? Of course not. But can they be a lot better than they are now? Absolutely.

Leaders who invest personally in the process of developing future leaders are also building the most precious of organisational assets. The long-term success of leaders cannot be measured by whether they win today or tomorrow. The measure will be whether or not their company is still winning 15 years from now, when a new generation of leaders has taken over.

— Noel Tichy

Robert D. Hisrich has identified a few more capabilities or personal characteristics that an entrepreneur should possess. According to him, the entrepreneur must have an adequate commitment, motivation and skills to start and build a business. The entrepreneur must determine if the management team has the necessary complementary skills to succeed. Some key characteristics of a successful entrepreneur are:

Motivator: An entrepreneur must build a team, keep it motivated and provide an environment for individual growth and career development.

Self-confidence: Entrepreneurs must have belief in themselves and the ability to achieve their goals.

Long-term Involvement: An entrepreneur must be committed to the project with a time horizon of five to seven years. No ninety-day wonders are allowed.

High energy level: Success of an entrepreneur demands the ability to work long hours for sustained periods of time.

Persistent problem-solver: An entrepreneur must have an intense desire to complete a task or solve a problem. Creativity is an essential ingredient.

Initiative: An entrepreneur must be able to set challenging but realistic goals.

Moderate risk-taker: An entrepreneur must be a moderate risk-taker and learn from failures.

These personal traits go a long way in making an entrepreneur successful. However, no entrepreneur possesses total strength. In such cases, he acquires and/or associates and thus strengthens his enterprise.

Success Depends on...

Building value propositions for customer groups
Dealing with competitors as business partners
Tracking and analysing customer database for trends
Setting up strong front-end solutions units

Potential Pitfalls are...

The absence of product-specific sales teams
Managing culturally diverse alliance partners
Focusing on volumes rather than profits
Keeping up the pace of new product launches

Table 21.1 Characteristics of Entrepreneurs

Small-scale Entrepreneurs	Large-scale Entrepreneurs
1. Youngmen	1. Middle-aged Professionals
2. Ambitious	2. Professional Specialists
3. Intelligent	3. Shareholders contribute Venture Capital
4. Energetic	4. Energetic
5. Enthusiastic	5. Outsourcing
6. Minimum education	6. Networkers
7. Hard-working	7. Ability to get along with people
8. Confident	8. Tolerant
9. Passionate	9. Risk-takers
10. Dedicated	10. Large Assets controlled
11. Practical	11. Engaged in Diversified Activities
12. Goal-oriented	12. Diversified products
13. Mobile	13. Multiple activities
14. Adaptable	14. Easy access to institutional finance
15. Able	15. Leverages
16. Aggressive	16. Well connected with Politics Bureaucrats
17. Innovative	17. Trend-setters
18. Well-mannered	18. Demand creators
19. Self-made person	19. Value-driven
20. Disciplined	20. Corporate Philosophy
21. Zealous	21. Ambitious
22. Flexible	22. Drive to go ahead
23. Courageous	23. Self-confident
24. Skilful	24. Innovative/immitative
25. Creative	25. Adaptable

26.	Experienced	26.	Trained
27.	Meagre capital	27.	Large capital
28.	Small operation	28.	Large operation
29.	Employ few people	29.	Skilled manpower
30.	Small turnover	30.	Large turnover/sales/profit
31.	Honest	31.	Honest
32.	Progressive	32.	Progressive
33.	Patient	33.	Pragmatic
34.	Perseverance	34.	Perseverance
35.	Self-reliant	35.	Self-reliant
36.	Commonsense	36.	Abundant common sense
37.	Adaptive	37.	Competitive
38.	Ability to strive	38.	Versatile
39.	Compassionate	39.	Quality conscious
40.	Dreamer	40.	Visionaries
41.	Conscious	41.	Focussed
42.	Intuitive	42.	Singleness of purpose
43.	Practical	43.	Ability to change
44.	Imaginative	44.	Educated
45.	Achiever	45.	A strong need to achieve
46.	Hopeful	46.	Passionate
47.	Independent	47.	Analytical
48.	Self-starter	48.	Optimistic
49.	Individualist	49.	Organisation man
50.	Sensitive	50.	Loyal
51.	Perceptive	51.	Pleasing personality
52.	Quality conscious	52.	Dynamic
53.	Desire to share experience	53.	Tolerant
54.	Ability to change	54.	Active
55.	Money-oriented	55.	Contributor
56.	Driven by values	56.	Knowledgeable
57.	Intrapreneurial	57.	Motivator
58.	Facilitator	58.	Strategist
59.	Learner	59.	Goal conscious
60.	Opportunist	60.	Compassionate
61.	Ability to strive	61.	Leader
62.	Task master	62.	Scanner-looking for opportunities
63.	Striving Richness	63.	Planner
64.	Gut-feeler	64.	Thinker
65.	Dictator	65.	People Manager

Entrepreneurial Initiative

Recent data on entrepreneurial initiative and self-employment reveal a few problems. To overcome these problems, it is essential to develop entrepreneurial skills for which the entrepreneur has to initiate the process of development. This is a challenging task. This unprecedented, perpetual change with unlimited barriers makes entrepreneurial initiative in the future more significant and more dynamic.

This means that entrepreneurial initiative is a strategic process which embodies calculated strategic choices. There are strategies open to the entrepreneur himself in terms of industry choice and individual and resource-task fit, and there are strategies open to the regulators and support agencies in terms of industrial policy tools, incentive and explicit stimulation of industrial sector or branches. A conceptual framework that contains both dimensions will provide a convenient base for analysis and possible policy action.

Encouraging entrepreneurial initiative is an issue applicable to both developed and developing countries and the search for effective means is proceeding in earnest. The analysis has dealt with a way of viewing the constraints embodied in the process of creating a new business or manufacturing operation.

The slow pace of the propensity to enterprise is mainly due to the existence of a tangible set of barriers prohibiting the process of entry into, continuity in, and an eventual exit from a business venture of a would-be entrepreneur if it is a function of forces that one may view as barriers limiting full-fledged business performance. There may be *entry barriers, survival barriers and exit barriers*.

Entry barriers are those forces limiting access to identified business opportunities and capitalisation on these opportunities. Survival barriers are constraints on the conditions essential for the small business entity. Exit barriers are constraints limiting the termination of small industrial ventures that have outlived their business viability or the growth of such ventures to a different size category.

The existing entry barriers are:

1. A cultural bias in identifying and managing the entrepreneurial development process.
2. Limited industry-specific data and insufficient market information.
3. Limited effectiveness of the infrastructural base.
4. Existence of visible and invisible obstacles to entry of a specific societal group (e.g., women) into business.
5. Unorganised capital market and traditional feasibility assessment processes.
6. Unsympathetic and cumbersome government attitude.
7. Hostile environment.
8. Limited access to technology.

Observed survival barriers include the following:

1. A behavioural pattern that could impair basic managerial practices.
2. Constraining practices within the capital market.
3. The threatening shadow of changing technology.
4. Limited learning.
5. The cultural management of resources.
6. Failure of guidance agencies to guide.
7. Scarce information and limited dissemination of that information.

Identified exit barriers include:

1. The emotional commitment of the entrepreneur to his venture.
2. Specialised assets, sunk funds.
3. The increasing demand for managerial skills.
4. Fear of failure.

Barriers, single or combined are said to have an impact on to strategic and long-term planning perspective of the small entrepreneur and could, equally, have an impact on the government's promotional policies within the sector. Low entry and low survival industries (or industrial branches) could provide policymakers with an area for quick and intensive intervention. At the other extreme, industries with high entry barriers and high survival barriers, can probably be regarded as low priority areas that deserve a different kind of attention, i.e., barrier adjustment instead of enterprise development. The relationship between entry and exit barriers could lead to a similar set of conclusions. One of those conclusions is the advisability of the management of enterprise flow and the early identification of the potential for switching (a form of exit), or planned divestment. Again this can prove valuable for government policies for small industry promotion at the national and regional levels.

Progress in economic development and technological diversification does not happen accidentally or haphazardly. In a hyper competitive environment, the economic renaissance of an area depends on a city's or region's ability to address critical needs. To sustain the momentum of positive economic growth, communities must establish programmes for investment in a viable public-private infrastructure. This includes not only meeting the other essential infrastructural needs such as roads, water, and services but also providing for educational needs and diversified cultural amenities.

A vibrant financial environment is essential for continued economic development. This includes sophisticated banking community that understands the unique problems and needs of emerging companies, especially technologically-based companies, and an expanding venture capital industry that can address the requirements of high-risk ventures. Only in this way can an area ensure diversified opportunities for entrepreneurs.

A pool of capable people hold the responsibility for economic development. A community, therefore, has to find ways to ensure a locally-trained workforce with a minimum reliance on imported services. As needs are supplied locally there are more opportunities for entrepreneurs. By responding to a rapidly changing environment, it engenders a dynamic entrepreneurial spirit.

Motivation

Motivation is an indispensable function of management. When man is at work, he cannot be forced to work like a machine. He is a human being who has his dignity, self-respect, values, sentiments and aspirations apart from the economic status. Under such circumstances, the efficiency of the enterprise is related not merely to the efficiency of sophisticated machines installed but more importantly upon the satisfaction and the spontaneous desire of man to put his mind and heart into the work. This spontaneous urge to involve in work is not merely relate to monetary awards or assignment of position or the direction to perform the duty or even the fear of punishment but to the mechanics and system of motivation.

Motivation encompasses complex aspects of human behaviour to which contribution has been made by sociologists, social anthropologists, psychologists and business executives. This concept has its roots in motives within a person which induce him to behave in a particular manner. Generally speaking, the concept of motivation is by and large psychological which "relates to those forces operating within the individual employee or subordinate which impel him to act or not to act in certain ways".

"Motivation refers to the way in which urges, drives, desires, aspirations, strivings or needs direct, control or explain the behaviour of human beings."

This is a deep-seated definition of motivation. It includes three things:

(i) The urges, drives, desires, aspirations, strivings or needs of human beings influence human behaviour.
(ii) The factors which influence human behaviour – psychological, sociological, economic or managerial.
(iii) The efficiency of such behaviour – this may be tested by the resultant action. Whether this behaviour has directed, controlled or implemented the desired action.

If the entrepreneur feels motivated, his behaviour will bring about the desired action.

Here, one reaches the most crucial point in the Regional or District Development Strategy of the underdeveloped regions. The development agency with all the institutions concerned, will have to formulate a motivation programme and by continuous and ingenious methods, involve people in the process of development so that they acquire new attitudes and confidence to enter into new activities and to show the propensity of enterprise. Appropriate values will have to be inculcated and risking capacity be cultivated. Unless this aspect is given its due weightage in the Development Plan, in spite of all the incentives, most of the projects will hardly make much progress. Development is the consequence of motivated people.

Motivational factors constitute the inner urge present in an individual which continuously demands from him to do something new and unique as also to perform better than others. The motivational factors again are compressed of three basic elements – entrepreneurial motivation, personal efficiency and coping capability. The achievement motivation is also termed *efficiency motivation*. McClelland and Winter have made considerable studies and concluded that what motivates a person to do something new or something to seek better is the inner urge which directs him towards such ends. This urge also force a person to use the resources efficiently than to be negligent of it. Also important is the power of motivation which is really the urge to have control over others and to direct their course of activities towards the end which one seeks to attain. These motivational factors induce the person to undertake entrepreneurial activities which relate to creating a new business where there was none. This also means to excel the performance in carrying out any activity by striving through persistent efforts unlike others who do not have sufficient capacity for hardwork.

What Makes Entrepreneurs?: A Survey

Access to capital, positive attitude, and favourable regulations, says an Accenture survey.

THIS SHOULD COME AS NO SURPRISE: The US is perceived as the most enterprising country. And neither should this: India is seen as the most enterprise-unfriendly nation. So, what accounts for this huge disparity in entrepreneurial success? According to a survey done by Accenture on entrepreneurship, no matter where is the world a company is located or does business, certain basic aspects must be in place for an entrepreneurial climate to evolve, these include: access to capital, the right regulatory and tax environment, and positive social and cultural attitudes towards entrepreneurship.

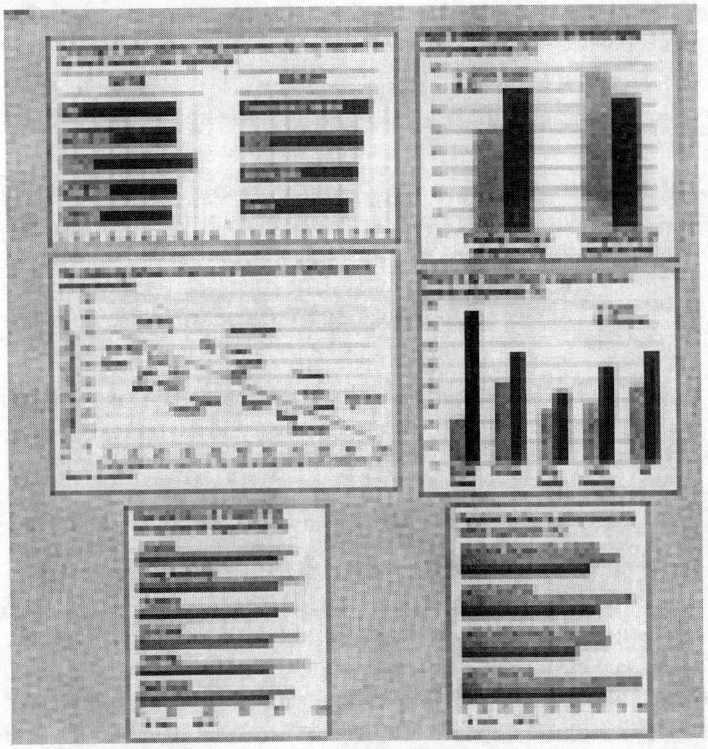

The survey – which spanned 18 months and 22 countries, including India – reveals that the US is overwhelmingly seen as the most entrepreneurial country, with Japan coming a clear, albeit distant, second. Interestingly, while executives in the US chose their country as the most entrepreneurial nation, very few Japanese executives thought likewise of their country, and virtually no other executives of other countries chose their own country.

Countries that stand out as having positive social attitudes to entrepreneurship include the US, Canada, Singapore, Taiwan and Netherlands. Art of the social acceptability of entrepreneurs is tied up with cultural attitudes to wealth and success. For instance, in India, when talking about entrepreneurs and their will to succeed, the chairman of Triveni Engineering, Dhruv Sawhney, says: "As a society we tend to suspect motives rather than encourage them."

According to the survey, most executives in India do not perceive their country to be highly entrepreneurial. Only five per cent mentioned India as the most entrepreneurial country, with half citing the US, while over four-fifths thought that India was far behind the country they regarded as the most entrepreneurial.

Bureaucratic problems are seen by three-quarters of Indian executives as one of the impediments to progress, with 78 per cent citing a lack of incentives against a global average of 63 per cent. Also, in India, entrepreneurship seems to be associated above all with leadership. Top executives see entrepreneurial organisations as those driven by strong leaders with propensity for risk-taking. The survey doesn't say this, but give India another decade for entrepreneurship to take risk.

What Makes an Entrepreneur?

What makes an entrepreneur is the combination of various factors that have enabled the personality formation right from the childhood as also the psychological urge that exists intensively in the person. These psychological processes which lead men to set up on their own a successful business enterprise beginning the very early life and have cumulative effect. The influence of early childhood and other social roles are determinate factors for the formation of that personality which motivates an individual towards becoming an independent businessman or entrepreneur.

In the case of persons who take up jobs, it has always been found that they have secured success in the established organisations. These people do not have a rejection towards the established institutions and neither do they attempt to rebel against the traditional path to success. On the other hand, an entrepreneur fails to achieve educational success through the established organisations and this is because of the general rejection of the established organisations at all levels. People who tend to like security and not uncertainty gets more satisfied by taking up jobs which are less risk-oriented and hence are not motivated towards building up their own industrial enterprise.

Men who establish new business are men who have right from the childhood faced a different set of environment in their family, school and other social situations. Research studies have indicated that successful entrepreneurs identify a crisis before they venture into new entrepreneurial activities. Even in their childhood most of them had threatening, non-supportive and disgusting adult figures who had much say in their social and economic life. Most of these have a childhood of imperverishment and stress. Economic deprivation also works as a motivational factor towards creating something on their own and free oneself from the clutches of oppressing forces which attempt to kill their spirit of individualism. Thus, it has been found that creating a successful new business is not due to an isolated incidence in the life of an individual but it has been as a result of learned response to their total social, emotional and economic environment.

The family background plays an important role in building up personality necessary for turning into an entrepreneur later in life. In family situations where security and non-risk bearing activities are encouraged right from childhood, the individual likes to be more security-oriented rather than attempt on his own in areas where adventures and uncertainty conditions prevail. Also in families where deep attachments and emotional relationships are encouraged, it has been found that the child growing under such situations tends to take up activities which are more security-oriented than risk-oriented. Since in most of the middle-class families, attachment and security-oriented activities are encouraged despite seeking academic excellence, it itself does not help the person to develop a deep urge to be independent and create a framework required for enjoying autonomy.

As a result of this attitude building, many bright graduates shy away from placing themselves in open positions but instead choose to stay in the established organisations because they have developed a favourable attitude towards the establishment. On the other hand, the entrepreneurial personality would rather face the impersonal forces of the economy than cope with interpersonal relations of the established organisations. Due to this characteristic of an entrepreneur, they tend to shift from job to job till they have finally found a field of activity in which they will ultimately have a say and also enjoy the happenings of events by their sheer will, determination and efforts.

While people who take up jobs prefer to see success in the traditional and highly structured roles in the established undertakings, entrepreneurs, on the other hand, prefer to have a different approach toward success and be unique in their own way. They find more satisfaction in their creative faculties getting an opportunity to express themselves fully satisfacted, rather than submitting themselves to forces which are already structured and rigid. The bright graduates may very often lack creativity and are not in a position to break through the undifferentiated mask of circumstances and make something of their own.

The entrepreneurs, on the other hand, find such situations extraordinarily challenging and attempt with determination and persistence to come out of this web of oppressing factors, which tend to keep him in the rigid framework. Thus, we find entrepreneurial characteristics are formed through a combination of various social, economic and psychological factors to which the person becomes subjected right from childhood. These factors reinforce in him the urge to excel others and seek satisfaction in creating on his own a new enterprise instead of seeking a security-oriented job, in the absence of these reinforcing elements which go into the formation of the entrepreneurial personality, however bright a person may be in the academic life, it is not a guarantee that he would also become a successful entrepreneur. Something more than mere academic excellence is a prerequisite for becoming an entrepreneur of success and repute. These requisites are embodied in the various qualities that the entrepreneur must have basically within himself in order to establish himself as a successful entrepreneur. But many graduates do lack in these qualities.

Qualities of an Entrepreneur

A true entrepreneur besides possessing functional qualities, must also possess a broad personality which help in developing initiative and drive to accomplish great tasks and face challenges squarely.

James J. Berne has stressed the following qualities of a good entrepreneur:

1. He is an enterprising individual, is energetic, hard-working, resourceful, aware of new opportunities and able to adjust himself to changing conditions with ease and willing to assume risks involved in change.
2. He is interested in an advancing technologically and in improving the quality of his product or service.
3. He is interested in expanding the scale of his operations by reinvesting his earnings.
4. He visualises changes and adapts to changing conditions.
5. He is a firm believer in planning and systematic work.
6. He works for the society at large and for the good of his fellow-beings.

These qualities sum up, what is usually implied from the phrase, the "spirit of enterprise". It is difficult to conceive of a first-rate industrial entrepreneur who is not adaptable to change, anxious to grow large and improve technologically.

Entrepreneurship appears as a personal quality which enables certain individuals to make decision with far-reaching consequences. The personal qualities that contribute to the success of an entrepreneur are as follows:

1. *Motivation Towards Achievement:* A successful entrepreneur should be a good administrator. He should know the art of getting things done by other people without hurting their feelings or self-respect. He should have a strong motivation towards the achievement of a task and must be able to exert considerable efforts in getting things done by others.

2. *Creativity:* Mental ability consists of intelligence, an analytical approach and creative things. An entrepreneur should have creative thinking and be able to engage in the analysis of various problems and situations in order to deal with them. The entrepreneur should anticipate changes and must be able to study various situations in which decisions may have to be made.
3. *Clarity:* An entrepreneur should have clear objective as to the exact nature of the business, the nature of the goods to be produced and the subsidiary activities to be undertaken.

The qualities of an entrepreneur are given in Fig. 21.2.

Kilby has rightly numerated the following activities for a successful entrepreneur in an underdeveloped economy:

1. Perception of market opportunities (novel or imitative).
2. Gaining command over scarce resources.
3. Purchasing of inputs.
4. Marketing of the product and responding effectively to competition.
5. Dealing with public bureaucracy as regards concessions, licences, taxes, etc., provided through the various fiscal policies of the government.
6. Management of the human relations within the enterprise.
7. Management of customer and supplier relations.
8. Financial management.
9. Production management, including control through written records, supervision, coordinating input flows with orders, maintenance.
10. Acquiring and overseeing assembly of the plant.
11. Taking care for minimising inputs for a given production process.
12. Maintaining the production process and improving the quality of the product.
13. Introduction of new production techniques and product-lines.

From the above discussion and definitions, it can be stated that entrepreneurial activities encompass those factors right from the perception of the profitable opportunity to its translation into reality through establishing a successful enterprise and further leading to its growth and development. Especially in an underdeveloped economy, the expectations from entrepreneurial units are much more varied and related to many dimensions, including socio-economic objectives. This is because this type of economy is characterised by a majority of low income strata than the developed economy characterised by high income.

Entrepreneurial Skills

To deal with entrepreneurial skills is to concern oneself with a wide coverage of aspects of setting up an enterprise and its management. It is not confined to visualisation, planning, setting-up and risk-taking. The skills which an entrepreneur includes are his ability to deal with view situations, organisations and social and economic forces as they emerge from time to time. The skills to deal with a situation fore-visualised or suddenly emerging must be an essential characteristic of an entrepreneur.

The small entrepreneur must have skills to positive response from administrators, bankers, infrastructure institutions, clients and employees.

The entrepreneur is rarely a master of the management skills, and yet is usually directly responsible for all aspects of business. Often he or she has to be the general manager, production manager, purchasing manager, personnel manager, controller and research organiser for the business all rolled into at least during its early years. The entrepreneur therefore has to have an understanding of marketing, quality control, finance, banking, commercial law, government regulations and procedures, and human relation as each of them has a vital bearing on the health of the enterprise.

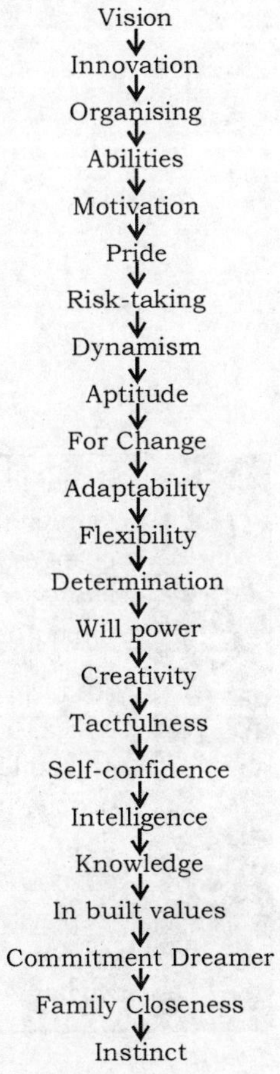

Fig. 22.2: Qualities of a Successful Entrepreneur

Need for Skills

We often talk of transfer of technology. As a matter of fact, the whole world is talking about it. There is hardly any international event at the global and regional level where this subject does not come up for discussion. The poor nations demand technology and resources from industrialised and rich countries and rightly so. The developing countries would rather export semi-finished and finished products which are value added than export raw materials. The development of entrepreneurial skill must precede transfer of technology if we do not desire to keep such technologies and equipment serving such technologies idle. One has also to realise that technologies are developing very fast and the skills are to match with this dynamic growth.

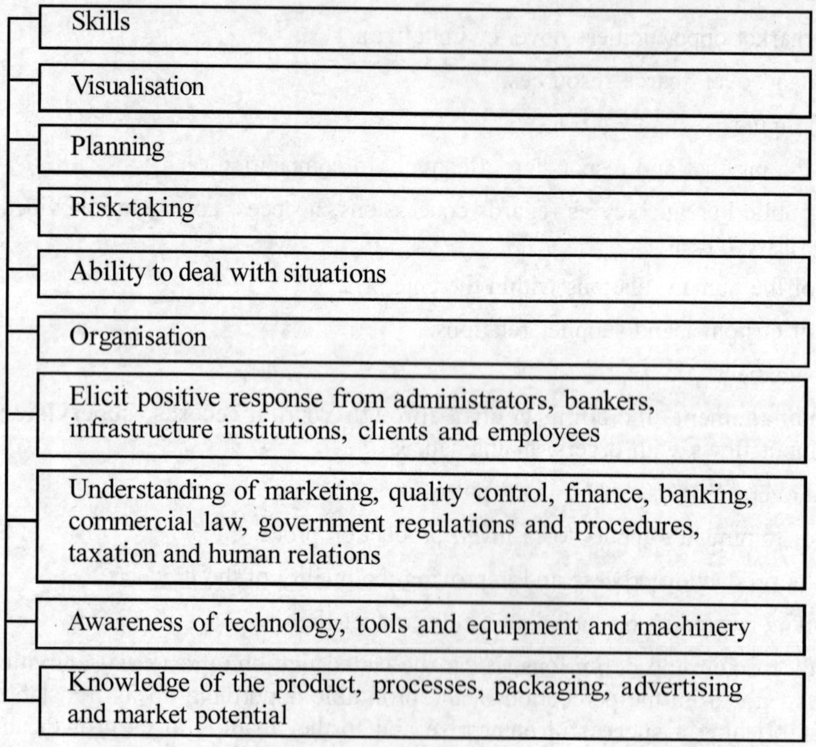

Fig. 21.3 Entrepreneurial Skills

CONCLUSION

A number of entrepreneurial managers have attempted to identify the true nature of entrepreneurs and entrepreneurship in the post-industrial revolution. The definition has, therefore, undergone changes with the changes in the socio-economic environment and will continue to undergo changes with the changing times. However, some basic concepts of innovation, risk-taking, vision and organising skills continue to be the four pillars on which the edifice of entrepreneurial concept has to be perceived from time-to-time.

An ideal entrepreneur is one who confines values in the market economy, that profits do not somehow preclude ethical behaviour, that growth is possible even if political patronage is not used to bend rules and cut corners, and quite simply that pursuit of wealth can be grateful and mannerly one. He takes with him the interest of his people, his country, his natural resources, the ecology and see that his enterprise becomes a catalytic agent of development. There is, thus, a need of true entrepreneurs, who do not opt for incentives, infrastructure, government support: but build his enterprises, harness the available resources and develop. They adopt a responsible value-driven corporate philosophy for their enterprises and/or business activities. As such, there is no dispute among economists and social thinkers about the urgent need for the emergence of an entrepreneurial society as a forerunner of accelerated development of the economy in an integrated manner.

ANNEXURE-I

Characteristics of a Successful Entrepreneur

A successful entrepreneur is a person who has started the business where there was none before. A successful entrepreneur is essentially an enterprising individual who is able to recognise the potential profitable opportunity and who initiates to produce marketable products by combining the various technologies and through organising together the people, finance, material resources marketing tools, in order to ultimately translate the idea in the minds to physical realities. In short, entrepreneur is a person who initiates, establishes, maintains and expands a new enterprise. He is basically an innovator, creator and accomplisher.

According to research studies, there are more than 50 personality traits and all these traits and attitudes constitute the characteristic of a successful entrepreneur. Though all the characteristics cannot be found in single entrepreneur yet the presence of greater number of these characteristics in an individual makes him an entrepreneur and only then it is possible for him to be successful to achieve the goals of entrepreneurship. Some of the characteristics or qualities of an entrepreneur are discussed below:

(1) Need for achievement, (2) Risk-taking, (3) Need for independence, (4) Sense of effectiveness, (5) Social consciousness, (6) Need for extension, (7) Optimistic, (8) Open minded, (9) Non-fatalist, (10) Low affiliation, (11) Pragmatist, (12) Aggressive, (13) Persistent, (14) Commitment and conviction, (15) Capacity to analyse, (16) Initiative, (17) Hopeful, and (18) Efficiency.

(1) Need for Achievement: The urge to achieve or the urge to excel others is the forceful psychological factor which is an essential characteristic found in almost all the individuals with enterprising qualities. McClelland Winter have through their research studies indicated that this is the single critical factor present in the entrepreneurs. Entrepreneurs belong to that category of people who are willing to work hard and to achieve something excellent despite the challenges and threats in the environment. Under such challenging and threatening forces, many people would lose or give up and would not care at all for achieving something better. But the high need of achievement present in the entrepreneurs drive them to excel others. This trait also indicates the urge to be different from others and strive to achieve the goals which are difficult to be achieved by other ordinary people. At the same time, these people do not aim at practically impossible goals. The goals set are achievable in reality. The high need of achievement urge results in a high drive in individuals and as a result high activity levels are present in these persons. As a consequence of this driving force, thought processes are always linked with the problems of doing things better than the others. Unless the persons possesses this urge to accomplish, excel or achieve through a balanced sense autonomy and tolerance, it is difficult to be a successful entrepreneur.

(2) Risk-taking: Risk-taking is another attribute of entrepreneurs. Entrepreneurs like to take risks which are calculated and not extreme ones. They undertake challenging risks which are difficult to overcome but are not impossible. They do not have the attitude of depending upon chance factors to get the expected results, instead they would like their own efforts to give the desired results. By this way of influencing the results by their own efforts, they like to enjoy the sense of having accomplished the tasks by their own efforts. In this process, the risks involved are calculated risks. To ensure success in the accomplishment of the goals, entrepreneurs see to it that they spend lot of time in planning their enterprises and ensure success before actually launching the project. This is done by studying in detail the various interfering forces and obstacles and keeping ready the solutions to overcome these interferences. Moderate risk-taking and safeguarding against anticipated difficulties are the qualities that can be found in successful entrepreneurs.

(3) Need for Independence and Autonomy: The strong need to be an independent or autonomous individual is another driving force associated with the entrepreneurs. The entrepreneurs dislike controls from outsiders as a result, conformations to set ideas and standards are not, their forte to appreciate. This non-conformative attitude is also responsible for their starting a new enterprise based on new ideas of their own. Autonomy coupled with a sense of determination is an essential characteristic of entrepreneurs.

(4) Sense of Effectiveness: Entrepreneurs like to see the problem solved through their involved efforts. They do not like to avoid the problems but like to be effective and instrumental in solving problems rather than avoiding them. Their attitudes towards a problem is always one of directing the efforts and finding ways and means to give solutions to such problems. Since they are full of confidence in their own capacities, they tend to be action-oriented rather than being passive conformists.

(5) Social Consciousness: Rightful entrepreneurs tend not to take undue advantage of social and economic conditions of the society in general. Instead there is a universal urge among the entrepreneurs for social change and economic development. As a result, entrepreneurs are always on the lookout for new methods of producing or developing new products that would create jobs for many. Hence, the pursuit of such business activities are directed to achieve social goals on larger interest than personal goals of individual interest.

Entrepreneurs in the real sense do not patronage or indulge in anti-social activities like black marketing, hoarding, profiteering and such other malpractices which causes considerable damages to interests of the consumers as a whole. They dislike economic backwardness of the society which is the result of such anti-social and unfair business practices. Instead they direct their energies in the eradication of the underside implications by finding new suitable opportunities of business and by providing the services at prices, the community can afford. An entrepreneur hence is socially concerned and respects labour. They spread the message of dignity of manual labour through their own example. They have very low resistance towards doing a work manually. They are ever ready to get the work done through their own hands if the situation demands without any hesitation. This kind of respecting labour enables them to work in cooperation with the people by generating high morale among the people with whom they work. Persons who hesitate to do the work with their own hands will find it difficult to succeed as an entrepreneur. Hence, this quality of respecting labour is also a driving force which enables them to be successful by setting examples of doing the work manually. The examples set by them enable others to learn and follow suit. Cooperation therefore becomes easy and effective under such situations.

(6) Need for Extension: An entrepreneur though likely to be self-centred in the pursuit of his goals so that his urge for achievement is satisfied, yet in the true sense he is not so. Many entrepreneurs understand the importance of industrialisation and faster economic development through rapid growth and expansion of the industries, hence they tend to share their experiences with others who have similar attributes and accomplish the task through joining hands with the suitable persons. But the degree of such participations by entrepreneurs in the developing economy is very low, hence by giving appropriate training the entrepreneurs should be motivated towards this goal of expansion through joint ventures. In a country like India, the need of the entrepreneurs for the rapid development in every field for the economy is more a necessity and therefore government efforts should be directed towards this end.

(7) Optimistic: The entrepreneurs have the quality of being optimistic and hoping to succeed rather than experiencing failure. This hope to succeed would enable a sense of determination which will boost their confidence in carrying out the task successfully. Hence, this quality of being optimistic is nonetheless important. As a consequence of their self-confidence, they are more successful in their efforts than those with pessimistic attributes.

Thus, pessimistic approach or fear of failure does not find place in their mind and they undertake all the tasks after careful planning and with the hope of succeeding with their efforts.

(8) Non-fatalist: Entrepreneurs, though they have faith in God or in the power of nature, yet disapprove the belief that outside forces will change the environment towards the desired needs. They would like to be instrumental through their own efforts rather than to be dependent upon chance factors or luck or those forces which are beyond their control, for attaining desired goals. Man's destiny can be changed by man himself by his own efforts is their strong belief. Psychologically this type of an attribute is called internal locus of control. This drives them to do things with extra vigour and help them to change the happenings by their own efforts and enjoy the feeling of making things to happen. This nature helps them to accept the mistaken efforts in any case and to attempt to bring about improvements in their approaches in future actions.

(9) Open-minded: Entrepreneurs develop the habit of learning from experience the limitations of achievements. They modify the goals according to the environmental challenges and threats. This modification does not mean avoiding the problems or the tasks, instead they like to face it. The modification is done in order to make it possible to achieve the goal within the given environmental conditions. They always like to get the feedback of their efforts and effectiveness of the programmes modified so that changes or modifications if needed can be effected as and when required. Entrepreneurs in a sense, therefore, always test their capabilities and for that purpose they tend to keep their mind open to receive information on their abilities or otherwise to achieve the desired goals.

(10) Low Affiliation: Entrepreneurs do not get attached emotionally with the people with whom they work. They know that if they do get into emotional involvement with the people they would be working more for the people with whom they are working rather than for the institutions which they intend to build. But even with this attribute they can show concern for their employees by checking, or restraining the behaviour that tends to show obviously their true reactions.

(11) Need for Power and Influencing: Entrepreneurs always feel the need to influence people and implement the ideas so that the organisation takes the shape in actuality. Excellence is no doubt a criteria for the entrepreneurs but leading others and influencing them to a great extent though the effective dealing is not secondary to an entrepreneur. Since they have a strong belief in their own capacity, they tend to a very high sense of morale which ultimately help to influence others to their own way of thinking and action. Here, the entrepreneur takes the role of a successful manager and influencing others in the accomplishment of the goals.

(12) Aggressive and Persistent: These are also the characteristics which help the entrepreneurs to continue with the drive till the goals are achieved. Aggressiveness indicates the presence of a driving force which enables the efforts to come out with full vigour through persistent attempts. This quality, therefore, indicates that entrepreneurs are not problem avoiders. They pursue the goals till they are achieved by modifying the same as and when required as also by removing the obstacles in the way so that the goals are finally achieved. With every failure, the entrepreneur learns to improve the method of approach rather than being passive in the face of frustrating experiences.

(13) Pragmatists: Another attribute of an entrepreneur is to be concerned with the present than the past or future. Though he learns from the past and intends to change the future through his visions and dreams yet he is downright a practical person living in the present. He is a pragmatist who lives in the present effectively. He is not a man of merely day dreams or one who is overhelmed by the past achievements or failures. Though entrepreneurs may at times give the impression of past-oriented personalities by narrating their pasts profusely, yet really speaking they are pragmatists who cannot easily be overwhelmed by either the past or the future orientations.

Other characteristics of a successful entrepreneur are high expectations from their employees, pleasing personality, dynamic opportunity seeker, self-starter, individualist, sensitive and perceptive of the environment, high tolerance towards ambiguities and uncertain happenings, materialist tendencies, always hoping and believing in the existence of a better way of doing things, many interests, mentally very active, courageous, etc.

(14) Commitment and Conviction:

- Fully commits himself to the project and rests only when achieved.
- Leaves no effort to complete the task in time.

(15) Capacity to Analyse:

- Knows the need for information, its relevance, where and how to find it.
- Has a thought process for diagnosing problems, conceiving and comparing alternative courses of action and approaches in that direction to solve rather than avoid.

(16) Initiative:

- Takes initiative and does not wait for the other to do first.
- Likes to lead rather than being led
- Likes to act on his own rather than follow others' directions.

(17) Hopeful about future and search for good business environment:

- Reasonably optimistic and tends to look at future with hope.
- Tends to search the environment in order to seek answers to questions.
- Sets goal and plans his line of operations.
- Perceives opportunities.

(18) High personal efficiency:

- Has a sense of effectiveness, and
- Presents himself with ability to do things with higher degree of efficiency.

There could be a long series of characteristics, but in my opinion, these are some of the very important and essential ones which should fit into the profile of a successful entrepreneur. It is actually not necessary that he may have high degree of all these traits but a fairly good combination of these is required to be reasonably available. The level of degrees could, however, be increased by motivation and proper training through entrepreneurship development programmes.

ANNEXURE-II

The Success Audit

Take the success audit for enterprise success:

1.	Do you contribute creatively to any business function other than your own?	Yes	No
2.	Do you consciously attempt to network with other professionals in your field?	Yes	No
3.	Do you have an overall perspective of the industry you are in?	Yes	No
4.	Do you understand your company's business goals, and how your job fits into them?	Yes	No
5.	Do you understand the needs and constraints of the different business functions?	Yes	No
6.	Can you cope with upgraded software packages without professional help?	Yes	No
7.	Would you volunteer for a challenging long-term overseas assignment?	Yes	No
8.	Do you make a conscious effort to keep abreast of international trends in your field?	Yes	No
9.	At a pinch, can you take over for a colleague in the event of his sudden illness?	Yes	No
10.	Do you often enroll for courses that deal with subjects that are supplementary to yours?	Yes	No

The Scoring

Give yourself 10 points for every YES, and 0 for every No.

Total

The Rating:

0-30	Take those blinkers off. Else, you could get left behind in the career-stakes.
40-70	Wishy-washy. You have the potential, just get more focused.
80-100	Congrats! You're in a pole position in the corporate grand prix.

ANNEXURE-III

Business Skills Inventory

The following inventory will help you to assess your strengths and weaknesses as a future small business owner. In this exercise, you need to identify how much knowledge and/or experience you have in relation to each of the skills listed in the inventory. These are the most important skills that you will need to start and run your future contracting business. They have been grouped under various management functions representing the key roles that you will have to play as a business owner.

It is important to realistically examine your background knowledge and your experience in these key roles. The success of your business depends on how well you are prepared to assume these roles.

Rate yourself on a four-point scale and circle the figure that you feel most accurately represents your explanation of each category:

- No knowledge, no experience
- Some knowledge, but no experience
- Some experience, and
- Much experience

Question: How much knowledge or experience do you have in relation to each skill listed in the inventory?

I. Marketing the Construction Firm Your Rating

- Identify the Construction Firm. 1 2 3 4
- Determine the territory within which you will operate. 1 2 3 4
- Determine the types of customers you will serve. 1 2 3 4
- Use Statistics of India as information to assess the size of the target market. 1 2 3 4
- Design a questionnaire to identify potential customers and their needs. 1 2 3 4
- Choose a location for the business. 1 2 3 4

Give yourself an overall rating reflecting your level of competency in identifying your target markets. 1 2 3 4

II. Competing with Others

- Find out how well your competitors are doing. 1 2 3 4
- Analyse how the competitors obtain their contracts. 1 2 3 4
- Determine how your firm will be different from the competition. 1 2 3 4

Give yourself an overall rating reflecting your level of competency in competing with others. 1 2 3 4

1. *Pricing Your Service*

- Set a competitive hourly labour rate. 1 2 3 4
- Prepare an estimate of the costs for providing your services. 1 2 3 4
- Submit bids with/without cost-escalating clauses. 1 2 3 4
- Negotiate contracts with other parties. 1 2 3 4

Give yourself an overall rating reflecting your level of competency in properly pricing your services. 1 2 3 4

2. *Promoting Your Business*

- Develop a promotional strategy. 1 2 3 4
- Design promotional materials 1 2 3 4
- Prepare a budget for advertising. 1 2 3 4
- Use quality of workmanship and customer service as a promotional tool. 1 2 3 4

Give yourself an overall rating reflecting your level of competency in promoting your future construction firm. 1 2 3 4

III. Managing Finances

1. *Borrowing Money*

- Determine how much money is needed to start and run your business. 1 2 3 4
- Forecast the need for additional capital or cash. 1 2 3 4

• Identify appropriate sources for short-term/long-term financing.	1 2 3 4
• Negotiate loans.	1 2 3 4
Given yourself an overall rating reflecting your level of competency in borrowing money.	1 2 3 4
2. *Managing Money*	
• Do bookkeeping.	1 2 3 4
• Establish and use financial controls.	1 2 3 4
• Set up a cost control system for separate jobs or contracts.	1 2 3 4
• Analyse overhead costs.	1 2 3 4
• Prepare profit and loss statements and balance sheets.	1 2 3 4
• Prepare budgets.	1 2 3 4
Give yourself an overall rating reflecting your level of competency in managing money.	1 2 3 4
3. *Analysing Financial Statements*	
• Prepare a cash flow analysis.	1 2 3 4
• Prepare a break-even analysis.	1 2 3 4
• Understand profit and loss statements and balance sheets.	1 2 3 4
Give yourself an overall rating reflecting your level of competency in analysing financial statements.	1 2 3 4
4. *Handling Credit and Collection*	
• Understand current credit policies in the construction industry set by subcontractors, general contractors and developers.	1 2 3 4
• Design accounts payable and receivable ageing systems.	1 2 3 4
• Use various collection techniques.	1 2 3 4
• Know-how and when to commence legal action, file a lien, go to Small Claim Court.	1 2 3 4
Give yourself an overall rating reflecting your level of competency in handling credit and collection.	1 2 3 4
IV. Organising the Business	
1. *Handling Legal Issues*	
• Choose the appropriate: proprietorship, partnership, incorporation.	1 2 3 4
• Write a partnership agreement	1 2 3 4
• Write a valid contract with general contractors, subcontractors and/or clients.	1 2 3 4
• Determine appropriate terms for a leasing agreement.	1 2 3 4
• Use the litigation process or other alternatives to resolve construction disputes.	1 2 3 4
• Choose a lawyer who can understand your legal problems.	1 2 3 4
Give yourself an overall rating reflecting your level of competency in handling legal issues.	1 2 3 4
2. *Complying with Government Regulations*	
• Obtain appropriate business licenses and permits.	1 2 3 4
• Comply with federal, provincial and municipal tax laws.	1 2 3 4
• Comply with the Labour Code: minimum wage, payment of wages, holidays, hours of work, Human Rights Code, Worker's Compensation Board.	1 2 3 4
Give yourself an overall rating reflecting your level of competency in complying with government regulations.	1 2 3 4
3. *Insuring your business*	
• Purchase proper insurance coverage for important business risks.	1 2 3 4
• Select an insurance broker or company.	1 2 3 4
• Obtain performance bonds.	1 2 3 4
Give yourself an overall rating reflecting your level of competency in insuring your business.	1 2 3 4

V. Managing Business Operations

- Buy supplies from the best sources at the best price possible (including discount). 1 2 3 4
- Buy reliable equipment with adequate warranties. 1 2 3 4
- Negotiate contracts with suppliers. 1 2 3 4
- Use techniques for controlling materials inventories. 1 2 3 4
- Set-up quality control procedure to ensure quality of workmanship. 1 2 3 4
- Coordinate own work schedule with the schedule of other trade people on the same project. 1 2 3 4
- Set-up a system for recording work orders.

Give yourself an overall rating reflecting your level of competency in managing your business operations. 1 2 3 4

VI. Managing People

- Develop a job description. 1 2 3 4
- Interview applicants for jobs available. 1 2 3 4
- Provide employees with feedback on their performance. 1 2 3 4
- Supervise and motivate employees. 1 2 3 4
- Train employees. 1 2 3 4
- Schedule workers on a daily or weekly basis. 1 2 3 4
- Work effectively with other trades on a construction job. 1 2 3 4

Give yourself an overall rating reflecting your level of competency in managing people. 1 2 3 4

The skills for which you have rated yourself as 1 or 2 represent your weaknesses. Before you start your business, you should plan on acquiring these skills or find a partner who has such an expertise. You must also plan to improve those skills which are rated 3.

In any case, attempting to develop or improve your skills as you run your business may be very costly and lead to bankruptcy. There will be numerous tasks to accomplish and they will put high demands on your ability to make your business profitable. If you are not sufficiently prepared and organised to have them done, you will soon fall behind and the problems will rapidly pile up with no relief in sight.

The skills which you rated as 4 represent the strengths that will contribute to the success of your future contracting business.

You should not expect to be equally strong in all the functions necessary for operating a business. However, knowing your weaknesses will allow you to see assistance for solving problems requiring those skills.

Consult the overall rates you have assigned to the main functions listed in the inventory (there are 13 overall rates). List your four strongest management functions and your four weakest management functions.

Strongest management functions: ____________________

____

Weakest management functions: ____________________

____

ANNEXURE-IV

Ranking Entrepreneurial Traits Centre

No single entrepreneur possesses all the traits or characteristics described earlier, nor are all those characteristics needed to be successful. But which of the traits and characteristics are most commonly shared and most important for success?

In order to assess what you believe to be important entrepreneurial abilities, complete the following quiz. Rate the characteristics on a scale of 1 to 5. A rating of 1 indicates little importance, and a rating of 5 indicates great importance.

Characteristics	*Little importance*			*Great importance*	
	1	*2*	*3*	*4*	*5*
1. A strong need to achieve					
2. A visionary					
3. A need to associate closely with others					
4. Ability to focus on people and process					
5. An ability to get along with employees					
6. Ability to motivate and build relationship					
7. A willingness to tolerate uncertainty					
8. Good physical health					
9. A high level of energy					
10. Singleness of purpose					
11. A willingness to take risks					
12. Drive to be ahead of others					
13. Ambitions					
14. Self-confidence					
15. Innovation					
16. Ability to chart a course of direction					
17. Ability to lead effectively					
18. Patience					
19. Ability to strive					
20. A strong desire for money					
21. Being well-organised					
22. Thirst for knowledge and adequate reading habits					
23. A desire to create					
24. A desire to adopt active attitudes towards goals					
25. A need for power					
26. Perseverance					
27. Commitment and hardwork					
28. Self-reliance					
29. Abundant common sense					
30. Desire and willingness to take the initiative					
31. Competitiveness					
32. Versatility					
33. Desire to share knowledge/experience					
34. Quality conscious					
35. Desire to add value					
36. Honesty					

37. Progressive
38. Flexibility
39. Ability to change, and
40. Uniqueness.

Now that you have rated the various entrepreneurial characteristics, rank the characteristics in order of importance in your opinion under one of the following three categories:

(a) Most important for success (include those characteristics that you numbered 4 and 5)

(b) Important for success (include those characteristics that you gave a rating of 3)

(c) Least important for success (include those characteristics that you rated as 1 and 2)

Most Important	Important	Least Important
....	....	....
....	....	....
....	....	....
....	....	....
....	....	....
....	....	....
....	....	....

The idea is not just work to finish a task but rather to work well and to savour each step you take up the mountain you've chosen. Then, when you reach the top, you won't feel spent from all the effort. In fact, you won't even feel you've arrived. Instead, you'll feel refreshed and invigorated by what you've accomplished, and you'll find yourself looking for the next peak to conquer.

Taken together, mission, vision and a set of unique traits forms the bedrock of entrepreneurship. They allow them to help shape their future. Mastering the discipline of innovation will require organisations to learn from one another.

Ranking entrepreneurial traits will definitely guide the entrepreneurs, particularly the first generation entrepreneurs to build-up their deficiencies and move ahead with speed in this competitive entrepreneurial environment.

22 CHAPTER

CLASSIFICATION AND TYPES OF ENTREPRENEURS

LEARNING OBJECTIVES

"The only thing that distinguishes your company from another is the quality of your people"

Ajay Piramal
CEO,
Morarjee Goculdas

The principle objective is to discuss the various types of entrepreneurs and explore the potential for entrepreneurial activities in accelerating the process of sustainable development, wherein an entrepreneur can play a crucial role.

First, an attempt had been made to classify entrepreneurs from the points of economic, sociological, psychological, anthropological, geographical ways.

Entrepreneurs are also classified into business community and others. Of late, a new breed of entrepreneurs have emerged. They are innovators and enterprising people. They build, operate and transfer enterprises. This cycle continues.

The students should keep on updating his/her knowledge on types of entrepreneurs on an ongoing process.

Creative
Problem Solving Logical
Reasoning Adaptability
Adroitness Agility
Efficacy Acumen
Intution Ingenuity
Sensitivity Proficiency
Ideation Dedication
Prudence Visionary
Enerprising Perseverance
Steadfastness Deliverance
Distinctive Congenial Equanimity
Equipoise Diligence Convivial Judicious
Decisiveness Wisdom Eloquence
Resilience Techno-savvy Teamwork
Conitive Precision Innovative Instinct
Punctilious Meticulous Prifligacy
Perceptive Imaginative Ambition
Transactional Transcendence
Intelligent Dynamic
Motivated Levelheaded

Crafting managers for global enterprises

INTRODUCTION

In the previous chapter, we have analysed the concept of entrepreneurship and its understanding over the centuries, particularly in the post-industrial revolution. In modern times, stress has been laid on the entrepreneur. Entrepreneurial development is the thrust area of development planners, economic thinkers and policymakers. What is more, the entrepreneur has emerged as a kingpin of development.

"Entrepreneur is a person who discovers new ideas and business opportunities, brings together funds to establish a business, organises and manages its operations in order to provide economic goods and services, for the public. Entrepreneurs have strong convictions, self-motivation, the will to grow and prosper tremendously and also the courage to go bankrupt if they fail in their venture. But in majority of the cases, they start with nothing but entrepreneurial ability and end with positive results."

By and large, entrepreneurs are found in every economic system and in every form of economic activity as well as in other social and cultural activities. They are found amongst artisans, labourers, artists, importers, exporters, engineers, supervisors, bankers, industry, professionals, etc. They are also found among farmers, fishermen, forest workers, tribals and so on. Some writers have also identified entrepreneurs among politicians, theologists, philosophers and bureaucrats.

Box 22.1 A Fair Success Path

Sunita Ramnathkar, a chemistry graduate and housewife, set up a factory in Andheri, a distant suburb of Mumbai with a net capital of ₹ one lakh in 1982. In a span of 12 years, the compnay, Fem Care Pharma Pvt. Ltd., has come a long way and has crossed ₹ 33.5 crore turnover mark with its key products. Its first product was 'Fem Instobleach'. Today, the company has broadened its product base. Fem has succeeded in carving a niche for itself in all its product-lines. While the distribution of the other products in the Fem range are handled by 450 stockists, sales and marketing for the Pharma range is via medical representatives and is restricted to Karnataka, Maharashtra and Madhya Pradesh and Fem has been developing its expertise in niche marketing developing into a fine art.

After all, whatever the generic name of the product, success of a brand depends on how the consumer values it.

Broadly, entrepreneurs are classified into business community and others. This chapter attempts to analyse different types of entrepreneurs in business as well as in different faculties of understanding. On the basis of his study of American agriculture, Clarence Danhof classified entrepreneurs into four categories, namely Innovative Entrepreneur, etc. The other classification is based on technology, economic activity and market economy.

Economists' View

In economic analysis, entrepreneurial functions are supposed to be directed towards the materialistic objective of maximisation though its foundations may be of a high order such as spiritual, patriotic, social, psychological or ethnic. Entrepreneurial activity is a form-giving activity – giving form to the wishes of the society, to ideas, to the efforts of factors and to the raw materials to be processed through.

Jean Baptiste Say states that to rationally combine the forces of production into a new producing organisation is the function of the entrepreneur. J.S. Mill lists superintendence, control and direction as entrepreneurial functions.

Superintendence: to assemble the means, turnout maximum at minimum cost and to supervise the work.

Control: the flow of goods, use of finance, utilisation of machinery and the activities of the subordinates.

Direction: He is a goal-oriented person; he has to keep the organisation constantly on the path of his objective. His activity of producing in the present what the future will demand. John Stuart also emphasised managerial and administrative functions of an entrepreneur according to Marshall. Organisation building capacity is the most critical skill expected of an entrepreneur according to Alfred. He assigns to the entrepreneur the functions of risk-bearing, innovation and management. To Cantillion, an entrepreneur is an uncertainty-bearer buying at a fixed price and selling at an uncertain one.

Israle M., viewed the entrepreneur as a disequilibrating force. It is the alertness to unnoticed opportunities which creates a tendency of the ever-circular flow of equilibrium. Harvey Leibenstenin states, "Entrepreneur is an individual or group of individuals with four major characteristics. He connects different markets; he is capable of making up market deficiencies (gap-filling); when his input complete and he creates or expands time-binding, input-transforming entities (firms)."

To Joseph A., innovation is the sole function of an entrepreneur. It covers the introduction of new goods, a new method of production, a new market, a new source of supply of raw materials or half-manufactured goods and a new organisation of any industry for the creation of a monopoly position or breaking it. The function of the entrepreneur is to reform or revise the pattern of production. So, Schumpeter has given a social context to the activity, a psychological objective to be attained and a functionality spearheading development of the community. Lazarfeld as also Meier and Baldwin concur with Schumpeter.

Bert F. Hoselitz reports, "The primary function of entrepreneurship is the investment of time, capital and energy in economically significant pursuit; the emphasis is on decision-making in its various aspects."

Frederick Fritz enumerates four functions: the undertaking or managing of risks and handling of economic uncertainty; planning and innovation; coordination, administration and control and routine supervision. Ability to build an organisation is, perhaps, Harbinson adds, the most precious of all entrepreneurial skills. Redlich's threefold division of function is: (i) capitalist – employing the factors and buying raw material, setting up the organisation; (ii) managerial – innovation, supervision and coordination of productive activities, and (iii) entrepreneurial – decision-making. Benjamin Higgins lists seeing opportunities for introduction of new techniques, new products and exploitation of new resources and organising factors of production into an enterprise to take advantage of these opportunities as essential for economic development.

B.C. Tandon discusses the function of an entrepreneur in a developing economy in the context of economic, legal, political and cultural environment. Accordingly, the entrepreneur must possess: (a) capacity to assume risk and self-confidence; (b) technological knowledge, alertness to know opportunities, willingness to accept change and ability to initiate; (c) ability to marshal resources, and (d) ability of organisation and administration. He has to have tact, patience, sagacity, power of observation and ability of discrimination. He should have the capacity to pick and choose associates and subordinates and wisely delegate authority to inspire loyalty. He must be able to multiply 'himself' effectively. Tandon describes the entrepreneur as an 'ideal-type' rather than as 'social-type'. Frank H., identifies entrepreneurship with control and responsibility.

Economic functions described above isolate the entrepreneur from the economic environs, social milieu and political ethos in which he functions. Maximisation is taken as the pole star in his voyage. It seems to be conveniently assumed that he is abundantly provided with all the resources and the market readily absorbs what he put into it. Reality is, however, full of bottlenecks and hurdles which are ignored in the above-mentioned works. Small industry is a natural habitat of the entrepreneur where his role is like that of a stoker who keeps the fire burning. Economic functioning takes no notice of this.

Sociologists' View

Sociologists consider the entrepreneur as a role performer corresponding to the role expected by the society. Wishes of the society are exhibited through customs and taboos, rewards and restraints, ethnic values and child-rearing practices, nationalistic attitude and patriotic inculcations and protestant ethics. He is conditioned by the social milieu to which he belongs. According to Peter Marris, to assemble or reassemble from what is available, very concrete kind of imagination, to see what others have missed, sensitivity to business and social environment, zest in industrial development and entrepreneurial courage are the factors that make an entrepreneur. According to Flavia Derossi, coordination at every stage – inception, maintenance and expansion – is the function of an entrepreneur. She feels an entrepreneur needs two qualities: (i) Optimistic outlook that there is a possibility of change, the environment can be mastered and he himself can introduce the required change. He finds difficulties challenging and stimulating; he thrives on them, and (ii) In a share as in the dynamic industry, new problems are seized upon as opportunities for testing one's own capabilities.

According to T.C. Cochran, the entrepreneur give represents society's model personality. His performance depends upon his own attitudes towards his occupation, the role expectations of sanctioning groups and the occupational requirements of the job. Society's values are the most important determinant of attitudes and role expectations.

Arthur, H. Cole, states that entrepreneurship should not be studied by focusing on individual entrepreneur but rather by looking at the enterprise. Special attention was often paid to the social relations within the enterprise and to the relations between the enterprise and its surroundings.

Everett, E. Hagen also concluded that entrepreneurs have emerged from certain communities and castes. Thus, Hagen disregard the complicated institutional environment that surrounds the entrepreneur.

Psychologists' View

Among psychologists, Frank Young describes an entrepreneur as a change-agent. K.L.Sharma maintains that entrepreneurs are men who exhibit qualities of leadership is solving persistent professional problems; but those persons likewise demonstrate eagerness to seize unusual opportunities. They have a business gambler's itch. T.V. Rao and Udai Pareek describes entrepreneurship as a creative and innovative response to the environment. The entrepreneur is goal-oriented rather than means-oriented. He must not only have a high capacity of risk-taking but must also have a high capacity of risk-sustaining which is a function of a high degree of self-confidence.

Joseph Schumpeter states that the entrepreneur is mainly motivated and driven by three things:

(i) 'the dream and the will to find a private kingdom';

(ii) 'the will to conquer';

(iii) 'the joy of creating'.

J. Schumpeter's formulation can be translated as:

(i) the desire for power and independence;

(ii) the will to succeed;

(iii) the satisfaction of getting things done.

According to him, money is not what ultimately motivates the entrepreneur. 'Entrepreneurs', according to Schumpeter, 'are certainly not economic men in the theoretical sense'.

According to David, McClelland, entrepreneurship has to do with an individual's so-called need for achievement (referred to nAchievement). He identified three features of entrepreneurs that were related to their need for achievement: (1) desire to accept responsibility for solving problems, setting goals and reaching the goals; (2) a willingness to accept moderate risks; (3) a desire to know the outcomes of their decisions. It was widely believed that a high achievement motivation has a strong likelihood of predicting entrepreneurial behaviour. Individuals with high achievement motive tend to take keen interest in situations of high risk, desire for responsibility and a desire for a concrete measure of task performance.

According to Fredrik Barth, entrepreneurship has essentially to do with connecting two spheres in the society, between which there exists a difference in value. Something which is cheap in one sphere, may be expensive in another sphere. Barth, one of the leading anthropologists of the world, states that entrepreneurial behaviour means to connect two different spheres in the society, between which there is a huge discrepancy in value.

In sum, the foregoing description of the functions of an entrepreneur presents the profile of a functionary. Economists present him as a perceiver of otherwise unnoticed opportunity, organisation builder, adaptor of new profitable activity and beneficiary thereof. Sociologists present him as a personality moulded by various practices of social enforcement and values imbibed in him. Psychologically, entrepreneurship is a vigorous application of the person's energies towards the long-cherished goals.

CLASSIFICATION OF ENTREPRENEURS

The entrepreneurs in business are broadly classified according to the types of business, use of professional skill, motivation, growth and stages of development. Clarence Danhof classifies entrepreneurs on the basis of stage of economic development; some others have classified on the basis of their functions and characteristics. The former reflects the role played by the entrepreneurs in the economic development, and later type reflects the degree of their involvement. The various types of entrepreneurs have been shown in Fig. 22.1.

According to the types of business
1. Business entrepreneur
2. Trading entrepreneur
3. Industrial entrepreneur
   (i) Large
   (ii) Medium
   (iii) Small, and
   (iv) Tiny
4. Corporate entrepreneur
5. Agricultural entrepreneur
   (i) Plantation
   (ii) Horticulture
   (iii) Dairy
   (iv) Forestry
   (v) Floriculture
   (vi) Animal Husbandry
   (vii) Poultry
   (viii) Seeds
6. Retail entrepreneur
7. Service entrepreneur
8. Fauzi entrepreneur
9. Health entrepreneur
10. Re-engineering entrepreneur

According to the use of technology
1. Technical entrepreneur
2. Non-technical entrepreneur
3. Professional entrepreneur
4. High-tech entrepreneur
5. Low-tech entrepreneur
6. IT entrepreneurs
7. E-entrepreneurs
8. BPO entrepreneurs
9. KPO entrepreneurs
10. LPO entrepreneurs

According to the motivation
1. Pure entrepreneur
2. Induced entrepreneur
3. Motivated entrepreneur
4. Spontaneous entrepreneur

According to the growth
1. Growth entrepreneur
2. Super Growth entrepreneur
3. Aspiring entrepreneur
4. Lifestyle entrepreneur

According to the stages of development
1. First generation entrepreneur
2. Modern entrepreneur
3. Classical entrepreneur
4. Generation-next entrepreneur
5. Inherited entrepreneur

According to area
1. Urban entrepreneur
2. Rural entrepreneur
3. Local entrepreneur
4. Global entrepreneur

According to gender and age
1. Men entrepreneurs
2. Women entrepreneurs
3. Young entrepreneurs
4. Old entrepreneurs
5. Middle-aged entrepreneurs

Others or Unclassified
1. Professional entrepreneurs
2. Non-professional entrepreneurs
3. New Modern entrepreneurs
4. Traditional entrepreneurs

5. Skilled entrepreneurs
6. Non-skilled entrepreneurs
7. Imitating entrepreneurs
8. Serial entrepreneurs
9. Forced entrepreneurs
10. National entrepreneurs
11. International entrepreneurs
12. Bureaucratic entrepreneurs
13. Entrepreneur entrepreneurs
14. Immigrant entrepreneurs
15. Innovative entrepreneurs
16. Philonthropreneurs
17. Entertainment entrepreneurs
18. Creative entrepreneurs
19. Knowledge entrepreneurs
20. Education entrepreneurs
21. Intrapreneurs
22. Ultrapreneurs
23. Mompreneurs
24. Alterpreneurs
25. Artapreneurs
26. Joint entrepreneurs
27. Generous entrepreneurs
28. Promoter entrepreneurs
29. Multifaced entrepreneurs
30. Entrepreneur employees
31. Accidental entrepreneurs
32. Orthodox entrepreneurs
33. Social entrepreneurs
34. Edupreneurs
35. Mentorpreneurs
36. Mobile entrepreneurs
37. Upcountry entrepreneurs
38. Foodrepreneurs
39. Executive entrepreneurs
40. Green entrepreneurs
41. Change entrepreneurs
42. Level headed entrepreneurs
43. Student entrepreneurs
44. Farmapreneurs
45. Forced entrepreneurs
46. Accidental entrepreneurs
47. Achieveing entrepreneurs
48. Successful entrepreneurs
49. Visionary entrepreneurs
50. Zealous entrepreneurs

According to Organisation

1. Individual entrepreneurs
2. Group entrepreneurs
3. Institutional entrepreneurs
4. Private entrepreneurs
5. Public entrepreneurs
6. Government entrepreneurs

Fig. 22.1 Classification of Entrepreneurs

The above classification of entrepreneurs is not exhaustive, for it aims at highlighting the broad range of entrepreneurs found in various businesses and professions. We shall now discuss in brief, each type of entrepreneur.

According to the Type of Business

Entrepreneurs are found in various types of businesses occupation of varying size. We may broadly classify them as follows:

Business Entrepreneur: They are individuals who conceive an idea for a new product or service and then create a business to materialise their idea into reality. They tap both production and marketing resources in their search to develop a new business opportunity. They may set up a big establishment or a small business unit. They are called *small business entrepreneurs* when found in small business units such as printing press, textile processing house, advertising agency, ready-made garments or confectionery. In a majority of cases, entrepreneurs are found in small trading and manufacturing business and entrepreneurship flourishes when the size of the business is small.

Trading Entrepreneur: He undertakes trading activities and is not concerned with the manufacturing work. He identifies potential markets, stimulates demand for his product-line and creates a desire and interest among buyers to go in for his product. He is engaged in both domestic and overseas trade. Britain, due to geographical limitations, has developed trade through trading entrepreneurs. These entrepreneurs demonstrated their ability in pushing many ideas ahead which promoted their business.

Industrial Entrepreneur: Industrial entrepreneur is essentially a manufacturer who identifies the potential needs of customers and tailors products or services to meet the marketing needs. He is a product-oriented man who starts in an industrial unit because of the possibility of making some new product. The entrepreneur has the ability to convert economic resources and technology into a considerably profitable venture. He is found in any industrial units such as the electronic industry, textile unit, machine tools or video cassette making and the like.

Corporate Entrepreneur: This entrepreneur is a person who demonstrates his innovative skill in organising and managing a corporate undertaking. A corporate undertaking is a form of business organisation which is registered under some statute or Act which gives it a separate legal entity. A trust registered under the Trust Act, or a company registered under the Companies Act are examples of corporate undertakings. He is thus an individual who plans, develops and manages a corporate body.

Agricultural Entrepreneur: Agricultural entrepreneurs are those who undertake such agricultural activities as raising and marketing of crops, fertilisers and other inputs of agriculture. They are motivated to raise the productivity of agriculture through mechanisation, irrigation and application of technologies for dry land agriculture. They cover a board spectrum of the agricultural sector and include agriculture and allied occupations.

Social Entrepreneur

Ashoka-Innovators for the public, a global non-profit organisation committed to nurturing social entrepreneurship, says a social entrepreneur is one who recognises the part of society which is stuck and provides new ways to get it unstuck. Be it dedicated efforts for child upliftment, fighting for the conservation of Assam's rainforests, working for the betterment of the blind or initiatives to empower women, the entrepreneur's passion is so strong that the can't let "the opportunity to make a difference" go by.

Ashoka was the idea of one man, William Drayton. His key insight was that there exist people in all countries who, like business entrepreneurs, have vision, creativity and tenacity, but who are possessed with a need to make a difference, to change society. He dubbed these people "social entrepreneurs". Social entrepreneurs, he explained, were "rare men and women who possess the vision, creativity and extraordinary determination of the business entrepreneur but who devote these qualities to introducing new solutions to societal problems". He also realised that a little investment in such people would go farther in terms of their social impact than simply giving money for projects would. "It is arrogant to think that well-meaning outsiders can make a dent in the horrendous social problems besetting every country in the world ... We empower social entrepreneurs from the communities and get out of their way. It is amazing how effective they become in finding their own solutions."

Like the visionary social entrepreneurs, Verghese Kurien of Amul, Rippan Kapur of CRY, Jeroo Billimoria of Childline (where children in trouble in numerous Indian cities can pick up a phone and make a toll-free call for help) and many others, a social entrepreneur approach to implement ideas in creative, innovative and unconventional. It's their sensitivity and the ability to voice and take a stand which differentiates them from others.

What Can be Achieved?

For a social entrepreneur, the potential to change lives is enormous. For instance, Dream Catcher, a Mumbai-based NGO, conducts a 6-week workshop for underprivileged children to give with a space to ask questions, seek answers and initiate a reconnection with their innerselves. But the achievable goes beyond this. Says Sonali Ojha, founder director of Dream Catcher, "To generate a complete leap of faith, from fear and doubt, embitterment and helplessness to a sense of possibility and self-worth."

Support Framework

If you want to unleash your social spark in a business-like fashion, there are a lot of funding agencies and boards that will help. For example, Ashoka & CRY have fellowships, which provide financial and non-financial aid. These come in the form of a stipend, capacity building and infrastructure support, sharing of ideas and information, networking with other fellows, mentoring, etc. You may learn more about these on www.ashoka.org and www.cry.org.

Other organisations like UNESCO, UNICEF, Aga Khan Foundation, Ford Foundation, Infosys, Tata Foundation and Azim Premji Foundation could be possible sources of funding too. What you need is an idea, a solution to a social problem/ need and plan of action.

According to the Use of Technology

The application of new technology in various sectors of the national economy is essential for the future growth of business. We may broadly classify these entrepreneurs on the basis of the use of technology as follows:

Technical Entrepreneur: A technical entrepreneur is essentially an entrepreneur of 'craftsman type'. He develops new and improved quality of goods because of his craftsmanship. He concentrates more on production rather than marketing. He does not care much to generate sales by applying various sales promotional techniques. He demonstrates his innovative capabilities in matters of production of goods and rendering services. The greatest strength which the technical entrepreneur has is his skill in introduction techniques.

Non-technical Entrepreneur: Non-technical entrepreneurs are those who are not concerned with the technical aspects of the product in which they deal. They are concerned only with developing alternative marketing and distribution strategies to promote their business.

Professional Entrepreneur: Professional entrepreneur is a person who is interested in establishing a business but does not have interest in managing or operating it once it is established. A professional entrepreneur sells out the running business and starts another venture with the sales proceeds. Such an entrepreneur is dynamic and he conceives new ideas to develop alternative projects.

According to Motivation

Motivation is the force that influences the efforts of the entrepreneur to achieve his objectives. An entrepreneur is motivated to achieve or prove his excellence in job performance. He is also motivated to influence others by demonstrating his power, thus, satisfying his ego.

Pure Entrepreneurs: A pure entrepreneur is an individual who is motivated by psychological and economical rewards. He undertakes an entrepreneurial activity for his personal satisfaction in work, ego or status.

Induced Entrepreneurs: The entrepreneur is the one who is induced to take up an entrepreneurial task due to the policy measures of the government that provides assistance, incentives, concessions and necessary overhead facilities to start a venture. Most of the entrepreneurs belong to this category and enter business due to financial, technical and several other facilities provided to them by the state agencies to promote entrepreneurship. A person with a sound project is provided package assistance to his project. Today, import restrictions and allocation of production quotas to small units have induced many people to start a small-scale industry.

Motivated Entrepreneurs: New entrepreneurs are motivated by the desire for self-fulfilment. They come into being because of the possibility of making and marketing some new products for the use of consumers. If the product is developed to a saleable stage, the entrepreneur is further motivated by reward in terms of profit.

Spontaneous Entrepreneurs: These entrepreneurs start their business out of their natural talents. They are the persons with initiative, boldness and confidence in their ability which motivate them to undertake entrepreneurial activity. Such entrepreneurs have a strong conviction and confidence in their ability.

According to Growth

The development of a new venture has a greater chance of success. The entrepreneur enters a new and open field of business. The customer's approval to the new product gives them psychological satisfaction and enormous profit. The industrial units are identified as high growth, medium growth and low growth industries and as such we have 'Growth Entrepreneur' and 'Super Growth Entrepreneur'.

Growth Entrepreneur: He necessarily takes up a high growth industry and choose an industry which has sustained growth prospects.

Super Growth Entrepreneur: This category of entrepreneurs are those who have shown enormous growth of performance in their venture. The growth performance is identified by the liquidity of funds, profitability and gearing.

According to Stages of Development

Entrepreneurs may also be classified as the first generation entrepreneur, modern entrepreneur and classical entrepreneur, depending upon the stage of development.

First Generation Entrepreneur: A first generation entrepreneur is one who starts an industrial unit by means of an innovative skill. He is essentially an innovator, combining different technologies to produce a marketable product or service.

Modern Entrepreneur: A modern entrepreneur is one who undertakes those ventures which go well along with the changing demand in the market. They undertake those ventures which suit the current marketing needs.

Classical Entrepreneur: A classical entrepreneur is one who is concerned with the customers and marketing needs through the development of self-supporting ventures. He is a stereotype entrepreneur whose aims to maximise his economic returns at a level consistent with the survival of the firm with or without an element of growth.

Women Entrepreneurs' Enterprises

In 1988, for the first time, the definition of Women Entrepreneurs' Enterprise was evolved that termed an SSI unit/ industry-related service or business enterprise, managed by one or more women entrepreneurs in proprietary concerns, or in which she/they individually or jointly have a share capital of not less than 51 per cent as partners/shareholders/directors of a private limited company/members of a cooperative society, as a Woman Enterprise.

Women entrepreneurs have been on the Indian business scene for quite sometime now and have achieved remarkable success. However, their number in relation to the overall number of small-scale enterprises is still very small. One of the reasons for this is the initial hesitation and inhibition, both familial and social, due to the traditional perception of the women's role. Moreover, like any other entrepreneur, any first generation woman entrepreneur has to compete in the business against those already well established.

Women entrepreneurs, as a group, came into prominence in the late 1970s. The information contained in the Second All India SSI Census 1987-88 shows that about 7.7 per cent of the small enterprises were owned by women. Industry group-wise, the most popular activity of women entrepreneurs was food processing followed by garment making. Realising the great untapped potential, the government has been making concerted efforts to channelise the skills and talent of women towards economic and business generating activities.

Box 22.2 Kiran Mazumdar Shaw

Age: 51 years

Designation: CMD, Biocon India

Education: B.Sc., Brewmistress

Strengths: A down-to-earth person with no delusions about herself. Operates on the basis of common sense and with a strong integrity.

Weakness: Tends to be very sensitive at most times

Business Icons: N.R.Narayana Murthy, Azim Premji, Jack Welch

Time off: Goes for art shows, plays golf, spends time with family and friends.

Kiran Mazumdar Shaw entered the biotech field by accident. In fact, armed with an Australian degree from Melbourne's Ballarat University, this qualified brewmi – stress had initially planned to work in a brewery. In 1978 came her biggest break

yet - the opportunity to set up a biotech venture. This despite the fact that she was inexperienced and lacked a business background, so to speak. In a country where women entrepreneurs usually come to the forefront through family businesses, Mazumdar has carved out her own niche in the uncharted waters of biotech. That appears to be the best decision she has made - to start Biocon and to marry her Scottish husband, John Shaw.

With a small amount of ₹ 10,000, Muzumdar started her business in a garage, working on enzymes that could be used for fermenting liquor. Today, this garage outfit is one of the leading biotechnology companies in the country, the ₹ 520 crore Bangalore-based Biocon India. Mazumdar recently took her company public, offering one crore shares of face value ₹ 5 at ₹ 315. The issue was oversubscribed 33 times "My biggest challenge was raising money, and establishing my credibility to financial institutions. In those days, biotech was an alien sector and the concept of a woman entrepreneur was alien too," she says.

Biocon is India's pioneering biotech venture, set up in 1978 as a joint venture with Biocon Biopharmaceuticals of Ireland to make industrial enzymes. While its Irish partner is no longer in its original entity. Mazumdar has transformed Biocon into a valuable organisation, with a global standing in enzymes and pharmaceuticals. From an enzyme producer (among the top five worldwide), Biocon has transformed itself into a biopharma company. Mazumdar's main achievements are to get Biocon's own bioreactor patented. And launching its human insulin in both, domestic and global markets.

Over the next five years Mazumdar wants Biocon to be a global major, one that will be considered a world-class enterprise. Before the end of the decade, Mazumdar wants Biocon to be a billion-dollar company among the top 10 biotech enterprises in the world.

Box 22.3 Zia Mody

Age: 47 years

Designation: Partner, CAB Partners

Education: LL.M.

Strengths: Hardwork

Weakness: Too much attention to detail

Time off: Spends it with family, does some Baha'i work

For Zia Mody, becoming a lawyer was an osmotic decision. Seeing her father, noted lawyer Soli Sorabjee, at work, his ability to argue each point clearly and convincingly, caught Mody's interest. "I never had the thought of engaging in any other profession. Law was always the number one choice," says Mody.

After studying law in Cambridge, and getting an LL.M. degree from Harvard University, Mody passed her New York Bar exams in 1980. Her biggest break was being employed as a corporate associate at the New York office of Baker & McKenzie, one of the largest law firms in the world. To be in New York, take the examinations and qualify, and then spend five years in an international environment, was a wonderful opportunity.

In a male-dominated profession, the challenge was to initially face a much more hesitant bar, one that was not so willing to give a break to women in this tough profession. An attitude which made Mody feel that she always had to try and to do better and work harder. Today, this glass ceiling has been broken to a certain extent.

Mody has been practising law since 1984, when she set up her proprietor firm, Chambers of Zia Mody. It was in 2002 that she made the shift from a proprietorship to a partnership structure with CZB Partners or Chudasama, Zia, Behram Partners.

Mody is one of the foremost corporate lawyers in the country. In the 15 years that she has been a counsel, Mody has been involved in litigation and arbitration in various matters relating to commercial and company law, constitutional law, and indirect tax. She has also been involved in both, domestic and international arbitration. Her work encompasses acquisitions, joint ventures, restructuring of companies, foreign-inward-investment-related practice, and corporate law. These have been in sectors as varied as offshore funds, venture capital, mutual funds, project finance, and oil & gas. In fact, the 2001-2002 edition of *Asia Pacific Legal* names her as one of the leading individuals in the project finance and energy sector.

Through hardwork and looking after her clients, Mody has for the most part succeeded in getting where she intended to be, that is, a successful lawyer. The quality of her work has received accolades. In fact, the 2002-2003 edition of *The World's Leading Lawyers* by Chambers and Partners rates Mody first among the leading individuals (corporate/M&A) in India with "a glowing recommendation for producing excellent work".

However, five years down the line she will hopefully hand over the baton to competent people in the firm and focus on maintaining quality, rather than the day-to-day execution.

Her best decision yet - to have children. And they are her three princesses — Anjali, Aarti and Aditi.

Others

Innovating Entrepreneurs: Innovating entrepreneurship is characterised by aggressive assemblage of information and analysis of results, deriving from a novel combination of factors. Men/women in this group are generally aggressive in experimentation who exhibit cleverness in putting attractive possibilities into practice. One need not invent but convert even old established products or services, by changing their utility, their value, their economic characteristics, into something new, attractive and utilitarian. Therein lies the key to their phenomenal success. Such an entrepreneur is one who sees the opportunity for introducing a new technique of production process, a new commodity, a new market, a new service or even reorganisation of an existing enterprise.

Adoptive or Imitating Entrepreneurs: Imitative entrepreneurship is characterised by readiness to adopt successful innovation inaugurated by innovating entrepreneurs. In other words, imitators follow the innovators later after observing how the latter fare. These groups are also revolutionary entrepreneurs with the difference that they do not innovate the changes themselves. They just imitate techniques and technology innovated by others. Such entrepreneurs are particularly important in developing countries because they contribute significantly to the development of such economies. Imitative entrepreneurs are most suitable for the developing regions because in such countries people prefer to imitate the technololgy, knowledge and skill already available in more advanced countries.

Table 22.1 Women-Owned Proprietory Enterprises

Industry Group	Rural	Urban	Total	%
Food Products	161.72	40.88	202.60	9.49
Beverages, Tobacco and Tobacco Products	396.61	131.41	528.02	24.72
Cotton Textiles	202.24	44.29	246.53	11.54
Wood, Silk and Synthetic Fibre Textiles	33.40	10.13	43.53	2.04
Jute, Hemp and Mesta Textiles	33.36	7.84	41.20	1.93
Hosiery and Garments	324.28	44.50	368.78	17.27
Wood Products	292.47	58.29	350.76	16.42
Paper Products and Printing	10.81	17.87	28.68	1.34
Leather Products	0.83	5.31	6.14	0.29
Rubber and Plastic Products	47.85	49.40	96.85	4.54
Chemical and Chemical Products	5.53	7.05	12.58	0.59
Non-Metallic Mineral Products	11.77	4.98	16.75	0.78
Basic Medical Industries	0.07	0.44	0.51	0.02
Metal Products	1.03	5.16	6.19	0.29
Machinery Parts Except Elect.	0.04	1.10	1.14	0.05
Electrical Machinery and Parts	0.37	0.87	1.24	0.06
Transport Equipment and Parts	0.03	0.66	0.69	0.03
Miscellaneous Mfg. Industries	127.91	46.96	174.87	8.19
Service Not Elsewhere Classified	0.42	2.62	3.04	0.14
Repair Services	1.87	3.59	5.46	0.26
Other Repair Services	0.07	0.09	0.16	0.01
Total	**1652.28**	**483.44**	**2135.72**	**100.00**

(**Source:** Survey of Manufacturing Enterprises, 1994-95)

The reason for the backwardness of the underdeveloped countries lies in the fact that they are deficient in innovating and imitating entrepreneurs when they are found in abundance in developed countries. Men are needed who can imitate the technologies and products to the particular conditions prevailing in such countries. And at times, there is a need of changing and adjusting the new technologies to their special conditions. Such countries, primarily need imitators who are responsible for transforming the system with the limited resources they possess.

Fabian Entrepreneurs: Fabian entrepreneurship is characterised by great caution and septicism in practising any change. Such entrepreneurs have neither will to introduce new changes nor desire to adopt new methods innovated by the most enterprising entrepreneurs. Such entrepreneurs are shy and lazy. Their dealings are determined by customs, religion, tradition and past practices. They are not much interested in taking risk and they try to follow the footsteps of their predecessors.

Drone Entrepreneurs: Drone entrepreneurship is characterised by a refusal to adopt and use opportunities to make changes in production. Such entrepreneurs may even suffer losses but they do not make changes in production methods. They are laggards because they continue in their traditional way and in fields their product loses its marketability of their operation becomes uneconomical they are pushed out of the market.

Aspiring Entrepreneurs: Dream of starting a business; they hope for the chance to be their own bosses, but they have not yet made the leap from their current employment into the uncertainty of a start-up.

Growth Entrepreneurs: Have both the desire and ability to grow as fast and as large as possible.

Lifestyle Entrepreneurs: Have developed an enterprise that fits their individual circumstance and style of life. Their basic intention is to earn an income for themselves and their families.

The Executive Entrepreneur

A rare breed of entrepreneurs that stayed on executive position to run the business and at the same time run one or more ventures independently. This unique breed is known as executive entrepreneurs. Godrej Groups' A. Mahenedran may be one of the vanguards of executive entrepreneur, in addition to being managing Director of Godrej Sara lee has also have 4-5 independent ventures that are run by his wife and son.

It is a growing clan, close to 100 in 2009, who have sold out their ventures but stayed on long beyond the call of duty, or the duration of the transition contract.

IT Entrepreneurs

The new breed of IT entrepreneurs are creating a new business model that takes them straight to the top of the value chain. The empirical study suggests that they have two things in common — a narrowly defined niche and a skew towards products. They are confident, ambitious, innovative and acquired creativity in the competitive global environment. They are the brave new bunch of entrepreneurs who are raring to take on the world of information technology. They need to be encouraged and respected.

Box 22.4 The Sky is the Limit

His father did not talk to him for a month when, after qualifying as an army aviation pilot, he resigned in 22 days to set up a technology company. But as is the case with most 'inventors' — the category Rai puts his company in-practical considerations forced him to take a detour. From 1994-98, he ran another vanilla services company. In 1998, he decided to sell the company to a competitor for ₹ 20 lakh and dive headlong into his dream.

Sanjeev Rai

His company aims to be a design house on the Cisco model. It will design and patent products that it can then get produced by others. The 'big idea' for Are is to develop a chip that will allow interface between all 11 standards used by different operators across the globe at a price of around $5. In tech terms, that means a Universal Frequency Universal baseband Chip (named D-5) that is device independent and standards independent. As Rai explains: "The idea is to empower the wireless consumers with 100 mbps uplink and 20 mbps downlink that is accessible for computing and communication, right from the top of Everest to the Pacific."

Though the product is still under development, the company has already started licensing interfaces to various telecom equipment manufacturers. What it means is that using Are's technology, a CDMA phone operator can install a GPRS interface that will allow him to give locational services to his subscribers. According to Rai, D-5 has the potential to create a $15 billion market.

While looking for talent to build his research team. Rai realised the low availability of wireless talent. Towards the end of 1998, a Wireless Training and Certification Product was designed to cater to hiring needs. Today, the AreWP (Are Certified Wireless Professional) product is distributed through Prometric, which is a part of the $8 billion Thomson group, AceWP today accounts for 55 per cent of the company's revenues.

A New Class

In step with India's liberalisation process, entrepreneurship has received a boost. In the last two decades, even the composition of the entrepreneurial class has seen a sea change as an increasing number of a whole new class of entrepreneurs has been born. The new entrepreneur is educated, sometimes qualified abroad, is keyed into the frontiers of technology, aware of the latest in the production techniques, generally conscious of current management systems and is relatively well versed in marketing and quality control. He is thus, in full command of himself.

More importantly, this class of entrepreneurs is active all over the country and harvesting the fruits of a liberalised economy.

Box 22.5 The Java Men

Pramati Technologies

Founders: Jay Raghavendra Pullur and Vijay Prasanna Pullur

Niche: End-to-end Enterprise Java platform vendor

Revenues: NA

No. of Employees: 100

Brothers Jay-Vijay started off from an apartment in 1998. Both have worked with Wipro, a company that's a hotbed for entrepreneurs. Working for a decade, particularly in the early days, gave them the experience of dynamics of growth, building technology for US consumption, rapid changes in technology, and also a taste for Internet/Java in its very early days.

They wanted to use their experience in the technology services business and build branded products, as they believed the time had come for high-value software in India after its success in IT services.

Pramati is an enterprise Java technology, an area where you will not find many other Indian companies that pitches their products against global majors like IBM, Sun and Oracle.

Pramati's products are an imporant part of solutions across vertical domains. That is why they have customers in a variety of segments such as insurance, and health care. Their client list reads like a Who's Who of Indian and global companies: ICICI Bank, HDFC Bank, ABN Amro Securities, Rubbermaid, Gateway, Morgan Stanley and Ericsson.

1998: New breed of first-generation entrepreneurs born; IT professionals quit jobs to explore Net-based business opportunities. Venture capital firms pitch in.

1999: The spread of the Internet helps professionals set up SOHOs. Principal beneficiaries; Journalists, web designers, programmers, ad and PR people, copywriters, fund managers, research analysts.

2000: Dotcom bust wipes out many webpreneurs. Chastened, they return to the corporate world; VC activity slows down.

2001: Action in biotech and bioinformatics, select VCs, focus on these new areas; there's less hype now.

2002: Outsourcing spawns new business opportunities and start-ups in IT-enabled services. Also in the limelight: HR services like training and retirement benefits management.

2003: India ranks second among 37 countries in the annual Global Entrepreneurship. Monitor index for entrepreneurial activity, but government policy, infrastructure, finance remain big hurdles.

Entrepreneurship and Intrapreneurship

Intrapreneurship or intrapreneuring or corporate entrepreneurship is the process by which other new ventures are born within the confines of an existing corporation. It involves expansion by exploring new opportunities through new combination of existing resources. The concept of intrapreneurship requires that top executives inside the company should be encouraged to be entrepreneurs within the enterprise rather than go outside.

Entrepreneurship can be differentiated from intrapreneurship in the following ways:

1. An entrepreneur is an independent businessman, whereas an intrapreneur is semi-dependent on the promoters/ owners of the corporation.
2. An entrepreneur himself raises the necessary capital from various sources and guarantees the return to investors/ creditors. On the other hand, an intrapreneur neither raises the capital nor guarantees any returns to the suppliers of capital.
3. An entrepreneur bears full risks of his business, whereas an intrapreneur does not fully bear the risk of the business he develops and operates.
4. An entrepreneur operates from outside, whereas an intrapreneur is an organisation man operating from within the organisation.

Social Entrepreneur

Phaneesh Murthy

David Bornstein, the exponent of social innovations and entrepreneurship believes that the future belongs to social entrepreneurs. They are newsworthy and pose serious threats to the *status quo.*

In essence, they are both the same. However, while the former is concerned about profits, the latter is fanatical about a cause. So much so, that he or she is not happy solving an idea in one village or two villages. Yet at the same time, social entrepreneurs have got to be very systematic, are basically really good people, with a high streak of integrity. And finally, they are really self-effacing — always passing on the credit of their work to the team.

Vivek Paul

Most of these social entrepreneurs start with a higher base of education with greater access to information, and are more aware of problems around them in this era of the internet. Between 1970 and 1985, adult literacy rates have increased in the developed world from 43% to 60% and there has been a proliferation of the dot organisations too. Finally, there is more opportunity both politically and financially now, than ever before in history. Per capita incomes in free market economies have risen by more than 700% in the 20th century. So essenitally, freedom, wealth, exposure, social mobility and greater individual confidence are driving this huge wave of social innovation and entrepreneurship. After all people are tired with the inefficiency of governments and the indifference of corporates, and want to make a change and this is the case everywhere.

David Bornstein

Businesses must also realise that besides the cause, social entrepreneurs also allow them to tap a market which they themselves perhaps can never capture. Secondly, it is beneficial for employees to know that their workplace associates itself not only with profits, but also with social causes, where occasionally they can go and work too. Thirdly, business organisations have developed better competencies to understand a market over the years, developing distribution channels and also identifying target customers for example. They can help social entrepreneurs with these skills. Finally, organisations can also use their strengths to identify social entrepreneurs to associate with. For example, an architectural firm can associate with a person doing work on landscape beautification. An excellent example is how Tata Consultancy Services came forward to associate with Childline to create a nationwide database of destitute children – Childnet. It's quite simple – TCS used its software skills, Childline had the cause ready, together both beneficiary earning a good name for a noble cause.

The Serial Entrepreneur

KOPPAR: TAKING THE TOUGH CALL

BOT (Build, Operate, Transfer) is a phenomena that wouldn't have happened if it wasn't for the rise of the new age entrepreneur. The new age entrepreneurs today aren't the scions of rich business families diversifying into new areas. They are men and women who have earned their spurs as professionals. Raman Roy had run a similar business in GE and Amex before setting up Spectramind. Sanjeev Aggarwal had worked with Motorola and 3.com before he set up Daksh with another entrepreneur, Pavan Vaish. Among the younger lot, there are well educated ex-execs who have worked with blue chip companies. For example, Transwork's Rizwan Koita, is an ex-McKinsey consultant with an MIT and IIT background. Vision Health-source's Anurag Jain is an ex-Cap Gemini consultant and holds an Michigan University MBA. Indialife Hewitt's Manish Sabharwal is a Wharton MBA.

KOITA: SMART MOVE

ANURAG JAIN: HIGH ON MOTIVATION

BOT is an established way of business in highly entrepreneurial societies like the US where serial entrepreneurs abound.

Changing industry dynamics have played an important part in the rise of BOT model in India.

Many entrepreneurs have begun to realise that to grow and compete with big firms, they need scale and size.

Ready buyers, in the form of large companies in the acquisition mode and MNCs who wish to have a foothold in India have provided a sale exit route for these mid-sized companies.

SAHAI: TIME TO CASH OUT

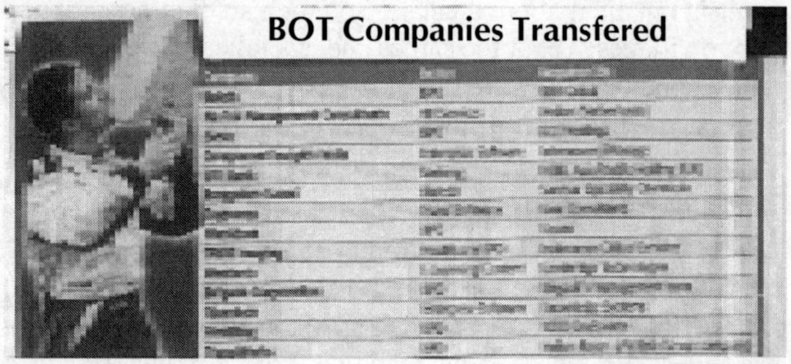

Venture capitalists have played a significant role in the emergence of the BOT model. Remember that many of these companies are funded by VCs and they have a large sTay in the future direction of these companies.

The New Age entrepreneurs are a different lot. They create world-class enterprises. But unlike the older generation of Indian businessmen, they do not hold on to their enterprises (babies) for life.

They believe in a company's first attitude and would happily set aside their egos and personal agendas for ensuring the good of their companies. So, the decision to sell out, though a painful one, is taken if it helps maximise value for all the shareholders, employees, investors, and clients. "It was a decision taken for the long-term benefit of all who mattered", says Koppar of Kshema. And, moreover, they don't have the 'know-all' attitude. "I realised that my strengths lay in building a business – growing the business further would need a different set of skill sets", acknowledges India World's Rajesh Jain, who now runs Netcore Solutions. Most tend to accept this fact and therefore, there are no ego battles after they have sold out, like the promoters of yore, even if they stay back within the company, "As long as there's clarity of thought on where you want to take the company and you are clear about your role, it's easy", says Koita. And, the entrepreneurial activity accelerates in new pastures.

INFORMATION: STRATEGIC CATALYST OF ENTREPRENEURIAL TRANSFORMATION

With all the recent attention paid to information as a strategic entrepreneurial resource, it is possible to overlook that which is simple and obvious: that information is a commodity that enterprises are run by people. Businesses do not make decisions, people do. The right information coming at the right time and place in an appropriate context leads to an informed decision, and an informed decision is always better than a blind one.

This in itself is not a new phenomenon. What is new is the requirement that entrepreneurs in every enterprise, intrapreneurs in every major corporation, government body or large institutions responsibly navigate their organisations through a more rapidly changing and complex environment, with more uncertainty, more viability, a greater number of stakeholders and wider range of choices than has ever been the case.

This kind of environment demands a leadership that can anticipate the future impact of relevant trends, current decisions and evolving possibilities. It requires that both leaders and followers be prepared to redirect and mobilise an organisation in quick response to the opportunities presented by shifting markets, diversifying needs, evolving technology and changing social norms.

In the past, we tended to think of human resources as only arms and legs. More recently and more importantly, we have begun to realise the tremendous potential represented by minds and their capacity to grow, adapt, learn and innovate. If we are to capitalise on the full capacity of people to think and create, then we must begin to view information, communication and the technology on which they are based as another critical human resource.

Another emerging aspect of the potential of human resources is the recognition that our employees are not the only human resources available to us. Instead, we should be viewing an expanded set of stakeholders and their human potential as well. It is a simple and obvious fact that our shareholders, customers, suppliers and the communities in which we operate are made up of people too. We tend to overlook the obvious potential role information can play in the development of mutually beneficial relationships with each of these stakeholder groups. All we have said about the value and potential of information and communications as human resource can be applied as well to our relationships with other organisations, public and the marketplace.

In the past few years, we have all seen numerous articles focussing on the concept of competitive advantage, but only a few have envisioned the power of using information as a competitive weapon. There seem to be two overriding strategies: one is to bundle information or technology with the company's products, electronically connecting with suppliers or with customers to place orders, invoice, pay bills and the like. This is the area where a number of well-known successes have been documented. A second way to achieve competitive advantage through information is by delivering information capacity that allows the business to lead, manage and utilise its resources in a manner superior to others in the industry.

Distinctiveness in the future will come from leveraging and creatively bringing to bear value-adding forms of information, communication and technology to achieve excellence in:

Strategic market intelligence, by combining factual, data-based trends with human judgement and learning;

Personal excellence as a result of leveraging the uniquely human qualities of judgements, experience, insight and creativity to our internal and external relationships;

Product and service excellence, by adding information components to the product or service bundles we offer in the marketplace;

Functioning excellence, by creating fluid networks unbounded by the constraints of time, technology, structure or geography; and

Stakeholder excellence, due to the extension of organisational boundaries to connect with external stakeholders in new ways, so as to add mutual value and influence.

The power of information to make an impact upon people, on an individual and collective basis is real. It is our challenge to apply new thinking to the extended uses of information as a catalyst for excellence. After all, it is thinking that drives behaviour, and behaviour in turn drives results; and it is information that moulds thinking towards new, higher results. We are all convinced that this in an integrated and escalating process that gains substance through time and that our challenge as leaders is to make this gain a reality.

CONCLUSION

It should be noted private entrepreneurship has to harmonise economic opportunities with social and moral responsibility. As our wise people have said, unless the pursuit of wealth in integrated with the pursuit of Dharma, there could be no lasting prosperity and peace, whether within a country or among nations. The highly developed countries have realised that aggressive entrepreneurship without an ethical base can produce more harm than good, more misery than happiness and more destruction than creation. Harmonised planning of economic and moral values is a long-drawn-out process, but the goal has to be kept in mind constantly. One should remain optimistic that entrepreneurship in India will develop on these lines, to promote India's economic development on a sound basis, as an integral part of the world economy. The burst of creativity and innovation in emerging technological industries holds tremendous promise for economic development and technological business growth. When talent is linked with technology, people recognise and then push viable ideas and the entrepreneurial process is underway.

Liberalisation and the new economic policy have thrown open the doors for every entrepreneur to seek its own fortunes and thus contribute his mite to the growth of the economy. In a way, the new economic policy has been fostering the spirit of entrepreneurship. The human capital and infrastructure provide the two major assets in a global economy. The states are striving to provide a framework that will improve investment, infrastructure, agriculture and industry. They have endeavoured to dovetail industrial growth with creation of employment and balanced development. The country has a vast pool of skilled manpower and there is no dearth of entrepreneurs.

In this time of rapid economic development and technological change, entrepreneurial spirit can be unique and of important advantage, but only if we learn to use it. The entrepreneurs are the agents of change and our hope for the future. In fact, the entrepreneur always searches for change, responds to it and exploits it as an opportunity.

23 CHAPTER

WOMEN ENTREPRENEURS

"The stage is set for social take-off for women from a low development path to an accelerated ace in achieveing higher level of self-sustaining economic growth...... Women entrepreneurs have to graduate from a state of dependence on subsidies/concessions to that of seizing opportunities as they emerged in an open economy."

LEARNING OBJECTIVES

"It is the holistic application of putting together the jigsaw that gives it the edge of sustainability."

Shashi Khanna
Management Consultant

The main objective is to discuss the various facets of women entrepreneurs.

The chapter *inter alia* discusses:

- Women in business world.
- Women entrepreneurship in India.
- Successful women entrepreneurs.
- Woman intrapreneur.
- Professional women.
- Profile of a woman entrepreneur.
- Leadership qualities.
- Psycho-social barriers.
- The new thrust.
- Basic problems.
- New awareness.

INTRODUCTION

The emergence of entrepreneurs in a society depends to a great extent on the economic, social, religious, cultural and psychological factors prevailing in the society. In the advanced countries of the world, there is a phenomenal increase in the number of self-employed women after the World War II. In the US, women own 25 per cent of all businesses, even though their sales on an average are less than two-fifths of those of other small businesses. In Canada, one-third of small businesses are owned by women and in France it is one-fifth. In UK, since 1980, the number of self-employed women has increased three times, as fast as the number of self-employed men.

Women entrepreneurs have been making a significant impact in all segments of the economy in Canada, Great Britain, Germany, Australia and the United States. The areas chosen by women are retail trade, restaurants, hotels, education, cultural, cleaning, insurance and manufacturing. They have made their mark in business for the following reasons:

(i) They want new challenges and opportunities for self-fulfilment.

(ii) They want to prove their mettle in innovative and competitive jobs.

(iii) They want the change to control the balance between their family responsibilities and their business lives. Dina Lavoie, a Professor of Entrepreneurship, Montreal observes that, "women business owners hire an average of two or three employees, whereas men are more likely to have nine employees or more. Often, a micro-business fits a woman's lifestyle. Expansion might mean a loss of control or disruption in the amount of time she invests in other facets of her life. She may also want to oversee and control every aspect of her life. She may also want to oversee and control every aspect of her business and may feel she will lose that opportunity if she grows to the point where she cannot."

WOMEN OF SUBSTANCE

Sudha Murthy

Nita Ambani

Parmesh Godrej

Anita Kaul Basu

Malavika Sanghvi

Priya Paul

Statistical Evidence

Globally women own between one-quarter and one-third of businesses in the formal sector and are likely to play an even greater role in the informal sector.

In Russia, women business owners are involved in international trade at a higher rate (19%) than in the US (13%).

In Brazil, Mexico and Argentina, 22-32% of women business owners are involved in international trade.

In a recent study, economist Catherine Swift, has mentioned that women face tougher security requirements on their lines of credit than do men. However, she also explains that other identified differences such as higher interest rates, lower

credit approval rates and espousal cosignature requirements are primarily attributable to the fact that women operate younger and smaller firms that are known to meet with such financing problems, whether they are owned by men or women.

The percentage of business started and operated by women in the US is less than those started by men. However, the number is increasing at a rapid rate. For example, the number of female sole proprietorships was 3,104,029 or 22 per cent of all sole proprietorships, according to the Internal Revenue Service, whereas the Bureau of Labour Statistics has indicated that between 1974 and 1984, the number of self-employed women grew 74 per cent or six times faster than self-employed men.

Table 23.1 Survey on Women Entrepreneurs

Country	Years	% Increase	Number of Women Entrepreneurs	
			Employed (in lakh)	Independent (in lakh)
USA	1977-1983	56	3.3	5.4
Canada	1987	50	4.3	1.3
Australia	1987	45	2.0	6.0
Germany	1987	25	0.6	0.8
Norway	1987	29	3.9	1.1
Sweden	1972-82	9	2.3	8.7
England	1986	25	0.6	6.3
France	1987	25	0.8	6.5
Holland	1979-85	36	0.5	4.5

Women get independent job more easily in these countries. All people working independently have been classified or termed as entrepreneurs. The highest number of women are found in laundries, dry cleaning, hairdressing, private nurseries, hotels, etc. According to the table above, the highest number of self-employed women were in Sweden followed by England, France and the USA.

New Age Women

In barely one generation, our culture has experienced two momentous changes in tandem. Rigid work-structures that provided relative stability and prosperity for 150 years have given way to a more fluid post-industrial economy. Women are, for the first time, assuming positions of influence in business and public life, the confluence of these transformations has enormous indications for the future. The study of women's lives assesses the impact that social and economic revolutions are having in at least 3 realms of public life: career development and training, commercial and social entrepreneurship, and the new physical, social, and spiritual communities that are reshaping cultures.

The new meaning of careers: Most women today are, have been, or will be part of the paid workforce. They may take 2, or 5, or even 10 years away from their jobs to raise children, to work part-time, or to volunteer for community organisations, but most eventually return to full-time work. In a rigid industrial system, where one gets an education, works for 35 years, and then retires, taking several years off is destructive to one's work-life. But, women's traditional pattern of taking time away from work give them an edge in adapting to the difficult, but increasingly common career-transitions. Women who have chosen to make a career change after taking a few years off often reexamine the nature of their work in the light of more mature personal and professional goals. When they return to the workplace, they have a better sense of who they are, and what they want to do.

The new market for training: The demand for continuing educational programmes among well-educated adults is growing. Although men receive most of the dollars spent on corporate training, according to the US Department of Labour, women are the largest consumers of outside training, whether public seminars, college courses, or personal development programmes. Women more actively seek out such training opportunities. They are more willing to spend their own money and, thus, take responsibility for their own training.

Cities on the edge: The profound changes in how we live and work are closely tied to where we live and work. Today, the massive commercial, office, and residential developments in outlying areas – dubbed edge cities by writer Joel Garreau – dominate the landscape. These communities are much more complex and self-contained than the suburbs of the 1950s, and provide a new stage for the twin revolution of gender participation, and technological and economic transformation.

The new forms of affiliation: Many people are approaching their current jobs as an opportunity to lay the foundation for a second or third career. People who rely for their sense of pride, enjoyment, and personal mastery on their work are not going to want to bow out at 70. One outlet for displaced employees and women, in particular is entrepreneurship. More than one-third of all small business are now owned by women. They are a manifestation of what Charles Handy calls the work portfolio, encompassing the many jobs we will hold in our lives as well as the family and educational commitments we will pursue. Often, these social and commercial ventures are done part-time at home as people cobble together diverse casserole careers that suit their own needs and interests. Again, women are leading this social shift.

Community and non-profit: Volunteer work is beginning to assume a non-professionalism character. This is evident among women who manage the home problems of a child or family-member. The result is an unparalleled growth in influence and sophistication of volunteer enterprises. The challenge for organisation is to engage the hearts and minds of their people at this level to draw the same kind of commitment and energy that people devote to their voluntary activities.

The intentional community: The dual revolutions in social and economic behaviour are having a clear impact on individuals and organisations. As never before, people are defining their own vocations – sometimes, 2 or 3 at a time – as well as organisational affiliations. The most accomplished people see themselves as of a self-selected network; yet, as also being larger than that network. The organisations, such once-peripheral issues such as flexitime, child care family led employee-training and development, community-service, and work-redesigned emerging as important competitive tools. That these were largely dismissed women's issues just a few years ago is indicative of the extent to which women leading today's workplace revolution.

In the end, women's greatest contribution to our changing world may be insistence on breaking the mould rather than just fitting in. This has forced to devise new strategies and improvisations that are collectively reshaping our work.

Rita Singh: Woman Entrepreneur in the Business World

Rita Singh, founder of the M'escos (Mid-east Shipping Company) group, is one of the first women entrepreneurs to make it big in the business world.

Rita's business venture is a rags to riches story. Starting from scratch about 20 years ago, she now exports trendy M'escos shoes, owns a fleet of state-of-the-art helicopters and ships, and a ₹ 450 crore steel plant.

The M'escos group with an annual turnover of over ₹ 1,500 crore, employs more than 7,000 people.

The only daughter of a Punjabi college professor who migrated from Sargodha in Pakistan to Nagpur after partition, with only a degree in Science, she set up a small dairy farm with two buffaloes near the Hind on air station and a sulphur plant at Hapur. She sold off their small farm and started exporting rice and tapioca. Then she went into shipping in a small way. Within a year, her annual income crossed the ₹ 50 lakh mark. In the coming years, she entered into steel, aviation, etc.

What are the factors behind her success? "Attribute my success to one thing – never run away from life. Face it boldly. Dare to be different."

Why aren't there many women entrepreneurs in the big league? Singh feels that a false sense of security and fear of failure are the main stumbling blocks in the path of success. " It hardly matters whether you are a man or a woman if you are insecure inside. I have never been bothered about security."

Designing Dreams

Name	:	Neeru Kumar
Education	:	B.Sc. (Chemistry), Ahmedabad University, 1974; Graduate, National Institute of Design, Ahmedabad, 1980
Experience	:	Designer, Fab India, 1980-81
Track Record	:	Turnover has grown from zero in 1984 to ₹ 3 crore in 1994-95
Investment	:	₹ 10,000
Employees	:	10
Work Style	:	Hands-on
Work Philosophy	:	Keep experimenting
Hobbies	:	Collecting old Indian textiles and antique furniture

Spinning off her old job into a new business was really not on Neeru Kumar's mind. Until, that is, the 1980 graduate of the National Institute of Design, Ahmedabad, was handed a ₹ 1 lakh contract from Tata Exports to develop a fabric for soft furnishings. "I started with their advance of ₹ 10,000," recalls Kumar. It allowed her to set up a small unit, with overheads comprising a monthly rent of ₹ 1,500 and a daily wage bill of ₹ 25 for each of the two weavers she hired to craft woollen carpets. Today, her enterprise, Tal, rakes in ₹ 3 crore annually, selling its products through an exclusive retail outlet in the capital as well as upmarket stores in the UK, US, and France.

Exclusive Accessories Business

Make silk purse out of a thoroughbred's ear. That's what Ruty Birdy, the managing partner of the low-profile Christina, has managed to do over the past decade.

WOMEN ENTREPRENEURS

Quite successfully too, the sales of this tiny chain of accessories boutiques galloping past the ₹ 1 crore mark last year. However, nine years ago, when Birdy first dabbled with a line of leather and silk accessories, she chose as the inspiration for her brand name – of all things – a horse.

With Christina accessories now emerging as the racegoer's delight, Birdy's gamble has more than paid off. To be sure, she had an unfair advantage. Not only was Birdy's father a bookkeeper at the Mahalaxmi Race Course in Mumbai, she practically grew up on the turf. An ardent racegoer, it was only natural that Birdy would chose the feminine version of Christoff – her favourite among the four racehorses her family once owned – to christen her own start-up.

THE THREE WOMEN ON THE LIST WHO HAVE FOUNDED COMPANIES HAVE ACTUALLY CREATED INDUSTRIES

3 Number of founders on the list. **Villoo Morawala Patel** (left), **Kiran Muzumdar Shaw** (centre), and **Shahnaz Husain.**

Fact File

Name	: Ruty Birdy
Education	: Presentation Convent, Kodaikanal, 1964; dropped out of St. Xavier's College, Mumbai, in 1965
Work Experience	: Designer, Star Industries; set up Christina in 1987
Initial Investment	: ₹ 40,000
Track Record	: Turnover grew from ₹ 40 lakh in 1989-90 to ₹ 1.28 crore in 1994-95
Work Style	: Hands-on
Management Philosophy	: Enjoy your work and treat your employees as family
Hobbies	: Reading, riding

Women Entrepreneurship in India

Out of total 940.98 million people in India, in the 1990s, females comprise 437.10 million representing 46.5 per cent of the total population. There are 126.48 million women workforce (representing 28.9 per cent of the female population), but as per the 1991 Census, only 1,85,900 women accounting for only 4.5 per cent of the total self-employed persons in the country were recorded. Majority of them are engaged in the unorganised sector like agriculture, agro-based industries, handicrafts, handlooms, and cottage-based industries. Participation of women as industrial entrepreneurs, however, is comparatively a recent phenomenon – commencing from the 70s onwards. There were more than 2,95,680 women entrepreneurs claiming 11.2 per cent of the total 2.64 million entrepreneurs in India during 1996-97. This is almost double the percentage of women (5.2%) among the total population of self-employed during 1981. Of this, a majority were concentrated in low-paid, low-skilled, low-technology and low-productivity jobs in the rural and unorganised sector. 90% (79.4 million) women workers were in the rural areas as against only 10% (8.6 million) in urban areas. Only 2.5 million women workers were in the organised sector – a mere 12.4% of the total employed.

Table 23.2 Women-owned Proprietary Enterprises

(units in '000)

Industry Group	Rural	Urban	Total	%
Food Products	161.72	40.88	202.60	9.49
Beverages, Tobacco, and Tobacco Products	396.61	131.41	528.02	24.72
Cotton Textiles	202.24	44.29	246.53	11.54
Wool, Silk and Synth. Fibre Textiles	33.40	10.13	43.53	2.04
Jute, Hemp and Mesta Textiles	33.36	7.84	41.20	1.93
History and Garments	324.28	44.50	368.78	17.27
Wood Products	292.47	58.29	350.76	16.42
Paper Products and Printing	10.81	17.87	28.68	1.34
Leather Products	0.83	5.31	6.14	0.29
Rubber and Plastic Products	47.45	49.40	96.85	4.54
Chemical and Chemical Products	5.53	7.05	12.58	0.59
Non-metallic Mineral Products	11.77	4.98	16.75	0.78
Basic Metal Industries	0.07	0.44	0.51	0.02
Metal Products	1.03	5.16	6.19	0.29
Machinery and Parts Except Elect.	0.04	1.10	1.14	0.05
Electrical Machinery and Parts	0.37	0.87	1.24	0.06
Transport Equipment and Parts	0.03	0.66	0.69	0.03
Miscellaneous Mfg. Industries	127.91	46.96	174.87	8.19
Services Not Elsewhere Classified	0.42	2.62	3.04	0.14
Repair Services	1.87	3.59	5.46	0.26
Other Repair Services	0.07	0.09	0.16	0.01
Total	**1652.28**	**483.44**	**2135.72**	**100.00**

(**Source:** Survey of Manufacturing Enterprises, 1994-95.)

During the Eighth Five Year Plan, the number of SSIs expected to rise from 1.7 million to 2.5 million, adding 0.8 million in the five-year period or 1.6 0 lakh every year. The rough estimate showed that amongst the SSI entrepreneurs, approximately 9% were women entrepreneurs. Their participation, however, is increasing. Considering the trend, women participation in another five years was 20% more, raising the number of women entrepreneurs to about 5,00,000. Therefore, one could aim at developing at least 3,50,000 women entrepreneurs during Eighth Five Year Plan through training and other developmental efforts. The present rate of 30% success in EDP training was likely to go up to 45% with growing experience and improved techniques of training and follow-up. Based on this assumption, for getting 3.5 lakh women entrepreneurs, it was necessary to train and support about 7.78 lakh entrepreneurs during the Eighth Five Year Plan. Besides the SSI women entrepreneurs, a large number of women entrepreneurs particularly in district and rural areas were likely to be developed for small business. Even assuming a very modest target of 335 women entrepreneurs per district, the number of women entrepreneurs would have come to 1,42,375 per year. These women were to be given training in self-employment/entrepreneurship of shorter duration as well as some training in trade and skill areas. In order to mobilise such percentage of women entrepreneurs, a number of activities such as motivational drive, preparation of information material; conducting training; creation of women industrial estates/areas/sheds; creation of common marketing exposition centres; training of trainers/promoters; and use of mass media, etc., are required. Combined effect of all these is bound to accelerate the process of women entrepreneurship development.

Woman Entrepreneurs in Several Industries

Today, we find women in different types of industries, traditional as well as non-traditional, such as engineering, electronics, ready-made garments, fabrics, eatables, handicrafts, doll-making, poultry, plastics, soap, ceramics, printing, toy making, nurseries, crèches, drugs, textile designing, dairy, canning, knitting, jewellery design, solar cooker, etc. What motivates women to aspire for career in business is an interesting thing to explore and analyse. According to Mclelland and Winter, motivation is a critical factor that leads one towards entrepreneurship. This apart, the challenge and adventure to do something new, liking for business and wanting to have an independent occupation are some of the attractive leverages for women. These factors indicate a relatively deeper commitment to entrepreneurial profession on the part of the entrepreneur. Responsibility thrust, due to death or incapacitation of a near relation, tax benefit for self and for relations are the push factors. In addition, special qualifications attained for running a concern, identifying the demand from the market, external motivation, employment to needy and destitutes to set up an ancillary unit or business already in the family are some of the factors which gave stimulus to women entrepreneurs to start their own business.

Successful Women Entrepreneurs

Although the list of successful women entrepreneurs is quite long, a selected representative women entrepreneurs are mentioned here. Among some accomplished women entrepreneurs, Smt. Sumati Morarji of Shipping Corporation been seen as beacon to women entrepreneurs. Smt. Sharayu Daftary of Automobile Radiators, Smt. Yamutai Kirloskar of Mahila Udyog Limited, Smt. Vimal Pitre, manufacturer of surgical instruments, Smt. Manik Vandrekar of leather crafts, Smt. Radanika Pradhan of Plastic Industries, Smt. Gogate for Drugs, Smt. Swati Bhatija in engineering industries, Smt. Prerang Thakore of Jayant Vitamins Limited, Smt. Nargis Wadia of Inter Publicity, Smt. Neena Malhotra in Exports, Smt. Rajani Aggarwal in engineering, Smt. Shahnaz Hussain in beauty products and cosmetics, Smt. Wadia in fabrics, Smt. Waheeda Rahman in fast foods, all stand out as successful women entrepreneurs. Other outstanding women entrepreneurs are – Smt. Priya Khanna, Smt. Savitri Debi, Smt. Raman Suri, Smt. Madhura Chatrapathy, Smt. Prabha Thakkar, Smt. Sunanda Pant.

What is more, since the inception of the National Awards to small entrepreneurs instituted in 1983, 10 women entrepreneurs have received special recognition awards. They have attributed their success in their enterprise to hardwork, perseverance, dedication, devotion, determination, integrity and confidence in themselves. However, there are still others striving to get their enterprises established. Behind every successful women entrepreneurs, there is a man and *vice versa*.

A Success Story

She certainly has been the most powerful woman of Indian origin living in the United States. Roman Malkani was listed by the respected *Washingtonian* magazine as one of the 100 most powerful women living in the US capital, along with the likes of Jeane Kirkpatick, Carla Hills and Elizabeth Dole. And more importantly, her success has been in an area which even in the US has traditionally been male-dominated: of specialised high technology communication systems.

Malkani left India in 1967 when her father, a professor of engineering at Roorkee University, went on a Fulbright scholarship to the University of Virginia. In 1979, father and daughter, who by then had a master's degree in computers, founded Information System and Network Corporation (ISN). Roman, who look over full charge a year later, has since turned the company into an largest woman-owned US government contractor.

With a revenue of over $60 million (Philosophy ₹ 105.21 crore) and an employee strength of 580, ISN was listed by the chic US women's monthly *Savvy* as the 43rd largest, female-owned and run company in that country, and the only one in the top 60 involved in manufacturing telecommunication systems.

Lakshmi G. Menon, 47, could not resist a challenge. When the top slot at the Madras-based Hindustan Teleprinters Limited (HTL) fell vacant, she applied of it. After an interview with the Public Enterprises Selection Board, she was selected – to become the first ever woman chief executive of a public sector organisation.

"I am an electronics person. I love to be in the thick of things, planning, specifying, installing and manufacturing systems in the telecommunications arena", she said. The electronics bug had bit her as a student at Trivandrum University. On graduating with a B.Sc. in 1961, she headed for the Madras Institute of Technology, and in 1964, acquired a post-graduate diploma in electronic engineering.

Box 23.1 Biocon Rising

Kiran Mazumdar Shaw has quietly transformed her company from a small maker of enzymes into an integrated biopharma player that's aiming for the global leagues. It could be the Infosys of biotech sector

Kiran Mazumdar, is the face of modern India. A self-made woman, an entrepreneur, an international success story, in the hi-tech field of biotechnology, which is undoubtedly the growth business for the twenty first century.

Kiran's Biocon is an amazing success story, almost without parallel in India. A young educated middle-class twenty-five-year old lady started a small company twenty-five years ago. The company grew steadily for years and then suddenly a few years ago transformed itself, based on its accumulated skills from an industrial biotechnology company into a pharma biotech company. Suddenly, it mushroomed into a major international pharma player.

Few people, even in corporate India have heard of Biocon. The company is expected to cross ₹ 500 crore in sales in March 2004, with a profit of ₹127 crore. And this is just for starters. And it is now well accepted worldwide that biotechnology is a field hotter than IT. This is even though few biotechnology companies in the world make any real money. This makes Biocon attract attention from pharma companies all over the world. There is little doubt that biotechnology is the science of the twenty-first century. Most of the big breakthroughs in scientific discovery in this century will be in this field. Understanding and altering biological processes will bring about revolutionary changes, whether in increased food production or whether in new drugs or whether in new medical procedures that do away with invasive surgeries. In the late eighties and early nineties, many in the West felt that the age of biotechnology had arrived and there were spurt of biotech ventures, most of which ultimately collapsed. But after recent breakthroughs in decoding the human genome, all of which would have taken much longer without the availability of hitech computing which also became available only in the nineties, the stage is set for the real growth in biotechnology.

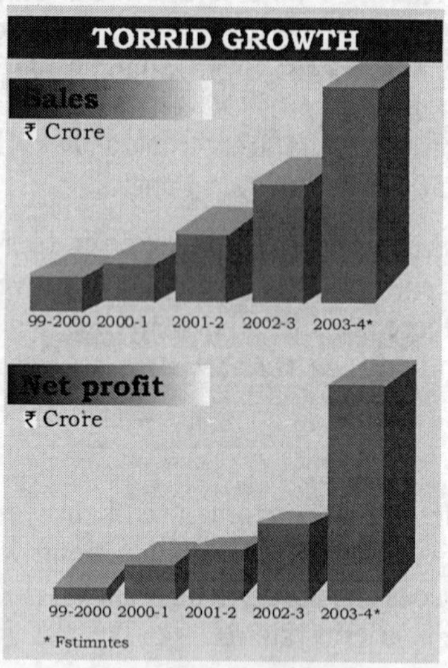

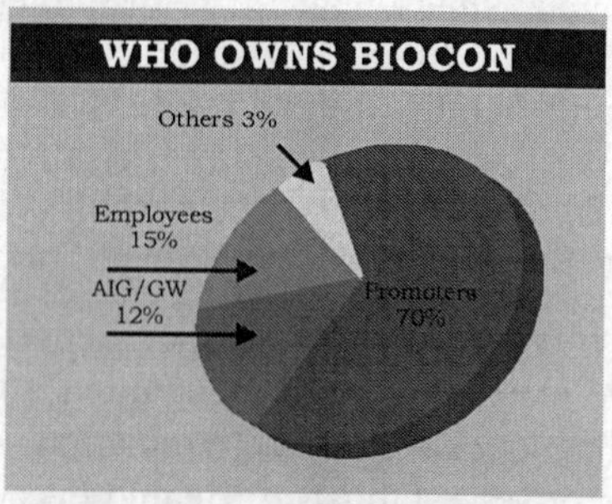

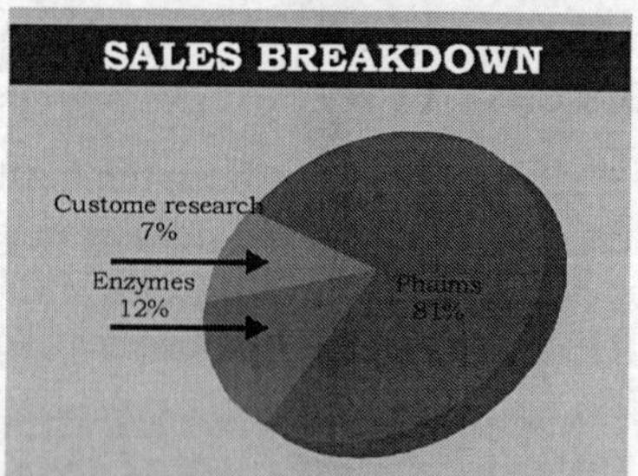

Fortunately we in India, once again have an enormous advantage in this field too. With our large base of science teaching colleges and our large human talent base, given the right government encouragement and policies India can emerge as a powerhouse in the field of biotechnology too. We can expect many science entrepreneurs wanting to enter this brave new world.

Kiran is planning a public offering for Biocon in the first quarter of next year. Given the companies growth and earnings and given the high price earnings ratios that successful biotech companies enjoy, Biocon will enter the top tier companies in India. It will also make Kiran the richest woman in India.

Few people even in the business world recognise Kiran Mazumdar's success. But soon Kiran and Biocon will be spoken about in the same tones as people speak about Azim Premji of Wipro or Narayana Murthy of Infosys. Many young people will see her as a role model and will seek to build to their lives following her footsteps.

Kiran Mazumdar is truly the face of modern India.

Menon has been known to initiate a lot of enthusiasm to her job, and Hindustan Teleprinters was in need of it. This company's performance at that time has been dismal. Though sales increased to ₹ 27 crore in 1988 as against ₹ 19 crore in 1987-88, net profit had come down to ₹ 184 crore. The company's electronic teleprinter capacity, still 50 per cent underutilised, and the original target turnover of ₹ 100 crore expected to be achieved in 1989-90 was pruned down to ₹ 50 crore. But Menon stood unfazed. "My primary concern is to decide on the best course of action for HTL, which will diversify in the telecommunications field. A corporate plan is being formulated", she said.

D. Jayalakshmi Devaraj

Smt. Jayalakshmi Devaraj was just like any other housewife till June 1983, when her husband Mr. Devaraj, founder of the Sri Vigneshwara Group of Industries died. Instead of closing down the companies in despair, she rose to the occasion and took up the challenge of running the industry started by her husband.

The total sales turnover of the foundary has been recorded as ₹ 33 lakh in 1984-85 to nearly ₹ 50 lakh in 1988-89. Smt. Jayalakshmi has been responsible for providing employment to nearly 200 persons through her various concerns.

She was the winner of the CODISSIA Award 1989 for the best women entrepreneur.

Women Intrapreneurs

Karthy Inamdar, a graduate of the Indian Institute of Management (IIM), Ahmedabad, started her career with a two-and-a-half year stint at Citibank in Bombay. Then she moved to Citibank, Delhi, had a family and went back to work for a year before deciding to take a break in her career. Six years later, after raising two children to school-going age, she joined American Express Bank in Delhi as a senior accounts manager.

Another entrepreneur in Jamshedpur, Rekha Marsalamani, also an IIM graduate, had opted out of her job as assistant manager, management development, at Tata Engineering and Locomotive Company (TELCO). For five years, she reared two children before taking up a job as executive assistant to Telco's resident director there.

Box 23.2 Women in Motion - I

The Internet as a business is a myth, says Ramesh

Ramesh, 36, is a career Wiproite. Joining the company in 1988 as a customer support executive straight from the Indian Institute of Management, Ahmedabad, the computer science engineer from Anna University moved on to become marketing services manager, production manager, southern regional manager (manufacturing segment), regional business manager and 6-Sigma facilitator, changing designations at two-year intervals. The reason she has shifted so many departments is that she finds her interest flagging after two years and begins looking for new challenges – which she has always found, thanks to Wipro's flexibility.

In April 2000, she launched 01 markets. To fulfil her immediate goal of making 01 markets India's top e-procurement service provider, she has designed a business model where nearly 90 per cent of the work is done offline. "I realised that the internet as a business is a myth, it doesn't work!" she says.

At home, Ramesh is supermom personified – helping Abhinav and Pranav with their homework, teaching them Carnatic music, and playing blind man's buff with them. An early riser, she enjoys her daily morning walks, which she sees as stress-busters. She is also an avid reader and enjoys her Agatha Christie and P.G. Wodehouse, which give her a much-needed break. She loves to paint and is also a Carnatic music aficionado. But she has no regrets about her stressful schedule: she believes that the balancing act helps enhance her capability and make her more methodical. Back at work, Ramesh believes that a leader should be able to "visualise the road ahead and also see the stones that one is stepping on". Her stepping-stones seem sure to take her up the right road. Only, going by past standards, her two-year "time's up" soon!

Both women entrepreneurs symbolised a small but growing phenomenon: women who quit relatively well-paid jobs to raise children, before returning to the job market. And it's a phenomenon that's cutting a broad swathe across industries as diverse as computers, communications, advertising and banking.

As most professional women have confirmed, it's easier to make a comeback in sunrise professions like marketing, advertising, management and perhaps even banking.

Professional Women

At Tata Steel in Jamshedpur, 33-year-old Rupa Mahanty is an example, who, after eight years with the organisation and different responsibilities, has held post of the deputy manager, human resources planning. Her job is to chalk out a detailed plan for career development of more than 4,000 officers at Tata Steel.

With a bachelor's degree in Statistics from Mumbai, Mahanty studied Management at IIM, Kolkata before joining Tata Steel in 1981. And she has struck a long record with the company because "here we are neither discriminated against nor favoured, but taken as we are".

"Aggressive marketing", according to her "is the name of the game". The marketing manager of Poona Industrial Hotels (PIH) Ltd., has significantly contributed to raising the sales of this Kirloskar Company to ₹ 10 crore during her tenure.

As an MBA from Pune University, she joined PIH as a trainee in 1984 and rose to the managerial level in two years. PIH owns Blue Diamond, a five-star hotel in Pune and Hotel Pearl in Kolhapur and she has boosted her company's sales tremendously when she initiated setting up a number of retail outlets – Banker's Basket – and also the flight catering services at Pune airport. In addition, Uttaamchandani opened offices in Mumbai and Delhi for more business. She was involved in setting up a chain of smaller hotels in the towns of interior Maharashtra.

Box 23.3 Women in Motion - II

Ruth's Delight

Ruth Varsulkar, 33, vice-president, sales and marketing, Le Royal Meridien Hotel in Mumbai, is having a ball. She is in charge of overall sales and marketing operations of the hotel and enjoys every bit of her job. "We believe in guest delight", she says. "That means our guests are not just happy, but delighted, with our service and they leave with fond memories and mean to return to us."

Varsulkar graduated in commerce from Delhi University and moved into the hotel industry. "I thought it was glamorous", she says. She very nearly did launch into an airline career, lured by the glamour of the industry, soon after she completed her graduation. "I'm glad I was not selected. I would not be anywhere else", she says. "What I'm doing is 50 times more interesting." She is responsible for formulating sales and marketing policies.

She has been familiar with sales for over 12 years. She began her career with Le Meridien in Delhi in 1988, as a sales executive. Then she joined Holiday Inn Delhi Crowne Plaza as an assistant sales manager in 1991 and moved to Hotel Leela Venture Limited as assistant sales manager, became the membership manager at the Cyclone, the hotel's discotheque. By 1999, Varsulkar was regional manager at the hotel and she began the new millennium with Le Royal Meridien where she joined as director, sales and marketing. Throughout her career, she found her thrills from getting her company business and seeing guests satisfied, their needs anticipated.

When she is not working she likes to read. She likes Jeffrey Archer and possesses most of his books, but her favourite read is *The Client* by John Grisham. The pressure of work leaves her little time for travel – besides trips to offices in Delhi, Kolkata and Bengaluru – or music. Yet, when she does get a spare moment, she relaxes to the sound of the *jaltarang* and strains of Indian classical music.

From Microbes to Mall

What does a postgraduate in Microbiology do after standing first in Mumbai University? Well, if it is Bhavna Jasra, 29, bacteria and viruses can take a breather. After receiving scholarships and a position in the nuclear medicine department of Hinduja Hospital in Mumbai as honorary research assistant, Bhavna's life took an unexpected turn. "Our family had to relocate in the Middle East for business reasons and I had to move with the family", she says.

So, she used her people skills and swiftly moved into marketing. She joined *Gulf News*. A year later she started her own event management and public relations firm in the Middle East, launching fashion guru Hemant Trivedi's Taj Mahal Collections with designer wear from the house of Sheetal and a music concert with diva Suneeta Rao. She also marketed events for other companies, besides handling product launches for the Regal Group and fashion multinationals such as Bossini and Mikura Pearls.

Marriage to Gautam Jasra of Jasra Graphics, India's premier pre-press house, brought her back to Mumbai and a new turn in her career. The age of the shopping mall has arrived in India and Landmark builders offered her the opportunity to help to create a shopping landmark on Bandra's Linking Road, called Suburbia – The Mall, due to open this Diwali. Her consultancy included helping to conceptualise the scope of the mall and its public persona and marketing of the project. She is also responsible for event management, public relations, and corporate communications. "As the mall culture is in its natal stage in India, it is critical for us continuously relearn and reinvent, along with attention to detail", she says. A good start for Suburbia and for Bhavna Jasra.

ANGELS IN BUSINESS

These are the angels who have been lending a supporting wing to budding entrepreneurs long before the technology boom made it fashionable to do so. Built around the concept of one successful entrepreneur guiding other newcomers, there's a thriving network of facilitating agencies across the country that nurtures women entrepreneurs and helps them grow.

Indira Gowada
Tending to a diabetic led her to producing health food. She worked out of AWAKE till the business qualified for a loan.

Indira Gowda (45), was a housewife when she walked into the Bangalore office of AWAKE in response to an advertisement for an entrepreneurship development course focussing on the food industry. Gowda had been caring for a diabetic relative and had an idea that she could build a brand of therapeutic foods with the cereal ragi. Buoyed by her enthusiasm, AWAKE allowed her to test a sample product at its newly opened Business Incubation Centre. Says Reddy: "Gowda was our very first incubation centre user and she is among our most successful businesswomen today".

Working out of AWAKE's incubation unit, Gowda produced and retailed a variety of ragi-based foods till 1996. By then, the business had grown enough for her to approach the Karnataka State Financial Corporation for a term loan of ₹ 8 lakh, with which she set her first manufacturing unit. In the next two years, both her sons joined the business. The family now operates three manufacturing units producing a range of jams, sauces, ketchups, chutneys, pickles and convenience foods under the brand name "Granny's Treat". The business started with an investment of ₹ 500, and today has a turnover of about ₹ 6 lakh per month. Say Gowda: "By operating under the AWAKE umbrella, I could use their food products registration number for the first year. This allowed me to sell at all retail outlets and build a brand at no extra cost". Now, as chairperson of the Business Incubator Unit at AWAKE, Gowda takes time to counsel fresh entrepreneurs and run an idea-generation seminar for fresh entrants in the food industry.

Special Projects. Initiatives like the ₹ 4 crore Biotech Park are the new approach to entrepreneurship support. The Park, set up with technical support from the M.S. Swaminathan Research Centre and project guidance from Tidco, offers 1,000 sq. ft. sheds (at ₹ 5,000) or land modules for biotech projects. About eight entrepreneurs have already started production in biotech areas as diverse as fertilisers, cosmetics, spices and aquaculture, with most projects requiring a minimum start-up capital of ₹ 10 lakh.

Profile of a Woman Entrepreneur

Who is this woman entrepreneur? What are her qualities?

She is a woman of commitment, independently employed, she has a close relationship with her father and, after obtaining an undergraduate and subsequently a graduate degree in some area of liberal arts, marries, has children and starts her first significant entrepreneurial venture in the service area in her late 30s or early 40s. Her biggest problems at start-up later in the venture reflect a lack of business training and generally in the financial area.

Table 23.3 Profit of a Woman Entrepreneur and Her Business
First-born child of middle-class parents
Father and/or mother in independent business
College-educated
Married
Early 30s for the first significant venture
Previous experience in new venture
Desires independence
Motivated by desire for independence and job satisfaction
Small and young business
Self-confident
Moderate risk-taker

High tolerance for ambiguity
High energy level
Biggest problems in start-up
Lack of business training
  Obtaining credit
  Availability of information
  Obtaining seed capital
  Marketing
Personnel management
Biggest problems in current operations:
  Lack of experience in financial planning
  Weak collateral position
  Cash flow management
  Taxation

With education and training, the women have gained confidence to do all work, which was the prerogative of man and do it excellently, rather better than men. Over the years, the educated women have become ambitious, acquired experience and basic skills of competency and self-assurance.

Leadership Qualities

Some of the outstanding qualities of women entrepreneurs are:

Accept challenges	Ambitious
Drive	Enthusiastic
Hardwork	Patience
Industrious	Motivator
Skilful	Potential optimism
Adventurous	Conscious
Educated	Determination to excel
Keenness to learn and imbibe new ideas	Experienced
Intelligent	Perseverance
Studious	

Psycho-social Barriers

Although some women entrepreneurs have excelled in their enterprise, the fear of success haunts women in general. Some psycho-social factors impeding the growth of women-related entrepreneurship are as follows:

(i) Poor self-image of women
(ii) Inadequate motivation
(iii) Discriminating treatment
(iv) Faulty socialisation
(v) Role conflict
(vi) Cultural values
(vii) Lack of courage and self-confidence
(viii) Inadequate encouragement
(ix) Lack of social acceptance
(x) Unjust social, economic and cultural system

(xi) Lack of freedom of expression

(xii) Afraid of failures and criticism

(xiii) Susceptible to negative attitudes

(xiv) Non-persistent attitude

(xv) Low dignity of labour

(xvi) Lacking in leadership qualities, i.e., planning, organising, controlling, coordinating and directing.

The New Trust

Earlier researches undertaken indicate that several women are now willing to become entrepreneurs due to various factors. These factors can be broadly classified under two headings namely "Pull factors" and "Push factors". Under the first category, women entrepreneurs choose a profession as a challenge and an adventure with an urge to do something new, liking for business and to have an independent occupation. The other category of women takes up business enterprises to get over financial difficulties and responsibility is thrust on them due to family circumstances. However, the latter category forms a negligible percentage of the total women entrepreneurs.

The new thrust given to the process of economic development of the country by the new dynamic leadership has created an all-round enthusiasm and the new slogan of "March towards the twenty-first century" gained popularity. But in this new enthusiasm, a very vital sector of the society which can contribute substantially towards the economic development of the country is not given enough attention – women entrepreneurs. In fact, Harvard School experts feel that the basic quality of efficient management is futuristic outlook and a capacity to nurture and plan for the future or unknown. This comes naturally to women. Therefore, they feel that successful managers will be those who combine this feminist attribute of nurturing and futuristic planning with male aggressiveness. But this inherent management talent of woman and her entrepreneurial skills go unrecognised and unaccounted as it does not show profit or loss in monetary terms.

With the spread of education and new approaches/awareness, women entrepreneurs are achieving higher level of 3Es, namely, engineering, electronics and energy, though the number of such units is not as large as it should be. But the very fact that women are putting up units to manufacture solar cookers as in Gujarat, small foundries in Maharashtra and T.V. capacitors in the industrially backward areas of Orissa show that women, if trained and given opportunities, can venture in non-traditional industries. Even the so-called socially tabooed industrial activities of wine-making and selling is being done by women entrepreneurs in Mumbai. So, today no field is unapproachable to the trained and determined modern Indian women.

Basic Problems of Women

The basic problem or difficulty of a woman entrepreneur is that she is a woman – this pertains to her responsibility towards family, society and work. With joint families breaking up, many women simply don't have the support of elders in the family. Women have been confronted by such dilemmas ever since they stated leaving home for the workplace. On the other hand, the attitude of society towards women and constraints in which they has to live and work are not very conducive. In spite of the constitutional equality, in practice, the attitude of men is not only tradition-bound but even of those who are responsible for decision-making, planning and research is not of equality. They still suffer from reservations. This attitude of reservation creates difficulties and problems for women at all levels. Women in rural areas equally suffer. They have to face not only resistance or reservation from men but also from elderly women who are orthodox in their attitude. In rural areas, joint families are still the norm. The overbearing presence of elders restrain even young men from venturing out; so one can imagine how much a young girl needs to put up to become economically independent. Though in rural areas women are working along with men since times immemorial, their contributions in monetary terms remains unaccounted for, or if at all accounted, it is given a very low value. They are mostly engaged in low-paid, heavy agricultural activities or act as helpers in handicrafts.

It is not that women do not have skills or capacity but they are not properly trained or initiated in craftsmanship because it is taken as a taboo – it is wasted because when she gets married, she takes the skills with her. Therefore, a woman was confined at home and not given many opportunities. She was not allowed to function independently. Training is basic for any entrepreneurship. Facilities are available, many institutions have been imparting training under various schemes but again social attitudes do not appreciate this independence and thus keep women away from them – both in urban and rural areas.

At the government level, the licensing authorities and labour officers and sales tax inspectors ask all sorts of questions like what technical qualifications you have, how will you manage labourers, how will you manage both house and business, does your husband approve your going out for working, etc.

The most important question is asked regarding strategies for marketing – both of raw material and of finished goods. To market her product, she has to be at the mercy of middlemen who go away with a big chunk of profit. Besides the middlemen try to exploit women entrepreneurs at both ends. They deny them discount or give the minimum discount in the purchase of raw material and on the other hand, try to extract maximum credit discount and commission on purchase of finished products from them.

If she decides to eliminate middlemen, it involves a lot of footwork. Secondly, in these days of stiff competition, a lot of money is required for using advertisement. If the product is targeted at a consumer, then it takes time to win people away from other products and make this product popular. And then there is a tendency to question the quality of the product produced by women entrepreneurs, though many agree that they are most sincere in maintaining the quality and time schedule.

New Awareness

The new industrial policy of the Government of India has specially highlighted the need for special entrepreneurship programmes for women entrepreneurs in the nature of product-process oriented courses – to enable them to start small-scale industries. It further adds that the objective of this course is to give representation to women in the field of small industry development with a view to uplifting their status in the economic and social fields.

Due to the aforesaid fillip, growth of industrialisation, urbanisation, education and democratic system in the country, the tradition-bound Indian society has seen a major technological change and the women are now seeking gainful employment in several fields in increasing numbers. The women entrepreneurship movement has taken off the ground and it is felt that the moment has cross the state of transition. It is only during the last 15 years women have started becoming entrepreneurs and started industries and business and they have yet to go a long way to be on par with men. The fact, however, cannot be denied that women have to play a dual role as a home-maker and also as an income-earner. Thus, arises a role conflict in many women, which prevents them from taking a prompt decision in entering business. Despite the modernisation and other factors mentioned above, the weight of tradition and the responsibilities of the family tends to slow down this movement. Further, occupational backgrounds of the families and the educational attainment of the husbands have a direct bearing on the development of women entrepreneurship. The development of kindergartens, day nurseries and creches and limiting the size of the family help the women entrepreneurs to some extent enter business in such a manner that their husbands' prestige is enhanced.

Some of the major conclusions and recommendations made at a seminar on "Woman and Rural Entrepreneurship" held at Madurai-Kamaraj University early in September, 1990 were: Women are not weak, but very strong; the industrial and business opportunities are many – electronics (printed circuit boards, floppy discs), engineering (winding, machinery manufacturing), plastic injection moulding, (film-making), chemicals (golden paste and laboratory chemicals), food and allied products (protein biscuits and cake mixture); rubber, pharmaceuticals, machinery and equipment, energy, fuel, etc.

A majority of women entrepreneurs are from the middle-class families but have low technical education, less family responsibilities (owing to the joint family system) but desire to become entrepreneurs. This potential should be identified and tapped.

Adequate infrastructural support by one single coordinating or nodal agency to facilitate flow of adequate working capital, technology, electricity, land and marketing for rural women entrepreneurs may be helpful and mobile training centres should be opened. Post-training follow-up is vital for the success of entrepreneur development programmes.

Box 23.4 At Your Service

Agencies giving women entrepreneurs a leg up.

Typically, facilitating agencies such as AWAKE and FLO do not extend credit facilities. What they do is offer credit referrals to lending agencies, assist in drawing up loan proposal and guide women entrepreneurs through the process. On the other hand, BYST, which functions with the administrative support of CII (Confederation of Indian Industry), extends loans up to ₹ 50,000 at prevailing bank rate without down payments or collateral from the entrepreneurs.

Under this scheme from the Small Industries Development Bank of India (SIDBI), loans are given to women to set up tiny and small sector projects. Expansion, modernisation and technology upgradation schemes are also funded.

The cost of project cannot exceed ₹ 10 lakh. SIDBI provides a soft loan or seed capital of up to 25 per cent of the project cost, subject to a maximum of ₹ 2.5 lakh per project. The entrepreneurs put up 10 per cent, and the soft loan component comes with a service charge of 1 per cent p.a. The repayment period is 10 years for the soft loan and 8 years for the term loan component. Mahila Udyam Nidhi schemes are available in all states, and are disbursed by the state financial corporations and scheduled commercial banks.

Scheme for Women Entrepreneurs, Maharashtra

The Maharashtra State Financial Corporation (MSFC) also offers an IDBI scheme. Under this, IDBI provides training and extension services, and offers term loans of 12.5 per cent to 15 per cent of the project cost (up to ₹ 90 lakh) to women entrepreneurs to set up units in the small-scale industries (SSI) sector. The repayment period is eight years, including a two-year moratorium.

Magalir Udavi Scheme, Pondicherry

This scheme is organised by the Pondicherry Industrial Promotion Development and Investment Corporation (PIPDIC) for women entrepreneurs to set up SSI units or tiny projects. The project cost cannot exceed ₹ 20 lakh. PIPDIC offers a term loan of 75 per cent of the project cost, at a concessional interest 2 percentage points less than the normal interest rate.

Bharatiya Yuva Shakti Trust

For young entrepreneurs, men and women between 18 and 35 years of age, the Bharatiya Yuva Shakti Trust gives a loan of ₹ 50,000 (at bank lending rate for small business), with no down payment or collateral.

Facilitators

AWAKE (Association of Women Entrepreneurs of Karnataka), B-76, Industrial Estate, Rajajinagar, Bengaluru-44, Ph: 080-33899964, awakener@blr.vsnl.net.in

FLO (Ficci Ladies Orgn) Federation House, Tansen Marg, New Delhi-1, Ph: 011-237338760-70, floindia@bol.net.in

Bharatiya Yuva Shakti Trust, C/o CII, 23, Institutional Area, Lodi Road, New Delhi-3, Ph: 011-24629994 byst.delhi@ciionline.org

Golden Jubilee Biotech Park for Women, Siruseri, Inside SIPCOT-IT Park, Old Mahabalipuram Road, Navalpur PO, Kanchipuram Dist, 603 103, Ph: 954114 475028, biotechpark@vsnl. net

CONCLUSION

Today, there is a greater awakening among women. Given an opportunity, they will deliver the results. In education, they have not only excelled but also become top makers. Likewise, in office and industry, many have shown brilliant results. Even in rural India with education, women have shown better performance. educating women is absolutely essential in straightening her personality. The need of the hour is to provide an opportunity in a conducive atmosphere free from gender difference. The need for awareness motivation to be an active member of the society and courage to correct the faults of male counterparts are great challenges today. It is, therefore, encouragement of the growing intensity of motivation amongst educated young women for coming in the entrepreneurial stream and extend support with scientifically designed packages of the technical and financial assistance. The non-governmental organisations have a bigger role in stimulating and nurturing the spirit of entrepreneurship amongst women. Towards this end, an integrated approach is necessary for making the movement of women entrepreneurship a success. For this purpose, both the government and non-government agencies have to play a vital role.

24 CHAPTER
THE ROLE OF ENTREPRENEURS

Focusing on the 'who'

"When a company is very small, you focus on the who, the what and the how... When it was just me, I focused on all three. Overtime you give up on the how, then you give up on the what and focus on the who."

— Jeff Bezos, Founder, Amazon.com

LEARNING OBJECTIVES

The chapter focuses on the unique role of entrepreneurs in establishing enterprises and managing them to create wealth, generating employment and thereby ushering in economic growth. The discussion veers round:

- Entrepreneurial Qualities
- Decisions
- Role
- Entrepreneur and Enterprises
- Environment for Entrepreneurship
- Entrepreneur versus Entrepreneurship
- Attributes of Entrepreneurs
- Functions
- Innovations
- Managers versus Entrepreneurs
- Growth of Entrepreneurs
- Entrepreneurial Initiative
- Entrepreneurial Skills
- Vision for the Future

Leading with EQ

"Great communicators have an appreciation for positioning. They understand the people they're trying to reach and what they can and can't there. They send their message in through an open door rather than trying to push it through a wall."

— John Kotter, expert on leadership at Harvard Business School

INTRODUCTION

The world is rapidly changing, and unless we are also to change our attitudes and approaches, there is a real danger that a country of India's size and potential will become peripheral in the context of world's economy. The process of development includes creation of infrastructure and setting up and management of public utilities. Non-conventional energy sources have to be developed on a commercial scale. Similarly, application of modern scientific techniques in agriculture and horticulture is essential for providing a sound base for a more rapid growth of employment and income generation. There is also a need for rapid growth of industries well distributed and in a multi-directional way. Apart from land, labour and capital, there is greater need for entrepreneurs to strive for growth on an ongoing basis. In this context, an attempt has been made in this chapter to analyse the nature and importance of entrepreneurs.

ENTREPRENEURIAL QUALITIES

The entrepreneurial qualities are to some extent innate. But not all of them are entirely innate. Some can be enhanced by training, or simply by experience. For example, analytical ability and computational skills can be enhanced by education at school and university, while practical knowledge and foresight skills can be enhanced by the general experience of everyday life. Entrepreneurial careers will be strongly influenced by the desire to enhance qualities which are scarce, yet difficult to obtain through delegation because of the problems involved in screening for them. Of the two indispensable qualities of the entrepreneur, imagination is almost entirely innate, while foresight, though to some extent innate, can be enhanced by a varied experience. Imagination and foresight are the scarce qualities which are difficult to analyse and quantify. Delegation skill and organisational skill, though not essential, are highly desirable whenever large-scale decision-making is contemplated. These too are qualities which can be enhanced through experience.

Entrepreneurial Functions

A successful entrepreneur recognises the commercial potential of a product or service, designs operating policies in marketing, production, product development and the organisational structure. He carries out the whole set of activities of the business. He has a high capacity for taking calculated risks and has faith in his own capabilities.

According to some writers, the functions of an entrepreneur are coordination of an business management enterprise, risk-taking, controlling the enterprise, innovation for change, motivation and other related activities. In reality, an entrepreneur has to carry out a combination of these in keeping with time and environment. Truly, the entrepreneur has to react to new ideas, demands and exploit the opportunities, and thereby contribute to technical progress. He is thus a nucleus of high growth of the enterprise.

An entrepreneur is expected to perform the following functions:

1. **Assumption of Risk:** The entrepreneur assumes all possible risks of business. A business risk also involves the risk due to the possibility of changes in the tastes of consumers, techniques of production and new inventions. Such risks are not insurable. If they materialise, the entrepreneur has to bear the loss himself. Thus, risk-bearing or uncertainty still remains the most important function of an entrepreneur. An entrepreneur tries to reduce the uncertainties by his initiative, skill and good judgement.
2. **Business Decisions:** The entrepreneur has to decide the nature and type of goods to be produced. He enters the particular industry which offers him the best prospects and products and produces whatever commodities he thinks will pay him the most and employs those methods of production which he considers most profitable. He affects suitable changes in the size of the business, its location, techniques of production and does everything that is needed for the development of his business.
3. **Managerial Functions:** The entrepreneur performs the managerial functions which are different from entrepreneurial functions. He formulates production plans, arranges finance, purchases raw materials, provides production facilitates, organises sales and assumes the task of personnel management. In a large establishment, these functions are delegated to the paid managerial personnel.
4. **Function of Innovation:** An important function of an entrepreneur is 'innovation'. He conceives that idea for the improvement in the quality of production-line. He considers economic viability and technological feasibility in bringing about improved quality. The introduction of different kinds of electronic gadgets is an example of such an innovation of new products. Innovation is an ongoing function rather than once for all, or possibly intermittent activity.

The entrepreneurial functions can be performed by different kinds of people under different economic systems. In principle, the entrepreneur could be a planner in a socialist economy, or even a priest or king in a traditional society. In practice, entrepreneurship is closely identified with private enterprise in a market economy.

An entrepreneur performs many useful functions. He undertakes a venture, assumes risk and earns profit. He is the man having a strong motivation to achieve success. He is self-confident in his entrepreneurial abilities and exploits opportunities wherever and whenever they arise.

The entrepreneur can identify opportunities to start a business either as a manufacturer or as a distributor, for entrepreneurship exists in every field of economic endeavour. Manufacturing activities require a relatively high capital investment and a greater degree of entrepreneurial abilities than distribution activities. Entrepreneurship has also been developed in the trading sector. Britain, for example, has developed trading entrepreneurship while Germany and Japan have developed industrial entrepreneurship. A manufacturing entrepreneur demonstrates his entrepreneurial talents by bringing out new products while a trading entrepreneur performs his entrepreneurial functions in creating demand for the business in which he deals.

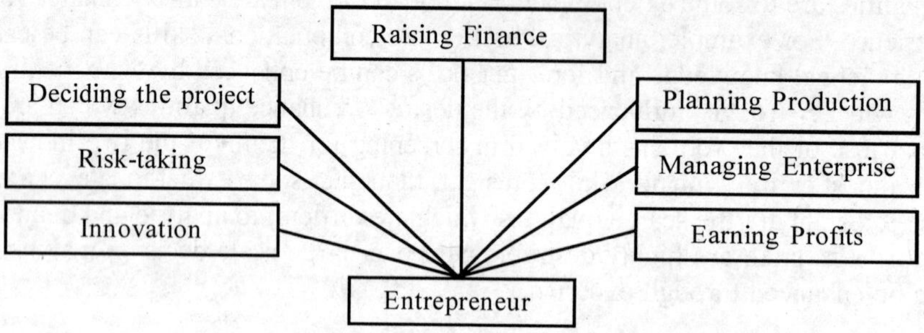

Fig. 24.1 Entrepreneurial Functions

Decision-maker

Arther H. Cole described an entrepreneur as a decision-maker and attributed the following functions:

The determination and change of objectives of the enterprise as required by changing conditions or made advantageous;

The development of an organisation, including efficient relations with subordinates and all employees;

Securing adequate financial resources and maintaining good relations with the existing and potential investors;

The requisition of efficient technological equipment and its revision as new machinery appeared;

The development of a market for the products and the devising of new products to meet or anticipate consumers' demand; and

The maintenance of good relations with public authorities and with the society at large.

Modern writers on this subject have outlined the following three broad functions of an entrepreneur:

Innovation

Risk-taking, and

Organisation and management of business so as to have leadership and control over it.

Innovation means "doing new things or the doing of things that are already being done in a new way." It includes new processes of production, introduction of new products, creation of new markets, discovery of a new and better form of industrial organisation. Risk-bearing means making provisions for capital in order to enable the entrepreneur to establish and run the enterprise. An important function of an entrepreneur is to reduce uncertainty in his plan of investment and expansion of the enterprise. Thus, innovation may occur in the following forms:

Introduction of a new good, that is, one which consumers are not yet familiar with or of a new quality of a product.

Introduction of a new method of production, that is one not yet tested by experience in the branch of manufacture concerned, which by no means needs to be founded upon a discovery scientifically new and can also exist in a new way of handling a commodity commercially.

Opening of a new market, that is, a market into which the particular branch of manufacture of the country in question has not previously entered, whether or not his market has existed before.

Conquest of a new source of supply of raw materials or half-manufactured goods, irrespective of whether this source already exists or whether it has first to be created.

Carrying out of the new organisation of any industry, like the creation of a monopoly position (for example, through trustification) or the breaking of a monopoly position.

Before coming to other functions, it is necessary to clarify how innovation differs from the two other notions with which it is sometimes confused: *research and invention.*

The aim of research is to produce knowledge, that of innovation to produce objects which work and can be sold. Since it is inspired by different objectives, innovation can be completely independent of research. It is not based on the same skills. Even the relevant information required on markets, on patents and on management has little to do with research. Innovation may be based on the application of knowledge produced by research but it may also be purely empirical: indeed practice often precedes theory and innovation may open the way to research (the steam engine for thermodynamics, or the computer for programing). Moreover, many innovations are not based on research but on ingenious combinations of existing materials and components.

Invention too is different for innovation. An invention becomes an innovation only when it is embodied in a product which can be successfully marketed. History abounds in examples of bankrupt inventors whose brainchild was born years later. The innovator, on the other hand, is the person who comes on the scene at the right moment to find the missing element in an invention which will make it eminently marketable. Thus, it is always difficult to identify the true innovator. Several individuals or organisations may simultaneously claim the authorship of ideas or inventions which have given rise to innovation.

Innovation cannot be confined to a simplistic scheme. Facts show that small and medium firms, at least in some countries, can make a very significant contribution to technical prosperity. For instance, it is estimated that firms of less than 1,000 workers and individual inventors were responsible for more than 40 per cent of the major innovations appearing in the United States in the early 1970s. This innovation potential can be explained by the advantages enjoyed by small firms over large ones.

Steps to Improved Innovation

Innovation means differently to different people. For some, it means new product ideas or new manufacturing processes that lower delivered costs. The manager may define it broadly as a strategic and profitable management of change. Still others think in terms of developmental stages: idea, implementation and diffusion throughout the marketplace. Many entrepreneurs appreciate the need for innovative thinking and implementation in every area, from human resources management to transportation. All these require special planning, implementation, and control. More importantly, the entrepreneurs today recognise that careful management of innovation can go a long way towards assuring real growth, competitiveness and profitability.

Arthur Young and the Institute for Innovation have created a group of powerful analytical tools that assist the entrepreneurs to innovate and change.

Role of Entrepreneurs

Entrepreneurs, on the hand, as Schumpeter and many others have pointed out, are distinct from business owners and managers. They are essentially strategic innovators, seeking profitability with growth. Promoting entrepreneurship, in that sense, is intrinsically different from promoting small-scale industry.

If any small business in the developed countries has received special attention, it is because it has been the fountainhead of innovation and creativity. Studies have brought out that a large number of innovations have come from small, rather than large businesses. As these innovative firms entered the market, they made profits and created jobs. In the US, Presidents Jimmy Carter and Gerald Ford emphasised that small businesses created 60 per cent of the new jobs in the United States. And this employment generation was due to its better financial performance. Similarly, the Bolton Committee, 1971, and the Wilson Committee, 1979, also concluded that the small business in UK had higher profitability than any large business.

The studies on entrepreneurship also point out that, "most of the risk in entrepreneurial management lies not in misperception of opportunity, but in trying to pursue opportunity, without adequate resources. One of the fundamental errors of large corporations, on the other hand, is overcommitment of resources".

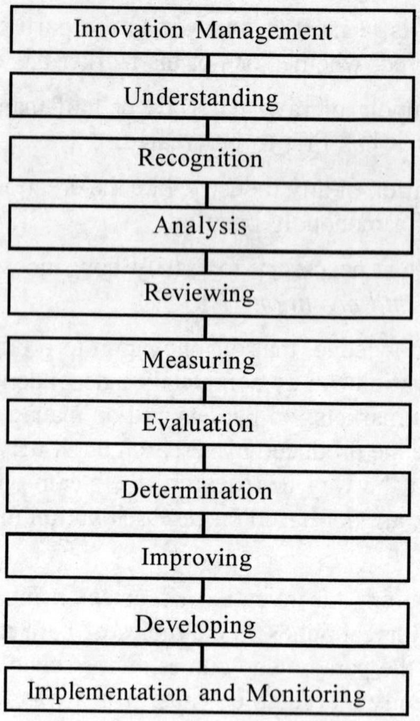

Fig. 24.2 Ten Commandments of Improved Innovation Management

MANAGERS AND ENTREPRENEURS

Both managers and entrepreneurs are answerable for producing results. The results are, of course, different. In their respective result areas, the buck stops with them. While they can delegate, they are finally accountable.

Both have to produce results through people working with them though they deal with different sets of people. They are not effective in the long run, if they are loners.

Both are decision-makers but the decisions are different as their tasks vary.

Both have to operate under constraints which are also understandably different.

To be effective in their respective roles, both have to follow sound principles of management like planning, staffing, delegation and control. The focus of these management tools may vary depending upon the ultimate purpose.

Table 24.1 summarises the similarities, focussing on the different perspectives within each similarity.

A successful organisation needs both enterprise and management. The entrepreneurial role may be played by the Chief Executive and his team of top-level executives, the managerial role by the middle-level and joint-level executives.

The entrepreneur differs from the professional manager in that the former undertakes a venture for his personal gratification. As such he cannot live within the framework of occupational behaviour set by others. He may engage a professional manager to perform some of his functions such as setting of objectives, policies, procedures, rules, strategies and formal communication network. However, the entrepreneurial functions of innovation, assumption of business risk cannot be delegated to the manager. Failure to the professional executive may mean a little more than locating a new job perhaps even at a higher salary, whereas failure of an entrepreneur in his efforts would mean a devastating loss to his career. The professional manager has to work within the framework of policy guidelines laid down by the entrepreneur.

Table 24.1 Similarities Between Managers and Entrepreneurs

Area of Similarity	Differing Focus: Managers	Differing Focus: Entrepreneurs
To produce results	Results of today, this month, this year. Short-term and medium-term	Result of tomorrow, next year and coming five years. Long-term and very long-term.
To produce results through people	Have usually to handle people-oriented to day-to-day management of nitty-gritty and nuts and bolts type – Men of details	Have to deal with people who can conceptualise with aggregate perspectives – Strategists.
To take decisions	Operational and administrative decisions, which have a bearing on short-term and medium-term results.	Mostly strategic decisions, involving growth through expansion, diversification, take-overs and mergers.
To cooperate under *constraints*	The constraints are usually organisational, i.e., those within an organisation like machine capacity, labour productivity, routing and scheduling, information availability, financial limitations, etc.	The constraints are usually environmental which lie outside an organisation like the policy of financial institutions, import policy, licencing policy, infrastructural constraints, etc.
To follow sound principles of management	The principles are more oriented towards internal administration and controls like delegation, accountability, responsibility, planning, budgeting, reporting and information system.	The principles are with reference to macro-social aspects like social responsibility equal-opportunity employment, ethical advertisement practices, adherence to government policies, etc.

Distinctive Features of Traditional Managers and Entrepreneurs

	Managers	Entrepreneurs
Primary motives	Wants promotion and traditional corporate rewards. Power motivated.	Wants freedom, goal-oriented, self-reliant and self-motivated.
Time orientation	Responds to quotas and budgets, weekly, monthly, quarterly, annual planning horizons, the next promotion or transfer.	End goals of 5-10 years growth of business in view as guides. Takes action now to move the next step along the way.
Action	Delegates action. Supervising and reporting take most of energy.	Gets hands dirty. May upset employees by suddenly doing their work.
Skills	Professional management. Often business-school trained. Abstract analytical tools, people-management, and political skills.	Knows business intimately. More business acumen than managerial or political skill. Often technically trained if in technical business. May have had former P&L responsibility in corporation.
Courage and Destiny	Sees others in charge of his or her destiny. Forceful and ambitious, but may be fearful of other's ability.	Self-confident, optimistic, courageous.
Attention	Primarily on events inside the corporation	Primarily on technology and marketplace.
Risk	Careful.	Likes moderate risk. Invests heavily, but expects to succeed.
Market Research	Has market studies done to discover needs and guide product conceptualisation.	Creates needs. Creates products that often can't be tested with market research – potential customers don't yet understand them. Talks to customers and forms own opinions.

Status	Cares about status symbols (corner office, etc.).	Happy sitting on an orange crate if job is getting done.
Failure and mistakes	Strives to avoid mistakes and surprises. Postpones recognising failure.	Deals with mistakes and failures as learning experiences.
Decisions	Agrees with those in power. Delays decision until he gets a feel of what bosses want.	Follows private vision. Decisive and action-oriented.
Who serves	Please others.	Pleases self and customers.
Attitude towards the system	Sees system as nurturing and protective, seeks position within it.	May rapidly advance in a system, then, when frustrated, reject the system and form his or her own.
Problem-solving style	Works out problem within the system.	Escapes problem in large and formal structures by leaving and starting over on his own.
Family history	Family members worked for large organisations.	Entrepreneurial small-business, professional or farming background.
Relationship with parents	Independent of mother, good relations with father, but slightly dependent.	Absent father or poor relations with father.
Socio-economic background	Middle-class background.	Lower-class background in some early studies, middle-class in more recent ones.
Educational level	Highly educated.	Less well educated in earlier studies, some graduate work but not Ph.D. in later ones
Relationship with others	Hierarchy as basic relationship.	Transactions and deal making as basic relationship.

Entrepreneur and Enterprises

Entrepreneur is the fourth factor of enterprise. According to Noah Webster, entrepreneur is "one who assumes the risk and management of business".

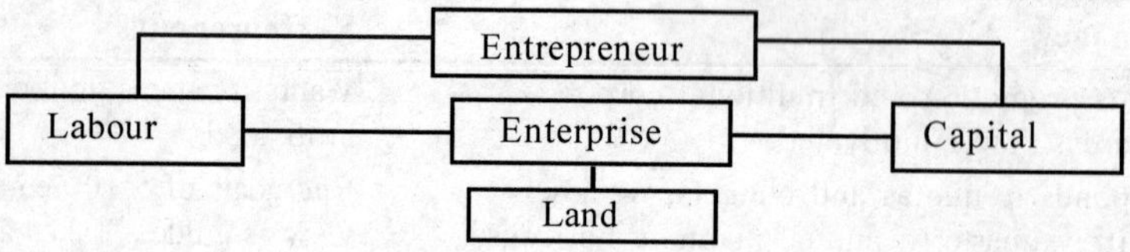

Fig. 24.3 Four Factors of an Enterprise

The enterprise is the basic unit of an economic organisation. It produces goods and services worth more than the resources used. Thus, any development effort for it to bear fruit, must ultimately affect directly or indirectly the individual enterprise. Enterprise is an undertaking, especially one which involves activity, courage, energy. It involves the willingness to assume risks in undertaking an economic activity. It also involves innovation. It always involves risk-taking and decision-making. Thus, entrepreneur and enterprise are interlinked, enterprise being the offshoot of an entrepreneur. Its success is dependent on the entrepreneur. Peter Drucker observes: "Innovation is the specific tool of entrepreneurs, the means by which they exploit change as an opportunity for a different business or a different service. It is capable of being practised".

Growth of Entrepreneurs

In terms of benefitting the people, the development of small and medium-scale industries and businesses offered many advantages. Most important perhaps, amid the mounting unemployment, are the small and medium enterprises which generate more jobs and often use labour-intensive methods of production. Industries and businesses of smaller size also promote better income distribution and development of entrepreneurship and general skills, in addition to such broader benefits as rural industrialisation and increased export earnings.

One of the most potentially fruitful areas of human resources development for small and medium-sized enterprises is the training of entrepreneurs and managers. Such training programmes should be as well rounded as possible, covering not only the basis of business, technology and so forth but also helping the trainees to identify their aptitudes, motivating them, encouraging innovative thinking and helping to develop personalities and attitudes geared for success. Indeed, small industries and businesses are ideally suited for capitalising on entrepreneurial skill initiative and talent and thus assisting in building a dynamic private sector in the developing countries.

Box 24.1 India has Most Start-ups: Study

India, with more than 85 million businesses, is the most entrepreneurial country by volume, says a new study. But the 2003 Global Entrepreneurship Monitor findings also say that because of the country's population of more than one billion, India was ranked as part of the second most entrepreneurial group of countries.

Worldwide, about 297 million people in the 41 countries surveyed were trying to develop 192 million businesses past their initial launch, estimated the study compiled by researchers at Babson College in Wellesley, Massachusetts, and the London Business School at the University of London. The Monitor, financed by the Ewing Marion Kauffman Foundation in Kansas City, found that 300 million people worldwide tried to launch firms in 2003.

Entrepreneurial activity in the US rose slightly in 2003, and optimism in the global economy was growing, said the fifth annual Monitor report.

Considering the number of start-ups and young firms, as well as existing firms anticipating growth, the most entrepreneurial countries listed were: Chile, South Korea, New Zealand, Uganda and Venezuela.

The study divided the 41 countries surveyed into five groups, ranging from the most entrepreneurial to the least. The US fell in the middle category with 14 other countries, including Britain, Canada, Australia, Singapore and Argentina. In the bottom group of least entrepreneurial were seven countries that included Poland, France, Russia and Japan.

The report, whose goal is to note the impact of entrepreneurial activity on national growth, made several suggestions about what governments could do to promote entrepreneurship, including reducing the scope of economic activities managed by the government, encouraging an increase in the annual number of hours worked and reducing the complexity and cost of registering a new business.

National experts in the countries studied said there was a universal perception that governments were ineffectual in promoting or assisting entrepreneurial activity.

The growth of entrepreneurship in the post-planning period has been significant. For example, between 1960 and 1989, the number of private companies went up from 26,000 to nearly 1,05,200. It will be seen that the maximum increase in the number of factories was in the case of industries which by virtue of their being in the small/medium-scale sector are less regulated than others. The increase in the number of factories in industries like tobacco and related products, wood and wood products, rubber and rubber products, jewellery, photographic and optical goods, watches and clothes, medical, surgical and scientific equipments, sports equipments, cold storage, etc., was more than forty times during the period 1959-2004.

There is a close relation between development of small-scale industries and the development of entrepreneurship. The entrepreneurial development paves the way for the development of small enterprises. This not only enhance employment opportunities but also reduces the concentration of economic power among few industrialists. An enthusiastic entrepreneur helps the process of development through optimal utilisation of available resorouces. The encouragement of entrepreneurs in setting up of enterprises enable the use of human capital more efficiently and also reduces the burden of unemployment which the country is facing at present.

The growth in the number of small entrepreneurs has been encouraging. The small-scale sector grew in volume from 16,000 units in 1950 to over 38 lakh units by the end of 2004. The range of items produced by the small-scale sector ranges from consumer goods to high precision items. This sector produces over 8,500 products.

The IT sector, biotechnology revolution and outsourcing (BPO) has opened new opportunities to professional entrepreneurs in a big way.

Not only has the number of entrepreneurs grown over a period of time but also the scope of entrepreneurship is getting broad-based. Earlier, for a large proportion of firms in India, the basic unit of entrepreneurship was the extended family. This tendency is now getting diluted. A study conducted a few years back by the Economic and Scientific Research Foundation (ESRF) indicated that out of a sample of entrepreneurs studied by them, around 1/5th of them were managers and engineers before they turned entrepreneurs. It was found that around 57 per cent of the new entrepreneurs in starting small-scale units were motivated by the experience that they had gained from the previous employment. Entrepreneurship in these cases was not necessarily inborn but largely acquired, and forced upon.

The year 1991 triggered a spurt of entrepreneurial energy that could have the consequences — ultimately — of doing more for the poor than all the well-intentioned activities of the state.

Box 24.2 Professional Managers

Vijay Singh, Vice-president (India), Sun Life Financial

Born: 1st December, 1945

Education: B.Com., Shri Ram College, Delhi, 1965; Chartered Accountancy

Career: IBM: business development and special projects, based in Canada, US, Singapore, and India, 1968-1992; country sales manager (Canada) for PC brand Ambra, 1992; manager (special projects) responsible for business development in Asia South, Singapore, 1993. **SLB Management Consulting:** President and CEO, Canada, 1995. **Sun Life Financial:** India, 1997.

W.S.Mukund, Managing Director, ACER India (Pvt.) Ltd.,

Born: 31st October, 1955

Education: Bachelor of Engineering (Electrical), Bangalore University, 1976; postgraduate diploma in management (Marketing), Indian Institute of Management, Ahmedabad, 1978.

Career: Management trainee, **Blue Star**, 1978; assistant manager, **Blue Star**, 1981; partner in **Home Specialities**, a Chennai-based marketing firm, 1983; regional sales manager, **Pertech Computer Ltd.**, 1988; general manager, sales, 1996; director, product and marketing, **ACER Computers, Dubai**, 1998; vice-president, sales and marketing, **ACER India**, May 2000; managing director, **ACER India**, January 2001.

Salil Parekh, Area Director, India, Cap Gemini, Ernst & Young, Consulting India Pvt. Ltd.

Born: 5th June, 1964

Education: B.Tech. (aeronautical engineering), IIT Mumbai, 1986; Master of Computer Science, Cornell University, New York, 1988; MBA (Finance), New York University, 1995

Career: Started software company Softouch in partnership with a friend, 1989. **Coopers & Lybrand:** consultant, New York, 1990. **Ernst & Young:** senior consultant, 1992; manager, 1994; senior manager, 1996; elected to partnership, 1998; CEO, April 1999.

Vishnu Deuskar, MD, ABN-Amro Securities (India) Private Ltd. and Head of Global Financial Markets

Born: 14th July, 1953

Education: B.A. Economics (Honours), Hindu College, Delhi, 1972; M.A. (Economics), Delhi School of Economics, 1974; MBA (Finance) University of Minnesota, US, 1976.

Career: Grindlays Bank, management trainee, 1976; head of trade finance, **BCCI Nigeria Ltd.**, 1981; Equities and options trader, BCC Emirates Ltd., Abu Dhabi, 1985; Controller of investment banking, **ANZ Grindlays Bank**, Mumbai, 1988; Chief manager, investments, investment banking division, 1990; Country treasurer, **ABN-Amro India**, 1994; MD, **ABN-Amro Securities (India)**, 1998.

The new entrepreneurs showed what Indians can do if allowed to pursue their natural talent for making money. Many of them were first generation entrepreneurs, and most did not belong to the traditional trading classes or groups or castes – further proof of the commercial acumen of Indians. The pioneers were risk takers. They had a sense of vision, a belief in themselves, and were exceptionally nimble in seizing the right business opportunity. They began with rags and ended with riches.

Such examples of commercial success, of innovation, drive, vision, determination, adaptability and adventure are anchored in the basic Indian openness to, and talent for, acquiring material wealth.

Though impressive in certain ways, the development accomplished so far, as indicated before, is inadequate and far from satisfactory when set against the needs as also the existing vast potential. In fact, according to Prof. Herbert Giersh, a noted economist, there is no shortage of entrepreneurial talent anywhere in the world , but the actual numbers depend on the demand conditions, i.e., the demand permitted, induced or actively provoked by the socio-economic structure and the politico-economic environment. According to him, a mixed capitalistic economy such as ours offers scope for development of entrepreneurial talent not only in the private sector but also in the government sector. The main disadvantage is that bureaucracy tends to limit the scope for entrepreneurial activity in the private sector.

Environment for Entrepreneurship

The entrepreneurs do not come spontaneously of their own. While the other factors of production are at least, in principle, hireable but enterprise is not. They have to come from different vocations. Even the educational system in most of the developing countries is designed in such a way as to create more of job-creators. In many countries, to sum up, entrepreneurs appear to have been motivated by a combination and interaction of the following factors of environment:

1. Socio-economic environment;
2. Family background;
3. Standard of education and technical knowledge;
4. Financial stability;
5. Political stability and government's policy;
6. Caste and religious affiliation;
7. Availability of supporting facilities
8. Achievement motivation; and
9. Personality and personal skill.

The environmental factors may be summarised as follows:

1. Entrepreneurship is not influenced by single factor but is the outcome of the interaction combination of various environmental factors.
2. By changing the environment, society can be recreated.
3. It is the 'desire to make money' that drives one to start an industry rather than the amount of money one owns, and
4. Encouraging government policy and social recognition influence a person to become an entrepreneur. As an educationist, we can think of modifying the educational system so as to produce more job-creators rather than job-seekers.

Box 24.3 Work Cultures of the Past and the Future

Work Culture of the Past	Work Culture of the Future
= individualism	= communitarianism
= independence	= interdependence
= autocracy	= democracy
= humanity against nature	= humanity part of nature
= unsustainable production	= sustainable production
= unsustainable consumption	= sustainable consumption
= patriarchy	= gender equality
= intercultural intolerance	= intercultural tolerance
= interreligious intolerance	= interreligious tolerance
= conflict resolution by confrontation	= conflict resolution by negotiation
= reliance on defense	= reliance on security
= reliance on rational intelligence	= reliance on emotional intelligence

Entrepreneurial Initiative

Recent data on entrepreneurial initiative and self-employment reflect a few problems. To overcome these problem to develop entrepreneurial skills, more importantly, the entrepreneur has to initiate the process of development overcoming the barriers. It is itself a challenging task. This unprecedented, perpetual change with unlimited barriers makes entrepreneurial initiative in the future more significant and infinitely, more dynamic.

The message is that stimulating entrepreneurial initiative is the strategic process that embodies calculated strategic choices. There are strategies open to the entrepreneur himself in terms of industry choice and individual and resource-task fit and there are strategies open to the regulators and support agencies in terms of use of industrial policy tools and incentives and explicit stimulation of industrial sectors or branches. A conceptual frame that contains both dimensions could provide a convenient base for analysis and possible policy action.

Encouraging entrepreneurial initiative is an issue common to both developed and developing countries and the search for effective means is proceeding in earnest. The analysis had dealt with a way of viewing the constraints embodied in the process of creating a new business or manufacturing operation.

The slow pace of the propensity to enterprise is mainly due to the existence of a tangible set of barriers prohibiting the process of entry into, continuity in and an eventual exit from a business venture of a would-be entrepreneur is a function of forces that one may view as barriers limiting a full-fledged business performance. There may be entry barriers, survival barriers and exit barriers.

Importance of an Entrepreneur

Entrepreneur is one of the most important inputs in the economic development of a country or of regions within the country. Entrepreneurial competence makes all the difference in the rate of economic growth. In India, state and private entrepreneurship coexist. The small-scale industrial sector and business are left completely to private entrepreneurs. It is, therefore, in this context that an increasingly important role has been assigned to the identification and promotion of entrepreneurs for this sector.

The need for a broad-based entrepreneurial class in India arises from the need to speed up the process of activating the factors of production, leading to a higher rate of economic growth, dispersal of economic activities, development of backward and tribal areas, creation of employment opportunities, improvement in the standard of living of weaker sections of the society and involvement of all sections of the society in the process of growth.

Several factors go into the making of an entrepreneur. Individuals who initiate, establish, maintain and expand new enterprises constitute the entrepreneurial class. The socio-political and economic conditions, the availability of industrial technology and know-how, the state-of-the-art and culture of business and trading, existence of markets for products and services and incentives and facilities available for starting an industry or business, all have a bearing on the growth of entrepreneurship. A conducive environment is created through the policies and interest of the government in economic and industrial development.

It is now well recognised that entrepreneurs can be developed through appropriately designed entrepreneurship development programmes. These programmes broadly envisage a three-tiered approach: developing achievement motivation and sharpening of entrepreneurial traits and behaviour, project planning and development and guidance on industrial opportunities, incentives and facilities and rules and regulations and developing managerial and operational capabilities. Various techniques and approaches have been developed and adopted to achieve these objectives, keeping in view the target-groups and/or target-areas. The structuring of the programmes and training methodology also necessitate consideration of the specific target-groups and target-areas. Methodology for selection of the prospective entrepreneurs as well as support services after training have a significant impact on the success of the entrepreneurs' development programmes.

Entrepreneur versus Entrepreneurship

The term 'entrepreneur' is often used interchangeably with 'entrepreneurship'. But conceptually, they are different, yet they are just like the two sides of a coin.

Entrepreneur and entrepreneurship are corelated.

The entrepreneur is the person who bears risks, unites various factors of production and carries out creative innovations. He is an individual or one of a group of individuals who tries to create something new. He always attempts to bring about change in terms of factor proportions which is known as innovation.

On the contrary, entrepreneurship is the set of activities performed by an entrepreneur. It is the process of identifying opportunities in the marketplace and marshalling the resources required to pursue these opportunities for long-term gains. It is an attempt to create value.

The Single Most Critical Ingredient that makes a successful entrepreneur is passion. Without passion, entrepreneur might succeed in managing an organisation but he can never succeed in inspiring his people. Unlike in art, where intense individual passion is enough to attain excellence, managing an organisation requires the leader to be able to infuse his whole team with that same passion.

Box 24.2 Visionary Achiever

Jamestji was an achiever India interested him, not Indian Politics. He left rhetoric to other; be built, piece by piece, the landmarks that would become beacons for future generations.

A beautiful analogy of the lifeblood that spirits the Tatas! For over 140 years, the Tata 'river' has flowed on, exhibiting the qualities of the great rivers of the world: long traction, turbulence, growing might, the ability to overcome obstacles, and the tendency to share its power for the happiness and prosperity of those on its banks.

As much as an institution it is a business conglomerate, the Tata group is unique in more ways than one. Established by Jamsetji Tata in the second half of the 19th century, 1868 to be precise, the group has grown into one of India's largest and most respected business organisations, thanks to its entrepreneurial vision, its commitment to ideals that put people before profits, and its fortitude in the face of adversity. There is a difference between making money for oneself and creating wealth for others. This enterprising spirit that creating wealth for others. This enterprising spirit that created wealth for a nation is alive in every aspect of Tata's contribution to India's growth and development.

Jamsetji Tata was more than merely an entrepreneur. Pioneer and a visionary, possessed of a spirit of entrepreneurial adventure and acumen never seen before, who helped India take her place in the league of industrialised nations. He was a patriot and a humanist whose ideals and vision shaped an exceptional business conglomerate. The nationalist in him believed unwaveringly that the fruits of his business success would deeply enrich his country.

The distinctive structure the Tata Group came to adopt after Jamsetji's passing, with a hung part of its assets being held by trusts devoted to ploughing money into social development initiatives, can be traced directly to the empathy embedded in the founder's philosophy of business.

There were certain deep-seated qualities about the Group that had become apparent by the time Jamsetji Tata, its Founder, passed away in 1904. The most outstanding of these were a passion for unconventional business ideas, a passion inventive business methods and a resolute adherence to business ethics.

Y.C. Deveshwar, ITC

An entrepreneur shares his passion with his term by translating it into a vision for the organisation. He needs to coax, cajole and inspire his people into sharing his vision. Alexander's soldiers grew tired and weary on more than one occasion, but were driven to great achievements by his passionate leadership. On the eve of each change, Alexander used his communication skills to psyche up his army.

The entrepreneur must also evoke trust among his followers. He should communicate with empathy and yet not deviate from his mission.

D.S. Brar, RANBAXY

Passion also generates courage of conviction, which acts as a source of strength in times of adversity. Mahatma Gandhi was convinced that the British rule in India was unjust and it was his moral duty to fight it out. It was this conviction that gave him the courage to take on the might of the Empire.

Organisations need leaders who are passionate institution-builders, institutions survive their builders and contribute enormously to the society. Dr. Vikram Sarabhai, the man behind the setting up of India's space research programme, IIM, Ahmedabad, the Physical Research Laboratory, and many other institutions, might not be around today, but his institutions continue to remind us of his contributions to the nation's progress.

Entrepreneurship is about understanding that an organisation will function effectively when it has the right mix of people, backgrounds, and experiences. This entails radical changes in recruitment policies. Entrepreneurship is a long journey and not a destination. It presupposes and presumes great preparation. To be an entrepreneur, one must have a sound grounding in preparation. It is the art of human relationships (ability to interact with other people). It also calls for growing mastery over the work and long hours of hardwork. The status and quality of entrepreneurship directly depends on these ingredient characteristics.

Above all, the entrepreneur should strive at all times to attain transparency in his organisation. Information should be freely given to those who need it. The entrepreneur should send out a message that information is not a source of power for an individual, but a power that contributes to the growth of an organisation.

The relationship between an entrepreneur and entrepreneurship is given in Table 24.2.

Table 24.2 The Relationship Between Entrepreneur and Entrepreneurship

Entrepreneur (PERSON)	Entrepreneurship (ACTION/ACTIVITY)
Administrator	Administration
Able	Ability
Aimer	Aim
Analyser	Analysis
Adopter	Adopting
Accelerator	Accelerating
Accountant	Accounting
Builder	Building
Balanced	Balancing
Believer	Belief
Brilliant	Brilliance
Bold	Boldness
Creator of value and trust	Creativity
Character	Values
Considerator	Consideration
Courageous	Courage
Communicator	Communication
Competitor	Competitive, Competence
Capitalist	Capital-venture, seed, working, Confidence/long-term, etc.
Confident cultured	Collaborative culture
Dreamer	Dreams
Designer	Designs
Director	Direction
Decision-maker	Decision-making
Delegator	Delegation
Dominant player	Focussed
Educator	Education
Empowerer	Empowerment
Excellor	Excelling
Ethical	Ethics
Facilitator	Facilitating, Fostering
Foresighter	Foresight
Futurist/Farsighted	Futuristic
Goal-setter	Goal-setting
Growth-fixer	Growth-oriented
Humble	Humility
Honest	Honesty
Human	Humanity

Initiator	Initiating, Initiative
Investor	Investing/Investment
Innovator	Innovation
Immitator	Immitating
Inspirer	Inspiring
Integrator	Integrity
Ignitor	Igniting
Imaginator	Imagination, Imagining
Intellectual (Driven by values)	Intelligence
Informer	Information
Knowledged	Knowledge
Leader	Leadership
Leverager	Leveraging
Learner	Learning
Mentor	Confidence building/Fostering
Motivator	Motivation
Marketeer	Marketing
Networker	Networking
Nurturer	Nurturing
Organiser	Organisation, Organising
Opportunist	Opportunities (Taking advantages of opportunities)
Planner	Planning
Programmer	Programming, Actions
Producer	Production
Performer	Performance
Partner	Partnership
Positioner	Positioning
Packager	Packaging
Promoter	Promotion
Passion-player	Passionate
Risk-bearing	Risk-taking
Responsible	Responsibility
Re-inventor	Re-inventing
Re-engineer	Re-ingineering
Skilled	Skills
Striver	Striving
Strategist	Strategy
Salesman	Selling
Talented	Talent
Trainer	Training
Trend-setter	Trend-setting
Technologist	Technology
Transformer	Transformation
Venturist	Venturing
Visionary	Vision
Visualiser	Visualisation
Wealth-creator	Wealth creation
Wizard	Specialist, Strategist, Diplomatic

Entrepreneurship management is basically concerned with the development and coordination of entrepreneurial functions. In a way, an entrepreneur precedes entrepreneurship.

Experience shows that entrepreneurship as an economic function is not a single point but rather a varied range of behaviour. There are six critical dimensions that distinguish entrepreneurial behaviour from more administratively-oriented behaviour: (i) strategic orientation; (ii) commitment to opportunity; (iii) the resource commitment process; (iv) the concept of control over resources; (v) the concept of management, and (vi) compensation policy.

		Desired future state involves growth or change	
		Yes	No
Sell-perceived Power to	Yes	Entrepreneur	Satisfied Manager
Achieve goals	No	Frustrated potential entrepreneurs	Bureaucratic functionary

Fig. 24.4 Manager's Opportunity Matrix

A matrix defining entrepreneurship is shown in Fig. 24.4. One can see how the present position influences whether one is entrepreneurial or not. It also clearly states that the particular skills, talents and attitudes towards risk influence the perception as to whether an outcome is feasible. Training, knowledge and self-confidence contribute to such perceptions.

The importance of this figure cannot be overemphasised since individuals place themselves in their particular box for rational reasons relating to their own lives; however, for the firms desiring to build the entrepreneurial spirit, action is required.

Creation of a Dream

Creating a dream gives entrepreneurs the energy and desire to become involved in its implementation and be willing to change. During the formulation of the dream, everyone participates (including the leaders), and this allows people to start seeing each other in a different light. How long they will maintain their commitment depends upon (i) how well the organisation's leaders function in their new role of facilitating resolution of the needs or issues that are at variance with the dream,(ii) how clearly the leaders articulate and share information about the business needs, and (iii) how well the leaders openly acknowledge their willingness to change in whatever fashion to fulfil the dreams.

The process of creating the dreams should be tailored to the situation with the objective of having the entire organisation ultimately own the dream. In a large organisation, there will be many dreams formulated by interdependent parts of the organisation. At some point, these should be integrated into a total organisational dream. We have found that creating a dream in a bottom-up manner where all organisational levels participate in some fashion is better than a tiered, top-down approach.

To illustrate the content of a typical dream, let us look at the leadership portion related to dreams from a Honeywell factory, which evolved as follows:

Leadership should be the ability of those leading work units (managers, supervisors, engineers, technical support and group leaders) to create an atmosphere of acceptance, openness and trust that will properly motivate members of the work units.

Interpersonal competence should be the ability to relate to people in a considerate and effective way.

This means that the leader:

1. *Cares*
   - (a) Gives positive feedback for a good job.
   - (b) Shows confidence in employees.
   - (c) Is fair and objective, not vindictive.
   - (d) Practices what is preached; does not ask or something that he or she would not be willing to do.
   - (e) Has a down-to-earth, person-to-person approach; acts as part of a team.
   - (f) Is compassionate and understanding; creates an atmosphere of acceptance and trust.

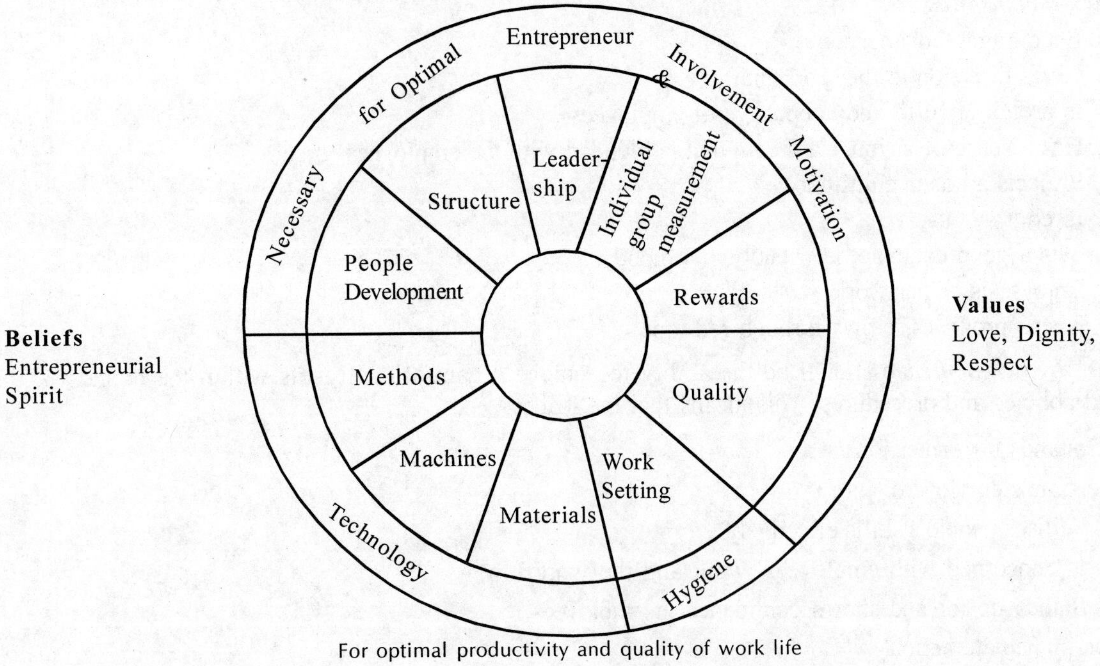

Fig. 24.5. Basic Elements — Entrepreneurial Involvement

2. *Communicates skilfully*
   - (a) Listens actively.
   - (b) Clarifies priorities.
   - (c) Is available.
   - (d) Links management with employees and *vice versa,* and employees with each other. He communicates effectively to all people on all shifts through all levels of the organisation.
   - (e) Provides feedback for both good and bad work.
   - (f) Talks openly and gives straight answers about what is happening.

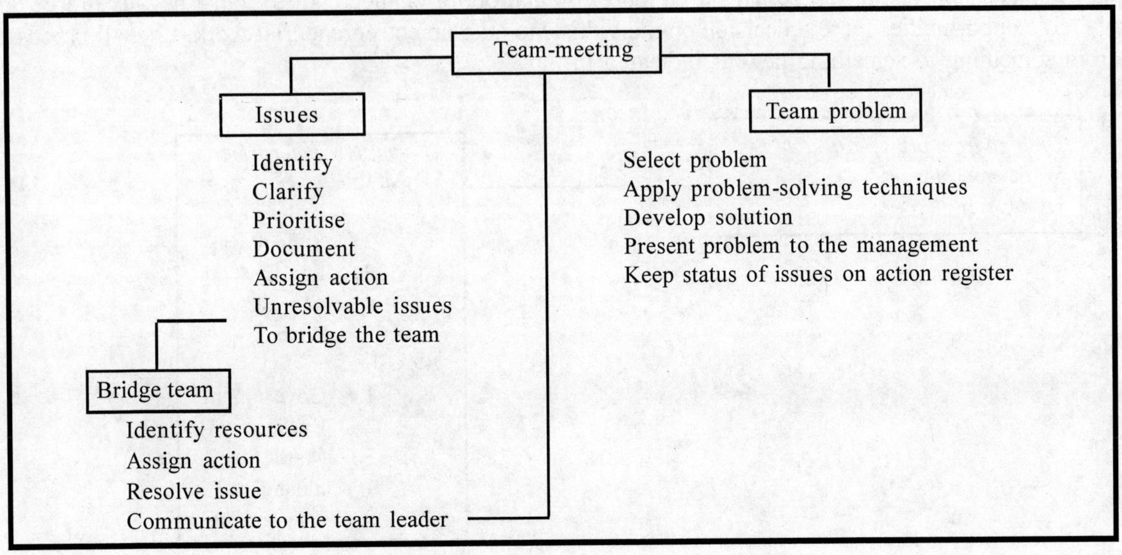

Fig. 24.6 Team Process

3. *Guides and inspires*
   (a) Encourages advancement.
   (b) Gives direction to the work unit.
   (c) Is proud, loyal to and supportive of employees.
   (d) Has a sense of vision – a dream that is blended with the employees' dream.
   (e) Projects a positive attitude.
   (f) Is courageous.
   (g) Sets a good example; is friendly, not moody.
   (h) Enjoys his or her work
   (i) Keeps promises, plows through red tape.

Administrative competence should be the ability to achieve organisational goals within the bounds of the business constraints and policies and procedures. This means that the leader:

1. Understands his or her job
2. Understands employees' jobs:
   (a) Utilises people's skills effectively.
   (b) Is concerned with employees' work and the workflow.
   (c) Stands up for and shows confidence in employees.
3. Takes immediate action
   (a) Does not ignore problems.
   (b) Follows up on promises.
   (c) Gets tough when necessary.
   (d) Takes action to remove poor performers.
   (e) Assures that the next in command knows his role and has authority to act.
   (f) Provides proper human resources for all shifts and all levels of an organisation.

Entrepreneurial Decision

Entrepreneurial decisions occur despite recession, inflation, high interest rates, lack of infrastructure, economic uncertainty, etc. Each of these decisions is a personal human process which, although unique, have some common characteristics. The impulsive motive to change his/her lifestyle and create something new and an inner urge to do something worthy, are the forces behind these decisions. At times, perhaps even more stimulation for change comes from a negative force disruption. At times, the available opportunities force a decision on individuals to take up entrepreneurial work. Like all processes, it entails movement from something to something new as indicated in Fig. 24.7.

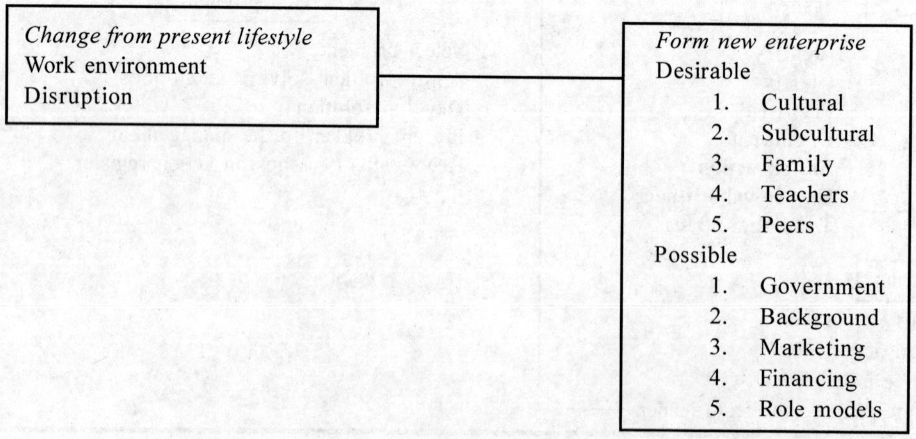

Fig. 24.7 Decision for a Potential Entrepreneur

What causes this change due to the work environment or disruption to result in a new company being formed instead of something else? The decision to start a new company occurs when an individual perceives that it is both desirable and possible.

The perception that starting a new company is desirable results from an individual's culture, subculture, teachers, family and peers. A culture that values an individual who successfully creates a new business will spawn more company formations than one that does not. For example, India places a high value on being your own boss, individual opportunity, being a success and making money – all aspects of entrepreneurship. What is more, many different subcultures that shape value, systems are operating within a cultural framework. More importantly, these subcultures support and even promote entrepreneurship. Thus, entrepreneurial decision has more bearing on sociological, cultural, subcultural, psychological and political environment, while satisfaction and adequate rewards are the optimistic goals.

Entrepreneurial Skills

To deal with entrepreneurial skills is to concern oneself with a wide coverage of aspects of setting up an enterprise and its management. It is not confined to visualisations, planning, setting up and risk taking. The skill which an entrepreneur possesses include his ability to deal with new situations, organisations and social and economic forces as they emerge from time-to-time. The skills to deal with a situation, fore-visualised or suddenly emerging, must be an essential characteristic of an entrepreneur.

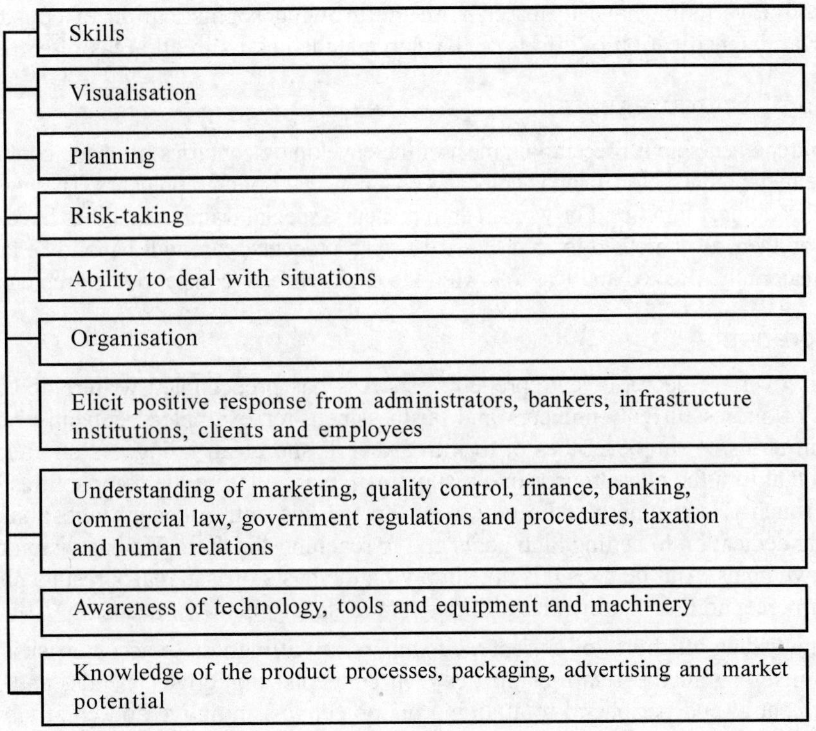

Fig. 24.8 Entrepreneurial Skills

The small entrepreneur must have the skill to elicit positive response from administrators, bankers, infrastructure institutions, clients and employees.

The entrepreneur is rarely a master of all management skills, and yet is usually directly responsible for all aspects of business. Often he or she has to be the general manager, production manager, purchasing manager, personnel manager, controller and research organiser for the business, all rolled into one, at least during its early years. The entrepreneur has, therefore, to have an understanding of marketing, quality control, finance, banking, commercial law, government regulations and procedures, and human relations as each of them has a vital bearing on the health of the enterprise.

Need for Skills

We often talk of transfer of technology. As a matter of fact, the whole world is talking about it. There is hardly any international event at the global and regional level where this subject does not come up for discussion. The poor nations demand technology and resources from industrialised and rich countries and rightly so. The developing countries would rather export semi-finished and finished products which are value added than export raw materials. The development of entrepreneurial skills must precede transfer of technology if we do not desire to keep such technologies and equipment serving such technologies idle. One has also to realise that technologies are developing very fast and skills also match with this dynamic growth. The entrepreneur has to be made aware of the imperative needs of updated technologies, modern tools and equipments, processes and systems and skills. In this task, his whole organisation, however, small it may be, has to join the exercise.

It is observed that in least developed countries, sophisticated equipment and machinery imported at heavy cost, often under pressure of international financial institutions or aid agreements, are lying unutilised for want of efficiently trained hands. It is obvious that the accelerated development of human resources and appropriate training of manpower must be concurrent with the transfer of technologies which are relevant to the needs of each developing country. This will call for an inventory of existing manpower, degree of their present skills, arrangements for proper imparting of skills needed. This should have a relation to natural endowment and resources and their optimum utilisation.

Types of Skills

Types of skills will vary according to location, products, clientele, etc. In the rural areas, a small enterprise making goods for local consumption based on local raw materials would need relatively simpler skills. In urban areas, the product, processes, packaging and advertising have to match with the growing sophistication of consumer goods, preference of needs, etc. They call for an intensification of efforts to develop matched skills in all areas of entrepreneurial activity.

Skills for New Class of Entrepreneurs

As stated earlier, entrepreneurship till recently in most of the developing countries has been confined to persons coming from the traditionally trade-oriented families. Now there is emphasis on a new class of entrepreneurs. These would include women, tribals and young men from non-traditional families. For women entrepreneurs, special training facilities have to be provided owing to the special difficulties faced by them as compared to men. For tribal entrepreneurs, care will have to be taken that their basic culture, crafts and skills are not materially affected and lost following the emergence of competitive entrepreneurship.

Attributes of Entrepreneurs

The attempts to discover the secret of entrepreneurs' success has preoccupied writers and analysts from a variety of disciplines. Biographies of successful entrepreneurs and businessmen, for example, frequently reflect the tendencies of the subject of such studies in terms of simple virtues of thrift, hardwork and clean living. As an alternative to the biographical models are those studies that turn the entrepreneur into a superman, manipulating the complexities of an uncertain world with a sure and omnipotent touch. Thus, emerges the notion of the 'genius entrepreneur' whose success is in large measure caused by his unswerving dedication to setting high goals and to reaching for them. He has vision on which he bases his own objectives and sets his own goals. And he does this not simply on the basis of last year's results plus some growth factor, but on the basis of this own perception, of his own capabilities and to satisfy his own needs.

Among other distinguishing attributes of entrepreneurship are a willingness to assume risks; a sense of acquisitiveness or unceasing curiosity; insight into the relationship between concepts, objectives, needs, and needs satisfaction; sound judgement as to what is central and peripheral to attaining his objectives; initiative and creativity; problem-solving ability; ability to marshal resources needed to achieve his objectives and goals; and the administrative ability to organise those resources to accomplish his goals and satisfy his minor needs.

Perceptions
Dedication
Vision
High Goals/objectives
Thrift
Vigorous energy
Hardwork
Clean living
Quest for new ideas
Willingness to Assume Risks
Unceasing curiosity
Urge to get going
Sense of acquisitiveness to get things done
Insight
Gambler's instinct
Initiative
Creativity
Zest to explore the unexplored
Problem-solving ability
Ability to marshal resources
To achieve one's objectives and goals
Administrative Ability

A good entrepreneur should act with self-confidence, avoid anger, take prompt and timely decisions on a rational basis, think clearly with maturity.

He should have adequate knowledge of human relation at all levels, objective analysis, ability to communicate effectively with passion and belief.

He is also capable to set challenging yet realistic and achievable goals and a passion to achieve such goals and have technical competence. Other important traits are:

- Emulative,
- Conceptual skills,
- High integrity and honesty,
- Flexibility of mind, and
- Ability to establish proper priorities.

A good entrepreneur must above all be a role model who can be emulated by the workers (employees).

Fig. 24.9 Attributes of an Entrepreneur

CONCLUSION

Entrepreneurs play an important role in the development of society. For example, the use of jeans in America has created the demand for it throughout the world. Similarly, Coca-Cola has been accepted as a social drink. The introduction of colour T.V. has provided the society a means of information and entertainment. The society has accepted the innovations of such entrepreneurs as Gillet, Wright Brothers, and Henry Ford. The inventions of these great entrepreneurs has revolutionised the lifestyle of men in the society today.

The role of entrepreneurs in economic development varies from economy to economy, country to country, depending upon its material resources, industrial climate and more importantly, the responsiveness of the political system to the growth of entrepreneurs. By and large, entrepreneurs' contribution to development and growth is relatively higher in favourable opportunities conditions and than in less favourable situations. The growth of an entrepreneurial society will bear fruitful results in a short span.

Entrepreneurship is a key driver of economic growth. However, entrepreneurial attributes are under threat in the wake of international competition. These threats provide immense opportunities for innovation, which holds the key to a country's ability to participate and reap the benefits of globalisation. A country that fosters innovation and supports entrepreneurs will emerge the strongest in the future.

Indians need to emulate the early pioneers and move towards opportunity-driven entrepreneurship. In jump-starting any such process, it would help immensely if successful entrepreneurs play the role of mentors and incubators to the late starters. This has succeeded in the IT industry, but the mentors and incubators have primarily been Indian-American entrepreneurs who have made it big in the Silicon Valley. India needs successful entrepreneurs within the country who will spread their knowledge and expertise across industries.

Entrepreneurship, the *de facto* barometer of overall economic, social and industrial growth, has brought revolutionary changes in the society. It is the *sine quo non* of an nation's progress. It has facilitated large-scale production and distribution. It has widened the area and scope of the marketing of goods and services. Perhaps it is for these reasons that the small business sector has been given priority in our national development programmes, for entrepreneurship flourishes when the size of business remains relatively small and viable.

Modern business studies have a distinct entrepreneurial discipline. The approach to the study of entrepreneurship is multidisciplinary. It images on such areas as demography, economic anthropology, business history, politics, sociology, psychology, marketing and finance. That is why entrepreneurship development becomes an integral part of the overall economic, social and industrial development of a country. This is what makes the identification and management of entrepreneurial functions a highly complex exercise.

25 CHAPTER

ENTREPRENEURIAL ENVIRONMENT

Mike's Mantra

"Budding entrepreneurs should have real zeal for the pursuit they are undertaking, and a deep personal yearning to succeed. They should have a deep conviction about their business, enormous drive, incredible work ethics and extraordinary frugality."

— Mike Moritz, Venture Capitalist

LEARNING OBJECTIVES

The nurturing of entrepreneurship largely depends on the motivation, passion, policies, infrastructure, economic situation, technology, innovation, rules and regulations and the entrepreneurial culture.

The chapter rightly dwells about the entrepreneurial environment.

The entrepreneurial environment refers to the various facets within which enterprises operate.

The entrepreneurial environment is broadly classified into six important segments: Political, Economical, Social, Technological, Legal and Cultural.

- Private enterprise and development
- Entrepreneurial urge
- Significance
- Infrastructural network
- Environmental analysis
- The green arm of the law
- Instrumental synergy
- Training
- Artisans' development
- The culture of change

INTRODUCTION

Entrepreneurship environment refers to the various facets within which enterprises — big, medium, small and others have to operate. The enterprise is, therefore, influenced by the environment. By and large, entrepreneurship is influenced by an environment created by political, social, economic, national, legal forces, etc.

Entrepreneurial environment is broadly classified into six important segments, namely, (1) Political environment, (2) Economic environment, (3) Social environment, (4) Technological environment, (5) Legal environment, and (6) Cultural environment. (See Fig. 25.1).

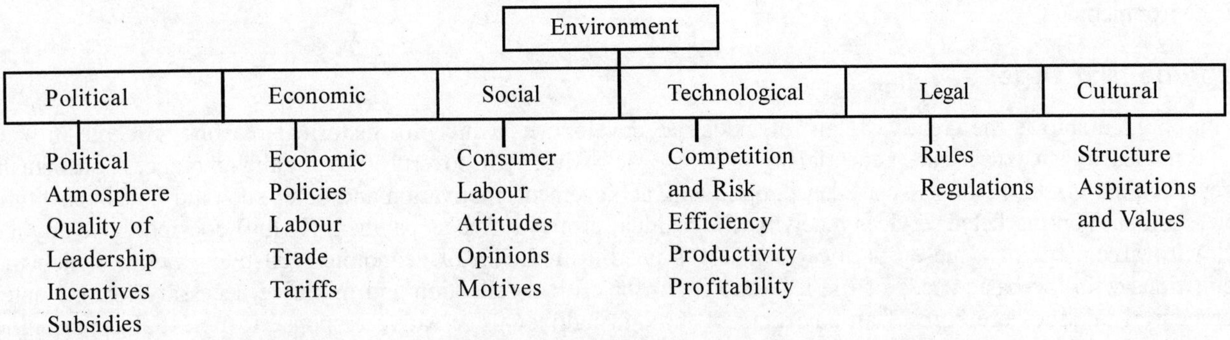

Fig. 25.1 Entrepreneurial Environment

PRIVATE ENTERPRISE AND DEVELOPMENT

The existence of uncertainty in the economic call for the attention of environment means that there are limits to planning. These limitations call for the attention of entrepreneurs to play a leading role in the growth process.

Individual entrepreneurs such as farmers and small businessmen and individual enterprises such as manufacturing, construction, transport, and wholesale enterprises and collective farms continually face risks. Whether they are privately or publicly owned, they must take account of uncertainty. Private entrepreneurs and the managers of private enterprises take risks, despite the heavy costs of failure because of the possibility of high profits or large bonuses. In any case, they must run their business efficiently if they are to make a profit and survive. The problem usually arises because major industrial decisions, which will affect the lives of thousands of ordinary people, are taken without proper planning and without public consultation. The result is that environmental activists have no choice but to fight a rear-guard action. This often gives the impression that environmental activists are against all growth and industry. In fact, they are more than conscious of the need for a balanced approach to growth and industry. All they say is that industrial decisions ought to be taken after considering the impact on environment and also that the public has a right to know all details.

Environmental activists have repeatedly pointed out they have caused by some of our petrochemical, heavy chemical, dyestuff and other polluting industries, as also the environmental damage caused by large-scale open mining, quarrying and deforestation, which will take decades to reverse. For their dogged determination, these environmentalists deserve our gratitude.

At the same time, it is now clear that technology has advanced significantly to allow efficient use of resources. Worldwide, industry has become conscious of the need to use renewable resources as far as possible and utilise non-renewable resources within planned limits. With potential developments taking place in the industry, we should learn from past incidences of industrial disasters leading environmental disaster and ensure further growth, consistent with environmental protection.

In contrast, the managers of public enterprises (whether directly or indirectly state-owned or collectively-owned) tend to be risk-averters. Indeed, risk-aversion is usually, and perhaps inevitably, the emphasis of public service training. Entrepreneurs and managers of these enterprises must be offered incentives to boost their efficiency and take risks. In this case, devising appropriate incentives become imperative. A variety of possible measures — some positive, such as bonuses for managers, and some negative, such as budget and operational controls — can be used in the public sector; even so, the problem often remains intractable.

If an economy is made up of a large number of entrepreneurial units, risks can be spread among them. Even though some enterprises may fail, others will be successful and the economy as a whole can grow rapidly. When inefficient units do not have access to subsidies or to other public assistance, they must improve their competitive position or disappear. Such failures need not be excessively costly because the economy's expansion creates job and income earning opportunities for entrepreneurs and employees of falling enterprises. Some of these may be in "informal" or small-scale activities and may not be counted in the formal employment sector. Nonetheless, they provide gainful employment.

Unfortunately, experience shows that private enterprises have to compete to survive. In most countries, public enterprises are protected from failure by implicit or explicit subsidies. Public enterprises are often expected to create employment opportunities for political reasons. But allowing public enterprises to operate inefficiently will mean very heavy costs in the long run. It affects not only a country's ability to produce efficiently but also its capacity to save and invest for future production.

Private enterprises and entrepreneurs can function smoothly and contribute to development only in an appropriate public policy environment.

Entrepreneurial Urge

Entrepreneurship is the creative 'elan' of industrial development which for historical reasons is feeble in backward areas. It is not feasible to expect entrepreneurial urge among people who live in poverty, illiteracy and ignorance. Conceptualisation of entrepreneurship in terms of self-confidence, optimism, achievement, motivation and other such attributes constituting the variable, residual non-marketed services receiving the residual profit income as payment (Kilby) does not have any meaning in backward areas; because these qualities themselves need a minimum of economic well-being below which the hard preoccupations with the basic needs of life leave no room for critical reflection and initiative necessary for any enterprise. Entrepreneurial qualities are born of an environment through individuals' creative response to potential opportunities. An entrepreneur needs a clear perception of economic opportunities and the investment capacity to pursue these opportunities. In backward areas where the basic struggle for existence is so tough, per capita income so low and where illiteracy or low level of education prevents access to business information or ideas, there is neither perception of opportunities nor the capacity to exploit these opportunities. Not only the environment is timid without brisk activities or aggressive ideas but also men are too deprived to have an urge to know and grow. When we think of the development of backward areas, we must think of the ascent of these lowly men to the capacity to participate in the development process, into the cosmetic growth of the soil by outsiders' investment and outsiders' profit. No effort will be successful to convert such people into entrepreneurs unless we realise the basic symbiotic nature of entrepreneurship so inextricably integrated with their total life-situation and environment. Therefore, in developing an environment and changing the life-situation, we take the first step to develop entrepreneurship.

Significance of Entrepreneurial Environment

A study of socio-political and economic environment has a great social and economic significance to the growth of entrepreneurship. Modern business is treated as a social and economic institution and is affected by the political, social and economic forces. The political environment, industrial policy, licensing policy, foreign exchange regulations, banking policy, technological development and social change form the framework within which an enterprise has to work. It is for these reasons that all business plans must be based on the immediate environment. An entrepreneurial plan cannot be framed and finalised for its implementation without its relevance to the political, social, economical and technological requirements. In fact, it is environment which regulates entrepreneurial activities. Business environment has a positive relationship with the development of entrepreneurship.

POLITICAL ENVIRONMENT

Political environment affects the entrepreneurial growth and accelerate the process of economic activity. Law and order is of high priority, followed by government policies in regard to the promotion of entrepreneurship, followed by incentives, encouragement and right institutional structure will go a long way in fostering entrepreneurship.

Economic Environment

The entrepreneurial growth and development is also governed by the economic environment. It encompass a wide spectrum of items, namely, land, availability of raw material, skilled labour, infrastructure, machinery, capital and so on.

Shortage of raw materials can much adversely affect the entrepreneurial environment and it has been affecting many industries. Shortage of raw materials, inferior quality, high price resulting in high cost of production are bringing bad name to the small industry. Without raw materials, no industry can run and no entrepreneurship would come up. The more favourable the conditions of raw materials are, better would be its influence on entrepreneurial emergence.

The role and importance of market and marketing should never be underestimated for the uprise of entrepreneurship. If the proof of pudding lies in eating, the proof of production lies in marketing. If the entrepreneur does not possess knowledge and various marketing techniques, he is unlikely to survive. The size and composition of market both influence entrepreneurship in their own ways.

The benefits of an improved and healthy market conditions in the environment of entrepreneurial growth are self-explanatory. Germany and Japan are examples where rapid improvement in market was followed by rapid entrepreneurial appearance.

A Brave New Marketing World

Markets have been changing faster than marketing. And marketing has to catch up with these changes. Today's customers are more price, quality, service and value sensitive. There's a proliferation of communication and distribution channels. There's a digital revolution affecting the speed with which we get information and the way we communicate.

Although the fundamental principles of marketing still apply, marketers are also adding additional perspectives. They are recognising the great value of building strong brands. According to Interbrand, Coca-Cola is worth $77 billion, far more than its tangible plant and equipment value. Companies are focusing more on customer lifetime value, not just the immediate earnings from a transaction. Companies are inviting their customers to collaborate in the creation of value. They are putting their messages on newer media. They are developing new metrics and hoping to measure the Rate of Interest RoI on marketing investments. Traditional marketing departments presumably are skilled in the basics of marketing research, advertising, sales promotion, and sales management. But in today's e-world, additional skills are needed in the marketing department. I would emphasise the following skills:

- Brand building skills and positioning skills
- Database management and data mining skills
- Customer and partner relationship management skills
- Customer profitability measurement skills
- Public relations and buzz marketing skills

Philip Kotler would count the following as some of his contributions to the field of marketing:

- Making the customer and customer value central to the thinking of marketers. Telling companies to design their firm from the customer backward.
- Broadening the concept of marketing to include not only goods and services but also the marketing of ideas, causes, places, persons, and whole organisations.
- Developing the field of not-for-profit marketing to cover museums, symphony orchestras, theatre groups, and so on.
- Developing the field of social marketing to help change people's behaviours in positive, life-enhancing ways.

The 4Ps remain a useful organising framework for marketing planning. There is nothing wrong with adding a few more Ps for emphasis, such as Packaging, People, Personnel, Politics, Public opinion, Product design positioning and Passion. All of these have been suggested. Those in services marketing have suggested three more Ps: people, process and physical evidence.

Even staying with the 4Ps I would advocate translating them into the four Cs which take a customer-based rather than a seller-based view. Product becomes Customer Value, Price becomes Customer Costs, Place becomes Customer Convenience, and Promotion become Customer Communication. Buyers want customer value, lower total costs, more convenience and honest communication.

Of course, the starting point is not the 4Ps but Segmentation, Targeting, and Positioning (STP). STP is strategic marketing and the 4Ps is tactical marketing. The old marketing doesn't work any more and the outlines of the new marketing are barely emerging. New marketing will require getting closer to the customers, developing more customer insight, working with fewer but more partnered suppliers and distributors, finding newer communication vehicles, and moving to high-tech marketing without losing a high touch.

The Most Important Growth Drivers

- A sharply designed, ambitious and well-communicated **growth vision**
- A **strategic reach** that protects, leverages and stretches the core
- A **strong leadership** team with specific, diversified experience and skills
- A clear **competence profile** that can be leveraged and stretched
- **Organisational excellence** with growth-related structure, processes, measurement and incentive systems
- A **growth-embedding**, open and progressing culture

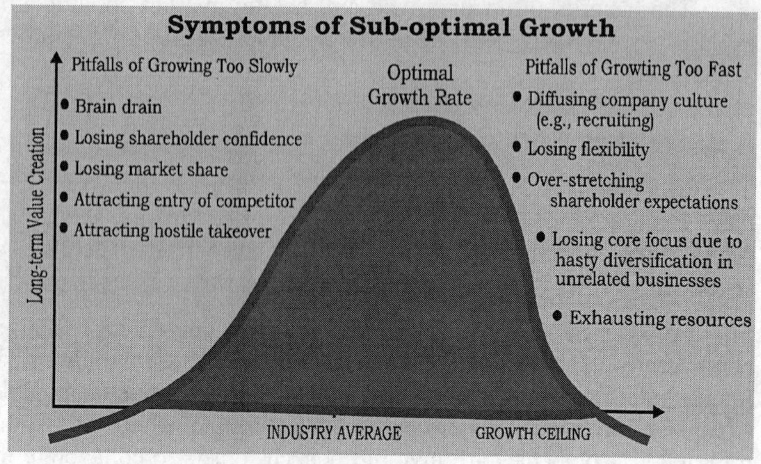

These growth drivers are propelled by vivid vision, leadership, communication, creativity, innovation fuel value building growth.

- Value – growers must pursue top performance, maintain stamina, redefine their businesses and markets, and continuously "push the envelope" even further.
- Profit seekers need to make a clean break from the profit trap-cost-cutting and control – and refocus on market and growth-oriented investments. This begins by developing a vision and reassessing the company's culture and incentive system.
- Simple growers typically need to refocus on core competencies while maintaining growth momentum.
- Underperformers may need fundamental restructuring and strategic reorientation.

SOCIAL ENVIRONMENT

Social environment strongly affect the entrepreneurial behaviour which contribute to entrepreneurial growth. The social factors can be: (i) family background, (ii) kith and kins (relatives, friends and teachers), (iii) religion, (iv) social status, (v) social mobility, and (vi) social marginality.

Family background greatly affects the entrepreneurial environment and maintenance of social system. Joint family or nuclear families have their own benefits and disadvantages. There is more sentimental attachment of family members of joint family as compared to nuclear family. But even in nuclear families, sentimental association or emotional bonds are stronger in India as compared to those in the Western countries where "out of sight out of mind" is the type of attitude of people. In the words of Desai, "the joint family is perhaps the most faithful in which he lays stress on generation depth and sentimental belongingness among the members of the family". The joint family according to him is a three and more generational group of final descendants.

The environment of the family also influences the entrepreneurship. If the father is a professional or a businessman or the like, the son is more likely to adopt the same occupation because of certain inherent advantages by virtue of his father being in the similar line.

The reference also affects the environment. A person is likely to adopt the guidelines or rules of the reference group to which he belongs. The reference group can be church groups, armed services and otherwise, informal circle of friends and relatives. The prospective entrepreneur would discuss his ideas with them and seek their advice while starting a new business.

Similarly, social status has its own role to play. Every human being aspires for a high social status and once he achieves a reasonable level, his aspirations and desires for it start getting multiplied. People, therefore, become quite responsible in the wake of protecting and developing their status. Chester Barnard said that the desire for improvement of status and especially the desire to protect status appears to be the basis of a sense of general responsibilities. People work hard to maintain their status as it also contributes to their entrepreneurial growth.

Caste and religion of entrepreneur are the contributory factors of entrepreneurial growth. History reveals that the entrepreneurial traits do not belong to a specific caste rather the entrepreneurs emerge from varied communities. James Berna conducted a study of 52 medium-scale manufacturing entrepreneurs and found that his firms had mostly grown from small beginnings and his entrepreneurs had come from a wide range of social and economic backgrounds. Many of his entrepreneurs had to face formidable obstacles but their enterprises did grow. But sociologists still claim that caste and religions do have an impact on the environment. For example, Parsis of Maharashtra, Jains of Rajasthan and Gujarat have been the mainsprings of entrepreneurial activity.

Social mobility involves the degree of social and geographical mobility and the nature of mobility channels within a system. There are varied opinions about the influence of social mobility on the entrepreneurial environment. Hoselitz and McClelland's need for openness of a system and flexibility in role relations respectively reveal an imperative role of mobility within a system for entrepreneurship development. Their viewpoint is that high degree of social mobility would help in the emergence of entrepreneurship. But Hagen's belief is that the lack of mobility possibilities promote entrepreneurship. Brozen's emphasis is that the system should neither be too flexible nor too rigid because the former would pull the entrepreneur away from his role and the latter would restrict the entrepreneur. However, social mobility does not work in the system in isolation but there are many other factors which influence the entrepreneurial environment.

Social marginality also positively influences entrepreneurship. Stauworth and Curran stress that a person belonging to a social group traditionally constrained to enter economic activity and barred from many other activities by the society is expected to choose the owner manager role in a small industry.

TECHNOLOGICAL ENVIRONMENT

Technology represents the application of scientific knowledge for practical purposes. While the 20th century and certainly the first half up to 1950 gave us a massive industrial base, shift from agriculture and rural life to urban life, utilisation of energy and power for our benefit, the ongoing progress of technology through R&D efforts have led to more comfortable lifestyles. The last three decades of the 20th century brought in what we call an Information Revolution.

Technological advancement has become a catalytic agent in the promotion of entrepreneurship growth of industrial and allied services. Thomas DeGregori sets forth thirty operational principles demonstrating that technology creates resources and that with intelligent policies in science our society can be sustainable and will continue to invent new resource creating technologies. Conversely, he argues, "living within limits: is a course that, if followed, would lead to certain decline and destruction." The technological impact on agriculture, industry are immense. Further, technology bring in cultural changes as well as the quality of life. Technological development continues to give fillip to entrepreneurship in multifaceted manner, affecting the life of the entrepreneurs as well as the common man. The entrepreneur's endeavour is to stay ahead technologically in products and services with a penchant for quality. This will not only enhance profits, but also maintain balance in the ecosystem.

Next two decades will see a Knowledge Revolution, leading to large-scale adoption of new technologies in India. Most of them will be based on information technology using tools such as computer and mobile phones for processing, storage and transfer of data, internet communication and e-commerce. Many new industries, arising out of application of new technologies, will flourish in countries of Asia, depending on their stage of economic and technological development.

The Knowledge Revolution has made it possible to routinise processes – a shift from the traditional manual control of conventional machinery for using the computer brain to operate the machinery. Computer software is an alternate way to reorganise traditional work processes, through application of overseeing knowledge aided by systematic, logical analysis.

LEGAL ENVIRONMENT

There are various rules and regulations applicable to different groups of industries, for various purposes. Some of them relate to: registration, licencing, pollution, location, acquisition, payment of wages and labour related laws, pollution and environmental rules, laws relating to organisation, product, patent, resource and taxes. According to a recent study, there are over 150 legal requirements an entrepreneur has to take care off.

Some legal entity – may be a business, a government agency, or a large non-profit organisation – may well contain in its fold a network of diverse autonomous organisations. The old model of corporations is fast becoming obsolete and is being replaced by new ones. We are witnessing the operation of Schumpeter's doctrine of "creative destruction" in practice. Traditional geocentric way of industrial operations are being replaced by innovative, multilocation industrial operations tapping the synergies of "outsiders" from different countries. This is happening in China and India now; and in countries like Korea, Singapore, Thailand and Malaysia this process began almost a decade or two ago. Indeed Australia, being closely aligned to the Western countries, had the advantage of a headstart.

CULTURAL ENVIRONMENT

Every organisation has an invisible quality – a certain style, a character; a way of doing things – that may be more powerful than the dictates of any one person or a formal system. This invisible quality 'the corporate culture' decides how effective the organisation is in the marketplace. Achieving cultural change to maintain a prime market position is the key preoccupation of every chief executive these days.

Max Weber emphasises that cultural factors have a crippling effect on entrepreneurial growth. Culture consists of (i) tangible man-made objects like furniture, buildings etc., (ii) intangible concepts like laws, morale, knowledge etc., and (iii) values and behaviour acceptable within the society. America is a capitalist country, Russia followed a socialist pattern, democracy has no touch in China, but Indian culture encourages democracy and accepts mixed economy. At the time of independence, India was in such a state that the economy could not be left in the hands of people. The government had to intervene and chalk out plans to take the country towards development. Culture of Hindus is to worship 'Ganesha' before undertaking any financial affair. Whether it is a superstition or not is a debatable point. While going on some long journey or on some special days or while tying up a nuptial knot, it is in our culture to seek the recommendations of priests, pandits or sufis.

Catalysing change in corporate cultures by managing people and talent better seems to be the new mantra on the Indian corporate landscape. Better people management is being recognised as the key to sustained success – from managing internal relationships to building corporate cultures that nurture the talent. It is no longer enough to be a blue chip IIT-IIM manager, it is equally necessary to update one's EQ to become emotionally engaged with employee and customer need.

Gone are the days when the dictat ran down from the top and the boss' words were carved out in stone. In place of fear and distruct of management policies, is creeping in, slowly but surely, a culture of inclusiveness and openness which starts at the very bottom of the ladder. There is a growing understanding that it is people-driven strategies that sow the seeds of consistent growth.

Hence, there is a growing demand for change managers and culture interventionists who are putting in place a wide range systems and templates which handle issues from employee attrition rates to the business perceptions within the company, to nurturing talent by matching people with the right jobs and bringing in new talent.

And most often these are people who have been associated with that company either as employees and consultants but have since become specialists in one or more areas of change management. Take Ashoke Maitra, former head of Tata Share Registry whose focus is on organisational development and institutional building.

Although he quit the Tata Group years ago, today he is mentor to three top MDs and CEOs of the group and is actively coaching them on a one-to-one basis on a wide spectrum from intra-organisation relationships to developing organisational structures. "It is often lonely at the top. There is no one to look up to or discuss things with. Having a mentor helps because he or she is also a sounding board. And it is always better if it is someone who knows the company and its culture."

Besides demographic advantages, other factors that will contribute to the shifts in economic power are cultural traits, lifestyles, new technologies, and globalisation. Demographically young nations capable of efficient absorption and application of new technologies enabling sharper competition in business, will not only thrive, but will emerge as key drivers of globalisation.

The pace of India's ascendancy will be accelerated, when India move up the value chain, supplying high-value products and services in the global market. The emergence of the internet will provide added thrust to the process.

It will be interesting to watch how the Western countries will respond to these changes. How will societies living with their old attitudes adapt to the new environment of changing equations? Will it mean increased tensions between nations on either side of the Digital Divide? Or will it give rise to occasional outbursts of frenzy, like the one we witnessed during two World Wars and later during the Cold War?

Infrastructural Network

It has been argued that the development of industries be preceded by development of agriculture which introduces certain economic changes that culminate in industrial activities. "A developed mass agriculture is normally needed before you can have widespread successful development in other sectors" (Michael Lipton: *Why Poor People Stay Poor?*). But we cannot, perhaps, wait that long till a "developed agriculture sector provides wage goods and savings capacity" needed to support rapid industralisation. If agricultural development does not create savings for industralisation, an industrial development process can be induced by substantial investments on certain selected nucleus industries, leading to a number of ancillary and other related industrial units. This method has gained wide acceptance. But before such nucleus industries are set up in backward areas, necessary infrastructural facilities have to be provided. Even then, the location of these industries may not necessarily lead to a development process in which the poor people of backward areas whose development is the real development area successfully participate – unless the choice of nucleus industries is such that it can utilise the available skills and capacities of a large number of small artisans or farmers. Otherwise, the entrepreneurial opportunities thrown up by such nucleus industries will be exploited by affluent entrepreneurs from outside who have the capacity to invest. It has been seen that entrepreneurs from developed areas have normally gravitated towards these backward areas which are *contiguous* to developed business centres with a view to availing themselves of the incentives and concessions. But such enterprises have not created any economic impact on the people of the backward areas except, perhaps, creating some negligible employment avenues.

It is, therefore, very important to ensure that the infrastructural facilities created to pave the way for nucleus industries are extended to cover a vast multitude of small artisans or farmers whose products can be processed in the nucleus industries. "An integrated infrastructural programme geared to the needs of small-holder farms and small-scale enterprises is the best means of promoting both types of productive activity." (J. Muller: *Promotion of the Manufacture of Rural Implements in the United Republic of Tanzania*). For example, if there are a number of small dairy farmers, a central refrigeration plant can serve all the farmers in the area by an active network of communication. As a result, each farmer can get the benefit of an assured market and an enhanced income. If a large number of farmers are producing soyabean, a central soyabil processing unit would serve as ideal nucleus plant. Such a step would not only integrate agricultural development with industrial development, it would also bring about a pervasive growth of both. On the other hand, if a unit manufacturing some sophisticated machinery is the nucleus plant, its ancillaries would also need the precision or sophistication which will not be possible to achieve within the capabilities of the target-beneficiary group whom we want to develop through the development of backward areas. As Paul Streeten has said, "Industry should produce consumer goods required by the people, the majority of whom live in the countryside, hoes and simple power-tillers and bicycles, not air-conditioners or expensive cars and equipments. Much of the recent criticism of inefficient, high cost industrialisation behind high walls of protection and quantitative restrictions should be directed at the types of product and technique which cater for a highly unequal income distribution and reflect entrenched vested interests" (Paul Streeten: "Industrialisation in a United Development Strategy," *World Development,* January, 1975). Actually the production of simple goods depends on the character and potential of a particular backward area; and the essential infrastructure so developed that it would be capable of sustaining active linkages between the subsidiary units in the villages and the central unit.

Environmental Analysis

This integrated approach which is the key to the development of backward areas implies a very careful environment analysis or research study of the target groups of beneficiaries, their activities and differential needs; and the practical modes of operation by which their activities can be linked with the covering enterprise. Unless these studies are made meticulously, the entire planning will only give unproductive results. Most of the development schemes fail to benefit the target clientele because elaborate linkages are not identified and built-up.

An imaginative study should —

1. Identify the beneficiaries or target groups;
2. Analyse the environment for immediate feasible enterprises in an integrated manner;
3. Delineate the linkages and institutional arrangements;
4. Recommend appropriate organisational structures to provide necessary promotional support.

Unfortunately, in most of the studies on backward areas, there is a tendency to make generalisations and ignore the specific details of really feasible projects. As a result, immediate perception of concrete opportunities by interested entrepreneurs is left in confusion. Sometimes "Area Studies" make a general statement of demand and resources and recommend certain enterprises which are not immediately feasible due to important reasons unaccounted for in such studies. It is also not seriously contemplated whether the recommended enterprises are feasible within the capabilities and investment capacity of the target-group. In short, most of the studies fail to discern the real issues of growth in the target area and fail to identify the concrete and specific needs of these endowments like resource, skill, etc., to flourish. Enunciation of general objectives and generic beneficiaries tend to blur the distinct contours of one homogeneous group from the other. Also, the extension of certain standard facilities or services does not serve their actual needs. All this possibly happens because in such basic studies, we fail to identify clearly the target-groups and their specific problems, and make theoretical studies on resources and demand in an impersonal manner, as a result of which even the schemes devised on the basis of such studies tend to become too impersonal and rigid. Sometimes, the schemes become so inflexible on account of a standardised petrified approach that in some most genuine cases demanding a certain departure from the fixed framework, the scheme is incapable of giving requisite help. It is, therefore, absolutely necessary that any action plan for a backward area must first identify the target-group, identify the specific services they need for monitoring their enterprises and devise an appropriate structural support for comprehensive coverage of their needs.

THE GREEN ARM OF THE LAW

Three important Indian legislations presently enjoin the industry to remain within the pollution control standards set by the government:

1. Water (Prevention and Control of Pollution) Act, 1974, with amendments made in 1988:
   - Following the 1988 amendments, permission is necessary to set up any industry which is considered environmentally hazardous — one that uses or discharges any poisonous, noxious or polluting matter. Standards must be those set by State Pollution Boards. Industries set up prior to the amendment need to obtain clearance within three months of its coming into force.
   - State Pollution Control Boards (PCBs) have the power to obtain information regarding the construction, installation or operation of any process of the industry.
   - After the 1988 amendments, the PCBs can issue directions or order for closure or stoppage of electricity or water supply, if standards are not being met by the polluting industry.
   - Penalties for non-compliance have been increased to ₹ 10,000 for defaulting and ₹ 5,000 per day for continued default.
2. Air (Prevention and Control of Pollution) Act, 1981, with 1987 amendments:
   - The definition of air pollutant was extended from harmful solid, liquid or gaseous substances present in the atmosphere to include noise pollution.
   - Unlike the practice earlier, now all air polluting industries must have the sanction of their respective PCBs to prevent any liabilities later.
   - Penalties are as those in the Water Act.
3. Environment (Protection) Act, 1986:
   - The Central Government has the power to take all such measures as it deems necessary for protecting the environment.

- Section 3 of EPA empowers the Central Government to: *(a)* restrict areas in which any industry, operations, process or class of industries can be carried out under certain safeguards; *(b)* lay down procedures and safeguards for the prevention of accidents which may cause environmental pollution and initiate remedial measures for them; *(c)* lay down procedures for handling hazardous substances; *(d)* examining manufacturing process and materials; and *(e)* widespread inspection powers.
- As in the other two Acts, the EPA gives the Centre wide powers to direct closure, prohibition and regulation of any industry if it contravenes the provisions of the Act.
- In addition, the Marpol Convention, pertaining to marine pollution control, was drawn up by the International Maritime Organisation, a United Nations agency, any ratified by India in 1978.
- The five annexures of this convention deal with the prevention of oil pollution; prevention of pollution by noxious liquid substances in bulk; prevention of pollution by noxious packaged substances; pollution from sewage and from garbage.
- The Indian government has ratified only the first two annexures. Thus, a vessel can be penalised for oil or chemical pollution. But the remaining forms of pollution are unchecked.

Instrumental Synergy

Comprehensive coverage of dynamic needs cannot be ensured unless this strategy incorporates the necessary organisational support. In the development of backward areas, two things are of fundamental importance. Firstly, the needs of the entrepreneurs or the target-groups are wider than those immediately related to an enterprise. Unless the complex structure of his private and social needs is understood, our assessment of his requirements which will have to be met to sustain him in a desired enterprise like a small industry or a farm will be unrealistic and lopsided. The amount sent on his enterprise tends to remain unproductive. Unless we support the entrepreneur in all his needs and exigencies till his enterprise yields profit, entrepreneurs are often coerced out of their enterprise during the initial years, because they lack the capacity to withstand inevitable risks, if any. In order to develop small enterprises and like small farmers in an integrated manner with an industrial project, the socio-economic conditions of these people have to be understood to appreciate their needs, and devise appropriate loan schemes. The weaker sections of the population are likely to benefit from a programme is designed to meet the varying needs of beneficiary groups *(Development Programme for the Door: Do Strategies Make a Difference?*, Samuel Paul and Ashok Subramaniam). Sometimes, even the consumption needs of the poor artisans have to be provided for in order to sustain in their work.

Secondly, an integrated approach to rural industrialisation which has to deal with a complex structure of differential needs requiring regular monitoring and timely intervention of promotional agencies calls for active coordination among institutions. "The more backward a country's economy, the greater was the part played by the special institutional factors designed to increase the supply of capital to nascent industries and in addition to provide them with less decentralised and better informed entrepreneurial guidance; the more backward the country, the more pronounced was the coerciveness and comprehensiveness of these factors." (A. Gershenkson: *Economic Backwardness in Historical Perspective).* In a backward place, the role of government institutions is of the highest significance. The institutions should not only cater to a variety of needs but also fulfil their role in the desired sequence so as to make the project work. This is what has been described by some as "synergistic effect or congruence". For example, small industrial units get term-loans from term-lending institutions but the desired working capital is not sanctioned at the right time as a result of which the entire scheme goes wrong. Similarly, if raw materials are not supplied for the essential utilities, the investment may remain idle, unproductive and eventually succumb to heavy accumulated liabilities. Various institutional supports must permit coverage in a synergy to make a success of an enterprise which needs all of them in a given order. In urban or developed areas, institutional asynergy can perhaps be overcome by the resilience of the entrepreneurs, but in backward areas, the staying power of the entrepreneurs is so feeble that they quickly wear out with the smallest obstruction. Institutional patronage must, therefore, be comprehensive, continuous and synergistic.

Training

It is only against this background that we can effectively plan out training programmes for the development of entrepreneurship in the backward areas. The basic difference between a backward area and a developed area is that unlike the latter, backward areas do not have a hidden reservior of potential entrepreneurs who through motivation, training and support can quickly become competent entrepreneurs. Entrepreneurs from the backward areas have to be given comprehensive functional training based on the specific conditions of the entrepreneur and the choice of the enterprise. The entrepreneurship development programme must deal with the following:

(1) On the basis of an elaborate action-plan based on environment analysis, various areas of entrepreneurial activities should be identified and specific projects formulated. These areas should be suitably assigned to develop the inherent skills of artisan groups and high school drop-outs, educated unemployed, farmers and men of other trades.

(2) For each area of activity, institutional linkages should be clearly spelt out. Simultaneous attempts where necessary, should be made to build new institutions which are needed to give financial marketing or other necessary support. For example, if we are promoting a large number of dairy farms, a central refrigeration plant in the area should simultaneously come up.

(3) On the basis of institutional linkages, thus worked out, an inter-agency team should be constituted to take up each identified group of entrepreneurs for training. Since the product of an entrepreneur of such a group is to manufacture is known, and his own socio-economic conditions are also known, a series of needs of each entrepreneur in implementing his project should be clearly identified by the agency to look after each need or group of needs in a time-bound programme.

(4) The training programme should briefly make the entrepreneurs by a multidisciplinary familiarisation course aware of the nature and problems of entrepreneurship in their context. Further, the training programme should discuss their schemes and proceed with the implementation. No training is more effective than the actual experience in implementation – the agencies must ensure that the entrepreneur gets all assistance and guidance in the implementation of his project. This would eliminate inter-agency disputes and the consequent delay which prove fatal to many entrepreneurs.

(5) There should be a nodal agency, preferably an agency which organises the training programme, to monitor the progress of the implementation of each trainee's project. This calls for coordination of the functions of various promotional agencies in order to make its specific services available to the entrepreneur in right time.

Training programmes for entrepreneurship development which involve all promotional agencies and financial institutions have proved to be the most successful. Involvement in the training programme does create a continuing interest to prove advantageous to the entrepreneurs among these agencies. And since for backward areas, project-oriented training programmes have been considered indispensable, the multi-agency involvement in the training programme helps in a better appraisal and quicker implementation. These agencies should work in a manner as if they are escorting an entrepreneur right from the conception of a project-idea to the state when the units starts production. Even after that stage, specific institutional arrangements have to be made to extend continuing marketing support.

Such a multi-agency "escort" approach compensates for many deficiencies which the entrepreneurs of backward areas are beset with by their birth and circumstances, and it helps engender entrepreneurial qualities among them through practical experience.

ARTISANS' DEVELOPMENT

An integrated approach to rural industrialisation calls for giving priority to the organised development of artisans – a formidable task beset with problems are not as simple as they often appear to be. They live in scattered places and do not constitute a homogeneous group. Their problems vary from place-to-place although the products may be the same. Their productivity is unremuneratively low, and the standard of their products is not always suitable for wider acceptability. Their input supply system is irregular and fragile, and the market is restricted. And above all, these artisans live in so much of want that their socio-economic needs keep them permanently as wage-earners almost in bondage to some middlemen. Unless their consumption needs and other social exigencies are properly taken care of, they cannot really come up as independent entrepreneurs. The incentives and assistance given to them often fail because the training programmes fail to provide for the varying needs of the artisans. Many artisans just cannot attend design development training programmes because they can neither afford to stay out of daily wage-earning routine and face financial crisis. Sometimes, they sell their highly value added works of art at throw away prices to middleman because they can neither afford to wait for long nor can they take them to the right market. As a result they choose to work as daily wage-earners and the profit of their highly value-added items accrues to the middleman who employs the capital. What we need, therefore, is not a set of incentives or concessions but an enveloping support to the entrepreneurs in the backward areas which can reasonably cater to their varying individual and social needs.

Besides providing for their needs, the strategy should be to establish cooperative societies or government agencies to provide raw materials to help them in making and marketing their products. But since they stay scattered, it is not easy to organise rural market centres under this strategy on a regular basis. It is, therefore, necessary that the supplies from this sector should be given preferential status in marketing and if necessary, competition from big manufacturers has to be banned. In that case, the total demand for such products in a region will have to be met from this artisan sector and more people can be inducted into this sector to increase output and even the underemployment of the existing artisans would disappear.

For example, if simple agricultural implements are only in the artisan sector, the total demand of a region can give so much work that the artisans no longer remain in financial crisis. The only problem is to organise this vast network to touch each atomic unit. But all this has to be done if the backward areas are to be easily awakened. "It is not argued that the village metalsmiths and tinsmiths should be promoted for any nostalgic or romantic reasons. On the contrary, these craftsmen, if supported, constitute a basis for rural industrialisation which will otherwise be wasted and by rural industrialisation is not meant the establishment of any industries in rural areas, it means the establishment of enterprises that are linked backward and forward to other productive activities within the rural communities" (J. Muller).

Appropriate technical and consultancy organisations must work constantly to introduce appropriate technological innovations to increase productivity without displacing labour. New designs and improvements can be introduced for decorative crafts to cater to sophisticated markets which are ever widening. It is just enough to allow the artisans to survive not to make them increasingly relevant to the changing needs. If more efficient agricultural implements are available, no one would buy old-fashioned implements, simply because they are the products of the artisans. Nor, would it be proper to upgrade their skill so as to enable them to produce more efficient equipments without adopting the stylistic changes and needs. Otherwise, the market for these products would quickly shrink. But it is not so easy to introduce these innovative changes among the illiterate or semi-literate artisans. In order to do this, we have to create active linkages between research organisations and these artisans on a permanent basis. Training programmes have to be organised which must expose their inadequacies and teach them to assimilate the innovative ideas. And this cannot be done unless their tradition, skill and quality of work are studied in depth and imaginative training programmes designed. Similarly, arrangements have to be made to market their products. Organisations sponsored by government should initially buy their products in order to ensure quick payment to the artisans and then release the profit when the product is ultimately sold to the real customer.

Innovation via creativity

"Leaders know how to bring out the best in people. They are able to create and maintain an environment where people feel valued, inspired and encouraged to share new ideas and diverse perspectives. Innovation requires attracting top talent and creative thinking. Diverse points of view lead to creativity. Creativity to innovation, and innovation to growth."

— CEO, Agilent Technologies.

After over 15 years in the electronics and telecom industries where he worked with giants such as Alcatel and Siemens, Mobile, Beat Brandle chose to put his skill to good use, in scouting for innovative ideas to fund in the mobile telephony space. He was in India recently to identify opportunities in areas like mobile portal solutions, design and behaviour tracking applications such as book readers, wireless, tools, for senior citizens and networking management solutions. AG in Switzerland, says India is a much preferred destination compared to China, and that has lot to do with the stronger entrepreneurial culture among Indians and of course, the ease of communicating in English. "The image of India is better than China", he says. Though he has been to China "more times than to India" Brandle says he finds it easier to contact people directly and form opinion about business here. Based on the presentations he made here are a few important tips on making that first meeting with the Angel a successful one:

- **Be open and don't hide facts:** A robust business plan should not only highlight your strengths but acknowledge weaknesses as well. This will help establish trust at the beginning of the relationship
- **Be clear about cash flows in your business:** How to manage them is crucial, so know your sources of inflows and outflows.
- **What is your abortion criteria and cost?** The plan should include conditions and costs for shutting down the business if it fails to meet certain predecided criteria and timeliness. It's measure of how well you have done your risk evaluation of the business.
- **Focus:** Either be big or be very niche. Anything in between is much less likely to succeed.
- **Of estimates and plans:** It usually takes double the time and money and half the volume you estimated. So, think through those numbers again!
- **Finally, remember that it's better to be conservative than optimistic:** Overambitious plans could turn off potential investors and ruin your chances of taking your project off the ground. Be realistic.

CONCLUSION

Entrepreneurship, therefore, will flourish only under the right atmosphere said to be conducive to the social, political and economic issues. Even though the urge to excel others and to create something new is inborn and psychologically oriented in the larger analysis, this urge to excel others will fail to obtain the full freedom of expression unless the right environment is available. Entrepreneurial environment, therefore, a high awareness of incorporates existing potentials and enough source of capital is available, and also where there are sufficient number of individuals and institutions which provide adequate help and advice for the establishment and growth of industrial enterprises.

Thus, since entrepreneurship involves a complex of economic and social behaviour, it can only survive where conditions are ideal in terms of political, economic, social and ethical concerns, and when economic changes are free from restraints — for the benefit of all concerned.

An integrated approach to backward area development requires a unified administrative machinery itself animated by a passion for distributive justice. And in no small measure, the proselytising entrepreneurial zeal of the deprived and the downtrodden is a reflection of that passion.

26 CHAPTER

IDENTIFICATION OF OPPORTUNITIES

Companies have now grasped the principles of good management in a competitive, uncertain scenario: cut costs, cut time, stay lean, build organisational capabilities, and empower people, to name a few. These guidelines are the bedrock of what management gurus call the 'competitive edge'. To put it differently, companies are now incorporating knowledge into their business, whatever business they may be in. The so-called 'old economy' in fact is as knowledge-intensive now as the so-called 'new economy' is. The change in attitudes is pervasive right through the corporate rank and file. For example, a finance manager does not see himself as an accountant. He likes to see himself as a 'business partner'; he sees himself not as a bookkeeper, but someone who provides valuable inputs to help steer the organisation on the right path. Factory workers no longer just turn screws or valves. They are continuously thinking of kaizens or small innovations.

LEARNING OBJECTIVES

Business opportunities galore. The chapter deals primarily to grab the right opportunity at a right time and convert it into a reality. The chapter discusses:

- The Power of Imagination
- Project identification – identification of methods to generate business ideas
- Art of spotting opportunities
- Choosing an idea
- Choice of a product
- Scanning of business environment
- Selection of a product
- The adoption process
- Criterias
- Project profile
- Product planning
- Revolutions for the future
- The golden age of bio-tech.

INTRODUCTION

Industrialisation is widely recognised not only as one of the important means to usher in socio-economic transformations and achieving industrial self-sufficiency but also for the accelerated development of agriculture, transport, trade, services and other potential sectors through the forward and backward linkages. It is a process which accelerates economic growth; affects structural changes in the economy, particularly in respect of resource utilisation, production functions, income generation, occupational pattern, population distribution and foreign trade; and induces social change. Jawaharlal Nehru had emphasised that "Real progress must ultimately depend on industrialisation. Throughout the world, industrialisation has indeed become the magic word of the mid-twentieth country".

Industrialisation is brought about by well-trained entrepreneurs. Entrepreneurship is one of the most important factors of industrialisation in the process of economic growth.

Project identification is the first step of a new venture. A right direction may take an entrepreneur to new heights. Otherwise, he has to undergo a number of hurdles in his way. It is, therefore, very crucial to entrepreneurs. We have made an attempt in this chapter to analyse the various aspects of project identification.

Theoretically, an entrepreneur has an infinitely wide choice with respect to his project. The important dimensions of choice are: Project/service, market, technology, equipment, scale of production, location, incentives and time phasing. The task of identifying a feasible and promising project is somewhat difficult. Moreover, it is interrelated with the government policies, infrastructural development and skills of people.

The Power of Imagination

Studies show that winning requires intense desire, relentless focus and flawless execution. Winning big requires dreaming big and taking bold steps to fulfil these dreams. Out of dreams, a vision emerges and an idea takes shape. In other words, creativity leads to innovation.

We need to start imagining about a new opportunity. This turns into a dream and a goal. In a way, vision captures the worth of business, integrating the goals, strategies and action plans.

Mission provides an orientation – not a checklist of accomplishments. It defines a direction – not a destination. It tells the members of an organisation why they are working together, how they intend to contribute to the work. But there is a big difference between having a mission statement and being mission-based. To be mission-based means that people can, and should object to edicts that they do not see as connected to the mission. It means that thinking about, and continually taken together, mission, vision, and assessment create an ecology, a set of fundamental relationships forming the bedrock of real leadership. They allow people, regardless to their designations, to help shape their future. Mastering the discipline of innovation will require organisation to learn from one another.

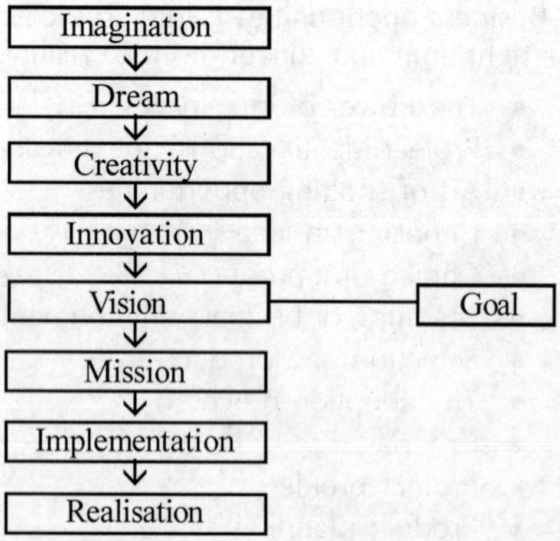

The lessons from success stories are similar. They are:

1. Imagination is a prerequisite for coping with apparent resource-constraints. We have to think outside the box, breaking both the conventional wisdom in India as well as the existing business models elsewhere. Strategy here is about discovery and innovation.

2. The business models that work in India are indigenously-developed.
3. Strong leadership-knowledge, persistence, belief, and commitment-pays.
4. Entrepreneurship is well and alive among the poorest. Government intervention, subsidies, and policies cannot accomplish what millions of entrepreneurs can.
5. The appropriate technology was state-of-the-art technology that was creatively adapted to Indian conditions. The task of deployment of the technology required as much innovation as the technology *per se*.
6. New organisational models are critical for India's development.
7. All transactions must be based on commercial considerations.
8. Accountability and transparency in performance is a prerequisite.
9. Indian operations can be world-class; in fact, it must strive to set global standards.
10. All useful initiatives will upset the power structure. Leaders must recognise that major innovations will meet with enormous resistance upfront.

The success of these efforts provide us with an understanding of how to transform the problem of the poor in India to the opportunity of a mass market.

Major Changes in Business

- Free movement of capital is making it easily accessible.
- Technology is no longer the preserve of a few companies.
- Unrestricted flow of information makes it available to all.
- Globalisation is creating one all-important quality standard.
- The world economy is increasingly becoming service-oriented.

And its main Advantages are:

- It uses only knowledge as a competitive advantage for survival.
- It constantly tries to attain total quality in every sphere.
- It builds evolutionary bonds with customers and vendors.
- It is best-suited to cope with incessant global change.
- It creates energised workforces that evolve with the organisation.

Project Identification

Project identification is concerned with the collection, compilation and analysis of economic data for the eventual purpose of locating possible opportunities for investment and with the development of the characteristics of such opportunities.

Opportunities according to Drucker are of three kinds: additive, complementary and breakthrough. Additive opportunities are those opportunities which enable the decision-maker to better utilise the existing resources without in any way involving a change in the character of business. Complementary opportunities involve the introduction of new ideas and as such do lead to a certain amount of change in the existing structure. Breakthrough opportunities, on the other hand, involve fundamental changes in both the structure and character of business. Additive opportunities involve the least amount of disturbance to the existing state of affairs and hence the least amount of risk. The element of risk is greater in the case of complementary opportunities but is the greatest in the case of breakthrough opportunities. As the element of risk increases, it becomes more and more important to precisely define the scope and nature of the project idea, to develop alternative solutions for achieving the project objectives and to select the best possible approach so as to minimise both resource consumption and risks and to optimise returns or gains.

The human mind had an infinite capacity to observe, to deduct and to innovate. Observation is one of the most important sources of project ideas. The observant mind continuously comes across situations which can be utilised to develop investment opportunities. The observation may be made during the course of one's routine occupation or otherwise. The dearth of a particular article or service may for instance lead to the development of an industry which can provide the article or service in short supply. The availability of a specified type of raw material or skill may lead to yet another type of industrial activity. The observant mind is always on the look out for opportunities which can form the existing processes which can sometimes lead to new opportunities and project ideas.

Box 26.2 Global Opportunities

There are several things Indian that helped me succeed. The work ethic inherent in India's culture provided a solid foundation; its philosophical roots, a sense of balance. There is also a big advantage to being an immigrant because new opportunities can be created only when one changes something in the system; it is sometimes easier to do that when you are an immigrant. Then, there's thrift. In India, most of us grew up with few resources and learnt to do with them. The ability to manage with little gives one the leverage to explore new opportunities and take risks. The pay-off is that if you win, you win big. Business in the US is, and has always been, a meritocracy.

If you look at people like me who moved to either the US or Canada in the 1970s you'll find several similarities. In the 1970s, we excelled in universities as graduate students. In the 1980s, we made a name for ourselves in universities, as distinguished researchers, and in industry, as technical leaders. In the early 1990s, we proved we could be technical managers, and by the end of the decade we had arrived. Indians were accepted as mangers in sales, marketing, and business and in general, as CEOs, as entrepreneurs, and as founders of companies.

What I have listed is a broad trend and several of us participated in it. It would have been very difficult to get a similar trend going in India. That it isn't impossible has been proved by the likes of Narayana Murthy. The result is that it is now possible to build profitable global companies in India.

Gururaj 'Desh' Deshpande
Co-founder and Chairman of
Sycamore Networks Inc.

Today, there isn't very much of a technology gap between India and the rest of the world. Advances in telecommunications have created a global economy and we are rapidly getting to a point where something has the same value anywhere in the world irrespective of where the 'value' he been added.

Over the last 10 years, India's success in software has proved that it can compete with the world's best in the knowledge-based service sector. As is evident from hectic industrial activity, this can be extended to call centres, business process outsourcing outfits, financial services back offices, and biotech research centres. India can continue to position itself as a low-cost provider of highly-skilled knowledge-based services. This will create huge opportunities for all kinds of business activity in India. I see several great entrepreneurs and great companies coming out of India in the next 10 years. There is an opportunity for Indian to become the world leader by applying advanced technology to solve problems vital to the global economy. The government, entrepreneurs, venture capitalists and scientists need to work to harness this opportunity.

This would for instance be the case when a processing unit decides to go in for the manufacture of the machines which it has so far been using for processing purpose only. The process of deduction is on many occasions used to supplement and rationalise the project ideas based on pure observations. In innovative units, it often becomes necessary to depend upon the deductive process for the development of new approaches to the solution of existing problems.

Trade and professional magazines provide a very fertile source of project ideas. The statistics and information thrown up by these magazines and reports and records of professional bodies often reveal opportunities which can be eventually developed into investment propositions. It is very important for every person who is involved in the process of development of new investment opportunities to remain in touch with the latest developments in his own field of specialisation. It is also necessary for him to keep in touch with developments in other fields which may be horizontally or even vertically linked with his own line of specialisation. Study of technical and professional literature, besides keeping a person *all constant* also stimulates and helps in the process of development of new project ideas.

Bulletins of Research Institutes are also a very fertile source of information for the development of new project ideas. These bulletins generally give broad outlines of the new processes or products developed by research institution and are very usefully in identification of new opportunities. The information made available in the Research Bulletin may not be adequate for concretisation of ideas. Further correspondence with the Research Institute may become necessary.

The Art of Spotting Opportunities:

India is like a blank canvas to the entrepreneur. Painting requires the ability to visualise the picture and the colours, gather the paints, and apply the brushstrokes. With the big picture increasingly clear to many, the opportunities will be snapped up like never before.

In most developing countries where planned development has been accepted as an approach towards the removal of proverty, the plan document published by the government provides a very useful source of project ideas. The plan document generally analyses the existing economic situation in a country and also pinpoints the investment opportunities which fit into the overall planning effort. Considerable information can, therefore, be gathered from the plan document.

Departmental publication of various departments of the government also provides useful information which can help in the development of new project ideas. These publications are either periodical in character or are issued on special occasions. The census document which is a periodical publication is a very useful source of information about the economic structure of the society and various trends in the growth of economy and purchasing power can be used to develop new ideas.

The project idea is the user's concept of what a project should be like. It is the raw expression of the desire of the project sponsoring body to achieve something. The exact form in which the project idea is expressed is immaterial. In order to avoid unnecessary communications between the project sponsoring body and the project formulation team, the project idea should indicate the broad objectives of the sponsor and limit these in time, space, function and structure. In case no limitations are envisaged, the sponsoring body should state so and leave the project formulation team in no doubt about it.

Choosing an Idea

Establishing yourself as a successful entrepreneur depends, in part, upon choosing a good idea. That idea must not only be good for the market, but good for the project and good for you. It means that the project is viable, profitable and socially good. It should also be manageable without much dependence on others. Importantly, the idea should be satisfactory to you.

At first, when you are searching for an idea worthy of your commitment, don't pursue one idea at a time. Develop five or ten in parallel until one emerges so strongly that it begins to dominate your thoughts and fantasies. To adopt one idea at a time has several disadvantages. First, because you are constantly receiving random information from what you read and from people you talk to, having a number of back-burner ideas gives you a greater likelihood of finding uses for information you pick-up. Second, if you are pursuing a single idea by feigning commitment before you feel it, you may put yourself into a tight corner. It is very hard to be objective when you are down to your last idea.

Choosing an idea is quite difficult and the entrepreneur has to weigh objectively his intrinsic capabilities in finalising an idea.

In the idea stage, suggestions for new products are obtained from all possible sources: customers, competitions, R&D, distributors and company employees. Frequently, one of the creative problem-solving techniques discussed below are used to develop marketable ideas. The suggested ideas need to be carefully screened to determine which are good enough to qualify for a more detailed investigation. Established objectives and defined growth areas provide a basis for developing these criteria.

Product Idea

It had been an exhausting day. Mansukhbhai had spent all morning cycling to and fro, hawking his home made goods in the lanes and bylanes of the crowded city. Now he sat outside a pan shop, trying to snatch a few minutes rest before starting another round.

As he sat there, he noticed how the customers at the pan shop kept growing, in number and impatience. Mansukhbhai saw the time it took to make each pan, the panwallah trying to attend to a dozen people at the same time. It occurred to him that if pan could be packaged and sold, it would instantly find a ready market.

And an idea was born. A man of the masses, with only his native shrewdness to guide him, had hit upon a marketing idea in a million. The kind that takes a genius to think of. That man was Mansukhbhai Mahadevbhai Kothari. The man behind Pan Parag Pan Masala.

The business ideas may be generated from internal and external sources.

Internal Sources of Business Ideas

Internal sources refer to the storehouse of knowledge built by a person over the years. These are as follows:

(a) Analysis of concepts in the light of existing problems and their solutions
(b) Search from memory to identify similarities and elements related to the concept
(c) Recombining the available elements in new and better ways
(d) Personal interests and hobbies of the individual
(e) Thinking of novel uses of existing product, e.g., use of rice husk for making hard boards, use of fly ash in making concrete and bricks, etc.
(f) Conceiving improvements in existing products
(g) Examining possibilities of anciliarisation to large-scale industry
(h) Knowledge of the potential customer needs

External Sources of Ideas for New Products

These are as under:

(i) List of items reserved by the government for exclusive production in the small sector
(ii) Items reserved for exclusive purchase for small-scale industries under the Central Store Purchase Programme of the government
(iii) Professional journals, trade journals, etc., catering to particular interests such as electronics, components, oils and vanaspati
(iv) Success stories of friends and relatives
(v) Trade fairs and exhibitions displaying new products
(vi) Government agencies like SIDO, NSIC, etc.
(vii) Market surveys to know trends in fashions
(viii) Technical and management consultants
(ix) Project profiles for various industries

Generation of business ideas or opportunities is also known as 'opportunity scanning and identification' (OSI). After generating ideas, it is necessary to evaluate them so as to identify the most appropriate idea/opportunity. This process is called "zeroing in process". Following factors should be considered while selecting the product to be manufactured:

(i) Market potential

(ii) Degree of competition

(iii) An innovative idea which has greater profit potential than an existing product

(iv) Availability of raw material and technology

(v) Resources and experience of the entrepreneur in the line

(vi) Government policies and regulations

(vii) Suitability of the product to market requirements

AN ILLUSTRATION: CHOICE OF A PRODUCT

Sanitary Napkins: The product was first introduced in the late 60s and the concept of sanitary napkin was popularised through the 70s while the 80s introduced new variations like the beltless napkins and tampons.

Since the very concept of a sanitary napkin was so new to India, one realised that conventional retailing alone was not enough to sell the product.

What was important was educating women about the product and about personal hygiene, so the manufacturers started with schools, screening films on menstruation and how to cope with it. This was followed up by free sampling.

Estimated to be a ₹ 30 crore industry (that's an astonishing 180 million pieces), with a growth rate of 10 to 15 per cent, manufacturers are unanimous that this is still just the tip of the iceberg. It is likely to scale new heights in the 90s. And the entry of Procter & Gamble with the much published dry weave technology for Whisper, the market is expected to double at the turn of the century.

The market leader and pioneer in the field is undoubtedly Johnson & Johnson with Carefree, Stayfree, OB Tampons and now Freshday Pantyliners. As things stand, the consumer does not yet have a real choice in terms of wide price variations, for instance. But the market is poised for a boom and even smaller manufacturers who admit that they earn 50 per cent of their income from his one product category alone, are doing well, though they are not advertising or retailing their product.

Starting with the base, which is still the belted napkin, the pyramid narrows to the apex consisting of products like tampons (3 per cent of the market share) and the just introduced Pantyliners. There is still a tremendous potential for expansion even at the base. The women population needing sanitary napkins is estimated to be around 20 crore, of which 5 crore lives in urban centres. There is thus scope for (₹ 840 crore industry) 500 crore pieces alone in urban centres. Right now, the Class I towns are prime targets for expansion and the huge rural market remains untapped. Given this scenario, the 90s will see and has seen many new brands and consequently more brand wars, hopefully resulting in the ideal napkin at the right price, for the consumer.

Observations

With the constant awareness campaign, the entrepreneurs have made an impact on the consumers. The product has a ready market. Technology is available, raw material is in plenty. With the widening of the market, the demand for the product will increase manifold. It is profitable, healthier, comfortable and socially accepted. Market is vast but tricky. The product is tempting to entrepreneurs/manufacturers to step into this field.

To Every Operation

Product design is an outcome of sustained personal innovation.

Manufacturing is the result of teamwork applied to technology.

Marketing is the sum of people-devised service added to products.

Restructuring is the redeployment of people and their knowledge.

TQM is the application of human intelligence to improve processes.

PROJECT IDEAS — SCANNING OF BUSINESS ENVIRONMENT AND IDENTIFYING A PROJECT

Project ideas could originate from various sources or due to different reasons like the success story of a friend/relative, experience of others in manufacture/sale of product, demand for certain products, changes of producing a substitute of an article imported for which there is good demand, etc., and of course, the motivation, background and skills of the entrepreneur and his associates.

One major aspect while choosing a project idea should be to ascertain the extent of the marketing of the product proposed to be manufactured, its general use, industries which use it, its end-use and its buyers. You should, therefore, study the demand and supply of the product over the last few years to estimate its future demand based on the past trends. While doing so, it would be necessary to take into consideration the anticipated changes in fashions, technology and levels of income of the people. If the product proposed to be manufactured has a market throughout the country, the study should take into account the demand and supply of the product for the whole country. However, if the market for the product would be confined to one/ two states/or a particular region, the study may be confined to the concerned states/region. Many units function as ancillaries to major industries. In such a case, their fortunes being very closely dependent and linked to that of the 'parent unit', it is very important that detailed analyses are made on various areas before the decision to become an ancillary is made, i.e., areas like, will the unit be totally dependent on the parent unit, the potential for reasonable profit and future growth, the experience of similar ancillary units, whether there are any problems in obtaining payments or supportive know-how, whether the investment in fixed assets will be such as to facilitate easy branching of into a new product line in case the ancillary arrangement does not yield anticipated benefits, etc.

Box 26.2 Innovate or Perish

Innovation is so critical to Wipro that the management articulated it in its promise statement in 1998, as one of its four values. The groundwork for the initiative, however, started only in January 2000 because other big initiatives such as Six Sigma, brand-building and SEI initiatives had to stabilise.

The initial days were spent studying the concept of innovation from books and the internet. The team entrusted with starting the initiative did a survey among selected employees to understand their perception and understanding of innovation. They also listed Wipro's past successes and failures.

The project was taken so seriously that the team travelled to study organisations such as 3M, Home Depot, Nike and Nokia which are known for their innovations. The team also met academicians and consultants who specialise on the subject.

In the end, these were the findings:

- All successful organisations are innovative.
- You cannot copy an organisation. Each organisation has its own culture, processes and customer relationship. You can certainly learn from them.
- Organisations who have succeeded in innovations are those who had a strong driver or a need to innovate. The innovation initiative is linked to the business.
- Top management commitment to the initiative is the starting point of the journey.
- Mistakes are part of the innovation journey. We must learn to accept and learn from them. We need the ability to take risk and kill fear of failure. There has to be a culture of forgiveness.
- You need to build a learning organisation.
- You need to have a lot of organisational support and most importantly perseverance in order to succeed.
- You need to have stability of people. High turnover hits innovation.
- Innovation as an initiative cannot have one framework or methodology that could be readily deployed.
- We need to develop our own framework and methodology that suits our organisation in order to succeed.
- Only when innovation is valued by the customer will it give returns, customer validation of the idea at various stages could be most essential.
- Walls and silos in the organisation kills innovation. Communication network is essential. Proximity of teams helps.
- The need to understand the unstated needs of the customer is a necessity for innovation.
- Idea implementation is far more challenging than idea generation.

Finally, Wipro came up with its own definition of innovation: "implementation of new idea resulting in marketable product or service".

It will be equally important to judge market demand even when you are setting up a 'general purpose' workshop or service industry. In such cases, it will be necessary to have a clear idea of the industrial environment, the type of job orders you may obtain, whether they will be repeated, who will be giving them local competition, whether there are any large projects/establishments which promise potential for assured orders, whether your unit will have specialisation in a particular type of work which will give an edge over competitors, etc.

An import-substitute product, basically, should have a good market in view of the general policy to encourage indigenous production. It would, however, be necessary to have a clear idea of the government's import policy, present demand, the landed price of the imported item and how your price will compare with it, quality differences, etc.

In order to arrive at reasonable estimates of the future demand for and supply of a product, information relating to the capacity of existing units manufacturing that product, the extent of its utilisation, the capacity of the units that have already been granted licences but are in the process of being established, import and export potentiality of the product, etc., should be taken into consideration.

Although it is a difficult exercise to arrive at a precise forecast for demand and supply of a particular product, specially since reliable and up-to-date information is difficult to obtain on the basis of the available data, it should be possible to decide on the future prospects of the item proposed to be selected by you. Towards this, capacity utilisation of the existing units could be taken as a broad indication of market for the product. Similarly, underutilisation of the exiting capacity could be taken as a single for little or no scope for setting up a new unit.

An SSI unit generally enters the market which is localised and already had existing manufacturers. The success of the new unit in competing with the existing manufacturers would depend on a combination of its capability to identify and approach its targeted customer group and its marketing features like price, quality, delivery schedule, sales promotion etc.

Box 26.3 **Big Business**

Chances are that you have never seen an ad for Sula wines. Ritu Beri or Rohit Bal couture and for the Athena or Olive restaurants. But most people have heard of them: The wine and couture industries and designer restaurants have all been built by the Page 3 culture. Take wine: The industry had been virtually non-existent a few yeas back. The *modus operandi* has been simple: celebrities endorsing hitherto unheard of wines, lengthy articles on the history of wine, extensive converge of new launches and wine tasting sessions all brought to you courtesy of Page 3. The industry is valued at a cool ₹ 50 crore today.

It is difficult to value the industries that are a creation of Page 3 but if one were to take the three above-mentioned businesses alone it would probably be in the range of ₹ 300-400 crore. This is not including a number of retail stores, fragrance brands, Swiss watches and the burgeoning Feng Shui business. Look at the hair colour business, while the cosmetics majors may advertise their products, the barrier to hair colouring was broken down by Page 3 which showed Indian celebrities with constantly changing hair colour.

Most of these brands are aspirational and reaching their audience through advertising is expensive. It's easier to associate themselves with celebrities and make sure that they find enough mention in Page 3 to reach out to the top end of Gen P 3. After all, the celebrities are not the ones who bring in the money it's Gen P 3 patronage which makes them success or failure. A favourable mention on Page 3 can make these unknown brands/restaurants/designers talking points. It works for a circle of art impresarios and gallery owners – Naresh Kapuria's efforts are minutely here – as well. Restaurants are constantly holding theme night and sending out invitations to the press with the hope that they will make it to Page 3. Wine sellers try and ensure that the brand name is mentioned in the copy about the celebrity and his drink. Fashion designers try and make sure that they point out all the people at a party who are wearing their creations.

It's difficult to estimate to what extent the economy is impacted by Page 3, but it's hard to argue that there are few brands that wouldn't give an arm and a leg to be seen there.

IMPORTANCE OF PROJECT IDENTIFICATION

Project identification is often of great importance for the following reasons:

1. They become the catalytic agents of economic development.
2. They initiate the process of development – production, employment, income generation and so on.
3. They have consequences which are long-term in nature.

4. Projects provide the framework of the future activities of the enterprises.
5. They also shape the future pattern of services.
6. Projects usually involve substantial financial outlays.
7. They also initiate development of basic infrastructure and environment.
8. Project commitments cannot be easily reversed.
9. Project identification brings necessary changes in society in course of time.
10. Projects accelerate the process of socio-cultural development.

Selection of a Product

At this stage, the entrepreneur is concerned with identifying a particular product that he hopes to market successfully at a reasonable profit. Therefore, the selection of the right product is very essential for being successful in the business venture. The right product here means that which can be marketed at a reasonable profit which will induce him to continue in the business. Various factors influence the entrepreneur in selecting the right product. These decisive factors are:

(i) Whether import restrictions or the items selected are banned items would considerably weigh favourably or otherwise in the selection of the products. This is because in the case of banned items, the domestic market offers considerable scope for selling as the demand for such a product would not be met by import. Thus, if the item selected falls in the category of banned import items, the entrepreneur would favour it and in the case of unrestricted import of the items, he would definitely not show his favour for selecting such a product.

(ii) If the entrepreneur himself or his partners have gathered substantial amount of experience in the manufacture and marketing of certain products, then the selection of such a product would be to their advantage. Therefore, most often the items selected are of those lines of products in which the entrepreneur or his colleagues have gathered enough experience. The line in which they are not experienced obviously would not be favoured much as to the will entail uncertain situations very often.

(iii) The selection of the product will also be based upon the degree of profitability that generally rules in the market. Such information can be obtained from banks, financial corporations or the market itself. The selection, therefore, will depend upon the information compiled for the particular line of product for its profitability.

(iv) Many concessions are available from the government for producing a product which serves as an import substitute or even an essential item. Hence, if a particular product enjoys a substantial amount of incentives, concessions and liberal taxation policies, obviously the entrepreneur will select such an item to enjoy these advantages conferred on the production of this particular type of product.

(v) Many products belong to the priority industries or the small-scale sector also; certain products are listed by the government for purchasing exclusively from the small-scale sector. As a result, if a particular product belongs to this category, the selection of such a product would be advantageous for the entrepreneur; therefore, these factors also must receive due consideration before the selection of a product.

(vi) The market for the product also plays a significant role in the selection of the product. If the product also has an export market, it widens the scope of marketing, hence such a product has its own advantages in the success of the enterprise.

(vii) Certain products are permitted for production only if the licence is obtained from the appropriate authority while others belong to the delicensed category. In the case of a licensed product, obtaining of licence would be a difficult proposition or the capacity required for the entire industry may also have been created fully by the government, as a consequence, the impossibility of seeking further permission for the production of such a product. A product belonging to the licensed category or delicensed category also is considered before selecting the product.

(viii) Many products enjoy specific advantages in regard to the scale of manufacture or carry locational advantage, e.g., if produced in a free trade zone or in the backward areas with special incentives and concessions which are made available for manufacturing such a product. Selection of a product, therefore, also depends upon these factors.

(ix) If a product belongs to an ancillary unit and serves as major competent for the parent industry, it provides a ready demands, hence the selection of this type of product entails easy marketability.

Finally, at this stage, the selection of a product would also be weighed in favour or against depending upon whether or not the machinery and the raw materials required would be imported or indigenous. Similarly, the selection would also be based upon the skilled and unskilled labour position as well as technical know-how which is available indigenously or would require a foreign collaboration.

The study of the project idea is the starting point of the feasibility analysis. The study is undertaken to identify the logic of the project, the tasks which must be performed for achieving the objectives and the inputs, outputs and process evolved in each activity. The ultimate aim is to identify the characteristics of the project. A project idea poses a problem, on the one hand and seeks a solution of the problem on the other. In other that the solution may be an appropriate one, it is necessary to examine and appreciate the nature and extent of the problem and to clearly identify its dimensions.

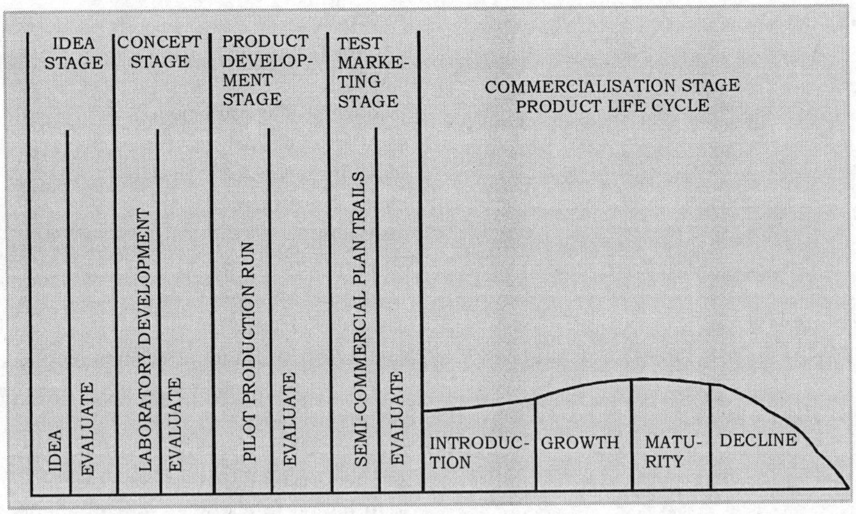

Fig. 26.1 Product Planning and Development

(**Source:** Adapted from Robert D. Hisrich and Michael P. Peters, *Marketing Decisions for New and Mature Products*, (Columbus, Ohio: Charles E. Merrill Publishing Co., 1984))

The Adoption Process

The adoption of an innovation demands planned management of change (overcoming the resistance to change). An adoption process is a process bringing about a change in a buyer's attitudes and perception. Consumer adoption process covers the steps that a consumer usually goes through in determining the feasibility of buying new products: (1) Awareness, (2) Interest, (3) Evaluation or mental trial, (4) Trial (physical), and (5) Adoption.

1. ***Awareness:*** A person learns about a new idea, product or practice. He has general information about it, e.g., through advertisement. He has, however, limited knowledge about special qualities, usefulness, performance, etc., regarding the innovation. He merely knows about its existence.
2. ***Interest:*** He now develops an interest in the innovation. He demands more detailed information about the new product, its utility, its performance, and so on. He listens with interest to jingles on the radio or TV ads, reads press ads, and learns more about it from others, and is now inclined to actively seek the desired information from salespersons, opinion leaders, peers, friends, etc.
3. ***Evaluation:*** The accumulated information and evidences are weighed by the person in order to assess the basic soundness or worth of the innovation. He tries to weigh the value of the new product and the extent to which it is good for him. In a sense, he conducts a mental trial of the new product.
4. ***Trial:*** The person now is ready to put the idea into practice. Competent personal assistance is necessary to put the innovation to use.
5. ***Adoption:*** It is the final stage in which he makes a decision to buy. The person now decides to adopt the new idea, product or practice for continued use. If post-purchase experience is good, he becomes a repeat buyer and a talking advertisement of the innovation.

Key performance areas	Key areas and variables
Market standing	Sales
	Production margin
	New orders
	Lost orders
	Lost customers
Innovation	Number of new products
	New markets
Productivity	Capacity utilisation
	Backlogs
	Back orders
	Manufacturing costs
	Yields
Physical and financial resources	Number of idle equipment
	Number of obsolete inventory items
	Accounts receivable turnover
	Inventory turnover
	Cash flow
	Working capital turnover
	Return on investment
Motivation and organisational development	Absenteeism trend
	Number of personnel problems going to arbitration
	Number of personnel attending training programmes
	Labour turnover
Public responsibility	Number of employees involved in community programmes
	Expenditure on pollution control
	Contribution to charitable organisations.

Criteria for Selecting a Particular Project

After gathering a large number of project profiles, the entrepreneur should consider the following criteria for selecting a particular project:

Investment Size: Professional managers, who have worked in multinational companies or large Indian companies, should think of starting medium-sized or large-sized units only. The investment size (project cost) should be at least ₹ 3 to 5 crore. They should not commit the common mistake of restricting the project size to less than ₹ 2 crore so that they need not go to all financial institutions. In fact, under the present circumstances, it will be much easier to get projects cleared by all-India institutions, requiring even lesser promoter's contribution.

Location: A new entrepreneur should locate his project to the extent possible, in and around state headquarters. There are many backward areas around such cities. It is necessary to have such a location to attract competent managers. This will also facilitate liaison with the State Electricity Board, State Industrial Development Corporation and various other agencies.

Technology: The first project should not be for a product which requires high technology, necessitating foreign technical collaboration. It is better to go in for a product with a proven technology that is indigenously available. It makes life easier to begin with.

Equipment: The entrepreneur should select the best equipment based on the advice of experienced technical consultants. He should not compromise on the quality of the equipment. Many entrepreneurs enter into some sort of a deal with the equipment manufactured for a 'kickback' and in the process sacrifice quality. Industry is a goose that lays golden eggs. One should not be shortsighted and come to grief by going in for poor quality equipment.

Marketing: It is not advisable to get into a project particularly the first, which would mean survival amidst cut-throat competition involving direct selling to the ultimate consumer. One should go in for products with a limited number (say 10 to 20) of industrial customers.

Checklist for Choosing Ideas

Fit with your skills and experience

- Do you believe in the product or service?
- Does the need arise and do you feel like attending personally?
- Do you like and understand the potential customers?
- Do you have experience in this type of business?
- Do the basic success factors of this business fit your skills?
- Are the tasks of the enterprise once you will enjoy doing yourself?
- Do you enjoy working with the people employed and supervising them?
- Has the idea begun to take over your imagination and spare time?
- Is the idea innovative to the extent of social benefit?
- Are you expecting good returns?

Fit with the Market:

1 Is there a real customer need?

- Can you get a price that gives you good margins?
- Would customers believe in the product coming from your company?
- Does the product or service you propose produce clearly perceivable customer benefit which is significantly better than that offered by competing ways to satisfy the same basic need?
- Is there a cost-effective way to get messages and the product to the customers?

Fit with the Enterprise

- Is there a reason to believe your enterprise could be very good at the business?
- Does it fit the enterprise culture?
- Can you imagine who might sponsor it?
- Does it look profitable (high margin – low investment)?
- Will it look to large markets and growth?

What to Do When Your Idea is Rejected?

Frequently, as an entrepreneur, you will find that your idea has been rejected and/or is not successful as envisaged. There are a few things you can do:

1. Give up and select a new idea.
2. Listen carefully, understand what is wrong, improve your idea and your presentation and try again.
3. Find someone else to whom you can present your idea by considering:
   - Who will benefit most if it works and can they be a sponsor?
   - Who are the potential customers and will they demand the product?
   - How can you get to the people who really care about entrepreneurial ideas?

Box 26.4 Businesses to be in Today

As long as you ask if your business has enough cash-paying customers.

Despite the prevailing gloom, the Internet is seen driving future growth enough to ensure that the technology dream stays alive. Craig Barrett, President and CEO, Intel Corp, sees the Indian success story in software development being replicated in IT-enabled services and inernet applications. Remember, investors are looking for companies that can create intellectual property, tap new trends and have cash-paying customers.

Some areas that look promising for the new-age entrepreneur.

IT-ENABLED SERVICES

This sector involves remote data management. In 2000-01, Indian software revenues totalled ₹ 37,760 crore of which ₹ 4,100 crore came from IT-enabled services, including call centres medical transcription, back-office automation, legal databases, data digitisation and digital content development. Of these, customer interaction alone will see global spends of $60 billion by 2003. The key here is scale of operations, and big is definitely beautiful.

SOFTWARE DEVELOPMENT

By 2008, Nasscom estimates that the total software exports from India will reach $ 50 billion, accounting for 7.7 per cent of GDP. The early nineties model was the onsite one, where Indian engineers went overseas to write software code at competitive costs. The sector has since evolved into a primarily offshore model, where value-added work is done at company development centres here. Offshore business rose to 44 per cent of the country's software exports in 2001 against 5 per cent in 1991. The focus now is on software development, integration and IT business consulting, done out of Indian offices. Investors expect start-ups to have the ability to create intellectual property and share royalty with vendors on software project components.

DIGITAL SIGNAL PROCESSING

The presence of very few niche players and the advent of gadgets with multifunctionality drives this space. Apart from Net telephone and cellphones, other digital appliances will be used to transfer text, voice and graphics, all requiring high computing power. By 2005, the DSP software and services market is expected to touch $9 billion, and the DSP silicon chip processor (the hardware) $5 billion. The tools will be used in computer companies, wireless communications, networking, and information storage markets.

E-LEARNING

This is a huge space with not many players at the high end of the value chain. International Data Corp ((IDC) estimates that the global e-earning market will grow from $ 1.1 billion in 2000 to $ 11.4 billion in 2003. Online education or web-based training is targeted at corporate employees, students and general consumers. In India, the growing collaboration between Indian universities and training centres with overseas partners, as well as industrial and academic tie-ups are expected to grow this market exponentially. Indian start-ups will need the ability to scale up business for both domestic and global markets.

COMMUNICATION SOFTWARE

These are software solutions for the mobile computing world-wireless or handheld solutions and the ability to build global markets is vital here. In Asia alone, the mobile commerce market will reach $ 36 billion by 2004, according to IDC projections, intellectual property and royalty sharing drives start-up growth in this space.

NETWORKING SPACE

The network infrastructure market is seen as the fastest growting segment in IT services. By 2005, the global demand for networking services will touch $ 39.8 billion. This will include the planning, installation and access provision of corporate and e-commerce networks, as well as project management and information security services. As more end-users demand greater access to information and services, networks will only grow bigger.

BIOTECHNOLOGY

Bioinformatics is the collation and analysis of data for development of biotech products in human pharma and plant genomics. By 2006, this market will touch an estimated $10 billion, and provide data analysis to speed up R&D cycles. Contract research or outsourcing low-cost R&D to Indian companies is a growing trend. Global spends on outsourced R&D is estimated at $7 billion, with 30 per cent annual growth rates. Opportunities lie in basic gene sequencing, genetic research for medical diagnostics, new crop varieties and early stage drug development.

SECURITY

As networks proliferate, security of corporate intranets and e-commerce sites is a growing business opportunity. IDC estimates the 3A (authentication, authorisation and administration) market at $7.7 billion by 2004. Equally, intrusion detection and vulnerability assessment of corporate networks will see revenues of $1 billion. With an established revenue model, this start-up segment is a hot pick among investors.

INFRASTRUCTURE

This comprises building the backbone for a networked environment. As businesses move to e-commerce, they need sophisticated storage software tools and management solutions for back-end functions like stacking, restoring and archiving data across platforms. By 2004, global revenues are expected to double from the present $2.5 billion.

PROJECT PROFILE

Ceiling Fan

1. General

(i) Profile.	New
(ii) Whether reserved for manufacture in small-scale sector.	No
(iii) Whether reserved for purchase from small-scale sector.	No

2. Product and its Uses

Ceiling fan is a household appliance and is used for circulating of air in the room.

3. Market Potential

With the increase in housing activity and construction of multi-storey building, the demand of ceiling fans will increase considerably.

4. Production Targets and Range

Ceiling fans (900 mm to 1,500 mm)	4,000 Nos. per.
Installed Capacity.	Annum per shift.

5. Basis and Presumption

No. of working days	300 days per Annum
No. of working hours	6 hrs per day
Size of fan taken for calculations	1,200 mm
Annual production	3,000 Nos. per annum per shift

6. Process of Manufacture and Production Details

The manufacturing process of the ceiling fans involves the following operations:

(i) The casting of the body are purchased and turned to the required size.

(ii) Core is assembled.

(iii) Coil winding is done on the automatic coil winding machines.

(iv) Shaft is turned to the required size.

(v) Fan body and the blades are painted.

(vi) All the parts/components are assembled.

(vii) The assembled fan is tested to IS specifications.

7. Pollution Control

The pollution control is not applicable.

8. Quality Control and Standardisation

IS: 347-1979	Specifications for Electric Ceiling Type Fans and Regulators.
IS: 1709-1960	Fans – Fixed Capacitors
IS: 648-1970	Specifications for Steel Sheet and Magnetic Circuits of Power Electrical Apparatus.
IS: 302-1979	General and Safety Requirements for Household Electrical Appliances.

9. Land and Building

	₹
(a) Land	
500 sq. metres @ ₹ 60/- per sq.m.	30,000.00
(b) Building	
(i) Workshed 15m × 20m = 300 sq.m. @ ₹ 1,000/- per sq. metre.	3,00,000.00
(ii) Office 4m × 5m – 20 sq.m. @ ₹ 1,200/- per sq.m.	24,000.00
(iii) Laboratory 4m × 5m – 20 sq.m. @ ₹ 1,200/- per sq m.	24,000.00
(iv) Room for air delivery test 8m × 8m @ ₹ 100 per sq. m.	64,000.00
(v) Cycle Stand, Lavatory Block and Boundry wall	20,000.00
	4,32,000.00

10. Machinery and Equipments

(a) Machinery

1. Lathe Machine 6'	Two	48,000.00
2. Automatic Coil Winding Machine for Fan Rotar	Two	40,000.00
3. Drill Machine Pedestal 1' cap	Two	6,000.00
4. Bench Grinder D.E.	One	2,000.00
5. Fly Press no. 4 (4' × 4' × 6')	Two	2,000.00
6. Hand Presses	Two	2,000.00
7. Electric Oven (4' × 2' × 2)	One	6,000.00
8. Electric Oven	One	4,000.00
9. Air Compressor	One	5,000.00
10. Hand Tools		2,500.00
		1,17,5000

(b) Testing Equipments

1. AC High Voltage Test Set 0-5000V.	One	6,000.00
2. A.C. Variac Transformer 0-300 V 5 Amp	One	2,000.00
3. Meggar 500 V	One	1,500.00
4. Watt meter	One	1,200.00
5. Wheat-stone Bridge	One	10,500.00
6. Test Panel Complete with Amp. Meter volt meter, watt meter.	One	7,800.00
7. Avo meter	One	2,000.00
8. Anemometer	One	5,000.00

9. Air Delivery Test Chamber	One	25,000.00
		61,000.00
(c) Office Equipment and Furniture.		10,000.00
(d) Installation and Electrification @ 10%		17,850.00
(e) Transportation, Packing, Forwarding and Sales tax @ 10%		17,850.00
		2,24,200.00

11. Total Fixed Cost

	₹
Land and Building	4,62,000.00
Machinery and Equipments	2,24,200.00
	6,86,200.00

12. Raw Materials per month

1. Stampings CRGO 250 kg @ ₹ 65/- per kg	16,250.00
2. C.I.Body 250 sets @ ₹ 40/- per set.	10,000.00
3. Ball Bearing 250 sets @ ₹ 45/- per set.	11,250.00
4. S.E. Copper wire 75 kg @ ₹ 110/- per kg	8,250.00
5. M.S.Rod 100 kg @ ₹ 10/- per kg	1,000.00
6. Blade Assembly 250 sets @ ₹ 25/- per set	6,250.00
7. Hanger 250 Nos. @ ₹ 6/- each	1,500.00
8. Canopy 250 sets @ ₹ 6/- per set	1,500.00
9. Condensers 2.5 MFD 250 Nos. @ ₹ 12/- each	3,000.00
10. Regulators 250 Nos. @ ₹ 10/- each	2,500.00
11. Black pipe 250 ft. @ ₹ 2/- per foot	500.00
12. Insulating materials @ ₹ 5/- per Fan	1,250.00
13. Paint/Varnish @ ₹ 5/- per Fan	11,250.00
14. Hardware @ ₹ 4/- per Fan	1,000.00
15. Packing Materials	1,000.00
	66,500.00

13. Staff and Labour per month

		₹
(a) Administrative and Supervisory		
1. Manager-cum-production Engineer	One	1,000.00
2. Sales man	One	750.00
3. Clerk-cum-storekeeper	One	750.00
4. Chowkidar	One	500.00
		3,000.00
(b) Technical		
1. Skilled workers @ ₹ 750/- each	3	2,250.00
2. Semi-skilled workers @ ₹ 600/- each	4	2,400.00
3. Helpers @ ₹ 500/-	3	1,500.00
		6,150.00
Perquisited @ 15% of total salaries		1,350
		8,500.00

14. Utilities per month

1. Power 30 HP @ ₹ 28/- per H.P.	840.00
2. Water	200
	1,040.00

15. Other Expenses per month

1. Postage, Stationery and Printing, etc.	250.00
2. Advertisement and Publicity	500.00
3. Consumable Stores	100.00
4. Transport Charges	250.00
5. Telephone	500.00
6. Repair and Maintenance	350.00
7. Sales Expenses	750.00
8. Miscellaneous Expenses	100.00
	2,800.00

16. Working Capital

(a) Per Month (12) + (13) + (14) +(15)	80,860.00
(b) For three months 16(a) × 3	2,42,580.00

17. Total Capital Investment

(a) Fixed Investment	6,86,200.00
(b) Working Capital for three months	2,42,580.00
	9,28,780.00

18. Cost of production per annum

1. Raw Materials	7,98,000.00
2. Staff and Labour	1,26,240.00
3. Utilities	12,480.00
4. Other Expenses	33,600.00
5. Depreciation on Building @ 50%	21,600.00
6. Depreciation on Machinery @ 10%	17, 850.00
7. Depreciation on Office Equipments @ 20%	2,000.00
8. Interest on total investment @ 15%	1,39,317.00
	11,51,087.00

19. Sales Proceeds per annum

By sales of 3,00 ceiling fans @ ₹ 450/- each	13,50,000.00

20. Profitability per annum

	₹
Profit	1,98,913.00
(a) Percentage of profit on sales	14.7%
(b) Percentage of Profit on Total Investment	21.42%

21. Break-even Analysis

	₹
Fixed Cost	
Depreciation on Building	21,600.00
Depreciation on Machinery	17,830.00

Interest on Capital	1,39,317.00
40% of Salary	50,496.00
40% of Other Expenses	13,440.00
	2,29,263.00

$$\text{BEP} = \frac{\text{Annual Fixed Cost} \times 100}{\text{Annual Fixed Cost} + \text{Profit}}$$

$$\frac{2,29,263 \times 100}{2,29,236 + 1,98,913} = \frac{2,29,263.00}{4,28,176} = 53.5\%$$

22. Addresses of Machinery and Equipment Suppliers

1. M/s. Batli Boi & Co. Ltd. M.I. Road, Jaipur - 302 001. — General Machines
2. M/s. Sri Ram Lathe House, Anba-bari, Jaipur - 302 202 — -do-
3. M/s. Perfect machine Tools Co., Bell building, Sir P.M. Road, Mumbai - 400 001. — -do-
4. M/s. Atlas Engineering Co., G.T. Road, Batala - 143 505 — -do-
5. M/s. BMP & Equipment Co., Block 16-B, Kurla Ind. Estate, Mumbai - 400 077. — Coil Winding Machine
6. M/s. Choudhary Trading Co., Bhagirath Place, Delhi - 110 006 — -do-
7. M/s. Gyro Laboratories Pvt. Ltd., 8, Gazdor Street, Thankudwar, Mumbai - 400 002 — Testing Equipments
8. M/s. Toshniwal Bros. Pvt. Ltd., M.G. Road, Ajmer - 305 007. — -do-
9. M/s. BHS India Pvt. Ltd., 304, Ashok Bhawan, Nehru Place, New Delhi - 110 024. — -do-

23. Addresses of Raw Material Suppliers

1. G.K.W. (Stamping Division), Gopi Nath Marg, Jaipur - 302 001 — Stampings
2. M/s. Golden Pressing Factory, 104, Ind. Area, Jhotwara, Jaipur - 302 012. — -do-
3. M/s. National Engineering Industries, Khatipura road, Jaipur - 302 006. — Ball bearing
4. M/s. Indian Cable Company Ltd., Ind. Assurance Building Chor Rasta, Gandhi Road, P.O. Box 33, Ahmedabad - 380 001. — Enameled wire
5. M/s. National Insulated Co. of India Ltd. Nicoo House, Hare street, Kolkata - 700 001. — -do-
6. M/s. National Casting & Industries, Sudershanpura, Ind. Area, Jaipur - 302 006. — C.I. Castings
7. M/s. Agarwal Engge. Works 125, Ind. Area, Jhotwara, Jaipur - 302 012. — -do-

Note: 1. Casting can be procured for any C.I. Foundry.
2. SE Copper wire, Bearings, Insulating materials etc. are available in open market

(Prepared by SISI Jaipur)

Many innovative ideas are needed to find one good idea worth for commercialisation and many new ideas fail to pass the screening stage. Few ideas are compatible with the corporate resources and goals. Finally, five ideas are eliminated for lack of profit potential. Finally, having profitability, only one new product idea becomes eligible for market introduction and officially enters its life cycle.

Product Planning and Development Process

There are seven steps in the planning and development of a new product:

1. **New Product Ideas:** We visualise the detailed features of a model product. Ideas may be contributed by scientists, professional designers, rivals, customers, sales force, top management, dealers, etc. We may need sixty new ideas to get one commercially viable product.
2. **Idea Screening:** We have to evaluate all ideas and inventions. Poor or bad ideas are dropped and through the process of elimination, only the most promising and profitable ideas are picked up for further detailed investigation and research.
3. **Concept Development and Testing:** All ideas that survive the process of screening (preliminary investigation) will be studied in detail. They will be developed into mature product concepts. We will have a precise description of the ideas and features of the proposed product. At this stage, we can incorporate consumer preference into our agenda for concept development and testing product ideas. Concept testing the company to choose the best among the alternative product concepts. Consumers are called upon to offer their comments on the precise written description of the product concept, *viz.,* the attributes and expected benefits.
4. **Business Analysis:** Once the best product concept is picked up, it will be subjected to rigorous scrutiny to evaluate its market potential, capital investment, rate of return on capital, etc. Business analysis is a combination of marketing research, cost-benefit analysis and assessment of competition. We have demand analysis, cost analysis and profitability analysis. Business analysis will prove the economic prospects of the new product concept. It will also prove the soundness and viability of the selected product concept from a business viewpoint. Now we can proceed to concentrate on product development programme. The proposed product must offer a realistic profit objective.

5. **Product Development Programme:** We have three steps in this stage when a paper idea is duly converted into a physical product: (a) prototype development, giving a visual image of the product, (b) consumer testing of the model or prototype, and (c) branding, packaging and labelling. Consumer testing of the model product will provide the ground for the final selection of the most promising model for mass production and mass distribution.
6. **Test Marketing:** The entire product marketing programme is tried out for the first time in a small number of well-selected test markets, i.e., test markets, i.e., test cities or areas. Test marketing is necessary to find out the viability of a full marketing programme for national distribution. Customer reactions can be tested under normal market conditions. It helps the company to learn through trial and error and to get additional valuable clues for product improvement and for modifications in our marketing mix. We can use test markets for testing the effectiveness of all ingredients of our marketing mix. Test marketing can answer such questions as: Is the new product labelled and packaged properly? Is the new product liked by the consumer? Is the firm justified in spending large sums on productive capacity? Has the communication (promotion) programme been right? Positive answers will reassure marketers.
7. **Commercialisation:** Once the test marketing gives the green signal for the product with or without expected modifications, the company can proceed to finalise all features of the product. Now marketing management can launch a full-fledged advertising and promotion campaign for mass distribution. Mass production will start and all distribution channels will be duly organised. The product is now born and will start its life cycle in due course.

Revolutions for the Future

1. **Health care:** Biotechnology has opened up a world of endless possibilities to mankind. Diseases that traumatise and kill people today will become a thing of the past. Surgery may be replaced with non-intrusive techniques that don't just repair, but grow new cells to heal. That in turn will have a dramatic impact on productivity and efficiency of workforce. But increasing longevity will create a market for new kinds of geriatric care.
2. **Environment:** Population growth in developed countries will begin to taper off, while that of Third World countries will continue to clip. Basic natural resources such as air, water, fuel will become big issues. Innovations aimed at squeezing more out of dwindling resources will hit the market. Increasing global incomes would increase the consumption of energy. Therefore, new ways of tapping green and renewable sources of fuel will be developed.
3. **Education:** In the new age, labour will increasingly be replaced by knowledge. Mechanical jobs will either be eliminated or entrusted to machines. Personal progress would be linked to education. With more people seeking education, the need will be for the service providers to reach out to them inexpensively but ubiquitously.
4. **Communications:** The demand for information and connectivity will grow exponentially. Media will converge with greater force, and more versatile communication devices will see the light of the day. Geographical distance would become meaningless, and the cost of communication ape the trend in information technology.
5. **Artificial Intelligence:** Robots built to think like humans will be everywhere: at road crossings, shop counters, offices, restaurants, and even in the cockpit of an aircraft. Highly developed user interface will allow such robots to talk to human beings and build their knowledge dynamically. In the short-term, artificial intelligence will potentially endanger all low-skill tasks currently carried out by human beings. In the long-run, it may play God.

The Golden Age of Biotech

Alzheimer's, Cancer, AIDS, Down's Syndrome, disease-free plants, regenerative body parts and, perhaps, human immortality. All these and much more would be on the radar of biotech scientists, now that they've constructed the human genome map. But to make repairs at cell level, scientists will have to understand how proteins in our genes work. Proteomics (the study of proteins) will create the next big wave in biotech. Once the protein mystery is solved, medicines will be able to do almost anything. Repair damaged neurons in an Alzheimer's patient, rebuild the immune system in an AIDS sufferer, or grow a new layer of skins for a burn victim.

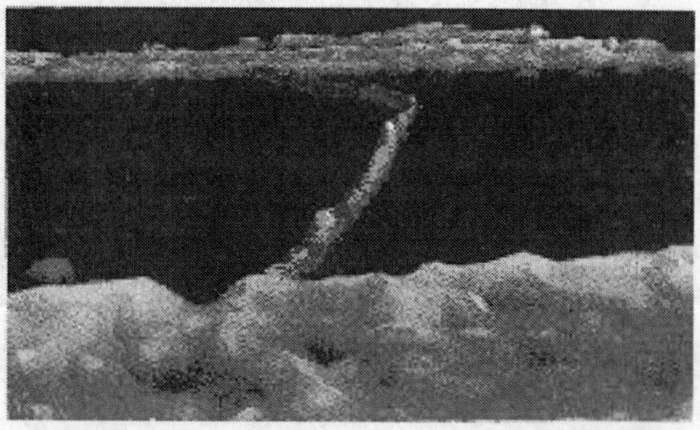

Circuits of the future: nanotubes draped across electrodes

Another revolution will be in terms of regrowing body parts. Scientists are battling ethical issues to experiment with stem cells – cells responsible for growing blood, muscles, and tissues – to find ways to regrow body parts. A breakthrough would mean amputees, deformity, and handicaps become a thing of the past.

Nanotechnology, which explores activities at subatomic level, is another exciting area. The premise is simple: since everything – human beings, potatoes, and diamonds – is made of atoms, it is theoretically possible to produce copies of them inexpensively and rapidly, if their chemical structures were replicated. So, sitting in a laboratory one could grow potatoes and diamonds.

Nanotechnology would also make it possible to make 'machines' that work at the subatomic level. In March this year, IBM researchers announced that they had succeeded in creating "a network of tiny transistors from nanotubes only a few atoms wide". Although its commercial application may be several years away, what it means is that Moore's Law will not only hold true in the future, but it may actually be bettered.

Starting the Venture

- [ ] **Translate Ideas into Business Opportunities**
- [ ] **Prepare an Opportunity Analysis and Learn the Five Steps to Success**
- [ ] **Know How to Protect Your Idea or Product**
- [ ] **Prepare a Cash Flow Forecast**
- [ ] **Design a Cash Flow Forecast**
- [ ] **Formulate a Successful Marketing Plan**
- [ ] **Prepare the Marketing Analysis and Plan**
- [ ] **Employ Successful Database Marketing Technology**
- [ ] **Define the Market Segmentation**
- [ ] **Conduct a Competitive Analysis**
- [ ] **Prepare the Pricing and Sales Strategy**
- [ ] **Penetrate the Market and sell the Product**
- [ ] **Take Advantage of Marketing and E-Commerce Opportunities**
- [ ] **Establish the Scope of the Business Plan**
- [ ] **Determine What Type of Business Plan is Best**
- [ ] **Determine What Steps are Involved in Writing the Business Plan**
- [ ] **Being the Process of Writing the Eight Business Plan Sections**
- [ ] **Estimate How Long Writing the Business Plan will take**
- [ ] **Locate Investors and Prepare a Presentation**
- [x] **Determine Which Form of Ownership is Best for Your Venture**
- [x] **Review the Business Start-up Checklist**
- [x] **Establish Employer-Employee Agreements**
- [x] **Establish Stock Option Agreements.**

CONCLUSION

During the past two decades, advance information and computer technologies have interconnected world economies. The globalisation of national economies has brought considerable benefits, and also thrown open plenty of opportunities to entrepreneurs at all levels. What is more important is that the service sector, IT sector and knowledge sectors are growing at a greater speed.

In an environment of wide range of opportunities, the search for a business idea and converting it into a successful venture is a continuous process. The responsibility of the entrepreneur is to build winning characteristics into the organisation so that achievement levels exceed normal expectations. Towards this end, "our dreams have to be bigger, our ambitions higher, our commitment deeper, and our efforts greater".

In short, India is a land of opportunity, where the economy is fast becoming global and the empowerment of ordinary people a reality. There is abundant scope to entrepreneurs to set up new ventures, open up new services, generate employment and create wealth. It is time for all of India's entrepreneurs, new and old, to shrug off the chains and play a leading role by grabing the opportunities by in converting into enterprises, services, etc.

27 CHAPTER

CONVERTING BUSINESS OPPORTUNITIES INTO REALITY

"Making Tough Choices"

"There's a fundamental distinction between strategy and operational effectiveness. Strategy is about making choices, trade-offs; it's about deliberately choosing to be different. Operational effectiveness is about things that you really shouldn't have to make choices on; it's about what's good for everybody and about what every business should be doing."

— Michael E. Porter, Management Guru

LEARNING OBJECTIVES

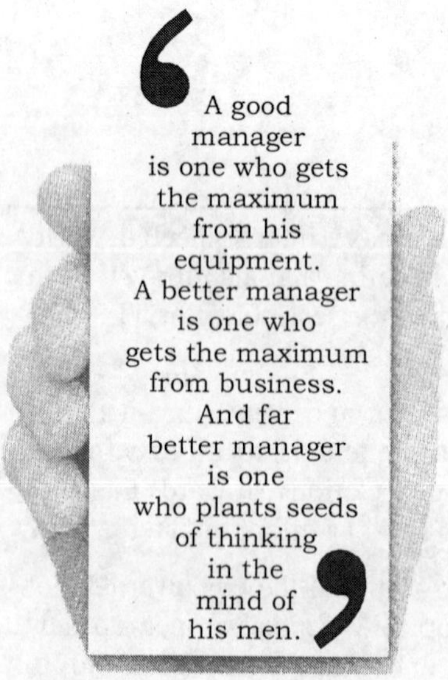

The chapter throws light on varied aspects involved in the process of converting business opportunities into reality – promotion of a venture.

- Basic Objectives
- Selection of an Enterprise
- Feasibility Analysis
- Break-even Analysis
- Registration
- Infrastructure
- Machinery
- Raw Materials
- Venture Capital, Working Capital, Long-term Funds, etc.
- Marketing
- Availing of Varied Incentives
- Lessons
- The Winning Edge
- The Strategy
- The Vision, Innovation

Five Steps to Success

1. Seize the opportunity.
2. Investigate the need through market research.
3. Develop the plan.
4. Determine the resources needed.
5. Manage the distinguishing features of the business.

INTRODUCTION

The success of a small-scale industry solely depends upon doing the right thing at the right time. In other words, a small-scale industrialist has to be conversant with the varied regulations governing the small-scale industry and the procedures to be followed in order to acquire the necessary assistance and incentives offered by the government from time-to-time.

The procedural aspects of the small-scale industry are quite formidable. Each and every entrepreneur is often overwhelmed by the multitude of procedures which help to face at every stage of the development of a small-scale industry. It is, therefore, necessary to emphasise here that the student should concentrate more on the purpose and the principles underlying the various procedural formalities than on such routine formalities as filling in various forms, applications, etc.

Basic Objectives

The basic objectives underlying the development of small-and medium-scale industries are the increase in the supply of manufactured goods, the promotion of capital formation, the development of indigenous entrepreneurial talents and skills and the creation of broader employment opportunities. In addition, they include socio-economic goals such as the decentralisation and dispersal of manufacturing activities from the metropolitan to the non-metropolitan and rural areas, the reduction of regional economic imbalances within a country and the diffusion of entrepreneurial and managerial abilities and skills and technology throughout the country.

In the Indian economy, cottage and small-scale industries have a significant role to play. With increasing pace of industrialisation and sophistication of the large-scale industries, a new orientation is inevitable in the relationship of the SSIs with the large and medium industries. This relationship calls for integration of the production methods, upgradation of the qualities of production, ability to meet stringent delivery schedules and very many other problems that arise in a changing environment.

Right Thing at the Right Time

Box 27.1 Are you Ready for Business?

Some questions to ask yourself before you take the entrepreneurial leap.

— Udayan Ray (30 Apr., 2001)

Bitten by the business bug? Remember, it's not easy to shake off the soporific security of a 9-to-5 job and perks to adopt a career that promises huge rewards but is rife with uncertainties. Ask yourself these questions before you make the leap.

Have the personality? You have to have passion but equally, you have to be a good general. You must attract great talent, and later get the best out of your team and motivate it.

Can you persevere? There will be setbacks: finance, labour, market downturns. You must have tremendous faith in yourself and your idea to weather these.

Have the big idea? First, evaluate your business idea. Is it unique or is it better/cheaper than the rest? It's a good idea to use informal market research to get feedback on the idea's viability.

What's your gameplan? Figure out your scale of operations: will you cater to a niche segment? Chart a road map of your business goals and timeframes.

Is it on paper? Make a sound business plan. This process will help you spot planning oversights early. If you're looking for loans, a business plan is mandatory.

Where is the money? Figure out how much you can raise from personal and other sources. Money from the wrong investors can be source of conflict.

Is cash flow in place? Cash flows must see you through contingencies and hidden costs, and help you stay afloat for at least six months after start-off. Don't make optimistic revenue projections.

Will revenues be stable? Get at least one or two anchor clients, the ones who will provide large, regular orders.

How lean can you get? Keep a tight leash on expenses till operations stabilise. Cut down on fixed costs, like high rentals, till your venture finds its feet.

Then act.

1. Evaluate your business idea and ensure your product/service is superior to what's available in the market.
2. Making a sound business plan will help you spot planning oversights early. Also essential if you want a loan.
3. How much money can you raise from personal sources? Will your cash flows see you through the initial period?
4. Attract talent and make the most of your team. And have enough faith in yourself, your idea and your team to weather initial setbacks.
5. Get at least two anchor clients who can provide large, regular orders. This should keep revenues stable.

In this chapter, the treatment of procedures – right from conceiving a small-scale industry until the repayment of creditors and ploughing back of profits – is based on the personal and practical experience of a small industrialist. In the latter part of the discussion, a reference has been made to the varied regulations that a small-scale industrialist has to abide by. They are mentioned later.

A discussion of the relevant procedures to be followed when setting up a small-scale industry has been dealt with reference to various phases of its development. These phases are:

(i) Selection of a small industry and preparation of feasibility and project reports;

(ii) Accommodation, power and other infrastructural facilities;

(iii) Machinery;

(iv) Raw materials;

(v) Finance;

(vi) Marketing; and

(vii) Securing various incentives offered for the development of the small-scale industry.

1. SELECTION OF A SMALL-SCALE INDUSTRY

The process of setting up a small-scale industry has been shown in Fig. 27.1, which has been drawn on the basis of practical experience gained in its promotion. It indicated all the important stages in setting up of a small-scale industry.

The objectives of the promotional regulation are to provide an impetus to the growth of a small-scale industry and regulate the supply of machinery, electricity, water, premises, finance, raw materials and markets. The process of production and marketing is governed by set rules and regulations. In a way, these regulations are a boon to the small entrepreneur.

The procedure for setting up a small-scale industrial unit is given below:

1. Selection of the product and preparation of project report.
2. Selection of site.
3. Selection of forms of ownership.
4. Direct purchase of land or obtaining land/shed in the industrial estates.
5. Registration in case of company or partnership type of organisation.
6. Agreement with collaborator, if any.
7. Obtaining letter of intent or provisional registration of SSI.
8. Preparation of detailed project feasibility report.
9. Obtaining import licence, customs, clearance, etc.
10. Applying for power connection to KSEB.

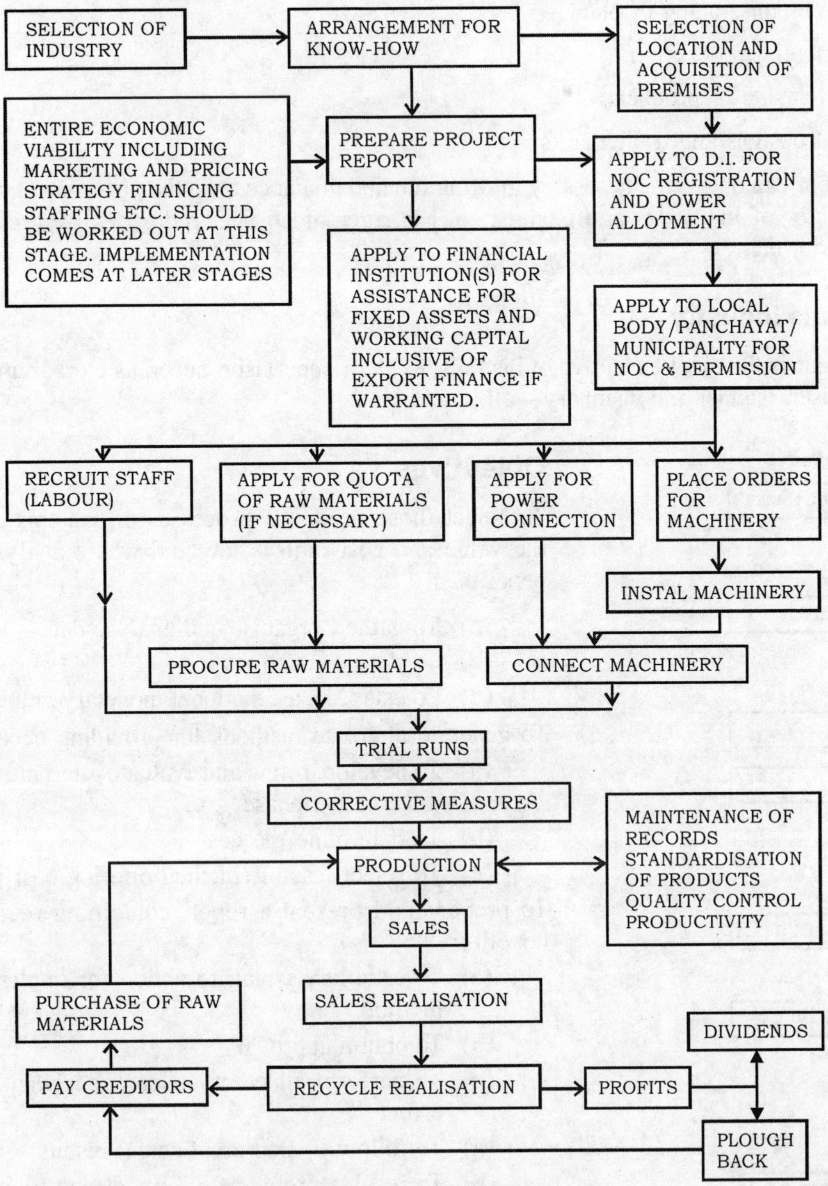

Fig. 27.1 Process of Setting-up a Small-scale Industry

11. Sanction by financial institutions.
12. Start of civil construction work after obtaining clearance from local authority or town planning officer.
13. Obtaining letter of credit for imported machinery, etc.
14. Selection of personnel, both administrative and technical.
15. Completion of civil works.
16. Delivery of imported and indigenous machinery.
17. Erection of machinery and equipments.
18. Obtaining clearance from pollution control board.
19. Obtain industrial licence or permanent SSI registration.
20. Arrangement of raw materials and unskilled labour.
21. Apply for getting grants/subsidies from the government.

22. Trial run and commissioning of plant.
23. Start of commercial production.
24. Arrangement for sale of products.
25. Registration of designs and trade marks.

A small entrepreneur can obtain the necessary information and guidance from the government departments, organisations and agencies like Director of Industries and Commerce, Manager of District Industries Centres, Kerala State Industrial Development Corporation, etc.

Starting a Small-scale Industry

A small entrepreneur is the chief executive of his unit, its floor supervisor, accounts clerk, purchase manager, salesman, legal and economic adviser, planner and visionary – all in one.

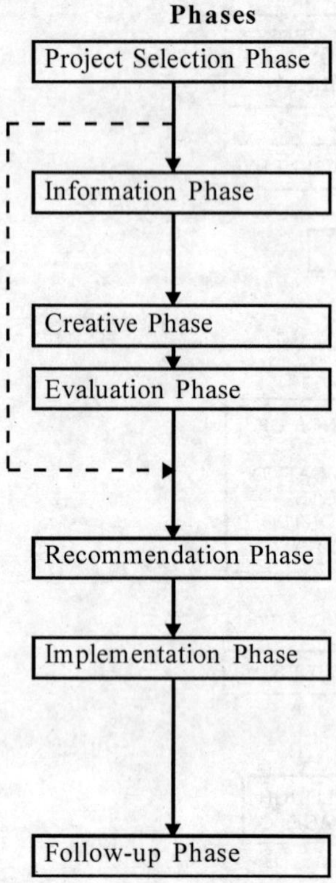

Objectives

To select those products, processes or systems in an organisation where the value and cost ratio is low and where analysis will lead to increased benefits.

(a) To gather, organise and analyse data
(b) To define functions
(c) To establish a functional monetary value

To generate alternate methods for providing necessary functions.

(a) To develop, refine and evaluate alternate methods generated during the creative phase
(b) To determine the cost
(c) To select feasible method offering best value

To prepare and present a report containing recommendation along with benefits.

(a) To establish a plan to action for implementation of the selected method
(b) To obtain approval
(c) To perform all other actions necessary to put the proposal into effect

(a) To follow-up and audit actual results
(b) To resolve problems, if any, during proposal implementation.

Fig. 27.2 Project Objectives

Every now and then, you will come across advertisements and announcements in newspapers, to set up small industries under the aegis of the State Small Industries Corporations, which promise you the world: a fully developed industrial shed with power and water, assistance in getting you raw materials, machinery on hire-purchase basis, common services facilities, training facilities and facilities in the marketing of your product. You are assured of term loans on attractive terms and working capital in time and at concessional rates. In backward areas, a number of additional subsidies are available.

An entrepreneur may be a qualified engineer. Even though he should not dream of becoming a small entrepreneur unless he is confident of meeting the following twelve essential requirements:

(i) The entrepreneur should be fully conversant with the product-line. It is not enough that he knows the method of manufacture; he has to know how to operate the machines, etc.
(ii) He should have adequate shop-floor experience to guide the machine operators in tool-setting techniques or the die-maker on the specific needs of his press tools.
(iii) He should be familiar with the raw materials he requires, their specifications, how to ensure their quality and where to get them at reasonable prices.

(iv) He should know how to keep accounts, how to maintain stores, how to prepare the balance sheet, etc.

(v) He should have knowledge of marketing channels, distribution network, agency practices, transport intricacies and the economics of packaging.

(vi) He should know how to ensure the stipulated quality of his product.

(vii) He should be well versed in taxation and other laws governing small-scale industries.

(viii) He should be willing to control polluted environments and small inconveniences.

(ix) He should be willing to put up with bureaucratic regulations and hurdles, and move with the wind.

(x) He should know how to avail himself of the various benefits available for the small-scale industry.

(xi) He should possess the following qualities – expertise, shrewdness, resourcefulness and most important, perseverance. There is no substitute for hardwork.

(xii) He should have the guts to withstand the polluted climate in which he has to build his unit.

Objectives: Any entrepreneur desirous of starting a small-scale industry should have a clear picture of the objective of his project. It is advisable to prepare a comprehensive checklist. Such a list, embracing all the important matters, has been given below for the guidance of prospective entrepreneurs. Students will get an insight into the various processes of a small-scale industry.

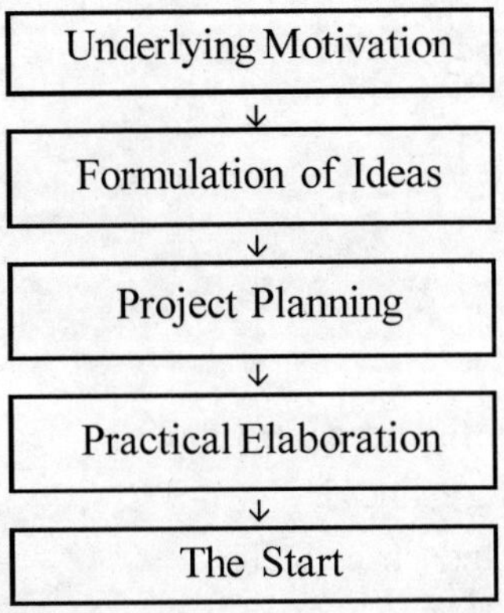

Fig. 27.3 Process of Starting a Small Enterprise Checklist

- Does your industry have scope for development? (Consult Director of Industries) — Yes/No
- Is there enough demand for the item you propose to manufacture? — Yes/No
- Do you have some experience of:
  - (a) Manufacturing — Yes/No
  - (b) Marketing? — Yes/No
- Have you studied the viability of your scheme? (Consult the Small Industries Service Institute) — Yes/No
- Is factory space available:
  - (a) In the Industrial Estate — Yes/No
  - (b) In an Industrial Area, or — Yes/No
  - (c) In some other approved place? — Yes/No
- Have you obtained the necessary licence from the municipality or the local body? — Yes/No
- Are the necessary raw materials available:
  - (a) Indigenously — Yes/No
  - (b) Are they to be imported? — Yes/No

- Are facilities available for:
  - (a) Tooling Yes/No
  - (b) Quality control? Yes/No
- Is necessary labour available:
  - (a) Of skilled workers Yes/No
  - (b) Of semi-skilled workers? Yes/No
- Have you the necessary technical background for:
  - (a) The manufacture of various parts Yes/No
  - (b) Operations? Yes/No
- Have you studied your product in respect of:
  - (a) The manufacture of the various parts Yes/No
  - (b) Production planning Yes/No
  - (c) Inspection and quality control Yes/No
  - (d) Assembly Yes/No
  - (e) Packing Yes/No
  - (f) Diversification? Yes/No
- Have you got the necessary finance:
  - (a) Are you a client of any bank? Yes/No
  - (b) Has any bank offered to lend you:
    - (i) Short-term loans? Yes/No
    - (ii) Long-term loans? Yes/No
  - (c) Have you any assets? Yes/No
  - (d) Are your assets adequate for obtaining the necessary funds? Yes/No
  - (e) Have you other sources/ways of raising money? Yes/No
  - (f) Have you approached the Director of Industries/State Financial Corporation for financial help? Yes/No
  - (g) Do you propose to approach the NSIC/SSIC for machinery on hire-purchase basis? Yes/No
  - (h) Have you adequate cash/bank arrangement to furnish the earnest money required by the NSIC? Yes/No
- What are your markets:
  - (a) Local Yes/No
  - (b) Country-wide Yes/No
  - (c) Export? Yes/No
- How would you market your product(s) through:
  - (a) Retailers Yes/No
  - (b) Wholesalers, or Yes/No
  - (c) Agents? Yes/No
- Are necessary transportation facilities available by:
  - (a) Road or Yes/No
  - (b) Rail? Yes/No
- Have you attended a course on:
  - (a) Production, Planning and Control Yes/No
  - (b) Purchasing and Marketing Yes/No

(c) Finance and Cost Control Yes/No
(d) Personnel Management Yes/No
(e) General Industrial Management? Yes/No

- Have you entered into a foreign collaboration agreement for:
  (a) Technical know-how Yes/No
  (b) Royalty/Commission on sales? Yes/No
  (c) Has your agreement been approved by the Government? Yes/No

Feasibility Report

Before starting a small-scale industry, one should consult the Director of Industries and the Small Industries Service Institute (SISI) located in one's state. The SISI guides entrepreneurs as to the type of industry to start, where to start and how to start it. The SISI helps them to select the various items of manufacture which have scope for development in different areas. It suggests the lines on which a project report for the proposed units should be prepared for the consideration of various financial institutions with a view to securing financial assistance. Similarly, technical help in the selection of proper raw materials and type of machinery is also provided. Apart from this, the SISI gives valuable information of the various incentives available to the small-scale industries from various organisations.

Project Feasibility Analysis

A project feasibility analysis includes market analysis, technical analysis, financial analysis and social profitability analysis. Although each feasibility analysis is different and is tailored to the product, its goal is to identify the strengths and weaknesses of the project.

The starting point of a project analysis is the establishment of the objectives to be attained. The next stage is the pre-selection stage – the advisability of having an in-depth study. The analysis stage consists mainly of three factors – market, technical and financial analysis. A market analysis is a method of screening project ideas as well as a means of evaluating a project's feasibility in terms of the market. A market analysis should cover the following areas:

(i) A brief description of the market including the market area, methods of transportation and existing rates of transportation. Channels of distribution and general trade practices are also included.

(ii) An analysis of past and present demands, including the determination of quantity and the value of consumption and identification of the major consumers of the product.

(iii) An analysis of past and present supply, broken down as to source (whether imported or domestic) as well as information which will assist in determining the competitive position of the product such as selling prices, quality and marketing practices of the competitors.

The technical analysis of a project feasibility study establishes whether the project is technically feasible or not, and whether it offers a basis for the estimation of costs. Moreover, it provides an opportunity for a consideration of the effect of various technical alternatives on employment, ecology, infrastructure demands, capital services, support or other industries, balance of payments and other factors. A technical analysis should contain a review of the techniques or processes to be applied and should incorporate:

(i) A description of the product, including specifications relating to its physical, mechanical and chemical properties, as well as uses of the product.

(ii) A description of the selected manufacturing process, showing detailed flow charts and presenting the alternative process which may have been considered and the justification for the adoption of the selected process.

(iii) A determination of the plant size and production schedule, which includes the expected volume for a given time-period on the basis of start-up and technical factors.

(iv) Selection of machinery and equipment, including specifications, equipment to be purchased and its origin, quotations from suppliers, delivery dates, terms of payment and a comparative analysis of alternatives in terms of cost, reliability, performance and spare parts availability.

(v) An identification of the plant's location and an assessment of its desirability in terms of its distance from raw material sources and markets. For a new project, this part may include a comparative study of different sites, indicating the advantages and disadvantages of each.

(vi) A design of the plant layout and an estimate of the cost of the erection of the proposed buildings and land improvements.

(vii) A study of the availability of raw materials and liabilities and utilities, including a description of physical and chemical properties, quantities needed, current and prospective costs, terms of payment, locations of sources of supply and continuity of supply.

(viii) An estimate of labour requirements, including a detailed breakdown of direct and indirect labour requirements, and the supervision required for the manufacture of the product.

(ix) A determination of the type and quantity of waste to be disposed of together with a description of the waste disposal method, its costs and the necessary clearance from proper authorities.

(x) An estimate of the production cost of the product.

In the financial analysis of a project feasibility study, emphasis is on the preparation of financial statements, so that the project may be evaluated in terms of the different measures of commercial profitability and the magnitude of financing required may be determined. The financial analysis requires the assembly of the market and technical costs estimated into various proforma statements. If it is necessary to have more information on which to base an investment decision, a sensitivity analysis or possibly, a risk analysis may be conducted. The financial analysis should concentrate on –

(i) Projects that involve new companies, statements of total project cost, initial capital requirements and cash flows relative to the project timetable;

For all projects, financial projections for future time periods including income statements, cash flows and balance sheet are imperative.

(ii) All projects, supporting schedules for financial projection, stating the assumption made as to the collection period of sales, inventory levels, payment period of purchases and expenses, and the element of production cost, selling, administrative and financial expenses.

(iii) All projects, prepare a financial analysis showing returns on investments, returns on equity, break-even volume and price analysis.

(iv) All projects, if necessary, a sensitivity analysis to identify items which have a substantial impact on profitability or possibly a risk analysis.

For the small entrepreneur, the studies conducted during the analysis stage of the project provide the material for an assessment. If positive results are obtained, the entrepreneur, in seeking finance will want to prepare an investment proposal. The planners or government officials, however, having obtained positive conclusion from the economic feasibility study, will want to evaluate the element of social profitability.

The purpose of the investment or loan application is to convince a lender (financial institution) that the project is a desirable investment; that it not only possesses the potential for profit but that the proposed management team has the capability to achieve the potential. The investment proposal normally contains:

(i) General information on the product, company history, the nature of the industry and the reputation and qualifications of the existing or proposed management.

(ii) A description of the period, which usually consists of extracts from economic feasibility studies and includes information on such items as market, production, selected manufacturing methods (with detailed indication of the cost of equipment and operational expenses) and a financial statement, and

(iii) Miscellaneous information, such as the steps taken for the implementation of the project and the qualifications of the technical partners envisaged or selected.

Break-even Analysis

Let us first address 'why break-even analysis? While discussing preparation of a project report of feasibility report, we stated that the level of estimated capacity utilisation, i.e., quantum of production in terms of goods or services as the case may be, needs to be spelled out in advance in the project report. Our business experience tells us that when the enterprise/business is actually started. In other words, the project is actually implemented, the projected or targeted level of capacity is not achieved due to various unforeseen reasons.

Such a situation entails financial implications. Then, the entrepreneur needs to decide to what extent the curtailment in production can be afforded to meet all its liabilities. Steinhoff and Burgess put it as "How much must I sell before I start making profit." The answer to this question is called the 'break-even analysis' where income exactly equals expenses. Let us now understand "What is break-even analysis? In simple words, it is an analysis of production point at which profit starts. This point is where income and expenses are exactly equal and the point is called 'break-even point,. Thus, break-even analysis is used to find the break-even point.

Having understood the concept of break-even analysis, we now intend to expose you to the mechanics involved in finding out break-even point. In carrying out any enterprise, profit comes from sale of goods or services as the case may be and expenses emerge out from the cost involved. Expenses to be incurred refer to cost. Cost is broadly divided into two types, *viz.,* (1) Fixed cost, and (2) Variable cost. What are these costs?

Fixed Cost: Fixed costs are defined as those that do not change with increase or decrease in production. No matter what the production is, the fixed cost remains the same. Examples of fixed costs could be the monthly rent paid for the factory, interest on long-term loan, administrative expenses, etc. Even if there is zero production, the fixed cost will remain unchanged. Say, if factory rent, i.e., ₹ 10,000 per month is the only cost, it will remain fixed at ₹ 10,000 if there is a production of 500 units or 200 units or even no production at all.

Variable Cost: In short, what is not fixed cost is variable cost. Variable cost is defined as expenses that change with the volume of production. It varies proportionately with changes in production. Thus, if production is zero, variable cost would be zero. The absolute total variable cost increases or decreases along with increases or decrease in production. But the variable cost per unit is constant at any level of production. The following example clears it.

There are some variable costs that do not vary proportionately with the change in production. In fact, these vary in varying degrees. As a result, such costs are called semi-variable. The popular examples of such costs could be telephone, electricity and gas charges if they are billed on a usage basis. In such cases that proportion of expenses which continue even if production falls are considered as fixed and expenses which increase or decrease as production increases or decreases are considered as variable cost.

After knowing sales and total cost in terms of fixed cost and variable cost, now the break-even point can be calculated.

According to the simplest method, Profit is the excess of sales over cost, i.e.:

Sales – Cost = Profit.

The calculation of break-even point involves four steps. These are:

1. Segregation of fixed and variable costs
2. Percentage of variable costs to sales
3. Calculate the contribution or margin, i.e., the difference between 100 and the percentage of variable cost to sales as worked out above.
4. Divide the fixed cost by the percentage of contribution or margin as worked out above.

Thus, the calculated figure will be 'break-even point'.

It will be better, at least for those of you who are coming across to the concept of break-even point for the first time, to calculate break-even point with the help of an example.

Once the industry is identified, the SISI prepares a feasibility report and project report, thus giving a comprehensive idea of an industry's prospects and profitability.

Licences: An impression seems to have gained round among some people that there are some restrictions on the setting up of small-scale industrial units and that licences from either the Central or State government have to be taken out before an entrepreneur can take steps to start a small-scale industrial unit. This impression is not correct. It is open to any entrepreneur to setup an industrial unit in the small-scale sector; no formal permission from the state or Central Government is necessary for this purpose. Also, industries employing less than 100 workers and having fixed assets of less than ₹ 10 lakh need not obtain any licence under the Industries (Development and Regulation) Act.

Small-scale units have, however, to conform to the rules and regulations prescribed by the state or local authority under the Factories Act, the Commercial Establishment Act, the Town Planning Rules made for the issue of quotas of raw materials, etc.

However, powerlooms do not come under the purview of the small-scale industries programme. For installing powerlooms, the prior permission of the Textile Commissioner, Government of India, Mumbai, is required.

(1) Registration of Small-scale Industries

In their own interest, all existing small-scale units or intending entrepreneurs employing more than 10 workers should get themselves registered with the Director of Industries in their state. A copy of this application for registration should be sent to the Director of Small Industries Service Institute in the concerned state. Such registration with the Director of Industries and the Small Industries Services Institute will be of considerable help to the small-scale unit in obtaining financial assistance from the government and for obtaining machinery on hire-purchase basis from the National Small Industries Corporation. Assistance in the supply of controlled raw materials, essentiality certificate for imported raw materials and components and facilities for export promotion, would then be easily made available to small-scale units registered with the State Director of Industries. The registration number is now required to be quoted while submitting import applications. Registration procedures have been substantially simplified. Revised forms of SSI have been introduced from 1.1.1994.

(2) Infrastructure

This pertains to approaching the Director of Industries and/or the SISI in the state to provide you with built-up factory space in an industrial estate or develop the factory site, power, etc. After the initial clearance from the State Director of Industries, the Municipality or the Panchayat issues a 'No Objection Certificate'. The procedure for obtaining the basic infrastructure facilities is given below.

The mechanics of establishing a new factory in Greater Bombay are:

(i) Apply to the Industries Commissioner, Industries and Labour Department, Government of Maharashtra, and obtain a 'No Objection Certificate'.

(ii) With a copy of the above NOC, apply, in Factory Form "A" to the Ward Engineer of BMC.

(iii) Clarification and submission of further details on the information supplied in Form 'A' may, follow.

(iv) The Sub-engineer will inspect the premises and submit Form No. '2' to his Assistant Engineer.

(v) The Assistant Engineer will scrutinise and confirm if the applicant's activity conforms to the zone and will intimate to the applicant in Form No. '3' if there is no objection or in Form No. '4' if there is any objection.

(vi) From 'B' will be received by the applicant if Form No. '3' is issued to him. This form should be filled in and submitted.

(vii) Within 21 days after the submission of Forms 'A', 'B' and the factory plans in triplicate, the Assistant Engineer will issue Form Nos. '5' and '6' in which he will specify:

  (a) The electric power sanctioned (thereafter the BEST provides electricity);

  (b) Adequate water facilities provided;

  (c) The various requirements, requisitions and conditions for operating the factory, including those required by the Chief Inspector of Factories.

Form 'C' will also be issued along with these forms. (Upon complying with the stipulation in Form 'B', the BMC should be informed thereof in writing).

Thereafter, permission to commence production will be given.

(3) Machinery

The small entrepreneur needs the requisite type of machines for production. He can get the necessary machinery from the National Small Industries Corporation (NSIC) under a hire-purchase scheme.

The scheme for the supply of indigenous and imported machines on hire-purchase basis was launched in March 1956 to enable small entrepreneurs without substantial means to avail themselves of assistance. The scheme is different from the credit operations scheme for entrepreneurs. The NSIC has acquired the necessary experience and expertise in the procurement of machines from the right sources. It also takes care of the problems up to the stage of delivery of machineries to the entrepreneurs. Also, while financial institutions look mainly to the creditworthiness of entrepreneurs, the NSIC would look primarily to the motivation of the individual applicant, his capacity, his technical competence and his managerial ability to run the enterprise.

The small entrepreneur should enlist himself as a member with the NSIC. His application form should be accompanied with the Registration Certificate and report of the Director of Industries. The application for obtaining machines under the hire-purchase scheme of the NSIC is quite comprehensive. The small entrepreneur has to provide full details along with the relevant documents.

The application form for hire-purchase machinery calls for information regarding the organisational set-up of a unit, its programme of production and marketability and profitability of the enterprise. It also calls for additional information regarding the cost of production, the infrastructure facilities available for the unit, the technical capability of the entrepreneur, etc. The details in the application are self-explanatory.

(4) Raw Materials

The raw materials required by small-scale units may broadly be classified asunder:

(i) Raw material components and spares, both indigenous and imported;

(ii) Non-ferrous materials – both indigenous and imported;

(iii) Iron and steel – both indigenous and imported; and

(iv) Chemical – indigenous and imported.

Under the liberalised scheme, the actual users are provided with adequate foreign exchange to meet their justifiable requirements of imported items of industrial materials. The 'priority' industries are assured of an adequate supply to the extent of their requirements by way of grant of rotational licences.

Small-scale units should apply directly to the Regional Licensing Authority, and not through the sponsoring authority, for import licences for raw materials, components and spares after utilising the previous set of licences to the extent of 90 per cent by way of opening their own credit or 60 per cent by way of actual import, covering six months' requirements of the unit. New units should submit their applications through their respective sponsoring authority.

The State Director of Industries allocates indigenous non-ferrous metals. Some of the non-ferrous items are canalised through the State Trading Corporation of India (STC). The raw materials imported by the STC are given to the SSI units in accordance with the recommendations of the Director of Industries concerned.

Iron and steel raw materials are canalised through the MMTC in accordance with the recommendations of the Director of Industries.

In times of difficulties, the decontrolled chemical raw materials are canalised through the DGTD in accordance with the recommendation of State Director of Industries. Indigenous controlled chemicals are allocated through the State DIS/SICs. Imported raw materials are canalised through the STC.

In short, controlled and imported raw materials are to be obtained through the State DIS, SICs (SSI).

(5) Finance

The financial function in a small-scale industry is similar to the financial function in any other organisation, but with this essential difference – that there are a host of banking and insurance regulations to be strictly adhered to and quite a few precautions to be taken.

The areas where finance would be needed, after the small-scale industrialist fixes the land accommodation are:

(i) Purchase and installation of machinery;

(ii) Procurement of raw materials and components and the manufacture of products;

(iii) Working funds; and

(iv) Availability of funds until the realisation of sales.

The State Director of Industries provides loans for block capital under the Industries Act. One should apply through the sponsoring authority. State Financial Corporations provide long-term credit for the purchase of fixed assets. The application should be submitted to the SFCs along with the following documents: (i) Project Report; (ii) Copy of Registration; (iii) Cash flow Statement, and (iv) Stock Statement.

In some states, the SFCs and the banks have agreed to process the common application for loans. For an amount of ₹ 2 lakh, the commercial bank provides medium-term instalment credit. It also provides loans for meeting needs for working capital for the purchase of raw materials as also for day-to-day requirements.

In order to get a loan from a commercial bank, the entrepreneur has to fill in an application form as per the specimen (Annexure VIII) and submit it to the bank along with the following documents:

(i) Authentic copies of Balance Sheets and Profit and Loss Accounts (if the industrial concern is a limited company or an industrial cooperative society).
(ii) A statement of assets and liabilities in the prescribed form (Appendix I of Annexure VIII) in the case of partnership and proprietary concerns.
(iii) Proforma statements in all other cases.
(iv) Copies of the affidavit in regard to the size of the unit.
(v) Technical Feasibility Report from the Small Industries Service Institute, the Director of Industries, if obtained, may also be enclosed.

(6) Marketing

The rationale of the Government Purchase Scheme of the Corporation lies in the fact that the Government of India is the largest single buyer; and by channelising these purchases in favour of small-scale units, it gives a tremendous boost to the marketing of their products.

Box 27.2 Finance – To take or not to take

FOCAL POINT

- Individuals wish to start off businesses but cannot due to lack of funds.
- Banks provide finance to entrepreneurs under many schemes.
- If your papers are in order, it is safe and fast to avail credit from a bank.
- Till you pay off the loan, banks are owners of your property.
- You have to be psychologically strong to be an entrepreneur.

Indians are known to be entrepreneurs. But to be one needs funds. A guide to bank funding for 'wanna-be' entrepreneurs....

Munira Mohta is an Architect-cum-interior designer who works for a famous Architect firm. She has had a good stint of three years at the same job and is itching to strike out on her own. But the big question that looms large in her head is how to fund for the office space and expenses till plum projects fall on her lap.

Sudenshu Gupta wants to start an auto ancillary unit. He has done his homework on the manufacturing side of the business as well as built report with a number of Auto Manufacturers who have assured him of regular orders... He knows his idea is sure fire if only....

If wishes were horses, all of the above would have been riding them as CEOs. But the biggest thorn on their future bed of roses is MONEY... or rather a lack of it.

In an ideal world, all of them would have Sugar Daddies to fund their dreams, if they decide to wait and save up till they shore up all the capital they require the business opportunity may no longer be a viable option. The only other option is of course a rich father in law or the Bank. Banks have lots of schemes for schemes for such entrepreneurs.

Term Loans: Normally, these loans are given to fund property and immovable assets like plant and machinery. The repayment is 3 to 5 years and the interest is in the range of 11% to 14%.

Working Capital Loans/Cash Credit: Simplistically this loan would finance the day-to-day running of your business. The interest charged is on the actual amount used and falls within the band of 10.5% to 12%.

Bill Discounting Facility: Say, you sell goods to X & Co. You raise a bill but give them credit for three months. If you want the money right away, the bank shall deduct some charges, pay you the bill amount and levy interest. After three months, the bank collects directly from X & Co.

Apart from the above, there are many schemes floated by the banks like small-scale liberalised schemes, Entrepreneur's Scheme, Schemes for Women Entrepreneurs, etc.

A composite, tailor-made package can also be devised for suitable customers. What are the pros and cons for availing this kind of a loan?

Pros:

- If you have a dream, this is most certainly the safest way to finance it.

  Alternatively, you can find people who also believe in you and finance you in terms of equity or extend a loan to you. In that case you make partners in your business or pay them interest just like a bank. The only hitch is that individuals can decide to pull out of your business at will, which just might leave you in the lurch.
- Banks will clear repayment and interest schedules making cash flow planning easy.
- Banks have technical teams that sometimes help you in assessing the viability of your projects.

Cons:

- There will be tons of administrative work, scores of forms to be filled.
- Normally, banks require the entrepreneur to bring in his own money into the business. This is called margin money.
- Banks will have a first charge on your assets. This means that till you pay the bank off completely, they are the owners of the property they have given a loan for.
- Banks ask for personal guarantee and/or guarantors. This means that if your business fails, your personal assets like house, etc., can be attached and/or your guarantors will be made to repay your loan.

If you can sleep peacefully at night after taking on a debt and you are sure your business will generate at least that much money to take care of the interest and loan repayment, you have the stomach of an entrepreneur. Go for it.

The salient features of the scheme are:

(a) The small-scale units, desiring to avail themselves of assistance, have to enlist themselves with the NSIC;

(b) Instead of purchasing tender sets from the DGS&D, the small units enlisted with the NSIC automatically gets them from it and its branches free of cost;

(c) If their prices are acceptable to the DGS&D, they are not required to pay a security deposit on the issue of a competency certificate by the NSIC;

(d) Price preference up to 15 per cent over the quotations of large-scale units is considered by the purchasing agency, depending on the merits of each case;

(e) Wherever they feel that injustice has been done to them, the NSIC takes up their cases with the DGS&D and other government departments such as Defence, the Railways and the P&T Department in order to find out the reasons for non-placement of the contract with the units, and tries to redress their grievances.

In the beginning, purchases in respect of only 16 items were reserved exclusively for the small-scale sector; the number of such items has steadily increased, and at present it is estimated to be at 379.

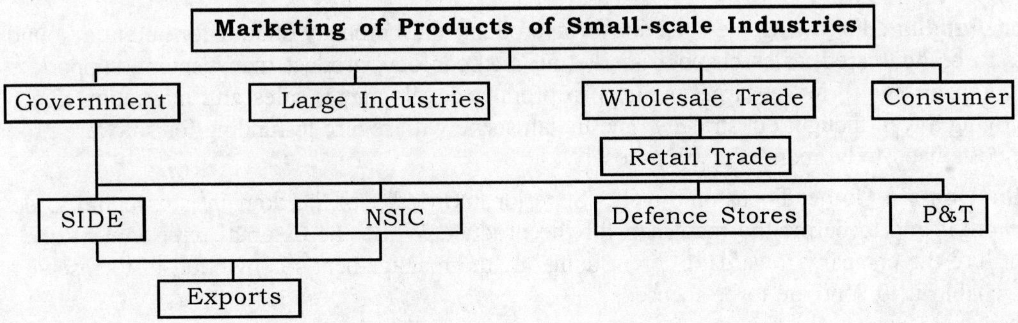

Fig. 27.4 Marketing of Products of SSIs

The Corporation also helps small-scale industries in securing contracts from other government departments such as Railways, Posts and Telegraphs, etc.

Hitherto, the purchase programme has been restricted purely to Central purchase houses like DGS&D, the P&T and the Railways. It is proposed to extend the base further to cover state government departments such as the State Electricity Boards, PWDs, etc., and provide liaison offices at each of the principal purchase centres of the state.

(7) Incentives

For availing the various incentives, it is advisable to seek the help of the SISI and/or the Director of Industries.

The Small Industries Development Organisation (SIDO), Ministry of Industry, Nirman Bhavan, New Delhi, coordinates policies and programmes at the national level and provides a comprehensive range of extension services through its network of sixteen Small Industries Services Institutes, nineteen Branch Institutes and forty-five Extension Centres.

At the state level, organisations like State Director of Industries, Small Industries Development Corporations and Finance Corporations cater to the needs of small industries; these needs include land, sheds, credit, power, raw materials, etc.

The National Small Industries Corporation (NSIC), Okhla, New Delhi, provides machines and equipment on hire-purchase basis to entrepreneurs, assists units to participate in stores purchase programmes and provides training and prototype development facilities.

Registration with the NSIC entitles the units to obtain facilities from Central or State government organisations. New units have to apply to the respective State Directors of Industries for provisional registration, which is given within a week. It enables the party to take the necessary steps to bring the unit into existence, i.e., apply for sheds in industrial estates or on developed sites for water and power connections and for credit facilities. After the party has taken all the steps, it can apply for registration.

SIDO provides technical consultancy on improved technical processes, use of modern machines and equipment and technical assistance on all aspects of production. Each SISI has attached workshops for common facility services, training of workers, demonstration of modern machines and processes, making of tools and dies, etc.

Lessons for Software Bravehearts

Building a software product company is an activity from the ground-up. There is hardly any guidance from an external entity like in the case of software services companies where the customer specifies the requirement, the technology, the platform and the tools. This unique situation makes building a software product company, a wonderful experience on one hand and one that constantly tests your sanity, on the other. This article does not purport to be a 'Guide to Sure Success in Software Products Business', since there are many ways to succeed in this business. So, this is only a collection of my experience at Subex.

Identifying the "Product": Products can be grouped into "absolutely-essential", "need-to-have", "nice-to-have" and "frill". One of the reasons for the bankruptcies of product companies during the tech downturn was that they were in the last two categories. How does one identify a potential product idea? Look around and choose a few areas in the domain that you are familiar with, apply filters to quality each one of these and arrive at a shortlist. Then meet potential users and apply a generous dose of "gut feel" to choose the product.

Strategy and Funding: Following the selection of a product, the company should formulate a sound strategy with regards to markets to be addressed, sales channel, marketing methodology, product management, support, etc. Although a software product company has to invest large amounts in product development, sales and marketing, the outflow can be controlled by employing a well thought out strategy. The Indian scene with regard to funding for software product companies is quite bleak. So, costs need to be monitored very closely.

Focus and the Domain Game: Focus on a niche. Superior knowledge of the domain is essential to develop products that will be future proof and to define the road map for the product. While the external environment and a multitude of opportunities might lure the company towards different domains, the management's conviction in themselves, their strategy and products must enable it to continue to be focused.

Personnel: Software product companies need people with certain unique skill-sets not common in India and also with mindsets that are different from those in services companies. Product management is a key function and personnel with that experience are scarce in India. In such a scenario, Indian companies must tap overseas markets or returning Indians for this critical function.

Referenceability: Gone is the adage 'Customer is King'. It now reads, 'Customer is Emperor'. Customers invest considerable amount of time and money in procuring products. The due diligence process is extensive and exhaustive. Unlike services business where customers can change vendors with minimal cost impact, after a trial, software products are tricky even for customers. Companies need to ensure that every customer is a good reference as they can be used as excellent ambassadors with potential customers.

Advantage India: Setting up software product companies in India is an attractive proposition given advantages like low cost of handling marketing, implementation and customer support, availability of high quality technical skill and a large domestic market for most products. A recent example of a Silicon Valley company that managed to get through two years of operations with only about $5 million (by depending on India) instead of about $15 to 20 million that they would've otherwise invested shows that it's time we take advantage of this unique situation too.

Building a software product company is actually an exhilarating experience. Herein lies the opportunity to be truly creative, innovative and be a true generator of value and wealth. India is today at the crossroads of an IT revolution. It is up to us to cock a snook at those who have labelled us as "techno coolies". However, we need to tread cautiously to avoid the pitfalls that have resulted in a high rate of mortality – seven out of ten software product companies fail. It is within us, to succeed in a grand scale provided we pay considerable attention to the cardinal principles of a software products business – a "need to have" product, well-honed strategy, razor-sharp focus, motivated and qualified personnel, eminently referenceable customers, tight cost control, commitment and above all, conviction that India can be the thought leader of tomorrow.

Box 27.3 Mind Your Business

The entrepreneurial road is paved with risks of every kind. How to anticipate them and risk-proof your small business.

Given the ease with which burglars broke into leather goods exporter Udai Piplani's gift accessories showroom in South Delhi in August 2003 and carted away merchandise worth ₹ 1.3 lakh, they may have felt they were plundering an unguarded fortress. But they would have been wrong.

It's of course true that there were serious breaches in the defence, and Piplani's business did suffer a material loss that could have dented it seriously. But the businessman wasn't entirely without a last line of defence. A silent, unseen army held the fort, and ensured that the Piplani empire's flag remained flying from its ramparts. It came in the form of a low-cost insurance policy that helped him bear the financial shock of the loss, and ensured that his business was not laid low by a common-enough risk.

"A small business is like a one-day cricket innings", says Piplani, with a touch of Sidhuism. "You can't avoid risk altogether – not if you want to score big – but there are ways of containing it." It was with this risk-containment objective that he secured a shopkeeper's cover for stocks and goods in his showroom, which would compensate him in the event of fire or theft. "For a small price – ₹ 4,500 as premium for ₹ 4.5 lakh of stocks plus about ₹ 10 lakh cover for the premises and ₹ 2 lakh worth of fittings – I insulated my business against a big risk and bought myself complete peace of mind," says he.

It was this policy that ensured he got ₹ 1 lakh as compensation for the material loss he suffered.

"Very few small businesses adequately understand the importance of risk management", says L. Ravindran, a Hyderabad-based risk management consultant. "And even those that do, fail to realise that with increasing scale of operations, the risks only get compounded."

And although there are a range of insurance covers that address specific kinds of risk, there are other business hazards for which the defences like outside the realm of financial products.

Insurable Risks

The risks that any business is susceptible to will vary with the nature of the business. Principally, the "insurable risks" – that is, risks for which there are defences in the form of insurance covers – relate to theft of or damage to assets, the risk of business interruption or breakdown, the loss of money or goods in transit, employee fraud, and legal liability towards employees or a third party. "It's important to identify the specific risks your business may face, and then buy appropriate cover – for the right amount.

Insurable Risks

- Cover your assets
- Never take a break
- Schedule the business process
- Know your liability
- Ensure high fidelity
- Insure goods in transit
- Non-insurable risks
- Have a plan 'B'
- Manage your cash flows

- Stick to a budget
- Do not borrow blind
- Master the art of business.

Cost of Managing Risk

In addition to the standard fire and allied perils policy for the premises and contents, there are a few must-have covers to contain your business risk. Here's what a trader in gift items, with a showroom for display and stocks worth ₹ 12 lakh, will pay as premium under various heads.

Section	Cover (₹)	Premium (₹)
Stocks cover		
For fire	12 lakh	2,700
For burglary	12 lakh	600
Breakdown cover		
Of electrical and mech.appliances	10,000	25
Of electronic appliances	1 lakh	1,030
Money cover		
In transit	50,000	250
In safe	50,000	100
In till	10,000	25
Employee fraud cover	25,000	150
Legal liability cover		
Towards third-party	10,000	10
Towards employees[1] lakh	980	
Total premium (inc.8% service tax)		6,340

[1]For four employees, based on nature of work.

Source: *Outlook Money,* 31 May, 2004.

The Winning Edge

The opening up of the Indian small industry sector to competition as well as the increase in the need to cater to the global market demands fresh perceptions to respond to the radical changes in the 90s. Consequently, the Indian small industry sector must change first to survive as well as restructure itself to meet the new challenges through a critical evaluation of the forces of free global trade and increased competition. These events demand quantum strategic changes in terms of industry culture, flattening of the organisational structure, employee empowerment as well as team-building. Only those organisations which can respond to these changes will be able to survive and retain a winning edge.

Some of the important characteristics that differentiate the successful organisations from the unsuccessful ones are:

1. The most important aspect of successful business is leadership. It calls for clear vision, goals and objectives, welldefined mission, dash and employees' participation.
2. Adequate but well-orchestrated control. Constant feedback of results as well as setting and adherence of high standards gives an organisation a cutting edge over others. Planning, foresight and analysis are also important qualities.
3. To able to extract the best from its employees through total involvement, the organisation put a lot of emphasis on proper internal communication and on training employees.
4. The successful organisation is one which is very close to the marketplace. The process of systematic market research is used to develop products or processes and to provide value for money to the customers. This helps to gain the market share.

5. The next most important characteristic of a winning business organisation is 'Zero Basing' or sticking to the last – knowing what business the company is in and swiftly recognising when it has diverted into an unsuitable path.
6. Another important characteristic for success is commitment to innovation which is vital in keeping ahead of the competition and perhaps the most difficult one to achieve. Yet, most of the organisations just pay lip service to creativity and innovation. They ask for new ideas and then quickly reject them and even when a new idea is accepted, the employee rarely gets a reward proportionate to the idea's worth.

Successful business organisation create a climate that encourages new ideas as a part of the employee's job. Anything that helps create the innovative culture and a natural curiosity, about how things are done in other companies will add value to the organisation.

The Strategy

It is therefore imperative that the vision of a company be shared across all levels. Effective communication of the vision statement across the organisation is the first step towards designing a focused work environment and a goal-oriented people force.

Translating goals into action calls for synergising individual effort and belief to create a single force. It requires an able team and equally able leaders who invoke a sense of camaraderie and team spirit and vision, both in terms of words and meaning. Simply preaching the vision will not alone achieve it, and this is where people management and the art of motivation becomes paramount. Taking the values of the company and what it seeks to become in the future, beyond the walls of the boardroom is important, but what is vital is for the team-members to feel that they are an integral part of this vision. This means involving them in setting goals which is the key to gaining their commitment to achieve and to excel.

One thing is certain that customer service excellence is the true differentiator and the secret of long-term success. Customer service is a passion that transcends all boundaries and is the glue of organisational goals and success.

Customers and their growing demands are at the forefront of our business models, supported by people sharing a common vision. With this combination, performance and success can't be far ahead. The test of true leadership is in executing the perceived future of success. This future will be won by capable people.

Given the ever-changing business situation today, it is indeed a herculean task for entrepreneurs to keep realigning services, products, methods and practices to match needs. They can, however, do it best by empowering their team-members to take calculated decisions as and when the need arises, and providing them with space for innovation at every touch point. This, apart from motivating employees to continuously strive for the better, makes them feel a part of each success story that the company can boast of.

A company that creates a customer-oriented culture where it sees every problem as an opportunity to serve the customer better, is the one that will survive the toughest competition today.

To be self-employed, one has to be a vision. To entrepreneurs who has it as one of the fundamental characteristics, vision is a vivid, dramatic and complete picture of what the company wants to be, and do. Crucially, this future is not one that can be reached in normal course; it needs a quantum leap.

Vision has been defined as the power of perceiving by imagination or by clear thinking. In the organisational context, vision is a picture of the future of the organisation. Vision is the hallmark of a forward looking organisation. It provides the motivation needed to get the best out of an organisation – enterprise and people. Vision inspires one to strive for better.

The founder of an organisation needs to paint a picture of the organisation as he sees it in the future. This encompasses primarily its scope as an organisation in terms of areas of business or products; the geographic boundaries and the value system by which it desires to attain the same, and a clarity of the relationships that it will develop with various members associated with the organisation.

It is important for an enterprise to have clarity of vision primarily because the organisation can stay focused, and not wander off into any unrelated areas that arise as a result of opportunities or apparent synergies. For instance, a company may feel that it can get into situations of vertical integration to optimise cost/returns, profitability, etc. While it may be profitable in the short run or may appear to be a strategically good move, it may not be optimal in the long-term if it is not in keeping with the corporate vision.

Box 27.4 The Enterprise Manual

Enterprise will never be the same again. The mega dotcom boom saw the initiation of big-ticket venture funding in the country, with an enormous infusion of capital into start-ups covering a whole gamut of industries – ranging from the ubiquitous IT to biotechnology and customer services.

Now the party is over, but that does not mean the demise of enterprise. What it does mean is that both funders and entrepreneurs now play a much more cautious game. As Sanjay Anadaram, managing director, Jumpstartup, says: "VCs will fund entrepreneurs who have failed before if the reasons for failure have nothing to do with issues like ethics and team-building skills".

After the dust has settled, what has emerged is a storehouse of start-up lessons that serve as signposts on the road to successful enterprise. The money is there, and so is the opportunity: but before taking the plunge, it helps to get a grip on the rules.

The DO's

- **Stay Low Profile.** Building a start-up from the idea stage to the cash-positive company is best done away from the mesmeric are lights. IT reseller Veritas Software grew from a single-vendor reseller into a ₹ 12 crore outfit in seven years, without ever using mass media. Says Asha Pandey, cofounder: "You would never have heard of us, we never made a noise".
- **Read the fine print.** Make sure you know the finer points of all the contracts signed with investors or customers; this can save.
- **From nasty surprises later.** Particularly if as founder, you are faced with the prospect of an abrupt exit from the start-up, as happened to Prakash Gurbaxani of 24/7 customer.com.
- **Network.** It's vital to keep your contacts intact, both within and outside the entrepreneurial ecosystem. Lovaii Navlakhi sent out a farewell mail to 300 names on his address list on his last day at indya.com; the replies helped convince him of the market for his new venture, Money Matters.
- **Take care of the pennies.** Cash is always at a premium for start-ups; don't be a guzzler. Money Matters is run from a home office; it helps the six-month-old outfit concentrate on building new business instead of meeting needless overhead expenses.
- **Make VCs your last resort.** Asha Pandey's Veritas Software used debt funding from commercial banks for a decade, as there was no significant knowledge equity that a VC could bring into the reselling space they were in. VC money is valuable only when it brings both intellectual and cash equity.

The DON'Ts

- **Follow the herd.** It was e-commerce yesterday and its call centres and business process outsourcing today. Following the herd without thinking your gameplan through can result in your being trampled underfoot by the competition. Gautam Agrawal launched formsindia.com at the height of the boom only to cash out in a distress sale seven months later.
- **Calculate just profits.** Instead of evaluating your business idea merely on potential profits, calculate the losses too to arrive at the real value of your investment. Nisheeth Srivastava signed a sweat-and-cash deal to get on board support, but has returned to the security of the corporate world after a tumultuous two years without cashing out his equity holding.
- **Ignore change.** Although Asha Pandey was running a tight ship at Veritas, as the internet transformed the business landscape, she realised her personal growth had been stunted. She cashed out to launch e-learning start-up onward Education.
- **Focus just on the long-term.** It is the short-term goals that build a company – paying customers, building the management team, making cash profits. These need to be in place first before the long-term goal of market expansion. Prakash Gurbaxani had to quit 24/ 7 customer.com ultimately because his long-term goals did not match those of his partners on the board.

Similarly, a firm's long-term interests in terms of developing a well-integrated organisation may not be served if it considers unrelated diversification just because an opportunity comes its way, or because the officials have specific contact with certain officials in the government.

The second important reason why clarity of vision is needed is because it develops a culture of learning within the organisation, in order to fulfil the clarified and stated vision. For instance, if an organisation's vision is to expand and become a global player in the market of the developing world, then the entire organisation could develop an interest in the specific industry sector and the geographic area and would, over a period of time, gain the knowledge to fulfil that vision.

Clarity of vision also enables the entire organisation to develop an inspirational force towards attaining a common goal, thus enhancing the team-building process in an organisation since the entire organisation as the team will perform even a simple task.

An organisation (entrepreneur) must develop its vision statement based on where it is today via a thorough analysis of *swot.*

Building a Vision: Stage I

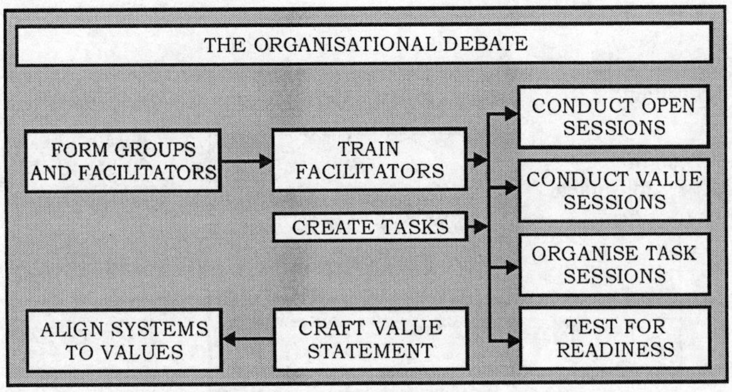

Increased Innovation

Innovation will provide the basis for the sustainability of an organisation. Richard Foster in his book *Innovation* has sketched the curve of performance versus effort for technological progress. The result is an S-shaped curve that moves from infancy to explosion and then a gradual maturation. The key to sustainability is the ability to glide through successive such S.curves, in other words, the ability to continually innovate. 3M, on account of its constant innovation (it has something like 60,000 products in its stable) has been able to glide smoothly through many successive S-curves and thus has built an incredible amount of staying power in the market.

Implicit in continuous innovation is the importance of cannibalisation. Intel is one of the few organisations that has perfected the art of cannibalisation. As the market of a processor begins to mature, Intel launches a superior processor, and tries to make the market graduate to its new offering. This not only pre-empts imitators, but also keeps margins high for Intel. In fact, with its continual innovation and cannibalisation, Intel has been able to create an artificial monopoly for itself.

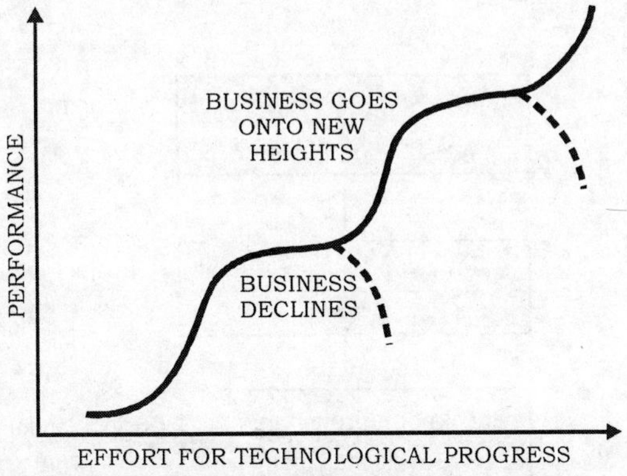

Fig. 27.5 The Successive S-curve

New Business Concept Generation and Gestation Process

Though there are no set rules, Rosebeth Moss Kanter, a Professor at Harvard University has suggested six characteristics of innovation:

- Uncertain
- Knowledge intensive
- Controversial
- Crosses boundaries
- Changes work relationships and hierarchical arrangements
- Conditions for organisation and innovation are different from those of adoption and diffusion.

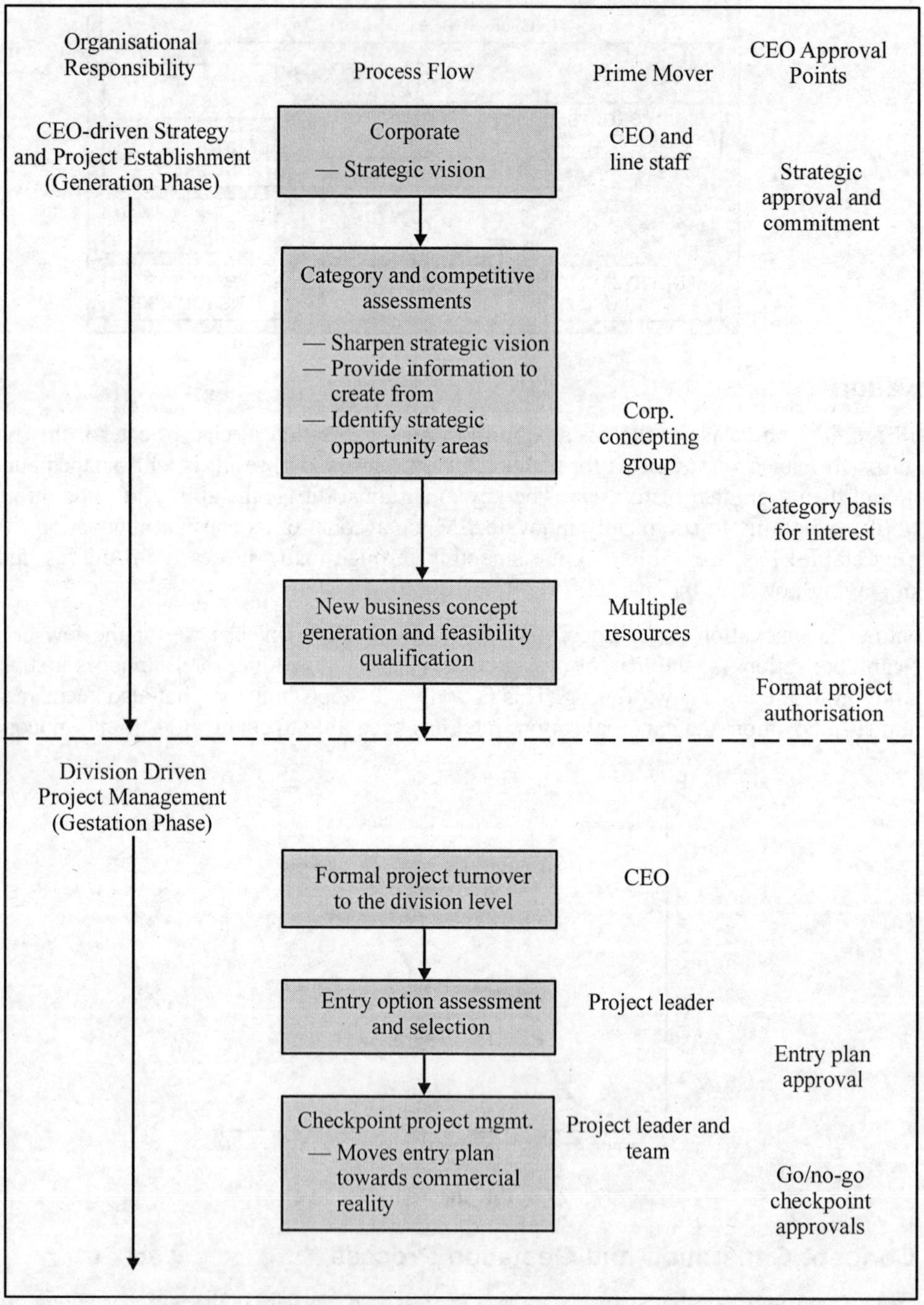

THE STEP THEORY

Attraction of new customers

Innovation of products and services

Innovation of value-delivery system

Acquisition and/or consolidation

Expansion into new geographies

Step outs into new competitive arenas

Current Business

Thus, "if innovation is uncertain, fragile, political and imperialistic (reaching out to other territories)," she adds, "then it is most likely to flourish where conditions allow flexibility, feedback, quick action and intensive care, coalition formation, and connectedness". Here Kanter also hints at the organisational environment that surrounds the entire process.

The innovation process involves at least five generic stages:

- Idea generation and concept definition
- Model development
- Limited/test production
- Full production and growth
- Diffusion and adoption

Innovation cannot be divorced from change. A technological innovation may bring a change in the materials, manufacturing process, shop-floor management, product packing and marketing strategies too. This change may be opposed by the people affected by it and this could initiate a debate or opposition which is seldom objective. Often restructuring in an organisation follows a major innovation or breakthrough. It is important to ensure that a minor innovation that could possibly take place at such a time is not ignored.

Peaks of Success

Fuelling ambitions and dreams. Breathing life into promising business ventures. Charting the course of incisive business ideas. Providing foresight with a fine sense of direction. Helping insightful, imaginative business ideas glide smoothly over rough passages. Helping vision and enterprise sight the target and achieve it with pinpoint accuracy. Complementing acumen and enterprise with a steady flow of resources. Partnering enterprises on the move, till they reach the peaks of success.

Steps of the Ladder

For starting an enterprise, an entrepreneur will have to climb the steps narrated on the next page, one by one; and for doing so, he would do well to give careful thought to the following considerations. This thought in advance may help him to avoid some mistakes. So, many things must be considered that unless some kind of a checklist is followed seriously, there is the danger of important matters being overlooked. And, once the entrepreneur has started the business, his getting busy with the urgency of the day-to-day details reduces the opportunity of thoughtful consideration to important questions.

Obviously, this list does not cover everything. It should be used as a starter. The list is designed with the object of focusing the entrepreneur's thought, on the different steps of the ladder he would have to climb. Carefully consider each one as it applies to your particular problem. Before deciding to ignore any question, completely satisfy yourself that it does not apply to your particular operation.

SUCCESS FACTORS FOR TODAY

- Total quality in manufacture, design and delivery
- Lean organisation
- Focus on core competence (market segments)
- Productivity (new product development)
- Global player
- Total customer satisfaction

SUCCESS FACTORS FOR TOMORROW

- More of all the above
- Risk management
- Survival skills
- New organisation
- Learning organisation
- Creativity

Although the ladder of success an entrepreneur has to climb in setting up an enterprise and run it consists of 34 steps, the ladder may undergo a change with the change in the environment and entrepreneurial climate. For an entrepreneur, work is worship. Leisure is a luxury. There is nothing like hardwork. A 14 to 18 hour work is the norm. He should have a killer instinct to push ahead in the competitive environment.

Steps of the Ladder the Entrepreneur has to Climb

It is a continuous process of industrialisation.

34. ANCILLARY DEVELOPMENT
33. GROW BIGGER
32. COMPETE WITH OTHERS
31. MODERNISATION
30. DIVERSIFICATION
29. PLOUGH-BACK PROFITS
28. KEEP UP-TO-DATE
27. SELL
26. PRODUCE
25. PLAN OUT RECORD-KEEPING
24. ORGANISE MARKETING
23. DECIDE ON PRICING POLICY
22. TRIAL RUN
21. RECRUIT PERSONNEL
20. PROCURE MATERIALS
19. INSTALL MACHINERY
18. PLAN BUYING
17. APPLY FOR MATERIALS (IF IMPORTED OR CONTROLLED)
16. PLACE ORDER FOR MACHINERY (PREFERABLY ON HIRE-PURCHASE)
15. PLAN SOURCES OF MACHINERY
14. PLAN FINANCE
13. OBTAIN CLEARANCE FROM CENTRAL, STATE AND LOCAL AUTHORITIES AND SSI REGN.NO.

12. MAKE SURE WHAT LAWS WILL PARTICULARLY AFFECT YOU
11. ARRANGE THE WORKSHED WITH FACILITIES (PREFERABLY ON RENT)
10. DECIDE ON LOCATION AND SITE
9. OBTIAN THE PROJECT REPORT FROM SISI OR ELSEWHERE OR PREPARE IT YOURSELF
8. DECIDE WHETHER TO PURCHASE A GOING CONCERN OR TO START A NEW ONE
7. DECIDE ON FORM OF OWNERSHIP [SOLE-PROPRIETARY/PARTNERSHIP/COOPERATIVE/COMPANY (PRIVATE/PUBLIC)]
6. CHOOSE A LINE
5. DATE WITH YOURSELF FOR A DECISION
4. DISCUSS WITH ALLAROUND YOU AND WITH SISI AND D.I. OFFICE
3. CONSULT PUBLICATIONS AND AGENCIES
2. DATE WITH YOURSELF FOR NEWER IDEAS
1. ANALYSE YOURSELF AND YOUR OBJECTIVES

CONCLUSION

As an entrepreneur, you have the pleasure of being in charge of your own business. And it is possible for you to exercise your individuality.

Employment generation, dispersal of industries in rural and semi-urban areas, utilisation of local resources and skills and development and widening of entrepreneurial base figure prominently in our plan priorities. Similarly, maximisation of exports has assumed added importance in the context of current balance of payments position. The prospects for export of non-traditional items such as ready-made garments, leather and marine products, processed food, plastics and engineering goods, etc., have improved.

As the main thrust of the new economic policy is to encourage competitiveness, characteristic of market-driven economy, small-scale units have to increasingly equip themselves to be on their own. Technology, together with quality promotion measures, holds the key to improved factor productivity and strengthening of competitiveness. An enlightened entrepreneurial class, fully conscious of the directions in which changes are taking place, can look forward with confidence to improve its market share, both within and in a global setting in recognition of the opportunities available for further growth.

But you may have to face some problems too. Raw materials may be scarce. Finding a market for your products may not always be easy. Procuring or executing really large orders may be virtually possible.

You would need assistance in such circumstances. And this can best come from organisations that are specially geared to assist small-scale units.

Primarily, it is necessary to decide on what to manufacture, where and how. Then follows the process of establishing a small-scale industry. But, till the dream is realised, there are a number of hurdles, which could be crossed over, if one takes care. Herein, one's perseverance is at least. Let us start the hurdle race. No, before participation in this hurdle as well as marathon race, let us prepare ourselves or be fit for the race.

If you are a novice in the field, the first exercise you should concentrate on is what items you can market either on your own or through a reliable selling agency. Once a product is decided, you can then take up for examination their manufacture, marketing, viability and profitability in the small-scale sector. You are just a pin — a small pin in the huge machine of industry. While exploring the market, please assess the element of competition. Please do not overlook competition to your products as well as the capacity of the competitors to outwit you by underselling. Bear always that the road is not smooth. Even the hurdles are of uneven nature, competition is taken for granted. Even the special institution will suggest to you to manufacture only such item which you can successfully market.

The age of continuous change has finally arrived. The choice is between two positions; either we can influence the same to the advantage of the firm, or end up as victims of the onslaught caused by the change. Accepting the *status quo* will directly lead to competitive decline. A better approach would be to shift the managerial and organisational mindset to the new paradigm stated above and thereby increase the overall capabilities of the firm to take charge of its own destiny.

ANNEXURE-I

Process of Setting up a Small-scale Industry - Guidelines

I. *Selection of Industry*	
Small Industries Service Institutes	They guide entrepreneurs in the selection of industries, areas, suitable raw materials and machinery.
Indian Investment Centre	It advises on foreign capital participation and technical collaboration.
Parliament Street, New Delhi-1	Provides guidance to entrepreneurs regarding government policies, procedures, available incentives and facilities for investment, economic size of unit and the magnitude of investments required, demand forecast, availability of raw materials, etc. Ministry of Industrial Development.
Ministry of Industrial Development and Affairs, New Delhi.	It approves the cases of foreign collaboration and Company
II. *District Industries Centres*	In each district, there would be one agency to deal with all requirements of small and village industries, which would be called the Districts Industries Centre. Under the single roof of the centre, all the services and support required by small and village entrepreneurs would be provided. The Centre would have a separate wing for looking after the special needs of cottage and household industries as distinct from the small industry. The Rural Industries Project and Rural Artisans Programme would be merged with the programme of the District Industries Centre. Each DIC would have a General Manager and seven managers of different disciplines for looking after planning and economic investigation, credit, marketing, etc.
III. *Factory Accommodation*	
Directors of Industries	They provide built-up factory space in industrial estates or developed factory sites, power, water, etc.(The building designs have to be approved by Municipalities or Corporations while power and water connections are sanctioned by State Governments/ Undertakings.
IV. *Industrial Estates*	There are more than 600 industrial estates in India which provide constructed accommodation in developed areas. Main facilities include common facility services, workshops, allotment of sheds on hire-purchase, concessional charges on water and power, exemption from octroi duty on building materials, etc.
V. *Registration*	Although it is not mandatory, it is certainly helpful to obtain the SSI Registration Number from the Director of Industries.
VI. *Machinery*	
Small Industries Service Institutes	They advise about the kind of machinery and equipment needed for the manufacture of different products.
National Small Industries Corporation, New Delhi	It supplies indigenous as well as imported machinery on hire-purchase basis.
State Small Industries Corporations	They provide indigenous machinery on deferred credit basis
Chief Controller of Imports Exports, New Delhi	He issues import licences for machinery of foreign origin on the recommendation of the Directors of Industries.
Consultants	Install machinery as per the layout drawn by them.
VII. *Raw Materials*	
Development Commissioner, Small-scale Industries, New Delhi.	He procures raw materials for the small industry and distributes them among state governments. He also arranges imports of raw materials through the Minerals and Metals Trading Corporation and the State Trading Corporation of India.
Directors of Industries	They allot quotas of scarce raw materials.
State Small Industries Corporations	They supply raw materials.

Chief Controller of Imports and Exports and His Port Offices	They issue licences for the import of raw materials.
VIII. Finance	
Small Industries Development	Small Industries Development Bank of India (SIDBI) has started operations through its 25 offices located in different states of the country. The SIDBI has been set up under an Act of Parliament as the principal financial institution for promotion, financing and development of industry in the tiny and the small-scale sector. The SIDBI is also expected to coordinate the functions of the institutions engaged in similar activities. The SIDBI is a wholly-owned subsidiary of the Industrial Development Bank of India (IDBI). It has taken over IDBI's financing activities relating to the small-scale sector.
State Financial Corporations	They provide long-term credit for the purchase of fixed assets.
State Directors of Industries	They provide loans under State Aid to Industries Act/Rules for block capital.
State Bank of India and its Subsidiaries	They sanction medium-term and instalment credit loans for the purchase of machinery and the construction of factory buildings. They also provide working capital for the purchase of raw materials and meeting other day-to-day requirements.
Commercial Banks	They sanction loans for working capital needs.
Small Industrial Service Institutes	They furnish technical reports to Institutes and the State Bank of India on the applicant units.
IX. Technical know-how	
Small Industries Service Institutes	They prepare improved designs and Institute's drawings for products. They assist in making tools, dies, jigs and fixtures. They help in the optimum utilisation of men, materials and machinery. They prepare management control charts for the maximisation of profits. They train managers and supervisors in industrial management. They train workers to upgrade their skill. They demonstrate modern technical processes.
National Small Industries Corporation, New Delhi.	They give advanced training in their prototype. Production-cum-Training Centres in the operation of modern machines.
Council of Scientific and Industrial Research, New Delhi.	It develops new technological processes and disseminates the same to the industry.
Productivity Councils	Train factory-owners to increase productivity.
Small Industry Extension Training Institute, Hyderabad	It gives full-time and management training to managers/proprietors in the small industry sector.
Central Institute of Tools Designs (CITD) Hyderabad.	Specialises in provision of technical consultancy and tool facilities, training in design and manufacture of tools.
Institute for Design of Electrical Measuring Instruments (IDEMI) Mumbai.	Provides technical know-how and testing, calibration laboratory, workshop and training facilities to electrical measuring instrument manufacturers.
X. Standardisation	
Small Industries Service Institutes	They provide technical guidance in the production of goods according to prescribed standards.
Indian Standards Institution	It prescribes specifications for the products and issues ISI certification.
Directors of Industries	They prescribe standards and give 'Q' Mark to the small industry's products.
Quality Control	Those in charge provide technical guidance in maintaining the quality of products.
XI. Marketing	
Small Industries Service Institutes	They conduct distribution and surveys for the benefit of small Industrialists. They enlist the units for participation in the Central Government Stores/Purchase Programme.

	They issue competency certificates to the units receiving government orders. They promote ancillary relationships with large and medium-scale units in public and private sectors.
National Small Industries Corporation, New Delhi	It secures contracts from the Director General of Supplies and Disposals, Railways, and Defence Departments for supply of manufactured goods by small-scale units.
State Small Industries Corporations	They secure orders from the state government and other semi-government organisations for the supply of stores.
XII. Export	
Small Industries Service Institutes	They enlist small units for participation under the Export Aid to Small Industry Scheme of the State Trading Corporation of India. They render technical counselling services for a satisfactory execution of export orders. They disseminate information about the items having export markets. They maintain a close liaison with specialised agencies like the Export Promotion Councils to have up to date knowledge about the products having export markets.
Chief Controller of Imports and Exports, New Delhi.	He issues licences for the export of products to foreign countries.
Directorate of Export Promotion, Udyog Bhavan, New Delhi	It collects and supplies information on foreign markets. It carries out market studies for particular products. It publishes Trade Directories, Brochures and Bulletins.
Export Promotion Councils	They organise exhibitions and showrooms. They maintain a close liaison between Indian exporters and foreign buyers. They settle commercial disputes. They frame special export promotion schemes.
State Trading Corporation of India, New Delhi	It registers units for participation under Export Aid to Small Industry Scheme. It helps the small-scale units in the preparation of sales leaflets, price lists, etc. It secures export orders for small industries.
Trade Fair Authority of India, New Delhi	Organises National Small-scale Industries Fairs. Conducts publicity work. Project image of the industry and assists in finding potential markets.
XIII. Inventions	
The Inventions Promotion Board, 39 Ring Road, Lajpat Nagar IV, New Delhi-110 014	It promotes workable inventions of practical utility through financial assistance and other incentives.
The Central Institute of Tools Design, Hyderabad.	It produces tools, jigs, fixtures, dies and moulds. It trains practising personnel in the design and manufacture of tools, etc.
XIV. Training	
Small-scale Industries Development Organisation	It trains practicing managers and technologists.
Small Industries Service Institutes	They conduct management courses for senior managerial personnel.
Extension Centres	They conduct regular and *ad hoc* training courses in various technological trades for skilled and semi-skilled workers.
Indian Investment Centre	Conducts regular entrepreneurial development programme courses. Assistance is given to the trainees in the identification of project reports. They are also helped in obtaining the necessary financial assistance from the financial institutions and guidance is also provided up to the stage of trial production.
Small Industry Extension Training Institute (SIET)	Offers training in industrial management and other aspects of small industries development; undertakes feasibility and research studies and collects and disseminates technical information through its Documentation Centre. Under assistance to Young Engineers programme, training is provided through specified agencies and interest subsidy, i.e., difference between interest rate of 7% per annum

	and the normal rate charged by the financial institutions is provided subject to a maximum of ₹ 20,000 per annum for a period of five years in backward areas and three years in other areas.
National Institute for Entrepreneurship and Small Business Development (NIESBUD)	NIESBUD is an apex body established in 1983 for coordinating and overseeing the activities of various institutes/agencies engaged in entrepreneurship development in the small industry and related business.
XV. Problems	
The Federation of Associations of Small Industries of India, Rohtak Road, New Delhi, Chambers of Commerce and Industry	They represent the problems faced by the small industries to the Government. They discuss the problems and represent them to the appropriate authorities.
XVI. Monitoring	
The National Alliance of Young Entrepreneurs (NAYE)	It is a national level apex organisation of entrepreneurs. It assists in promoting new enterprises through first-generation entrepreneurs. It also monitors the programmes of entrepreneurial development in India.
XVII. Other Voluntary Organisations	Association of Women Entrepreneurs of Karnataka (AWAKE) Women Entrepreneurs' Association of Maharashtra (WIMA) Self-employed Women's Association (SEWA) World Association of Small and Medium Enterprises (WASME) National Alliance of Young Entrepreneurs (NAYE) National Association of Software and Service Companies (NASSCO) Consortium of Women Enterprises of India (CWEI) etc.

CONTACT ADDRESSES
MINISTRY OF MICRO, SMALL AND MEDIUM ENTERPRISES

S. No.	Name and Address of the Organisation	Website	E-mail	Telephone	Fax
1.	Ministry of Micro Small Medium Enterprises, Udyog Bhavan, New Delhi- 110 107.	www.msme.nic.in www.msme.gov.in	dcmsmepublicity @yahoo.com	011- 23063800 23063802-06	011- 23062315 23061726 23061068
2.	Office of AS&DC (MSME), 7th Floor, A Wing Nirman Bhavan, New Delhi-110 108.	www.dcmsme.gov.in www.laghu-udyog.com; www.smallindustry.com	dc-msme@nic.in	011- 23063800 23063802-06	011- 23062315 23061726 23061068
3.	Khadi and Village Industries Commission, (KVIC),"Gramodaya" 3, Irla Road,Vile Parle (West), Maharashtra	www.kvic.qrg.in	kvichq@bom3.vsnl. net.in, ditkvic@bom3.vsnl. net.in, dit@kvic.gov.in	022- 26714320-25/ 26716323/ 26712324/ 26713527-9/ 26711073/ 26713675	022- 26711003
4.	Coir Board, "Coir House", M.G. Road, Ernakulam, Kochi-682016, Kerala.	www.coirboard.nic.in, www.coirboard.gov.in	coir@md2.vsnl.net.in coirboard@vsnl.com	0484- 2351807 2351788 2351954 2354397	0484- 2370034
5.	National Small Industries Corporation Limited (NSIC), NSIC Bahvan,Okhla Industrial Estate, New Delhi-110 020.	www.nsic.co.in	info@nisc.co.in, pro@nsic.co,in	011- 26926275 269109910 26926370	0120 2403057 2403062
6.	National Institute for Entrepreneurship and Small Business Development (NIESBUD), A-23- 24 , Sector-62, Institutional Area, Phase-II, NOIDA-201301, Uttar Pradesh.	www.niesbud.nic.in	info.niesbud@nic.in, rrsingh04@yahoo.com	0120- 2403051-54	0120- 2403057 2403062
7.	National Institute for Micro, Small and MediumEnterprises (NI-MSME), Yousuf Gauda, Hyderabad-500 045.	www.nimsme.org.in	registrar@nimsme. org	040- 23608544-46 23608316-19	040- 23608547 23608956 23541260
8.	Indian Institute of Entrepreneurship (IIE), 37 NH Bypass, Lalmati, Basistha Chariali, Guwahati-781 029, Assam.	www.iie.gov.in	iieindia1@sanchr net.in, iieindia1@bsnl.in	0361- 2302646 2300994 2300123 2300840	0361- 2300325

28 CHAPTER

LOCATION ISSUES

"Organisations that have world-class ambitions will need to nurture knowledge workers"

— V. Thyagarajan, Managing Director, Glaxo

A GREAT LEADER HAS THE ABILITY TO CRAFT A VISION,...

....effectively, articulate the same to those around him/her so as to make it into a rallying point which can galvanise the organisation and develop effective strategies that sets out the road map to realise the vision. A great leader inspires all around him/her and becomes a role model.

LEARNING OBJECTIVES

The main objective is to have an insight into the varied issues relating to the location. In this chapter, emphasis is being laid on the important aspects of:

- Need for enterprise location.
- Importance of location.
- Location policy.
- Economic considerations.
- Factors affecting location of an enterprise.
- Steps in location.
- Weber's Theory of industrial location.
- Selection of an economic site.
- Factors influencing the location.
- Industrial growth centres scheme.

The location of enterprise has a great effect on the success or failure of the operation of that plant. If the selection of the site is not proper, then all the money invested on factory building, machinery and their installation, etc., will go waste and the owner of the factory will have to suffer a great loss. Further, the cost of transferring it from one location to another would prove a very costly affair and pose problems which cannot be easily solved.

INTRODUCTION

Location considerations for the establishment of manufacturing plants is critical to the operation of the set-up in an uninterrupted and least resistant manner. Considerable emphasis is laid from the technical point of view regarding site locations.

The study of industrial location forms an important branch of economic geography which has engaged the attention of both economists and geographers. Economists judge from the point of view of profit, productivity and growth. Similarly, they may also look from the point of view of raw material, market, labour, finance, infrastructure, policy, costs, incentives, and subsidies.

In this chapter, an entirely different perspective of selection of site for an enterprise has been dealt with. The selection of site and equipment are important aspects of project to derive maximum operative economy and effectiveness.

An ideal site certainly contributes to the smooth and efficient functioning of an enterprise. It not only saves on costs but also enhances productivity and profits. An ideal location is a boon to a manufacturing unit to grow, diversify and prosper, as well as provide quality products on an ongoing basis.

Need for Enterprise Location

The need for plant location arises under the following circumstances:

(1) When a new enterprise is to be established.

(2) In the case of established enterprise, the need for enterprise location arises when expansion, decentralisation and diversification is undertaken to meet the increased demand for its products.

(3) Whenever the existing factory is not in a position to obtain renewal of lease.

(4) When an undesirable location is to be abandoned.

(5) When the tendency of shifting the market, depletion of raw materials, changes in transportation facilities, new processes requiring a different location are observed in a factory.

(6) When a new branch or branches are to be opened for increasing the volume of production or distribution or both.

Importance of Enterprise Location

The selection of an appropriate location enables the enterprise to operate smoothly, efficiently, and with the minimum cost; it is estimated that manufacturing and distribution costs may vary to an extent of 10 per cent simply by virtue of the choice of enterprise location. Wrong location leads to wastage in efforts and talents of the promoters with consequent uncertainty in results. The location of enterprise has a great effect on the success or failure of the operation of that plant. If the selection of the site is not proper, then all the money invested on factory will have to suffer a great loss. Further, the cost of transferring it from one location to another would prove a very costly affair and pose problems which cannot be easily solved. Therefore, while selecting a site, the owner must consider technical, commercial and financial aspects and then to select a suitable site that may provide maximum advantages.

Locational Policy

Locational policy has also been significantly amended. In locations other than cities of more than one million population, there is no requirement of obtaining industrial approvals from the Central Government except for the industries under compulsory licensing. In respect of cities with population exceeding one million, industries other than those of a non-polluting nature such as electronics, computer software and printing, may be located outside 25 kms of periphery of urban areas, except if they are located in designated industrial area, prior to 25.7.1991. Zoning and Land Use Regulations and Environmental Legislation's continue to regulate industrial locations.

Economic Size

For each project, there exists a certain minimum economic size below which the project will not be viable. It may so happen that in the case of some acute scarcity products, a project even below the economic size may appear to be viable in the immediate future, but if a long-term view is taken, it may not be viable. The minimum economic size of a project regarding products to be manufactured, complexity of the manufacturing process, size of the market, availability of raw materials, equipment and other factors of production, particularly capital and labour, are areas for assessing the economic feasibility of the project concerned. The concept of economic size of a project is also linked with inflationary pressures on the unit cost of investment and technology adopted.

In a continuous processing unit, the minimum size of a plant would be determined by technology as also the size of the plant/equipment available while in a jobbing unit, the size of the plant will depend on the product mix, location of the project, availability of skilled labour, cost of infrastructural input and quantum of bought-out finished and semi-finished components. The scale of a project is, therefore, examined keeping in view the technological efficiency, cost of production, size of the likely market and capital cost. The various factors may, however, be conflicting and therefore, while deciding upon the scale of operation, certain compromises may have to be made. For instance, when the likely demand for the product is not adequate to justify the size of the project, it would be necessary to compromise on the technological efficiency criteria and choose a lower scale of operation, sacrificing thereby a part of technological efficiency.

Various alternatives are often evaluated for project phasing in terms of either the size of the plant or the extent of integration. When eventually the market develops, the size of the project can be increased appropriately by backward or forward integration.

Other factors which have an important bearing on the economic size of the project are the cost structure and availability of infrastructure facilities. In view of these factors, it might often be necessary to compromise with projects of smaller capacity and shorter gestation period *vis-a-vis* large capacity plants involving huge investment and long gestation periods. Thus, in each and every case, the economic size of the project is analysed carefully by the appraising financial institution and it is ensured that neither the project is too small nor too ambitious. If a project is found to be of an uneconomic size, the borrower is advised at the initial stage itself so that it might be possible for him to modify his scheme and make it an economically viable and acceptable reposition. It may be mentioned here that the institutions also ensure that the licensed capacity of a plant is expressed in terms of physical quantities and not in terms of monetary value as per the directions of the Central Government.

LOCATION

Location is also an important factor determining the ultimate success or failure of a small-scale unit. On it may depend the small industry's ability to obtain an adequate and regular supply of its raw materials at a minimum cost, to maintain a sufficient labour force and to serve satisfactorily its customers. In spite of its importance, many small entrepreneurs in the past did not pay much attention to the problem of proper location of their units.

Location of any project is sometimes determined by government licensing regulation and not by the choice of the promoters. However, since location is an extremely important aspect for ensuring commercial success of an enterprise, appraisers evacuate location in relation to availability of raw materials, power, labour, fuel, transport, market and other infrastructure needs. The social infrastructure facilities such as availability of housing and education, medical and recreation facilities also become important, particularly if skilled personnel have to be attracted from outside. In the case of certain projects involving sophisticated technology, availability of testing and research facilities are also taken into consideration. The weightage given to different aspects depends upon the type of industry. Water and power availability, for example, are the major factors examined particularly in relation to a power-and water-intensive project. Generally, the power-intensive units are not encouraged to be set up in areas having a chronic power shortage. In the case of export-oriented projects, location near a port might prove advantageous.

Factors influencing selection of location may be shown in an exhibit as given below:

Table 28.1 Factors Affecting Location of an Enterprise

A. Selection of Region	B. Selection of Community	C. Selection of Site	D. Optimum Selection of Site
(i) Availability of raw materials (ii) Nearness to market (iii) Availability of power and fuel (iv) Transport	(i) Availability of labour (ii) Civic amenities for workers (iii) Existence of complementary and competing industries (iv) Finance and Research facilities	(i) Soil, size and topography (ii) Disposal of waste (iii) Price of land (iv) Expansion potential	Optimum site is selected on the basis of a comparative economic survey of the alternative sites in question.

(v) Suitability of climate	(v) Availability of water and the fighting facilities	(v) Commercial service
(vi) Government policy	(vi) Local taxes and restrictions	(vi) Communication
(vii) Competition among stages	(vii) Momentum of an early start	(vii) Availability of amenities
(viii) Meteorological conditions and topography	(viii) Personal factors	(viii) Health of locality
	(ix) Banking facility	(ix) Statutory consideration
	(x) Communication facility	(x) Flood and drought
	(xi) Cultural affinity	(xi) Right and title of the land
	(xii) Religious and social institutions	(xii) Good scenery
	(xiii) Educational environment	(xiii) Attitude of local people
	(xiv) Historical factors	(xiv) Technological know-how
	(xv) Political stability	(xv) State Assistance

Generally speaking, if the value-added component is not high, the project may be located near the source of raw material but for project manufacturing high value-added products; a wide choice in respect of location is available as the projects can bear the to-and-fro transportation cost of raw materials and finished products.

It has been found in a recent investigation that around 92 per cent of the small industrialists had selected the location of their units to the nearest point of their residence; and out of these about 90 per cent ignored the economies of the location of an industry. They did not bear in mind the fact that heavy recurring costs were involved in the purchase of their industries. In the case of some small industrial units, a particular type of climate, proximity to certain markets, a certain type of water or texture of the soil and proximity to rail or road transport is necessary, but no care had been taken in selecting a site with these locational advantages. The study concludes: "Due to the faulty selection of a site for the location of an industry, some 56 per cent of the small units failed within a period of five years of their start." This fact emphasises the importance of location as a primary consideration in planned production and control.

Production Channel of an Enterprise

The Project

The company has already set up a unit for re-refining of used/waste oils with an installed capacity of 10,500 KL/MT. The proposed issue is to part finance the company's expansion programme to manufacture blended lubricating oils, industrial waxes and jellies as well as to provide balancing equipments to the existing re-refining plant to improve capacity utilisation and plant efficiency. After the proposed expansion, the capacity will increase to 13,500 KL/MT per annum.

Location

The unit is located at Khopoli, Dist. Raigad, Maharashtra which is about 90 kms. from Mumbai. It is a 'C' category backward area having benefit of state subsidy.

The factors favouring this location are asunder:

1. Easy availability of raw materials from the surrounding areas in Maharashtra and Gujarat.
2. Proximity to the potential market of Mumbai.
3. Well established road network.
4. Easy availability of power, water, labour and general industrial infrastructure.

Land and Building

The company is situated on a freehold land at Village Honad, Taluka Khalapur, Dist. Raigad, and measuring about 10,789 sq.mtrs. As on March 31, 1992, the company had incurred an expenditure of ₹ 55 lakh approximately, towards purchase and development of land and construction of building.

The existing built-up area is 1,130 sq.mtrs. approximately. The built-up area after the proposed expansion will be 1,785 sq.mtrs and the civil construction contract has been awarded to M/s. Akcon Engineering Company.

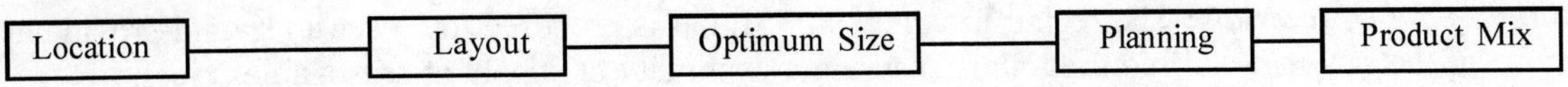

Fig. 28.1 Production Channel of an Enterprise

Steps in Location

According to Bethel, Atwater and Smith, enterprise location involves three main steps. They are: (1) selection of the region or general area; (2) selection of the particular community; and (3) selection of the exact plant site.

In choosing a plant location, the entrepreneur would do well to follow the undermentioned steps:

(a) Selection of the region;
(b) Selection of the locality or community;
(c) Selection of the exact site; and
(d) Selection of an optimum site.

Weber's Theory of Industrial Location

The Weber's theory of industrial location is based on the following basic assumptions:

(1) The materials used by an industry can be classified into ubiquitous and localised materials.

The ubiquities are those raw materials which are available everywhere, like brick, clay and water. The localised materials are those which are available in certain localities only, like minerals, fuels, etc.

The localised materials are further divided into: (i) weight-losing or gross materials, and (ii) pure materials. The weight-losing materials are those which considerably lose weight during the manufacturing process (e.g., coal and other minerals), as opposed to pure materials like cotton or wool.

(2) The situation and size of places of consumption are given, with the market comprising a number of separate points.

(3) There are certain fixed labour locations and labour is immobile. Wage rates may vary from location to location but in each location, supply of labour is unlimited at the given wage rate.

Weber's theory divides the factors influencing industrial location into the following two:

(i) The general regional factors of transport and labour costs. These general regional factors are regarded as the primary causes affecting industrial location.

(ii) The local factor of 'agglomerative' or 'deglomerative' forces regarded as the secondary causes responsible for redistribution of industries.

The location of an industry is determined by the interaction of the two sets of factors.

The limitations of the Weber's theory of industrial location are:

(1) The theory is based on three wrong assumptions about labour supply;
(2) Transport cost depend on the mode of transport, nature of goods, etc.;
(3) Location and size of markets may vary with changes in the economy;
(4) Non-economic factors also exert important influence on industrial location;
(5) The theory ignores the role of capital and entrepreneurship in industrialisation; and
(6) The classification of materials is not proper.

Selecting General Area

The important factors, which should be taken into account in the selection of a site, are: (i) availability of raw materials; (ii) availability of skilled and unskilled labour; (iii) nearness to the source of motive power; (iv) nearness to market; (v) availability of transport facilities; (vi) nuisance problem, and (vii) suitability of the climate.

(i) ***Availability of Raw Materials:*** The region in which an SSI unit is proposed to be set up should provide at least a greater part of the raw material required, thus ensuring a continuity of supply at reasonable prices.

(ii) ***Availability of Skilled and Unskilled Labour:*** It has to be seen whether proper labour required is available in the areas. If labour is brought from other areas, its cost would go up.

(iii) ***Nearness to the Source of Motive Power:*** The area should provide cheap power, soft water and sewage disposal facilities. Power failure has been one of the important reasons of industrial breakdowns in the small-scale sector.

(iv) ***Nearness to Market:*** If production is meant for self-consumption, the location of a small-scale industry is determined solely by considerations of the availability of raw materials, power and labour, if its production is for market, its nearness also has to be taken into account.

(v) ***Availability of Transport Facilities:*** Transport cost has often a decisive influence on the choice of location. In making a selection, the factor to be considered is the availability of transportation facilities at a reasonable cost.

(vi) ***Nuisance Problems:*** If there are any special 'nuisance' problems connected with an industry – smoke, noise, odour or smog – an arrangement for their control should either be available or necessary controls should be installed.

(vii) ***Suitability of Climate:*** Although the natural climate as a factor has lost its importance following rapid technological advances, small-scale industries have yet to pay adequate attention to this factor. Climate does influence the product and its quality.

The other important features to be considered are:

(1) Topography – flat, cheap or marshy land, sea, lake or river location. Vegetarian in the area, elevation above sea-level.

(2) Soil conditions – This determines the nature of foundation, nature and depth of piling required, steps to be taken with regard to corrosion to underground pipes, drainage requirements, quantity and cost of fill required.

(3) Water supply – surface or underground. Quality of water is important. Where water is extremely hard, additional plant for softening and treatment may be required.

(4) Waste disposal – Local regulations may require additional facilities for treatment of effluents prior to discharge to main stream.

(5) Position of plant to local transport facilities; nearness to rail connections or highway.

(6) Availability of homes for workers.

(7) Local legislations and municipal laws including sanitation, air and steam pollution and other factors.

(8) Living conditions for labour and management which include consideration of climate, recreational facilities, quality of schools, religious institutions, medical facilities, hospitals and other factors.

(9) Community directives and community attitude towards manufacturing activities and outside investors.

(10) Tax concessions and other incentives applicable to area/site.

It is very important to ascertain the general development surrounding the site. Whenever a construction activity is launched, it is useful to have ancillary support available in the area. Availability of construction facilities like rental of cranes, earthmoving equipments, welding sets, etc., in the vicinity reduces the cost of construction as well as the time of project implementation.

The extent of industrialisation has as much bearing as its impact on unionisation. Location of sites closer to the concentration of industries has significant fallouts in terms of interference from external elements. The usual outcome of such interactions are comparison of notes and the germination of seeds of dissatisfaction, which even if not directed towards one's organisation, has a potent effect of acting as a source of 'learning' to others. In such situations, any manipulation tends to could thinking and often leads to industrial strike without cause.

Table 28.2 Criteria for Choosing Site Location

		Selection of Region	Selection of Locality	Selection of Site
1.	Availability of raw materials	XXX		
2.	Nearness to markets	XXX		
3.	Availability of power	XXX		
4.	Transport facilities	XXX		
5.	Suitability of climate	XXX		
6.	Government policy	XXX		
7.	Competition between states	XXX		
8.	Availability of labour		XXX	
9.	Civic amenities for workers		XXX	
10.	Finance and research facilities		XXX	
11.	Availability of water and firefighting facilities		XXX	
12.	Local taxes and restrictions		XXX	
13.	Momentum of an early start		XXX	
14.	Personal factors		XXX	
15.	Soil, size and topography			XXX
16.	Disposal of waste			XXX
17.	Housing facilities for workers			XXX
18.	Unencumbered land			XXX
19.	Good scenery			XXX
20.	Road, rail and water connections			XXX

Having decided upon the location, the selection of a suitable site for the project is important. Factors taken into consideration in the selection of a site are:

Soil test indicating type and load-bearing capacity of the soil at various depths, water table, terrain, etc.;

Extent of site development required;

Climatic conditions, namely temperature, rainfall, humidity, etc.;

Presence of mineral deposits;

Proneness to natural and structural disturbance; and

Leasehold or freehold nature of land/compensation, mode of acquisition, etc.

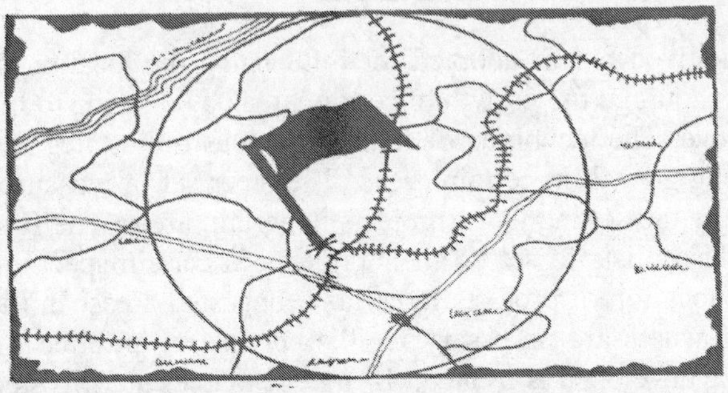

Fig. 28.2 Site Perspectives

For a proper assessment of the locational features of a project, the borrowers are asked to enumerate the locational advantages and are also required to furnish copies of the location map, site plan showing the contour lines, internal roads, power receiving station, railway siding, tubewell, factory layout providing for flow of raw materials and finished products, etc. While appraising the project, it is examined whether the land at site is sufficient not only for the immediate but also for its future requirements. Care is also taken to ensure that the formalities connected with the acquisition of land are completed before the appraisal of the project.

SELECTION OF MOST ECONOMIC SITE

According to Kimball and Kimball, the "most advantageous location is that at which the cost of gathering material and fabricating it plus the cost of distributing the finished product to the customer will be a minimum". This statement can better be explained with the help of the following diagram.

Let A and B represent the two sources of supply of materials. Let C stand for the marketplace; and let D represent the site of the factory. If the site of the factory is located at the marketplace C, then only the transportation cost of raw materials will have to be paid. Instead, if the factory site is located either at A or B, then only the distribution cost of finished goods is to be incurred. If the site is located at an intermediate point D, then only transportation cost on incoming raw materials and outgoing finished goods will have to be incurred. In order to arrive at the final decision for the most economic site, a comparative statement of total cost is to be prepared for an alternative site. This is illustrated below:

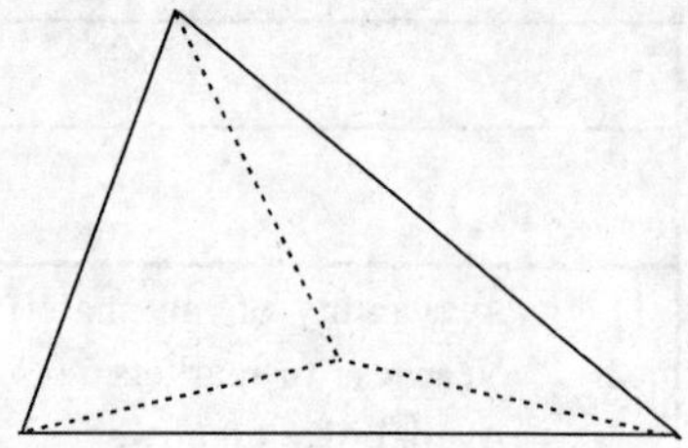

Fig. 28.3 Economic Size

Table 28.3 Selection of Actual Site

Items of Cost	Cost per unit at site		
	Site A	Site B	Site C
Fixed Capital			
1. Land acquisition cost			
2. Building construction cost			
3. Equipment installation cost			
Total of fixed cost			
Cost of Production and Distribution			
1. Materials cost:			
(a) Direct Materials			
(b) Indirect Materials			
2. Labour cost:			
(a) Direct labour cost			
(b) Indirect labour cost			
3. Overheads:			
(a) Factory insurance			
(b) Factory taxes			
(c) Factory depreciation			
(d) Office salaries			
(e) Selling overheads			
(f) Distribution overheads			
Total			

FACTORS INFLUENCING THE LOCATION OF PROJECTS

Broadly speaking, there are two types of measures that may be advocated or adopted for influencing the location of projects. The first set of measures may be called *positive measures* to encourage the growth of certain areas by offering to the industrialists various inducements, some of which have been listed above. The technique of setting up industrial estates and export processing zones has been widely used as a means of stimulating growth in certain areas. The other set of measures to be adopted by the authorities include *negative measures* to discourage the setting up of projects in certain areas. The first set of measures refers to the various inducements extended to the industrialists to set up their projects in certain specified areas, whereas the second set of measures imposes restrictions on the location of projects in certain congested areas. In the actual operation of the policy, as experience suggests, both sets of measures are necessary for the purpose of an effective location policy. During a given period, the total number of projects to be developed is limited. If more resources are invested in projects in one region, less resources will be available for investment of resources in projects in some regions of the country. Thus, a combined use of both positive and negative measures is of importance.

If a policy of industrial location with a view to achieving decentralisation and dispersal is accepted on economic, social, political and environmental grounds, then there is strong case for setting up a machinery for the administration of the policy. The machinery should exist at the central, regional and local levels to deal with the problems of regional or local industrial development. Naturally, the Central Ministry of Industry which has most to do with industrial matters, should be in charge of the overall administration of the policy. Various ministries and agencies are concerned with the problems of industrial development. Coordination, therefore, becomes extremely important. The Ministry of Industry in charge of administration of the policy will be in a better position to coordinate the various aspects of the policy through an inter-ministerial or inter-departmental panel competent to take decisions on the location of projects with speed and efficiency on sound economic and social grounds. There is the need for similar organisation at the regional and local levels to deal with the problems of industrial development in a particular region and locality. At the regional and local levels also, the responsibility for the administration of the policy should rest with the regional office of the department in industry. Here also a large number of departments and agencies will be concerned with industrial matters and the task of coordination may be achieved through the inter-departmental regional panel which will promote dispersal of industries even in hitherto background areas.

Among the important factors relating to industrial location, state incentives also play a key role. Although central incentives and subsidies assist the growth of enterprises in the country, it is the state incentives which attract entrepreneurs to set up their enterprises in particular States/Union Territories. The objectives of state incentives is to provide assistance and facilities to allure and motivate techno-entepreneurs, intrapreneurs and first generation entrepreneurs to locate their ventures in their region. State incentives must be so devised as to synchronise private incentives with social return in an efficient, cost-effective manner that simultaneously promotes moral imperatives. To the extent state incentives are a tool, no less than a programme, they make industrialisation and growth of entrepreneurship a reality. The nature of assistance, however, varies from state-to-state.

STATE INCENTIVES

Incentives offered	Small-scale industries	Medium and large-scale industries
(1) Feasibility study subsidy	Subsidy to a ceiling of 75% of the cost of preparing the report up to a maximum of ₹ 5,000.	Loan of 75% of the cost of preparing feasibility report up to a maximum of ₹ 50,000
(2) Investment subsidy	10% of value of fixed assets, subject to a ceiling of ₹ 5 lakh.	10% of the value of fixed assets, subject to a ceiling of ₹ 10 lakh.
(3) Development loan	Overall ceiling of 25% of the value of fixed assets.	For Zone II, 10% of the value of fixed assets to a maximum of ₹ 50 lakh and for Zones III and IV, 15% of the value of fixed assets, subject to a maximum of ₹ 50 lakh.
(4) Working capital loan	Interest-free loan offered, subject to a ceiling of 25% of the value of fixed assets or the development loan taken whichever is less.	Interest-free loan, subject to a maximum of ₹ 50 lakh.
(5) Procurement of know-how	It shall be reimbursed in full, subject to a maximum of ₹ 25,000.	50% of fees paid by new units for procurement of know-how shall be subsidised up to a ceiling of ₹ 1 lakh.
(6) Stamp duty exemption and reduction in registration fee	Exemption on a stamp duty for executing agreement with KSFC. There is also reduction fee of ₹ 1 per ₹ 100 for registering the agreement deeds.	Same as in the case of small-scale industries.
(7) Subsidy on housing	Subsidy at the rate of ₹ 1,500 per house of built-up area of not less than 300 sq.ft. shall be offered for the new units, who have plans to build houses for the employees.	Same as in the case of small-scale industries.

Curbs on Location of Units Eased

The government has eased restrictions on location of industries and also announced guidelines for industrial license applications received for industries falling outside compulsory licensing but involving locational constraints.

A notification issued by the Ministry of Industry mentioned that under the new industrial policy, industrial licensing exemption granted to all industries except the 18 specified categories were subject to certain locational restrictions.

These include that the proposed project should not be located within 25 kms from the periphery of the standard urban areas limits of a city with a population of more than a million, as per the 1991 Census.

But if the industrial units were to be located in an area designated as an 'industrial area' by the concerned state government before July 25, 1991, this restriction on location would not apply, the notification said.

Industrial units other than electronics, computer software or printing, which are to be located outside such a designated 'industrial area' and within the 25 kms limit would, however, require an industrial license even if they are otherwise delicensed.

The applications are being received for grant of industrial licenses from industries for relaxation of the locational angle.

However, it is only the environmental, safety, land use, urban planning and related factors that were kept in view while considering the industrial licence applications received for such industries.

Industrial Growth Centres Scheme

For the promotion of industries in the backward areas, the scheme of establishing growth centres was envisaged in 1988 for the establishment of 100 growth centres around the country. The criteria for location of centres is asunder:

(i) Outside 50 kms of cities with a population above 2.5 million.

(ii) Outside 30 kms of cities with a population of above 1.5 million but below 2.5 million.

(ii) Outside 15 kms of cities with a population of 0.75 million but below 1.5 million.

The objective of the scheme has been to provide the best of the infrastructure facilities in these growth centres nation-wide. The other criteria for the establishment of growth centres were: (i) the proximity to rail heads, national or state highway and (ii) access to adequate and dependable sources of water, power, telecommunication facilities, educational and health facilities and sufficient land for the development of housing and for the promotion of tertiary activities. Growth centres should not be located in ecologically sensitive areas and the location for such centres should cover an area of the radius of 20-25 kms. The state governments/UTs have been furnishing proposals for the final selection of growth centres.

BUTIBORI – A NEW INDUSTRIAL AREA

On 5th December, 1992, Shri C. Subramaniam, the Governor of Maharashtra formally inaugurated the upcoming industrial area at Butibori, just 17 kms away from Sonegaon airport of Nagpur, which is the winter capital of the state of Maharashtra.

Butibori, expected to be one of the biggest industrial estates in Asia was to be developed in three stages covering an expanse of 2,440 hectares of land, of which 717.77 hectares have already been developed as a part of the first stage. The estimate situated at the junction of the main North-South National Highway No. 3 is 26 kms for Nagpur city which is at the centre of India, enjoying direct access to all four metropolitan and other major cities of the country.

For the benefit of those who wish to set up their industrial ventures in Butibori, we offer a glimpse into its industrial infrastructure with promises of more to come in near future.

Butibori – A Glimpse

Location: 8,559 kms by road and 837 kms by rail from Mumbai. Nearest airport Sonegaon, Nagpur is just 17 kms away.

Land: 2,440 hectares MIDC industrial area on Nagpur-Hyderabad Highway No.7.

Water: Wadgaon dam is under construction. This permanent water supply scheme of MIDC will supply 61 million litres of filtered water per day.

Power: Three to four substations of 220 KV/66 VK/33 KV will supply power to the area.

Telecommunications: MIDC has booked 1,000 telephones. The capacity of the existing Telephone Exchange will be augmented to 3,000 lines.

Internal Transport: ST bus services between Nagpur and Butibori.

Social Amenities: Proximity to Nagpur opens many recreational avenues and provides access to all the social amenities such as schools including 20 English medium; 48 colleges and the Nagpur University with 32 departments, a dental college; modern hospitals, including the Government Medical College and Hospital, the biggest in Asia, private clinics; 3 and 5-star hotels; clubs and several housing colonies.

Prominent Industries: ACC Nihon Castings Ltd., Indo Rama Synthetics (I) Ltd., The Associated Tyre Machinery Co. Ltd.

INDUSTRIAL LOCATION POLICY FOR BMR MODIFIED

The Government of Maharashra has brought about radical changes in the existing Industrial Location Policy (ILP) for the Bombay metropolitan region with emphasis on containing pollution and taking into consideration, the need for generating employment opportunities to take care of the declining employment in Mumbai and its suburbs. The policy has been in force for nearly two decades now, revisions in it being made from time-to-time depending on the need. The last such revision was made in February 1984.

The revised policy is to be applicable to all industries in the BMR excluding cotton textile industries, godowns, service industries and service industrial estates. The locational clearance, however, shall be subject to environmental approvals from the Central and State governments as also provisions of the regional plan for BMR, the Development Plan and Development Control Regulations.

For purposes of implementation to the policy, the BMR was divided into three zones:

Zone I consisting of Greater Bombay and areas of Thane Municipal Corporation and Mira-Bhayandar Municipal Council;

Zone II consisting areas of Kalyan and Navi Mumbai Municipal Corporations, Ulhasnagar, Ambernath, Kulagaon-Badlapur Municipal Councils, Bhivandi and Uran subregions and Vasai-Virar subregion; and

Zone III consisting of the remaining areas of the BMR excluding the areas covered under Zones I and II.

Industries are classified in three categories, namely: (i) non-polluting high-tech or high value-added units as listed in Schedule I, (ii) highly polluting, hazardous or obnoxious units as listed in Schedule II, and (iii) units other than these.

The main industries covered under Schedule I are electronics, white goods such as refrigerator, freezer, washing machine, microwave oven, air-conditioner, etc. Plastic products, watches and clocks, gems and jewellery, textile products, excluding dyeing and processing of cloth, food and food products, paper products, printing and publishing, leather and fur products excluding tanning, curing and processing of hides and wood products excluding manufacture of plywood, blackwood and saw-milling. Setting up any new unit under this category will be allowed freely in Zone I while no other industry will be allowed. Expansion, modernisation or diversification of an existing unit will also be allowed for these industries in Zone I and II as well as for those not covered by Schedule I and II up to permissible FSI, provided additional power is limited to 25% of authorised connected load on 4th May, 1993. Proposed industrial estate or construction of an open plot as well as expansion of approved industrial estates (having final NOC), division of gala or structure for housing only these industries will be allowed in Zone I and II all the industries other than those mentioned in Schedule II, in Zone II.

The list of industries under Schedule II include manufacturing and refining of sugar, manufacture of hydrogenated oils, blending of spirit, manufacture of pulp/pare or newsprint, tanning of leather, manufacture of cement, petroleum and coal products, chemical and chemical products, asbestos and asbestos products, etc. Any new unit or expansion under this category will be allowed only in MIDC areas in Zone II.

Environmental Problems

Environmental problems in India can be classified into two broad categories:

(a) Those arising from conditions of proverty and underdevelopment, and

(b) Those arising as negative effects of the very process of development.

The first category has to do with the impact on the health and integrity of our natural resources (land, soil, water, forests, wildlife, etc.) as a result of poverty and the inadequate availability, for a large section of our population of the mankind to fulfil basic human needs (food, fuel, shelter, employment, etc.)

CONCLUSION

Among other things, the entrepreneur has to give special emphasis to the location of this project, equipment and layout to derive maximum benefits. Selection of site and equipment is governed by various variables. Taking into consideration all these aspects, the entrepreneur have to select the site and equipment for his enterprise.

The selection of the most economical site is possible where an entrepreneur prepares a comparative cost statement, taking into account the different sites available. Certain recent trends in plant location are now discernible. These are: (a) To locate plants away from cities; (b) The development of industrial estates; (c) Competition among states to develop industries; (d) Trend towards decentralisation; (e) Pollution control; (f) Location of industries leading to balanced regional development; and (g) Growth of multinational firms, thereby transcending the geographical area of the country.

Location of an industrial enterprise plays an important role in the development of the industry. Location affects the cost-structure, growth potential and profitability of an enterprise. A location that is most beneficial and enterprising in all respects is known as an *optimum location*. An optimum location is essentially an idealistic concept. Such a location is difficult to obtain and still more difficult to retain. The location decision is a complex process because of varied factors and their impact on the industry. Taking into consideration the ground realities and the basic needs of an enterprise, the entrepreneur has to select the best among the lot and then develop the areas as the needs to be. It is, therefore, very necessary to weigh the merits and demerits of location factors before setting up of an industrial enterprise. In fact, location is the most important factor, next only to the choice of an industry/product, in laying a sound foundation for an industrial enterprise. A critical evaluation of the industrial location policies reveals that a thorough overhauling is required in the approach towards location of industries based on economies of scale and marketing.

In the years ahead, industrial location will be guided primarily by commercial considerations and sustainability rather than by regulatory or social demands alone. An investment which does not maximise the generation of surpluses cannot contribute to the country's social goals. Thus, location in backward regions where there is a great deal of willingness and native skill amongst the first generation workers provides a very attractive scenario to the decaying environment of cities where industry has been traditionally located.

ANNEXURE-I

Checklist

The location of an enterprise has to be carefully selected. A wrong choice may prove fatal for the enterprise. The selection of a suitable locality depends on a number of factors. Further, each factor is to be undertaken by the entrepreneur before he selects a particular site. The following checklist prepared by the United States Department of Commerce will help the entrepreneur in the appraisal of the basic location factors.

Checklist for considering basic industrial location factors

I. Location of production (raw) materials

A. What production materials exist in the area?

B. In what volume are the production materials available?

C. What is the quality of each production material?

D. How accessible are the available material?

Does the nature of such production materials (quantity, bulk, perishability, etc.), or any unusual advantage attendant thereto definitely favour plant location at or near site or source?

II. Labour

A. What is the labour force of the area?

B. What is the quality of the available labour force?

C. What is the character of the labour force?

D. What quantity of labour is reasonably available?

1. Is a large supply necessary?
2. Are special skills required?

III. Sites

A. How much land is available for industrial expansion?

B. What are the soil and topographic features?

C. At what cost and terms can land be purchased or leased?

D. What facilities are now or will be available?

E. What industrial floor space is or will be available in existing structures?

1. Is a large area needed?
2. Must the site have special features, such as topographic soil conditions, transportation facilities, low costs, etc.?

IV. Industrial Fuel

A. What industrial fuel is available for additional industry?

B. How dependable is the supply?

C. At what cost is the fuel available?

1. Is low cost heat a major factor in processing?
2. Is a particular fuel required?

V. Transportation Facilities

A. What transportation facilities are available?

B. What is the rate situation?

1. Do materials and/or product require prompt and/or low cost movement?
2. Does product or raw material require a special type of transportation?

VI. Market

A. What is the trading area generally served by this location?

B. What is the general quality of this market?

1. Are time and distance vital matters to reach the market?
2. Is price of quality a vital market factor?

VII. Distribution Facilities

A. What agencies and services are available?

1. Are there channels for marketing complex and do they require special financing inspection, warehousing, storage or terminal facilities?

VIII. Power

A. What kind of industrial power is available?

B. How dependable is the power supply?

C. At what cost is the power available?

1. Is power a significant factor?
2. Is sufficient surplus power available?

IX. Water

A. How much water is available for additional industry?

B. What is the quality of the water supply?

1. Is significant quality of low-cost water required in processing?
2. Whether the required quantity is available?

X. Living Conditions

A. Are adequate facilities available for education, recreation, shopping, religious and social life, health and professional service?

B. Is sufficient housing available?

1. Will the industry employ enough people to make housing and environment significant factors?

XI. Laws and Regulations

A. What laws and regulations are of significance to prospective industries?

1. Is the industry subject to special local and/or state regulation?

XII. Tax Structure

A. How favourable is the tax structure to industry?

1. Is the capital investment of such a size that the tax rate or assessment policy will be important?

XIII. Climate

A. What are the climatic characteristics of the area?

29 CHAPTER

ENVIRONMENTAL PROBLEMS

"Business today is built, and grows, around human resources. So, people are the key resource."

— Sushil Handa, CEO, Core Healthcare

LEARNING OBJECTIVES

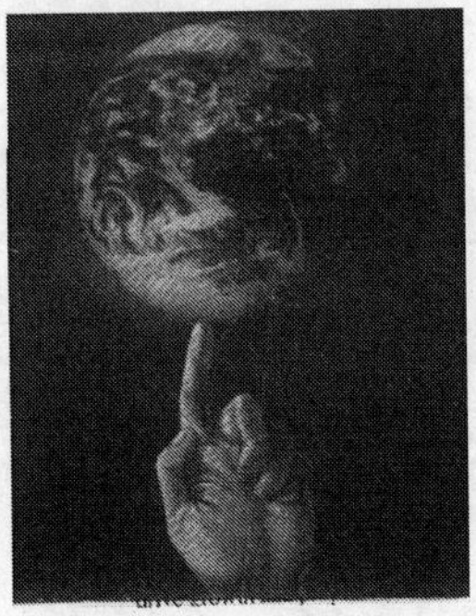

The prime objective of this chapter is to focus on the effects of environmental degradation, spread of awareness and knowledge among students, teachers and the entrepreneurs. For a progressive sustainable development, businessmen, professionals and students should be educated well.

Indian corporations/entrepreneurs need to gear themselves urgently to address the environmental imperatives facing them, and integrate environmental perspectives within their corporate strategies for organisational development.

The chapter approaches the issue in a pragmatic way and covers:

- Environmental policy.
- State of the environment.
- Laws.
- Measures.
- Environmental action.
- Polluting units.
- Environmental clearance and management.

INTRODUCTION

The differences in economic activities may be partly explained by the interaction between man and his environment. Although physical environment does not, absolutely determine the character of economic life, it does exercise a control over it which is more apparent in integrated development. Environment offers certain opportunities which man may or may not utilise. His abilities in exploiting the resources of the environment depend upon their knowledge, intelligence and culture as well as on the social structure of the country they live in. The environment and human ability together determine the economic growth of the country.

The environment is considered an integral part of planning, policy framing and development. It plays a crucial role in economic planning, improving productivity, growth and above all, in maintaining the ecological balance as it affects each segment of our economic and social life. In recent years, the planners and economists have focussed their attention on the environment, more so on the acute environmental problems and this becomes clear only if the concern for environmental protection is understood in its proper context.

Corporate concern for the environment is not merely a social obligation, or a fashionable 'flavour-of-the-month' recipe to which lip service needs to be paid, but a hardcore business proposition. What is required, therefore, is a change in the mindset of corporate managers today, and an understanding of business and environment on the part of graduate students undergoing business education. After all, on them rests the responsibility to manage growth and development in a sustainable world – one in which future generations are not left to pay the price for the follies committed by their forebears. Whilst environmentalists the world over are concerned about the gross inequities being perpetrated and are quite radical in their approach to the problem, corporations need to imbibe a more rational approach which balances the need for environmental preservation on the one hand, with concern for economic development and business viability on the other.

National Environmental Policy

Life owes its existence and obtains its sustenance, growth and fulfilment from the environment which is the product of complex and dynamic interactions of physical, chemical, biological and social systems. The quality of life is linked with the quality of environment. Man is continuously altering the environment to satisfy his needs and aspirations. Nature has, however, finite capacity to accommodate such changes without degradation. Pressures of the growing population and technological capacities often inflict undesirable and irreversible changes, outstripping nature's regenerative capacity. In many cases, these have adversely support systems. Conservation and improvement of the environment are vital for the survival and well-being of man. National resources of land, air and water have to be used wisely as a trust to ensure a healthy environment for the present and future generations.

Environmental pollution in many cities and larger towns has been increasing rapidly. Pollution affects river water and land, besides polluting air and posing health risks to the inhabitants. Industrial units contribute to pollution through solid wastes, liquid effluents and gases. The inappropriate handling of industrial wastes creates problems for the human and the natural environment. Increasing industrialisation without proper treatment of effluents has been considered a major cause of pollution. Further, poor working conditions in the SSIs are often the cause of occupational health hazards. Small industries tend to cause more pollution due to inefficient production methods, inferior equipment, poor housekeeping and the inability to adopt proper treatment technologies. In order to encourage cleaner production, the Government of India extends incentives like custom duty waiver, soft loans, etc., and provides other concessions for installation of pollution control equipment in industrial units.

The National Environment Policy (NEP) must ensure effective and judicious use of resources – natural, man-made and human – to meet the needs of the population without undermining the carrying capacity of the environment or pre-empting future choices. The Government of India, therefore, had resolved that the objectives of the National Environmental Policy shall be to:

(i) Conserve and develop a safe, healthy, productive and aesthetically satisfying environment.

(ii) Upgrade, develop and manage rural and urban settlements to enhance the quality of life.

(iii) Plan development on sound ecological principles with environmental impact assessments and incorporating appropriate environmental safeguards.

(iv) Promote environmental safety technologies, recycling of resources and utilisation of wastes.

(v) Conserve the biotic diversity in the country by creating nature reserves and sanctuaries for specific habitats such as mountains, rainforests, pastures, deserts, wetlands, lakes, beaches, mangroves, estuaries, lagoons and islands.

(vi) Safeguard the environment within the national maritime Exclusive Economic Zone.

(vii) Evolve environmental norms and establish effective mechanisms for monitoring surveillance and collection and dissemination of information.

(viii) Preserve scenic landscapes and cultural monuments and their environs.

(ix) Promote environmental education at all levels and create public awareness

(x) Encourage research of environmental sciences and technological and social investigations to conserve and improve the environment.

(xi) Develop adequate manpower within the country of ecologists, environmental scientists, planners and managers of the highest quality and recognise their work as an important component of national development.

Environmental problems in India can be classified into two broad categories:

(a) Those arising from conditions of proverty and underdevelopment, and

(b) Those arising as negative effects of the very process of development.

The first category has to do with the impact on the health and integrity of our natural resources (land, soil, water, forests, wildlife etc.), as a result of poverty and inadequate availability, for a large section of our population to fulfil basic human needs (food, fuel, shelter, employment, etc.). The second category has to do with the unintended side-effects of efforts to achieve rapid economic growth and development. In this, the latter category would fall on the distortions imposed on national resources from poorly planned development projects and programmes as well as from lack of attention to long-term concerns by commercial and vested interests. Thus, it is clear that a concern for environment is essentially a desire to see that national development proceeds along rational sustainable lines.

India's focus on industrial progress has apparently consumed unlimited resources of air and water, which play a vital role in industrial processing. They bring about the necessary chemical and physical transformations required for converting the raw materials into products and for product separation, isolation and purification in downstream processing.

The residuals of the manufacturing activities together with the undesired products of side reactions and chemical intermediate constitute the three principle categories of industrial wastes – process waste water, atmospheric emission, sludges and solid residues. These contribute to the problems of water pollution, air pollution and solid waste management problems of the industries.

While it is generally acknowledged that the generation of some wastes or residuals is inevitable in any industry, it is necessary to utilise the available resources in an effective integrated manner for multiproduct activities. This will minimise the total quantum of process residuals.

Industries are now engaged in implementing waste minimisation strategies through better plant operation, process modification and by-product development through recovery and reuse schemes. In addition to these, recent worldwide developments targeted towards a cleaner process technology to reduce the pollution potentials have also been adopted. Environmental management and pollution control pose a major concern to all.

State of the Environment

At present, pollution of air, water, land, noise, radiation and odour affect the quality of life in India. Most of the environmental and ecological problems are mainly due to the pressure on land and adoption of technology which releases effluents in a larger quantity than nature can neutralise by physical, chemical and biological processes without losing the ecosphere's equilibrium. For example, the petrochemical technology has become a menace to environmental stability since their effluents are invulnerable to enzyme attack and are thus inherently bio-nondegradable. Similarly, chemical fertilisers and other modern industries have been adding various oxides affecting the health of the living species.

Environment Protection Laws

Environmental pollution as a subject matter of legislation did not find a place in the Indian law books until as late as 1974. Prior to 1974, the only recourse available to citizens against pollution of any nature was under the provisions of the Indian Penal Code. Suits claiming damages for tortuous liability were also possible. However, there was nothing in the nature of regulatory or preventive enactments as far as environmental pollution was concerned. All that the law provided for was to proceed under civil or criminal law after the damage to environment took place.

The procedural requirements of a regular civil court made relief very difficult. Very often cases were lost on account of mere procedural and technical irregularities. It was only in the year 1974 that the Water (Prevention and Control of Pollution) Act, 1974 was enacted. Then came the Water (Prevention and Control of Pollution) Act, 1977, the Air (Prevention and Control of Pollution) Act, 1981.

Until 1981, the legislation with regard to environmental pollution were drawn up piecemeal. Moreover, even these legislations were only punitive in nature and not preventive. Whatever little regulatory measures were provided for in the laws were never implemented. There was no clear demarcation of powers of the various authorities under the Acts and this often led to further confusion.

The Environmental (Protection) Act, 1986, was the first comprehensive legislation with regard to environmental pollution. It evoked encouraging response and support from all environmental groups. It was widely acclaimed as the first legislation to tackle the problem of pollution. But the Act itself was a major disappointment as it was not very comprehensive in its scope and was not provided with sufficient powers to effectively bring to book offenders and control environmental pollution.

There are two major statutes that govern water and air pollution control. The majority of SSI units in the country do not fall within the ambit of these pollution control laws. However, certain highly polluting industries are required to obtain a No Objection Certificate (NOC) prior to establishing a unit, even in the SSI sector.

The Water (Prevention and Control of Pollution) Act, 1974:

The Act applies to all establishments discharging effluents into water or on land. A unit while making the project report is required to meet pollution control requirements and obtain an NOC (from the State Pollution Control Board) before setting up the unit. The effluents so discharged have to be managed at all times or else there are penalty provisions under the Act for violations. Further, the unit is not permitted to install any new or altered outlet for discharge of effluents/sewage into a stream or well, without prior consent of the Board. In a major initiative to reduce industrial waste pollution, the Government of India in partnership with the World Bank (WB), Washington, has launched an Industrial Pollution Control Project for assisting clusters in setting up common effluent treatment plants.

The Air (Prevention and Control of Pollution) Act, 1981:

The Act applies to all industries, which have to declare air pollution control points and instal necessary equipment. At the time of making the project report, provision has to be made for pollution control requirements and an NOC is to be obtained before establishing the unit. During operation of the unit, discharges into the air are to be managed within the prescribed standards at all time, failing which penalty provisions will be applicable.

Environmental Measures in SSIs

Specific attempts have been made to liberalise environmental laws wherever possible as applicable to small-scale industries. In fact, except for 17 categories of polluting industries in other areas, small-scale industries have only to file a memorandum of information which will serve the purpose of consent.

Specific areas where measures for pollution control are urgently required to be taken in the small-scale sector were identified. These are dye-stuffs, pesticides formulation, storage batteries, lead oxides, reclamation of used lubricating oils, manufacture of chromic acid, sodium dichromates, chrome pigments, basic chrome, chrome sulphates acid — slurry and blown bitumen. A paper of pollution control on safely aspects of synthetic detergent industry was prepared for circulation. Similarly, the areas have been identified for energy conservation that include design improvements in the boilers attached to different chemical groups of industries, improved design for evaporation/distillation process and improved design for ball mill/ grinding equipment for paint industry.

There is environmental awareness among the small-scale industries and are acting thereupon within the available resource at their disposal.

Environmental Action

Liberalisation of Industrial Licensing Policy has necessitated greater attention being paid to environmental related issues of industrial development both because of resultant increase in industrial activity and freedom being given to entrepreneurs for location of industrial enterprises. Suitable measures are required to be taken to abate industrial pollution and for conservation of natural resources through promoting suitable technologies.

Following actions have been/are being taken with respect to environment:

1. Monitoring of pollution control measures being undertaken by different industries.
2. Ensuring adherence to environmental guidelines issued by the Ministry of Environment for location of industries wherever applicable.
3. Efforts are being made to introduce the concept of Common Effluent Treatment Plant in industrial estates developed by the state government. One such cluster approach has been successfully executed in Ambur, Tamil Nadu. More such clusters are being taken up in Vaniyambadi, Ambur, etc.

4. An Inter-departmental Fuel Efficiency Committee has already worked out fuel efficiency standards for the various industrial sectors including the automobile industries.
5. Based on the recommendations of the Inter-departmental Task Force headed by Department of Industrial Development, the National Strategy on Phasing out of Ozone Depleting Substance has been formulated by the Ministry of Environment.
6. National Productivity Council (NPC), an autonomous organisation under this department, has pioneered significant steps in the field of pollution prevention and control especially in the small and medium-scale industries. NPC provides pollution control and prevention services to the small-scale industries.

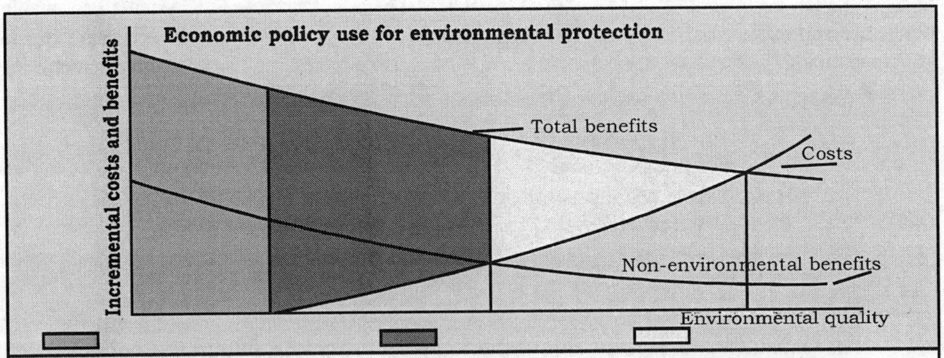

Policies that have no net financial costs for governments and contribute to both economic efficiency and environmental protection, elimination, of subsidies for energy inputs, pesticides, fertiliser and irrigation water
- elmination of subsidies for logging and ranching
- clarification of farmer's right to lands
- taxes on urban road congestion

Public and private investment that have positive net economic benefits even when environmental benefits are excluded
- investments in water supply and sanitation
- investments in soil conservation
- improvements in the education of women

Policies and investments that address market failures and that have positive net economic benefits when environmental effects are included
- taxes on emissions and wastes
- regulations on disposal of hazardous wastes
- piece for timber attraction

Note: This figure is not drawn to scale. The relative size of the shaded area is not intended to show the importance of each set of policies and investments.

Source: World Development Report, 1992.

Approach to Pollution Control

Measures needed for prevention of pollution include: (i) policy approach, emphasising regulations for use of less polluting materials, introducing clean technologies and recycling of waste streams – either on site or as a useful by-product, (ii) technical assistance approach, emphasising training, technology transfer and development, and (iii) financial assistance approach, support for fulfilling environmental conditions and technical incentives for research and development facilities.

For controlling the level of pollution in the SSI sector, support is needed both from the government as well as from the NGOs in the matter of: (i) raising awareness of risks, occupational health and pollution, and providing training at enterprise level, (ii) providing representation to Industries Association in the policy formulation committees to fill the gap between policy level and enterprise level cooperation, and (iii) coordination of environmental policy incentives and programmes for a sustained development.

POLLUTING UNITS

Over 9,000 industrial units in Delhi have been notified by the Central Pollution Control Board (CPCB) to be shifted out of Delhi, in compliance with the Supreme Court order of March 24, 1995. Most of these are small-scale units, employing locals.

Pollution is undoubtedly a major problem, which concerns all. But while dealing with a problem which involves the livelihood of lakh of people, the human angle should always be kept in mind. Logically, first of all, these small units should not have been allowed to come up. Again, the units which were set up before the master plan for Delhi came into force should have been asked to shift their activities to safer places, but these were not done.

Environmental Statement

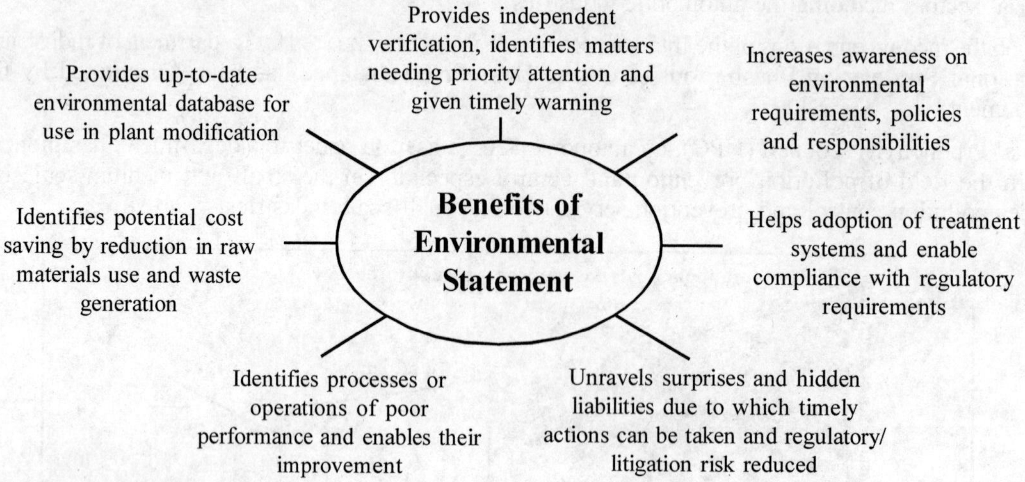

The Green Arm of the Law

Three important Indian legislations presently enjoin the industry to remain within the pollution control standards set by the government:

1. Water (Prevention and Control of Pollution) Act, 1974, with amendments made in 1988:
   - Following the 1988 amendments, permission is necessary to set up any industry which is 'polluting' – one that uses or discharges any poisonous, noxious or polluting matter. Standards must be those set by state pollution boards. Industries set up prior to the amendment need to obtain clearance within three months of its coming into force.
   - State pollution control boards (PCBs) have the power to obtain information regarding the construction, installation or operation of any process of the industry.
   - After the 1988 amendments, the PCBs can issue directions or order for closure or stoppage of electricity or water supply, if standards are not being met by the polluting industry.
   - Penalties for not-compliance have been increased to ₹ 10,000 for defaulting and ₹ 5,000 per day for continued default.
2. Air (Prevention and Control of Pollution) Act, 1981, with 1987 amendments:
   - The definition of air pollutant was extended from harmful solid, liquid or gaseous substances present in the atmosphere to include noise pollution.
   - Unlike the practice earlier, now all air polluting industries must have the sanction of their respective PCBs.
   - After amendments, powers have been given to PCBs to issue directions which include the closure, prohibition, stoppage of electricity, etc., for violation of standards set.
   - Penalties are as those in the Water Act.
3. Environment Protection Act (EPA), 1986:
   - The Central Government has the power to take all such measures as it deems necessary or expedient for protecting the environment.
   - Section 3 of EPA empowers the Central Government to: (a) restrict areas in which any industry, operations, process or class of industries can be carried out under certain safeguards; (b) lay down procedures and safeguards for the prevention of accidents which may cause environmental pollution and remedial measures for them; (c) lay down procedures for handling hazardous substances; (d) examining manufacturing process and materials, and (e) widespread inspection powers.
   - As in the other two Acts, the EPA gives the Centre wide powers to direct closure, prohibition and regulation of any industry if it contravenes the provisions of the Act.
   - In addition, the Marpol Convention, pertaining to marine pollution control, was drawn up by the International Maritime Organisation, a United Nations agency, and ratified by India in 1978.

- The five annexures of this convention deal with: prevention of oil pollution; prevention of pollution by noxious liquid substances in bulk; prevention of pollution by noxious packaged substance; pollution from sewage and from garbage.
- The Indian government has ratified only the first two annexures. Thus, a vessel can be penalised for oil or chemical pollution. But the remaining forms of pollution go unchecked.

The ecological environment of business is slowly but surely emerging as an important factor in the decision-making process of corporate enterprises. It will become central to cost considerations and product development and critical to ensure access to global markets. No longer can any country, public agency or corporate enterprise insulate itself from the effects of environmental degradation and ecological imbalances, caused by itself or by others.

The environment is indivisible. It is difficult to appropriate the ownership or cost of its exploitation and degradation. Since environmental impacts are not limited to the regions where actions causing them were initiated, the task has become formidable.

The key principles of environmental systems are as follows:

- Recognise that environmental management is among the highest corporate priorities.
- Establish and maintain communications with internal and external interested parties.
- Determine the legislative requirements and environmental aspects associated with the organisation's activities, products and services.
- Develop management and employee commitment to the protection of the environment, with clear assignment of accountability and responsibility.
- Encourage 'cradle-to-grave' environment strategic planning, i.e., throughout the product or process life cycle.
- Establish disciplined management process for achieving targeted performance levels.
- Provide appropriate and sufficient resources, including training to achieve targeted performance levels on an ongoing basis.
- Evaluate environmental performance against appropriate policies, objectives and targets, and seek improvement where appropriate.
- Establish a management process to review and audit the EMS and to identify opportunities for improvement of the system and resulting environmental performance.
- Encourage contractors and suppliers to establish an EMS (Environment Management System).

Environmental Clearance Procedures

Under the Environment (Protection) Act, 1986, 24 categories of projects and industries require environmental clearance from the Central Government. In addition, any project proposed to be located within 10 kms of the boundary of a reserved forest or a designated ecologically sensitive area or within 25 kms of the boundary of a national park or sanctuary require environmental clearance from the Central Government. For all other projects, environmental clearance need to be obtained from the state government. Clearance is required from the environmental (for site clearance) and pollution control angle, which has to be obtained by all units other than certain specified non-polluting units in the small-scale sector. No objection certificate for the site clearance usually involves clearance from the concerned State Pollution Control Board. NOC is also required for adequacy of pollution control measures. In general, the State Pollution Control Board is the authority concerned which usually specifies certain pollution control measures to be taken by the unit.

The Environment Rules

1. Apply to the Union Ministry of Environment and Forests for obtaining a pollution clearance certificate.
2. Obtain a No Objection Certificate from the office of the State Pollution Control Board.
3. Provide a copy of the Project Report to the State Pollution Control Board.
4. Provide a copy of the Risk Analysis Report to the Union Ministry of Environment and Forests.
5. Submit a comprehensive rehabilitation programme to the ministry if more than 1,000 people will be displaced.
6. Provide evidence of water supply connection to the ministry.
7. Provide evidence of electricity connection to the ministry.

8. Submit Form XIII for the consent of the ministry to establish an industrial unit under the Water (Prevention and Control of Pollution) Act, 1974.
9. Submit Forms I and XII for the consent of the ministry to establish and operate an industrial unit under the Air (Prevention and Control of Pollution) Act, 1981.
10. Provide evidence of installing an Effluent Treatment Plant (ETP) on the factory premises to the ministry.
11. Provide a chart of the manufacturing process to the ministry.
12. In case the industrialist is an importer of environment-sensitive items, apply to the DGFT for an import licence.

Environment Management

The small-scale sector which accounts for a significant portion of the total industrial production in the country is yet to adopt pollution control measures on a significant scale. Environment management has, therefore, been identified by the Bank as a thrust area for assisting the SSI units in complying with pollution control norms. Taking cognizance of the limitations in ensuring unit-level pollution abatement measures by the small-scale units, the route common to treatment facilities is being encouraged especially in case of homogeneous group of units located in clusters.

ISO 14000: Environmental Management Systems

ISO 9000, the corporate *mantra* that has swept India over the last five years has made corporations aware of the quality of products and processes required to attain world-class standards. But not any more... By March 1996, when the ISO 14000 draft for Environment Management Systems (EMS) superseding the ISO 9000 is expected to be finalised, the mad rush for accreditation under this system will begin. An audit of the corporation's EMS will be essential for exporting to the European Community, NAFTA, APEC, and other trade blocs.

An EMS provides order and consistency to organisational efforts that address environmental concerns through allocation of resources, assignment of responsibilities, and ongoing evaluation of practices, procedures and processes. As environmental management is part of an organisation's overall responsibility, its structure, process, policies and objectives need to be integrated with current efforts in other areas such as operations, finance, quality, marketing, etc.

Image Damage	**Low**	**High**
High	Reactive threat driven	Reactive legislation driven
Low	Discretionary management driven	Reactive communications driven

As in the case of ISO 9000, the ISO 14000 framework has the following components: Commitment and Policy, Planning, implementation, Measurement and Evaluation, Review and Improvement. The key principles for managers, as enumerated in the draft include:

The quality paradigm has helped managers refocus their mindsets from one that viewed defects as an inevitable by-product of the manufacturing process to one that viewed defects as a result of inefficiencies in product and process design. Similarly, the environment paradigm will hopefully refocus managerial mindsets from one that is focussed on pollution control for one that focusses on environment management, by changing over from the view that effort on pollution reduction and prevention adds to costs, slows down progress and makes companies uncompetitive to one that regards pollution as a result of incomplete, inefficient or ineffective use of resources, and enables companies to increase competitiveness by improving their resource utilisation.

CONCLUSION

The entrepreneur's concern for the environment is not merely a social obligation, but a hardcore business proposition. Indian entrepreneurs need to awaken themselves urgently to the environmental imperatives facing them, and integrate environmental perspectives within their business strategies for organisational development. Environment is a key issue of sustained industrial growth.

30 CHAPTER
ENTREPRENEURIAL DEVELOPMENT

"The strategic use of human resources will differentiate better-run firms from the rest."

— H. Mafatlal, CEO, Mafatlal Industries

LEARNING OBJECTIVES

Entrepreneurship development and training is one of the key elements for development of micro, small and medium enterprises (MSMEs), particularly the first generation entrepreneurs.

The main objective of this chapter is to enlighten the students/teachers with the varied gamut of entrepreneurial development. It focusses on knowledge, vision, education, training, etc.

The Chapter discusses:

- Approaches – Human Resource Development.
- The need.
- Appropriate design.
- Objectives.
- Structuring.
- Discipline.
- Issues, and
- Strategy

EDP is an effective technique aimed at developing human resources, particularly in strengthening skills and capabilities to succeed in translating one's dreams into a reality. And, more importantly to lead by example.

INTRODUCTION

Entrepreneurship development and training is one of the key elements for development of micro, small and medium enterprises (MSMEs), particularly, the National Institute of Small Industry Extension Training (NISIET), Hyderabad. The Indian Institute of Entrepreneurship (IIE), Guwahati, and the National Institute of Entrepreneurship and Small Business Development (NIESBUD), Noida have been set up as national-level institutions for promotion of MSMEs through training and entrepreneurship development. To promote and assist entrepreneurship development in the country, the Ministry has also been implementing (in addition to the schemes of SIDO) two important schemes, namely, promotion of entrepreneurship development institutions (EDI) and scheme of National Entrepreneurship Development Board (NEDB). The main objective of these programmes are: (i) promoting entrepreneurship for creating self-employment through enterprise creation; (ii) facilitating creation of training in infrastructure; and (iii) supporting research of entrepreneurship related issues.

An entrepreneur is one of the most important inputs in the economic development of a country or of regions within the country. Entrepreneurial competence makes all the difference to the rate of economic growth. In India, state and private entrepreneurship coexist. The small-scale industrial sector and business are left completely to private entrepreneurs. Entrepreneurship development and small-scale industry development are the obverse and reverse of the same coin. The small-scale enterprise is a breeding ground for entrepreneurship. Conversely, that the rapid growth of small-scale sector is mainly due to the entrepreneurship development is also true. It is, therefore, in this context that an increasingly important role has been assigned for the identification and promotion of entrepreneurs to this sector.

Box 30.1 Starting from Scratch

All successful programmes and initiatives for developing leadership talent within an organisation are created for one single purpose: to support important business needs. These programmes are an integral part of running the day-to-day business of the company. They fuel growth while fulfilling the needs of human capital and leadership.

Most companies are not sure where to begin, others don't believe they can build leadership from scratch. Yet others start from scratch, launch costly initiatives with a variety of programmes, but with no real plan to build a system that will sustain good leadership.

The truth is: great leadership programmes are not programmes at all. They are essential processes for driving the business.

Everything in leadership begins and ends with business. A leadership strategy needs to define how you will support your business strategy. It is a fundamental part of running the business, and needs to run across selecting, developing, assessing and compensating your leaders.

Identifying Critical Capabilities

First, you need to identify the critical capabilities you will need in your leaders so that you realise your long-term business goals. Each organisation is different and these differences will dictate a different and unique competency model. However, while good processes allow executive teams to assess their needs and rethink their strategy, they need to be kept in perspective.

A good competency model is a starting place for a dialogue and discussion of what's required, and its sole function should be to add clarity to expectations. You need to choose the critical behaviours that will define the success of your leaders, which will create clarity of what's really important for your business and industry.

Two factors decide how well a leader fits with his or her role: the business strategy and the amount of change in the environment.

Business Strategy

There is no universal best-leader model that describes ideal leadership characteristics and strategies. Business strategy can be broadly classified into two – growth strategy and return strategy. Having a growth strategy means you pursue profits primarily by expanding sales, while having a return strategy means you will compete on the basis of having a more efficient organisation than your competitors. Both these strategies require different sets of skill and capabilities from the leadership team.

Starting from scratch isn't easy, but it can be done. Sometimes, it's easier to start from scratch than to dismantle bad processes and then workout a new strategy.

Finding and developing leaders will become more challenging in the future than it is today. The future poses new challenges and greater speed and complexity, but also opportunities to develop leadership capability more effectively.

The great companies of the future will be those that recognise the new challenges early, and respond aggressively with the help of a strong senior team, a focus on their best talent and doing the right programmes the right way.

Source: *The Economic Times,* 28 November, 2003.

Peter Drucker, the well-known management expert, defines an entrepreneur as one who always searches for change, responds to it and exploits it as an opportunity. Entrepreneurs innovate and innovation is a specific instrument of entrepreneurship, according to one definition that has emerged very recently, and an entrepreneur is a person who senses opportunity for economic gains in the socio-economic spheres around him and initiates activity leading to production/distribution/service, through interaction of men and materials. Entrepreneurship involves taking risks or making investment under conditions of uncertainty and to innovate, plan and take decisions so as to increase production, productivity and profits. Growth-oriented development is the cornerstone of entrepreneurs.

APPROACHES TO ENTREPRENEURSHIP DEVELOPMENT

There are various approaches to entrepreneurship development which policymakers, planners, trainers and other officials involved in development may choose. Such development could be achieved within the conceptual framework in which the various strategies and policies of an entrepreneurship development programme are evolved or formulated. There is need for a thorough discussion of the various theories and their implications for the organisation's resources and capabilities. But however it is approached, entrepreneurship development should be viewed in the total perspective and should integrate entrepreneurial training, provision of incentives, consultancy services, sectoral development and other essential strategies of intervention. There are at least four major approaches.

HUMAN RESOURCES DEVELOPMENT

The issue of human resources development is very important in small-scale industries. Since it is people-oriented and labour-intensive, developing the human resource is a *sine qua non* in the development. Human resources development as defined by Harbison and Myer, "is the process of increasing the knowledge, the skills and the capacities of all the people in society. In economic terms, it could be described as the accumulation of human capital and its effective investment in the development of an economy". It is achieved more effectively through training, education, information and scholastic exchange, but also as the supply and demand of manpower, with a view to improving employment generation and income distribution and supporting the expanded socio-economic development activities of the country. Human resources development is the key to the growth of small-scale industries.

The Meaning

Entrepreneurial Development Programme (EDP) means programme designed to help a person in strengthening his entrepreneurial motive and in acquiring skills and capabilities necessary for playing his entrepreneurial role effectively. Towards this end, it is necessary to promote his understanding of motives, motivation pattern, their impact on behaviour and entrepreneurial value. A programme which seeks to do this can qualify to be called an EDP. This has to be stressed here, because there are a number of programmes which aim at providing informational or managerial inputs or focus on preparation of a project. Although all these inputs are required by a new entrepreneur, a programme not touching entrepreneurial motivation and behaviour cannot be called an EDP.

The Need

The need for a broad-based entrepreneurial class in India arises from the need to speed up the process of activating the factors of production, leading to a higher rate of economic growth, dispersal of economic activities, development of backward and tribal areas, creation of employment opportunities, improvement in the standard of living of the weaker sections of the society and involvement of all sections of the society in the process of economic growth.

In India, some of the management schools at the top end of the ladder do have some courses for SSE promotion in their regular MBA programmes. But taken together, they are doing pretty little for the development of entrepreneurship.

In advanced countries like the United States or Britain, small business study forms a significant part of management education.

Generally, small business studies are offered as optional in the second half of the programme. During the course of the study, not only various aspects of small business management are discussed, but the students prepare their business plans (project reports) and make tie-ups with financial institutions.

Thus, the MBA course offers him a sound education in general management with special orientation in small business enterprises. Recognising the importance of SSEs, it was only recently that the National Westminster Bank instituted a chair for a Small Business Professor at the Cornfield School of Management in Britain.

Though EDP has been recognised as an effective human resource development tool, many a times there are many expectations from a single programme, like removing unemployment, enhancing industrial development, promoting small-scale industries, developing industrially underdeveloped regions, etc.

EDP is primarily meant for developing those first generation entrepreneurs, who on their own cannot become successful entrepreneurs. It covers three major variables: location, target group and enterprise (entrepreneurial activities). Any of these can become the focus or starting point for initiating and implementing an EDP. The remaining two then will follow by making proper synthesis with the first. As for example, if the objective is to promote women entrepreneurs, suitable location and proper entrepreneurial activities must match or if the objective is to develop North-East region, then the potential target group and feasible entrepreneurial ventures must follow.

EDP by itself therefore aims at achieving the specific objectives of the programmes and therefore cannot create any magical result. It is a continuous process of training and motivating then to set up profitable enterprises in large measure.

Appropriate Design

It is now well recognised that entrepreneurs can be developed through appropriately designed entrepreneurship development programmes. These programmes broadly envisage a three-tiered approach: developing achievement motivation and sharpening of entrepreneurial traits and behaviour, project planning and development and guidance on industrial opportunities, incentives and facilities and rules and regulations, and developing managerial and operational capabilities. Various techniques and approaches have been developed and adopted to achieve these objectives, keeping in view the target-groups and/or target-areas. The structuring of the programmes and training methodology also necessitate the consideration of the specific target-groups and target-areas. Methodology for selection of the prospective entrepreneurs as well as support services after the training have a significant impact on the success of the entrepreneur development programmes.

Combined Courses May Help

In our management schools too, full-time courses in small business management should be offered in the MBA programme. These courses should focus on manufacturing and service sectors. Management schools can also help existing SSEs through part-time courses. As many of the management schools are located near the technological institutions, it is possible to have combined programmes for both technological and managerial areas. This will also enable technology students intending to start ventures to have adequate management education.

Possibly, in the long-run, association with SSEs can lead to short courses and consultancy, not only to bridge the gap between theory and practice, but also as a source of revenue.

It is not claimed here that all the problems of SSE development can be solved by the introduction of small business studies in management schools. Far from it, the idea is to remove as many constraints as possible for industrial development. These programmes oriented to entrepreneurship. Creativity and innovation can help sustain a healthy growth of small business.

ENTREPRENEURSHIP DEVELOPMENT PROGRAMME

Past endurance has shown that industrial promotion by provision of facilities, technical assistance, management training and consultancy, industrial information and other services alone are not sufficient to develop entrepreneurs. It was concluded that the focal point should be aimed at the overlooked entrepreneurial spirit and entrepreneurial characteristics of the people to be developed. The EDP package was therefore launched.

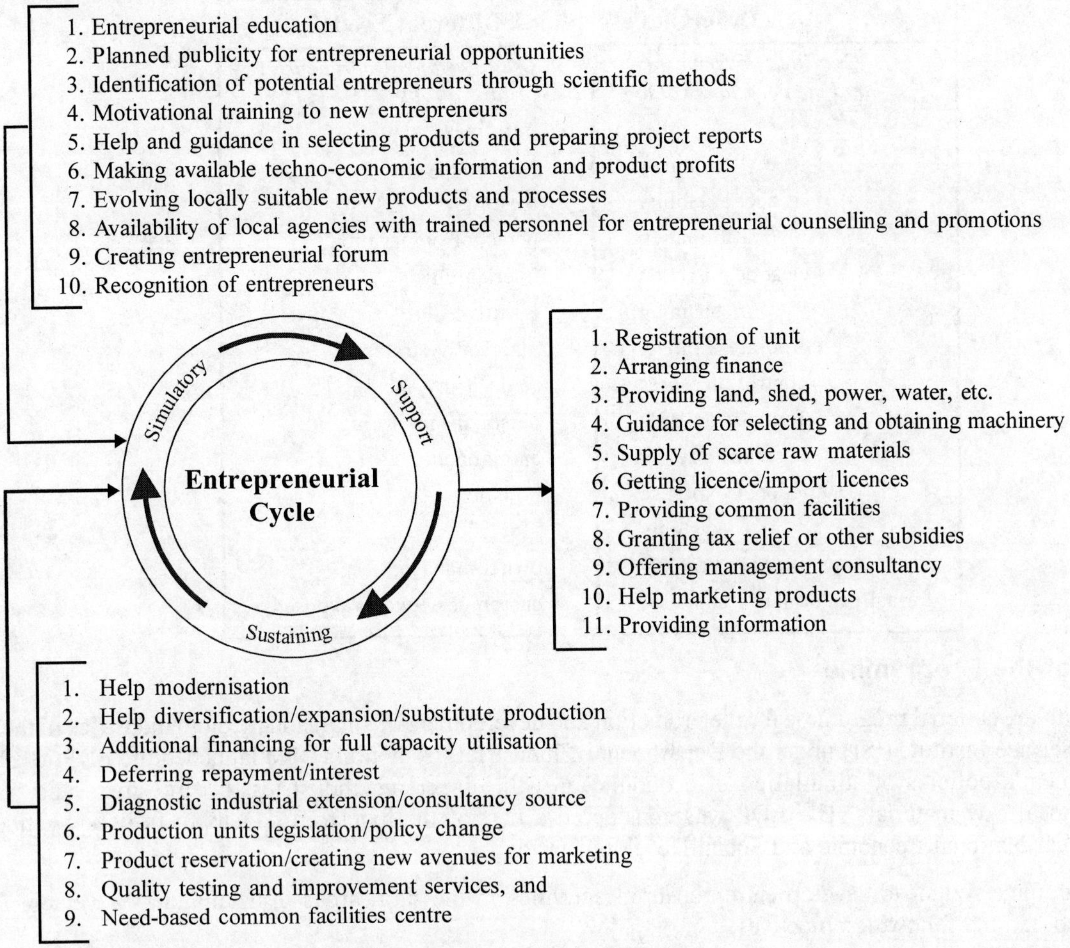

Fig. 30.1 Entrepreneurial Development Cycle

A Complex Phenomenon

Entrepreneurial development is a complex phenomenon. Entrepreneurs play a key role in the economic development of a country. Importance of the development of entrepreneurship as an ingredient of economic development has been recognised a long time back. It was as early as 1950 that the need for entrepreneurial development was first felt and since then a substantial amount of research has gone into this sphere. It is a well-known fact that entrepreneurs are not born and can be made in the sense that the quality can be improved. In our country where human resources are to be found in plenty, we can identify individuals in all segments of the population who have the requisite entrepreneurial skills. But it requires to mould them, motivate them and train them through proper Entrepreneurial Development Programmes (EDPs) for undertaking risk-bearing ventures. Thus, the EDPs become a vital approach for harnessing the vast untapped human skills, to channelise them into accelerating industrialisation in general and growth of the small-scale sector in particular. It is also observed by several scientists like McClelland, that with proper training provided to the right kind of persons, entrepreneurship could be developed.

Of late, entrepreneurship development has become extremely important in achieving the goals of all-round development in the country. Consequently, many entrepreneurial opportunities are emerging in various fields. Be it electronic, medicine, engineering, agriculture, communication, atomic energy, telecommunication, food technology and packaging, entrepreneurial opportunities have surfaced at rapid pace in all these and many other areas. Such opportunities, however, become more perceptible to entrepreneurs if they are exposed to the latest development in the respective fields either in terms of technology, use or style of living. Accessibility and understanding of such information widens the base of opportunity sensing by potential entrepreneurs.

Different Perceptions, Different Needs	
Qualities governments and corporations value vs.	*Qualities of entrepreneurial organisations*
order	untidiness
formality	informality
accountability	trusting
information	personal observation
clear demarcation	overlapping
planning	intuitive
corporate strategy	"tactically strategic"
control measures	"I do it my way"
formal standards	personal monitoring
transparency	ambiguous
functional expertise	holistic
systems	"feely"
positional authority	owner managed
formal performance appraisal	customer/network exposed

Objectives of the Programme

In line with the national programme for the promotion and development of small and medium industries in the countryside, the Industrial Service Institute (ISI) under the Department of Industrial Promotion (DIP) launched the EDP to give substance to the government's policies of stimulation of economic growth, dispersing industries to rural areas and promoting the processing of local raw materials. The EDP was considered a part of the industrial development policy articulated in the present Five-Year National Economic and Social Development Plan.

The programme sought to develop entrepreneurial activities in the rural areas of Thailand as a vehicle for economic growth and also had the following objectives:

(a) To promote the development of small and medium enterprises that would encourage self-employment among potential entrepreneurs;

(b) To provide, in the rural areas, special programmes designed to stimulate new ventures and encourage expansion of existing activities of small and medium industries;

(c) To generate employment and self-employment in the processing of indigenous raw materials for local consumption and for export;

(d) To develop entrepreneurial capabilities for potential entrepreneurs and upgrade managerial skills of existing entrepreneurs.

From a sound training programme for entrepreneurship development in India, the expert group constituted by the NIESBUD accepted that it must be able to help selected entrepreneurs to:

(a) Develop and strengthen their entrepreneurial quality/motivation;

(b) Analyse environment related to both small industry and small business;

(c) Select project/product;

(d) Formulate projects;

(e) Understand the process and procedure of setting up of small enterprise;

(f) Know and influence the source of help support needed for launching the enterprise.

(g) Acquire the basic management skills;

(h) Know the pros and cons of being an entrepreneur; and

(i) Acquaint and appreciate the needed social responsibility/entrepreneurial disciplines.

Some of the other important aspects of entrepreneurial training are:

(i) To let him set or reset the objectives of his business and work individually and along with his group for their realisation.

(ii) To prepare him for accepting totally unforeseen risks of business for a long time after such training.

(iii) To enable him to take strategic decisions.

(iv) To enable him to build an integrated team equal to the demands of tomorrow.

(v) To communicate fast, clearly and effectively.

(vi) To develop a broad vision to see the business as a whole and to integrate his function with it.

(vii) To enable him to relate his product and industry to the total environment; to find what is significant in it and to take it into account in his decisions and actions.

(viii) To enable him to cope with and coordinate the different types of paperwork, most of which is statutorily obligatory.

(ix) To make him subscribe to industrial democracy, that is, accepting workers as partners in enterprise.

(x) To strengthen his passion for integrity, honesty and compliance with law which is the key to success in the long-run.

Entrepreneurial Behaviours

- grasping opportunity
- taking initiative
- solving problems creatively
- managing autonomously
- taking responsibility for, and ownership of things
- seeing things through
- networking effectively to manage interdependence
- putting things together creatively
- using judgement to take calculated risk.

Entrepreneurial Attributes

- achievement orientation and ambition
- self-confidence and self-esteem
- perseverance
- high internal locus of control (autonomy)
- action orientation
- preference for learning by doing
- hard-working
- determination
- creativity

Entrepreneurial Skills

- creative problem-solving
- persuading
- negotiating
- selling
- proposing
- holistically managing business/projects/situations
- strategic thinking

- intuitive decision-making under uncertainty
- networking.

STRUCTURING ENTREPRENEURIAL DEVELOPMENT PROGRAMMES

The above case studies bring out certain features important for the success of entrepreneurial development programmes. The training programme aims at identification and careful selection of entrepreneurs (using advanced series of psychological tests), developing the motivation and entrepreneurial capabilities of the trainees, equipping the trainees to identify viable industrial projects and to prepare project profiles or brief project reports, equipping the trainees with basic enterprise-building skills, imparting basic managerial skills required for the successful management of the unit and helping the trainees to secure the necessary financial, infrastructural and related assistance during the implementation of the project. Skill training formed a vital and major component of this programme.

Entrepreneurship development model/promotion are prerequisites for entrepreneurial development programme training.

The entire infrastructure of an area should be reviewed. Entrepreneurs require various levels of assistance and support in arranging finance, plant and machinery, land, ready-made sheds, power, raw materials and finally information relating to the industry. The support activities provide nurturing and help entrepreneurship to grow and survive. The inadequacy of the support system may impede provision of timely help to entrepreneurs. The coordinator of the entrepreneurial training programme may convene a meeting of various developmental agencies to elicit their cooperation.

Survey of Entrepreneurial Opportunities

It consists of identifying viable industrial activities and enterprises based on demand and resources and the extent of competition. Although the emphasis is to be given to demand of an area, the adjoining areas having linkages and the requirement of a region should also be considered. The objective of a survey is to identify opportunities in industries and other activities which offer a promising future for entrepreneurs.

Selection of Entrepreneurs

Selection methodology is a critical input in the entrepreneurship development scheme. If the entrepreneurs are not properly selected, the entire programme can be affected; and this has a direct bearing on the success rate to stand guarantee for the young entrepreneurs. Continuous and sustained follow-up action was undertaken. This was the responsibility of the project officer and the assistant project officer. A success rate of 60 per cent was attained. The state government later gave assistance to the institutes for conducting entrepreneurial development programmes for unemployment engineers, diploma holders, graduates and ITI trained boys and the institute has done fairly well.

Experiences in EDPs Abroad

It will not be out of place to touch upon the experiences of some foreign countries in the area of entrepreneurship development. In a recent workshop organised by the East-West Centre Technology Institute, Hawaii, the EDP experiences of various countries were discussed which revealed that training made positive contributions in the performance of entrepreneurs. The non-entrepreneurial participants were motivated to start a business. The general conclusion was that EDPs could be developed as a valid substitute for natural institutions (i.e., business families). The experiences of other institutions like Development Technology Centre, Institute of Technology, Bandung Institute of Psychology, University of Indonesia, Jakarta also reiterate that EDPs have a great scope in increasing the number of new entrepreneurs to accelerate the process of industrialisation.

The basic features of the EDP has gone through several modifications overtime as:

(a) Identification and careful selection of entrepreneurs for training;

(b) Developing the entrepreneurial capabilities of the trainee;

(c) Equipping the trainee with the basic managerial understanding and strategies;

(d) Ensuring a viable industrial project for each potential entrepreneur;

(e) Helping him to secure the necessary financial, infrastructural and related assistance; and

(f) Training cost is highly subsidised and only token fee is charged. A deposit is, however, taken to ensure commitment of participants.

Entrepreneurial Discipline

Entrepreneurs who are developed and promoted at social cost have a certain responsibility to the society that promotes and supports them. The society expects adequate returns from these people. Towards this end, entrepreneurs are expected to follow a certain discipline which is essential for entrepreneurial career. This covers subjects like:

1. Repayment behaviour – Financial management.
2. Response to tax and statutory requirement – Law and compliances.
3. Progressive outlook towards labour – Labour management.
4. Care for ecology and environment – Environment management.

Issues of Entrepreneurial Development Programmes

The present stage of development of EDP as a factor continuation to the industrialisation of backward and other areas needs a proper direction and organisation for making it more effective and purposeful. The contribution of EDP is very uneven among regions and definite programmes need to be chalked out to bring about some degree of uniformity and upgradation. Before this is tackled, some important issues need immediate attention. They are detailed below for consideration.

1. Structure and Composition of EDPs: The structure and content of EDPs, taking into account the regional variations, need to be streamlined. The programme should have a practical content and needs a lot of inter-institutional organisational arrangement to make it a success. The successful EDPs have, at their base, the inter-institutional cooperation or an institution such as Gujarat Centre of the State Bank of India, which besides conducting the programmes also arranges for finance and other input for the entrepreneurs. The EDPs conducted in isolation would dissipate resources and talents. The issue, therefore, for effective functioning of EDPs is to have financial agency strongly backing up efforts of the Entrepreneurial Development. The place and role of Technical Consistency Organisations (TCOs) need to be reviewed and their activities suitably accelerated. Who should conduct an EDP is an important issue.

2. Areas of Operation: As has been stated earlier, in the North-Eastern area, entrepreneurial development activities are lacking the support activities of the financial institutions. In these areas, programmes have to be linked with support activities.

3. Fixing Priorities: Another area of fixing the priorities of EDPs is to consider their working in terms of efficiency and social need (justice) criteria. Evaluation of EDPs have revealed that those who have business experience, education and skills are proving successful entrepreneurs. This source should be tapped first and then go to the stratum to cover entrepreneurs from the non-traditional class, i.e., without business and industrial experience, but having the potential of becoming successful entrepreneurs. Next come the entrepreneurs belonging to backward and other communities who have to overcome many additional handicaps to become successful entrepreneurs. A proper course counter of EDPs has to be developed to meet the specific requirements of each of these three strata of entrepreneurs in proper balance, without sacrificing the efficiency criteria.

4. Lack of Specialists' Support: Entrepreneurship is a comparatively new area of study requiring inter-disciplinary efforts by people from different disciplines. A large number of organisations/agencies engaged in entrepreneurship development in India do not have in-house specialists required and have to depend upon external faculty. The number of specialists available in the country for developing small-scale industries is not very large. As a result, many a time organisations are unable to locate/ avail services of experts. On the other hand, there are specialists who have time to spare in which they can render their services to the organisations.

This apart, the ED programmes in India are afflicted with a number of operational problems. As such, though there are many institutions to train entrepreneurs, the growth of entrepreneurs is inhibited by these problems. The operational problems of EDP are as follows:

(a) Inherent inability,

(b) Diverse opinions,

(c) No proper strategy,

(d) Low institutional commitment,

(e) No local support,

(f) Non-availability of inputs,
(g) Poor follow-up,
(h) No adequate research facilities,
(i) Ill-planned training methodology,
(j) Inconsistent programme design,
(k) Perpetual ambiguity,
(l) No clear-cut objective,
(m) Lack of clarity in approach, and
(n) Lack of creativity and commitment.

- There appears to be inherent inability to identify the need of the institution and differences of opinion prevailing amongst the practitioners and also amongst the trainers.
- There seems to be low institutional commitment for local support to entrepreneurs and there is low involvement of marketing, voluntary and financial institutions in the programme, except for a few.
- Non-availability of various inputs, i.e., raw materials, power, etc., and infrastructural support entwined with poor follow-up by the primary monitoring institution, results in the failure of EDP.
- There seems to be ill-planned training methodology, inconsistency in programme design, its content, sequence and themes and focus of the programme is not clear.
- Training institutions do not show much concern for objective identification and selection of entrepreneurs and the follow-up training.
- Some of the institutions seem to be still debating whether to look for proper identification and selection of entrepreneurs for making successful entrepreneurs.
- Those involved and concerned with the 'selection and follow-up' activities have either limited manpower support or a narrow linkage with other support agencies.
- There does not appear to be standard course curricula even in terms of broad module being adopted by such institutions.
- Majority of the institutions engaged in EDP are themselves not convinced of what they are doing as a task delegated by the government of helping the policy in attaining its social objectives.
- Perceptual ambiguity of the EDP objective seems to have percolated to grassroot level with a significant distortion both in terms of content and intent.

To conclude, it can be stated that many of the issues related to an EDP are conceptual in nature, many are practical and operational and many are in the borderline between concept and practice. Research and studies, building sophisticated skills and expertise, coordinating, collaborating, corroboration of ideas and actions are necessary strategies that should be continuously pursued to confront these issues.

In the post-independence period, the nation laid stress and put its faith in science and technology. The country has made tremendous investments in scientific institutions and scientific and technical manpower. These investments need to be harvested. We have learnt that the managerial skills necessary to harvest businesses are different from the skills required to create businesses. Similarly, to create technology enterprises, we may also require a different breed of managers in our institutions. Development of technical entrepreneurship and the management of science and technology cannot be dealt with in mutual exclusion.

Strategy for Entrepreneurship Development

Keeping this background in view, the following strategies of entrepreneurship development in India may be suggested:

(i) Public entrepreneurship should remain confined only to those industries and sectors where private enterprise, individual or corporate, is generally not attracted. Existing public entrepreneurship should be improved through better management and by putting relatively greater emphasis on research and development. There is need to streamline the R&D wing of public sector enterprises.

(ii) All possible efforts be made very seriously for the development of an industrial culture. It should be realised that the central core of entrepreneurship is the motive force since an appropriate entrepreneurship implies positive action and initiative. Motivated individuals with combination of abilities and attributes can pursue their goal with enthusiasm. One can easily give examples of men like J.N. Tata or Ranchodlal Chhotalal who established their enterprises against heavy odds in the country under British rule. Without motivation, an individual cannot become a successful entrepreneur even though he may have access to finance. Individual qualities of vision, vigour, leadership and enterprise need to be inculcated.

(iii) There is a need to develop management education and industrial training. In modern times, management education is being viewed as an effective supplement to the development of entrepreneurship since entrepreneurial decisions have to be effectively supported by managerial decisions. Quite often, the entrepreneur functions a manager especially in small-scale industries where the entrepreneur is his own technician and manager. This fact justifies the route of formal education and necessitates the establishment of business schools and management institutes in the country, where relevant courses may be introduced. Happily, some such institutions have come up but they should further be strengthened and developed into first-class institutions comparable with their counterparts in developed countries. In addition, facilities should be provided on an increasing scale for sending talented young men and women to business schools abroad. But, strategies should be chalked out to give a conducive environment for them to come back to India and apply this knowledge in a suitable manner. Besides, industrial training programmes should be frequently organised. This will help in widening the mental horizon toward practical business and industrial problems. New industrial training centres well equipped may as well be established. Education and training will very much help in developing and augmenting a race of new entrepreneurs needed to harness and utilise the scarce resources for economic development.

(iv) The development of backward regions/areas constitutes a new challenge. Programmes for their development be drawn up and should be effectively implemented. Such programmes await new entrepreneurs whose technical expertise and managerial competence would bring about the desired development and fulfil social needs.

(v) Adequate measures are a must for mobilising and fostering entrepreneurial talent in the country. In this context, it should be realised that entrepreneurs are not the gift of a particular class. For instance, in Japan, innovators came from the underprivileged classes as the affluent classes had hardly any incentive to innovate. "Innovating entrepreneurs have frequently come from those classes of people normally barred from advancement to status-bearing positions."

(vi) Economic administration by the state should be improved and made more effective so that objectives of economic policies may be fully achieved in the overall interest of the country's economy. Better economic administration would go a long way in ensuring and increasing entrepreneurship. Monopoly benefits to a few big entrepreneurs is an evil and must be checked. The general policy of encouraging the small entrepreneur will go a long way in activating and broadening the leadership potential. Improvement in business climate by the state through its well-designed economic policies, be it fiscal, commercial, industrial or agricultural will benefit the entrepreneurs in a changing technological society and thus facilitate healthy development of entrepreneurship.

(vii) Institutional framework should work towards meeting major industrial or economic needs or goals. Such framework, in addition to its several facets, must place entrepreneurial development and its objectives in a proper and meaningful perspective following which entrepreneurs may plan their business activities within the bounds of such a framework for the desired coordinated development.

(viii) Greater emphasis should be put on research relating to processes and enhancement of the value of indigenous techniques. This would have an encouraging impact on entrepreneurship and technology at the domestic level. As a general rule, Indianisation of entrepreneurship should be effected in place of foreign collaboration. However, general guidelines should be stated for cases in which foreign collaboration with well-known foreign companies may be allowed.

(ix) Financial institutions should provide adequate and timely credit and technical assistance, especially to small and medium-sized enterprises. They should also impart knowledge about the needs of the economy and they should file their massive data in terms of growth of new entrants or entrepreneurs in the field of industry. These may as well be dwelt upon at length in their reports and other publications. All this will go a long way in inculcating and sustaining entrepreneurial spirit in the newly-emerging classes.

(x) Now, special categories of entrepreneurs, viz., women, retired army personnel, handicapped persons, educated youths, Non-resident Indians (NRIs), displaced persons, etc., have appeared on the economic scene. Their emergence is more directly conditioned by economic and industrial factors and not only by social factors of caste, community and social approval or disapproval. Factors like access to capital, business experience, opportunity to acquire technical and managerial competence have played a crucial role. For instance, in the case of light engineering products, electronics, computers and in several other new products, the entrepreneurial source is generally not traceable to any specific caste or community background. The entrepreneurs in such fields are usually technologists and in their endeavour to establish manufacturing units, they reveal a multiple basis of entrepreneurship, viz., foreign collaboration, diversification, etc. Conducive working environment should be ensured for the healthy development of such entrepreneurs in future. It is only then that their qualities of vision, vigour, leadership and enterprise can be well utilised for the industrial development of the country.

Entrepreneurship is not confined to industry and is needed in all activities. Its existence in agriculture among the cultivators, small and large, is seen by all today. The growing farm of today in many parts of the country is a proof of such entrepreneurship. The need for entrepreneurship is even greater in management of the government, more so as it is the largest entrepreneur.

India has a proud record of entrepreneurship. Its present growing status in the industrial world is its proof. It has now to prepare itself for entrepreneurship of a different order. Tremendous advances of science and technology will have to be harnessed and incorporated requiring on the part of the people and the government a more mature approach to be on par with advanced countries. Philips, Sony, Honda, Ford are the signposts of entrepreneurship today for all to emulate. Some of these have come up only in recent years and from small beginnings. In India, too, one sees glimpses of such entrepreneurship.

CONCLUSION

It is now well recognised that entrepreneurs can be developed through appropriately designed entrepreneurship development programmes. These programmes broadly envisage a three-tiered approach: developing achievement motivation and sharpening of entrepreneurial traits and behaviour, project planning and development and guidance on industrial opportunities, incentives and facilities and rules and regulations, and developing managerial and operational capabilities. Various techniques and approaches have been developed and adopted to achieve these objectives, keeping in view the target-groups and/or target-areas. The structuring of the programmes and training methodology also necessitate consideration of the specific target-groups and target-areas. Methodology for selection of the prospective entrepreneurs as well as support services after the training have significant impact on the success of the entrepreneur development programmes.

More importantly, the government and the financial institutions are in forefront in entrepreneurial development. However, it is said that various training programmes of these institutions work at training people for self-employment to acquire gainful employment. Thus, the very purpose of developing entrepreneurial talent among the youths is defeated. This calls for a critical evaluation of EDPs and of personnel with conviction and commitment to undertake the task of planning, designing and implementing programmes in this area. More importantly, entrepreneurial programmes must be attuned to Indian economic environment and be made available in regional languages. The need of the hour is to develop genuine and not imitative entrepreneurs to accelerate the process of industrialisation. The need of the hour is for stimulating innovation and the entrepreneurial spirit to support the development of new ideas through new and mature enterprises.

The entrepreneurs themselves constitute the human factors and their needs as a human being must, therefore, not be overlooked. Being the kingpin in the whole small enterprise development game, the human factors involved in the small and medium-scale industry must be analysed, assisted to grow and develop.

The success of small industries depends upon the entrepreneurial and managerial capabilities of those involved in the business. Because of its size and unique operational characteristics, a small industry requires a management approach which is also unique. In general, small industries are managed in a personalised fashion. Their managers or entrepreneurs tend to know all the employees personally. They participate in all aspects of managing the business and there is usually no sharing in the decision-making process. As far as the scope and scale of operations are concerned, small industries, generally serve a local or regional market rather than a national or international one. They also tend to have a very limited share of any given market. These special characteristics must, therefore, be taken into account in the planning of small industries development on a national scale.

The human factor or the entrepreneur should also be considered. The entrepreneurial spirit, as mentioned earlier, involves not only a desire to gain monetary benefits but also an admixture of the characteristics of a high achiever, and social, family and service motives. Long-term involvement with a goal which the entrepreneur has set for himself creates the need to persist with an undertaking even in the face of difficulties.

Management and entrepreneurial skill must, therefore be blended in the small industry owner's total make-up as these will spell the difference between success and failure. The ideal would be to find a person who is both efficient and effective. Without the latter capabilities, a person may simply be a good manager. He still has to be developed into an effective manager by inculcating the entrepreneurial spirit in him. A small enterprise development programme, therefore, must take into consideration upgrading the managerial and entrepreneurial skills in the whole country in order to create a pool of enlightened entrepreneurs who can form a strong small industry sector in the business community of the country concerned.

31 CHAPTER

ENTREPRENEURIAL TRAINING

"Making a real difference"

"For creating budding entrepreneurs, get a great bunch of people around you. Go into businesses that you have a fascination for – and only go into businesses where you think you can make a real difference. Try to create the best quality businesses in whatever area you go into – and the best value."

— Richard Branson, CEO, Virgin Airlines

LEARNING OBJECTIVES

"Only the learning organisations can cater to today's dramatic demands quickly"

Pradip Khandwalla
Director, IIM-A

The main objective of this study is to focus attention on entrepreneurial training leaders as well as the led. Training is an integral input of entrepreneurs. The aim is to encourage, empower and educate potential as well as aspiring entrepreneurs to create their own business or social enterprise as well as enable them to nurture it through.

Training provides a competitive advantage that is eternally sustainable.

The chapter discusses the following subjects:

- Importance
- Objectives
- Principles
- Design
- Finance and technical support
- Inputs
- Methods
- Course content
- German and Japanese approach
- EDP organisations
- Manpower training

Training is basically to enhance skills – communications, computer literacy – and building competencies — leadership, teamwork.

Building Human Capital

"A great company has to invest in human resources, and that means being very selective about who you recruit, and getting people who meet the right profile in terms of attitudes as well as skills. You must also distinguish between who must be hired versus who can be trained."

— Christopher Lovelock, Service Management Expert

Now is the time to change the world.

Now is the time to connect lives.

Now is the time to break new ground.

Now is the time to explore opportunities.

INTRODUCTION

Training is an integral input of managerial development. The lack of adequate and skilled personnel is one of the bottlenecks in a developing economy. Staff training is essential for entrepreneurs and workers employed in small enterprises.

WHAT IS TRAINING?

Training is the systematic instruction of staff at all levels in new attitudes or new skills; random bits of continuing education or mere learning on-the-job cannot be called *training*: the term implies a scheme of instruction which is more-or-less formal and ongoing, which is planned, systematic, consistent, pervasive and monitored to measure its effectiveness. Although it may be usually reactive to a response to a perceived demand or pressure, it should be developed to become proactive – an advance response, instigating new services, skills and methods, identifying unsuspected problems and leading the way towards an improved standard of service. As a term, it implies a trainer and a trainee; it suggests an institutional context, but it is in fact open to anybody to be a trainee and we should not mislead ourselves into assuming that an institution is essential.

Why Should We Train Staff?

Very few individuals indeed do their jobs in an 'ideal' way, many jobs are done for the wrong reasons or in the wrong place, or by the wrong staff and many jobs that should be done are overlooked. Currently, the pressures on the public sector make any of these 'mistakes' unsupportable. The costs of staff are so great and their role in a service profession so crucial that their work must be demonstrably effective. Effective staff do not happen; they must be created through training.

A service profession must enjoy a careful relationship with its public; attitudes of the staff towards their clientele is the most vital area of training. Banks are becoming more market-oriented; there is change in emphasis and to cope with this, the staff need training to understand the need to change and to become familiar with the needs of their clientele.

All individuals have a need for training; new recruits need induction into the rationale and objectives of their jobs, and need to be trained in specific skills and routines. New professional staff many need additionally a programme of training to enable them to obtain their professional qualifications. Certain individuals may need training for a specific purpose, the development of a new service, taking on a new role in the organisation, preparing for retirement.

But, in a world where development and promotion happen more rarely, everyone still needs training, or rather needs it even more; if a job at any level becomes drudgery, then it cannot be effectively performed. The role of training is to develop the critical awareness of staff and prevent in growth. An employee who can make some appraisal of her or his role, can compare the situation of colleagues elsewhere, and can feel that management promotes this process, is likely to experience satisfaction in the job, however, great the constraints on achievement, And job satisfaction is a clear way towards effectiveness; if individuals at all levels can contribute towards the formulation of goals, then those goals are more likely to be the most appropriate in this context.

Importance of Training

The importance of training employees results in the following advantages:

(i) It makes sure the availability of skilled workers at all levels of management.

(ii) It increases the potential abilities of workers and thus to improve their performance to the maximum attainable level through the training process.

(iii) It enables the workers to perform the work more efficiently and precisely so as to maintain the quality of products.

(iv) It minimises excessive scraps, defects and wastage in the production process.

(v) It minimises the number of accidents, as unskilled and semi-skilled workers are more prone to industrial accidents.

(vi) Training reduces fatigue.

(vii) Training enables the workers to work speedily and thus increases the earning of employees.

(viii) When the speed of production increases, overtime work can be avoided and therefore, the payment of overtime does not arise.

(ix) A trained worker does not feel the need to join other factories and thus reduces the labour turnover.

(x) Training improves the good relations between employees and the management.

(xi) New techniques can be easily adopted through trained employees.

(xii) Standardisation can be adopted in a factory where trained employees are available.

(xiii) Team spirit and teamwork can be promoted when employees are fully trained.

(xiv) Training enable employees to occupy higher position of authority.

(xv) As trained workers do not require any consolation and because of less spoilage resulting from their performance, the supervision cost can be minimised.

Objectives of Training

The training programme is designed to subserve the following objectives:

(i) To impart basic knowledge about the industry, product and production methods;

(ii) To build the necessary skills of new entrepreneurs and workers;

(iii) To assist the entrepreneur/worker to function more effectively in his present position by exposing him to the latest concept, techniques and information;

(iv) To build up a second line of workers and prepare them to shoulder additional responsibility and/or watch on the production of a new product, if there is any diversification;

(v) To expose the entrepreneur to the latest developments which directly or indirectly affect him;

(vi) To broaden the vision of entrepreneurs by providing them suitable opportunities for an interchange of experiences within and outside an industry:

(vii) To impart customer education; and

(viii) To impart knowledge of the marketing goods.

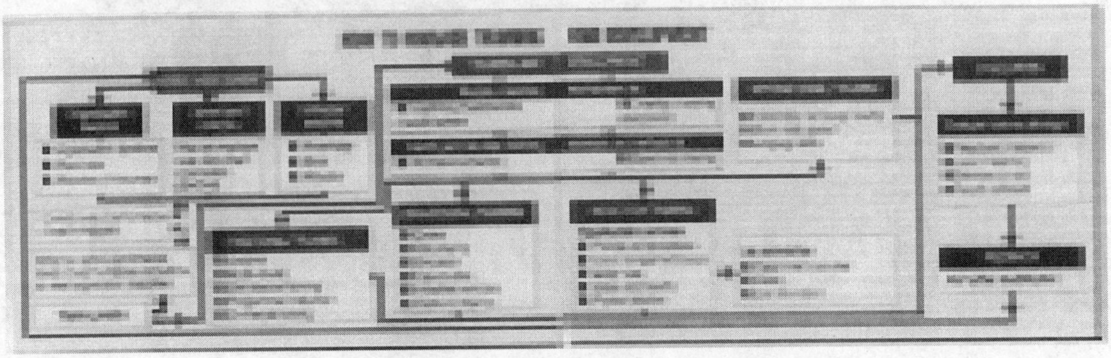

Fig. 31.1 How to Manage Training and Development

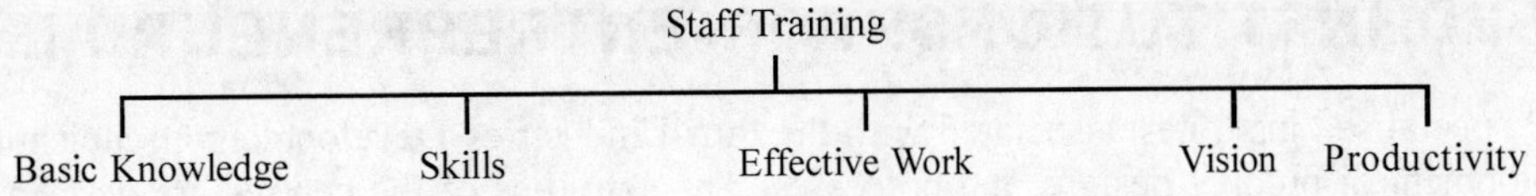

Fig. 31.2 Objectives of Training

The principles of training may be enumerated asunder:

(i) Training should be given in a proper atmosphere and that too systematically through duly qualified and trained instructors.

(ii) Training should be of reasonably long duration so as to enable the workers understand the theory and develop skills for managing the job accurately.

(iii) Training should be given at all levels. This means training programme of a factory should include induction training, job training, training for promotion and refresher training.

(iv) The level of training should be high. It must be comprehensive and the participant should be made familiar with the latest trends in production technology.

(v) Training should consist not only of theory; it should be supplemented by practical training and made interesting to all participants.

Achievement motivation training is designed to increase the achievement orientation of the trainees with the idea that positive behaviour, such as striving for excellence, learning from feedback and moderate risk-taking is required. Likewise, it strengthens the ability of an individual to generate alternatives as well as to solve problems creatively. It also develops the ability to define and set goals in life. As such, entrepreneurship development is viewed as behaviour-oriented. One of the factors contributing to the success of this training intervention in entrepreneurship development is that it is based on experience. In entrepreneurship training, learning by discovery is usually preferred. Here, one is able to learn from one's actions and behaviour in training. The learning process becomes a positive reinforcement.

Although there are some variations of and/or models for this intervention, the overall objective of any achievement motivation training is the transformation of the entrepreneur into a new person as a result of the training. The training intervention may also take the form of management skills development. Most entrepreneurs show lack of managerial skills and unfamiliarity with the management techniques needed to deal with the management problems of the enterprise. Therefore, for any entrepreneurship development programme to succeed, it is important not only to motivate the trainees but also to provide them with all the skills necessary to run their business successfully. In Malaysia, where this training intervention is utilised in entrepreneurship development programmes, Majlis Amanah Rakyat (MARA) maintains a pool of small enterprises to act as hot to the trainees. For two weeks, trainees work in the factories where they obtain practical know-how and guidance on how to manage and operate an enterprise. In turn, MARA hosts the cost of training.

Nurturing Leaders: Mentor-in-chief N.R. Narayana Murthy Addressing Infoscions

SPECIALISED INSTITUTIONS: FOR ENTREPRENEURIAL TRAINING

There are 19 specialised institutes associated with the Small Industries Development Organisation (SIDO) for training research and development of product designs and processes. The activities of the centres are described in the table below:

Table 31.1 Specialised Training Institutes

Name of Institute	Place	Activities
National Institute of Small Industry Extension Training (NISIET)	Hyderabad	Training Research and Consultancy activities
National Institute for Entrepreneurship and Small Business Development (NIESBUD)	New Delhi	Coordinating and overseeing activities of various institutes/agencies engaged in entrepreneurship development
Indian Institute of Entrepreneurship (IIE)	Guwahati	Training and entrepreneurship development with focus on North East
Integrated Training Centre (Industries)	Nilokheri	Integrated training in different trades. Conducts EDP Courses.
Institute for Design of Electrical Measuring Instruments (IDEMI)	Mumbai	Render services to the Instrument Industry
Central Institute of Hand Tools	Jalandhar	Aims at rapid growth of the Hand Tool Sector
Hand Tool Design Development and Training Centre	Nagpur	Assistance for improvement in productivity and betterment in quality, high value addition in making hand tools
Central Tool Room	Ludhiana	Provide services in the area of consultancy, tool design and manufacture and technical training
Central Tool Room and Training Centre Central Institute of Tool Design (CITD)	Kolkata	Training, design and manufacture of complicated precision tools for the telecom industry and other Common Facility Services
Product-cum-Process Development Centre for Sports Goods	Hyderabad	Training, CAD/CAM Centre for postgraduate trainees, automatic process control unit, etc.
	Meerut	Training, process and product development of sports goods, R&D
Product-cum-Process Development Centre for Essential Oils Fragrance and Flavour Development Centre	Kannauj (UP)	Modernise and upgrade technology status for the essential oils and perfumery industry
Product-cum-Process Development Centre for Foundry and Forging Units	Agra	Provide better technology to small-scale foundry and forging units, process and product development, provision of design for melting equipment, testing facilities
Electronic Service and Training Centre	Ramnagar	Training, technical and consultancy services
Centre for the Improvement of Glass Industry	Firozabad	Development and adoption of new technologies and products – technical training and consultancy
National Small Industries Corporation (5 Prototype Development Training Centres at Delhi, Howrah, Rajkot, Chennai, Hyderabad)	New Delhi	Supply of machinery, marketing assistance and training Several vocations and development of prototype machines.
Central Footwear Training Institute	Agra	Training in leather and footwear products, footwear technology
Small Entrepreneur Promotion Training Institute	Tiruvalla	Skill-oriented entrepreneurial development and training

Source: Office of the DC (SSI).

Designing an Entrepreneurship Training Programme

Designing the training programme involves setting training objectives, developing the course content and choosing appropriate training methods. The programme design is prescribed by the training needs of the target clientele. The training objectives should be stated clearly, be trainee-centred, employ observable action words concerned with ends rather than means. When objectives are set, the course content can be developed. The elements of content are knowledge, habits, skills and control of emotion. The materials to be included should be accorded priority according to its relative degree of importance to achieving training objective. Certain sequences can be followed in arranging the content. Developing the course contents involves several steps, starting from analysing training needs and starting the outcomes. In choosing the appropriate training methods, the factors to be considered are the subject area, the nature of learning, the trainee population, the trainers themselves and time and material factors. There are three processes involved in designing the training programme: setting training objectives, developing the course content or curriculum and choosing appropriate training methods.

Setting Training Objectives: The training objectives make up the framework of the programme on which other training decisions, including the course content itself as well as the methods to be used, will be based. Setting training objectives stems primarily from the results of the training needs assessment.

Training Objectives: Training objectives are statements that describe what the trainees will be able to do upon completion of the training or at any designated point during the training. In other words, they represent the goals which the entrepreneur aims to reach. Once he has clearly decided where he wants to go, then it will be reasonably easy to determine how to achieve the goals.

Developing Course Content: After the training objective have been clearly set, the course content can be developed. While the training objectives serve as the skeletal framework of the course, the content represents its flesh and blood. It embodies the subject matter or learning points that will be put across to enable the trainees to attain the training objectives.

Again, in formulating the content, the planner must be guided by the results of the training needs, assessment and analysis, and of course, by the training objectives.

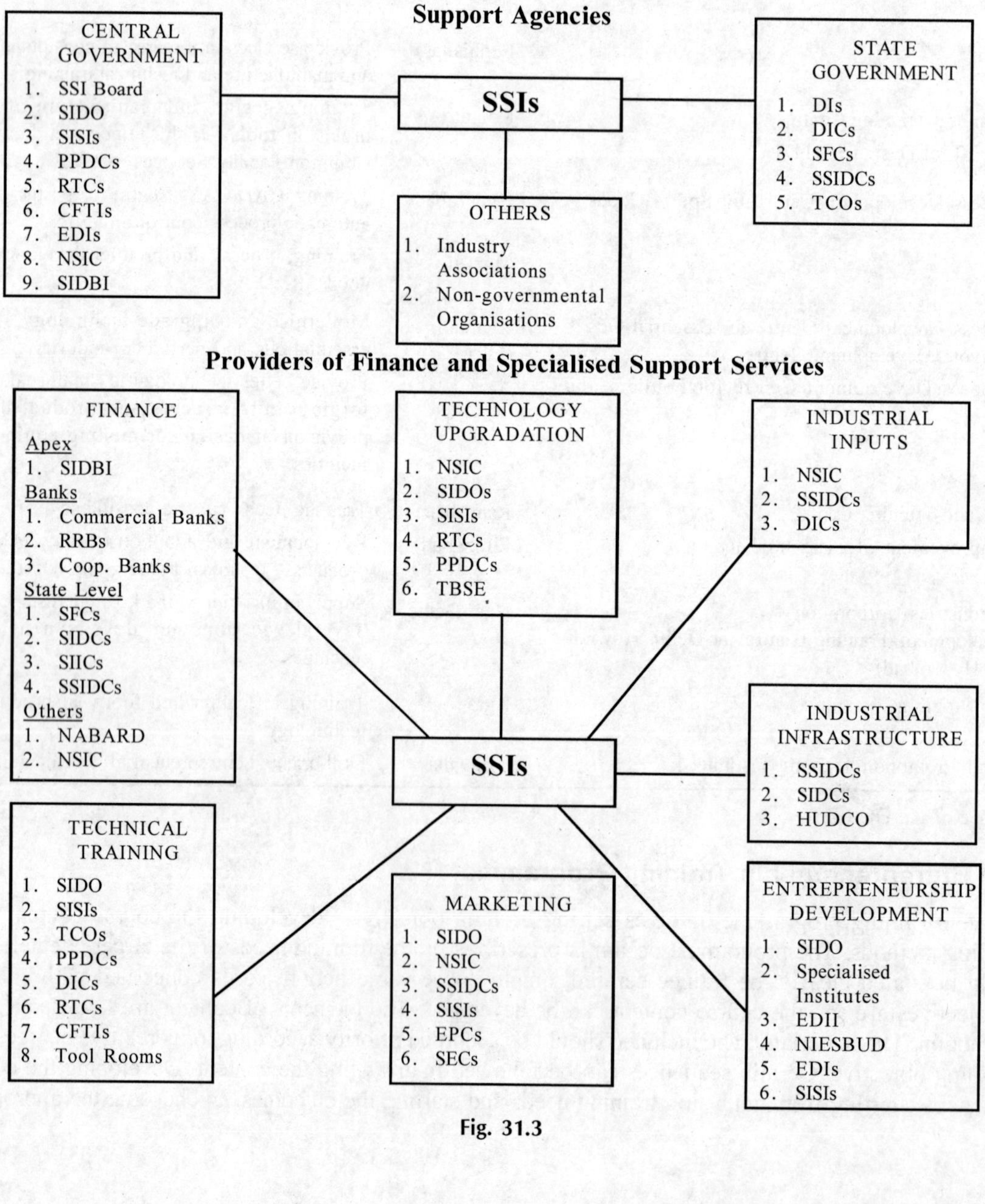

Fig. 31.3

The data on training need analysis which will help the planner to identify the specific knowledge habits, skills, etc., that the trainees should acquire. Training objectives on the other hand will indicate the specific behaviour expected of the trainees at the end of the training.

FINANCIAL AND TECHNICAL SUPPORT PROGRAMMES FOR ENTREPRENEURSHIP DEVELOPMENT

The financial problems cited by the entrepreneurs include lack of collateral guarantee for obtaining loans, unorganised finance sectors which offer loans at higher interest rates, poor credit collection, inadequate loans, short repayment periods, red tape and voluminous paper requirements.

Development of the Practice-oriented Training Programme

The aforementioned principles, concepts and approaches can be projected upon the actual interventions that have taken place in the project area. The activities were developed in such a manner that it become gradually evident that the various steps to be taken and already taken were inter related logically and reflected the methodology described in this paper. The steps taken can be identified as follows:

(a) Identification of problems and prospects of general nature (in selected sectors):
  (i) general assessment;
  (ii) data collection, and
  (iii) identification of specific problems and prospects of both the entrepreneurs and the enterprise.

(b) Identification of specific problems and prospects:
  (i) by enterprise in selected sectors by means of action survey techniques (a continuous process).

(c) Identification of (technical) resources available, a process undertaken simultaneously with (b).

(d) Forming groups of participants/trainers;

(e) Execution and implementation of the work plan (also is a continuous process).

(f) Follow-up and evaluation. (See Fig. 31.4 below).

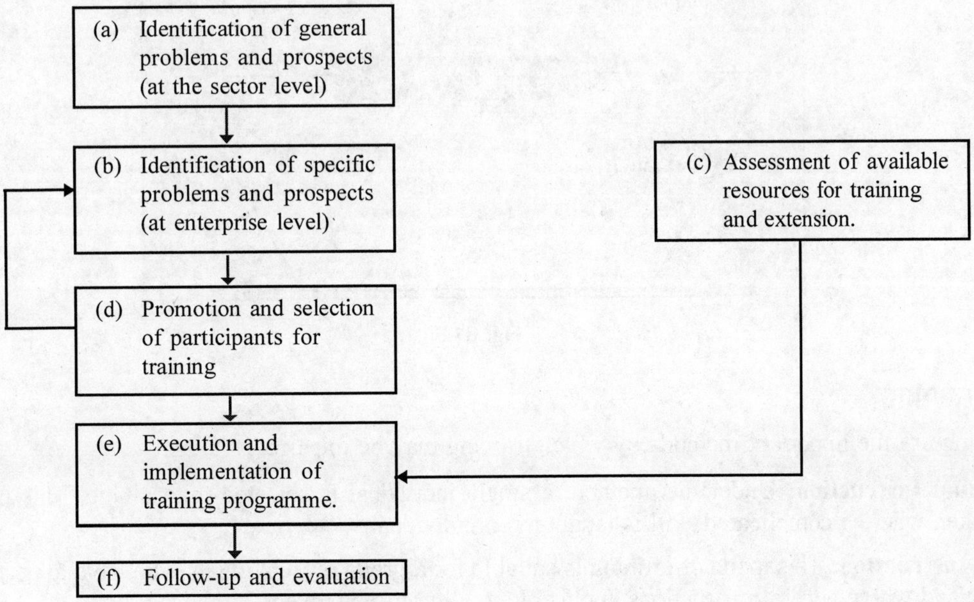

Fig. 31.4 Building Up an Action-oriented Training Programmes

Inputs for Entrepreneurship Development Training

The objective of the programme of training in entrepreneurship development is to develop motivation of potential entrepreneurs, help them in taking up suitable enterprises and activities, enable them to prepare economically viable and technically feasible project reports and enhance their enterprise-building skills. The motivational inputs include psychological games, tests, goal setting exercises and role-play. The objective of these inputs is to enable the participants to understand their own entrepreneurial personality and behaviour and bring about thorough self-study changes in self-concept, values and skills leading to positive entrepreneurial behaviour.

The training programme further enables entrepreneurs to develop skills in identifying suitable items for manufacture or other self-employment ventures. The technique of conducting studies, market survey and research should further be covered in the programme of training based on which project reports have to be prepared. For organising an industry, information on government policies and programmes is helpful to the entrepreneurs. A number of institutional agencies offer finance, raw materials, ready-made sheds, power, machinery and equipment and water, etc. Some countries have also introduced schemes of incentives and concessions available to entrepreneurs. A programme for training for entrepreneurship development should also cover information on programmes of assistance and support systems.

Any programme of training should not only develop proper entrepreneurial motivation and skills for project preparation but should also ensure that entrepreneurs are able to develop their enterprises well by application of scientific managerial techniques in various fields of management. The managerial contents of programme of training should be considered as vital for developing enterprise-building skills and as such various aspects of management such as financial management, marketing management, production management, inventory control, labour laws and taxation should be covered in the programme. There is also the need for visits to the industrial units, consistent with the items identified by the entrepreneurs, to gain more knowledge on production processes and machines required for the purpose. Facilities for inplant training will further heighten the usefulness of the programme, particularly when the enterprises are very small or in areas where there is paucity of skilled personnel.

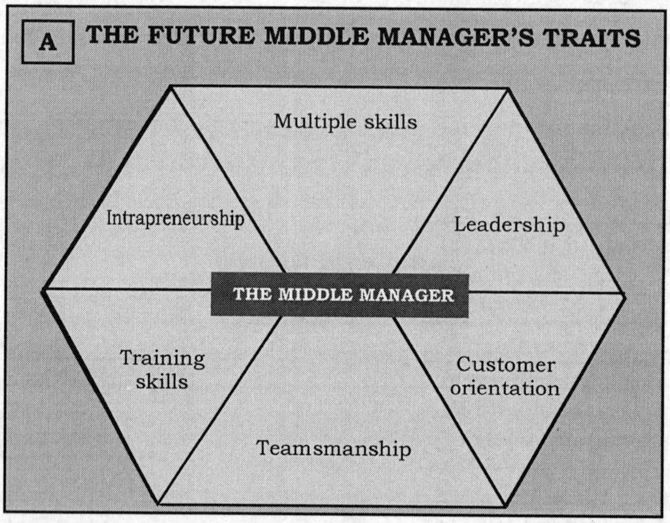

Fig. 31.5

Methods of Training

The following are the important methods by which training may be imparted:

(i) **Individual Instruction:** Under this method, a single individual is selected for training. This mode of training is undertaken where a complicated skill is taught to an individual.

(ii) **Group Instruction:** This mode of training is suitable for a group of individuals who have to perform a similar type of work and where general instructions applicable to all are to be given.

(iii) **Lecture Method:** Here the instructor orally communicates the practice to be followed by the learners. Under this method, whenever there are any doubts, they may be clarified on the spot.

(iv) Demonstration Method: Where the performance of work is to be shown physically by the instructor for better understanding, this method can be followed. This is more concerned with the practical than theoretical aspect.

(v) Written Instructional Method: This medium of training is followed where a future reference is to be made by the learners. This method is mostly followed where a standardised production system is followed.

(vi) Conference: Conferences are frequently organised wherein experts in the field share their ideas and bring to the notice of learners the new ideas and techniques that can be used to increase production.

(vii) Meetings: Meetings are a mode of training involving a group of people who discuss the various problems confronting them. They involve exchanging ideas and views and later on, coming to a firm conclusion based on the various proposals and alternatives.

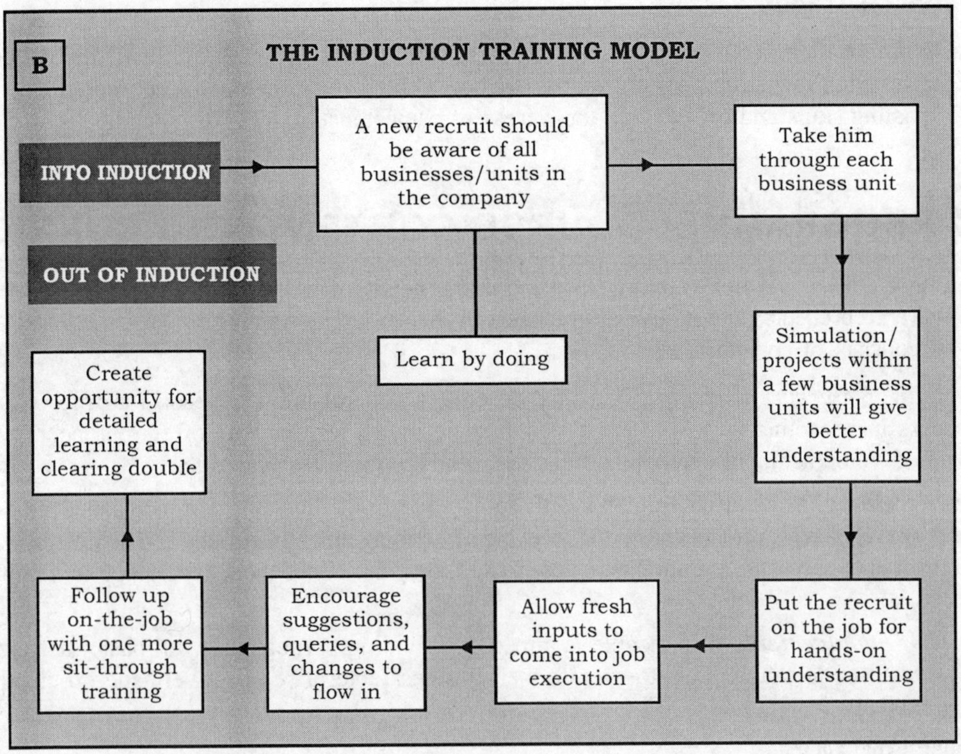

Fig. 31.6

Small-scale industries in India suffer from various handicaps compared to large-scale industries; one of the most important among these is the non-availability of technical and managerial personnel of the required calibre. Large industries can employ qualified staff who are specialised in different areas of production and management. Further, they can afford to retain from time-to-time their own supervisory personnel and workers. As against this, the small industrialist cannot afford to employ workers and supervisors having a sound educational background and the requisite experience in production and in trade. Besides, they do not have the equipment and resources to train their own staff. To meet this lacuna, the training of small industrialists and their workers has been taken up as an important part of the Industrial Extension Service rendered by the Development Commissioner and Small-scale Industries Organisations (DCSSIO). The courses provided are designed to familiarise small industrialists and their workers with the latest tools and techniques in their respective fields. The object of the training of personnel for and from small-scale industries is to equip them with improved management/technical know-how and to appraise them the kinds of assistance available from various government organisations. The training programme of such personnel is suitably geared to the needs of individuals with different background and performing different functions.

The training of instructors at various levels was *sine qua non* of the programme. Besides training officers of the DCSSIO, it became imperative that state government officers, entrusted with the development of small-scale industries, should be given similar training, since the development of small industries is a state subject under the Constitution. Indeed, the training programmes of this organisation commenced with orientation training for its own officers in charge of the Pilot (industrial) Projects under the Community Development Programme. The Small-scale Industries Organisation has extended the benefit of its training resources and programmes to other developing countries, which being interested in the development programmes of small-scale industries, have been deputing their officers for participation in training programmes, study visits, etc., specially arranged by it for them.

In the post-independence period, the nation laid stress and put its faith in science and technology. The country has made tremendous investments in scientific institutions and scientific and technical manpower. These investments need to be harvested. We have learnt that the managerial skills necessary to harvest business are different from the skills required to create businesses. Similarly, to create technology enterprises, we may also require different kinds of managers in our science and technology institutions. Development of technical entrepreneurship and the management of science and technology cannot be dealt with in mutual exclusion.

Training in Technical Trades

Regular and *ad hoc* training courses in various technical trades are conducted by Small Industries Service Institutes, SISI's Extension Centres and Production Centres for artisans, both skilled and semi-skilled, sponsored by small-scale industries for upgrading their existing skills and broadening their areas of competence to meet the specific requirements of small-scale industries.

TRAINING PROGRAMME: COURSE CONTENT AND CURRICULUM

The EDP training will be set up according to the training needs of participants, who are both existing and potential entrepreneurs, and industrial prospects of the area. The training programme lasts for four weeks, and consists of six modules.

(a) ***Introduction of entrepreneurship:*** This module covers general knowledge on the role of entrepreneurs in economic factors affecting small-scale industries, the role of entrepreneurs in economic development, entrepreneurial behaviour and the facilities available.

(b) ***Motivation training:*** Motivation training is a three-day live-in-module aimed at increasing the participant's level of achievement and confidence and developing the right attitude and behaviour toward business. Successful entrepreneurs are invited to speak about their experience in setting up and running a business.

(c) ***Essentials of management:*** This module is aimed at providing participants with basic management and technical know-how required to enable them to operate their business enterprise effectively and efficiently. It consists of the following subjects.

(i) General management.

(ii) Marketing management.

(iii) Production management.

(iv) Financial management.

(d) ***Fundamentals of project feasibility study:*** This ratio provides guidelines on the effective analysis of feasibility of the project in view of marketing, organisation, technical, financial and social aspects.

(e) ***Organising the business:*** The purpose of this module is to enable participants to know the environment in which they will operate their business. This covers such aspects as government incentives, industrial opportunities, policies, business laws and regulations, etc.

(f) ***Plant visit:*** Plant visits are necessary to familiarise the participants with real-life situations in small business. Such trips also provide participants with opportunities, to learn more about an entrepreneur's behaviour, personality, thoughts and aspirations, including his plans and projects.

The training method is a combination of group dynamics, lecture discussions, case studies, actual preparation of project assignment, and workshop exercise.

German Experience

The worldwide acclaim achieved by the German companies has been due to the rapid adaptation to change and restructuring the training accordingly. The common features of restructuring are:

1. Broad-based training to start with, followed by specialisation. This has led to a reduction in the number of trades.
2. Development of multicraft skills.
3. Development of unique training modules and units.
4. Industry's lead and initiative in restructuring the training.
5. Change in complexion of the workforce leading to more skilled workers.
6. Retraining programmes for skill upgradation of the existing workforce.
7. The overall personality development of the workforce through emphasis on 'key qualifications' which will equip the workforce with the ability to cope with change. This is illustrated in the diagram.

Two important recommendations emerged when there was an interchange of German and Indian experiences, through a workshop organised by the Confederation of Engineering Industry.

Multiskill Concept

1. The pattern of Indian training system needs to be overhauled. This is needed particularly in respect of offering broad training with limited number of trades and offering specialised modules in tune with the hi-tech requirements. Also, the multiskilled concept which is fast emerging as a response to hi-tech needs would necessitate this approach.
2. At the operational level, the modification of the existing training programmes to include the allied elements. In particular, the maintenance aspect has been much stressed, whether it be mechanical, electrical, electronics or the processing sector.

To make training successful, the German experiences point to the absolute necessity for developing good training materials and updating the instructors on their use.

Japanese Approach

In total contrast to the German approach, the Japanese place little accent on formalised institution training. On the other hand, tremendous emphasis is laid on "on-the-job" training. The primary objective of job training is to bring about a change — an increase in knowledge, the acquisition of a skill, or the development of confidence and good judgement. Job training is not successful unless the person can do something new or different or demonstrate a change in behaviour.

There are three dimensions in each job that an employee must master in order to perform effectively knowledge, skill and ability.

Knowledge refers to the information that is needed to perform a set of activities efficiently and effectively. Skill refers to the techniques, the approaches, and the styles of translating knowledge into action or practice. Ability refers to the intangible qualities or characteristics that are necessary for performance and are often referred to under the umbrella of 'motivation' or 'attitude'.

Job training is structured to consist of both formal and informal activities that address each of these three dimensions – knowledge, skill and ability – and the goals of training made clear enough so that the trainee understands what outcome or behaviour is desired.

In trying to solve job-related problems, often the Japanese employees are encouraged to communicate their own training needs so that these can be arranged. This is in direct contrast to the practices prevalent in many factories here, wherein every one participates in determining the training needs of a person excepting the person himself.

For example, through the participation as members of Quality Circles, in the process of problem-solving, the employees may identify specific skill needs to improve product quality. These are then arranged to be provided.

Table 32.2 New Training Tools

No.	Level	Tool	Use
1.	Top & senior levels	ZOPP	Realistic organisational diagnosis and action plans to overcome problems.
2.	Middle level managers	Blockage concept	Identifying and helping to remove blockage to competency, "empowering" them for greater effectiveness.
3.	Workforce	Modular training	Adaptation to hi-tech integrated approach to operation and maintenance.
4.	Cross-functional	The New Seven tools of QC	To ensure better product quality and meeting customer expectations.

Entrepreneurship Development Programme Organisations

There are several organisations engaged in conducting entrepreneurship development programme in India. The lead in the matter was given by the Small Industries Development Organisation through its service centres. Entrepreneurial development in Gujarat has been conducted for a long time, and sophisticated selection techniques and training methodology have been developed. The programme has integrated identification and training of potential entrepreneurs, identification of viable industrial projects and developing managerial capabilities. Institutional support in the areas of finance, infrastructure, etc., is also linked with the programme.

Other organisations that have been actively conducting entrepreneurship development programmes are State Bank of India; financial institutions such as IDBI; Entrepreneurial Motivation Training Centre in Northern-Eastern Region; Xavier Institute of Social Service, Ranchi; industrial consultancy organisations in various states; Centre for Entrepreneurship Development, Ahmedabad; State Financial Corporations; the Centre for Entrepreneurship Development, Hubli; Small Industries Extension Training Institute, Hyderabad; National Science and Technology Entrepreneurship Development Board, etc.

The need for a national organisation to serve as an apex body to coordinate training programmes of various centres and organisations in the country, to train trainers and motivators in entrepreneurship development, to prepare model syllabi training for various target-groups and target-areas, etc., was felt, with a view to evolve an integrated national approach to this subject.

Benefits of the Training Process

(a) The training: The combination of on-the-job training and consultancy with group training during rather a short time (three weeks) is an effective strategy.

— The entrepreneurs/participants demonstrate a willingness to improve existing working methodology and techniques and learned the possibilities or limitations in the use of equipment;

— They are more aware of the need to develop and introduce new products and production techniques; and relationship of theory to the situation in their workplace;

— They demonstrate a growing awareness of the relationship between technical problems in their enterprises and management and control.

— During the group training, an opportunity is created to exchange experiences and problems and questions that were observed or arisen during the visits to the enterprises.

(b) Level of instruction: Through the mix of on-the-job training and group training, but mostly through direct contact between the entrepreneur and the instructor at the work floor of the former, the instructor usually speaks the language of the entrepreneur. The instructor had to adapt himself to the client, to the entrepreneur, and to think at his level while searching for new methodologies and solutions for problems observed. This contrasts with formal training programmes where the participants have to adjust themselves to the trainer and his environment, and where the participants are left afterwards with the burden of reentry into their system with the new knowledge. The entrepreneur feels himself more at ease in his own environment where he is the boss; and with that self-confidence he often feels more comfortable in questioning the trainer/instructor about the things he himself considers to be of interest.

Box 31.1 Entrepreneurship Training Institutes

The activities of Entrepreneurship Training Institutes are, however, briefly described below:

National Institute for Small Industry Extension and Training

National Institute for Small Industry Extension and Training (NISIET) at Hyderabad, has been imparting training to entrepreneurs, managers and various development functionaries of state governments, financial institutes and other agencies. NISIET organises about 45 national level and 15 international level programmes every year. It also acts as an important resource and information centre for small units and undertakes research and consultancy for small industry development.

Entrepreneurship Development Institute of India

Entrepreneurship Development Institute of India (EDII), Ahmedabad is an autonomous not-for-profit institution, set up in 1983 and sponosred by financial institutions, such as Industrial Development Bank of India, Industrial Finance Corporation of India, Industrial Credit and Investment Corporation of India, and the State Bank of India. The Government of Gujarat has also provided assistance for setting up of EDII.

EDII has been spearheading an entrepreneurship movement in the country and takes up activities like augmenting the supply of trained entrepreneurs, generating multiplier effect on opportunities for self-employment, improving the managerial capabilities of small-scale industries and producing trained motivators for entrepreneurship development. The institute participates in institution-building efforts, besides promoting micro-enterprises at a rural level. It has designed and implemented several national and international training programmes and workshops for the academic community and for the youth. The special training programmes that EDII organises include informal Micro Credit Delivery Systems, management programme for strengthening the participation of NGOs in the area of informal credit, etc. It organises trainers' meets and chief executives' meets to foster linkages among trainers and chief executives of entrepreneurship development organisations to facilitate experience sharing.

National Institute for Entrepreneurship and Small Business Development

The National Institute for Entrepreneurship and Small Business Development (NIESBUD), which started functioning from July 1983 is an apex body established by the Ministry of Industry, Government of India for coordinating and overseeing the activities of various institutions/agencies engaged in entrepreneurial development in small industry and small business. The activities of the institute include: (i) Evolving effective training strategies and methodology, standardising model syllabi for training various target groups; (ii) Formulating scientific selection procedures, developing training aids, manuals and tools, facilitating and supporting Central State and other agencies in executing Entrepreneurship Development programmes; (iii) Conducting such programmes for promoters, trainers and entrepreneurs which are commonly not undertaken by other agencies; and (iv) Maximising the benefits and accelerating the process of entrepreneurship development.

Indian Institute of Entrepreneurship

The Indian Institute of Entrepreneurship (IIE), Guwahati was established in 1993 by the Ministry of Industry, Government of India to undertake training, research and consultancy activities in the field of Small-scale Industries. SIDBI is a copromoter of the institute. IIE has adopted a multipronged approach in entrepreneurship development with a special focus in the northern region. The main activities of the institute are: (i) To organise and conduct training for entrepreneurship development; (ii) To evolve strategies and methodologies for different target-groups and locations and field test them, (iii) To identify training needs and offer training programmes to government and non-governmental organisations engaged in promoting and supporting entrepreneurship, (iv) To organise seminars, workshops and conferences, etc., for providing a form for interaction and exchange of views by various agencies and entrepreneurs; and (v) To conduct research to generate knowledge for accelerating the process of entrepreneurship development.

National Institute of Fashion Technology

The National Institute of Fashion Technology (NIFT), New Delhi was registered as an Autonomous Society in 1986. It is a government-funded institution under the Ministry of Textiles with Secretary (Textiles) as Chairman of the Board of Governors, besides the Chairman, there are 17 members on the Board of NIFT.

NIFT was established in collaboration with the Fashion Institute of Technology (FIT), New York. The genesis of the NIFT was in the idea of an apex institution to cater to the growing needs of India's evolving fashion industry. Over the years, NIFT has emerged as the premier training institute in India nurturing and creating a bright and able generation of professionals in different areas of fashion technology, meeting the human resource requirements of this vital industry. Its high level of interaction and collaboration with the leading fashion institutions of the world has enhanced the stature and scope for the fashion industry in India to meet the challenges of the industrial competitiveness on a global place.

EDPs of SIDBI

The aim of SIDBIs EDPs is to build and nurture a reservoir of entrepreneurs. Such EDPs are conducted through the specialised agencies, i.e., Entrepreneurship Development Institute of India, Institute of Entrepreneurship Development, Centre for Entrepreneurship Development, Technical Consultancy Organisations and Non-Government Organisations.

Management deficiency and a low level of skill and technology have been some of the major weaknesses of small industries. SIDBI is constantly endeavouring to address these problems by bringing reputed management and technical institutions to the small-scale industries and arranging specially designed programmes, *viz.*, Small Industries Management Programme and Skill-cum-technology Upgradation Programme. The objective of SIMAP is to develop a cadre of industrial managers specifically trained to assist the SSI entrepreneurs in their multiple responsibilities. STUP is structured to improve the performance of existing SSI units by developing strengthening managerial skills and the technical competence of the entrepreneurs and senior executives of the small enterprise.

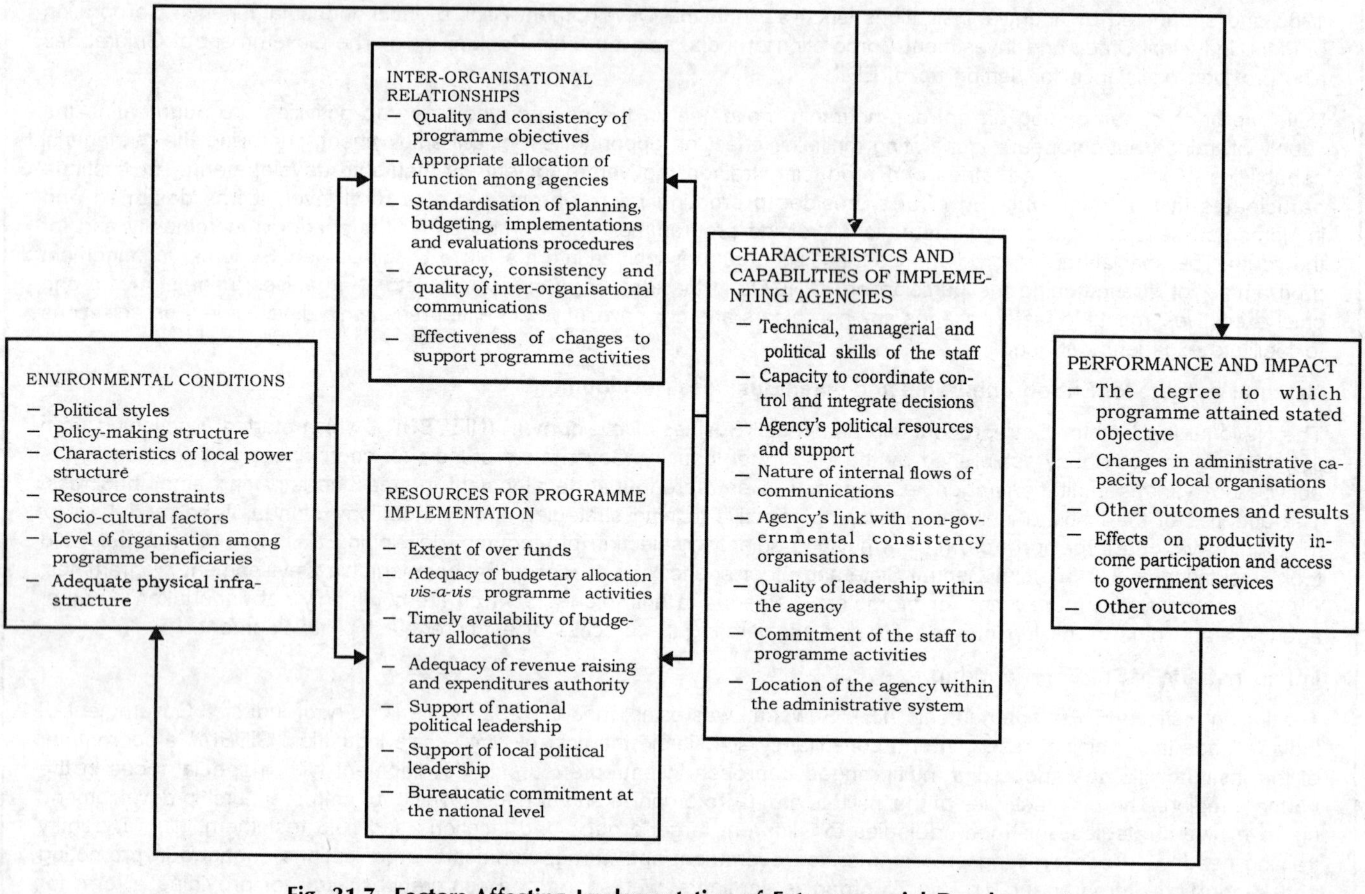

Fig. 31.7 Factors Affecting Implementation of Entrepreneurial Development

(c) Mobilisation of resources: Within a limited time, the identification of the pertinent resources on contract terms for the training programme was initiated. Successful negotiation with a state technical training institute resulted in the contracting of three professionals for the three weeks of the course. This was mainly possible through the availability of a budget, and the possibility to decide on the use of that budget without approvals and endorsements of third parties or higher authorities. With this the mobilisation of resources through contracts approved at local level directly was made. Furthermore, the contribution of the larger industries was ensured, which resulted in the release of one instructor for a three-week period at no cost. Although his participation was of high value, his release by the large industry was a marginal cost, and was seen as a contribution to the development of the area (social investment by the large industry, also to improve their general image). Unfortunately, it was not possible to use the workshop facilities of a particular industry.

It became evident that even governmental services could be mobilised and integrated into the programme at the working level. Approaching the government at higher level for official approval and release would have been less attractive, because such activities are normally not foreseen in annual plans and budgets, nor do the budget cater for such additional expenditures.

(d) Cost-effectiveness: One of the major objections raised against the individualised training approach (albeit for a group of trainees) like the one described here, is related to the cost aspects. It is often claimed that the costs of group training alone (without consultancy and the like) are considerably less than the consultancy-cum-instruction technique. This, however, is not at all that obvious.

In the field of training in the small-scale enterprise sector, we see the following principles being adopted more and more:

- Training of entrepreneurs is seen more as a process of transfer of know-how.
- More attention is being paid to the process of adult learning instead of just setting university and college courses.
- Training programmes are more individualised, with special attention to the individual training needs.
- Training programmes are becoming more practice-oriented, with more attention being paid to on-the-job training aspects.
- Consultancy and extension are seen more and more as a part of the process of transfer of know-how.

Table 31.3 Cost Aspect of Training through Subcontractors Vs. Training by the Institution Itself

		Subcontracting arrangements		Institutionalised operations	
		Recurrent cost	Incidental cost	Recurrent cost	Incidental cost
1	Professional manpower	Low	High	High	Low
2	Administrative	Relatively High	Low	Low	Low
3	Logistic support	Low	Low	High	Low
4	Material cost	Low	Low	High	Low
5	Follow-up	High	Low	High	Low
6	Staff training	Low	Low	High	High

- More attention is being paid to ensuring active participation of both the entrepreneur and the "instructor".
- Training should cover both the entrepreneurs and workers (labour) and future programmes should be built up at the Central and state government levels through the FDIs.
- Various institutes providing training for small-scale entrepreneurs should be brought under the umbrella of the National Entrepreneurship Development Board to provide uniformity in training and avoid duplication of efforts.
- Syllabi of various training courses/modules should be regularly updated. For this purpose, a standing committee should be constituted by the institutes and the industry associations should also be given a role.
- Efforts should be made by the government to avail of external sources of funding for training and EDPs. Training for self-employed persons should be encouraged.

Indian Diamond Institute

The Indian Diamond Institute, located at Surat, registered under the Societies Registration Act, was established in 1978 with the objective of strengthening and improving the availability of trained manpower for the gems and jewellery industry by conducting various Diploma/Postgraduate Diploma level courses in the field concerned. The institute is financed by the Government of India, Ministry of Commerce and the Gems and Jewellery Export Promotion Council.

Manpower Training

Training for the development of technical skills of manpower required in the small-scale industries sector is being imparted in different technical vocations for technicians and workers in various workshops attached to SISs. Besides, other institutions such as testing centres, toolrooms, CFTI, etc., also impart training for improving the skill of the workers of small-scale industries by organising regular and part-time courses. National Small Industries Corporation has also been supplementing the training requirements of workers through its Prototype Development and Training Centres (PDTCs). There are five PTDCs located at Delhi, Howrah, Rajkot, Chennai and Hyderabad. These centres, under the control of NSIC, have been providing assistance to industrial units at respective locations. Approximately 100 small units, on a selective basis, have been assisted under the Modernisation Implementation Programme whereby, a large number of these units have been able to get ISI and other related quality marks. These centres train manpower in several vocations and develop prototypes of machines.

To help SSIs, PDTCs are providing Common Facility Services that are normally out of the reach of individual small units. These services have been extended to various areas like raw material testing, physical and chemical testing, precision machining, casting, heat treatment, electroplating, wood working, etc. Through these testing facilities and consultancy services, many of the products manufactured by SSI units have been brought within the purview of Indian Standards, besides resulting in substantial business growth for the SSIs.

CONCLUSION

In any set-up, the typical ways of enhancing knowledge are reading, networking, and, lately, accessing the Internet, but each of these are self-directed and without a structure. On the other hand, a course is structured towards providing specific theoretical knowledge, skills like making presentations, or even an attitudinal change.

An annual process of assessing training needs and scheduling courses is the hallmark of any progressive organisation. Conversely, putting out an annual calendar of its programmes is necessary for a training provider so it is not out of the reckoning at any stage. Most human resource managers will not mind if training budgets are exceeded, as these assessments are merely indicative.

Training refers to the process of increasing knowledge and skills of an employee for doing a particular job. Soon after a worker is selected and inducted into a job, we may not expect full contribution from him in attaining the objective of the factory, as he is just a 'raw' human resource. For ensuring satisfactory job performance, training is essential at all levels of management. Training serves not only the purpose of motivation but also as a means of developing various methods of work. The terms 'training' and 'development' are often synonymously used. But there is a difference between the two. While training is viewed as a process by means of which the aptitudes, skills and capabilities of an individual employee to perform a specific job are enhanced, development implies the nature and direction of change induced in the employee through the process of education and training. Several factors have contributed to the increased adoption of training and the development scheme of factories.

As the value of constant training was realised in the West earlier, probably the pool of available trainers may be higher in those countries. But with increasing exposure, Indian institutions can catch up on infrastructure provided. Training styles may differ and these largely reflect the philosophy of the institute. IIM, Ahmedabad and the Harvard Business School, for instance, rely extensively on the case study method. Exercises, case studies, and simulation are a typical mode of training.

It is obvious from the foregoing that the achievement in rural areas is contingent upon the evaluation of a national training policy, the creation of a national training infrastructure, the formulation of suitable coordinative mechanisms at all levels, the acceptance of manpower planning and budgeting as the basis for training programmes, the developments of multiple skill courses, the acceptance of area planning approach for training institutions at district and block levels and the participation of people through their own organisations, especially at the cutting edge level. Unless a massive training programme is organised to support ambitious rural development programmes, the goal of full employment may not be achieved within the stipulated period of time.

More importantly, the government and the development financial institutions are in the forefront of entrepreneurial development. However, experience shows that the various training programmes of these institutions are aimed at training people to either take up self-employment, some small venture or acquire gainful employment. Thus, the very purpose of developing entrepreneurial talent among the youth is defeated. This calls for a critical evaluation of EDPs and to develop personnel with conviction and commitment to undertake the task or planning, designing and implementing programmes for entrepreneurship development. More importantly, entrepreneurial programmes must be attuned to the Indian economic environment and be made available in regional languages. The need of the hour is to develop genuine entrepreneurs and not imitative entrepreneurs to accelerate the process of industrialisation. The need of the hour is for stimulating innovation and entrepreneurial spirit to support the development of new ideas through new and mature enterprises.

APPENDIX-I

A Programme of Training Small Industry Entrepreneur – Managers

Types of Individual to receive training	Types of training measures required	Sources of personnel to staff training facilities	Means of training the Trainees
FULL-TIME			
Typical managers of small factories or others planning to establish such factories	Short courses	(a) Staff members of advisory services operated by governments, associations or other bodies	(a) Joint use can be made of facilities provided for manager training, e.g., short courses, advanced management courses, self-educational measures.
Exceptional managers of rapidly expanding semi- modern factories	Advanced management courses (either national regional or international).	(b) Staff members of educational institutions, development corpo-rations, banks.	(b) Specialised training can be given to management training personnel in the institutions – either national or foreign – designed for large industry; e.g., in business, engineering or economics.
Manager candidates	Preparatory courses	(c) Foreign specialists	(c) Internships may be possible in large industrial plan – national or foreign to give practical training to prospective staff members.
PART-TIME			
All types	Self-education measures	(d) Managers of modern small factories. (e) Managers of medium and large-sized factories, banks, utilities, etc. (f) Government officials (g) Members of professions.	(d) Same as: (a), (b), or (c) above

32 CHAPTER

INSTITUTIONS IN AID OF ENTREPRENEURSHIP DEVELOPMENT

"Research is the word which moves me. It gives me all kinds of perspectives in my mind. In the larger sense of the word, research looks upon it as something more than that: as something leading a community or country forward or humanity forward in its march towards the goal that it has."

— Jawaharlal

LEARNING OBJECTIVES

The chapter discusses the new concept for harnessing the vast untapped human resources.

The Entrepreneurial Development Programmes (EDPs) are presently one of the most talked about social development activities. The chapter deals with:

Focus of EDPs

Entrepreneurial Development Programme Organisations

Management Development Institute (MDI)

NIESBUD

- Entrepreneurial Qualities
- Objectives
- Activities

EDI

- Training Programmes

IED

- STEPs
- CED

Role of Development Banks

Role of Business Schools

EDPs of SIDBI

Role of Commercial Banks

Phases of Entrepreneurship Development

- Role of NAYE

INTRODUCTION

Since 1950, a substantial volume of study has gone into the different facets of entrepreneurial development in India to accelerate the process of industrialisation. The study showed that entrepreneurs are born and can also be made — their skills sharpened, quality of an enterprise improved and generated in good number. It is possible to identify individual in all communities, in rural and urban areas, among men and women with entrepreneurial talent, to motivate and train them through properly organised programmes undertaking risk-bearing innovative activities for raising the growth rate in agriculture, in industry as well as in the service sector.

The Entrepreneurial Development Programmes (EDPs) thus became a new concept for harnessing the vast untapped human resources. The EDPs are presently one of the most talked about social development activities which many organisations have taken up in right earnest. It strikes a welcome note in respect of change in perception and recognition of the critical role the entrepreneurs play in industrial development by creating potential avenues for self-employment.

FOCUS OF EDPs

While organising EDPs, it should be remembered that entrepreneurs cannot be created like degreeholders in a university and that it would be necessary to eliminate those who do not possess the basic capabilities for entering into business ventures, weed out such persons and help develop latent facilities of those who possess the potential for becoming entrepreneurs.

As the quality of entrepreneurship differs from region to region, the type of inputs that a particular group of entrepreneurs would require should be understood clearly and the training programmes tailored accordingly. Training should be not only to set up an industrial venture but also to enable the trainee to run it successfully. The focus of EDP should be on the person rather than on the project and this calls for proper counselling facilities available to the trainees. These programmes should be conducted in places where necessary infrastructure for training is available and proximity of the support agencies is assured. This would underline the need for proper selection of the trainees. It should be ensured that the trainees show interest in setting up industries and that they do not treat the ED as a stop Ps gap arrangement for taking up a job subsequently. For this purpose, we should think new techniques to make the process of selection more appropriate. Poor involvement on the part of the institutions as also trainees and an incorrect selection of target-groups contribute largely to the failure of a number of EDPs. One of the objects of training should be on changing the attitude and set of mind of young people from security-oriented activities to risk-taking through entrepreneurship development.

ENTREPRENEURSHIP DEVELOPMENT PROGRAMME ORGANISATIONS

There are several organisations engaged in conducting entrepreneurship development programmes in India. The lead in the matter was given by Small Industries Development Organisation through its Small Industries Service Centres.

In the area of creation of the institutional infrastructure for entrepreneurship development, the first step of Indian financial institutions including IFCI was the establishment of Entrepreneurship Development Institute of India (EDII) in March, 1983, at Ahmedabad as a resource organisation at the national level. The Central Government also established in the same year the National Institute for Entrepreneurship and Small Business Development (NIESBUD) at New Delhi, with the objective of coordinating activities related to entrepreneurship and small business development. Both these organisations are working hand-in-hand for giving a fillip to the entrepreneurship development movement.

In addition, institutions established by the government are: Rural Entrepreneurship Development Institute (REDI) at Ranchi in 1983, Rural Management and Management Centres (RMDCs) at Maharashtra and Training-cum-Development Centres (EDCs) aim increasing interaction between entrepreneurs and enterprise.

This apart, a host of management institutions various universities have included entrepreneurship development in their curriculum.

Other organisations that have been actively conducting entrepreneurship development programmes are State Bank of India; financial institutions such as IDBI; Entrepreneurial Motivation Training Centre in Northern-Eastern Region; Xavier Institute of Social Services, Ranchi; industrial consultancy organisations in various states; Centre for Entrepreneurship Development, Ahmedabad; state financial corporations; the Centre for Entrepreneurship Development, Hubli; Small Industries Extension Training Institute, Hyderabad; National Science and Technology Entrepreneurship Development Board, etc.

For institutionalising the entrepreneurship development activities at the state level, Institutes of Entrepreneurship Development (IED) in Uttar Pradesh, Bihar and Orissa have already come into existence with the support of India's financial institutions, concerned state governments and banks, and are carrying on their activities on a full-fledged basis. During the period under review, a Centre for Entrepreneurship Development (CED) was registered in Madhya Pradesh on 17th November, 1988, taken up later by IFCI. An Institute for Entrepreneurship Development was also set up at Goa under DB on the same pattern as other IEDs. A proposal to set up an IED for North-Eastern Region was also under consideration by the North-Eastern Council. A few state governments of Karnataka, Andhra Pradesh, Rajasthan, etc., have also expressed the desire to set up CEDs in their respective states. The proposals of these state governments to be considered on their merits by the financial institutions in due course, while the focus of the national organisations like EDII, NIESBUD, etc., continued to be on: *(a)* institutional entrepreneurship activities, *(b)* generating, sharpening and sharing knowledge through research documentation and publication, *(c)* creating and developing professionals in the discipline of "entrepreneurship" to emerge and flourish, and *(e)* developing new products and pursuing market segments for carrying the entrepreneurship development in priority areas and sections of the people. The state-level institutes/CEDs endeavoured to carry out at the grassroot level to provide the support of human resources to various State and district EDPs level organisations engaged in entrepreneurship. The state-level organisations also continued to provide industrial extension motivation services, business opportunities guidance, project counselling, etc., and helped in initiating entrepreneurship at school level in the career planning of the younger generation. For this these organisations conducted, during the period under review, a number of workshops, seminars, conferences and brought out well researched publications, for training of entrepreneurs. The organisations also produced a number of video films as audio-visual aids for training the entrepreneurs and motivating them towards enterprise setting and operating the same on sound and healthier lines.

MANAGEMENT DEVELOPMENT INSTITUTE (MDI)

For developing and improving the quality of day-to-day management, which is so crucial for the success of any industrial venture, as also, with a view to encouraging professionalisation in management, IFCI had sponsored in 1973, the Management Development Institute (MDI) at Gurgaon (Haryana) near Delhi. MDI is now a cornucopia of management training, research and consultancy, its prime goal being to improve managerial effectiveness in the industry/government and banking sectors of the economy. Research studies undertaken by MD are in both macro areas of economic and industrial development as also in micro areas relevant to a specific industry or economic activity.

A mention was made in the last year's Annual Report about MD having been chosen by the Government of India, Department of Personnel and Training as an agency for conducting the first-ever intensive 15-month National Management Programme (NMP) for government officers belonging to IAS/Group 'A' Services as well as executives from public and private sector organisations having potential to acquire top positions.

MDI conduct Management Development Programmes in various disciplines. These programmes included the programmes for officers of the Indian Economic Service (IES), Indian Administrative Service (IAS) and for the executives of a number of PSUs of, like Oil & Natural Gas Commission (ONGC), Bharat Heavy Electrical Ltd., (BHEL), Bharat Aluminium Co. Ltd., (BALCO), Export Credit Guarantee Corporation of India (ECGC), Bureau of Indian Standards (BIS), Hindustan Zinc Ltd., (HZL), Hindustan Machine Tools Ltd., (HMT), Indian Drugs & Pharmaceuticals Ltd., (IDPL), Uttar Pradesh State Industrial Development Corporation Ltd., (UPSIDC), Madhya Pradesh Financial Corporation (MPFC), etc.

MDI also had conducted in Karnataka a programme on Identification, Promotion and Implementation of Industrial Projects (IPIIP) specially catering to the needs of officers of District Industries Centres (DICs), State-level Promotional and Financial Institutions, Commercial Banks, etc. In addition, a number of programmes, particularly in concerning strategic planning, marketing of new products, strengthening of cooperative short-term credit system, marketing and sales, management consultancy, development banking, labour-management relations, human resources development, small industries financing performance evaluation, role of directors, merchant banking, leasing, working capital financing, technology transfer, management, documentation and recovery practices of Development Financing Institutions, etc., were carried out by MDI and its subsidiary Development Banking Centre (DBC). As many as 23 workshops were conducted by MDI under the Planning Commission International Labour Organisation, United Nations Development Programme, In-house Management Consultancy Development Project (Phase II).

A major effort was also made by MDI during the period in the area of consultancy and research — focus was not only on developing management consultancy through training programmes and workshops but also undertaking process consultancy assignments in large complex organisations and directing efforts to develop in-house management consultancy teams in public utilities. The Consultancy and Research Wings of MDI have done extensive work in areas like corporate planning, evaluation of appraisal systems, feasibility studies, job structuring, management information systems, manpower planning, marketing appraisal, capital markets, offshore banking, inter-firm comparison, seed capital, technology — its relevance, assessment and diffusion, etc.

THE NATIONAL INSTITUTE FOR ENTREPRENEURSHIP AND SMALL BUSINESS DEVELOPMENT (NIESBUD)

The need for a national organisation to serve as an apex body to coordinate the training programmes of various centres and organisations in the country, to train a larger number of trainers and motivators in entrepreneurship development, to prepare model syllabuses of training for various target-groups and target- areas, etc., was felt for further accelerating training in entrepreneurship.

The Delhi-based National Institute for Entrepreneurship and Small Business Development (NIESBUD), established by the Government of India, is an apex body for coordinating and overseeing the activities of various institutions and agencies engaged in entrepreneurship development particularly in the area of small industry and small business. The Institute, registered as a Society under Government of India Societies Act, XXI of 1860, started functioning from 6th July, 1983.

Over the years, the institute stands devoted to evolving model syllabi for training various target-groups — by effective training strategies, methodology, manuals and tools; facilitating and supporting Central/State governments and other agencies in executing programmes of entrepreneurship and small business development; maximising benefit and accelerating entrepreneurship development; conducting programmes for motivators, trainers and entrepreneurs which are commonly not undertaken by other agencies. Above all organising those that help in developing entrepreneurial culture is worth appreciation in society. The institute is also the secretariat of the National Entrepreneurship Development Board (NEDB), the apex body which determines policy for entrepreneurship development in the country. The institute, therefore, performs the task of processing the recommendations made by the Board.

Objectives

The main objectives of the institute are:

- To accelerate the process of entrepreneurship development ensuring its impact throughout the country and among all segments of the society.
- To help/support institutions/agencies in carrying out activities relating to entrepreneurship development with greater success.
- To evolve standardised process of selection, training support and sustenance to potential entrepreneurs enabling them to set up and run their enterprise successfully.
- To provide vital information support to trainers, promoters and entrepreneurs by organising documentation and research work relevant to entrepreneurship development.
- To provide functional forums for interaction and exchange of experiences helpful for policy formulation and modification at various levels.

Since development of entrepreneurship and self-employment is basically a promotional and industrial extension activity, the programmes organised by the institute are mostly by the founded government. However, the institute's training activities are restricted to areas in which either demand for programmes is very great or there is absence of such training programmes. For organisations directly or indirectly engaged in promoting entrepreneurship and self-employment in the country, the NIESBUD's role is that of a catalyst as it helps in developing the effectiveness of all these organisations. Programmmes initiated/sponsored by the NIESBUD are constantly evaluated and revised to suit the changing needs in the area of entrepreneurship and small business development. The institute is engaged in creating a climate conducive for entrepreneurship and in developing favourable attitude amongst the general public in support of those who opt for entrepreneurial career.

Activities

The activities of the institute include evolving effective training strategies and methodology; standardising model syllabi for training various target-groups; formulating scientific selection procedures; developing training aids, manuals and tools;

facilitating and supporting Central/State/other agencies in executing entrepreneurship development programmes; maximising the benefits and accelerating the process of entrepreneurship development.

The major activities of the institute are:

1. Evolving model syllabi for training various target-groups;
2. Providing effective training strategies, methodology, manuals and tools;
3. Facilitating and supporting Central/state governments and other agencies in executing programmes of entrepreneurship and small business development; and
4. Conducting programmes for motivators, trainers and entrepreneurs who are commonly not undertaken by other agencies and organising activities which helps in developing an entrepreneurial culture in the society functions.

The various functions which the National Institute has been called upon to perform are as follows:

- To serve as an apex national level institute;
- To organise and conduct training programmes;
- To coordinate the training activities of various institutes and organisations in the country imparting training in entrepreneurship;
- To affiliate institutes and organisations conducting entrepreneurship training;
- To identify, train and assist potential entrepreneurs amongst technical and non-technical personnel in setting up self-employment ventures in small industries including service industries;
- To hold examinations and tests and confer certificates and diplomas on the trainers as well as trainees;
- To undertake documentation and research in the field of entrepreneurship and small business development;
- To conduct workshops, seminars and conferences, etc., for promotion and development of entrepreneurship in small-scale industries and small business;
- To publish literature for furtherance of entrepreneurship and small business development;
- To provide a forum for interaction and exchange of view with agencies engaged in various aspect of entrepreneurship in small industries and small business development.
- To assist in setting up of regional and state level training institutes for entrepreneurship and small business development.

The institute interacts with all other organisation centres engaged in conducting entrepreneurship development programmes in the country and provides them support in various areas including funding of programmes wherever necessary and feasible. The institute addresses itself to working with them in enhancing the efficiency and utility of entrepreneurship development programmes bringing about coordination.

With the setting up of this institute, entrepreneurship development in India through organised training has assumed added significance particularly for training educated unemployed youth for taking up self-employment ventures.

Entrepreneurship Development Institute of India (EDII)

Entrepreneurship Development Institute of India (EDII), Ahmedabad, is an autonomous non-profit institution, set up in 1983, sponsored by financial institutions such as Industrial Development Bank of India (IDBI), Industrial Finance Corporation of India (IFCI), Industrial Credit and Investment Corporation of India (ICICI) and the State Bank of India (SBI). The Government of Gujarat has also provided assistance for the setting up of EDII.

EDII has been spearheading an entrepreneurship movement throughout the nation with a belief that entrepreneurs need not necessarily be born; they can be developed through well-conceived and well-directed activities.

In consonance with this belief, the objectives of the EDII are to:

- augment the supply of trained entrepreneurs through training;
- generate a multiplier effect on opportunities for self-employment;
- improve managerial capabilities of small-scale industries;
- contribute to the dispersal of business ownership and thus expand the social base of Indian entrepreneurial class;

- contribute to the creation and dissemination of new knowledge and insight into entrepreneurial theory and practice through research;
- augment the supply of trainer-motivators for entrepreneurship development;
- participate in institution-building efforts;
- sensitise the support environment to facilitate potential as well as existing entrepreneurs to establish and manage their enterprises;
- promote micro-enterprises at the rural level;
- inculcate the spirit of 'Entrepreneurship' amongst youth, and
- collaborate with similar organisations in India and other developing countries to accomplish the above objectives.

Training Programmes

The training programmes of the institute are grouped under four heads:

- Entrepreneurship in education;
- Micro-finance and micro-enterprise development;
- Performance and growth of existing entrepreneurs, and
- Performance improvement of ED institutions and ED programmes.

The educational environment and policy framework offer opportunities for sustainable self-employment to ensure the contribution of the workforce to the industrial economy. Entrepreneurship, self-employment and enterprise creation thus provide a solution to the crisis of both unemployment and disguised unemployment. With this in view, the EDII has designed and successfully implemented several national and international training programmes and workshops for the academic community and for the youth.

EDII organises training programmes on Informal Micro Credit Delivery Systems (IMCDS) and management for strengthening the participating NGOs in the area of informal credit. To strengthen NGOs through building their managerial capabilities, the EDII has launched a programme on the sustainability of NGOs through better management. It also provides a platform to NGCOs and bankers with the objective of facilitating the access of the poor to credit.

The small industry sector is required to gear up to face the challenges of liberalisation and globalisation. The EDII in 1984 initiated Performance Improvement Programmes in anticipation of the need of management strategy and growth-oriented awareness and competencies. These programmes focus on functional management inputs and strategic techniques, thereby channelising entrepreneurial competencies to rejuvenate enterprises.

The institute conceptualises and designs several strategic programmes through innovative training techniques and updated information and documentation. It regularly organises trainers' meets and chief executives' meets to foster linkages among trainers and chief executives of ED organisations to facilitate and experience sharing.

EDII has supported the creation of centres for Entrepreneurship Development and Institutes of Entrepreneurship Development in various states of the country to achieve institutionalisation of ED activities.

INSTITUTES FOR ENTREPRENEURSHIP DEVELOPMENT (IED)

As part of a strategy of giving special attention to entrepreneurship development needs of the more backward states, IDBI had announced the proposal to set up Institutes for Entrepreneurship Development (IED) in association with other financial institutions and banks and the state governments. IED's set-up in Uttar Pradesh, Bihar and Orissa have become operational and the proposed IED in Madhya Pradesh has already been registered.

IED in the UP had conducted 16 EDPs covering 664 trainees, besides training state-level trainers. It also has conducted programmes on industrial extension motivation, business opportunity guidance and project counselling for women, entrepreneurial awareness workshop for ex-serviceman, state-level meet of EDP conducting agencies, studies on "Factors inhibiting and facilitating turnaround possibilities in small sector" and "Relevance of hill wool scheme". IED in Orissa had conducted 11 EDPs which benefited 307 trainees. It also conducted four management development programmmes, four entrepreneurship awareness camps and lecture-cum-discussion session on "Problems and Prospects of Indo-US Trade and Investment". IED in Bihar conducted two EDPs and organised an entrepreneurs' meet during the period under review.

SCIENCE AND TECHNOLOGY ENTREPRENEURSHIP PARKS (STEPs)

As part of the programme for supporting the setting up of 15 STEPs jointly with other institutions, IDBI over the years has assisted seven STEPs, viz., those sponsored by the Birla Institute of Technology (BIT), Ranchi; National Entrepreneurs' Chemical Park (NECP); The Regional Engineering College (TREC), Trichy; Harcourt Butler Technological Institute (HBTI), Kanpur; Sri Jayachamarajendra College of Engineering (SJCE), Mysore; Guru Nanak Engineering College, Ludhiana and Maulana Azad College of Technology, Bhopal with the aggregate assistance of ₹ 6.2 crore. While the first five STEPs were sanctioned assistance prior or 1988-89, the last two were sanctioned assistance during the reporting period. STEPs proposed by Guru Nanak Engineering College will specialise in machine tools and electro-mechanical control equipment while the STEP sponsored by the Maulana Azad College of Technology will be specialising in electronics and power engineering.

BIT-STEP has developed a unique technology for automatic wire length measurement system and import substitutive stainless steel wedge wire screen, besides other technologies for industrial applications. NECP is engaged in the preparation of project profiles of selected imported drugs. TREC-STEP has developed technology for hit-tech paints for nuclear applications, besides other hi-tech and import-substitutive products. Commercial production had already been started by seven TREC-STEP entrepreneurs. Student entrepreneurs of HBTI-STEP are working on projects which include fibre reinforced concrete and plastic components. SJCE-STEP has already transferred technology of liquid level pump controller to one of its entrepreneurs for commercial exploitation and eight of the STEP entrepreneurs have established their units.

The Centre for Entrepreneurship Development (CED)

Development of entrepreneurs on a systematic basis started in 1970. A number of specialised institutions came up to provide training to various target-groups — educated unemployed persons, women, technicians, foremen, rural artisans, physically handicapped persons, etc. The Centre for Entrepreneurship Development (CED), Ahmedabad was sponsored by the state government and public sector corporations concerned with industrial development in the state. This centre conducts entrepreneurship development programmes. Persons were selected from amongst the employees, workers, merchants and graduates and training was imparted at six centres. The following are some of the significant features of the programme of training:

(a) Before conducting the programme of training, a survey of investment opportunity was made for identifying industries having good scope in the area.

(b) Appropriate linkage was developed with various agencies which provide support and service to entrepreneurs in getting finance, ready-made sheds, raw materials and other inputs;

(c) Entrepreneurs were selected through behavioural tests. Due weightage on experience was given rather than education or unemployment.

(d) Programmes of training included theoretical and practical coverage, including visits to industrial units consistent with the items identified by the entrepreneurs.

(e) Follow-up action was taken by the full-time project leader and individual attention was given to each entrepreneur trainee.

The success rate of CED programmes is reported to be of the order of 66 per cent.

The Entrepreneurial Motivation Centre, set up in Assam in the north-eastern region of India, conducts entrepreneurial development programmes. In the earlier stages 28, officers drawn from various departments of the state government were given training in entrepreneurial motivation, economic investigation and survey, management of small enterprise, etc., in the Small Industries Extension Training Institute in Hyderabad. These officers then joined the various branches of the Entrepreneurial Motivation Training Centres in six districts.

The Entrepreneurial Motivation Training Centre gave wide publicity to the entrepreneurial development programmes and invited applications from educated unemployed persons. Selection was made based on psychological tests and personal interviews. Selected entrepreneurs were given preliminary motivation training of two weeks for developing or strengthening the motivation for self-employment, managerial and economic aspects of entrepreneurial development. The entrepreneurs were further assisted in selecting enterprises for themselves, conducting guided market surveys and preparing economically viable and feasible projects reports. The Centre acted as link agency and helped the entrepreneurs in obtaining finance from banks and other institutions, and ready-made sheds as working space. The Centre further provided 10 per cent of the sanctioned amount as seed money wherever necessary. An evaluated revealed that by March 1975, the number of entrepreneurs trained came to 1,550, of which 1,053 entrepreneurs (68 per cent) completed their project reports and 581 were given in-plant training. Among those who completed the project reports, 310 entrepreneurs were assisted in obtaining sanction of financial assistance. Of these 310 entrepreneurs, 279 (90 per cent) actually established their enterprises and started functioning.

Central Manufacturing Technology Institute, Bengaluru

The Xavier Institute of Social Service in Ranchi was involved with tribals and people from the villages in training to become entrepreneurs. A group of young tribal youths constituted into a local organisation for promotion of socio-economic and health schemes (known as Vikas Maitry) received some funds from the Indo-German Social Service Society in New Delhi in 1975. They desired that an entrepreneurship development programme be run for them. A project leader who himself was a tribal was appointed. The programme was organised and 20 candidates were selected, all belonging to tribal areas. In selecting, little importance was given to academic qualifications. Clarity of presentation of goals and determination to reach that goal were the important considerations. Four months' full-time training was arranged. During the day, the entrepreneurs worked as apprentices in shops of the type they intended to set up themselves. In the evening, they got a grounding in the basis of achievements, motivation, leadership and communication, management, finances, costing, laws and taxation, marketing and project preparation. After completion of the training course, the entrepreneurs went back to their respective villages and made mini-market surveys. They brought back the field data and worked these into a project proposal for financing by the bank. The financing was undertaken through the intermediary of Vikas Maitri Kalyan Sangh and the organisation undertook to stand guarantee for the young entrepreneurs. Continuous and sustained follow-up action was undertaken. This was the responsibility of the project officer and assistant project officer. A success rate of 60 per cent was attained. The state government later gave assistance to the institute for conducting entrepreneurial development programmes for unemployed engineers, diplomaholders, graduates and ITI trained boys and the institute has done well.

Role of Development Banks

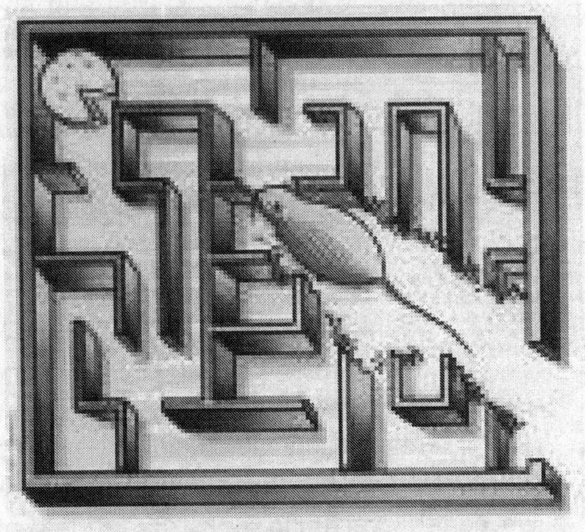

Various development banks in India have introduced "special capital" and "seed capital" schemes to provide equity of assistance to new and technically-skilled entrepreneurs who lack financial resources of their own. In view of the long-term benefits to society from the emergence of a new class of entrepreneurs, development banks have been actively involved in entrepreneurship development programmes and in establishing a set of institutions which identify and train potential entrepreneurs. The promotional activities like carrying out industrial potential surveys, identification of potential entrepreneurs, conducting entrepreneurship development programmes and providing technical consultancy services have contributed in a significant manner to the process of industrialisation and effective utilisation of institutional finance by industry. In recent years, the development banks have initiated special measures for the creation of specialised institutions for the training of entrepreneurs and research in this field.

Role of Business Schools
Can any B-school actually teach Entrepreneurship?

To the would-be MBA entrepreneur, 'O' no longer spells opportunity as much as opportunity cost. Yet, interest in entrepreneurship as a subject is growing steadily in Indian B-school campuses. They have entrepreneurship cells, business plan contests, elective courses and, in some cases, full-fledged entrepreneurship centres, some going so far as to provide 'incubation support'. The question remains: can entrepreneurship really be 'taught'? And the case study method answer is: it depends.

Originally, entrepreneurship courses were meant to literally 'produce entrepreneurs'. In 1947, Harvard Business School (HBS) developed an elective titled 'Management of Small Enterprises' for students eager to start their own businesses after World War II. The real thrust into teaching and research in the area came in the early 1980s when HBS graduate and pioneering venture capitalist Arthur Rock funded the first professorship in the field of entrepreneurship at HBS.

Under legendary Professor Howard H. Stevenson, entrepreneurship came to be defined not just as an 'innate trait' but a particular type of managerial behaviour available to virtually all managers in organisations of all kinds and sizes. Today, HBS requires its 900 first-year students to take a course called 'The Entrepreneurial Manager', and offers almost 20 elective courses in the area to its second-year students. American B-schools, including the likes of Wharton, offer entrepreneurial management as a major, "preparing students for careers as autonomous entrepreneurs, family-business entrepreneurs, or entrepreneurs in corporate setting". Entrepreneurship centres have also become an integral feature at campuses in the US, thanks to corporates and individuals who are keen to fund them. The University of Michigan, for example, got $10 million to set up such a centre in 1999.

In contrast, Indian B-schools have made a more modest foray into entrepreneurship education. Every self-respecting B-school offers at least one elective in the area as part of the second year of the postgraduate programme (PGP). And interest from students is high. At IIM Lucknow, the 'New Venture Planning' (NVP) course has seen an enrolment as high as 70 per cent in some years. The course gives perspectives from all functional areas like marketing, finance, operations, strategy and also preparation of business plans. IIM Bengluru offers as many as four electives covering the entire gamut — from the regulation 'Managing New Ventures' to the gung-ho 'Entrepreneurship from the Trenches: A Real World Perspective'. Further, a course in 'Social Entrepreneurship' is being introduced. In March 2002, IIM-B set up the Nadathur S. Raghavan Centre for Entrepreneurial Learning (NSRCEL) with a generous grant from N. S. Raghavan, one of the cofounders of Infosys Technologies (See 'Incubation, The New Buzzword').

In addition to supporting teaching and research, NSRCEL has a state-of-the-art incubator "to help entrepreneurs launch their business plans into commercially viable products and services". The problem is, students of the PGP seem to be showing little interest (so far) in utilising its facilities. "Most of the entrepreneurship courses are not taken seriously as they are taught in the fifth and sixth term when marks are not counted for placements", a second-year student points out. "There is a 'Start-up Club' as well in the campus, but its activities are infrequent and limited to a few VC lectures and games."

Box 32.1 Incubation, The New Buzzword

In sync with the global trends, Indian B-schools are jumping on to the wealth creation bandwagon. Entrepreneurship centres offering research, training and incubation facilities are coming up all over the place.

- IIM-A set up the Centre for Innovation, Incubation and Entrepreneurship (CIIE) in 2001 through grants from the Gujarat government and National Innovation Foundation, and its own funds.
- IIM-C set up a Centre for Entrepreneurship and Innovation to spearhead activities to promote, train and incubate entrepreneurial ventures, especially in high-tech areas.
- Mumbai's K.J. Somaiya Institute of Management Studies and Research is setting up the Centre of Excellence in Entrepreneurship with Strathclyde University's Hunter Centre for Entrepreneurship.
- The ICFAI Centre for Entrepreneurship Development at Hyderabad offers training as well as incubation facilities. (It presently supports one company.)
- Mudra Institute of Communications, Ahmedabad (Mica) has set up an entrepreneurship development centre (EDC).
- ISB Hyderabad's Wadhwani Centre for Entrepreneurial Development aims to "inspire the next generation of entrepreneurs to create 1,000 new businesses over the next 10 years". It is funded and chaired by Romesh Wadhwani, former vice-chairman, i2 Technologies.

On paper, everything looks great. Most of the centres plan to cater to the in-house student community, as well as offer services and training to outsiders. IIM-C hopes to network with other top educational institutions in the eastern region, and all the incubators are open to evaluating proposals from 'anyone with a viable business plan'. However, the centres haven't been able to enthuse their students – not even those with entrepreneurial ambitions.

But that might be changing. At Mica, Raunica Sethi, a 2004 graduate, is the first student whose dream is being supported by the centre on campus. Sethi plans to set up a 'Career Exploration, Training and Counselling' centre to guide students. She is spending a year as a project associate at Mica's EDC — time that she is using to put her ideas into practice. And for the very first time, Anveshan, a national search for innovation by IIM-A's CIIE, has thrown up a second-year student from the campus as a winner. 'Biosynthesis of Nanomaterials', a project submitted by Kunal Upadhyaya (IIM-A) and Dr. Murali Sastry (National Chemical Laboratory, Pune) bagged third place in the 'Innovation/Prototype in search of an 'enterprise' category.

CIIE is offering incubation support to Upadhyaya as well as a team from IIIT Gwalior which won gold in the 'business plan' category. This means not just working space and computers, but mentoring as well as networking to see the idea through to the commercialisation stage. Says CIIE coordinator Somnath Chatterjee: "The dream is that one day we will have not just banks and consultants, but VCs chasing our students on Day 1." Amen.

While the NSRCEL incubator can house about 10 teams of up to six members each, it currently supports just two-education BPO Meta-i Technologies and software company EmbedX. Neither of the two boasts any IIM-B students or alumni. There are some practical issues adding to the problem. For instance, the NSRCEL Board meets only once in six months to evaluate new entrepreneurial ideas. But at the heart of the matter lies the same old argument: IIMs are a platform to get lucrative jobs, which you won't get once you are out of this place.

This very attitude is being attacked head on with remarkable success with 'Laboratory in Entrepreneurial Motivation' (LEM), an elective course at IIM Ahmedabad. Taught since 1992 by IIM-A alumnus and entrepreneur Sunil Handa, the course has no textbook, no readings, no quizzes, no test, no exams. No funds on how to apply for loans or make project reports students can always figure that out later. LEM simply targets the 'fear factor' involved in spurning or giving up a job to start out on your own.

EDPs OF SIDBI

The aim of SIDBI's EDPs is to build and nurture a reservoir of entrepreneurs. Such EDPs are conducted through the specialised agencies in Entrepreneurship Development Institute of India, Institutes of Entrepreneurship Development (IED), Centre for Entrepreneurship Development (CED), Technical Consultancy Organisations (TCOs) and Non-governmental Organisations (NGOs).

Management deficiency and a low level of skills and technology have been some of the major weaknesses of small industries. SIDBI is constantly endeavouring to address these problems by bringing reputed management and technical institutions close to the small-scale industries and arranging specially designed programmes, *viz.:* Small Industries Management Assistants Programme (SIMAP) and Skill-cum-Technology Upgradation Programme (STUP). The objective of SIMAP is to develop a cadre of industrial managers specifically trained to assist the SSI entrepreneurs in their multiple responsibilities. STUP is structured to improve the performance of the existing SSI units by developing/strengthening managerial skills and the technical competence of the entrepreneurs and senior executives of the small enterprises.

The Institutes of Entrepreneurship Development (IED) set up with Bank's support in Bihar, Orissa, Madhya Pradesh and Uttar Pradesh, continued to make good progress.

SIDBI's strategy for entrepreneurship development involves support to specially designed programmes covering the target-groups like rural poor, women, scheduled castes/tribes, ex-servicemen, etc. In tune with the renewed policy initiatives on rural development, the bank has given thrust to promote rural entrepreneurs. This is evident from the fact that of 102 EDPs supported during the 1994-95 for various target groups, 66 were exclusively targeted at rural entrepreneurs. Besides rural EDPs conducted during the current year, SIDBI supported 30 EDPs for women and 8 for other groups having special focus on North-Eastern and other backward areas. A few specialised technical institutes like Central Institute of Plastic Engineering and Technology at Bhopal, Patna, Lucknow and Madras; Rural Technology Institute, Ahmedabad and UP Electronics Corporation, Lucknow were extended assistance for conduct of product specific EDPs. To back-up the EDP efforts, the Bank has been compiling project profiles on viable project ideas suitable for tiny and rural entrepreneurs. A compendium of Profiles on Food Processing and Agro-based Industries, prepared by Central Food Technological Research Institute, Mysore, on behalf of SIDBI, was brought out during the year. Two more compendia — one on new hi-tech projects prepared by various CSR laboratories in collaboration with National Research Development Corporation and the other on location neutral projects (Volume-II), prepared by Gujarat Industrial and Technical Consultancy Organisation Ltd., have been published.

Role of Commercial Banks

The State Bank of India at that time was the only bank amongst commercial banks to come out with a comprehensive programme for entrepreneurship development. From the orthodox role of commercial banks, the State Bank of India pioneered as a premier banking institution in India by assuming the role of a development bank. The sixties and early seventies saw many important strides towards the fulfilment of this objective. The bank recognised the importance of small-scale industries in industrial development and started financing small-scale industries on a large scale. To cater to the specific needs of this sector, a package of schemes and programmes was formulated by the bank. These are in: (*i*) Liberalised scheme of financing small-scale industries wherein 75 per cent of the project cost is met as bank loan; (*ii*) Entrepreneur scheme for financing technically-qualified persons where the entire project cost could be financed by way of term loan; and (*iii*) Equity Fund Scheme for providing interest-free loan to meet the equity gap up to ₹ 1 lakh.

Approach Modifications

Looking to the characteristics of the small-scale industries, it must be realised that these are basically owner-manager-oriented and need special attention and support. The norms for financing such industries were, therefore, liberalised and a need-based approach was evolved — a major departure from earlier security-oriented approach.

Non-financial Support

In spite of liberalisation in financing policy and government incentives, the progress in industrialisation was not so rapid. Realising that mere provision of financial support was not sufficient for bringing about that desired change, the need was felt for evolving a policy of providing for non-financial assistance. A number of measures were thereafter initiated— development of management skills of the SSI borrowers through Management Development Programmes and Management Appreciation Programmes. The bank went to the extent of conducting training programmes for development of entrepreneurial attitude and financing such entrepreneurs. It was indeed the beginning of a new banking era.

To set up an industry, the ability to meet the margin money requirements of the small-scale project itself is not enough, but entrepreneurial characteristics have to be identified and reinforced in the entrepreneur of that industry. Thus, the important characteristics of the entrepreneur, namely, psychological, economic, social and managerial characteristics, have to be learnt, understood and digested by every prospective entrepreneur. For the success of the industry, the man behind the project is more important than its fixed assets; the entrepreneur has to be trained well. Industrial and Technical Consultancy Organisation Limited (ITCO), as subsidiary of Industrial Development Bank of India, having a professional experience in counselling the entrepreneurs, identifying the project ideas and preparing detailed project reports, conducting EDPs with the following objectives:

(1) Assess and develop entrepreneurial abilities required to become a successful industrialist.

(2) Dissemination of information on the formalities and procedures to be followed for starting small-scale industries.

(3) Dissemination of information on the facilities and incentives available for starting small-scale industries.

(4) Guidance in selecting projects suitable for different trainees based on their investment, educational background, technical expertise, proficiency, aptitude, etc.

(5) Acting as a liaison between the various officers/organisation engaged in industrial promotional activities in the state and trainees for availing of necessary facilities available in their projects.

(6) Dissemination of information on how to plan and manage a small-scale industry successfully.

These programmes cover all educated unemployed youths —

(1) Having a strong desire to set up an industry and having the confidence of its success.

(2) With basic technical qualification of S.S.C. with 5 years' industrial experience.

(3) In the age group of 21 to 35 years.

(4) Able to invest the required share capital (25 per cent of project cost) to the selected project.

(5) With independent thinking and decision-making status.

(6) Claiming nativity of the district.

This course is intended to give a working knowledge of industrial promotional agencies, project report preparation, general management of small-scale industries, besides transforming the prospective entrepreneurs by achievement motivation. These programmes include the academic inputs necessary for the purpose.

SBI's Programmes

The State Bank of India formulated an elaborate plan to conduct the EDPs, particularly in the backward areas and started conducting such programmes since 1978. As per the bank's model, the EDPs consist of one month's intensive training in Behavioural Sciences, Aspects of Management and Field Training. During this period, the entire cost of boarding and lodging is borne by the Bank. In this year, the bank had conducted 7 EDPs covering 11 districts in Madhya Pradesh (7 lead districts plus Surguja, Bhind, Morena, and Gwalior districts) and a total of 156 candidates were trained under these programmes. A total loan of ₹ 121 lakh has been sanctioned to 44 such trained persons.

Phases of Entrepreneurship Development

In broad terms, the EDP consists of three basic phases:

(i) *Initiation Phase:* For creating awareness about the entrepreneurial opportunities.

(ii) *Development Phase:* Through training programmes in developing motivation and management skills.

(iii) *Support Phase:* Counselling, encouragement and infrastructural support for establishing and running an enterprise.

In the initiation phase, it is aimed at identifying persons with a potential for development of entrepreneurial disposition. The development phase aims at infusing motivation through achievement motivation training, supported with adequate management and technical knowledge. But finally, the most important is the support phase as from the entrepreneurial point of view, the most crucial stage is the start-up period.

The development of entrepreneurship depends very much on organisation, education, stimulation and motivation of the clientele through a concerted and systematic approach, focusing on individuals and groups. Entrepreneurial development, is essential not only to solve the problem of industrial development, but also to solve the long existing problems of unemployment, unbalanced area development concentration of economic power, and diversion of profits from traditional avenues of investment. Therefore, one can notice some attempts made by the government's agencies and other institutions to undertake the task of entrepreneurial promotion. Most of the promotional activities are directed towards the financial and physical facilities with a strong belief that there will be a conglomeration of entrepreneurs if such facilities are created in the economically backward states of India. Financial and physical facilities are not the only crucial inputs in the development of entrepreneurship but there are other inputs also which one has to consider in any model for entrepreneurial development. In this study, a quantitative survey of entrepreneurship development in India has been presented. The study says that in spite of abundant natural resources, the pace of industrial and entrepreneurial development is slow not only because of lack of basic facilities and financial institutions, but also due to untapped entrepreneurial talent in the country and suggests that timely action by the government and other agencies should be taken for the entrepreneurship development in the country.

ROLE OF NAYE (NATIONAL ALLIANCE OF YOUNG ENTREPRENEURS)

NAYE has been a pioneer in promotion and development of entrepreneurship among women. In keeping with the emerging trends, then NAYE had set up a Women's Wing in 1975, the internationally acknowledged Women's Year. NAYE convened a Conference of Women Entrepreneurs in November 1975 in New Delhi to discuss at length steps to be taken to make women self-reliant and to raise their status in the society. Since then three International Conferences and eight National Conventions of Women Entrepreneurs have been organised in different cities in the country.

Women's wing of NAYE assists women entrepreneurs in:

(a) getting better access to capital, infrastructure and markets;

(b) development of management and production capabilities;

(c) identifying investment opportunities;

(d) attending to problems by taking up individual cases with appropriate authorities;

(e) sponsoring delegations, participation in trade fairs, exhibitions, buyer-seller, specialised conferences, etc.;

(f) organising seminars, workshops and training programmes for giving them wider exposure to available facilities and developing their entrepreneurial capabilities;

(g) lobbying for them in Press, Parliament, State legislatures and other forums;

(h) advocating effectively for securing their rightful place in the Indian economy.

In addition, the Association of Women Entrepreneurs of Karnataka (AWAKE), Women Entrepreneurs' Association of Maharashtra (WIMA) and Self-employed Women's Association (SWWA) are not only fighting for their rights but also striving to promote entrepreneurship among women.

Set up in May 1985, WIMA — the Association of Women Industrialists/Entrepreneurs of Maharashtra has 400 members all over Maharashtra, with its head office in Pune, and branches at Mumbai, Aurangabad, Nasik and Dhulia. NAYE of which WIMA forms a part, presented the organisation with a national award in 1988 for promoting entrepreneurship among women. WIMA aims to help 1,000 women all over Maharashtra.

WIMA's main objective has been to provide a form for members and to help them sell their products. But making is their main problem. WIMA also has training programmes.

There should be a curriculum change along with proper career guidance in women's polytechnics, which will shape the students to become capable entrepreneurs in future. There should also be some reservation for admission of women to disciplines like engineering, medicine, law, agriculture and architecture, with some concessions in regard to the qualification marks. It will be worthwhile to consider the institution of special scholarship schemes for meritorious women students. As far as the Sbtate and Central Governments are concerned, a scheme could be evolved for extending additional concessions for women entrepreneurs for setting up industrial units. As in the case of weaker sections of society, the financial institutions and banks should consider feasibility of waiving collateral security, because women do not possess any land or other property. Women should also be given property rights and an equal share in their fathers' property.

Although the rate of interest then charged by banks on loans extended to women entrepreneurs slightly lower than that charged on the normal loans, what is more important is further reduction and the reorientation by the Reserve Bank of India. In order to ensure that there was adequate credit flow to women entrepreneurs, a sub-goal was considered under the priority sector advances by the banks as is being done presently for advances to weaker sections and other special sectors. More importantly, the condition of a guarantor in the case of women entrepreneurs should be waived by the banks.

INSTITUTIONS IN AID OF ENTREPRENEURSHIP DEVELOPMENT

Arms for Progress: The Ministry of SSI implements its programmes for small-scale sector growth through three organisations under its umbrella.

Ministry of SSI

Small Industries Development Organisation (SIDO)
- Support Services in Entrepreneurship Development
- Management Training
- Project Profiles, Testing Services, Feasibility Reports, Marketing Support

Small Industries Service Institutes (SISIs)
- Interface between States and Central Government
- Technical Support
- Consultancy Services

National Small Industries Corporation (NSIC)
- Loans for Equipment Purchase
- Lease Facility
- Assists in procurement of Raw Materials, Marketing, Technology Transfer

In order to ensure that development of women entrepreneurship takes place, as fast as possible, there is a case for setting up apex bodies at the state capital level and organisations at district levels which could be affiliated to the apex body. Separate industrial cooperative estates for women in different cities may be set up. And 15% to 20% of the purchases of the state governments should be made from women entrepreneurs.

Women entrepreneurs in rural and backward regions need special assistance and incentives from the government and other associate agencies. What is more, training of lakh of women entrepreneurs in the coming decade is a Herculean task for various agencies.

Although it is still in the growing stage, there is unquestionably a business revolution in the works across the nation — and women are a major part of it. Whether they opt to remain on a micro-level, or move to expand on a major scale, they are making their impact felt on the society.

Indian Institute of Management, Ahmedabad

Established in 1961, it was one of the first three management education centres to be established across the country. Starting modestly with support help and guidance from the Harvard Business School, today IIMA is considered to be the best of all other centres.

IIMA pioneered management education by first introducing its executive development programmes for working managers and following it up with its graduate diploma programme a year later in 1962. Following the case study method of teaching, over the years, it has in its collection, more than 2,000 Indian cases developed by its own faculty.

In 1991, IIMA introduced student exchange programmes. This cross-cultural approach is desirable especially when students are vying for overseas placement after graduation.

Even though it falls under the Ministry of Education, IIMA enjoys functional and academic autonomy. Although there is a common admission test for all IIM centres, each centre applies different selection criterion and IIMA's selection procedure is totally internal, i.e., IIMA faculty do the evaluation at all stages.

Besides a two-year postgraduate programme, IIMA also offers a fellow programme in management, faculty development programme and its executive development programmes are considered to be the best.

Indian Institute of Management, Ahmedabad - 380015.
Tel: (079)6327241
Fax: (079)6326896
Website: www.iimahd.ernet.net.in

National Institute of Design (NID) , Ahmedabad

Like IIMA, NID was started in 1961 as a part of post-independence government initiative of establishing educational institutions across the country. Today, NID is most recognised for its quality – quality of its professionals as well as training. It functions autonomously as a part and parcel of the Ministry of Commerce and Industry and as an institute of excellence in education, research, service and training.

The primary focus is on design education encompassing a number of fields such as industrial design, communication design, textile and apparel design and exhibition design, making it the only one offering so many disciplines under a single umbrella. All these are the broad disciplines under which further specialisations are offered.

The strong point of NID, which is a must for any design institute, is its unique mode of inculcating learning by doing. At the end of the course, it is this bank of experience accumulated over the period of five or more years that helps each student from his own set of views, beliefs and opinions of a good design.

NID does not work in isolation from the changing global environment. Its collaboration with other prestigious design institutions across the world prove ideal for its students. As part of its information technology initiatives, it has already entered into strategic alliance with other institutes as a mechanism to reinforce IT in its design curriculum.

National Institute of Design,
Paldi, Ahmedabad - 380007.
Tel: (079)6639692
Fax: (079)6605342
E-Mail: info@nid.edu
Website: www.nid.edu

Indian Institute of Technology (IIT), Kharagpur

The first in a chain of six IITs, it was established in 1950 following the recommendations of the Sarkar Committee, to cater to the need for skilled manpower in the country. From a modest start in the dilapidated Hijli jail building, in an idyllic, sylvan setting IIT Kharagpur has been engaged in a virtually continuous process of development to let the creative edges of the budding engineers run free. Maulana Abul Kalam Azad adopted the present name 'Indian Institute of Technology' before the formal inauguration of the institute on August 18, 1951. The handsome main building with its majestic tower was inaugurated in 1956. It was aptly described by Pandit Jawarharlal Nehru at the first convocation address that, "Hijli Detention Camp stands this fit monument of India, representing India's urges, India's future in the making". IIT Kharagpur started its journey in the old Hijli Detention Camp where some of our great freedom fighters toiled and sacrificed their lives for the independence of our country. This is possibly one of the very few institutions all over the world which started life in a prison house. A large amount of financial help was available for procuring a number of machine tools from the ministry of industry and supply. The institute workshop was supposed to be one of the best in the country. Today, IIT Kharagpur has come a long way to its present position of pre-eminence with eighteen academic departments, eight multidisciplinary centres, a school of management, a school of telecommunications and several sophisticated central facilities. It is the largest and most diversified among all the IITs. In a study sponsored by the Department of Science and Technology, Government of India, it was found to have the highest relative employment productivity index among the IITs and is the top supplier of fresh engineers and technologists to the public and private sector industries. It also ranked first among the IITs in the production of science and engineering Ph.Ds. From this modest start in 1950, IIT Kharagpur has been engaged in a steady process of development with about 18 academic departments, five centres of excellence. IIT Kharagpur, the premier institute of technology in the country, promotes the pursuance of academic excellence in disciplines ranging from Aerospace Engineering to Biotechnology; Computer Science Engineering to Agriculture and Food Engineering through its various departments centres and central facilities and special R&D cells which offer 22 undergraduate and 50 postgraduate courses. Over the last four decades of its existence, IIT Kharagpur has redefined its aims, broadened its objectives, and introduced major changes in its programmes and priorities. The syllabi and the curricula are constantly updated and modified keeping in pace with technological developments. Consolidation and diversification of academic efforts to relate the entire educational endeavour to the larger context of the national development process, constitute the focus of its dynamic educational philosophy. A special cell for Sponsored Research and Industrial Consultancy (SRIC) was set up in the institute more than two decades ago to promote sponsored and industrial R&D. The activities have grown phenomenally during the last decade. With the surging of the international collaborative projects, both the students and faculty are looking up to horizons of new possibilities that still await the optimum technological excellence.

Address: Indian Institute of Technology, Kharagpur-721302, India.

E-mail: iitkgp.emet.in

Structuring Entrepreneurial Development Programmes

The above case studies bring out certain features important for the success of entrepreneurial develoment programmes. The training programme aims at identification and careful selection of entrepreneurs (using advanced series of psychological tests), developing the motivation and entrepreneurial capabilities of the trainees, equipping the trainees to identify viable industrial projects and to prepare project profiles or brief project reports, equipping the trainees with basic enterprise-building skills, imparting basic managerial skills required for the successful management of the unit and helping the trainees to secure the necessary financial, infrastructural and related assistance during the implementation of the project. Skill training formed a vital and major component of this programme.

CONCLUSION

Economic activities could be directly linked with the entrepreneurial level of a nation and, therefore, entrepreneurship development be considered as a critical input for industrial and business development efforts of a country. In this process, institutions play a catalytic role in entrepreneurship development.

Entrepreneurship is one of the pillars of economic growth. Development of economy is impacted by the entrepreneurial level and the spread of the entrepreneurial culture in the country. The myth that entrepreneurs are born, no more holds good, rather it is well recognised now that the entrepreneurs can be created and nurtured through appropriate interventions in the form of entrepreneurship development programmes.

Entrepreneurial development in India has now been conducted for a long-time, and sophisticated selection techniques and training methodology have been developed. The programme integrates identification and training of potential entrepreneurs, identification of viable industrial projects and developing managerial capabilities. Institutional support in the areas of finance, infrastructure, etc., is also linked with the programme.

The role of EDPs in accelerating industrialisation of a state or a region can hardly be over-emphasised. All those who are engaged in the administration of this programme must fully realise the enormous responsibility entailed in seeking to assist those without much influence, managerial ability or capability to bear risks. No tangible results can, therefore, be expected unless all the agencies involved in the task work with determination, zeal and a sense of dedication and commitment. Entrepreneurship development is to be attuned to economic needs. It is, therefore, necessary to recognise the importance of entrepreneurship as an aspect of social life.

Similarly, entrepreneurship education should be made more socially utilitarian. It is, nevertheless, imperative to restructure the entire curriculum — should identify the area of entrepreneurship and to motivate young people to start their own business at an early age in their chosen field of interest, for entrepreneurship exists in every profession, irrespective of its size. This will generate self-employment, which is always more satisfying than working for others.

ANNEXURE-I

Syllabus for Entrepreneurship Development Programme

Duration: 3 months

Specific subjects

I. Micro Laboratory

(1) Tests – achievement successful experience

— Ring toss game

— Individual

— Group

— Group with stake

(2) Scoring achievement stories

Interpretation of results of achievement and ring toss

(3) Interpretation of stories and games

Problem showing game

Boat building game

Block building game

(4) Group discussions

Life goal exercises

II. (1) Role of small-scale industries, need for small industries, problems and prospects.

III. (1) Development programme for small industries and selected small industries having prospects for development.

(a) Engineering industries

(b) Chemicals

(c) Rubber and plastics

(d) Electrical and electronics

(e) Leather

(f) Ceramics

(g) Ancillaries

IV. Financial and Physical Facilities for Small Industries.

(1) Risk capital – long-term and short-term loans, financing of entrepreneurs by banks, other agencies/corporations (filling out applications forms, etc.)

(2) Role of industrial estates/industrial areas, availability of built-up sheds, developed areas in the state, procedure and formalities required.

(3) Assistance provided by state industries development corporations.

(4) (a) Procedures and formalities in obtaining raw materials (indigenous/imported).

(b) Availability of power, water, municipal licence, etc.

(c) Marketing assistance programme, etc.

(d) Export possibilities and assistance.

(e) Project selection and preparation of project report, preliminary report, technical consultancy discussions with officers, institutions, etc.

V. Library Consultations

(1) Experience of successful entrepreneurs drawn from mechanical, chemical and othe trades in small-scale sector.

VI. Study Visits to Industrial Units and In-plant Training

(1) This tour is mainly intended to broaden the outlook of entrepreneurs by actual observations and discussions with small industrialists regarding managerial and technical problems.

(2) Trainees should also visit industrial units of their own choice relating to the lines chosen by them. The participants in the course should be taken in a group to a few well-organised large and small-scale industrial units with a view to exposing them to modern techniques of management, etc., and training. As far as possible, arrangements may be made for in-plant training in industrial units or production centres of importance.

VII. Industrial and Other Tax Acts Regulating:

(a) Working hours

(b) Minimum wages

(c) Employees' insurance

(d) Industrial disputes

(e) Income tax

(f) Sales tax

(g) Other aspects.

VIII. Practice of Management

(1) Functions of management, planning, organisation, coordination, direction, control and motivation, definition of organisation, organisational structures, line and staff, functional role of committees, etc.

(2) Practice of management, organisation and structure of an enterprise, problem of maintaining team spirit, modern office management, automation and management, research in management techniques and practices, etc.

(3) Types of organisations.

(4) Scope and functions of O&M selection and initiation of assignment, method study, design and control of forms, layout, office environment and design of functional furniture, etc.

IX. Functional Areas of Management

(1) Production, planning and control.

(2) Creative marketing, planning, policies and strategies, etc.

(3) Finance and costing, etc.

X. Project Finalisation

(1) To conduct an explorative survey individually by the trainees by contacting dealers, consumers, established agencies and manufacturers in line for collecting factual market data concerning the production lines chosen by them. Efforts should also be made to collect details about the availability of machinery and terms and conditions of their supply, etc.

(2) How to create market for the production line chosen, processing and compilation of market data in consultation with the different development agencies and technical officers.

(3) Finalisation of the project report and its presentation.

XI. Evaluation and Workshop for Project Registration and an Approval with DIs/Banks, etc.

(1) Evaluation of the progress achieved by the trainees during the course.

(2) Workshop and group discussions.

(Management adjustment can be resorted to by the training institute in respect of allotment of number of working hours to each one of the major topics covered, keeping in view that the approach should be conceptual and oriented more towards practical aspects rather than theory).

ANNEXURE-II

Important Guidelines

(A) Entrepreneurial Quality/Identity Development

1. Number of sessions range from 20-30 covering 4 sessions a day up to a maximum 6 days.
2. It varies with the number of participants because EMT Lab demands individual attention.
3. The above sequence has been largely in a chronological order. However, certain areas need to be spread over a number of days as indicated above.
4. In the case of rural entrepreneur activity, data may be generated in the beginning at stretches followed with TAT. Analysis need not precede activity exercise.
5. Sessions on coping mechanisation, influencing ability and other aspects of entrepreneurial behaviour can be incorporated during enterprise launching or afterwards fitting it with the language of enterprise.
6. In order to develop identity of entrepreneur, EMT trainer cannot be just concerned with the first week's input or behaviour input; trainer has to provide a linkage and integrate it with the entire syllabus. Entrepreneurial process integration can emerge with appropriate interventions at various points in different programmes. Trainer has to use his own discretion in this.
7. Goal-setting and action plan may need more time.
8. Public statement on proposed action plan may enhance the commitment to entrepreneurial goal.

(B) Enterprise Launching and Resourcing

1. Each session would be of 90 minutes' duration.
2. Lecture notes would be based on the lectures delivered.
3. Reading material would be additional literature.
4. Wherever available, appropriate films would be shown.
5. Audio-visual aids to be used wherever necessary.
6. All exercises related to enterprise launching should be related to the selected enterprise. In case the entrepreneurs have not selected a project during training, a separate one-week period may be allotted for preparing actual project report after field visit. Selected references have been indicated separately.

(C) Enterprise Management

1. Additional sessions can be added, depending on the entrepreneur's background, size and type of enterprise introducing to computer/information management.
2. Production planning, systematic control, etc., can be included accordingly.

(D) Social Responsibility and Entrepreneurial Discipline

1. The topic indicated under this may be treated simultaneously with other topics or may be taken up separately at one place.

This can also be done by discussing pros and cons of entrepreneurial career or in the need and scope of entrepreneurship in the present economic context.

Field Visits/Inplant Study

Depending on the level of enterprises, both the field visits and in-plant studies of 4-6 days' duration each can be organised as a part of the EDTP. However, a field study of 4-6 days' duration will always help provide practical experience and is recommended as part of the general entrepreneurship course.

(**Source:** Model Syllabi for Entrepreneurship Development Training Programmes.)

ANNEXURE-III

Course code: Entrepreneurship 100

Course title: Entrepreneurship and Economic Development in the Philippines.

Course Description

The first part is concerned with the presentation of a firm. It also presents and discusses the current business outlook in relation to the prevailing social, political and economic conditions of the country.

The second part aims at increasing the level of confidence and achievement orientation among the students, thereby developing in them proper psychological preparation for and mental attitude to business.

Course Outline

Part 1

Topic	No.of Hours
1.1 Entrepreneurship Defined	1
1.2 Attitudinal Factors in the Development of Entrepreneurs	3
1.2.1 Psychological	
1.2.2 Social	
1.2.3 Others	
1.3 Environmental Factors Affecting Entrepreneurial Performance in the Philippines	6
1.3.1 Social	
1.3.2 Political	
1.3.3 Economic	
1.3.4 International	
1.3.5 Others	
1.4 The Role of Entrepreneurs in Economic Development	9
1.4.1 Starting own Business	
1.4.2 Motivating Others to Engage in Nusiness	
1.4.3 Assisting Others in Managing Business	
1.5 The Social Responsibilities of an Entrepreneur	
2.1 Goal-setting	5
2.1.1 Definition of Goals	
2.1.2 General and Specific Objectives	
2.2 Risks in Business	8
2.2.1 Definition	
2.2.2 Kinds of Risk	

33 CHAPTER

ALL ABOUT RELEVANT ACTS

"Shoring up the bottom line"

"At the end of the day, it's the bottom line that will count, and the entire refocussing is aimed at shoring up the bottom line. The focus should be on actual execution of strategy and also on how we look in terms of the competitive environment relative to what other people are doing, rather than just in the abstract of what we are doing"

— *Niall Booker, CEO, HSBC India*

LEARNING OBJECTIVES

"The focus of effective learning should not be what, but how a company learns."

Madhukar Shukla
Professor, XLRI

The basic objective of this study is to provide a minimum knowledge about the relevant laws that the entrepreneur has to bear in mind.

Every business, whether small or big is governed by a set of rules and regulations enacted by the government in the best interest of the society. The entrepreneur is bound by these laws at all stages of his activities from start-up to running the venture on an ongoing basis.

In the present context of globalisation, liberalisation, the entrepreneur has to give special attention to patent laws, intellectual property rights, environmental laws so that one can withstand competition, and concentrate on innovation and creativity.

It is timely to channelise rules and laws to increase productivity, profit and growth.

The chapter discusses a few of the relevant acts.

INTRODUCTION

Regulations are the basis of steady growth. In a society, regulations are the governing factors, ensuring that everything occurs in conformity with the plans and policy adopted, the instructions issued and the principles established. They pinpoint the weaknesses and errors so that they may be rectified and their recurrence may be prevented. They operate on everything – people, objects and actions. Thus, a regulation is a process by which we may check whether or not plans are being adhered to, whether or not proper progress is being made towards the objectives, whether the environment is saved from pollution, whether law and order is maintained or not, whether the interests of the workers are safeguarded or not, whether the small entrepreneurs are getting the raw materials or not, and whether there are any deviations for which a corrective action needs to be taken.

Objectives

The basic objective behind the whole process of regulations is to ensure that the results of operations conform as closely as possible to established standards of goods, specified procedures or instructions. The small-scale industry has to develop as an important segment of society; as such it has to adhere to the rules of the land, i.e., it has to be subject to the various regulations. Regulations governing the small-scale industry are of two types: (i) Protective, and (ii) Promotional. Protective regulations are in the nature of various safeguards, while promotional regulations are in the nature of giving a push to the small-scale industry, i.e., they are growth-oriented.

The regulation and promotion of industries constitutionally is envisaged in such a manner that the industries sector forms a part of the concurrent list of the Constitution. The Industries (Development and Regulation) Act of 1951 is a Central Act under which small-scale industries have been defined. The Act/rules and regulations are formulated by various authorities at the Central Government level, state government level and by local authorities. These legal regulations are further classified into:

- labour-related issues,
- tax-related issues,
- finance-related issues,
- location-related issues,
- product-related issues,
- environment-related issues, and
- safety, security, hygiene, health and welfare-related issues, etc.

Which Regulations Affect Your Business?

Each category of business/service will have differing regulations. However, it is up to you to seek local information as to which regulations will affect your venture in your state and district.

- Business Registration
- Licensing Requirements
- Sales Tax
- Income Tax
- Labour Legislations
- Environment Laws – Pollution, etc.
- Patent Laws

Registration/licensing – Industries with an investment of less than ₹ 100 lakh in plant and machinery are small-scale industries. They may be registered with GM District Industries Centres of the district concerned to get benefits.

Ancillary unit (SSI) is defined as having capital investment in plant and machinery not exceeding ₹ 100 lakh which produces parts, components, subassemblies and makes supplies against known or anticipated demand of one or more large units manufacturing/assembling complete product and which is not a subsidiary or controlled by any large unit in regard to the negotiation of contract for supply of its goods to any large unit. This will not however, preclude an ancillary unit from entering into agreement with a large unit giving it the first option to take the former output.

The unit primarily set up for the replacement market falls within its scope. Manufacture of tools, dies, jigs and fixtures is also recognised as an ancillary industry. These ancillary units (SSI) can also get themselves registered with GM District Industries Centres of the district concerned.

Regulations: Right from the beginning, a small-scale industry is regulated and governed by the following regulations: (a) State Industries Acts; (b) The Factories Act, 1948; (c) Shops and Establishment Act, 1948; (d) Indian Boiler Act (if applicable); (e) Payment of Wages Act, 1936; (f) Minimum Wages Act, 1948; (g) Workmen's Compensation Act, 1923; (h) Employees' Provident Fund Act, 1952; (i) Employees State Insurance Act, 1948; (j) Income Tax Act, 1961; (k) Central Sales Tax Act and State Sales Tax Act; (l) Drugs Control Act; (m) The Payment of Bonus Act, 1978; (n) The Industrial Employment (Standing Orders) Act, 1926, and (o) Industrial Disputes Act, 1947.

In addition, the small-scale entrepreneur has to be well-versed in excise, customs procedures and export and import regulations and procedures. He should always seek assistance from the following professionals: (a) Inspecting staff of Government, (b) Labour consultants, and (c) Financial consultants.

The salient features of the regulations governing the small-scale industries are summarised below:

INDUSTRIAL DEVELOPMENT (REGULATION) ACT (IDRA)

The IDRA is an instrument in the hands of the government for the control and direction of private sector industrial investment through the mechanism of the industrial licensing system, which enables it to exert pressure on the applicants in a variety of ways. Conceptually, the government ought to direct further industrial investment in such product-lines as would better serve the overall national interest and in such geographical areas which need it the most.

It is a complicated, time-consuming and costly exercise to acquire an industrial licence. Sometimes, it takes years before it can be obtained. Obviously, it cannot be the intention of the government to extend this procedure to the small-scale sector because it would be impossible to work towards implementation. A small unit cannot even prepare an application for an industrial licence; and there is nobody to help it in preparing it. There is no agency which is capable of checking the veracity of what the applicant says in his application, much less comment thereon.

In recent years, there has been quite a clamour from various associations of small-scale industries for their legislative protection. In August 1971, the Small-Scale Industries Board, at its 29th meeting, had recommended to the government to set up a committee to examine the feasibility of enacting suitable legislations for the development of small-scale industries. Always eager to form committees, the government speedily acceded to the recommendation of the Board and constituted a committee in January 1972 under the chairmanship of Mr. A.R. Bhat to draft legislations for the small-scale sector. It was, moreover, required to identify specific areas where legislation was considered necessary and to submit drafts for the purpose.

In its reports submitted in August 1972, the Bhat Committee prepared a total of five draft legislations for the government's approval. They were: the Small Industries Development Act, which included a definition of the small-scale industry; the Restricted Partnership Act; the Small Industries Reservation Act; the Small-Scale Ancillary Industries Act and the Public Stores Purchase and Disposal Act for small industries.

The committee has quoted extensively from similar legislative enactments in the USA and Japan. However, though well over nine years have passed since the recommendations were submitted to it, the government has not been able to take any decision on them, perhaps because it has reservations on the desirability of enacting such a legislation. If this is so, it should come out in the open and share its viewpoint with others.

The small-scale sector in this country is an important sector, for it is capable of meeting the consumer goods needs of the community. It is, therefore, only fair that the government should keep the interests of the community uppermost in mind while extending legislative protection to the small-scale sector. At the same time, the small-scale sector must fulfil social and moral obligations if it desires protection against large houses. It should, on its part, safeguard the interests of millions of those who depend on it for their livelihood.

FACTORIES ACT, 1948

(i) **Definition of a factory:** Section 2 (m) defines a factory as any place wherein ten or more persons are working and in which a manufacturing process is carried on with the aid of motive power supplied by steam, oil or electricity. Premises in which power is not used come under the term of a factory if twenty or more persons are working in them. This definition brings a greater number of places under the purview of this Act than was the case under the Act of 1934.

(ii) Employment of children: The Act fixes the minimum age of persons who can enter a factory for work at 14 years, It prohibits the employment of children up to the age of 13.

The Act further lays down that a qualified surgeon must certify that a person has completed the age of 14. Such certificates must be obtained by a factory manager and must be available for inspection by a factory inspector.

(iii) Hours of work for children: The Act reduces the hours of work for children between the ages of 14-17 from 5 hours a day to 4½ hours a day. It also prohibits work at night for such persons.

(iv) Hours of work for adult female and male workers: The Act prohibits employment of women in factories between 6 p.m. to 7 a.m. It reduces the hours of work for adult men and women workers from 54 to 48 per week and from 9 hours to 8 hours a day.

The Act also lays down that the eight hours of work will be spread over a period of not more than 10½ hours. Further, it provides that no worker shall work for more than 5 hours before he has had an interval or rest of at least half an hour. Lastly, the Act lays down that those workers who are made to work for more than 8 hours a day or 48 hours a week shall be paid for the extra hours at the rate of twice their ordinary rates of wages.

(v) Cleanliness: The Act lays down that every factory shall be kept clean and free from effluvia arising from any drain, privy of other nuisance. Accumulation of dirt and refuse shall be removed daily from the floor and the benches of workrooms, from staircases and passages, and disposed of in the suitable manner.

The floor of every workroom in a factory shall be cleaned once a week.

All inside walls, ceilings and partition shall be whitewashed at least once in fourteen months; if they are painted or varnished, they shall be repainted or revarnished once in five years.

Effective arrangements shall be made in every factory for the disposal of wastes arising out of the manufacturing process carried on therein.

(vi) Ventilation and temperature: Effective and suitable provision shall be made in every factory for securing and maintaining in every workroom adequate ventilation by the circulation of fresh air and the maintenance of such temperature as will secure therein reasonable conditions of comfort for those working there. Where excessively high temperatures are necessary for technical reasons, adequate measures shall be taken by the management to protect the workers from such temperatures.

The state government may prescribe a standard of adequate ventilation and reasonable temperature for any factory or class of factories and can suggest ways and means for reducing excessively high temperatures.

In any factory, where dust or fumes injurious to the health of workers arise in any manufacturing process, effective measures shall be taken to prevent their inhalation or accumulation in any workroom.

(vii) Artificial Humidification: In factories where humidity is artificially increased, the state government may ensure:

(a) Prescribing standards of humidification;

(b) Regulating methods used for humidification;

(c) Directing prescribed tests for determining humidity, and directing that such tests are carried out – their results recorded; and

(d) Prescribing methods to be adopted for securing adequate ventilation and cooling of the air in those rooms where artificial humidity is introduced.

Water used for the purpose of humidification shall be such as has been certified by the municipal authorities as fit for drinking.

(viii) Overcrowding: To prevent overcrowding in a factory, the Act lays down that, in factories built before the passing of this Act, there shall be a space of at least 350 cubic feet per worker and in factories built after the Act came into force, it shall be at least 500 cubic feet. To arrive at these figures, a height above 14 feet shall not be taken into consideration. In accordance with this rule, the Chief Inspector of Factories will communicate each factory manager the maximum number of workers that may be employed on any premises. He has, however, the power to exempt any factory or workroom from this rule, if he is satisfied that the observance of this rule is not necessary in the interest of the workers employed therein.

(ix) Lighting: It is the duty of the management of a factory to maintain sufficient and suitable lighting, natural or artificial or both, in a factory and in all the workrooms.

All glazed windows and skylights shall be kept clean on both the inner and outer surfaces, and effective measures shall be taken for the prevention of glare and formation of any shadows which may cause eye-strain or create a risk of accidents.

The state government may make rules as to what is sufficient and suitable lighting, for a factory or a class of factories.

(x) Drinking water: In every factory, effective arrangements shall be made to provide, at suitable points conveniently situated for all workers employed therein, a sufficient supply of wholesome drinking water.

In every factory, where more than 253 workers are ordinarily employed, provision shall be made for cool drinking water during the hot weather.

(xi) Toilets: In every factory, sufficient toilet facilities of the precribed types, shall be provided at places which are conveniently situated and are easily accessible to workers at all times while they are at the factory.

The state government may prescribe the number of public toilet services to be provided in any factory in proportion to the number of male and female workers ordinarily employed therein.

(xii) Provision of spittoons: In every factory, there shall be provided a sufficient number of spittoons in convenient places and they shall be maintained in a clean and hygienic condition.

(xiii) Safety provisions: According to the Act of 1934, a factory manager cannot afford to wait till an Inspector of Factories gave instructions as to what ought to be done to ensure the safety of workers. The Act of 1948 has placed the responsibility for safety matters on the shoulders of the occupier or the manager of a factory. He must comply with all the safety provisions without waiting for the inspectors's instructions.

Secondly, the Act places legal responsibility on the management for the maintenance and use of safety guards. It is its duty to supervise the use of these guards by the workers.

The specific provisions for safety are as follows: in every factory, all dangerous parts of all machines, such as the moving parts of prime movers, flywheels, electric generators, motors, rotary converters, etc., shall be securely fenced by safety guards of substantial construction which shall be kept in position while the parts of machinery they fence are in motion.

(xiv) Dangerous fumes: Adequate provision shall be made in a factory where dangerous fumes are present in any chamber, tank, pipe, etc., for the egress of such fumes.

(xv) Explosive gases, dust, fume: If, in any factory, the manufacturing process raises dust, gas, fume or vapour which is likely to explode on ignition, all measures shall be taken to prevent any such explosion by –

(a) Providing an effective enclosure of the plant or machinery used in the process, or

(b) The removal or prevention of accumulation of such dust, gas or fumes.

(xvi) Safety of factory building and machinery: If it appears to the inspector that any building or part of factory is in such a condition that it is dangerous to human life or safety, he may serve on the manager of the factory an order in writing specifying the measures that should be adopted and the specific date by which they should be carried out to ensure the safety of the building or factory. He may also serve an order on the manager, prohibiting its use until proper repairs or alterations have been carried out.

(xvii) Welfare provisions: *(a) Facilities for washing:* In every factory, adequate and suitable facilities for washing shall be provided and maintained for the workers. Adequately screened facilities for washing shall be provided for male and female workers separately. Such facilities shall be conveniently accessible and shall be maintained and kept clean.

(b) Storing and drying clothes: The State Government may require any factory or class of factories to make provision therein of suitable places for keeping clothes not worn during working hours and for drying wet clothing.

(c) Facilities for sitting: In every factory, suitable arrangements for sitting shall be provided and maintained for all workers obliged to work in a standing position in order that they may take advantage of any opportunity for rest which may occur in the course of their work.

(d) First-aid appliances: First-aid boxes, equipped with the prescribed contents, which will be really accessible during all working hours, shall be provided and maintained in every factory. The number of such boxes shall not be less than one for every one hundred and fifty workers.

(xviii) **Penalties for breach of provision of the act:** For any contravention of the provisions of the Act, the occupier and the manager of a factory shall each be guilty of an offence and be punishable with imprisonment for a term not exceeding three months or with a fine up to ₹ 500 or with both.

If any person, who has been convicted of any offence punishable under the provisions of this Act, is again found to be guilty of an offence involving contravention of the same provision within a period of two years from the date of conviction with imprisonment up to six months or with a fine up to ₹ 1,000 or with both. This Act, for the time, provides that if any worker contravenes any provision of this Act or any rules or orders, such as the use of safety guards, spitting only in spittoons provided for the purpose, he shall be punishable with fine up to ₹ 20.

India's ratification of International Labour Convention No. 90 prohibiting the employment of young persons in factories at night necessitated an amendment of the relevant sections of the Factories Act, 1948. This was achieved by passing an Amendment Act in April 1954. This Act added a new chapter on "Annual Leave with Wages" to the Factories Act, 1948. It lays down a period of 240 days as the minimum attendance necessary during a calendar year to qualify for leave with wages. It also prohibits employment of young persons on cleaning, lubricating or adjusting any prime mover or transmission machinery while it is in motion, if such work exposes them to a risk of injury.

INCOME TAX ACT

The tax concessions provided in the Income-tax Act for small-scale industries are of minor significance. Under Section 80 HHA of the Act, which came into effect from the assessment year 1978-79, an assessee is entitled to a deduction in respect of profits and gains derived from new small-scale industrial undertakings set up in any rural area at the rate of 20 per cent for the first ten assessment years. One of the conditions is that the unit should have commenced its manufacturing activity after September 30, 1977. This concession is discriminatory, for there is no justification for denying the benefit to those units which commenced manufacturing activity before September 30,1977. Moreover, the units in urban areas have been neglected. Unless we have correct statistics of the proportion of small-scale units in rural areas to those in urban areas and the proportion of the tax collected from rural units to the tax collected from urban ones, the significance of such a discriminatory tax concession cannot be evaluated.

Another incentive is the investment allowance under Section 32A of the Act, under which a small-scale unit is entitled to a deduction at the rate of 25 per cent of the cost of plant and machinery installed after March 31, 1976. This allowance is capital-oriented, whereas most of the small-scale units are capital-saving and labour-oriented.

At present, there is no Central Government definition of the term *small-scale industrial undertaking* – a fact which indicates how unimportant these undertakings are in the eyes of the tax department. According to the definitions given under sections 32 A and 80 HHA, the term is used to mean an industrial undertaking whose aggregate value of machinery and plant – other than tools, jigs, dies and moulds – installed on the last day of the previous year for the purpose of the business of the undertaking, does not exceed ₹ 10 lakh. In Section 58 A of the Companies Act, however, the term is defined as any industrial undertaking registered with the Directorate of Industries or the Directorate of Small-scale Industries.

THE INDUSTRIAL EMPLOYMENT (STANDING ORDERS) ACT, 1946

The absence of standing order clearly defining the rights and obligations of the employer and the workers in respect of recruitment, discharge, disciplinary action, holidays, leave, etc., was one of the most frequent causes of friction between management and workers. On the recommendations of the Tripartite Labour Conferences held in 1943, 1944, 1945, the Government of India passed the Industrial Employment (Standing Orders) Act in 1946. This Act provides for the framing of standing orders in all establishments employing 100 or more persons. It requires employers to submit within six months of the enactment of the law standing orders covering the classification of workmen (permanent, temporary, etc.), the manner of intimating to them their hours of work, holidays, pay days and wage rates, the procedure to be followed while applying for leave and holidays in the termination of employment for notice of discharge and for disciplinary action. In pursuance of this Act, the Central Government published the Central rules in 1946 which were applicable to the Commissioner's provinces and to the undertaking under the Central Government. Its lead was promptly followed by all state governments. In the state of Maharashtra, it has been made applicable to establishments in which fifty or more persons are employed.

THE INDIAN TRADE UNION ACT, 1926

The experience of the working of the system of free enterprise in the industrial field revealed that though theoretically both the employers and workers were free to enter into a contract and to agree upon the wages to be paid and received, in point of fact, for various reasons, this freedom did not benefit the workers in any way. Firstly, the commodity that a worker has to sell is highly perishable in the sense that if he refuses to work on a particular day because the wages offered are low, he cannot store up his labour of that day to be used the next day. This compels him to accept work even if the wages offered are unsatisfactory. Secondly, as his income is very low, he is not able to accumulate any savings on which he can fall back upon if and when he refuses to work. The only alternative to refusal to work because of low wages is, therefore, starvation. These two factors compel a worker to accept low wages and so the theoretical freedom of contract is not of much use to him. Lastly, the fact that a worker is a small-scale seller and the employer is a large-scale buyer reduces his bargaining power to a very great extent. It is possible for the employer to refuse the wage which a worker demands because it is possible for him to engage somebody else who is willing to work on a lower wage. It is, however, relatively difficult for a worker to find an alternative employer who would pay him the wage he demands. His weak bargaining position thus compels him to accept whatever wages are offered to him.

Rules of a trade union: The rules of a union must contain the following provisions: (a) the name, (b) the objects for which it has been established, (c) the purpose for which its general funds will be applicable, (d) maintenance of the list of members for inspection by officers and members of the union, (e) the admission of ordinary members who shall be persons engaged in the industry with which the union is connected and also the admission of honorary members to form the executive of the union, (f) the conditions under which members are entitled to the benefits ensured by the rules and under which fines or forfeiture may be imposed on them, (g) the manner in which any rule shall be amended, altered or rescined, (h) the manner in which the members of the executive and other officers of the union shall be appointed and removed, (i) the safe custody of the funds of the union, the audit of accounts and inspection of the account books by the officers and members, and lastly (j) the manner in which the union will be dissolved.

Rights of Registered Trade Unions

A registered trade union has a right:

(a) To collect membership fees on the premises of the factory without interference from the management;

(b) To put up notices of the meetings of the union and of other activities of the union on the premises of the factory;

(c) To use the general funds for specific purposes;

(d) To raise funds for political purposes at the option of the members;

(e) To go on strike by peaceful methods;

(f) To be exempted from the provisions of Section 120B, Sub-section (2) of the Indian Penal Code if the members conduct a peaceful strike;

(g) To appoint outsiders in a number which is not more than one half of the total number of office-bearers to the executive of the union, and

(h) To send to the Registrar, every year, an audited statement of receipts and expenditure.

THE PAYMENT OF WAGES ACT, 1936

The payment of wages to factory workers in a particular form and at regular intervals without any unauthorised deductions is the objective of this Act.

Scope of the Act

The provisions of the Act are applicable to workers engaged in factories as defined by the Factories Act of 1948, and to persons employed on any railway by contractor or subcontractor. The state government may, after giving three months' notice of its intention of doing so by a notification in the Official Gazette, extend the provisions of this Act to any class of persons employed in any industrial establishment. The provisions of this Act are applicable to those persons whose wages do not exceed ₹ 400 per month.

The Date of Payment of Wages

The wages of every person employed in a factory, industrial establishment or a railway, where less than 1,000 persons are employed, shall be paid before the expiry of the seventh day after the completion of the wage period, generally a month; the wages for a month, for example, shall be paid before the seventh day of the next month. In the factories in which more than a thousand persons are employed, the wages shall be paid before the expitry of the tenth day of the next month. The wages of a person whose services have been terminated shall be paid on the next working day after such termination.

The payment of wages shall be made on a working day.

Authorised Deductions

The Act authorises an employer to make deductions from wages for the following purposes only: (a) fines, (b) absence from duty, (c) damage to or loss of goods or money, where such damage or loss is due to the negligence or default on the part of the employee, (d) housing accommodation supplied by the employer, and (e) such amenities and services supplied by the employer as the state government may authorise.

(i) Fines shall be imposed for those acts of commission and omission which the employer, with the approval of the State Government, may have specified by notice to his employees.

(ii) Fines shall not be imposed on any employee unless he has been given an opportunity to show cause why the fine should not be imposed.

(iii) No fine shall be imposed on persons below the age of fifteen.

(iv) A fine imposed on any employee in any wage period shall not exceed an amount of half an anna or three naye paise in the rupee of the wages payable to him for the period, (i.e., 3%).

(v) The fine so imposed shall be recovered in instalments or after the expiry of sixty days from the day on which it was imposed.

(vi) The fine and the actual amount recovered shall be recorded in a separate register in the prescribed form and all amounts of fines realised shall be utilised only for such purposes as are beneficial to the employees and as are approved by the prescribed authority. Applications for the recovery of fines, or of deductions not authorised under the Act, for delay in payment of wages shall be presented within six months of the date on which such fines were imposed or deductions were made or wages were due.

THE WORKMEN'S COMPENSATION ACT, 1923

Within the installation of machinery operated by motive power, the number of accidents in factories have increased considerably. Many times, workers were incapacitated and in some cases even their lives while working on machines in factories. This meant the loss of earnings for those who were involved in accidents and in cases where a worker died, his dependants were in financial difficulties. From a purely humanitarian point of view, it would be natural to expect that employers should give some compensation to such workers or their dependants. Further, even on economic grounds, it could be argued that the amount of compensation is a legitimate element of the cost of production under the factory system and, therefore, neither society nor employers should grudge to pay it whenever workers were involved in accidents. Some enlightened employers did pay compensation to their employees when they suffered accidents; but a large majority was not willing to accept this responsibility. The workers, however, could not claim compensation as a matter of right; and even when compensation was paid, there was bound to be an honest difference of opinion between an employer and an employee as regards the fairness of the amount paid. In order to provide some bases for a statutory claim for compensation to be paid to the disabled factory worker, Workmen's Compensation Acts have been passed in almost all the countries.

The following are the provisions of the Indian Workmen's Compensation Act:

Employer's Liability for Compensation

If a personal injury is caused to a worker by an accident arising out of and in the course of his employment, his employer shall be liable to pay compensation in accordance with the provisions of this Act.

When Employer is not Liable

The employer, however, shall not be liable if: (a) the injury results in a partial or total disablement of the worker for less than three days; (b) if the injury can be directly attributed to the worker having been under the influence of drink or drugs; (c) if the injury can be directly attributed to the wilful disobedience by the worker of an order expressly given, or (d) if the injury can be directly attributed to the wilful removal or disregard by the worker of any safety guard or other device which he knew has been provided for the purpose of securing his safety.

Occupational Diseases

If a worker engaged in any employment which involves the handling of wool, hair bristles or animal carcasses or loading or unloading of such merchandise, or in processes carried on in compressed air, or in processes which involve the use of lead or tetraethyl or in processes involving exposure to nitrous fumes, contracts diseases like anthrax, compressed-air illness, lead poisoning or poisoning by nitrous fumes respectively; or when engaged continuously for not less than six months in any employment specified in Part B of Schedule III, contracts any disease specified in this schedule as an occupational disease, the contacting of such a disease shall be regarded as an injury by accident and shall be deemed to have arisen out of and in employment. The state governments in the case of employments specified in Part C of the schedule may make additions to the list of employments in Schedule III and specify the corresponding diseases after giving three months' notice in the Gazette.

Types of Injuries

Injuries for the purposes of this Act have been classified into the following categories: (i) death, (ii) permanent total disablement, (iii) permanent partial disablement, and (iv) temporary disablement, partial or total.

Amount of Compensation

The Act provides for compensation for these categories of injuries in Schedules I to IV.

Medical Examination

A worker who has given notice of an accident shall submit himself to a medical examination, if the employer insists on it by a qualified medical practitioner and free of charge. Similarly, a worker who is in receipt of half-monthly payments under this Act shall submit himself to such medical examination from time-to-time.

If a worker refuses to submit himself to such a medical examination without sufficient cause, his right to compensation shall be suspended.

THE EMPLOYEES' STATE INSURANCE ACT, 1948

Experience in the working of the Workmen's Compensation Act, 1923 revealed that the benefits conferred by it upon factory workers in many cases, did not reach them. This was due to various reasons. Firstly, a claim for compensation for injury had to be filed in an ordinary court of law and the lack of finance often made impossible for a worker to file such a suit and fight it out. Secondly, armed with expert legal advice, it was often possible for an employer to prove that the accident either did not arise out of and in the course of employment or that it was due to the worker concerned being under the influence of drink or drug at the time of the accident, or that it was due to his negligence or his disobedience of safety rules. In such conditions, workers were generally unwilling to go to court of law, and referred to accept whatever compensation employers chose to payout of a sense of pity or charity. The Employees' State Insurance Act, 1948 was framed to prevent such victimisation of the worker by the employer.

Contributions

Every person, who is employed for wages in or is in connection with the work of a factory or establishment to which this Act applies, shall be insured. All the insured workers, except those who earn wages of less than fifty rupees per day, shall pay their contribution to the Employees' State Insurance Corporation at the rates specified in the First Schedule to the Act. The employers shall pay their contributions at the rates specified in the above schedule.

Distribution of Benefits under the Act

The insured persons or as the case may be, their dependants shall be entitled to the following benefits namely:

(a) **Sickness Benefits:** Periodical payments, to any insured person in case of his sickness certified by a duly appointed medical practitioner;

(b) **Maternity Benefits:** Periodical payments, in case of confinement, to an insured woman certified to be eligible for such payments, by an authority specified in this behalf by the regulations;

(c) **Disablement Benefits:** Periodical payment to an insured person suffering from disablement as a result of an injury sustained in the course of his employment;

(d) **Dependants' Benefits:** Periodical payment to such dependants of an insured person who dies as a result of an injury sustained in the course of his employment, and

(e) **Medical Benefits:** Medical treatment for an attendance on an insured person.

The Corporation may at the request of Government of India, extend medical benefits to the family of the insured person. Accordingly, these benefits have been so extended from 1st January, 1962.

A person who is in receipt of sickness or disablement benefit, must observe the following conditions:

(a) He shall remain under medical treatment at dispensary, hospital, clinic or any other institution provided under this Act and shall carry out the instructions of the medical officer or medical attendant in charge thereof;

(b) He shall not, while under treatment, do anything which might retard or prejudice his chances of recovery;

(c) He shall not leave the area in which medical treatment provided under this Act is being given without the permission of the medical officer or such other authority as may be specified in this behalf under the rules framed for this purposes; and

(d) He shall allow himself to be examined by any duly appointed medical officer or any other person authorised by the corporation in this behalf.

Penalties

If a person makes a false statement for the purpose of causing any increase in payment or benefit or for the purpose of causing any payment of benefit to be made where no payment or benefit is authorised, or for the purpose of avoiding any payment to be made by himself, he shall be punishable with imprisonment for a term upto three months or with fine up to ₹ 500 or with both.

If any person fails to pay any contribution which he is liable to pay, or deducts from the wages of an employee the whole or any part of the employee's contribution or reduce the wages or any privileges or benefits admissible to an employee, dismisses, discharges, reduces or otherwise punishes an employee in contravention of Section 73, fails or refuses to submit any return required by the regulations or makes a false return, or obstructs any inspector or other official of the corporation in the discharge of his duties, is guilty of contravention of, and non-compliance with any of the requirements of this Act, he shall be punishable with imprisonment up to a period of three months or with fine up to ₹ 500 or with both.

Industrial Disputes Act, 1947

Industrial disputes, strikes and lockouts were not very common occurrences in India till 1914. It was, however, during the Great War of 1914-18 that the strike came to be regarded as an ordinary weapon of industrial warfare. During the War, while the cost of living went on rising, the wages did not keep pace with it. This gave rise to serious discontent among industrial workers and led to a series of strikes, notably in the textile industry in Mumbai, in the post-war period. In addition to low wages, there were many other causes which were partly responsible for the outbreak of strikes during this period. The more important of these were long hours of work, bad conditions, insanitary housing conditions, absence of any provision till 1922 for compensation for injuries sustained in the course of employment, absence till 1925 of the right to form a trade union, ill-treatment of workmen by foremen or other mill officials, etc.

The important provisions of the Industrial Disputes Act of 1947 are:

(i) If any industrial dispute exists or is apprehended, the appropriate government may, by order in writing, (a) refer the dispute to a board for promoting a settlement thereof; or (b) refer any matter appearing to be connected with or relevant to the dispute to a Court of Inquiry, or (c) refer the dispute to a tribunal for arbitration.

(ii) If either of the parties to a dispute or both of them apply to the government to refer a dispute to a Board, Court or Tribunal, the appropriate government, if satisfied that the person applying represents majority of each party, shall make the reference accordingly.

(iii) If a dispute has been referred to a board or a tribunal, the government may prohibit the continuance of any strike or lockout in connection with such a dispute.

(iv) A settlement arrived at in the course of conciliation proceedings under the Act, or an award which is declared by the government as binding on all the parties to the dispute for at least six months.

(v) An award declared by a government shall come into operation on such date as may be specified by the government and shall remain in operation for a period of one year, or a shorter period, if so fixed by the government.

(vi) Workers employed in public utility industries shall not go on a strike and the employers in such industries shall not resort to lockouts –

(a) without giving a fourteen days' notice and before the period of notice expires, or

(b) during the pendency of conciliation proceedings.

(vii) Workers employed in any industrial establishment shall not go on strike –

(a) during the pendency of conciliation proceeding; or

(b) during the pendency of proceeding before a Labour Court, Tribunal or National Tribunal; or

(c) during a period in which a settlement or award is in operation.

A strike or a lockout, in contravention of any of these provisions shall be illegal.

No person shall knowingly expend or apply any money in direct furtherance or support of any illegal strike or lockout.

Penalties

Any worker who commences, continues or acts in furtherance of an illegal strike shall be punishable with imprisonment up to one month or with fine up to ₹ 50 or both.

THE EMPLOYEES' PROVIDENT FUND ACT, 1952

The Act provides for the institution of a contributory provident fund in any establishment in which 20 or more persons are employed. The contribution, which shall be paid by the employer to the fund, shall be eight-and-one-third per cent of the basic wage and the dearness allowance payable to each employee, while the employee's contribution shall be equal to the contribution payable by the employer.

THE INDIAN BOILERS ACT, 1923

An owner of a boiler shall not use it or permit it to be used:

(a) Unless it has been registered in accordance with the provisions of this Act;

(b) In the case of a boiler transferred from one state to another, until the transfer has been reported in the prescribed manner;

(c) Unless certificate or provisional order authorising the use of the boiler is obtained under this Act;

(d) At a pressure higher than the maximum pressure recorded in such certificate or provisional order:

(e) Unless the boiler is in charge of a person holding a certificate of competency.

Procedure

The owner of a boiler may apply to the inspector to have the boiler registered. Every such application shall be accompanied by the prescribed fee. The inspector shall examine the boiler and submit a report to the chief inspector in the prescribed form. The permit is a 'must' for boilers.

THE INDIAN ELECTRICITY ACT, 1910

The Act relates to the supply and use of electricity energy.

Issue of Licence: A state government may, on an application made in the prescribed form and on the payment of the prescribed fee, grant a licence to supply energy in any specified area and also to lay electric supply lines for the transmission of energy.

The Water (Prevention and Control of Pollution) Act, 1974 mention of other Environmental Acts follow below:

It applies to all establishments discharging effluents into water or on land. A unit while making the project report is required to meet pollution control requirements and obtain an NOC (from State Pollution Control Board) before the setting up of the unit. The effluents so discharged have to be managed at all times or else there are penalty provisions under the Act for violations. Further, the unit is not permitted to install any new or altered outlet for the discharge of trade effluents sewage into a stream or river, without prior consent of the board. In a major initiative to reduce industrial waste pollution, the Government of India, in partnership with the World Bank, has started the Industrial Pollution Control Project for assisting clusters in setting up common effluent treatment plants.

The Air (Prevention and Control of Pollution) Act, 1981 applies to all industries, which have to declare air pollution control areas and install necessary equipments. At the time of making the project report, provision has to be made for pollution control requirements and an NOC is to be obtained before establishing the unit. During the operation of the unit, discharges into the air are to be managed within prescribed standards at all times, failing which penalty provisions are applicable.

The National Environment Tribunal Act addresses the issue of compensation-cum-relief to accident victims and for environmental damages. Separate notifications have been issued prohibiting the handling of 70 Azo dyes (mostly manufactured by the SSI sector) and the open burning of waste oil.

In the case of SSIs, the SSI Board, in its meeting held on 24 August, 1992, had decided to petition the Ministry of Environment and Forests for the relaxation of the provision of the two Acts on pollution prevention and control. Consequently, SSIs have to obtain the consent from the Central Pollution Control Board only in the case of 17 industries (which have been categorised as heavy polluting) listed below:

1. Fertilisers (Nitrogen/Phosphate)
2. Sugar
3. Cement
4. Fermentation and Distillery
5. Aluminium
6. Petrochemicals
7. Thermal Power
8. Oil Refining
9. Sulphuric Acid
10. Tanneries
11. Copper Smelter
12. Zinc Smelter
13. Iron and Steel
14. Pulp and Paper
15. Dye and Dye Intermediates
16. Pesticides Manufacturing and Formulation
17. Basic Drugs and Pharmaceuticals

For industries other than those listed above, the acknowledgement by the State Pollution Control Board of the application form would serve as consent for SSIs. There would also be no need for the industry to obtain a periodic renewal of consent till such time that a unit modifies/ changes its processes. The State Pollution Control Board or the Committee specified by the Central Government (for Union Territories) might conduct checks or call for information from any SSI and making a formal consent order, prescribing conditions, etc., as may be required.

INTELLECTUAL PROPERTY RIGHTS

The 1994 agreement on Trade Related Aspects of Intellectual Property Rights (TRIPS) provides for the establishment of standards for intellectual property rights, protection and the enforcement of those standards within nations and at the border. Industrialised countries were given one year for implementation from the entry into force of the agreement on July 1, 1995. Developing countries and those shifting from centrally planned economies to market economies were given until January 1,2000 for implementation. Least-developed countries will have until 2006 to comply. The TRIPS Agreement is administered by the World Trade Organisation.

What is Intellectual Property?

Countries with innovative local industries almost invariably have laws to foster innovation by regulating the copying of inventions, identifying symbols, and creative expressions. These laws encompass four separate and distinct types of intangible property, namely patents, trademarks, copyrights, and trade secrets, which collectively are referred to as "intellectual property".

Intellectual property shares many of the characteristics associated with real and personal property. For example, intellectual property is an asset, and as such it can be bought, sold, licensed, exchanged, or gratuitously given away like any other form of property. Further, the intellectual property owner has the right to prevent the unauthorised use or sale of the property. The most noticeable difference between intellectual property and other forms of property, however, is that intellectual property is intangible, that is, it cannot be defined or identified by its own physical parameters. It must be expressed in some discernible way to be protectable.

All four types of intellectual property are protected on a national basis. Thus, the scope of protection and the requirements for obtaining protection will vary from country to country. There are, however, similarities between national legal arrangements. Moreover, the current worldwide trend is towards harmonising national laws.

Some people confuse patents, copyrights, and trademarks. Although there may be some similarities among these kinds of intellectual property protection, they are different and serve different purposes.

What is a patent?: A patent for an invention is the grant of a property right to the inventor, issued in the US by the Patent and Trademark office. The term of a new patent is 20 years from the date on which the application for the patent was filed in the United States or, in special cases, from the date and earlier related application was filed, subject to payment of maintenance fees. US patent grants are effective only within the US, its territories, and possessions.

The right conferred by the patent grant is, in the language of the statute and of the grant itself, "the right to exclude others from making, using, offering for sale, or selling" the invention in the United States or "importing" the invention into the United States. What is granted is not the right to make, use, offer for sale, sell or import, but the right to exclude others from making, using, offering for sale, selling or importing the invention.

What is a trademark or service mark?: A trademark is a word, name, symbol or device which is used in trade with goods to indicate the source of the goods and to distinguish them from the goods of others. A service mark is the same as a trademark except that it identifies and distinguishes the source of a service rather than a product. The terms "trademark" and "mark" are commonly used to refers to both trademarks and service marks.

Trademark rights maybe used to prevent others from using a confusingly similar mark, but not to prevent others from making the same goods or from selling the same goods or services under a clearly different mark. Trademarks which are used in interstate or foreign commerce may be registered with the Patent and Trademark office.

What is a copyright?: Copyright is a form of protection provided to the authors of "original works of authorship" including literary, dramatic, musical, artistic, and certain other intellectual works, both published and unpublished. The 1976 Copyright Act generally gives the owner of the copyright the exclusive right to reproduce copyrighted work, to prepare derivative works, to distribute copies or recordings of the copyrighted work, to perform the copyrighted work publicly, or to display the copyrighted work publicly.

The copyright protects the form of expression rather than the subject matter of the writing. For example, a description of a machine could be copyrighted, but this would only prevent others from copying the description: it would not prevent others from writing a description of their own or from making and using the machine.

The Nature of Property	
Tangible property	**Intellectual property**
A "brand X" television set	The circuit design for all "brand X" television sets
A photograph named "Trees"	The pictorial work embodied in all copies of the photograph "Trees"
A phonorecord with the song "Misty" recorded on it	The musical composition embodied in all phonorecords with "Misty" on them
A copy of the local telephone book	The particular arrangement of names in the literary work known as the local telephone book.
A bottle of "Chemical Z"	A method of manufacturing "Chemical Z"
A microbe containing "gene Y"	The process of engineering "gene Y"

(**Source:** US Office of Technology Assessment, Intellectual Property Rights in an Age of Electronics and Information, Washington, DC, April 1986).

Box 33.1 The International Intellectual Property System

The international system for protecting intellectural property, as it exists today, had its foundations in the late 19th century, and it has been quite stable since that time. Unlike other international agreements that are periodically readapted or completely revised, the interlocking conventions that constitute the international intellectual property system provide a permanent legal framework, although it can be amended and revised if required.

The system is complex and structured around many different conventions and agreements to which different groups of countries adhere. Nevertheless, these conventions share several characteristics, including the harmonisation of disparate national intellectual property systems, the principle of national treatment, and the establishment of minimum rights.

Within the intellectual property system, two principal agreements govern copyrights. The first is The Berne Convention for the Protection of Literary and Artistic Works, which was adopted in 1886 and has been revised on seven occasions during its 100-year existence, most recently in 1971. There are 75 member countries under the Berne Convention, not including the United States, although legislation to permit US adherence to the convention has been introduced in the US Congress.

As is stated in article II of the Berne Convention, it "obliges Contracting States to protect the expression of literary and artistic works (which include) every production in the literary, scientific, and artistic domain whatever may be the mode or form of its expression, such as books, pamphlets, and other writings: lectures, addresses, sermons, and other works of the same nature; dramatic or dramatico-musical works; choreographic works and entertainment in dumb show; musical compositions with or without words; cinematorgraphic works to which are assimilated words expressed by a process analogous to cinematography; works of drawing, painting, architecture, sculpture, engraving, and lithography; photographic works to which are assimilated works expressed by a process analogous to photography; works of applied art; illustrations, maps, plans, sketches, and three-dimensional works relative to geography, topography, architecture, or science".

The second principal copyright agreement is the Universal Copyright Convention, which was adopted in 1957 and updated once, in 1971. It has 78 member countries. Article I of this agreement states that "Each Contracting State undertakes to provide for the adequate and effective protection of the rights of authors and other copyright proprietors in literary, scientific, and artistic works including writing, musical, dramatic, and cinematographic works and paintings, engravings, and culpture".

Yet other, narrower agreements in the area of copyright include the Rome Convention for the Protection of Performers, Producers of Phonograms, and Broadcasting Organisations; the Convention for the Protection of Producers of Phonograms Against the Unauthorised Duplication of Their Phonograms; the Convention Relating to Distribution of Program — Carrying Signals Transmitted by Satellite; and six Inter-American Copyright Conventions.

The principal agreement governing patents and trademarks is the Paris Convention for the Protection of Industrial Property, which was adopted in 1883 and has been revised half-a-dozen times since, most recently in 1967. This agreement encompasses 91 countries.

According to article I of the Paris Convention, "The protection of industrial property has as its object patents, utility models, industrial designs, trademarks, service marks, trade names, indications of source or appellations of origin, and the repression of unfair competition. Industrial property shall be understood in the broadest sense and shall apply not only to industry and commerce proper, but likewise to agricultural and extractive industries and to all manufactured or natural products........Patents shall include the various kinds of industrial patents recognised by the laws of the countries of the Union, such as patents of importation, patents of improvement, patents and certificates of addition, etc".

INDIAN PATENT ACT, 1970

The Indian Patent Act, 1970, is applicable uniformly to all industries – large or small. To patent their products, brands or manufacturing processes, industrial units in the small and medium scale sector are required to observe the same procedural hassles as their large-scale counterparts.

Headquartered in Kolkata, the Indian Patent Office administers the Patent Act along with the Design Act, 1911 and the Trade and Merchandise Marks Act, 1958 with branches in New Delhi, Mumbai and Chennai under the Department of Industrial Development of the Union Industry Ministry.

The department brings out an annual report on patents where a list of patent applications and approvals is given for a particular year. However, the list does not indicate how many patents have been sanctioned to applicants belonging to the SME sector.

Finally, India has shifted its patent paradigm, with the Administration joining the Paris Convention, 1967, for the Protection of Intellectual Property. And, by extension, the Patent Cooperation Treaty (PCT) 1970. The biggest benefit an investor who has already filed for a patent in one of the 147 member countries can claim priority when subsequently filing in other countries. Agrees R.A. Mashelkar,55, Director-General, Council of Scientific and Industrial Research: "This will help cut costs." Of course, as a signatory to the agreement on Trade Related Intellectual Property Rights (a.k.a. TRIPS), India had to comply with the Paris convention in any case. And with the April 1999, deadline for amending patent laws looming closer, India's patent on delaying intellectual property legislation is close to expiring.

The New Patents Framework

What The Indian Patents Act, 1970, said...

- Inventors must wait for a minimum of 6 weeks before obtaining clearance to apply for patents abroad.
- Product patents are not granted for food, medicines, drugs, and chemicals. The patenting of life-forms is not allowed.
- Patent protection is not always granted to products imported from or developed in other countries.

What The Paris Convention, 1967, states....

- Inventors can establish a priority date for securing patents in several countries simultaneously.
- Protection is extended to all forms of industrial property, including plant varieties and microorganisms.
- There can be no discrimination between the protection granted to an imported product and a domestic. product.

The dimension of the problem is reflected in the fact that no less than 38,000 patent cases relating to different PCT member countries are now pending with the Indian patent office for examination and final approval by the authorities concerned before these foreign countries can sell their patented products and manufacturing processes or both in the Indian market.

Apart from this huge pile up of foreign patent cases, the Indian Patent Office in Kolkata is receiving no less than 10,000 applications an average every year from indigenous corporate and individual applicants. Patent examiners take four to five years to approve or cancel a patent application which requires related trials and examination before final approval. This is one of the reasons for piling up of patent cases.

As a result of all these operational constraints, the experience of small-scale entrepreneurs seeking patents is far from happy. For them, it is a long-drawn and cumbersome process and the time and money spent in patenting their products or manufacturing processes do not justify the commercial benefits that come from it.

As such, most SMEs are reluctant to go for patents except those who have some compelling reasons to do so, for example, those in drugs and pharmaceuticals.

Four Ways of Going Global

There are four entry level options for Indian players seeking a global market. The first route which is the most basis, and one followed by the majority of Indian players, entails a local manufacturer to serve as a *sourcing agent* for local distributors in that country. However, this is at best a short-term strategy susceptible to the whims of distributors.

The second entry option is a collaborative effort wherein local agents provide the distribution and marketing input to the Indian company. This is a route followed by most Indian players including Titan, Balsara, Maruti Udyog Ltd., and Bajaj Auto.

The Indian company retains control over key marketing and branding issues. Clearly a long-term entry option, the arrangement gives the marketer a controlling interest and an assurance of a commonality of product messaging and packaging irrespective of the country the brand is being sold in. In such an arrangement, the Indian marketer provides development material and business promotion options to local distributors, and media costs are shared jointly by the two parties involved.

Marketers opting to follow the third route make a solo entry through independent distributors in a manner similar to the route followed in India. However, this route is usually followed only in countries that offer a consumer profile closest to India since it is a highly expensive route and open to failure.

The fourth more convenient and easily accessible alternative is to start as a private label supplier at the lower price end through the mass merchandising outlets of foreign buyers. Balsara is probably the best example of an Indian company taking the private label route particularly in the North American and European toothpaste markets. Of late, however, market analysts claim that this route is no longer as viable as it once was with private label marketing wars rampant in the US. Moreover, private label manufacture can at best be called global suppliers.

REGULATORY LAWS FOR SSI UNITS

The vision for the 21st century for SSEs cannot be realised with plethora of laws and rules and regulations governing this sector and there is need for a Single Unified Act governing promotion and development of small-scale enterprises in the country.

There should be a separate Small Enterprises Development Act for SSEs similar to the Industrial Development and Regulation (IDR) Act. This comprehensive Act may cover all aspects relating to regulation and growth of SSEs.

The Small Business Administration (SBA) of United States has a comprehensive single law governing SMEs. On the same lines, there should be a separate comprehensive law for SSI Units, which has been long pending demand of SSI units.

The SSE units should be free from laws/procedures which cause undue harassment. As far as possible, inspection should be replaced by self-certification and procedures should be transparent and hassle-free. Broadly, the existing laws could be classified in three categories: (a) Laws governing setting of industries; (b) Laws governing working of the industry; and (c) Laws relating to labour and their welfare.

The laws relating to labour and welfare have been found more deterrent and troublesome because the small entrepreneurs are not able to comply with the requirement of maintaining a large number of registers, forms, returns, etc. Further, the labour strength of small enterprises may vary as per availability of orders, which increases difficulties of small enterprises to comply with the labour laws. In view of the above difficulties experienced by the SSI entrepreneurs, especially tiny units, it is felt necessary to recommend exemption from all laws/regulations to tiny units. This would leave more time for entrepreneurs to pay attention to their work and make efforts for increasing productivity and profitability.

Other important measures are:

- To replace inspections by self-certification
- To exempt tiny units from all laws regulations except those which relate to safety of human beings and the environment
- To simplify regulations procedures for SSI units and all inspections to be held only on one day in a quarter
- To club jurisdiction of various sections clauses and departments so that only one or two inspectors are required to visit the SSI unit
- To arrange single window clearances for new units irrespective of whether they relate to clearances from Central Authorities or State Authorities or Local Authorities.

The major impact of all the regulations will probably be in the amount of forms you will have to fill up on a regular basis and the records you will need to maintain. From time-to-time, your business will have to be audited by a competent chartered accountant or provincial agencies, and your books will be carefully examined. It is strongly recommended that as soon as possible, you establish a system for keeping proper books and records to avoid any unpleasant surprises in the future. Additional legislation affects the conduct of small businesses in specific areas, such as the securing of bad debts, the formation of contracts, negligent actions, etc.

Checklist of legal requirements: Depending on the locality where the business is started, there is need to collect legal requirements of that area. Based on that, a checklist is to be prepared for necessary follow-up action.

Good public relations: Regulations can be overwhelming and at times may be unfairly applied to you. It pays to have some contact with the sources of power or the people in power, who can make changes for you. This is not to say that you have to go out and bribe somebody, but it pays to know how to get some influence when you need it. There are many ways but the best is to take an interest in your local community and to meet some of the people who are in power (power buttons). In a democratic society, it is usually possible to contact your elected representative and ask for assistance if you have a problem and it is often surprising how effective the results can be, as politicians do tend to scare bureaucrats. It usually pays to belong and be active in local community and business associations developing contacts and relationships that can help you. You will find that the voice of an association is much more powerful than that of a lone individual when a complaint has to be presented. Elected politicians are elected to represent you (regardless of whether you voted for them or not) and usually feel a great responsibility to their constituents and take pride in solving bureaucratic problems. Use them. It is always beneficial if you are a member of professional bodies/associations formed to protect the interests of business/owners/entrepreneurs like you. You need to adopt strategies or methods which draw the attention of officials of the government to your genuine problems. Adopt a persuasive approach and avoid confrontation as far as possible.

Table 33.1 A Sample of a Directory of Resources

Legislated Area/Department	Agency/Ministry	Phone Number
Apprenticeship training		
Building requirement		
Provident fund		
Pension plan		
Health and Safety Regulations		
Factory inspection		
Labour welfare		
Income tax		
Sales tax		
Municipal/Panchayat Officer		
Municipal taxes		
• Property taxes		
• Business taxes		
Registration of Business		
• District Industrial Centre		
• Industry Department		
Trade Practices		
• Provincial		
• Federal		
Employees' State Insurance Officer		
Wages		
Minimum wages		
Payment of wages		
Annual holidays		
Hours of work		
Trade Union		
Workers' Compensation Board		
Pollution Board		
Workers' Education Programmer		
Others		

Beyond the Obvious

Having begun his entrepreneurial journey at age 14, and spending over a decade in the uber competitive leather apparel exports business where he supplied to top global brands like Donna Karan and Eddie Bauer, Sunil Kalra clearly comes across as the hard-nosed investor he's meant to be.

And he makes no bones about it. "When you go with risk money it's akin to going to Las Vegas," he says. Right now it's a problem of plenty as far as ideas for angel investing are concerned: "India suffers from too many entrepreneurs." That has resulted in evaluation becoming tougher and more stringent. And while he follows basic evaluation norms like any other investor, Kalra insists that it's usually the small things that matter most. "An angel is used to risks and is a good judge of character," he says.

Bullish on health care, logistics, infrastructure and education, he has recently launched a new firm in the Ayurvedic space, which will look at "modern approaches to traditional medicine". A cautious investor by his own admission, Kalra says he has reduced his exposure to the equity markets from 60% to below 20% over the past few months, and is looking at investing more in start-ups. His advice:

- **Education is not a prerequisite:** It's the passion that counts. You must be the best at what you do.
- **Set realistic targets:** You will be held accountable at each step for what you promise.
- **Reputation is key:** Remember, the networks that work well for you can also quickly spread the negative news fast.
- **Be consistent and keep working towards the plan:** Remember, you are as good as your last delivery.
- **Impressions are formed in the first 15 seconds:** If you have done your homework are well-prepared with the answers, it will show. So, will drive and commitment.
- **Body language and subliminal messages:** Be open, don't try to hide, and address issues headlong.
- **Persistence pays:** If a potential investor hasn't returned your call or message, do not take that as a rejection. Be creative in how you follow-up.
- **What's your HR plan?** What are you doing to build teams, retain talent, and empower your colleagues? Do you show respect for people at all levels?
- **Learn to share wealth:** Kalra recounts an entrepreneur duo who promptly went and gifted themselves gleaming new BMWs after receiving their first funding. The investor called off the deal. "You will have to exercise self-control. Your lifestyle will go down a notch or two. Expect your life to get tougher," he says.
- **Build a safety net:** Save enough cash to sustain for three years, if the business were to fail, even before you start.

CONCLUSION

Rules and regulations governing small-scale industries act as a governor ensuring steady growth of the industry as well as the environment (ecosystem) and the labour force. It not only ensures healthy growth but also rapid growth. The basic objective of rules and regulations governing small-scale industries is to ensure that the results of operations confirm as closely as possible to establish standards of goods, specified procedures or instructions. The need for rules and regulations are meant to develop small-scale industries, enabling them to move on the successful track.

They are the directions for excellence, growth and development and regulations is a monitoring mechanism of rules. Since the small-scale enterprise is concerned with land, environment, goods, people and consumers, rules and regulations have been formulated to safeguard these varied interests. If there is greater awareness among the entrepreneurs, these rules and regulations have minimum effect and disturbance. Thus, rules and regulations ensure steady and rapid growth of small-scale industries, develop new products and markets, produce quality goods and promote healthy development of human resources. More importantly, small industries are located nearer to the natural resources and human resources, do not pollute or degrade the ecosystem, intimidate and exploit labour and cheat the consumer on all counts. Rules and regulations are, therefore, the basic components of small-scale industries. They are like the lamp post directing the growth of this sector on a firm ground.

ANNEXURE-I

Inspector Raj: The Great Survivor

The licence-quota raj may be over but the inspector raj still reigns supreme. Industry may have been delicensed in 1991 but is still highly regulated. Each industrial unit is visited by between 40 and 60 inspectors in the course of a month. The following is an illustrative, and not an exhaustive, list of inspectors. There may be several more inspectors depending on the kind of manufacturing activity. As a result, small and medium enterprises are forced to shell out bribes to these officers or else face harassment.

Ministry	No. of inspectors	Work Done
Industry equipment.	5	Check registration, inventories, tax payment, quality control, safety
Home	2	Check fire protection facilities and compliance with Explosives Act.
Planning and Statistics	1	Collect data on production, manpower, manhours utilised and lost.
Finance	12	Five for income tax (three of them checking the same records for three different departments); seven from excise department.
Separate Revenue	5	Enforcement, verification and recovery of sales tax; enrolment of professional tax; weights and measures.
Revenue Department (State government) Tax	1	Registration of professionals.
Labour	8	Checking compliance with different labour laws, checking the same records.
Municipal Corporations	2	Municipal bylaws.
Power and Energy	1	Electricity connections.
Health and Family Welfare	2	Hygiene and occupational health.
Urban Affairs and Employment	1	Sanitation.
Environment and Forest	2	Pollution control.
Communications	1	Telecom facilities.
Local Self-government	2	Octroi and mass raids.
Food and Drug Administration	1	Safety standards.

ANNEXURE-II

A. Acts Affecting an Industrial Unit

1. The Agricultural Produce (Grading and Marketing) Act,1937
2. The Aluminium (Control) Order
3. The Arms Act, 1959
4. The Art-silk Textiles (Production and Distribution) Order, 1962
5. The Beer and Wine Prohibition Act, 1956
6. The Central Excise and Salt Act, 1944
7. The Cigarette (Regulation of Production and Distribution) Act, 1975
8. The Cinema Carbons (Control) Order, 1961
9. The Coffee Act, 1942
10. The Coir Reeling (Licensing) Order, 1968
11. The Cold Storage Order, 1980
12. The Commercial Vehicles/Tractors/Motor Cars (Distribution and Sales) Control Order, 1971
13. The Copper (Prohibitions of Use in Manufacture of Electric Cables and Wires) Order, 1970
14. The Cotton Textiles (Control) Order, 1948
15. The Dangerous Drugs Act, 1983
16. The Drugs and Cosmetics Act, 1940
17. The Drugs and Magic Remedies (Objectionable Advertisement) Act, 1954
18. The Drugs (Price Control) Order, 1979
19. The Essential Commodities Act, 1946
20. The Ethyl Alcohol (Price Control) Order, 1966
21. The Fertiliser Control Order, 1957
22. The Foodgrains (Prohibition of Use in Manufacture of Starch) Order, 1966
23. The Fruit Products Order, 1955
24. The Gold (Control) Act, 1968
25. The Household Electrical Appliances (Quality Control) Order, 1976
26. The Indian Boilers Act, 1923
27. The Indian Explosive Act, 1884
28. The Indian Forest Act, 1927
29. The Indian Standard Institute (Certificate Mark) Act, 1952
30. The Insecticides Act, 1968
31. The Iron and Steel (Control) Order, 1956
32. The Jute Textiles (Control) Order, 1961
33. The Kerosene/Light Diesel Oil/Furnace Oil (Fixation of Selling Prices) Order, 1973
34. The Meat Food Products Order, 1973
35. The Medical and Toilet Preparations (Excise Duties) Act, 1956
36. The Minerals (Regulation and Development) Act, 1957
37. The Molasses (Control) Order, 1961
38. The Non-ferrous Metals (Control) Order, 1958
39. The Packaged Commodities (Regulation) Order, 1975
40. The Paper (Control of Production) Order, 1974
41. The Paraffin Wax (Supply, Distribution and Price Fixation) Order, 1972

42. The Press and Registration of Books Act, 1971
43. The Prevention of Food Adulteration Act, 1954
44. The Rice Milling Industry (Regulation) Act, 1958
45. The Rubber Act, 1947
46. The Solvent Extracted Oil, Deoiled Meal and Edible Flour (Control) Order, 1967
47. The Sugar (Control) Order, 1966
48. The Sugar (Price Determination) Order, 1972
49. The Sugarcane Press Mud (Control) Order, 1961
50. The Textile Machinery (Production and Distribution) Control Order, 1962
51. The Textiles (Production by Knitting, Embroidery, Lacemaking and Printing Machines) Order, 1962
52. The Textiles (Development and Regulation) Order, 1992
53. The Textiles (Production by Handlooms) Control Order, 1956
54. The Tobacco Act, 1978
55. The Vegetable Oil Products (Control) Order, 1947
56. The Weights and Measures Act, 1958
57. The Wheat Roller Flour Milling (Licensing and Control) Order, 1957
58. The Woollen Textiles (Production and Distribution) Act, 1962

B. Labour Legislation

1. The Apprenticeship Act, 1961
2. The Contract Labour Act, 1970
3. The Employees' Provident Funds and Family Pension Fund Act, 1952
4. The Employees' State Insurance Act, 1948
5. The Employment Exchange (Compulsory Notification of Vacancies) Act, 1959
6. The Employment of Children's Act, 1938
7. The Equal Remuneration Act, 1976
8. The Factories Act, 1948
9. The Industrial Disputes Act, 1947
10. The Industrial Disputes (Amendment) Act, 1956
11. The Industrial Employment Act, 1946
12. The Industrial Relations Act, 1946
13. The Maternity Benefit Act, 1961
14. The Minimum Wages Act, 1948
15. The Payment of Bonus Act, 1978
16. The Payment of Gratuity Act, 1972
17. The Payment of Wages Act, 1936
18. The Sales Promotion Employees Act, 1976
19. The Shops and Establishment Act and Rules, 1948
20. The Trade Unions Act, 1926
21. The Workmen's Compensation Act, 1923

C. Other Acts Meant for Specific Industries

1. The Beedi and Cigar (Conditions of Employment) Act, 1966
2. The Coal Mines Labour Welfare Fund Act, 1947
3. The Coal Mines Provident Fund and Bonus Scheme Act, 1948
4. The Dock Workers (Regulation of Employment) Act, 1948

5. The Indian Dock Labourers Act, 1934
6. The Indian Ores Mines Labour Welfare Cess Act, 1961
7. The Industrial Disputes (Banking and Insurance Companies) Act, 1949
8. The Industrial Disputes (Banking Companies) Decision Act, 1955
9. The Limestone and Dolomite Mines Welfare Fund Act, 1972
10. The Mica Mines Labour Welfare Fund Act, 1946
11. The Motor Transport Workers Act, 1961
12. The Plantation Labour Act, 1951
13. The Working Journalists (Conditions of Services) and Miscellaneous Act, 1955

D. Taxation

1. The Central Sales Tax Act, 1956
2. The Profession Tax Act, 1959
3. The Gift Tax Act, 1958
4. The Income-tax Act, 1961
5. The State Sales Tax Act, 1956
6. The Wealth Tax Act, 1957

E. Regulation of Industries

1. The Indian Partnership Act, 1932
2. The Indian Companies Act, 1956
3. The Industries (Development and Regulation) Act, 1951
4. The Emblems and Names (Prevention of Improper Use) Act, 1950
5. The Companies (Acceptance of Deposits) Rules, 1975
6. The Capital Issue (Control) Act, 1947
7. The Monopolies and Restrictive and Trade Practices Act, 1969
8. The Land Acquisition Act, 1894
9. The Urban Land (Ceiling and Regulation) Act, 1976
10. The Water (Prevention and Control of Pollution) Act, 1974
11. The Prevention of Black Marketing and Maintenance of Supplies of Essential Commodities Act, 1980
12. The Conservation of Foreign Exchange and Prevention of Smuggling Activities Act, 1947
13. The Imports and Exports Control Act, 1947
14. The Securities Contracts (Regulation) Act, 1956
15. The Foreign Exchange Regulation Act, 1973
16. The State Aid to Industries Act, 1973
17. The Sick Industrial Combines (Special Provisions) Act, 1985
18. The Shops and Establishment Act, 1948
19. The Cement Control Order, 1967
20. The Jute Packing Materials Act, 1987
21. The Explosives Act, 1884
22. The Petroleum Act, 1934
23. The Inflammable Substances Act, 1952
24. The Patents Act, 1970
25. The Designs Act, 1911
26. The Trade and Merchandise Marks Act, 1958
27. The Smoke Nuisance Act, 1963

F. General Legislations

1. Banking Regulation Act, 1949
2. Negotiable Instruments Act, 1881
3. The Indian Stamp Act, 1899
4. The Indian Evidence Act
5. The Companies Law, 1956
6. The Indian Companies Act, 1956
7. The Indian Registration Act, 1908
8. The Limitation Act, 1963

Summary

Sl. No.	Type of Legislations	No.of Legislations
A	Acts affecting industrial units	58
B	Labour Legislations	21
C	Other Acts (Specific)	13
D	Taxation	6
E	Regulation of Industries	27
F	General	8
	Total	**133**

Note: *There are about 133 Acts and Orders about which the entrepreneur or his legal adviser should have some knowledge. The list is not exhaustive, but covers a good ground. For details, references may be made to the updated Acts/Orders in original wherever applicable.*

ANNEXURE-III

Applicability of Various Labour Acts

A table indicating the factories or establishments to which various Labour Acts are applicable is given below to enable the entrepreneur to know the Acts applicable to his enterprise:

Name of the Act	Factories or establishments to which applicable	Remarks
Apprenticeship Act, 1961	-	Apprenticeship Adviser shall give a notice in writing to the employer. It is permitted if work is intermitent or of sporadic nature.
Contract Labour (Regulation and Abolition) Act, 1970	Where contract labour is permitted. Establishment or contractors who employ or had employed 20 or more workers on any day in preceding 12 months.	Principal employer/contractor is required to seek registration/licence.
Employees' Provident Fund and Family Pension Fund Act, 1952	Factories employing 20 or more persons and those industries which are specified in the Schedule.	Employer required to furnish particulars to Regional Commissioner within 15 days of the application of the Act to his establishment. Those employees are eligible to become members whose wages do not exceed ₹1,000 per month.
Employees' State Insurance Act, 1948	Factories employing 20 or more persons, except specified seasonal factories.	
Employment Exchanges (Compulsory Notification of Vacancies) Act, 1959	Establishments where ordinarily 25 or more persons are employed.	Vacancies are to be notified to local Employment Exchange one week before the date on which interviews/test is to take place.
Employment of Children Act, 1938	Workshops engaged in specified processes; these processes are 10 in number.	Employment of children in these processes is prohibited. Child is defined as one who has not completed his 14th year.
Equal Remuneration Act, 1976	-	Act enjoins every employer to pay equal remuneration to men and women workers.
Factories Act, 1948	Factories where 10 or more workers with the aid of power or 20 or more workers without aid of power are working or were working on any day in preceding twelve months and where manufacturing process is carried on.	Occupier is expected to obtain prior permission for construction of factory premises and seek licence for the factory. Act is applicable to other places where manufacturing process is carried on, even though number of workers is less than 10 or 20, if so notified by the state government.
Industrial Disputes Act, 1947	Any business, trade, undertaking, manufacture or cailing of employer and includes any handicraft, or industrial occupation.	It deals with procedures for settlement of disputes and stipulates compensation for lay-off, retrenchment and closure of establishments.
Industrial Employment (Standing Order) Act, 1961	Industrial establishments employing one hundred or more workmen.	Standing Orders relating to classification of workmen, terms and conditions of service, etc., are to be got approved from certifying officers.
Maternity Benefit Act, 1961	Factories where 10 or more workers with aid of power or 20 or more workers without aid of power are/were working; mines and plantations or other establishments notified by the state government.	Act is not applicable to any factory or establishment to which Employees' State Insurance Act applies. A woman is entitled to maternity benefit at the rate of average daily wages for 12 weeks (6 weeks before and 6 weeks after delivery) if she has worked for 160 days in 12 preceding months.
Minimum Wages Act, 1948	Certain specified employments or processes.	State governments have fixed minimum wages for skilled, unskilled, manual and clerical workers, and have specified other conditions of service. Payment of Wages Act, 1936 is also applicable to these specified employments and processes.

Payment of Bonus Act, 1965	Factories where 10 more more workers with aid of power or 20 or more workers without aid of power are/were working; and establishments employing 20 or more persons.	A minimum bonus 8.33% of the salary or wages earned or Rs.10, whichever is higher, is payable even if the establishment has made no profits. Maximum amount of bonus payable is 20 per cent of the salary or wage earned. Newly set up establishments are exempted from payment of bonus till they start deriving profit or for 5 years from their establishment, whichever is earlier.
Payment of Gratuity Act, 1972	Factories where 10 or more workers with aid of power or 20 or more workers without aid of power are/were working; and mines or plantations, and shops or establishments employing 10 or more persons.	An employer is required to furnish particulars to the controlling authority when Act becomes applicable, notify any change or closure of establishment. Gratuity is payable, after an employee has rendered five years of continuous service, at the rate of 15 days of wages for a year's service, subject to a maximum of 20 months' wages.
Payment of Wages Act, 1936	Factories where 10 or more workers with aid of power or 20 or more workers without aid of power are/were working; other industrial establishments as are specified; specified employments included in the Schedule to Minimum Wages Act.	The Act seeks to regulate timely payment of wages in respect of persons, whose wages average less than ₹ 1,000 a month.
Sales Promotion (Conditions of Service) Act 1976	Establishments engaged in Pharmaceutical industry.	-
Shops and Establishments Act of state governments	Shops, commercial establishments, residential hotels, restaurant, eating houses, etc.	Act is not applicable to such undertakings which are covered under Factories Act, 1948.
Workmen Compensation Act, 1923	Certain specified employments.	Compensation is payable to workmen, whose monthly wages do not exceed ₹ 1,000, for injury by accident or occupational disease.

ANNEXURE-IV

Applicability of Various Regulations to Small-scale Industries in India

A summary of the various Acts/Regulations that are applicable to small-scale industries is given below to enable the entrepreneur to know the Acts at a glance.

Name of the Act	Applicability	Remarks
Central Sales Tax Act	Any dealer engaged in interstate trade or commerce during any year is liable to pay tax on all such sales effected by him. [Sec.6(1),(A)]	Not liable to pay tax if the sale is for the purpose of export out of the territory of India. [Sec.6(12), (1A)]
Maharashtra Sales Tax Act	Every dealer who carries on business of buying and selling goods, except an agriculturist who sells agricultural produce grown on land cultivated by him personally, is liable to pay tax in respect of sales as purchase made by him. [Sec.(34)]	Every registered dealer has to display the certificate of registration or a copy thereof conspicously at each place of his business. [Rule 9] A dealer liable to pay tax shall get himself registered by making an application in the prescribed form to the sales tax officer and shall seek a certificate of registration. [Sec.141]
Delhi Sales Tax Act, 1975	Every dealer whose turnover from the commencement of any year exceeds the taxable quantum (₹ 30,000 in relation to any dealer who manufactures goods for sale regardless of the value of gods manufactured) shall become liable to pay tax on all sales effected by him after the day immediately following that day on which the turnover exceeded the taxable quantum. [Sec.3(2)(1)]	
Income Tax Act, 1961 Maharashtra State Tax on Professions, Trade and Employment Act, 1975	Income tax is leviable on profits and gains from business if it is carried on in the previous year. [Sec.2(13) or (36)] Individual, undivided Hindu family, firm, company, corporation, society, club or association. [Sec.5(1) and 2(c)]	In computing the taxable income from business or profession, following deductions are admissible: 1. Rents, land revenue, municipal taxes, cost of repairs, insurance premium etc. [Sec.(32)] 2. *Depreciation* in respect of buildings, plant as machinery and furniture and fixture on the basis of its actual cost. [Sec.32(1)] 3. *Investment Allowance:* 35% of actual cost of machinery or plant installed for the purposes of manufacturer or production after 30.6.1977 but before 1.4.1982. [Sec.32A(2B)] 4. Preliminary expenses, commission, etc. (a) Amortisation of preliminary expenses-restricted to 2 1/2 per cent of the cost. [Sec.35D] (b) Commission Bonus paid to employees. [Sec.36(i) & (ii)] (c) Contribution towards recognised Provident Fund & Gratuity. [Sec.36(i), (iv) & (v)] (d) Audit fee, commission, pension, compensation etc. [Sec.37) (e) Expenditure on scientific research related to assessee's business is admissible. [Sec.35] (f) Expenditure on acquiring patent rights or copyrights is allowed in 14 equal yearly instalments. [Sec.35A] 5. *Donations:* 50 per cent of qualifying amount of donation. [Sec.80G)

		6. *New undertakings in Backward Areas:* 20 per cent deduction in respect of Profit and gains. [Sec.80HH] 7. *Setting up small industrial undertakings in rural areas:* 20 per cent of the profits are eligible for deduction. [Sec.80HHA] 8. *Capital Allowance:* Deduction is allowed at 7.5 per cent per annum on capital employed for companies which begins manufacturing after 31.3.1976 for five years (otherwise it is 6 per cent). 9. *Publication of Books:* Publication of books (other than newspapers, journals and magazines etc.) are eligible for a deduction of 20 per cent of such profits and gains. [Sec.80QQ] 10. *Interest on borrowed capital.* [Sec.40A(8)] 11. Amalgamation of sick units with health units effective from 1.4.1978. [Sec.71A] 12. Rural Development
Maharashtra State Tax on Professions, Trade and Employment Act, 1975	Individual, undivided Hindu family, firm, company, corporation, society, club or association. [Sec.5(1) and 2(c)]	The employer has to deduct tax payable and furnish to the appropriate authority within 15 days of expiry of a month. [Sec.4 and 6]

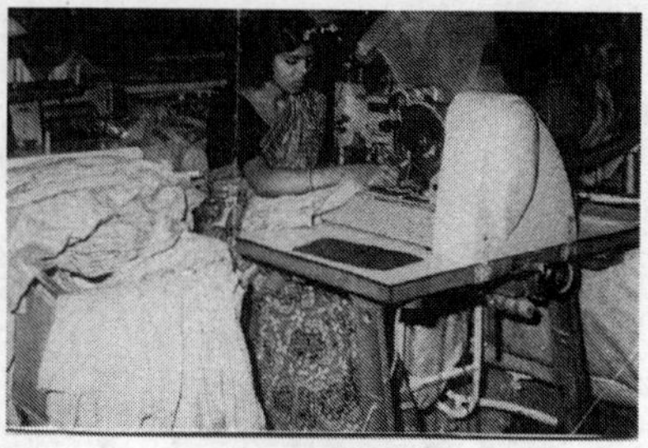

III SECTION

PROJECT WORK

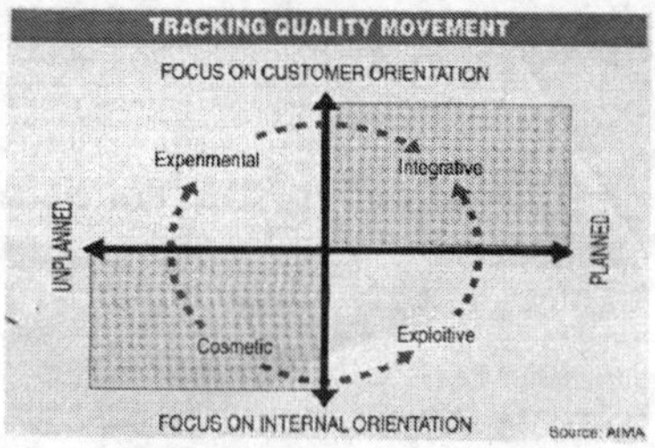

"The case study can be used to help students learn inductively by giving them information that simulates a complex business situation, and asking them to analyse it and choose a particular course of action."

THE CASE STUDY

Management education seeks to accomplish several objectives simultaneously. One is to develop a set of concepts so that students can understand the framework in which business decisions are made. The second is to operationalise those concepts with specific tools of analysis. These are fairly straightforward. But the more difficult part is providing a broad business perspective within which students can develop a perspective on the evolving nature of management, and begin to exercise judgements in situations where the choices and their consequences are not obvious.

Equally varied and diverse are the components of management education, like concepts, models, tools, and techniques. These are tangible. There are also intangibles, like perspectives, judgements, values, and ethics. Together, they enable an individual to develop confidence in her ability to cope with complex problems. Evidently, this cannot be accomplished with one event or one case study or one simulation or one game or one set of tools. It can be accomplished only through a series of components, a sequence of experiences, spread over a period of time.

When we are talking about the relevance of a particular component of management education, it is important to understand that no single component, *per se*, can transform an individual into a better manager. Besides, each has a diversity of its own. There are good cases and bad cases, long ones and short ones — just as there are good teachers who can draw valuable lessons from simple cases, and others who use good cases in a bad way.

In fact, the idea of case-oriented learning was not invented by the B-schools. Even at Harvard University, the concept did not originate in the B-school; it originated in the law school. If you look at medical schools around the world, they also use cases extensively. When a doctor takes his students to see a patient on his rounds, they deal with cases through which they learn to diagnose, use complex sets of data in order to arrive at a hypothesis, and prescribe a modality of treatment. They also acquire bedside manners. Even at law schools, officers learn from well-documented case studies, where it is even possible to create simulations for potential conflicts. The influence of the case is, thus, all-pervasive in a variety of fields.

The important thing to remember is that the case intervention is part of a broader initiative, and will only succeed if it is complemented and supported by other interventions aligned with the desired change.

This is not to say that the case study is a perfect tool. The case study can never fully substitute the learning that comes from real experiences, nor can it ever capture the full complexity of a managerial situation. But, imperfect as it may be, the case study remain the best way to train potential business leaders.

THE SHORTCOMINGS OF THE CASE STUDY

The concept of case-oriented learning was originated in the law school. Even in medical colleges case-oriented learning is in vogue. The same practice was introduced in management education.

In a perpetually changing global marketplace, where developmental stages, comparative advantages, cultural states, information flows, and technological innovation are constantly forcing the tenets of management theory to be rewritten, the case method may appear to be an anachronism. In the new millennium, will the case study be the best way of teaching managers/entrepreneurs how to manage better?

What is important in the competitive world is not what you know, but what you do with that knowledge. A case study helps you understand how to put knowledge to use. It enables managers to rely more on commonsense – which is what management is all about – rather than on external support systems. It exposes greenhorns to a range of situations that may take them a lifetime to experience on the job. And it trains an individual to dissect a problem to its fundamentals, arrive at the core, examine the alternatives, and formulate an action plan that works.

A good case study has several characteristics. It should generate extraordinary problems in an ordinary setting. It should not state the problems in a cut-and-dry fashion, which will lead logically to cut-and-dry solutions. Each problem should have subtle and unstated clues lurking in the narrative. The clues should lead to multiple analyses, leading to several equally.

THE BENEFITS

Application of Theory: The use of a simulated, but realistic problem forces managers to explore how to apply principles.

Customised Problem-solving: The objective is to elicit unique answers, not to apply pre-packaged solutions.

Core Focus: Instead of tackling symptoms, the idea is to identify the heart of the problem, and to tackle it at that level.

Plurality of Perspectives: The approach shows that there is no one answer, but many ways to solve the same problem.

Insistence on Alternatives: The aim is to work out a solution only after exploring all the possible options.

Small-scale Sector in India

The small-scale sector has been a prime contributor to the overall growth of the industrial sector in India. The growth rate recorded by this sector has normally been higher than that of the industrial sector as a whole. Maintaining the same trend, the sector registered to record a higher growth in the range of 7.5-8.5 per cent during 1999-2000 in comparison to the 6.5 per cent target growth in GDP during this period.

The Small-scale Industry (SSI) sector has emerged over five decades as a highly vibrant and dynamic sector of the Indian economy. Today, this sector accounts for about 95 per cent of the industrial units and is contributing about 40 per cent of value addition in the manufacturing sector, nearly 80 per cent of manufacturing employment and about 35 per cent of exports (both direct and indirect). More than 32 lakh units are spread all over the country producing over 7,500 items and generating employment for more than 178 lakh people.

Small enterprises, i.e., small-scale units, not only play a crucial role in providing large-scale employment opportunities at lower capital cost than large-scale industries, but also help in industrialisation of rural and backward areas, thereby reducing regional imbalance assuring more equitable distribution of national income and wealth. SSI units are supplementing and complimentary to large and medium-scale units as ancillary units. Considering the large employment level and backlog of creation of new jobs to provide employment to all able hands today, hopes are pinned on the small-scale sector. The government is making all efforts to provide a conducive atmosphere, a level playing ground and policy support to enable the SSI sector to achieve higher levels of production, exports and employment.

The Government of India has helped the small-scale sector through supportive policy measures since adoption of the planned economy model. The basic policy support for the SSI sector has its roots in the Industrial Policy Resolution of 1956. Further, the Industrial Policy Statement, 1977, laid emphasis on reservation of items. The reservation of economically viable and technologically feasible products to be exclusively manufactured by SSIs began with a list of 47 items which was gradually extended to many products. Presently, 811 items are on the reserved list. Other policy supports which could be listed are excise exemption, credit under the priority sector lending from banks and financial institutions, marketing through reservation of items for products from the SSI sector for government purchases, providing infrastructure facilities like sheds, plots in industrial estates, technological support, new management techniques, training and entrepreneurship development.

The Scope

The project work should be undertaken in the batches not exceeding five students in each batch:

1. Visit to Industrial Estates.
2. Study of problems of Finance and Marketing.
3. Visit to training institutes offering training for entrepreneurs in the small sector.
4. Study of environmental problem.
5. Influence of environment on the working of Small Industries.
6. Study of tax benefits available from time-to-time.
7. Preparation of project report in relation to opportunities available.
8. Preparation of feasibility report of a project.
9. Preparation of profile of successful entrepreneurs – Small Sector.
10. Study of sick units (in the small sector).
11. Survey of export-oriented small-scale units.
12. Visit to the banks to study financial assistance to small-scale industries.

Why Start Own Business?

This is aptly reflected in replies to a typical questionnaire from an entrepreneurship development institute for prospective entrepreneurs as follows:

I want to be on my own.

Demand is very high.

For economic gains.

Status in society.

Opportunity to serve society.

Somebody else is doing it successfully.

I want to do something new/better.

Somebody has promised to help me all the way.

I am tired of job/service.

Indian Scene

Small enterprises have distinct advantages, both economic and social. Some of these are:

(a) They create immediate and permanent employment at a relatively small capital cost.

(b) They meet a substantial part of increased demand for consumer goods, including mass consumption goods.

(c) They facilitate mobilisation of resources of capital and skills which often would remain inadequately utilised.

(d) They bring about integration of rural economy with large-scale enterprises.

(e) They offer a method of ensuring equitable distribution of national income.

(f) They involve a short gestation period.

(g) They do not require as heavy and costly infrastructure as the larger enterprises.

(h) They have a favourable capital-output ratio.

(i) The products of these enterprises earn a substantial foreign exchange.

(j) They assist the dispersal of industries and avoid problems which unplanned urbanisation tends to create.

Due to all these advantages, the development of small enterprises has been assigned a crucial role in India's five year plans. With a view to protect, support and promote small enterprises to become self-supporting and to facilitate a balanced growth of small and large sectors, a number of policy and promotional measures have been taken by the government. The policy measures include reservation of certain items for the exclusive production in the small-scale sector and exclusive purchase under the stores purchase policy and differential excise duty. Promotional measures have included development of entrepreneurship backed by a package of consultancy services, improvement in techniques, institutional support in respect of supply of credit and raw materials, factory accommodation in industrial estates, capital subsidy and rebates on the sales of certain products.

As a result of various measures taken by the government, these enterprises have come to occupy a crucial place in the national economy. It has been estimated that the share of small industries in the contribution made by the manufacturing sector is around 49 per cent in terms of gross value of output and 51 per cent of value-added. The share of this sector in the total exports represent one-third, and over 65 per cent of the total exports from the manufacturing sector. This sector provides employment to about 24 million, both full-time and part-time.

In the above context, the role of entrepreneurs assumes great significance in India. In August 1983, the late Prime Minister of India, Indira Gandhi had announced a scheme for providing self-employment to educated unemployed youth. The scheme aimed at assisting 2,00,000 to 2,50,000 educated unemployed youth through industry, service and business routes each year to set up their own ventures with a package of assistance. If 2,50,000 small enterprises are set up each year, these alone would provide employment to 2.5 million persons. The creation of more 'owners' as against 'employees' will go a long way in reducing the people's dependence on jobs, diversifying industrial ownership by developing entrepreneurs from non-traditional occupations and communities and balancing regional development by extending enterprise formation in less developed areas.

The identification, training and development of a large number of local entrepreneurs from among the emerging new sources such as technicians, employees, small traders, sons of agriculturists and educated and less-educated unemployed is strategic to the development of small enterprises and self-employment in rural and backward areas, small towns and metropolitan centres. Indigenous entrepreneurship development also provided the missing link in 'local resources' in the form of local entrepreneurs in areas which earlier had to depend upon entrepreneurs coming in from outside.

Entrepreneur development and training programmes were taken up in India in the early 1960s by a number of agencies, mostly governmental. The entrepreneurs required a whole range of information for setting up of a business and in that context, the contribution of these programmes was essentially in the area of dissemination of knowledge on financial, technical and managerial aspects. To that extent, these programmes were not directed towards imparting skills but were in the nature of supportive programmes for existing and new entrepreneurs. Most of these agencies generally lacked the faculty and orientation of inspiring and motivating young people, particularly from non-traditional sections to become entrepreneurs. The Government of India has recently established a National Institute for Entrepreneurship Development and Small Business in New Delhi. This institute will act as an apex body for coordinating entrepreneurship development programmes in the country, providing streamlined programmes to specific target-groups and target-areas and course material, organising and conducting programmes for motivators, trainers and entrepreneurs.

The Government of India has also set up a National Entrepreneurship Development Board to determine policies for entrepreneurship development and advise on schemes for promotion of entrepreneurship and self-employment in small industries. The Science and Technology Board also has been set up for development of entrepreneurship among scientific and technical graduates.

As is the case in India, in most developing countries, the entrepreneurship development programmes have either been sponsored by government or semi-government agencies and hence suffer from inherent inadequacies arising out of bureaucratic set-up. These programmes should be a joint effort of the government, financial institutions, including banks, educational institutions, voluntary organisations and others concerned.

A few case studies are presented here to give an insight for Project Work.

1. TECHNOCRAT-ENTREPRENEUR

Here is a case of a technocrat-entrepreneur, who took to jobbing through a mechanical workshop. Mr. Saha is one of the first technocrats who were assisted by a bank under its special scheme. He is a highly qualified mechanical engineer, with postgraduate degrees and diplomas in industrial management and industrial engineering from some leading universities of the world, including the famous MIT. He also has had a considerable amount of practical experience in leading companies in the United States, Britain, and India. At the time he approached the bank for assistance to start his own industry, he was drawing a salary of about ₹ 2,500 per month. Quite an impressive background indeed!

The project submitted by Mr. Saha envisaged the manufacture of a stationery item – staple removers – and job work on ancillary items and precision turned and pressed parts. The machinery required by him was: a power press, an automat and toolroom equipment, i.e., a lathe, a milling machine, a shaping machine, a bench grinder, etc. The project was estimated to cost asunder:

Plant and Machinery	₹ 136,000
Working Capital	₹ 56,000
Deposit for shed	₹ 10,000
Total	₹ 2,02,000

Of this amount, the borrower offered to bring in ₹ 10,000. The bank sanctioned the remaining amount by way of:

Loan against hypothecation of machinery	₹ 1,36,000
Cash Credit against hypothecation of stock	₹ 30,000
Clean Loan	₹ 1,92,000

The entrepreneur anticipated an annual sales of ₹ 4.27 lakh with a pre-tax profits of ₹ 83,000.

Mr. Saha was looking for a shed admeasuring 2,000 sq.ft., for he had an eye on future expansion, although his immediate need was for about 1,000 sq.ft. However, for quite some time after the sanction of the loan, he could not locate a suitable shed. With permission of the bank, he decided to take delivery of his automat, to operate which he had adequate job orders in hand and installed in a friend's shed as a stop-gap arrangement. Pending the finalisation of the arrangements for his own shed, he shelved his programme to manufacture staple removers.

After a month's working, he found to his surprise and annoyance that most of his products were rejected by his customers. He became furious and let loose his wrath upon his workers. Matters did not improve in the second month either. Soon raw materials worth ₹ 15,000 were used up and no revenue worth the name was generated. Unfortunately, this particular branch of the bank was deposit-oriented. Initially, therefore, no stock inspection was carried out, and raw material bills were paid without questions. However, the head office soon came into the picture, and assisted the branch in supervising the account. From then onwards, disbursements were made only with the sanction of the head office.

Before the expiry of six operational months, the sanctioned working capital limits had been utilised; but there were hardly any assets except bills receivable. To keep the unit operating, an additional facility of ₹ 20,000 by way of book debts was sanctioned by the bank in January 1972. About this time, Mr. Saha had moved into his own shed on a long-term basis and on a monthly rent of ₹ 1,800. He was now confident that with all the facilities he had, he would have no difficulty in controlling the production and that the rejections would not exceed 5 per cent.

However, this was not to be. Rejections continued as before, and the responsibility for these was once again thrown upon the workers. A senior engineer, with a salary of ₹ 1,200 p.m. and inspectors for quality control were appointed. Mr. Saha himself was drawing a living allowance of ₹ 1,500 p.m. plus car expenses. But, in spite of all his care and high expenditure, he did not realise more than 50 per cent of his bills.

The financial structure was crumbling; therefore in September 1972, his book debt limit was raised to ₹ 40,000. The production picked up to some extent. The monthly output crossed ₹ 20,000, but with heavy overheads, the break-even amount was as high as ₹ 28,000 p.m. The progress in output, however, was maintained for a few months; it even improved a little, touching a maximum of ₹ 24,000.

In the meantime, the customers of the borrower started delaying the payment of his bills, and the book debts started mounting. The book debts account was overdrawn by about ₹ 13,000. Finding the unit in difficulties once again, and having regard to the slight improvement in the output and confidence in the integrity of Mr. Saha, the book debts limit was raised to ₹ 80,000 in February 1973. At this time, the bank did not have any misgivings about the ability of the borrower to manage the unit successfully. Nevertheless he was told that this would be his last chance. Till then, 100 per cent finance had been adjusted against book debts. But now a margin of 20 per cent was deducted and adjusted against past bills, so that they could be gradually liquidated.

Sometime after this, a new situation arose. Mr. Saha lost all his customers, and the unit was starving for orders. But despite the difficulties he had passed through, Mr. Saha refused to economise and change his lifestyle. He was advised to let out a part of his shed, half the area of which was not utilised, move to a cheaper residential flat – he was paying ₹ 900 p.m., – and sell off his car. But this advice fell on deaf ears.

Finally, he managed to enter into a contract for a job with a new customer, who supplied him the raw materials to keep his entire workshop, including the power press, busy for 2 working shifts. Mr. Saha did not initially inform the bank about this arrangement. He thought he had discovered a gold mine and that, in a few months, his affairs would not only be put in order but his debts would be completely paid-off. However, during a routine inspection, the new arrangement was discovered by the bank and he agreed to deposit some funds in the account after paying off his day-to-day working capital needs. At this stage, the bank hoped that the tide had turned in Saha's favour.

But alas, this was not to be! The contract with the new party was revoked after about four or five months. Mr. Saha did not communicate this fact to the bank. Again, the situation was discovered during a periodic inspection. At this stage, the bank firmly told him that there was no question of any further assistance to him. He was asked to look for a partner to share with him the responsibilities of the unit. His drawbacks were pointed out to him. Saha scoffed at the idea; in his over-confidence, he was too greedy to share the fruits of his hard work with someone else. It was several months after the bank had put its foot down that he finally decided to look for a partner. By this time, his liabilities totalled ₹ 4.5 lakh against a realisable value of assets of ₹ 1.5 lakh. Who would be foolish enough to enter into a partnership with him at that stage? Naturally, not even his closest friends – not that were many – would have anything to do with.

By the end of 1973, some of his creditors had filed legal proceedings against him. Somehow, consent decrees were obtained to the effect that he would liquidate his liabilities in instalments. In October 1973, he was so cross with the branch which had patiently associated with him for nearly three years, that he asked for a transfer of his account to another branch. Unluckily for him, the agent here was a tough guy, and Saha could not cut much ice with him. With the concurrence of the head office, he was firmly told that his pressure tactics and arrogance would no longer be tolerated and that unless he changed his ways and showed some positive results without any further assistance from the bank, there was no hope for him.

The question of recalling the advance, filing a suit against Mr. Saha and invoking the Reserve Bank of India guarantee is now under the consideration of the bank.

Let us now analyse the causes of the failure of this very highly qualified technocrat, who seemed so promising when the bank sanctioned a loan for him.

(a) The following points of weakness on the part of the bank can be identified:

- (i) Despite the glittering background of the proponent, the bank appears to have placed too much confidence in his ability to succeed;
- (ii) The reasons why he had changed jobs once too often in the past were not given due weight before the loan was sanctioned;
- (iii) The bank sanctioned a project at nil margin (almost), though it was much larger than a small but economical unit;
- (iv) The marketability of and marketing arrangements for his product, *viz.,* staple removers, were not fully assessed. Later, Mr. Saha could not arrive at any settlement with his dealers; and
- (v) The bank's confidence in his ability to succeed was carried too far.

(b) The following weakness of the borrower may be identified:

(i) He is very arrogant, self-centred and an individualistic person;

(ii) His public/human relations are very immature. He could not get on with any one – his workers, his bankers and raw material suppliers and his customers. As a result, he erected a barrier between himself and all he had to deal with. Obviously he could not depend on the cooperation of his employees, and he could not cultivate any worthwhile relationship with his customers;

(iii) He was over-confident and used to a life of luxury, and would not economise even in adversity;

(iv) He was used to the style of working in large organised companies and tried to apply the same standards in his small-scale unit, with disastrous results;

(v) He was absolutely unimaginative;

(vi) Initially, he had not explored the market well enough and failed to meet the orders of the market. His was a case of many opportunities lost;

(vii) In spite of having qualified in industrial engineering and administration, he did not apply his knowledge to the practical business of running his unit successfully;

(viii) On at least two occasions, he failed to take the bank into confidence.

2. FINANCIAL ASSISTANCE

The prime force behind the 'small' trading corporation is the major partner, P.D. Narayana Menon, who had taken to entrepreneurship after achieving the status of an inventor. This is a rare case, where an inventor has successfully converted his invention into a commercial enterprise. The opportunity to assist such an enterprise is unique and an example of successful entrepreneurship.

Background to the Invention: Narayana Menon is an employee of Hindustan Petroleum. An inventor is always said to be on the look ut for a solution to a problem, may be of a day-to-day nature. In Menon's case, the problem was how to pour a liquid from its container into another without the help of a funnel, without spilling and wasting even a single drop. The answer to this question did not present itself to Menon in a jiffy. Night-after-night, he worked far into the wee hours of the morning in a laboratory which was nothing nobler than his two room tenement. There could not be a more appropriate place for playing with liquids – as it were here.

Menon's efforts were purely personal. He was not backed by his employers or supported by any institution or the government. In fact, no one was aware of his activities. When he was successful in his experiments, Menon mentioned the fact to his employers – a multinational firm who was surprised. Here was a solution to a problem which they had been looking for a long time. Eminent scientists had failed to come upon the simple device which Menon had invented. So, Menon, who was in the company's Accounts Department, realised that the problem was not only his, but that of the entire world. The company placed an order with him for the supply of liquid pourers to fit their containers. It even encouraged and guided him into obtaining a patent for this invention.

History of the Unit: He established a 'small' trading corporation in 1969 to manufacture and sell his liquid pourer, known technically as the safety cap pourer (SCP). He had a set of dies manufactured by an injection moulding unit. At that time, he was mainly engaged in marketing and developing new items rather than in fabricating them. In 1972, however, he decided to manufacture them. So, he purchased a machine, but used it in the premises of his well-wishers. It was only in 1976 that he took up his present production shed on a rental basis. Till that stage, he had not borrowed money from any source but had managed entirely with his own savings and the small surplus he had put by from his business. During this period, he zealously guarded his patent right.

The Product: The liquid pourer (SCP) is practically a household and industries item today. This simple device had been developed suitably for pouring liquid from all types of containers of all sizes and shapes: glass bottles, cans, plastic jerry cans, drums, jugs, etc. Presently, there are about 20 different sizes and designs in each category of pourers, all of which are protected by patent rights.

The safety pourer plus which Menon has introduced has a great safety factor in the handling of dangerous liquids. It is a plug-cum-pourer. We are all aware of the plastic plug, which is fitted to the mouth of plastic, glass or metal containers, on top of which there is a cup. First the cup and then the plug has to be removed when a liquid is poured out. His plug-cum-pourer need not be removed for this purpose. The pesticide industry has taken to this innovation in a big way being positive of the safety factor involved in its use. The SCP has been further developed to provide an additional service to stop the flow of the liquid once its desired level has been achieved in the receiving container.

Location and Infrastructure: To fabricate his products, Menon acquired a shed in the Bombay Talkies Compound at Malad, which has been patronised by a large number — about 400 – of small-scale industrial units. The shed is an independent structure, with an area of about 2,400 sq.ft. Its monthly rent is ₹ 750. It is made of brick masonry walls up to a height of about 15 ft., and is covered with a roof of asbestos cement sheets supported on a timber structure and trusses. The rent receipt is in the name of Mini Trading Corporation. The electric power bills and receipts are also in the name of the unit. It has a power allocation of 30 HP. The water supply is adequate. There is a nearby well from which supplies are drawn to cool the machines. Drinking water is also available.

Menon made an application to the Directorate of Industries for the registration of his unit. The location is suitable for the unit's programme, since the Mumbai market is most economical and easily accessible, both for the supply of raw materials and the sale of his products.

Raw Materials: The unit requires high density polyethylene, PVC, rubber, etc., all of which are easily available in the market. The monthly requirement is about 2.5 tonnes, valued at ₹ 40,000 for the scale of production, which is expected to be achieved shortly. With Indian Petrol Chemicals Ltd., (IPCL) going into production, there will be no dearth of raw materials.

Process Know-how: The products are made by the injection moulding process. Plastic injection moulding has become quite common nowadays, and skilled operators to man hand-operated, semi-automatic and fully automatic machines are available in the required numbers. Menon and his son, Ramesh, who have now been in this line for more than three years, have adequate know-how. The very fact that Menon has developed many patented products is a testimony to his technical capability and his inventiveness.

Machinery: A list of the items of machinery installed by the unit is attached. It may be noticed that, as the unit progressed, Menon has added facilities to his establishment. New machinery was purchased in 1978 in order to meet the sizeable orders that are expected following his efforts since 1977. The machinery is a standard product which has proved itself in the market over many years. Its present depreciated value is ₹ 1,37,679, including the latest addition of a 3-oz automatic machine.

Market: Menon is so involved in pouring devices that he has become an expert in the field. He has modified the devices to suit the various requirements of large companies, mainly multinationals such as Bayer, Cyanamid (India), BASP, Hoechst, Sandoz, Rallies India, Hindustan Petroleum, Metal Box, Bharat Pulverizing Mills, etc. Since each design has been patented by Menon, these companies have no alternative but to place their orders with him for their requirements of these products and their requirements are indeed very large, running into lakh of pieces. Menon has been now negotiating with other companies as well.

In addition to the above which are for patented products, the Mini Trading Corporation manufactures conventional items of household consumption such as bottle/jar caps, tumblers, brushes, etc. Some dies were introduced for the manufacture of pocket torches and bottle openers, which are expected to be introduced in the market within the next three months. The bottle opener will be unique in that it is an item of novelty and will also be the first one available in plastic. All these items have been introduced mainly in the local market through employed salesmen. Menon has also appointed regional distributors in Delhi, Chennai and Kerala. For his household items, he has under consideration a sales campaign in collaboration, if necessary, with the Tatas, Hindustan Lever, Godrej, Cyanamid, Bayer, etc., who market such consumer products as edible oils, petroleum products, household chemicals and pesticides. The nature of the patented products is such that an immense monopoly market can be created for it. The export market is also wide open for Menon.

Administrative and Managerial Competence: Although Menon has been in business for more than three years, he has not applied his mind so far to a proper administrative set-up for his unit, because his attention was concentrated on product development. Records, therefore, except those needed for financial accounting, are at present practically non-existent. He knows that a proper maintenance of all the records pertaining to purchase, production, despatches, sales, etc., are essential for a systematic and effective control of the affairs of his business. He has, therefore, turned his attention to this aspect of his enterprise. Already, the financial accounts of the unit are being written up by a chartered accountant.

Inventory: Menon is a man of many ideas. He has utilised this quality not only to develop new products, but also to improve those items which are already in the market. As regards the latest set of items, he has chosen a strategy to manufacture them in bulk and then release them in the market, so that he will have the initial advantage before others copy his product and cut him down in competition. As a result, he has at present a sizable stock of finished products, which he plans to introduce in the market during the next few weeks. Such items will be released only in the local market and against cash sales, so that the money is quickly realised. The apprehension that the improved product may not have consumer appeal is well taken care of by Menon, for he places an order for a die for a product only after he has thoroughly studied consumer needs and tastes.

Working Capital: The unit shortly expects to be able to go into full capacity production, considering that substantial orders for the patented items from reputed companies are in the pipeline. On a single shift working, the production capacity of the unit may be estimated at a conservative figure of ₹ 60,000 p.m. The working capital requirements for this level of production may be estimated asunder:

	₹
Raw material stocks – (1 month)	48,000
Goods in process, packing materials, etc. (1 week)	12,000
Finished stocks – (15 days)	30,000
1 month's recoverable (peak level)	60,000
Total working capital	1,50,000

Working capital assistance to the unit may, therefore, be provided asunder:

Facility	*Limit*	*Margin*
Pledge of stocks	₹ 1,00,000	20% on materials
Bills Purchase – Usance	₹ 50,000	30% on finished goods
30 days (acceptance)		10%

Raw materials are purchased on cash and hence there is no purchase credit. This estimate is based on a production level of finished goods of the sales valued at ₹ 60,000 p.m.

3. CASE STUDY OF A SMALL-SCALE SICK UNIT AND NURSING PROGRAMME

M/s Indian Electronics: A Small-scale Sick Industry nursed by a Nationalised Bank

(This is a true case study of a small-scale unit which was sick and was nursed back to health by a nationalised bank. Only the name of the company and the names of the partners have been changed. Small-scale entrepreneur students of small-scale industries and management students would find immense wealth of additional materials in this case study.)

Background: Indian Electronics, a small-scale industrial unit, was started as a partnership concern in 1957. Its partners included Mr. Lalwani, Mr. Kaka, Mr. Shukla, Mr. S. Lalwani.

The partners are of fair means and adequately trained for the work. All of them are well trained in different faculties – technical, cost accountancy, sales and advertisement and expansion.

In the initial period, the unit took up the manufacture of radio sets, amplifiers, public address systems, etc. Simultaneously, development work on sophisticated electronic items was undertaken. The unit's scheme for the manufacture of oscilloscope was approved by the Development Commissioner, SSI, in 1965. The unit successfully developed oscilloscopes, and the equipments were successfully demonstrated to such institutions as the TIFR, BARC, PRL (Ahmedabad), BEL (Bengaluru), NPL (Delhi), etc. BEL purchased a number of items from the unit.

In 1970, the unit wanted to venture into a new field – the manufacture of television receivers. Subsequently, a licence for the manufacture of 2,500 TV sets per annum was obtained. Keeping in view the tremendous demand for TV receivers in Mumbai, the unit decided to go ahead and implement the TV project. It placed orders for capital equipment and imported the necessary raw materials.

Production and Sales

Table 1 Trends in Production, Sales and Stock of Goods

	Production		Sales		Stock	
	No. of Units	Amount (₹ in lakh)	No. of Units	Amount (₹ in lakh)	No. of Units	Amount (₹ in lakh)
1973	8	10.16	-	-	8	0.16
1974	222	4.44	211	4.22	19	0.38
1975	308	6.16	300	6.00	27	0.54
1976	407	8.14	200	4.00	234	4.68
1977	128	2.56	52	1.04	310	7.20
1978	15	0.30	20	0.40	305	7.10

The other problems that affected the unit were:

The production of TV receivers accelerated during the second and third year, and reached the peak in 1976. At this crucial time, sales, which had picked up in the initial two years, declined sharply in 1976, resulting in the building up of large stocks. As a result of the sharp decline in sales, the production of TV receivers was slowed down in 1977. Sales declined further. The small-scale unit had 305 pieces of finished TV receivers valued at ₹ 7.10 lakh (cost price) at the end of 1978. The unit faced financial difficulties during 1976, with a drop in sales. The difficulties were further aggravated by the escalation in the cost of production and accumulated interest on unsold finished goods.

Signs of Sickness

(a) Increase in Cost of Capital Equipment: Because of the heavy booking of television equipment in India and from other developing countries, the supply of equipment was somewhat delayed. During this delay, the rupee was devalued and the cost of imported components went up substantially, increasing the capital outlay.

(b) Higher Cost of Imported Materials: Because of the devaluation of the rupee and the increase in the rate of duty from 50 per cent to 120 per cent, the raw material cost increased by more than two times.

(c) Indigenous Raw Materials Price Escalation: The prices of indigenous raw materials – valves, resistors, condensers, etc., also increased to a considerable extent.

(d) Non-availability of components: A quota for picture tubes was allotted to small-scale units by the Electronic Commission. However, BEL, the only manufacturer of TV picture tubes, never kept their promise to supply them. Practically, all the TV manufacturers suffered badly on this account. Also, it was difficult to find suitable cabinet manufacturers in Mumbai who would supply a small quantity, say 50 to 100 cabinets per month. All the cabinet manufacturers were supplying cabinets to large TV manufacturers – for example, so Standard, Televise, etc., and other reputed manufacturers, and were not in a position to oblige small units requiring a small number of cabinets.

(e) Excise Duty: As the unit started production in 1973 in spite of all these constraints, an increase in excise duty (from 10 per cent to 20 per cent) in 1974 came as a blow. The final blow came in 1975, when the government made a statement that the price of TV sets would go down. This statement brought about a complete lull in sales right up to 1976, when the government announced its new policy of reduction in excise duty on cheap sets costing ₹ 1,800 or less. This also affected the unit's sales of TVs costing more than ₹ 1,800 per receiver. It took a considerable time for the unit to introduce the Janata set, which attracted an excise of only 5 per cent. However, the profit margin on the Janata sets is much less and the unit could not achieve an economically viable sales turnover. As a cumulative result of all these factors, the sales were badly affected. It overdrew on the bank's sanctioned limits by ₹ 2.30 lakh. The position of different accounts at that juncture was:

Table 2 Trends in Production, Sales and Stock of Goods

(₹ in lakh)

		Sanctioned Limit	Outstanding
1.	Cash Credit Hypothecation of Stocks	3.25	4.01
2.	Cash Credit Hypothecation of Book Debts	0.50	0.62
3.	Loan Hypothecation of Plant and Machinery	1.68	2.85
4.	Loan Pledge of Stocks	2.25	2.50
		7.68	9.98

(All accounts were grossly out of order.)

At this stage, the unit decided to discontinue the production of TV sets and went back to the production of oscilloscopes and moved into the production of other electronic products.

Rearrangement and Nursing

During the depression period, the unit quoted a tender for double beam oscilloscope, based on solid design, to the Ministry of Defence. The price quoted was very competitive and offered all the facilities required by the Defence Authority. The unit was successful in securing this prestigious defence order against steep competition from such multinationals as Philips and ECIL. It also developed a radio frequency signal generator which is free from radiation problems faced by other available makes in the market. M/s. Philips India was pleased with the design and performance of this signal generator and wanted to market this produce under their own brand name. At this time, a nationalised bank visualised the potential of this unit in spite of its setback in TV manufacturing, rendered it all kinds of assistance, including the technical know-how required for the execution of the defence order. The unit took up Philips order. The nationalised bank helped it with a package deal – with technical, financial, managerial and consultancy services.

The bank sanctioned additional limits, amounting to ₹ 10.19 lakh (including the guarantee for ₹ 4.69 lakh) and provided working capital to enable the unit to continue production and fulfil the orders in hand:

A. Defence Order	
(i) Cash Credit Hypothecation of stocks	₹ 100,000/-
(ii) Pledge of Stocks	₹ 365,000/-
(iii) Guarantee (Clean) (Performance)	₹ 469,000/-
B. Philip's Assignment	
(i) Cash Credit Hypothecation of stocks	₹ 45,000/-
(ii) Cash Credit Hypothecation of Book Debts	₹ 40,000/-

Results

As a result of the bank's timely assistance in providing additional working capital and performance guarantee, the unit successfully completed the defence order for 70 pieces of oscilloscopes (sale value amounting to ₹ 12 lakh). It also supplied a few hundred signal generators to M/s Philips, which are widely used for servicing radios throughout the country. M/s Phillips subsequently showed interest in offloading some of their own equipment – the oscilloscope, the FM generator, the soldering gun, etc., – to this unit and active negotiations for the purpose are in progress. The unit is prepared to undertake more sophisticated defence orders.

A power of attorney was registered with the Ministry of Defence to enable the bank receive the sales amount directly. The amount received from the defence order was properly utilised to bring all the accounts of the unit in order.

Table 3 shows the detailed position of different accounts before and after the adoption of the nursing programme.

It is evident from this table that only the loan hypothecation of machinery a/c is still out of order. Since the unit has stopped the production of television sets, the bank has proposed that the plant and machinery for their manufacture should be disposed of. The unit has finalised an arrangement with a local customer to dispose of television equipment worth ₹ 1.17 lakh.

The power of attorney has since been registered with the customer. The equipment was delivered and the amount received, reducing the outstanding balance loan (machinery) account by ₹ 1.17 lakh to ₹ 1.98 lakh. The outstanding balance were to be paid back in six half-yearly equal instalments of ₹ 33,000 each, commencing from March 1979.

Table 3 Trends in Production, Sales and Stock of Goods

(*₹ in lakhs*)

Types of Facility	Sanctioned Limit	Outstanding before Adoption of Nursing Programme	Present Drawing Limit	Present Outstandings	Remarks
A. Old Limits					
1. C/C Hypo. of Stocks (TV)	3.25	4.01	2.63	2.14	In order
2. C/C Hypo. of Book Debts (TV)	0.50	0.63	-	-	In order
3. Loan Pledge (TV)	2.25	2.50	1.78	1.78	In order
4. Loan Hypo. of Machinery	1.68	2.84	0.91	3.15	Out of order
B. Additional Limits					
1. C/C Hypo. of Stocks (Philips)	0.45	-	0.39	0.23	In order
2. C/C Book Debts (Philips)	0.40	-	0.40	0.40	In order
3. C/C Hypo. of Stocks (Defence)	1.00	-	-	-	In order
4. Pledge (Defence)	3.65	-	0.31	0.31	In order
5. Guarantee (Defence)	4.69	-	4.68	4.68	In order

It would be worthmentioning that M/s Indian Electronics is the first of its kind in the small-scale industries sector to execute defence orders for oscilloscopes. The unit is now out of difficulties and it is expected that, with a repeat order from the Ministry of Defence, which is expected shortly, it would be able to generate adequate internal resources to wipe out all the accumulated losses incurred during the early part of 1979.

4. NURSING A SICK UNIT

A/c: Foto Friction Components (India) Pvt. Ltd., Nagpur.

Small-scale Industry Established in June, 1972

Bank: Nagpur Industrial Bank, Nagpur

As desired by the Regional Manager, Nagpur, and approved by the Deputy General Manager (Operations), the undersigned. Mr. R.P. Kogle and Mr. P.S. Bhat, inspected the company's factory at Nagpur and had discussions with Mr. B.R. Dhore, Managing Director of the company, from 26th to 29th June, 1978. The Branch Manager, Shri Patil, was also present. The object of the inspection and discussion was to assess the company's present position and future prospects in the light of its past performance and the present situation, and to suggest a future course of action for the recovery of its dues to the bank, aggregating ₹ 50.34 lakh as on 26th June, 1978, including the outstanding guarantee of ₹ 0.49 lakh.

Briefly, the company's poor performance so far is due to delays in the commissioning of the project, overrun in project cost, delayed and insufficient allotment of imported resins resulting in substantial idle/underutilisation of capacity, a steep hike in the price of imported resins, the time taken to get the company's products, *viz.,* brakelines approved by the Road Transport Corporations which happen to be its only customers at present: and they will continue to be so for sometime to come.

The company has claimed to have lost 6½ months of production in 1978 due to non-availability of imported resins, which arrived only in the last week of July 1978. Production on a single shift basis was resumed from the second week of July 1978.

Marketing

(i) The introduction of its products in the market has been one of the biggest stumbling blocks of the unit, leading to its poor performances so far. Until the products are tested by the users and its quality proven, none would venture to place an order with new unit, since the safety of a vehicle depends to a very large extent on the performance of the brakeliners it has been fitted with. The Managing Director informed me that, very recently, the company had secured recognition from the Association of All India State and Municipal Road Transport Corporations and Undertakings for the supply of brakeliners to its members, about 46 in number, who had a total fleet strength of 59,679 vehicles as on 31st March, 1977.

(ii) The company intends to initially confine its sales to the members of the aforesaid Association, particularly the State Road Transport Corporations of Maharashtra and other Western states and thereby enjoy the advantages of making bulk supplies to a small number of customers, which will involve every little marketing effort. Its competitors are Hindustan Ferodo, Rane, The TVS Group, etc., who are all in the large sector, catering to the diverse requirements of manufacturers as well as users of both light and heavy vehicles. The Managing Director said that the company is the only small-scale manufacturer of brakeliners in the entire country and the only manufacturer of the product in Maharashtra. He, therefore, expects to receive preferential cooperation from the Maharashtra State Road Transport Corporation (MSRTC) insofar as orders for brakeliners are concerned. The unit expects to receive orders worth 60 per cent of MSRTC's requirements (₹ 30 lakh per annum). The SRTCs will place orders not through tenders but directly on the basis of the approval accorded by the apex association and the rates quoted by the company and accepted by the latter (i.e., on an annual rate contract basis).

(iii) At that time, the company had seven orders in hand, all from the MSRTC, for supply of 7,515 sets of brakeliners at rates varying from ₹ 78.61 per cent to ₹ 120.19 per cent. The total value of the orders is ₹ 6,91,500. The dates of the orders vary from 27th October, 1977 to 20th March, 1978. All the orders had to be executed by the end of August 1978. The company expects to receive, before the end of June 1978, three more orders from the Delhi Transport Undertakings, the Pallavan Transport Corporation and the Madras and Kottabomman Transport Corporation of an aggregate value of about ₹ 6 lakh.

(iv) For canvassing orders, the company employed two field officers who are, most of the time, away meeting the Purchase Managers/Officers of the MSRTC, while the Managing Director meets the top officials of the various State Road Transport Corporations (SRTCs) periodically. The company anticipated no problem in selling its full monthly production of ₹ 25,000 pieces of brakeliners when it achieves this production rate on a two-shift basis.

Infrastructure

The factory is located in the Industrial Estate, Nagpur. Facilities of power, water, telephone/telex, banking services and sanitation are available in the state. Only the disposal of waste is a problem. The solid waste comprising of ground asbestos fibres, etc., is presently dumped in the open space outside the shop-floor in the unit's compound. The municipal authorities object to this practice on the ground that it endangers the health of the people in the neighbourhood. Eventually, the unit will have to find a way to dispose of this waste. The approach road to the factory is in good condition. The estate is situated about 10 kms to 15 kms from Nagpur city and is close to the national highway.

Land and Building

The factory is situated on a plot of land and measuring about 4,800 sq. yards. The buildings comprise the administrative office, the shop-floor and the worker' canteen. The size of the shop-floor is adequate for a proper layout of plant and machinery and the movement of men and materials. There are two storerooms, one on either side of the entrance to the shop-floor. The room on the right is used to store raw materials, *viz.,* asbestos and resins, and it is air-conditioned so as to keep the resins in good condition. The room on the left is used to store finished goods. There is a mezzanine floor just above the two storerooms, on which the company's quality control laboratory is situated. This floor is not fully utilised.

Plant and Machinery

(i) The major items comprise a tumbler-mixer, a cyclone-mixer, 3 hydraulic presses, an air-press, a dielectric heater, 2 ovens, a cutting machine, 3 grinders, 3 drilling machines, an air-conditioner and dust-removing equipments.

(ii) At the time of inspection, the plant and machinery were found to be in good condition, except for the fact that one oven was not in use for want of adequate tooling. The managing director stated that the necessary tooling would be ready by July/August 1978 and the second oven would be started by the end of August. He said that a sum of

₹ 30,000, sanctioned by the General Manager, Mr. K.K. Desai, during his recent visit to the unit, would be adequate for this purpose.

(iii) The processing capacities of the different sections are not balanced. The banking section comprising of the 2 ovens has the minimum capacity, namely, 250 pieces/oven/shift. It is, therefore, evident that the 2 ovens control the production rate of the factory as a whole. At the time of inspection, the factory was working on a single shift basis; and only one oven was working. The production rate was about 250 pieces per day. The managing director said that the oven would be used in 2 shifts from the second week of May 1978 to step up production to 500 pieces per day. He also said that the second oven would be commissioned in the last week of August or the first week of September, thereafter the production would be 1,000 pieces per day. We are satisfied that the unit would achieve this capacity. However, to be on the safer side, its profitability has been worked out on the basis of production of 400 pieces per day up to August 1978, 800 pieces per day from September 1978 to December 1979, 900 pieces per day during 1980 and 1,000 pieces per day from 1981.

Raw Materials

(i) The major raw materials required by the company are asbestos, resins and minerals. The company stated that, for producing 3 lakh pieces of brakeliners annually, the raw material requirement would be 70 tonnes of asbestos, 24 tonnes of resins and about 20 tonnes of minerals. At the time of inspection, the company had in stock 64 tonnes of asbestos, 9 tonnes of resins and 10 tonnes of minerals. The Managing Director stated that the present stocks of asbestos would last till March 1979, and of resins till end of July 1978. However, the second oven was expected to be commissioned only by the end of August 1978. Consequently, the rates of consumption of raw materials for these four months will be half to that when both the ovens start working in two shifts. The present stocks of asbestos and resins should therefore last for at least 2 to 3 months more than the period expected by the company.

(ii) The company has indigenised its entire requirement of resins, leading to a reduction of about 50 per cent in the cost and a proportionate reduction in the requirements of the inventory value thereof. In future, it will procure resins mainly from Beck and Co. (India) Ltd., Pimpri, and other suppliers. Orders have to be placed for 3 months' requirements at a time, about two months in advance. The managing director stated that the first order of about ₹ 2.50 lakh would have to be placed by the end of May 1978 at the latest. However, as stated above the existing stock of resins may last up to the end of September 1978 and, therefore, the first order will have to be placed only towards the end of July 1978. Although the suppliers have not yet insisted on payment through L/C, the company has requested for a suitable provision to be made in this regard to avoid a last-minute rush. However, before opening any L/C, the branch should satisfy itself about the genuineness of the need, having regard to the production rate achieved, the production rate that would be expected on a realistic basis, and the likely rate of consumption of raw materials.

(iii) Asbestos will have to be imported from Canada. It has been decanalised, and importers can place orders directly with overseas suppliers. Orders have to be placed three months in advance. The company has asked that it may hold six months' requirements of asbestos, which is considered reasonable. As payment is through L/Cs, and an import L/C limit of ₹ 1.5 lakh has been requested for the purpose. Depending on the production rates achieved by the company and the consequent rate of consumption of asbestos, the first L/C may have to be opened anytime between December 1978 and February 1979.

(iv) Although the necessary minerals – barytes, alusil and philback – were reported to be easily available, the company desires to have three months' stock (value ₹ 25,000) so as to avoid any interruptions in production on this account.

Inventory

(i) All the stocks of raw materials – asbestos, resins, barytes, alusil – were physically checked, and the quantity thereof was found to tally with the records of the company. As regards finished goods, the list furnished by the company contained 36 different types of brakeliners. Nineteen items with 80 per cent of the total value of the stocks held in the pledge godown were physically checked and found to tally with the records.

(ii) Both the raw materials and finished goods are pledged to the bank, except the stocks of raw materials required for the day-to-day working of the factory. However, most of the bags of abestos were found to be lying on the shop-floor. The company should try to have these stored under the bank's lock and key, if necessary by making another room available for the purpose; but any capital expenditure, even for this purpose, should not be incurred at this stage or in the near future without the bank's prior permission.

(iii) It has been observed that a good part of the stocks of finished goods, held in pledge, have not moved for a very long time. This has been discussed with the company, which has explained the position as follows:

Trial production of all the items, for which tooling have been made, was made in the presence of the collaborators' representatives. This had to be done to prove the accuracy of the toolings. Production could not be phased out to match the orders received, because the representatives' stay could not be prolonged for obvious reasons. However, steps have been taken to dispose of the slow-moving stocks as a result of which, their level has come down considerably low – from ₹ 4.26 lakh on 31st March, 1987 to ₹ 2.5 lakh on 30th April 1978. The company also admitted an error of judgement in producing one particular item – ash coloured HI/7/2-276 – worth ₹ 37,000 (approx.), in consideration of its popularity in Western countries, but which has been found to be very unpopular in India because of past bad experiences. Shir Nair said that he was negotiating with a New Delhi-based dealer for the sale of these stocks, even at a lower rate. In any case, a bulk of the stocks is expected to be cleared during this month, and most of the rest by the end of June.

The company's explanation appears to be satisfactory. It has accepted our comment that before taking up the production of the item – ash coloured HI/7/2-276 – they should have made market enquiries.

Quality Controls

(i) Brakeliners are friction materials and are used as a safety component for lining the brakes of cars, trucks, buses, etc. The safety of pedestrians and passengers depends on them. The importance of quality control in the brakelining industry, therefore, cannot be overestimated.

(ii) The company's quality control involves the measurement of the physical properties of the product at every stage of production, as also its ash content at various stages. Any piece, which does not meet with all the requirements, is rejected. The company's production records for the period from 15th May, 1978 to 25th May, 1978 were checked; and it was observed that the rejections were about five per cent of the output, although the company has stated that the average rate of rejections is 10 per cent.

Organisation

The organisational structure of the company comprises of the Chairman and Managing Director, to whom the General Manager and the Marketing and Administration Manager report. All the three of them are brothers. Under the General Manager is the plant supervisor, while there is a Chief Accounts Officer who reports to the Marketing and Administration Manager. Till recently, Mr. N. Shore was Director (Marketing); but he is reported to have requested to be relieved of his assignment as he intends to start some business of his own. He will, however, continue to be Director of the Company.

Technical Know-how and Managerial Abilities

(i) In view of the collaboration, the know-how available to the unit is adequate. This has been proved by the fact that its products have been accepted by the users. The formulations for the raw materials mix is a secret with all the manufacturers of friction materials. Here too, the secret is shared between the managing director and the general manager and this arrangement is satisfactory.

(ii) As regards managerial abilities, the past experience of the bank indicates that the company had committed errors of judgement in deciding the priorities, which have contributed, at least partially, to the unit's present unenviable position. It is only to be hoped that the directors have learnt from past experience and will now take decision more wisely.

(iii) It appeared from the discussions that the directors are genuinely interested in the welfare of the unit and are working hard to lift it from the present state, which is one factor that is favourable and offers a ray of hope.

Accounts

It was observed that the company was maintaining proper books of accounts which were found to be written up-to-date.

Break-even Point

Fixed Expenses: The annual fixed expenses of the Company for 1979 are estimated at ₹ 12 lakh asunder:

Fixed Expenses	₹ in lakh
Salaries and Wages	3.00
Repairs and Maintenance	0.10
Electricity	0.05
Insurance	0.05
Advertisement and Travelling Expenses	0.50
Postage, Stationery, Telephone, Telex, etc.	0.15
Depreciation	2.15
Bank Interest	6.00
Total Fixed Expenses	12.00

Sales: The average sales price of 1 set of brakeliners is about ₹ 81.80.

Variable Expense: The unit variable expenses are ₹ 34.58 per unit asunder:

	₹
Raw materials	28.63
Consumables	0.64
Power	1.02
Packing and Forwarding Charges	1.02
Royalty	3.27
Total Unit Variable Expenses	34.58

Unit Sale Price = Average Sales Price – Unit Variable Expenses

= 81.80 – 34.58 = ₹ 47.22 lakh

Therefore, the break-even volume of sales

$$= \frac{\text{Fixed Expenses}}{\text{Unit Contribution}}$$

$$= \frac{12.00\,\text{lakh}}{47.22}$$

= 25,412 sets

say, 26,000 sets

= ₹ 21.27 lakh per annum.

The break-even point calculated above is only a rough guide. It may increase from year-to-year, for both fixed and variable expenses may increase with the passage of time because of the rise in the prices of raw materials, wage rates, etc. But there may not be a proportionate increase in the selling price because of competition, market resistance, etc.

Working Capital Requirement

Working capital requirements for the year 1979 have been estimated on the basis of the projected level of sales and expenses. However, at the time of inspection, the company had stocks worth about ₹ 14.02 lakh (₹ 12.37 lakh in pledge + ₹ 1.65 lakh in hypothecation). Any sudden reduction in the cash-credit limits, operative at present, may be continued at least up to the end of this year so that the company may have a reasonable time to bring down the inventory to normal levels. A reduction in working capital limits may be considered at the time of the next review. However, an import L/C limit of ₹ 1.50 lakh and an inland L/C limit of a maximum ₹ 2.50 lakh may become necessary; and these would be adequate.

Profitability

The projected profitability of the unit has been summarised below:

(₹ in lakh)

	1978	1979	1980	1981	1982	1983	1984
Sales	16.00	32.00	36.00	40.00	40.00	40.00	40.00
Profit before tax	-5.10	6.45	9.80	12.90	13.55	14.10	14.85
C/F loss	16.00	21.10	14.65	4.85	-	-	-
Taxable profit	-	-	-	8.05	13.55	14.10	14.85
Tax @ 60%	-	-	-	4.85	8.15	8.45	8.90
Profit after tax	-6.10	6.45	9.80	8.05	5.40	5.65	5.95
Depreciation	2.50	2.15	1.80	1.55	1.30	1.10	0.95
Surplus/Deficit	-2.60	8.60	11.60	9.60	6.70	6.75	6.90

Present Financial Position

Except the bills purchase and guarantee accounts, all the accounts of the company are out of order. The total out-of-order position is of the order of ₹ 28.71 lakh. Besides, the total value of security (₹ 29.67 lakh) – primary security (₹ 27.22 lakh) + collateral security (₹ 2.45 lakh) – falls short of the total outstanding of ₹ 49.15 lakh in borrowed accounts by ₹ 19.48 lakh. The stock position of the company is good; therefore, the unit does not need – nor has it asked for – any additional facilities. On the other hand, in order to reduce the heavy out of the order position of the accounts, and particularly in order to repay the accumulated interest of ₹ 12.24 lakh, the company – as the managing director, Shri B.R. Dhore, – is considering raising finance from the market by converting itself into a public company.

Shri B.R. Dhore is very hopeful of a good response, particularly from his relatives and close friends, who are working abroad – in the Middle-East and South-East Asian countries. According to him, the minimum amount that is expected is ₹ 5 lakh to ₹ 6 lakh, although the possibility of receiving a sum as high as ₹ 10 lakh to ₹ 12 lakh cannot be ruled out. However, Shri Dhore's expectations are optimistic of the present position of the company's finances and that in view of the fact that company is not likely to declare any worthwhile dividends in the next 5 to 7 years.

Borrowers' Claim Against the Bank Power to Attorney

(i) The borrowers have filed a claim with the bank for an amount of about ₹ 5 lakh, which they claim they have lost because of the stoppage of production as a result of the delay on the part of the bank in opening an L/C for ₹ 1.45 lakh to enable them to import resins from abroad. The correspondence on this subject was seen. The branch has clarified that the facility could not be sanctioned at their level immediately upon receipt of the request, but had to be forwarded to the Regional Office. The bank has explained to the borrowers that the unit should plan their requirements of raw materials in advance, and give to the bank adequate time for processing its requests. In view of the fact that the accounts of the unit are very much out of order, any requests have to be properly looked into at the appropriate level for a decision; and this usually takes time. The borrowers are aware of this fact, and, therefore, their charge against the bank is unfounded.

(ii) The gross out-of-order position of the accounts appears to have created some friction between the branch and the borrowers. The branch's advice to the borrowers to execute a power of attorney in the bank's favour and register it with the unit's customers has added to the strain in the relation between the two. The managing director has taken the stand that if a power of attorney (P.A.) is registered with the MSRTC, the present rapport between himself and the MSRTC will be lost and the prompt payments now being received will be unduly delayed. He contends that if he is forced to register the P.A., he will not be able to follow-up the payments from MSRTC, and it will be the bank's responsibility to collect such dues; he will not be responsible for the resulting delay.

(iii) The managing director was informed of the bank's practice of obtaining the power of attorney. He was told that his apprehension of delay in payments was unfounded and that he should have no difficulty in pursuing the question of payments with the MSRTC.

(iv) The borrowers have also taken the stand now that the bank should have obtained refinance from the IDBI for the demand loan accounts – which would have given them the benefit of a lower rate of interest. It was clarified that the advances were sanctioned in accordance with the then prevailing policy of the bank and that the term of the sanction of the advances were indicated to, and accepted by, the borrowers. Any objectives raised by the borrowers at this stage had no validity.

Future Prospects

(i) Having regard to the facts that:

(a) The government has decanalised the import of asbestos, making it easier for manufacturers to get it more easily;

(b) The unit has indigenised its requirements of resins, thereby getting them at a much lower cost;

(c) The unit's products have been recently approved for quality and price by the All-India Association of Road Transport Corporations;

(d) The unit already has orders in hand worth ₹ 7 lakh, and is expecting shortly more orders worth ₹ 4 lakh; and

(e) The profitability as discussed earlier, is quite attractive.

It is evident that the main reasons for the unit's poor performance so far does not submit any more and that the unit has a fair chance of recovery. In view of the bank's present gross out-of-order position, if the advances are recalled at this stage, it is likely to suffer a considerable loss. It would therefore, be in the interests of the bank to exercise patience and nurse the unit to normal health. This would enable the bank to recover its dues fully.

(ii) Shri B.R. Dhore has categorically stated that the unit at present does not anticipate any obstacle in its smooth production programme and that, by the end of 1978, it is expected to reach the targeted level of production of 1,000 pieces per day. For this reason, he does not seek any additional funds.

NURSING PROGRAMME

The following proposal may be considered for nursing the company:

(i) Sanction of a partly secured demand loan limit of ₹ 36.30 lakh asunder:

	(₹ in lakh)
Out of order position in all accounts	28.73
Drawing limit in existing demand loan account	4.37
Two instalments of ₹ 30,000, each falling due for payment in term loan account on 30.7.78 and 30.10.78	0.60
Non-payment of interest due to gross loss expected during 1978	2.60
Total	**36.30**

(ii) The existing demand loan account may then be closed.

(iii) Reschedule the remaining instalments in the term loan account after obtaining the prior approval of the IDBI.

(iv) Irrespective of whether or not the repayment schedule in the term loan account is revised, the remaining instalments (₹ 3.63 lakh) may be paid on due dates to the debit of the new demand loan account. This is, however, not expected to increase the outstanding in this account beyond the proposed limit because of the continual appropriation of the surplus generated by the company, as indicated below.

(v) Although the outstanding in the new demand loan account will not exceed ₹ 36.30 lakh at any time, the repayment programme has to provide for the repayment of ₹ 39.33 lakh, i.e., ₹ 36.30 lakh *plus* ₹ 3.36 lakh, being the balance in the term loan account, the instalments of which would be debited to the new demand loan account as and when they fall due. The outstandings in the new demand loan account may be repaid by the appropriation of a specified percentage of each bill purchased or sent on collection basis from 1st January, 1979, subject to the specified ceilings for each year asunder:

Year	% of Each Bill Amount to be Appropriated	Maximum Annual Appropriation (₹ in lakh)
1979	30%	7.00
1980	30%	10.00
1981	30%	8.00
1982	15%	5.00
1983	15%	5.00
1984	15%	4.95
	Total	39.93

(vi) The Cash Credit pledge limit of ₹ 8.35 lakh and clean bills purchase limit of ₹ 3 lakh may be considered on a regular basis until the next review.

(vii) The rate of interest may be reduced to 12.5 per cent per annum on all the borrowal accounts, other than the term loan account, with IDBI refinance, till the accumulated losses are wiped out.

(viii) The Import L/C limit of ₹ 1.59 lakh and Inland L/C limit of ₹ 2.59 lakh may be considered.

(ix) The company should submit progress reports to the branch every fortnight, giving particulars of production, sales, opening stock, purchases, closing stock, trade debtors at the beginning and close of the period, sales realisations, programme for the next fortnight, etc.

(x) Every month, an officer from the Regional Office, Maharashtra may visit the factory to review the progress of the company, sort out any problems that are faced by it, etc. Once in three months, the managing director of the company should meet our regional manager at Nagpur and appraise him of the progress made by the company and its plants for future action.

5. PROJECT PLANNING: A CASE STUDY

Setting up one's own business is no easy matter. From the start, the entrepreneur-to-be is pitilessly confronted with many problems inherent in the initial phase. Many are inadequately prepared and quickly fall by the wayside; indeed, enthusiasm alone is no sufficient guarantee of success, as business demands a professional approach and admits of no improvisation at the beginning.

In recent years, resources have been allocated to help ease the independent company through its early stages, and interesting initiatives to promote small-scale enterprises have been taken up by both the authorities and the private sector in Belgium, as well as in neighbouring countries: among the initiatives have been the provision of small business centres, sponsorship and consultancy help, as well as offering of financial spurs. The article reviews and weighs up these endeavours, though not before first briefly taking a look at the consecutive initial stages of a small enterprise.

The Scenario for Starting a Business

According to the degree of specification, the process of establishing a small enterprise can be broken down into various stages, the official start of the business thereby being considered as the resultant of previous negotiations and decisions.

There is no doubt that a variety of personal motives and external factors play a part in the decision to set up in business. In practical, all surveys, however, the same key elements return, namely the desire to achieve something, the wish to be creative, freedom and independence, while financial earning and profits are usually deemed to be of less importance as initial incentives. Besides this, there are also factors which, right from the start, work against any decision to establish and business, for example, the not so infrequent negative attitude of parents and family (an import consideration for those working or involved in the management of a larger company) and the financial risks. For all these reasons, becoming an entrepreneurs remains, for many, limited to vague intentions and desires.

A minority takes the plunge, their urge expressing itself in a concrete formulation of ideas. The incentive to establish a new enterprise ideally finds its origin in the development of a new product or in identifying a gap in the market. Opportunities continually arise for young Small Manufacturing Enterprises (SMEs), given that big industries ignore particular branches as they are interested only in products having a considerable market or because they deem the commercialisation of certain products to be incompatible with their corporate strategy. Moreover, because of negative effects of scale, some commercial activities, production processes or services are better performed by small companies.

But before even the most promising business idea can be put into practice, it has to be tested for *feasibility*, implying that the potential market should certainly be plumbed. Following a positive result, a *business plan*, which includes a commercial and financial plan, is worked out. As the starting-up process progresses, moreover, the tasks become more specific. Gradually, a definitive stage is reached, i.e., negotiating with financial institutions, identifying interested purchasers or suitable subcontractors and deciding on a location for the business. Probably the least exhilarating but nevertheless necessary task is to take care of the various administrative requirements (the notarial Act detailing the form of company chosen, application for the VAT number, the trade register entry, arranging Social Security status, etc). Their completion can be taken as the definitive signalling of the new enterprise's start.

The Big Help the Small

One of the most tangible hindrances to establishing new enterprises is the shortage of sufficient *starting capital*. Understandably enough, the banks and other traditional moneylenders regard the often very high initial risks askance; indeed, normal lending to existing companies already entails sufficient risk and eventually, has always to be practically completely financed with risk-shunning capital , i.e., deposits and medium-term bonds. Too great an accumulation of risk on the assets side of a banks balance sheet, therefore cannot be justified. Promising new entrepreneurs can expect help from venture capitalists. These last wittingly attempt to obtain stakes in young or fast-growing companies where the risk may be high, but so too is the potential medium-term profit accompanying them. Financial resources are usually made available in return for shares, thus making a full partner so the venture capitalist. The original initiators, receive founder or deferred shares in order that they should identify themselves to the utmost with the economic interest to the company. Subsequentially, after 5 to 10 years, the venture capitalist sells his stake so as to collect, via the gain in value that has meanwhile accrued if the project has been successful, a considerable profit in return for the risk taken.

To surmount the problem of finding starting capital, there is, moreover, the not-to-be-ignored *government aid* in the form of subsidies and fiscal advantages. For the government, indeed, a person setting up on his own represents an improvement to the unemployment figures and a means of promoting economic growth, and young jobless establishing themselves as self-employed have the possibility of calling on a special subordinated loan. This loan represents an advance on the unemployment allowance that they would normally receive over a period of three years, though up to a maximum of BEF 500,000. In passing, it should be said that it is also possible for those out of work to set up as self-employed while retaining their right to unemployment allowance should their enterprise not be successful within the space of six years. Moreover, and not just for the unemployed, there is the Waarborgfonds (Guarantee Fund) which can act to make up any shortfall in guarantees *vis-a-vis* credit institutions. Thus, a loan that appears initially impossible to extend because of over-great risks can indeed be granted. Naturally, besides this there are still the interest subsidies and capital investment grants, provincial allowances, etc. Among other things, the fiscal measures include a deduction for investment, accelerated deprecations, exemption from the obligation to pay tax in advance and a benefit on the first employee being taken on. Many of these measures stem originally from the government's concern for existing SMEs, but, usually new enterprises can also make use of these facilities.

Many young entrepreneurs who have successfully negotiated the financial hurdle very quickly find that they lack *management experience*. Large firms wishing to pass on part of their *corporate culture* can make a contribution here, examples of this being found in other Western European countries. Thus, in the UK, the private sector makes a substantial contribution to the growth and success of SMEs in the process of starting up, and in the local enterprise agencies, big companies work closely with the local authorities to encourage the creation of new small-scale businesses. Much is done, besides, in the way of support, whereby the big companies conduct the new SMEs through the difficult phase of starting and expanding – in other words, a sort of active sponsorship. Thus, since 1979, the London Enterprise Agency has given help to already more than 2,000 enterprises; more than 700 new companies have been set up, leading to 3,000 new jobs. Similar initiatives have been undertaken in the Netherlands, among others the 'Kleinood' foundation which was established at the end of the seventies and with which 25 large companies are involved; so far, about 400 small concerns have been given management advice.

Support, in fact, can take various forms. Sponsoring companies can make experienced members of their own staff available or the entrepreneur can follow the training courses organised by these companies for their own personnel: further, support could be legal, administrative, commercial or financial. Examples are legion: help in obtaining subsidies, in applications for patents, in the drafting of international sale contracts, etc. It is often the case that the young entrepreneur puts too much emphasis on technical know-how, and therefore, to this will be added an awareness of market aspects, as well as a common sense approach to budgeting and financial planning.

From the supporting firm's angle, all this is usually done in understandable self-interest. Big and small complement each other, and this provides the larger company with flexibility in eventually contracting out work and the opportunity to follow the progress of such work closely. What is also fine about this approach is that the staff of the larger firm who are providing the expertise come into contact with the spirit and daily work of entrepreneurs. Lastly, sponsorship gives large companies the opportunity to polish up their social image. Nowadays, the big firms are no longer able to provide much of a boost to employment – on the contrary – and therefore sponsorship provides a counterweight to this.

Small Business Centres

Active SME sponsorship is something that lends itself to development at the locate level so as to stimulate local activity. A somewhat different approach to getting new enterprises off the ground is that within the framework of the so-called small business centres, a concept like others, has been imported from Belgium's neighbours (Great Britain, West Germany, The Netherlands). Such a centre can be described as a collection of small business areas under one roof, which are put at the temporary disposal of entrepreneurs just setting up on their own. The actual premises can just as well be a disused industrial building as custom built, and besides this are provided communal services and utilities such as telephone, telex, secretariat, reception and conference rooms, the practical and most tangible advantage being the *cost-saving*. Every concert has a number of minimum requirements which can be a considerable burden in the beginning, but cannot be done without; in a smaii business centre, however, these initial operating costs are kept to a minimum, there being no over burdensome concerning commercial rent to be paid, but a modulated price as well as a flexible system for giving notice. The entrepreneur is charged a reduced rate for communal services, and then only for those made use of (typing, translation, despatch, etc.). At the same time, the whole bestows a professional cachet on the enterprise.

However, a small business centre has still more to offer, as there is also the permanent presence of a manager who takes care of the professional organisation of the centre and provides expert advice for the resident enterprises. These latter operate autonomously, but can always refer their problems to the coordinator who gives advice on the basis of his own experience or calls on well-disposed companies or on institutions at the disposal of the self-employed and SMEs. Lastly, maximum period of residence is sent in advance for the companies in the Centre.

The first small business centres have now been established in Belgium (Kortrijk, Bruges, Zaventem) and there has already been a decision in favour of setting up centres in the provinces of Antwerp and Limburg; others are expected to follow. Projects currently under way depend on cooperation among government institutions, semi-public bodies and the private sector; the respective Regional Development Companies normally take a minority participation in the starting capital of the small business centre, while the remaining resources required are provided by private companies, financial institutions or semi-official bodies.

Up to now, the 'Naamloze Vennootschap' (Limited Company) has always been adopted as the legal form for the co-operation between the various partners, and it is the aim that the initiatives should be at least self-supporting, otherwise they would set a sorry example to the firms being given guidance. For backing, the centres in Flanders can count on the co-operation of the Flemish Regional Government (maximum support for expansion, exemption from withholding tax during a period of five years, accelerated deprecations). For budgetary reasons and to prevent uncontrolled growth, the number of participations for each Flemish Regional Development Company is restricted to four. Recently too, the first small business centres supported entirely by private initiative have been set up.

A variant to this type of centre is formed by the Business Technology Centres where the emphasis is placed on co-operation between science and industry. Such research parks are mostly established in the vicinity of universities or high schools and naturally enough concentrate on high technology (microelectronic, telecommunications, biotechnology); one or two such centres have already been set up in Belgium.

Experience gained so far in business centres abroad is positive, small craft companies in particular, taking advantage of the opportunity offered to them. Nevertheless, neither in Belgium nor in other countries, has there been much analysis of the effects on long-term employment which would normally follow from such an initiative; indeed, no details exist about companies once they have left the centre. It can be taken, though, that many small companies have been able to weather the difficult early years better because of their having passed them in a small business centre, whereby the chances for a successful continuation to the venture are considerably enhanced.

Too Much of a Good Thing?

Besides the initiatives already mentioned, there are also the 'support cells' for the newly self-employed, established by some Chambers of Commerce and Industry. Universities too, make people available to provide expert help. In addition, there are training centres and trading class organisations, many training seminars, information meetings, colloquia, etc., which clearly don't lack well-intentioned initiatives.

In the case of substantial subsidising and government aid right from the start, there is inevitably the risk of distortion and disturbance of normal competition; such bounty to people just starting up does little to further the interests of those already established. However, the consequences of such distortion need to be evaluated at the sectoral level. In various branches of industry, with high entry barriers, subsidising new entrants can contribute towards healthy competition.

Another danger presented by government subsidy is that the incentives produced other than the expected effects, with those on employment being more felt among consultants subsidy and fiscal experts and government services rather than at the level of new entrepreneurs. Moreover, the exact group aimed at is often not reached just by providing subsidies. By definition, becoming an entrepreneur is for motivated people who dare; and escaping from unemployment appears to be a rather weak motive for setting up one's own business. Besides this, quick-witted newcomers will adapt their planning to the subsidies they can draw, whereas it is market conditions that ought to be the decisive factor.

Finally, the government has little apparatus to test the efficiency and efficacy of its aid; relevant statistics are too sparse and, moreover, the government itself appears hardly to be interested in thorough testing.

A last objection is that the apparatus for instruction and advice threatens to lose somewhat in efficiency as a result of the gradual blurring of the structure and the multiplicity of the bodies active in it. Before long, the newly self-employed will have to make their own market analyses to determine the best and most interesting form of support.

Towards a More Integrated Setting up Policy

The value of some local initiatives does not lessen the need for a *general stimulative policy towards enterprises just getting under way*. What is needed in the first place here is a macroeconomic situation wherein the entrepreneur can find sufficient new and attractive opportunities. Further, there have to be enough potential entrepreneurs possessing inventiveness and market insight; this is not just a question of training, but more of the value society places on entrepreneurship, implying climate benevolent towards business and a reasonable return on risk capital. It is only when these requirements are satisfied that the need for support and advice has to be considered.

Nor can a policy for setting up new companies be divorced from one for winding them up. Obsolete companies ought no longer than necessary hinder the progress of young enterprises, while government aid to moribund companies is usually no more than waste.

This does not complete the list of *favourable contextual factors* to be striven for. There are a number of positive facts relevant to this to be perceived, for example, the efforts being made to give a new suitable legal form to the small company. The present government is contemplating the introduction of the 'one-man business with limited liability', a difference being made between what is impersonally owned and what is working capital, implying the protection of personal goods in the case of bankruptcy. A (modest) start has also been made with doing away with the suffocating administrative redtape — indeed which entrepreneur or entrepreneur-to-be is not discouraged by the labyrinth of rules and regulation? In France, recently, the administrative obligations to be complied with in setting up a company have been drastically reduced, as has been the time previously required to give legal form to the company in the process of starting up. Among other factors liable to reform in Belgium, are the social security status and the law relating to commercial practices.

Too Much Made of the SME?

A wind of change has been blowing for some years now, revitalising the entrepreneurial spirit. Entrepreneurs are being feted and the prizes for the most successful among them are exceeding all bounds, the enthusiasm applying particularly to small concerns. Politicians and entrepreneurs sometimes wax lyrical about small and medium-sized firms, description such as 'dynamic', 'creative' and 'human' beings frequently handed about.

SME advocates point fervently to reports about successful newcomers to Silicon Valley, but it is easily forgotten that the concept 'small and medium-sized' has a much wider meaning overseas, companies with less than 1,000 employees also being considered as 'small businesses'. However, to bestow a similar revitalising role on Belgian traders and SMEs exhibits a certain overoptimism.

On the other hand, this is not to detract from the fact that small and medium-sized enterprises will continue to fulfil an essential and irreplaceable role in Belgium's social and economic system.

6. CASE STUDY OF A SMALL-SCALE UNITS

M/s NCL

(This is a true case study of a small-scale unit which was sick because of various causes. The unit was rehabilitated by the entrepreneur with the help of government departments and this bank. This case study reflects on the positive characteristics of the entrepreneurs and their role in nursing sick units. In fact, the entrepreneur is the kingpin in nursing a small-scale unit and bringing it back to health and vitality. The case study shows that the entrepreneur is responsible for turning a healthy small-scale unit into a sick unit and that he alone can revive it by following the right path. In fact, the health of the unit solely depends upon the entrepreneurs himself.)

Background

The NCL was established in 1971 to manufacture cosmetic and beauty products. It was promoted by two persons; one a technocrats and the other who had experience in general administration. Its factory-cum-office was located in a rented shed in an industrial estate building in Central Bombay. In 1972, NCL was granted financial assistance by a public sector bank – ₹ 40,000 for the purchase of machinery and ₹ 80,000 for working capital. The advances were guaranteed by a marketing executive of a big business house in the cosmetic line. In 1973, the technocrat director resigned and son of the guarantor jointed the NCL as director. In 1974, the other original directors also resigned.

Irregularities

The NCL had not submitted any financial statements to the bank, which could not, therefore, review its performance. The bank account became irregular; and in the absence of any review, the bank did not extend further credit facilities to the NCL. But the latter carried on its skeleton production activities by availing itself of certain credit facilities from another bank.

Later, the advances of the second bank were adjusted on persuasion by the original bank. In 1976, the guarantor to the bank's advances, on retirement from his executive post, joined the NCL as executive director and assumed complete control. The balance sheet submitted by the NCL, as on December 1980, read as follows:

Balance Sheet			
			(Rupees in thousands)
Liabilities		**Assets**	
Share Capital	253.00	Fixed Assets	46.00
Bank Loans	106.00	Stocks and Debtors	104.00
Loans from directors and shareholders	104.00	Deposits Advances	22.00
Other loans	60.00	Accumulated Losses	373.00
Creditors	10.00		
Sales Tax Payable	12.00		
	545.0		545.00

Erosion

The owners' funds of ₹ 2,53,000 and their loan of ₹ 1,04,000 were completely wiped out as a result of the accumulated losses of ₹ 3,73,000. Assuming that the assets are worth the value attached to them, losses of ₹ 16,000 were carried to the creditors other than the owners of the company.

NCL's liquidity position was glaringly negative, mainly because of accumulated losses and investment of short-term funds in long-term assets.

The Causes: In the light of this background, the causes of the sickness of the NCL are diagnosed. It was evident that:

(i) Its directors were not conversant with the selling techniques of the products they were manufacturing. Selling in the cosmetic industry calls for a sophisticated strategy. About four initial but crucial years were lost, during which its management did not come to grips with its marketing problems.

The NCL, had anticipated a spurt in its share of the market as a sequel to a purported change in the government's policy of easing out the giants in the line. But this policy did not materialise.

(ii) The directors who promoted NCL did not possess the requisite degree of perseverance to withstand the crises which normally arises in any new unit, but which are particularly acute in a unit entering the cosmetic product-line as a small unit.

(iii) Four products formed the product range; but there was no proper planning. Lack of planning was noticeable in production and in marketing, and in different batches/types of production.

The Rehabilitation Plan: The new executive director, with his vast experience and down-to-earth approach to the problems faced by the company, was able to secure orders to run the factory at an operating level which would enable the NCL to cover the cost. Realising the limitations of his company, he changed the strategy of selling his products.

Taking advantage of the liberal concession of the government for the encouragement of small-scale units, he concentrated on government departments for orders. Ultimately, the new executive director succeeded in securing small orders from canteen stores department. The value of the order was expected to go up to ₹ 30,000 per month. At this stage, the executive director of the NCL received further financial support from this bank.

Financial Assistance

The bank promptly extend ₹ 54,000 and agreed to further extend finance up to ₹ 80,000 on the basis of a fresh appraisal of the working capital requirements for the execution of the new orders. It also agreed to convert the outstanding in the working capital/cash credit account into a term loan account repayable in easy instalments. However, it wanted the NCL to feed it with information on its performance on a regular basis to enable it to monitor the account.

The building up a reasonable internal information system – the maintenance of proper books of accounts, production, and stock and sales data – was made a part of the rehabilitation plan.

The fulfilment of this condition resulted in cost to the unit; but the cost was considered to be unavoidable, for it was necessary to keep track of the direction in which the unit was going. The latest results indicate that the NCL is out of the wood and is one its way to health.

Entrepreneurial Characteristics: This brief review of NCL's history indicates that it had entered a very sophisticated industry, but its management was nowhere near the task. Marketing was its main problem.

The unit's managing director dream it of becoming an industrialist; but the path leading to the destination was too strenuous to tread; and he was not prepared for it. Certain characteristics of the owner-managers of this unit are worthnoting.

They were possessed of the need for achievement. This is evident from the fact that the owners, who were earlier in employment, left their jobs to set up an industrial unit. It is reasonable to infer that they did this on perceiving the environmental opportunities, including the encouragement of the small-scale industry on the part of the government, the credit facilities available on easy terms from financial institutions, and the likely change in the government's policy which was likely to favour smaller units in that particular industry against the larger ones. The owner-managers also showed the ability to accept challenges and take the risks.

However, they were lacking in certain entrepreneurial characteristics, which are very vital for the success of a cosmetic unit. One such characteristic was the need for involvement. When they encountered problems in the implementation of the project, the original directors started leaving the unit one by one.

They were also lacking in confidence to succeed in the business. They accepted the challenge; but they did not have the capacity to face the turmoil of business activity.

In other words, the commitment to the project and perseverance in seeing it through thick and thin was lacking in the project sponsors. An entrepreneur should possess the characteristic of changing his environment, or he should believe that he is capable of living with it. Openness to feedback on project implementation, say, from the banker and well-wishers, was yet another characteristic which the owner-managers did not possess.

Sufficient hints had been available from the financing bank that something was wrong with the implementation of the project. But the unit reacted to these hints by going to another bank for assistance. Moreover, the approach and the manner of working of the owner-managers were similar to the traditional executive pattern rather than that of a small entrepreneurs.

Because of all these facts, the weaknesses inherent in the project had not been evaluated realistically in the initial stage. The reality is that a small-scale industry entails work for 24 hours a day. The deficiencies observed in the initial owner-managers were taken care of by the present incumbent: and that is the prime reason for the unit's recovery from sickness.

NCL entered a sophisticated industry to produce shampoo, shaving cream, hair oil and white tooth powder. The challenge in the marketing of these products in competition with large established companies, including a few multinational corporations, should not have been overlooked at the project-idea-stage.

The Industry

The NCL started entering the consumer market by trying to sell through the sales points dealers in competition with large units in different parts of the country. But its ability to open sales points through the dealers proved to be grossly inadequate. Moreover, it could not match the resources of the giants in advertising campaigns and other marketing strategies.

The marketing strategy should have involved a publicity campaign and a simultaneous opening of sales points. This could not be done by a unit whose resource base was abysmally small.

The marketing strategy followed by the resourceful units in the industry could not possibly be adopted by small units like the NCL. This was realised by it very late – only when the present incumbent took over charge. That is how he turned to the canteen stores department of the defence department for rescue!

The present owner-manager's attempted to push sales through departmental stores like the Janata Bazaars proved to be costly, for his presence could not be ensured at the production point at his factory and in the department stores.

The appointment of salesman was futile because inexperienced persons cannot accomplish this task; and the NCL could not attract experienced persons.

The Strengths

The quality of the products was comparable to any in the industry. There were no major production or technical problems.

The sincerity and the integrity of the owner-managers could not be questioned. Apart from wiping out the capital brought in by the owners as a result of accumulated losses, they never attempted to divert funds from the business.

The overhead expenses, especially of the owners were kept at the minimum possible level. In fact, the present incumbent injected fresh funds by way of deposits in the name of his wife (who is also a director) on a reasonable rate of interest.

He did not effect any withdrawals for his family's maintenance and sustained himself on his retirement benefits. A check on overhead costs by the owner-manager and the decision of the financing bank to write off a part of the interest on the loans have made it possible for the unit to achieve its break-even sales at a lower level of operation.

This is a vital factor because the unit was not in a position to increase the prices of its products. In fact, its prices have been kept lower than those of others because it does not have the advantage of brand names. And these prices are lower because the cost of production has been pegged down.

In other words, the overhead costs, which are crucial in keeping down the cost of production, were kept in check at some sacrifice on the part of the owner-manager and the financing bank.

There was no labour trouble in the unit. The number of workers was small and the relations with them were cordial. The owner's human approach and considerate attitude to labour has been very helpful in running the unit without labour trouble, which normally afflicts a sick unit.

The Banker's Role

The financing bank agreed to draw up a rehabilitation plan in the conviction that it would be implemented by the owner-manager in all sincerity and seriousness. The present owner-manager of the NCL was considered an excellent moral risk by the bank, other creditors and labour. Adequate funds were made available to the unit on the basis of its comprehensive reappraisal, and a rehabilitation plan was drawn up.

This was done when the owner-manager had succeeded in getting steady orders from the canteen stores department. His characteristics were the dominant factors which weighted with the bank when it made a reappraisal study and established the viability of the unit.

However, one may reasonably ask whether it would not have been better for the financing bank to put the unitwise in the initial stage itself by drawing the attention of the owner-managers to the weaknesses of the project!

Summing Up

The analysis of the factors involved in the rehabilitation of this sick unit would indicate that the key role in the entire exercise has been played by the entrepreneur himself. Others, like government departments and the banker played the role of felicitators. The health and vitality of the unit is nothing but the reflection of the positive characteristics of the entrepreneur.

7. CED PROGRAMMES

(1) Development of entrepreneurs on a systematic basis started in 1970. A number of specialised institution came up to provide training to various target-groups – educated unemployed persons, women, technicians, foremen, rural artisans, physically-handicapped persons, etc. The Centre of Entrepreneurship Development (CED), Ahmedabad, was sponsored by the state government and public sector corporations concerned with industrial development in the state. This Centre conducts entrepreneurship development programmes. Persons were selected from amongst the employees, workers, merchants and graduates and the training was imparted at six centres. The following are some of the significant features of the programme of training:

(a) Before conducting a programme of training, a survey of investment opportunities was made for identifying industries having a good scope in the areas.

(b) Appropriate linkage was developed with the various agencies which provide support and service to entrepreneurs in getting finance, ready-made sheds, raw materials and other inputs.

(c) Entrepreneurs were selected through behavioural tests. Due weightage on experience was given rather than education or unemployment.

(d) Programmes of training included theoretical and practical coverage, including visits to industrial units consistent with the items identified by the entrepreneurs.

(e) Follow-up action was taken by a full-time project leader and individual attention was given to each entrepreneur trainee.

The success rate of CED programmes is reported to be of the order of 66 per cent.

(2) The Entrepreneurial Motivation Centre, set up in Assam in the north-eastern region of India, conducts entrepreneurial development programmes. In the earlier stages, 28 officers drawn from various departments of the state government were given training in entrepreneurial motivation, economic investigation and survey, management of small enterprise, etc., in the Small Industries Extension Training Institute in Hyderabad. These officers then joined the various branches of the Entrepreneurial Motivation Training Centres in six districts.

The Entrepreneurial Motivation Training Centre gave wide publicity to the entrepreneurial development programmes and invited applications from educated unemployed persons. Selection was made on psychological tests and personal interviews. Selected entrepreneurs were given preliminary motivation training of two weeks for developing or strengthening the motivation of self-employment managerial and economic aspects of entrepreneurial development. The entrepreneurs were further assisted in selecting enterprises for themselves, conducting guided market surveys and preparing economically viable and feasible project reports. The Centre acted as a link agency and helped them in obtaining finance from banks and other institutions, and ready-made sheds as working space. The Centre further provided 10 per cent of the sanctioned amount as seed money wherever necessary.

(3) The Xavier Institute of Social Services in Ranchi was involved with tribals and people from the villages in training to become entrepreneurs. A group of young tribal youths constituted into a local oranisation for promotion of socio-economic and health schemes (known as Vikas Maitry) received some funds from the Indo-German Social Service Society in New Delhi in 1975. They desired that an entrepreneurship development programme be run for them. A project leader who himself was a tribal was appointed. The programme was organised and 20 candidates were selected, all belonging to the tribal areas. In selecting, little importance was given to academic qualification. Clarity of presentation of goal and determination to reach that goal were the important considerations. Four months' full-time training was arranged. During the day, the entrepreneurs worked as apprentices in shops of the type they intended to set up themselves. In the evening, they got a grounding on the basis of achievement, motivation, leadership and communication, management, finances, costing, laws and taxation, marketing and project preparation. After completion of the training course, the entrepreneurs went back to their respective villages and made mini-market surveys. They brought back the field data and worked these into a *project proposal* for financing by the bank. The financing was undertaken though the intermediary of Vikas Maitry Kalyan Sangh and the organisation undertook to stand guarantee for the young entrepreneurs. Continuous and sustained follow-up action was undertaken. This was the responsibility of the project officer and assistant project officer. A success area of 60 per cent was attained. The state government later gave assistance to the institute for conducting entrepreneurial development programmes for unemployed engineers, diplomaholders, graduates and ITI trained boys and the institute has done fairly well.

8. FIXING THE PRICE

Price cutting procedures are like a greasy pole where the climber slips back two feet for every one foot he climbs up. Frankly, the buyers who only consider price are of no permanent value to the manufacturer. No goodwill can be built up with such buyers because they move from one supplier to another. On the other hand, the buyer who is faithful to his suppliers and who considers quality, presentation and service above price is the buyer who is likely to have a more permanent business and whose custom is of real value. This type of buyer may even be antagonised by low prices and he may even be suspicious of the goods if the price is, in his estimation, too low. He will say to himself, "it can't be any good if it is as cheap as that" and will refuse to buy unless the manufacturer has a ready and legitimate explanation as to why he can manage to offer good quality and low prices at the same time.

The second method of fixing the price at the highest the market can stand also has its defects. It is difficult, even impossible, to keep a new idea exclusive. Any new product which has reasonable sales potential will attract imitators. The higher the price, the more imitators there will be. Other manufacturers will examine the proposition, and seeing that there is a good profit margin in it, will rush into its manufacture like bees flock around a honeycomb. To fix the price too high is to invite not only competition but also price cutting. Nor is it a legitimate argument for a manufacturer to say that he will start with a high price and reduce it later when competition appears. The customer can be permanently lost if he finds out that the manufacturer has been selling to him at a higher prices than necessary and only bring down the price to a proper level when forced to do so.

Prices must be fixed on a properly scientific basis. Any manufacturer is in business to earn a profit and there is no point in his being in business unless he can earn a better profit on his investment than the return which he would get if he invested his money in securities. Therefore, he must price his products in a way which shows him the requisite profit on his investment. If he cannot sell his goods at such a price, then he had better withdraw from business or at least take up the manufacturer of a better line of products. It is all very nice to have a large sales turnover; but it must be remembered that it is true to say that the larger the sales the larger the loss when the prices is uneconomical.

Prices must be calculated from the bottom up, i.e., by finding out first what the product is going to cost to produce. For the small manufacturer, it may not be possible to have a precisely detailed cost system but there must be some form of costing which will give reliable results and which will give a reliable idea of what the cost of the product is. The manufacturers know how to account for raw materials, labour overheads, and other elements in arriving at a legitimate ex-works cost and now it must be decided how much has to be added to arrive at a sensible price and to show a proper proportion of the net profit.

Example 1: A factory producing 6 ft. lathes has a total capital of ₹ 2,00,000 and is producing and selling four lathes per month at an ex-works cost of ₹ 2,000 each. There is a certain amount of risk owing to competition and possible fluctuations of government sponsored hire-purchase schemes and the proprietor considers that he is entitled to a net return of 12½ per cent on his investment. Therefore, he will require to make an annual profit of ₹ 25,000. Because he estimates his continued sales at 48 lathes per year, he must provide for the addition of ₹ 521 per lathe which is equivalent to a percentage of 26 per cent on ex-works cost. This appears a high percentage but is no more than is legitimate on the investment.

Example 2: A factory producing assorted size and brands of hair oils has a total capital of ₹ 35,000 and it is estimated that the cost of annual sales will be ₹ 80,000. The risk is considered to be fairly high on this type of business and return of 17½ per cent may be required on the capital investment, so that a total annual provision of ₹ 6,125 will be necessary. If this amount is divided by 80,000, the answer is 0.77 or in other words, 7¾ per cent to the ex-factory cost of any item whatever its cost.

The addition for profit described above is calculated on the assumption that there will be no more than the normal usage of working capital. The availability of capital is one of the prime factors in deciding whether or not the business can be expanded. If customers take longer credit than is normally provided for, this is the same as if they were borrowing money to finance their enterprise. If the manufacturer is making or planning to make 12 per cent net profit, then the giving of one months' extra credit will cost him 1 per cent and the customer should pay this. On the other hand, if the customer is prepared to pay at an earlier date, the manufacturer should be prepared to pass that customer a concession or reward for such early payment.

Now all the elements of cost are accounted for and the price at which the manufacturer should sell his goods is said to be: — ex-works cost + carriage or distribution cost + publicity cost + sales cost + profit + credit cost: — and this may be termed the basic price.

These costs may well be calculated on the basis of production and distribution of the smallest economical quantity. For manufacturers of specialised equipment of reasonable sized machine tools, for instance, the smallest economical quantity may will be one item but for manufacturers of consumer goods and repetition items, the smallest economical quantity will be determined by the number of units which it is worth packing or the number of units which constitute a standard pack, or the number of items which make up the minimum value which is it worth a representative or salesman spending selling time upon customers.

If customers order larger quantities than the minimum economical quantity, certain saving will accrue to the manufacturer. For instance, the sales expenses, (i.e., sales office costs, salesman's salary and travelling and daily allowances) may well be the same on a large order as they are on a small order although commission will increase proportionately. Carriage costs will reduce with larger orders and also raw material purchases may well be cheaper if large quantities can be ordered to fulfil larger orders. Larger orders also mean longer production runs and, in consequence, lower works costs. It is only right, therefore, that there should be some inducement to the customer to place orders in excess of the lowest economical quantity and this inducement is usually in the form of increasing discounts from the basic price of increasingly larger orders. Such quantity discounts may be arranged in relation to the total value of the order if the manufacturer is producing an assortment of goods with varying prices.

At this stage, it is necessary for the manufacturer to decide as to what extent he is going to fix prices for his goods. Where the manufacturer is selling direct to the actual user, there is no difficulty and he will price his goods in accordance with the considerations already studied. Where, however, the goods are to reach the user via wholesale and retail dealer channels, the manufacturer will need to decide whether he will fix his price only to the customer who buys from him and leave that customer to mark up the prices to other buyers in the channel of sale or whether he will fix prices for each buyer in the channel irrespective of whether he has direct dealing or not.

If the manufacturer sells to wholesalers and only fixes his price to them, he may well find that different wholesalers are fixing different mark-ups on his prices with the result that there is unhealthy competition between the various wholesalers; because the less reputable wholesalers may work on a minimum mark-up in order to obtain the dealers' custom in the easiest way. In Western countries, it is usual for the manufacturer to decide to price at which the product will be sold to the eventual use irrespective of the number of trade channels by way of distributors, wholesalers and retail dealers who handle the product. This is done by adding on to the cost the amounts necessary to provide the margins required by the intermediate traders and to quote prices in terms of user's prices less trade and wholesale discounts. The price at which the product is to be sold to the public or actual user is most frequently marked on the item itself. For instance, a manufacturer of a certain consumer product will quote his price on the following lines:

Shino Hair Oil 4 II. oz. Bottles – ₹ 2 each.

Trade (dealers) price ₹ 24 per dozen less 25 per cent. Wholesale price ₹ 24 per dozen less 25 per cent and less 20 per cent.

It is believed that this method of pricing helps to prevent price cutting. If the dealers are quoted ₹ 18 per dozen for one dealer may sell at ₹ 1.75 per bottle and think he is doing well to make 25 paise on each whilst another dealer may think he is doing well if he makes 20 paise per bottle and accordingly sell at ₹ 1.80 paise. If the same two dealers are quoted ₹ 2 less 25 per cent, there is a good chance that they will both sell at the same price and be less anxious to undercut as they will lose a profit they might have made if they do so.

Most buyers are suspicious that the manufacturer is trying to charge them more than is really necessary and this feeling is heightened by the absence of any regular form of price list. All manufacturers are well advised that when they have fixed their prices and have decided upon the discounts to be allowed for quantities and prompt payment, to publish these prices and details in a proper manner. Handwritten and typewritten price lists often cause buyer suspicion and there is no substitute in helping the schedule of prices, discounts and payment terms. Many small manufacturers are reticent to publish their prices and accounts for fear of being copied by competitors but if they want to find out the manufacturer's prices they will do so any way and this should not deter the manufacturer from publishing an authentic price list.

GUTS AND GLORY

Passion Works Wonders

Being a successful entrepreneur, some say, has a simple recipe. Spot an opportunity, take risk, think big, sell the vision to various stakeholders and in between all this, hire great people. Then, just focus, execute and course correct when necessary.

This list of first generation entrepreneurs have made it big only in the recent past; and they have managed to achieve it mostly on their own. What sets them apart is their passion to perform, their ability to sail through highs and lows, and their never-say-die attitude.

Cool Operator: Sunil Mittal

At age 14, Sunil Bharti Mittal had made up his mind to do something exceptional in life, though he didn't know what. But the second son of politician Sat Paul Mittal had decided he would be in business, not politics. That fire in the belly to do something different has been the driving force in Mittal's life.

Armed with a graduate degree from Punjab University, Mittal started his first business venture at 18 years of age in the manufacturing sector with a capital of a ₹ 20,000. This was in 1976, and his choices in Ludhiana were limited; so he tried his hand at manufacturing crankshafts and cycle parts. Then feeling the need for a bigger canvas, Mittal moved to New Delhi in 1978. With no big industrial family to fall back on, trading seemed to be the best option and he was soon importing portable generators. But in a turn of events, the government banned import of generators, and Mittal soon had nothing to fall back on.

Six months later, Mittal happened to visit a trade fair in Taiwan where he was introduced to push-button telephones, and he soon began importing them to India. It was this foray into the fringes of the telecom industry that got Mittal excited. And it was the listing on the bourses that brought Mittal into the limelight. Today, his empire is a conglomerate (₹ 72,000 crore by market cap, with a customer base of 18.5 million GSM subscribers and 1.3 million broadband and fixed line customers). His plans are now to diversify into the food retail sector, with an initial investment of ₹ 6,000 crore.

The Buzz in Biotech: Kiran Mazumdar-Shaw

One April morning in 2004, Bangalore's leading biotech player Biocon listed on the National Stock Exchange. Its market capitalisation hit $1 billion and as the largest shareholder, Kiran Mazumdar-Shaw became a much richer woman in a matter of minutes. Starting out as a small enzyme maker in 1978, she built Biocon into a biopharmaceutical company of global reckoning, piece by piece. Luck no doubt had something to do with it, but mainly it was perseverance and plain old hardwork that got her to where she is.

Moreover, she had no business background – her father was a brewmaster with the UB group – nor did she have a management degree. Mazumdar-Shaw like Azim Premji and N.R. Narayana Murthy, built her company by leveraging intellectual capital and creating a knowledge businesses. For the longest time, biotech was a black box which few people could fathom. So, Biocon's business model was not widely understood. From making enzymes for an Irish partner, Mazumdar-Shaw progressed to developing proprietary manufacturing technology, moved into contract research and drug development, creating the building blocks for Biocon's future in biopharmaceuticals.

In a worldwide poll conducted by *Nature* magazine. Mazumdar-Shaw was recently voted as the most influential person who has distinguished herself in biotech outside the US and Europe. She is in the company of greats — the American nominee is Arthur Levinson of biotech giant Genentech and the European winner is Dan Vasella of Novartis. That Mazumdar-Shaw overtook Philip Yeoh of Singapore's EDB who is chairman, Agency for Science, Technology and Research as also Eli Hurvitz of Teva Pharmaceuticals, makes this sweet victory indeed. Curiously, this biotech icon got fewer votes in India, prompting *Nature* to comment that she seems to be more popular outside her home country. Mazumdar-Shaw takes that in her stride. "This is a huge recognition for Indian biotech," she declares modestly.

No-frills Man: Captain G.R. Gopinath

Gorur Ramaswamy Gopinath came from a small remote village called Gorur in Karnataka. A graduate from the National Defence Academy, he started his career as a commissioned officer in the Indian army; but returned to his village with ₹ 6,000 in his pocket, saw an opportunity in agriculture, and later won a 'Rolex award for Enterprise', for breaking new ground in ecological silk farming.

In 1995 however, Gopinath moved to Bangalore to secure his children's education and it was here that he began his tryst with the airline industry; setting up Deccan Aviation, India's first private heli-charter company. Encouraged by its commercial success, he set up Air Deccan in 2003 with one 48-seater ATR turboprop aircraft that connected low-traffic destinations. Not that Gopinath had it easy. A few seconds before the inaugural take-off, the aircraft engine caught fire and passengers had a miraculous escape. Then came in opposition from other airlines on parking rights, check-in-counters and flight timings. Even today, with its balance sheet continuing to bleed, critics say the company is going about in a haphazard manner.

But despite the occasional skid or two, what cannot be dismissed is that Gopinath has led the no-frill and low-cost strategy in Indian air travel. And Air Deccan has increased to 221 flights, its route network stretches to 51 airports, it has carried about three million passengers to date, and has an average load factor of 85 per cent.

Riding the Bull Wave: Sameer Gehlaut

Unlike Gopinath, 30-something Sameer Gehlaut did not start small. A mechanical engineer from IIT, Delhi, he had a successful earth-moving business – Mackenna Minerals and Equipment. With money saved from this, and from his earlier jobs at oilfield services companies Schlumberger and Halliburton, he bought a seat on the Bombay Stock Exchange in 1998-99 through Inorbit Securities.

By year 2000, friends Rajiv Rattan and Saurabh Mittal, whom he had worked with at Schlumberger and Halliburton, joined in, and Inorbit was renamed Indiabulls. When the company listed on the bourses in 1999, it cost ₹ 19 a share. This mind you, was followed by the dot.com bust; and it wouldn't have been unreasonable for many to consider it part of just that.

But remarkably, the company diversified and is today a leader in retail financial services, with a network of over 270 offices in over 90 cities. Along with its subsidiary companies, it offers consumer loans, brokerage and depository services, mutual funds, personal loans and home loans.

INHERITING ENTREPRENEURSHIP

"Innovation is the specific instrument of entrepreneurship… the act that endows resources with a new capacity to create wealth."

Management Guru, Peter Ducker

For the first time, Ernst & Young's Entrepreneur of the Year World Summit will after Youth Entrepreneurship Workshops. These workshops are for children, aged 10-18, of Entrepreneur of the Year winners. Junior Achievement Europe and past Entrepreneur of the Year winners will lead the sessions, aimed at introducing children to the world of business.

Over the day-to-day period, youth participants will attend a series of instructional sessions designed to teach them about various aspects of entrepreneurship. As part of the experience, competitive activities will be conducted to reinforce the instructional content. The curriculum specifically targets the age groups listed, and all sessions will be conducted in English.

Jupiter Mills for ₹ 276 crore, is paying off.

The Indiabulls share now trades at about ₹ 220. And with a 15 per cent shareholding, Gehlaut, remains its single-largest shareholder.

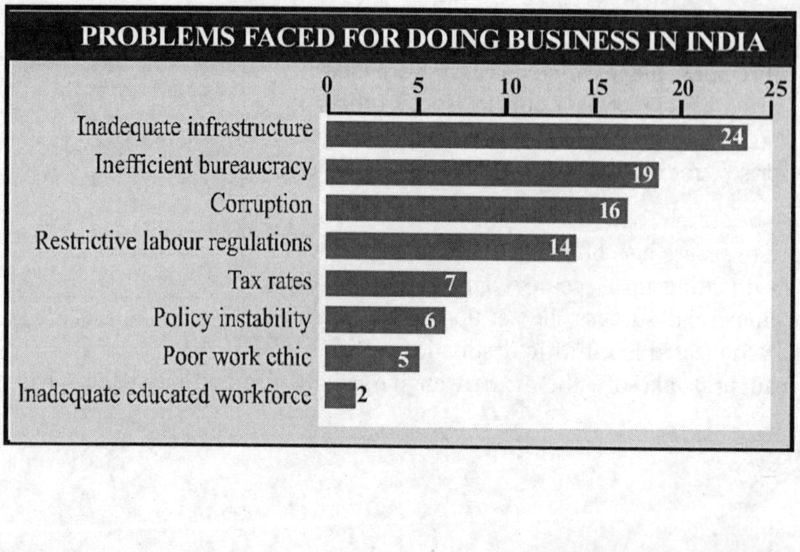

High and Lows: Avnish Bajaj

It isn't easy being an entrepreneur at times, and Bajaj at 34, knows this well. A B.Tech. in computer science from IIT, Kanpur, Bajaj moved to the US to further pursue education, and passed out as Baker Scholar from Harvard Business School. He then went on to work with Goldman Sachs. In the year 2000, he returned to India to form Baazee.com along with fellow Harvard Business graduate Suvir Sujan. Like Gehlaut, he too survived the dot.com bust. In four years' time, Baazee.com established itself as the only auction Website in India with a sound business model. Baazee.com was bought out eventually by e-Bay for $50 million.

But the lowest ebb in Bajaj's career was yet to come. In the year 2004, accused of facilitating the sale of 'obscene material' through his website, Bajaj was arrested and had spend more than a week in Tihar jail, just like another undertrail would. The industry's strong reaction to his arrest is a known story, and it still stands by his side. There is an amendment in the IT Act that is being pushed for, which insists on equitable liability between the host and the uploader of content.

But even all the education in the world and the money made, do not guarantee an entrepreneur a smooth ride. For Bajaj, it was quick recovery that was essential. "On average, life is fair," he says. "Yet, this happens when one takes a long enough period of time into consideration – over short periods it can swing either way."

Today, Bajaj is on a short sabbatical in the US, but has not lost faith in the Indian story (he continues as chairman, e-Bay India). Meanwhile, he is building up his investments in the Indian stock markets as a small investor, and his bets are on the pharma sector.

DREAMING BIG

Entrepreneur achievers who write their own success stories have, a clear Vision; Desire to excel; Clear-cut strategy.

Ask venture capitalists what they look for in a company they say like to fund and the first thing they say is the market they are in and vision, second: people; and third: a unique value proposition.

In India, today, few other sector receives as much early- and mid-stage investment as information technology. The companies below are IT start-ups who've been through the initial struggle, and have managed to convince others to be big money on their small ventures. More importantly, as venture capitalist puts it, they have "their skin in the game".

This required many to give up cushy jobs, and risk it out in the hope of making it big. All have one problem in common: building a good team. Will they succeed? Watch this space.

Makemytrip.com, Delhi

When Deep Kalra graduated from IIM Ahmedabad (1992), his carrier choice was obvious the corporate sector – and he joined ABN-Amro. Thereon he moved to AMF Bowling (which introduced the concept of pool and bowling in many parts of the Indian subcontinent) after which he joined GE in business development. "Somewhere along the line I got restless and wanted to do something of my own. In 1998, I planned a trip to Thailand and the bookings were made on the net – which turned out to be 30 per cent cheaper and was also very convenient. That's when I decided to set up a travel portal of my own," says Deep Kalra, founder and CEO of MakeMyTrip.com.

E-Ventures invested close to ₹ 10 crore in the business, from which he began to cater to the US market. "Subsequently, E-Ventures decided to close shop in India as the partners wanted to set out on their own overseas. We brought back our equity which was backed by a small group of investors," says Kalra. Then came the next stage – of setting up a portal for the India-based customers.

Today, Markemytrip has grown from 42 people (when we started six years back) to over 200 people. "We will met our projected revenue of ₹ 190 crore by end March 2006. Besides, there is ₹ 20 crore in cross commission that would come to our kitty," adds Kalra.

Ocimum Biosolutions, Hyderabad

Anuradha Acharya, after studying physics for five years at IIT, Kharagpur, moved to the US to acquire a master's degree in management information system and a master's in physics. " But when you know you can't be best in a field, it is important to move out at the right time." she says.

So Acharya, along with a friend, formed Ocimum Biosolutions (Ocimum in layman's terms means tulsi) in the US and then established a base in Hyderabad. What started out as a contract research firm in year 2000 has developed into a company with several products. In fact, Ocimum's product optgene – a gene optimising tool – won an award from Nasscom: 'IT Innovation of Year award'.

She recently acquired a small company in Germany, and says that it is the company's customer base that has come of help the most. Ocimum is today a complete life science R&D enabling company with focus areas in BioIT, microarrays and contract research. Acharya is close on the heels of raising $5.5 million in private equity, money she wants to use more inorganic growth.

Gridlogics, Pune

Girish Sinha raised $600,000 recently in VC funding from IndiaCo Ventures. Sinha, an engineering graduate from Ranchi, worked with the erstwhile Hughes Software (now Flextronics) in New Delhi for three-and-a-half years before setting up Gridlogics in end-2003 to help companies and institutions meet their growing computing requirements. "I was looking around for incubators and came across IndiaCo," he says.

Grid computing, Sinha explains, is "binding multiple computers to act as one, with all their power combined". "There's whole lot of data which needs to be run every five seconds or so and evaluated for action," he says.

The money Sinha has just raised will help him enhance his products, develop marketing and sales operations and take a strategic interest in a couple of applications companies. "Our products don't have a direct route to the market," he points out. "We provide components for the grid infrastructure, which need to be bundled with an applications for end-users like banks, universities, R&D establishments, energy vendors."

Vegayan Systems, Mumbai

Girish P. Saraph spent 13 years in the US after he decided to return to India to work as an associate professor with the Indian Institute of Technology, Mumbai, in the department of electrical engineering. Here he invented a routing technology that he claims improves significantly the flow of pockets of data. Based on the MPLS (multi-protocol lable switching) model, it gives network operators flexibility in diverting and routing traffic around link failure, congestion and bottlenecks.

Saraph calls this the VS routing scheme, and says it is highly scalable and dynamic. Despite it being a more expensive proposition, he has filed for international IP protection. Vegayan recently raised $ 75,000 as venture capital funding from the California-based Draper Fisher Jurveston (it was one of the two companies selected out of 125). "The funding is most welcome," he says, "but a large part will go in building a team and paying high salaries, that even Indians are now getting used to."

NEC Technologies, Bengaluru

There was another company that Draper Fisher funded $75,000 with recently, Mukesh Hedge (in blue), also an IIT graduate, moved to Bengaluru recently and set up NEC Technologies, which runs Devsquare.com that, based on a java platform, enables developers to create products online.

"This saves the visitor start-up costs involved in setting a development atmosphere – the server, technology and all the little things that go with it," says Hedge. The user can log in, take programming tests, and is allowed to access and manipulate training content. While the site is limited to Java-based applications, Hedge is developing technology to develop a platform that supports all and any kind of online development. How will he use the money? "In ramping up our hosting infrastructure and development team," he says.

CSS Group, Chennai

Softbank Asia Information Fund (SAIF) partners recently announced its plan to invest $22.5 million in the Chennai operations of the San Joes headquartered CSS Group. CSS was started in 1997 by three partners in San Jose, headed by CEO and co-promoter the 32-year-old Shiva Ramani.

Today, the CSS group has under its fold SlashSopport (technology support), Ready-TestGo (software testing), CSS Inc (software services) and Synaptris (software products) with over 3,000 professionals working across nine geographies. Ramani says he'd like CSS to grow into the world's largest technology and support company. The infusion from SAIF happened when the initial funding from ING Bearings had to be retired. SAIF stepped in with $22.5 million.

Source: *Business India*

SUNRISE INDUSTRIES

Driving the boom in the job markets are several sunrise industries that are growing at an extraordinary pace. *Business India* takes a look at emerging opportunities in some of the burgeoning industries.

The Sky is the Limit

Indian aviation is finally taking off. In the past two years, three new airlines have taken to the skies and 13 more are waiting in the wings. Paramount Airways is beginning operations soon and the Nusli Wadia backed 'Go' airlines just took off. Existing players such as jet Airways, on the other hand, are busy spreading their wings across the globe.

The Centre for Asia-Pacific Aviation predicts that in the next five years, the country will acquire around 215 aircrafts to grow to 450-500 fleet from the current fleet of 185. India was already among the largest buyers (of civilian airplanes) in the world at the recent air show in Paris. Of the 280 aircrafts ordered at the meet, 150 orders came from Indian buyers. According to the Centre for Asia-Pacific Aviation, the aviation industry will create employment for 3,000-4,000 pilots, a similar number of maintenance crew and 7,000-8,000 cabin crew, not to mention the large numbers of indirect employment it will create in the form of ground staff, security staff, and air-traffic controllers. Moreover, with the privatisation of the Mumbai and Delhi airports as well as the greenfield airports of Bengaluru and Hyderabad, retail business at the airports will flourish creating jobs for a million others.

The burgeoning aviation industry is creating waves in the Indian tourism industry. Domestic tourism is pegged at 19 million currently and is expected to jump to 45 million by 2010. Similarly, inbound tourism is expected to grow at 6.5 million by 2010 from the current number of 3.69 million. Tourism is among the biggest employers in the world. In India, according to the World Travel and Tourism Council, the travel and tourism economy is estimated to account for 2,42,65,500 jobs — 5.5 per cent of the country's total employment figures in 2005. The council anticipates this to increase to 2,60,77,700 jobs by 2015. Travel and tourism industry is growing at 10 per cent this year and at 8.6 per cent per annum, in real terms, between 2006 and 2015.

Retail Revolution

The retail industry is also witnessing a similar resurgence. With the industry growing at 6-7 per cent per annum and organised retail growing at 25-30 per cent a year, KSA Technopak estimates the industry to create anywhere up to 50,000 jobs in the next few years. What's more, the jobs are spanned across the levels. "If any industry can make a claim to adding employment to the country, it's retail," asserts Nagesh of Shoppers' Stop. "We will create job opportunities across the levels, from the front-end shop-floor salespeople to the back-end mid-level managerial jobs."

Anil Nagpal, manager, retail of KSA Technology agrees, "WalMart is the largest employer in the world," he says. "In fact, retail is probably the largest employer in India, if you include the unorganised sector. And, with the organised sector growing so rapidly, retail will create a lot of employment. To cite an example, every 300 sq.ft. of mall space requires one front-end person. About 50 million sq.ft. of space is expected to come up by 2008," he adds. Shoppers' Stop is adding four stores' to its stable in the next four months, and intends to grow to 39 stores in the next three-and-a-half years. "We will recruit between 2,000-2,500 people for this purpose and around a 1,000 for our Hypercity stores," says Nagesh of Shoppers' Stop.

The RPG group is also pacing itself for the future. "Retail is an important sector for us. We are gearing up for the human resource challenges for the coming years," says Harsh Goenka of RPG. Several foreign players are also eyeing the retail segment in India. Costa Coffee, Guess, WalMart, and another coffee chain are already firming up their plans to foray into the Indian retailscape. Many domestic corporate houses such as Godrej (in collaboration with Adhar) and DCN Sriram (with Hariyali) are also taking the plunge into retail. "Retail is where the future is. It's a scaleable industry that is going to be the growth driver for companies," says Nagpal.

APPENDIX

APPENDIX-I

Key Proposals of The Direct Tax Code 2010 for Small Enterprise

SMALL-SCALE INDUSTRIES are an important and crucial segment of the Indian industry sector. The Indian government has accorded high priority to this sector as it plays a vital role in balanced and sustainable economic growth. The government has offered a variety of packaged incentives for the last six decades for its accelerated development. And, taxation benefits are the key components of these incentives programme.

In the current context of rapid economic development, one must view taxation benefits in relation to the need for increasing investment in small-scale and ancillary industries.

Here are a few key proposals of the Direct Tax Code, 2010, (DTC).

Income-Expense Model

In terms of the DTC., besides the presumptive and special taxation regimes for specified businesses, the profits from all other businesses will be equal to gross earnings from the business minus the amount of allowable deduction.

Gross Earnings from the Business

All accruals and receipts from business, besides those derived from businesses assets, make up the gross earnings of the business of the tax payer. For instance, profit on sale of an undertaking under a slump sale; advance or security deposit on long-term lease of business asset; or reimbursement of any expennditure, etc.

Allowable Deduction

Generally, all operating expenses incurred essentially for business purposes are deductible from gross total income. The requisite for deductibility of expenses must be wholly and exclusively incurred or paid during the previous year and supported by pertinent papers and records.

Expenses of a personal and capital nature, remuneration payable to a "non-working participant", any unascertained liabilities, etc. are not deductible.

Expenditure incurred by way of land revenue, local rates or municipal taxes, sales tax, duty, cess, fees, bonus or commission to employees, leave encashment is deductible in the financial years in which the liability arose only if paid in the financial year or by the due date of filling the return of tax bases for that financial year. Otherwise it will be allowed in the financial year in which it is actually paid.

Expenditure incurred by way of interest on loans or borrowings from permitted financial institutions is deductible in the year of accrual or payment, whichever is later.

Depreciation on business capital assets (including acquired by the lessee under financial lease) is calculated on the declining balance method and is based on the "block of assets". The 'block of assets' concept suggest aggregation of all assets with the same depreciation rate into a common block for calculation of depreciation. Depreciation is computed at varying rates as prescribed and in the year of purchase, is available for the full year if an asset is used for more than 180 days. In other cases, depreciation is allowed at half the normal rates.

Besides depreciation, a manufacturer or producer of an article or thing is allowed initial depreciation on new machinery and plant (expect office appliances and assets not installed in office premises, guest house or any other residential premises) at the rate of 20% of the original cost of the asset for the full year if the asset is used for more than 180 days. In other cases, initial depreciation is allowed at half the normal rates.

Deferred revenue expenditure by way of, i.e., non-compete fee, premium paid on lease or rental asset, amount paid to an employee under voluntary retirement scheme, expenses incurred by an Indian company wholly and exclusively, preliminary expenditure, etc., will be allowed deduction in six financial years starting the year of actual payment, or year of business reorganisation, or year of start of business, extension of business or set-up of new business, as the case may be.

Tax Holidays

The DTC has grandfathered, though restrictive, the tax holiday to all Special Economic Zone units for the unexpired period out of 15 years, including new such units that start operations on or before 31 March, 2014. The tax holiday will be computed on the lines discussed in the above model with two exceptions namely: capital expenditure and expenditure incurred prior to the start of business.

Unfortunately, there is no exception for SEZ units from MAT. Absence of MAT exemption under DTC would mean that SEZ units would need to pay a minimum tax of 20% on book profits.

Business Reorganisation

It covers transactions between two or more residents involved in amalgamation or de-merger. Reorganisation, ordinarily being tax netutral is subject to 'test of continuity of business', and other conditions as are necessary to prevent abuse of the Code.

The successor of business will pass the 'test of continuity of business' if he: (i) continuously holds at least 75% of the book value of the fixed assets of the predecessor acquired through business re-organisation for at least five financial years immediately succeeding the year in which the business reorganisation takes place; (ii) continues the business of the predecessor for at least five financial years immediately succeeding the financial year in which the business reorganisation takes place; and (iii) meets such other conditions as may be prescribed to ensure the revival of the business of the predecessor or to ensure that the business reorganisation is for genuine business purpose.

In the case of demerger, the resulting company must issue only its equity shares to the shareholders of the demerged company on a proportionate basis to avail of tax exemption and benefit of carry forward of unabsorbed tax losses.

Allowable Deduction

Besides depreciation, a manufacturer or producer of an article or thing is allowed initial depreciation on new machinery and plant (except 'office appliances' and assets not installed in office premises, guest house or any other residential premises) at the rate of 20% of the original cost of the asset for the full year if the asset is used for more than 180 days. In other cases, initial depreciation is allowed at half the normal rates.

Tips on Time Management for Entrepreneurs

1. Keep your to-do list short. Do not go beyond 6-8 things to do. When you finish ticking each item on the list, you will have a feeling of accomplishment.
2. At the end of the day, organise your desk and e-mails so that you do not waste time next morning.
3. Identify time wasters — internet, e-mails, forwards, phone calls — before planning your day.
4. Learn to prioritise. Complete most important tasks first.
5. When you have identified and prioritised your tasks, set a time limit and stick to it.
6. Take regular breaks to get back focus. It gets difficult to concentrate when you are at something for too long.
7. Keep business and family separate. When at wrok, concentrate on it.
8. Partner with a virtual assistant for administrative tasks that can be delegated. This would let you spend more time in attending to clients.
9. There are a number of tasks which are repetitive. Develop a routine around them to be more productive.
10. Allow time between tasks to reevaluate priorities.

APPENDIX-II

The Entrepreneurship Ecosystem

There is now enough evidence out there which proves that entrepreneurship is the sure way to development. It contributes disproportionately to rapid job creation, GDP growth, and long-term productivity and a lot of the things that societies are struggling to get right. Dan Isenberg of Babson College suggests to launch an entrepreneurial revolution. People who have true entrepreneurial spirit do not wait for the situation to improve to get moving. In fact, often the most effective practices come from remote corners of the earth, where resources — as well as legal frameworks, transparent governance, and democratic values — may be scarce.

"There are some natural characteristics of an entrepreneur like curiosity and a constant pursuit of different ways of doing things but education is most certainly important because there are a lot of skills that have to be learned. More importantly, an entrepreneurial climate must be created to support the entrepreneurial growth strategy.

Prof. Isenberg evolved the entrepreneurship ecosystem to launch an entrepreneurial revolution.

While charting out the future course of action, the entrepreneur will have to remember that to get a competitive edge on a sustainable basis five things are essential — increased productivity, improved quality, innovation in the market, a deep understanding of customer needs and delivery of world-class service.

THE 13 PILLARS OF THE ENTREPRENEURSHIP ECOSYSTEM

The entrepreneurship components are grouped into 13 pillars which is shown on the next page.

Basic Systems

- Leadership
- Government
- Culture
- Infrastructure

} Key for shaping entrepreneurship

Efficiency Enhancers

- Human Capital
- Financial Capital
- Non-government Institutions
- Educational Institutions

} Key for efficiency-driven growth

Other Factors

- Economic Clustures
- Networks
- Support Services
- Early Customers

} Key for sustained growth

The Entrepreneurship Ecosystem

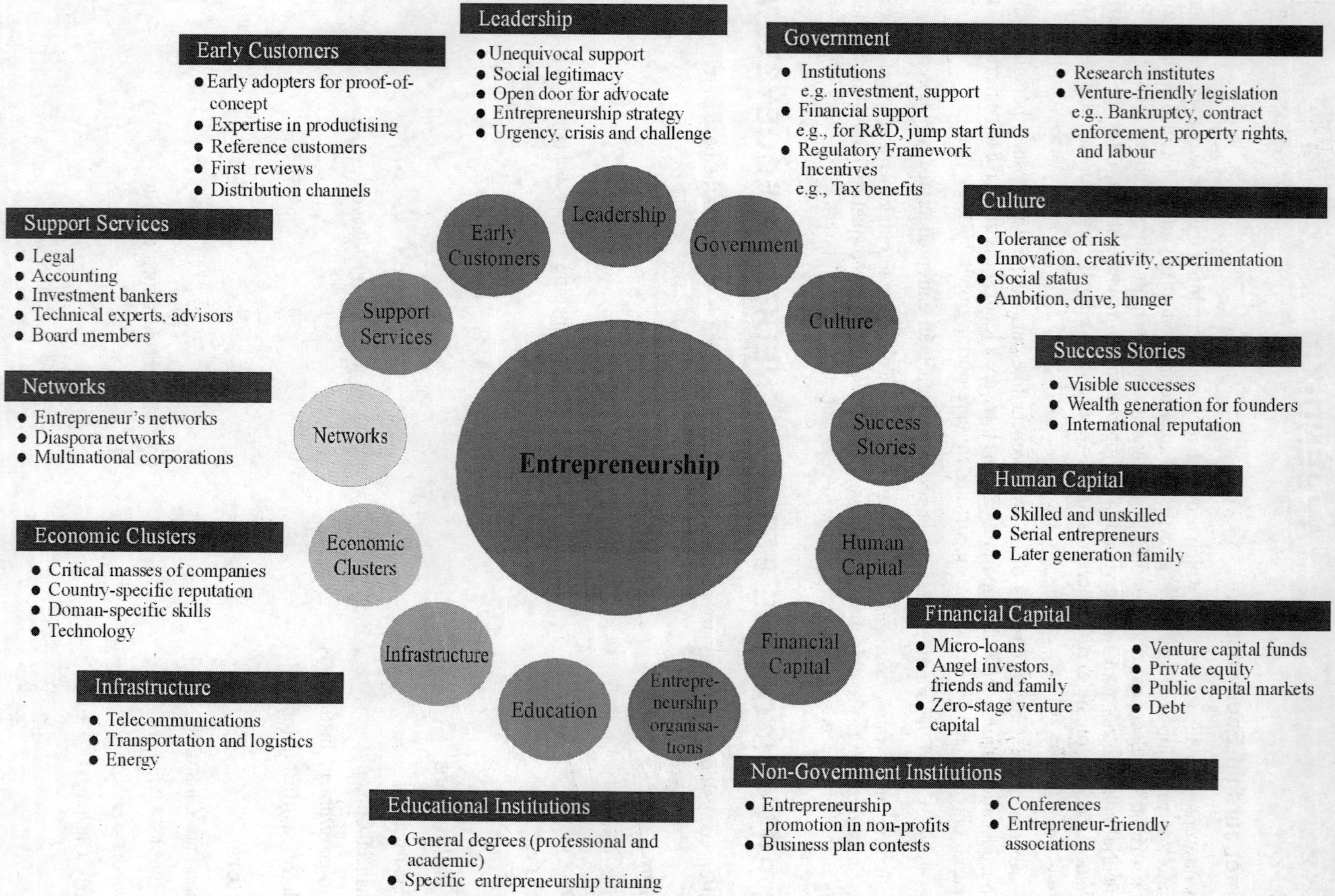